XSLT 2.0 and XPath 2.0
Programmer's Reference
4th Edition

XSLT 2.0 and XPath 2.0
Programmer's Reference
4th Edition

Michael Kay

WILEY

Wiley Publishing, Inc.

XSLT 2.0 and XPath 2.0 Programmer's Reference
4th Edition

Published by
Wiley Publishing, Inc.
10475 Crosspoint Boulevard
Indianapolis, IN 46256
www.wiley.com

To Anyone Who Uses This Book
To Make the World a Better Place

About the Author

Michael Kay has been working in the XML field since 1997; he became a member of the XSL Working Group soon after the publication of XSLT 1.0, and took over as editor of the XSLT 2.0 specification in early 2001. He is also a member of the XQuery and XML Schema Working Groups, and is a joint editor of the XPath 2.0 specification. He is well known not only through previous editions of this book but also as the developer of the open source Saxon product, a pioneering implementation of XSLT 2.0, XPath 2.0, and XQuery 1.0.

In 2004 the author formed his own company, Saxonica, to provide commercial software and services building on the success of the Saxon technology. Previously, he spent three years with Software AG, working with the developers of the Tamino XML server, an early XQuery implementation. His background is in database technology: after leaving the University of Cambridge with a Ph.D., he worked for many years with the (then) computer manufacturer ICL, developing network, relational, and object-oriented database software products as well as a text search engine, and held the position of ICL Fellow.

Michael lives in Reading, England, with his wife and daughter. His hobbies (reflected in his choice of examples) include genealogy and choral singing, and once included chess. Since completing the previous edition he has found time to improve his croquet handicap to 6.

Credits

Director of Acquisitions
Jim Minatel

Development Editor
Maureen Spears

Technical Editor
Sam Judson

Production Editor
Angela Smith

Copy Editor
Foxxe Editorial Services

Editorial Manager
Mary Beth Wakefield

Production Manager
Tim Tate

Vice President and Executive Group Publisher
Richard Swadley

Vice President and Executive Publisher
Joseph B. Wikert

Project Coordinator, Cover
Lynsey Stanford

Proofreader
Nancy Carrasco

Indexer
Robert Swanson

Acknowledgments

There are two groups of people I must thank: those who contributed to the book, and those who supported me in writing it.

In the first group, I am indebted to readers of previous editions who have pointed out my errors, and have told me what they liked and didn't like. I hope readers of this edition will do the same. Also to the (by now numerous) reviewers and editors engaged first by the original Wrox team in the UK, and more recently by their successors in Wiley, who have done so much of the legwork of testing example code and finding continuity errors, not to mention handling the unseen production processes that turn a heap of word-processed text into a finished book. Then my colleagues on the working groups, who provided the subject matter for me to write about, and those who taught me how to use the language — if you find a programming pearl that you particularly like in this book, the chances are I stole the idea from someone. James Clark in particular, who invented the XSLT language and showed me how it worked.

In the second group, I must once again acknowledge the patience of my family, who sighed resignedly when I suggested the prospect of retreating to my study for half a year to produce a new revision, and the generosity of my past employers who provided the time to get the project off the ground in the first place.

Contents

Contents

Contents

Contents

Contents

Contents

Contents

Contents

Part III: Exploitation

Contents

Part IV: Appendices

Contents

Introduction

This book, as the title implies, is primarily a practical reference book for professional XSLT developers. It assumes no previous knowledge of the language, and many developers have used it as their first introduction to XSLT; however, it is not structured as a tutorial, and there are other books on XSLT that provide a gentler approach for beginners.

Who This Book Is For

The book does assume a basic knowledge of XML, HTML, and the architecture of the Web, and it is written for experienced programmers. There's no assumption that you know any particular language such as Java or Visual Basic, just that you recognize the concepts that all programming languages have in common.

I have tried to make the book suitable both for XSLT 1.0 users upgrading to XSLT 2.0, and for newcomers to XSLT. This is easier to do in a reference book, of course, than a tutorial. I have also tried to make the book equally suitable whether you work in the Java or .NET world.

As befits a reference book, a key aim is that the coverage should be comprehensive and authoritative. It is designed to give you all the details, not just an overview of the 20 percent of the language that most people use 80 percent of the time. It's designed so that you will keep coming back to the book whenever you encounter new and challenging programming tasks, not as a book that you skim quickly and then leave on the shelf. If you like detail, you will enjoy this book; if not, you probably won't.

But as well as giving the detail, this book aims to explain the concepts, in some depth. It's therefore a book for people who not only want to use the language but who also want to understand it at a deep level. Many readers have written to me saying that they particularly appreciate these insights into the language, and it's my sincere hope that after reading it, you will not only be a more productive XSLT programmer, but also a more knowledgeable software engineer.

What This Book Covers

The book aims to tell you everything you need to know about the XSLT 2.0 language. It gives equal weight to the things that are new in XSLT 2.0 and the things that were already present in version 1.0. The book is about the language, not about specific products. However, there are appendices about Saxon (my own implementation of XSLT 2.0), about the Altova XSLT 2.0 implementation, and about the Java and Microsoft APIs for controlling XSLT transformations, which will no doubt be upgraded to handle XSLT 2.0 as well as 1.0. A third XSLT 2.0 processor, Gestalt, was released shortly before we went to press, too late for us describe it in any detail. But the experience of XSLT 1.0 is that there has been a very high level of interoperability between different XSLT processors, and if you can use one of them, then you can use them all.

In the previous edition we split XSLT 2.0 and XPath 2.0 into separate volumes. The idea was that some readers might be interested in XPath alone. However, many bought the XSLT 2.0 book without its XPath companion and were left confused as a result; so this time, we've brought the material back together. The XPath reference information is in self-contained chapters, so it should still be accessible when you use XPath in contexts other than XSLT.

The book does not cover XSL Formatting Objects, a big subject in its own right. Nor does it cover XML Schemas in any detail. If you want to use these important technologies in conjunction with XSLT, there are other books that do them justice.

How This Book Is Structured

This book contains twenty chapters and eight appendixes (the last of which is a glossary) organized into four parts. The following section outlines what you can find in each part, chapter, and appendix.

Part I: Foundations

The first part of the book covers essential concepts. I recommend reading these before you start coding. If you ignore this advice, as most people do, then I suggest you read them when you get to that trough of despair when you find it impossible to make the language do anything but the most trivial tasks. XSLT is different from other languages, and to make it work for you, you need to understand how it was designed to be used.

Chapter 1: XSLT in Context

This chapter explains how XSLT fits into the big picture: how the language came into being and how it sits alongside other technologies. It also has a few simple coding examples to keep you alert.

Chapter 2: The XSLT Processing Model

This is about the architecture of an XSLT processor: the inputs, the outputs, and the data model. Understanding the data model is perhaps the most important thing that distinguishes an XSLT expert from an amateur; it may seem like information that you can't use immediately, but it's knowledge that will stop you from making a lot of stupid mistakes.

Chapter 3: Stylesheet Structure

XSLT development is about writing stylesheets, and this chapter takes a bird's-eye view of what stylesheets look like. It explains the key concepts of rule-based programming using templates, and explains how to undertake programming-in-the-large by structuring your application using modules and pipelines.

Chapter 4: Stylesheets and Schemas

A key innovation in XSLT 2.0 is that stylesheets can take advantage of knowledge about the structure of your input and output documents, provided in the form of an XML Schema. This chapter provides a quick overview of XML Schema to describe its impact on XSLT development. Not everyone uses schemas, and you can skip this chapter if you fall into that category.

Chapter 5: The Type System

XPath 2.0 and XSLT 2.0 offer strong typing as an alternative to the weak typing approach of the 1.0 languages. This means that you can declare the types of your variables, functions, and parameters, and use this information to get early warning of programming errors. This chapter explains the data types available and the mechanisms for creating user-defined types.

Part II: XSLT and XPath Reference

This section of the book contains reference material, organized in the hope that you can easily find what you need when you need it. It's not designed for sequential reading, though if you're like me, you might well want to leaf through the pages to discover what's there.

Chapter 6: XSLT Elements

This monster chapter lists all the XSLT elements you can use in a stylesheet, in alphabetical order, giving detailed rules for the syntax and semantics of each element, advice on usage, and examples. This is probably the part of the book you will use most frequently as you become an expert XSLT user. It's a "no stone unturned" approach, based on the belief that as a professional developer you need to know what happens when the going gets tough, not just when the wind is in your direction.

Chapter 7: XPath Fundamentals

This chapter explains the basics of XPath: the low-level constructs such as literals, variables, and function calls. It also explains the context rules, which describe how the evaluation of XPath expressions depends on the XSLT processing context in which they appear.

Chapter 8: XPath: Operators on Items

XPath offers the usual range of operators for performing arithmetic, boolean comparison, and the like. However, these don't always behave exactly as you would expect, so it's worth reading this chapter to see what's available and how it differs from the last language that you used.

Chapter 9: XPath: Path Expressions

Path expressions are what make XPath special; they enable you to navigate around the structure of an XML document. This chapter explains the syntax of path expressions, the 13 axes that you can use to locate the nodes that you need, and associated operators such as union, intersection, and difference.

Chapter 10: XPath: Sequence Expressions

Unlike XPath 1.0, in version 2.0 all values are sequences (singletons are just a special case). Some of the most important operators in XPath 2.0 are those that manipulate sequences, notably the «for» expression, which translates one sequence into another by applying a mapping.

Chapter 11: XPath: Type Expressions

The type system was explained in Chapter 5; this chapter explains the operations that you can use to take advantage of types. This includes the «cast» operation which is used to convert values from one type to another. A big part of this chapter is devoted to the detailed rules for how these conversions are done.

Chapter 12: XSLT Patterns

This chapter returns from XPath to a subject that's specific to XSLT. Patterns are used to define template rules, the essence of XSLT's rule-based programming approach. The reason for explaining them now is that the syntax and semantics of patterns depends strongly on the corresponding rules for XPath expressions.

Chapter 13: The Function Library

XPath 2.0 includes a library of functions that can be called from any XPath expression; XSLT 2.0 extends this with some additional functions that are available only when XPath is used within XSLT. The library has grown immensely since XPath 1.0. This chapter provides a single alphabetical reference for all these functions.

Chapter 14: Regular Expressions

Processing of text is an area where XSLT 2.0 and XPath 2.0 are much more powerful than version 1.0, and this is largely through the use of constructs that exploit regular expressions. If you're familiar with regexes from languages such as Perl, this chapter tells you how XPath regular expressions differ. If you're new to the subject, it explains it from first principles.

Chapter 15: Serialization

Serialization in XSLT means the ability to generate a textual XML document from the tree structure that's manipulated by a stylesheet. This isn't part of XSLT processing proper, so (following W3C's lead) we've separated it into its own chapter. You can control serialization from the stylesheet using an `<xsl:output>` declaration, but many products also allow you to control it directly via an API.

Part III: Exploitation

The final section of the book is advice and guidance on how to take advantage of XSLT to write real applications. It's intended to make you not just a competent XSLT coder, but a competent designer too. The best way of learning is by studying the work of others, so the emphasis here is on practical case studies.

Chapter 16: Extensibility

This chapter describes the "hooks" provided in the XSLT specification to allow vendors and users to plug in extra functionality. The way this works will vary from one implementation to another, so we can't cover all possibilities, but one important aspect that the chapter does cover is how to use such extensions and still keep your code portable.

Chapter 17: Stylesheet Design Patterns

This chapter explores a number of design and coding patterns for XSLT programming, starting with the simplest "fill-in-the-blanks" stylesheet, and extending to the full use of recursive programming in the functional programming style, which is needed to tackle problems of any computational complexity. This provides an opportunity to explain the thinking behind functional programming and the change in mindset needed to take full advantage of this style of development.

Chapter 18: Case Study: XMLSpec

XSLT is often used for rendering documents, so where better to look for a case study than the stylesheets used by the W3C to render the XML and XSLT specifications, and others in the same family, for display on the Web? The resulting stylesheets are typical of those you will find in any publishing organization that uses XML to develop a series of documents with a compatible look-and-feel.

Chapter 19: Case Study: A Family Tree

Displaying a family tree is another typical XSLT application. This time we're starting with semi-structured data — a mixture of fairly complex data and narrative text — that can be presented in many different ways for different audiences. We also show how to tackle another typical XSLT problem, conversion of the data into XML from a legacy text-based format. As it happens, this uses nearly all the important new XSLT 2.0 features in one short stylesheet. But another aim of this chapter is to show a collection of stylesheets doing different jobs as part of a complete application.

Chapter 20: Case Study: Knight's Tour

Finding a route around a chessboard where a knight visits every square without ever retracing its steps might sound a fairly esoteric application for XSLT, but it's a good way of showing how even the most complex of algorithms are within the capabilities of the language. You may not need to tackle this particular problem, but if you want to construct an SVG diagram showing progress against your project plan, then the problems won't be that dissimilar.

Part IV: Appendices

Appendix A: XPath 2.0 Syntax Summary

Collects the XPath grammar rules and operator precedences into one place for ease of reference.

Appendix B: Error Codes

A list of all the error codes defined in the XSLT and XPath language specifications, with brief explanations to help you understand what's gone wrong.

Appendix C: Backward Compatibility

The list of things you need to look out for when converting applications from XSLT 1.0.

Appendix D: Microsoft XSLT Processors

Although the two Microsoft XSLT processors don't yet support XSLT 2.0, we thought many readers would find it useful to have a quick summary here of the main objects and methods used in their APIs.

Appendix E: JAXP: The Java API for XML Processing

JAXP is an interface rather than a product. Again, it doesn't have explicit support yet for XSLT 2.0, but Java programmers will often be using it in XSLT 2.0 projects, so we decided to include an overview of the classes and methods available.

Appendix F: Saxon

At the time of writing Saxon (developed by the author of this book) provides the most comprehensive implementation of XSLT 2.0 and XPath 2.0, so we decided to cover its interfaces and extensions in some detail.

Appendix G: Altova

Altova, the developers of XML Spy, have an XSLT 2.0 processor that can be used either as part of the development environment or as a freestanding component. This appendix gives details of its interfaces.

Appendix H: Glossary

Index

What You Need to Use This Book

To use XSLT 2.0, you'll need an XSLT 2.0 processor: at the time of writing that means Saxon, AltovaXML, or Gestalt, though Gestalt appeared on the scene too late for us to give it much coverage. You can run these products in a number of different ways, which are described as part of the "Hello World!" example in Chapter 1 (pages 11–18).

If in doubt, the simplest way to get started is probably to download Kernow (`http://kernowforsaxon .sourceforge.net/`), which has Java SE 6 as a prerequisite. Kernow comes complete with the Saxon XSLT engine. The only other thing you will need is a text editor.

Conventions

To help you get the most from the text and keep track of what's happening, we've used a number of conventions throughout the book.

There are two kinds of code examples in this book: *code fragments* and *worked examples*.

Code fragments are incomplete and are not intended to be executed on their own. You can build them into your own stylesheets if you find them useful, but you will have to retype the code.

Worked examples are provided in the form of complete stylesheets, accompanied by sample source XML documents to which they can be applied, and an illustration of the output that they are expected to produce. You can download these examples and try them out for yourself. They generally appear in a box like this:

A Specimen Example

Source

This section gives the XML source data, the input to the transformation. If the filename is given as `example.xml`, you will find that file in the archive that you can download from the Wrox website at `http://www.wrox.com/`, generally in a subdirectory holding all the examples for one chapter.

```
<source data="xml"/>
```

Stylesheet

This section describes the XSLT stylesheet used to achieve the transformation. Again, there will usually be a filename such as `style.xsl`, so you can find the stylesheet in the Wrox download archive.

```
<xsl:stylesheet...
```

Output

This section shows the output when you apply this stylesheet to this source data, either as an XML or HTML listing, or as a screenshot.

```
<html...</html>
```

Occasionally, for reasons of space, we haven't printed the whole of the source document or the stylesheet in the book, but instead refer you to the website to fetch it.

> **Boxes like this one hold important, not-to-be forgotten information that is directly relevant to the surrounding text.**

Notes, tips, hints, tricks, and asides to the current discussion are offset and placed in italics like this.

As for styles in the text:

❑ We *highlight* new terms and important words when we introduce them.

❑ We show keyboard strokes like this: Ctrl+A.

❑ We show filenames, URLs, and code within the text like so: persistence.properties.

❑ We show code within the text as follows: Element names are written as <html> or <xsl:stylesheet>. Function names are written as concat() or current-date(). Other names (for example of attributes or types) are written simply as version or xs:string. Fragments of code other than simple names are offset from the surrounding text by chevrons; for example, «substring($a, 1, 1)='X'». Chevrons are also used around individual characters or string values, or when referring to keywords such as «for» and «at» that need to stand out from the text. As a general rule, if a string is enclosed in quotation marks, then the quotes are part of the code example, whereas if it is enclosed in chevrons, the chevrons are there only to separate the code from the surrounding text.

❑ We present code in two different ways:

```
For blocks of code we usually use gray highlighting.
```

```
But for individual lines of code we sometimes omit the highlighting.
```

Downloading the Code

All of the source code referred to in this book is available for download at http://www.wrox.com. Once at the site, simply locate the book's title (either by using the Search box or by using one of the title lists) and click the Download Code link on the book's detail page to obtain all the source code for the book.

Because many books have similar titles, you may find it easiest to search by ISBN; this book's ISBN is 978-0-470-19274-0.

Once you download the code, just decompress it with your favorite compression tool. Alternately, you can go to the main Wrox code download page at http://www.wrox.com/dynamic/books/download.aspx to see the code available for this book and all other Wrox books.

Errata

We make every effort to ensure that there are no errors in the text or in the code. However, no one is perfect, and mistakes do occur. If you find an error in one of our books, such as a spelling mistake or faulty piece of code, we would be very grateful for your feedback. By sending in errata you may save another reader hours of frustration and at the same time you will be helping us provide even higher-quality information.

To find the errata page for this book, go to http://www.wrox.com and locate the title using the Search box or one of the title lists. Then, on the book details page, click the Book Errata link. On this page you can view all errata that have been submitted for this book and posted by Wrox editors. A complete book list, including links to each book's errata, is also available at www.wrox.com/misc-pages/booklist.shtml.

If you don't spot "your" error on the Book Errata page, go to www.wrox.com/contact/techsupport.shtml and complete the form there to send us the error you have found. We'll check the information and, if appropriate, post a message to the book's errata page and fix the problem in subsequent editions of the book.

p2p.wrox.com

For author and peer discussion, join the P2P forums at p2p.wrox.com. The forums are a Web-based system for you to post messages relating to Wrox books and related technologies and interact with other readers and technology users. The forums offer a subscription feature to e-mail you topics of interest of your choosing when new posts are made to the forums. Wrox authors, editors, other industry experts, and your fellow readers are present on these forums.

At http://p2p.wrox.com you will find a number of different forums that will help you not only as you read this book but also as you develop your own applications. To join the forums, just follow these steps:

1. Go to p2p.wrox.com and click the Register link.
2. Read the terms of use and click Agree.
3. Complete the required information to join as well as any optional information you wish to provide, and click Submit.
4. You will receive an e-mail with information describing how to verify your account and complete the joining process.

You can read messages in the forums without joining P2P but in order to post your own messages, you must join.

Once you join, you can post new messages and respond to messages other users post. You can read messages at any time on the Web. If you would like to have new messages from a particular forum e-mailed to you, click the Subscribe to this Forum icon by the forum name in the forum listing.

Here are some tips for writing a question if you want a good answer:

1. Choose your subject line carefully. Not just "XSLT question".

2. Don't use text shorthand. Not everyone has English as their first language, but if you take care over writing your question, it's much more likely that someone will take care over answering it.

3. Show a complete source document, a complete example of your required output, and if you want to know why your code doesn't work, your complete code — but only after paring the problem down to its essentials. Don't ask people to debug code that they can't see.

4. If you tried something and it didn't work, say exactly what you tried and exactly how it failed (including details of what products you are using).

For more information about how to use the Wrox P2P, be sure to read the P2P FAQs for answers to questions about how the forum software works as well as many common questions specific to P2P and Wrox books. To read the FAQs, click the FAQ link on any P2P page.

List of Examples

This list includes all the worked examples in the book: that is, the examples consisting of entire stylesheets, for which working code can be downloaded from http://www.wrox.com/. It does not include the many examples that are provided as incomplete snippets.

The purpose of this list is to help you out when you know that you've seen an example somewhere that is relevant to your current problem, but you can't remember where you saw it.

Chapter 1

Chapter 2

continued

Chapter 6

continued

List of Examples

continued

List of Examples

Chapter 12

Chapter 13

continued

List of Examples

Chapter 15

Chapter 16

Chapter 17

Chapter 18

Chapter 19

Chapter 20

Appendix F

Part I
Foundations

1

XSLT in Context

This chapter is designed to put XSLT in context. It's about the purpose of XSLT and the task it was designed to perform. It's about what kind of language it is, how it came to be that way, and how it has changed in version 2.0; and it's about how XSLT fits in with all the other technologies that you are likely to use in a typical Web-based application (including, of course, XPath, which forms a vital component of XSLT). I won't be saying very much in this chapter about what an XSLT stylesheet actually looks like or how it works: that will come later, in Chapters 2 and 3.

The chapter starts by describing the task that XSLT is designed to perform — **transformation** — and why there is the need to transform XML documents. I'll then present a trivial example of a transformation in order to explain what this means in practice.

Next, I discuss the relationship of XSLT to other standards in the growing XML family, to put its function into context and explain how it complements the other standards.

I'll describe what kind of language XSLT is, and delve a little into the history of how it came to be like that. If you're impatient you may want to skip the history and get on with using the language, but sooner or later you will ask "why on earth did they design it like that?" and at that stage I hope you will go back and read about the process by which XSLT came into being.

What Is XSLT?

XSLT (Extensible Stylesheet Language: Transformations) is a language that, according to the very first sentence in the specification (found at http://www.w3.org/TR/xslt20/), is primarily designed for transforming one XML document into another. However, XSLT is also capable of transforming XML to HTML and many other text-based formats, so a more general definition might be as follows:

> *XSLT is a language for transforming the structure and content of an XML document.*

Why should you want to do that? In order to answer this question properly, we first need to remind ourselves why XML has proved such a success and generated so much excitement.

XML is a simple, standard way to interchange structured textual data between computer programs. Part of its success comes because it is also readable and writable by humans, using nothing more complicated than a text editor, but this doesn't alter the fact that it is primarily intended for communication between software systems. As such, XML satisfies two compelling requirements:

❏ **Separating data from presentation:** the need to separate information (such as a weather forecast) from details of the way it is to be presented on a particular device. The early motivation for this arose from the need to deliver information not only to the traditional PC-based Web browser (which itself comes in many flavors) but also to TV sets and handheld devices, not to mention the continuing need to produce print-on-paper. Today, for many information providers an even more important driver is the opportunity to syndicate content to other organizations that can republish it with their own look-and-feel.

❏ **Transmitting data between applications:** the need to transmit information (such as orders and invoices) from one organization to another without investing in one-off software integration projects. As electronic commerce gathers pace, the amount of data exchanged between enterprises increases daily, and this need becomes ever more urgent.

Of course, these two ways of using XML are not mutually exclusive. An invoice can be presented on the screen as well as being input to a financial application package, and weather forecasts can be summarized, indexed, and aggregated by the recipient instead of being displayed directly. Another of the key benefits of XML is that it unifies the worlds of documents and data, providing a single way of representing structure regardless of whether the information is intended for human or machine consumption. The main point is that, whether the XML data is ultimately used by people or by a software application, it will very rarely be used directly in the form it arrives: it first has to be transformed into something else.

In order to communicate with a human reader, this something else might be a document that can be displayed or printed: for example, an HTML file, a PDF file, or even audible sound. Converting XML to HTML for display is probably still the most common application of XSLT, and it is the one I will use in most of the examples in this book. Once you have the data in HTML format, it can be displayed on any browser.

In order to transfer data between different applications, we need to be able to transform information from the data model used by one application to the model used by another. To load the data into an application, the required format might be a comma-separated-values file, a SQL script, an HTTP message, or a sequence of calls on a particular programming interface. Alternatively, it might be another XML file using a different vocabulary from the original. As XML-based electronic commerce becomes widespread, the role of XSLT in data conversion between applications also becomes ever more important. Just because everyone is using XML does not mean the need for data conversion will disappear.

There will always be multiple standards in use. As I write there is a fierce debate between the protagonists of two different XML representations of office documents: the ODF specification from the Open Office community, and the OOXML specification from Microsoft and its friends. However this gets resolved, the prospects of a single XML format for all word processor documents are remote, so there will always be a need to transform between multiple formats.

Even within the domain of a single standard, there is a need to extract information from one kind of document and insert it into another. For example, a PC manufacturer who devises a solution to a customer problem will need to extract data from the problem reports and insert it into the documents issued to field engineers so that they can recognize and fix the problem when other customers hit it. The field engineers, of course, are probably working for a different company, not for the original manufacturer. So, linking up enterprises to do e-commerce will increasingly become a case of defining how to extract and combine data from one set of XML documents to generate another set of XML documents, and XSLT is the ideal tool for the job.

During the course of this chapter, we will come back to specific examples of when XSLT should be used to transform XML. For now, I just wanted to establish a feel for the importance and usefulness of transforming XML. If you are already using XSLT, of course, this may be stale news. So let's take a look now at what XSLT version 2.0 brings to the party.

Why Version 2.0?

XSLT 1.0 came out in November 1999 and was highly successful. It was therefore almost inevitable that work would start on a version 2.0. As we will see later, the process of creating version 2.0 was far from smooth and took rather longer than some people hoped. However, XSLT 2.0 was finally published as a W3C Recommendation (that is, a final specification) in January 2007, and user reaction has been very favorable.

It's tempting to look at version 2.0 and see it as a collection of features bolted on to the language, patches to make up for the weaknesses of version 1.0. As with a new release of any other language or software package, most users will find some features here that they have been crying out for, and other additions that appear surplus to requirements.

But I think there is more to version 2.0 than just a bag of goodies; there are some underlying themes that have guided the design and the selection of features. I can identify four main themes:

❑ **Integration across the XML standards family:** W3C working groups do not work in isolation from each other; they spend a lot of time trying to ensure that their efforts are coordinated. A great deal of what is in XSLT 2.0 is influenced by a wider agenda of doing what is right for the whole raft of XML standards, not just for XSLT considered in isolation.

❑ **Extending the scope of applicability:** XSLT 1.0 was pretty good at rendering XML documents for display as HTML on screen, and for converting them to XSL Formatting Objects for print publishing. But there are many other transformation tasks for which it proved less suitable. Compared with report writers (even those from the 1980s, let alone modern data visualization tools) its data handling capabilities were very weak. The language was quite good at doing conversions of XML documents if the original markup was well designed, but much weaker at recognizing patterns in the text or markup that represent hidden structure. An important aim of XSLT 2.0 was to increase the range of applications that you can tackle using XSLT.

❑ **More robust software engineering:** XSLT was always designed to be used both client-side and server-side, but in many ways XSLT 1.0 optimized the language for use in the browser. However, people write large applications in XSLT, containing 100K or more lines of code, and this needs a more rigorous and robust approach to things such as error handling and type checking.

❑ **Tactical usability improvements:** Here we *are* into the realm of added goodies. The aim here is to achieve productivity benefits, making it easier to do things that are difficult or error-prone in version 1.0. These are probably the features that existing users will immediately recognize as the most beneficial, but in the long term the other themes probably have more strategic significance for the future of the language.

Before we discuss XSLT in more detail and have a first look at how it works, let's study a scenario that clearly demonstrates the variety of formats to which we can transform XML, using XSLT.

A Scenario: Transforming Music

As an indication of how far XML has now penetrated, Robin Cover's index of XML-based application standards at `http://xml.coverpages.org/xmlApplications.html` today runs to 594 entries. (The last one is entitled *Mind Reading Markup Language*, but as far as I can tell, all the other entries are serious.)

I'll follow just one of these 594 links, *XML and Music*, which takes us to `http://xml.coverpages.org/xmlMusic.html`. On this page we find a list of no less than 18 standards, proposals, or initiatives that use XML for marking up music.

This diversity is clearly unnecessary, and many of these initiatives are already dead or dying. Even the names of the standards are chaotic: there is a Music Markup Language, a MusicML, a MusicXML, and a MusiXML, all quite unrelated. There are at least three really serious contenders: the Music Encoding Initiative (MEI), the Standard Music Description Language (SMDL), and MusicXML. The MEI derives its inspiration from the Text Encoding Initiative, and has a particular focus on the needs of music scholars (for example, the ability to capture features found in different manuscripts of the same score), while SMDL is related to the HyTime hypermedia standards and takes into account requirements such as the need to synchronize music with video or with a lighting script (it has not been widely implemented, but it has its enthusiasts). MusicXML, by contrast, is primarily focused on the needs of composers and publishers of sheet music.

Given the variety of requirements, it's unlikely that the number of standards in use will reduce any further. The different notations were invented with different purposes in mind: a markup language used by a publisher for printing sheet music has different requirements from the one designed to let you listen to the music from a browser.

In the first edition of this book, back in 2001, I introduced the idea of using XSLT to transform music as a theoretical possibility, something to make my readers think about the range of possibilities open for the language. By the time I published the second edition, PhD students were showing that it could actually be done. Today, MusicXML is a standard part of over 80 software applications including industry leaders such as Sibelius and Finale, and XSLT is routinely used to manipulate the output. The MEI website publishes XSLT stylesheets for converting between MEI and MusicXML in either direction.

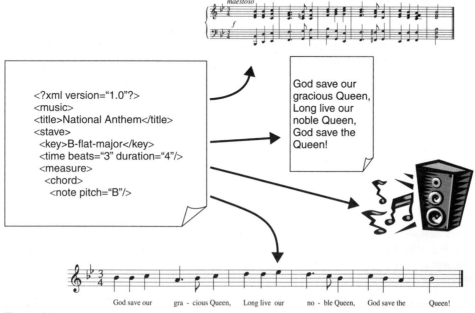

Figure 1-1

6

As it happens, MusicXML itself provides two ways of representing a score. In one the top-level subdivision in the XML hierarchy is by instrumental part or voice; in the other the top-level structure is the timeline of the music. XSLT stylesheets are provided to convert between the two formats.

Figure 1-1 shows some of the possibilities. You could use XSLT to:

❑ Convert music from one representation to another, for example from MEI to SMDL.

❑ Convert music from any of these representations into visual music notation, by generating the XML-based vector graphics format SVG.

❑ Play the music on a synthesizer, by generating a MIDI (Musical Instrument Digital Interface) file.

❑ Perform a musical transformation, such as transposing the music into a different key or extracting parts for different instruments or voices.

❑ Extract the lyrics, into HTML or into a text-only XML document.

❑ Capture music from non-XML formats and translate it to XML (XSLT 2.0 is especially useful here).

As you can see, XSLT is not just for converting XML documents to HTML.

How Does XSLT Transform XML?

By now you are probably wondering exactly how XSLT goes about processing an XML document in order to convert it into the required output. There are usually two aspects to this process:

1. The first stage is a structural transformation, in which the data is converted from the structure of the incoming XML document to a structure that reflects the desired output.

2. The second stage is formatting, in which the new structure is output in the required format such as HTML or PDF.

The second stage covers the ground we discussed in the previous section; the data structure that results from the first stage can be output as HTML, as a text file, or as XML. HTML output allows the information to be viewed directly in a browser by a human user or be input into any modern word processor. Plain text output allows data to be formatted in the way an existing application can accept, for example comma-separated values or one of the many text-based data interchange formats that were developed before XML arrived on the scene. Finally, XML output allows the data to be supplied to applications that accept XML directly. Typically, this will use a different vocabulary of XML tags from the original document: for example, an XSLT transformation might take the monthly sales figures as its XML input and produce a histogram as its XML output, using the XML-based SVG standard for vector graphics. Or, you could use an XSLT transformation to generate Voice XML output, for aural rendition of your data.

Information about VoiceXML can be found at `http://www.voicexml.org/`.

Let's now delve into the first stage, transformation — the stage with which XSLT is primarily concerned and which makes it possible to provide output in all of these formats. This stage might involve selecting data, aggregating and grouping it, sorting it, or performing arithmetic conversions such as changing centimeters to inches.

XSLT is not the only way of processing or transforming XML. For example, you can write applications in Java or C# that build a tree-like representation of an XML document (using the W3C-defined Document

Object Model, or other similar models such as JDOM or XOM). Your program could interrogate this tree structure to find the specific information needed. It would do so by defining a specific *sequence of steps* to be followed in order to produce the required output.

So, how is using XSLT to perform transformations on XML better than writing custom applications? Well, the design of XSLT is based on a recognition that these programs are all very similar, and it should therefore be possible to describe what they do using a high-level *declarative* language rather than writing each program from scratch in Java or C#. The required transformation can be expressed as a set of rules. These rules are based on defining what output should be generated when particular patterns occur in the input. The language is declarative in the sense that you describe the transformation you require, rather than providing a sequence of procedural instructions to achieve it. XSLT describes the required transformation and then relies on the XSLT processor to decide the most efficient way to go about it.

XSLT still relies on an XML parser — it might be a DOM parser or a SAX-compliant one, or one of the new breed of "pull parsers" — to convert the XML document into a tree structure. It is the structure of this tree representation of the document that XSLT manipulates, not the document itself. If you are familiar with the DOM, then you will be happy with the idea of treating every item in an XML document (elements, attributes, processing instructions, and so on) as a node in a tree. With XSLT we have a high-level language that can navigate around a node tree, select specific nodes, and perform complex manipulations on these nodes.

> *The XSLT tree model is similar in concept to the DOM, but it is not the same. The full XSLT processing model is discussed in Chapter 2.*

The description of XSLT given thus far (a declarative language that can navigate to and select specific data and then manipulate that data) may strike you as being similar to that of the standard database query language, SQL. Let's take a closer look at this comparison.

XSLT and SQL: An Analogy

In a relational database, the data consists of a set of tables. By themselves, the tables are not of much use, the data might as well be stored in flat files in comma-separated values format. The power of a relational database doesn't come from its data structure; it comes from the language that processes the data, SQL. In the same way, XML on its own just defines a data structure. It's a bit richer than the tables of the relational model, but by itself it doesn't actually do anything very useful. It's when we get a high-level language expressly designed to manipulate the data structure that we start to find we've got something interesting on our hands, and for XML data the main language that does that is XSLT.

Superficially, SQL and XSLT are very different languages. But if you look below the surface, they actually have a lot in common. For starters, in order to process specific data, be it in a relational database or an XML document, the processing language must incorporate a declarative query syntax for selecting the data that needs to be processed. In SQL, that's the SELECT statement. In XSLT, the equivalent is the *XPath expression*.

The XPath expression language forms an essential part of XSLT, though it is actually defined in a separate W3C Recommendation (http://www.w3.org/TR/xpath) because it can also be used independently of XSLT (the relationship between XPath and XSLT is discussed further on page 22).

The XPath syntax is designed to retrieve nodes from an XML document, based on a path through the XML document or the context in which the node appears. It allows access to specific nodes, while preserving the hierarchy and structure of the document. XSLT instructions are then used to manipulate the results of these queries, for example by rearranging selected nodes and constructing new nodes.

There are further similarities between XSLT and SQL:

- ❑ Both languages augment the basic query facilities with useful additions for performing arithmetic, string manipulation, and comparison operations.

- ❑ Both languages supplement the declarative query syntax with semiprocedural facilities for describing the processing to be carried out, and they also provide hooks to escape into conventional programming languages where the algorithms start to get too complex.

- ❑ Both languages have an important property called *closure*, which means that the output has the same data structure as the input. For SQL, this structure is tables, for XSLT it is trees — the tree representation of XML documents. The closure property is extremely valuable because it means operations performed using the language can be combined end-to-end to define bigger, more complex operations: you just take the output of one operation and make it the input of the next operation. In SQL you can do this by defining views or subqueries; in XSLT you can do it by passing your data through a series of stylesheets, or by capturing the tree produced by one transformation phase in a variable and using that variable as the input of another transformation phase. This last feature is new in XSLT 2.0, though most XSLT 1.0 processors offered a similar capability as a language extension.

In the real world, of course, XSLT and SQL have to coexist. There are many possible relationships, but typically, data is stored in relational databases and transmitted between systems in XML. The two languages don't fit together as comfortably as one would like, because the data models are so different. But XSLT transformations can play an important role in bridging the divide. All of the major relational database vendors have released extensions that allow XML data to be stored and manipulated directly within what is still nominally a relational database.

Before we look at a simple working example of an XSLT transformation, we should briefly discuss a few of the XSLT processors that are available to effect these transformations.

XSLT Processors

The job of an XSLT processor is to apply an XSLT stylesheet to an XML source document and produce a result document.

With XSLT 1.0, there are quite a few good XSLT processors to choose from, and many of them can be downloaded free of charge (but do read the licensing conditions).

If you're using Microsoft technology, there is a choice of two products. The most widely used option is MSXML (Google for "Download MSXML" to find it — the current version is MSXML 6). Usually, I'm not Microsoft's greatest fan, but with this processor it's generally agreed that they have done an excellent job. This product comes as standard with Internet Explorer and is therefore the preferred choice for running transformations in the browser. For the .NET environment, however, Microsoft developed a new processor. This doesn't have a product name of its own, other than its package name within the .NET framework, which is `System.Xml.Xsl`. This processor was initially said to be significantly slower than the MSXML product, but that seems to be no longer true, and if you're writing your application using .NET technologies such as C# and ASP.NET, it's probably the one that you'll find more convenient.

In the Java world, there's a choice of Xalan-J product. There's my own Saxon product (version 6.5.5 is the version that supports XSLT 1.0) available from `http://saxon.sf.net/`, and there's the Xalan-J product which is bundled with Sun's Java JDK software from JDK 1.4 onwards. There's also an Oracle implementation, and a new processor from Intel.

For C and C++ the most popular processor is the `libxslt` engine (`http://xmlsoft.org/XSLT/`).

Most of these products are XSLT interpreters, but there are two well-known XSLT compilers: XSLTC, which is distributed as part of the Xalan-J package mentioned earlier, and Gregor, from Jacek Ambroziak (`http://www.ambrosoft.com/gregor.html`). At the top end of the market, for those with a large budget, you can also get hardware-accelerated engines from IBM and Intel.

With XSLT 2.0, at the time of writing, the choice is more limited. There are currently three XSLT 2.0 processors available:

❏   My own Saxon product. This is available in two variants, corresponding to the two conformance levels defined in the W3C specification: Saxon-B 9.x (`http://saxon.sf.net/`) is an open-source implementation of a basic XSLT 2.0 processor, and Saxon-SA 9.x (`http://www.saxonica.com/`) is a commercial implementation of a schema-aware XSLT processor. Both variants are available for both the Java and .NET platforms. You can run most of the examples in this book, using a basic XSLT processor, but Chapter 4 and Chapter 11 focus on the additional capability of XSLT when used with XML Schemas, with examples that will only run with a basic XSLT processor.

❏   Saxon as delivered offers a command line interface and a Java or .NET API. A number of toolsets provide graphical user interfaces on top: the simplest is the open-source Kernow product (`kernowforsaxon.sourceforge.net`); other options are the comprehensive Stylus Studio development environment (`www.stylusstudio.com`) and the oXygen XML editor (`www.oxygenxml.com`), both of which support step-by-step Saxon debugging.

❏   Altova (`www.altova.com`) have released their own XSLT 2.0 processor, which is available either as a freestanding COM component with a command line interface and Windows API, or built in to the popular XML Spy development environment. As a standalone component the product is free (but not open source), and offers both schema-aware and non-schema-aware processing. The level of conformance of the Altova product has been improving with each release, and nearly all the examples in this book run successfully with the 2008 edition of this product.

❏   Gestalt is an open-source XSLT 2.0 processor written in the Eiffel language by Colin Adams (`http://sourceforge.net/projects/gestalt`). The product is work in progress, and although the software is under active development, the documentation is a little sketchy and this implementation is unlikely to appeal to you unless you are something of an Eiffel enthusiast. We have not tested the examples in this book against the Gestalt processor.

By reading papers published at research conferences and blog postings by employees, you can make an educated guess that implementations are underway within IBM, Oracle and Microsoft, but none of these companies has announced any official product plans or release dates at the time of writing — and of course, not everything those companies do in their research labs sees the light of day as a product.

I think it's a little unlikely that there will be quite as many XSLT 2.0 processors as there are for XSLT 1.0 (there is bound to be some shakeout in a maturing market), but I'm confident there will be four or five, which should be enough.

Meanwhile, you can use Altova or Saxon, and those are the primary vehicles I will be using for all the examples in this book.

A Simple XSLT Stylesheet

We're now ready to take a look at an example of using XSLT to transform a very simple XML document.

Example: A "Hello, world!" XSLT Stylesheet

Kernighan and Ritchie in their classic *The C Programming Language* (Prentice-Hall, 1988) originated the idea of presenting a trivial but complete program right at the beginning of the book, and ever since then the `Hello world` program has been an honored tradition. Of course, a complete description of how this example works is not possible until all the concepts have been defined, and so if you feel I'm not explaining it fully, don't worry — the explanations will come later.

Input

What kind of transformation would we like to do? Let's try transforming the following XML document.

```
<?xml version="1.0" encoding="iso-8859-1"?>
<?xml-stylesheet type="text/xsl" href="hello.xsl"?>
<greeting>Hello, world!</greeting>
```

This document is available as file `hello.xml` in the download directory for this chapter.

A simple node-tree representation of this document is shown in Figure 1-2.

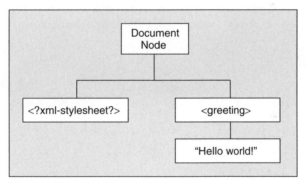

Figure 1-2

There are four nodes in this tree: a document node that represents the document as a whole; an `<?xml-stylesheet?>` processing instruction that identifies the stylesheet to be used; the `<greeting>` element; and the text within the `<greeting>` element.

The document node in the XSLT model performs the same function as the document node in the DOM model (it was called the root node in XSLT 1.0, but the nomenclature has been brought into line with the DOM). The XML declaration is not visible to the XSLT processor and, therefore, is not included in the tree.

I've deliberately made it easy by including an `<?xml-stylesheet?>` processing instruction in the source XML file. Many XSLT processors will use this to identify the stylesheet if you don't specify a different stylesheet to use. The `href` attribute gives the relative URI of the default stylesheet for this document.

Output

Our required output is the following HTML, which will simply change the browser title to `"Today's Greeting"` and display whatever greeting is in the source XML file:

```
<html>
<head>
   <title>Today's greeting</title>
</head>
<body>
   <p>Hello, world!</p>
</body>
</html>
```

XSLT Stylesheet

Without any more ado, here's the XSLT stylesheet `hello.xsl` to effect the transformation. This is an XSLT 1.0 stylesheet, hence the «version = "1.0"» in the `<xsl:stylesheet>` element.

```
<?xml version="1.0" encoding="iso-8859-1"?>
<xsl:stylesheet
   version="1.0"
   xmlns:xsl="http://www.w3.org/1999/XSL/Transform">

<xsl:template match="/">
   <html>
   <head>
      <title>Today's greeting</title>
   </head>
   <body>
      <p><xsl:value-of select="greeting"/></p>
   </body>
   </html>
</xsl:template>

</xsl:stylesheet>
```

Running the Stylesheet

There are a number of ways you can run this stylesheet, which we'll look at in the following sections. It may be worth trying several of the different approaches, to find out which you are most comfortable with — familiarity with the tools will help you master the examples in the rest of the book, as well as making you a more proficient XSLT developer.

Whichever approach you use, the first stage is to download the sample code for this book from the Wrox web site (`www.wrox.com`), as explained in the Introduction. The code is organized by chapter, so you'll find the two files `hello.xml` and `hello.xsl` in the directory `ch01`.

If you're a serious XSLT developer then your company may well have invested in an XML development environment such as XML Spy, Stylus Studio, or oXygen. All these products have the capability to run XSLT 2.0 stylesheets: XML Spy uses Altova's XSLT 2.0 processor (though it can also be configured to run Saxon), while Stylus Studio and oXygen both use Saxon. We won't cover the use of these development environments in this book.

Using the Browser

The easiest way to run this example is simply to load the XML file `hello.xml` into any recent version of Internet Explorer or Firefox (right-click the file and select `Open With...`). The browser will recognize the `<?xml-stylesheet?>` processing instruction and will use this to fetch the stylesheet and execute it. The result is a display like the one in Figure 1-3.

Figure 1-3

We can run this example in the browser because it is actually an XSLT 1.0 stylesheet. Most modern browsers support XSLT 1.0 processing in this way, but at the time of writing none yet supports XSLT 2.0.

Using Saxon from Kernow

We'll be running most of the XSLT 2.0 examples in this book using Saxon, and one of the easiest ways to run Saxon is by using a graphical front-end called Kernow. You can download Kernow from `http://kernowforsaxon.sourceforge.net/`. It includes the Saxon JAR files, so the only prerequisite is that Java itself is installed. You will need Java Standard Edition 6 or later, which you can get from `http://java.sun.com/`. (Saxon itself works with JDK 1.4 or later, the requirement for Java SE 6 comes from Kernow.)

To install Kernow, the only thing you need to do is to unzip the download file into a suitable directory, and if you are running Windows you can then start the product by double-clicking the `Run.bat` file. In the dialog box that appears, select the "Single File" tab, and browse to the source and stylesheet files. Then click Run to run the transformation. The output is as shown in Figure 1-4.

Note that this time, the result is shown in terms of raw HTML. If you want to see what the HTML looks like in a browser, you can always save it to a file and then open the file in your browser. But Kernow is designed for developers, not for end users, and as a developer you need to see the HTML that you have generated. I wouldn't advise anyone to do serious XSLT development by testing directly in a browser, because it's hard to see what's gone wrong when you make a mistake.

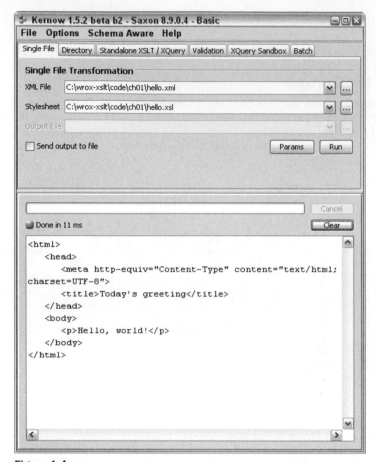

Figure 1-4

Using Saxon on Java from the Command Line

If you're a professional software developer then you're probably not averse to running utilities from the command line, which is the natural way to test your stylesheets when you use Saxon "out of the box." The steps are as follows:

1. Ensure you have Java installed on your machine. Saxon will work with JDK 1.4 or later. Saxon is pure Java code, and so it will run on any platform that supports Java, but I will usually assume that you are using a Windows machine.

2. Download the Saxon-B processor from `http://sf.net/saxon`. Choose the most recent version of Saxon-B for Java, and unzip the download file into a suitable directory, for example `c:\saxon`.

3. Bring up an MSDOS-style console window (use Start ➪ Run, and type "cmd").

4. Type the following at the command prompt:

```
java -jar c:\saxon\saxon9.jar -a -s:hello.xml
```

5. Admire the HTML displayed on the standard output.

If you want to view the output using your browser, simply save the command line output as an HTML file, in the following manner:

```
java -jar c:\saxon\saxon8.jar -a -s:hello.xml -o:hello.html
```

(Using the command prompt in Windows isn't much fun. If you're a Unix fan, install Cygwin. Most editors have the ability invoke a command line processor that is generally much more usable than the one provided by the operating system. I use UltraEdit, but there are many other choices available.)

Using Saxon on .NET

The Saxon XSLT processor also runs on the .NET platform. You'll need to make sure that .NET (either version 1.1 or 2.0) is installed — if it's not already present on your machine, it's a free download from Microsoft. Download the latest version of Saxon-B for .NET from `http://sf.net/saxon`, and unzip the download file into a directory such as `c:\saxon`.

You can then run it using the command line:

```
c:\saxon\Transform -a -s:hello.xml -o:hello.html
```

If you want to develop applications with this product, you'll need to install Saxon in the Global Assembly Cache, but for running from the command line, this isn't necessary.

Using the Altova XSLT processor

You can obtain the freestanding AltovaXML product from `www.altova.com`. The current version at the time of writing is AltovaXML 2008. This includes separate XSLT 1.0 and 2.0 processors, and an XQuery engine. The product installs by default into `c:\Program Files\Altova\AltovaXML2008`. Assuming this directory is on your PATH, you can then run our example transformation with the command line:

```
AltovaXML -in hello.xml -xslt2 hello.xsl -out hello.html
```

Using XMLSpy

If you have installed XMLSpy, use File ➪ Open to open the stylesheet file `hello.xsl`, then F10 (or the XSL Transformation icon) to run a transformation. In the next dialog box, select the source file `hello.xml`, and click OK. The output is displayed as shown in Figure 1-5. You can switch between the `Text` and `Browser` tabs at the bottom of the output window to see either the generated HTML or the result as it will appear in the browser.

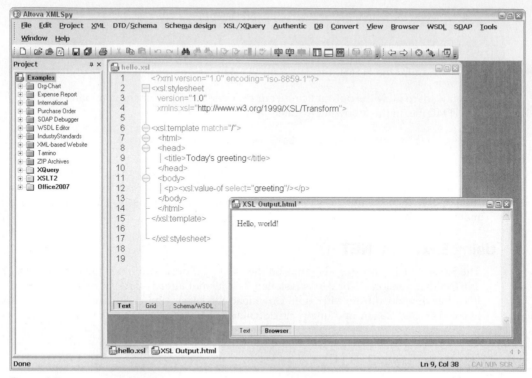

Figure 1-5

Using Stylus Studio

Stylus Studio uses its own built-in XSLT processor by default. This only supports XSLT 1.0, but that's fine for this example.

First open the stylesheet using File ⇨ Open. The next step is to create a scenario (that is a transformation task). Click the "..." button next to the "Create Scenario" drop-down box. In the resulting dialog box (shown in Figure 1-6), define a name for the scenario (so that next time you run the task you can simply select it from the drop-down) and browse to the source XML file in the "Source XML URL" box. Then click the green triangle icon (with hover text "Preview Result") to run the transformation. The output appears in a new window, and you can again switch between a source HTML view and a browser view, or an Explorer-style tree view of the result tree if you prefer.

If you want to use XSLT 2.0 with Stylus Studio, choose the Processor tab in the Create Scenario dialog, and choose the most recent version of Saxon from the list of processors offered (one of the nice features of Stylus is that you can use it to test that your code is portable across a range of different processors). You can then click the Settings... button to select from a range of Saxon-specific options (for example, you can choose whether or not to use schema-aware processing.) These correspond to options that are available on the Saxon command line.

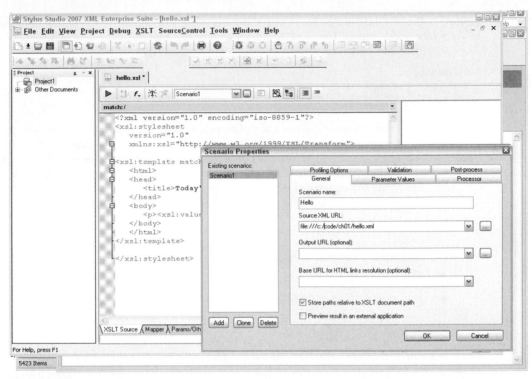

Figure 1-6

How It Works

If you've succeeded in running this example, or even if you just want to get on with reading the book, you'll want to know how it works. Let's dissect it.

```
<?xml version="1.0" encoding="iso-8859-1"?>
```

This is just the standard XML heading. The interesting point is that an XSLT stylesheet is itself an XML document. I'll have more to say about this later in the chapter. I've used `iso-8859-1` character encoding (which is the official name for the character set that Microsoft sometimes calls "ANSI") because in Western Europe and North America it's the character set that most text editors support. If you've got a text editor that supports UTF-8 or some other character encoding, feel free to use that instead.

```
<xsl:stylesheet
    version="1.0"
    xmlns:xsl="http://www.w3.org/1999/XSL/Transform">
```

This is the standard XSLT 1.0 heading. In XML terms it's an element start tag, and it identifies the document as a stylesheet. The `xmlns:xsl` attribute is an XML namespace declaration, which indicates that the prefix `xsl` is going to be used for elements defined in the W3C XSLT specification. XSLT makes extensive use of XML namespaces, and all the element names defined in the standard are prefixed with this namespace to avoid any clash with names used in your source document. The `version` attribute indicates that the stylesheet is designed to work with an XSLT 1.0 processor.

Let's move on.

```
<xsl:template match="/">
```

An `<xsl:template>` element defines a template rule to be triggered when a particular part of the source document is being processed. The attribute «match = "/"» indicates that this particular rule is triggered right at the start of processing the source document. Here «/» is a pattern that identifies the *document node* of the document: an XML document has a hierarchic structure, and in the same way as Unix uses the special filename «/» to indicate the root of a hierarchic file store, XPath uses «/» to represent the root of the XML content hierarchy.

```
<html>
<head>
   <title>Today's greeting</title>
</head>
<body>
   <p><xsl:value-of select="greeting"/></p>
</body>
</html>
```

Once this rule is triggered, the body of the template says what output to generate. Most of the template body here is a sequence of HTML elements and text to be copied into the output file. There's one exception: an `<xsl:value-of>` element, which we recognize as an XSLT instruction because it uses the namespace prefix `xsl`. This particular instruction copies the textual content of a node in the source document to the output document. The `select` attribute of the element specifies the node for which the value should be evaluated. The XPath expression «greeting» means "find the set of all `<greeting>` elements that are children of the node that this template rule is currently processing." In this case, this means the `<greeting>` element that's the outermost element of the source document. The `<xsl:value-of>` instruction then extracts the text of this element and copies it to the output at the relevant place — in other words, within the generated `<p>` element.

All that remains is to finish what we started.

```
</xsl:template>

</xsl:stylesheet>
```

Why would you want to place today's greeting in a separate XML file and display it using a stylesheet? One reason is that you might want to show the greeting in different ways, depending on the context; for example, it might be shown differently on a different device, or the greeting might depend on the time of day. In this case, you could write a different stylesheet to transform the same source document in a different way. This raises the question of how a stylesheet gets selected at runtime. There is no single answer to this question; it depends on the product you are using.

With Saxon, we used the -a option to process the XML document using the stylesheet specified in its <?xml-stylesheet?> processing instruction. Instead, we could simply have specified the stylesheet on the command line:

```
java -jar c:\saxon\saxon8.jar -s:hello.xml -xsl:hello.xsl -o:hello.html
```

Having looked at a very simple XSLT 1.0 stylesheet, let's now look at a stylesheet that uses features that are new in XSLT 2.0.

An XSLT 2.0 Stylesheet

This stylesheet is very short, but it manages to use four or five new XSLT 2.0 and XPath 2.0 features within the space of a few lines. I wrote it in response to a user enquiry raised on the xsl-list at http://www .mulberrytech.com/ (an excellent place for meeting other XSLT developers with widely varying levels of experience); so it's a real problem, not an invention. The XSLT 1.0 solution to this problem is about 60 lines of code.

Example: Tabulating Word Frequencies

The problem is simply stated: given any XML document, produce a list of the words that appear in its text, giving the number of times each word appears, together with its frequency.

Input

The input can be any XML document. I will use the text of Shakespeare's *Othello* as an example; this is provided as othello.xml in the download files for this book.

Output

The required output is an XML file that lists words in decreasing order of frequency. If you run the transformation using Kernow, the output appears as shown in Figure 1-7.

Stylesheet

Here is the stylesheet that produces this output. You can find it in wordcount.xsl.

```
<?xml version="1.0" encoding="iso-8859-1"?>
<xsl:stylesheet
    version="2.0"
    xmlns:xsl="http://www.w3.org/1999/XSL/Transform">
<xsl:output method="xml" indent="yes"/>

<xsl:template match="/">
  <wordcount>
    <xsl:for-each-group group-by="." select="
        for $w in //text()/tokenize(., '\W+')[.!=''] return lower-case($w)">
      <xsl:sort select="count(current-group())" order="descending"/>
      <word word="{current-grouping-key()}"
            frequency="{count(current-group())}"/>
```

```
        </xsl:for-each-group>
      </wordcount>
    </xsl:template>
  </xsl:stylesheet>
```

Let's see how this works.

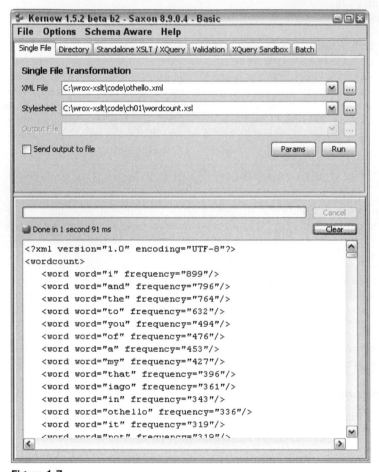

Figure 1-7

The `<xsl:stylesheet>` element introduces the XSLT namespace, as before, and tells us that this stylesheet is designed to be used with an XSLT 2.0 processor.

The `<xsl:output>` element asks for the XML output of the stylesheet to be indented, which makes it much easier for humans to read.

There is one `<xsl:template>` element, as before, which defines the code to be executed when the document node of the source document is encountered. This generates a `<wordcount>` element in the result, and within this it puts the word frequencies.

To understand the `<xsl:for-each-group>` instruction, which is new in XSLT 2.0, we first need to look at its `select` attribute. This contains the XPath 2.0 expression

```
for $w in //text()/tokenize(., '\W+')[.!=''] return lower-case($w)
```

This first selects «`//text()`», the set of all text nodes in the input tree. It then tokenizes each of these text nodes, that is, it splits it into a sequence of substrings. The tokenizing is done by applying the regular expression «\W+». Regular expressions are new in XPath 2.0 and XSLT 2.0, though they will be very familiar to users of other languages such as Perl. They provide the language with greatly enhanced text handling capability. This particular expression, «\W+», matches any sequence of one-or-more "non-word" characters, a convenient category that includes spaces, punctuation marks, and other separators. So the result of calling the `tokenize()` function is a sequence of strings containing the words that appear in the text. Because there are text nodes that contain nothing of interest, the result also includes some zero-length tokens, and we filter these out by applying the predicate «`[.! = '']`»

The XPath «for» expression now applies the function `lower-case()` to each of the strings in this sequence, producing the lower-case equivalent of the word. (Almost everything in this XPath expression is new in XPath 2.0: the `lower-case()` function, the `tokenize()` function, the «for» expression, and indeed the ability to manipulate a sequence of strings.)

The XSLT stylesheet now takes this sequence of strings and applies the `<xsl:for-each-group>` instruction to it. This processes the body of the `<xsl:for-each-group>` instruction once for each group of selected items, where a group is identified as those items that have a common value for a grouping key. In this case the grouping key is written as «`group-by="."`», which means that the values (the words) are grouped on their own value. (In another application, we might have chosen to group them by their length, or by their initial letter.) So, the body of the instruction is executed once for each distinct word, and the `<xsl:sort>` instruction tells us to sort the groups in descending order of the size of the groups (that is, the number of times each word appears). For each of the groups, we output a `<word>` element with two attributes: one attribute is the value we used as the grouping key; the other is the number of items in the group.

Don't worry if this example seemed a bit bewildering: it uses many concepts that haven't been explained yet. The purpose was to give you a feeling for some of the new features in XSLT 2.0 and XPath 2.0, which will all be explained in much greater detail elsewhere in this book.

Having dipped our toes briefly into some XSLT code, I'd now like to take a closer look at the relationship between XSLT and XPath and other XML-related technologies.

The Place of XSLT in the XML Family

XSLT is published by the World Wide Web Consortium (W3C) and fits into the XML family of standards, most of which are also developed by W3C. In this section I will try to explain the sometimes-confusing relationship of XSLT to other related standards and specifications.

XSLT and XSL Formatting Objects

XSLT started life as part of a bigger language called *XSL (Extensible Stylesheet Language)*. As the name implies, XSL was (and is) intended to define the formatting and presentation of XML documents for display on screen, on paper, or in the spoken word. As the development of XSL proceeded, it became clear that this was usually a two-stage process: first a structural transformation, in which elements are selected, grouped and reordered; and then a formatting process in which the resulting elements are rendered as ink on paper, or pixels on the screen. It was recognized that these two stages were quite independent, so XSL was split into two parts: XSLT for defining transformations; and "the rest" — which is still officially called XSL, though most people prefer to call it *XSL-FO (XSL Formatting Objects)* — for the formatting stage.

XSL-FO is nothing more than another XML vocabulary, in which the objects described are areas of the printed page and their properties. Since this is just another XML vocabulary, XSLT needs no special capabilities to generate this as its output. XSL-FO is outside the scope of this book. It's a big subject. XSL-FO provides wonderful facilities to achieve high-quality typographical output of your documents. However, for many people translating documents into HTML for presentation by a standard browser is quite good enough, and that can be achieved using XSLT alone, or if necessary, by using XSLT in conjunction with Cascading Style Sheets (CSS or CSS2), which I shall return to shortly.

> *It's best to avoid the term XSL, because it's used with so many different meanings. It's the proper name for XSL Formatting Objects, but many people use it to mean XSLT. It's also used in older Microsoft documents to refer to their obsolete WD-xsl language, which was issued as part of Internet Explorer 4 before XSLT was standardized in 1999.*

XSLT and XPath

Halfway through the development of XSLT 1.0, it was recognized that there was a significant overlap between the expression syntax in XSLT for selecting parts of a document and the XPointer language being developed for linking from one document to another. To avoid having two separate but overlapping expression languages, the two committees decided to join forces and define a single language, *XPath*, which would serve both purposes. XPath 1.0 was published on the same day as XSLT 1.0, November 16, 1999.

XPath acts as a sublanguage within an XSLT stylesheet. An XPath expression may be used for numerical calculations or string manipulations, or for testing Boolean conditions, but its most characteristic use (and the one that gives it its name) is to identify parts of the input document to be processed. For example, the following instruction outputs the average price of all the books in the input document:

```
<xsl:value-of select="avg(//book/@price)"/>
```

Here, the `<xsl:value-of>` element is an instruction defined in the XSLT standard, which causes a value to be written to the output document. The `select` attribute contains an XPath expression, which calculates the value to be written: specifically, the average value of the `price` attributes on all the `<book>` elements. (The `avg()` function too is new in XPath 2.0.)

Following its publication, the XPath specification increasingly took on a life of its own, separate from XSLT. Several DOM implementations (including Microsoft's) allowed you to select nodes within a DOM tree structure, using a method such as `selectNodes(XPath)`, and this feature is now included in the current version of the standard, DOM3. Subsets of XPath are used within the XML Schema language and in XForms for defining validation conditions, and bindings of XPath to other languages such as

Perl are multiplying. Perhaps most important of all, the designers of XQuery decided to make their language a pure superset of XPath. The language has also proved interesting to academics, and a number of papers have been published analyzing its semantics, which provides the basis for optimized implementations.

XSLT and XML Namespaces

XSLT is designed on the basis that *XML namespaces* are an essential part of the XML standard. So when the XSLT standard refers to an XML document, it always means an XML document that conforms to the XML Namespaces specification, which can be found at `http://www.w3.org/TR/REC-xml-names`.

Namespaces play an important role in XSLT. Their purpose is to allow you to mix tags from two different vocabularies in the same XML document. We've already seen how a stylesheet can mix elements from the target vocabulary (for example HTML or XSL-FO) with elements that act as XSLT instructions. Here's a quick reminder of how namespaces work:

❏ Namespaces are identified by a Uniform Resource Identifier (URI). This can take a number of forms. One form is the familiar URL, for example `http://www.wrox.com/namespace`. Another form, not fully standardized but being used in some XML vocabularies, is a URN, for example `urn:biztalk-org:biztalk:biztalk_1`. The detailed form of the URI doesn't matter, but it is a good idea to choose one that will be unique. One good way of achieving this is to use the domain name of your own website. But don't let this confuse you into thinking that there must be something on the website for the URI to point to. The namespace URI is simply a string that you have chosen to be different from other people's namespace URIs; it doesn't need to point to anything.

❏ The latest version, XML Namespaces 1.1, allows you to use an International Resource Identifier (IRI) rather than a URI. The main difference is that this permits characters from any alphabet (for example, Chinese); it is no longer confined to ASCII. In practice, most XML parsers have always allowed you to use any characters you like in a namespace URI.

❏ Since namespace URIs are often rather long and use special characters such as «/», they are not used in full as part of the element and attribute names. Instead, each namespace used in a document can be given a short nickname, and this nickname is used as a prefix of the element and attribute names. It doesn't matter what prefix you choose, because the real name of the element or attribute is determined only by its namespace URI and its local name (the part of the name after the prefix). For example, all my examples use the prefix `xsl` to refer to the namespace URI `http://www.w3.org/1999/XSL/Transform`, but you could equally well use the prefix `xslt`, so long as you use it consistently.

❏ For element names, you can also declare a default namespace URI, which is to be associated with unprefixed element names. The default namespace URI, however, does not apply to unprefixed attribute names.

A namespace prefix is declared using a special pseudo-attribute within any element start tag, with the form:

```
xmlns:prefix = "namespace-URI"
```

This declares a namespace prefix, which can be used for the name of that element, for its attributes, and for any element or attribute name contained in that element. The default namespace, which is used for elements having no prefix (but not for attributes), is similarly declared using a pseudo-attribute:

```
xmlns = "namespace-URI"
```

XML Namespaces 1.1 became a Recommendation on February 4, 2004, and the XSLT 2.0 specification makes provision for XSLT processors to work with this version, though it isn't required. Apart from the largely cosmetic change from URIs to IRIs mentioned earlier, the main innovation is the ability to undeclare a namespace, using syntax of the form «xmlns:prefix="""». This is particularly intended for applications like SOAP messaging, where an XML payload document is wrapped in an XML envelope for transmission. Without namespace undeclarations, there is a tendency for namespaces used in the SOAP envelope to stick to the payload XML when this is removed from the envelope, which can cause problems — for example, it can invalidate a digital signature attached to the document.

XSLT and CSS

Why are there two stylesheet languages, XSL (that is, XSLT plus XSL Formatting Objects) as well as Cascading Style Sheets (CSS and CSS2)?

It's only fair to say that in an ideal world there would be a single language in this role, and that the reason there are two is that no one was able to invent something that achieved the simplicity and economy of CSS for doing simple things, combined with the power of XSL for doing more complex things.

CSS is mainly used for rendering HTML, but it can also be used for rendering XML directly, by defining the display characteristics of each XML element. However, it has serious limitations. It cannot reorder the elements in the source document, it cannot add text or images, it cannot decide which elements should be displayed and which omitted, neither can it calculate totals or averages or sequence numbers. In other words, it can only be used when the structure of the source document is already very close to the final display form.

Having said this, CSS is simple to write, and it is very economical in machine resources. It doesn't reorder the document, and so it doesn't need to build a tree representation of the document in memory, and it can start displaying the document as soon as the first text is received over the network. Perhaps, most important of all, CSS is very simple for HTML authors to write, without any programming skills. In comparison, XSLT is far more powerful, but it also consumes a lot more memory and processor power, as well as training budget.

It's often appropriate to use both tools together. Use XSLT to create a representation of the document that is close to its final form, in that it contains the right text in the right order, and then use CSS to add the finishing touches, by selecting font sizes, colors, and so on. Typically, you would do the XSLT processing on the server and the CSS processing on the client (in the browser); so, another advantage of this approach is that you reduce the amount of data sent down the line, which should improve response time for your users and postpone the next expensive bandwidth increase.

XSLT and XML Schemas

One of the biggest changes in XSLT 2.0, and one of the most controversial, is the integration of XSLT with the XML Schema language. XML Schema provides a replacement for DTDs as a way of specifying the structural constraints that apply to a class of documents; unlike DTDs, an XML Schema can regulate the content of the text as well as the nesting of the elements and attributes. Many of the industry vocabularies being used to define XML interchange standards are specified using XML Schema definitions. For example, several of the XML vocabularies for describing music, which I alluded to earlier in the chapter, have an XML Schema to define their rules, and this schema can be used to check the conformance of individual documents to the standard in question.

When you write a stylesheet, you need to make assumptions about the structure of the input documents it is designed to process and the structure of the result documents it is designed to produce. With

XSLT 1.0, these assumptions were implicit; there was no formal way of stating the assumptions in the stylesheet itself. As a result, if you try applying a stylesheet to the wrong kind of input document, the result will generally be garbage.

The idea of linking XSLT and XML Schema was driven by two main considerations:

❑   There should, in principle, be software engineering benefits if a program (and a stylesheet is indeed a program) makes explicit assertions about its expected inputs and outputs. These assertions can lead to better and faster detection of errors, often enabling errors to be reported at compile time that otherwise would only be reported the first time the stylesheet was applied to some test data that happened to exercise a particular part of the code.

❑   The more information that's available to an XSLT processor at compile time, the more potential it has to generate optimal code, giving faster execution and better use of memory.

So why the controversy? It's mainly because XML Schema itself is less than universally popular. It's an extremely complex specification that's very hard to read, and when you discover what it says, it appears to be full of rules that seem artificial and inconsistent. It manages at the same time to be specified in very formal language, and yet to have a worryingly high number of bugs that have been fixed through published errata. Although there are good books that present XML Schema in a more readable way, they achieve this by glossing over the complications, which means that the error messages you get when you do something wrong can be extremely obscure. As a result, there has been a significant amount of support for an alternative schema language, Relax NG, which as it happens was co-developed by the designer of XSLT and XPath, James Clark, and is widely regarded as a much more elegant approach.

The XSL and XQuery Working Groups responded to these concerns by ensuring that support for XML Schema was optional, both for implementors and for users. This has largely silenced the objections.

The signs are that XML Schema is here to stay, whether people like it or not. It has the backing of all the major software vendors such as IBM, Oracle, and Microsoft, and it has been adopted by most of the larger user organizations and industries. And like so many things that the IT world has adopted as standards, it may be imperfect but it does actually work. Meanwhile, to simplify the situation rather cruelly, Relax NG is taking the role of the Apple Mac: the choice of the cognoscenti who judge a design by its intrinsic quality rather than by cold-blooded cost-benefit analysis.

As I've already mentioned, W3C is not an organization that likes to let a thousand flowers bloom. It is not a loose umbrella organization in which each working group is free to do its own thing. There are strong processes that ensure the working groups cooperate and strive to reconcile their differences. There is therefore a determination to make all the specifications work properly together, and the message was that if XML Schema had its problems, then people should work together to get them fixed. XSLT and XML Schema come from the same stable, so they were expected to work together. And now that the specs are finished and products are out, I think users are starting to discover that they can work together beneficially.

Chapter 4 provides an overview of how stylesheets and schemas are integrated in XSLT 2.0, and Chapter 19 provides a worked example of an application that uses this capability. When I first developed this application for the book (which I did at the same time as I developed the underlying support in Saxon), I was pleasantly surprised to see that I really was getting benefits from the integration. At the simplest level, I really liked the immediate feedback you get when a stylesheet generates output that does not conform to the schema for the result document, with error messages that point straight to the offending line in the stylesheet. This makes for a much faster debugging cycle than does the old approach of putting the finished output file through a schema validator as a completely separate operation.

XSLT and XQuery

XQuery is a separate specification from W3C, designed to allow data in XML documents to be queried. It can operate on single documents, or on collections containing millions of documents held in an XML database.

Functionally, XQuery offers a subset of the capabilities of XSLT. You could regard it as XSLT without the template rules, and without some of the extra features such as the ability to do grouping, or to format dates and times, or to import modules and selectively override them. It would be a mistake, however, to think that being a smaller language makes XQuery a poor relation. The relative simplicity of XQuery does indeed make it harder to write large and complex applications, but it does bring two significant advantages: the language is easier to learn, especially for those coming from a SQL background, and it is easier to optimize, especially when running against gigabytes of data preloaded and preindexed in an XML database.

XQuery has XPath 2.0 as a subset. This makes it very much a member of the same family as XSLT. The two languages have a great deal in common, most importantly their type system. There are no formal facilities in the W3C specifications that allow XSLT and XQuery to be mixed in a single application, but because the processing models are so closely aligned, many implementations allow one language to be called from the other. Saxon in fact implements both languages as different surface syntaxes for the same underlying processing engine.

There are some applications for which XSLT is definitely better suited, particularly document publishing. There are others where XQuery is the only sensible choice, notably searching for data in large XML databases. There's a third class of applications, especially message conversion, where either language will do the job, and where the choice is largely a matter of personal preference. My advice would be to use XQuery if it's a very small application and XSLT if it's bigger, largely because in my experience it's easier to write XSLT code that's adaptable to change and reusable in different applications.

The History of XSL

Like most of the XML family of standards, XSLT was developed by the World Wide Web Consortium (W3C), a coalition of companies orchestrated by Tim Berners-Lee, the inventor of the Web. There is an interesting page on the history of XSL, and styling proposals generally, at http://www.w3.org/Style/History/.

> *Writing history is a tricky business. Sharon Adler, the chair of the XSL Working Group, tells me that her recollections of events are very different from the way I describe them. This just goes to show that the documentary record is a very crude snapshot of what people were actually thinking and talking about. Unfortunately, though, it's all that we've got.*

Prehistory

HTML was originally conceived by Berners-Lee (www.w3.org/MarkUp/draft-ietf-iiir-html-01.txt) as a set of tags to mark the logical structure of a document; headings, paragraphs, links, quotes, code sections, and the like. Soon, people wanted more control over how the document looked; they wanted to achieve the same control over the appearance of the delivered publication as they had with printing and paper. So, HTML acquired more and more tags and attributes to control presentation; fonts, margins, tables, colors, and all the rest that followed. As it evolved, the documents being published became more and more browser-dependent, and it was seen that the original goals of simplicity and universality were starting to slip away.

The remedy was widely seen as separation of content from presentation. This was not a new concept; it had been well developed through the 1980s in the development of *Standard Generalized Markup Language* (*SGML*).

Just as XML was derived as a greatly simplified subset of SGML, so XSLT has its origins in an SGML-based standard called *DSSSL (Document Style Semantics and Specification Language)*. DSSSL (pronounced *Dissel*) was developed primarily to fill the need for a standard device-independent language to define the output rendition of SGML documents, particularly for high-quality typographical presentation. SGML was around for a long time before DSSSL appeared in the early 1990s, but until then the output side had been handled using proprietary and often extremely expensive tools, geared toward driving equally expensive phototypesetters, so that the technology was really taken up only by the big publishing houses.

Michael Sperberg-McQueen and Robert F. Goldstein presented an influential paper at the WWW '94 conference in Chicago under the title *A Manifesto for Adding SGML Intelligence to the World-Wide Web*. You can find it at `http://tigger.uic.edu/~cmsmcq/htmlmax.html`.

The authors presented a set of requirements for a stylesheet language, which is as good a statement as any of the aims that the XSL designers were trying to meet. As with other proposals from around that time, the concept of a separate transformation language had not yet appeared, and a great deal of the paper is devoted to the rendition capabilities of the language. There are many formative ideas, however, including the concept of fallback processing to cope with situations where particular features are not available in the current environment.

It is worth quoting some extracts from the paper here:

> *Ideally, the stylesheet language should be declarative, not procedural, and should allow stylesheets to exploit the structure of SGML documents to the fullest. Styles must be able to vary with the structural location of the element: paragraphs within notes may be formatted differently from paragraphs in the main text. Styles must be able to vary with the attribute values of the element in question: a quotation of type "display" may need to be formatted differently from a quotation of type "inline"...*

> *At the same time, the language has to be reasonably easy to interpret in a procedural way: implementing the stylesheet language should not become the major challenge in implementing a Web client.*

> *The semantics should be additive: It should be possible for users to create new stylesheets by adding new specifications to some existing (possibly standard) stylesheet. This should not require copying the entire base stylesheet; instead, the user should be able to store locally just the user's own changes to the standard stylesheet, and they should be added in at browse time. This is particularly important to support local modifications of standard DTDs.*

> *Syntactically, the stylesheet language must be very simple, preferably trivial to parse. One obvious possibility: formulate the stylesheet language as an SGML DTD, so that each stylesheet will be an SGML document. Since the browser already knows how to parse SGML, no extra effort will be needed.*

> *We recommend strongly that a subset of DSSSL be used to formulate stylesheets for use on the World Wide Web; with the completion of the standards work on DSSSL, there is no reason for any community to invent their own style-sheet language from scratch. The full DSSSL standard may well be too demanding to implement in its entirety, but even if that proves true, it provides only an argument for defining a subset of DSSSL that must be supported, not an argument for rolling our own. Unlike home-brew specifications, a subset of a standard comes with an automatically predefined growth path. We expect to work on the formulation of a usable, implementable subset of DSSSL for use in WWW stylesheets, and invite all interested parties to join in the effort.*

In late 1995, a W3C-sponsored workshop on stylesheet languages was held in Paris. In view of the subsequent role of James Clark as editor of the XSLT Recommendation, it is interesting to read the notes of his contribution on the goals of DSSSL, which can be found at `http://www.w3.org/Style/951106_Workshop/report1.html#clark`.

Here are a few selected paragraphs from these notes:

> *DSSSL contains both a transformation language and a formatting language. Originally the transformation was needed to make certain kinds of styles possible (such as tables of contents). The query language now takes care of that, but the transformation language survives because it is useful in its own right.*

> *The language is strictly declarative, which is achieved by adopting a functional subset of Scheme. Interactive stylesheet editors must be possible.*

> *A DSSSL stylesheet very precisely describes a function from SGML to a flow object tree. It allows partial stylesheets to be combined ("cascaded" as in CSS): some rule may override some other rule, based on implicit and explicit priorities, but there is no blending between conflicting styles.*

James Clark closed his talk with the remark:

> *Creating a good, extensible style language is hard!*

One suspects that the effort of editing the XSLT 1.0 Recommendation didn't cause him to change his mind.

The First XSL Proposal

Following these early discussions, the W3C set up a formal activity to create a stylesheet language proposal. The remit for this group specified that it should be based on DSSSL.

As an output of this activity came the first formal proposal for XSL, dated August 27, 1997. Entitled *A Proposal for XSL*, it lists 11 authors: James Clark (who works for himself), five from Microsoft, three from Imso Corporation, one from ArborText, and one (Henry Thompson) from the University of Edinburgh. The document can be found at `http://www.w3.org/TR/NOTE-XSL.html`.

The section describing the purpose of the language is worth reading.

> *XSL is a stylesheet language designed for the Web community. It provides functionality beyond CSS (e.g. element reordering). We expect that CSS will be used to display simply structured XML documents and XSL will be used where more powerful formatting capabilities are required or for formatting highly structured information such as XML structured data or XML documents that contain structured data.*

> *Web authors create content at three different levels of sophistication given as follows:*

> ❑ *markup: relies solely on a declarative syntax*

> ❑ *script: additionally uses code "snippets" for more complex behaviors*

> ❑ *program: uses a full programming language*

> *XSL is intended to be accessible to the "markup" level user by providing a declarative solution to most data description and rendering requirements. Less common tasks are accommodated through a graceful escape to a familiar scripting environment. This approach is familiar to the Web publishing community as it is modeled after the HTML/JavaScript environment.*

The powerful capabilities provided by XSL allow:

❏ *formatting of source elements based on ancestry/descendency, position, and uniqueness*

❏ *the creation of formatting constructs including generated text and graphics*

❏ *the definition of reusable formatting macros*

❏ *writing-direction independent stylesheets*

❏ *extensible set of formatting objects*

The authors then explained carefully why they had felt it necessary to diverge from DSSSL and described why a separate language from CSS (Cascading Style Sheets) was thought necessary.

They then stated some design principles:

❏ XSL should be straightforwardly usable over the Internet.

❏ XSL should be expressed in XML syntax.

❏ XSL should provide a declarative language to do all common formatting tasks.

❏ XSL should provide an "escape" into a scripting language to accommodate more sophisticated formatting tasks and to allow for extensibility and completeness.

❏ XSL will be a subset of DSSSL with the proposed amendment. *(As XSL was no longer a subset of DSSSL, they cannily proposed amending DSSSL so it would become a superset of XSL.)*

❏ A mechanical mapping of a CSS stylesheet into an XSL stylesheet should be possible.

❏ XSL should be informed by user experience with the FOSI stylesheet language.

❏ The number of optional features in XSL should be kept to a minimum.

❏ XSL stylesheets should be human-legible and reasonably clear.

❏ The XSL design should be prepared quickly.

❏ XSL stylesheets shall be easy to create.

❏ Terseness in XSL markup is of minimal importance.

As a requirements statement, this doesn't rank among the best. It doesn't read like the kind of list you get when you talk to users and find out what they need. It's much more the kind of list that designers write when they know what they want to produce, including a few political concessions to the people who might raise objections. But if you want to understand why XSLT became the language it did, this list is certainly evidence of the thinking.

The language described in this first proposal contains many of the key concepts of XSLT as it finally emerged, but the syntax is virtually unrecognizable. It was already clear that the language should be based on templates that handled nodes in the source document matching a defined pattern, and that the language should be free of side effects, to allow "progressive rendering and handling of large documents." I'll explore the significance of this requirement in more detail on page 34, and discuss its implications on the way stylesheets are designed in Chapter 17. The basic idea is that if a stylesheet is expressed as a collection of completely independent operations, each of which has no external effect other than generating part of the output from its input (for example, it cannot update global variables), then it becomes possible to generate any part of the output independently if that particular part of the input changes. Whether the XSLT language actually achieves this objective is still an open question.

The first Working Draft of XSL (not to be confused with the Proposal) was published on August 18, 1998, and the language started to take shape, gradually converging on the final form it took in the November 16, 1999 Recommendation through a series of Working Drafts, each of which made radical changes, but kept the original design principles intact.

> **A Recommendation is the most definitive of documents produced by the W3C. It's not technically a standard, because standards can only be published by government-approved standards organizations. But I will often refer to it loosely as "the standard" in this book.**

Saxon

At this point it might be a good idea to clarify how I got involved in the story. In 1998 I was working for the British computer manufacturer ICL, a part of Fujitsu. Fujitsu, in Japan, had developed an object database system, later marketed as Jasmine, and I was using this technology to build content management applications for large publishers. We developed a few successful large applications, but found that it was too complex for people who wanted something in six weeks rather than six months. So I was asked to look at what we could do with XML, which was just appearing on the horizon.

I came to the conclusion that XML looked like a good thing, but that there wasn't any software. So I developed the very first early versions of Saxon to provide a proof-of-concept demonstration. At that stage Saxon was just a Java library, not an XSLT processor, but as the XSL standards developed I found that my own ideas were converging more and more with what the W3C working group was doing, and I started implementing the language as it was being specified. ICL had decided that its marketing resources were spread thinly over too many products, and so the management took the imaginative decision to make the technology available as open source. Seventeen days after the XSLT 1.0 specification was published in November 1999, I announced the first conformant implementation. And on the day it was published, I started work on the first edition of this book.

When the book was published, the XSL Working Group invited me to join and participate in the development of XSLT 1.1. Initially, being based in the United Kingdom and with limited time available for the work, my involvement was fairly sporadic. But early in 2001 I changed jobs and joined Software AG, which wanted me to take a full role in the W3C work. The following year James Clark pulled out of the Working Group, and I stepped into his shoes as editor.

The reason I'm explaining this sequence of events is that I hope it will help you to understand the viewpoint from which this book is written. When I wrote the first edition I was an outsider, and I felt completely free to criticize the specification when I felt it necessary. I have tried to retain an objective approach in the present edition, but as editor of the language spec it is much more difficult to be impartial. I've tried to keep a balance: it wouldn't be fair to use the book as a platform to push my views over those of my colleagues of the working group, but at the same time, I've made no effort to be defensive about decisions that I would have made differently if they had been left to me.

Software AG continued to support my involvement in the W3C work (on the XQuery group as well as the XSL group), along with the development of Saxon and the writing of this book, through till February 2004, at which point I left to set up my own company, Saxonica.

Beyond XSLT 1.0

After XSLT 1.0 was published, the XSL Working Group responsible for the language decided to split the requirements for enhancements into two categories: XSLT 1.1 would standardize a small number of urgent features that vendors had already found necessary to add to their products as extensions, while XSLT 2.0 would handle the more strategic requirements that needed further research.

A working draft of XSLT 1.1 was published on December 12, 2000. It described three main enhancements to the XSLT 1.0 specification: the ability to produce multiple output documents, the ability to use temporary trees to create a multi-pass transformation, and standard bindings to extension functions written in Java or ECMAScript.

For a number of reasons XSLT 1.1 never got past the working draft stage. This was partly because of controversy surrounding the Java language bindings, but more particularly because it was becoming clearer that XSLT 2.0 would be a fairly radical revision of the language, and the Working Group didn't want to do anything in 1.1 that would get in the way of achieving the 2.0 goals. There were feelings, for example, that the facility for temporary trees might prejudice the ability to support sequences in 2.0, a fear which as it happens proved largely unfounded.

Convergence with XQuery

By the time work on XSLT 2.0 was starting, the separate XQuery Working Group in W3C had created a draft of its own language.

While the XSL Working Group had identified the need for a transformation language to support a self-contained part of the formatting process, XQuery originated from the need to search large quantities of XML documents stored in a database.

Work on an XML Query Language had started as early as 1998. A workshop was held in December 1998, and you can find all 66 position papers presented at this workshop at `http://www.w3.org/TandS/QL/QL98/pp.html`. It's interesting to see how the participants saw the relationship with XSL, as it was then known. The Microsoft position paper states the belief that a query language could be developed as an extension of XSLT, but in this it is almost alone. Many of the participants came from a database background, with ideas firmly rooted in the tradition of SQL and object database languages such as OQL, and to these people, XSL didn't look remotely like a query language. But in the light of subsequent events, it's interesting to read the position paper from the XSL Working Group, which states in its summary:

1. The query language should use XSL patterns as the basis for information retrieval.

2. The query language should use XSL templates as the basis for materializing query results.

3. The query language should be at least as expressive as XSL is, currently.

4. Development of the pattern and transformation languages should remain in the XSL Working Group.

5. A coordination group should ensure either that a single query language satisfies all working group requirements or that all W3C query languages share an underlying query model.

(Remember that XPath had not yet been identified as a separate language, and that the expressions that later became XPath were then known as patterns.)

This offer to coordinate, and the strong desire to ensure consistency among the different W3C specifications, can be seen as directly leading to the subsequent collaboration between the two working groups to define XPath 2.0.

The XQuery group started meeting in September 1999. The first published requirements document was published the following January (`http://www.w3.org/TR/2000/WD-xmlquery-req-20000131`). It included a commitment to compatibility with XML Schema, and a rather cautiously worded promise to "take into consideration the expressibility and search facilities of XPath when formulating its algebra and query syntax." July 2000 saw a revised requirements document that included a selection of queries that the language must be able to express. The first externally visible draft of the XQuery language was published in February 2001 (see `http://www.w3.org/TR/2001/WD-xquery-20010215/`), and it was at this stage that the collaboration between the two working groups began in earnest.

The close cooperation between the teams developing the two languages contrasts strangely with the somewhat adversarial position adopted by parts of the user community. XSLT users were quick to point out that XSLT 1.0 satisfied every single requirement in the first XQuery requirements document, and could solve all the use cases published in the second version in August 2000. At the same time, users on the XQuery side of the fence have often been dismissive about XSLT, complaining about its verbose syntax and sometimes arcane semantics. Even today, when the similarities of the two languages at a deep level are clearly apparent, there is little overlap between their user communities: I find that most users of the XQuery engine in Saxon have no XSLT experience. The difference between XSLT and XQuery is in many ways a difference of style rather than substance, but users often feel strongly about style.

The Development of XSLT 2.0 and XPath 2.0

The requirements for XSLT 2.0 and XPath 2.0 were published on February 14, 2001. In the case of the XPath 2.0 requirements, the document was written jointly by the two working groups. You can find the documents at the following URLs:

```
http://www.w3.org/TR/2001/WD-xslt20req-20010214
```

```
http://www.w3.org/TR/2001/WD-xpath20req-20010214
```

Broadly, the requirements fall into three categories:

❑   Features that are obviously missing from the current standards and that would make users' lives much easier, for example, facilities for grouping related nodes, extra string-handling and numeric functions, and the ability to read text files as well as XML documents.

❑   Changes desired by the XML Query Working Group. The difficulty at this stage was that the Query group did not just want additions to the XPath language; they wanted fundamental changes to its semantics. Many members of the XQuery group felt they could not live with some of the arbitrariness of the way XPath handled data types generally, and node-sets in particular, for example the fact that «a = 1» tests whether there is some «a» that equals one, whereas «a − 1 = 0» tests whether the first «a» equals one.

❑   Features designed to exploit and integrate with XML Schema. The W3C XML Schema specification had reached an advanced stage (it became a Candidate Recommendation on October 20, 2000), and implementations were starting to appear in products. The thinking was that if the schema specified that a particular element contains a number or a date (for example), then it ought to be possible to use this knowledge when comparing or sorting dates within a stylesheet.

The development of XSLT 2.0, culminating in the Recommendation of January 23, 2007, proved to be a long drawn out process. There were early delays getting agreement with the XQuery group on the details of XPath 2.0. This took a long time firstly, because of the number of people involved; secondly, because of the very different places where people were coming from (the database community and the document community have historically been completely isolated from each other, and it took a lot of talking before people started to understand each others' positions); and finally, because of the sheer technical difficulty of finding a workable design that offered the right balance between backwards compatibility and rigorous, consistent semantics. Later, when the specification appeared to be all but finished, it still took a couple of years to get through the public reviews demanded by the W3C process, which generated thousands of detailed comments.

But that's all history now. Let's look next at the essential characteristics of XSLT 2.0 as a language.

XSLT 2.0 as a Language

What are the most significant characteristics of XSLT as a language, which distinguish it from other languages? In this section I shall pick five of the most striking features: the fact that it is written in XML syntax, the fact that it is a language free of side effects, the fact that processing is described as a set of pattern-matching rules, the fact that it has a type system based on XML Schema, and the fact that it is a two-language system in which one language (XPath) is embedded in another (XSLT).

Use of XML Syntax

As we've seen, the use of SGML syntax for stylesheets was proposed as long ago as 1994, and it seems that this idea gradually became the accepted wisdom. It's difficult to trace exactly what the overriding arguments were, and when you find yourself writing something like:

```
<xsl:variable name="y">
   <xsl:call-template name="f">
      <xsl:with-param name="x"/>
   </xsl:call-template>
</xsl:variable>
```

to express what in other languages would be written as «y = f(x);», then you may find yourself wondering how such a decision came to be made.

The most obvious arguments for expressing XSLT stylesheets in XML are perhaps as follows:

❑   There is already an XML parser in the browser; so it keeps the footprint small if this can be reused.

❑   Everyone had got fed up with the syntactic inconsistencies between HTML/XML and CSS and didn't want the same thing to happen again.

❑   The Lisp-like syntax of DSSSL was widely seen as a barrier to its adoption; so it would be better to have a syntax that was already familiar in the target community.

❑   Many existing popular template languages (including simple ASP and JSP pages) are expressed as an outline of the output document with embedded instructions; so this is a familiar concept.

❑   The lexical apparatus is reusable, for example Unicode support, character and entity references, whitespace handling, namespaces.

❑   Visual development tools remove the inconvenience of typing lots of angle brackets.

❑   It's often useful to have a stylesheet as the input or output of a transformation; so it's a benefit if a stylesheet can read and write other stylesheets.

In my experience, the most pervasive argument is the last one: it's surprising how often complex applications construct or modify stylesheets on the fly. But like it or not, the XML-based syntax is now an intrinsic feature of the language that has both benefits and drawbacks. It does make the language verbose, but in the end, the number of keystrokes has very little bearing on the ease or difficulty of solving particular transformation problems.

In XSLT 2.0, the long-windedness of the language has been reduced considerably by increasing the expressiveness of the non-XML part of the syntax, namely XPath expressions. Many computations that required five lines of XSLT code in 1.0 can now be expressed in a single XPath expression. Two constructs in particular led to this simplification: the conditional expression (if..then..else) in XPath 2.0; and the ability to define a function in XSLT (using <xsl:function>) that can be called directly from an XPath expression. To take the example discussed earlier, if you replace the template «f» by a user-written function «f», you can replace the five lines in the example with:

```
<xsl:variable name="y" select="f($x)"/>
```

The decision to base the XSLT syntax on XML has proved its worth in several ways that I would not have predicted in advance:

- ❑ It has proved very easy to extend the syntax. Adding new elements and attributes is trivial; there is no risk of introducing parsing difficulties when doing so, and it is easy to manage backwards compatibility. (In contrast, extending XQuery's non-XML syntax without introducing parsing ambiguities is a highly delicate operation.)

- ❑ The separation of XML parsing from XSLT processing leads to good error reporting and recovery in the compiler. It makes it much easier to report the location of an error with precision and to report many errors in one run of the compiler. This leads to a faster development cycle.

- ❑ It makes it easier to maintain stylistic consistency between different constructs in the language. The discipline of defining the language through elements and attributes creates a constrained vocabulary with which the language designers must work, and these constraints impose a certain consistency of design.

No Side Effects

The idea that XSL should be a declarative language free of side effects appears repeatedly in the early statements about the goals and design principles of the language, but no one ever seems to explain *why*: what would be the user benefit?

A function or procedure in a programming language is said to have side effects if it makes changes to its environment; for example, if it can update a global variable that another function or procedure can read, or if it can write messages to a log file, or prompt the user. If functions have side effects, it becomes important to call them the right number of times and in the correct order. Functions that have no side effects (sometimes called pure functions) can be called any number of times and in any order. It doesn't matter how many times you evaluate the area of a triangle, you will always get the same answer; but if the function to calculate the area has a side effect such as changing the size of the triangle, or if you don't know whether it has side effects or not, then it becomes important to call it once only.

I expand further on this concept in the section on Computational Stylesheets in Chapter 17, page 985.

It is possible to find hints at the reason why this was considered desirable in the statements that the language should be equally suitable for batch or interactive use, and that it should be capable of *progressive rendering*. There is a concern that when you download a large XML document, you won't be able to see anything on your screen until the last byte has been received from the server. Equally, if a small change were made to the XML document, it would be nice to be able to determine the change needed to the screen display, without recalculating the whole thing from scratch. If a language has side effects, then the order of execution of the statements in the language has to be defined, or the final result becomes unpredictable. Without side effects, the statements can be executed in any order, which means it is possible, in principle, to process the parts of a stylesheet selectively and independently.

What it means in practice to be free of side effects is that you cannot update the value of a variable. This restriction is something many users find very frustrating at first, and a big price to pay for these rather remote benefits. But as you get the feel of the language and learn to think about using it the way it was designed to be used, rather than the way you are familiar with from other languages, you will find you stop thinking about this as a restriction. In fact, one of the benefits is that it eliminates a whole class of bugs from your code. I shall come back to this subject in Chapter 17, where I outline some of the common design patterns for XSLT stylesheets and, in particular, describe how to use recursive code to handle situations where in the past you would probably have used updateable variables to keep track of the current state.

Rule-Based

The dominant feature of a typical XSLT stylesheet is that it consists of a set of template rules, each of which describes how a particular element type or other construct should be processed. The rules are not arranged in any particular order; they don't have to match the order of the input or the order of the output, and in fact there are very few clues as to what ordering or nesting of elements the stylesheet author expects to encounter in the source document. It is this that makes XSLT a declarative language, because you specify what output should be produced when particular patterns occur in the input, as distinct from a procedural program where you have to say what tasks to perform in what order.

This rule-based structure is very like CSS, but with the major difference that both the patterns (the description of which nodes a rule applies to), and the actions (the description of what happens when the rule is matched) are much richer in functionality.

Example: Displaying a Poem

Let's see how we can use the rule-based approach to format a poem. Again, we haven't introduced all the concepts yet, and so I won't try to explain every detail of how this works, but it's useful to see what the template rules actually look like in practice.

Input

Let's take this poem as our XML source. The source file is called poem.xml, and the stylesheet is poem.xsl.

```
<poem>
    <author>Rupert Brooke</author>
    <date>1912</date>
    <title>Song</title>
```

```
      <stanza>
         <line>And suddenly the wind comes soft,</line>
         <line>And Spring is here again;</line>
         <line>And the hawthorn quickens with buds of green</line>
         <line>And my heart with buds of pain.</line>
      </stanza>
      <stanza>
         <line>My heart all Winter lay so numb,</line>
         <line>The earth so dead and frore,</line>
         <line>That I never thought the Spring would come again</line>
         <line>Or my heart wake any more.</line>
      </stanza>
      <stanza>
         <line>But Winter's broken and earth has woken,</line>
         <line>And the small birds cry again;</line>
         <line>And the hawthorn hedge puts forth its buds,</line>
         <line>And my heart puts forth its pain.</line>
      </stanza>
   </poem>
```

Output

Let's write a stylesheet such that this document appears in the browser, as shown in Figure 1-8.

Stylesheet

It starts with the standard header.

```
<xsl:stylesheet
   xmlns:xsl="http://www.w3.org/1999/XSL/Transform"
   version="1.0">
```

Now we write one template rule for each element type in the source document. The rule for the `<poem>` element creates the skeleton of the HTML output, defining the ordering of the elements in the output (which doesn't have to be the same as the input order). The `<xsl:value-of>` instruction inserts the value of the selected element at this point in the output. The `<xsl:apply-templates>` instructions cause the selected child elements to be processed, each using its own template rule.

```
<xsl:template match="poem">
   <html>
   <head>
      <title><xsl:value-of select="title"/></title>
   </head>
   <body>
      <xsl:apply-templates select="title"/>
      <xsl:apply-templates select="author"/>
      <xsl:apply-templates select="stanza"/>
      <xsl:apply-templates select="date"/>
   </body>
   </html>
</xsl:template>
```

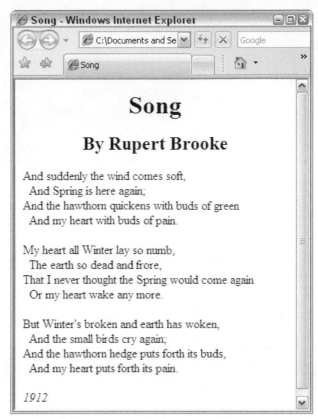

Figure 1-8

In XSLT 2.0 we could replace the four `<xsl:apply-templates>` instructions with one, written as follows:

```
<xsl:apply-templates select="title, author, stanza, date"/>
```

This takes advantage of the fact that the type system for the language now supports ordered sequences. The «,» operator performs list concatenation and is used here to form a list containing the `<title>`, `<author>`, `<stanza>`, and `<date>` elements in that order. Note that this includes all the `<stanza>` elements, so in general this will be a sequence containing more than four items.

The template rules for the `<title>`, `<author>`, and `<date>` elements are very simple; they take the content of the element (denoted by «select = "."»), and surround it within appropriate HTML tags to define its display style.

```
<xsl:template match="title">
   <div align="center">
      <h1><xsl:value-of select="."/></h1>
   </div>
</xsl:template>
```

```
<xsl:template match="author">
   <div align="center">
      <h2>By <xsl:value-of select="."/></h2>
   </div>
</xsl:template>

<xsl:template match="date">
   <p><i><xsl:value-of select="."/></i></p>
</xsl:template>
```

The template rule for the `<stanza>` element puts each stanza into an HTML paragraph, and then invokes processing of the lines within the stanza, as defined by the template rule for lines:

```
<xsl:template match="stanza">
   <p><xsl:apply-templates select="line"/></p>
</xsl:template>
```

The rule for `<line>` elements is a little more complex: if the position of the line within the stanza is an even number, it precedes the line with two non-breaking-space characters (` `). The `<xsl:if>` instruction tests a boolean condition, which in this case calls the `position()` function to determine the relative position of the current line. It then outputs the contents of the line, followed by an empty HTML `<br>` element to end the line.

```
<xsl:template match="line">
   <xsl:if test="position() mod 2 = 0">  </xsl:if>
   <xsl:value-of select="."/><br/>
</xsl:template>
```

And to finish off, we close the `<xsl:stylesheet>` element:

```
</xsl:stylesheet>
```

Although template rules are a characteristic feature of the XSLT language, we'll see that this is not the only way of writing a stylesheet. In Chapter 17, I will describe four different design patterns for XSLT stylesheets, only one of which makes extensive use of template rules. In fact, the Hello World stylesheet I presented earlier in this chapter doesn't make any real use of template rules; it fits into the design pattern I call *fill-in-the-blanks*, because the stylesheet essentially contains the fixed part of the output with embedded instructions saying where to get the data to put in the variable parts.

Types Based on XML Schema

I have described three characteristics of the XSLT language (the use of XML syntax, the principle of no side-effects, and the rule-based processing model) that were essential features of XSLT 1.0 and that have been retained essentially unchanged in XSLT 2.0. The fourth characteristic is new in XSLT 2.0, and creates a fundamental change in the nature of XSLT as a language. This is the adoption of a type system based on XML Schema.

There are two aspects to the type system of any programming language. The first is the set of types that are supported (for example, integers, strings, lists, tuples), together with the mechanisms for creating user-defined types. The second aspect is the rules that the language enforces to ensure type-correctness.

XSLT 1.0 had a very small set of types (integers, booleans, strings, node-sets, and result tree fragments), and the rules it applied were what is often called "weak typing": this means that the processor would always attempt to convert the value supplied in an expression or function call to the type that was required in that context. This makes for a very happy-go-lucky environment: if you supply an integer where a string is expected, or vice versa, nothing will break.

XSLT 2.0 has changed both aspects of the type system. There is now a much richer set of types available (and this set is user-extensible), and the rules for type checking are stricter.

We will look at the implications of this in greater detail in Chapters 4 and 5.

A Two-Language System: XSLT and XPath

The final characteristic of XSLT that I want to explore is its use of XPath as an embedded sublanguage. This is not unlike the way SQL is often embedded in other languages, and it is done for the same reason — it allows XPath to be used in many different contexts.

The fact that XPath was designed to be embedded in other language has some specific consequences:

❏ An embedded language does not need to have every conceivable piece of functionality. In the language of computer science, it does not need to be computationally complete. In more practical terms, it can be restricted to being able to access variables but not to declare them, to call functions but not to define them, to navigate around nodes in a tree but not to create new nodes.

❏ An embedded language can depend on a context established by the host language in which it is embedded. If an embedded language is to be well integrated with a host language, then they should share information so that the user does not need to declare things twice, once for each language. The information that XPath shares with its host language is called the context. This can be divided into information that's available at compile time (the static context), and information that's not available until runtime (the dynamic context). Both aspects of the XPath context are described in Chapter 7 of this book.

❏ An embedded language can be called by its host language, but cannot make calls in the other direction. XSLT can invoke XPath, but not the other way around. This means that there is incomplete composability of expressions when the XSLT language is considered as a whole. However, XPath can invoke XSLTindirectly by means of function calls. Some functionality, notable conditional and iteration constructs, are duplicated in XSLT and XPath.

The syntax of XPath has some unusual features, which reflect the fact that it amalgamates ideas from a number of different sources. One can identify three different syntactic styles within XPath expressions:

❏ **Conventional programming expressions:** This allows the same kind of expressions, infix operators, and function calls as many other programming languages; an example is an expression such as «$x + 1 = round($y) mod 3». Such expressions trace their roots via programming languages such as Algol and Fortran back to the notations of elementary mathematics.

❏ **Path expressions:** These perform hierarchic selection of a node within a tree, an example is «/a/b//c». These expressions can be seen as a generalization of the syntax used by operating systems to identify files within a hierarchic filestore.

❏ **Predicate logic:** This includes the «for», «some» and «every» expressions, for example «for $i in //item[@price > 30] return $i/@code». These expressions, which are new in XPath 2.0, derive from the tradition of database query languages (SQL, the object database language OQL, and precursors to XQuery), which can be seen as adaptations of the notation of mathematical symbolic logic.

Some other factors that have influenced the design of the XPath syntax include:

❑ A decision that XPath should have no reserved words. This means that any name that is legal as an XML element name (which includes names such as «and» and «for») should be legal in a path expression, without any need for escaping. As a result, all names used with some other role, for example function names, variable names, operator names, and keywords such as «for», have to be recognizable by their context.

❑ In both the original applications for XPath (that is, XSLT and XPointer), the language was designed to be embedded within the attributes of an XML document. It therefore has no mechanisms of its own for character escaping, relying instead on the mechanisms available at the XML level (such as numeric character references and entity references). This also made the designers reluctant to use symbols such as «&&», which would require heavy escaping. This principle has been abandoned in XPath 2.0 with the introduction of the operators «<<» and «>>»; however, these operators are not likely to be used very often.

❑ There was originally an expectation that XPath expressions (especially in an XPointer environment) would often be used as fragment identifiers in a URI. This usage of XPointer never really took off, but it meant there was a reluctance to use special characters such as «#», «%», and «?» that have special significance in URIs.

Despite its disparate syntactic roots and its lexical quirks, XPath has managed to integrate these different kinds of expression surprisingly well. In particular, it has retained full composability within itself, so any kind of expression can be nested inside any other.

Summary

This introductory chapter answered the following questions about XSLT:

❑ What kind of language is it?

❑ How is it used?

❑ Where does it fit into the XML family?

❑ Where does it come from and why was it designed the way it is?

You now know that XSLT is a declarative high-level language designed for transforming the structure of XML documents; that it has two major applications: data conversion and presentation; and that it can be used at a number of different points in the overall application architecture, including at data capture time, at delivery time on the server, and at display time on the browser. You also have some idea why XSLT has developed in the way it has.

Now it's time to start taking an in-depth look inside the language to see how it does this job. In the next chapter, we look at the way transformation is carried out by treating the input and output as tree structures, and using patterns to match particular nodes in the input tree and define what nodes should be added to the result tree when the pattern is matched.

2

The XSLT Processing Model

This chapter takes a bird's-eye view of what an XSLT processor does. We start by looking at a system overview: what are the inputs and outputs of the processor?

Then we look in some detail at the data model, in particular the structure of the tree representation of XML documents. An important message here is that XSLT transformations do not operate on XML documents as text; they operate on the abstract tree-like information structure represented by the markup.

Having established the data model, I will describe the processing sequence that occurs when a source document and a stylesheet are brought together. XSLT is not a conventional procedural language; it consists of a collection of template rules defining output that is produced when particular patterns are matched in the input. As seen in Chapter 1, this rule-based processing structure is one of the distinguishing features of the XSLT language.

Finally, we look at the way in which variables and expressions can be used in an XSLT stylesheet, and also look at the various data types available.

XSLT: A System Overview

This section looks at the nature of the transformation process performed by XSLT, concentrating on the inputs and outputs of a transformation.

A Simplified Overview

The core task of an XSLT processor is to apply a stylesheet to a source document and produce a result document. This is shown in Figure 2-1.

As a first approximation we can think of the source document, the stylesheet, and the result document as each being an XML document. XSLT performs a *transformation* process because the *output* (the result document) is the same kind of object as the *input* (the source document). This has immediate benefits: for example, it is possible to do a complex transformation as a series of simple transformations, and it is possible to do transformations in either direction using the same technology.

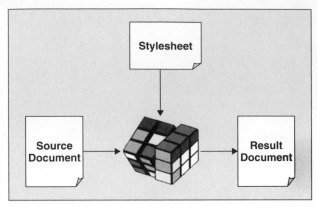

Figure 2-1

The choice of Rubik's cube to illustrate the transformation process is not entirely whimsical. The mathematics of Rubik's cube relies on group theory, which is where the notion of closure comes from: every operation transforms one instance of a type into another instance of the same type. We're transforming XML documents rather than cubes, but the principle is the same.

The name *stylesheet* has stuck for the document that defines the transformation, despite the fact that XSLT is often used for tasks that have nothing to do with styling. The name reflects the reality that a very common kind of transformation performed using XSLT is to define a display style for the information in the source document, so that the result document contains information from the source document augmented with information controlling the way it is displayed on some output device.

Trees, Not Documents

In practice, we don't always want the input or output to be XML in its textual form. If we want to produce HTML output (a very common requirement), we want to produce it directly, rather than having an XML document as an intermediate form. When the Firefox browser displays the result of an XSLT transformation, it doesn't serialize the result to HTML and then parse the textual HTML; rather, it works directly from the result tree as a data structure in memory. Similarly, we might want to take input from a database or (say) an LDAP directory, or an EDI message, or a data file using comma-separated-values syntax. We don't want to spend a lot of time converting these into serial XML documents if we can avoid it, nor do we want another raft of converters to install.

Instead, XSLT defines its operations in terms of a data model (called XDM) in which an XML document is represented as a *tree*. The tree is an abstract data type. There is no defined application programming interface (API) and no defined data representation, only a conceptual model that defines the objects in the tree, their properties, and their relationships. The XDM tree is similar in concept to the W3C DOM, except that the Document Object Model (DOM) does have a defined API. Some implementors do indeed use the DOM as their internal tree structure. Others use a data structure that corresponds more closely to the XDM specification, while some use optimized internal data structures that are only distantly related to this model. It's a conceptual model we are describing, not something that necessarily exists in an implementation.

The data model for XSLT trees is shared with the XPath and XQuery specifications, which ensures that data can be freely exchanged between these three languages (it also means you can take your pick as to what the "X" in "XDM" stands for). With XSLT and XPath, this is of course essential, because XSLT always retrieves data from a source document by executing XPath expressions. There is a description of this data model later in this chapter, and full details are in Chapter 4.

Taking the inputs and output of the XSLT processors as trees produces a new diagram (see Figure 2-2). The formal conformance rules say that an XSLT processor must be able to read a stylesheet and use it to transform a source tree into a result tree. This is the part of the system shown in the oval box. There's no official requirement to handle the parts of the process shown outside the box, namely the creation of a source tree from a source XML document (known as *parsing*), or the creation of a result XML document from the result tree (called *serialization*). In practice, though, most real products are likely to handle these parts as well.

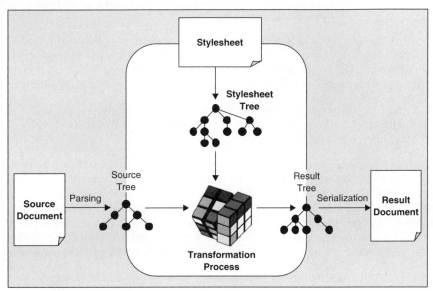

Figure 2-2

Different Output Formats

Although the final process of converting the result tree to an output document is outside the conformance rules of the XSLT standard, this doesn't mean that XSLT has nothing to say on the subject.

The main control over this process is the `<xsl:output>` element. This element defines four output formats or methods, namely `xml`, `html`, `xhtml`, and `text`. In each case a result tree is written to a single output file.

❑ With the `xml` output method, the output file is an XML document . We'll see later that it need not be a complete XML document; it can also be an XML fragment. The `<xsl:output>` element allows the stylesheet writer some control over the way in which the XML is written, for example, the character encoding used and the use of CDATA sections.

❑ With the `html` output method, the output file is an HTML document, typically HTML 4.0, though products may support other versions if they wish. With HTML output, the XSLT processor recognizes many of the conventions of HTML and structures the output accordingly. For example, it recognizes elements such as `<hr>` that have a start tag and no end tag, as well as the special rules for escape characters within a `<script>` element. It may also (if it chooses) generate references to built-in entities such as «é».

- ❑ Selecting html as the output method doesn't in any way automate the process of creating valid HTML, nor does it cause the processor to check that the output is valid HTML (with one exception — it will report the presence of characters that aren't allowed in HTML). All it does is to tell the serializer to use HTML conventions when turning the nodes in the tree back into markup.

- ❑ The xhtml output method, as one might expect, is a compromise between the xml and html output methods. Generally speaking, it follows the rules of the xml output method, but sticks to the conventions described in the XHTML specification that are designed to make the output display properly in browsers that were written to handle HTML. Such conventions include, for example, outputting an empty <br> element as
 (with a space before the «/»), and outputting an empty <p> element as <p></p>.

- ❑ The text output method is designed to allow output in any other text-based format. For example, the output might be a comma-separated-values file, a document in Microsoft's Rich Text Format (RTF), or in Adobe's Portable Document Format (PDF); or, it might be an electronic data interchange message, or a script in SQL or JavaScript. It's entirely up to you.

If the <xsl:output> element is omitted, the processor makes an intelligent guess, choosing HTML if the output starts with an <html> element in the null namespace, XHTML if it starts with an <html> element in the XHTML namespace, and XML otherwise.

Implementations may include output methods other than these four, but this is outside the scope of the standard. One mechanism provided by several products is to feed the result tree to a user-supplied document handler. In the case of Java products, this will generally be written to conform to the ContentHandler interface defined as part of the SAX2 API specification (which is part of the core class library in Java). Most implementations also provide mechanisms to capture the result as a DOM tree. Remember that if you use the result tree directly in this way, the XSLT processor will not serialize the tree, and therefore nothing you say in the <xsl:output> declaration will have any effect.

So, while the bulk of the XSLT Recommendation describes the transformation process from a source tree to a result tree, there is one section that describes another process, serialization. Because the serialization of a document tree as a file is a process that is relevant not only to XSLT but also to XQuery and potentially other applications in the future, the detail is no longer in the XSLT 2.0 Recommendation, but forms a W3C specification in its own right (see http://www.w3.org/TR/xslt-xquery-serialization/). For similar reasons, it has a chapter of its own in this book (Chapter 15). The name *serialization* is used because it turns a tree structure into a stream of characters or bytes, but it mustn't be confused with serialization in distributed object systems such as Component Object Model (COM) or Java, which produces a serial file representation of a COM or Java object. XSLT processors can implement this at their discretion, and it fits into our diagram as shown in Figure 2-3.

Multiple Inputs and Outputs

In real life, the processing model is further complicated because there can be multiple inputs and outputs. Specifically:

- ❑ There can be multiple input documents. The stylesheet can use the doc() or document() functions (described in Chapter 13, page 750) to load secondary input documents, based on URI references held in the source document or the stylesheet. Each input document is processed as a tree in its own right, in exactly the same way as the principal input document. It is also possible to supply additional input documents as parameters to the stylesheet, or to read an entire collection of documents using the collection() function.

❑ The stylesheet may also consist of multiple documents. There are two declarations that can be used in the stylesheet, `<xsl:include>` and `<xsl:import>`, to load additional stylesheet modules and use them as extensions of the principal module. Splitting a stylesheet in this way allows modularity: in a complex environment different aspects of processing can be described in component stylesheets that can be incorporated into several different parent stylesheets. There is a detailed discussion of how to split a stylesheet into modules in Chapter 3.

❑ A single run of the XSLT processor can produce multiple output documents. This allows a single source document to be split into several output files: for example, the input might contain the text of an entire book, while the output contains one HTML file for each chapter, all connected using suitable hyperlinks. This capability, which is provided by the `<xsl:result-document>` element described in Chapter 6, is new in XSLT 2.0, though many vendors provided similar facilities as extensions to their XSLT 1.0 processors.

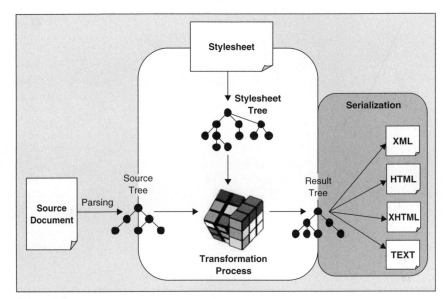

Figure 2-3

The XDM Tree Model

Let's now look at the tree model used in XSLT and XPath, in a little more detail. It's defined in the W3C Specification *XQuery 1.0 and XPath 2.0 Data Model (XDM)* (http://www.w3.org/TR/xpath-datamodel): you can read XDM as standing for either XQuery Data Model or XPath Data Model (or even XML Data Model) as you prefer.

The XDM tree model is similar in many ways to the XML DOM. However, there are a number of differences of terminology and some subtle differences of detail. I'll point some of these out as we go along.

XML as a Tree

In this section, I will describe the XDM tree model of an XML document, and show how it relates to textual XML files containing angle brackets.

This isn't actually how the XDM specification does it: it adopts a more indirect approach, showing how the data model relates to the XML InfoSet (an abstract description of the information content of an XML document), and the Post Schema Validation Infoset (PSVI), which is defined in the XML Schema specifications to define the information that becomes available as a result of schema processing. The InfoSet is described in a W3C specification at `http://www.w3.org/TR/xml-infoset/`. *The PSVI is described in the W3C Schema recommendations at* `http://www.w3.org/TR/xmlschema-1/`.

At a simple level, the equivalence of the textual representation of an XML document with a tree representation is very straightforward.

Example: An XML Tree

Consider a document like this:

```
<definition>
   <word>export</word>
   <part-of-speech>vt</part-of-speech>
   <meaning>Send out (goods) to another country.</meaning>
   <etymology>
      <language>Latin</language>
      <parts>
      <part>
         <prefix>ex</prefix>
         <meaning>out (of)</meaning>
      </part>
      <part>
         <word>portare</word>
         <meaning>to carry</meaning>
      </part>
      </parts>
   </etymology>
</definition>
```

We can consider each piece of text as a leaf node, and each element as a containing node, and build an equivalent tree structure, as shown in Figure 2-4. I show the tree after the stripping of all whitespace nodes (in XSLT this can be achieved using the `<xsl:strip-space>` declaration; in other environments, it may be something you can control from the processor's API). In this diagram each node is shown with potentially three pieces of information:

❑   In the top cell, the *kind* of node

❑   In the middle cell, the *name* of the node

❑   In the bottom one, its *string value*

For the document node and for elements, I showed the string value simply as an asterisk; in fact, the string value of these nodes is defined as the concatenation of the string values of all the element and text nodes at the next level of the tree.

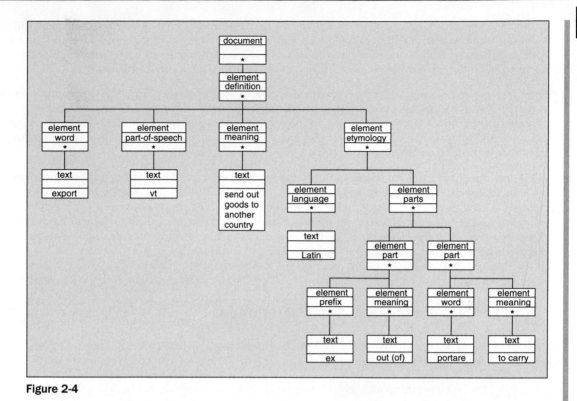

Figure 2-4

It is easy to see how other aspects of the XML document, for example, attributes and processing instructions, can be similarly represented in this tree view by means of additional kinds of nodes.

At the top of every tree, there is a *root* node (trees in computer science always grow upside down). Usually the root will be a document node, but we will look at other cases later on.

> *The terminology here has changed since XPath 1.0. What was the root node in XPath 1.0 is now called a document node. In XPath 2.0, it is possible to have element nodes, or indeed any kind of node, that have no parent. Any node that has no parent, whatever kind of node it is, can be considered to be the root of a tree. So the term "root" no longer refers to a particular kind of node, but rather to any node that has no parent, and is therefore at the top of a tree, even if that tree contains just one node.*

An XDM document node performs the same function as the document node in the DOM model, in that it doesn't correspond to any particular part of the textual XML document, but you can regard it as representing the XML document as a whole. The children of the document node are the top-level elements, comments, processing instructions, and so on.

In the XML specification the outermost element is described as the "root or document element." In XDM this element is not the root of the tree (because it has a parent, the document node), and the term "document element" is not normally used, because it is too easily confused with "document node." I prefer to call it the "outermost element," because that seems to cause least confusion.

The XDM tree model can represent every well-formed XML document, but it can also represent structures that are not well-formed according to the XML definition. Specifically, in well-formed XML, there must be a single outermost element containing all the other elements and text nodes. This element can be preceded and followed by comments and processing instructions, but it cannot be preceded or followed by other elements or text nodes.

XDM does not enforce this constraint — the document node can have any children that an element might have, including multiple elements and text nodes in any order. The document node might also have no children at all. This corresponds to the XML rules for the content of an *external general parsed entity*, which is a freestanding fragment of XML that can be incorporated into a well-formed document by means of an entity reference. I shall sometimes use the term *well balanced* to refer to such an entity. This term is not used in the XDM specification; rather, I have borrowed it from the largely forgotten XML fragment interchange proposal (`http://www.w3.org/TR/xml-fragment.html`). The essential feature of a well-balanced XML fragment is that every element start tag is balanced by a corresponding element end tag.

Example: Well-balanced XML Fragment

The following example shows an XML fragment that is well balanced but not well formed, as there is no enclosing element:

```
The <noun>cat</noun> <verb>sat</verb> on the <noun>mat</noun>.
```

The corresponding XDM tree is shown in Figure 2-5. In this case it is important to retain whitespace, so spaces are shown using the symbol ♦.

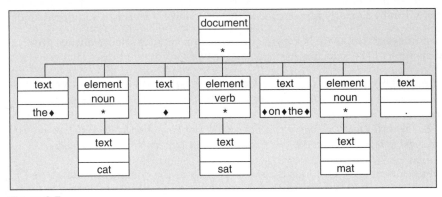

Figure 2-5

The string value of the document node in this example is simply:

```
The cat sat on the mat.
```

In practice the input and output of an XSLT transformation will usually be well-formed documents, but it is very common for temporary trees constructed in the course of processing to have more than one element as a child of the document node.

Nodes in the Tree Model

An XDM tree is made up of nodes. There are seven kinds of node. The different kinds of node correspond fairly directly to the components of the source XML document:

Node Kind	Description
Document node	The document node is a singular node; there is one for each document. Do not confuse the document node with the document element, which in a well-formed document is the outermost element that contains all others. A document node never has a parent, so it is always the root of a tree.
Element node	An element is a part of a document bounded by start and end tags, or represented by a single empty-element tag such as `<TAG/>`. Try to avoid referring to elements as tags: elements generally have two tags, a start tag and an end tag.
Text node	A text node is a sequence of consecutive characters in a PCDATA part of an element. Text nodes are always made as big as possible: there will never be two adjacent text nodes in the tree, because they will always be merged into one. (This is the theory. Some implementations don't always follow this rule)
Attribute node	An attribute node includes the name and value of an attribute written within an element start tag (or empty element tag). An attribute that was not present in the tag, but which has a default value defined in the DTD or Schema, is also represented as an attribute node on each separate element instance. A namespace declaration (an attribute whose name is «xmlns» or whose name begins with «xmlns:») is, however, *not* represented by an attribute node in the tree.
Comment node	A comment node represents a comment written in the XML source document between the delimiters «<!--» and «-->»
Processing instruction node	A processing instruction node represents a processing instruction written in the XML source document between the delimiters «<?» and «?>». The PITarget from the XML source is taken as the node's name and the rest of the content as its value. Note that the XML declaration `<?xml version="1.0"?>` is not a processing instruction, even though it looks like one, and it is not represented by a node in the tree.
Namespace node	A namespace node represents a namespace declaration, except that it is copied to each element that it applies to. So each element node has one namespace node for every namespace declaration that is in scope for the element. The namespace nodes belonging to one element are distinct from those belonging to another element, even when they are derived from the same namespace declaration in the source document.

There are several possible ways of classifying these nodes. We could distinguish those that can have children (element and document nodes), those that can have a parent (everything except the document node), those that have a name (elements, attributes, namespaces, and processing instructions) or those that have their own textual content (attributes, text, comments, processing instructions, and namespace nodes). Because each of these criteria gives a different possible class hierarchy, the XDM model instead leaves the hierarchy completely flat, and defines all these characteristics for all nodes. Where a characteristic isn't applicable to a particular kind of node, XDM generally defines its value as an empty sequence, though sometimes when you access the property from a real XPath expression what you actually get back is a zero-length string.

So if we show the class hierarchy in UML notation, we get the simple diagram shown in Figure 2-6.

UML (the Unified Modeling Language) provides a set of diagrammatic conventions for object-oriented analysis and design. For information about UML, see `http://www.uml.org/`.

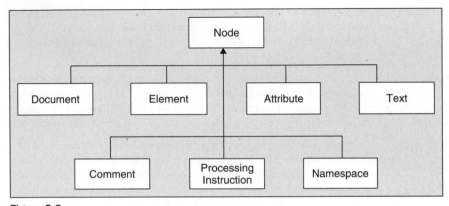

Figure 2-6

This diagram looks superficially similar to the tree we saw earlier, but this time I'm not showing a specific tree, I'm showing a class hierarchy: the boxes represent classes or types, and the arrow represents an *is-a-kind-of* relationship; for example a comment *is-a-kind-of* node. The earlier diagram was just one example of a particular tree, whereas now we are considering the structure of all possible trees.

I've already hinted at some of the properties and relationships of these nodes. Let's look at the properties and relationships in more detail, and then add them to the diagram.

The Name of a Node

In general, a node has a name. Nodes can (and often do) have simple names, but in the general case, node names are qualified by the namespace they are in.

An element or attribute name as written in a textual XML document is a *lexical QName*. (QName stands for Qualified Name.) A lexical QName has two parts: the prefix, which is the part of the QName before the «:» as written in the source XML, and the local part, which is the part of the QName after the «:». If there is no colon, the prefix is the zero-length string. For example, «xsl:stylesheet» is a lexical QName, with prefix «xsl» and local-name «stylesheet».

In XDM, however, a name is represented by an *expanded QName*. This is an atomic value whose type is xs:QName. The expanded QName has three parts, though there is no explicit syntax for displaying it. The three parts are the prefix, the namespace URI, and the local part.

The namespace URI is derived from the prefix used in the source document, by finding the namespace declarations that are in scope where it is used, while the local name is again the part of the lexical QName after the «:». The prefix is retained as part of the expanded name, to allow a document to be serialized using the author's original choice of prefixes, but it is not considered to be a significant part of the name. So the expanded QName corresponding to the lexical QName «xsl:stylesheet» has namespace URI http://www.w3.org/1999/XSL/Transform (assuming the standard namespace declarations are used), and local part «stylesheet», while also retaining the prefix «xsl» for display purposes.

The name of an element or attribute node is accessible, as an xs:QName value, using the node-name() function defined in Chapter 13. The namespace URI and local-name parts of the name are also separately accessible (as strings) using the functions namespace-uri() and local-name(). If you want the original lexical QName, it can be obtained using the name() function.

Document nodes, comments, and text nodes have no name, and for these, the node-name() function returns the empty sequence, which is the XDM equivalent of a null value. (Note that this differs from the DOM, where names such as «#comment» are used.)

The name of a processing instruction is the *PITarget* from the source XML: this contains a local name but no namespace URI, as processing instruction names are not subject to namespace rules.

The name of a namespace node is, by convention, the namespace prefix from the original namespace declaration (without the «xmlns:» part). For example, the namespace declaration «xmlns:acme="http://acme.com/xml"» generates a namespace node with name «acme», while the default namespace declaration «xmlns="http://acme.com/xml"» generates a namespace node whose name is effectively null (represented as an empty sequence). The name of a namespace node, like the name of any other node, is an xs:QName, but the namespace URI part of this xs:QName is always null, while the local-name part holds the namespace prefix.

The String Value of a Node

Every node has a string value, which is a sequence of Unicode characters. The string value depends on the kind of node, as shown in the table below:

Node Kind	String Value
Text	The text as it appears in the source XML document, except that the XML parser will have replaced every end-of-line sequence (for example, CRLF as used on Windows platforms) by a single newline (x0A) character.
Comment	The text of the comment, minus the delimiters.
Processing instruction	The data part of the source processing instruction, not including the whitespace that separates it from the PITarget. For example, given the processing instruction <?ignore this?>, the string value is «this».
Attribute	The string value is the value of the attribute as written, modified by any whitespace normalization done by the XML parser and schema processor. The detailed rules for whitespace normalization of attributes depend on the attribute type.
Document or element	The concatenation of the string values of all the element and text children of this node. Or, to look at it another way: the concatenation of all the PCDATA contained in the element (or for the document node, the entire document) after stripping out all markup. (This again differs from the DOM, where the nodeValue property in these cases is null.)
Namespace	By convention, the URI of the namespace being declared.

The string value of a node can be obtained by using the `string()` function described in Chapter 13. This should not be confused with the `xs:string()` constructor, which works differently when applied to a node: it extracts the typed value of the node, as described in the next section, and then converts the typed value to a string. This might not give precisely the same result. For example, if the attribute is declared as an `xs:boolean`, and the actual attribute is written as «ok="1"», then the result of «string(@ok)» will be the string «1», while the result of «xs:string(@ok)» will be the string «true».

In XPath 2.0, most operations use the typed value of a node, which is discussed in the next section. The only time the string value is used directly is when you explicitly call the `string()` function, or one or two other functions such as `string-length()` or `normalize-space()`. But the result differs from the typed value only if the node has been validated using a schema.

The Typed Value of a Node

The typed value of a node reflects the content of the node as it appears after schema validation. The typed value is available using the `data()` function described in Chapter 13; it is also obtained implicitly as the result of the process of atomization, described on page 165.

Schema validation only applies to element and attribute nodes, so let's get the other kinds of nodes out of the way first. For every other kind of node, the typed value is the same as the string value, which is defined in the previous section. However, for document nodes, namespace nodes, and text nodes, the value is labeled as `xs:untypedAtomic`, while for comments and processing instructions it is labeled as `xs:string`. There is, as one might expect, some tortuous logic behind this apparently arbitrary distinction: labeling a value as `xs:untypedAtomic` enables the value to be used in contexts where a value other than a string is required, whereas a value labeled as `xs:string` can only be used where that is the type expected. There are plausible scenarios where one might want to use the content of document nodes, namespace nodes, and text nodes in non-string contexts, but it's hard to think of similar justifications for comments and processing instructions.

Let's return to elements and attributes, which are the cases where the typed value comes into its own.

First of all, if you're working on a document that has no schema, or that has not been validated against a schema, or if you're using an XSLT processor that doesn't support schema processing, then the typed value of an element or attribute is the same as the string value, and is labeled with the type `xs:untypedAtomic`. This is very close to the situation with XPath 1.0, which didn't support schema processing at all. It means that when you use an expression that returns an element or attribute node (for example, path expressions like «title» or «@price»), then they take on the type expected by the context where you use them. For example, you can use «@price» as a number by writing «@price * 0.8», or you can use it as a string by writing «substring-after(@price, '$')». The typed value of the attribute, which is simply the string value as written in the source document, will be converted to a number or to a string as required by the context. If the conversion fails, for example, if you try to use the value as an integer when it isn't a valid integer, then you get a runtime error.

If you have processed the document using a schema, things get more interesting. The situation where the typed value is most useful is where the schema defines a simple type for the element or attribute (or in the case of elements, a complex type with simple content — which means that the element can have attributes, but it cannot have child elements). As we will see in Chapter 4, simple types in XML Schema allow atomic values or lists of atomic values, but they don't allow child elements.

- ❏ The simple type may be an atomic type, such as xs:integer or xs:date, in which case the typed value will be the result of converting the string value to an xs:integer or xs:date value according to the rules defined by XML Schema. The value must be a valid xs:integer or xs:date, or it wouldn't have passed schema validation.

- ❏ The schema may also define the type as being a list; for example, a list of xs:integer or xs:date values. In this case the typed value is a sequence of zero or more atomic values, again following the rules defined in XML Schema.

- ❏ Another possibility is that the schema defines a union type; for example, it may allow either an xs:integer or an xs:date. The schema validator tries to interpret the value as an xs:integer (if that is the first possibility listed), and if that fails, it tries to validate it as an xs:date. The typed value returned by the data() function may then be either an xs:integer or an xs:date value.

- ❏ Lists of a union type are also allowed, so you can get back a sequence containing (say) a mixture of integers and dates.

For attributes, all types are simple types, so the above rules cover all the possibilities. For elements, however, there are additional rules to cover non-simple types:

- ❏ If the schema defines the element as having mixed content, then the typed value is the same as the string value, labeled as xs:untypedAtomic. Note that the deciding factor is that the schema allows mixed content (a mixture of element and text node children), not that the element in question actually has mixed content: in reality it might have element children, or text children, or both or neither. This is identical to the rule for processing without a schema, which means that in many cases, narrative or document-oriented XML (as opposed to data-oriented XML) will be processed in exactly the same way whether there is a schema or not. Narrative XML is characterized by heavy use of mixed content models.

- ❏ If the schema defines the element as having empty content (that is, the element is not allowed to have either element nodes or text nodes as children, though it can have attributes), then the typed value is an empty sequence.

- ❏ If the schema defines the element as having an element-only content model (that is, it can contain element nodes as children but not text nodes), then there is no typed value defined, and attempting to retrieve the typed value causes an error. This error is classified as a type error, which means it may be detected and reported either at compile time or at evaluation time. The reason that this is an error is that the typed value must always be a sequence of atomic values, and there is really no way of doing justice to the content of a structured element by representing it as such a sequence. The content is not atomic, because it only makes sense when considered in conjunction with the names of the child elements. Element-only content models tend to feature strongly in "data-oriented" XML applications.

The Type Annotation of a Node

As well as having a typed value, a node also has a type annotation. This is a reference to the type definition that was used to validate the node during schema processing. It is not available directly to applications, but it affects the outcome of a number of type-sensitive operations. For example, when you select all attributes of type xs:date by writing the path expression «//attribute(*, xs:date)» (this is described in Chapter 11), the system looks at the type annotations of the attributes to see which nodes qualify.

In the XDM specification, the type annotation is modeled as an `xs:QName` holding the name of the type in the case where the type is a globally declared schema type, or an invented name in the case where it is locally declared (not all types defined in a schema need to be named). It's reasonable to treat this as polite fiction, designed to tie up loose ends in the specification in an area where the practical details will inevitably vary from one implementation to another. Any real schema-aware XPath processor will need to have some kind of access to schema information both at compile time and at runtime, but the W3C specifications have not tried to model exactly what this should look like. In practice, the type annotation on a node is likely to be implemented as some kind of pointer into the metadata representing the cached schema information. But for defining the semantics of constructs like «`//attribute(*, xs:date)`», it's enough to assume that the node contains just the type name.

The type annotation defines the type of the content of the node, not the type of the node itself. This is an important distinction, and we'll have more to say about it when we discuss the XPath type system in Chapter 5.

You might imagine that the type annotation is redundant, because the typed value is itself an atomic value, and the atomic value itself has a label identifying its type. Very often, the type annotation of the node will be the same as the label on its typed value. However, this only works for nodes whose typed value is a single atomic value. In cases where the schema type is a list type, or a union type, the type annotation on the node is the name of the list or union type, which is not the same as the type of the individual atomic values making up the typed value. For example, if the schema type of an attribute is `xs:IDREFS` (which is defined as a list of `xs:IDREF` values), then the type annotation on the attribute node will be `xs:IDREFS`, but the items in the typed value will be labeled `xs:IDREF`. If the typed value is an empty sequence, there will be no items to carry a label, but the containing node can still be annotated as being of type `xs:IDREFS`. Similarly, if the schema type of an element allows attributes as well as integer content, the typed value will be labeled as `xs:integer`, while the element node itself will have a type annotation that refers to the name of a complex type in the schema.

There is, however, a strong relationship between the string value, the typed value, and the type annotation. In fact, with knowledge of the schema and access to a schema validator, the typed value can always be reconstructed from the string value and the type annotation.

If an element or attribute node has not been validated using a schema processor, then the type annotation will be `xs:untypedAtomic` in the case of an attribute node, or `xs:untyped` in the case of an element node.

For document, comment, processing-instruction, and namespace nodes, there is no type annotation (the value of the type annotation is an empty sequence). For text nodes, the type annotation is `xs:untypedAtomic` (but there is nothing in the language that makes use of this fact).

The Base URI of a Node

A node has a base URI. This should not be confused with its namespace URI. The base URI of a node depends on the URI of the source XML document it was loaded from, or more accurately, the URI of the external entity it was loaded from, since different parts of the same document might come from different XML entities. The base URI is used when evaluating a relative URI reference that occurs as part of the value of this node, for example an `href` attribute: this is always interpreted relative to the base URI of the node it came from.

It is possible to override this by specifying an explicit base URI using the `xml:base` attribute. For example, if an element has the attribute «`xml:base="../index.xml"`», then the base URI for this element, and for all its descendants provided they are in the same XML external entity, is the `index.xml` file in the parent directory of the file that would otherwise have provided the base URI.

The base URI is maintained explicitly only for document nodes, element nodes, and processing instruction nodes. For attributes, text nodes, and comments, and for elements and processing instructions without an explicit base URI of their own, the base URI is the same as the URI of its parent node.

For a namespace node the base URI is «()», the empty sequence. The system doesn't attempt to go to the parent node to find its base URI. This is rather a curiosity. The only time you might be interested in the base URI of a namespace node is if you are using the namespace URI as the URI of a real resource, for example a schema. But even then, the base URI will only be needed if this is a relative URI reference. W3C, after fierce debate, decided that a relative namespace URI was deprecated and implementation defined, so the working groups steered clear of defining an interpretation for it.

The fact that text nodes don't have their own base URI is a little ad hoc, because a text node need not come from the same external entity as its parent element, but it reflects the decision that text nodes should be joined up irrespective of entity boundaries.

The base URI of a node in a source document is used almost exclusively for one purpose: to resolve relative URI references when loading additional input documents using the `doc()` or `document()` functions, described in Chapter 13. The base URI is accessible using the `base-uri()` function, which is also described in Chapter 13.

The Children of a Node

A node has a sequence of child nodes. This one-to-many relationship is defined for all nodes, but the list will be empty for all nodes other than document nodes and element nodes. So you can ask for the children of an attribute, and you will get an empty sequence returned.

The children of an element are the elements, text nodes, processing instructions, and comments contained textually between its start and end tags, provided that they are not also children of some lower-level element.

The children of the document node are all the elements, text nodes, comments, and processing instructions that aren't contained in another element. For a well-formed document the children of the root node will be the outermost element plus any comments or processing instructions that come before or after the outermost element.

The attributes of an element are not regarded as children of the element; neither are its namespace nodes.

The Parent of a Node

Every node, except a node at the root of a tree, has a parent. A document node never has a parent. Other kinds of node usually have a parent, but they may also be parentless. The parent relationship is *not* the exact inverse of the child relationship: specifically, attribute nodes and namespace nodes have an element node as their parent, *but they are not considered to be children of that element*. In other cases, however, the relationship is symmetric: elements, text nodes, processing instructions, and comments are always children of their parent node, which will always be either an element or the document node.

Two nodes that are both children of the same parent are referred to as being *siblings* of each other. (In case you are not a native English speaker, the word "sibling" means "brother or sister.")

The Attributes of a Node

This relationship only exists in a real sense between element nodes and attribute nodes, and this is how it is shown on the diagram at the end of this section. It is a one-to-many relationship: one element has zero or more attributes. The relationship `hasAttributes` is defined for all nodes, but if you ask for the attributes of any node other than an element, the result will be an empty sequence.

The Namespaces of a Node

This relationship only really exists between element nodes and namespace nodes, and this is how it is shown on the diagram. It is a one-to-many relationship: one element has zero or more namespace nodes. Like the `hasAttributes` relationship, the relationship `hasNamespaces` is defined for all nodes, so if you ask for the namespaces of any node other than an element, the result will be an empty sequence.

Note that each namespace node is owned uniquely by one element. If a namespace declaration in the source document has a scope that includes many elements, then a corresponding namespace node will be generated for each one of these elements. These nodes will all have the same name and string value, but they will be distinct nodes for the purposes of counting and using the «is» operator (which tests whether its two operands are references to the same node: see Chapter 8).

Completing the UML Class Diagram

It's now possible to draw a more complete UML class diagram, as shown in Figure 2-7. In this version:

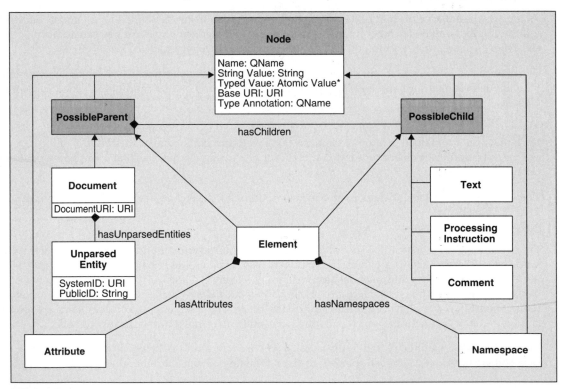

Figure 2-7

❑ I brought out `PotentialParent` and `PotentialChild` as separate (abstract) classes, to group those nodes that can be parents (document and element nodes) and those nodes that can be children (elements, text nodes, comments, and processing instructions). Abstract classes are shown as shaded boxes on the diagram. Note that elements fall into both categories. This grouping is for illustration only, and in reality the relationships `hasChildren`, `hasAttributes`, and `hasNamespaces` are available for all kinds of node, they just return an empty sequence when the node is not a document or element node.

❑ I identified the `hasChildren` relationship between an element or document node and its children.

❑ I identified the separate relationships between an element and its attributes, and between an element and its namespace nodes.

❑ I identified the additional class `UnparsedEntity`. This is not itself a node on the tree. It corresponds to an unparsed entity declaration within the document's DTD. Unparsed entities are exposed by the functions `unparsed-entity-uri()` and `unparsed-entity-public-id()` available in XSLT (see Chapter 13), but they are second-class citizens, because there is no way to create an unparsed entity in an output document.

It's worth mentioning that XDM never uses null values in the sense that SQL or Java use null values. If a node has no string value, then the value returned is the zero-length string. If a node has no children, then the value returned is the empty sequence, a sequence containing no items.

Let's look briefly at some of the other features of this model.

Document Order

Nodes within a tree have an ordering, called *document order*. Where two nodes come from the same tree, their relative position in document order is based on their position in the tree, which in turn is based on the ordering of the underlying constructs in the original textual XML document. For example, an element precedes its children in document order, and sibling nodes are listed in the same order as they appear in the original source document. By convention an element node is followed by its namespace nodes, then its attributes, and then its children, but the ordering of the namespace nodes among themselves, and of the attribute nodes among themselves, is unpredictable.

Where two nodes come from different trees, they still have a document order, but it is not predictable what it will be. In fact, any sequence of nodes can be sorted into document order, whether the nodes come from the same document or different documents, and if you sort the same sequence into document order more than once, you will always get the same result, but in the case of nodes from different documents, you can't predict which one will come first. The spec does say, however, that nodes from different documents will not be interleaved: a node from document A will never come after one node from document B and before another node from document B.

There are a number of XPath expressions that always return nodes in document order. These include all path expressions (any expression using the «/» operator), step expressions such as «ancestor::*», and expressions using the operators union (or «|»), intersect, and except. If you want to sort a sequence $seq into document order, you can do this with the trivial path expression «$seq/.», or by forming a union with the empty sequence: «$seq|()».

XPath 2.0 also includes operators to test whether one node is before or after another in document order: the expressions «$a<<$b» and «$b>>$a» both test whether node $a is before $b in document order.

When a node is copied, for example using the XSLT instruction `<xsl:copy-of>`, the new node has a new position in document order that is quite unrelated to the position of the old node.

Names and Namespaces

XSLT and XPath are designed very much with the use of XML namespaces in mind, and although many source documents may make little or no use of namespaces, an understanding of the XML Namespaces Recommendation (found in `http://www.w3.org/TR/xml-names11`) is essential.

I'll start with an overview of how namespaces work, and then get into more detail of how they are represented in the XDM data model.

Namespaces: An Overview

Expanding on the description in Chapter 1 (page 23), here's a summary of how namespaces work:

❏ A namespace declaration defines a namespace prefix and a namespace URI. The namespace prefix needs to be unique only within a local scope, but the namespace URI is supposed to be unique globally. Globally here really does mean globally — not just unique in the document, but unique across all documents around the planet. To achieve that, the advice is to use a URI based on a domain name that you control, for example, `http://www.mega-utility.com/namespace/billing`. The W3C specifications are a little ambivalent about whether the namespace name really must be a valid absolute URI, but this is good practice and some products insist on it. In most of our examples we'll use URIs beginning with «http://».

❏ Some people also recommend using a URI that leads human readers to a document on the Web that defines and documents the namespace, but this isn't mandatory. The namespace URI does not have to identify any particular resource, and even if it does, XML and XSLT processors won't go looking for it. Two namespace URIs are considered equal if they contain the same sequence of Unicode characters. This means that the two strings `file:///c:/this.dtd` and `file:///c:/THIS.DTD` are both legal namespace URIs, whether or not there is actually a file of this name, and they represent different namespaces even though when read as filenames they might identify the same file.

❏ To emphasize the point: The fact that every XSLT stylesheet uses the namespace URI `http://www.w3.org/1999/XSL/Transform` doesn't mean that you need an Internet connection before you can run a transformation. The name is just an elaborate constant, it's not the address of something that the processor has to go and fetch.

❏ A namespace declaration for a non-null prefix is written as follows. This associates the namespace prefix `my-prefix` with the namespace URI `http://my.com/namespace`:

```
<a xmlns:my-prefix="http://my.com/namespace">
```

❏ A namespace declaration may also be present for the null prefix. This is known as the default namespace. The following declaration makes `http://your.com/namespace` the default namespace URI:

```
<a xmlns="http://your.com/namespace">
```

❏ In the absence of such a declaration, an unprefixed element name is not in any namespace. I will often describe such a name as being in the null namespace, though this is not the officially correct terminology.

❏ The default namespace applies only to element names, not to attribute names; an unprefixed attribute name is always in the null namespace.

❑   You can undeclare the default namespace like this:

```
<a xmlns="">
```

This puts you back in the position you were in at the outermost level of the document: an element name with no prefix is in the null namespace.

❑   The latest version of the XML Namespaces Recommendation, version 1.1, also allows you to undeclare other namespaces, like this:

```
<a xmlns:my-prefix="">
```

This has the effect that the prefix becomes unavailable for use within this element. This feature is not widely used, but XDM allows for it.

❑   The scope of a namespace declaration is the element on which it appears plus all its children and descendants, excluding any subtree where the same prefix is undeclared or redeclared to associate it with a different URI. This scope defines where the prefix is available for use. Within this scope, any name with the given prefix is automatically associated with the given namespace URI.

Namespaces in the Data Model

A namespace-qualified name is referred to as a QName. When a QName appears in a textual XML document, it is written in the form *prefix:local-part*. For example, in the name `xsl:template`, the prefix is «xsl» and the local part is «template». XSLT refers to this form as a *lexical QName*. The real underlying name, however, is the combination of the namespace URI and the local part. When two names are compared, they are considered equivalent if they have the same namespace URI and the same local part; it is irrelevant whether or not they were written with the same prefix. The combination of a namespace URI and a local name is referred to as an *expanded QName*. An expanded QName also retains the original prefix, but this is "for information only": it is never used when names are compared.

An expanded QName is never written directly in XPath, it is purely an internal value manipulated by the system. However, in some APIs and in error messages you might sometimes see expanded QNames written out in the form «{http://my.com/namespace}local-name». This format is sometimes called Clark notation, after James Clark, the editor of the XSLT 1.0 and XPath 1.0 specifications.

The job of converting element and attribute names from lexical QNames into expanded QNames is done by the XML parser. The namespace URI of the name is found from the innermost element that carries a namespace declaration of the relevant prefix. If a name has no prefix, then its namespace URI is considered to be the default namespace URI in the case of an element name, or a null URI in the case of an attribute name.

A namespace node represents the binding of a namespace prefix to a namespace URI: it uses the node name to hold the prefix, and the string value of the node to represent the URI. In many cases, namespace nodes are redundant — you could reconstruct them from other information, such as the expanded names of elements and attributes, or from the namespace nodes on the parent element. In fact, a real implementation might well construct many namespace nodes on the fly in this way. But in some cases namespace nodes hold essential information; the explanation for this appears in the section "Namespace Sensitive Content" on the next page.

For any element, it is possible to determine all the namespace declarations in force for that element, by retrieving the associated namespace nodes. These are all made available as if the namespace declarations were repeated on that specific element. The application cannot determine where the namespace declaration actually occurred in the original document, but if there is a namespace node present for a particular element, then it follows that there was a namespace declaration either on that element or on some containing element.

Namespace undeclarations, for example «xmlns=""», or in XML Namespaces 1.1 «xmlns: ppp=""», are not represented as namespace nodes; rather they result in the *absence* of a namespace node for the namespace that has been undeclared. Without the undeclaration, the parser would create a namespace node for that namespace for every element within its scope, whether the element used it or not; the namespace undeclaration stops this happening.

Although the namespace declarations are originally written in the source document in the form of XML attributes, they are not retained as attribute nodes on the tree, and cannot be processed by looking for all the attribute nodes. Similarly, it is not possible to generate a namespace node on the result tree by creating an attribute with a name such as «xmlns:p»: such names are reserved for namespace declarations. In the data model, namespaces and attributes are quite distinct animals. XSLT 2.0 has a special instruction, <xsl:namespace>, for creating namespace nodes on the rare occasions that you need to do so.

Namespace Sensitive Content

Namespace nodes are needed because of the possibility that elements or attributes will contain namespace-sensitive content. If namespace prefixes were only ever used in element and attribute names, it would be possible to reconstruct all the namespace declarations simply by looking at the prefixes and URIs held in the expanded QNames of the elements and attributes.

Unfortunately, it is quite common for XML documents to contain references to element or attribute names within the content of the document. The obvious examples of XML documents that use this technique are XSLT stylesheets and XML schemas. When you see a stylesheet containing an attribute such as «select="html:table"», or a schema containing the attribute «type="xs:date"», you are looking at namespace-sensitive content. Similarly, the attribute «xsi:type="xs:short"» appearing in an instance document is using namespaces both in the attribute name and in the attribute content. Stylesheets and schemas are not the only XML documents to use this technique, but they are probably the ones you will encounter most frequently.

In general, the XML parser can't convert these values from lexical QNames to expanded QNames because it doesn't know that they are special. XML Schema has tried to address the problem by defining a data type «xs:QName» that declares the content of an element or attribute to be a QName, but this doesn't solve the whole problem, for a number of reasons:

❑ There can be namespace-sensitive content other than simple QNames; for example, an attribute might contain an XPath expression, which is also namespace sensitive, but there is no schema-defined type for it.

❑ There are documents that have no schema.

❑ Although knowing the data type means that a schema processor can convert the lexical QName used in the string value of these attributes to the expanded QName used as the typed value, this only works if the schema processor knows the mapping of prefixes to namespace URIs. So if you want to be able to construct a tree and then pass it to a schema processor for validation, you need some way of representing the namespace information on the tree before this can work.

❑ The definition of the xs:QName data type says that an unprefixed QName is assumed (like an unprefixed element name) to be in the default namespace. Unfortunately, at least one heavy user of QName-valued attributes, namely the XSLT specification, had already decided that an unprefixed QName (like an unprefixed attribute name) should be in the null namespace. This means that if the attribute were defined as an xs:QName, a schema processor would allocate the wrong namespace URI. So you will find that in the schema for XSLT 2.0 (the schema that can be used to validate XSLT stylesheets), the xs:QName data type isn't actually used.

So, namespace nodes exist primarily so that namespace prefixes appearing in namespace-sensitive content can be handled. Although this might seem a minor requirement, they cause significant complications.

The way namespace nodes are represented in the data model hasn't changed significantly between XPath 1.0 and XPath 2.0. What has changed, though, is that namespace nodes are now semi-hidden from the application. To be precise, the only way that you could actually get your hands on a namespace node in XPath 1.0 was by using the namespace axis; and in XPath 2.0, the namespace axis has been deprecated, which means that some implementations may continue to support it for backward-compatibility reasons, but they aren't required to. Instead, two functions have been provided, in-scope-prefixes() and namespace-uri-for-prefix(), that provide access to information about the namespaces that are in scope for any element. These functions are described in Chapter 13. The significance of this change is that it gives implementations the freedom to maintain namespace information internally in a form that is much more efficient than the formal description of namespace nodes in XDM would imply: remember that the data model is just a model, not a description of a real implementation.

As far as XSLT and XPath are concerned, don't worry too much about namespace nodes — all you need to know is that there are functions you can call to resolve namespace prefixes found in element or attribute content. When you construct new trees, however, understanding what namespace nodes are present on the new tree sometimes becomes more important.

IDs and IDREFs

An ID is a string value that identifies an element node uniquely within a document. If an element has an ID, it becomes easy and (one hopes) efficient to access that element if the ID value is known. Before XML Schemas came along, the ID always appeared as the value of an attribute declared in the DTD as being of type ID. XML Schema has retained this capability, but also allows the content of an element to be used as an ID value. This is done by declaring its type as xs:ID, which is a type derived by restriction from xs:string.

In XDM, every element has at most one ID value and (if the document is valid, which is not necessarily the case) every ID value identifies at most one element.

For example, in an XML dataset containing details of employees, each <employee> element might have a unique ssn attribute giving the employee's Social Security number. For example:

```
<personnel>
<employee ssn="SSN-123-45-6789">
   <name>John Doe</name>
   ...
</employee>
<employee ssn="SSN-123-45-6890">
   <name>Jane Stagg</name>
   ...
</employee>
</personnel>
```

As the ssn attribute is unique, it can be declared in the DTD as an ID attribute using the following declaration:

```
<!ATTLIST employee ssn ID #REQUIRED>
```

Alternatively, an ID attribute can be declared in a schema:

```
<xs:element name="employee">
  <xs:complexType>
    <xs:sequence>
      <xs:attribute name="ssn" type="xs:ID"/>
      ...
    </xs:sequence>
  </xs:complexType>
</xs:element>
```

More recently, a third way of defining ID attributes has been defined. Simply name the attribute xml:id, and it will automatically be recognized as an ID attribute. (Note, however, that if you validate your documents against a DTD or schema, it is still necessary to declare this as a permitted attribute name.)

An ID value is constrained to take the form of an XML NCName. This means, for example, that it must start with a letter, and that it must not contain characters such as «/», «:», or space.

Attributes can also be defined as being of type IDREF or IDREFS if they contain ID values used to point to other elements in the document (an IDREF attribute contains one ID value, an IDREFS attribute contains a whitespace-separated list of ID values). XPath provides a function, id() (see page 802), which can be used to locate an element given its ID value. This function is designed so that an IDREF or IDREFS attribute can be used as input to the function, but equally, so can any other string that happens to contain an ID. However, IDREF and IDREFS attributes are treated specially by the idref() function (see page 804), which follows IDREF links in the opposite direction — given an ID value, it finds all the nodes of type IDREF or IDREFS that refer to it.

There is a slight complication with the use of ID values, in that XPath is not constrained to process only valid XML documents. If an XML document is well formed (or merely well balanced) but not valid, then values that are supposed to be IDs may be duplicated, and they might not obey the syntactic rules for an XML NCName. Similarly, attributes might be marked as IDREF attributes, but actually contain broken links (values that don't match the ID of any element in the document). The XDM specification says that if an ID value appears more than once, all occurrences except the first are ignored. If the ID value contains invalid characters such as spaces, the id() function will fail to find the element but will otherwise appear to work correctly. If you use ID values, it's probably a good idea to use a validating XML parser to prevent this situation occurring.

XSLT offers another more flexible approach to finding elements (or other nodes) by content, namely keys. With keys you can do anything that IDs achieve, other than enforcing uniqueness. Keys are declared in the stylesheet using the <xsl:key> element, and they can be used to find a node by means of the key() function.

Characters in the Data Model

In the XML Information Set definition (http://www.w3.org/TR/xml-infoset), each individual character is distinguished as an object (or *information item*). This is a useful model conceptually, because it allows one to talk about the properties of a character and the position of a character relative to other characters, but it would be very expensive to represent each character as a separate object in a real tree implementation.

XDM has chosen not to represent characters as nodes. It would be nice if it did, because the XPath syntax could then be extended naturally to do character manipulation within strings, but the designers chose instead to provide a separate set of string-manipulation functions. These functions are described in Chapter 13.

A string (and therefore the string value of a node) is a sequence of zero or more characters. Each character is a Char as defined in the XML standard. Loosely, this is a Unicode character. In XML 1.0 it must be one of the following:

- ❑ One of the four whitespace characters tab x09, linefeed x0A, carriage return x0D, or space x20.

- ❑ An ordinary 16-bit Unicode character in the range x21 to xD7FF or xE000 to xFFFD.

- ❑ An extended Unicode character in the range x010000 to x10FFFF. In programming languages such as Java, and in files using UTF-8 or UTF-16 encoding, such a character is represented as a *surrogate pair*, using two 16-bit codes in the range xD800 to xDFFF. But as far as XPath is concerned, it is one character rather than two. This affects functions that count characters in a string or that make use of the position of a character in a string, for example the functions string-length(), substring(), and translate(). Here XPath differs from Java, which normally counts a surrogate pair as two characters.

> *Unicode surrogate pairs are starting to be increasingly used for specialist applications. For example, there is a full range of musical symbols in the range x1D100 to x1D1FF. Although these are unlikely to be used when typesetting printed sheet music, they are very important in texts containing musical criticism. They also have some of the most delightful names in the whole Unicode repertoire: Who can resist a character called* Tempus Perfectum cum Prolatione Perfecta? *If you're interested, it looks like a circle with a dot in the middle.*

Note that line endings are normalized to a single newline x0A character, regardless of how they appear in the original XML source file.

XML 1.1 allows additional characters, notably control characters in the range x01 to x1F. XSLT 2.0 and XPath 2.0 processors are not obliged to support XML 1.1, but many are likely to do so eventually. XML 1.1 also recognizes line ending characters used on IBM mainframes and converts these to the standard x0A newline character.

It is not possible in a stylesheet to determine how a character was written in the original XML file. For example, the following strings are all identical as far as XDM is concerned:

- ❑ >
- ❑ &gt;
- ❑ &#62;
- ❑ &#x3E;
- ❑ &#x003E;
- ❑ <![CDATA[>]]>

The XML parser handles these different character representations. In most implementations, the XSLT processor couldn't treat these representations differently even if it wanted to, because they all look the same once the XML parser has dealt with them.

What Does the Tree Leave Out?

The debate in defining a tree model is about what to leave out. What information from the source XML document is significant, and what is an insignificant detail? For example, is it significant whether the CDATA notation was used for text? Are entity boundaries significant? What about comments?

Many newcomers to XSLT ask questions like "How can I get the processor to use single quotes around attribute values rather than double quotes?" or "How can I get it to output « » instead of « »?" The answer is that you can't, because these distinctions are considered to be things that the recipient of the document shouldn't care about, and they were therefore left out of the XDM model.

Generally, the features of an XML document fall into one of three categories: definitely significant, definitely insignificant, and debatable. For example, the order of elements is definitely significant, the order of attributes within a start element tag is definitely insignificant, but the significance of comments is debatable.

The XML standard itself doesn't define these distinctions particularly clearly. It defines certain things that must be reported to the application, and these are certainly significant. There are other things that are obviously significant (such as the order of elements) about which it says nothing. Equally, there are some things that it clearly states are insignificant, such as the choice of CR-LF or LF for line endings, but many others about which it stays silent, such as choice of «"» versus «'» to delimit attribute values.

One result of this is that different standards in the XML family have each made their own decisions on these matters, and the XDM specification is no exception.

The debate arises partly because there are two kinds of applications. Applications that want only to extract the information content of the document are usually interested only in the core information content. Applications such as XML editing tools tend also to be interested in details of how the XML was written, because when the user makes no change to a section of the document, they want the corresponding output document to be as close to the original as possible.

One attempt to define the information content of an XML document is the W3C InfoSet specification (http://www.w3.org/TR/xml-infoset/). This takes a fairly liberal view, retaining things such as CDATA section boundaries and external entity references in the model, on the basis that some users might attach importance to these things.

Another attempt appears in the specification of Canonical XML (http://www.w3.org/TR/xml-c14n). This specification approaches the question by defining a transformation that can be applied to any XML document to turn it into canonical form, and if two documents have the same canonical form, they are considered equivalent.

The process of turning a document into canonical form is summarized as follows:

1. The document is encoded in UTF-8.
2. Line breaks are normalized to x0A.
3. Attribute values are normalized, depending on the attribute type.
4. Character references and parsed entity references are expanded.
5. CDATA sections are replaced with their character content.

6.   The XML declaration and document type declaration (DTD) are removed.

7.   Empty element tags (`<a/>`) are converted to tag pairs (`<a></a>`).

8.   Whitespace outside the document element and within tags is normalized.

9.   Attribute value delimiters are set to double quotes.

10.   Special characters in attribute values and character content are replaced by character references.

11.   Redundant namespace declarations are removed.

12.   Default attribute values defined in the DTD are added to each element.

13.   Attributes and namespace declarations are sorted into alphabetical order.

Canonical form discards some of the original content that the InfoSet retains, for example CDATA sections. However, this specification has a gray area too: canonical form may or may not retain comments from the original document.

XDM leans more towards the minimalist view of the Canonical XML specification. Figure 2-8 illustrates the resulting classification: the central core is information that is retained in canonical form (comments being on the boundary since the spec leaves the question open); the "peripheral" ring is information that is present in the Infoset but not in canonical XML, while the outer ring represents features of an XML document that are also excluded from the InfoSet. XDM sticks essentially to the Core features (including comments), with a couple of minor additions: XSLT also recognizes unparsed entities, and also makes available the base URI (which is a rather peculiar property, since it can't actually be determined from the content of the XML document, only from its location).

From Textual XML to a Data Model

I've explained the data model so far in this chapter by relating the constructs in XDM (such as element nodes and text nodes) to constructs in a textual XML document. This isn't actually how the W3C specs define it. There are two important differences:

❑   The W3C specifications don't describe the model in terms of textual XML; they describe it in terms of the XML Infoset, as mentioned in the previous section, together with the PSVI (Post Schema Validation Infoset), which describes an augmented Infoset containing not only the information in the raw XML but also the additional information that becomes available as a result of schema validation.

❑   Although the W3C specifications describe a mapping from the Infoset and PSVI to XDM, this mapping is non-normative (which is standards-speak for saying that it's not officially part of the standard). Products aren't required to provide any particular way of constructing the XDM tree from raw XML. This was also true in XSLT 1.0, and it is an issue that has caused some controversy, because it means there is no guarantee that two XSLT processors will give the same answer when applied to the same source document.

❑   The main reason for putting this mapping outside the conformance boundary of the specification is to allow XPath and XSLT to be used in as wide a variety of contexts as possible, for example in environments where the data model is not constructed from textual XML at all, but is rather a view of non-XML information. Unfortunately, this also means that where the data model is constructed in the conventional way by parsing textual XML files, different processors are allowed to do it in different ways.

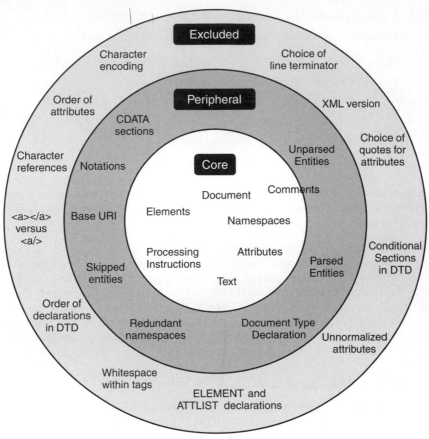

Figure 2-8

Examples of the variations that have arisen in this area between different 1.0 processors are:

❑ The standard way of building a data model using Microsoft's MSXML processor, if all options are set to their default values, causes whitespace-only text nodes to be removed from the model. The standard mapping keeps these nodes present. Microsoft's decision has some rationale: in many cases the extra whitespace nodes simply get in the way; they make the XPath user's life more difficult, and they take up space for no useful reason. Unfortunately, there are some cases where the whitespace is actually significant, and more importantly, this decision means that it's not uncommon for an XSLT stylesheet to produce a different result under MSXML than the result produced under every other processor.

❑ One XSLT vendor (Fourthought: see www.fourthought.com) decided that it would be a good idea to expand any XInclude directives in the source XML as part of the process of building the data model. There is nothing in the spec to say whether XInclude should be expanded or not, and it's something that some users might want to happen and other users might not want to happen. So they were entirely within their rights to make this decision. But again, it creates a problem because different processors are no longer compatible.

XDM leaves additional scope for variations between processors. Because the model is designed to support XQuery as well as XSLT, the range of possible usage scenarios is greatly increased. Many XQuery vendors aim to offer implementations capable of searching databases containing hundreds of gigabytes of data, and in such environments performance optimization becomes a paramount requirement. In fact, database products have traditionally treated performance as a more important quality than standards conformance, and there are indications that this culture is present among some of the XQuery vendors. Examples of the kind of variations that may be encountered include the following:

❑   Dropping of whitespace text nodes (again!).

❑   Storing only the typed value of elements and attributes, and not the string value.

❑   Dropping comments and processing instructions.

❑   Dropping unused namespace declarations.

It remains to be seen how most vendors will handle these problems. Hopefully, vendors will offer any optimizations as an option that the user can choose, rather than as the default way that source XML is processed when loading the data.

Controlling Serialization

The transformation processor, which generates the result tree, generally gives the user control only over the core information items and properties (including comments) in the output. The output processor or serializer gives a little bit of extra control over how the result tree is converted into a serial XML document. Specifically, it allows control over the following:

❑   Generation of CDATA sections

❑   XML version

❑   Character encoding

❑   The standalone property in the XML declaration

❑   DOCTYPE declaration

Although you get some control over these features during serialization, one thing you can't do is copy them from the source document unchanged through to the result. The fact that text was in a CDATA section in the input document has no bearing on whether it will be represented in as a CDATA section in the output document. The tree model does not provide any way for this extra information to be retained.

The Transformation Process

I've described the essential process performed by XSLT, transformation of a source tree to a result tree under the control of a stylesheet, and looked at the structure of these trees. Now it's time to look at how the transformation process actually works, which means taking a look inside the stylesheet.

Invoking a Transformation

The actual interface for firing off a transformation is outside the scope of the XSLT specification, and it's done differently by different products. There are also different styles of interface: possibilities include an API that can be invoked by applications, a GUI interface within a development environment, a command line interface, an interface from a pipeline processor such as XProc or a build tool such as ant, as well as the use of an <?xml-stylesheet?> processing instruction within a source document, which is described in Chapter 3 (see page 99). There's a common API for Java processors that was initially called

TrAX, then became part of JAXP, and since JDK 1.4 has been part of the standard Java class library. For browsers, Microsoft and Firefox each have their own API, but there is at least one project (Sarissa, see http://sarissa.sourceforge.net/) that provides a common API that can be used on both these browsers as well as Opera, Safari, and Konqueror.

What the XSLT 2.0 specification does do is to describe in abstract terms what information can be passed across this interface when the transformation is started. This includes the following:

❑ *The stylesheet itself*: Many products provide separate API calls to compile a stylesheet and then to run it, which saves time if the same stylesheet is being used to transform many source documents.

❑ *A source document*: This can be identified by any node in the document, which acts as the initial context node for the transformation. This will usually be the document node at the root of the tree, but it doesn't have to be. In fact, you don't have to supply an initial context node at all; the stylesheet can then fetch any data it needs from stylesheet parameters or from calls on the document() function.

❑ *An initial named template*: This acts as the entry point to the stylesheet and is needed when you don't supply an initial context node, but it is also possible to supply both. If an initial named template is identified, the transformation starts with that template; otherwise, it starts by searching for a template rule that matches the initial context node, as described in the next section.

❑ *An initial mode*: Modes are described later in this chapter, on page 78. Normally, the transformation starts in the default (unnamed) mode, but you can choose to start in a different mode if you prefer. When the template rules in a stylesheet use a named mode, it becomes easier to combine two stylesheets into a single multiphase transformation, as described on page 85, and this feature ensures that you can still use the rules for each processing phase independently.

❑ *Parameters*: A stylesheet can define global parameters using <xsl:param> elements, as discussed on page 425. Interfaces for invoking a transformation will generally provide some kind of mechanism for setting values for these parameters. (A notable exception is that when you invoke a transformation using the <?xml-stylesheet?> processing instruction in a source document, there is usually no way of setting parameters.)

❑ *A base URI for output documents*: Many stylesheets will produce a single result document, and this URI effectively defines where this result document will be written. If the stylesheet produces multiple result documents, then each one is created using an <xsl:result-document> instruction with an href attribute, and the href attribute, if it is relative, is interpreted as a location relative to this base URI.

Template Rules

As we saw in Chapter 1, most stylesheets will contain a number of template rules. Each template rule is expressed in the stylesheet as an <xsl:template> element with a match attribute. The value of the match attribute is a pattern. The pattern determines which nodes in the source tree the template rule matches.

For example, the pattern «/» matches the document node, the pattern «title» matches a <title> element, and the pattern «chapter/title» matches a <title> element whose parent is a <chapter> element.

When you invoke an XSLT processor to apply a particular stylesheet to a particular source document, the first thing it does is to read and parse these documents and create internal tree representations of them in memory. Once this preparation is complete, the transformation process can start.

The first step in the transformation process is usually to find a template rule that matches the document node of the source tree. If there are several possible candidates, there is a conflict resolution policy to choose the best fit (see page 79 for details). If there is no template rule that matches the document node, a built-in template is used. The XSLT processor then evaluates the contents of this template rule.

> *XSLT 2.0 also allows you to start the transformation by supplying an initial node other than the document node. As discussed in the previous section, you can even start the transformation without supplying an initial node at all, by providing the name of the first template to be evaluated.*

Contents of a Template Rule

The content of an `<xsl:template>` element in the stylesheet is a sequence of elements and text nodes. Comments and processing instructions in the stylesheet are ignored, as are whitespace text nodes, unless they belong to an `<xsl:text>` element or to one with an appropriate `xml:space` attribute. This sequence of elements and text nodes is called a *sequence constructor*, because the result of evaluating it is itself a sequence.

Elements in the sequence constructor can be classified as either instructions or data, depending on their namespace. Text nodes are always classified as data. When the sequence constructor is evaluated, the instructions are evaluated, and the result of each instruction is added to the result sequence. The data nodes are copied to the result tree. Elements that are classified as data are officially termed *literal result elements*.

Consider the following template rule:

```
<xsl:template match="/">
    <xsl:message>Started!</xsl:message>
    <xsl:comment>Generated from XSLT</xsl:comment>
    <html>
        ...
    </html>
    The end
</xsl:template>
```

The body of this template rule consists of two instructions (`<xsl:message>` and `<xsl:comment>`), a literal result element (the `<html>` element), and some text («The end», preceded and followed by significant whitespace). When this template is evaluated, the instructions are executed according to the rules for each individual instruction, and literal result elements and text nodes are copied (as element nodes and text nodes, respectively) to the result sequence.

It's simplest to think of this as a sequential process, where evaluating a sequence constructor causes evaluation of each of its components in the order they appear. Actually, because XSLT is largely side-effect-free, they could be executed in a different order, or in parallel. The important thing is that after evaluating this sequence constructor, the result sequence will contain a comment node (produced by the `<xsl:comment>` instruction), an `<html>` element node (produced by the `<html>` literal result element), and the text node «The end». The order of these items in the result sequence corresponds to the order of the instructions in the stylesheet, although in principle the XSLT processor is free to execute the instructions in any order it likes.

> `<xsl:message>` *is an exception to the rule that XSLT is side-effect-free. Evaluating an* `<xsl:message>` *instruction doesn't cause anything to be added to the result sequence; it merely causes the side effect of writing a message to some external device (perhaps standard output, or a log file). If there are*

several `<xsl:message>` *instructions in a sequence constructor, then the order in which the messages appear is not guaranteed.*

If I hadn't included the «...» within the `<html>` element, this would be the end of the matter. But when a literal result element such as `<html>` is evaluated, its content is treated as a sequence constructor in its own right, and this is evaluated in the same way. It can again contain a mixture of instructions, literal result elements, and text. As we'll see in the next section, the result sequence produced by this sequence constructor is used to create the nodes that are attributes and children of the new `<html>` element.

Sequence Constructors

Sequence constructors play such an important role in the XSLT 2.0 processing model that it's worth studying them in some detail.

As we have seen, the content of an `<xsl:template>` element, after any parameter definitions contained in `<xsl:param>` elements, is a sequence constructor. In XSLT 1.0, a sequence of instructions was officially called a *template*, though few people used the term correctly. The new name *sequence constructor* reflects a change in the way the processing model is described, and a change in its capability: a sequence of instructions can now be used to produce any sequence of items, not necessarily a sequence of sibling nodes in a tree.

Many other XSLT elements are also defined to have a sequence constructor as their content. For example, the contents of an `<xsl:variable>` or `<xsl:if>` element follow exactly the same rules as the content of an `<xsl:template>` (ignoring `<xsl:param>` elements), and these too are sequence constructors. It follows that one sequence constructor may be contained within another. For example, consider the following template rule:

```
<xsl:template match="para">
   <xsl:if test="position()=1">
      <hr/>- o - 0 - o -<hr/>
   </xsl:if>
   <xsl:apply-templates/>
   <xsl:if test="position()=last()">
      <hr/>- o - 0 - o -<hr/>
   </xsl:if>
</xsl:template>
```

Viewed as a tree, using the notation introduced earlier in this chapter, this has the structure shown in Figure 2-9. There are three sequence constructors, indicated by the shaded areas. Within the sequence constructors on this tree, there are four kinds of nodes: text nodes, XSLT instructions (such as `<xsl:if>`), attributes (`test="position()=last()"`, not shown), and literal result elements (such as `<hr>`), which are elements to be written to the result tree.

A sequence constructor is the nearest equivalent in XSLT to a block or compound statement in a block-structured programming language such as C or Java, and like blocks in C or Java, it defines the scope of any local variables declared within the block.

A sequence constructor is a sequence of sibling nodes in the stylesheet. Comment and processing instruction nodes are allowed, but the XSLT processor ignores them. The nodes of interest are text nodes and element nodes.

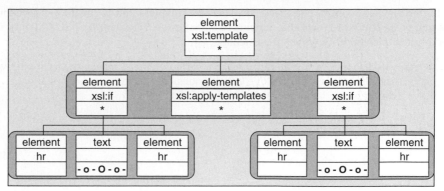

Figure 2-9

When a sequence constructor is evaluated, the result is, in general, a sequence of items. Many instructions such as <xsl:element>, <xsl:copy-of>, and <xsl:number> create new nodes; a couple of the new instructions introduced in XSLT 2.0 such as <xsl:sequence> and <xsl:perform-sort> can also return references to existing nodes in a source document. It is also possible for the sequence to contain atomic values: these can be produced using the <xsl:sequence> and <xsl:copy-of> instructions.

Most likely, the sequence returned by a sequence constructor will be used to build the content of an element node in the result tree. In the example shown in Figure 2-9:

❑   The sequence constructors contained in the <xsl:if> elements always (if they are evaluated at all) produce a sequence of three nodes: two empty <hr> elements and a text node.

❑   The sequence constructor contained in the <xsl:template> instruction returns a sequence that is the concatenation of the nodes returned by the first <xsl:if> instruction, then the nodes returned by the <xsl:apply-templates> instruction, and finally the nodes returned by the second <xsl:if> instruction. The result of the template is this sequence of nodes.

Suppose that the template rule in our example is invoked using a construct such as the following:

```
<div>
    <xsl:apply-templates select="para"/>
</div>
```

The <xsl:apply-templates> instruction results in the sequence of nodes produced by evaluating the selected template rule. In fact, this instruction can select several <para> elements, and the template rule is invoked once for each one. The resulting nodes are all concatenated into a single sequence. Because the <xsl:apply-templates> instruction is the only instruction in the sequence constructor contained by the <div> element, the final sequence delivered to the <div> element contains the results of expanding the template rule for each of the selected <para> elements in the source document.

The <div> element is a literal result element, which when evaluated constructs a new element node. The name of this node will be <div>, and the content will be formed from the sequence produced by evaluating the sequence constructor contained within the literal result element in the stylesheet. In our example, this sequence contains elements and text nodes, and these are copied to form the content of the new <div> element.

This is by far the most common scenario: instructions are evaluated to produce a sequence of nodes, and the nodes are copied to form the contents of a result tree. However, in XSLT 2.0 it is also possible to process the sequence in other ways. In particular:

❑   A generated sequence can be captured in a variable. For example, the following variable will have a value that is a sequence of element nodes. These elements are not attached to a tree; they have no parent, and they are not siblings of each other:

```
<xsl:variable name="months" as="element()*">
  <month>January</month>
  <month>February</month>
  <month>March</month>
</xsl:variable>
```

❑   You can then refer to the third element in this sequence as «$months[3]». But don't try doing «$months/month»; the $months variable holds a sequence of <month> elements, and the path expression «$months/month» (which is short for «$months/child::month») tries to find children of these elements that are named <month>. It won't find any.

This kind of variable is constructed when the «as» attribute is present to define the required type of the items in the sequence. If the «as» attribute were omitted, the <month> elements would be added to a temporary document, and the variable $months would refer to the document node of this tree. For more information, see the section "Temporary Documents" on page 85.

❑   A generated sequence can also be returned by a function. Rather than defining the sequence of month elements in a variable, it could equally well be defined in a function.

```
<xsl:function name="m:months" as="element()*">
  <month>January</month>
  <month>February</month>
  <month>March</month>
</xsl:function>
```

❑   You could then refer to the third month as «m:months()[3]». Note that user-defined functions must always be in a namespace, to avoid conflicts with system-defined functions.

❑   There is a subtle difference between using a variable and a function to capture the sequence: the variable will return the same elements every time, whereas the function will create new elements every time you call it. For example, this means that the expression «$months[3] is $months[3]» will be true, while «m:months()[3] is m:months()[3]» will be false. (The «is» operator in XPath 2.0 tests whether the values of the two operands are references to the same node.) In practice, you would want to use a function only if you were supplying parameters, because the data that came back depended on the parameters in some way.

Text nodes appearing within a sequence constructor are copied to the result sequence when the sequence constructor is evaluated. However, text nodes that consist entirely of whitespace will be ignored, unless the xml:space attribute is used on an enclosing element to define them as significant.

Text nodes containing whitespace only are also significant if they appear as the content of an <xsl:text> *element, but in that case they are not part of a sequence constructor.*

For more information on the treatment of whitespace see Chapter 3, page 141.

Nested Sequence Constructors

Suppose the template rule actually looks like this:

```
<xsl:template match="/">
    <xsl:message>Started!</xsl:message>
    <xsl:comment>Generated from XSLT</xsl:comment>
    <html>
        <head>
            <title>My first generated HTML page</title>
        </head>
        <body>
            <xsl:apply-templates/>
        </body>
    </html>
    The end
</xsl:template>
```

Here the `<html>` element contains two child elements, `<head>` and `<body>`. These are both literal result elements, so they are evaluated by copying them from the stylesheet to the result sequence.

Evaluating the `<head>` element in turn causes the sequence constructor within the `<head>` element to be evaluated. This sequence constructor contains a single literal result element, the `<title>` element, which in turn contains a sequence constructor containing a single text node, whose value is the string «My first generated HTML page».

What happens here (as far as the formal definition of the processing model is concerned) is a bottom-up process of tree construction. The sequence constructor containing the text node is evaluated to produce a result sequence containing a copy of the text node. The `<head>` element is then evaluated to produce a new `<head>` element node, which has this text node as its only child.

When the `<body>` element is evaluated, things get more interesting because it contains an XSLT instruction, namely `<xsl:apply-templates/>`. This particular instruction has critical importance: when written as here, without any attributes, it means "select all the children of the current node in the source tree, and for each one, find the matching template rule in the stylesheet, and evaluate it."

What actually happens at this point depends both on what is found in the source document, and on what other template rules are present in the stylesheet. Typically, because we are currently processing the root node of the source document tree, it will have just one child node, namely the document element (the outermost element of the source XML document). Suppose this is a `<doc>` element. Then the XSLT processor will search the stylesheet looking for a template rule that matches the `<doc>` element.

The simplest situation is where it finds just one rule that matches this element, for example one declared as:

```
<xsl:template match="doc">
```

If it finds more than one matching template rule, it has to use its conflict resolution policy to choose the best fit. The other possibility is that there is no matching template rule: in this case it invokes the built-in template rule for element nodes, which simply executes `<xsl:apply-templates/>`: in other words, it selects the children of this element, and tries to find template rules that match these children. There's also a built-in template rule for text nodes, which copies the text node to the output. If the element has no children, `<xsl:apply-templates/>` does nothing.

Whatever happens, however, the result of evaluating the `<xsl:apply-templates>` instruction is a sequence, usually a sequence of nodes. These nodes are added to the result of the sequence constructor contained by the `<body>` instruction, and are used to form the children (and potentially also the attributes) of the new `<body>` element. The new `<head>` and `<body>` elements now form a sequence that's used to make the children of the `<html>` element; and because this template rule was the first one to be activated, the transformation is now complete and the tree with this `<html>` element at the top becomes the final result tree of the transformation. (The `<html>` element is automatically wrapped in a document node, to complete the process.)

Hopefully, you never actually need to analyze what's going on to this level of detail. The name *template* was chosen because you can think of the whole process as producing a simple fill-in-the-blanks copy of the elements in the stylesheet as elements in the result tree. In the case of literal result elements and literal text, they are copied across unchanged; in the case of XSLT instructions, some processing is performed to fetch data from a source document for insertion at this point in the result tree.

Push Processing

The simplest way to process a source tree is thus to write a template rule for each kind of node that can be encountered, and for that template rule to produce any output required, as well as to call `<xsl:apply-templates>` to process the children of that node.

Example: Push Processing

This example demonstrates the push processing technique: a rule-based stylesheet in which there is one template rule to process each different kind of node.

Input

The source document, `books.xml`, is a simple book catalog:

```xml
<?xml version="1.0"?>
<books>
    <book category="reference">
        <author>Nigel Rees</author>
        <title>Sayings of the Century</title>
        <price>8.95</price>
    </book>
    <book category="fiction">
        <author>Evelyn Waugh</author>
        <title>Sword of Honour</title>
        <price>12.99</price>
    </book>
    <book category="fiction">
        <author>Herman Melville</author>
        <title>Moby Dick</title>
        <price>8.99</price>
    </book>
    <book category="fiction">
        <author>J. R. R. Tolkien</author>
        <title>The Lord of the Rings</title>
        <price>22.99</price>
    </book>
</books>
```

Stylesheet

Say you want to display this data in the form of a sequentially numbered booklist. The following stylesheet, books.xsl, will do the trick:

```
<xsl:stylesheet version="2.0"
   xmlns:xsl="http://www.w3.org/1999/XSL/Transform">

<xsl:template match="books">
  <html><body>
    <h1>A list of books</h1>
    <table width="640">
      <xsl:apply-templates/>
    </table>
  </body></html>
</xsl:template>

<xsl:template match="book">
  <tr>
    <td><xsl:number/></td>
    <xsl:apply-templates/>
  </tr>
</xsl:template>

<xsl:template match="author | title | price">
  <td><xsl:value-of select="."/></td>
</xsl:template>

</xsl:stylesheet>
```

What's happening here? There's no template rule for the document node, so the built-in template gets invoked. This processes all the children of the document node.

There's only one child of the document node, the <books> element. So the template rule for the <books> element is evaluated. This creates some standard HTML elements on the result tree, and eventually calls <xsl:apply-templates/> to cause its own children to be processed. These children are all <book> elements, so they are all processed by the template rule whose match pattern is «match="book"». This template rule outputs an HTML <tr> element, and within it a <td> element, which it fills by executing the <xsl:number/> instruction whose effect is to get the sequence number of the current node (the <book> element) within its parent element. It then calls <xsl:apply-templates/> once again to process the children of the <book> element in the source tree.

The children of the <book> element in the source document are all <author>, <title>, or <price> elements; so as it happens they all match the template rule whose match pattern is «match="author | title | price"» (you can read «|» as "or"). This template rule outputs an HTML <td> element that it fills by executing an instruction <xsl:value-of select="."/>. This instruction evaluates an XPath expression, and writes its result (a string) as text to the result tree. The expression is «.», which returns the string value of the current node, that is the textual content of the current <author>, <price>, or <title> element.

This template makes no further call on <xsl:apply-templates>, so its own children are not processed, and control returns all the way up.

Output

```
<html>
  <body>
     A list of books</h1>
     <table width="640">
        <tr>
           <td>1</td>
           <td>Nigel Rees</td>
           <td>Sayings of the Century</td>
           <td>8.95</td>
        </tr>
        <tr>
           <td>2</td>
           <td>Evelyn Waugh</td>
           <td>Sword of Honour</td>
           <td>12.99</td>
        </tr>
     etc..
        </table>
     </body>
</html>
```

This style of processing is called *push* processing. It is driven by the `<xsl:apply-templates>` instruction, as if the processor is pushing the nodes out of the door, saying "is anyone interested in dealing with this one?"

In this description I occasionally talk of instructions writing to the result tree. This is how the process was described in XSLT 1.0, and it accounts for the name push. It's a convenient way to think about what's going on. Technically, as we have seen, instructions don't write to the result tree; they are evaluated to produce a sequence (usually a sequence of nodes, but occasionally atomic values) and this sequence is then used by the calling instruction, often to construct the children of a new element. The importance of this model is that in XSLT 2.0, there are some situations in which the result of a sequence constructor is not used directly to build part of a result tree, but can be used in some other way, for example as the result of an XPath function call.

In such situations it is possible for an XPath expression to encounter nodes such as attributes and text nodes that have no parent, because they have not yet been attached to a result tree.

Controlling Which Nodes to Process

Simple push processing works very well when the data in the output is to have the same structure and sequence as the data in the input, and all we want to do is add or remove a few tags or perform other simple editing of values as we go along.

In the previous example, it wouldn't work so well if the properties of each book were less predictable, for example if some of the books had no price, or if the title and author could appear in either order. In this case the HTML table that we generated wouldn't be nicely arranged in columns any more, because generating a new cell for each property we encounter is not necessarily the right thing to do.

In such circumstances, there are two choices:

- ❏ Be more precise about which nodes to process, rather than just saying *process all children of the current node*.

- ❏ Be more precise about how to process them, rather than just saying *choose the best-fit template rule*.

Let's try the first option.

Example: Controlling the Sequence of Processing

We can gain greater control over *which* nodes are to be processed by changing the `<book>` template in `books.xsl`, as follows:

```
<xsl:template match="book">
   <tr>
     <td><xsl:number/></td>
     <xsl:apply-templates select="author, title, price"/>
   </tr>
</xsl:template>
```

Instead of selecting all child elements and finding the appropriate template rule for each one, this now explicitly selects first the `<author>` child element, then the `<title>` child element, and then the `<price>` child element.

This will still work, and it's more robust than our previous attempt, but it will still produce a ragged table if there are any `<book>` elements without an `<author>` (say), or with more than one.

The comma operator used in the expression «`select="author, title, price"`» is new in XPath 2.0. It simply concatenates several sequences (which might be single items, but could also be empty, or contain multiple items) into a single sequence, in the order specified.

As we want a regular structure in the output and because we know a lot about the structure of the source document, we'd probably be better off in this situation defining all the processing in the `<book>` template rather than relying on template rules to match each of its child elements.

Example: Selecting Nodes Explicitly

We can gain greater control over *how* nodes are to be processed by writing the `<book>` template rule in the following manner.

```
<xsl:template match="book">
  <tr>
    <td><xsl:number/></td>
    <td><xsl:value-of select="author"/></td>
    <td><xsl:value-of select="title"/></td>
    <td><xsl:value-of select="price"/></td>
  </tr>
</xsl:template>
```

Some people call this *pull* processing, because instead of the template pushing nodes out of the door to be picked up by another template, it is pulling the nodes in and handling them itself.

The pattern-matching (or push) style of processing is the most characteristic feature of XSLT, and it works very well in applications where it makes sense to describe the handling of each type of node in the source document independently. However, there are many other techniques available, all of which are equally valuable. From within a template rule that is processing one particular node, the main alternatives if you want access to information in other nodes are as follows:

- ❑ Call `<xsl:apply-templates>` to process those nodes using their appropriate template rules.

- ❑ Call `<xsl:apply-templates>` in a particular *mode* (see later) to process those nodes using the template rules for the relevant mode.

- ❑ Call `<xsl:value-of>` to extract the required information from the nodes directly.

- ❑ Call `<xsl:for-each>` to perform explicit processing of each of the nodes in turn.

- ❑ Call `<xsl:call-template>` to invoke a specific template by name, rather than relying on pattern matching to decide which template to invoke.

Further discussion of the different approaches to writing a stylesheet is included in Chapter 17, *Stylesheet Design Patterns*.

Modes

Sometimes you want to process the same node in the source tree more than once, in different ways. The classic example is to produce a table of contents. When generating the table of contents, you want to handle all the section headings in one way, and when producing the body of the document, you want to handle them in a different way.

One way around this problem is to use push processing on one of these passes through the data, and pull processing on all the other occasions. However, this could be very constraining. Instead, you can define different modes of processing, one for each pass through the data. You can name the mode of processing when you call `<xsl:apply-templates>`, and the only template rules that will be considered are those that specify the same mode. For example, if you specify:

```
<xsl:apply-templates select="heading-1" mode="table-of-contents"/>
```

Then the selected template rule might be one defined as:

```
<xsl:template match="heading-1" mode="table-of-contents">
...
</xsl:template>
```

Further details of how to use modes are in Chapter 6, page 242 and a real-life case study showing how to use them to generate a table of contents is in Chapter 18, page 1019.

Built-In Template Rules

What happens when `<xsl:apply-templates>` is invoked to process a node, and there is no template rule in the stylesheet that matches that node?

A *built-in template rule* is invoked.

There is a built-in template rule for each kind of node. The built-in rules work as follows.

Node Kind	Built-In Template Rule
Document	Call `<xsl:apply-templates>` to process the children of the document node, in the same mode as the calling mode.
Element	Call `<xsl:apply-templates>` to process the children of this element, in the same mode as the calling mode.
Attribute	Copy the attribute value to the result tree, as text — not as an attribute node.
Text	Copy the text to the result tree.
Comment	Do nothing.
Processing instruction	Do nothing.
Namespace	Do nothing.

The built-in template rules will only be invoked if there is no rule that matches the node anywhere in the stylesheet.

There is no way to override the built-in template for namespace nodes, because there is no pattern that will match a namespace node. If you call `<xsl:apply-templates>` to process namespace nodes, nothing happens. If you want to process all the namespace nodes for an element, use:

```
<xsl:for-each select="namespace::*">
```

Conflict Resolution Policy

Conversely, what happens when there is more than one template rule whose pattern matches a particular node? As I mentioned earlier, the conflict resolution policy comes into play.

This works as follows:

- ❏ First the *import precedence* of each rule is considered. As Chapter 3 will show, one stylesheet may import another, using the `<xsl:import>` declaration, and this part of the policy basically says that when stylesheet A imports stylesheet B, the rules in A take precedence over the rules in B.

- ❏ Then the *priority* of each rule is examined. The priority is a numeric value, and the higher the number, the higher the priority. You can either specify the priority explicitly in the `priority` attribute of the `<xsl:template>` element or leave the system to allocate a default priority. In this case, the system allocates a priority that is designed to reflect whether the pattern is very general or very specific: for example the pattern «subsection/title» (which matches any `<title>` element whose parent is a `<subsection>` element) gets higher priority than the pattern «*», which matches any element. System-allocated priorities are always in the range –0.5 to +0.5: user-allocated priorities will normally be 1 or more, but there are no restrictions. For more details see the description of the `<xsl:template>` element in Chapter 6, page 483.

- ❏ Finally, if there is more than one rule with the same import precedence and priority, the XSLT processor has a choice: it can either report an error, or choose whichever rule appears last in the stylesheet (some processors do both: they give you a warning, and then carry on processing).

Different processors will behave differently in this situation, which gives you a slight portability problem to watch out for: it is best to ensure this ambiguity never happens, which you can achieve by setting explicit priorities on your template rules.

Error Handling

There are two kinds of error that can occur during an XSLT transformation: static errors and dynamic errors. Static errors occur while the stylesheet is being compiled, and dynamic errors occur while the transformation is actually running. If you invoke the transformation using a single-shot interface that doesn't distinguish compilation from execution then you may not notice the difference, but it is there all the same.

XSLT 1.0 was designed to minimize the number of things that could cause runtime errors. This was done largely by defining fallback behavior. For example, if you supplied the string "Africa" as input to an arithmetic operator, you would get the result NaN (not-a-number). This might not be a very useful result, but the thinking was that it was better than producing a pop-up on the browser saying "Error in stylesheet." For many runtime errors, implementors were in fact given a choice of reporting an error, or taking some defined fallback action.

The thinking in XSLT 2.0 has shifted significantly. There are now many more conditions that cause runtime errors, and most of these are not recoverable. There is also no try/catch mechanism to trap the errors when they occur: if a runtime error does occur in a stylesheet, it is fatal. In practice this means that you have to design your stylesheet to prevent them from occurring. This means that you have to test whether the input data is valid before using it in an operation that could cause errors if it isn't. For example, before trying to convert a string to an integer using the `xs:integer()` constructor function, it is a good idea to test whether the conversion is possible using a construct such as «`if ($x castable as xs:integer) then ...`».

Although the language specification is very precise about what constitutes an error and what doesn't, there may well be variations between processors as to whether runtime errors are actually reported in particular circumstances. This is partly because for some errors the choice of reporting the error or taking fallback action is still there, as in XSLT 1.0, and it is also because the order of execution of instructions (or of subexpressions within an XPath expression) is not precisely defined. Suppose you write an expression such as «`exists(//employee[@retirement-date=current-date()])`» (which finds out whether any employees are retiring today). One XSLT processor might find such an employee, and return `true`. Another might find an employee whose `retirement-date` attribute is not a date (perhaps it is the string `"unknown"`) and report a runtime error. Processors are never required to do extra work just to look for runtime errors. In this example, the processor is allowed to stop searching the employees as soon as it finds one that satisfies the required conditions.

What if there are no employees retiring today, and there are some employees whose retirement dates are not valid dates? Does the processor have to raise a runtime error, or can it return `false`? A straightforward reading of the specification suggests that it has to report an error in this case. However, the rules that allow the processor to devise an optimal execution strategy are drawn up so broadly that I think an implementor could argue that returning `false` was conformant.

Variables and Expressions

The system of data types lies at the core of any language, and the way expressions are used to compute values and assign these to variables is closely tied up with the type system. The XSLT type system interacts closely with XML Schema. We'll look in more detail in Chapter 4 at how stylesheets and schemas interact, and we'll survey the detailed repertoire of built-in types in Chapter 5. In this section, however, we'll assume some basic principles about types, and look at the way they are used in variables and expressions.

Variables

XSLT allows global variables to be defined, which are available throughout the whole stylesheet, as well as local variables, which are available only within a particular sequence constructor. The name and value of a variable are defined in an `<xsl:variable>` element. For example:

```
<xsl:variable name="width" select="50" as="xs:integer"/>
```

This defines a variable whose name is `width` and whose value is the number `50`. The variable can subsequently be referenced in an XPath expression as `$width`. If the `<xsl:variable>` element appears at the top level of the stylesheet (as a child of the `<xsl:stylesheet>` element), then it declares a global variable; if it appears within the body of an `<xsl:template>` or `<xsl:function>` element, then it defines a local variable.

The use of variables is superficially very similar to their use in conventional programming and scripting languages. They even have similar scoping rules. However, there is one key difference: *once a value has been given to a variable, it cannot be changed*. This difference has a profound impact on the way programs are written, so it is discussed in detail in the section *Programming without Assignment Statements* in Chapter 17, page 985.

The «as» attribute is optional, and defines the data type of the variable as being an integer. In this example, this doesn't add much: you can tell that it's an integer by looking at the value, and so can the XSLT processor. But there are cases where it's useful to specify the type. The `select` attribute doesn't have to be a constant, as it is in the previous example — it might, for example, be a call on a function. The «as» attribute acts both as an assertion about the type of the value (if the value is of the wrong type, you'll see an error message, either at compile time or at runtime) and also as a request to perform certain limited conversions from the supplied value to the specified type.

The type conversions that are possible in XSLT can be categorized as strong conversions and weak conversions. In a context like this, only weak conversions are applied. The weak conversions include the following:

❑ Treating a value of type T as a value of a supertype of T, for example an `xs:integer` as an `xs:decimal`, or an `xs:ID` as an `xs:string`.

❑ Extracting the typed value of a node, in cases where the supplied value is a reference to a node and the required type is atomic. This process is called *atomization*. The typed value of a node has the type determined by schema validation, for example if the node has been validated as an integer, you can use its value where an integer is expected, but not where (say) an `xs:anyURI` is expected. If there is no schema, then the typed value is the same as the string value.

❑ Numeric promotion of an `xs:integer` or `xs:decimal` to an `xs:float` or `xs:double`, and of an `xs:float` to an `xs:double`. In XML Schema, `xs:float` is not defined as a subtype of `xs:double`, but XPath and XSLT behave largely as if it were.

❑ Promotion of `xs:anyURI` values to `xs:string`. Again, XPath and XSLT behave largely as if `xs:anyURI` were a subtype of `xs:string`, even though XML Schema doesn't define it that way.

❑ Conversion of untyped atomic values (which usually arise as the values of nodes in documents, or parts of documents, that have not been schema-validated) to the required type. This conversion uses the rules defined in XML Schema: for example, if the required type is `xs:date`, then the

81

supplied value must have the correct lexical form for an xs:date, as defined in the XML Schema specifications (that is, YYYY-MM-DD with an optional timezone).

These weak conversions are applied to the values of variables and parameters, and they are also used when converting the arguments supplied in a function call to the types declared in the function signature.

Strong conversions can be achieved by use of constructor functions; for example, you can convert a string to an integer with the function «xs:integer($s)». Generally in XSLT 2.0, strong conversions are not applied automatically; you have to ask for them. Strong conversion is also referred to as *casting*, and the rules for casting are given in Chapter 11.

In the case of function calls, strong conversions are sometimes applied implicitly if you run the stylesheet in backward-compatible mode. This is described in Chapter 3 on page 128. You can select backward-compatible mode by specifying «version="1.0"» on the <xsl:stylesheet> element. However, even in backward-compatible mode strong conversions are not applied to variables and parameters in the stylesheet. This is because in XSLT 1.0 it was not possible to declare the type of a variable or parameter, so there is no requirement here for backward compatibility.

Parameters

Parameters in XSLT are very similar to variables. They are declared with an <xsl:param> element instead of <xsl:variable>, and they differ in that the value can be supplied externally. There are three places you can use parameters in a stylesheet:

❑ *Stylesheet parameters* (also known as global parameters) are supplied when the transformation is invoked, and they can be referenced from anywhere in the stylesheet. They are set from outside the stylesheet (for example, from the command line or from an API — the actual mechanism is implementation defined).

❑ *Template parameters* are defined within an <xsl:template> element, and are available only during the evaluation of that template. They are set by means of <xsl:with-param> elements within the instruction (for example <xsl:call-template> or <xsl:apply-templates>) that invokes the template. These parameters can take different values each time the template is invoked.

❑ *Function parameters* are defined within an <xsl:function> element, and are available only during the evaluation of that function. Functions are very similar to named templates, except that they are invoked not by means of XSLT instructions but by evaluating a function call within an XPath expression. The parameters to a function are supplied as part of this function call.

As with variables, the expected type of a parameter can be declared using an «as» attribute. Here it's especially useful to declare the expected type, because you can then fail cleanly if the caller supplies the wrong type of value, rather than crashing or producing wrong answers. It's also very valuable to the XSLT compiler to know in advance what type of value will be supplied, because it means that it can generate tighter code that doesn't have to deal with as many runtime possibilities. You don't have to declare the types of parameters, and if you don't, then any type of value will be accepted — but I would recommend as good programming practice always to declare the types. I certainly find that it catches many of my sillier programming mistakes.

Expressions

The syntax of expressions is defined in the XPath 2.0 Recommendation, and is described in detail in Chapters 7 through 11.

XPath expressions are used in a number of contexts in an XSLT stylesheet. They are used as attribute values for many XSLT elements, for example:

```
<xsl:value-of select="($x + $y) * 2)"/>
```

In this example $x and $y are references to variables, and the operators «+» and «*» have their usual meanings of addition and multiplication.

Many XPath expressions, like this one, follow a syntax that is similar to other programming languages. The one that stands out, however, and the one that gave XPath its name, is the *path expression*.

A path expression defines a navigation path through the document tree. Starting at a defined origin, usually either the current node or the document node, it follows a sequence of steps in defined directions. At each stage the path can branch, so for example you can find all the attributes of all the children of the origin node. The result is always a sequence of nodes in a fixed order (known as document order) with no duplicates. It might be empty or contain only one node, but it is still treated as a sequence.

The directions of navigation through the tree are called *axes*. The various axes are defined in detail in Chapter 9. They include the following:

❑ The child axis, which finds all the children of a node.

❑ The attribute axis, which finds all the attributes of a node.

❑ The ancestor axis, which finds all the ancestors of a node.

❑ The following-sibling axis, which finds the nodes that come after this one and share the same parent.

❑ The preceding-sibling axis, which finds the nodes that come before this one and share the same parent.

As well as specifying the direction of navigation through the tree, each step in a path expression can also qualify which nodes are to be selected. This can be done in several different ways:

❑ By specifying the name of the nodes (completely or partially).

❑ By specifying the kind of nodes (for example, elements or processing instructions).

❑ By specifying the schema-defined type of the nodes (for example, elements of type person, or attributes of type xs:date).

❑ By defining a predicate that the nodes must satisfy — an arbitrary boolean expression.

❑ By defining the relative position of the node along the axis: for example, it is possible to select only the immediately preceding sibling.

The syntax of a path expression uses «/» as an operator to separate the successive steps. A «/» at the start of a path expression indicates that the origin is the document node; otherwise, it is generally the context node (we'll be looking at the notion of context in the next section). Within each step, the axis is written first, separated from the other conditions by the separator «::». However, the child axis is the default, so it may be omitted; and the attribute axis may be abbreviated to «@».

For example:

```
child::item/attribute::category
```

is a path expression of two steps; the first selects all the child `<item>` elements of the current node, and the second selects their `category` attributes. This can be abbreviated to:

```
item/@category
```

Predicates that the nodes must satisfy are written in square brackets, for example:

```
item[@code='T']/@category
```

This selects the `category` attributes of those child `<item>` elements that have a `code` attribute whose value is «T».

There are many ways of abbreviating path expressions to make them easier to write, but the basic structure remains the same. The full detail appears in Chapter 9.

Context

The way in which XPath expressions are evaluated is to some extent context dependent. For example, the value of the expression $x depends on the current value of the variable x, and the value of the expression «.» depends on which node is currently being processed in the source document.

There are two aspects to the context: the static context, which depends only on where the expression appears in the stylesheet; and the dynamic context, which depends on the state of processing at the time the expression is evaluated.

The static context for an expression includes the following:

❑   The set of namespace declarations in force at the point where the expression is written. This determines the validity and meaning of any namespace prefixes used in the expression. As well as defining the namespace prefixes that are available, the context also defines the default namespace that will be used for unqualified element names appearing in path expressions.

❑   The set of variable declarations (that is, `<xsl:variable>` and `<xsl:param>` elements) in scope at the point where the expression is written. This determines the validity of any variable references used in the expression. As well as checking at compile time that the variable has been declared, the processor can also make checks on its type; for example, it would be an error to use a variable of type `xs:date` as an argument to the `round()` function, and the processor can often detect such errors and report them at compile time.

❑   The functions that are available to be called. These always include the core library of functions defined in the XSLT and XPath specifications, and the constructor functions for built-in atomic types such as `xs:date`. They also include user-defined functions written using the `<xsl:function>` declaration, constructor functions for user-defined types in an imported schema (as described in Chapter 4), vendor-defined extension functions, and user-defined extension functions linked in to the stylesheet using vendor-defined mechanisms.

❑   The base URI of the stylesheet element containing the XPath expression. This only affects the result if the expression uses functions such as `document()` that make explicit use of the base URI.

All of these aspects of the static context for XPath expressions can be controlled from within the stylesheet, and may be different for different XPath expressions. There are other aspects of the XPath context that cannot be controlled using XSLT itself, but where implementors are likely to allow you some control via the API of their individual products. The most important example in this category is the set of URIs that are available for identifying collations (that is, rules for sorting and comparing strings according to the conventions of different languages).

The dynamic context is set only at stylesheet execution time. It consists of the following:

❑ The current values of all the variables that are in scope for the expression. These may be different each time the expression is evaluated.

❑ The focus, which reflects the current state of processing in the stylesheet. The focus comprises the following:

    ❑ The *context item*. This is the item (often a node in the source tree) that is currently being processed. An item becomes the context item when it is selected using the `<xsl:apply-templates>` or `<xsl:for-each>` instructions. The context item can also be set by the XPath processor when evaluating a subexpression. The context item can be referenced using the expression «.». In addition, the `current()` function (defined in Chapter 13) can always be used to reference the item that's the context item at the XSLT level, ignoring any changes made at the XPath level.

    ❑ The *context position*. This is an integer ($\geq$1) that indicates the position of the context item in the sequence of items currently being processed. The context position can be referenced using the `position()` function. When `<xsl:apply-templates>` or `<xsl:for-each>` are used to process a sequence of items, the context position takes the values 1 . . . *n* as each of the items in the list is processed. Similarly, when a predicate is used within a path expression, the context position is the position of the node being tested within the set of nodes being tested. For example, «`child::a[position() !=1]`» selects all the child elements named `<a>`, except the first.

    ❑ The *context size*. This is an integer ($\geq$1) that indicates the number of items in the sequence of items currently being processed (that is, the highest value that `position()` will reach). The context size can be referenced using the `last()` function. For example, «`child::a[position() !=last()]`» selects all the child elements named `<a>`, except the last.

❑ The set of documents that can be accessed using the `doc()` and `document()` functions is also regarded as being part of the dynamic context. This might include the whole of the Web, or it might be restricted by security policies to the server from which the stylesheet was loaded, or (if, say, the transformation is running on an embedded processor controlling the engine of your car) it might contain no documents at all. Modeling the set of addressable documents as part of the context is a formal device for describing the language semantics (it's a way of saying that the result of the `document()` function is defined by the environment in which the stylesheet runs, not by the language specification itself), and it turns out to be quite a neat device for distinguishing those aspects of these functions that are defined by the language spec from those that depend on the implementation.

Some system functions that can be used in XPath 2.0 expressions have other dependencies on the stylesheet context; for example, the effect of the `key()` function depends on the set of `<xsl:key>` declarations in force; but the list given earlier covers all the context information that is directly accessible to user-written expressions.

Temporary Documents

As we described at the beginning of the chapter, a transformation takes a source tree as input (or perhaps more than one source tree) and produces a result tree (or several result trees) as output.

Very often, however, the easiest way to write a complex transformation is to split it into a number of phases, each of which performs one task. Like pipes in Unix, this creates a powerful way of reusing modules of code — on the basis that each module does only one job. For example, if your stylesheet involves selecting input records, sorting them, grouping them, numbering them, and then formatting the result as HTML, you could potentially carry out each of these five steps in a separate transformation phase. One benefit is that if you wanted to change the output from HTML to PDF, the first four steps would be completely reusable.

One way of doing this is to write five separate stylesheets, and couple them together into a processing pipeline. This can be done using the Java JAXP API, described in Appendix D, or by using the new XProc pipeline language being developed by W3C. You can even do it (less efficiently) with a shell script or using ant. But often, you want rather closer coupling than this. So the alternative is to write all the phases of the transformation in a single stylesheet, using *temporary documents* to represent the intermediate results between one phase of processing and the next.

A temporary document is created by using an `<xsl:variable>` element with no «as» attribute, containing a sequence constructor to create the content of the tree. For example:

```
<xsl:variable name="author">
  <person>
    <first>Michael</first>
    <last>Kay</last>
    <nationality>British</nationality>
  </person>
</xsl:variable>
```

In this example, the value of the variable is a document node, which contains the `<person>` element as its only child node.

One popular way to use a temporary document is as a lookup table. The following stylesheet fragment uses data held in a temporary document to get the name of the month, given its number held in a variable $mm.

```
<xsl:variable name="months">
  <name>January</name><name>February</name><name>March</name>
  <name>April</name><name>May</name><name>June</name>
  <name>July</name><name>August</name><name>September</name>
  <name>October</name><name>November</name><name>December</name>
</xsl:variable>
...
  <xsl:value-of select="$months/name[position()=$mm]"/>
```

Of course, the sequence constructor does not have to contain constant values as in these two examples; it can also contain instructions such as `<xsl:value-of>` and `<xsl:apply-templates>` to build the content of the temporary document dynamically. This is shown in the following example:

```
<xsl:variable name="tree">
  <xsl:text>AAA</xsl:text>
  <xsl:element name="x">
    <xsl:attribute name="att">att-value</xsl:attribute>
    <xsl:text>BBB</xsl:text>
  </xsl:element>
  <xsl:element name="y"/>
  <xsl:text>CCC</xsl:text>
</xsl:variable>
```

This creates the tree illustrated in Figure 2-10. Each box shows a node; the three layers are respectively the node kind, the node name, and the string value of the node. Once again, an asterisk indicates that the string value is the concatenation of the string values of the child nodes.

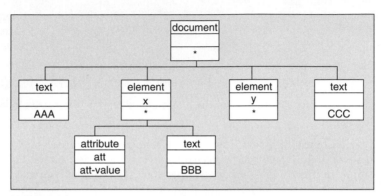

Figure 2-10

In XSLT 1.0, temporary documents went under the name of *result tree fragments*. I introduced the term *temporary tree* in an earlier edition of this book, because I felt that the phrase *result tree fragment* undervalued the range of purposes to which these structures can be applied. In fact, result tree fragments in XSLT 1.0 were very limited in their capability because of a quite artificial restriction that prevented them being accessed using path expressions. Most vendors ended up circumventing this restriction using an extension function generally named xx:node-set(), where xx refers to the vendor's particular namespace. In XSLT 2.0, the restriction is gone for good, and temporary documents can now be used in exactly the same way as any source document: they can be used as the result tree for one phase of transformation, and the source tree for the next.

The restrictions in XSLT 1.0 were defined by making result tree fragments a separate data type, with a restricted range of operations available. In XSLT 2.0, a temporary document is a tree rooted at a document node just like any other, and is manipulated using variables or expressions that refer to its root node. (In XSLT 2.0 you can also have trees rooted at elements, or even at attributes or text nodes — though in that case there will only be one node in the tree. In fact, you might sometimes prefer to use a sequence of parentless elements rather than a document. But because of the XSLT 1.0 legacy, a temporary document is what you get when you declare an <xsl:variable> element with no «as» attribute.)

A temporary document does not necessarily correspond to a well-formed XML document, for example the document node can own text nodes directly, and it can have more than one element node among its children. However, it must conform to the same rules as an XML external parsed entity; for example, all the attributes belonging to an element node must have distinct names.

The ability to use temporary documents as intermediate results in a multiphase transformation greatly increases the options available to the stylesheet designer (which is why the xx:node-set() extension function was so popular in XSLT 1.0). The general structure of such a stylesheet follows the pattern:

```
<xsl:variable name="phase-1-output">
  <xsl:apply-templates mode="phase-1"/>
</xsl:variable>

<xsl:variable name="phase-2-output">
  <xsl:apply-templates select="$phase-1-output" mode="phase-2"/>
</xsl:variable>

<xsl:result-document>
  <xsl:apply-templates select="phase-2-output" mode="phase-3"/>
</xsl:result-document>
```

Some people prefer to use local variables for the intermediate results, some use global variables; it makes little difference.

One way that I often use multiphase transformations is to write a preprocessor for some specialized data source, to convert it into the format expected by an existing stylesheet module that renders it into HTML. For example, to create a glossary as an appendix in a document, you may want to write some code that searches the document for terms and their definitions. Rather than generating HTML directly from this code, you can generate the XML vocabulary used in the rest of the document, and then reuse the existing stylesheet code to render this as phase two of your transformation. This coding style is sometimes referred to as a micro-pipeline.

Because multiphase transformations are often used to keep stylesheets modular, some discipline is required to keep the template rules for each phase separate. I generally do this in two ways:

❑ Keep the rules for each phase of transformation in a separate stylesheet module. Stylesheet modules are discussed in Chapter 3.

❑ Use a different mode for each phase of the transformation. Modes were described earlier in this chapter, on page 78.

Summary

In this chapter we explored the important concepts needed to understand what an XSLT processor does, including the following:

❑ The overall system architecture, in which a stylesheet controls the transformation of a source tree into a result tree.

❑ The tree model used in XSLT, the way it relates to the XML standards, and some of the ways it differs from the DOM model.

❑ How template rules are used to define the action to be taken by the XSLT processor when it encounters particular kinds of node in the tree.

❑ The way in which expressions, data types, and variables are used in the XSLT language to calculate values.

The next chapter looks at the structure of an XSLT stylesheet in more detail.

3

Stylesheet Structure

This chapter describes the overall structure of a stylesheet. In the previous chapter we looked at the processing model for XSLT and the data model for its source and result trees. In this chapter we will look in more detail at the different kinds of construct found in a stylesheet such as declarations and instructions, literal result elements, and attribute value templates.

Some of the concepts explained in this chapter are tricky; they are areas that often cause confusion, which is why I have tried to explain them in some detail. However, it's not necessary to master everything in this chapter before you can write your first stylesheet — so use it as a reference, coming back to topics as and when you need to understand them more deeply.

The topics covered in this chapter are as follows:

❑   *Stylesheet modules*. We will discuss how a stylesheet program can be made up of one or more stylesheet modules, linked together with `<xsl:import>` and `<xsl:include>` elements.

❑   The `<xsl:stylesheet>` (or `<xsl:transform>` element). This is the outermost element of most stylesheet modules, and it defines various attributes that control how other constructs in the module behave.

❑   The `<?xml-stylesheet?>` processing instruction. This links a source document to its associated stylesheet, and allows stylesheets to be embedded directly in the source document whose style they define.

❑   A brief description of the *declarations* found in the stylesheet, that is, the immediate children of the `<xsl:stylesheet>` or `<xsl:transform>` element. The full specifications are in Chapter 6.

❑   A brief description of each *instruction* that can be used in a stylesheet. In the previous chapter, I introduced the idea of a *sequence constructor* as a sequence of instructions that can be evaluated to produce a sequence of items, which will usually be nodes to be written to the result tree. This section provides a list of the instructions that can be used, with a quick summary of the function of each one. Full specifications of each instruction can be found in Chapter 6.

❑   *Simplified stylesheets*, in which the `<xsl:stylesheet>` and `<xsl:template match = "/">` elements are omitted, to make an XSLT stylesheet look more like the simple template languages that some users may be familiar with.

❑ *Attribute value templates*. These define variable attributes not only of literal result elements but of certain XSLT elements as well.

❑ Facilities allowing the specification to be extended, both by vendors and by W3C itself, without adversely affecting the portability of stylesheets.

❑ Handling of *whitespace* in the source document, in the stylesheet itself, and in the result tree.

Changes in XSLT 2.0

The important concepts in this chapter are largely unchanged from XSLT 1.0. The most significant changes are as follows:

❑ There are some terminology changes. Top-level elements are now called declarations. Templates (or *template bodies* as I called them in previous editions of this book) are now called sequence constructors — most people used the word template incorrectly to refer to an `<xsl:template>` element, and the new terminology bows to popular usage. Some of the terms previously used in this book but not in the official specification are now official (an example is the term *stylesheet module*).

❑ Some new declarations and instructions have been introduced.

❑ The concept of backward-compatibility mode has been introduced. This is invoked when a stylesheet specifies «version = "1.0"» and causes certain constructs to be handled in a way that is compatible with XSLT 1.0.

❑ The `use-when` attribute is introduced to allow parts of a stylesheet to be conditionally included or excluded at compile time.

❑ In other areas, there has been a general tightening up of the rules. For example, the effect of specifying «xml:space = "preserve"» in a stylesheet is now described much more precisely.

The Modular Structure of a Stylesheet

In the previous chapter, I described the XSLT processing model, in which a stylesheet defines the rules by which a source tree is transformed into a result tree.

Stylesheets, like programs in other languages, can become quite long and complex, and so there is a need to allow them to be divided into separate modules. This allows modules to be reused, and to be combined in different ways for different purposes: for example, we might want to use two different stylesheets to display press releases on-screen and on paper, but there might be components that both of these stylesheets share in common. These shared components can go in a separate module that is used in both cases.

We touched on another way of using multiple stylesheet modules in the previous chapter, where each module corresponds to one phase of processing in a multiphase transformation.

One can regard the complete collection of modules as a *stylesheet program* and refer to its components as *stylesheet modules*.

One of the stylesheet modules is the *principal stylesheet module*. This is in effect the main program, the module that is identified to the stylesheet processor by the use of an `<?xml-stylesheet?>` processing instruction in the source document, or whatever command-line parameters or application programming interface (API) the vendor chooses to provide. The principal stylesheet module may fetch other stylesheet modules, using `<xsl:include>` and `<xsl:import>` elements. These may in turn fetch others, and so on.

The following example illustrates a stylesheet written as three modules: a principal module to do the bulk of the work, with two supporting stylesheet modules, one to obtain the current date, and one to construct a copyright statement.

Example: Using `<xsl:include>`

Source

The input document, `sample.xml`, looks like this:

```
<?xml version="1.0" encoding="iso-8859-1"?>
<document>
    <author>Michael Kay</author>
    <title>XSLT 2.0 Programmer's Reference</title>
    <copyright/>
    <date/>
    <abstract>A comprehensive guide to the XSLT 2.0
      recommendation published by the World Wide Web Consortium
    </abstract>
</document>
```

Stylesheets

The stylesheet uses `<xsl:include>`. The effect of this stylesheet is to copy the source document unchanged to the result, except that any `<date>` elements are set to the current date, and any `<copyright>` elements are set to a string identifying the copyright owner.

There are three modules in this stylesheet program: `principal.xsl`, `date.xsl`, and `copyright.xsl`. The `date.xsl` module uses the XSLT 2.0 function `current-date()`; the other modules will work equally well with XSLT 1.0 or 2.0.

When you run the transformation, you only need to name the principal stylesheet module on the command line — the other modules will be fetched automatically. The way this stylesheet is written, all the modules must be in the same directory.

When an XSLT 2.0 processor sees a module that specifies «version = "1.0"», it must either run that module in backward-compatibility mode, or it must reject the stylesheet. The latest versions of Saxon and AltovaXML both support backward-compatibility mode, so this is not a problem. Saxon displays a health warning, required by the W3C specifications, which you can safely ignore in this instance.

If you try to run the stylesheet in XMLSpy, it will fail, reporting an error in the date.xsl module. This is because XMLSpy uses «version = "1.0"» as a signal to invoke its XSLT 1.0 processor, but the module date.xsl uses XSLT 2.0 features.

principal.xsl

The first module, `principal.xsl`, contains the main logic of the stylesheet.

```
<?xml version="1.0" encoding="iso-8859-1"?>
<xsl:stylesheet
     xmlns:xsl="http://www.w3.org/1999/XSL/Transform"
     version="1.0"
>
<xsl:include href="date.xsl"/>
<xsl:include href="copyright.xsl"/>
<xsl:output method="xml" encoding="iso-8859-1" indent="yes"/>
<xsl:strip-space elements="*"/>

<xsl:template match="date">
   <date><xsl:value-of select="$date"/></date>
</xsl:template>
<xsl:template match="copyright">
   <copyright>
       <xsl:call-template name="copyright"/>
   </copyright>
</xsl:template>
<xsl:template match="*">
   <xsl:copy>
       <xsl:copy-of select="@*"/>
       <xsl:apply-templates/>
   </xsl:copy>
</xsl:template>
</xsl:stylesheet>
```

It starts with two `<xsl:include>` elements to bring in the other modules. The `<xsl:output>` element indicates that the output should be in XML format, using the ISO 8859/1 character set (which makes it easy to view with a text editor), and with indentation to show the XML structure. The `<xsl:strip-space>` element indicates that whitespace nodes in the source document are to be ignored: I'll have a lot more to say about whitespace handling later in this chapter. Then there are three template rules, one for `<date>` elements, one for `<copyright>` elements, and one for everything else.

The template rule for `<date>` elements outputs the value of the variable named $date. This variable isn't defined in this stylesheet module, but it is present in the module date.xsl, so it can be accessed from here.

The template rule for `<copyright>` elements similarly calls the template named copyright. Again, there is no template of this name in this module, but there is one in the module copyright.xsl, so it can be called from here.

Finally, the template rule that matches all other elements («match = "*"») has the effect of copying the element unchanged from the source document to the output. The `<xsl:copy>` (page 287) and `<xsl:copy-of>` (page 292) instructions are explained in Chapter 6.

date.xsl

The next module, date.xsl, declares a global variable containing today's date. This calls the current-date() function in the standard XPath 2.0 function library, and the XSLT 2.0 format-date() function, both of which are described in Chapter 13.

```
<xsl:stylesheet
    xmlns:xsl="http://www.w3.org/1999/XSL/Transform"
    version="2.0"
    xmlns:xs="http://www.w3.org/2001/XMLSchema"
>
<xsl:variable name="date" as="xs:string"
    select="format-date(current-date(), '[MNn] [D1o], [Y]')"/>

</xsl:stylesheet>
```

Although this is a rather minimal module, there's a good reason why you might want to separate this code into its own module: it's dependent on XSLT 2.0, and you might want to write an alternative version of the function that doesn't have this dependency. Note that we've set «version = "2.0"» on the <xsl:stylesheet> element to document this dependency; the other modules in this stylesheet have «version = "1.0"».

Earlier releases of AltovaXML had incomplete support for the format-date() *function: the date was output, but not in the requested format. This is fixed in the 2008 release.*

copyright.xsl

Finally, the module copyright.xsl contains a named template that outputs a copyright statement. This template is called by the <xsl:call-template> instruction in the principal stylesheet. The template uses a variable $owner to construct the copyright statement; we'll see later how this is useful.

```
<?xml version="1.0" encoding="iso-8859-1"?>
<xsl:stylesheet
    xmlns:xsl="http://www.w3.org/1999/XSL/Transform"
    version="1.0">

<xsl:variable name="owner">John Wiley and Sons</xsl:variable>

<xsl:template name="copyright">
   <xsl:text>Copyright © </xsl:text>
   <xsl:value-of select="$owner"/>
   <xsl:text> 2007</xsl:text>
</xsl:template>

</xsl:stylesheet>
```

The reason for separating this stylesheet program into three modules is that the date.xsl and copyright.xsl modules are reusable in other stylesheets. Functionally, the stylesheet would have exactly the same effect if the variable $date and the template named copyright were defined directly in the principal stylesheet module.

```
<?xml version="1.0" encoding="iso-8859-1"?>
<document>
    <author>Michael Kay</author>
    <title>XSLT 2.0 Programmer's Reference</title>
    <copyright>Copyright © John Wiley and Sons 2007</copyright>
    <date>October 3rd, 2007</date>
    <abstract>A comprehensive guide to the XSLT 2.0 recommendation
published by the World Wide Web Consortium </abstract>
</document>
```

There is no syntactic difference between a principal stylesheet module and any other module; in fact any module can be used as a principal module.

This means that `<xsl:include>` and `<xsl:import>` can be used in any module, not only the principal module. So the stylesheet program is actually a tree of stylesheet modules, with the principal module at its root.

A stylesheet module is generally a complete XML document (the exception, an *embedded stylesheet*, will be described later on page 102). The document element (the outermost element of the XML document) is then either an `<xsl:stylesheet>` element or an `<xsl:transform>` element; the two names are synonymous. The elements immediately subordinate to the `<xsl:stylesheet>` or `<xsl:transform>` element are called *declarations*. The XSLT-defined declarations are listed on page 105.

The `<xsl:include>` and `<xsl:import>` declarations are always children of the `<xsl:stylesheet>` or `<xsl:transform>` element. Usually, declarations can appear in any order, but `<xsl:import>` is an exception: it must appear before any other declaration. Both elements take an `href` attribute whose value is a URI. Most commonly, it will be a relative URI, defining the location of the included or imported stylesheet module relative to the parent module. For example, `<xsl:include href = "mod1.xsl"/>` fetches the module `mod1.xsl` located in the same directory as the parent module.

The difference between `<xsl:include>` and `<xsl:import>` is that conflicting definitions are resolved differently:

❑ `<xsl:include>` effectively does a textual inclusion of the referenced stylesheet module, minus its containing `<xsl:stylesheet>` element, at the point where the `<xsl:include>` element is written. The included module is treated exactly as if its top-level elements, with their contents, appeared in the parent module in place of the `<xsl:include>` element itself.

❑ `<xsl:import>` also incorporates the top-level elements from the referenced stylesheet module, but in this case the declarations in the imported module have lower *import precedence* than the declarations in the parent module. If there are conflicting declarations, the one with higher import precedence will generally win. The detailed rules actually depend on the type of definition, and are given in the specification of `<xsl:import>` on page 357 in Chapter 6. Importing a module is thus rather like defining a subclass, in that the parent module can use some declarations unchanged from the imported module, and override others with declarations of its own.

It may not come naturally to think of the importing module as a subclass of the imported module, because in a class hierarchy, the most general classes are near the root of the tree, whereas in the <xsl:import> tree, the most general classes are at the leaves of the tree. Nevertheless, this is how <xsl:import> should be used: general-purpose modules should always be imported into special-purpose modules, not the other way around.

The most common kind of declaration is the definition of a template rule, using an <xsl:template> element with a match attribute. As we saw in the previous chapter, if there are several template rules that match a particular node in the source tree, the first step in deciding which to use is to look at their import precedence, and discard all those with import precedence less than the highest. So a template rule defined in a particular stylesheet module will automatically take precedence over another matching rule in a module that it imports.

Where one module A imports two others, B and C, as shown in Figure 3-1, then A takes precedence over both B and C, and C also takes precedence over B, assuming that the <xsl:import> element that loads B precedes the <xsl:import> element that loads C.

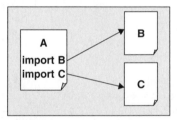

Figure 3-1

When a stylesheet incorporates another using <xsl:include>, the declarations in the included stylesheet have the same import precedence as those in the parent stylesheet.

Where two declarations have the same import precedence (because they were in the same stylesheet module, or because one was in a module incorporated in the other using <xsl:include>), the rules for resolving conflicts depend on the kind of declaration. In some cases, for example declarations of named templates or variables, duplicate declarations with the same name are always reported as an error. In other cases, for example declarations of template rules, the implementor has the choice of reporting an error or choosing the declaration that occurs later in the stylesheet. Some implementors may pass this choice on to the user. The detailed rules are given in Chapter 6 for each kind of declaration, and they are summarized in the section for <xsl:import>, page 357.

Example: Using <xsl:import>

This extends the previous <xsl:include> example, showing how to use <xsl:import> to incorporate the declarations in another stylesheet module while overriding some of them.

Source

The input document for this example is sample.xml.

Stylesheet

Recall that the `copyright.xsl` module used a variable, `$owner`, to hold the name of the copyright owner. Suppose that we want to use the `copyright` template, but with a different copyright owner. We can achieve this by writing a revised principal stylesheet as follows (this is called `principal2.xsl` in the downloadable sample files).

This stylesheet uses `<xsl:import>` instead of `<xsl:include>` to incorporate the `copyright.xsl` module, and it then contains a new declaration of the `$owner` variable, which will override the declaration in the imported module. Note that the `<xsl:import>` element must come first.

```xml
<?xml version="1.0" encoding="iso-8859-1"?>
<xsl:stylesheet
    xmlns:xsl="http://www.w3.org/1999/XSL/Transform"
    version="1.0"
>
<xsl:import href="copyright.xsl"/>
<xsl:variable name="owner">John Wiley Inc.</xsl:variable>
<xsl:include href="date.xsl"/>

<xsl:output method="xml" encoding="iso-8859-1" indent="yes"/>
<xsl:strip-space elements="*"/>

<xsl:template match="date">
   <date><xsl:value-of select="$date"/></date>
</xsl:template>
<xsl:template match="copyright">
   <copyright><xsl:call-template name="copyright"/></copyright>
</xsl:template>

<xsl:template match="*">
   <xsl:copy>
      <xsl:copy-of select="@*"/>
      <xsl:apply-templates/>
   </xsl:copy>
</xsl:template>
</xsl:stylesheet>
```

Output

```xml
<?xml version="1.0" encoding="iso-8859-1" ?>
<document>
   <author>Michael Kay</author>
   <title>XSLT Programmer's Reference</title>
   <copyright>Copyright © John Wiley Inc 2007</copyright>
   <date>April 28th, 2007</date>
   <abstract>A comprehensive guide to the XSLT 2.0 recommendation
published by the World Wide Web Consortium </abstract>
</document>
```

This example wouldn't work if you used `<xsl:include>` rather than `<xsl:import>`. It would complain that the variable `$owner` was declared twice. This is because with `<xsl:include>`, the two declarations have the same import precedence, so neither can override the other.

It is an error for a stylesheet module to import or include itself, directly or indirectly, because doing so would define an infinite loop.

It isn't an error, however, for a stylesheet module to be included or imported at more than one place in the stylesheet program. The following isn't an error.

```
<xsl:stylesheet xmlns:xsl="http://www.w3.org/1999/XSL/Transform" version="2.0">
    <xsl:import href="date.xsl"/>
    <xsl:import href="date.xsl"/>
</xsl:stylesheet>
```

This may seem rather pointless, but in a highly modular structure it can sometimes happen by accident and be harmless. For example, several of your stylesheet modules might independently reference a commonly used module such as `date.xsl`. The effect is simply to load two copies of all the declarations in `date.xsl`, exactly as if two identical files with different names had been imported.

If the same module is fetched twice using `<xsl:include>`, the included declarations will have the same import precedence, which is likely to cause an error. If, for example, the included module defines a global variable or a named template, duplicate declarations will be reported. In other cases, for example where the file uses the `<xsl:attribute-set>` element to define named attribute sets, the duplicate declarations are harmless (the `<xsl:attribute-set>` element is described on page 266, in Chapter 6). However, if there is a risk of loading the same module twice, it makes sense to use `<xsl:import>` rather than `<xsl:include>`.

Note that with both `<xsl:include>` and `<xsl:import>`, the `href` attribute is fixed: it is possible for a stylesheet compiler to assemble all the modules in a stylesheet well before a source document is supplied to actually run the transformation. People often ask for some kind of facility to load stylesheet modules dynamically, based on a decision made while the transformation is running. The simple answer is that you can't do this: you have to construct the whole stylesheet before you can start running it.

Sometimes, this requirement arises when people try to use `<xsl:import>` "the wrong way round." It's fairly natural to think in terms of writing a general-purpose stylesheet G that imports A in some circumstances (say if the user is French) and imports B in other circumstances (if the user is Spanish). But that's the wrong way to do it: you should select A or B as the principal stylesheet module, and have both of these import the general-purpose module G. The special-purpose stylesheet module should always import the general-purpose module.

Although you can't make a runtime decision on what modules to import or include, you can use compile-time conditional logic. For example, you can write:

```
<xsl:include href = "mod1.xsl"
             use-when = "system-property('xsl:vendor') = 'Altova GmbH'"/>.
```

97

This allows conditional inclusion of a module based on information that is known at compile time. There is more information on the use-when *attribute later in the chapter: see the section ''Writing Portable Stylesheets'' on page 127.*

The <xsl:stylesheet> Element

The <xsl:stylesheet> element (or <xsl:transform>, which is a synonym) is the outermost element of every stylesheet module.

The name <xsl:stylesheet> is a conventional name. The first part, xsl, is a prefix that identifies the namespace to which the element name belongs. Any prefix can be used so long as it is mapped, using a namespace declaration, to the URI http://www.w3.org/1999/XSL/Transform. There is also a mandatory version attribute. So the start tag of the <xsl:stylesheet> element will usually look like this:

```
<xsl:stylesheet
    xmlns:xsl="http://www.w3.org/1999/XSL/Transform"
    version="2.0"
>
```

The <xsl:stylesheet> element can also be written as <xsl:transform> if you prefer to think of XSLT as doing transformations rather than styling. The two names are completely interchangeable, but I usually use <xsl:stylesheet> for familiarity. Everything I say about the <xsl:stylesheet> element applies equally to <xsl:transform>.

As a general principle, it's advisable to specify «version = "2.0"» if the stylesheet module uses any facilities from XSLT 2.0 or XPath 2.0, and «version = "1.0"» if it relies only on XSLT 1.0 and XPath 1.0 features. This isn't purely documentary; as we'll see later (see page 128), XSLT processors have some subtle differences in behavior, depending on the setting of this attribute.

If you encounter a stylesheet that uses the namespace URI http://www.w3.org/TR/WD-xsl, *then the stylesheet is written in a Microsoft dialect based on an early working draft of the XSLT 1.0 standard. There are many differences between this dialect and XSLT 1.0, and even more differences between WD-xsl and XSLT 2.0. Although it has been obsolete for some years, you may still come across it occasionally.*

The other attributes that may appear on this element are described under <xsl:stylesheet> in Chapter 6, page 465. Specifically, they are as follows:

❏   id identifies the stylesheet when it appears as an embedded stylesheet within another document. Embedded stylesheets are described in the next section.

❏   extension-element-prefixes is a list of namespace prefixes that denote elements used for vendor-defined or user-defined extensions to the XSLT language.

❏   exclude-result-prefixes is a list of namespaces used in the stylesheet that should not be copied to the result tree unless they are actually needed. I'll explain how this works in the section *Literal Result Elements* on page 112.

❏   xpath-default-namespace is a namespace URI, which is used as the default namespace for unprefixed element names used in path expressions within the stylesheet, and also for unprefixed type names. This attribute is handy when all the elements in your source document are in a particular namespace, because it saves you having to use a namespace prefix every time you refer to an element in this namespace. Without this attribute, element names with no prefix are assumed to refer to names in the null namespace (neither the default namespace declared using «xmlns = "uri"» in the stylesheet, nor the default namespace declared in the source document, has any effect on names used in path expressions).

❑ default-validation takes one of the values «preserve» or «strip». This attribute is used by a schema-aware processor to determine whether any schema-derived type annotations are retained when elements and attributes are copied. You will find more details of how result trees are validated against a schema in Chapter 4.

❑ default-collation defines how strings are to be compared and sorted. There are many different conventions for sorting strings, depending on the language and sometimes on the whims of a publisher. The value of this attribute is simply a URI that acts as a name for the set of conventions to be used; the values you can use for this attribute will vary from one XSLT processor to another. For more details on collations, see <xsl:sort> on page 459 in Chapter 6.

❑ input-type-annotations takes one of the values «preserve», «strip», or «unspecified». This attribute is used by a schema-aware processor to determine whether any schema-derived type annotations are retained in the input document.

With the exception of input-type-annotations, these attributes affect only the stylesheet module in which this <xsl:stylesheet> element appears; they do not affect what happens in included or imported stylesheet modules.

The <xsl:stylesheet> element will often contain further namespace declarations. Many stylesheets are likely to reference the names of types defined in XML Schema, in which case the XML Schema namespace needs to be declared. If the result tree uses a namespace (perhaps XSL-FO or SVG), then that namespace too will often be declared. Also, if the extension-element-prefixes or exclude-result-prefixes attributes are used, then any namespace prefixes they mention must be declared by means of a names-pace declaration on the <xsl:stylesheet> element. So, if you want to declare «saxon» as an extension element prefix, the start tag of the <xsl:stylesheet> element might look like this.

```
<xsl:stylesheet
    xmlns:xsl="http://www.w3.org/1999/XSL/Transform"
    xmlns:xs="http://www.w3.org/2001/XMLSchema"
    xmlns:fo="http://www.w3.org/1999/XSL/Format"
    xmlns:saxon="http://saxon.sf.net/"
    version="2.0"
    extension-element-prefixes="saxon"
    exclude-result-prefixes="xs"
>
```

Namespace declarations on the <xsl:stylesheet> element, and indeed anywhere else in the stylesheet, apply only to the stylesheet module in which they appear. They are not inherited by included or imported modules.

The <?xml-stylesheet?> Processing Instruction

This processing instruction is not a part of the XSLT or XPath standard; rather it has a short W3 C Recom-mendation all to itself, which you can find at http://www.w3.org/TR/xml-stylesheet. XSLT mentions it, but only in an example, so there is no implication that an XSLT processor is required to support it. However, many processors do, at least in its most basic form.

The `<?xml-stylesheet?>` processing instruction is used within a source XML document to identify the stylesheet that should be used to process it. There can be several `<?xml-stylesheet?>` processing instructions present, defining different stylesheets to be used under different circumstances.

This way of controlling a transformation is particularly useful if you want to run the transformation on the client side (that is, in the browser). This is supported by most browsers, including Internet Explorer, Firefox, Safari, and Opera. It means you can simply send an XML file to the browser, with a processing instruction to identify the stylesheet to be used, and the browser will automatically invoke a transformation and then display the resulting HTML. No special script is needed to control the process, which means the solution is very portable. Unfortunately, at the time of writing, none of the major browsers includes support for client-side transformation using XSLT 2.0.

On the server side, which is where you are more likely to be using XSLT 2.0, it's less likely that you will want to control the transformation using this processing instruction. It's much more likely that you will want either to drive the process from the operating system command line or to use an API such as the Microsoft or Java APIs (described in Appendices D and E, respectively). These APIs give you much more control: they allow you to apply different stylesheets to the same documents on different occasions, to set parameters, and to compile a stylesheet once and then use it repeatedly.

So it's quite likely you can skip this section for now; but for completeness, I think it's still important to describe this mechanism.

The `<?xml-stylesheet?>` processing instruction has an `href` attribute whose value is the URI of the stylesheet (that is, the principal stylesheet module), and a `type` attribute that indicates the language in which the stylesheet is written. This doesn't have to be an XSLT stylesheet; it could be a Cascading Style Sheet (CSS).

There's considerable confusion about what the correct value of the `type` attribute should be in the case of XSLT. Until recently there was no registered media type (often called MIME type) for XSLT stylesheets, so Microsoft invented one: `text/xsl`. This has never been made official, and the XSLT 2.0 Recommendation instead registers the name `application/xslt+xml`. However, the use of `text/xsl` is now so widespread that it is unlikely to go away.

> *Technically, XML processing instructions do not contain attributes; they contain a name (here* `xml-stylesheet`*) followed by character data. But in this case the character data is structured as a sequence of* `name = "value"` *pairs, like the attributes in an element start tag, and the xml-stylesheet recommendation refers to these pairs as pseudo-attributes.*

Following is the full list of pseudo-attributes in the `<?xml-stylesheet?>` processing instruction.

Attribute Name	Value	Meaning
`href` (mandatory)	URI	The URI of the stylesheet. This may be an absolute or relative link to the XML document that contains the stylesheet, or it may contain a fragment identifier (for example `#styleB`) used to locate the stylesheet within a larger file. See the section *Embedded Stylesheets* on page 102.
`type` (mandatory)	MIME type	Identifies the language in which the stylesheet is written; typically «`application/xslt+xml`» or «`text/xsl`» (see the discussion earlier).

continued

Attribute Name	Value	Meaning
title (optional)	String	If there are several <?xml-stylesheet?> processing instructions, each should be given a title to distinguish them. The user can then be allowed to choose which stylesheet is wanted. For example, there may be special stylesheets that produce large print or aural rendition.
media (optional)	String	Description of the output medium, for example «print», «projection», or «aural». The list of possible values is defined in the HTML 4.0 specification. This value can be used to select from the available stylesheets.
charset (optional)	Character encoding	This attribute is not useful with XSLT stylesheets, since as XML documents they define their character encoding themselves.
alternate (optional)	"yes" or "no"	If «no» is specified, this is the preferred stylesheet. If «yes» is specified, it is an alternative stylesheet to be selected at user option.

As far as I have been able to discover the only attributes that influence Internet Explorer or Firefox are the media, href, and alternate attributes, and alternate is not very useful, because both browsers choose the «alternate = "no"» stylesheet without giving the user any opportunity to override the choice.

An <?xml-stylesheet?> processing instruction must appear, if it appears at all, as part of the document prolog, that is, before the start tag of the document element. The href attribute identifies the location of the stylesheet by an absolute or relative URI reference. For example:

```
<?xml-stylesheet type="text/xsl" href="../style.xsl"?>
```

According to the W3C spec, it is possible to have several <?xml-stylesheet?> processing instructions that match the required criteria. The idea is that, as with CSS, the different stylesheets should be merged. Again, however, the practical reality seems to be different: it appears that Internet Explorer uses the first stylesheet specified, and Firefox uses the last. (Because this might be a bug that could be fixed at any time, I would advise against relying on this observation in the design of your application.)

It isn't mandatory to use the <?xml-stylesheet?> processing instruction, and most products will offer some other way of saying which stylesheet you want to apply to a particular document. It's mainly useful when you want to apply a stylesheet to an XML document within the browser; specifying this processing instruction means that the browser can apply a default stylesheet to the document, without any extra scripting being needed.

Clearly, one of the reasons for separating the stylesheet from the source XML document is so that the same information can be transformed or presented in different ways depending on the user, their equipment, or the particular mode of access. The various attributes of the <?xml-stylesheet?> processing instruction are designed to define the rules controlling the selection of an appropriate stylesheet. The mechanism is geared toward stylesheets that are used to display information to users; it has less relevance to the more general use of XSLT for performing data transformations.

Embedded Stylesheets

There is one exception to the rule that the stylesheet module must be an XML document. The principal stylesheet module can be *embedded* within another XML document, typically the document whose style it is defining.

The ability to embed stylesheets within the source document is best regarded as a carryover from CSS. It can be useful if you have a freestanding document that you want to distribute as a self-contained unit, but in most situations it is better to use an external stylesheet that can be used for many different source documents. I sometimes use an embedded stylesheet when I have a "one-of-a-kind" document such as a diary of events to be displayed on a Web site, as it simplifies things to keep the stylesheet and the data together. Some people like to embed stylesheets to reduce download time, but this can be counterproductive, because it means the browser cannot spot that the stylesheet is already present in its cache.

> **Not all products support embedded stylesheets. The example below works in Firefox but not in Internet Explorer.**

The outermost element of the stylesheet is still an `<xsl:stylesheet>` or `<xsl:transform>` element, but it will no longer be the outermost element of the XML document (that is, the document element). The `<xsl:stylesheet>` element will generally have an `id` attribute to identify it and will be referenced within its containing document using the `<?xml-stylesheet?>` processing instruction, as shown in the following example.

Example: Embedded Stylesheets

This example shows a stylesheet embedded within an XML source document containing a list of books.

Source

The data file, `embedded.xml`, containing both source document and stylesheet, is as follows:

```
<?xml version="1.0"?> <!DOCTYPE books [
  <!ATTLIST xsl:stylesheet id ID #REQUIRED>
]>
<?xml-stylesheet type="text/xsl" href="#style1"?>
<books>
  <book category="reference">
    <author>Nigel Rees</author>
    <title>Sayings of the Century</title>
    <price>8.95</price>
  </book>
  <book category="fiction">
    <author>Evelyn Waugh</author>
    <title>Sword of Honour</title>
    <price>12.99</price>
  </book>
  <book category="fiction">
    <author>Herman Melville</author>
```

```
        <title>Moby Dick</title>
        <price>8.99</price>
    </book>
    <book category="fiction">
        <author>J. R. R. Tolkien</author>
        <title>The Lord of the Rings</title>
        <price>22.99</price>
    </book>
    <xsl:stylesheet id="style1" version="1.0"
        xmlns:xsl="http://www.w3.org/1999/XSL/Transform">
    <xsl:template match="xsl:stylesheet"/>
    <xsl:template match="books">
        <html><body>
            <h1>A list of books</h1>
            <table>
                <xsl:apply-templates/>
            </table>
        </body></html>
    </xsl:template>

    <xsl:template match="book">
        <tr><xsl:apply-templates/></tr>
    </xsl:template>
    <xsl:template match="author | title | price">
        <td><xsl:value-of select="."/></td>
    </xsl:template>
    </xsl:stylesheet>
</books>
```

You can run this stylesheet either by simply opening it in Firefox or by using Saxon with a command of the form:

```
java -jar c:\saxon\saxon9.jar -a embedded.xml
```

The -a option tells Saxon to look for an <?xml-stylesheet?> processing instruction in the supplied source document, and to process the source document using that stylesheet. Saxon doesn't allow you (when using the command line interface) to specify the criteria for selecting a specific stylesheet, so if there are several, it uses a composite stylesheet that imports all of them.

Saxon will recognize the relative URI «#style1» only if it refers to the value of an attribute of type ID. The «id» attribute of the <xsl:stylesheet> element therefore needs to be declared as having this type; this is the purpose of the short <!DOCTYPE> entry. This isn't sufficient to invoke validation of the document (if you do try to invoke validation, by specifying the -v option on the command line, you will get a string of error messages referring to undeclared elements), but it is sufficient to register the attribute type of the «id» attribute.

This example doesn't work with Saxon on the .NET platform; this is because the Microsoft XML parser on .NET doesn't notify ID attributes unless you do DTD validation. An alternative is to use the xml:id *attribute, which doesn't depend on a DTD. In the downloaded code, the file* embedded2.xml *illustrates this variation.*

Output

The output of this embedded stylesheet, when viewed in a Web browser, is shown in Figure 3-2.

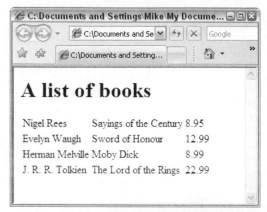

Figure 3-2

Note the empty template rule that matches the `<xsl:stylesheet>` element. This is needed because without it the stylesheet will try to process itself along with the rest of the document. The empty template rule ensures that when the `<xsl:stylesheet>` element is matched, no output is generated and its child elements are not processed. You may need to take care to avoid matching other elements in the stylesheet as well. For example, if the stylesheet looks for book titles using an expression such as «//title», this could accidentally match a `<title>` literal result element within the embedded stylesheet.

An embedded stylesheet module will generally be used as the principal stylesheet module. The standard doesn't explicitly say whether or not an embedded stylesheet can be included or imported into another. In practice, the details of what is supported are likely to vary from one product to another; few of the current products have much to say about embedded stylesheets in their documentation.

If namespace declarations occur outside the embedded stylesheet, they will still be in scope within the embedded stylesheet, which may result in extra namespace nodes being copied into the result tree. You can suppress such namespaces, using the `exclude-result-prefixes` attribute on the `<xsl:stylesheet>` element. If you are using an XML 1.1 parser, another solution would be to undeclare these namespaces (that is, to remove them from the set of namespaces that are in scope) by using a namespace undeclaration of the form «xmlns:prefix = "">». (With XML 1.0, the only namespace that can be undeclared is the default namespace.)

Declarations

All elements that are immediate children of the `<xsl:stylesheet>` or `<xsl:transform>` element are called *top-level elements*. The top-level elements that are defined in the XSLT specification, and whose names are in the XSLT namespace, are called *declarations*. Those that are not defined in the XSLT specification are called user-defined data elements, and I will consider these in two categories: elements defined by the vendor of the XSLT processor and elements defined by the stylesheet author.

It is not permitted to have text nodes as immediate children of the `<xsl:stylesheet>` or `<xsl:transform>` element, unless they consist entirely of whitespace characters. Processing instructions and comments may appear, and the XSLT processor will ignore them.

Top-level elements can appear in any order in the stylesheet, except that if there are any `<xsl:import>` declarations, these must come first. In most cases the order in which the elements appear is of no significance; however, if there are conflicting definitions, the XSLT processor sometimes has the option of either reporting an error or taking whichever definition comes last. If you want your stylesheet to be portable, you cannot rely on this behavior, and should ensure that conflicting declarations don't arise.

Let's now examine the three categories of elements that may appear as children of `<xsl:stylesheet>`.

- ❏ XSLT-defined declarations
- ❏ Implementor-defined declarations
- ❏ User-defined data elements

XSLT-Defined Declarations

An XSLT-defined declaration must be one of the following:

```
<xsl:attribute-set>
<xsl:character-map>
<xsl:decimal-format>
<xsl:function>
<xsl:import>
<xsl:import-schema>
<xsl:include>
<xsl:key>
<xsl:namespace-alias>
<xsl:output>
<xsl:param>
<xsl:preserve-space>
<xsl:strip-space>
<xsl:template>
<xsl:variable>
```

No other XSLT element (that is, no other element with the namespace URI `http://www.w3.org/1999/XSL/Transform`) may be used as a child of an `<xsl:stylesheet>` element.

The `<xsl:param>` and `<xsl:variable>` elements are exceptional in that they can be used both as declarations (of global variables and parameters) and as instructions within a sequence constructor.

The following table gives a quick introduction to the purpose of each of these declarations.

Declaration	Effect
`<xsl:attribute-set>`	Defines a named set of attribute nodes that can be added to any element in the result tree
`<xsl:character-map>`	Defines how individual characters in the result tree are to be output by the serializer

continued

Declaration	Effect
`<xsl:decimal-format>`	Defines a display format for numbers, used by the `format-number()` function described in Chapter 13
`<xsl:function>`	Defines a stylesheet function that can be invoked from any XPath expression
`<xsl:import>`	Incorporates declarations from another stylesheet module, with lower precedence than the declarations in the importing module
`<xsl:import-schema>`	Incorporates definitions from an XML Schema
`<xsl:include>`	Incorporates declarations from another stylesheet module, with the same precedence as the declarations in the including module
`<xsl:key>`	Defines a key that may be referenced using the `key()` function (described in Chapter 13) to give fast access to elements if their key values are known
`<xsl:namespace-alias>`	Defines a translation from namespaces used in the stylesheet to namespaces used in the result tree
`<xsl:output>`	Defines how a result tree should be serialized
`<xsl:param>`	Defines a stylesheet parameter, a value that can be set from outside the stylesheet and accessed from anywhere within it
`<xsl:preserve-space>`	Defines a list of elements that contain whitespace text nodes that need to be retained
`<xsl:strip-space>`	Defines a list of elements that contain whitespace text nodes that must be removed
`<xsl:template>`	Defines a template that can be invoked either when specific nodes are matched, or explicitly by name
`<xsl:variable>`	Defines a global variable whose value can be accessed from anywhere in the stylesheet

The meaning of each of these elements is explained in full detail in Chapter 6.

Implementor-Defined Declarations

An implementor-defined declaration must belong to a namespace with a non-null URI, different from the XSLT namespace. This will generally be a namespace defined by the vendor: for example with the Saxon product, the relevant namespace URI is `http://saxon.sf.net/`. The meaning of elements in this category is entirely at the discretion of the vendor, though the specification states a rule that such elements must not be used to change the meaning of any standard XSLT constructs, *except to the extent that the behavior is implementation defined*. This is a very important caveat, because there are a great many things in XSLT that are implementation defined, and this clause allows vendors to use top-level elements to give the user control over the choices that are exercised. For example, they might be used to control the following:

❑   Binding of extension functions and extension instructions

❑   Collations used for sorting

- ❏ Details of result-tree serialization
- ❏ Localization of messages
- ❏ Options applied when building source trees, for example whether or not schema validation is performed
- ❏ Performance trade-offs, for example switches to control optimization or generation of diagnostics
- ❏ Error recovery policy

Note that these top-level elements are not technically extension instructions, so their namespace does not have to be declared in the `extension-element-prefixes` attribute for them to be effective.

Several vendors supply top-level elements that allow you to define extension functions that can be invoked from XPath expressions in the stylesheet (for example, Microsoft has an element called `<msxsl:script>` that can be used to define JavaScript functions to be called during the transformation). Others might use such elements to define debugging or tracing options. Saxon also provides a top-level element to describe details of collations used for sorting, and another to import functions from an XQuery library module. Such extensions are described in the vendor's documentation for the particular product.

If the processor doesn't recognize the namespace used for an implementor-defined declaration, it simply ignores it. This means you can safely mix different vendors' extensions in the same stylesheet.

User-Defined Top-Level Elements

A *user-defined top-level element* must also belong to a namespace with a non-null URI, different from the XSLT namespace, and preferably different from the namespace URI used by any vendor. These elements are ignored by the XSLT processor.

With XSLT 1.0, user-defined top-level elements were useful as a place to put lookup data, error messages, and the like. It is possible to reference these elements from within the stylesheet, by treating the stylesheet as an additional source document, and loading it using the `document()` function, which is described in Chapter 13. If the first argument to this function is an empty string, it is interpreted as a reference to the stylesheet module in which the `document()` function appears.

So, for example, if the stylesheet contains a user-defined top-level element as follows:

```
<user:data xmlns:user="http://acme.com/">
   <message nr="1">Source document is empty</message>
   <message nr="2">Invalid date</message>
   <message nr="3">Sales value is not numeric</message>
</user:data>
```

then the same stylesheet can contain a named template to display a numbered message as follows:

```
<xsl:template name="display-message">
   <xsl:param name="message-nr"/>
   <xsl:message xmlns:user="http://acme.com/">
      <xsl:value-of
       select="document('')/*/user:data/message[@nr=$message-nr]"/>
   </xsl:message>
</xsl:template>
```

The `<xsl:value-of>` element evaluates the XPath expression in its `select` attribute as a string, and writes the value to the result tree. In this case the XPath expression is a path expression starting with «`document('')`», which selects the root node of the stylesheet module, followed by «`*`», which selects its first child (the `<xsl:stylesheet>` element), followed by «`user:data`», which selects the `<user:data>` element, followed by «`message[@nr = $message-nr]`», which selects the `<message>` element whose nr attribute is equal to the value of the `$message-nr` parameter in the stylesheet.

The advantage of this technique is that it gathers all the messages together in one place, for ease of maintenance. The technique can also be readily extended to use different sets of messages, depending on the user's preferred language.

With XSLT 2.0 this technique is no longer necessary, because it becomes more convenient to define fixed data as part of a global variable definition. Instead of writing:

```
<user:data xmlns:user="http://acme.com/">
    <message nr="1">Source document is empty</message>
    <message nr="2">Invalid date</message>
    <message nr="3">Sales value is not numeric</message>
</user:data>
```

you can write:

```
<xsl:variable name="data">
    <message nr="1">Source document is empty</message>
    <message nr="2">Invalid date</message>
    <message nr="3">Sales value is not numeric</message>
</xsl:variable>
```

and instead of:

```
<xsl:value-of select="document('')/*/user:data/message[@nr=$message-nr]"/>
```

you can write:

```
<xsl:value-of select="$data/message[@nr=$message-nr]"/>
```

The XSLT 1.0 technique still works, and you may want to continue using it when you write stylesheets that are to be portable between 1.0 and 2.0 processors.

Instructions

We saw in the previous chapter that a stylesheet is evaluated by a process that involves identifying template rules, evaluating the instructions contained in a template rule to produce nodes, and then adding the nodes to a result tree. This section explores in more detail the instructions that can be evaluated to produce nodes in the result tree.

The content of an `<xsl:template>` declaration, and of various other XSLT elements, is known as a *sequence constructor*. Element nodes within a sequence constructor are one of three kinds: XSLT instructions, extension elements, and literal result elements. I'll describe these in the next three sections.

XSLT Instructions

An XSLT instruction is one of the following elements.

`<xsl:analyze-string>`	`<xsl:for-each-group>`
`<xsl:apply-imports>`	`<xsl:if>`
`<xsl:apply-templates>`	`<xsl:message>`
`<xsl:attribute>`	`<xsl:namespace>`
`<xsl:call-template>`	`<xsl:next-match>`
`<xsl:choose>`	`<xsl:number>`
`<xsl:comment>`	`<xsl:perform-sort>`
`<xsl:copy>`	`<xsl:processing-instruction>`
`<xsl:copy-of>`	`<xsl:result-document>`
`<xsl:document>`	`<xsl:sequence>`
`<xsl:element>`	`<xsl:text>`
`<xsl:fallback>`	`<xsl:value-of>`
`<xsl:for-each>`	`<xsl:variable>`

No other element in the XSLT namespace may appear directly in a sequence constructor. Other XSLT elements, for example `<xsl:with-param>`, `<xsl:sort>`, and `<xsl:otherwise>`, are not regarded as instructions, because they cannot appear directly in a sequence constructor — they may appear only in very specific contexts. The `<xsl:param>` element is anomalous as it can appear as a child of an `<xsl:template>` element, but it is constrained to appear before other elements, and is therefore not considered to be part of the sequence constructor. So, it is not classified as an instruction. The same is true of an `<xsl:sort>` element appearing within `<xsl:for-each>` or `<xsl:for-each-group>`.

The following table gives a brief introduction to the effect of each XSLT instruction.

Instruction	Effect
`<xsl:analyze-string>`	Applies a regular expression to a string, causing subsidiary instructions to be evaluated for each matching and nonmatching substring.
`<xsl:apply-imports>`	Searches imported stylesheets for another template rule to apply to the context node.
`<xsl:apply-templates>`	Selects a sequence of nodes and for each of these nodes identifies the template rule to be used to process that node, invokes the template rule, and returns the results.
`<xsl:attribute>`	Constructs an attribute node.
`<xsl:call-template>`	Invokes a named template and returns its result.
`<xsl:choose>`	Chooses one of a number of instructions to evaluate, based on boolean conditions.
`<xsl:comment>`	Constructs a comment node.

continued

Instruction	Effect
`<xsl:copy>`	Copies the context node. This is a shallow copy; the content of the new node is determined by the contained instructions.
`<xsl:copy-of>`	Returns a deep copy of selected nodes or atomic values.
`<xsl:document>`	Constructs a document node.
`<xsl:element>`	Constructs an element node.
`<xsl:fallback>`	Defines fallback behavior to use if a particular instruction is not available.
`<xsl:for-each>`	Invokes the contained instructions once for each item in a sequence of items.
`<xsl:for-each-group>`	Selects a sequence of items and divides these into groups according to specified criteria; invokes the contained instructions once for each group of items.
`<xsl:if>`	Evaluates the contained instructions if and only if a specified condition is true.
`<xsl:message>`	Outputs a message to a system-defined destination.
`<xsl:namespace>`	Constructs a namespace node.
`<xsl:next-match>`	Selects another template rule that applies to the context node and invokes it.
`<xsl:number>`	Generates a sequence number for the context node and formats it for output.
`<xsl:processing-instruction>`	Constructs a processing instruction node.
`<xsl:perform-sort>`	Selects a sequence of items and sorts them according to specified criteria.
`<xsl:result-document>`	Constructs a document node to act as the root of a result tree and optionally serializes it to a specified output destination.
`<xsl:sequence>`	Produces a sequence of nodes and/or atomic values.
`<xsl:text>`	Constructs a text node from literal text in the stylesheet, preserving whitespace.
`<xsl:value-of>`	Constructs a text node.
`<xsl:variable>`	Defines a local variable whose value can be accessed from other instructions within its scope.

All of these XSLT instructions are explained in full detail in Chapter 6.

If an unknown element in the XSLT namespace is encountered in a sequence constructor, the action taken depends on whether *forward-compatible mode* is enabled. This is discussed later on page 130.

Extension Instructions

An *extension instruction* is an instruction defined by the vendor or the user, as distinct from one defined in the XSLT standard. In both cases, they are recognized as extension elements because they belong to a namespace that is listed in the [xsl:]extension-element-prefixes attribute of this element or of a containing element. (The prefix «xsl:» is used on this attribute only when it appears on an element that is *not* in the XSLT namespace. Most commonly, this attribute — without the «xsl:» prefix — appears on the <xsl:stylesheet> element itself.)

In practice, extension instructions are more likely to be defined by vendors than by users. With XSLT 1.0, several vendors provided extension instructions to direct the stylesheet output to multiple output files (with XSLT 2.0, this is superseded by a standard facility, the <xsl:result-document> instruction). The Saxon product also provided the <saxon:group> extension element, which has been superseded by the <xsl:for-each-group> instruction in XSLT 2.0. An example of an extension that has not been superseded by any XSLT 2.0 feature is Saxon's <sql:query> element, which returns the result of performing a query on a relational database.

The following example shows an <acme:instruction> element that would be treated as a literal result element were it not for the xsl:extension-element-prefixes attribute, which turns it into an extension instruction.

```
<acme:instruction
    xmlns:acme="http://acme.co.jp/xslt"
    xsl:extension-element-prefixes="acme"/>
```

The way in which new extension instructions are implemented is not defined in the XSLT specification and is likely to vary for each vendor. Not all products allow users to implement their own extension instructions, and with those that do, it may well involve some rather complex system-level programming. In practice, it is usually simpler to escape to user-written code by using extension functions, which are much easier to write. Extension functions are discussed later in this chapter, on page 134.

However, all XSLT processors are required to recognize an extension instruction when they see one, and distinguish it from a literal result element.

What happens if a stylesheet that uses an extension instruction defined in the Xalan product (say) is processed using a different product (say Microsoft's)? If the processor encounters an extension instruction that it cannot evaluate (typically because it was invented by a different vendor), the action it must take is clearly defined in the XSLT standard: if the stylesheet author has defined an <xsl:fallback> action, it must evaluate that; otherwise, it must report an error. The one thing it must not do is to treat the extension instruction as a literal result element and copy it to the result tree.

The <xsl:fallback> instruction allows you to define how an XSLT processor should deal with extension instructions it does not recognize. It is described in more detail on page 141, and full specifications are on page 316 in Chapter 6.

Any element found in a sequence constructor that is not an XSLT instruction or an extension instruction is interpreted as a *literal result element* (for example, the <hr/> elements in the example discussed earlier). When the sequence constructor is evaluated, the literal result element will be copied to the result sequence.

So in effect there are two kinds of nodes in a sequence constructor: instructions and data. Instructions are obeyed according to the rules of the particular instruction, and data nodes (text nodes and literal result elements) are copied to the result sequence.

Literal result elements play an important role in the structure of a stylesheet, so the next section examines them in more detail.

Literal Result Elements

A literal result element is an element within a sequence constructor in the stylesheet that cannot be interpreted as an instruction, and which is therefore treated as data to be copied to the current output destination.

The notation I'm using here to describe literal result elements will be used extensively in Chapter 6, so it's worth explaining it.

❑ The *Format* section explains where the element can appear in the stylesheet; it lists the permitted attributes and their meanings and defines what child elements can appear in this element, if any. For each attribute it gives the name of the attribute, states whether the attribute is mandatory or optional, gives the permitted values for the attribute, and explains how the attribute is used. It also indicates whether the attribute may be an attribute value template.

❑ The *Effect* section defines what the element does

❑ The *Usage* section explains how the element is used in practice.

❑ The *Examples* section gives examples of how the element is used. In some cases, especially where an element has several distinct usages, the examples are merged into the *Usage* section.

Format

A literal result element can have any name, provided it is not in the XSLT namespace and is not in a namespace declared to contain extension instructions.

Position

A literal result element always appears directly within a sequence constructor.

Attributes

Name	Value	Meaning
xsl:use-when (optional)	An XPath expression that can be evaluated at compile time	Allows the element to be conditionally excluded from the stylesheet.
xsl:default-collation (optional)	A URI identifying a collation supplied by the vendor	Defines the default collation to be used within this part of the stylesheet.
xsl:exclude-result-prefixes (optional)	Whitespace-separated list of namespace prefixes (see the following note)	Each prefix in the list must identify a namespace that is in scope at this point in the stylesheet module. The namespace identified is not to be copied to the result tree.

continued

Name	Value	Meaning
xsl:extension-element-prefixes (optional)	Whitespace-separated list of namespace prefixes (see the following note)	Each prefix in the list must identify a namespace that is in scope at this point in the stylesheet module. Elements that are descendants of this literal result element, and whose names are in one of these identified namespaces, are treated as extension instructions rather than literal result elements.
xsl:inherit-namespaces (optional)	«yes» or «no» (Default is «yes»)	Indicates whether the constructed element will inherit the namespaces of its parent.
xsl:version (optional)	Number	The value «1.0» invokes backward-compatible processing for this element and its descendants (see page 129). A value greater than 2.0 enables forward-compatible processing (see page 130).
xsl:use-attribute-sets (optional)	Whitespace-separated list of QNames identifying named <xsl:attribute-set> elements (see the following note)	The attributes defined in the named attribute sets are instantiated and copied as attributes of this literal result element in the constructed sequence.
xsl:type (optional)	The name of a global type (simple type or complex type), which is either a built-in type such as xs:date, or a type defined in an imported schema	The constructed element in the result tree will be validated against this type definition. If it is valid, the element will be annotated with this type; if not, the transformation will fail.
xsl:validation (optional)	One of the values «strict», «lax», «strip», or «preserve»	Describes the validation action to be performed. This attribute cannot be combined with the xsl:type attribute. The value «strict» or «lax» causes the processor to look in the available schemas for an element declaration that matches the name of the literal result element, and to validate the constructed element against this declaration. *Validation* is described in more detail in Chapter 4.
Other attributes (optional)	Attribute value template	Any XPath expressions occurring between curly braces in the value are evaluated, and the resulting string forms the value of an attribute copied to the result sequence. *Attribute Value Templates* are described on page 122.

Several of the attributes take the form of whitespace-separated lists. This is simply a list of names (or prefixes) in which the various names are separated by any of the XML-defined whitespace characters: tab, carriage return, newline, or space. For example, you could write:

```
<TD xsl:use-attribute-sets = "blue italic centered"/>
```

Here the names blue, italic, *and* centered *must match the names of* <xsl:attribute-set> *elements elsewhere in the stylesheet.*

Content

The content of a literal result element is a sequence constructor. It may thus contain XSLT instructions, extension elements, literal result elements, and/or text nodes.

Effect

A new element is created, whose expanded name (that is, local name and namespace URI) is the same as the name of the literal result element. In nearly all cases the prefix will also be the same. The sequence constructor contained in the literal result element is evaluated, and this sequence is used to form the content of the new element. The new element is then returned as the result of the instruction, to be combined with other items produced by sibling instructions in the stylesheet.

The way attributes and namespaces are handled is described in subsequent sections.

Usage

Consider a sequence constructor containing a single literal result element.

```
<TD>Product code</TD>
```

In this case a <TD> element will be written to the result tree with a child text node whose content is «Product code». When the result tree is output to an XML or HTML file, it will regenerate the text as it appeared in the stylesheet — or something equivalent. There is no guarantee that it will be character-for-character identical, for example the processor may add or remove whitespace within the tags, or it may represent characters using character or entity references.

If the literal result element has content, then the content must be another sequence constructor, and this sequence constructor is itself evaluated; any nodes generated in the result sequence in the course of this process will become children of the element created from the literal result element.

For example, if the sequence constructor is:

```
<TD><xsl:value-of select="."/></TD>
```

then when the <TD> element is evaluated, its content will also be evaluated. The content in this case is a sequence constructor consisting of a single XSLT instruction, and the effect is that this instruction is evaluated to create a text node that will be a child of the <TD> element in the result tree. The instruction <xsl:value-of select = "."/> outputs the typed value of the current node in the source tree, converted to a string. So if this value is «$83.99», the result would be as follows:

```
<TD>$83.99</TD>
```

It is tempting to think of this as a sequence of three steps:

❑ The <TD> start tag causes a <TD> start tag to be written to the output.

❑ The <xsl:value-of> element is evaluated, and the result («$83.99») is written to the output.

❑ The </TD> end tag causes a </TD> end tag to be written to the output.

However, this is not a true picture of what is going on, and it is best not to think about it this way; otherwise, you will start wondering, for example, how to delay writing the end tag until some condition is encountered in the input.

> The transformation process writes nodes to the result tree; it does not write tags to a text file. The `<TD></TD>` element in the stylesheet causes a `<TD></TD>` element to be written to the result tree. You cannot write half a node to the tree — the start and end tags are not written as separate operations. The `<TD>` and `</TD>` tags are generated only when the result tree is serialized as XML or HTML.

Figure 3-3 helps illustrate this.

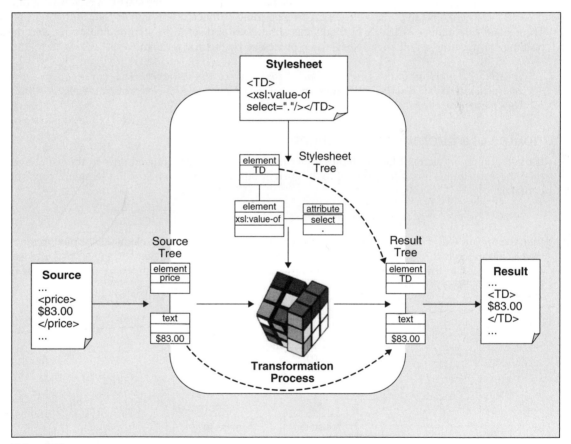

Figure 3-3

If you do find yourself thinking about where you want tags to appear in the output, it is a good idea to draw a sketch showing the required shape of the result tree and then think about how to write the stylesheet to produce the required nodes on the tree. Because the element in the result tree will always be produced by evaluating one sequence constructor in the stylesheet, this amounts to asking "what condition in the input tree should cause this result element to be generated?"

For example, suppose you want to generate an HTML table with five columns, arranging the <item> elements from the source XML five to a row. Then the condition in the source XML that causes an output row to be generated is an <item> element whose position is 1, 6, 11, and so on. The logic can be written:

```
<xsl:template match="item[position() mod 5 = 1]">
<tr>
  <xsl:for-each select=".,  following-sibling::item[position() lt 5]">
    <td><xsl:value-of select="."/></td>
  </xsl:for-each>
</tr>
</xsl:template>
<xsl:template match="item"/>
```

The first template rule matches <item> elements that should appear at the start of a new row; it outputs the <tr> element, and five <td> elements corresponding to this <item> and its four following siblings. The second rule matches <item> elements that should *not* appear at the start of a new row, and does nothing, because these will already have been processed by the first template rule.

In XSLT 2.0 problems like this one can also be solved conveniently using the <xsl:for-each-group> instruction, which is described with examples in Chapter 6 on page 326. However, for simple cases like this, the approach shown above works just as well.

Attributes of a Literal Result Element

If the literal result element has attributes, other than the special xsl-prefixed ones in the list above, then these attributes too will be copied to the current output destination. So if the sequence constructor contains:

```
<TD><IMG src="picture1.gif"/></TD>
```

then the output will contain a copy of this whole structure. The outer <TD> element is copied to the result tree as before, and this time its content consists of another literal result element, the <IMG> element, which is copied to the result tree as a child of the <TD> element, along with its src attribute. This time both the stylesheet tree and the result tree take the form shown in Figure 3-4.

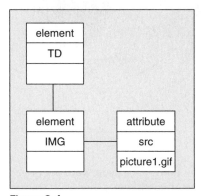

Figure 3-4

If the value of an attribute of a literal result element contains curly braces («{» and «}»), then it is treated as an *attribute value template* (discussed further in the next section). The text between the curly braces is treated as an XPath expression, and is evaluated as a string; the attribute written to the result tree contains this string in place of the expression. For example, suppose we apply the following template to the books.xml file used earlier:

```
<xsl:template match="/">
  <xsl:for-each select="//book">
    <div id="div{position()}">
      <xsl:value-of select="title"/>
    </div>
  </xsl:for-each>
</xsl:template>
```

Because the position() function takes the values 1, 2, 3, and 4, as we move through the set of books, the output will take the following form:

```
<div id="div1">Sayings of the Century</div>
<div id="div2">Sword of Honour</div>
<div id="div3">Moby Dick</div>
<div id="div4">The Lord of the Rings</div>
```

It is also possible to generate attributes for a literal result element by two other mechanisms:

❑   The attribute can be generated by an <xsl:attribute> instruction. This instruction does not need to be textually within the content of the literal result element in the stylesheet, but attributes generated in the result sequence must appear before any child nodes (elements or children).

The reason for this rule is to allow the XSLT processor to avoid building the result tree in memory. Many processors will serialize XML syntax directly to an output file as the nodes are generated, and the rule that attributes must be generated before child elements or text nodes ensures that this is possible. Technically, it's not the order in which the instructions are evaluated that matters (that's up to the implementation); rather, the rule is that attribute nodes in the result of evaluating a sequence constructor must appear earlier in the sequence than nodes to be used as children.

❑   A collection of attributes can be generated by use of a named attribute set. The literal result element must contain an xsl:use-attribute-sets attribute that names the attribute sets to be incorporated: these names must correspond to <xsl:attribute-set> declarations at the top level of the stylesheet. The named attribute sets each contain a sequence of <xsl:attribute> instructions, and these cause attributes to be added to the generated element as if they were present directly in the content of the literal result element. Named attribute sets are useful to maintain a collection of related attributes such as font name, color, and size, which together define a style that will be used repeatedly in the output document; they are a direct parallel to the styles found in simpler languages such as CSS.

Attributes are added to the generated element node in a defined order: firstly, attributes incorporated using xsl:use-attribute-sets, then attributes present on the literal result element itself, and finally attributes added using <xsl:attribute> instructions. The significance of this sequence is that if two or more attributes with the same name are added, it is the last one that counts. It doesn't mean that they will necessarily appear in this order when the result tree is serialized.

Namespaces for a Literal Result Element

The namespace nodes of a literal result element are also copied to the result sequence of the sequence constructor. This is often the source of some confusion. The literal result element in the stylesheet will have a namespace node for every namespace declaration that is in scope: that is, every «xmlns» or «xmlns:*» attribute on the literal result element itself, or on any of its ancestor elements in the stylesheet. The only exception is that the attribute «xmlns = ""» does not act as a namespace declaration, rather it cancels any earlier declaration for the default namespace.

With XML Namespaces 1.1, it is also possible to cancel declarations of non-default namespaces, using an attribute of the form «xmlns:prefix = ""». This undeclaration, if supported by the XSLT processor, ensures that the literal result element will not have a namespace node for that namespace prefix.

In the result tree, the element created from the literal result element is guaranteed to have a namespace node for every namespace node that was present on the literal result element in the stylesheet, except the following:

❏ A namespace node for the XSLT namespace URI http://www.w3.org/1999/XSL/Transform will not be copied.

❏ A namespace node for a namespace declared as an extension instruction namespace will not be copied. A namespace is declared as an extension instruction namespace by including its prefix in the value of the [xsl:]extension-element-prefixes attribute of the literal result element, or of any enclosing element in the stylesheet. (The attribute must be prefixed with the XSLT namespace if it appears on a literal result element, but must be unprefixed if it appears on an XSLT element.)

❏ A namespace node for an excluded namespace will not be copied. A namespace is declared as an excluded namespace by including its prefix in the value of the [xsl:]exclude-result-prefixes attribute of this literal result element or of any ancestor element in the stylesheet. (Again, the attribute must be in the XSLT namespace when it appears on an element that is *not* in the XSLT namespace.)

These exceptions don't apply if the name of the element, or the name of one of its attributes, actually uses one of these namespaces. The system will always ensure that the namespaces used for the element and attributes in the result tree are declared, however hard you try to prevent it. If this isn't what you want, then the chances are you should be generating the element in a different namespace to start with. To achieve this, you might need to use the <xsl:element> instruction instead of using literal result elements.

Consider the following stylesheet:

```
<xsl:stylesheet xmlns:xsl="http://www.w3.org/1999/XSL/Transform"
    version="2.0"
    xmlns:Date="java:java.util.Date"
>

<xsl:template match="/" xmlns="urn:acme-com:gregorian">
    <date><xsl:value-of select="$today"/></date>
</xsl:template>

<xsl:param name="today" select="Date:toString(Date:new())"/>

</xsl:stylesheet>
```

There are three namespaces in scope for the `<date>` element, namely the XSLT namespace, the namespace «`java:java.util.Date`», and the default namespace «`urn:acme-com:gregorian`». The XSLT namespace is not copied to the result tree, but the other two are. So, the `<date>` element added to the result tree is guaranteed to have these two namespaces in scope: «`java:java.util.Date`», and «`urn:acme-com:gregorian`».

> *This stylesheet uses two extension functions «`Date:new()`» and «`Date:toString()`». This means that it will not be portable between different XSLT processors.*

If the `$today` parameter is supplied as the value «`2008-03-18`», the output would be as follows (regardless of the source document):

```
<date xmlns="urn:acme-com:gregorian"
      xmlns:Date="java:java.util.Date">2008-03-18</date>
```

The first namespace declaration is necessary, because it defines the namespace for the element name `<date>`. However, you probably don't really want the `xmlns:Date` declaration here. It's not doing any harm, but it's not doing any good either. It's there because the XSLT processor can't tell that it's unwanted. If you want this declaration to be omitted, use the `xsl:exclude-result-prefixes` attribute as follows:

```
<xsl:stylesheet
    xmlns:xsl="http://www.w3.org/1999/XSL/Transform"
    version="2.0"
    xmlns:Date="java:java.util.Date"
>

<xsl:template match="/" xmlns="urn:acme-com:gregorian">
      <date xsl:exclude-result-prefixes="Date">
          <xsl:value-of select="$today"/>
      </date>
</xsl:template>

<xsl:param name="today" select="Date:toString(Date:new())"/>

</xsl:stylesheet>
```

Alternatively, if your processor supports XML Namespaces 1.1, you can write `<date xmlns:Date = "">...</date>`.

The fact that an element in the result tree has a namespace node does not necessarily mean that when the result tree is written out as an XML document, the corresponding element will have a namespace declaration for that namespace. The XSLT processor is likely to omit the namespace declaration if it is redundant, in other words, if it duplicates a namespace declaration on a containing element. It can't be omitted, however, simply on the basis that it is not used. This is because namespace declarations might affect the meaning of the data in the output document in a way that the XSLT processor is unaware of. Applications are perfectly entitled to use namespace declarations to scope identifiers and names appearing in attribute values or text.

> *The `xsl:exclude-result-prefixes` attribute is used to remove namespace declarations that are unused and unwanted. It can't be used to remove the declaration of namespace prefixes that are actually used in the result tree. And it isn't used to remove duplicate namespace declarations, as most processors will do that automatically.*

Namespace Inheritance

By default, when an element is generated in the result tree, it will automatically acquire copies of the namespace nodes attached to its parent in the result tree. Suppose your stylesheet has the following form:

```
<xsl:template match="product" xmlns:p="urn:acme-com:product">
  <p:product>
    <xsl:call-template name="generate-description"/>
  </p:product>
</xsl:template>

<xsl:template name="generate-description">
  <text>This product is brilliant!</text>
</xsl:template>
```

The result of applying these two rules to a `<product>` element in the source document will generally look like this:

```
<p:product xmlns:p="urn:acme-com:product">
    <text>This product is brilliant!</text>
</p:product>
```

Note that in this serialized output, the namespace «urn:acme-com:product» is in scope for the `<text>` element. Suppose, however, that you are using XML Namespaces 1.1, and you want the result tree to be serialized as follows:

```
<p:product xmlns:p="urn:acme-com:product">
    <text xmlns:p="">This product is brilliant!</text>
</p:product>
```

To achieve this, you need to do two things. Firstly, you need to ensure when constructing the `<text>` element that it doesn't acquire a namespace node for the «urn:acme-com:product» namespace. Secondly, you need to ensure that the serializer generates the namespace undeclaration «xmlns:p = ""».

The first step is achieved by setting the attribute «xsl:inherit-namespaces = "no"» on the `<p:product>` literal result element. This switches off the normal behavior during tree construction, by which a child element automatically inherits the namespaces of its parent element.

The second step is achieved by setting the following declaration in the stylesheet:

```
<xsl:output method="xml" version="1.1" undeclare-prefixes="yes"/>
```

In this example, the namespace undeclaration is largely cosmetic. But if the `<p:product>` element were the envelope of a SOAP message, and the `<text>` element were the payload of the SOAP message, then the namespace undeclarations could be useful: the effect is that if the recipient of the SOAP message extracts the payload using another XSLT transformation, it will be in precisely its original form, not polluted with any declarations of SOAP namespaces.

For information about SOAP, see http://www.w3.org/TR/soap12-part0/.

Namespace Prefixes

When a literal result element is copied to the result tree, the element name and attribute names of the new nodes in the result tree will have the same expanded name (that is, local name and namespace URI) as the corresponding nodes in the stylesheet. Unless there is a conflict, the names that are eventually output will also use the namespace prefix that was used in the stylesheet.

There are unusual circumstances when the XSLT processor may need to change the prefix of an element or attribute. Consider the following contrived example:

```
<p:output xmlns:p="http://domain-a.com/">
    <xsl:namespace name="p">http://domain-b.com/</xsl:namespace>
</p:output>
```

The generated output in this case will look something like this:

```
<ns0:output
    xmlns:ns0="http://domain-a.com/"
    xmlns:p="http://domain-b.com/"/>
```

Here the literal result element and its contained `<xsl:namespace>` instruction are in conflict: they are trying to establish different bindings for the same namespace prefix «p». The specification is clear that the `<xsl:namespace>` instruction wins, so the element acquires an arbitrary prefix allocated by the system.

When namespace nodes are copied from the source or stylesheet tree to the result tree, the namespace prefix and namespace URI are both copied unchanged. When element or attribute nodes are copied, the expanded name of the element or attribute (that is, its local name and namespace URI) is always preserved, but the namespace prefix may occasionally need to be changed. If this happens, however, an extra namespace node will be added to the result tree to associate the new namespace prefix with the correct namespace URI.

Namespace Aliasing

In some circumstances, instead of changing the namespace prefix when a literal result element is copied to the result tree, it is necessary to change the namespace URI.

The most obvious situation where this arises is when the output document is itself a stylesheet. This isn't as esoteric a requirement as it may appear — generating a stylesheet can be a very useful technique. For example, if your company changes its house style to use different fonts and colors, you could write an XSLT transformation to convert all your existing stylesheets to the new standard.

When you generate a stylesheet, you will want to generate XSLT elements such as `<xsl:template>` in the result tree, but you can't include such elements as literal result elements in the stylesheet, because they would be mistaken for instructions. One approach is to generate these elements using the `<xsl:element>` instruction instead of literal result elements. But there is another way of doing it: you can include them in the stylesheet with a different namespace and then declare in an `<xsl:namespace-alias>` element that the URI should be changed when the literal result element is copied to the result tree.

For more details of this mechanism, see `<xsl:namespace-alias>` in Chapter 6, on page 394.

Attribute Value Templates

As we've seen, an attribute value template is a special form of parameterized attribute value. There are two ways they can be used:

❑ On a literal result element, an attribute value template provides a way of generating an attribute whose value is computed at runtime rather than always taking the same value, for example `<td width = "{$width}">`. You could achieve the same effect with the `<xsl:attribute>` instruction, but attribute value templates are easier to write and understand.

❑ On some XSLT elements, certain attributes can be computed at runtime. For example, when sorting, instead of writing «order = "ascending"» or «order = "descending"», you could write «order = "{$order}"» so that the order varies, depending on a runtime parameter.

Note that there are very few attributes where this facility is available. They are listed later in this section.

The term *template* here has nothing to do with `<xsl:template>` elements. Attribute value templates simply provide a notation for embedding variable components into an otherwise fixed attribute value.

An attribute value template is a string in which XPath expressions may be embedded within curly braces («{» and «}»). The XPath expression is evaluated, and in general the result will be a sequence. This sequence is processed using the same rules as for an `<xsl:attribute>` instruction, explained in detail on page 254 in Chapter 6: in short, adjacent text nodes are merged, nodes are atomized, atomic values are converted to strings, and the strings are then concatenated, with a single space character inserted as a separator between each string. The resulting concatenated string is substituted into the attribute value in place of the original XPath expression and curly braces.

If backward-compatibility mode is in use (that is, if «version = "1.0"» is specified), then all strings after the first in the sequence are discarded; only the first string is included in the output. See the section Version Compatibility on page 128 for details.

For example, suppose you have a set of images representing an alphabet such as the following, and you want to use these to represent the first character of a paragraph of text.

fancy

fancyA.gif	fancyB.gif	fancyC.gif	fancyD.gif	fancyE.gif

You could write a template rule to achieve this as follows (ignoring practical details such as how to deal with paragraphs that don't start with a capital letter). It uses the substring() function, which is described in Chapter 13.

```
<xsl:template match="para">
   <p><img src="fancy{substring(.,1,1)}.gif" style="float:left"/>
   <xsl:value-of select="substring(.,2)" /></p>
</xsl:template>
```

122

A paragraph that starts with the letter A (like this one) will cause the `src` attribute of the `<img>` element to be evaluated as «img src = "fancyA.gif"», so it will be displayed in the browser as shown in Figure 3-5.

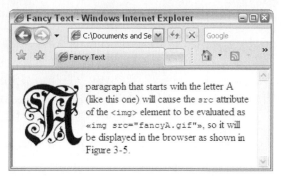

Figure 3-5

If you want to include the characters «{» or «}» in an attribute value with their ordinary meaning, they should be doubled as «{{» or «}}». This is sometimes necessary when generating dynamic HTML, and it also happens often with the `regex` attribute of the `<xsl:analyze-string>` instruction, whose value is a regular expression. However, you should do this only in an attribute that is being interpreted as an attribute value template. In other attributes, curly braces have no special meaning.

Curly brackets can never be nested. You can use them only to include an XPath expression in the text of a stylesheet attribute; they cannot be used within an XPath expression itself. You can always achieve the required effect some other way; for example, instead of:

```
<a href="#{id('A{@nr}')}"> <!-- WRONG -->
```

write:

```
<a href="#{id(concat('A', @nr))}">
```

The `concat()` function, described in Chapter 13, performs concatenation of strings.

Attribute value templates cannot be used anywhere you like in the stylesheet. They can be used only for those attributes that are specifically identified as attribute value templates in the XSLT Recommendation. The following table gives a complete list of all the places you can use attribute value templates.

Element	Attributes Interpreted as Attribute Value Templates
Literal result elements	All attributes except those in the XSLT namespace
Extension elements	As defined by the specification of each extension element
`<xsl:analyze-string>`	`regex`, `flags`
`<xsl:attribute>`	`name`, `namespace`, `separator`
`<xsl:element>`	`name`, `namespace`
`<xsl:for-each-group>`	`collation`
`<xsl:message>`	`terminate`

continued

Element	Attributes Interpreted as Attribute Value Templates
`<xsl:namespace>`	`name`
`<xsl:number>`	`format, lang, letter-value, ordinal, grouping-separator, grouping-size`
`<xsl:processing-instruction>`	`name`
`<xsl:result-document>`	`format, href, method, byte-order-mark, cdata-section-elements, doctype-public, doctype-system, encoding, escape-uri-attributes, include-content-type, indent, media-type, normalization-form, omit-xml-declaration, standalone, undeclare-prefixes, output-version`
`<xsl:sort>`	`lang, order, collation, data-type, case-order`
`<xsl:value-of>`	`separator`

In all other contexts, don't even think of trying to use them because the curly braces will either be ignored or cause an error to be reported. It can be very tempting, if you want to use `<xsl:call-template>`, for example, and the name of the template you want to call is in a variable, to want to write:

```
<!-- WRONG -->
<xsl:param name="tname"/>
<xsl:call-template name="{$tname}"/>
<!-- WRONG -->
```

However, you can't, because the `name` attribute (or any other attribute of `<xsl:call-template>` for that matter) of `<xsl:call-template>` is not in the above list of places where attribute value templates can be used.

Why are attribute value templates rationed so severely? The restrictions are there deliberately to make life easier for the XSLT processor:

❑ Attribute value templates are never allowed for attributes of declarations. This ensures that the values are known before the source document is read, and are constant for each run of the stylesheet.

❑ Attribute value templates are never allowed for attributes whose value is an XPath expression or a pattern. This ensures that expressions and patterns can be compiled when the stylesheet is read, and do not need to be re-parsed each time they are evaluated.

❑ Attribute value templates are generally not allowed for attributes whose value is the name of another object in the stylesheet, for example a named template or a named attribute set (an exception is the `format` attribute of `<xsl:result-document>`). This ensures that references from one stylesheet object to another can be resolved once and for all when the stylesheet is first read. They are allowed, however, for names of nodes being written to the result tree.

❑ Attribute value templates are not recognized when attributes such as `xml:space`, `xml:lang`, `xml:base`, or `xsi:type` are interpreted by the XML parser or schema validator. This also applies to namespace declarations (`xmlns` and `xmlns:prefix`). This is because the XML parser reads the value before the XSLT processor gets a chance to expand it. The XSLT processor won't stop you from using curly braces in such an attribute when it appears on a literal result element, but the chances are that some other software will throw an error before you get that far.

When an XPath expression within an attribute value template is evaluated, the context is the same as for any other expression in the stylesheet. The idea of an expression having a context was introduced in Chapter 2, on page 84: it determines the meaning of constructs such as «.», which refers to the context node, and «position()», which refers to the context position. Variables and namespace prefixes may be used within the expression only if they are in scope at that point in the stylesheet. The context item, context position, and context size are determined from the sequence being processed in the most recent call of <xsl:apply-templates>, <xsl:for-each>, or <xsl:for-each-group>. Outside such a call (for example, while a global variable is being evaluated), the context item is set to a value supplied by the caller of the stylesheet (generally the document node of the source document), and the context position and size are set to 1 (one).

Simplified Stylesheets

A simplified stylesheet uses an abbreviated syntax in which the <xsl:stylesheet> element and all the top-level declarations are omitted.

The original purpose of this facility was to allow people with HTML-authoring skills but no programming experience to write simple stylesheets with a minimum of training. A simplified stylesheet has a skeleton that looks like the target document (which is usually HTML, although it doesn't have to be), and uses XSLT instructions to fill in the variable parts.

A stylesheet module is interpreted as a simplified stylesheet if the outermost element is not <xsl:stylesheet> or <xsl:transform>. The outermost element can have any name, provided it is not in the XSLT namespace. It must still contain a declaration of the XSLT namespace, and it must have an xsl:version attribute. For XSLT 2.0 the value should be «1.0» or «2.0» (use «2.0» if your stylesheet depends on features defined in XSLT 2.0, or «1.0» if you also want it to work with XSLT 1.0 processors). When the xsl:version attribute is greater than «2.0», forward-compatible processing mode is enabled. This is discussed later in this chapter on page 130.

Example: A Simplified Stylesheet

This example shows a stylesheet that takes the form of an HTML skeleton page, with XSLT instructions embedded within it to pull data from the source document. The stylesheet is in the download file under the filename simplified.xsl, and can be used together with the data file books.xml.

The complete stylesheet is as follows:

```
<html xmlns:xsl="http://www.w3.org/1999/XSL/Transform"
      xsl:version="2.0">
<head><title>A list of books</title></head>
<body>
<h1>A list of books</h1>
    <table border="2">
    <xsl:for-each select="//book">
        <xsl:sort select="author"/>
        <tr>
          <td><xsl:value-of select="author"/></td>
          <td><xsl:value-of select="title"/></td>
```

```
          <td><xsl:value-of select="@category"/></td>
          <td><xsl:value-of select="price"/></td>
        </tr>
     </xsl:for-each>
     </table>
  </body>
  </html>
```

When you run this against the file `books.xml` (which is listed on page 74 in Chapter 2), the output is a sorted table showing the books (see Figure 3-6).

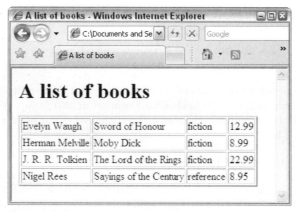

Figure 3-6

A simplified stylesheet is equivalent to a stylesheet in which the outermost element (typically the `<html>` element) is wrapped first in an `<xsl:template>` element with «match = "/"», and then in an `<xsl:stylesheet>` element. The `xsl:version` attribute of the outermost element becomes the `version` attribute of the `<xsl:stylesheet>`. So the expanded form of the above example would be as follows:

```
<xsl:stylesheet xmlns:xsl="http://www.w3.org/1999/XSL/Transform"
                version="2.0">
<xsl:template match="/">
<html>
<head><title>A list of books</title></head>
<body>
<h1>A list of books</h1>
   <table border="2">
   <xsl:for-each select="//book">
      <xsl:sort select="author"/>
      <tr>
        <td><xsl:value-of select="author"/></td>
        <td><xsl:value-of select="title"/></td>
        <td><xsl:value-of select="@category"/></td>
        <td><xsl:value-of select="price"/></td>
      </tr>
```

```
        </xsl:for-each>
      </table>
    </body>
  </html>
</xsl:template>
</xsl:stylesheet>
```

The significance of «match = "/"» is that this identifies the template rule as the first one to be processed when the stylesheet is activated. As we saw in Chapter 2, processing generally starts at the root node of the source document tree, and whichever template rule matches this root node is the first one to be invoked. The match pattern «/» matches a document node. In a simplified stylesheet, this will be the only template rule invoked.

There are many things a simplified stylesheet cannot do, because it cannot contain any declarations. For example, a simplified stylesheet can't include or import another stylesheet, it can't have global variables or parameters, and it can't define keys. But when you need these extra capabilities, you can always "unsimplify" the stylesheet by adding the surrounding <xsl:stylesheet> and <xsl:template> elements.

It is possible in theory for a stylesheet to include or import a simplified stylesheet, which would be expanded exactly as described above — but it would be a rather unusual thing to do.

Writing Portable Stylesheets

In this section we will examine a range of facilities that are included in XSLT to help you write portable stylesheets; that is, stylesheets that can run across different XSLT processors, possibly supporting different versions of the XSLT language.

We will look at the question of version compatibility; that is, how to write stylesheets that work with both XSLT 1.0 and XSLT 2.0. Then we will look at how to use vendor extensions, without sacrificing portability. But before we do either of these things, I will describe a new feature that has been added to XSLT 2.0 to aid portability, namely the use-when attribute, which allows you to include or exclude stylesheet code conditionally at compile time.

Conditional Compilation

The use-when attribute serves a similar purpose to #ifdef in the C language: it allows you to define conditions under which a section of the stylesheet can be conditionally included or excluded at compile time.

The use-when attribute can be used on any XSLT element. This includes declarations and instructions, and other elements such as <xsl:sort> and <xsl:with-param>. Written as «xsl:use-when», it is also allowed on literal result elements and extension instructions. The value of the attribute is a condition to be evaluated at compile time. If the condition is false, then the element and the subtree rooted at that element are effectively eliminated from the stylesheet, before any further processing takes place: it is as if the element and its content were not there. One consequence is that no XSLT errors will be reported in respect of this element or its descendants.

Here is an example, which defines two alternative entry points, one for an XSLT 1.0 processor and one for an XSLT 2.0 processor. This assumes that the <xsl:stylesheet> element specifies «version = "2.0"». This means that an XSLT 1.0 processor will be running in forward-compatible mode (explained in the next section) and will therefore ignore attributes such as use-when that it does not understand. An XSLT 1.0 processor will use the first template rule as the entry point, because it has higher priority. An XSLT 2.0 processor, however, will behave as if the first template rule is not present, and will use the second one, which differs in that it invokes schema validation of the result document.

```
<xsl:template match="/" priority="2"
              use-when="system-property('xsl:version')='1.0'">
  <xsl:apply-templates/>
</xsl:template>

<xsl:template match="/" priority="1">
  <xsl:result-document validation="strict">
    <xsl:apply-templates/>
  </xsl:result-document>
</xsl:template>
```

The expression contained in the use-when attribute can be any XPath expression, but it is constrained to have a very restricted evaluation context. This means there is no context item, there are no variables available, and no access to external documents. In practice, this means that the only things the expression can usefully do is to examine the results of functions such as system-property(), element-available(), and function-available(), to see what environment the stylesheet is running in. These three functions are fully described in Chapter 13.

One important reason for the introduction of the use-when attribute was to allow stylesheets that work both on schema-aware and non-schema-aware XSLT processors to be written. For example, you can use the system-property() function in a use-when attribute on the <xsl:import-schema> declaration so that a schema is imported only when using a schema-aware processor. For details of how schemas are imported into a stylesheet, see Chapter 4.

Version Compatibility

Version compatibility is about how to achieve resilience to differences between versions of the XSLT standard.

There are currently two versions of the XSLT Recommendation, versions 1.0 and 2.0 (the many intermediate working drafts don't count). So compatibility between versions has now become an issue. However, the language designers had the foresight to anticipate that it would become an issue, and made provision even in version 1.0 to allow stylesheets to be written in a portable way.

The stylesheet is required to carry a version number (typically «version = "1.0"» or «version = "2.0"») as an attribute of the <xsl:stylesheet> element. Specifying «version = "1.0"» declares that the stylesheet is designed primarily for use with XSLT 1.0 processors, while specifying «version = "2.0"» indicates that it is designed for XSLT 2.0.

The term *backward compatibility* refers to the ability of version N of a language to accept programs or data that worked under version $N - 1$, while *forward compatibility* refers to the ability of programs that worked under version N to move forward to version $N + 1$. The two concepts are therefore opposite sides of the same coin. However, the XSLT language specification distinguishes carefully between them. As far as an XSLT 2.0 processor is concerned, a stylesheet that specifies «version = "1.0"» is operating in backward-compatible mode, while a stylesheet that specifies «version = "3.0"» is operating in forward-compatible mode.

If you specify «version = "1.0"» in the stylesheet, then you are signaling the fact that the stylesheet was designed to be run under XSLT 1.0, and that in some specific cases where XSLT 2.0 defines different behavior from 1.0, the 1.0 behavior should be used. For example, if you supply a sequence of nodes as the value of the `select` attribute of `<xsl:value-of>`, the XSLT 1.0 behavior is to output the first value in the sequence and ignore the others; the XSLT 2.0 behavior is to output all the values, space separated.

Specifying «version = "1.0"» does *not* mean that you cannot use facilities that were newly introduced in XSLT 2.0. It only means that an XSLT 2.0 processor should use the 1.0 behavior in certain specific cases where there are incompatibilities.

> *XSLT 2.0 processors are not required to implement backward-compatibility mode. If they don't provide this feature, they must reject any stylesheet that specifies* «version = "1.0"». *Some products, such as XMLSpy, use the version number to decide whether to invoke an XSLT 1.0 processor or an XSLT 2.0 processor.*

If you specify «version = "2.0"» in a stylesheet, and then run it under an XSLT 1.0 processor, you are indicating that the stylesheet makes use of facilities that were newly introduced in XSLT 2.0, and that the 1.0 processor should not treat these constructs as an error unless they are actually evaluated. The stylesheet can use various mechanisms to avoid evaluating the constructs that depend on XSLT 2.0 when these features are not available. This only works, of course, because the need for it was anticipated in the XSLT 1.0 specification, and even though no details were known of what new features would be introduced in a later version of the language, XSLT 1.0 processors were required to behave in a particular way (called forward-compatibility mode) when the `version` attribute was set to a value other than «1.0». XSLT 2.0 similarly carries forward these provisions so that when the time comes, stylesheets that take advantage of new features in XSLT 3.0 or beyond will still be able to run under an XSLT 2.0 processor.

If you use facilities defined in XSLT version 1.0 only, but want your stylesheet to run under both XSLT 1.0 and 2.0 processors, then you should specify «version = "1.0"», and every conformant XSLT processor will then handle the stylesheet correctly, provided (a) that you're not using an XSLT 2.0 processor without support for backward-compatible mode, and (b) that you're not using one of the few constructs that are incompatible even in backward-compatible mode. There is a list of these in Appendix C, and for the most part they are things that reasonable users would not do.

If you use facilities that are new in XSLT version 2.0, and you don't need the stylesheet to run under an XSLT 1.0 processor, then it's best to specify «version = "2.0"». If there are parts of the stylesheet that you haven't converted from XSLT 1.0, where you want backward-compatible behavior to be invoked, then you can leave those parts in a separate stylesheet module that specifies «version = "1.0"». It's quite OK to mix versions like this. In fact, XSLT 2.0 allows you to specify the `version` attribute at any level of granularity, for example on an `<xsl:template>` element, or even on an element that encloses one small part of a template. If you use it on a literal result element, the attribute should be named `xsl:version` to distinguish it from user-defined attributes. Bear in mind, however, that XSLT 1.0 processors allow the `version` attribute to appear only on the `<xsl:stylesheet>` element, or, as `xsl:version`, on a literal result element: it's not permitted, for example, on `<xsl:template>`.

If you use facilities that are new in XSLT version 2.0, but you also want the stylesheet to run under an XSLT 1.0 processor, then you may need to write it in such a way that it defines fallback behavior to be invoked when running under 1.0. There are various techniques you can use to achieve this. You can use the `element-available()` function to test whether a particular XSLT instruction is implemented; you can use `<xsl:fallback>` to define what the processor should do if a construct is not available; or you can use the `system-property()` function (described in Chapter 13) to test which version of XSLT is supported, and execute different code, depending on the result. Whichever technique you use, you need to ensure that those parts of the stylesheet that use XSLT 2.0 facilities are within the scope of an element that specifies «version = "2.0"», otherwise an XSLT 1.0 processor will reject them at compile time.

The following sections look in more detail at the rules for backward-compatible and forward-compatible behavior.

Forward Compatibility in XSLT 1.0

At present, you are probably more concerned with migration of XSLT 1.0 stylesheets to XSLT 2.0 than with migration from 2.0 to 3.0, so it makes sense to look at the forward-compatibility rules as they were defined in the XSLT 1.0 specification. The rules have changed a little in XSLT 2.0 to reflect the introduction of the [xsl:]use-when attribute, so if you are reading this perhaps in 2012 and planning the transition to a new version 3.0, most of the advice should still be relevant, but you will be able to achieve most of what you need using [xsl:]use-when instead.

Forward-compatibility mode is invoked, as far as an XSLT 1.0 processor is concerned, by setting the version attribute on the <xsl:stylesheet> element to any value other than «1.0» (even, surprisingly, a value lower than «1.0»). For an XSLT 2.0 processor, forward-compatibility mode is invoked by a version attribute greater than «2.0».

This mode has static scope rather than dynamic scope: it affects the instructions in the stylesheet that are textually within the element that carries the relevant version attribute. It only affects the behavior of the compiler; it does not alter the way that any instruction or expression is evaluated at runtime.

In forward-compatible mode, the XSLT processor must assume that the stylesheet is using XSLT facilities defined in a version of the standard that has been published since the software was released. The processor, of course, won't know what to do with these constructs, but it must assume that the stylesheet author is using them deliberately. It treats them in much the same way as vendor extensions that it doesn't understand:

❑   It must report an error for XSLT elements it doesn't understand only if they are actually evaluated, and if there is no child <xsl:fallback> instruction.

❑   It must ignore attributes whose name it doesn't recognize. One particular consequence of this is that if the stylesheet specifies «version = "2.0"», then an XSLT 1.0 processor will ignore any «use-when» attributes that it finds on XSLT elements.

❑   In XSLT 1.0, there were some additional rules for forward-compatible mode that have been dropped in 2.0:

  ❑   If an XPath expression uses a function that's not defined in XPath 1.0, an XSLT 1.0 processor running in forward-compatible mode must report an error only if the function is actually called. You can avoid this error condition by using function-available() to test whether the function exists before calling it.

  ❑   Similarly if an XPath expression uses syntax that isn't allowed in XPath 1.0, the processor must report an error only if the expression is actually evaluated.

  ❑   There's also a provision in XSLT 1.0 that the processor should ignore optional attributes whose value isn't recognized, for example <xsl:message terminate = "maybe" />. It seems that many XSLT 1.0 processors ignored this rule, so it might be unwise to rely on it.

This behavior occurs only if the <xsl:stylesheet> element specifies a version other than «1.0» (or for XSLT 2.0, a value greater than «2.0»). Forward-compatible mode can also be specified for a portion of a stylesheet by specifying the xsl:version attribute on any literal result element, and in the case of

XSLT 2.0, by specifying the version attribute on any XSLT element. If forward-compatible mode is not enabled, then any use of an XSLT element, attribute, or function that isn't in the version of XSLT that the processor supports, or any use of XPath syntax that isn't in the corresponding XPath specification, is an error and must be reported, whether it is actually executed or not.

If you specify «version = "1.0"» and then use XSLT 2.0 facilities such as <xsl:result-document>, then an XSLT 1.0 processor will reject this as an error. An XSLT 2.0 processor, however, will process your stylesheet successfully. An XSLT 2.0 processor when given a stylesheet that specifies «version = "1.0"» is not expected to check that the stylesheet actually conforms to XSLT 1.0.

> *This is the theory. The rules for forward-compatibility mode were simplified in XSLT 2.0 after the XSL Working Group discovered that implementation of this feature in 1.0 processors was patchy. Altova's 1.0 processor, for example, allows unknown functions but rejects unknown attributes; the Saxon XSLT 1.0 implementation accepts both of these but often rejects unknown values for known attributes.*

Forward-compatible processing was specified to allow you to write a stylesheet that exploits facilities in version 2.0 while still behaving sensibly when run with an XSLT processor that supports version 1.0 only, or, at some point in the future, to use facilities in version 3.0 and still behave sensibly with an XSLT 2.0 processor. To achieve this, you can use the system-property() function (described on page 890, in Chapter 13) to discover which version of XSLT the processor implements, or which processor is being used. For example, you could write code such as the following:

```
<xsl:if test="system-property('xsl:version')=2.0 or
      starts-with(system-property('xsl:vendor'), 'xalan')">
   <xsl:new-facility/>
</xsl:if>
```

Relying on the version number this returns is a rather crude mechanism: there are likely to be processors around that implement some of the new features in XSLT 2.0 but not yet all of them. Testing which vendor's processor is in use is therefore handy for portability, especially when vendors have not kept strictly to the conformance rules. Another possibility is to use the element-available() and function-available() functions described later in the chapter: although these are primarily intended to allow you to test whether particular vendor or user-defined extensions are available, they can also be used to test for the availability of specific XSLT instructions and functions in the core language.

Technically, a processor that implements some of the new XSLT 2.0 features but not all of them doesn't conform either to XSLT 1.0 or to XSLT 2.0. But because many XSLT processors are developed incrementally with new releases every few weeks, you might well find products that occupy this no man's land. A product will presumably return «2.0» as the value of «system-property('xsl-version')» when the vendor is confident that the product is "almost" conformant: past experience suggests that different vendors will interpret this in different ways.

> *There was a suggestion that one should ban processors from returning «2.0» unless they are fully conformant with the spec. But there is little point in such a prohibition, because a product that isn't fully conformant with the spec is by definition doing things that the spec doesn't allow.*

Backward Compatibility in XSLT 2.0

For an XSLT 2.0 processor, you can invoke backward-compatibility mode by setting the version attribute on the <xsl:stylesheet> element (or on any other XSLT element) to the value «1.0». In fact, any value less than «2.0» will do. You can also set the xsl:version attribute on a literal result element in the same way.

Like the switch for forward-compatibility mode, this has static scope: it applies to all instructions and XPath expressions contained within the element where the version attribute is set. Unlike forward-compatibility mode, however, this mode affects the results of evaluating instructions and expressions, rather than being purely a compile-time switch.

XSLT 2.0 processors aren't obliged to support backward-compatible processing. If they don't, they must reject any attempt to specify «version = "1.0"» as an error. The reason the facility was made optional was that the language designers expected that the need for it would gradually decline as XSLT 1.0 receded into history. However, some vendors may decide that their customers don't need the facility at all, as it's not actually that difficult to change the few constructs in a stylesheet whose behavior is different under XSLT 2.0.

How does backward compatibility actually affect the results of the stylesheet? One thing that it does *not* do is to say "process this according to the rules in the XSLT 1.0 specification." This wouldn't work, because the parts of the stylesheet that use 2.0 facilities and the parts that use backward-compatibility mode need to work with the same data model, and the data model used by an XSLT 2.0 processor is the 2.0 data model, not the 1.0 data model. Instead, backward-compatibility mode changes the behavior of a small number of specific XSLT and XPath constructs, in quite specific ways.

Here is a checklist of the things that are done differently. The left-hand column indicates the normal XSLT 2.0 (or XPath 2.0) behavior, the right-hand column the behavior in backward-compatibility mode.

First, the differences covered by the XSLT 2.0 specification are given as follows.

2.0 Behavior	1.0 Behavior
When the value selected by the <xsl:value-of> instruction is a sequence, all the values are output, separated by spaces.	When the value selected by the <xsl:value-of> instruction is a sequence, the first value is output, and the rest are ignored.
When the value produced by an expression in an attribute value template is a sequence, all the values are output, separated by spaces.	When the value produced by an expression in an attribute value template is a sequence, the first value is output, and the rest are ignored.
When the value returned by the expression in the value attribute of <xsl:number> is a sequence, all the numbers in the sequence are output, according to the format described in the format attribute.	When the value returned by the expression in the value attribute of <xsl:number> is a sequence, the first number in the sequence is output, and the rest are discarded.
When the value of a sort key is a sequence containing more than one item, a type error is reported.	When the value of a sort key is a sequence containing more than one item, the first item is used as the sort key, and remaining items are ignored.
When <xsl:call-template> supplies a parameter that's not defined in the template being called, a static error is reported.	When <xsl:call-template> supplies a parameter that's not defined in the template being called, the extra parameter is ignored.
Values used as keys are compared as supplied, for example as numbers or dates.	When keys are used, values are always converted to strings before being compared.
When the first element output is an <html> element in the XHTML namespace, the output method defaults to XHTML.	When the first element output is an <html> element in the XHTML namespace, the output method defaults to XML.

Backward-compatibility mode also affects the way that XPath expressions in the stylesheet are evaluated. Here are the differences.

2.0 Behavior	1.0 Behavior
When a function expects a single node or a single item as an argument, and the supplied value of the argument is a sequence containing more than one item, a type error is reported.	When a function expects a single node or a single item as an argument, and the supplied value of the argument is a sequence containing more than one item, all items except the first are ignored.
When a function expects a string or a number as an argument, and the supplied value is of the wrong type, a type error is reported.	When a function expects a string or a number as an argument, and the supplied value is of the wrong type, the system converts the supplied value using the `string()` or `number()` function as appropriate.
When one of the operands to an operator such as « = » or « < » is a number, and the other is not, a type error is reported.	When one of the operands to an operator such as « = » or « < » is a number, and the other is not, the non-numeric operand is converted to a number using the `number()` function.
When one of the operands of an arithmetic operator such as «+» or «*» is a sequence containing more than one item, a type error is reported.	When one of the operands of an arithmetic operator such as «+» or «*» is a sequence containing more than one item, all items except the first are ignored.
When the operands of an arithmetic operator such as «+» or «*» have types for which this operator is not defined, a type error is reported.	When the operands of an arithmetic operator such as «+» or «*» have types for which this operator is not defined, the supplied operands are converted to numbers using the `number()` function.
Arithmetic may be carried out in integer, decimal, float or double depending on the operands.	Arithmetic is always carried out in double-precision floating point.
In an expression such as «A and B» or «A or B», the operands may be evaluated in either order.	In an expression such as «A and B» or «A or B», the first operand is evaluated first, and the other operand is not evaluated if not needed.

My personal preference when moving forward to a new software version or language version is to take the pain of the conversion all at once, and try to make the program or stylesheet look as if it had been written for the new version from the word go. Most of the changes listed above are to reflect the fact that XSLT 2.0 and XPath 2.0 no longer use the "first node" rule when a sequence is supplied in a context where a singleton is needed. You can always get the effect of selecting the first item in the sequence, by using the predicate «[1]». For example, if an XSLT 1.0 stylesheet contains the instruction:

```
<xsl:value-of select="following-sibling::*"/>
```

then it should be changed to:

```
<xsl:value-of select="following-sibling::*[1]"/>
```

But doing the conversion all at once is a luxury that you can't always afford. Backward-compatibility mode is there to allow you to spread the cost of making the changes by doing it gradually.

Extensibility

Bitten by years of experience with proprietary vendor extensions to HTML, the W3C committee responsible for XSLT took great care to allow vendor extensions in a tightly controlled way.

The extensibility mechanisms in XSLT are governed by several unstated design principles:

❑ Namespaces are used to ensure that vendor extensions cannot clash with facilities in the standard (including facilities introduced in future versions), or with extensions defined by a different vendor.

❑ It is possible for an XSLT processor to recognize where extensions have been used, including extensions defined by a different vendor, and to fail cleanly if it cannot implement those extensions.

❑ It is possible for the writer of a stylesheet to test whether particular extensions are available, and to define fallback behavior if they are not. For example, the stylesheet might be able to achieve the same effect in a different way, or it might make do without some special effect in the output.

The principal extension mechanisms are extension functions and extension instructions. However, it is also possible for vendors to define other kinds of extensions, or to provide mechanisms for users or third parties to do so. These include the following:

❑ XSLT-defined elements can have additional vendor-defined attributes, provided they use a non-null namespace URI, and that they do not introduce nonconformant behavior for standard elements and attributes. For example, a vendor could add an attribute such as `acme:debug` to the `<xsl:template>` element, whose effect is to pause execution when the template is evaluated. But adding an attribute «`acme:repeat = "2"`» whose effect is to execute the template twice would be against the conformance rules.

❑ Vendors can define additional top-level elements; again provided that they use a non-null namespace URI, and that they do not cause nonconformant behavior for standard elements and attributes. An example of such an element is Microsoft's `<msxsl:script>` element, for defining external functions in VBScript or JScript. Any processor that doesn't recognize the namespace URI will ignore such top-level elements.

❑ Certain XSLT-defined attributes have an open-ended set of values, where vendors have discretion on the range of values to be supported. Examples are the `lang` attribute of `<xsl:number>` and `<xsl:sort>`, which provides language-dependent numbering and sorting; the `method` attribute of `<xsl:output>`, which defines how the result tree is output to a file; and the `format` attribute of `<xsl:number>`, which allows the vendor to provide additional numbering sequences beyond those defined in the standard. The list of system properties supplied in the first argument of the `system-property()` function is similarly open-ended.

Extension Functions

Extension functions provide a mechanism for extending the capabilities of XSLT by escaping into another language such as Java or JavaScript. The most usual reasons for doing this are as follows:

❑ To improve performance

❑ To exploit system capabilities and services

❏   To reuse code that already exists in another language

❏   For convenience, as complex algorithms and computations can sometimes be verbose when written in XSLT

XSLT 2.0 allows functions to be written using the `<xsl:function>` declaration in a stylesheet (these are referred to as stylesheet functions, and they are not considered to be extension functions). This facility, together with the increase in the size of the core function library, greatly reduces the need to escape into other programming languages. However, it is still necessary if you need access to external resources or services from within the stylesheet.

The term *extension function* is used both for functions supplied by the vendor beyond the core functions defined in the XSLT and XPath standards (those described in Chapter 13 of this book), and also for functions written by users and third parties.

The XSLT Recommendation allows extension functions to be called, but does not define how they are written, or how they should be bound to the stylesheet, or which languages should be supported. This means that it is quite difficult to write extension functions that work with more than one vendor's XSLT processor, even though in the Java world there are some conventions that several vendors have adopted.

> In December 2000 the XSL Working Group in W3C published a working draft for XSLT 1.1, which proposed detailed conventions for writing extension functions in Java and JavaScript. These proposals met a rather hostile reception, for a variety of reasons. The working draft was subsequently withdrawn, and the work hasn't been taken forward. It is still available, if you are interested, at http://www.w3.org/TR/xslt11.

A function name in the XPath expression syntax is a QName, that is, a name with an optional namespace prefix. Under XSLT, the default namespace for functions (the namespace that is assumed when the function name has no prefix) is always the namespace for the core function library. This function library includes the a repertoire of over a hundred functions defined in the XPath 2.0 specifications, together with another twenty or so that are available only for use in XSLT. These are all described in Chapter 13 of this book. For example the core function not() can be invoked as follows:

```
<xsl:if test="not(@name = 'Mozart')">
```

If the function name has a prefix, the function can come from a number of other sources, depending on its namespace:

❏   Functions in the XML Schema namespace http://www.w3.org/2001/XMLSchema (traditionally associated with the prefix «xs», though «xsd» is also used) are used to construct values of built-in types. For example, the function call «xs:date('2004-02-29')» is used to convert a string to an xs:date value. You can also use such functions to construct values of user-defined types in an imported schema. These are referred to as constructor functions.

❏   XSLT vendors will often provide additional functions in their own namespace. For example, Saxon provides a number of functions in the namespace http://saxon.sf.net/. An example is saxon:evaluate(), which allows an XPath expression to be constructed dynamically from a string, and then executed.

❏   Third parties may also define function libraries. Of particular note is the EXSLT library at http://www.exslt.org/. This provides, among other things, a useful library of mathematical functions. (It also provides capabilities such as date and time handling, and regular expression processing, that have largely been overtaken by standard facilities in XSLT 2.0 and XPath 2.0.) This is primarily a library of function specifications, but implementations of the functions are available for many popular XSLT processors, either from the XSLT vendor or from some other party. This ensures that you can use these functions in a stylesheet and still retain portability across XSLT processors. Note, however, that implementations of these functions are not generally portable: an implementation of `math:sqrt()` that's written for MSXML3 won't work with Xalan, for example.

❑ You can write your own functions in XSLT, using the `<xsl:function>` declaration. These will be completely portable across XSLT 2.0 implementations, but, of course, they are restricted to things that can be coded in XSLT and XPath. These functions can be in any namespace apart from a small number of reserved namespaces. The namespaces that are reserved are the obvious ones such as the XSLT, XML, and XML Schema namespaces.

❑ The `<xsl:function>` element has an attribute `override` that can be set to «yes» or «no» to indicate whether the stylesheet function should override any vendor-defined function of the same name. This is useful because there might be a portable cross-platform implementation of a function such as `math:sqrt()` specified in a third-party library such as EXSLT, as well as a native implementation provided by the XSLT vendor. This attribute allows you to choose which implementation is preferred.

❑ Finally, if the XSLT processor allows it, you may be able to write functions in an external programming language. Microsoft's XSLT processors, for example, allow you to invoke functions in scripting languages such as JavaScript, and all the Java-based processors such as Xalan-J and Saxon allow you to invoke methods written in Java. Saxon also allows you to call functions written in XQuery, and when used on the .NET platform it allows access to methods defined in any loadable .NET assembly, regardless of the source language. Other processors will tend to support the native language of the processor: Xalan-C++ allows you to write extension functions in C++ (you need to be aware that installing these is lot more complex than in the case of Java), while the 4XSLT processor (`http://4suite.org`) focuses on Python, and Gestalt (`http://sf.net/projects/gestalt`) on Eiffel.

The language specification says nothing about how extension functions are written, and how they are linked to the stylesheet. The notes that follow are provided to give an indication of the kind of techniques you are likely to encounter.

In the case of Java, several processors have provided a mechanism in which the name of the Java class is contained in the namespace URI of the function, while the name of the method is represented by the local name. This mechanism means that all the information needed to identify and call the function is contained within the function name itself. For example, if you want to call the Java method `random()` in class `java.lang.Math` to obtain a random number between 0.0 and 1.0, you can write:

```
<xsl:variable name="random-number" select="Math:random()"
    xmlns:Math="ext://java.lang.Math"/>
```

Unfortunately, each processor has slightly different rules for forming the namespace URI, as well as different rules for converting function arguments and results between Java classes and the XPath type system, so it won't always be possible to make such calls portable between XSLT processors. But the example above works with both Saxon and Xalan.

This example calls a static method in Java, but most products also allow you to call Java constructors to return object instances, and then to call instance methods on those objects. To make this possible, the processor needs to extend the XPath type system to allow expressions to return values that are essentially wrappers around external Java objects. The XSLT and XPath specifications are written to explicitly permit this, though the details are left to the implementation.

For example, suppose you want to monitor the amount of free memory that is available, perhaps to diagnose an "out of memory" error in a stylesheet. You could do this by writing:

```
<xsl:message>
    <xsl:text>Free memory: </xsl:text>
    <xsl:value-of select="rt:freeMemory(rt:getRuntime())"
                  xmlns:rt="ext://java.lang.Runtime"/>
</xsl:message>
```

Again, this example is written to work with both Saxon and Xalan.

There are two extension function calls here: the call on `getRuntime()` calls a static method in the class `java.lang.Runtime`, which returns an instance of this class. The call on `freeMemory()` is an instance method in this class. By convention, instance methods are called by supplying the target instance as an extra first parameter in the call.

Another technique that's used for linking an extension function is to use a declaration in the stylesheet. Microsoft's processors use this approach to bind JavaScript functions. Here is an example of a simple extension function implemented using this mechanism with Microsoft's MSXML3/4 processor and an expression that calls it.

```
<xsl:stylesheet version="1.0"
    xmlns:xsl="http://www.w3.org/1999/XSL/Transform"
    xmlns:ms="javascript:my-extensions">

<msxsl:script
    xmlns:msxsl="urn:schemas-microsoft-com:xslt"
    language="VBScript"
    implements-prefix="ms"
>
Function ToMillimetres(inches)
    ToMillimetres = inches * 25.4
End Function
</msxsl:script>

<xsl:template match="/" >
    <xsl:variable name="test" select="12"/>
    <size><xsl:value-of select="ms:ToMillimetres($test)"/></size>
</xsl:template>
</xsl:stylesheet>
```

This is not a particularly well-chosen example, because it could easily be coded in XSLT, and it's generally a good idea to stick to XSLT code unless there is a very good reason not to; but it illustrates how it's done.

People sometimes get confused about the difference between script in the stylesheet, which is designed to be called as part of the transformation process, and script in the HTML output page, which is designed to be called during the display of the HTML in the browser. When the transformation is being done within the browser, and is perhaps invoked from script in another HTML page, it can be difficult to keep the distinctions clearly in mind. I find that it always helps in this environment to create a mock-up of the HTML page that you want to generate, test that it works as expected in the browser, and then start thinking about writing the XSLT code to generate it.

Sometimes you need to change configuration files or environment variables, or call special methods in the processor's API to make extension functions available; this is particularly true of products written in C or C++, which are less well suited to dynamic loading and linking.

In XSLT 2.0 (this is a change from XSLT 1.0), it is a static error if the stylesheet contains a call on a function that the compiler cannot locate. If you want to write code that is portable across processors offering different extension functions, you should therefore use the new `use-when` attribute to ensure that code containing such calls is not compiled unless the function is available. You can test whether a particular extension function is available by using the `function-available()` function. For example:

```
<xsl:sequence xmlns:acme="http://acme.co.jp/xslt">
   <xsl:value-of select="acme:moonshine($x)"
                 use-when="function-available('acme:moonshine')"/>
   <xsl:text use-when="not(function-available('acme:moonshine'))"
         >*** Sorry, moonshine is off today ***</xsl:text>
</xsl:sequence>
```

Extension functions, because they are written in general-purpose programming languages, can have side effects. For example, they can write to databases, they can ask the user for input, or they can maintain counters. At one time Xalan provided a sample application to implement a counter using extension functions, effectively circumventing the restriction that XSLT variables cannot be modified in situ. Even the simple `Math:random()` function introduced earlier has side effects, because it returns different results each time it is called. However, extension functions with side effects should be used with great care, because the XSLT specification doesn't say what order things are supposed to happen in. For example, it doesn't say whether a variable is evaluated when its declaration is first encountered, or when its value is first used. The more advanced XSLT processors adopt a lazy evaluation strategy in which (for example) variables are not evaluated until they are used. If extension functions with side effects are used to evaluate such variables, the results can be very surprising, because the order in which the extension functions are called becomes quite unpredictable. For example, if one function writes to a log file and another closes this file, you could find that the log file is closed before it is written to. In fact, if a variable is never used, the extension function contained in its definition might not be evaluated at all.

Before writing an extension function, there are a number of alternatives you should consider:

❑   Can the function be written in XSLT, using an `<xsl:function>` element?

❑   Is it possible to supply the required information as a stylesheet parameter? Generally this provides a cleaner and more portable solution.

❑   Is it possible to get the result by calling the `document()` function, with a suitable URI? The URI passed to the `document()` function does not have to identify a static file; it could also invoke a web service. The Java JAXP API allows you to write a `URIResolver` class that intercepts the call on the `document()` function, so the `URIResolver` can return the results directly without needing to access any external resources. The `System.Xml` namespace in the Microsoft .NET framework has a similar capability, referred to as an `XmlResolver`.

Extension Instructions

An extension instruction is an element occurring within a sequence constructor that belongs to a namespace designated as an extension namespace. A namespace is designated as an extension namespace by including its namespace prefix in the `extension-element-prefixes` attribute of the `<xsl:stylesheet>` element, or in the `xsl:extension-element-prefixes` attribute of the element itself, or of a containing extension element or literal result element. For example, Saxon provides an extension instruction

`<saxon:while>` to perform looping while a condition remains true. There is no standard XSLT construct for this because without side effects, a condition once true can never become false. But when used in conjunction with extension functions, `<saxon:while>` can be a useful addition.

Example: Using an Extension Instruction

The following stylesheet (`sysprops.xsl`) uses the `<saxon:while>` element to display the values of all the Java system properties. It does not use a source document, and can be run in Saxon by using the option `-it:main` on the command line.

Stylesheet

The stylesheet calls five methods in the Java class library:

❑   `System.getProperties()` to get a `Properties` object containing all the system properties

❑   `Properties.propertyNames()` to get an `Enumeration` of the names of the system properties

❑   `Enumeration.hasMoreElements()` to determine whether there are more system properties to come

❑   `Enumeration.nextElement()` to get the next system property

❑   `Properties.getProperty()` to get the value of the system property with a given name. For this method, the `Properties` object is supplied as the first argument, and the name of the required property in the second

```
<xsl:stylesheet version="2.0"
   xmlns:xsl="http://www.w3.org/1999/XSL/Transform"
>
<xsl:output indent="yes"/>
<xsl:template name="main">
  <system-properties
      xmlns:System="ext://java.lang.System"
      xmlns:Properties="ext://java.util.Properties"
      xmlns:Enumeration="ext://java.util.Enumeration"
      xsl:exclude-result-prefixes="System Properties Enumeration">
    <xsl:variable name="props"
                select="System:getProperties()"/>
    <xsl:variable name="enum"
                select="Properties:propertyNames($props)"/>
    <saxon:while test="Enumeration:hasMoreElements($enum)"
        xsl:extension-element-prefixes="saxon"
        xmlns:saxon="http://saxon.sf.net/">
      <xsl:variable name="property-name"
                  select="Enumeration:nextElement($enum)"/>
      <property name="{$property-name}"
          value="{Properties:getProperty($props, $property-name)}"/>
    </saxon:while>
  </system-properties>
</xsl:template>
</xsl:stylesheet>
```

Note that for this to work, «saxon» must be declared as an extension element prefix; otherwise, `<saxon:while>` would be interpreted as a literal result element and would be copied to the output. I've chosen to declare it with the smallest possible scope, to mark the parts of the stylesheet that are non-portable. The `xsl:exclude-result-prefixes` attribute is not strictly necessary, but it prevents the output being cluttered with unnecessary namespace declarations.

Technically, this code is unsafe. Although it appears that the extension functions are read-only, the `Enumeration` object actually contains information about the current position in a sequence, and the call to `nextElement()` modifies this information; it is therefore a function call with side effects. In practice you can usually get away with such calls. However, as optimizers become more sophisticated, stylesheets that rely on side effects can sometimes work with one version of an XSLT processor, and fail with the next version. So you should use such constructs only when you have no alternative.

A tip: with Saxon, the `-TJ` option on the command line can be useful for debugging. It gives you diagnostic output showing which Java classes were searched to find methods matching the extension function calls. Another useful option is `-explain`, which shows how the optimizer has rearranged the execution plan.

As with extension functions, the term *extension instruction* covers both nonstandard instructions provided by the vendor and nonstandard instructions implemented by a user or third party. There is no requirement that an XSLT implementation must allow users to define new extension instructions, only that it should behave in a particular way when it encounters extension instructions that it cannot process.

Where a product does allow users to implement extension instructions (two products that do so are Saxon and Xalan), the mechanisms and APIs involved are likely to be rather more complex than those for extension functions, and the task is not one to be undertaken lightly. However, extension instructions can offer capabilities that would be very hard to provide with extension functions alone.

If there is an extension instruction in a stylesheet, then all XSLT processors will recognize it as such, but in general some will be able to handle it and others won't (because it is defined by a different vendor). As with extension functions, the rule is that a processor mustn't fail merely because an extension instruction is present; it should fail only if an attempt is made to evaluate it.

There are two mechanisms to allow stylesheet authors to test whether a particular extension instruction is available: the `element-available()` function and the `<xsl:fallback>` instruction.

The `element-available()` function works in a very similar way to `function-available()`. You can use it in a `use-when` attribute to include stylesheet code conditionally. In this case, however, you can also do the test at evaluation time if you prefer, because calls to unknown extension instructions don't generate an error unless then are executed. For example:

```
<xsl:choose xmlns:acme="http://acme.co.jp/xslt">
   <xsl:when test="element-available('acme:moonshine')">
     <acme:moonshine select="$x" xsl:extension-element-prefixes="acme"/>
   </xsl:when>
   <xsl:otherwise>
```

```
        <xsl:text>*** Sorry, moonshine is off today ***</xsl:text>
    </xsl:otherwise>
</xsl:choose>
```

Note that at the time `element-available()` is called, the prefix for the extension element (here «acme») must have been declared in a namespace declaration, but it does not need to have been designated as an extension element.

The `<xsl:fallback>` instruction (which is fully described on page 316, in Chapter 6) provides an alternative way of specifying what should happen when an extension instruction is not available. The following example is equivalent to the previous one.

```
<acme:moonshine select="$x"
    xmlns:acme="http://acme.co.jp/xslt"
    xsl:extension-element-prefixes="acme">
    <xsl:fallback>
        <xsl:text>*** Sorry, moonshine is off today ***</xsl:text>
    </xsl:fallback>
</acme:moonshine>
```

When an extension instruction is evaluated, and the XSLT processor does not know what to do with it, it should evaluate any child `<xsl:fallback>` element. If there are several `<xsl:fallback>` children, it should evaluate them all. Only if there is no `<xsl:fallback>` element should it report an error. Conversely, if the XSLT processor can evaluate the instruction, it should ignore any child `<xsl:fallback>` element.

> *The specification doesn't actually say that an extension instruction must allow an `<xsl:fallback>` child to be present. There are plenty of XSLT instructions that do not allow `<xsl:fallback>` as a child, for example, `<xsl:copy-of>` and `<xsl:value-of>`. However, an extension instruction that didn't allow `<xsl:fallback>` would certainly be against the spirit of the standard.*

Vendor-defined or user-defined elements at the top level of the stylesheet are not technically extension instructions, because they don't appear within a sequence constructor; therefore, the namespace they appear in does not need to be designated as an extension namespace.

Whitespace

Whitespace handling can be a considerable source of confusion. When the output of a stylesheet is HTML, you can get away without worrying too much about it, because except in some very specific contexts HTML generally treats any sequence of spaces and newlines in the same way as a single space. But with other output formats, getting spaces and newlines where you want them, and avoiding them where you don't, can be crucial.

There are two issues:

❏ Controlling which whitespace in the source document is significant and therefore visible to the stylesheet.

❏ Controlling which whitespace in the stylesheet is significant, because significant whitespace in the stylesheet is likely to get copied to the output.

Whitespace is defined as any sequence of the following four characters.

Character	Unicode Codepoint
Tab	x09
Newline	x0A
Carriage Return	x0D
Space	x20

The definition in XSLT is exactly the same as in XML itself. Other characters such as non-breaking-space (xA0), which is familiar to HTML authors as the entity reference « », may use just as little black ink as these four, but they are not included in the definition.

There are some additional complications about the definition. Writing a character reference « » is in many ways exactly the same as hitting the space bar on the keyboard, but in some circumstances it behaves differently. The character reference « » will be treated as whitespace by the XSLT processor, but not by the XML parser, so you need to understand which rules are applied at which stage of processing.

The XML standard makes some attempt to distinguish between significant and insignificant whitespace. Whitespace in elements with element-only content is considered insignificant, whereas whitespace in elements that allow #PCDATA content is significant. However, the distinction depends on whether a validating parser is used or not, and in any case, the standard requires both kinds of whitespace to be notified to the application. XSLT 2.0 (unlike 1.0) says that by default, if the source document is validated against a DTD or schema, insignificant whitespace (that is, whitespace in elements with element-only content) is ignored. In other cases, handling of whitespace can be controlled from the stylesheet (using the `<xsl:strip-space>` and `<xsl:preserve-space>` declarations, which are fully described in Chapter 6).

The first stages in whitespace handling are the job of the XML parser and are done long before the XSLT processor gets to see the data. Remember that these apply both to source documents and to stylesheets:

❑ End-of-line appearing in the textual content of an element is always normalized to a single newline «x0A» character. This eliminates the differences between line endings on Unix, Windows, and Macintosh systems. XML 1.1 introduces additional rules to normalize the line endings found on IBM mainframes.

❑ The XML parser will normalize attribute values. A tab or newline will always be replaced by a single space, unless it is written as a character reference such as «	» or «
»; for some types of attribute (anything except type CDATA), a validating XML parser will also remove leading and trailing whitespace, and normalize other sequences of whitespace to a single space character.

This attribute normalization can be significant when the attribute in question is an XPath expression in the stylesheet. For example, suppose you want to test whether a string value contains a newline character. You can write this as follows:

```
<xsl:if test="contains(address, '&#x0A;')">
```

It's important to use the character reference «
» here, rather than a real newline, because a newline character would be converted to a space by the XML parser, and the expression would then actually test whether the supplied string contains a space.

What this means in practice is that if you want to be specific about whitespace characters, write them as character references; if you just want to use them as separators and padding, use the whitespace characters directly.

> **The XSLT specification assumes that the XML parser will hand over all whitespace text nodes to the XSLT processor. However, the input to the XSLT processor is technically a tree, and the XSLT specification claims no control over how this tree is built. If you use Microsoft's MSXML, or Altova's XSLT processor, then the default action of the parser while building the tree is to remove whitespace text nodes. If you want the parser to behave the way that the XSLT specification expects, you must set configuration options to make this happen; see the vendors' documentation for details.**

Once the XML parser has done its work, further manipulation of whitespace may be done by the schema processor. This is more likely to affect source documents than stylesheets, because there is little point in putting a stylesheet through a schema processor. For each simple data type, XML Schema defines whitespace handling (the so-called whitespace facet) as one of three options:

- ❑ **Preserve:** All whitespace characters in the value are preserved. This option is used for the data type xs:string.

- ❑ **Replace:** Each newline, carriage return, and tab character is replaced by a single-space character. This option is used for the data type xs:normalizedString and types derived from it.

- ❑ **Collapse:** Leading and trailing whitespace is removed, and any internal sequence of whitespace characters is replaced by a single space. This option is used for all other data types (including those where internal whitespace is not actually allowed).

When source documents are processed using a schema, the XDM rules say that for attributes, and for elements with simple content (that is, elements that can't have child elements), the typed value of the element or attribute is the value after whitespace normalization has been done according to the XML Schema rules for the particular data type. The *string* value of an element or attribute may either be the value as originally written or the value obtained by converting the typed value back to a string — implementations are allowed to choose either approach. In the latter case, insignificant leading and trailing whitespace may be lost. However, the string() function itself is almost the only thing that depends on the string value of a node; most expressions use the typed value.

Finally, the XSLT processor applies some processing of its own. By this time entity and character references have been expanded, so there is no difference between a space written as a space and one written as « »:

- ❑ Adjacent text nodes are merged into a single text node (*normalized* in the terminology of the DOM).

- ❑ Then, if a text node consists entirely of whitespace, it is removed (or *stripped*) from the tree if the containing element is listed in an <xsl:strip-space> definition in the stylesheet. The detailed rules are more complex than this, and also take into account the presence of the `xml:space` attribute in the source document; see the `<xsl:text>` element on page 492 in Chapter 6 for details.

This process never removes whitespace characters that are adjacent to non-whitespace characters. For example, consider the following:

```
<article>
   <title>Abelard and Heloise</title>
   <subtitle>Some notes towards a family tree</subtitle>
   <author>Brenda M Cook</author>
   <abstract>
      The story of Abelard and Heloise is best recalled nowadays from the stage drama
of 1970 and it is perhaps inevitable that Diana Rigg stripping off for Keith Mitchell
should be the most enduring image of this historic couple in some people's minds.
   </abstract>
</article>
```

Our textual analysis will focus entirely on the whitespace — the actual content of the piece is best ignored.

There are five whitespace-only text nodes in this fragment, one before each of the child elements `<title>`, `<subtitle>`, `<author>`, and `<abstract>`, and another between the end of the `<abstract>` and the end of the `<article>`. The whitespace in these nodes is passed by the XML parser to the XSLT processor, and it is up to the stylesheet whether to take any notice of it or not. Typically, in this situation this whitespace is of no interest and it can be stripped from the tree by specifying `<xsl:strip-space elements = "article"/>`.

The whitespace within the `<abstract>` cannot be removed by the same process. The newline characters at the start and end of the abstract, and at the end of each line, are part of the text passed by the parser to the application, and it is not possible in the stylesheet to declare them as being irrelevant. If the `<abstract>` element is defined in the schema as being of type `xs:token` (or a type derived from this), then the schema processor will remove the leading and trailing whitespace characters and convert the newlines into single spaces. But if it is of type `xs:string`, or if no schema processing is done, then all the spaces and newlines will be present in the tree model of the source document. What you can do is to call the `normalize-space()` function when processing these nodes on the source tree, which will have the same effect as schema processing for a type that specifies the `collapse` option (that is, it will remove leading and trailing whitespace and replace all other sequences of one or more whitespace characters by a single space). The `normalize-space()` function is described in Chapter 13.

> The processing done by a schema processor for data of type `xs:normalizedString` is to replace each newline, tab, and carriage return by a single space character. This is not the same as the processing done by the `normalize-space()` function in XPath. The term normalization, unfortunately, does not have a standard meaning.

So we can see that XSLT makes a very firm distinction between text nodes that consist of whitespace only, and those that hold something other than whitespace. A whitespace text node can exist only where there is nothing between two pieces of markup other than whitespace characters.

To take another example, consider the following document:

```
<person>
   <name>Prudence Flowers</name>
```

```
          <employer>Lloyds Bank</employer>
          <place-of-work>
              71 Lombard Street
              London, UK
              <zip>EC3P 3BS</zip>
          </place-of-work>
      </person>
```

Where are the whitespace nodes? Let's look at it again, this time making the whitespace characters visible.

```
<person>↵
→<name>Prudence Flowers</name>↵
→<employer>Lloyds Bank</employer>↵
→<place-of-work>↵
→♦♦♦71 Lombard Street↵
→♦♦♦London, UK↵
→♦♦♦<zip>EC3P 3BS</zip>♦↵
→<place-of-work>↵
</person>
```

The newline and tab between `<person>` and `<name>` are not adjacent to any non-whitespace characters, so they constitute a whitespace node — so do the characters between `</name>` and `<employer>`, and between `</employer>` and `<place-of-work>`. However, most of the whitespace characters within the `<place-of-work>` element are in the same text node as non-whitespace characters, so they do not constitute a whitespace node. To make it even clearer, let's highlight the whitespace characters in whitespace nodes and show the others as ordinary spaces.

```
<person>↵
→<name>Prudence Flowers</name>↵
→<employer>Lloyds Bank</employer>↵
→<place-of-work>
      71 Lombard Street
      London, UK
      <zip>EC3P 3BS</zip>♦↵
→</place-of-work>>↵
</person>
```

Why is all this relevant? As we've seen, the `<xsl:strip-space>` element allows you to control what happens to whitespace nodes (those shown in the immediately preceding example), but it doesn't let you do anything special with whitespace characters that appear in ordinary text nodes (those shown as ordinary spaces).

Most of the whitespace nodes in this example are immediate children of the `<person>` element, so they could be stripped by writing:

```
<xsl:strip-space elements="person"/>
```

This would leave the remaining whitespace node intact (the one after the end tag of the `<zip>` element). Whitespace nodes are retained on the source tree unless you ask for them to be stripped, either by using `<xsl:strip-space>`, or by using some option provided by the XML parser or schema processor during the building of the tree.

The Effect of Stripping Whitespace Nodes

There are two main effects of stripping whitespace nodes, as done in the `<person>` element in the earlier example:

❑ When you use `<xsl:apply-templates/>` to process all the children of the `<person>` element, the whitespace nodes aren't there, so they don't get selected, which means they don't get copied to the result tree. If they had been left on the source tree, then by default they would be copied to the result tree.

❑ When you use `<xsl:number>` or the `position()` or `count()` functions to count nodes, the whitespace nodes aren't there, so they aren't counted. If you had left the whitespace nodes on the tree, then the `<name>`, `<employer>`, and `<place-of-work>` elements would be nodes 2, 4, and 6 instead of 1, 2, and 3.

There are cases where it's important to keep the whitespace nodes. Consider the following.

```
<para>
Edited by <name>James Clark</name>♦<email>jjc@jclark.com</email>
</para>
```

The diamond represents a space character that needs to be preserved, but because it is not adjacent to any other text, it would be eligible for stripping. In fact, whitespace is nearly always significant in elements that have mixed content (that is, elements that have both element and text nodes as children). Figure 18-3 on page 1005 shows a live example of what goes wrong when such spaces are stripped.

If you want to strip all the whitespace nodes from the source tree, you can write:

```
<xsl:strip-space elements="*"/>
```

If you want to strip all the whitespace nodes except those within certain named elements, you can write:

```
<xsl:strip-space elements="*"/>
<xsl:preserve-space elements="para h1 h2 h3 h4"/>
```

If any elements in the document (either the source document or the stylesheet) use the XML-defined attribute «xml:space = "preserve"», this takes precedence over these rules: whitespace nodes in that element, and in all its descendants, will be kept on the tree unless the attribute is canceled on a descendant element by specifying «xml:space = "default"». This allows you to control on a per-instance basis whether whitespace is kept, whereas `<xsl:strip-space>` controls it at the element-type level.

Whitespace Nodes in the Stylesheet

For the stylesheet itself, whitespace nodes are all stripped, with two exceptions, namely whitespace within an `<xsl:text>` element, and whitespace controlled by the attribute «xml:space = "preserve"». If you explicitly want to copy a whitespace text node from the stylesheet to the result tree, write it within an `<xsl:text>` element, like this:

```
<xsl:value-of select="address-line[1]"/>
<xsl:text>&#xA;</xsl:text>
<xsl:value-of select="address-line[2]"/>
```

The only reason for using «
» here rather than an actual newline is that it's more clearly visible to the reader; it's also less likely to be accidentally turned into a newline followed by tabs or spaces. Writing the whitespace as a character reference doesn't stop it being treated as whitespace by XSLT, because the character references will have been expanded by the XML parser before the XSLT processor gets to see them.

Another way of coding the previous fragment in XSLT 2.0 is to write:

```
<xsl:value-of select="address-line[position() = 1 to 2]"
               separator="&#xA;"/>
```

You can also cause whitespace text nodes in the stylesheet to be retained by using the option «xml:space = "preserve"». Although this is defined in the XML specification, its defined effect is to advise the application that whitespace is significant, and XSLT (which is the application in this case) will respect this. In XSLT 1.0, this sometimes caused problems because certain elements, such as <xsl:choose> and <xsl:apply-templates>, do not allow text nodes as children, even whitespace-only text nodes. Many processors, however, were forgiving on this. XSLT 2.0 has clarified that in situations where text nodes are not allowed, a whitespace-only text node is now stripped, despite the xml:space attribute. (However, an element that must always be empty, such as <xsl:output>, must be completely empty; whitespace-only text nodes are not allowed within these elements.)

Despite this clarification of the rules, I wouldn't normally recommend using the xml:space attribute in a stylesheet, but if there are large chunks of existing XML that you want to copy into the stylesheet verbatim, the technique can be useful.

Solving Whitespace Problems

There are two typical problems with whitespace in the output: too much of it, or too little.

If you are generating HTML, a bit of extra whitespace usually doesn't matter, though there are some places where it can slightly distort the layout of your page. With some text formats, however (a classic example is comma-separated values) you need to be very careful to output whitespace in exactly the right places.

Too Much Whitespace

If you are getting too much whitespace, there are three possible places it can be coming from:

- ❏ The source document
- ❏ The stylesheet
- ❏ Output indentation

First ensure that you set «indent = "no"» on the <xsl:output> element, to eliminate the last of these possibilities.

If the output whitespace is adjacent to text, then it probably comes from the same place as that text.

- ❏ If this text comes from the stylesheet, use <xsl:text> to control more precisely what is output. For example, the following code outputs a comma between the items in a list, but it also outputs a newline after the comma, because the newline is part of the same text node as the comma:

```
<xsl:for-each select="item">
  <xsl:value-of select="."/>,
</xsl:for-each>
```

❏ If you want the comma but not the newline, change this so that the newline is in a text node of its own, and is therefore stripped.

```
<xsl:for-each select="item">
  <xsl:value-of select="."/>,<xsl:text/>
</xsl:for-each>
```

❏ If the text comes from the source document, use normalize-space() to trim leading and trailing spaces from the text before outputting it.

If the offending whitespace is between tags in the output, then it probably comes from whitespace nodes in the source tree that have not been stripped, and the remedy is to add an <xsl:strip-space> element to the stylesheet.

Too Little Whitespace

If you want whitespace in the output and aren't getting it, use <xsl:text> to generate it at the appropriate point. For example, the following code will output the lines of a poem in HTML, with each line of the poem being shown on a new line:

```
<xsl:for-each select="line">
    <xsl:value-of select="."/><br/>
</xsl:for-each>
```

This will display perfectly correctly in the browser, but if you want to view the HTML in a text editor, it will be difficult because everything goes on a single line. It would be useful to start a newline after each <br> element — you can do this as follows:

```
<xsl:for-each select="line">
    <xsl:value-of select="."/><br/><xsl:text>&#xa;</xsl:text>
</xsl:for-each>
```

Another trick I have used to achieve this is to exploit the fact that the non-breaking-space character (#xA0), although invisible, is not classified as whitespace. So you can achieve the required effect by writing:

```
<xsl:for-each select="line">
    <xsl:value-of select="."/><br/> 
</xsl:for-each>
```

This works because the newline after the « » is now part of a non-whitespace node.

Summary

The purpose of this chapter was to study the overall structure of a stylesheet, before going into the detailed specification of each element in Chapter 6. We've now covered the following:

❏ How a stylesheet program can be made up of one or more stylesheet modules, linked together with <xsl:import> and <xsl:include> declarations. I described how the concept of import precedence allows one stylesheet to override definitions in those it imports.

❏ The <xsl:stylesheet> (or <xsl:transform>) element, which is the outermost element of most stylesheet modules.

❏ The `<?xml-stylesheet?>` processing instruction, which can be used to link from a source document to its associated stylesheets, and which allows a stylesheet to be embedded directly in the source document whose style it defines.

❏ The declarations found in the stylesheet, that is, the immediate children of the `<xsl:stylesheet>` or `<xsl:transform>` element, including the ability to have user-defined or vendor-defined elements here.

❏ How the `<xsl:stylesheet>` and `<xsl:template match = "/">` elements can be omitted to make an XSLT stylesheet look more like the simple template languages that some users may be familiar with.

❏ The idea of a sequence constructor, a structure that occurs throughout a stylesheet, which is a sequence containing text nodes and literal result elements to be copied to the result tree, and instructions and extension elements to be executed. This led naturally to a discussion of literal result elements and of attribute value templates, which are used to define variable attributes not only of literal result elements but of certain XSLT elements as well.

❏ How the W3C standards committee has tried to ensure that the specification can be extended, both by vendors and by W3C itself, without adversely affecting the portability of stylesheets. You saw how to make a stylesheet work even if it uses proprietary extension functions and extension elements that may not be available in all implementations.

❏ How XSLT stylesheets handle whitespace in the source document, in the stylesheet itself and in the result tree.

The next chapter describes how to use XSLT stylesheets together with an XML Schema for the source and/or result documents. If you are not interested in using schemas, you can probably skip that chapter and move straight to Chapter 5, which gives detailed information about the data types available in the XDM model and the ways in which you can use them.

Stylesheets and Schemas

One of the most important innovations in XSLT 2.0 is that stylesheets can take advantage of the schemas you have defined for your input and output documents. This chapter explores how this works.

This feature is an optional part of XSLT 2.0, in two significant ways:

❑ Firstly, an XSLT 2.0 processor isn't required to implement this part of the standard. A processor that offers schema support is called a *schema-aware processor*; one that does not is referred to as a *basic processor*.

❑ Secondly, even if the XSLT 2.0 processor you are using is a schema-aware processor, you can still process input documents, and produce output documents, for which there is no schema available.

There is no space in this book for a complete description of XML Schema. If you want to start writing schemas, I would recommend you read *XML Schema* by Eric van der Vlist (O'Reilly & Associates, 2002) or *Definitive XML Schema* by Priscilla Walmsley (Prentice Hall, 2002). XML Schema is a large and complicated specification, certainly as large as XSLT itself. However, it's possible that you are not writing your own schemas, but writing stylesheets designed to work with a schema that someone else has already written. If this is the case, I hope you will find the short overview of XML Schema in this chapter a useful introduction.

XML Schema: An Overview

The primary purpose of an XML Schema is to enable documents to be validated: they define a set of rules that XML documents must conform to, and enable documents to be checked against these rules. This means that organizations using XML to exchange invoices and purchase orders can agree on a schema defining the rules for these messages, and both parties can validate the messages against the schema to ensure that they are right. So the schema, in effect, defines a type of document, and this is why schemas are central to the type system of XSLT.

In fact, the designers of XML Schema were more ambitious than this. They realized that rather than simply giving a "yes" or "no" answer, processing a document against a schema could make the application's life easier by attaching labels to the validated document indicating, for each element and attribute in the document, which schema definitions it was validated against. In the language of XML Schema, this document with validation labels is called a Post Schema Validation Infoset, or PSVI. The XDM data model used by XSLT and XPath is based on the PSVI, but it only retains a subset of the information in the PSVI; most importantly, the type annotations attached to element and attribute nodes.

We begin by looking at the kinds of types that can be defined in XML Schema, starting with simple types and moving on to progressively more complex types.

Simple Type Definitions

Let's suppose that many of your messages refer to part numbers, and that part numbers have a particular format such as ABC12345. You can start by defining this as a type in the schema:

```
<xs:simpleType name="part-number">
  <xs:restriction base="xs:token">
    <xs:pattern value="[A-Z]{3}[0-9]{5}"/>
  </xs:restriction>
</xs:simpleType>
```

Part number is a simple type because it doesn't have any internal node structure (that is, it doesn't contain any elements or attributes). I have defined it by restriction from `xs:token`, which is one of the built-in types that come for free with XML Schema. I could have chosen to base the type on `xs:string`, but `xs:token` is probably better because with `xs:string`, leading and trailing whitespace is considered significant, whereas with `xs:token`, it gets stripped automatically before the validation takes place. The particular restriction in this case is that the value must match the regular expression given in the `<xs:pattern>` element. This regular expression says that the value must consist of exactly three letters in the range A to Z, followed by exactly five digits.

Having defined this type, you can now refer to it in definitions of elements and attributes. For example, you can define the element:

```
<xs:element name="part" type="part-number"/>
```

This allows documents to contain `<part>` elements whose content conforms to the rules for the type called `part-number`. Of course, you can also define other elements that have the same type, for example:

```
<xs:element name="subpart" type="part-number"/>
```

Note the distinction between the name of an element and its type. Many element declarations in a schema (declarations that define elements with different names) can refer to the same type definition, if the rules for validating their content are the same. It's also permitted, though I won't go into the detail just yet, to use the same element name at different places within a document with different type definitions.

You can also use the same type definition in an attribute, for example:

```
<xs:attribute name="part-nr" type="part-number"/>
```

You can declare variables and parameters in a stylesheet whose values must be elements or attributes of a particular type. Once a document has been validated using this schema, elements that have been validated against the declarations of `part` and `subpart` given above, and attributes that have been validated against the declaration named `part-nr`, will carry the type annotation `part-number`, and they can be assigned to variables such as:

```
<xsl:variable name="part1" as="element(*, part-number)">
```

```
<xsl:variable name="part2" as="attribute(*, part-number)">
```

The variable part1 is allowed to contain any element node that has the type annotation part-number. If further types have been defined as restricted subtypes of part-number (for example, Boeing-part-number), these can be assigned to the variable too. The «*» indicates that we are not concerned with the name of the element or attribute, but only with its type.

There are actually three *varieties* of simple types that you can define in XML Schema: atomic types, list types, and union types. Atomic types are treated specially in the XPath/XSLT type system, because values of an atomic type (called, naturally enough, atomic values) can be manipulated as freestanding items, independently of any node. Like integers, booleans, and strings, part numbers as defined above are atomic values, and you can hold a part number or a sequence of part numbers directly in a variable, without creating any node to contain it. For example, the following declaration defines a variable whose value is a sequence of three part numbers:

```
<xsl:variable name="part" as="part-number*"
              select="for $p in ('WZH94623', 'BYF67253', 'PRG83692')
                      return $p cast as part-number"/>
```

Simple types in XML Schema are not the same thing as atomic types in the XPath data model. This is because a simple type can also allow a sequence of values. For example, it is possible to define the following simple type:

```
<xs:simpleType name="colors">
  <xs:list>
    <xs:simpleType>
      <xs:restriction base="xs:NCName">
        <xs:enumeration value="red"/>
        <xs:enumeration value="orange"/>
        <xs:enumeration value="yellow"/>
        <xs:enumeration value="green"/>
        <xs:enumeration value="blue"/>
        <xs:enumeration value="indigo"/>
        <xs:enumeration value="violet"/>
      </xs:restriction>
    </xs:simpleType>
  </xs:list>
</xs:simpleType>
```

There are actually two type definitions here. The inner type is anonymous, because the <xs:simpleType> element has no name attribute. It defines an atomic value, which must be an xs:NCName, and more specifically, must be one of the values «red», «orange», «yellow», «green», «blue», «indigo», or «violet». The outer type is a named type (which means it can be referenced from elsewhere in the schema), and it defines a list type whose individual items must conform to the inner type.

This type therefore allows values such as «red green blue», or «violet yellow» or even «red red red». The values are written in textual XML as a list of color names separated by spaces, but once the document has been through schema validation, the typed value of an element with this type will be a sequence of xs:NCName values.

The term *simple type* in XML Schema rules out types involving multiple attribute or element nodes, but it does allow composite values consisting of a sequence of atomic values.

Elements with Attributes and Simple Content

One thing that might occur quite frequently in an invoice or purchase order is an amount in money: there might be elements such as:

❑   `<unit-price currency = "USD">50.00</unit-price>`

❑   `<amount-due currency = "EUR">1890.00</amount-due>`

What these two elements have in common is that they have a `currency` attribute (with a particular range of allowed values) and content that is a decimal number. This is an example of a complex type. I defined `part-number` as a simple type because it didn't involve any nodes. The `money-amount` type is a complex type, because it involves a decimal number and an attribute value. You can define this type as follows:

```
<xs:simpleType name="currency-type">
  <xs:restriction base="xs:token">
    <xs:enumeration value="USD"/>
    <xs:enumeration value="EUR"/>
    <xs:enumeration value="GBP"/>
    <xs:enumeration value="CAD"/>
  </xs:restriction>
</xs:simpleType>

<xs:complexType name="money-amount">
  <xs:simpleContent>
    <xs:extension base="xs:decimal">
      <xs:attribute name="currency" type="currency-type"/>
    </xs:extension>
  </xs:simpleContent>
</xs:complexType>
```

Here I have defined two new types in the schema, both of which are named. The first defines the type of the `currency` attribute. I could have used the same name for the attribute and its type, but many people prefer to keep the names of types distinct from those of elements and attributes, to avoid confusing the two. In this case I've chosen to define it (again) as a subtype of `xs:token`, but this time restricting the value to be one of four particular world currencies. In practice, of course, the list might be much longer. The `currency-type` is again a simple type, because it's just a value; it doesn't define any nodes.

The second definition is a complex type, because it defines two things. It's the type of an element that has a `currency` attribute conforming to the definition of `currency-type`, and has content (the text between the element start and end tags) that is a decimal number, indicated by the reference to the built-in type `xs:decimal`. This particular kind of complex type is called a *complex type with simple content*, which means that elements of this type can have attributes, but they cannot have child elements.

Again, the name of the type is quite distinct from the names of the elements that conform to this type. You can declare the two example elements above in the schema as follows:

```
<xs:element name="unit-price" type="money-amount"/>
<xs:element name="amount-due" type="money-amount"/>
```

But although the type definition doesn't constrain the element name, it does constrain the name of the attribute, which must be «currency». If the type definition defined child elements, it would also constrain these child elements to have particular names.

In an XSLT 2.0 stylesheet, you can write a template rule for processing elements of this type, which means that all the logic for formatting money amounts can go in one place. For example, you could write:

```
<xsl:template match="element(*, money-amount)">
  <xsl:value-of select="@currency, format-number(., '#,##0.00')"/>
</xsl:template>
```

This would output the example `<amount-due>` element as «EUR 1,890.00». (The `format-number()` function is described in Chapter 13, on page 788). The beauty of such a template rule is that it is highly reusable; however much the schema is extended to include new elements that hold amounts of money, this rule can be used to display them.

Elements with Mixed Content

The type of an element that can contain child elements is called a *complex type with complex content*. Such types essentially fall into three categories, called *empty content*, *mixed content*, and *element-only content*. Mixed content allows intermingled text and child elements, and is often found in narrative XML documents, allowing markup such as:

```
<para>The population of <city>London</city> reached
  <number>5,572,000</number> in <year>1891</year>, and had risen
  further to <number>7,160,000</number> by <year>1911</year>.</para>
```

The type of this element could be declared in a schema as:

```
<xs:complex-type name="para-type" mixed="true">
  <xs:choice minOccurs="0" maxOccurs="unbounded">
    <xs:element ref="city"/>
    <xs:element ref="number"/>
    <xs:element ref="year"/>
  </xs:choice>
</xs:complex-type>
```

In practice, the list of permitted child elements would probably be much longer than this, and a common technique is to define *substitution groups*, which allow a list of such elements to be referred to by a single name.

Narrative documents tend to be less constrained than documents holding structured data such as purchase orders and invoices, and while schema validation is still very useful, the type annotations generated as a result of validation aren't generally so important when the time comes to process the data using XSLT; the names of the elements are usually more significant than their types. However, there is plenty of potential for using the types, especially if the schema is designed with this in mind.

When schemas are used primarily for validation, the tendency is to think of types in terms of the form that values assume. For example, it is natural to define the element `<city>` (as used in the example above) as a type derived from `xs:token` by restriction, because the names of cities are strings, perhaps consisting of multiple words, in which spaces are not significant. Once types start to be used for processing information (which is what you are doing when you use XSLT), it's also useful to think about what the value actually means. The content of the `<city>` element is not just a string of characters, it is the name of a geographical place, a place that has a location on the Earth's surface, that is in a particular country, and that may figure in postal addresses. If you have other similar elements such as `<county>`, `<country>`, and `<state>`, it might be a good idea to define a single type for all of them. Even if this type doesn't have any particular purpose for validation, because it doesn't define any extra constraints on the content, it can potentially be useful when writing XSLT templates because it groups a number of elements that belong together semantically.

Elements with Element-Only Content

This category covers most of the "wrapper" elements that are found in data-oriented XML. A typical example is the outer `<person>` element in a structure such as:

```
<person id="P517541">
  <name>
    <given>Michael</given>
    <given>Howard</given>
    <family>Kay</family>
  </name>
  <date-of-birth>1951-10-11</date-of-birth>
  <place-of-birth>Hannover</place-of-birth>
</person>
```

The schema for this might be:

```
<xs:element name="person" type="person-type"/>

<xs:complexType name="person-type">
  <xs:sequence>
    <xs:element name="name" type="personal-name-type"/>
    <xs:element name="date-of-birth" type="xs:date"/>
    <xs:element name="place-of-birth" type="xs:token"/>
  </xs:sequence>
  <xs:attribute name="id" type="id-number"/>
</xs:complexType>

<xs:complexType name="personal-name-type">
  <xs:sequence>
    <xs:element name="given" maxOccurs="unbounded" type="xs:token"/>
    <xs:element name="family" type="xs:token"/>
  </xs:sequence>
</xs:complexType>

<xs:simpleType name="id-number">
  <xs:restriction base="xs:ID">
    <xs:pattern value="[A-Z][0-9]{6}"/>
  </xs:restriction>
</xs:simpleType>
```

There are a number of ways these definitions could have been written. In the so-called *Russian Doll* style, the types would be defined inline within the element declarations, rather than being given separate names of their own. The schema could have been written using more top-level element declarations, for example the `<name>` element could have been described at a top level. When you use a schema for validation, these design decisions mainly affect your ability to reuse definitions later when the schema changes. When you use a schema to describe types that can be referenced in XSLT stylesheets, however, they also affect the ease of writing the stylesheet.

In choosing the representation of the schema shown above, I made a number of implicit assumptions:

❑   It's quite likely that there will be other elements with the same structure as <person>, or with an extension of this structure: perhaps not at the moment, but at some time in the future. Examples of such elements might be <employee> or <pensioner>. Therefore, it's worth describing the element and its type separately.

❑   Similarly, personal names are likely to appear in a number of different places. Elements with this type won't always be called <name>, so it's a good idea to create a type definition that can be referenced from any element.

❑   Not every element called <name> will be a personal name, the same tag might also be used (even in the same namespace) for other purposes. If I were confident that the tag would always be used for personal names, then I would probably have made it the subject of a top-level element declaration, rather than defining it inline within the <person> element.

❑   The elements at the leaves of the tree (those with simple types) such as <date-of-birth>, <place-of-birth>, <given>, and <family> are probably best defined using local element declarations rather than top-level declarations. Even if they are used in more than one container element, there is relatively little to be gained by pulling the element declarations out to the top level. The important thing is that if any of them have a user-defined type (which isn't the case in this example), then the user-defined types are defined using top-level <xs:simpleType> declarations. This is what I have done for the id attribute (which is defined as a subtype of xs:ID, forcing values to be unique within any XML document), but I chose not to do the same for the leaf elements.

XSLT 2.0 allows you to validate elements against either a global element declaration or a global type definition, so you'll be able to validate an element provided that either the element declaration or the type definition is global. If you're planning to use XQuery with your schema, however, it's worth bearing in mind that XQuery doesn't allow validation against a type definition, so validation is only possible if the element declaration is global. It's useful to be able to validate individual elements because you can then assign the elements to variables or function parameters that require an element of a particular type. The alternative is to defer validation until a complete document has been constructed.

Defining a Type Hierarchy

Using top-level type definitions is very handy when you have many different elements using the same type definitions. I've come across an example of this in action when handling files containing genealogical data. A lot of this data is concerned with recording events: events such as births, baptisms, marriages, deaths, and burials, but also many other miscellaneous events such as a mention in a newspaper, enrollment at a school or university, starting a new job, receiving a military honor, and so on. Traditionally, this data is recorded using a file format called GEDCOM, which predates XML by many years, but can very easily be translated directly into XML and manipulated using XSLT, as we will see in Chapter 19.

The GEDCOM specification defines about 30 kinds of event such as BIRTH, DEATH, and MARRIAGE, and then provides a general catch-all EVENT record for anything else you might want to keep information about. All these records have a common structure: they allow information about the date and place of the event, the sources of information about the event, the participants and witnesses, and so on. In other words, they are all different elements with the same type.

In XSLT 1.0, the only way of referring to elements was by name. This meant that if you wanted to write a template rule to process any kind of event, you had to know all the element names representing events, and write a union expression of the form «BIRTH|DEATH|MARRIAGE|...» to select them. This is tedious to say the least, and it is also inextensible: when new kinds of event are introduced, the stylesheet stops working.

XSLT 2.0 introduces the ability to refer to elements by type: you can now write a template that specifies «match = "element (*, EVENT)"», which matches all elements of type EVENT. The «*» indicates that you don't care what the name of the element is, you are interested only in its type. This is both more convenient and more flexible than listing all the different kinds of event by name.

You can go beyond this, and define a type hierarchy. In a genealogical database, in addition to recording events in a person's life, you can also record properties of a person such as their occupation, religion, state of health, or (if you want) their height or eye color. GEDCOM hasn't modeled these particularly well; it treats them as events, which isn't a particularly good fit. They have a lot in common with events, in that you want to record the evidence for the information, but they tend to be independent of place and to be applicable over some extended period of a person's life. So in an ideal world we would probably model these using a separate type called, say, ATTRIBUTE (not to be confused with XML attributes, of course). The things that EVENT and ATTRIBUTE have in common could be defined in a third type from which both of these inherit: let's call this DETAIL. Then in an XPath expression, I can find all the events and all the attributes for a person with the single expression «element (*, DETAIL)».

Sometimes you get the chance to write a schema with schema-aware XSLT and XQuery processing in mind. More often, however, you have to work with a schema that already exists, and which was written primarily for validation. In this case, it might not contain any very useful type hierarchies. But there's another device in XML Schema that allows elements to be referred to generically, namely substitution groups, and we'll look at what these have to offer in the next section.

Substitution Groups

The type of an element or attribute tells you what can appear inside the content of the element or attribute. Substitution groups, by contrast, classify elements according to where they can appear.

There is a schema for XSLT 2.0 stylesheets published as part of the XSLT Recommendation (see http://www.w3.org/2007/schema-for-xslt20.xsd). Let's look at how this schema uses substitution groups.

Firstly, the schema defines a type that is applicable to any XSLT-defined element, and that simply declares the standard attributes that can appear on any element:

```
<xs:complexType name="generic-element-type" mixed="true">
  <xs:attribute name="default-collation" type="xsl:uri-list"/>
  <xs:attribute name="exclude-result-prefixes" type="xsl:prefixes"/>
  <xs:attribute name="extension-element-prefixes"
                type="xsl:prefix-list-or-all"/>
  <xs:attribute name="use-when" type="xsl:expression"/>
  <xs:attribute name="xpath-default-namespace" type="xs:anyURI"/>
  <xs:anyAttribute namespace="##other" processContents="lax"/>
</xs:complexType>
```

There's a good mix of features used to define these attributes. Some attributes use built-in types (xs:anyURI), while some use user-defined types defined elsewhere in the schema (xsl:prefixes). The <xs:anyAttribute> at the end says that XSLT elements can contain attributes from a different namespace, which are laxly validated (that is, the processor will validate the attribute if and only if a schema definition is available for it.)

Every XSLT element except the <xsl:output> element allows a standard version attribute (the <xsl:output> element is different because its version attribute is defined for a different purpose and has a different type). So the schema defines another type that adds this attribute:

```
<xs:complexType name="versioned-element-type">
  <xs:complexContent>
    <xs:extension base="xsl:generic-element-type">
      <xs:attribute name="version" type="xs:decimal" use="optional"/>
    </xs:extension>
  </xs:complexContent>
</xs:complexType>
```

The XSLT specification classifies many XSLT elements as *instructions*. This is not a structural distinction based on the attributes or content model of these elements (which varies widely), it is a distinction based on the way they are used. In particular, instruction elements are interchangeable in terms of where they may appear in a stylesheet: If you can use one instruction in a particular context, you can use any instruction. This calls for defining a substitution group:

```
<xs:element name="instruction"
            type="xsl:versioned-element-type"
            abstract="true"/>
```

Note that although the substitution group is defined using an element declaration, it does not define a real element, because it specifies «abstract = "true"». This means that an actual XSLT stylesheet will never contain an element called <xsl:instruction>. It is a fictional element that exists only so that others can be substituted for it.

What this declaration does say is that every element in the substitution group for <xsl:instruction> must be defined with a type that is derived from xsl:versioned-element-type. That is, every XSLT instruction allows the attributes default-collation, exclude-result-prefixes, extension-element-prefixes, use-when, xpath-default-namespace, and version, as well as any namespace-prefixed attribute. This is in fact the only thing that XSLT instructions have in common with each other, as far as their permitted content is concerned.

Individual instructions are now defined as members of this substitution group. Here is a simple example, the declaration of the <xsl:if> element:

```
<xs:element name="if" substitutionGroup="xsl:instruction">
  <xs:complexType>
    <xs:complexContent mixed="true">
      <xs:extension base="xsl:sequence-constructor">
        <xs:attribute name="test" type="xsl:expression" use="required"/>
      </xs:extension>
    </xs:complexContent>
  </xs:complexType>
</xs:element>
```

This shows that the <xsl:if> element is a member of the substitution group whose head is the abstract <xsl:instruction> element. It also tells us that the content model of the element (that is, its type) is defined as an extension of the type xsl:sequence-constructor, the extension being to require a test attribute whose value is of type xsl:expression — this is a simple type defined later in the same schema, representing an XPath expression that may appear as the content of this attribute.

The type xsl:sequence-constructor is used for all XSLT elements whose permitted content is a *sequence constructor*. A sequence constructor is simply a sequence of zero or more XSLT instructions, defined like this:

```
<xs:complexType name="sequence-constructor">
  <xs:complexContent mixed="true">
    <xs:extension base="xsl:versioned-element-type">
      <xs:group ref="xsl:sequence-constructor-group" minOccurs="0"
                                                     maxOccurs="unbounded"/>
    </xs:extension>
  </xs:complexContent>
</xs:complexType>

<xs:group name="sequence-constructor-group">
  <xs:choice>
    <xs:element ref="xsl:variable"/>
    <xs:element ref="xsl:instruction"/>
    <xs:group ref="xsl:result-elements"/>
  </xs:choice>
</xs:group>
```

The first definition says that the xsl:sequence-constructor type extends xsl:versioned-element-type, whose definition we gave earlier. If it didn't extend this type, we wouldn't be allowed to put <xsl:if> in the substitution group of <xsl:instruction>. It also says that the content of a sequence constructor consists of zero or more elements, each of which must be chosen from those in the group sequence-contructor-group. The second definition says that every element in sequence-contructor-group is either an <xsl:instruction> (which implicitly allows any element in the substitution group for <xsl:instruction>, including of course <xsl:if>), or an <xsl:variable>.

The <xsl:variable> element is not defined as a member of the substitution group because it can be used in two different contexts: either as an instruction or as a top-level declaration in a stylesheet. This is one of the drawbacks of substitution groups: they can't overlap (this limitation disappears in XML Schema 1.1). The schema defines all the elements that can act as declarations in a very similar way, using a substitution group headed by an abstract <xsl:declaration> element. It's not possible in XML Schema 1.0 for the same element, <xsl:variable>, to appear in both substitution groups, so it has been defined in neither, and needs to be treated as a special case.

If you need to use XSLT to access an XSLT stylesheet (which isn't as obscure a requirement as it may seem; there are many applications for this), then the classification of elements as instructions or declarations can be very useful. For example, you can match all the instructions that have an attribute in the Saxon namespace with the template rule:

```
<xsl:template match="schema-element(xsl:instruction)[@saxon:*]">
```

assuming that the namespace prefix «saxon» has been declared appropriately. Here the expression «schema-element(xsl:instruction)» selects elements that are either named <xsl:instruction> or are in the substitution group with <xsl:instruction> as its head element, and the predicate «[@saxon:*]» is a filter that selects only those elements that have an attribute in the «saxon» namespace.

The penalty of choosing a real schema for our example is that we have to live with its complications. As we saw earlier, the <xsl:variable> element isn't part of this substitution group. So we might have to extend the query to handle <xsl:variable> elements as well. We can do this by writing:

```
<xsl:template match=
  "(schema-element(xsl:instruction)|schema-element(xsl:variable))[@saxon:*]">
```

A detailed explanation of the syntax used by this match pattern can be found in Chapter 12.

So, to sum up this section, substitution groups are not only a very convenient mechanism for referring to a number of elements that can be substituted for each other in the schema, but they can also provide a handy way of referring to a group of elements in XSLT match patterns. But until XML Schema 1.1 comes along they do have one limitation, which is that elements can only belong directly to one substitution group (or to put it another way, substitution groups must be properly nested; they cannot overlap).

At this point I will finish the lightning tour of XML Schema. The rest of the chapter builds on this understanding to show how the types defined in an XML Schema can be used in a stylesheet.

Declaring Types in XSLT

As we saw in Chapter 3, XSLT 2.0 allows you to define the type of a variable. Similarly, when you write functions or templates, you can declare the type of each parameter, and also the type of the returned value.

Here is an example of a function that takes a string as its parameter and returns an integer as its result:

```
<xsl:function name="my:length" as="xs:integer">
  <xsl:param name="in" as="xs:string"/>
  <xsl:sequence select="max((string-length(upper-case($in)),
                             string-length(lower-case($in))))"/>
</xsl:function>
```

And here's a named template that expects either an element node or nothing as its parameter, and returns either a text node or nothing as its result:

```
<xsl:template name="sequence-nr" as="text()?">
  <xsl:param name="in" as="element()?"/>
  <xsl:number level="any" select="$in" format="i"/>
</xsl:template>
```

You don't have to include type declarations in the stylesheet: If you leave out the «as» attribute, then as with XSLT 1.0, any type of value will be accepted. However, I think it's a good software engineering practice always to declare the types as precisely as you can. The type declarations serve two purposes:

❑ The XSLT processor has extra information about the permitted values of the variables or parameters, and it can use this information to generate more efficient code.

❑ The processor will check (at compile time, and if necessary at runtime) that the values supplied for a variable or parameter match the declared types, and will report an error if not. This can detect many errors in your code, errors that might otherwise have led to the stylesheet producing incorrect output. As a general rule, the sooner an error is detected, the easier it is to find the cause and correct it, so defining types in this way leads to faster debugging. I have heard stories of users upgrading their stylesheets from XSLT 1.0 to XSLT 2.0 and finding that the extra type checking revealed errors that had been causing the stylesheet to produce incorrect output which no one had ever noticed.

These type declarations are written using the «as» attribute of elements such as <xsl:variable>, <xsl:param>, <xsl:function>, and <xsl:template>. You don't need to use a schema-aware processor to use the «as» attribute, because many of the types you can declare (including those in the two examples above) are built-in types, rather than types that need to be defined in your schema. For example, if a function parameter is required to be an integer, you can declare it like this:

```
<xsl:param name="in" as="xs:integer"/>
```

which will work whether or not your XSLT processor is schema-aware, and whether or not your source documents are validated using an XML Schema.

The rules for what you can write in the «as» attribute are defined in XPath 2.0, not in XSLT itself. The construct that appears here is called a *sequence type descriptor*, and it is explained in detail in Chapter 11. Here are some examples of sequence type descriptors that you can use with any XSLT processor, whether or not it is schema-aware:

Construct	Meaning
xs:integer	An atomic value labeled as an integer
xs:integer *	A sequence of zero or more integers
xs:string ?	Either a string, or an empty sequence
xs:date	A date
xs:anyAtomicType	An atomic value of any type (for example integer, string, and so on)
node()	Any node in a tree
node() *	Any sequence of zero or more nodes, of any kind
element()	Any element node
attribute() +	Any sequence of one or more attribute nodes
document-node()	Any document node

The types that are available in a basic XSLT processor are shown in Figure 4-1, which also shows where they appear in the type hierarchy:

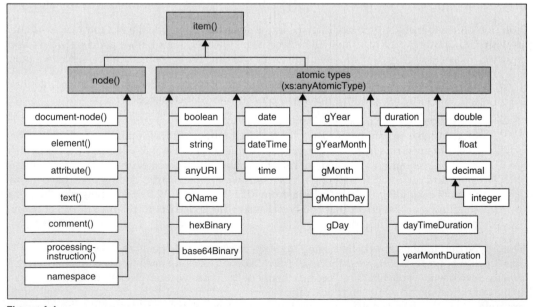

Figure 4-1

The shaded boxes show abstract types, and the clear boxes represent concrete types. The difference is that a value can never belong to an abstract type unless it also belongs to one of the concrete subtypes of that type.

The most general type here is «item()», which allows any kind of item. The two kinds of items are nodes, shown on the left-hand branch of the type hierarchy, and atomic values, shown on the right-hand branch.

In a sequence type descriptor, any of the item types listed in Figure 4-1 may be followed by one of the occurrence indicators «*», «+», or «?». The occurrence indicator defines how many items (of the given item type) may appear in the value. They have the following meanings:

Occurrence indicator	Meaning
*	Zero or more occurrences allowed
+	One or more occurrences allowed
?	Zero or one occurrence allowed

If there is no occurrence indicator, then the value must contain exactly one item of the specified type.

In a schema-aware processor, this type hierarchy is extended in the following two ways:

❑ Firstly, all the built-in atomic types defined in the XML Schema specification become available. These include the additional primitive type xs:NOTATION, and types derived from xs:string and xs:integer, such as xs:normalizedString and xs:nonNegativeInteger. A full list of these types, with explanations of their meanings, is given in Chapter 5.

❑ Secondly, user-defined types can be imported from an XML Schema definition.

To make user-defined types available for use in type declarations in a stylesheet, the schema must first be imported into the stylesheet. This can be done with an <xsl:import-schema> declaration, which might take the form:

```
<xsl:import-schema namespace="http://acme.org/ns"
                   schema-location="acme.xsd"/>
```

The <xsl:import-schema> declaration is described in more detail later in this chapter (see page 180). You can import any number of schema documents into a stylesheet, provided that the namespaces do not clash. If you want to refer to types defined in a schema by name, then you must import that schema into the stylesheet using an <xsl:import-schema> declaration. However, you don't need to import a schema simply because you are using it to validate source or result documents.

The types defined in a schema are either complex types or simple types, and simple types in turn divide into three varieties: union types, list types, and atomic types.

When atomic types are imported from a schema, they can be used in a stylesheet in just the same way as the built-in atomic types. For example, if the schema defines an atomic type mf:part-number as a subtype of xs:string constrained to conform to a particular pattern, then in the stylesheet you can declare a variable:

```
<xsl:variable name="part" as="mf:part-number" select="EXPRESSION"/>
```

which informs the system that the value of the $part variable will always be a part number. The expression in the select attribute must return a valid part number according to these rules, or the transformation will fail.

Note that to conform to this type, it's not enough to supply a string that matches the schema-defined pattern. The value must actually be labeled as an `mf:part-number`*. To achieve this, you typically have to convert the value to the required type using a constructor function. For example, you could write:*

```
<xsl:variable name="part" as="mf:part-number"
              select="mf:part-number('BFG94623')"/>
```

Atomic values can exist independently of any node in a document, which is why you can use an atomic type directly as the type of a value. In contrast, instances of complex types, union types, and list types can exist only as the content of a node in a document. This means that the names of these types can't be used directly in an «as» attribute defining the type of a variable or parameter. You can use them, however, to qualify a type that describes a node. Examples of such sequence type descriptors are shown in the table below:

Construct	Meaning
`element(*, mf:invoice)`	An element node validated against the complex type `mf:invoice` defined in an imported schema
`attribute(*, xs:NMTOKENS)`	An attribute validated against the built-in schema list type `xs:NMTOKENS`
`document-node(element(*, mf:invoice))`	A document node representing a well-formed XML document whose outermost element has been validated against the complex type `mf:invoice` defined in an imported schema

Often the structure of an element is defined in the schema not by creating an explicitly named `<xs:complexType>` definition, but rather by means of an `<xs:element>` declaration that contains an unnamed `<xs:complexType>`. Here's a typical example, taken from the schema for XSLT 2.0 stylesheets:

```
<xs:element name="apply-imports" substitutionGroup="xsl:instruction">
  <xs:complexType>
    <xs:complexContent>
      <xs:extension base="xsl:versioned-element-type">
        <xs:sequence>
          <xs:element ref="xsl:with-param" minOccurs="0" maxOccurs="unbounded"/>
        </xs:sequence>
      </xs:extension>
    </xs:complexContent>
  </xs:complexType>
</xs:element>
```

To allow for the fact that many of the types defined in a typical schema are anonymous, there is another form of the `element()` test that is used to refer to elements conforming to this named element declaration. If you write:

```
<xsl:param name="ai" as="schema-element(xsl:apply-imports)"/>
```

then you are saying that the value of the parameter must be an element that has been validated against the element declaration `xsl:apply-imports` in this schema. The name of the element passed as the parameter must either be `xsl:apply-imports`, or must match an element defined in the schema to be a member of the substitution group of `xsl:apply-imports`.

You can similarly refer to top-level attribute declarations in the schema using the syntax «schema-attribute(nnn)», though this form is not seen very often because it is unusual to find top-level attribute declarations in a schema.

Sequence type descriptors can also be used within XPath expressions. The expressions that use them are described in Chapter 11, which also defines the syntax and semantics in much greater detail than defined here. The operators that use sequence type descriptors are as follows:

❑ «instance of», which tests whether a given value is an instance of a given type. For example, «@dob instance of attribute(*, xs:date)» returns true if the attribute @dob is labeled with the type annotation xs:date (or a type derived from xs:date), which will be true only if the attribute contains a valid date and has been validated using a schema that declares the type of the attribute as xs:date.

❑ «treat as», which asserts that a given value is an instance of a given type, causing a runtime failure if it is not. This operator is useful mainly with XPath processors that do strict static type-checking, which is unlikely to apply in an XSLT environment unless the processor has a diagnostic mode to do this extra level of checking.

Validating the Source Document

Validation is the process of taking a raw XML document and processing it using an XML Schema. The most obvious output of this process is a success or failure rating: the document is either valid or invalid against the schema. But this is not the only output. Validation also annotates the document, marking each element and attribute node with a label indicating its type. For example, if validation checks that a <shippingAddress> element is valid according to the «us-postal-address» type in the schema, then this element will be annotated as having the type «us-postal-address». There are various ways the stylesheet can then use this information:

❑ Many operations on nodes extract the typed value of the nodes. This process is called *atomization*, and it is sensitive to the type annotations on the nodes. For example, when you compare two attributes using an expression such as «@discount gt $customer/@max-discount», the values that are compared are the typed values of @discount and @max-discount respectively. If the schema defines these values to be numbers (for example, using the type xs:decimal), then they will be compared numerically, so the value «10.00» will be considered greater than the value «2.50». If the same values were compared as strings, «10.00» would be less than «2.50». Adding type annotations to nodes, through the process of schema validation, enables operations on the values of the nodes to be performed more intelligently.

❑ There are many operations that only make sense when applied to a particular kind of data. At the top level, the stylesheet as a whole might be designed to process purchase orders, and will produce garbage if you make the mistake of feeding it with input that's actually a delivery note. At a more fine-grained level, you might have a stylesheet function or template rule that's designed to process US postal addresses, and that won't work properly if you give it a phone number instead. XSLT 2.0 allows you to define the type of data that you expect your functions and template rules to process, and to define the type of result that they produce as their output. A schema-aware processor will then automatically check that when the function or template is actually called, the data is of the right type, and if it isn't, the error will be reported.

At times these errors can become frustrating. But remember, every time you get one of these error messages, it tells you about a programming mistake that might otherwise have been much harder to track down. With XSLT 1.0, most programming mistakes don't give you an error message, they simply give you wrong output (or no output at all), and it can be a tortuous process debugging the stylesheet to find out where you went wrong. With XSLT 2.0, if you choose to define data types for your stylesheet functions and templates, you can get error messages that make it much clearer where the mistake lies.

You don't request validation of the input document from within the stylesheet. It's assumed that you will request this as part of the way you invoke the transformation, and details of how you do this will vary from one XSLT processor to another. (With Saxon you can use the -val:strict option on the command line; with Altova you need an xsi:schemaLocation attribute in the source document.) Within your stylesheet, what you can do is to test whether the input has actually been validated. I often write two template rules in the stylesheet as follows:

```
<xsl:template match="/">
  <xsl:message terminate="yes">
     Source document is not a validated purchase order
  </xsl:message>
</xsl:template>

<xsl:template match="document-node(schema-element(purchase-order))">
  <xsl:apply-templates/>
</xsl:template>
```

The effect of writing the template rules this way is that if the stylesheet is presented with a document that is not a validated purchase order, it will immediately fail and display an error message, rather than trying to process it and producing garbage output.

Note the carefully chosen phrase *a validated purchase order*. It's not enough to supply an XML document that would be deemed valid if you tried to validate it. To pass this test, the document must already have been through a schema processor, and must have passed validation.

If you prefer, you could code the stylesheet to invoke the validation explicitly, by writing the following:

```
<xsl:template match="/">
  <xsl:variable name="input">
    <xsl:copy-of select="*" type="purchase-order-type"/>
  </xsl:variable>
  <xsl:apply-templates select="$input"/>
</xsl:template>
```

This defines a variable to hold a copy of the input document. The «type» attribute on the <xsl:copy-of> instruction asks the XSLT processor to invoke schema validation on the document, and if this succeeds, the element and attribute nodes in the new copy will have type annotations reflecting the result of this process. There is no explicit logic here to test whether validation has succeeded. It isn't needed, because a validation failure will always cause the transformation to be aborted with an error message.

However, I wouldn't normally recommend this approach. Creating a copy of the input document is likely to be expensive. It's better to do the validation on the fly while the input document is being parsed in the first place.

The value of the «type» attribute in this example, like the type named in the «instance of» expression in the previous example, is a type that's defined in a schema. Like any other type that's referred to by name in a stylesheet, it must be defined in a schema that has been imported using the <xsl:import-schema> declaration.

Here's an example of a complete stylesheet written to process a validated source document.

Example: Validating the Source Document

This example shows how a stylesheet can make use of the schema for the source document.

Source

The source document is a poem such as `theHill.xml`, which starts:

```
<poem xmlns="http://poetry.org/ns"
      xsi:schemaLocation="http://poetry.org/ns poem.xsd"
      xmlns:xsi="http://www.w3.org/2001/XMLSchema-instance">
   <author>
      <name>Rupert Brooke</name>
      <birth>1887-08-03</birth>
      <death>1915-04-23</death>
   </author>
   <date>1912</date>
   <title>The Hill</title>
   <stanza>
      <line>Breathless, we flung us on the windy hill,</line>
      <line>Laughed in the sun, and kissed the lovely grass.</line>
      <line>You said "Through glory and ecstasy we pass;</line>
      <line>Wind, sun, and earth remain, and birds sing still,</line>
      <line>When we are old, are old...." "And when we die</line>
      <line>All's over that is ours; and life burns on</line>
      <line>Through other lovers, other lips" said I,</line>
      <line>"Heart of my heart, our heaven is now, is won!"</line>
   </stanza>
```

The `xsi:schemaLocation` *attribute tells the processor where to find a schema for this document. This isn't needed with Saxon, which will validate the document against the schema imported into the stylesheet, provided that validation is requested on the command line. With AltovaXML, the* `xsi:schemaLocation` *attribute acts as an implicit request for document validation, and is therefore necessary for this example to work.*

The `xsi` *namespace is defined in the XML Schema specification and contains four attributes:* `xsi:schemaLocation`, `xsi:noNamespaceSchemaLocation`, `xsi:type`, *and* `xsi:nil`. *The prefix* `xsi` *is conventional, but the namespace URI must be* `http://www.w3.org/2001/XMLSchema-instance`.

Schema

The schema for poems is in `poem.xsd`:

```
<?xml version="1.0" encoding="UTF-8"?>
<xs:schema xmlns:xs="http://www.w3.org/2001/XMLSchema"
elementFormDefault="qualified" targetNamespace="http://poetry.org/ns"
xmlns:p="http://poetry.org/ns">
   <xs:element name="poem">
      <xs:complexType>
         <xs:sequence>
```

```
            <xs:element ref="p:author"/>
            <xs:element ref="p:date"/>
            <xs:element ref="p:title"/>
            <xs:element maxOccurs="unbounded" ref="p:stanza"/>
        </xs:sequence>
      </xs:complexType>
    </xs:element>
    <xs:element name="author">
      <xs:complexType>
        <xs:sequence>
            <xs:element ref="p:name"/>
            <xs:element ref="p:birth"/>
            <xs:element ref="p:death"/>
        </xs:sequence>
      </xs:complexType>
    </xs:element>
    <xs:element name="name" type="xs:string"/>
    <xs:element name="birth" type="p:date"/>
    <xs:element name="death" type="p:date"/>
    <xs:element name="date" type="p:date"/>
    <xs:element name="title" type="xs:string"/>
    <xs:element name="stanza">
      <xs:complexType>
        <xs:sequence>
            <xs:element maxOccurs="unbounded" ref="p:line"/>
        </xs:sequence>
      </xs:complexType>
    </xs:element>
    <xs:element name="line" type="xs:string"/>
    <xs:simpleType name="date">
      <xs:union memberTypes="xs:date xs:gYear xs:gYearMonth"/>
    </xs:simpleType>
</xs:schema>
```

Stylesheet

The following stylesheet is in `poem-to-html.xsl`. It relies on the source document being validated.

```
<?xml version="1.0" encoding="iso-8859-1"?>
<xsl:stylesheet version="2.0"
      xmlns:xsl="http://www.w3.org/1999/XSL/Transform"
      xmlns:xs="http://www.w3.org/2001/XMLSchema"
      xpath-default-namespace="http://poetry.org/ns"
      exclude-result-prefixes="xs">

<xsl:import-schema namespace="http://poetry.org/ns"
                   schema-location="poem.xsd"/>
<xsl:output method="html" indent="yes"/>

<xsl:template match="/">
  <xsl:message terminate="yes">Input must be a validated poem</xsl:message>
</xsl:template>
```

```xsl
<xsl:template match="document-node(schema-element(poem))">
    <html>
      <head>
        <title><xsl:value-of select="poem/title"/></title>
      </head>
      <body>
        <h1><xsl:value-of select="poem/title"/></h1>
        <p><i>by </i><xsl:value-of select="poem/author/name"/>
          (<xsl:apply-templates select="poem/author/birth"/>
          - <xsl:apply-templates select="poem/author/death"/>)</p>
        <p><xsl:apply-templates select="poem/date"/></p>
        <xsl:for-each select="poem/stanza">
          <p>
            <xsl:for-each select="line">
              <xsl:value-of select="."/>
              <xsl:if test="position() != last()"><br/></xsl:if>
            </xsl:for-each>
          </p>
        </xsl:for-each>
      </body>
    </html>
</xsl:template>
<xsl:template match="element(*, gendate)">
  <xsl:variable name="date-value" select="data(.)"/>
  <xsl:choose>
    <xsl:when test="$date-value instance of xs:date">
      <xsl:value-of select="format-date($date-value, '[D] [MNn] [Y]')"/>
    </xsl:when>
    <xsl:otherwise>
      <xsl:value-of select="$date-value"/>
    </xsl:otherwise>
  </xsl:choose>
</xsl:template>
</xsl:stylesheet>
```

Notice how the template rules in this example are matching nodes by their type. The first rule catches unvalidated documents to report an error. The second rule matches the document node of a poem, while the third matches any element that is typed as a gendate — a user-defined type that can be an xs:date, an xs:gYearMonth, or an xs:gYear. There are three elements in the schema that use this type, but we don't need to name them in the stylesheet; the rule can be used to format any element of this type, regardless of its name.

Output

This example can be run using Saxon-SA, by using the command (on one line):

```
java net.sf.saxon.Transform -val:strict -s:theHill.xml ↵
-xsl:poem-to-html.xsl -o:theHill.html
```

It can also be run using the AltovaXML 2008 processor, with the command:

```
AltovaXML -in theHill.xml -xslt2 poem-to-html.xsl
```

Figure 4-2 shows what the output looks like in the browser.

Figure 4-2

Try some experiments with this, so that you can see what effect schema-aware processing has when you make errors. For example, change the path expression on line 23 from «poem/author/name» to «poem/poet/name». Saxon-SA gives you the warning:

```
Warning: on line 23 of .../code/ch04/poem-to-html.xsl:
   The complex type of element poem does not allow a child element named poet
```

When you're dealing with a complex schema it's very easy to make this kind of mistake in your path expressions, and allowing the XSLT processor to check your code against the schema can make a big difference to the ease of diagnosing such errors. Note that it's only a warning, not an error: the expression is actually legal, but Saxon-SA is warning you that it selects nothing. AltovaXML, at the time of writing, doesn't do this level of checking.

Validating the Result Document

We've seen what you can achieve by using knowledge of the schema for the source document. You can also request validation of the output of the transformation. For example, if you have written the stylesheet to generate XHTML, you can ask for it to be validated by writing your first template rule as follows:

```
<xsl:template match="/">
  <xsl:result-document validate="strict">
    <xsl:apply-templates/>
  </xsl:result-document>
</xsl:template>
```

In this example, there is nothing that says what the expected type of the output is. What «validate = "strict"» means is that the outermost element of the result document (for example, <xhtml:html>) must correspond to an element declaration that's present in some schema known to the system, and the system is then required to check that the contents of the element conform to the rules defined in that element declaration.

You could argue that validating the output from within the stylesheet is no different from running the transformation and then putting the output through a schema processor to check that it's valid. However, once you try developing a stylesheet this way, you will find that the experience is very different. If you put the output file through a freestanding schema processor once the transformation is complete, the schema processor will give you error messages in terms of a position within the result document. You will then have to open the result document in a text editor, find out what's wrong with it, find the instruction in the stylesheet that generated the incorrect output, and then correct the stylesheet. Working with a schema processor that's integrated into your XSLT processor is much more direct: In most cases the error message will tell you directly which instruction in the stylesheet needs to be changed. This makes for a much more rapid development cycle.

There is another advantage — in many cases it should be possible for a schema-aware XSLT processor to tell you that the output will be invalid before you even try running the stylesheet against a source document. That is, it should be able to report some of your errors at compile time. This gives you an even quicker turnaround in fixing errors, and more importantly, it means that the ability to detect bugs in your code is less dependent on the completeness of your test suite. Stylesheet programming is often done without much regard to the traditional disciplines of software engineering — testing tends to be less than thorough. So anything that reduces the risk of failures once the stylesheet is in live use is to be welcomed.

The following example shows how this works.

Example: Validating the Result Document

This example shows how validation of a result document can be invoked from within the stylesheet.

Source

The source document is a poem such as theHill.xml, which is listed (in part) on page 167.

Stylesheet

The following stylesheet poem-to-xhtml.xsl is designed to format this poem into XHTML, checking as it does so that the output is valid XHTML. It contains a deliberate error: see if you can spot it.

```
<xsl:stylesheet version="2.0"
       xmlns:xsl="http://www.w3.org/1999/XSL/Transform"
       xpath-default-namespace="http://poetry.org/ns"
       xmlns="http://www.w3.org/1999/xhtml">

<xsl:import-schema namespace="http://www.w3.org/1999/xhtml"
       schema-location="http://www.w3.org/2002/08/xhtml/xhtml1-strict.xsd"/>
```

```
<xsl:output method="xhtml" indent="yes"/>
<xsl:template match="/">
  <xsl:result-document validation="strict">
    <html>
      <head>
        <title><xsl:value-of select="poem/title"/></title>
      </head>
      <body>
        <h1 align="center"><xsl:value-of select="poem/title"/></h1>
        <p align="center"><i>by </i><xsl:value-of select="poem/author/
name"/>
          (<xsl:value-of select="poem/author/(birth,death)"
                         separator="-"/>)</p>
        <xsl:for-each select="poem/stanza">
          <p>
            <xsl:for-each select="line">
              <xsl:value-of select="."/>
              <xsl:if test="position() != last()"><br/></xsl:if>
            </xsl:for-each>
          </p>
        </xsl:for-each>
      </body>
    </html>
  </xsl:result-document>
</xsl:template>
</xsl:stylesheet>
```

Note that this stylesheet validates the output, but doesn't require validating the input. The only reason for this is to demonstrate one feature at a time, and to show that input validation and output validation are quite independent of each other.

This stylesheet fetches the XHTML schema from the W3C web site. That's not a practical thing to do for something that you run frequently. If you run behind a proxy server then it will probably be cached automatically, but in other cases you may prefer to make a local copy.

Output

When this stylesheet is run using Saxon-SA 9.0, the output is:

```
Error on line 17 of .../code/ch04/poem-to-xhtml.xsl:
  XTTE1510: Attribute align is not permitted in the content model of
the complex type of element h1. Failed to compile stylesheet. 1 error
detected.
```

The error message should be clear enough: the align attribute is not permitted in strict XHTML. You could fix it by using the schema for transitional XHTML rather than strict XHTML, or better, by replacing the align attribute with «style = "text-align: center"».

Previous releases of Saxon reported this error as a runtime validation error, while still pinpointing the line in the stylesheet where the problem occurred. The XSLT specification isn't prescriptive about this: it allows implementations to do the validation either at compile-time or at runtime.

AltovaXML reports the error at runtime, like this:

```
Validation Error
Attribute 'align' is not allowed in element <h1>
...\code\ch04\poem-to-xhtml2.xsl Line 11, Character 4
```

Like Saxon-SA, it gives a clear message about what is wrong, though it's not quite so precise in identifying the location in the stylesheet of the offending instruction (line 11 is the `<xsl:result-document>` instruction).

Validation of a result document can be controlled using either the `validation` attribute or the `type` attribute of the `<xsl:result-document>` element. You can use only one of these: they can't be mixed. The `validation` attribute allows four values, whose meanings are explained in the table below.

Attribute value	Meaning
strict	The result document is subjected to strict validation. This means that there must be an element declaration for the outermost element of the result document in some schema, and the structure of the result document must conform to that element declaration.
lax	The result document is subjected to lax validation. This means that the outermost element is validated against a schema if a declaration for that element name can be located; if not, the system assumes the existence of an element declaration that allows any content for that element. The children of the element are also subjected to lax validation, and so on recursively. So any elements in the tree that are declared in a schema must conform to their declaration, but for other elements, there are no constraints.
preserve	This option means that no validation is applied at the document level, but if any elements or attributes within the result tree have been constructed using node-level validation (as described in the next section), then the type annotations resulting from that node-level validation will be preserved in the result tree. These node annotations are only relevant, of course, if the result tree is passed to another process that understands them. If the result tree is simply serialized, it makes no difference whether type annotations are preserved or not.
strip	This option means that no validation is applied at the document level, and moreover, if any elements or attributes within the result tree have been constructed using node-level validation (as described in the next section), then the type annotations resulting from that node-level validation will be removed from the result tree. Instead, all elements will be given a type annotation of `xs:untyped`, and attributes will have the type annotation `xs:untypedAtomic`.

The other way of requesting validation of the result tree is through the `type` attribute. If the `type` attribute is specified, its value must be a QName, which must match the name of a global type definition in an imported schema. In practice this will almost invariably be a complex type definition. The rules to pass validation are as follows:

1. The result tree must be a well-formed document: That is, it must contain exactly one element node, and no text nodes, among the children of the document node. (In the absence of validation, this rule can be relaxed. For example, it is possible to have a temporary tree in which the document node has three element nodes as its children.)

2. The document element (that is, the single element node child of the document node) must validate against the schema definition of the specified type, according to the rules defined in XML Schema.

3. The document must satisfy document-level integrity constraints defined in the schema. This means:

   ❑ Elements and attributes of type `xs:ID` must have unique values within the document.

   ❑ Elements and attributes of type `xs:IDREF` or `xs:IDREFS` must contain valid references to `xs:ID` values within the document.

   ❑ Any constraints defined by `<xs:unique>`, `<xs:key>`, and `<xs:keyref>` declarations in the schema must be satisfied.

Document-level validation rules must also be satisfied when validation is requested using the option «validation = "strict"» or «validation = "lax"».

The language of the XSLT specification that describes these rules is somewhat tortuous. This is because XSLT tries to define what validation means in terms of the rules in the XML Schema specification, which means that there is a need to establish a precise correspondence between the terminologies of the two specifications. This is made more difficult by the fact that XML Schema is not defined in terms of the XSLT/XPath data model, but rather in terms of the XML Infoset and the Post Schema Validation Infoset (PSVI), which is defined in the XML Schema specification itself. To make this work, the XSLT specification says that when a document is validated, it is first serialized, and then re-parsed to create an Infoset. The Infoset is then validated, as defined in XML Schema, to create a PSVI. Finally, this PSVI is converted to a document in the XPath data model using rules defined in the XDM specification. However, you should regard this description of the process as a purely formal device to ensure that no ambiguities are introduced between the different specifications. In practice, an XSLT processor is likely to have a fairly intimate interface with a schema processor, and both are likely to share the same internal data structures.

If you request validation by specifying «validation = "strict"» or «validation = "lax"», this raises the question of where the XSLT processor should look to find a schema that contains a suitable element declaration. The specification leaves this slightly open. The first place a processor will look is among the schemas that were imported into the stylesheet using `<xsl:import-schema>` declarations: see *Importing Schemas* on page 180. The processor is also allowed (but not required) to use any `xsi:schemaLocation` or `xsi:noNamespaceSchemaLocation` attributes that are present in the result document itself as hints indicating where to locate a suitable schema. My advice, however, would be to make sure that the required schemas are explicitly imported.

Validating a Temporary Document

In the previous two sections, we have seen how you can validate a source document that is to be processed by the stylesheet, and how you can validate result documents produced as output by the stylesheet. It's also possible to apply validation to temporary documents created and used internally during the course of stylesheet processing.

The most common way to create a temporary document is by using <xsl:variable> with no «as» attribute, for example:

```
<xsl:variable name="temp">
  <xsl:apply-templates select="." mode="phase-1"/>
</xsl:variable>
```

The value of this variable will be the document node at the root of a newly constructed temporary tree. The body of the tree in this case is produced by the <xsl:apply-templates> instruction.

The example above can be regarded as shorthand for the more detailed construction:

```
<xsl:variable name="temp" as="document-node()">
  <xsl:document>
    <xsl:apply-templates select="." mode="phase-1"/>
  </xsl:document>
</xsl:variable>
```

This shows more explicitly how the sequence constructor contained in the <xsl:variable> element creates a single document node, whose content is populated by the <xsl:apply-templates> instruction.

If you expand the variable definition in this way, you can also use the attributes validation and type on the <xsl:document> instruction to invoke validation of the temporary document. These attributes work exactly the same way on <xsl:document> as they do on <xsl:result-document>, which produces a final result tree.

Another way of creating temporary documents is by copying an existing document node using either of the instructions <xsl:copy> (which makes a shallow copy) or <xsl:copy-of> (which makes a deep copy). These instructions both have validation and type attributes, and when the instructions are used to copy a document node, these attributes work the same way as the corresponding attributes on the <xsl:document> and <xsl:result-document> instructions.

Because a temporary document exists only locally within your stylesheet, it sometimes makes sense to validate it using a schema that is also local to the stylesheet. To this end, XSLT allows you to write a schema document inline as the content of the <xsl:import-schema> element. For example, if the temporary document has the form:

```
<months xmlns="http://www.acme.com/ns/local/months">
  <month name="January" abbr="Jan"/>
  <month name="February" abbr="Feb"/>
  ...
</months>
```

then the <xsl:import-schema> declaration might be:

```
<xsl:import-schema>
  <xs:schema targetNamespace="http://www.acme.com/ns/local/months"
             xmlns:m="http://www.acme.com/ns/local/months">
  <xs:element name="months">
    <xs:complexType>
```

```
      <xs:sequence>
        <xs:element ref="m:month" minOccurs="12" maxOccurs="12"/>
      </xs:sequence>
    </xs:complexType>
  </xs:element>
  <xs:element name="month">
    <xs:complexType>
      <xs:attribute name="name" type="xs:string"/>
      <xs:attribute name="abbr" type="xs:string"/>
    </xs:complexType>
  </xs:element>
  </xs:schema>
</xsl:import-schema>
```

For the complete stylesheet, see `inline.xsl` in the download files for this chapter. If you use inline schema documents, it's good practice to use a unique namespace, to ensure that the schema definitions don't conflict with any other schema definitions that might be loaded.

Validating Individual Elements

Rather than applying validation at the document level, it is possible to invoke validation of specific elements as they are constructed. This can be useful in a number of circumstances:

❑ Sometimes you do not have a schema definition for the result document as a whole, but you do have schema definitions for individual elements within it. For example, you may be creating a data file in which the contents of some elements are expected to be valid XHTML.

❑ If you are running a transformation whose purpose is to extract parts of the source document, then you may actually know that the result document as a whole is deliberately invalid — the schema for source documents may require the presence of elements or attributes, which you want to exclude from the result document, perhaps for privacy or security reasons. The fact that the result document as a whole has no schema should not stop you from validating those parts that do have one.

❑ You may be creating elements in temporary working storage (that is, in variables) that are to be copied or processed before incorporating them into a final result document. It can be useful to validate these elements in their own right, to make sure that they have the type annotations that enable them to be used as input to functions and templates that will only work on elements of a particular type.

❑ You may have templates or functions that declare their return types using sequence type descriptors such as `element(*, us-postal-address)`. The only way to generate new content that satisfies such a return type is to put it through schema validation.

The usual way of creating a new element node in XSLT is either by using a literal result element or by using the `<xsl:element>` instruction.

The `<xsl:element>` instruction has attributes `validation` and `type`, which work in a very similar way to the corresponding attributes of `<xsl:result-document>` and `<xsl:document>`; however, in this case it is only element-level validation that is invoked, not document-level validation.

The same facilities are available with literal result elements. In this case, however, the attributes are named `xsl:validation` and `xsl:type`. This is to avoid any possible conflict with attributes that you want copied to the result document as attributes of the element you are creating.

For example, suppose you want to validate an address. If there is a global element declaration with the name `address`, you might write:

```
<address xsl:validation="strict">
  <number>39</number>
  <street>Lombard Street</street>
  <city>London</city>
  <postcode>EC1 3CX</postcode>
</address>
```

If this matches the schema definition of the element declaration for `address`, this will succeed, and the resulting element will be annotated as an address — or more strictly, as an instance of the type associated with the address element, which might be either a named type in the schema, or an anonymous type. In addition, the child elements will also have type annotations based on the way they are defined in the schema, for example the `<number>` element might (perhaps) be annotated as type `xs:integer`. If validation fails, the whole transformation is aborted.

What if there is no global element declaration for the `<address>` element (typically because it is defined in the schema as a local element declaration within some larger element)? You can still request validation if the element is defined in the schema to have a named type. For example, if the element is declared as:

```
<xs:element name="address" type="address-type"/>
```

then you can cause it to be validated by writing:

```
<address xsl:type="address-type">
  <number>39</number>
  <street>Lombard Street</street>
  <city>London</city>
  <postcode>EC1 3CX</postcode>
</address>
```

If neither a top-level element declaration nor a top-level type definition is available, you can't invoke validation at this level. The only thing you can do is either:

❑ change the schema so that some of the elements and/or types are promoted to be globally defined, or

❑ invoke validation at a higher level, where a global element declaration or type definition is available.

You don't need to invoke validation at more than one level, and it may be inefficient to do so. Asking for validation of `<address>` in the above example will automatically invoke validation of its child elements. If you also invoked validation of the child elements by writing, say:

```
<address xsl:type="address-type">
  <number xsl:type="xs:integer">39</number>
  ...
```

then it's possible that the system would do the validation twice over. If you're lucky the optimizer will spot that this is unnecessary, but you could be incurring extra costs for no good reason.

If you ask for validation of a child element, but don't validate its parent element, then the child element will be checked for correctness, but the type annotation will probably not survive the process of tree construction. For example, suppose you write the following:

177

```
<address>
  <number xsl:type="xs:integer">39</number>
  <street>Lombard Street</street>
  <city>London</city>
  <postcode>EC1 3CX</postcode>
</address>
```

Specifying the `xsl:type` attribute on the `<number>` element causes the system to check that the value of the element is numeric, and to construct an element that is annotated as an integer. The result of evaluating the sequence constructor contained in the `<address>` element is thus a sequence of four elements, of which the first has a type annotation of `xs:integer`. Evaluating the literal result element `<address>` creates a new `<address>` element, and forms children of this element from the result of evaluating the contained sequence constructor: The formal model is that the elements in this sequence are copied to form these children. The `xsl:validation` attribute on the `<address>` element determines what happens to the type annotations on these child elements. This defaults to either `preserve` or `strip`, depending on the `default-validation` attribute of the containing `<xsl:stylesheet>` (which in turn defaults to `strip`). If the value is `preserve`, the type annotation on the child element is preserved, and if the value is `strip`, then the type annotation on the child element is replaced by `xs:untyped`.

The type of an element never depends on the types of the items used to form its children. For example, suppose that the variable `$i` holds an integer value. Then you might suppose that the construct:

```
<xsl:element name="x">
  <xsl:sequence select="$i"/>
</xsl:element>
```

would create an element whose type annotation is `xs:integer`. It doesn't — the type annotation will be `xs:untyped`. Atomic values in the sequence produced by evaluating the sequence constructor are always (at least conceptually) converted to strings, and any type annotation in the new element is obtained by validating the resulting string values against the desired type.

> *This might not seem a very satisfactory design — why discard the type information? The working groups agonized over this question for months. The problem is that there are some cases like this one where retaining the type annotation obviously makes sense; there are many other cases, such as a sequence involving mixed content, where it obviously doesn't make sense; and there are further cases such as a sequence containing a mixture of integers and dates where it could make sense, but the definition would be very difficult. Because the working group found it difficult to devise a clear rule that separated the simple cases from the difficult or impossible ones, they eventually decided on this rather blunt rule: everything is reduced to a string before constructing the new node and validating it.*

Note that when you use the `xsl:type` attribute to validate an element, the actual element name can be anything you like. There is no requirement that it should be an element name declared in the schema. It can even be an element name that is declared in the schema, but with a different type (though I can't see any justification for doing something quite so confusing, unless the types are closely related).

All the same considerations apply when creating a new element using the `<xsl:element>` or `<xsl:copy>` instruction rather than a literal result element. The only difference is that the attributes are now called `validation` and `type` instead of `xsl:validation` and `xsl:type`.

The value of the `type` or `xsl:type` attribute is always a lexical QName, and this must always be the name of a top-level complex type or simple type defined in an imported schema. This isn't the same as the «as» attribute used in declaring the type of variables or functions. Note the following differences:

❑ If the «as» attribute is a QName, the QName must identify an atomic type. The «type» attribute is always a QName, and this may be any type defined in an imported schema: complex types are allowed as well as all three varieties of simple type; that is list types, union types, and atomic types.

❑ The «as» attribute can include an occurrence indicator («?», «*», or «+»). The «type» attribute never includes an occurrence indicator.

❑ The «as» attribute may define node kinds, for example «node()», «element()», or «comment()». Such constructs are never used in the «type» attribute.

This means that to create an element holding a sequence of IDREF values, you write:

```
<xsl:element name="ref" type="xs:IDREFS"
    select="'id001 id002 id003'"/>
```

whereas to declare a variable holding the same sequence, you write:

```
<xsl:variable name="ref" as="xs:IDREF*"
    select="xs:IDREF('id001'), xs:IDREF('id002'), xs:IDREF('id003')"/>
```

In the case of <xsl:copy>, note that the option «validation = "preserve"» applies to the children (and attributes) of the copied element, but not to the copied element itself. This instruction does a shallow copy, so in general the content of the new element will be completely different from the content of the old one. It doesn't make sense to keep the type annotation intact if the content is changing, because this could result in the type annotation becoming inconsistent with the actual content.

By contrast, the <xsl:copy-of> instruction does a deep copy. Because the content remains unchanged, it's safe to keep the type annotation unchanged, and the option «validation = "preserve"» is useful in achieving this.

When you request validation at the element level, the system does not perform any document-level integrity checks. That is, it does not check that ID values are unique, or that IDREF values don't point into thin air. To invoke this level of validation, you have to do it at the document level. The specification as published also says that it does not check identity constraints defined by <xs:unique>, <xs:key>, and <xs:keyref> definitions in the schema, but this was a mistake and has been fixed in an erratum.

Validating Individual Attributes

XSLT 2.0 also allows you to request validation at the level of individual attributes. The <xsl:attribute> instruction, like <xsl:element>, has attributes validation and type, which can be used to validate an attribute node independently of its containing element.

It's relatively unusual for a schema to contain global attribute declarations, so the options «validation = "strict"» and «validation = "lax"» are unlikely to be very useful at the attribute level. Also, because attributes don't have children, the options «validation = "strip"» and «validation = "preserve"» both mean the same thing: the new attribute node will be annotated as «xs:untypedAtomic». The most useful option for attributes is to specify «type» to validate the attribute value against a specific type definition in the schema. This will always be the name of a simple type, and in many cases it will be the name of a built-in atomic type, for example «type = "xs:date"» or «type = "xs:ID"». But it can also be a list or union type, for example «type = "xs:IDREFS"».

If «xsl:copy» or «xsl:copy-of» is used to create attribute nodes by copying nodes from a source document, attribute-level validation can be invoked using the validation and type attributes in the same way. Unlike the situation with elements, «preserve = "yes"» on either of these instructions means what it says: the attribute is copied together with its type annotation.

There are special rules in the language specification concerning the validation of attributes whose type is xs:QName or xs:NOTATION. Since these types require a namespace context to perform the validation, you can't validate standalone attributes that have these types. They can only be validated as part of an element that has the appropriate namespaces in scope.

The default-validation Attribute

The default-validation attribute on the <xsl:stylesheet> element can take one of the two values «preserve» or «strip», and it defines the default that is used on any of the instructions <xsl: attribute>, <xsl:copy>, <xsl:copy-of>, <xsl:document>, <xsl:element>, and <xsl:result-document> when neither a type nor a validation attribute is specified explicitly.

You can't set the default to «strict» or «lax». Allowing the value «strict» would give you problems unless every element and attribute that you create were declared globally in a schema, which would be unusual. Allowing «lax» would be more likely to give acceptable results, but could lead to performance problems through excessive validation.

The default value for the default-validation attribute is «strip». Personally, I would stick with this default. Changing it to «preserve» may lead to rather patchy results in terms of which elements and attributes carry a type annotation, and which are left as untyped. Preserving type annotations makes most sense when you are explicitly copying data from one document to another, and it's probably best to request it explicitly on the instructions that do the copying.

But there may well be situations I haven't thought of, and if you find yourself using the same value of the validation attribute throughout the stylesheet, then defining a default at the stylesheet module level may turn out to be a useful thing to do.

Importing Schemas

The facilities that we've been discussing in this chapter work only if schema information is available to the XSLT processor. The primary way that the processor gets this information is through the <xsl:import-schema> declaration, which can be used at the top level of any stylesheet module.

The <xsl:import-schema> declaration is modeled on the <xs:import> element within the XML Schema specification, but with some concessions to the XSLT house style (for example, the schemaLocation attribute in <xs:import> becomes schema-location in XSLT). Importantly, it adopts the same deliberate vagueness about exactly where the schema comes from, giving implementations the freedom to implement local schema caches or catalogs.

The most important attribute is the namespace attribute. This gives the target namespace of the schema being imported. If the attribute is omitted, this represents a request for a schema with no target namespace. You should import a schema for each namespace that contains a type definition, element declaration, or attribute declaration that your stylesheet refers to by name. Importing a schema that in turn imports another schema isn't good enough: The only names that become available for use in your stylesheet are those in namespaces that you import explicitly. The XSLT processor is given some leeway to implicitly import schemas that aren't requested explicitly in the stylesheet. This is intended particularly for use in highly controlled environments, such as running a transformation within an XML database engine where the available schemas are all known in advance. But it's unwise to rely on this if you want your stylesheet to be portable.

The `schema-location` attribute of `<xsl:import-schema>` defines a URI where the schema document can be located. This is described in the specification as a hint, which means that if the XSLT processor knows a better place to look, it is free to do so. For example, it might already have a precompiled copy of the schema held in memory. If you don't supply a `schema-location` attribute, then the schema import will work only if the XSLT processor already knows where to look. It's possible, for example, that some XSLT processors might have built-in knowledge of common schemas such as the XHTML schema, so they never need to fetch the XML source. However, if you want your stylesheet to be portable, it's probably a good idea to specify the schema location.

You don't need to import schemas into every stylesheet module individually. Importing a schema into one stylesheet module makes its definitions available in all stylesheet modules. (This is a notable difference from the equivalent facility in XQuery.)

What happens if you have two `<xsl:import-schema>` declarations for the same namespace URI (or, more probably, for the null namespace)? This can easily happen when different stylesheet modules are combined into a single stylesheet. Firstly, the system chooses the one with the highest import precedence, as explained in Chapter 3. If this leaves more than one, then they are all used. The XSLT specification explains how conflicts are resolved by reference to the XML Schema specification: it's defined to be the same as if you have two `<xs:import>` declarations for the same namespace in a schema document. This is rather passing the buck, as it happens, because XML Schema leaves a lot of latitude to implementations in deciding how far they will go in analyzing two different schemas for conflicts. It's best not to do it. Because the processor is perfectly entitled to ignore the `schema-location` hint, it is also entitled to assume that if it already has a schema for a given namespace loaded, then this is the one that the user wanted.

As with validation, the XSLT specification describes the semantics of schema import by means of a rather artificial device: it describes an imaginary schema document that is assembled to contain `<xs:import>` declarations representing each of the `<xsl:import-schema>` declarations in the stylesheet. The reason for this artifice is that it provides a way of invoking the rules of XML Schema and saying that they apply equally to XSLT, without actually copying the rules and repeating them, which would inevitably lead to inconsistencies. No real implementation is likely to integrate the XSLT processor and the schema processor in the clumsy manner described in the spec.

You don't need to import a schema merely because it is used to validate source documents. However, I would recommend doing so. If you don't, this creates the possibility that a source document will contain type annotations that mean nothing to the XSLT processor. There are various ways an XSLT processor can deal with this problem (no less than four possible approaches are described in the specification, one of which is to raise an error), but the simplest approach is to avoid the problem by ensuring that all the schemas used in your transformation are explicitly imported.

> *With AltovaXML 2008, source documents are validated only if they contain an* `xsi:schemaLocation` *attrbibute that identifies the schema to be used.*

Using xsi:type

I haven't yet mentioned the use of `xsi:type` in this chapter (I did mention `xsl:type`, but that's a completely different thing, despite the similar name). In fact, the XSLT 2.0 specification mentions `xsi:type` only in notes and examples, which means that it plays no formal role in the XSLT language.

The `xsi:type` attribute is defined in the XML Schema specification — the prefix `xsi` is conventional, but the namespace URI must be `http://www.w3.org/2001/XMLSchema-instance`.

You can use `xsi:type` as an attribute on an element within a document that's being assessed by a schema processor. Its effect is to ask the schema processor to apply a stricter check to the element than it would otherwise. An `xsi:type` can't override the constraints defined in the schema, but it can make assertions about the document content that go beyond what the schema requires. For example, if the schema allows a particular element (by means of a union type) to contain either an integer or a QName, then specifying «`xsi:type = "xs:QName"`» will cause it to be validated as if only a QName were allowed. This can also result in the element node acquiring a more specific type annotation than would otherwise be the case.

The effect of `xsi:type` on schema validation applies just as much when the validation is happening under the control of XSLT as it does in freestanding schema processing. If you write an `xsi:type` attribute to the result tree (which you can do in exactly the same way as you write any other attribute), then the element will be validated against that type definition.

Although I started by saying that `xsi:type` and `xsl:type` were quite different things, this description shows that there are cases where their effects are very similar. For example, writing:

```
<cost xsi:type="xs:decimal">23.44</cost>
```

and:

```
<cost xsl:type="xs:decimal">23.44</cost>
```

can both produce a `<cost>` element validated and annotated as being of type `xs:decimal`. However, there are some important differences:

❑ `xsl:type` (or `type`) invokes validation as well as specifying the expected type of the element. `xsi:type` specifies the expected type, but it is ignored unless validation is requested by some other mechanism.

❑ The `xsi:type` attribute is copied to the result document; the `xsl:type` and `type` attributes are not.

❑ The `xsi:type` attribute can only be used to specify the type of element nodes. A `type` attribute (when it is used on the `<xsl:attribute>` instruction) can also control the type of attribute nodes.

Nillability

The `xsi:nil` attribute was defined in XML Schema because there were some people from the relational database tradition who felt that omitting an element or attribute from an XML document was not an adequate way of representing the SQL concept of null values. I have to say I find the facility completely unnecessary: null was invented in SQL so that a cell in a table could hold no data, but XML already has perfectly good ways of representing absence of data, namely an absent element or attribute. But `xsi:nil` exists, and it can't be uninvented, and you may need to use it if it has been built in to the semantics of the vocabulary for your source or result documents.

As with `xsi:type`, the `xsi:nil` attribute is mentioned in the XSLT specification only in notes and examples. However, it gets a rather more detailed treatment in the XPath formal semantics, because it has a significant effect in complicating the rules for type matching.

You can use `xsi:nil` on an element only if the schema defines the element as nillable. If you do set «`xsi:nil = "true"`» on an element, then the element is valid only if it is empty; moreover, it is allowed to be empty in this case even if the content model for the element would otherwise not permit it to be empty.

The possibility of encountering an `xsi:nil` potentially plays havoc with the type safety of your stylesheet. If you write a function that is designed to process valid book elements, and every book must have an ISBN, then the function should be allowed to access the ISBN without adding conditional logic to check that it is there. For this reason, a function or variable that accepts nilled elements has to declare that it does so. If a function parameter is declared with the type «`as = "element(*, book-type)"`», then passing the element `<book xsi:nil = "true"/>` to this function will cause a type error. If you want to write a function that accepts this element, you must instead write «`as = "element(*, book-type?)"`» to show that your function can handle this input.

Apart from this, `xsi:nil` behaves in XSLT just like any other attribute.

You do need to be a little careful if you want to put your stylesheets through a schema processor (which you might do, for example, if you store your stylesheets in an XML database). The schema processor attaches a special meaning to attributes such as `xsi:nil`, `xsi:type`, and `xsi:schemaLocation`, even though XSLT does not. It's therefore best to avoid using these attributes directly on literal result elements. Two possible ways round this problem are:

- ❑ Generating these attributes using the `<xsl:attribute>` instruction instead.
- ❑ Using a namespace alias for the `xsi` namespace: See the description of the `<xsl:namespace-alias>` declaration in Chapter 6 (page 394).

Summary

Firstly, a reminder of something we said at the beginning of the chapter, and haven't touched on since: schema processing in XSLT 2.0 is optional. Some XSLT 2.0 processors won't support schema processing at all, and even if you are using a processor that is schema-aware, you can still use it to transform source documents that have no schema into result documents that have no schema.

We started this chapter with a very quick tour of the essentials of XML Schema, describing the main concepts of element and attribute declarations and simple and complex types, and discussing the role that they play in XSLT processing.

There are two main roles for schemas in XSLT, which are strongly related. Firstly, XML Schema provides the type system for XSLT and XPath, and as such, you can define the types of variables, functions, and templates in terms of types that are either built into XML Schema, or defined as user-defined types in a specific schema.

Secondly, you can use an XML Schema to validate your source documents, your result documents, or intermediate working data. This not only checks that your data is as you expected it, which helps debugging, but also annotates the nodes in the data model, which can be used to steer the way the nodes are processed, for example by defining template rules that match particular types of node.

The mechanism that binds a stylesheet to one or more schemas is the `<xsl:import-schema>` declaration, and we looked in some detail at the way this works.

In the next chapter we will look more closely at the way types are used in XSLT and XPath processing, including a survey of the built-in types that are available whether or not you use a schema.

5

Types

This chapter looks in some detail at the XPath type system; that is, the types of the values that can be manipulated by XPath expressions and XSLT instructions.

XPath is an expression language. Every expression takes one or more values as its inputs, and produces a value as its output. The purpose of this chapter is to explain exactly what these values can be.

Chapter 2 presented the XDM tree model with its seven node kinds — that's part of the picture, because XPath expressions will often be handling nodes in a tree. The other half of the picture is concerned with atomic values (strings, numbers, booleans, and the like), and it's these values that we'll be studying in this chapter.

One of the things an expression language tries to achieve is that wherever you can use a value, you can replace it with an expression that is evaluated to produce that value. So if «2 + 2» is a valid expression, then «(6−4) + (1 + 1)» should also be a valid expression. This property is called *composability*: expressions can be used anywhere that values are permitted. One of the important features that make a language composable is that the possible results of an expression are the same as the possible inputs. This feature is called *closure*: every expression produces a result that is in the same space of possible values as the space from which the inputs are drawn.

The role of the data model is to describe this space of possible values, and the role of the type system is to define the rules for manipulating these values.

What Is a Type System?

Let's make sure that when we talk about a type system, we're talking the same language.

Every programming language has some kind of type system. A language manipulates values, and the values are of different types. At the simple level, they might be integers, booleans, and strings. Then the language might support various kinds of composite types; for example, arrays or records or lists. Most modern languages also allow users to define their own types, on top of the basic types provided "out of the box".

So, types are used to classify the values that can be manipulated by expressions in the language, and the type system defines the basic types provided by the language as well as the facilities for defining new types by combining and refining existing types.

A type serves two main purposes. Firstly, it defines a set of permissible values. For example, if you say that a function expects a positive integer as its first argument, then the phrase "positive integer" tells you what the valid values for the first argument are.

Secondly, a type defines a set of possible operations. Integers can be added, lists can be concatenated, booleans can be combined using the operators «and», «or», and «not».

Not only does the type tell you whether a particular operation is permitted on a value of that type, it determines how that operation will be performed. So integers, strings, dates, and high school grades can all be sorted into order, but the way they are sorted depends on their type. Operations that are performed in different ways depending on the type of their operands are called *polymorphic* operations (from Greek words meaning *many shapes*).

Types are useful in programming languages for a number of reasons:

❑   Types allow errors to be detected, including programming logic errors and data errors. Because a type defines a set of permissible values, the system can give you an error message when you try to use a value that is not permissible. And because a type defines a set of allowed operations, the system can also give you an error message if you try to apply an operation to the wrong kind of value.

❑   Types allow polymorphic operations to be defined. At a simple level, this allows «A < B» to mean different things depending on whether A and B are numbers or dates or strings. At a more sophisticated level, it allows the kind of inheritance and method overriding which is such a powerful tool in object-oriented programming.

❑   Types allow optimization. To make expressions in a language such as XPath run as fast as possible, the system does as much work as it can in advance, using information that is available at compile time from analysis of the expression itself and its context. A lot of the reasoning that can be done at this stage is based on analysis of the types of values that the expression will process. For example, XPath has a very powerful «=» operator, in which the operands can not only be any type of value (such as integers or strings) but can also be sequences. Handling the general case, where both operands are arbitrary sequences containing items of mixed types, can be very expensive. In most cases the operands are much simpler; for example, two integers or two strings. If the system can work out in advance that the operands will be simple (and it often can), then it can generate much more efficient code and save a lot of work at runtime.

Enough of this introduction to type systems in programming languages: let's get down to details.

Changes in 2.0

XPath 1.0 only supported three atomic types: boolean, double-precision floating point, and string. This has been generalized to allow all the types defined in XML Schema.

XPath 1.0 supported node-sets (unordered collections of nodes, with no duplicates). XPath 2.0 generalizes this to support sequences, which are ordered and may contain duplicates, and which may contain atomic values as well as nodes.

The thinking on types has changed considerably between XPath 1.0 and XPath 2.0. In 1.0, there were very few types, and very little type checking. Almost all operations were permitted, and runtime errors were very rare. That sounds good on the surface, but what it actually means is that if you make a mistake, you don't get an error message — you just get the wrong answer back (or no answer at all, which can be even more bewildering). This approach to language design generally goes under the name *dynamic typing* or *weak typing*, and it is found most often in scripting languages such as JavaScript and Perl. XPath 2.0 has made a significant shift toward the other approach to language design, based on *static typing* or *strong typing*, which is more characteristic of compiled languages such as C or Java. It has to be said that not everyone is happy with the change, though there are good reasons for it, essentially the fact that XSLT (and its cousin, XQuery) are starting to be used to tackle much bigger problems where a more robust engineering approach is needed.

Actually, the really innovative thing about XPath 2.0 is that it tries to accommodate multiple approaches to typing within a single language. Because XML itself is used to handle a very wide spectrum of different kinds of document, from the very rigidly structured to the very flexible, XPath 2.0 has been designed to accommodate both very flexible and dynamic approaches, where you have no idea what the data is going to look like in advance, to highly structured queries where the structure of the data is regular and predictable and the expression can be optimized to take advantage of the fact. That's the theory, anyway; in practice, as one might expect, there are a few wrinkles.

Sequences

Sometimes object programming languages introduce their data model with the phrase "everything is an object". In the XPath 2.0 data model, the equivalent statement is that every value is a *sequence*.

By *value*, we mean anything that can be the result of an expression or an operand of an expression. In XPath 2.0, the value of every expression is a sequence of zero or more items. Of course XPath, like other languages, can use atomic values such as integers and booleans. But in XPath, an atomic value is just a special case of a sequence: it is a sequence of length one.

The items in a sequence are ordered. This means that the sequence (1, 2, 3) is different from the sequence (2, 3, 1). The XPath 2.0 data model does not have any direct means of representing unordered collections. Instead, where ordering is unimportant, it makes this part of the definition of an operator on sequences: for example, the `distinct-values()` function returns a number of values with no defined ordering, and with duplicates disallowed, but the result is still presented as a sequence. The ordering might sometimes be arbitrary and left to the implementation to determine, but there is always an ordering.

The items in a sequence are always numbered starting at 1. The number of items in a sequence (and therefore, the number assigned to the last item in the sequence) can be obtained using the `count()` function. (The functions available in XPath 2.0, such as `count()` and `distinct-values()`, are listed in Chapter 13.)

Sequences have no properties other than the items they contain. Two sequences that contain the same items are indistinguishable, so there is no concept of a sequence having an identity separate from its contents.

A sequence can be empty. Because two sequences that contain the same items are indistinguishable, there is no difference between one empty sequence and another, and so we often refer to *the* empty sequence rather than to *an* empty sequence. An empty sequence, as we shall see, is often used to represent absent data in a similar way to nulls in SQL.

The items in a sequence are either `atomic values`, or `nodes`. An atomic value is a value such as an integer, a string, a boolean, or a date. Nodes have already been described in Chapter 2. We will examine atomic values in much greater detail later in this chapter. Most sequences either consist entirely of nodes, or entirely of atomic values, but it's quite legitimate (and occasionally useful) to have a sequence that consists, say, of two strings, an integer, and three element nodes.

Types

The relationships between sequences, items, atomic values and nodes are summarized in the simple UML diagram in Figure 5-1.

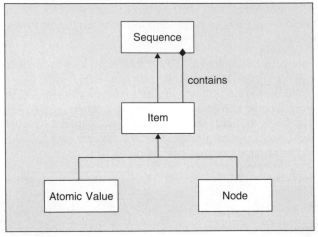

Figure 5-1

This shows that:

❑   A sequence contains zero or more items

❑   An item is itself a sequence

❑   An atomic value is an item

❑   A node is an item

Although we talk about a sequence containing nodes, this doesn't mean that a node can only be in one sequence. Far from it. It might be less confusing if we spoke of the sequence containing references to nodes rather than containing the nodes themselves, or if we used a verb other than "contains" — but sadly, we don't.

A sequence can only contain individual items; it cannot contain or reference other sequences. This is an aspect of the data model that some people find surprising, but there are good reasons for it. The usual explanations given are:

❑   Sequences in the XDM model are designed primarily to represent lists as defined in XML Schema. For example, XML Schema allows the value of an attribute to be a list of integers. These lists cannot be nested, so it wouldn't make sense to allow nested lists in XDM either.

❑   Sequences that contain sequences would allow trees and graphs to be constructed. But these would bear no relationship to the trees used to represent XML documents. In XDM we need a representation of trees that is faithful to XML; we don't need another kind of tree that bears no relationship to the XML model.

The effect of this rule is that if you need a data structure to hold something more complicated than a simple list of items, it's best to represent it as an XML document. (This is easy when you are using XSLT or XQuery, which allow you to construct nodes in new trees at any time. It's less easy in standalone XPath, which is a read-only language.)

The simplest way of writing an XPath expression whose value is a sequence is by using a comma-separated list: for example, «1, 2, 3» represents a list containing three integers. In fact, as we will see in Chapter 10, the comma is a binary operator that concatenates two sequences. Remember that a single integer is a sequence. So «1, 2» concatenates the single-item sequence «1» and the single-item sequence «2» to create the two-item sequence «1, 2». The expression «1, 2, 3» is evaluated as «(1, 2), 3», and it concatenates the two-item sequence «1, 2» with the one-item sequence «3» to produce the three-item sequence «1, 2, 3». This definition of comma as an operator means that it is also possible to write sequences such as «$a, $b», which concatenates two arbitrary sequences represented by the variables $a and $b.

> *Sometimes a list of values separated by commas needs to be enclosed in parentheses to prevent ambiguity, for example when it is used as an argument in a function call. For details, see Chapter 10, page 635.*

Some of the important XPath operations defined on sequences are:

❑   «count($S)» counts the items in a sequence.

❑   «$S, $T» concatenates two sequences.

❑   «$S[predicate]» selects those items in a sequence that satisfy some condition.

❑   «$S[number]» selects the Nth item in a sequence.

❑   «for $item in $SEQ return f($item)» applies the function «f» (which can actually be any expression) to every item in the sequence $SEQ, and returns the results as a new sequence. (In list processing languages, this is known as a *mapping* expression).

We will study these operators in much greater depth later in the book.

Sequences also play an important role in navigating trees, as we shall see. The result of a *path expression* such as «/book/chapter/section» is a sequence of nodes. All operators that apply to sequences in general (including those listed above) can therefore be used to manipulate sequences of nodes selected using path expressions.

So, there are two kinds of item that can be found in a sequence, namely atomic values and nodes. We've already studied nodes in some detail in Chapter 2, so now it's time to look at atomic values.

Atomic Values

It's easiest to explain what an atomic value is by example: they are things like integers, floating-point numbers, booleans, and strings.

Every atomic value has a type (it is either an integer, or a string, or a boolean...). Broadly speaking, the types that are available are the 19 primitive types defined in XML Schema, such as xs:double, xs:string, or xs:date, which we will examine in this chapter, and types derived from these.

An atomic value either belongs directly to one of these primitive types, or to a type that is defined by restricting one of these primitive types. This may be a built-in type such as xs:NMTOKEN, which is defined in the XML Schema specification itself as a restriction of xs:string, or a type defined in a user-written schema. For example, if you have a schema that defines mf:part-number as a restriction of xs:string, then you can have atomic values whose type is mf:part-number.

A type definition determines the set of possible values allowed for items of that type. For example, the type xs:boolean has two possible values, called true and false. For a restricted type, the set of possible values is always a subset of the values allowed for its base type. So a type that is defined by restricting «xs:integer» might allow only the values 1 to 20.

An atomic value carries its type with it as a kind of label. If «PY03672» is an mf:part-number, then because of the way the type is defined, it is also an xs:string. This means it can be used anywhere that an xs:string can be used. However, its label still identifies it as an mf:part-number. Conversely, if you write the string literal «"PY03672"» in an XPath expression, the value will be labeled as an xs:string, and even though it meets all the rules that would make it a valid mf:part-number, you cannot use it in places where an mf:part-number is required, because it has the wrong label. To create a value labeled as an mf:part-number, you need to use the constructor function «mf:part-number("PY03672")».

So the two properties of an atomic value are the value itself, and the type label. If two atomic values are the same in these two respects, then they are indistinguishable. Atomic values do not have any kind of identity separate from their value and their type; there is only one number 42, and only one string "Venice".

In particular, this means that atomic values are not in any way attached to a particular XML document. Atomic values can be extracted from nodes in an XML document, through a process called *atomization*, described on page 165; but once extracted, they have no residual connection with the document where they originated. Atomic values can also be derived quite independently of any document; for example, as the result of an arithmetic expression.

The full set of primitive atomic types that are available in XPath (that is, types that are not derived by restriction from another type) has been left slightly open-ended. There is an assumption that by default, the 19 primitive types defined in XML Schema will be available. These are:

xs:boolean	xs:date
xs:decimal	xs:dateTime
xs:float	xs:time
xs:double	xs:duration
xs:string	xs:gYear
xs:QName	xs:gYearMonth
xs:anyURI	xs:gMonth
xs:hexBinary	xs:gMonthDay
xs:base64Binary	xs:gDay
xs:NOTATION	

> *Throughout this book we use the namespace prefix xs to refer to the namespace* http://www.w3.org/2001/XMLSchema, *which is the namespace in which these types are defined.*

However, XPath is designed to be used in a wide variety of different environments, and host languages (that is, specifications that incorporate XPath as a sublanguage) are allowed to tailor this list, both by omitting types from the list and by adding to it. The host language we are primarily concerned with in this book is XSLT 2.0, and this defines two conformance levels: a *basic* XSLT processor supports all the above 19 types with the exception of xs:NOTATION, while a *schema-aware* XSLT processor recognizes the full list.

The type `xs:integer` is unusual. On the one hand it has a special status in the XPath language (it is one of the few types for which values can be written directly as literals). On the other hand, it is actually not a primitive type, but a type that is derived as a restriction of `xs:decimal`. This is because the set of all possible `xs:integer` values is a subset of the set of all possible `xs:decimal` values.

In fact there are four types for which XPath provides a syntax for defining literal constants:

Type	Example literals
`xs:string`	"New York", 'Moscow', ""
`xs:integer`	3, 42, 0
`xs:decimal`	93.7, 1.0, 0.0
`xs:double`	17.5e6, 1.0e-3, 0e0

A number can always be preceded by a plus or minus sign when it appears in an XPath expression, but technically the sign is not part of the numeric literal, it is an arithmetic operator.

Values of type `xs:boolean` can be represented using the function calls `false()` and `true()`, listed in the library of functions described in Chapter 13. Values of any other type can be written using constructor functions, where the name of the function is the same as the name of the type. For example, a constant date can be written as «`xs:date("2004-07-31")`».

There is one other type we need to mention in this section: the type `xs:untypedAtomic`. This type is defined not by XML Schema, but in the XPath specifications (in working drafts it was also in a different namespace, with the conventional prefix `xdt`, which you may still find used in some products). This type is used to label values that have not been validated using any schema, and which therefore do not belong to any schema-defined type. It is also used to label values that have been validated against a schema, in cases where the schema imposes no constraints. The set of possible values for this type is exactly the same as the value space for the `xs:string` type. The values are not strictly strings, because they have a different label (`xs:untypedAtomic` is not derived by restricting `xs:string`). Nevertheless, an `xs:untypedAtomic` value can be used anywhere that an `xs:string` can be used. In fact, it can be used anywhere that a value of any atomic type can be used; for example, it can be used where an integer or a boolean or a date is expected. In effect, `xs:untypedAtomic` is a label applied to values whose type has not been established.

If an `xs:untypedAtomic` value is used where an integer is expected, then the system tries to convert it to an integer at the time of use. If the actual value is not valid for an integer, then a runtime failure will occur. In this respect `xs:untypedAtomic` is quite different from `xs:string`, because if you try to use a string where an integer is expected, you will get a type error regardless whether it could be converted or not.

Atomic Types

We've been talking about atomic values and we've introduced the 19 primitive atomic types. In this section we'll look at these types more closely, and we'll also see what other atomic types are available.

Notice that we're talking here about atomic types rather than simple types. In XML Schema, we use an `<xs:simpleType>` declaration to define any type other than a complex type; that is, any type that doesn't permit attributes or child elements. Attributes always have simple types, and elements may have simple types if they don't allow child elements or attributes. But simple types are not necessarily atomic types, because they allow lists. For example, consider the type definition (taken from the schema for XSLT 2.0):

```
<xs:simpleType name="prefixes">
  <xs:list itemType="xs:NCName"/>
</xs:simpleType>
```

This defines a simple type whose value allows a list of names (the type `xs:NCName` defines a name that follows the XML rules: `NCName` means no-colon-name). An example of an attribute conforming to this type might be «a = "h1 h2 h3"». This is a simple type, but it is not an atomic type. Atomic types do not allow lists.

XML Schema also allows simple types to be defined as a choice; for example, a simple type might allow either a decimal number, or the string «N/A». This is referred to as a union type. Like list types, union types are simple types, but they are not atomic types.

Atomic types come from a number of sources.

As well as the 19 primitive types, the XML Schema specification defines 25 derived types that can be used in any schema; together these are referred to as the built-in types. Like the primitive types, these types are all in the XML Schema namespace `http://www.w3.org/2001/XMLSchema`.

There is also a second namespace for schema-defined types, called `http://www.w3.org/2001/XMLSchema-datatypes`. Frankly, this namespace is best forgotten. It doesn't provide anything that you don't get by using the ordinary XML Schema namespace, and it creates some technical problems because the types in this namespace are not exact synonyms of the types in the ordinary namespace. My advice is, don't go anywhere near it.

XPath 2.0 adds four more atomic types: `xs:dayTimeDuration`, `xs:yearMonthDuration`, `xs:anyAtomicType`, and `xs:untypedAtomic`. We've already covered `xs:untypedAtomic` in the previous section. The two duration types are described on page 205, later in this chapter.

The type `xs:anyAtomicType` is simply an abstract supertype for all the other atomic types. It is used mainly in function signatures, when you want to write a function that can handle atomic values of any type (the `min()` and `max()` functions are examples).

In a basic XSLT processor (as distinct from one that is schema-aware), the only built-in derived types that are recognized are `xs:integer`, `xs:dayTimeDuration`, `xs:yearMonthDuration`, `xs:anyAtomicType`, and `xs:untypedAtomic`.

In a schema-aware processor, all the built-in types are available, and you can also define your own atomic types in a schema. As we saw in Chapter 4, a type defined in a schema becomes available for use in a stylesheet when the schema is imported using an `<xsl:import-schema>` declaration.

Implementors can also add their own atomic types. There are a number of reasons they might want to do this. The most likely reason is to make it easier for XPath expressions to make calls on external functions; for example, functions written in C# or Java. The XPath specification doesn't say how this is done, and leaves it to implementors to define. Another reason implementors might want to add extra types is to support XPath access to some specialized database, for example, an LDAP directory. XPath is defined in terms of a data model with an obvious relationship to XML, but there is no reason why other sources of data cannot be mapped to the data model equally well, and doing this effectively might involve defining some custom types. (I mentioned LDAP because it is a hierarchic database, which provides a particularly good fit to the XPath data model.) Generally, any extra types added by the implementor will have names that are in some implementation-controlled namespace.

In the sections that follow, I will describe the built-in atomic types in a number of groups. These are my own categories, not anything that comes from the specifications themselves:

❏ *The major atomic types*: `xs:anyURI`, `xs:boolean`, `xs:date`, `xs:dateTime`, `xs:decimal`, `xs:double`, `xs:integer`, `xs:QName`, `xs:string`, `xs:time`, `xs:dayTimeDuration`, and `xs:yearMonthDuration`. These are the only atomic types that are directly supported in the XPath library of functions and operators for anything but the most trivial of operations. They are therefore the ones you are likely to be using most of the time.

❏ *The minor atomic types*: These are defined as primitive types in XML Schema, but they are not well supported by XPath, and you are unlikely to use them very often. These are `xs:gYear`, `xs:gYearMonth`, `xs:gMonth`, `xs:gMonthDay`, `xs:gDay`, `xs:duration`, `xs:float`, `xs:hexBinary`, `xs:base64Binary`, and `xs:NOTATION`.

❏ *The derived numeric types*: These are defined by restriction from the `xs:integer` type. They all define integers with a limited range of values, for example, `xs:positiveInteger`, `xs:short`, `xs:unsignedByte`.

❏ *The derived string types*: These are defined by restriction from `xs:string`. They include types like `xs:token` and `xs:NCName` that restrict the syntax of the string and define the treatment of whitespace.

❏ *The type* `xs:untypedAtomic`: This represents values whose type is unknown, because the value has not been validated by a schema processor. This is a chameleon type, whose values can be used freely in any context, provided that the value can be converted at runtime to the type that's expected.

There are two ways to use these atomic types:

❏ You can use them in a schema to define the types of elements and attributes. When you do this, the result of validating an XML document against this schema will be that the elements and attributes acquire a type annotation of the appropriate atomic type, and the typed value of the nodes (which is what you typically get when you use the node as input to an operation such as addition) will be the atomic value of the relevant type.

❏ You can manipulate atomic values of these types in your XPath expressions. For example, if you compare two strings, the result is a boolean, that is, a value of type `xs:boolean`. This value has never been anywhere near an XML document, let alone an XML Schema validator, but it is an `xs:boolean` all the same.

The Major Atomic Types

This section describes the most important atomic types used in XPath expressions, in alphabetical order. These types are chosen because they are the ones that are supported in the standard library of functions and operators defined in XPath, in particular the functions listed in Chapter 13. They are probably the types you will use 95% of the time.

xs:anyURI

This type is intended to hold URIs, in the widest sense of the term. This includes:

❏ Absolute URIs such as «`http://www.w3.org/`»

❏ Relative URI references such as «`../index.html`»

❏ URIs with a fragment identifier at the end, separated by a «`#`» character: for example «`http://www.w3.org/TR/xpath20#Introduction`» or simply «`#Introduction`»

❏ Unescaped URIs such as «file:///My Documents/biog.doc». Technically, this is not a URI because it contains a space character. To make it into a URI, the space must be escaped so it appears as «file:///My%20Documents/biog.doc». A number of specifications such as XML Linking explicitly allow a URI to be held in its unescaped form (because it isn't a real URI until it is escaped, I sometimes refer to it as a *wannabe-URI*). And although these aren't real URIs, XML Schema explicitly allows them to appear in an xs:anyURI value.

Most types in XML Schema are rather specific about exactly what is allowed in the value space of the type (for example, xs:boolean has two values, true and false), and how these values may be written in a source document (the lexical representation: with xs:boolean the values «0», «1», «true», and «false» are permitted). Most types also define a *canonical lexical representation* for each value in the value space, which is the representation that will be chosen when a typed value is converted to a string.

For the xs:anyURI type, these definitions have been fudged. Though the wording makes it clear that the intention is for xs:anyURI items to hold a URI as defined in the relevant internet RFCs (the most recent is http://www.ietf.org/rfc/rfc3986), they stop short of saying that a schema validator is expected to check that the contents actually conform with these rules. There is good reason for this reticence: many commonly used URIs don't actually conform with the rules in the RFC, and in any case, the rules in the RFC are not always clear.

I have read some books on XML Schema that suggest that in the value space of xs:anyURI, the value is always escaped (as in the example «file:///My%20Documents/biog.doc») and that conversion from the lexical form used in a source document to the value space should therefore cause this escaping to happen. This would mean that when you compare two xs:anyURI values, differences caused by one of them being escaped and the other not don't matter. This appears to be an incorrect interpretation of the spec. In practice schema processors often allow any string to be used as an xs:anyURI value, and they leave the string unchanged when converting it to its internal representation. This interpretation is endorsed by the draft XML Schema 1.1 specification, which clarifies the intention.

Although xs:anyURI is a primitive type in XML Schema, the XPath type system treats it almost as if it were a subtype of xs:string. In particular, you can pass an xs:anyURI value to any function or operator that expects a string, and it will be implicitly converted. Many of the functions in the standard library that you might expect to take xs:anyURI arguments (an example is the resolve-URI() function) in fact have a function signature that requires a string to be supplied. The special rule for promotion of xs:anyURI to xs:string ensures that either type is accepted.

Similarly, the promotion rule means that it is possible without formality to compare an xs:anyURI value to a string literal. The only downside of this pragmatic approach is that comparisons between xs:anyURI values are performed using the default collation, which might be quite inappropriate for comparing URIs. But this applies equally to some types derived from xs:string, such as xs:NCName. If you want a strict comparison, you can use the function codepoint-equal() instead of the «eq» or «=» operators.

xs:boolean

This is the simplest type defined in XML Schema. It has two values in the value space, referred to as true and false, and each of these has two permitted lexical representations: «1» and «true», «0» and «false».

Although it's so simple, there are some interesting quirks in the way XML Schema and XPath handle this type.

❏ As far as XML Schema is concerned, the xs:boolean type has no ordering. But in XPath, there is an ordering: false is considered to be less than true. XPath 2.0 has taken this position largely for backward compatibility with XPath 1.0, and also because it can actually be useful; for example, a stylesheet might use the expression «age < 18» as a sort key, which will output the adults first, then the children.

❑ There are two ways of converting a string to a boolean. An XML Schema processor interprets «1» and «true» as true, «0» and «false» as false. This behavior also occurs when you use the xs:boolean() constructor (described in Chapter 11). But if you use the boolean() function (or fn:boolean() if you want to write it with a namespace prefix), as described in Chapter 13, then a zero-length string translates to false, and everything else to true. This is also the result you get if you do an implicit conversion of a string to a boolean by using a string in a context such as «if (S) then A else B», where S is a string.

Again, the difference is partly historic: the XPath 1.0 rules were invented before XML Schema came along. But the convention of equating a zero-length string to false also has a long history in weakly typed programming languages, and is very convenient in some recursive algorithms that need to terminate when the argument is a zero-length string.

xs:date

The xs:date type represents a date. The lexical representation of the date (that is, the way it appears in a textual XML document) is always the representation defined in the ISO 8601 standard, that is YYYY-MM-DD (for example, «1999-11-16» for November 16, 1999). This format is chosen because it is unambiguous; the theory is that XML documents should represent information in a neutral form that is independent of how different users might want to see the information formatted.

For formatting dates and times in a user-friendly way, XSLT provides the format-date() function, which is described in Chapter 13. This isn't available in standalone XPath expressions (or in XQuery).

A rather quirky feature of the xs:date type is that as well as holding the date itself, it can also hold a timezone. This is something that ISO 8601 itself doesn't allow. The idea is that a date actually represents a period of 24 hours starting at midnight in a particular timezone, and ending at the following midnight in the same timezone. The date November 16, 1999 represents a different period of 24 hours in New York from the period it represents in London, Tokyo, or Los Angeles, so the schema designers came up with the idea of adding a timezone to the date to indicate exactly when the date begins and ends. In the lexical representation, the timezone is added after the date part, for example «1999-11-16-05:00» represents a date in the timezone that is five hours behind UTC (the timezone used in the Eastern United States during the winter months). The timezone is optional; it is also possible to have a date value with no timezone, in which case the precise beginning and end of the 24-hour period represented by the value are considered to be unknown.

XML Schema doesn't define how dates are represented internally in the system, but it does define a *value space* for every type. If two different lexical values translate into the same value in the value space, then they are completely equivalent (to the extent that when you copy an element or attribute, the original lexical representation won't necessarily be retained). For dates (as distinct from times) the XML Schema and XPath specifications agree that the timezone is part of the value space: that is, «1999-11-16-05:00» represents a different xs:date value from «1999-11-16+01:00». However, «1999-11-16+13:00» (used in Tonga) is equivalent to «1999-11-15-11:00» (used in nearby Samoa), because both dates start at the same instant.

This gives the problem of deciding whether a date that specifies a timezone (for example «1999-11-16-12:00») comes before or after a date that doesn't specify a timezone (for example «1999-11-16») when you want to perform comparison operations or sorting. If both dates have timezones, the answer is clear enough: the dates are sorted in order of their starting instants. And if neither has a timezone, you

195

can assume that they relate to the same timezone. But if one has a timezone and the other doesn't, it's not obvious what the answer should be. XML Schema takes a rather purist view, saying that dates are *partially ordered*, which means that for some pairs of dates you don't know which one comes first. For an expression language like XPath, partial ordering is a nightmare: the system has to come up with some kind of answer. The answer chosen was that the system environment contains an implicit timezone that can be used as a default, and when dates with no timezone have to be compared or sorted, the system will assume that they refer to this implicit timezone. We look more closely at the implicit timezone when we examine the XPath evaluation context in Chapter 7.

The operations you can perform on a date include:

❏   Comparing and sorting dates

❏   Converting dates to and from strings

❏   Extracting the component parts of a date (year, month, day, timezone)

❏   Adding a duration to a date (or subtracting a duration) to get another date

❏   Determining the difference between two dates, as a duration

❏   Converting the value to an `xs:dateTime` (the result is the starting instant of the date)

❏   In XSLT only, formatting a date for human consumption (for example, as «Wednesday 16th November»)

Dates held using this type are always supposed to be Gregorian dates, even if they predate the introduction of the Gregorian calendar (which happened at different times in different countries). In principle, historic events are supposed to have their dates adjusted to represent them using the modern calendar.

Negative dates (BC dates) are supported, but they are a minor disaster area in XML Schema. According to XML Schema 1.0, the year zero is not allowed, and the year before 0001 is represented as −0001. However, shortly before XML Schema 1.0 was published, a new edition of ISO 8601 came out that stated that the year before 0001 should be represented as 0000. The draft XML Schema 1.1 specification has changed to match this, despite the fact that this affects the meaning of data in existing documents, and the results of queries. In practice, I would advise against using this type for historical dates. For most applications it's probably better to represent them using their original calendar.

xs:dateTime

The `xs:dateTime` type represents the combination of a date and time, that is, it represents an instant in time. The lexical representation is again based on ISO 8601, for example it might be «2008-04-12T13:05:00Z» to represent five minutes past one in the afternoon of April 12, 2008, in the timezone Z (Z represents Coordinated Universal Time, abbreviated to UTC, and often still referred to by its older name of Greenwich Mean Time, or GMT).

The seconds part of an `xs:dateTime` can contain a fractional part. The number of significant digits that are retained is implementation-defined, but must be at least three.

As with `xs:date`, the complications with dates and times are all to do with timezones (if only the world could agree to synchronize its clocks, the problem would disappear). XML Schema takes the view that the value space of `xs:dateTime` represents instants in time, and that «2008-04-12T13:05:00Z» and «2008-04-12T08:05:00-05:00» are the same instant in time (five past one in London is five past eight in New York), and are therefore indistinguishable.

The XSLT and XQuery working groups didn't feel it was acceptable that the original timezone information written in the source XML document should be simply thrown away. It didn't seem right, for example, that a transformation that copies a source document containing the value «2008-04-12T08:05:00-05:00» should produce the value «2008-04-12T13:05:00Z» in the result document. Although it's right to consider the two values as being equal (in the same way that 1 and 01 are equal) it seems that there is some information content in the timezone that the user probably wants to hold on to. So, after much agonizing and debate between the working groups, the XDM model defines a value space that retains the original timezone as well as the "instant in time". This doesn't affect the test whether two xs:dateTime values are equal, but it does affect other operations, for example the operation of converting an xs:dateTime value to a string (which will reconstitute the original timezone).

Like xs:date values, xs:dateTime values don't need to specify a timezone, and XPath adopts the same solution: they are assumed to apply to an implicit timezone taken from the evaluation context.

The operations you can perform on an xs:dateTime include:

❏ Comparing and sorting dateTimes

❏ Converting dateTimes to and from strings

❏ Extracting the component parts of a dateTime (year, month, day, hour, minutes, seconds, timezone)

❏ Adding a duration to a dateTime (or subtracting a duration) to get another dateTime

❏ Determining the difference between two dateTimes, as a duration

❏ Extracting the date or time part separately

❏ Adjusting the timezone: that is, creating an equivalent dateTime with or without a timezone, or with a different timezone (see the adjust-dateTime-to-timezone() function on page 715)

❏ In XSLT only, formatting a dateTime for human consumption (for example, as «Wednesday 16th November, 1.30p.m.»)

xs:decimal

The xs:decimal type represents numbers that can be accurately expressed in decimal notation. This type is useful for values such as amounts of money, where the actual value space is discrete rather than continuous, and where the rounding errors that arise with binary formats such as xs:double and xs:float are undesirable.

In a user-defined subtype of xs:decimal, the values can be restricted in terms of the total number of allowed digits, and the number of digits allowed after the decimal point. If the built-in type xs:decimal is used without restriction, the number of digits allowed must be at least 18, though it can be greater than this if the implementation chooses. Some implementations may use an unlimited-precision representation (Saxon does, for example).

Any numeric literal written with a decimal point in XPath 2.0 (but without using exponential notation) represents an xs:decimal value, for example the literal «3.50». Note that this represents exactly the same xs:decimal value as the literal «3.5»: in general, trailing zeros after the decimal point will be lost when xs:decimal values are manipulated, which can be a bit awkward when you are handling amounts of money. For example, the result of «2.44 + 2.56» is displayed as «5». XSLT has a function format-number() that allows you to control the way values are formatted; for example, you can use a picture of «0.00» to ensure that there are always two digits after the decimal point. But there is no equivalent to this in XPath or XQuery.

XPath 2.0 offers a full range of arithmetic operators and functions on xs:decimal values. These are summarized in the entry for xs:double which follows this entry. The arithmetic operators are described in more detail in Chapter 8, and the functions are listed in Chapter 13. When you apply these operators and functions to `xs:decimal` operands, the result is generally also an `xs:decimal`. In the case of operators with two operands, you can mix `xs:decimal` with other numeric types; if the other operand is an `xs:float` or `xs:double`, then the `xs:decimal` is converted to an `xs:float` or `xs:double` as appropriate, and the result will also be an `xs:float` or `xs:double`.

The main operation that can cause problems is division. The division operator in XPath is `div`, because «/» is reserved for use in path expressions. Division by zero is a fatal error. When you perform a division that does not have an exact decimal result, for example «10 div 3.0», the precision of the result is implementation-defined. One implementation might give you 3.333333, another might give you 3.333333333333. An implementation could even claim to be conformant if it gave you the answer 3, though it might not prove popular in the marketplace if it did that.

When a decimal number is displayed as a string, it is shown as an integer if there are no significant digits after the decimal point. So the result of «2.5 + 2.5» is displayed as «5».

xs:double

The `xs:double` type represents double-precision floating-point numbers. This was the only numeric type supported in XPath 1.0, and it is therefore the default for some operations where backward compatibility is important; in particular, if you apply numeric operations to the value of a node in a schemaless document, the system will try to convert the contents of that node to an `xs:double` value.

An `xs:double` is a double-precision (64-bit) floating-point number, and its behavior is defined to follow the IEEE 754 standard. This standard (*IEEE Standard for Binary Floating-Point Arithmetic. ANSI/IEEE Std. 754-1985*) has been widely implemented by many microprocessors for some years, but it is only through its adoption in the Java language that it has become familiar to high-level language programmers. If you understand how floating point behaves in Java, the contents of this section will be quite familiar; if not, they may be rather strange.

XPath 2.0 introduces the ability to use scientific notation for floating-point numbers, either on input or on output. If you want to enter the number one trillion, you can now write `1.0E12`. In fact, if you want to write an `xs:double` as a literal in an XPath expression, you must write it in scientific notation: otherwise, it will be treated as an `xs:decimal` (if it has a decimal point) or as an `xs:integer` (if not).

On output, that is when you convert an `xs:double` to a string, scientific notation is used only if the absolute value is smaller than 0.000001, or greater than 1,000,000. This means that most everyday numbers will be formatted in ordinary decimal notation on output. In XSLT, you can control the format of numeric output more precisely by using the `format-number()` function, which is described in Chapter 13.

In general, I recommend using `xs:double` for numbers that are on a continuous scale (for example, distances, weights, or temperatures), and using `xs:decimal` for numbers that represent discrete quantities, such as sums of money. But this is only rough guidance.

IEEE 754 defines the following range of values for a double-precision number:

Value	Description
Finite nonzero values	These are values of the form $s \times m \times 2^e$, where s (the sign) is +1 or −1, m (the mantissa) is a positive integer less than 2^{53}, and e (the exponent) is an integer between −1075 and 970, inclusive
Positive zero	This is the result of subtracting a number from itself. It can also result from dividing any positive number by infinity, or from dividing a very small number by a very large number of the same sign.

continued

Value	Description
Negative zero	This is the result of dividing any negative number by infinity. It can also result from dividing a positive number by minus infinity, or from dividing a very small negative number by a very large positive number, or vice versa.
Positive infinity	This is the result of dividing any positive number by zero. It can also result from multiplying two very large numbers with the same sign. Note that division by zero is not an error: it has a well-defined result.
Negative infinity	This is the result of dividing any negative number by zero. It can also result from multiplying two very large numbers with different signs.
NaN	Not a Number. This is the result of attempting to convert a non-numeric string value to a number. It can also be used to mean "unknown" or "not applicable", like the SQL null value.

These values cannot all be written directly as XPath constants. However, they can be expressed as the result of expressions, for example:

Value	XPath expression
Negative zero	−0e0
Positive Infinity	1 div 0e0
Negative Infinity	−1 div 0e0
NaN	number("NaN")

Technically, negative numbers cannot be written directly as constants: «-10» is an expression rather than a number, but in practice it can be used anywhere that a numeric constant can be used. The only thing you need to be careful of is that a space may be needed before the unary minus operator if you write an expression such as «$x div -1».

Except for NaN, number values are *ordered*. Arranged from smallest to largest, they are:

❑ Negative infinity

❑ Negative finite non-zero values

❑ Zero (positive and negative zero are equal to each other)

❑ Positive finite non-zero values

❑ Positive infinity

This ordering determines the result of less-than and greater-than comparisons, and in XSLT it determines the result of sorting using `<xsl:apply-templates>` or `<xsl:for-each>` with a sort key specified using `<xsl:sort data-type = "number">`.

NaN is *unordered*, so the operators «<», «<=», «>», and «>=» return false if either or both operands are NaN. However, when `<xsl:sort>` is used to sort a sequence of numeric values that includes one or more NaN values, NaN values are collated at the start of the sequence (or at the end if you choose descending order).

Positive zero and negative zero compare equal. This means that the operators «=», «<=», and «>=» return true, while «!=», «<», and «> » return false. However, other operations can distinguish positive and negative zero; for example, «1.0 div $x» has the value positive infinity if $x is positive zero, and negative infinity if $x is negative zero.

The equals operator «=» returns false if either or both operands are NaN, and the not-equals operator «!= » returns true if either or both operands are NaN. Watch out for the apparent contradictions this leads to; for example, «$x = $x» can be false, and «$x < $y» doesn't necessarily give the same answer as «$y > $x».

The simplest way to test whether a value $x is NaN is:

```
if ($x!=$x) then ...
```

If this seems too obscure for your taste, then provided you know that $x is numeric you can write:

```
if (string($x)='NaN') then
```

If you are familiar with null values in SQL, some of this logic might seem familiar, but there are some subtle differences. For example, in SQL the condition «null = null» has the value null, so that «not(null = null)» is also null, while in XPath «NaN = NaN» is false, so that «not(NaN = NaN)» is true.

XPath provides a number of operators and functions that act on or return numeric values:

- ❏ The numerical comparison operators « < », « <= », « > », and « >= ». Within a stylesheet, you may need to use XML escape conventions to write these, for example, « < » in place of « < ».
- ❏ The numerical equality operators «=» and «!= ».
- ❏ The unary minus operator «-».
- ❏ The multiplicative operators «*», «div», and «mod».
- ❏ The additive operators «+» and «-».
- ❏ The number() function, which can convert from any value to a number.
- ❏ The string() function, which converts a number to a string.
- ❏ The boolean() function, which converts a number to a Boolean.
- ❏ The abs() function returns the absolute value of a number.
- ❏ The functions round(), ceiling(), floor(), and round-half-to-even(), which convert a number to an integer.
- ❏ The aggregate functions sum(), avg(), max(), and min(), which produce a single xs:double value when applied to a sequence of xs:double values.

Operators on numbers behave exactly as specified by IEEE 754. XPath is not as strict as Java in defining exactly what rounding algorithms should be used for inexact results, and in what sequence operations should be performed. In fact XPath 2.0 is more liberal than XPath 1.0, in that it allows any of the options permitted by IEEE 754 to be chosen. These include, for example, producing an error on overflow rather than returning positive or negative infinity.

Many implementations, however, are likely to follow the Java rules. In this case, numeric operators and functions never produce an error. An operation that overflows produces positive or negative infinity, an operation that underflows produces positive or negative zero, and an operation that has no other sensible result produces NaN. All numeric operations and functions with NaN as an operand produce NaN as a result. For example, if you apply the sum() function to a sequence, then if the sequence contains a NaN value, the result of the sum() function will be NaN.

xs:integer

The xs:integer type supports the positive and negative natural numbers. Neither XML Schema nor XPath 2.0 dictate what the maximum value of an integer is. XML Schema has a rule that implementations must support at least 18 decimal digits. But one of the subtypes of xs:integer, namely xs:unsignedLong, supports values in the range 0 to 18,446,744,073,709,551,615. This requires 20 digits, so an implementation that stops at 18 is going to struggle to pass some of the conformance tests.

Unlike all the other types that I classify as major types, xs:integer is not a primitive type but a derived type. It is derived by restriction from xs:decimal. This means that every valid xs:integer is also a valid xs:decimal, and anywhere that an xs:decimal can be used, an xs:integer can be substituted. The actual nature of the restriction is that the xs:integer type contains all xs:decimal values that have no significant digits after the decimal point.

The xs:integer type follows the pattern of the other numeric types, in that all the arithmetic operators and functions, when applied to an xs:integer argument (or to two xs:integer operands) produce an xs:integer as their result.

The main exception to this is division. XPath 2.0 provides two division operators. The div operator treats integer operands as xs:decimals, and produces an xs:decimal result (so «5 div 2» is 2.5). The idiv operator (for integer division) produces an xs:integer result, so «5 idiv 2» is 2. Closely related to this is the avg() function: the average of a sequence of xs:integer values is an xs:decimal.

xs:QName

The xs:QName type is a rather specialized type whose values hold XML qualified names.

An xs:QName has two forms. In its lexical form, it consists of either a simple local name (such as «product») or a local name qualified by a namespace prefix (such as «mfg:product»). In its expanded form, it holds two significant components: a namespace URI (possibly null) and a local name, but it also retains the prefix so that the original lexical representation can be reconstituted on output.

There is no direct string representation of the expanded value, though in some interfaces (for example in the Java JAXP interface) expanded QNames are represented in a notation devised by James Clark, of the form «{namespace-uri}local-name»; for example, «{http://www.mfg.org/ns}product».

This type is unusual (and, one might add, a great nuisance) because it is not possible to translate between the lexical form and the internal value space without having additional context information. A schema validator gets this context information from the namespace declarations that surround the element or attribute where the QName appears. For XSLT processors, which have the job of extracting parts of a document and copying them into different places, this dependency on context information causes no end of hassle: it isn't safe to copy a QName to a new location unless you also copy its context information. This is why the spec devotes so much attention to the arcane matter of namespace nodes. It's also for this reason that there are restrictions on what you can do with an xs:QName — for example, you can't have a parentless attribute node of type xs:QName because there would be nowhere to put the namespace bindings.

To reduce the problems associated with xs:QName, the XPath type differs from the XML Schema definition by maintaining the namespace prefix as part of the value. The prefix plays no part in comparisons, but

5

Types

201

it is used when converting the value to a string. This means that `xs:QName` values, like all other atomic values, can always be converted to a string, which greatly reduces the number of special rules needed to handle tree construction and serialization.

One of the ideas behind defining `xs:QName` as a primitive type in XML Schema was so that the XML infrastructure would know which parts of the document have dependencies on namespace declarations, and would therefore be able to ensure that the relevant namespace declarations are kept around when data is copied. Unfortunately this doesn't work, because you can have namespace-sensitive data in a document without declaring it as an `xs:QName`. For example, if your document contains XPath expressions (which it will do if it happens to be a stylesheet, but it's not uncommon to find them in other kinds of document as well), then it will necessarily contain namespace-sensitive content that isn't flagged as such, because an XPath expression is more complex than a simple `xs:QName`.

What operations does XPath support on `xs:QName` values?

- ❑ You can compare two QNames for equality. This sounds trivial, but it is probably the most important reason for using them. The comparison checks both the namespace URI and the local name, and it ignores the prefix. Moreover, the proper rules are used for this comparison; it's not subject to the uncertainties that arise when comparing strings; for example, whether accents are significant and whether lower case compares equal to upper case. For example, the test:

    ```
    node-name(.) = QName("http://www.mfg.org/ns", "product")
    ```

    is comparing two `xs:QName` values. This is much more reliable than the test:

    ```
    name(.) = "mfg:product"
    ```

    which could go wrong for two reasons: it's dependent on the choice of namespace prefix, and it's doing a string comparison using the default collation, which might compare strings such as «product» and «Product» as equal if that's the way it's been set up. There's more detail on collations in the next section, which discusses the `xs:string` type.

- ❑ You can convert a QName to a string. This uses the prefix held as part of the value, if there is one, or returns an unprefixed name otherwise.

- ❑ You can construct an expanded QName from the namespace URI and local-name using the `QName()` function shown above, and you can extract these two components using the rather clumsily named functions `local-name-from-QName()` and `namespace-uri-from-QName()`.

You can convert a string to a QName, but only if you write it as a string literal. For example, you can write «xs:QName("mfg:product")», which will produce the expanded QName whose local-name is «product», and whose namespace URI is the namespace URI corresponding to the «mfg» prefix. The reason for this restriction is to ensure that the conversion can be done at compile time, when the namespace context is known. In XSLT there are plenty of other places where the namespace context has to be retained at runtime, so it would have been no great hardship for implementors to avoid limiting it this way; but the restriction isn't a great hardship for users either because the `QName()` function provides the ability to construct any QName dynamically knowing the namespace and local name.

xs:string

A string value in XPath is any sequence of zero or more characters, where the alphabet of possible characters is the same as in XML: essentially the characters defined in Unicode.

String values can be written in XPath expressions in the form of a literal, using either single quotes or double quotes, for example «'John'» or «"Mary"». In theory, the string literal can contain the opposite quote character as part of the value, for example «"John's"». In practice, certainly in XSLT, XPath expressions are written within XML attributes, so the opposite quote character will generally already be in use for the attribute delimiters. For more details, see the section *StringLiteral* in Chapter 7, page 532.

There is no special null value, as there is in SQL. Where no other value is appropriate, a zero-length string or an empty sequence is used. These are not the same thing: an empty sequence is a sequence containing no items («count($x)» returns 0), while a zero-length string is a sequence containing a single item, whose type is xs:string and whose value has a string-length of zero («count($x)» returns 1, «string-length($x)» returns 0). However, although zero-length strings and empty sequences aren't the same thing, most of the functions in the standard library (see Chapter 13) give the same answer when an empty sequence is supplied as when a zero-length string is supplied.

> *The specifications try always to use the term zero-length string for the value «""», to avoid any possible confusion, but occasionally the terms null string and empty string slip in by mistake.*

The actual set of Unicode characters permitted in XML changes between XML 1.0 and XML 1.1. The XPath 2.0 specifications leave it to the implementor to decide which version of XML to align with.

In XML 1.0, the only ASCII control characters permitted (codes below x20) are the whitespace characters x09, x0A, and x0D (tab, newline, and carriage return). In XML 1.1, all control characters other than x00 are allowed, though you have to write them using XML character references rather than in their native encoding. For example, the BELL character, which in former times was used to ring the bell on a teletype machine, but nowadays is more likely to result in an irritating electronic beep, is represented as «&#x07;». The requirement to use this form is because some of these control characters have special meaning in communications protocols that may be used to carry XML documents. The exclusion of the x00 character (sometimes called NUL) is probably a concession to programmers writing XML parsers and related software in C, where this character is treated as a string delimiter. It also has the effect — probably deliberate — that you still can't use XML directly to convey binary data, you have to encode it as characters. As we will see (on page 208), XML Schema provides two types to help with this, xs:hexBinary and xs:base64Binary.

Unicode was originally defined so that all characters would fit in two bytes (the highest code point was 65,535), but it has since outgrown that limit, and now defines characters using code points up to 1,114,111. In programming languages such as Java, there is poor support for Unicode characters above 65,535, and they appear in the application as a *surrogate pair*: two char values that have to be processed as a pair. (Java 5 provides library support for higher codepoints, but the basic types char and String have not changed). In XPath, you don't have to worry about surrogate pairs. Each character, even those above 65,535, is counted as a single character. This affects functions such as string-length(), which counts the number of characters in a string, and substring(), which extracts the characters at particular positions in the string.

Strings may be compared using the «=» and «!=» operators, as well as «<», «>», «<=», and «>=». The exact way in which these work is context-dependent. Strings are always compared using a collation, and it is up to the collation to decide, for example, whether the two strings «naive» and «naïve» are equal or not (spot the difference). XPath itself doesn't define what the default collation is (and neither does XSLT), it leaves the choice to the user, and the way you select it is going to depend on the configuration options for your particular XSLT processor. If you want more control over the choice of a collation, you can use the compare() function, which is described in detail in Chapter 13 (see page 727).

The handling of the « < » and « > » operators is not backward compatible with XPath 1.0. In XPath 1.0, these operators, when applied to two strings, attempted to convert both strings to numbers, and compared them numerically. This meant, for example, that «"4" = "4.0"» was false (because they were compared as strings), while «"4" >= "4.0"» was true (because they were compared as numbers). In XPath 2.0, if you want to compare strings as numbers, you must convert them to numbers explicitly, for example by using the number() function.

The library of functions available for handling strings is considerably expanded from XPath 1.0. It includes:

❏ concat() and string-join() to concatenate strings with or without separators

❏ contains(), starts-with(), and ends-with() to test whether a string contains a particular substring

❏ substring(), substring-before(), and substring-after() to extract part of a string

❏ upper-case() and lower-case() to change the case of characters in a string

❏ string-length() to find the length of a string

❏ normalize-space() to remove unwanted leading, trailing, and inner whitespace characters

❏ normalize-unicode() to remove differences in the way equivalent Unicode characters are represented (for example, the letter «ç» with a cedilla can be represented as either one Unicode character or two)

Perhaps the most powerful addition to the string-handling capability in XPath 2.0 is the introduction of support for regular expressions, familiar to programmers using languages such as Perl. Regular expressions provide a powerful way of matching and manipulating the contents of a string. They are used in three functions:

❏ matches() tests whether a string matches a particular regular expression. For example, «matches("W151TBH", "^[A-Z][0-9]+[A-Z]+$")» returns true. (This regular expression matches any string consisting of one uppercase letter, then one or more digits, and then one or more letters.)

❏ replace() replaces the parts of a string that match a given regular expression with a replacement string. For example, «replace("W151TBH", "^[A-Z]([0-9]+)[A-Z]+$", "$1")» returns «151». The «$1» in the replacement string supplied as the third argument picks up the characters that were matched by the part of the regular expression written in parentheses.

❏ tokenize() splits a string into a sequence of strings, by treating any character sequence that matches the regular expression as a separator. For example, «tokenize("abc/123/x", "/")» returns the sequence «"abc", "123", "x"».

All these functions are described in detail in Chapter 13. The syntax of regular expressions is described in Chapter 14.

xs:time

The xs:time type represents a time of day, for example, 12:15:00. Like an xs:dateTime, it can represent the fractional number of seconds to an arbitrary precision determined by the implementation (at least three decimal digits are required), and it can optionally include a timezone. A time with a timezone is written, for example, as «12:15:00+01:00» to indicate a timezone one hour ahead of UTC (as used in much of continental Europe during the winter months, and in Britain during the summer).

Like `xs:date` and `xs:dateTime` values, `xs:time` values without an explicit timezone are assumed to apply to an implicit timezone taken from the evaluation context.

Operations you can perform on an `xs:time` include:

- ❑   Comparing and sorting times
- ❑   Converting times to and from strings
- ❑   Extracting the component parts of a time (hour, minutes, seconds, timezone)
- ❑   Adding a duration to a time (or subtracting a duration) to get another time
- ❑   Determining the difference between two times, as a duration
- ❑   Combining the time with a date to create an `xs:dateTime`
- ❑   Adjusting the timezone: that is, creating an equivalent time with or without a timezone, or with a different timezone (see the `adjust-time-to-timezone()` function on page 715)

Although timezones are complex enough already, one problem that the XPath model doesn't tackle is daylight savings time (also known as summer time). If you want to use `xs:time` values to represent, say, a schedule of flights departing from Logan Airport in Boston, then you probably want to use the value «`13:15:00`» to mean "a quarter past one, in Boston's time zone". Specifying this as «`13:15:00-05:00`» would be incorrect, because for half the year Boston is five hours behind UTC, and for the other half it is only four hours behind. My recommendation in this situation would be not to store a timezone with the value itself, but to use some other way of representing the information (for example, a `timezone` attribute on the containing element). Alternatively, it might be better to hold all times internally in UTC (sometimes called Zulu time) and only convert them to a local timezone for display purposes.

A particular problem that is unique to `xs:time` values is comparison and sorting, because the natural ordering is cyclic. For example, most people would agree that `18:00:00` is before `23:59:00`, but is it before `00:00:00`? And is `20:00:00-05:00` (8 p.m. in New York) before or after `00:30:00Z` (half past midnight in London)?

There is no correct answer to this question, but the rule that XPath has adopted is chosen to give the least number of surprises. The rule is to take an arbitrary date (the example used in the spec is 1972-12-31), and treat both times as representing `xs:dateTime` values on this date; then compare the resulting `xs:dateTime` values. So `18:00:00-05:00` (6 p.m. in New York) is before `22:00:00-05:00` (10 p.m. in New York) because `1972-12-31T18:00:00-05:00` was earlier than `1972-12-31T22:00:00-05:00`. Less predictably, `20:00:00-05:00` (8 p.m. in New York) is after `00:30:00Z` (half past midnight in London) because `1972-12-31T20:00:00-05:00` is the same instant as `1973-01-01T01:00:00Z`, which is well after `1972-12-31T00:30:00Z`.

xs:dayTimeDuration and xs:yearMonthDuration

XML Schema provides a primitive type `xs:duration`, which we will discuss briefly on page 208. A duration represents a period of time, expressed in years, months, days, hours, minutes, seconds, and fractions of a second.

Durations that mix these different units are difficult to handle because the length of a month is variable. For example, what should be the result of comparing a duration of one month with a duration of 30 days? XML Schema addresses this problem by defining a partial ordering for durations, which means that some durations are clearly longer than others, but for some pairs of durations (like the example just cited), the relative magnitude is undefined.

The idea of a partial ordering makes life rather difficult for a language like XPath. Operations like «=» and «<» need to produce a yes-or-no answer, introducing a "maybe" would complicate the language immensely. For this reason, XPath decided to introduce two new duration types, which are defined as subtypes of xs:duration. The xs:dayTimeDuration handles durations expressed in days, hours, minutes, seconds, and fractions of a second, while xs:yearMonthDuration handles durations in years and months. These behave much more cleanly: an xs:dayTimeDuration is just a decimal number of seconds, and an xs:yearMonthDuration is just an integer number of months.

You can manipulate these two duration subtypes using arithmetic operators and functions; for example, you can add and subtract two durations to give another duration, you can multiply or divide a duration by a number to get another duration, and you can divide one duration by another to get the ratio between the two durations as a number (more specifically, as an xs:double). You can also use functions such as sum() and avg() to get the total or average of a sequence of durations.

I personally prefer to use numbers for most of these operations. There's no reason why you can't use an xs:double to represent a duration in seconds, just as you would use one to represent a distance, a weight, a temperature or a voltage. Many calculations in fact become easier when you represent durations as numbers: for example, there is no way to divide a distance by a duration to obtain an average speed, except by converting the duration to a number. Similarly, if you want to work out how much to pay someone who has worked for five hours at $10/hour, it's no use multiplying the duration five hours by 10: the answer will be 2 days and 2 hours, not $50.

To convert a dayTimeDuration to a number of seconds, divide it by xs:dayTimeDuration('PT1S'). Similarly, to convert a number of seconds to a dayTimeDuration, multiply it by xs:dayTimeDuration ('PT1S').

Where the duration types do prove useful is when they are used in conjunction with dates and times. You can add a duration to a date or time to get another date or time, and you can subtract one date or time from another to get a duration.

Durations are written lexically in the notation defined by the ISO 8601 standard. The general form is the letter «P», followed by one or more of the components nY for the years, nM for the months, nD for days, nH for hours, nM for minutes, and nS for seconds. A «T» is used as a separator between the days and the hours. All the values are integers except for the seconds, which may be fractional. Zero components may be omitted (though at least one component must be present), and a negative duration may be written with a leading minus sign. So «P10Y6M» is 10 years 6 months, while «PT10H30M» is 10 hours, 30 minutes. XML Schema 1.0 treats the values «P12M» and «P1Y» as distinct (an enumeration facet that permits one of these forms will not permit the other), but XPath treats them as equal, and will not retain any distinction between the two forms when converting the typed value back to a string value. XML Schema 1.1 follows XPath by normalizing the values.

XPath provides no functions to format durations in a user-friendly output representation. Instead there are six functions years-from-duration(), months-from-duration(), days-from-duration(), hours-from-duration(), minutes-from-duration(), and seconds-from-duration(), which allow the components to be extracted. These will be the components after normalizing the value: for example if the duration is supplied as «P18M», then extracting the components will give you one year and six months. If the duration is negative, then all the components will be supplied as negative numbers.

The Minor Atomic Types

The previous section covered the major types of XPath 2.0, the ones that are well supported by functions and operators in the language: specifically, xs:anyURI, xs:boolean, xs:date, xs:dateTime, xs:decimal, xs:double, xs:integer, xs:QName, xs:string, xs:time, xs:dayTimeDuration, and xs:yearMonthDuration.

In this section I will briefly survey what I call the minor atomic types. These are defined as primitive types in XML Schema, but they are not well supported by XPath, and you are unlikely to use them very often. These are xs:gYear, xs:gYearMonth, xs:gMonth, xs:gMonthDay, xs:gDay, xs:duration, xs:float, xs:hexBinary, xs:base64Binary, and xs:NOTATION.

The Partial Date Types

This category refers to the five types xs:gYear, xs:gYearMonth, xs:gMonth, xs:gMonthDay, and xs:gDay. They essentially represent dates in which one or two of the components are missing.

It has to be said that these types have been treated with a certain amount of derision by commentators. I have heard them referred to as the *gHorribleKludge* types, or (after the pronunciation of "gDay"), the *Strine* types. I have rarely seen them used in real applications, and it does seem fairly extraordinary that these types, even if someone finds them useful, should be considered as primitive types on the same level as string, boolean, and double. For my part, if I want to design an XML database that includes information about the vintage years of my favorite wines, I think I can do it without using the xs:gYear type, let alone an xs:gYear with a timezone.

But for better or worse, they are there — so we might as well describe them and move on.

The lexical representation of these values follows ISO 8601 conventions, using hyphens to represent missing components. ISO 8601 does not allow timezones on these values; this is an extra addition by the XML Schema working group. The allowed formats are shown using examples in the table below.

Type	Without timezone	With timezone
xs:gYear	2008	2008+08:00
xs:gYearMonth	2008-07	2008-07+08:00
xs:gMonth	--07	--07+08:00
xs:gMonthDay	--07-31	--07-31+08:00
xs:gDay	---31	---31+08:00

For the xs:gYear and xs:gYearMonth types, an optional leading minus sign is allowed to indicate BC dates.

The format of xs:gMonth values was shown incorrectly in the original XML Schema Recommendation as «--MM--». The error was corrected in a subsequent erratum, but in the meantime it has found its way into many books on XML Schema and a number of software products.

XPath 2.0 allows conversion of these values to and from strings. It allows them to be compared with each other using the «=» and «!=» operators, but they cannot be sorted or compared using «<» and «>». Comparison uses the implicit timezone if the value itself has no timezone. This means that two xs:gYear values are not equal to each other if they are in different timezones. (If you ever come across an application that relies on this, let me know.)

XPath 2.0 also allows casting from an xs:dateTime or xs:date to any of these five types: the relevant components (including the timezone) are extracted, and the other components are discarded. The full rules for casting between different types are given in Chapter 11.

Binary Types

XML Schema supports two types for holding binary data (for example, images or sound clips). These are `xs:base64Binary` and `xs:hexBinary`. Binary data cannot be held in an XML document directly, so it is always encoded as characters, and these two types support the two most popular encodings.

Base 64 encoding is defined by reference to Internet mail standards in RFC 2045 (`http://www.ietf.org/rfc/rfc2045`), though the format was originally described in RFC 1421. The basic idea is that the binary stream is split into 24-bit chunks (3 bytes), and each chunk is then considered as four groups of 6 bits. Each 6-bit group is then considered to be the code representing a character in an alphabet of 64 characters, and this character is used to represent the value in the lexical representation. The 64-character alphabet consists of A–Z, a–z, 0–9, «+», and «/». One or more «=» characters may occur at the end to indicate padding to a whole number of 8-bit bytes, and newlines may appear to break up the total sequence (according to the RFC, the maximum line length is 76 characters).

The `hexBinary` encoding is simpler but less compact: it simply takes each octet of the binary stream, and represents it as two hexadecimal digits.

XPath 2.0 doesn't offer any very useful functionality for these two types. In particular, it doesn't provide you with any way to convert the values to or from an actual stream of octets. What you can do is to compare the values for equality, convert them to and from strings, and convert between the two types, in either direction. If you need more than that, Saxon offers some extension functions.

Single-Precision Floating Point

Unlike the other types that I've classified as minor, `xs:float` is well supported by functions and operators in XPath 2.0; in fact, any operator or function that can be applied to an `xs:double` can also be applied to an `xs:float`.

There is no numeric literal for `xs:float` values. You have to create them using a constructor function, for example «`xs:float(3.14159)`».

The real reason I have classified `xs:float` as a minor type is that I can't see any reason why anyone should want to use it. Compressing a floating-point number into 32 bits made sense in the 1960s, but it makes little sense nowadays, and the loss of precision when performing numeric calculations is far too severe for most applications to justify the space saving. The only justification I have heard for including this type in XML Schema is for compatibility with other (older) type systems such as SQL.

In XML Schema, `xs:float` is not defined as a subtype of `xs:double`. Its value space is a strict subset of `xs:double`, but the working group decided to make it a primitive type apparently because of the difficulty of defining the nature of the restriction, which would have required the invention of new facets. In XPath, however, `xs:float` can be considered for most practical purposes to be a subtype of `xs:double`. It won't pass explicit tests such as «`$F instance of xs:double`» that it would pass if it were a true subtype, but you can pass an `xs:float` value to any function or operator that expects an `xs:double`, and it will be converted automatically (this particular kind of conversion is referred to as numeric promotion).

When you mix `xs:float` and `xs:double` in a calculation, the result is `xs:double`. If you mix `xs:float` and `xs:decimal`, however, the result is `xs:float`.

The xs:duration Type

The `xs:duration` type is one of the primitive types in XML Schema, but as we've already seen, XPath decided to avoid the difficulties it posed by introducing the two subtypes `xs:yearMonthDuration` and xs:dayTimeDuration. You can still use the xs:duration type in your schema and in your documents, but there is relatively little support for it in XPath. You can compare one xs:duration to test whether it is equal to another, but you can't apply any ordering tests, and you can't perform any arithmetic operations. You can extract the components of the duration — it will be normalized so that P18 M is treated as one year six months, and PT36H is treated as one day 12 hours, but months will never be converted to days or vice versa. A few conversions are also allowed: you can convert a string to an xs:duration, and convert an xs:duration to a string. You can also convert an xs:duration to an xs:yearMonthDuration or xs:dayTimeDuration, which is done by removing the components that aren't applicable to the target type.

The xs:NOTATION Type

The xs:NOTATION type is perhaps the weirdest primitive type in the whole armory. It's provided to give backward compatibility with a rarely used feature in DTDs.

In a DTD you can define an unparsed entity like this:

```
<!ENTITY weather-map SYSTEM "weather.jpeg"
    PUBLIC "-//MEGACORP//WEATHER/" NDATA JPEG>
```

This example refers to a binary file weather.jpeg, and the NDATA part tells you that its format is JPEG. The keyword NDATA can be read as "Non-XML Data".

This declaration is only valid if JPEG is the name of a notation defined somewhere in the DTD, for example:

```
<!NOTATION JPEG SYSTEM "image/jpeg" >
<!NOTATION GIF SYSTEM "image/gif" >
```

The theory is that the system identifier tells the application what the name JPEG actually means. Unfortunately, there is no standardization of the URIs you can use here, so this doesn't work all that well in practice. I've used the registered media type (or MIME type) for JPEG as if it were a URI, but this isn't universal practice.

Elsewhere in the DTD you can define an attribute whose value is required to be one of a number of specified notations, for example:

```
<!ELEMENT map EMPTY>
<!ATTLIST map
    format NOTATION (JPEG|GIF) "JPEG"
    src ENTITY #REQUIRED
>
```

This defines an element, <map>, whose content is empty, and which has two attributes: a format attribute of type NOTATION, whose value must be JPEG or GIF, with the default being JPEG, and a src attribute, whose value must be the name of an unparsed entity defined in the DTD.

You can't actually declare unparsed entities in a schema (for that, you need to continue using a DTD), but you can declare attributes whose values must be entity names or notation names. The schema equivalent to the DTD declarations above would be:

```
<xs:notation name="JPEG" system="image/jpeg"/>
<xs:notation name="GIF" system="image/gif"/>
```

```
<xs:element name="map">
  <xs:complexType>
    <xs:attribute name="format" type="image-notation" default="JPEG"/>
    <xs:attribute name="src" type="xs:ENTITY"/>
  </xs:complexType>

<xs:simpleType name="image-notation">
  <xs:restriction base="xs:NOTATION">
    <xs:enumeration value="JPEG"/>
    <xs:enumeration value="GIF"/>
  </xs:restriction>
</xs:simpleType>
```

Note that you can't declare an attribute whose type is xs:NOTATION, it must be a subtype of xs:NOTATION that is restricted to a specific list of allowed values. This all mirrors the rules for use in DTDs, and is all designed to ensure that users whose document types make use of unparsed entities and notations aren't prevented from taking advantage of XML Schema.

Although notations were added to XML Schema for backward compatibility reasons, the schema working group added an extra feature: they made notation names namespace-aware. In the schema above, the notation name «JPEG» is interpreted as a local name defined within the target namespace of the containing schema. If the target namespace is anything other than the null namespace, then the notation name actually used in the source document (and in the <xs:enumeration> elements) will need to be qualified with a namespace prefix.

So, how is xs:NOTATION supported in XPath 2.0? The answer is, minimally. There are two things that are allowed:

❑   You can compare two xs:NOTATION values to see if they are equal, or not equal.

❑   You can cast an xs:NOTATION value to a string.

Casting a string to a subtype of xs:NOTATION (but not to xs:NOTATION itself) is allowed provided that the string is supplied as a literal, so that the operation can be done at compile time. There is no way of constructing an xs:NOTATION value dynamically within an XPath expression; the only way you can get one is by reading the content of an attribute whose type annotation is xs:NOTATION.

This completes our survey of the "minor" types: that is, the types that are defined in XML Schema as primitive types, but which have fairly specialized applications (to put it politely). The next two sections deal with the two families of derived types that are predefined in XML Schema: the derived numeric types, and the derived string types.

Derived Numeric Types

XML Schema defines a range of types defined by restriction from xs:integer. They differ in the range of values permitted. The following table summarizes these types, giving the permitted value range for each one.

Type	Value	Minimum	Maximum
xs:byte		−128	127
xs:int		−2147483648	2147483647
xs:long		-2^{63}	$2^{63}-1$
xs:negativeInteger		no minimum	−1
xs:nonNegativeInteger		0	no maximum
xs:nonPositiveInteger		no minimum	0
xs:positiveInteger		1	no maximum
xs:short		−32768	32767
xs:unsignedByte		0	255
xs:unsignedInt		0	4294967295
xs:unsignedLong		0	$2^{64}-1$
xs:unsignedShort		0	65535

The type hierarchy for these types is shown in Figure 5-2.

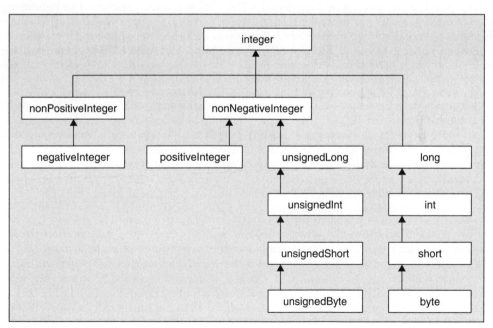

Figure 5-2

The range of values permitted in an xs:integer is unspecified. The specification says that at least 18 digits must be supported, but since the maximum value of an xs:unsignedLong is 18,446,744,073,709,551,615, it is clear that 18 digits is not actually sufficient. Some implementations (Saxon for example) allow arbitrary length integers.

I'm not a great enthusiast for these types. Their ranges are matched to the capacity of bits and bytes in the hardware, rather than to value ranges that actually occur in the real world. If you want to hold a percentage, and its value is an integer in the range 0 to 100, I would recommend defining a type with that specific range, rather than using an off-the-shelf type such as unsignedByte. This then leaves the question of which type to derive it from. There are 10 types in the above list that you could choose from. My own choice would be to derive it directly from xs:integer, on the grounds that any other choice is arbitrary. However, if you are using a data binding tool that generates Java or C# types equivalent to your schema types, then xs:int may work better.

As far as schema validation is concerned, it really doesn't matter very much what the type hierarchy is: if you define your percentage type with a minInclusive value of 0 and a maxInclusive value of 100, then the validator will do its work without needing to know what type it is derived from. When it comes to XPath processing, however, the type hierarchy starts to become more significant. For example, if a function is defined that accepts arguments of type xs:positiveInteger, then a value of type my:percentage will be accepted if my:percentage is derived by restriction from xs:positiveInteger, but not if my:percentage is derived from xs:int. The fact that every valid percentage is also a valid xs:int doesn't come into it; the value is substitutable only if the type is defined as a subtype of the required type in the type hierarchy.

In the standard function library, there are a number of functions that return integers, for example count(), position(), and month-from-Date(). There are also a few functions that require an integer as one of the arguments, for example, insert-before(), remove(), and round-half-to-even(). All these functions are described in Chapter 13. In all cases the type that appears in the function signature is xs:integer, rather than one of its subtypes. In many cases a subtype could have been used; for example, count() could have been defined to return an xs:nonNegativeInteger, while position() could have been defined to return xs:positiveInteger. But this wasn't done, and it's interesting to see why.

Firstly, consider functions that accept an integer as an argument, such as remove(). Here the integer represents the position of the item to be removed. This could have been defined as an xs:positiveInteger, because the only values that make sense are greater than zero (positions in a sequence are always numbered from one). But if this were done then the function call «remove($seq, 1)» would give a type error, on the curious grounds that 1 is not an xs:positiveInteger. This is because, when you supply a value in a context where a particular type is required, the type checking rules rely on the label attached to the value, they don't consider the value itself. The type label attached to the integer literal «1» is xs:integer, and xs:integer is not a subtype of xs:positiveInteger, so the call fails.

Secondly, consider functions that return an integer, such as month-from-date(). Here the result is always in the range 1 to 12. So the result could have been defined as an xs:byte or an xs:integer or an xs:positiveInteger or several other types. Alternatively, a new type, xs:month-value, could have been defined with the specific range 1 to 12. Defining it as xs:byte would have been helpful to people who want to use the returned value in a call to a function that expects an xs:byte, while defining it as an xs:positiveInteger would have helped people who want to call functions that expect that type. Defining a custom type just for this purpose would have been overkill. It's not possible to please everyone, so the plain vanilla type xs:integer was chosen to stay neutral.

The fact of the matter is that numeric ranges don't naturally fall into a hierarchy, and type checking by looking at the labels rather than the actual value doesn't work particularly well in this situation. Choosing a type such as xs:int may give performance advantages on some systems compared with xs:long, but they are likely to be miniscule. My advice would be either to define a type that reflects the actual semantics of the value, for example percentage or class-size or grade, or just use the generic type xs:integer. If you write general-purpose functions in XSLT or XQuery, then declare the expected type as xs:integer, and check the validity of the actual value within the code of your function.

> *Some people advocate defining numeric types for different units of measure; for example, inches or centimeters. If you find this useful to document the intended usage, then that's fine, but don't expect the type system to do anything clever with the values as a result. It won't stop you adding an inches value to a centimeters value, for example. My personal preference is to model units of measure as complex types, typically using an element whose content is the numeric value, and with a fixed, defaulted attribute to denote the unit of measure. Subtypes are designed to be used where values of the subtype are substitutable for values of the parent type, which means they aren't appropriate if you want to restrict the operations that are permissible.*

Derived String Types

As well as types derived from xs:integer, the repertoire of types that come as standard with XML Schema include a family of types derived from xs:string. The type hierarchy is shown in Figure 5-3.

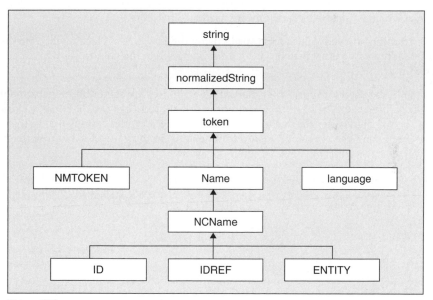

Figure 5-3

Most of these types restrict the set of characters that are allowed to appear in the string, but they also have other purposes:

❑   Some affect the way that whitespace within the value is normalized

❑   Some such as xs:ID and xs:IDREF trigger special validation rules that apply to the document as a whole

The processing of whitespace within an element or attribute value is controlled in XML Schema using the xs:whiteSpace facet on the type. There are three possible values: preserve, replace, and collapse. These work as follows:

❑   preserve leaves the value intact.

❑   replace replaces each tab, carriage return, or newline character with a single space.

❑   collapse removes leading and trailing whitespace, and replaces any sequence of internal white-space characters by a single space character. (*Whitespace* here means any of the characters x09, x0A, x0D, and x20, while *space* means the character x20.)

Validation of a source document against a schema only happens after XML parsing is complete, so this level of whitespace processing only comes into play after the XML parser has already done its work. The XML parser replaces any end-of-line sequence (for example, x0Dx0A) by a single newline character (x0A), unless it is written using character references such as «», and it also normalizes attribute values using the replace rule above. Specifying preserve in the schema won't stop the XML parser replacing tabs in an attribute value by spaces, unless you write them as «	».

In practice, you choose the whitespace processing you want not by specifying an explicit xs:whiteSpace facet, but by deriving your type definition from xs:string if you want preserve, xs:normalizedString if you want replace, and xs:token if you want collapse. (The type xs:token is a notorious misnomer, it actually represents a sequence of tokens separated by whitespace, and the assumption is that it makes no difference which whitespace characters are used as separators.)

You can restrict the allowed values for a string using the xs:pattern facet, which provides a regular expression that the value must match. The pattern is applied to the value after whitespace processing has been carried out.

Patterns can also be used for types other than strings, but they are rather blunt instruments. For example, if you try to define a subtype of xs:decimal with the pattern «[0-9]+\.[0-9]{2}», which states that there must be two digits after the decimal point, then any attempt to cast a value to this type is likely to fail — the system isn't clever enough to add trailing zeros to the value just because the pattern requires them.

Oddly, XML Schema doesn't define a type for strings in which spaces are not allowed, such as part numbers. It's often handy to define such a type as a user-defined type, from which many other application-oriented types can be derived. You can define it like this:

```
<xs:simpleType name="my:singleToken">
  <xs:restriction base="xs:token">
    <xs:pattern value="[^\s]+"/>
  </xs:restriction>
</xs:simpleType>
```

This pattern also restricts the value to contain at least one non-space character (a zero-length string is not allowed).

The meaning of each of the types is summarized in the table below.

Type	Usage
xs:string	Any sequence of characters, in which whitespace is significant.
xs:normalized-String	Any sequence of characters, in which whitespace acts as a separator, but no distinction is made between different whitespace characters.

continued

Type	Usage
xs:token	A sequence of tokens separated by whitespace.
xs:language	A value that follows the rules for the xml:lang attribute in XML.
xs:NMTOKEN	A sequence of characters classified as name characters in the XML specification. This includes letters, digits, «.», «-», «_», and «:», and a few other special characters.
xs:Name	An NMTOKEN that starts with a character classified as an initial name character in the XML specification. These include letters, «_», and «:».
xs:NCName	A Name that does not include a «:» (a no-colon-name).
xs:ID	The value of an ID can be any valid NCName, but it is constrained to be unique among all the ID values in a document.
xs:IDREF	The value of an IDREF can be any valid NCName, but it is constrained to be the same as some ID value somewhere in the same document.
xs:ENTITY	The value of an ENTITY can be any valid NCName, but it is constrained to the same as the name of an unparsed entity defined in the DTD.

XPath 2.0 doesn't handle any of these types specially; it just treats them as strings. If you try to cast a value to one of these types, it will first apply the whitespace rules for that type, and it will then check that the value conforms to the rules for the type. (This means for example, that calling «xs:token($s)» has pretty well the same effect as calling «normalize-space($s)»; the only difference is that in the first case, you end up with a value labeled as an xs:token, and in the second case, it is labeled xs:string.)

Confusingly, the normalize-space() function (which is carried forward from XPath 1.0 and is described in Chapter 13 of this book), *collapses* whitespace, while the xs:normalizedString type in XML Schema *replaces* whitespace.

The special validation rules for xs:ID, xs:IDREF, and xs:ENTITY are not invoked when you create atomic values of these types, as they only make sense in the context of validating an entire document.

This concludes our tour of the built-in atomic types defined in XML Schema. Before finishing, we need to look at the special type xs:untypedAtomic, and at the three list types xs:NMTOKENS, xs:IDREFS, and xs:ENTITIES.

Untyped Atomic Values

It might seem perverse to have a type called xs:untypedAtomic, but that's the way it is. This isn't a type defined by XML Schema, it is a type used to label data that hasn't been validated against an XML Schema.

XML is a technology whose unique strength is its ability to handle everything from completely unstructured data, through semi-structured data, to data that has a completely rigid and formal structure. XPath needs to work with XML documents that fit anywhere in this spectrum. Indeed, it's not unusual to find documents where one part is rigidly structured and another is completely free-form.

One way of handling this would be to say that everything that isn't known to have a specific type is simply labeled as a string. But to enable more accurate type checking of expressions and queries, the language designers wanted to be more precise than this, and to distinguish data that's known to be a string because it has been validated against a schema, from data that's handled as a string because we don't know any better.

The value space of xs:untypedAtomic is the same as that of xs:string; in other words, any sequence of Unicode characters permitted in XML can be held as an xs:untypedAtomic value. So in terms of the values they can represent, there's no difference between xs:untypedAtomic and xs:string. The difference is in how the values can be used.

xs:untypedAtomic is a chameleon type: it takes its behavior from the context in which it is used. If you use it where a number is expected, it behaves like a number; if you use it where a date is expected, it behaves like a date, and so on. This can cause errors, of course. If the actual value held in the xs:untypedAtomic value isn't a valid date, then using it as a date will fail.

In XPath 1.0, all data extracted from a source document was untyped in this sense. In some ways this makes life easy for the programmer, it means that you can do things like «@value + 2» without worrying about whether @value is a number or a string. But occasionally, this freedom can lead to confusion. For example, in XPath 1.0, «boolean(@value)» tests whether the value attribute exists; «boolean (string(@value))» tests whether it exists and is not an empty string, while «boolean(number (@value))» tests whether it exists and has a numeric value that is not zero. To make these kind of distinctions, you need to understand the differences between types.

With XPath 2.0, if your source documents have gone through schema validation, the elements and attributes will be annotated with a type. This label tells the system what operations are legitimate on the type, and may also be used to select different ways of implementing the same operation. For example, testing «@A < @B» will give different results depending on whether the attributes A and B have been defined in the schema as strings, numbers, or durations.

Data labeled as xs:untypedAtomic continues to behave as all data did in XPath 1.0; it has no intrinsic type of its own and is converted to whatever the default type is for the context in which it is used. If you supply an xs:untypedAtomic value as an argument to a function call, it is converted (cast) to the type defined in the function signature. If you use it as an operand of an arithmetic operator such as «+» then the system tries to convert it to a number (actually, an xs:double). If you use it as an operand of «=» or «<» then it first tries to convert it to the type of the other operand, which means that «@A > 4» and «@A > '4'» may give you different answers (if the attribute value is «10», for example, the first test will return true, the second false). If both operands are of type xs:untypedAtomic, then they will be compared using the rules for strings.

One thing that can trip you up if you aren't using schemas, and are therefore used to most of your data being untyped, is that the result of an operation is never untyped. This means, for example, that you can write «string-length(@chap-num)», and the value of @chap-num will be treated as an xs:string, which is what the string-length() function requires. You can also write «@chap-num + 1», and «@chap-num» will be treated as a number, which is what the «+» operator requires. But you can't write «string-length(@chap-num + 1)», because the result of «@chap-num + 1» is not untyped, it is an xs:double, and the string-length() function requires an xs:string. You have to do the conversion explicitly, like this: «string-length(string(@chap-num + 1))».

Values can be labeled as xs:untypedAtomic even when they come from a document that has been validated against a schema, if the validation rules in the schema caused that part of the document to be skipped. It will also happen when an element or attribute declaration in the schema does not define a type, or when the type is given as xs:anyType, xs:anySimpleType, or xs:anyAtomicType. This situation can arise with documents that are part rigid structure, part free-form.

Although untyped values arise most commonly when you extract the value of an unvalidated node in a source document, you can also construct an untyped value explicitly, in the same way as any other atomic value, by using a constructor function or cast. For example, the function call «`xs:untypedAtomic(@date)`» extracts the value of the `@date` attribute, and returns an untyped value regardless whether the original attribute was labeled as a date, as a string, or as something else. This technique can be useful if you need to process data that might or might not have been validated, or if you want to exploit the chameleon nature of `xs:untypedAtomic` data by using the value both as a string and as a date.

xs:NMTOKENS, xs:IDREFS, and xs:ENTITIES

This section of the chapter is about atomic types, but it would not be complete without mentioning the three built-in types defined in XML Schema that are not atomic, namely `xs:NMTOKENS`, `xs:IDREFS`, and `xs:ENTITIES`. These all reflect attribute types that were defined in DTDs, and are carried forward into XML Schema to make transition from DTDs to schemas as painless as possible.

In the sense of XML Schema, these are list types rather than atomic types. XML Schema distinguishes complex types, which can contain elements and attributes, from simple types which can't. Simple types can be defined in three ways: directly by restricting an existing simple type, by list, which allows a list of values drawn from a simple type, or by union, which allows a choice of values from two or more different simple types. But when it comes down to actual values, an instance of a simple type is either a single atomic value or a list of atomic values. Single atomic values correspond directly to atomic values in the XPath data model, as described in the previous chapter, while lists of atomic values correspond to sequences.

If an element or attribute is defined in the schema to have a list type such as `xs:NMTOKENS`, then after validation the element or attribute node will have a type annotation of `xs:NMTOKENS`. But when an XPath expression reads the content of the element or attribute node (a process called atomization), the result is not a single value of type `xs:NMTOKENS`, but a sequence of values, each of which is an atomic value labeled as an `xs:NMTOKEN`.

For example, you can test an attribute to see whether it is of type `xs:NMTOKENS` like this:

```
if (@A instance of attribute(*, xs:NMTOKENS)) ...
```

or you can test its value to see if it is a sequence of `xs:NMTOKEN` values like this:

```
if (data(@A) instance of xs:NMTOKEN * ) ...
```

What you cannot do is to test the attribute node against the sequence type «`xs:NMTOKEN*`», or the value contained in the attribute against the list type «`xs:NMTOKENS`». Both will give you syntax errors if you attempt them. For more information on using the «`instance of`» operator to test the type of a value, see Chapter 11.

Schema Types and XPath Types

The preceding discussion about list types demonstrates that while the XPath type system is based on XML Schema, the types defined in XML Schema are not exactly the same thing as the types that XPath values can take. This is best illustrated by looking at the two type hierarchies and seeing how they compare. The type hierarchy in XML Schema is shown in Figure 5-4.

This type hierarchy contains all the types that can be used as type annotations on nodes. The boxes that are shown unshaded are concrete types, so they can be used directly; the shaded boxes are abstract types,

Types

which can only be used via their subtypes. Some of the abstract types are named, which means you can refer to them in an XPath expression (for example you can write «element(*, xs:anySimpleType)» which will match any element whose type annotation shows that its type is a simple type). Others are unnamed, which means you cannot refer to them directly.

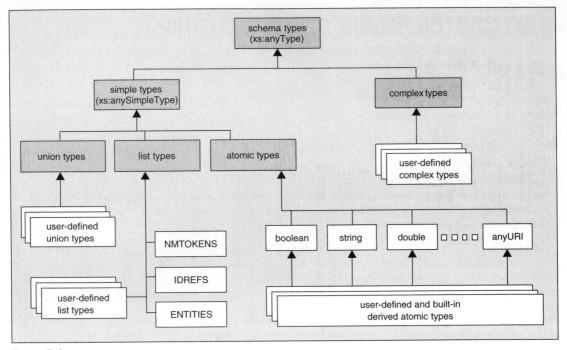

Figure 5-4

There is another type hierarchy, which represents the types of XPath items. This type hierarchy is shown in Figure 5-5.

This reflects the structure we described at the start of the chapter: every item in an XPath sequence is either a node or an atomic value; there are seven kinds of node, and the atomic types are either the built-in atomic types defined in the XML Schema specification, or user-defined atomic types.

Comparing these two diagrams:

❑ Atomic types appear in both. Atomic types can be used either as annotations on nodes, or as the type of a freestanding XPath item.

❑ Complex types, list types, and union types appear on the first diagram, but not the second. These types can be used as node annotations, but you can never have a freestanding XPath item that belongs directly to one of these types.

❑ Node kinds appear on the second diagram only. You can have an item in an XPath sequence that is an element or a comment or a processing instruction, but these types never appear as type annotations on element or attribute nodes.

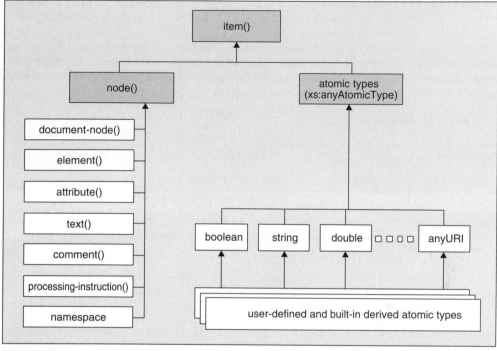

Figure 5-5

It's a little unfortunate that the boxes on both these diagrams are all referred to as types, when we are actually dealing with two different (but overlapping) categories: I call the first category *schema types* and the second category *item types*. The W3C specification for functions and operators attempts to depict both of these categories on a single type hierarchy diagram, but in my view this is likely to confuse more people than it enlightens. Apart from anything else, when you do this you find that xs:anyAtomicType, which appears on both diagrams, has two different supertypes.

Item types and schema types are used in different ways in XPath:

❑ You can test whether an item $V belongs to a particular item type T by writing «$V instance of T».

❑ You can test whether a node $N has a type annotation that is a particular schema type S by writing «$N instance of attribute(*, S)» or «$N instance of element(*, S)».

Because atomic types such as xs:integer belong to both categories, they can be used in either of these two ways. But item types such as «comment()» can only be used in the first of these roles, while non-atomic schema types such as xs:IDREFS can only be used in the second role.

The Type Matching Rules

The purpose of a type system in a language, as we saw, is to define which operations are legitimate for which types of value. In this section we will examine the way that XPath defines these rules.

Types

It's easiest to start with the rules for function calling. XPath expressions can call functions written in XSLT or XQuery, as well as the functions provided in the core function library that comes with the language. Each of these functions has a signature, which defines the types of each of the arguments expected by the function. The rules described in this section define whether or not a particular value can be used in a function call, given a particular type used in the function signature. It turns out that the rules are exactly the same as those for binding values to variables in XSLT (the "weak conversions" that we introduced in Chapter 2, page 81).

For example, the signature of the function `remove()` is given in Chapter 13 as follows:

Argument	Type	Meaning
sequence	`item()*`	The input sequence
position	`xs:integer`	The position of the item to be removed
Result	`item()*`	A sequence containing all the items in the input sequence except the item at the specified position

This shows that the function expects two arguments. The names of the arguments are irrelevant: these names are purely for reference within the documentation, they are not used in an actual function call. The important thing here is the type expected for each argument.

The first argument has a type of «`item()*`». There are two parts to this: the item type and the cardinality. The item type in this case is «`item()`», which is the most general item type of all, and accepts any node or atomic value. The cardinality is «`*`», which means that the argument can be a sequence containing zero, one or more items. Taken together, this means that the first argument of `remove()` can be any sequence whatsoever.

The second argument has a type of `xs:integer`. There is no cardinality specified, which means that the default cardinality is used: the effect of this is that the sequence supplied as the argument value must contain exactly one item. The item type for this argument is `xs:integer`, which means that the supplied value must be an atomic value labeled as an `xs:integer`, or as a subtype of `xs:integer` (for example, it might be labeled as an `xs:positiveInteger`). Supplying any other value would lead to a type error, which might be reported either when the expression is compiled or when it is subsequently evaluated.

Actually, the type system is not quite as rigid as this. Instead of supplying an `xs:integer` for the second argument, you can also supply:

❏ An untyped atomic value, provided that it takes a form that can be converted to an integer

❏ A node, provided that the typed value of the node is either an `xs:integer`, or an untyped atomic value

However, you cannot supply a string (even a string that obviously contains an integer, such as `"17"`), and you cannot supply a value of a different numeric type, such as `xs:decimal` or `xs:double`. You can use an `xs:integer` where an `xs:double` is expected, but not the other way around.

When the function call expects an atomic value and the supplied value is a node, the system goes through a process called *atomization* to extract the typed value of the node. Atomization is applied to the supplied value (a sequence) to produce a derived value (the atomized sequence). The rules are:

❏ Any atomic value in the supplied sequence is added to the atomized sequence unchanged.

❑ For any node in the supplied sequence, the typed value is extracted, as described in Chapter 2 (see page 52). The typed value is in general a sequence of zero or more atomic values, and the values in this sequence are added to the atomized sequence. If the node has not been validated against a schema, these atomic values will be untyped (they will have the type label `xs:untypedAtomic`); if they have been validated, they are likely to have some other type such as `xs:integer` or `xs:date`.

❑ For some kinds of node, extracting a typed value is not possible: specifically, this is true for elements that are labeled with a type that has complex element-only content. Supplying such a node where the function expects an atomic value is an error, and the XPath evaluation will fail.

The atomized sequence is then checked against the type given in the function signature. The cardinality of the sequence as a whole must match the cardinality constraints given in the function signature, and each item in the sequence must match the item type given.

The detailed syntax for describing the allowed type of each function argument is given in Chapter 11, where it is referred to as a sequence type descriptor. The detailed rules for deciding whether a particular value is allowed as an argument to a function call, and the way it is converted to the required type when necessary, are given in Chapter 7, in the section describing function calls on page 544.

Function calls are not the only place where a value needs to be checked against a required type. We've already seen that the same rules apply to XSLT variables and parameters. Many of the XPath operators, such as «+», «-», and «|», also have rules saying what type of operands are acceptable. These rules are based on the rules for function calls, but they are slightly different because XPath allows operators to be polymorphic: that is, the same operator can mean different things depending on the types of the arguments supplied. This is not currently allowed for function calls. For each operator, the rules are therefore slightly different, and they are described in this book in the section dealing with each operator. The non-trivial examples are the «=» family of operators and the arithmetic operators, which are all described in Chapter 8.

> *XQuery chose not to use the function calling rules for variable assignment, but instead applies a stricter criterion. When you write in XQuery «`let $x as xs:integer* := my:function(12)`», the result of «`my:function(12)`» must actually be a sequence of integers; no conversions such as atomization, or casting of untyped atomic values, are permitted in this context.*

Static and Dynamic Type Checking

As I said in the introduction to this chapter, one of the major purposes of the type system in a programming language is to enable programming errors to be detected and corrected. The best time to do this, where possible, is at compile time.

Very often, you will compile and execute an XSLT stylesheet, or an individual XPath expression, as a single indivisible operation. You may therefore feel that there isn't much difference between detecting an error at compile time and detecting it at runtime. Indeed, if you use XPath expressions from a programming language such as Java, it's likely that the XPath expressions won't be compiled until the Java program is executed, so in a sense all errors become runtime errors. However, there is still a big difference, because an error that's detected at compile time doesn't depend on the input data. This means that it will be reported every time you process the XPath expression, which means it can't remain lurking in the code until some chance condition in the data reveals a latent bug that got through all your tests.

I had a real-life example of this recently. In Chapter 20, there is a stylesheet whose task is to perform a knight's tour of the chessboard: a tour, starting from a user-specified square, in which the knight visits every square on the chessboard exactly once. I published an XSLT 1.0 version of this stylesheet in an earlier edition of this book, and I have also written an XQuery 1.0 version, which is published with the Saxon software distribution. Part of the algorithm involves backtracking when the knight gets stuck in a blind alley; however, I never found a way of testing the backtracking, because in every case I tried, the knight got all the way around the board without ever getting stuck. In fact, I said in the book that although I couldn't prove it, I believed that the backtracking code would never be invoked.

Three years after I first wrote the code, one of my readers discovered that if the knight starts on square f1, it gets stuck on move 58 and has to retrace its steps. The same user has since reported that this is the only starting square where this happens. The way he made the discovery was that in the XQuery version of the algorithm, the backtracking code was wrong. I had coded two arguments to a function call the wrong way around, and when the function call was executed, this was detected, because one of the values had the wrong type. So type checking detected the error, but static type checking (that is, compile time checking) could potentially have detected it three years earlier.

But static type checking also has a downside: it makes it much harder to cope with unpredictable data. With strict static type checking, every expression must satisfy the compiler that it can never fail at runtime with a type error. Let's see what happens if, for example, you have a price attribute whose value is either a decimal number, or the string «N/A». You can define this in XML Schema as follows:

```
<xs:attribute name="price">
  <xs:simpleType>
    <xs:union memberTypes="xs:decimal price-NA"/>
  </xs:simpleType>
</xs:attribute>

<xs:simpleType name="price-NA">
  <xs:restriction base="xs:string">
    <xs:enumeration value="N/A"/>
  </xs:restriction>
</xs:simpleType>
```

Now let's suppose that you want to find the average price of those products where the price is known. Your first attempt might look like this:

```
avg( product/@price[. != "N/A"] )
```

This looks sensible, but under strict static type checking, it will fail to compile. There are two reasons. Firstly, you can't compare a number with a string, so the expression «. != "N/A"» isn't allowed, on the grounds that the value of «.» (that is, the typed value of the price attribute) might be a number. Secondly, although you and I can tell that all the attributes that get through the filter in square brackets will be numeric, the compiler isn't so clever, and will report an error on the grounds that some of the items in the sequence being averaged might be strings rather than numbers.

The first of these two errors will be reported even if type checking is delayed until runtime, so in this case the static type checker has done us a service by reporting the error before it happened. The second error is a false alarm. At runtime, all the attribute values being averaged will actually be numeric, so the error of including a string in the sequence will never occur.

This example is designed to illustrate that static type checking is a mixed blessing. It will detect some errors early, but it will also report many false alarms. The more you are dealing with unpredictable or semi-structured data, the more frequent the false alarms will become. With highly structured data, static type checking can be a great help in enabling you to write error-free code; but with loosely structured data, it can become a pain in the neck. Because XML is designed to handle such a wide spectrum of different kinds of data, the language designers therefore decided that static type checking should be optional.

Whether you use static or dynamic type checking, the first error in our example above will need to be corrected. One way to do this is to force the value of the attribute to be converted to a string before the comparison, like this:

```
avg(product/@price[string(.) != "N/A"])
```

For the other error (the false alarm) we don't need to take any further action in the case of a system that only does dynamic type checking. However, if we want the expression also to work with systems that do static type checking, we will need to change it. The simplest approach seems to be:

```
avg(product/xs:decimal(@price[string(.) != "N/A"]))
```

The cast to xs:decimal here doesn't actually do anything at runtime, because the operand will always be an xs:decimal already. But it keeps the static type checker happy, because the system can now tell at compile time that the values input to the avg() function will all be xs:decimal values.

Looking back at the example:

```
avg(product/@price[. != "N/A"])
```

it might have occurred to you that under XPath 1.0, apart from the fact that the avg() function was not available, this would have worked quite happily, with neither static or dynamic errors. That's because XPath 1.0 treated all data in source documents as being untyped. You could compare the value of an attribute to a string, and it would treat it as a string, and you could then take an average, and it would treat the same value as a number. You can do the same thing in XPath 2.0, simply by switching off schema processing: if there is no schema, or if you switch off schema processing, then the attributes are going to be treated as xs:untypedAtomic values, and will adapt themselves to whatever operation you want to perform, just as with XPath 1.0. If you like this way of working, there is nothing to stop you carrying on this way. However, you should be aware of the consequences: many programming errors in XPath 1.0 go undetected, or are very difficult to debug, because the system in effect tries to guess what you meant, and it sometimes guesses wrong. For example, if you compare a string to a number using the «=» operator, XPath 1.0 guesses that you wanted a string comparison (so «4 = "04"» is false), while if you compare a string to a number using the « <= » operator, XPath 1.0 guesses that a numeric comparison was intended (so «4 <= "04"» is true). Sooner or later, this is going to trip you up. With a schema-aware XPath 2.0 processor, you have to be explicit about whether you want a string comparison or a numeric comparison, by explicitly converting one of the operands to the type of the other.

The XPath 2.0 Recommendation distinguishes static type checking from dynamic type checking. A product that offers static type checking is pessimistic: it assumes that if things can go wrong, they will go wrong. For example, if the operand of «+» is known at compile time to be either a string or an integer, the compiler will report a failure, because the pessimistic assumption is that sooner or later, the actual value of the operand will turn out to be a string. Remember that XPath 2.0 can be used in many environments other than XSLT. The XSLT specification largely assumes that implementors won't choose to provide pessimistic static typing, though it's not entirely ruled out.

In XSLT I think you are more likely to encounter a half-way house, which I will call *optimistic* static type checking. Here, you will only get an error message at compile time if the system knows that an expression cannot possibly succeed. An example of such an expression is:

```
current-date() = "2004-01-01"
```

Here the operand on the left will always be an `xs:date`, and the operand on the right will always be an `xs:string`. Comparison of a date to a string can never succeed, so even an optimistic type checker can report the error at compile time. To correct the error, you need to write:

```
current-date() = xs:date("2004-01-01")
```

It's worth pointing out that neither static nor dynamic type checking can catch all errors. Going back to my knight's tour where two parameters to a function call were coded in the wrong order, the error was only caught because the two arguments had different types. If both arguments had had a type of `xs:integer`, say, the function call would have succeeded, and the query would have gone on to produce garbage output.

A great deal depends in practice on how carefully you specify your types. Specifying the types of function parameters and of variables is done at the XSLT level, and it is this type information that forms the basis of the type checking performed by the XPath processor. If you choose not to specify any types at all, this is rather like declaring every Java variable or function with the generic type `Object`: you will get no compile time errors but an awful lot of runtime errors. I find that it's good programming discipline always to declare the types of variables and of function arguments. However, it's generally best to avoid over-constraining them. It can be tempting to declare types such as `xs:positiveInteger`, rather than `xs:integer`, if the value will always be positive; but as we've seen, this doesn't just constrain the value to be positive; it means that it actually has to be labeled as an `xs:positiveInteger`. The value represented by the XPath numeric literal «3» is an `xs:integer`, but it is not an `xs:positiveInteger`, because it has the wrong type label. So I tend to steer clear of using such types, because they create too much inconvenience.

Summary

The type system is probably the most innovative and the most controversial aspect of XPath 2.0, and it is very different in concept from the type system of XPath 1.0. We started this chapter with a brief rationale for introducing a type system based on XML Schema, and we ended the chapter with a discussion of the different forms of type checking that XPath 2.0 processor can apply, and some hints and tips to enable you to choose the right options.

In between, we looked in detail at each of the built-in atomic types defined in the XML Schema specification. We then saw how the type hierarchy in XML Schema relates to the type hierarchy in the XPath data model: they are strongly related, but they are not the same thing.

We also outlined how the type checking rules operate when calling an XPath function.

We're now moving into the section of the book that provides detailed reference information for each construct in the XSLT and XPath languages. Until now you may well have been reading the book sequentially. The next chapter, however, is a long one — it contains a detailed alphabetical reference of all the XSLT elements you can use in a stylesheet — and I would suggest that rather than reading it from start to finish, you dip into the sections describing the specific instructions that you need to understand.

Part II
XSLT and XPath Reference

6

XSLT Elements

This chapter provides an alphabetical list of reference entries, one for each of the XSLT elements. Each entry gives:

❑ A short description of the purpose of the element

❑ *Changes in 2.0*: A quick summary of changes to this element since XSLT 1.0

❑ *Format*: A pro forma summary of the format, defining where the element may appear in the stylesheet, what its permitted attributes are, and what its content (child elements) may be

❑ *Effect*: A definition of the formal rules defining how this element behaves

❑ *Usage*: A section giving usage advice on how to exploit this XSLT element

❑ *Examples*: Coding examples of the element, showing the context in which it might be used (where appropriate, the *Usage* and *Examples* sections are merged into one)

❑ *See also*: Cross-references to other related constructs

The *Format* section for each element includes a syntax skeleton designed to provide a quick reminder of the names and types of the attributes and any constraints on the context. The format of this is designed to be intuitive: it only gives a summary of the rules, because you will find these in full in the *Position*, *Attributes*, and *Content* sections that follow.

There are a number of specialized terms used in this chapter, and it is worth becoming familiar with them before you get in too deeply. There are fuller explanations in Chapters 2 and 3, and the descriptions in the following table are really intended just as a quick memory-jogger.

For a more comprehensive definition of terms, refer to the glossary.

Term	Description
attribute value template	An attribute whose value may contain expressions nested with curly braces, for example «url="../{$href}"». The term *template* here has nothing to do with any other kind of template in XSLT. Embedded expressions may only be used in an attribute value (or are only recognized as such) if the attribute is one that is explicitly designated as an attribute value template. Attribute value templates are described in more detail in Chapter 3, page 122.

continued

Term	Description
document order	An ordering of the nodes in the source tree that corresponds to the order in which the corresponding items appeared in the source XML document: an element precedes its children, and the children are ordered as they appeared in the source.
expression	Many XSLT elements have attributes whose value is an *expression*. This always means an XPath expression: a full definition of XPath Expressions is given in Chapters 7 to 11, and a summary is given in Appendix A. An expression returns a value, which may be any sequence of items (nodes, atomic values, or a mixture of the two). These types are described fully in Chapter 2.
Extension instructions	Any element used in a sequence: specifically, an XSLT instruction, a literal result element, or an extension element. The `<xsl:if>` element is an instruction, but `<xsl:strip-space>` isn't, because `<xsl:if>` appears in a sequence constructor and `<xsl:strip-space>` doesn't. Extension instructions are described in Chapter 3, page 111.
literal result element	An element in the stylesheet, used in a *sequence constructor*, which is copied to the output document: for example (if you are generating HTML) `<p>` or `<td>`. Literal result elements are described in Chapter 3, page 112.
pattern	Some XSLT elements have attributes whose value must be a pattern. The syntax of patterns is defined in Chapter 12. A pattern is a test that can be applied to nodes to see if they match. For example, the pattern «title» matches all `<title>` elements, and the pattern «text()» matches all text nodes.
lexical QName	An XML name, optionally qualified by a namespace prefix. Examples of lexical QNames with no prefix are «color» and «date-due». Examples of prefixed QNames are «xsl:choose» and «html:table». The adjective *lexical* is used to distinguish a QName in this form from a value of type `xs:QName`, which contains a namespace URI and a local name. Where the lexical QName has a prefix, this must always match a namespace declaration that is in scope at the place in the stylesheet where the QName is used. For more information on namespaces see Chapter 2, page 58.
stylesheet	In general, references to the *stylesheet* mean the principal stylesheet module plus all the stylesheet modules incorporated into it using `<xsl:include>` and `<xsl:import>` elements. When I want to refer to one of these components individually, I call it a *stylesheet module*.
sequence constructor	A sequence of instructions and literal result elements contained within (that is, that are children of) another XSLT element. Many XSLT elements, such as `<xsl:template>`, `<xsl:if>`, and `<xsl:variable>`, have a sequence constructor as their content.
SequenceType	A number of XSLT elements take an «as» attribute whose value is a `SequenceType`. This is a sequence type descriptor such as «xs:integer*», or «node()?», or «element(part,*)». The syntax for sequence type descriptors is given in Chapter 11.
template rule	An `<xsl:template>` element that has a `match` attribute.
XSLT element	Any of the standard elements in the XSLT namespace listed in this chapter, for example `<xsl:template>` or `<xsl:if>`.

The elements in this chapter are listed alphabetically rather than on functional lines, for ease of reference. This is fine when you know what you are looking for, but if you are using this book as your introduction to XSLT, it does create the problem that related things won't be found together. And if you try to read sequentially, you'll start with `<xsl:analyze-string>`, which is not one of the instructions that you are likely to use every day of the week.

So here's an attempt at some kind of ordering and grouping, to suggest which entries you might look at first if you're new to the subject. The following table includes all the more common elements, but leaves out a few that can only be classified as "miscellanous".

Grouping	Elements

Elements defining the structure of the stylesheet	`<xsl:stylesheet>`
	`<xsl:include>`
	`<xsl:import>`
	`<xsl:import-schema>`

Elements used to define template rules and functions and control the way they are invoked	`<xsl:template>`
	`<xsl:apply-imports>`
	`<xsl:apply-templates>`
	`<xsl:call-template>`
	`<xsl:function>`
	`<xsl:next-match>`

Elements used to create nodes	`<xsl:element>`
	`<xsl:attribute>`
	`<xsl:comment>`
	`<xsl:document>`
	`<xsl:namespace>`
	`<xsl:processing-instruction>`
	`<xsl:text>`
	`<xsl:value-of>`

Elements used to define variables and parameters	`<xsl:variable>`
	`<xsl:param>`
	`<xsl:with-param>`

Elements used to copy information from the source document to the result	`<xsl:copy>` `<xsl:copy-of>`

Elements used for conditional processing and iteration	`<xsl:if>`
	`<xsl:choose>`
	`<xsl:when>`
	`<xsl:otherwise>`
	`<xsl:for-each>`
	`<xsl:for-each-group>`

Elements to control sorting, searching, and numbering	`<xsl:perform-sort>`
	`<xsl:sort>`
	`<xsl:number>`
	`<xsl:key>`
	`<xsl:decimal-format>`

Elements used to control the output of the stylesheet	`<xsl:output>`
	`<xsl:result-document>`
	`<xsl:character-map>`
	`<xsl:output-character>`

xsl:analyze-string

The `<xsl:analyze-string>` instruction is used to process an input string using a regular expression (often abbreviated to *regex*). It is useful where the source document contains text whose structure is not fully marked up using XML elements and attributes, but has its own internal syntax. For example, the value of an attribute might be a list of numbers separated by commas.

I use the term *regex* to refer to regular expressions in this section, because it helps to avoid any confusion with XPath expressions.

Changes in 2.0

This instruction is new in XSLT 2.0.

Format

```
<xsl:analyze-string
  select = expression
  regex = { string }
  flags? = { string }>
  <!-- Content: (xsl:matching-substring?,
                 xsl:non-matching-substring?,
                 xsl:fallback*) -->
</xsl:analyze-string>
```

Position

`<xsl:analyze-string>` is an instruction, and it is always used within a sequence constructor.

Attributes

Name	Value	Meaning
select mandatory	XPath Expression	The input string to be analyzed using the regex. A type error occurs if the value of the expression cannot be converted to a string using the standard conversion rules described on page 505.
regex mandatory	Attribute value template returning a regular expression, as defined below	The regular expression (regex) used to analyze the string. See warning below regarding curly braces.
flags optional	Attribute value template returning regex flags, as defined below	Flags controlling how the regex is interpreted. Omitting the attribute is equivalent to supplying a zero-length string (no special flags).

The construct *expression* (meaning an XPath expression) is defined in Chapter 7.

The syntax of regular expressions permitted in the `regex` attribute is the same as the syntax accepted by the functions `matches()`, `replace()`, and `tokenize()` in XPath 2.0. This is described fully in Chapter 14, and is summarized below. It is based on the syntax used for regular expressions in XML Schema, with some extensions.

> **Warning: The `regex` attribute is an attribute value template. This makes it possible to construct the regex at runtime, using an XPath expression. For example, the regex can be supplied as a stylesheet parameter. The downside of this is that curly braces within the attribute value must be doubled if they are to be treated as part of the regex, rather than having their special meaning for attribute value templates. For example, to match a sequence of three digits, write «regex="[0-9]{{3}}"».**

The `flags` attribute controls how the regex is to be interpreted. Four flags are defined, each denoted by a single letter, and they can be written in any order. Like the `regex` attribute, `flags` may be written as an attribute value template. The meaning of the flags is defined in detail in Chapter 14 and is summarized below.

Flag	Meaning
i	Selects case-insensitive mode. In simple terms, this means that «X» and «x» will match each other.
m	Selects multiline mode. In this mode, the metacharacters «^» and «$» match the beginning and end of each line; otherwise, they match the beginning and end of the entire string.
s	Selects dot-all mode. In this mode the metacharacter «.» matches any character, whereas normally it matches any character except a newline (x0A).
x	Allows whitespace to be used as an insignificant separator within the regex.

Content

Either an `<xsl:matching-substring>` element or an `<xsl:non-matching-substring>` element, or one of each in that order. Followed by zero or more `<xsl:fallback>` elements.

An XSLT 2.0 processor will ignore any `<xsl:fallback>` instructions; they are allowed so that a stylesheet can specify fallback actions to be taken by an XSLT 1.0 processor when it encounters this element, if it is working in forward-compatible mode.

The elements `<xsl:matching-substring>` and `<xsl:non-matching-substring>` take no attributes, and their content is in each case a sequence constructor.

Effect

The XPath expression given in the `select` attribute is evaluated and provides the input string to be matched by the regex. A type error occurs if the value of this expression can't be converted to a string using the standard conversion rules described on page 505.

The regex must not be one that matches a zero-length string. This rules out values such as «regex=""» or «regex="[0-9]*"». The reason for this rule is that languages such as Perl have different ways of handling this situation, none of which are completely satisfactory, and which are sensitive to additional parameters such as `limit`, which XSLT chose not to provide.

The input string is formed by evaluating the `select` expression, and the processor then analyzes this string to find all substrings that match the regex. The substrings that match the regex are processed using the instructions within the `<xsl:matching-substring>` element, while the intervening substrings are processed using the instructions in the `<xsl:non-matching-substring>` element. For example, if the regex is «[0-9]+», then any consecutive sequence of digits in the input string is passed to the <xsl:matching-substring> element, and any consecutive sequence of non-digits is passed to the <xsl:non-matching-substring> element.

Within the <xsl:matching-substring> or <xsl:non-matching-substring> element, the substring in question can be referenced as the context item, using the XPath expression «.». It is also possible within the <xsl:matching-substring> element to refer to the substrings that matched particular parts of the regex: see *Captured Groups* below.

Because the instruction changes the context item, it's often useful to bind a variable to the context node before entering the instruction, so that you can refer to it within the <xsl:matching-substring> and <xsl:non-matching-substring> elements. If you forget to do this, a likely consequence is an error message along the lines "the context item is not a node".

Neither a matching substring nor a nonmatching substring will ever be zero-length. This means that if two matching substrings are adjacent to each other in the input string, there will be two consecutive calls on the <xsl:matching-substring> element, with no intervening call on the <xsl:non-matching-substring> element.

Omitting either the <xsl:matching-substring> element or the <xsl:non-matching-substring> element causes the relevant substring to be discarded (no output is produced in respect of this substring).

In working its way through the input string, the processor always looks for the first match that it can find. That is, it looks first for a match starting at the first character of the input string, then for a match starting at the second character, and so on. There are several situations that can result in several candidate matches occurring at the same position (that is, starting with the same character in the input). The rules that apply are:

❏   The quantifiers «*» and «+» are *greedy*: They match as many characters as they can, consistent with the regular expression as a whole succeeding. For example, given the input «Here [1] or there [2]», the regex «\[.*\]» will match the string «[1] or there [2]».

❏   The quantifiers «*?» and «+?» are *non-greedy*: They match as few characters as they can, consistent with the regular expression as a whole succeeding. For example, given the input «Here [1] or there [2]», the regex «\[.*?\]» will match the strings «[1]» and «[2]».

❏   When there are two alternatives that both match at the same position in the input string, the first alternative is preferred, regardless of its length. For example, given the input «size=5.2», the regular expression «[0-9]+|[0-9]*\.[0-9]*» will match «5» rather than «5.2».

Regular Expression Syntax

The regular expression syntax accepted in the regex attribute is the same as that accepted by the match(), tokenize(), and replace() functions, and it is fully described in Chapter 14. This section provides a quick summary only; it makes no attempt to define details such as precedence rules.

The following table summarizes the more important constructs found in a regex. In this summary, capital letters A and B represent arbitrary regular expressions. n and m represent a number (a sequence of digits). a, b, c represent an arbitrary character, which is either a normal character, or one of the metacharacters «.», «\», «?», «*», «+», «{», «}», «(», «)», «[» or «]» escaped by preceding it with a backslash «\», or one of the symbols «\n», «\r», «\t» representing a newline, carriage return, or tab, respectively.

Construct	Matches a string S if . . .
A|B	S matches either A or B.
AB	The first part of S matches A and the rest matches B.
A?	S either matches A or is empty.
A*	S is a sequence of zero or more strings that each match A.
A+	S is a sequence of one or more strings that each match A.
A{n,m}	S is a sequence of between n and m strings that each match A.
A{n,}	S is a sequence of n or more strings that each match A.
A{n}	S is a sequence of exactly n strings that each match A.
Q?	Where Q is one of the regular expressions described in the previous six rows: matches the same strings as Q, but using nongreedy matching.
(A)	S matches A.
c	S consists of the single character c.
[abc]	S consists of one of the characters a, b, or c.
[^abc]	S consists of a single character that is not one of a, b, or c.
[a-b]	S is a character whose Unicode codepoint is in the range a to b.
\p{prop}	S is a character that has property prop in the Unicode database.
\P{prop}	S is a character that does not have property prop in the Unicode database.
.	S is any single character (in dot-all mode) or any single character other than a newline (when not in dot-all mode).
\s	S is a single space, tab, newline, or carriage return.
\S	S is a character that does not match \s.
\i	S is a character that can appear at the start of an XML Name.
\I	S is a character that does not match \i.
\c	S is a character that can appear in an XML Name.
\C	S is a character that does not match \c.
\d	S is a character classified in Unicode as a digit.
\D	S is a character that does not match \d.
\w	S is a character that does not match \W.
\W	S is a character that is classified in Unicode as a punctuation, separator, or "other" character.
^	Matches the start of the input string, or the start of a line if in multiline mode.
$	Matches the end of the input string, or the end of a line if in multiline mode.

6

XSLT Elements

The most useful properties that may be specified in the «\p» and «\P» constructs are described below; for a full list see Chapter 14.

Property	Meaning
L	All letters.
Lu	Uppercase letters, for example, A, B, Š, Σ.
Ll	Lowercase letters, for example, a, b, ñ, λ.
N	All numbers.
P	Punctuation (full stop, comma, semicolon, and so on).
Z	Separators (for example, space, newline, no-breaking space, en space, em space).
S	Symbols (for example, currency symbols, mathematical symbols, dingbats, and musical symbols).

Captured Groups

Within the `<xsl:matching-substring>` element, it is possible to refer to the substring that matched the regular expression as «.», because it is provided as the context item. Sometimes, however, it is useful to be able to determine the strings that matched particular parts of the regular expression.

Any subexpression of the regular expression that is enclosed in parentheses causes the string that it matches to be available as a *captured group*. For example, if the regex «([0-9]+)([A-Z]+)([0-9]+)» is used to match the string «13DEC1987», then the three captured groups will be «13», «DEC», and «1987». If the regular expression were written instead as «([0-9]+)([A-Z]+([0-9]+))», then the three captured groups would be «13», «DEC1987», and «1987». The subexpression that starts with the *n*th left parenthesis in the regular expression delivers the *n*th captured group in the result.

Some parenthesized subexpressions might not match any part of the string. For example, if the regex «([0-9]+)|([A-Z]+)» is used to match the string «12», the first captured subgroup will be «12» and the second will be empty.

A parenthesized subexpression might also match more than one substring. For example, if the regex «([0-9]+)(,[0-9]+)*» is used to match the string «12,13,14», then the second part in parentheses matches both «,13» and «,14». In this case only the last one is captured. The first captured group in this example will be «12», and the second will be «,14».

While the `<xsl:matching-substring>` element is being evaluated, the captured groups found during the regular expression match are available using the `regex-group()` function. This takes an integer argument, which is the number of the captured group that is required. If there is no corresponding subexpression in the regular expression, or if that subexpression didn't match anything, the result is a zero-length string.

Usage and Examples

Many tasks that require regex processing can be accomplished using the three functions in the core function library (see Chapter 13) that use regular expressions: `matches()`, `replace()`, and `tokenize()`. These are used as follows:

Function	Purpose
matches()	Tests whether a string matches a given regular expression
replace()	Replaces the parts of a string that match a given regular expression with a different string
tokenize()	Splits a string into a sequence of substrings, by finding occurrences of a separator that matches a given regular expression

There are many ways to use these functions in an XSLT stylesheet. For example, you might write a template rule that matches customers with a customer number in the form 999-AAAA-99 (this might be the only way, for example, that you can recognize customers acquired as a result of a corporate takeover). Write this as:

```
<xsl:template
  match="customer[matches(cust-nr, '^[0-9]{3}-[A-Z]{4}-[0-9]{2}$')]">
```

There is no need to double the curly braces in this example. The match attribute of <xsl:template> is not an attribute value template, so curly braces have no special significance.

The <xsl:analyze-string> instruction is more powerful (but also more complex) than any of these three functions. In particular, none of the three XPath functions can produce new elements or other nodes. The <xsl:analyze-string> instruction can do so, which makes it very useful when you want to find a non-XML structure in the source text (for example, the comma-separated list of numbers mentioned earlier) and convert it into an XML representation (a sequence of elements, say). This is sometimes called up-conversion.

There are two main ways of using <xsl:analyze-string>, which I will describe as single-match and multiple-match applications. I shall give an example of each.

A Single-Match Example

In the single-match use of <xsl:analyze-string>, a regex is supplied that is designed to match the entire input string. The purpose is to extract and process the various parts of the string using the captured groups. This is all done within the <xsl:matching-substring> child element, which is only invoked once. The <xsl:non-matching-substring> element is used only to define error handling, to deal with the case where the input doesn't match the expected format.

For example, suppose you want to display a date as 13th March 2008. To achieve this, you need to generate the output «13thMarch 2008» (or rather, text nodes and element nodes corresponding to this serial XML representation). You can achieve the basic date formatting using the format-date() function described in Chapter 13, but to add the markup you need to post-process the output of this function.

Here is the code (for the full stylesheet see single-match.xsl in the download archive):

```
<xsl:analyze-string
          select="format-date(current-date(), '[D1o] #[MNn] #[Y]')"
          regex="^([0-9]+)([a-z]+)#([A-Z][a-z]+)#(.*)$">
  <xsl:matching-substring>
```

```
            <xsl:value-of select="regex-group(1)"/>
            <sup><i><xsl:value-of select="regex-group(2)"/></i></sup>
            <xsl:text> </xsl:text>
            <xsl:value-of select="regex-group(3)"/>
            <xsl:text> </xsl:text>
            <xsl:value-of select="regex-group(4)"/>
        </xsl:matching-substring>
        <xsl:non-matching-substring>
            <xsl:value-of select="."/>
        </xsl:non-matching-substring>
    </xsl:analyze-string>
```

Note that the regex is anchored (it starts with «^» and ends with «$») to force it to match the whole input string. Unlike regex expressions used in the pattern facet in XML Schema, a regex used in the `<xsl:analyze-string>` instruction is not implicitly anchored.

In this example I chose in the `<xsl:non-matching-substring>` to output the whole date as returned by `format-date()`, without any markup. This error might occur, for example, because the stylesheet is being run in a locale that uses an unexpected representation of ordinal numbers. The alternative would be to call `<xsl:message>` to report an error and perhaps terminate.

A Multiple-Match Example

In a multiple-match application, you supply a regular expression that will match the input string repeatedly, breaking it into a sequence of substrings. There are two main ways you can design this:

1. Match the parts of the string that you are interested in. For example, the regex «[0-9]+» will match any sequence of consecutive digits, and pass it to the `<xsl:matching-substring>` element to be processed. The characters that separate groups of digits are passed to the `<xsl:non-matching-substring>` element, if there is one (you might choose to ignore them completely).

There is a variant of this approach that is useful where there are no separators as such. For example, you might be dealing with a format such as the one used for ISO 8601 durations, which look like this: «P12H30M10S», with the requirement to split out the components «12H», «30M», and «10S». The regex «[0-9]+[A-Z]» will achieve this, passing each component to the `<xsl:matching-substring>` element in turn.

2. Match the separators between the parts of the string that you are interested in. For example, if the string uses a comma as a separator, the regex «,\s*» will match any comma followed optionally by spaces. The fields that appear between the commas will be passed, one at a time, to the `<xsl:non-matching-substring>` element, while the separators (if you want to look at them at all) are passed to the `<xsl:matching-substring>` element.

The following example (`multiple-match.xsl`) blends these techniques. It analyzes an XPath expression and lists all the variable names that it references. The regex chosen is one that matches things you're interested in (the variable names), but it also uses parentheses to provide access to a captured group from which the leading «$» sign is left out. It's not an industrial-quality solution to this problem; for example, it doesn't try to ignore the content of comments and string literals. But it does allow for the fact that a space is permitted between the «$» sign and the variable name. You can extend it to handle these extra challenges if you like. (And if you are really keen, you can extend it to extract the namespace prefix from the variable name, and look up the corresponding namespace URI using the `get-namespace-uri-for-prefix()` function.)

```
<xsl:analyze-string select="$param" regex="\$\s*(\i\c*)">
    <xsl:matching-substring>
        <ref><xsl:value-of select="regex-group(1)"/></ref>
    </xsl:matching-substring>
</xsl:analyze-string>
```

Note in this example that a «$» sign used to represent itself must be escaped using a backslash, and that we are taking advantage of the rather specialized regex constructs «\i» and «\c» to match an XML name. The output is a sequence of `<ref>` elements containing the names of the referenced variables.

See Also

<xsl:matching-substring> on page 386
<xsl:non-matching-substring> on page 402
matches() on page 828 (Chapter 13)
replace() on page 862 (Chapter 13)
tokenize() on page 894 (Chapter 13)
regex-group() on page 860 (Chapter 13)
Regular expression syntax, Chapter 14

xsl:apply-imports

The `<xsl:apply-imports>` instruction is used in conjunction with imported stylesheets. A template rule in one stylesheet module can override a template rule in an imported stylesheet module. Sometimes, you want to supplement the functionality of the rule in the imported module, not to replace it entirely. `<xsl:apply-imports>` is provided so that the overriding template rule can invoke the overridden template rule in the imported module.

There is a clear analogy here with object-oriented programming. Writing a stylesheet module that imports another is like writing a subclass, whose methods override the methods of the superclass. `<xsl:apply-imports>` behaves analogously to the `super()` function in object-oriented programming languages, allowing the functionality of the superclass to be incorporated in the functionality of the subclass.

Changes in 2.0

In XSLT 2.0, the instruction is extended to allow parameters to be passed using enclosed `<xsl:with-param>` elements.

XSLT 2.0 also introduces a new `<xsl:next-match>` instruction, which will often be a more suitable solution in situations where `<xsl:apply-imports>` might have previously been used.

Format

```
<xsl:apply-imports>
    <!-- Content: xsl:with-param* -->
</xsl:apply-imports>
```

Position

`<xsl:apply-imports>` is an instruction, and it is always used within a sequence constructor.

Attributes

None.

Content

The element may be empty, or it may contain one or more `<xsl:with-param>` elements.

Effect

`<xsl:apply-imports>` relies on the concept of a *current template rule*. A template rule becomes the current template rule when it is invoked using `<xsl:apply-templates>`, `<xsl:apply-imports>`, or `<xsl:next-match>`. Using `<xsl:call-template>` does not change the current template rule. However, using `<xsl:for-each>` makes the current template rule null, until such time as the `<xsl:for-each>` terminates, when the previous value is reinstated. The current template rule is also null while global variables and attribute sets are being evaluated.

Closely associated with this is the *current mode*. When a template rule is invoked using `<xsl:apply-templates>`, the mode specified on the `<xsl:apply-templates/>` instruction becomes the current mode (if no mode is named, then the default unnamed mode becomes the current mode). The current mode reverts to the default (unnamed) mode when a stylesheet function is called.

`<xsl:apply-imports>` searches for a template rule that matches the current node, using the same search rules as `<xsl:apply-templates>`, but considering only those template rules that (a) match the current mode and (b) are defined in a stylesheet module that was imported into the stylesheet module containing the current template rule. For details of import precedence, see `<xsl:import>` on page 357. If no template rule is found, the built-in template rule is used (see page 243).

Note that the instruction doesn't examine all template rules with lower precedence than the current rule. For an example that illustrates this, see Figure 6-4 on page 360. If the current template rule is in module C on that diagram, then `<xsl:apply-imports>` will search for rules in module H, but not in modules B, D, F, or G: although those modules have lower import precedence than C, they were not imported into C.

> *The specification defines what this means in terms of the import tree. If a stylesheet module A includes another module B using `<xsl:include>`, then A and B are part of the same stylesheet level. If any module in stylesheet level L imports a module in stylesheet level M, then M is a child of L in the import tree. The template rules that are considered are those that are defined in a stylesheet level that is a descendent of the stylesheet level containing the current template rule.*

It is possible to specify parameters to be supplied to the called template, using `<xsl:with-param>` elements contained within the `<xsl:apply-imports>` element. These work in the same way as parameters for `<xsl:call-template>` and `<xsl:apply-templates>`; if the name of the supplied parameter matches the name of an `<xsl:param>` element within the called template, the parameter will take that value; otherwise, it will take the default value supplied in the `<xsl:param>` element. It is not an error to supply parameters that don't match any `<xsl:param>` element in the called template rule, they will simply be ignored. However, if the called template specifies any parameters with «required="yes"», then a runtime error occurs if no value is supplied for that parameter.

Usage and Examples

The intended usage pattern behind `<xsl:apply-imports>` is illustrated by the following example.

One stylesheet, `a.xsl`, contains general-purpose rules for rendering elements. For example, it might contain a general-purpose template rule for displaying dates, given as follows:

```
<xsl:template match="date">
   <xsl:value-of select="day"/>
   <xsl:text>/</xsl:text>
   <xsl:value-of select="month"/>
   <xsl:text>/</xsl:text>
   <xsl:value-of select="year"/>
</xsl:template>
```

A second stylesheet, `b.xsl`, contains special-purpose rules for rendering elements. For example, you might want it to display dates that occur in a particular context in the same way, but in bold face. It could be written as:

```
<xsl:template match="timeline/date">
   <b>
   <xsl:value-of select="day"/>
   <xsl:text>/</xsl:text>
   <xsl:value-of select="month"/>
   <xsl:text>/</xsl:text>
   <xsl:value-of select="year"/>
   </b>
</xsl:template>
```

However, this involves duplicating most of the original template rule, which is a bad idea from a maintenance point of view. So, in `b.xsl` we could import `a.xsl`, and write instead:

```
<xsl:import href="a.xsl"/>
<xsl:template match="timeline/date">
   <b>
   <xsl:apply-imports/>
   </b>
</xsl:template>
```

Note that the facility only allows a template rule to invoke one of lower *import precedence*, not one of lower *priority*. The import precedence depends on how the stylesheet module was loaded, as explained under `<xsl:import>` on page 357. The priority can be specified individually for each template rule, as explained under `<xsl:template>` on page 483. The code above will work only if the «timeline/date» template rule is in a stylesheet module that directly or indirectly imports the «date» template rule. It will not work, for example, if they are in the same module but defined with different priority. In this respect, `<xsl:apply-imports>` differs from `<xsl:next-match>`.

In many situations the same effect can be achieved equally well by giving the general-purpose template rule a name and invoking it from the special-purpose template rule by using `<xsl:call-template>` (see page 271). But this approach doesn't work if you want one rule that overrides or supplements many others. One example I encountered was a developer who had a working stylesheet but wanted to add the rule "output an HTML `<a>` tag for any source element that has an `anchor` attribute." Rather than modifying every rule in the existing stylesheet, this can be achieved by defining a new stylesheet module that imports the original one, and contains the single rule:

```
<xsl:template match="*[@anchor]">
  <a name="{@anchor}"/>
  <xsl:apply-imports/>
</xsl:template>
```

There is a more complete example of the use of `<xsl:apply-imports>` in the section for `<xsl:import>`.

See Also

`<xsl:import>` on page 357
`<xsl:next-match>` on page 399
`<xsl:param>` on page 425
`<xsl:with-param>` on page 517

xsl:apply-templates

The `<xsl:apply-templates>` instruction defines a set of nodes to be processed and causes the system to process them by selecting an appropriate template rule for each one.

Changes in 2.0

The `mode` attribute may now take the value «#current» to continue processing in the current mode.

Built-in template rules now pass parameters through unchanged.

Format

```
<xsl:apply-templates
  select? = expression
  mode? = token>
  <!-- Content: (xsl:sort | xsl:with-param)* -->
</xsl:apply-templates>
```

Position

`<xsl:apply-templates>` is an instruction, and it is always used within a sequence constructor.

Attributes

Name	Value	Meaning
select optional	XPath Expression	The sequence of nodes to be processed. If omitted, all children of the context node are processed.
mode optional	Lexical QName or «#current»	The processing mode. Template rules used to process the selected nodes must have a matching mode. If omitted, the default (unnamed) mode is used. The value «#current» indicates that the current mode should be used.

Content

Zero or more `<xsl:sort>` elements and zero or more `<xsl:with-param>` elements, in any order.

Effect

The `<xsl:apply-templates>` element selects a sequence of nodes in the input tree and processes each of them individually by finding a matching template rule for that node. The sequence of nodes is determined by the `select` attribute; the order in which they are processed is determined by the `<xsl:sort>` elements (if present); and the parameters passed to the template rules are determined by the `<xsl:with-param>` elements (if present). The behavior is explained in detail in the following sections.

The select Attribute

If the `select` attribute is present, the *expression* defines the nodes that will be processed. This must be an XPath expression that returns a sequence of (zero or more) nodes. For example, `<xsl:apply-templates select="*"/>` selects the element nodes that are children of the context node. Writing `<xsl:apply-templates select="@width+3"/>` would cause a type error, because the value of the expression is a number, not a sequence of nodes.

The expression may select nodes relative to the context node (the node currently being processed), as in the example above. Alternatively, it may make an absolute selection from the root node (for example `<xsl:apply-templates select="//item"/>`), or it may simply select the nodes by reference to a variable initialized earlier (for example `<xsl:apply-templates select="$sales-figures"/>`).

If the `select` attribute is omitted, the nodes processed will be the children of the context node: that is, the elements, text nodes, comments, and processing instructions that occur directly within the context node. It's then an error if the context item isn't a node. Text nodes that consist only of whitespace will be processed along with the others, unless they have been stripped from the tree; for details, see `<xsl:strip-space>` on page 465. In the XDM tree model (described in Chapter 2) attribute nodes and namespace nodes are *not* regarded as children of the containing element, so they are not processed: If you want to process attribute nodes, you must include an explicit `select` attribute; for example, `<xsl:apply-templates select="@*"/>`. However, it is more usual to get the attribute values directly using the `<xsl:value-of>` instruction, described on page 495.

For each node in the selected sequence, in turn, one template rule is selected and the sequence constructor contained in its body is evaluated. In general, there may be a different template rule for each selected node. Within this sequence constructor, this node becomes the new context node, so it can be referred to using the XPath expression «.».

The called template can also discover the relative position of this node within the list of nodes selected for processing: specifically, it can use the `position()` function to give the position of that node in the list of nodes being processed (the first node processed has `position()`=1, and so on), and the `last()` function to give the number of nodes in the list being processed. These two functions are described in detail in Chapter 13. They enable the called template to output sequence numbers for the nodes as they are processed, or to take different action for the first and the last nodes, or perhaps to use different background colors for odd-numbered and even-numbered nodes.

Sorting

If there are no child `<xsl:sort>` instructions, the selected items are processed in the order of the sequence produced by evaluating the `select` expression. If the `select` expression is a path expression, the nodes will be in *document order*. In the normal case where the nodes all come from the same input document this means they will be processed in the order they are encountered in the original source document; for example, an element node is processed before its children. Attribute nodes belonging to the same element, however, may be processed in any order, because the order of attributes in XML is not considered significant. If there are nodes from several different documents in the sequence, which can happen when you use the `document()` function (described in Chapter 13, page 754), the relative order of nodes from different documents is not defined, though it is consistent if the same set of nodes is processed more than once.

> *The direction of the axis used to select the nodes is irrelevant. (The direction of different axes is described in Chapter 9.) For example, «select="preceding-sibling::*"» will process the preceding siblings of the current node in document order (starting with the first sibling) even though the preceding-sibling axis is in reverse document order. The axis direction affects only the meaning of any positional qualifiers used within the select expression. For example, «select="preceding-sibling::*[1]"» will select the first preceding sibling element in the direction of the axis, which is the element immediately before the current node, if there is one.*

Although most XPath expressions return nodes in document order, not all do so. For example, the expression «title, author, publisher» returns a sequence containing first the child title elements, then the child author elements, and then the child publisher elements of the context node, regardless of the order that these nodes appear in the source document. The nodes returned by the XPath expression will be processed in the order of the sequence that is returned, not necessarily in document order.

If there are one or more <xsl:sort> instructions as children of the <xsl:apply-templates> instruction, the selected nodes are sorted before processing. Each <xsl:sort> instruction defines one sort key. For details of how sorting is controlled, see <xsl:sort> on page 455. If there are several sort keys defined, they apply in major-to-minor order. For example, if the first <xsl:sort> defines sorting by country and the second by state, the selected nodes will be processed in order of state within country. If two selected nodes have equal sort keys (or if the same node is included more than once in the sequence), they will be processed in the order that they appeared in the original result of the select expression, unless the first <xsl:sort> element specifies «stable="no"», in which case there are no guarantees.

Choosing a Template Rule

For each node to be processed, a template rule is selected. The choice of a template rule is made independently for each selected node; they may all be processed by the same template rule, or a different template rule may be chosen for each one.

The template rule selected for processing a node will always be either an <xsl:template> element with a match attribute, or a built-in template rule provided by the XSLT processor.

An <xsl:template> element will be used to process a node only if it has a matching *mode*: That is, the mode attribute of the <xsl:apply-templates> element must match the mode attribute of the <xsl:template> element. An <xsl:template> element can define a list of modes that it matches, or it can specify «#all» to indicate that it matches all modes. If the <xsl:template> element has no mode attribute, or if its mode attribute includes the keyword «#default», then the template rule matches the default mode, which is the mode that is used when <xsl:apply-templates> has no mode attribute. If the mode name contains a namespace prefix, it is the namespace URI that must match, not necessarily the prefix itself. Alternatively, the <xsl:apply-templates> instruction can specify «mode="#current"» to continue processing in the current mode. This is useful when the instruction is contained in a template rule that can be invoked in a number of different modes. The concept of the *current mode* is explained more fully in the section for <xsl:apply-imports>.

Note that if the mode attribute is omitted, it makes no difference what mode was originally used to select the template rule containing the <xsl:apply-templates> instruction. The mode is not sticky; it reverts to the default mode as soon as <xsl:apply-templates> is used with no mode attribute. If you want to continue processing in the current mode, either specify the mode explicitly, or set «mode="#current"».

An `<xsl:template>` element will be used to process a node only if the node matches the pattern defined in the `match` attribute of the `<xsl:template>` element.

If there is more than one `<xsl:template>` element that matches a selected node, one of them is selected based on its *import precedence* and *priority*, as detailed under `<xsl:template>` on page 483.

If there is no `<xsl:template>` element that matches a selected node, a built-in template rule is used. The action of the built-in template rule depends on the kind of node, as follows:

Node Kind	Action of Built-In Template Rule
Document node Element node	Call `apply-templates` to process each child of the selected node, using the mode specified on the call to `<xsl:apply-templates>`. This is done as if the contents of the template were `<xsl:apply-templates mode="#current"/>`. The parameters passed in the call of `<xsl:apply-templates>` are passed transparently through the built-in template to the template rules for the child elements.
Text node Attribute node	Copy the string value of the node to the result sequence, as a text node. This is done as if the contents of the template were `<xsl:value-of select="string(.)">`.
Comment node Processing Instruction Namespace node	No action.

For the document node and for element nodes, the built-in template rule processes the children of the selected node in document order, matching each one against the available template rules as if the template body contained an explicit `<xsl:apply-templates>` element with no `select` attribute. Unlike the situation with explicit template rules, the mode is sticky; it is carried through automatically to the template rules that are called. So if you execute `<xsl:apply-templates mode="m"/>` for an element that has no matching template rule, the built-in template rule will execute `<xsl:apply-templates mode="m"/>` for each of its children. This process can, of course, recurse to process the grandchildren, and so on.

In XSLT 2.0, the built-in template rules not only pass on the mode they were called with, they also pass on their parameters. This is a change from XSLT 1.0.

Parameters

If there are any `<xsl:with-param>` elements present as children of the `<xsl:apply-templates>` element, they define parameters that are made available to the called template rules. The same parameters are made available to each template rule that is evaluated, even though different template rules may be invoked to process different nodes in the list.

Each `<xsl:with-param>` element is evaluated in the same way as an `<xsl:variable>` element, as described on page 500. Specifically:

❑ If it has a `select` attribute, this is evaluated as an XPath expression.

❑ If there is no `select` attribute and the `<xsl:with-param>` element is empty, the value is a zero-length string, unless there is an «as» attribute, in which case it is an empty sequence.

❏   Otherwise, the value of the parameter is determined by evaluating the sequence constructor contained within the `<xsl:with-param>` element. If there is an «as» attribute, this sequence forms the value of the parameter; if not, a temporary document is constructed from this sequence, and the document node is passed as the value of the parameter. Tree-valued variables are described under `<xsl:variable>` on page 500.

If the `<xsl:with-param>` element has an «as» attribute, then the value of the parameter must match the type specified in this attribute, and if necessary the value is converted to this type using the standard conversion rules described on page 505. In theory it is possible for a parameter value to be converted twice, first to the type defined on the `<xsl:with-param>` element and then to the type defined on the corresponding `<xsl:param>` element.

It is not defined whether the parameter is evaluated once only or whether it is evaluated repeatedly, once for each node in the sequence. If the value isn't needed (for example, because the `select` expression selected no nodes or because none of the nodes matches a template that uses this parameter) then it isn't defined whether the parameter is evaluated at all. Usually this doesn't matter, because evaluating the parameter repeatedly will have exactly the same effect each time. But it's something to watch out for if the parameter is evaluated by calling an extension function that has a side effect, such as reading the next record from a database.

If the name of a child `<xsl:with-param>` element matches the name of an `<xsl:param>` element in the selected template rule, then the value of the `<xsl:with-param>` element is assigned to the relevant `<xsl:param>` variable name.

If the `<xsl:with-param>` element specifies «tunnel="yes"», then the parameter is available not only to the immediately called templates, but to templates at any depth in the call stack, provided they declare the parameter with `<xsl:param tunnel="yes"/>` and a matching name. Tunnel parameters are described more fully on page 429.

If there is a child `<xsl:with-param>` element that does not match the name of any `<xsl:param>` element in the selected template rule, then it is ignored. This is not treated as an error.

If there is an `<xsl:param>` element in the selected template rule with no matching `<xsl:with-param>` element in the `<xsl:apply-templates>` element, then the parameter is given a default value: see `<xsl:param>` on page 425 for details. This is an error only if the `<xsl:param>` element specifies «required="yes"».

If the selected template rule is a built-in rule, then any parameters that are supplied are passed on to any template rules called by the built-in rule, in the same way that the mode is passed on. This is a change from XSLT 1.0. For example, consider:

```
<xsl:template match="section">
<ol>
  <xsl:apply-templates>
    <xsl:with-param name="in-section" select="true()"/>
  </xsl:apply-templates>
</ol>
</xsl:template>

<xsl:template match="clause">
  <xsl:param name="in-section" select="false()"/>
  ...
</xsl:template>
```

When a `<clause>` is contained directly within a `<section>`, the parameter `$in-section` will of course take the value «true» as expected. If there is an intervening element, with no explicit template rule, so that the `<clause>` is the grandchild of the `<section>` element, the `<clause>` template rule will still be invoked, and the parameter `$in-section` will still have the value «true». The reason is that the built-in template rule for the intermediate element calls `<xsl:apply-templates>` to process its `<clause>` children, supplying all the parameters that were supplied when it itself was invoked.

Result

The result of evaluating the `<xsl:apply-templates>` instruction is an arbitrary sequence, which may include both nodes and atomic values. This sequence is formed by concatenating the sequences produced by each of the template rules that is invoked. These sequences are concatenated in the order of the selected nodes (after any sorting), so that if the selected nodes after sorting were (A, B, C), and the template rule for node A generates the sequence T(A), then the final result sequence is (T(A), T(B), T(C)).

This doesn't mean that the XSLT processor has to process the nodes sequentially. It can process them in any order it likes, or in parallel, as long as it assembles the results in the right order at the end.

Usually, `<xsl:apply-templates>` is used to produce a sequence of nodes that become siblings in the result tree. This is what happens when `<xsl:apply-templates>`, or any other instruction, is used in the sequence constructor within an element such as an `<xsl:element>` instruction or a literal result element. But `<xsl:apply-templates>` is not confined to such uses. For example, the following code (which is written to take an XSLT stylesheet as input) uses `<xsl:apply-templates>` to decide in which version of XSLT the current element was first introduced:

```
<xsl:template match="*">
  <xsl:variable name="version" as="xs:decimal">
    <xsl:apply-templates select="." mode="get-version"/>
  </xsl:variable>
  <xsl:if test="$version=2.0">
    ...
  </xsl:if>
</xsl:template>

<xsl:template mode="get-version" as="xs:decimal"
      match="xsl:analyze-string | xsl:for-each-group |
        xsl:character-map | xsl:next-match | ...">
  <xsl:sequence select="2.0"/>
</xsl:template>

<xsl:template mode="get-version" as="xs:decimal" match="*">
  <xsl:sequence select="1.0"/>
</xsl:template>
```

In this example, the result returned by `<xsl:apply-templates>` is a single decimal number.

Note that it's quite legitimate to use `<xsl:apply-templates>` within the body of a global variable definition, for example:

```
<xsl:variable name="table-of-contents">
  <xsl:apply-templates mode="toc"/>
</xsl:variable>
```

In this situation the context node is taken as the root of the principal source document, so the `<xsl:apply-templates>` processes the children of the root node. If the transformation is invoked without supplying a principal source document, this causes a runtime error. There will also be an error reported if a template rule that is invoked attempts to access the value of the global variable currently being defined: This kind of error is referred to in the specification as a *circularity*.

Usage and Examples

First, some simple examples are given below.

Construct	Effect
`<xsl:apply-templates/>`	Processes all the children of the context node
`<xsl:apply-templates` `    select="para"/>`	Processes all the `<para>` elements that are children of the context node
`<xsl:apply-templates` `    select="//*" mode="toc"/>`	Processes every element in the document in mode «toc»

`<xsl:apply-templates`
`    select="para">`
`  <xsl:with-param name="indent"`
`    select="$n+4"/>`
`</xsl:apply-templates>`
	Process all the `<para>` elements that are children of the context node, setting the value of the indent parameter in each called template to the value of the variable $n plus 4

`<xsl:apply-templates`
`    select="//book">`
`  <xsl:sort select="@isbn"/>`
`</xsl:apply-templates>`
	Process all the `<book>` elements in the document, sorting them in ascending order of their isbn attribute

The following sections give some hints and tips about using `<xsl:apply-templates>`. First, I'll discuss when to use `<xsl:apply-templates>` and when to use `<xsl:for-each>`. Then I'll explain how to use modes.

<xsl:apply-templates> versus <xsl:for-each>

`<xsl:apply-templates>` is most useful when processing an element that may contain children of a variety of different types in an unpredictable sequence. This is a *rule-based* design pattern: the definition of each individual template rule declares which nodes it is interested in, rather than the template rule for the parent node defining in detail how each of its children should be processed. The rule-based approach works particularly well when the document design is likely to evolve over time. As new child elements are added, template rules to process them can also be added, without changing the logic for the parent elements in which they might appear.

This style of processing is sometimes called *push* processing. It will be familiar if you have used text-processing languages such as awk or Perl, but it may be unfamiliar if you are more used to procedural programming in C++ or Visual Basic.

Where the structure is more regular and predictable, it may be simpler to navigate around the document using `<xsl:for-each>`, or by accessing the required data directly using `<xsl:value-of>`. This is sometimes called *pull* processing. The `<xsl-value-of>` instruction allows you to fetch data from the XML document using an arbitrarily complex XPath expression. In this sense it is similar to a SELECT statement in SQL.

A unique strength of XSLT is the ability to mix these two styles of programming. I'll discuss both approaches, and their relative merits, in more detail in Chapter 17.

Modes

Modes are useful where the same data is to be processed more than once.

A classic example is when building a table of contents. The main body of the output can be produced by processing the nodes in default mode, while the table of contents is produced by processing the same nodes with «mode="TOC"».

The following example does something very similar to this: it displays a scene from a play, adding at the start of the page a list of the characters who appear in this scene:

Example: Using Modes

This example uses a mode to create a list of characters appearing in a scene of a play.

Source

The source file, scene.xml, contains a scene from a play (specifically, Act I Scene 1 of Shakespeare's *Othello* — marked up in XML by Jon Bosak).

It starts like this:

```
<?xml version="1.0"?>
<SCENE><TITLE>SCENE I. Venice. A street.</TITLE>
<STAGEDIR>Enter RODERIGO and IAGO</STAGEDIR>
<SPEECH>
<SPEAKER>RODERIGO</SPEAKER>
<LINE>Tush! never tell me; I take it much unkindly</LINE>
<LINE>That thou, Iago, who hast had my purse</LINE>
<LINE>As if the strings were thine, shouldst know of this.</LINE>
</SPEECH>

<SPEECH>
<SPEAKER>IAGO</SPEAKER>
<LINE>'Sblood, but you will not hear me:</LINE>
<LINE>If ever I did dream of such a matter, Abhor me.</LINE>
</SPEECH>
etc.
</SCENE>
```

Stylesheet

The stylesheet scene.xsl is designed to display this scene in HTML. This is how it starts:

```
<xsl:transform
    xmlns:xsl="http://www.w3.org/1999/XSL/Transform"
    version="2.0">
```

```
<xsl:template match="SCENE">
<html><body>
   <xsl:apply-templates select="TITLE"/>

   <xsl:variable name="speakers" as="element()*">
     <xsl:for-each-group select="//SPEAKER" group-by=".">
       <xsl:sequence select="current-group()[1]"/>
     </xsl:for-each-group>
   </xsl:variable>

   <h2>Cast: <xsl:apply-templates select="$speakers"
                                   mode="cast-list"/></h2>
   <xsl:apply-templates select="* except TITLE"/>
</body></html>
</xsl:template>
```

The template rule shown above matches the <SCENE> element. It first displays the <TITLE> element (if there is one) using the appropriate template rule. Then it sets up a variable called «speakers» to be a sequence containing all the distinct <SPEAKER> elements that appear in the document. This is constructed by grouping all the <SPEAKER> elements using the <xsl:for-each-group> instruction and then taking the first one in each group. The result is a list of the speakers in which each one appears once only.

The template rule then calls <xsl:apply-templates> to process this set of speakers in mode «cast-list» (a nice side effect is that they will be listed in order of appearance). Finally, it calls <xsl:apply-templates> again, this time in the default mode, to process all elements («*») except <TITLE> elements (because the title has already been processed).

The stylesheet carries on as follows:

```
<xsl:template match="SPEAKER" mode="cast-list">
    <xsl:value-of select="."/>
    <xsl:if test="not(position()=last())">, </xsl:if>
</xsl:template>
```

This template rule defines how the <SPEAKER> element should be processed when it is being processed in «cast-list» mode. The sequence constructor has the effect of outputting the speaker's name, followed by a comma if this is not the last speaker in the list.

Finally, the remaining template rules define how each element should be output, when processed in default mode. Note that there are two different rules for STAGEDIR, depending on where it appears:

```
<xsl:template match="TITLE">
<h1><xsl:apply-templates/></h1>
</xsl:template>

<xsl:template match="SCENE/STAGEDIR">
<p><i><xsl:apply-templates/></i></p>
</xsl:template>
```

```
<xsl:template match="STAGEDIR">
<i><xsl:apply-templates/></i>
</xsl:template>

<xsl:template match="SPEECH">
<p><xsl:apply-templates/></p>
</xsl:template>

<xsl:template match="SPEAKER">
<b><xsl:apply-templates/></b><br/>
</xsl:template>

<xsl:template match="LINE">
<xsl:apply-templates/><br/>
</xsl:template>
</xsl:transform>
```

There is potentially a simpler solution to this requirement: the cast list can be constructed using the expression «string-join(distinct-values(//SPEAKER), ', ')». However, using <xsl:for-each-group> gives a guarantee that the speakers will be listed in order of first appearance, whereas the result order of distinct-values() is undefined.

Output

The precise layout of the HTML depends on which XSLT processor you are using, but apart from layout details it should start like this:

```
<html>
    <body>
        <h1>SCENE I. Venice. A street.</h1>
        <h2>Cast: RODERIGO, IAGO, BRABANTIO</h2>
        <p><i>Enter RODERIGO and IAGO</i></p>
        <p>
            <b>RODERIGO</b><br>
            Tush! never tell me; I take it much unkindly<br>
            That thou, Iago, who hast had my purse<br>
            As if the strings were thine, shouldst know of this.<br>
        </p>
        <p>
            <b>IAGO</b><br>
            'Sblood, but you will not hear me:<br>
            If ever I did dream of such a matter, Abhor me.<br>
        </p>
        ...
    </body>
</html>
```

It is sometimes useful to use named modes, even where they are not strictly necessary, to document more clearly the relationship between calling templates and called templates, and to constrain the selection of template rules rather more visibly than can be achieved by relying on template rule priorities. This might even improve performance by reducing the number of rules to be considered, though the effect is likely to be marginal.

For example, suppose that a `<poem>` consists of a number of `<stanza>` elements, and that the first `<stanza>` is to be output using a different style from the rest. The orthodox way to achieve this would be as follows:

```
<xsl:template match="poem">
. . .
    <xsl:apply-templates select="stanza"/>
. . .
</xsl:template>
<xsl:template match="stanza[1]">
. . .
</xsl:template>
<xsl:template match="stanza">
. . .
</xsl:template>
```

This relies on the default priority rules to ensure that the correct template rule is applied to each stanza — as explained in Chapter 12, the default priority for the pattern «stanza[1]» is higher than the default priority for «stanza».

Another way of doing this, perhaps less orthodox but equally effective, is as follows:

```
<xsl:template match="poem">
. . .
    <xsl:apply-templates select="stanza[1]" mode="first"/>
    <xsl:apply-templates select="stanza[position()>1]" mode="rest"/>
. . .
</xsl:template>
<xsl:template match="stanza" mode="first">
. . .
</xsl:template>
<xsl:template match="stanza" mode="rest">
. . .
</xsl:template>
```

Another solution, giving even finer control, would be to use `<xsl:for-each>` and `<xsl:call-template>` to control precisely which template rules are applied to which nodes, avoiding the pattern-matching mechanisms of `<xsl:apply-templates>` altogether.

Which you choose is largely a matter of personal style, and it is very hard to argue that one is better than the other in all cases. However, if you find that the match patterns used in defining a template rule are becoming extremely complex and context dependent, then you probably have both a performance and a maintenance problem on your hands, and controlling the selection of template rules in the calling code, by using modes or by calling templates by name, may well be the answer.

Simulating Higher Order Functions

In functional programming languages, a very useful programming technique is to write a function that accepts another function as an argument. This is known as a higher order function. For example, you might write a function that does a depth-first traversal of a tree and processes each node in the tree using a function that is supplied as an argument. This makes it possible to use one tree-walking routine to achieve many different effects (you might recognize this as the *Visitor Pattern*).

In XSLT (and XPath), functions are not first-class objects, so they cannot be passed as arguments to other functions. The same is true of templates. However, the template-matching capability of `<xsl:apply-templates>` can be used to simulate higher order functions.

This use of `<xsl:apply-templates>` has been developed to a fine art by Dimitre Novatchev in his FXSL library (`http://fxsl.sourceforge.net/`), which provides many examples of the technique.

A simple example of a higher order function found in many functional programming languages is the `fold` function. Given as an argument a function that adds two numbers, `fold` will find the sum of all the numbers in a sequence. Given a function that multiplies two numbers, it will find the product of the numbers in the sequence. In fact, `fold` takes three arguments: the sequence to be processed, the function to process two values, and the initial value. It turns out that the `fold` function can be used, with suitable arguments, to perform a wide variety of aggregation functions on sequences.

The key to the Novatchev technique is that although you cannot pass a function or template as an argument to another function or template, you can pass a node, and you can use `<xsl:apply-templates>` to trigger execution of a template associated with that node.

Rather than show you how `fold` works, which you can find out on the FXSL Web site, I will use another example that makes greater use of the new capabilities in XSLT 2.0. A common problem is to check whether there are cycles in your data. For example, your data might represent a part explosion, and you want to check that no part is a component of itself, directly or indirectly. Or you might be checking an XSLT stylesheet to check that no attribute set is defined in terms of itself. (There is an example that shows how to do this conventionally, without a higher order function, under `<xsl:function>` on page 344.) The problem is that there are many ways one can represent a relationship between two nodes in XML, and we don't want to have to write a new function to check for cycles each time we come across a new way of representing a relationship. So we write a general higher order function that looks for cycles and pass it, as a parameter, a function (actually represented by a node that will trigger a template rule) that knows how a particular relationship is represented.

Example: Checking for Cycles in a Graph

This example provides a generic procedure to look for cycles in a graph and then applies this procedure to a data file to see if the ID/IDREF links are cyclic.

In essence, the algorithm to check for a cycle is this: given a function `links(A)` that returns the set of nodes to which A is directly linked, the function `refers(A,B)` is true if `links(A)` includes B (that is, if there is a direct reference) or if there is a node C in the result of `links(A)` such that `refers(C,B)` is true (this is an indirect reference via C). This is a recursive definition, of course, and it is implemented by a recursive function. Finally, you know that A participates in a cycle if `refers(A,A)` is true. In coding the function, we have to be careful to ensure that the implementation will never go into a loop, remembering that a node reachable from A might participate in a cycle even if A does not (for a simple example, consider a graph in which A refers to X and X refers to itself). To achieve this, we pass an extra parameter indicating the route by which a node was reached, and we ignore nodes that were already on the route (we could report a cycle if we find them; but we've actually written this code to test whether a specific node participates in a cycle, which isn't the same thing).

Stylesheet

The stylesheet that searches for cycles in a graph is in `cycle.xsl`.

You can implement the `refers` function like this:

```
<xsl:function name="graph:refers" as="xs:boolean">
   <xsl:param name="links" as="node()"/>
   <!-- $links is a node that represents the template to be called -->
   <xsl:param name="A" as="node()"/>
   <xsl:param name="B" as="node()"/>
   <xsl:param name="route" as="node()*"/>

   <!-- find the directly-connected nodes -->
   <xsl:variable name="direct" as="node()*">
      <xsl:apply-templates select="$links">
         <xsl:with-param name="from" select="$A"/>
      </xsl:apply-templates>
   </xsl:variable>

   <!-- return true if B is directly or indirectly connected from A -->
   <xsl:sequence select="exists($direct intersect $B) or
           (some $C in ($direct except $route)
                 satisfies graph:refers($links, $C, $B, ($route, $C)))"/>
</xsl:function>
```

When you call this higher order function, you need to supply a node as the `$links` argument that will always cause a particular template rule to be invoked. Let's do this for the case where the link is established by virtue of the fact that the first node contains an `idref` attribute whose value matches the `id` attribute of the node that it references. This is in `idref-cycle.xsl`:

```
<xsl:variable name="graph:idref-links" as="element()">
   <graph:idref-link/>
</xsl:variable>
<xsl:template match="graph:idref-link" as="node()*">
   <xsl:param name="from" required="yes" as="node()"/>
   <xsl:sequence select="$from/id($from/@idref)"/>
</xsl:template>
```

And now you can test whether the context node participates in a cycle like this:

```
<xsl:template name="check-context-node">
   <xsl:if test="graph:refers($graph:idref-links, ., .)">
     <xsl:message terminate="yes">Cycle detected!</xsl:message>
   </xsl:if>
</xsl:template>
```

Let's look at the details of how this works:

The higher order function is implemented using `<xsl:function>`. It can't actually take a function or a template as a parameter, so what it takes instead is a node, which uniquely identifies the specific code to be executed to follow a link.

The code to follow a link is implemented as a template rule, and is invoked using `<xsl:apply-templates>`. An element is created (`<graph:idref-link>`) whose sole purpose is to trigger the execution of the associated template rule. Note that because of the «as="element()"» attribute on the <xsl:variable> element, the variable holds a single (parentless) element node, not a document node.

Unlike conventional template rules that create new nodes, this particular rule returns a reference to a sequence of existing nodes: specifically, the nodes selected by the select attribute of the <xsl:sequence> instruction. The result of the <xsl:apply-templates> instruction is also captured in a variable with an «as» attribute, which means that the result of the variable is the sequence of nodes returned by the template. Without the «as» attribute, the nodes would be copied to make a temporary document, which wouldn't work, because the XPath intersect operator relies on the nodes in the variable $direct having their original identity (used in the way it is used here, it tests whether $B is one of the nodes in $direct).

The important thing about this stylesheet is that the module cycle.xsl is completely general purpose: it has no knowledge of how the links between nodes are represented, and can therefore be used to look for cycles in any graph, however it is implemented.

Source

Two source files are supplied: acyclic-data.xml and cyclic-data.xml. Here is the one containing a cycle:

```
<!DOCTYPE parts [
  <!ATTLIST part id ID #REQUIRED>
]>
<parts>
  <part id="p05" idref="p10"/>
  <part id="p10" idref="p20"/>
  <part id="p20" idref="p30 p40"/>
  <part id="p30"/>
  <part id="p40" idref="p10"/>
</parts>
```

Output

Running the stylesheet idref-cycle.xsl against the source file cyclic-data.xml simply produces an error message saying that the data contains a cycle.

Higher order functions such as this are a powerful programming technique, particularly when handling complex data structures.

See Also

<xsl:for-each> on page 322
<xsl:function> on page 344
<xsl:sequence> on page 452
<xsl:sort> on page 455
<xsl:template> on page 483
<xsl:with-param> on page 517

xsl:attribute

The `<xsl:attribute>` instruction constructs an attribute node and adds it to the result sequence.

Changes in 2.0

The content of the attribute can be specified using a `select` attribute, as an alternative to using a sequence constructor. The `separator` attribute can be used to format the attribute value when the content is supplied as a sequence.

With a schema-aware XSLT processor, the `type` and `validation` attributes can be used to control the type annotation given to the new attribute node.

Format

```
<xsl:attribute
  name = { qname }
  namespace? = { uri-reference }
  select? = expression
  separator? = { string }
  validation? = "strict" | "lax" | "preserve" | "strip"
  type? = qname>
  <!-- Content: sequence-constructor -->
</xsl:attribute>
```

Position

`<xsl:attribute>` may be used either as an instruction within a *sequence constructor*, or within an `<xsl:attribute-set>` element.

Attributes

Name	Value	Meaning
name mandatory	Attribute value template returning a lexical QName	The name of the attribute node to be generated
namespace optional	Attribute value template returning a URI	The namespace URI of the generated attribute node
select optional	XPath Expression	Provides the value of the attribute
separator optional	Attribute value template returning a string	Separator string to be inserted between items when the value is a sequence
validation optional	«strict», «lax», «preserve», or «skip»	Indicates whether and how the attribute should be subjected to schema validation
type optional	Lexical QName	Identifies a type declaration (either a built-in type, or a user-defined type imported from a schema) against which the new element is to be validated

The `type` and `validation` attributes are mutually exclusive: if one is present, the other must be absent.

Content

A sequence constructor, unless the `select` attribute is present, in which case the content must be empty.

Effect

The effect of this instruction is to create a new attribute node and to return this node as the result of the instruction. In the usual case where the sequence constructor containing the `<xsl:attribute>` instruction is used to construct the content of an element, the attribute must not be preceded in the result sequence by any node other than a namespace node or another attribute node. The name of the generated attribute node is determined using the `name` and `namespace` attributes. The way in which these attributes are used is described below in the section *The Name of the Attribute*.

The value of the new attribute node may be established either using the `select` attribute or using the sequence constructor contained in the `<xsl:attribute>` instruction. These are mutually exclusive: if the `select` attribute is present, the `<xsl:attribute>` element must be empty. If neither is present, the value of the attribute will be a zero-length string. The way the value of the attribute is established is described in more detail in the section *The Value of the Attribute*.

When a schema-aware XSLT processor is used, the new attribute may be validated to ensure that it conforms to a type defined in a schema. This process results in the new attribute node having a type annotation. The type annotation affects the behavior of subsequent operations on this attribute node even though it is not visible when the result tree is serialized as raw XML. The validation and annotation of the new attribute node are controlled using the `type` and `validation` attributes. This is described in the section *Validating and Annotating the Attribute*.

The Name of the Attribute

The name of an attribute node has three parts: the prefix, the local name, and the namespace URI. These are controlled using the `name` and the `namespace` attributes.

Both the `name` and the `namespace` attributes may be given as attribute value templates; that is, they may contain expressions nested within curly braces. One of the main reasons for using the `<xsl:attribute>` instruction in preference to attributes on a literal result element (described in the section *Literal Result Elements* in Chapter 3, page 112) is that `<xsl:attribute>` allows the name of the attribute node to be decided at runtime, and this is achieved by using attribute value templates in these two attributes.

The result of expanding the `name` attribute value template must be a lexical QName; that is, a valid XML name with an optional namespace prefix, for example, «code» or «xsi:type». If there is a prefix, it must correspond to a namespace declaration that is in scope at this point in the stylesheet, unless there is also a `namespace` attribute, in which case it is taken as referring to that namespace.

The local part of the name of the created attribute node will always be the same as the local part of the QName supplied as the value of the `name` attribute.

If the `<xsl:attribute>` instruction has a `namespace` attribute, it is evaluated (expanding the attribute value template if necessary) to determine the namespace URI part of the name of the created attribute node:

❑   If the value is a zero-length string, the attribute will have a null namespace URI. It will therefore be serialized without a prefix. Any prefix in the value of the `name` attribute will be ignored.

❑   Otherwise, the value should be a URI identifying a namespace. This namespace will be used as the namespace URI of the new attribute node. This namespace does not need to be in scope at this point in the stylesheet, in fact it usually won't be. The system may report an error if the namespace isn't a valid URI. The namespace URI associated with any prefix in the QName obtained from the name attribute will be ignored.

If there is no namespace attribute:

❑   If the supplied QName includes a prefix, the prefix must be a namespace prefix that is in scope at this point in the stylesheet: In other words, there must be an xmlns:prefix declaration either on the <xsl:attribute> instruction itself or on some containing element. The namespace URI in the output will be that of the namespace associated with this prefix in the stylesheet.

❑   Otherwise, the attribute will have a null namespace URI. The default namespace is *not* used.

Where possible, the prefix of the attribute name (or the absence of a prefix) will be taken from the prefix given in the name attribute. However, if it isn't possible to use this prefix, then the namespace fixup process (described on page 310) will allocate a different prefix. This arises, for example, if two attributes of the same element use the same prefix to refer to different namespaces, or if the attribute is in a namespace but no prefix is supplied, or if a reserved prefix such as xml or xmlns is used.

Namespace fixup is not performed at the level of an individual attribute node. This is because attributes can only be associated with namespace nodes via their parent element.

If the name attribute provides a name that has no prefix, but a namespace attribute is present so that the namespace URI is not null, then the system has no choice but to invent a namespace prefix for the attribute. For example, if you write:

```
<table>
  <xsl:attribute name="width" namespace="http://acme.org/">
    <xsl:text>200</xsl:text>
  </xsl:attribute>
</table>
```

then the output might be:

```
<table ns0001:width="200" xmlns:ns0001="http://acme.org/"/>
```

The XSLT specification explicitly states that you cannot use <xsl:attribute> to generate namespace declarations by giving an attribute name of «xmlns» or «xmlns:*». In the XPath data model, attributes and namespaces are quite different animals, and you cannot simulate a namespace declaration by creating an attribute node with a special name. Namespace declarations will be added to the output automatically whenever you generate elements or attributes that require them, and if you really need to, you can also force them to be generated using the <xsl:namespace> instruction.

Using the New Attribute Node

The new attribute node, when initially created, has no parent node. Usually, however, the result of the instruction will form part of a sequence that is used to construct the content of a new element node. This will always be the case when the parent of the <xsl:attribute> instruction is an <xsl:element> or <xsl:copy> instruction, or a literal result element, and it will also be the case when the <xsl:attribute> is contained in an <xsl:attribute-set>.

Very often the `<xsl:attribute>` instruction will be contained directly in the instruction that writes the element; for example:

```
<table>
   <xsl:attribute name="border">2</xsl:attribute>
</table>
```

but this is not essential, for example you could also do:

```
<table>
   <xsl:call-template name="set-border"/>
</table>
```

and then create the attribute from within the «set-border» template. Less commonly, parentless attribute nodes may be created and held in variables, for example:

```
<xsl:variable name="three-atts" as="attribute()*">
   <xsl:attribute name="color">red</xsl:attribute>
   <xsl:attribute name="color">green</xsl:attribute>
   <xsl:attribute name="color">blue</xsl:attribute>
</xsl:variable>
```

In this particular case, just to show what is possible, we have created a variable whose value is a sequence of three parentless attributes, each of which has the same attribute name. These attributes could later be added to elements using instructions such as:

```
<table>
   <xsl:copy-of select="$three-atts[2]"/>
</table>
```

Whether the attribute node is added immediately to an element, or whether it is perhaps stored in a variable and added to an element later, at the point where the attribute is attached to an element, it must appear in the sequence before any child nodes (text nodes, elements, comments, or processing instructions) that are being added to the same element node.

This rule is there for the convenience of implementors. It means that the XSLT processor can execute the stylesheet and build the result tree sequentially, if it wishes. If it does so, the attributes for an element will always be evaluated before the children of the element, which means that the processor doesn't actually need to build the result tree in memory. Instead, each node can be serialized to an XML file as soon as it is generated. If it weren't for this rule, the software wouldn't be able to write the first start tag until right at the end, because there would always be a chance of an attribute being added to it.

When a sequence of nodes containing several attribute nodes is used to form the content of an element, and several of the attributes have the same name, the one that is used is the one that appears last in the sequence. This is not an error: in fact, when named attribute sets are used to add attributes to an output element, it is an important mechanism. Named attribute sets are described under `<xsl:attribute-set>` on page 266.

XQuery does this differently. In XQuery 1.0, adding two attributes with the same name to the same element is an error.

The Value of the Attribute

The string value of the new attribute node is obtained by evaluating the `select` attribute or the sequence constructor. The value of the `separator` attribute, if present, also plays a role.

Whether the `select` attribute or the sequence constructor is used, it is evaluated to produce a sequence of items, and this sequence of items is processed as follows:

1. Adjacent text nodes in the sequence are merged, and zero-length text nodes are removed.

2. The sequence is atomized. Atomization is described in Chapter 2 (page 81). This process replaces any nodes in the sequence by their typed values.

3. Every value in the atomized sequence is converted to a string by applying the XPath casting rules.

4. The strings in the resulting sequence are concatenated, with an optional separator between adjacent strings. If the `separator` attribute is present, its value is used as the separator (this may be a zero-length string). If the `select` attribute is used, then the default separator is a single space; otherwise, it is a zero-length string — in other words, there is no separator.

5. The resulting string is used as the value of the new attribute node.

The following examples illustrate the effect:

Instruction	Result
`<xsl:attribute name="x" select="1 to 5"/>`	`x="1 2 3 4 5"`

`<xsl:attribute name="x">`
  `<xsl:sequence select="1 to 5"/>`
`</xsl:attribute>`
	`x="12345"`

`<xsl:attribute name="x" select="1 to 5"` `separator=","/>`	`x="1, 2, 3, 4, 5"`

`<xsl:attribute name="x" separator="-">`
  `<xsl:sequence select="1 to 5"/>`
`</xsl:attribute>`
	`x="1-2-3-4-5"`

`<xsl:attribute name="x" separator="-">`
  `<xsl:for-each select="1 to 5">`
    `<xsl:value-of select="."/>`
  `</xsl:for-each>`
`</xsl:attribute>`
	`x="12345"`
	There is no separator here because adjacent text nodes are merged before separators are added.

In XSLT 1.0, it was an error if evaluating the content of an attribute produced a node other than a text node. Processors were allowed to recover by ignoring such nodes. In XSLT 2.0, any kind of node is allowed and is handled by the atomization process. If your stylesheet contains this error, and your XSLT 1.0 processor chose to ignore it, then it will produce different results under XSLT 2.0.

Validating and Annotating the Attribute

This section is relevant only if you are using a schema-aware XSLT processor. With a non-schema-aware processor, you cannot use the `type` and `validation` attributes, and the type annotation on the new attribute node will always be `xs:untypedAtomic`, which you can effectively ignore because it imposes no constraints. This will also be the result with a schema-aware processor if you omit these two attributes.

With a schema-aware processor, you can validate the new attribute to ensure that it conforms to relevant definitions in a schema. If validation fails, a fatal error is reported. If it succeeds, the new attribute node will have a type annotation that reflects the validation that was performed. This type annotation will not affect the way the attribute node is serialized, but if you want to do further processing on the attribute, the type annotation may affect the way this works. For example, if you sort a sequence of attributes annotated with type `xs:integer`, you will get different results than if they are annotated as `xs:string`.

If you use the `type` attribute, its value must be a lexical QName that identifies a known type definition. Generally, this means that it must either be a built-in type such as `xs:string` or `xs:dateTime`, or it must be the name of a global simple type defined in a schema that has been imported using an `<xsl:import-schema>` declaration in the stylesheet. (That is, the local part of the QName must match the `name` attribute of a top-level `<xs:simpleType>` element in a schema document whose target namespace matches the namespace URI part of the QName.)

> *The XSLT specification allows the implementation to provide other ways of accessing type definitions, perhaps through an API or configuration file, and it also allows the type definition to originate from a source other than an XML Schema document, but since it provides no details of how this might work, we won't explore the possibility further.*

The processor validates that the value of the new attribute node conforms to the named type definition. If it does, the attribute is annotated with the name of this type. If it doesn't, processing fails.

Validating an attribute using the `type` attribute places no constraints on the name of the attribute. It doesn't need to be an attribute name that is defined in any schema, and it doesn't matter whether or not the attribute name is in a namespace. The validation is concerned with the content of the attribute and not with its name.

In contrast, validation using the `validation` attribute is driven by the attribute's name.

For symmetry with other instructions, the `validation` attribute has four possible values: «preserve», «strip», «strict», and «lax». However, in the case of `<xsl:attribute>`, «preserve» and «strip» have exactly the same effect: No validation takes place, and the type annotation on the attribute node will be `xs:untypedAtomic`. Let's focus on the other two options.

❑ «validation="strict"» causes the processor to look for an attribute declaration that matches the name of the attribute. That is, it looks for a top-level `<xs:attribute>` whose `name` attribute matches the local name of the attribute being validated, in a schema document whose target namespace matches the namespace URI of the attribute being validated. If it can't find such a definition, a fatal error is reported. Otherwise, the value of the attribute node is validated against the schema-defined rules implied by this attribute declaration. Because global attribute declarations are uncommon, this facility has rather limited use.

❑ If the attribute declaration in the schema refers to a named type definition, then on successful validation, the attribute is annotated with this type name. If the attribute declaration contains an inline (and therefore unnamed) type definition, the XSLT processor invents a name for this implicit type, and uses this invented name as the type annotation.

❑ «validation="lax"» behaves in the same way as «validation="strict"», except that no failure occurs if the processor cannot locate a top-level schema definition for the attribute. Instead of reporting an error, the attribute is annotated as `xs:untypedAtomic`.

Note that any type annotation created for the attribute may disappear once the attribute is added to an element, unless the element is itself validated, or is created using the option «validation= "preserve"».

XSLT does not provide any way of requesting validation of an attribute against a local attribute or type definition in a schema. The way around this is to request validation only when you create an element for which there is a top-level definition in the schema. This will then implicitly validate the whole subtree contained by that element, including elements and attributes that have local definitions in the schema.

You're not allowed to validate an attribute if its type is namespace-sensitive. This applies to the types xs:QName and xs:NOTATION and anything derived from these two. The reason for this restriction is that the validity of these types depends on the namespace context (prefixes in the QName or NOTATION must have been declared). This means it doesn't make sense to validate the attribute until it has been added to an element.

Usage

You will sometimes see stylesheets that use the `<xsl:attribute>` instruction whenever they need to output an attribute value. However, in XSLT there are several different ways of generating an attribute in the result tree. This section compares the different approaches. It then looks specifically at the problem of creating an attribute whose value is a QName, such as an «xsi:type» attribute.

Different Ways of Creating Attributes

Where an output element is generated using a literal result element, the simplest way to specify attributes is normally to include them as attributes on the literal result element itself. You can do this even when the value is derived from information in the source document, because the value can be generated using an attribute value template, for example:

```
<body bgcolor="#{@red}{@green}{@blue}">
```

This concatenates three attributes of the current node in the source tree to create a single attribute in the result tree. Attribute value templates are described in Chapter 3, page 122.

Using `<xsl:attribute>` gives you more control than writing the attribute directly using attribute value templates. It is useful where one of the following conditions applies:

❑ The parent element is output using `<xsl:element>` or `<xsl:copy>` (rather than a literal result element).

❑ There is conditional logic to decide whether to output the attribute or not.

❑ The name of the attribute is computed at runtime.

❑ There is complex logic to calculate the value of the attribute.

❑ The attribute is one of a set that can conveniently be grouped together using `<xsl:attribute-set>`.

❑ The output attribute belongs to a namespace that is not present in the source document or the stylesheet.

A third way to output attributes is to copy them from the source tree to the result tree by using `<xsl:copy>` or `<xsl:copy-of>`. This works only if the attribute you want to generate has the same name and same value as an attribute in the source.

`<xsl:copy>` can be used when the context node in the source document is an attribute node. It's not necessary that the owning element was output using `<xsl:copy>`; for example, the following code ensures that the width, height, and depth attributes of the source `<parcel>` element are copied to the output `<package>` element, but its value and owner attributes are discarded:

```
<xsl:template match="parcel">
<package>
   <xsl:apply-templates select="@*"/>
</package>
</xsl:template>

<xsl:template match="parcel/@width | parcel/@height | parcel/@depth">
   <xsl:copy/>
</xsl:template>

<xsl:template match="parcel/@value | parcel/@owner"/>
```

This example uses `<xsl:apply-templates>` to process all the attributes of the `<parcel>` element. Some of these match one template rule, which copies the attribute to the output element, while others match an empty template rule that does nothing.

The same effect could be achieved more easily with `<xsl:copy-of>`, as follows:

```
<xsl:template match="parcel">
  <package>
    <xsl:copy-of select="@width, @height, @depth"/>
  </package>
</xsl:template>
```

The select expression here selects a sequence containing all the width, height, and depth attributes of the context node, and the `<xsl:copy-of>` instruction copies this sequence. The «,» operator, described in Chapter 10, concatenates two sequences (or in this case, two nodes) to form a single sequence.

If you want to copy all attributes of the current node to the result tree, the simplest way to achieve this is `<xsl:copy-of select="@*"/>`. If you want to copy all the attributes except certain particular ones, you can use the XPath 2.0 «except» operator:

```
<xsl:copy-of select="@* except (@value, @owner)"/>
```

Finally, if you want to add a bundle of commonly used attributes to an element, a convenient mechanism is available in the form of attribute sets. These can be defined using an `<xsl:attribute-set>` declaration, described on page 266.

Creating an Attribute Whose Value Is a QName

XML Schema allows an attribute to have a value whose type is xs:QName. A typical example of such an attribute is «xsi:type="xs:decimal"», which happens to be an attribute whose meaning is defined in the XML Schema specification itself. But they can also be defined in any other XML vocabulary. In fact, QName-valued elements can also be defined, though I haven't come across them in practice.

If you are generating an XSLT stylesheet as the output of the transformation, you will often have to generate QNames in the content of attributes; not only attributes like the name attribute of `<xsl:template>` and `<xsl:variable>`, but any attribute that contains an XPath expression or a pattern. In fact, any attribute that is an attribute value template can potentially contain a QName.

The tricky thing about these attributes is that they contain a namespace prefix, and you need to ensure that the output document contains a namespace declaration that binds this prefix to the correct URI.

It turns out that the fact that the attribute is declared in the schema as an `xs:QName` doesn't help with this. Firstly, not all these attributes are declared as QNames (some of them contain entire XPath expressions). But even where the type is known to be an `xs:QName`, you can't rely on this to ensure that the right namespaces are declared. This is because the process of creating an attribute node for an element in XSLT is typically:

1. Evaluate the expression that delivers the attribute value; atomize the result of this expression and convert the resulting sequence to a single string. This process loses any type information associated with the values from which the string was constructed.

2. Create an attribute node with this string value.

3. When the attribute is attached to an element, perform namespace fixup on the element. Namespace fixup is described on page 310.

4. Finally, if required, perform schema validation on the element.

In this process, there is no type annotation associated with the attribute at the time namespace fixup is performed. The namespace nodes need to be in place before validation of the attribute as a QName will succeed, so the only way of constructing them automatically would be to do it during validation, which would require a rewrite of the (already hideously complex) rules defined in XML Schema for validating elements.

The consequence of all this is that when you construct one of these attributes, it is your responsibility firstly to choose a prefix and to output the attribute in its correct lexical form and secondly to ensure that the containing element node has a namespace node that maps this prefix to the required namespace URI. The simplest way to be sure of this is by using the `<xsl:namespace>` instruction described on page 390.

So to generate the element `<e xsi:type="xs:decimal">93.7</e>`, write:

```
<e>
  <xsl:attribute name="xsi:type"
               namespace="http://www.w3.org/2001/XMLSchema-instance"
               select="'xs:decimal'">
  <xsl:namespace name="xs"
               select="'http://www.w3.org/2001/XMLSchema'"/>
  <xsl:value-of select="93.7"/>
</e>
```

An alternative to using `<xsl:namespace>`, in a case like this where the containing element is generated using a literal result element, is simply to ensure that the literal result element has a namespace node that will be copied to the result tree. This can be achieved by writing:

```
<e xmlns:xs="http://www.w3.org/2001/XMLSchema">
  <xsl:attribute name="xsi:type"
               namespace="http://www.w3.org/2001/XMLSchema-instance"
               select="'xs:decimal'">
  <xsl:value-of select="93.7"/>
</e>
```

The cases where `<xsl:namespace>` is needed are (a) where the element is produced using `<xsl:element>` rather than a literal result element and (b) where the namespace prefix or URI is not known at compile time.

Note that it's not a good idea to generate special attributes such as `xsi:type` by including them directly as attributes on the literal result element. This is because if the stylesheet is ever passed through a schema processor, the schema processor will try to check that the content of the `<e>` element in the stylesheet is `xs:decimal`, and of course it isn't. You could avoid such problems by using namespace aliasing (see `<xsl:namespace-alias>` on page 394), but in my view generating the attribute using `<xsl:attribute>` is easier.

Examples

The following example outputs an HTML `<OPTION>` element, with a SELECTED attribute included only if the boolean variable `$selected` is true. (The XML output would be `<OPTION SELECTED="SELECTED">`, but the HTML output method will convert this to `<OPTION SELECTED>`.)

Example: Generating an Attribute Conditionally

This example shows the use of `<xsl:attribute>` in a situation where the attribute is generated only if certain conditions are true in the source data.

Source

The source file is `countries.xml`.

```
<?xml version="1.0"?>
<countries>
  <country name="France"/>
  <country name="Germany"/>
  <country name="Israel"/>
  <country name="Japan"/>
  <country name="Poland"/>
  <country name="United States" selected="yes"/>
  <country name="Venezuela"/>
</countries>
```

Stylesheet

The stylesheet file is `options.xsl`.

This is a complete stylesheet using the simplified stylesheet syntax described in Chapter 3, page 125. It outputs an HTML selection box in which the selected attribute is set for the option marked as «selected="yes"» in the XML source document.

```
<html xsl:version="1.0"
      xmlns:xsl="http://www.w3.org/1999/XSL/Transform">
<body>
<h1>Please select a country:</h1>
<select id="country">
```

```
<xsl:for-each select="//country">
  <option value="{@name}">
    <xsl:if test="@selected='yes'">
        <xsl:attribute name="selected">selected</xsl:attribute>
    </xsl:if>
    <xsl:value-of select="@name"/>
  </option>
</xsl:for-each>
</select>
<hr/>
</body>
</html>
```

Output

The output (shown with the selection box opened) is shown in Figure 6-1.

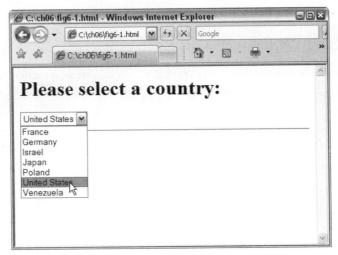

Figure 6-1

The following example outputs a `<promotion>` element with either a `code` or `reason-code` attribute, depending on the variable `$schema-version`. This kind of logic can be useful in an application that has to handle different versions of the output document schema.

Example: Deciding the Attribute Name at Runtime

This example shows the use of `<xsl:attribute>` in a situation where the name of the generated attribute is decided at runtime.

Source

This example uses no source file; it can be run by specifying `main` as the name of the initial template.

XSLT Elements

6

Stylesheet

The stylesheet can be found in the file `conditional.xsl`.

The stylesheet declares a global parameter «schema-version», which controls the name of the attribute used in the output file.

```
<xsl:stylesheet version="2.0"
      xmlns:xsl="http://www.w3.org/1999/XSL/Transform">
<xsl:param name="schema-version" select="4.0"/>
<xsl:template name="main">
  <promotion>
    <xsl:variable name="attname"
      select="if ($schema-version lt 3.0)
              then 'code'
              else 'reason-code'"/>
    <xsl:attribute name="{$attname}" select="17"/>
  </promotion>
</xsl:template>
</xsl:stylesheet>
```

Output

With the default value of the parameter «schema-version», the output is:

```
<promotion reason-code="17"/>
```

When run with the parameter «schema-version» set to 2.0, the output is:

```
<promotion code="17"/>
```

In XSLT 1.0, it was often necessary to use `<xsl:attribute>` because the value required a calculation. In the following example, the value of the `content` attribute is a whitespace-separated list of the `id` attributes of the child `<item>` elements of the context node:

```
<basket>
   <xsl:attribute name="content">
      <xsl:for-each select="item">
         <xsl:value-of select="@id"/>
         <xsl:if test="not(position()=last())">
            <xsl:text> </xsl:text>
         </xsl:if>
      </xsl:for-each>
   </xsl:attribute>
</basket>
```

In XSLT 2.0, the work can often be done at the XPath level. This example can now be written:

```
<basket content="{item/@id}"/>
```

because when the value of an expression in an attribute value template is given as a sequence, the processor will automatically convert the items in this sequence to strings and concatenate them using a single space as a separator.

See Also

<xsl:element> on page 306
<xsl:copy> on page 287
<xsl:copy-of> on page 292

xsl:attribute-set

The <xsl:attribute-set> element is a top-level XSLT declaration used to define a named set of attribute names and values. The resulting attribute set can be applied as a whole to any output element, providing a way of defining commonly used sets of attributes in a single place.

Changes in 2.0

None.

Format

```
<xsl:attribute-set
  name = qname
  use-attribute-sets? = qnames>
  <!-- Content: xsl:attribute* -->
</xsl:attribute-set>
```

Position

<xsl:attribute-set> is a declaration, so it must always occur as a child of the <xsl:stylesheet> element.

Attributes

Name	Value	Meaning
name mandatory	Lexical QName	The name of the attribute set
use-attribute-sets optional	Whitespace-separated list of lexical QNames	The names of other attribute sets to be incorporated into this attribute set

Content

Zero or more <xsl:attribute> elements.

Effect

Named attribute sets provide a capability similar to named styles in CSS.

The name attribute is mandatory and defines the name of the attribute set. It must be a lexical QName: a name with or without a namespace prefix. If the name uses a prefix, it must refer to a namespace declaration that is in scope at this point in the stylesheet, and as usual it is the namespace URI rather than the prefix that is used when matching names. The name does not need to be unique; if there are several attribute sets with the same name, they are effectively merged.

The `use-attribute-sets` attribute is optional. It is used to build up one attribute set from a number of others. If present, its value must be a whitespace-separated list of tokens each of which is a valid lexical QName that refers to another named attribute set in the stylesheet. For example:

```
<xsl:attribute-set name="table-cell"
   use-attribute-sets="small-font gray-background centered"/>
<xsl:attribute-set name="small-font">
   <xsl:attribute name="font-name">Verdana</xsl:attribute>
   <xsl:attribute name="font-size">6pt</xsl:attribute>
</xsl:attribute-set>
<xsl:attribute-set name="gray-background">
   <xsl:attribute name="bgcolor">#xBBBBBB</xsl:attribute>
</xsl:attribute-set>
<xsl:attribute-set name="centered">
   <xsl:attribute name="align">center</xsl:attribute>
</xsl:attribute-set>
```

The references must not be circular: if A refers to B, then B must not refer directly or indirectly to A. The order is significant: specifying a list of named attribute sets is equivalent to copying the `<xsl:attribute>` elements that they contain, in order, to the *beginning* of the list of `<xsl:attribute>` elements contained in this `<xsl:attribute-set>` element.

If several attribute sets have the same name, they are merged. If this merging finds two attributes with the same name, then the one in the attribute set with higher import precedence will take precedence. Import precedence is discussed under `<xsl:import>` on page 357. If they both have the same precedence, the one that came later in the stylesheet is used.

The order in which this merging process takes place can affect the outcome. When `use-attribute-sets` appears on an `<xsl:attribute-set>` or `<xsl:copy>` element, or `xsl:use-attribute-sets` on a literal result element, it is expanded to create a sequence of attribute nodes. This is essentially done by a recursive process:

1. To expand an `[xsl:]use-attribute-sets` attribute, use rule 2 to process each of the attribute set names in the order they are listed.

2. To process an attribute set name, use rule 3 to expand each of the `<xsl:attribute-set>` declarations having that name, taking them in increasing order of import precedence, and within each import precedence, in declaration order. For definitions of import precedence and declaration order, see `<xsl:import>` on page 357.

3. To expand an `<xsl:attribute-set>` declaration, use rule 1 to expand its `use-attribute-sets` attribute (if any), then add the attribute nodes generated by evaluating the contained `<xsl:attribute>` instructions to the result sequence.

It's best to illustrate this by an example. Suppose you have the following attribute-set definition:

```
<xsl:attribute-set name="B" use-attribute-sets="A1 A2">
  <xsl:attribute name="p">percy</xsl:attribute>
  <xsl:attribute name="q">queenie</xsl:attribute>
  <xsl:attribute name="r">rory</xsl:attribute>
</xsl:attribute-set>
```

If there is more than one attribute set named A1 these must be merged first (taking import precedence into account), and then the merged contents must be substituted into B.

Then the same process is applied to A2. The referenced attribute sets are expanded in order. The attributes that result from expanding A1 are output before those that result from expanding A2. This means that attributes from A2 take priority over those from A1 if there is a clash, because of the rule that when several attributes have the same name, the last one wins.

In turn, the attribute set B must be fully expanded before it is merged with any other attribute set called B. That is, the processor must replace the references to attribute sets A1 and A2 with an equivalent list of `<xsl:attribute>` instructions before it merges this B with other attribute sets of the same name.

When B is expanded, the attributes derived from A1 and A2 will be output before the attributes p, q, and r, so if expanding A1 and A2 generates any attributes called p, q, and r, these will be overwritten by the values specified within B (percy, queenie, and rory).

> *Normally when describing the processing model for XSLT instructions, we distinguish between the process of generating a sequence of nodes, and the subsequent process of attaching these nodes to a tree. Eliminating attribute nodes with duplicate names is technically part of the second process. However, attribute sets can only be expanded from instructions that create elements, so the resulting attributes will always be attached to an element. This means we can treat it as if generating the attribute nodes and attaching them to an element are done as a single process.*

Duplicate attribute names or attribute set names do not cause an error. If several attributes have the same name, the one that comes last (in the order produced by the merging rules given above) will take precedence.

Usage

The most common use of attribute sets is to define packages of attributes that constitute a display style, for example a collection of attributes for a font or for a table. They are often used when generating XSL-FO.

A named attribute set is used by referring to it in the use-attribute-sets attribute of the `<xsl:element>` or `<xsl:copy>` element or in the xsl:use-attribute-sets attribute of a literal result element or, of course, in the use-attribute-sets attribute of another `<xsl:attribute-set>`. The first three cases all create an element node and have the effect of adding the attributes in the named attribute set to that element node. Any attributes added implicitly from a named attribute set can be overridden by attribute nodes added explicitly by the invoking code.

An attribute set is not simply a textual macro. The attributes contained in the attribute set each have a select attribute or sequence constructor to define the value, and although this will often return a fixed value, it may also, for example, declare variables or invoke other XSLT instructions such as `<xsl:call-template>` and `<xsl:apply-templates>`.

The rules for the scope of variables, described under `<xsl:variable>` on page 500, are the same as anywhere else, and are defined by the position of the definitions in the source stylesheet document. This means that the only way to parameterize the values of attributes in a named attribute set is by reference to global variables and parameters: There is no other way of passing parameters to an attribute set.

However, the value of the generated attributes may depend on the context in the source document. The context is not changed when the attribute set is used, so the context item («.») as well as the context position and size are exactly the same as in the calling instruction.

Examples

The following example defines an attribute set designed for generated HTML `<table>` elements:

```
<xsl:attribute-set name="full-width-table">
    <xsl:attribute name="border">1</xsl:attribute>
    <xsl:attribute name="cellpadding">3</xsl:attribute>
    <xsl:attribute name="cellspacing">0</xsl:attribute>
    <xsl:attribute name="width">100%</xsl:attribute>
</xsl:attribute-set>
```

This attribute set can be used when generating an output element, as follows:

```
<table xsl:use-attribute-sets="full-width-table">
  <tr>...</tr>
</table>
```

This produces the following output:

```
<table border="1" cellpadding="3" cellspacing="0" width="100%">
  <tr>...</tr>
</table>
```

Alternatively it is possible to use the attribute set while overriding some of its definitions and adding others, for example:

```
<table border="2" rules="cols" xsl:use-attribute-sets="full-width-table">
  <tr>...</tr>
</table>
```

The output now becomes:

```
<table border="2" rules="cols" cellpadding="3" cellspacing="0" width="100%">
  <tr>...</tr>
</table>
```

If this combination of attributes is also used repeatedly, it could be defined as an attribute set in its own right, as:

```
<xsl:attribute-set name="ruled-table" use-attribute-set="full-width-table">
    <xsl:attribute name="border">2</xsl:attribute>
    <xsl:attribute name="rules">cols</xsl:attribute>
</xsl:attribute-set>
```

Then this new attribute set could also be invoked by name from a literal result element, an `<xsl:element>` instruction, or an `<xsl:copy>` instruction.

The next example shows that the values of the attributes in an attribute set need not be constants.

Example: Using an Attribute Set for Numbering

This is a rather untypical example, designed to show that attribute sets are more powerful than you might imagine. Suppose you want to copy an XML file containing a poem, but with the `<line>` elements in the poem output in the form `<line number="3" of="18">` within the stanza.

Source

The source file `poem.xml` has the following structure (I'm only showing the first stanza):

```
<?xml version="1.0"?>
<poem>
<author>Rupert Brooke</author>
<date>1912</date>
<title>Song</title>
<stanza>
<line>And suddenly the wind comes soft,</line>
<line>And Spring is here again;</line>
<line>And the hawthorn quickens with buds of green</line>
<line>And my heart with buds of pain.</line>
</stanza>
</poem>
```

Stylesheet

The stylesheet `number-lines.xsl` copies everything unchanged except the `<line>` elements, which are copied with a named attribute set:

```
<xsl:transform
 xmlns:xsl="http://www.w3.org/1999/XSL/Transform" version="2.0">
<xsl:strip-space elements="*"/>
<xsl:output method="xml" indent="yes"/>
<xsl:template match="*">
   <xsl:copy>
     <xsl:apply-templates/>
   </xsl:copy>
</xsl:template>
<xsl:template match="line">
   <xsl:copy use-attribute-sets="sequence">
     <xsl:apply-templates/>
   </xsl:copy>
</xsl:template>
<xsl:attribute-set name="sequence">
   <xsl:attribute name="number" select="position()"/>
   <xsl:attribute name="of" select="last()"/>
</xsl:attribute-set>
</xsl:transform>
```

Output

The output (again showing only the first stanza) looks like this:

```
<poem>
    <author>Rupert Brooke</author>
    <date>1912</date>
    <title>Song</title>
    <stanza>
        <line number="1" of="4">And suddenly the wind comes soft,</line>
        <line number="2" of="4">And Spring is here again;</line>
        <line number="3" of="4">And the hawthorn quickens with
                        buds of green</line>
        <line number="4" of="4">And my heart with buds of pain.</line>
    </stanza>
</poem>
```

See Also

<xsl:element> on page 306
<xsl:copy> on page 287
Literal Result Elements in Chapter 3, page 112

xsl:call-template

The <xsl:call-template> instruction is used to invoke a named template. Its effect is analogous to a procedure call or subroutine call in other programming languages.

Changes in 2.0

There are no syntactic changes to this instruction in XSLT 2.0. However, using the <xsl:sequence> instruction in the called template (see page 452) now allows the result of the <xsl:call-template> instruction to be any sequence, not only a sequence of nodes.

In many cases where it was appropriate to use <xsl:call-template> in XSLT 1.0, it may be more appropriate in 2.0 to call a stylesheet function defined using <xsl:function>, which is described on page 344.

Many problems that required recursive use of <xsl:call-template> to process a string can be solved more conveniently in XSLT 2.0 by using the <xsl:analyze-string> instruction (see page 230), and many problems that used recursion to process a sequence of nodes can now be tackled more easily by using <xsl:for-each-group>, described on page 326.

It is now a compile-time error to supply a parameter that the called template does not declare; in XSLT 1.0, such a parameter was silently ignored. To preserve backward compatibility, this rule is not enforced when the stylesheet specifies «version="1.0"».

Format

```
<xsl:call-template
  name = qname>
  <!-- Content: xsl:with-param* -->
</xsl:call-template>
```

Position

`<xsl:call-template>` is an instruction; it is always used within a sequence constructor.

Attributes

Name	Value	Meaning
name mandatory	Lexical QName	The name of the template to be called

Content

Zero or more `<xsl:with-param>` elements.

Effect

The sections below describe the rules for the template name, the rules for supplying parameters to the called template, and the way the context is affected.

The Template Name

The mandatory `name` attribute must be a lexical QName, and it must match the `name` attribute of an `<xsl:template>` element in the stylesheet. If the name has a namespace prefix, the names are compared using the corresponding namespace URI in the usual way. It is an error if there is no `<xsl:template>` element with a matching name.

If there is more than one `<xsl:template>` in the stylesheet with a matching name, they must have different import precedence, and the one with highest import precedence is used. For information about import precedence, see `<xsl:import>` on page 357.

The name of the template to be called must be written explicitly in the `name` attribute. There is no way of writing this name as a variable or an expression to be evaluated at runtime. If you want to make a runtime decision on which of several named templates to call, the only way to achieve this is to write an `<xsl:choose>` instruction. Alternatively, there is a technique for using template rules as if they were higher order functions; this is described under *Simulating Higher Order Functions* on page 250.

Parameters

If the name of a child `<xsl:with-param>` element matches the name of an `<xsl:param>` element in the called `<xsl:template>`, then the `<xsl:with-param>` element is evaluated (in the same way as an `<xsl:variable>` element), and the value is assigned to the relevant `<xsl:param>` variable name within that named template.

If the `<xsl:with-param>` element specifies «tunnel="yes"», then the parameter is available not only in the immediately called template but to templates at any depth in the call stack, provided they declare the parameter with `<xsl:param tunnel="yes"/>` and a matching name. Tunnel parameters are described more fully on page 429. In XSLT 2.0 a compile-time error is reported if there is a child `<xsl:with-param>` element that isn't a tunnel parameter and that doesn't match the name of any `<xsl:param>` element in the selected `<xsl:template>`. However, if the `<xsl:call-template>` instruction is in a part of the stylesheet that specifies «[xsl:]version="1.0"», the extra parameter is ignored as it was in XSLT 1.0.

If there is an `<xsl:param>` element in the selected `<xsl:template>` with no matching `<xsl:with-param>` element in the `<xsl:call-template>` element, then the `<xsl:param>` variable is given a default value. But if the `<xsl:param>` element specifies «required="yes"», this is a compile-time error. See `<xsl:param>` on page 425 for details.

Context

The selected `<xsl:template>` is evaluated with no change to the context: it uses the same context item, context position, and context size as the calling template. There is also no change to the *current template rule* (a concept that is used only by `<xsl:apply-imports>`, described on page 237, and `<xsl:next-match>`, described on page 399). The *current mode* is also unchanged.

Usage and Examples

The `<xsl:call-template>` element is similar to a subroutine call in conventional programming languages, and the parameters behave in the same way as conventional call-by-value parameters. It is useful wherever there is common logic to be called from different places in the stylesheet.

Using the Result

The result of an `<xsl:call-template>` instruction is the sequence returned by the sequence constructor inside the template that is called. Usually, this consists of nodes that are immediately added to the result tree. However, you can also capture the result by calling `<xsl:call-template>` from within an `<xsl:variable>` element, in which case the result of the called template becomes the value of the variable.

For example, the following template outputs the supplied string enclosed in parentheses:

```
<xsl:template name="parenthesize">
   <xsl:param name="string"/>
   <xsl:sequence select="concat('(',$string,')')"/>
</xsl:template>
```

This may be called as follows:

```
<xsl:variable name="credit-in-paren" as="xs:string">
   <xsl:call-template name="parenthesize">
      <xsl:with-param name="string" select="@credit"/>
   </xsl:call-template>
</xsl:variable>
```

If the value of the `credit` attribute is «120.00», the resulting value of the variable «$credit-in- paren» will be the string «(120.00)».

If you omitted the «as="xs:string"» from the `<xsl:variable>` element, the result would not be a string, but a temporary tree consisting of a document node that owns a single text node, and the contents of that text node would be «(120.00)»; but for all practical purposes the value could still be used as if it were a string. One difference is that you won't get such good type checking: For example, if you try to use the variable `$credit-in-paren` as defined above in a context where a number is required, this will be reported as an error, quite possibly at compile time. But if you leave off the «as» attribute, you will probably not get an error at all, just a wrong answer: The system will treat the value of the variable as NaN (not a number).

Changing the Context Item

If you want to use `<xsl:call-template>` to process an item that is not the context item, the easiest way to achieve this is to nest the `<xsl:call-template>` inside an `<xsl:for-each>` instruction. An alternative, however, is to give the target template a distinctive mode name and call it using `<xsl:apply-templates>` with the specified mode.

For example, suppose you have written a template that returns the depth of the current node (the number of ancestors it has). The template has been given a unique name and an identical mode name:

```
<xsl:template name="depth" mode="depth" match="node()">
   <xsl:sequence select="count(ancestor::node())"/>
</xsl:template>
```

Now, suppose you want to obtain the depth of a node other than the context node — let's say the depth of the next node in document order, which need not be on the same level as the context node. You can call this template in either of two ways.

Using `<xsl:call-template>`:

```
<xsl:variable name="next-depth" as="xs:integer">
   <xsl:for-each select="following::node()[1]">
      <xsl:call-template name="depth"/>
   </xsl:for-each>
</xsl:variable>
```

or using `<xsl:apply-templates>` with a special mode:

```
<xsl:variable name="next-depth" as="xs:integer">
   <xsl:apply-templates select="following::node()[1]" mode="depth"/>
</xsl:variable>
```

In both cases the variable $next-depth will, on return, hold a value, which is the depth in the tree of the node following the context node. If the context item is not a node, a runtime error will occur. Because the `<xsl:variable>` element has an «as» attribute, the result is of type `xs:integer`. Without the «as» attribute, the result would be a temporary document containing a single text node, whose value is the string representation of this integer. For details, see `<xsl:variable>` on page 500.

Recursion: Processing a List of Values

Named templates are sometimes used to process a list of values. As XSLT has no updateable variables like a conventional programming language, it also has no conventional *for* or *while* loop, because these constructs can only terminate if there is a control variable whose value is changing.

In XSLT 2.0 most processing of sequences can be done iteratively, using the XSLT `<xsl:for-each>` instruction or the XPath 2.0 «for» expression; for example:

```
sum(for $i in //item return $i/price * $i/quantity)
```

or more simply:

```
sum(//item/(price * quantity))
```

When things get difficult, it is possible to use functions such as `tokenize()` or `distinct-values()` to define the sequence that needs to be processed, and to use instructions such as `<xsl:analyze-string>` and `<xsl:for-each-group>` to do the processing. In XSLT 1.0 it was often necessary to write recursive templates to perform such calculations.

Recursion is still needed in XSLT 2.0 to handle more complex algorithms, particularly those that navigate a hierarchy or a graph, but it will often be done more conveniently using XPath function calls and stylesheet functions written using `<xsl:function>` rather than using `<xsl:call-template>`. Nevertheless, recursive use of `<xsl:call-template>` still has a role to play, so I will present a couple of examples.

The typical logic used to process a sequence using recursion is illustrated by the following pseudocode:

```
function process-sequence(sequence L) {
  if (not-empty(L)) {
    process(first(L));
    process-sequence(remainder(L));
  }
}
```

That is, the function does nothing if the sequence is empty; otherwise, it processes the first item in the sequence and then calls itself to process the sequence containing all items except the first. The net effect is that each item in the sequence will be processed and the function will then exit. This particular approach to writing recursive algorithms is often known as *head-tail recursion*.

There are two main kinds of sequence that this logic is applied to: sequences of nodes, and strings containing separator characters. I will show one example of each kind; more complex examples can be found in Chapters 17 and 20.

Example: Using Recursion to Process a Sequence of Nodes

Here's an example for processing a sequence of nodes. XPath 2.0 provides `min()` and `max()` functions for finding the minimum and maximum of a set of atomic values, but it doesn't provide a way of processing a set of nodes and returning the one whose value for some expression is least or greatest. This can be done by computing the value of the expression for each of the nodes, passing these values into the `min()` or `max()` function and then searching the nodes to see which of them had this value, but this approach is rather inefficient because it involves visiting each node and calculating the expression twice. So we'll do it ourselves, using a recursive scan of the nodes, in a single pass. The specific task we will tackle is to look for the longest speech in a scene of a play.

Conceptually it's trivial: the maximum value of a set of numbers is either the first number or the maximum of the set of the numbers after the first, whichever is larger. We use XPath predicates for manipulating the node sequences: in particular, «[1]» to find the first node in the sequence, and «[position()!=1]» to find the remainder.

Source

The source file `scene.xml` is the scene of a play. It starts like this:

```xml
<?xml version="1.0"?>
<SCENE><TITLE>SCENE I. Venice. A street.</TITLE>
<STAGEDIR>Enter RODERIGO and IAGO</STAGEDIR>

<SPEECH>
<SPEAKER>RODERIGO</SPEAKER>
<LINE>Tush! never tell me; I take it much unkindly</LINE>
<LINE>That thou, Iago, who hast had my purse</LINE>
<LINE>As if the strings were thine, shouldst know of this.</LINE>
</SPEECH>

<SPEECH>
<SPEAKER>IAGO</SPEAKER>
<LINE>'Sblood, but you will not hear me:</LINE>
<LINE>If ever I did dream of such a matter, Abhor me.</LINE>
</SPEECH>
etc.
</SCENE>
```

Stylesheet

The stylesheet `longest-speech.xsl` is shown below. It starts by defining a named template «max». This template takes a node sequence called «list» as its parameter.

The first thing it does is to test whether this node sequence is nonempty (`<xsl:when test="$list">`). If it isn't, it gets the number of `<LINE>` element children of the first node in the list into a variable «$first». Then the template calls itself recursively, passing all nodes except the first as the parameter, to determine the maximum value for the rest of the list. It then returns either the first value or the maximum for the rest of the list, whichever is greater. Finally, if the supplied list was empty, it returns zero.

The template rule for the root node of the source document simply calls the «longest-speech» template, passing the list of all `<SPEECH>` elements as a parameter.

```xml
<xsl:transform
 xmlns:xsl="http://www.w3.org/1999/XSL/Transform"
 xmlns:xs="http://www.w3.org/2001/XMLSchema"
 exclude-result-prefixes="xs"
 version="2.0"
>
<xsl:template name="longest-speech" as="element(SPEECH)?">
<xsl:param name="list" as="element(SPEECH)*"/>
  <xsl:choose>
   <xsl:when test="$list">
     <xsl:variable name="first" select="count($list[1]/LINE)"
                   as="xs:integer"/>
     <xsl:variable name="longest-of-rest" as="element(SPEECH)?">
       <xsl:call-template name="longest-speech">
         <xsl:with-param name="list"
```

```
                              select="$list[position()!=1]"/>
            </xsl:call-template>
          </xsl:variable>
          <xsl:choose>
          <xsl:when test="$first gt count($longest-of-rest/LINE)">
            <xsl:sequence select="$list[1]"/>
          </xsl:when>
          <xsl:otherwise>
            <xsl:sequence select="$longest-of-rest"/>
          </xsl:otherwise>
          </xsl:choose>
        </xsl:when>
        </xsl:choose>
    </xsl:template>
    <xsl:template match="/">
      <longest-speech>
        <xsl:call-template name="longest-speech">
          <xsl:with-param name="list" select="//SPEECH"/>
        </xsl:call-template>
      </longest-speech>
    </xsl:template>
    </xsl:transform>
```

Output

The output gives the text of the longest speech in this scene. It starts like this:

```
<?xml version="1.0" encoding="UTF-8"?>
<longest-speech>
<SPEECH><SPEAKER>IAGO</SPEAKER>
<LINE>O, sir, content you;</LINE>
<LINE>I follow him to serve my turn upon him:</LINE>
<LINE>We cannot all be masters, nor all masters</LINE>
<LINE>Cannot be truly follow'd. You shall mark</LINE>
<LINE>Many a duteous and knee-crooking knave,</LINE>
<LINE>That, doting on his own obsequious bondage,</LINE>
<LINE>Wears out his time, much like his master's ass,</LINE>
<LINE>For nought but provender, and when he's old, cashier'd:</LINE>
<LINE>Whip me such honest knaves...
```

Our version of AltovaXML 2008 gave the wrong answer on this stylesheet. Altova tell us there's a fix in the next release.

Note that this is taking advantage of several new features of XSLT 2.0. The template uses `<xsl:sequence>` to return a reference to an existing node, rather than creating a copy of the node using `<xsl:copy-of>`. It also declares the type of the parameters expected by the template, and the type of the result, which is useful documentation, and provides information that the XSLT processor can use for generating optimized code. I also found that while I was developing the stylesheet, many of my errors were trapped by the type checking. Note that the form «as="element(SPEECH)"» can be used even when there is no schema. The example could have been rewritten to make much heavier use of XSLT 2.0 features;

for example, it could have been written using `<xsl:function>` rather than `<xsl:template>`, and the `<xsl:choose>` instruction could have been replaced by an XPath 2.0 «if» expression. The result would have occupied fewer lines of code, but it would not necessarily have been any more readable or more efficient.

There is another solution to this problem that may be more appropriate depending on the circumstances. This involves sorting the node-set, and taking the first or last element. It goes like this:

```
<xsl:variable name="longest-speech" as="element(SPEECH)?">
   <xsl:for-each select="SPEECH">
     <xsl:sort select="count(LINE)"/>
     <xsl:if test="position()=last()">
       <xsl:sequence select="."/>
     </xsl:if>
   </xsl:for-each>
</xsl:variable>
```

In principle, the recursive solution should be faster, because it only looks at each node once, whereas sorting all the values requires more work than is strictly necessary to find the largest. In practice, though, it rather depends on how efficiently recursion is implemented in the particular processor.

Another case where recursion has traditionally been useful is processing of a list presented in the form of a string containing a list of tokens. In XSLT 2.0, most such problems can be tackled much more conveniently using the XPath 2.0 `tokenize()` function, which breaks a string into a sequence by using regular expressions, or by using the `<xsl:analyze-string>` instruction described on page 230. But although these functions are excellent at breaking a string into a sequence of substrings, they don't by themselves provide any ability to process the resulting sequence in a nonlinear way. Sometimes recursion is still the best way of tackling such problems.

Example: Using Recursion to Process a Sequence of Strings

Suppose that you want to find all the lines within a play that contain the phrase «A and B», where A and B are both names of characters in the play.

Source

There is only one line in the whole of *Othello* that meets these criteria. So you will need to run the stylesheet against the full play, `othello.xml`.

Stylesheet

The stylesheet `naming-lines.xsl` starts by declaring a global variable whose value is the set of names of the characters in the play, with duplicates removed and case normalized for efficiency:

```
<xsl:transform
  xmlns:xsl="http://www.w3.org/1999/XSL/Transform"
  xmlns:xs="http://www.w3.org/2001/XMLSchema"
  xmlns:local="local-functions.uri"
  exclude-result-prefixes="xs local"
  version="2.0"
>
```

```
<xsl:variable name="speakers" as="xs:string*"
  select="for $w in distinct-values(//SPEAKER) return upper-case($w)"/>
```

We'll write a function that splits a line into its words. This was hard work in XSLT 1.0, but it is now much easier.

```
<xsl:function name="local:split" as="xs:string*">
  <xsl:param name="line" as="xs:string"/>
  <xsl:sequence select="tokenize($line, '\W')"/>
</xsl:function>
```

The next step is a function that tests whether a given word is the name of a character in the play:

```
<xsl:function name="local:is-character" as="xs:boolean">
  <xsl:param name="word" as="xs:string"/>
  <xsl:sequence select="upper-case($word)=$speakers"/>
</xsl:function>
```

This way of doing case-independent matching isn't really recommended, it's better to use a collation designed for the purpose, but it works with this data. Note that we are relying on the "existential" properties of the «=» operator: that is, the fact that it compares the word on the left with every string in the $speakers sequence.

Now I'll write a named template that processes a sequence of words, and looks for the phrase «A and B» where A and B are both the names of characters.

```
<xsl:template name="scan-line">
  <xsl:param name="words" as="xs:string*"/>
  <xsl:if test="count($words) ge 3">
    <xsl:if test="local:is-character($words[1]) and
                  lower-case($words[2]) = 'and' and
                  local:is-character($words[3])">
      <hit>
        <xsl:value-of select="$words[position()=1 to 3]" separator=" "/>
      </hit>
    </xsl:if>
    <xsl:call-template name="scan-line">
      <xsl:with-param name="words"
                      select="$words[position() gt 1]"/>
    </xsl:call-template>
  </xsl:if>
</xsl:template>
```

Then comes the "main program," the template rule that matches the root node. This simply calls the named template for each <LINE> element in the document, which causes <hit> elements to be output for all matching sequences:

```
<xsl:template match="/">
  <naming-lines>
    <xsl:for-each select="//LINE">
```

```
        <xsl:call-template name="scan-line">
          <xsl:with-param name="words" select="local:split(.)"/>
        </xsl:call-template>
      </xsl:for-each>
    </naming-lines>
  </xsl:template>
</xsl:transform>
```

Output

The output is simply:

```
<?xml version="1.0" encoding="UTF-8"?>
<naming-lines>
   <hit>Othello and Desdemona</hit>
</naming-lines>
```

See Also

`<xsl:apply-templates>` on page 240
`<xsl:function>` on page 344
`<xsl:param>` on page 425
`<xsl:template>` on page 483
`<xsl:with-param>` on page 517

xsl:character-map

The `<xsl:character-map>` element is a top-level XSLT declaration used to provide detailed control over the way individual characters are serialized. A character map is used only when the result of the transformation is serialized, and when the `<xsl:output>` declaration that controls the serialization references the character map.

Changes in 2.0

Character maps are a new feature in XSLT 2.0, designed as a replacement for disable-output- escaping, which is now deprecated.

Format

```
<xsl:character-map
  name = qname
  use-character-maps? = qnames>
  <!-- Content: (xsl:output-character*) -->
</xsl:character-map>
```

Position

`<xsl:character-map>` is a top-level declaration, so it must always occur as a child of the `<xsl:stylesheet>` element.

Attributes

Name	Value	Meaning
name mandatory	Lexical QName	The name of this character map
use-character-maps optional	Whitespace-separated list of lexical QNames	The names of other character maps to be incorporated into this character map

Content

Zero or more `<xsl:output-character>` elements.

Effect

The «name» attribute is mandatory, and defines the name of the character map. It must be a lexical QName: a name with or without a namespace prefix. If the name uses a prefix, it must refer to a namespace declaration that is in scope at this point in the stylesheet, and as usual it is the namespace URI rather than the prefix that is used when matching names. If several character maps in the stylesheet have the same name, then the one with highest import precedence is used; an error is reported if this rule does not identify a character map uniquely. Import precedence is explained on page 359.

The character map contains zero or more `<xsl:output-character>` elements. Each `<xsl:output-character>` element defines a mapping between a single Unicode character and a string that is used to represent that character in the serialized output. For example, the element:

```
<xsl:output-character character=" " string=" "/>
```

indicates that the nonbreaking space character (Unicode codepoint 160) is to be represented on output by the string « ». This illustrates one of the possible uses of character maps, which is to render specific characters using XML or HTML entity references.

The `use-character-maps` attribute is optional. It is used to build up one character map from a number of others. If present, its value must be a whitespace-separated list of tokens, each of which is a valid QName that refers to another named character map in the stylesheet. For example:

```
<xsl:character-map name="NBSP">
    <xsl:output-character character=" " string=" "/>
</xsl:character-map>

<xsl:character-map name="latin-1-symbols">
    <xsl:output-character character="&#161;" string="&amp;iexcl;"/>
    <xsl:output-character character="&#162;" string="&amp;cent;"/>
    <xsl:output-character character="&#163;" string="&amp;pound;"/>
    <xsl:output-character character="&#164;" string="&amp;curren;"/>
    ...
</xsl:character-map>

<xsl:character-map name="latin-1-accented-letters">
    <xsl:output-character character="&#192;" string="&amp;Agrave;"/>
    <xsl:output-character character="&#193;" string="&amp;Aacute;"/>
    <xsl:output-character character="&#194;" string="&amp;Acirc;"/>
    <xsl:output-character character="&#195;" string="&amp;Atilde;"/>
```

6

XSLT Elements

281

```
    ...
</xsl:character-map>

<xsl:character-map name="latin-1-entities"
    use-character-maps="NBSP
                        latin-1-symbols
                        latin-1-accented-characters"/>
```

This example creates a composite character map called `latin-1-entities` that is effectively the union of three underlying character maps. The effect in this case is as if all the `<xsl:output-character>` elements in the three underlying character maps were actually present as children of the composite character map.

The rules for merging character maps are as follows. Firstly, there must be no circularities (a character map must not reference itself, directly or indirectly). The *expanded content* of a character map can then be defined (recursively) as the concatenation of the expanded content of each of the character maps referenced in its `use-character-maps` attribute, in the order in which they are named, followed by the `<xsl:output-character>` elements that are directly contained in the `<xsl:character-map>` element, in the order that they appear in the stylesheet. If the expanded content of a character map contains two mappings for the same Unicode character, then the one that comes last in this sequence is the one that is used.

Usage and Examples

Character maps have no effect on the XSLT transformation proper; they only affect the way that the result tree is serialized. If the result tree is used in some way other than passing it to a serializer (for example, if it is input to another transformation in a pipeline), then character maps have no effect.

For advice on using character maps as part of the serialization process, and worked examples, see Chapter 15 *Serialization*.

See Also

`<xsl:output>` on page 420
`<xsl:output-character>` on page 424
Character Maps in Chapter 15, page 941

xsl:choose

The `<xsl:choose>` instruction defines a choice between a number of alternatives.

If there are two alternatives it performs the equivalent of `if-then-else` in other languages; if there are more than two, it performs the equivalent of a `switch` or `select` statement.

Changes in 2.0

There are no changes to the syntax of `<xsl:choose>` in XSLT 2.0. However, by using `<xsl:sequence>` instructions within the `<xsl:when>` or `<xsl:otherwise>` branch, it is now possible to use `<xsl:choose>` in cases where the required result is an atomic value, or a reference to an existing node. In XSLT 1.0, the result always consisted of newly constructed nodes.

In many situations where `<xsl:choose>` was used in XSLT 1.0, it is now possible to use an XPath conditional expression (`if-then-else`) instead, which can sometimes make the code much more compact.

Format

```
<xsl:choose>
  <!-- Content: (xsl:when+, xsl:otherwise?) -->
</xsl:choose>
```

Position

`<xsl:choose>` is an instruction; it is always used within a sequence constructor.

Attributes

None.

Content

One or more `<xsl:when>` elements.

Optionally, an `<xsl:otherwise>` element, which must come last if it is present at all.

Effect

The `<xsl:choose>` element is evaluated as follows:

- ❑ The first `<xsl:when>` element whose test *expression* is true is selected. Subsequent `<xsl:when>` elements are ignored whether or not their test *expression* is true. The test expression is evaluated to obtain its *effective boolean value*; the rules for this are given under `<xsl:if>`, on page 354.

- ❑ If none of the `<xsl:when>` elements has a test *expression* that is true, the `<xsl:otherwise>` element is selected. If there is no `<xsl:otherwise>` element, no element is selected, and the `<xsl:choose>` element therefore has no effect (it returns an empty sequence).

- ❑ The selected child element (if any) is executed by evaluating its sequence constructor in the current context. So the effect is as if the relevant sequence constructor appeared in place of the `<xsl:choose>` instruction.

The test expression in `<xsl:when>` elements after the selected one is not evaluated.

Usage

The `<xsl:choose>` instruction is useful where there is a choice of two or more alternative courses of action. It thus performs the functions of both the `if-then-else` and `switch` or `Select Case` constructs found in other programming languages.

Using `<xsl:choose>` with a single `<xsl:when>` instruction and no `<xsl:otherwise>` is permitted and means exactly the same as `<xsl:if>`. Some people suggest writing every `<xsl:if>` instruction this way, to save rewriting it later when you discover that you want an `else` branch after all.

When `<xsl:choose>` is used within the body of an `<xsl:variable>` (or `<xsl:param>` or `<xsl:with-param>`) element, the effect is a conditional assignment: the relevant variable is assigned a different value depending on the conditions.

Examples

The following example returns the name of a state in the USA based on a two-letter abbreviation for the state. If the abbreviation is not that of a recognized state, it outputs the abbreviation itself.

```
<xsl:choose>
    <xsl:when test="state='AZ'">Arizona</xsl:when>
    <xsl:when test="state='CA'">California</xsl:when>
    <xsl:when test="state='DC'">Washington DC</xsl:when>
    ......
    <xsl:otherwise><xsl:value-of select="state"/></xsl:otherwise>
</xsl:choose>
```

An alternative way of coding such an expression is to use template rules, perhaps in a particular mode:

```
<xsl:template match="state[.='AZ']" mode="expand">Arizona</xsl:template>
<xsl:template match="state[.='CA']" mode="expand">California</xsl:template>
<xsl:template match="state[.='DC']" mode="expand">Washington DC</xsl:template>
```

The following example declares a variable called width and initializes its value to the width attribute of the current node, if there is one, or to 100 otherwise.

```
<xsl:variable name="width" as="xs:integer">
    <xsl:choose>
        <xsl:when test="@width">
            <xsl:sequence select="@width"/>
        </xsl:when>
        <xsl:otherwise>
            <xsl:sequence select="100"/>
        </xsl:otherwise>
    </xsl:choose>
</xsl:variable>
```

You might be tempted to write this as follows:

```
<!--WRONG-->
<xsl:choose>
    <xsl:when test="@width">
        <xsl:variable name="width" select="@width"/>
    </xsl:when>
    <xsl:otherwise>
        <xsl:variable name="width" select="100"/>
    </xsl:otherwise>
</xsl:choose>
<!--WRONG-->
```

This is legal XSLT, but it does not achieve the required effect. This is because both the variables called «width» have a scope that is bounded by the containing element, so they are inaccessible outside the <xsl:choose> instruction.

Everyone has personal preferences when coding. I tend to prefer constructs that are more compact than <xsl:choose>. I would usually write the above example as:

```
<xsl:variable name="width" select="(@width, 100)[1]" as="xs:integer"/>
```

See Also

<xsl:when> on page 515
<xsl:otherwise> on page 420
<xsl:if> on page 353

xsl:comment

The <xsl:comment> instruction is used to write a comment node to the result sequence.

Changes in 2.0

A select attribute is added in XSLT 2.0, allowing the content of the comment to be defined by an XPath expression rather than by a sequence constructor. It's no longer an error to include two adjacent hyphens in the value of a comment — the processor will insert a space to make it legal XML.

Format

```
<xsl:comment
  select? = expression>
  <!-- Content: sequence-constructor -->
</xsl:comment>
```

Position

<xsl:comment> is an instruction; it is always used within a sequence constructor.

Attributes

Name	Value	Meaning
select optional	XPath Expression	Defines the string value of this comment node

The select attribute and the sequence constructor are mutually exclusive; if one is present, the other must be absent.

Content

A sequence constructor.

Effect

The value of the comment is produced by evaluating either the select attribute or the sequence constructor. If neither is present, the comment will be empty.

The value is computed in the same way as for <xsl:attribute> (see page 254), except that the separator between adjacent values is always a single space. The resulting string forms the string value of the new comment node.

If the comment includes a hyphen that is immediately followed either by a second hyphen or by the end of the comment, a single space will be added after the offending hyphen to ensure that the comment follows the XML rules.

6

XSLT Elements

In XML or HTML output, the comment will appear as:

```
<!-- comment text -->
```

Usage

In theory, a comment has no meaning to the software that processes the output document — it is intended only for human readers. Comments are therefore useful to record when and how the document was generated, or perhaps to explain the meaning of the tags.

Comments can be particularly useful for debugging the stylesheet. If each `<xsl:template>` in the stylesheet starts with an `<xsl:comment>` instruction, you will find it much easier to trace back from the output to your stylesheet.

Comments in HTML output are used for some special markup conventions, for example surrounding Dynamic HTML scripts. The purpose of the comment here is to ensure that browsers that don't understand the script will skip over it rather than display it as text. An example is shown below.

Examples

Three examples follow.

Example 1: Showing the Date and Time of Transformation

The following example generates a comment showing the date and time at which the output file was generated, and identifying the XSLT processor that was used:

```
<xsl:comment>
    <xsl:text> Generated on: </xsl:text>
    <xsl:value-of select="format-dateTime(
                              current-dateTime(),
                              '[D] [MNn] [Y] at [H]:[m]:[s]')"/>
    <xsl:text> using </xsl:text>
    <xsl:value-of select="system-property('xsl:product-name')"/>
    <xsl:text> version </xsl:text>
    <xsl:value-of select="system-property('xsl:product-version')"/>
</xsl:comment>
```

Typical output might be:

```
<!-- Generated on: 23 March 2008 at 12:13:02 using SAXON version 9.0-->
```

Example 2: Generating Commented-Out JavaScript

The following example outputs a piece of client-side JavaScript to an HTML output file:

```
<script language="JavaScript">
    <xsl:comment>
        function bk(n) {
            parent.frames['content'].location="chap" + n + ".1.html";
        }
```

```
    //</xsl:comment>
  </script>
```

The output will look like this:

```
<script language="JavaScript">
  <!--
    function bk(n) {
      parent.frames['content'].location="chap" + n + ".1.html";
    }
  //--></script>
```

The comment cannot be written as a comment in the stylesheet, of course, because then the XSLT processor would ignore it entirely. Comments in the stylesheet are not copied to the output destination.

Example 3: Generating Comments Containing Markup

Sometimes you want to generate comments that contain markup, for example:

```
<!--[if lt IE 6]>
  <link rel="stylesheet" type="text/css" href="IE5style.css" />
<![endif]-->
```

It's not possible to do this by creating a result tree that contains an element node as a child of a comment node, because comment nodes can't have children. This leaves two possibilities: either create the serialized representation of the element "by hand", as a string, or trick the serializer into generating the comment delimiters by using character maps. The first approach looks like this:

```
<xsl:comment>[if lt IE 6]&gt;
  &lt;link rel="stylesheet" type="text/css" href="IE5style.css" /&gt;
&lt;![endif]</xsl:comment>
```

The alternative solution uses a character map:

```
<xsl:character-map>
  <xsl:output-character character="&if-lt-IE6;" string="&lt;!--[if lt IE 6]&gt;"/>
  <xsl:output-character character="&endif;" string="&lt;[endif]--&gt;"/>
</xsl:character-map>
```

where the two entities if-lt-IE6 and endif are defined in the DTD to map to arbitrary private-use-area characters, followed by:

```
<xsl:text>&if-lt-IE6;</xsl:text>
  <link rel="stylesheet" type="text/css" href="IE5style.css" />
<xsl:text>&endif;</xsl:text>
```

xsl:copy

The <xsl:copy> instruction copies the context item in the source document to the result sequence. This is a shallow copy; it does not copy the children, descendants, or attributes of the context node, only the context node itself and (if it is an element) its namespaces. For a deep copy, you need to use <xsl:copy-of>, see page 292.

Changes in 2.0

New attributes `copy-namespaces` and `inherit-namespaces` have been added, to allow finer control over whether namespace nodes for an element should be copied or not.

New attributes `validation` and `type` have been added to control whether and how a copied node is validated against a schema.

Format

```
<xsl:copy
  copy-namespaces? = "yes" | "no"
  inherit-namespaces? = "yes" | "no"
  use-attribute-sets? = qnames
  validation? = "strict" | "lax" | "preserve" | "strip"
  type? = qname>
  <!-- Content: sequence-constructor -->
</xsl:copy>
```

Position

`<xsl:copy>` is an instruction. It is always used within a sequence constructor.

Attributes

Name	Value	Meaning
copy-namespaces optional	«yes» or «no». (Default is «yes»).	Indicates whether the namespace nodes of an element should be copied.
inherit-namespaces optional	«yes» or «no». (Default is «yes»).	Indicates whether the children of a copied element will inherit its namespaces.
use-attribute-sets optional	Whitespace-separated list of lexical QNames	The names of attribute sets to be applied to a copied element.
validation optional	«strict», «lax», «preserve», or «skip»	Indicates whether and how the copied nodes should be subjected to schema validation, or whether existing type annotations should be retained or removed.
type optional	Lexical QName	Identifies a type declaration (either a built-in type, or a user-defined type imported from a schema) against which copied nodes are to be validated.

Content

An optional sequence constructor, which is used only if the item being copied is a document node or an element.

Effect

The action depends on the kind of context item, as follows:

Item kind	Action
atomic value	Adds the atomic value to the result sequence. (Atomic values have no identity, so there is no distinction between the original value and a copy of the value.)
document	A new document node is added to the result sequence. The sequence constructor is evaluated to provide the content for the document node. This works in the same way as the content of an `<xsl:document>` instruction, as described on page 303. The attributes `copy-namespaces`, `inherit-namespaces`, and `use-attribute-sets` are ignored. The `type` and `validation` attributes have the same effect as with `<xsl:document>`.
element	An element node is added to the result sequence, as if by a call on `<xsl:element>`. This will have the same name as the context node. The local name and namespace URI are guaranteed to be the same as the original, and the prefix will be the same unless there is a conflict. The namespace nodes associated with the current element node are copied to the new element, unless «copy-namespaces="no"» is specified. The namespace nodes are also copied to the new children of the element, unless «inherit-namespaces="no"» is specified. The `use-attribute-sets` attribute and the contained sequence constructor are then evaluated to create the attributes and children of the new element in the same way as for `<xsl:element>`. Namespace fixup is applied to the new element, to ensure that it has all the namespace nodes it needs, in the same way as for the `<xsl:element>` instruction. With a schema-aware processor, the new element may be validated and may acquire a type annotation; this depends on the values of the `type` and `validation` attributes, and works exactly as for `<xsl:element>` described on page 306. Note the surprising consequence that «validation="preserve"» does not cause the type annotation of the original element to be retained: This is not feasible, because the content of the element is not being copied.
text	A new text node is added to the result sequence, with the same string value as the context node. The attributes of the `<xsl:copy>` instruction and the sequence constructor are ignored.
attribute	A new attribute node is added to the result sequence, as if by a call on `<xsl:attribute>`. This will have the same name and value as the context node. The attributes `copy-namespaces`, `inherit-namespaces`, and `use-attribute-sets` are ignored. The local name, namespace URI, and string value of the output attribute are guaranteed to be the same as the original, and the prefix will be the same unless there is a conflict (for example, if two attributes added to the same element use the same prefix to refer to different namespace URIs). With a schema-aware processor, the new attribute may be validated and may acquire a type annotation: This depends on the values of the `type` and `validation` attributes, and works exactly as for `<xsl:copy-of>` described on page 292.
processing instruction	A processing instruction node is added to the result sequence, with the same name and value (target and data in XML terminology) as the context node. The attributes of the `<xsl:copy>` instruction and the sequence constructor are ignored.

continued

Item kind	Action
comment	A comment node is added to the result sequence, with the same content as the context node. The attributes of the `<xsl:copy>` instruction and the sequence constructor are ignored.
namespace	The namespace node is copied to the result sequence. The new namespace node will have the same name and value (that is, the same namespace prefix and URI) as the original. The attributes of the `<xsl:copy>` instruction and the sequence constructor are ignored.

Usage

The main use of `<xsl:copy>` is when doing an XML-to-XML transformation in which parts of the document are to remain unchanged. It is also useful when the source XML document contains XHTML fragments within it; for example, if the simple HTML formatting elements such as `<i>` and `<b>` are used within textual data in the source and are to be copied unchanged to an HTML output document.

Although `<xsl:copy>` does a shallow copy, it is easy to construct a deep copy by applying it recursively. The typical manner of use is to write a template rule that effectively calls itself:

```
<xsl:template match="@*|node()" mode="copy">
   <xsl:copy>
      <xsl:apply-templates select="@*|node()" mode="copy"/>
   </xsl:copy>
</xsl:template>
```

This is sometimes referred to as the *identity template*. This template rule matches any node except a namespace or document node. This is because «@*» matches any attribute node, and «node()», which is short for «child::node()», matches any node that is allowed to be the child of something (that is, an element node, text node, comment, or processing instruction). Once this template rule is applied to a node, it copies that node, and if it is an element node, it applies itself to its attributes and child nodes — on the assumption that there is no other template rule with `mode="copy"` that has a higher priority. An easier way of doing a deep copy is to use `<xsl:copy-of>`. However, the recursive use of `<xsl:copy>` allows modifications to be made to the tree while it is being copied, by adding further template rules. For example, if you want to copy the whole document except for the subtree rooted at a `<note>` element, you can achieve this with a stylesheet that contains the identity template as above, together with the rule:

```
<xsl:template match="note" mode="copy"/>
```

which does nothing when a `<note>` element is found. Because it does nothing, nothing is written to the result tree, so the `<note>` element is effectively deleted. There are many variations on this theme — whenever you want to copy most of the input document to the result, but making a few changes as you go, you can do it by writing a stylesheet that uses the identity template for elements that are to be copied unchanged, supplemented by more specific templates that match the nodes you want to handle specially.

A variant of the identity template is often used which copies attributes unconditionally rather than applying templates to them. Here it is:

```
<xsl:template match="*" mode="copy">
   <xsl:copy>
      <xsl:copy-of select="@*"/>
```

```
            <xsl:apply-templates mode="copy"/>
        </xsl:copy>
    </xsl:template>
```

Examples

The following template rule is useful if the source document contains HTML-like tables that are to be copied directly to the output, without change to the structure.

```
<xsl:template match=" table | tbody | tr | th | td ">
    <xsl:copy>
        <xsl:copy-of select="@*"/>
        <xsl:apply-templates/>
    </xsl:copy>
</xsl:template>
```

The effect is that all of these elements are copied to the output destination, along with their attributes, but their child elements are processed using whatever template rule is appropriate, which might be the same one in the case of a child element that is part of the table model, or it might be a different template for some other element.

The following template rule matches any elements in the source document that are in the SVG namespace, and copies them unchanged to the output, along with their attributes. The SVG namespace node itself will also be included automatically in the output tree. (SVG stands for Scalable Vector Graphics, which is an XML-based standard for representing diagrams.)

```
<xsl:template match="svg:*"
              xmlns:svg="http://www.w3.org/2000/svg">
    <xsl:copy copy-namespaces="no">
        <xsl:copy-of select="@*">
        <xsl:apply-templates/>
    </xsl:copy>
</xsl:template>
```

This example uses «copy-namespaces="no"» to avoid copying the namespace nodes attached to the SVG elements. It is safe to do this because SVG elements and attributes do not include data that depends on in-scope namespaces. The namespaces used in the element and attribute names will automatically acquire namespace nodes as a result of the namespace fixup process described on page 310. Getting rid of extraneous namespace nodes in this way can be useful. For example, if the SVG document is embedded in an XHTML document, and the purpose of the copy operation is to make it into a freestanding SVG document, then the default value «copy-namespaces="yes"» would mean that the freestanding SVG document would contain an unwanted reference to the XHTML namespace.

The option «inherit-namespaces="no"» is useful only when generating XML 1.1 output. XML 1.1 allows namespace undeclarations of the form «xmlns:p=""», which can be useful to indicate that a namespace used in the envelope of a message (for example, a SOAP envelope) is not required in the body of the message. The serializer will generate such a namespace undeclaration on a child element if two conditions are satisified: firstly, there must be a namespace node on the parent element that is not present on the child, and secondly the serialization parameters «version="1.1"» and «undeclare-prefixes="yes"» must both be set. To meet the first requirement, you need to specify «inherit-namespaces="no"» when generating the *parent* element.

See Also

`<xsl:copy-of>` immediately following.

xsl:copy-of

The main purpose of the `<xsl:copy-of>` instruction is to copy a sequence of nodes to the result sequence. This is a deep copy — when a node is copied, its descendants are also copied.

Changes in 2.0

A new `copy-namespaces` attribute is introduced: This gives you control over whether or not the unused namespaces of an element should be copied.

Two new attributes `validation` and `type` are available to control whether and how the copied nodes are validated against a schema.

Format

```
<xsl:copy-of
  select = expression
  copy-namespaces? = "yes" | "no"
  validation? = "strict" | "lax" | "preserve" | "strip"
  type? = qname />
```

Position

`<xsl:copy-of>` is an instruction. It is always used within a sequence constructor.

Attributes

Name	Value	Meaning
select mandatory	XPath Expression	The sequence of nodes or atomic values to be copied to the output destination
copy-namespaces optional	«yes» or «no». Default is «yes»	Indicates whether the namespace nodes of an element should be copied
validation optional	«strict», «lax», «preserve», or «skip»	Indicates whether and how the copied nodes should be subjected to schema validation, or whether existing type annotations should be retained or removed
type optional	Lexical QName	Identifies a type declaration (either a built-in type, or a user-defined type imported from a schema) against which copied nodes are to be validated

The `type` and `validation` attributes are mutually exclusive: if one is present, the other must be absent. These attributes are available only with a schema-aware processor.

Content

None; the element is always empty.

292

Effect

The result of evaluating the select expression can be any sequence, containing nodes, atomic values, or a mixture of the two. Each of the items is copied to the result sequence, as follows:

❑ If the item is an atomic value, it is copied directly to the result sequence. So the instruction `<xsl:copy-of select="1 to 5"/>` has exactly the same effect as the instruction `<xsl:sequence select="1 to 5"/>`.

❑ If the item is a text node, comment, processing instruction, or namespace node, then it is copied in exactly the same way as with the `<xsl:copy>` instruction. The new node has the same name and string value as the original, but it has a new identity. For example, `generate-id()` applied to the new node will give a different result from `generate-id()` applied to the original.

❑ If the item is an attribute node, then it is copied to create a new attribute node. The new attribute node has the same name and string value as the original, but has a new identity. The type annotation on the new attribute node depends on the values of the type and validation attributes. These work in the same way as for `<xsl:attribute>` as described on page 254, except for the value «validation="preserve"», which causes the type annotation to be copied from the existing node.

❑ If the item is an element node, then it is copied to create a new element node. This is a deep copy: All the attributes and children of the element node are also copied. The namespace nodes of this element, and of any descendant elements, are copied unless the copy-namespaces attribute is present with the value «no». The base URIs of copied element nodes are unchanged (which means that any relative URIs in the content of these nodes retain their original meaning).

❑ The type annotation of the new element node depends on the values of the type and validation attributes. If the type attribute is specified, or if validation is set to «strip», «strict», or «lax», then the effect is exactly as if new content were being constructed from scratch: Existing type annotations are discarded, and the copied content is revalidated to construct type annotations. In the case of «validation="preserve"», the existing type annotations are copied over to the new nodes.

❑ If the item is a document node, then it is copied to create a new document node. This is a deep copy: All the children of the document node are also copied. All copied nodes below this document node retain the name, string value, base URIs, and type annotations of their respective originals. If «validation="preserve"» is specified, then existing type annotations are copied unchanged; in other cases, document-level validation may occur to create new type annotations. This follows the rules for the `<xsl:document>` instruction, which means that it includes checks on ID/IDREF constraints as well as `<xs:unique>`, `<xs:key>`, and `<xs:keyref>`.

Usage and Examples

There are two principal uses for `<xsl:copy-of>`: it can be used when copying data to and from a temporary tree, and it can be used for copying a subtree unchanged from the input document to the output.

Copying Nodes to and from Temporary Trees

One use of `<xsl:copy-of>` in conjunction with temporary trees arises when you want to write the same collection of nodes to the output in more than one place. This might arise, for example, with page headers and footers. The construct allows you to assemble the required output fragment as the value of a variable and then copy it to the final output destination as often as required.

Example: Using `<xsl:copy-of>` for Repeated Output

This example constructs a table heading in a variable and then copies it repeatedly each time a new table is created.

Source

The source file `soccer.xml` holds details of a number of soccer matches played during the World Cup finals in 1998.

```
<?xml version="1.0"?>
<results group="A">
<match>
  <date>1998-06-10</date>
  <team score="2">Brazil</team>
  <team score="1">Scotland</team>
</match>
<match>
  <date>1998-06-10</date>
  <team score="2">Morocco</team>
  <team score="2">Norway</team>
</match>
<match>
  <date>1998-06-16</date>
  <team score="1">Scotland</team>
  <team score="1">Norway</team>
</match>
<match>
  <date>1998-06-16</date>
  <team score="3">Brazil</team>
  <team score="0">Morocco</team>
</match>
<match>
  <date>1998-06-23</date>
  <team score="1">Brazil</team>
  <team score="2">Norway</team>
</match>
<match>
  <date>1998-06-23</date>
  <team score="0">Scotland</team>
  <team score="3">Morocco</team>
</match>
</results>
```

Stylesheet

The stylesheet is in the file `soccer.xsl`.

It constructs an HTML table heading as a global tree-valued variable, and then uses `<xsl:copy-of>` every time it wants to output this heading. In this particular case the heading is fixed, but it could contain data from the source document, as long as the heading is the same each time it is output. If it contained calculated values, there would be a possible performance benefit by coding it this way rather than regenerating the heading each time.

```
<xsl:stylesheet version="2.0"
    xmlns:xsl="http://www.w3.org/1999/XSL/Transform">

<xsl:variable name="table-heading">
    <tr>
        <td><b>Date</b></td>
        <td><b>Home Team</b></td>
        <td><b>Away Team</b></td>
        <td><b>Result</b></td>
    </tr>
</xsl:variable>

<xsl:template match="/">
<html><body>
    <h1>Matches in Group <xsl:value-of select="/*/@group"/></h1>
    <xsl:for-each select="//match">
    <h2><xsl:value-of select="team[1], 'versus', team[2]"/></h2>
    <table bgcolor="#cccccc" border="1" cellpadding="5">
        <xsl:copy-of select="$table-heading"/>
        <tr>
        <td><xsl:value-of
          select="format-date(date, '[D] [MNn,1-3] [Y]')"/></td>
        <td><xsl:value-of select="team[1]"/></td>
        <td><xsl:value-of select="team[2]"/></td>
        <td><xsl:value-of
          select="team[1]/@score, '-', team[2]/@score" separator=""/></td>
        </tr>
    </table>
    </xsl:for-each>
</body></html>
</xsl:template>

</xsl:stylesheet>
```

6

XSLT Elements

Figure 6-2

> ## Output
>
> (Apologies to soccer fans who know that all these matches were played in France, on neither team's home territory. It's only an example!) See Figure 6-2.

Deep Copy

The other use for `<xsl:copy-of>` is that it provides a simple way of copying an entire subtree of the input document directly to the output. As `<xsl:copy-of>` does a deep copy, this is simpler than using `<xsl:copy>`, although it can only be used when the whole subtree is to be copied without change. For example, an XML document defining a product description might have an element called `<overview>` whose content is pure XHTML. You could copy this to the output HTML document with a template rule such as:

```
<xsl:template match="overview">
    <div>
        <xsl:copy-of select="node()"/>
    </div>
</xsl:template>
```

Unlike the examples using `<xsl:copy>`, there is no recursive application of template rules here: each child node of the `<overview>` element is copied to the output destination in a single operation, along with all its children.

The most common example of this technique is using `<xsl:copy-of select="@*"/>` to copy all the attributes of the current element. You can also use this selectively. To copy specific attributes use the following code:

```
<xsl:copy-of select="@name, @height, @width"/>
```

Copying all the attributes with specific exceptions is also straightforward using the new «except» operator in XPath 2.0:

```
<xsl:copy-of select="@* except @note"/>
```

Using `<xsl:copy-of>` only works if you want an exact copy of the subtree. If you want to change anything, for example removing some nodes or changing the namespace URI of the element names, you will need to walk the tree using a modified identity template as described under `<xsl:copy>` on page 287.

Copying Namespace Nodes

The `copy-namespaces` attribute provides a choice as to whether the namespace nodes in a tree are copied or not. By default, all the namespaces are copied.

If namespaces are used only in the names of elements and attributes, then there is no need to copy namespace nodes. In the new tree, all the necessary namespace nodes will be created by virtue of the namespace fixup process, which is described under `<xsl:element>` on page 306 but applies equally to elements constructed using `<xsl:copy>` or `<xsl:copy-of>`. Copying unwanted namespace nodes generally does no harm, but they are unnecessary and can clutter the result document, and in some cases they can cause DTD-based validation to fail.

The real problem arises when namespace prefixes are used in the values of attributes or text nodes. This happens, for example, if the document is an XSLT stylesheet containing XPath expressions, if it is an XML Schema, if it uses «xsi:type» attributes that identify schema-defined types (the value of this attribute is a QName, and therefore contains a namespace prefix), or if it uses any other XML vocabulary that contains references to the names of elements or attributes within the document content. Since the XSLT processor cannot know that these references exist, and since the references depend on the existence of namespace nodes to resolve namespace prefixes to a URI, it is unsafe to shed the namespace nodes.

There are some cases where losing namespace nodes is very desirable. For example, if an XML document is wrapped in a SOAP envelope and then subsequently removed from the envelope, the round trip can easily cause the SOAP namespaces defined for use in the envelope to stick to the content when it is extracted using <xsl:copy-of>. Under these circumstances, using «copy-namespaces="no"» can be useful to remove unwanted namespaces from the result. But it is only safe to use this option if you know that there are no namespace prefixes in the content of text nodes and attribute nodes.

Copying Type Annotations

The validation attribute of the <xsl:copy-of> instruction gives you four options on how to handle type annotations:

❑ The «strip» option removes all type annotations from the element and attribute nodes being copied, leaving them only with the generic type annotations xs:untyped and xs:untypedAtomic, respectively. The main advantage of doing this is that you know exactly where you stand. This is the default, unless overridden using the default-validation attribute of the <xsl:stylesheet> element, and it means that the behavior will be the same whether or not the processor is schema-aware.

❑ Sometimes the «strip» option is needed because the existing type annotations do not make sense in a new context. For example, you might be copying a price-range attribute from an element in which the name is constrained to be a sequence of two numbers, to an element in which any string is allowed. Retaining the type annotation would cause spurious effects, or errors, if the attribute in its new context is then used for comparisons or sorting.

❑ The «preserve» option leaves all the type annotations intact. One might expect that this would be the default, but the value «strip» was chosen for consistency with other instructions. Generally speaking, if the source nodes have been validated and annotated, this will often be the option that makes most sense on <xsl:copy-of>.

This option works because the validity of an element or attribute depends only on its content (that is, on its attributes, its descendant elements, and their attributes). Cross-validation constraints such as ID/IDREF constraints are not taken into account by the XPath type system. This means that if the source data has a particular type annotation, you can take it on trust that the data is valid against that type, and if you copy the whole subtree, then the new nodes will still be valid against these types.

❑ The «strict» and «lax» options discard all existing type annotations, and then invoke the schema processor to validate the copied nodes. The same happens when you use the type attribute instead of the validation attribute. The way that validation works is exactly as described for the <xsl:element> instruction in the case of element nodes (see page 312), or the <xsl:attribute> instruction in the case of attribute nodes (see page 258), or the <xsl:document> instruction in the case of document nodes (see page 304). For other nodes and atomic values the validation and type attributes are ignored.

There may be cases where the existing nodes had a specific type annotation, but where revalidating the copied subtree either fails, or produces a different type annotation from the original. This is because the validation context may be different. If the subtree was originally validated as part of some larger tree, then it is possible that local element and attribute declarations were used on that occasion, whereas top-level element and attribute declarations are used this time. The top-level declarations may be either more or less permissive than the local declarations.

See Also

<xsl:copy> on page 287
<xsl:variable> on page 500

xsl:decimal-format

The <xsl:decimal-format> element is used to define the characters and symbols used when converting numbers into strings using the format-number() function.

Note that <xsl:decimal-format> applies only to the format-number() function. It has no effect on the way <xsl:number> formats numbers for display, nor on the default number-to-string conversion used by the string() function, nor on the format used when <xsl:value-of> is used to output a number as a string.

Changes in 2.0

The specification of the format-number() function, which uses the <xsl:decimal-format> declaration, is substantially rewritten in XSLT 2.0, though users should notice few changes except in a few corner cases. The <xsl:decimal-format> declaration itself is unchanged.

Import precedence now applies to decimal formats in a similar way as to other declarations.

Format

```
<xsl:decimal-format
  name? = qname
  decimal-separator? = char
  grouping-separator? = char
  infinity? = string
  minus-sign? = char
  NaN? = string
  percent? = char
  per-mille? = char
  zero-digit? = char
  digit? = char
  pattern-separator? = char />
```

Position

<xsl:decimal-format> is a top-level declaration. It may appear any number of times in a stylesheet, but only as an immediate child of the <xsl:stylesheet> element.

Attributes

Name	Value	Meaning
name optional	Lexical QName	The name of this decimal format. If omitted, the attributes define the default decimal format.
decimal-separator optional	Character	Character to be used to separate the integer and the fraction part of a number. Default is «.» (x2E).
grouping-separator optional	Character	Character used to separate groups of digits. Default is «,» (x2C).
infinity optional	String	String used to represent the numeric value infinity. Default value is «Infinity».
minus-sign optional	Character	Character used as the default minus sign. Default is «-» (x2D).
NaN optional	String	String used to represent the numeric value NaN (not a number). Default value is «NaN».
percent optional	Character	Character used to represent a percentage sign. Default value is «%» (x25).
per-mille optional	Character	Character used to represent a per-mille (per-thousand) sign. Default value is «‰» (x2030).
zero-digit optional	Character	Character used in a format pattern to indicate a place where a leading or trailing zero digit is required, even if it is not significant. Default value is «0» (x30). This character must be one that is classified in the Unicode database as a digit character, with the numeric value zero.
digit optional	Character	Character used in a format pattern to indicate a place where a digit will appear, provided it is a significant digit. Default value is «#» (x23).
pattern-separator optional	Character	Character used in a format pattern to separate the subpattern for positive numbers from the subpattern for negative numbers. Default value is «;» (x3B).

Content

None; the element is always empty.

Effect

If a name attribute is supplied, the <xsl:decimal-format> element defines a named decimal format; otherwise, it defines attributes of the default decimal format. A named decimal format is used by the format-number() function when it is called with three arguments (the third argument is the name of a decimal format); the default decimal format is used when the format-number() function is called without a third argument.

It is possible to have more than one <xsl:decimal-format> element for the default decimal format, or more than one for a decimal format with a given name. The effective value of a given attribute (such as zero-digit) is taken from the declaration with the highest import precedence that specifies a value for the required attribute. It is an error if this selects more than one declaration, unless the values specified are the same.

The <xsl:decimal-format> element does not directly define the display format of a number. Rather it defines the characters and strings used to represent different logical symbols. Some of these logical symbols occur in the *picture string* used as an argument to the format-number() function, some of them occur in the final output number itself, and some are used in both. The actual display format of a number depends both on the picture string and on the choice of decimal format symbols.

For example, if there is an <xsl:decimal-format> element as follows:

```
<xsl:decimal-format name="european"
                    decimal-separator=","
                    grouping-separator="." />
```

then the function call:

```
format-number(1234.5, '#.##0,00', 'european')
```

will produce the output:

```
1.234,50
```

The use of the «.» and «,» characters in both the picture string and the output display is determined by the named <xsl:decimal-format> element, but the number of digits displayed, and the use of leading and trailing zeros, is determined solely by the picture string.

The structure of a picture string is defined in the description of the format-number() function in Chapter 13, page 788. The syntax of the picture string uses a number of special symbols: the actual characters used for these symbols are defined in the relevant <xsl:decimal-format> element. These symbols are:

decimal-separator

grouping-separator

percent

per-mille

zero-digit

digit

pattern-separator

The <xsl:decimal-format> element also defines characters and strings that are used, when required, in the actual output value. Some of these are the same as characters used in the picture string, others are different. These characters and strings are:

decimal-separator

grouping-separator

infinity

minus-sign

NaN

percent

per-mille

zero-digit

For example, if the <xsl:decimal-format> element defines the infinity string as «***», then the output of «format-number(1e0 div 0, $format)» will be «***», regardless of the picture string.

Usage

The <xsl:decimal-format> element is used in conjunction with the format-number() function to output numeric information. It is designed primarily to provide localization of the format for display to human readers, but it can also be useful when you need to produce an output data file using, for example, a fixed number of leading zeroes. It is typically used for numbers in the source data or computed from the source data, whereas the <xsl:number> element, which has its own formatting capabilities, is generally used to generate sequence numbers.

Each <xsl:decimal-format> element defines a style of localized numbering, catering for the variations that occur in different countries and languages, and for other local preferences such as the convention in the accountancy profession whereby parentheses are used to indicate negative numbers.

Examples

The tables in the following examples illustrate some of the effects achievable using the <xsl:decimal-format> element in conjunction with a different picture string.

Example 1: Comma as a Decimal Separator

This decimal format is used in many Western European countries; it uses a comma as a decimal point and a period (full stop) as a thousands separator, the reverse of the custom in Britain and North America.

The left-hand column shows the number as it would be written in XSLT. The middle column shows the picture string supplied as the second argument to the format-number() function. The right-hand column shows the string value returned by the format-number() function.

The patterns used in this example use the following symbols:

❑ «.», which I have defined as my thousands separator

❑ «,», which I have defined as my decimal point

❑ «#», which is a position where a digit can occur, but where the digit is omitted if it is an insignificant zero

❑ «0», which is a position where a digit will always occur, even if it is an insignificant zero

❑ «%», which indicates that the number should be expressed as a percentage

❑ «;», which separates the subpicture used for positive numbers from the subpicture used for negative numbers

```
<xsl:decimal-format decimal-separator="," grouping-separator="."/>
```

Number	Picture String	Result
1234.5	#.##0,00	1.234,50
123.456	#.##0,00	123,46
1000000	#.##0,00	1.000.000,00

continued

301

6

XSLT Elements

Number	Picture String	Result
−59	#.##0,00	59,00
1e0 div 0	#.##0,00	Infinity
1234	###0,0###	1234,0
1234.5	###0,0###	1234,5
.00035	###0,0###	0,0004
0.25	#00%	25%
0.736	#00%	74%
1	#00%	100%
42	#00%	4200%
−3.12	#,00;(#,00)	(3,12)
−3.12	#,00;#,00CR	3,12CR

Example 2: Non-Western Digits

This example shows how digits other than the Western digits 0–9 can be used. I will use the Indic Arabic digits (that is, the digits used in many Arabic countries, as distinct from the so-called Arabic digits used in the West):

```
<xsl:decimal-format zero-digit="&#x0660;"/>
```

Number	Format pattern	Result
12345	• (x0660)	١٢٣٤٥

The digits will be output in the output XML or HTML file in the usual order (most significant digit first). Displaying the number correctly when it appears as part of text that runs from right to left is the job of the browser or other display software, and you shouldn't worry about it at the XSLT level.

Example 3: NaN and Infinity

This example shows how the exceptional numeric values NaN and Infinity can be shown, for example in a statistical table.

```
<xsl:decimal-format NaN="Not Applicable" infinity="Out of Range"/>
```

Number	Format pattern	Result
number('a')	any	Not Applicable
1e0 div 0	any	Out of Range
-1e0 div 0	any	-Out of Range

See Also

format-number() function in Chapter 13, page 788

<xsl:number> on page 403

xsl:document

The `<xsl:document>` instruction creates a document node and adds it to the result sequence. The most likely reason for using it is to perform document-level validation on a temporary tree.

Changes in 2.0

This instruction is new in XSLT 2.0. It should not be confused with the `<xsl:document>` instruction described in the abandoned XSLT 1.1 working draft, which was the precursor to the `<xsl:result-document>` instruction in XSLT 2.0. The document created by `<xsl:document>` is a temporary document that becomes available for further processing within the stylesheet; the document created by `<xsl:result-document>` is a final output from the transformation.

Format

```
<xsl:document
  validation? = "strict" | "lax" | "preserve" | "strip"
  type? = qname>
  <!-- Content: sequence-constructor -->
</xsl:document>
```

Position

`<xsl:document>` is used as an instruction within a sequence constructor.

Attributes

Name	Value	Meaning
validation optional	«strict», «lax», «preserve», or «skip»	Indicates whether and how the document should be subjected to schema validation
type optional	Lexical QName	Identifies a type declaration (either a built-in type, or a user-defined type imported from a schema) against which the outermost element of the new document is to be validated

The `type` and `validation` attributes are mutually exclusive: if one is present, the other must be absent. These attributes are available only with a schema-aware XSLT processor.

Content

A sequence constructor.

Effect

The following sections describe firstly how the content of the document node is constructed and secondly how document-level validation works.

The Content of the Document

The `<xsl:document>` instruction creates a new document node. The content of the document is constructed by evaluating the sequence constructor within the `<xsl:document>` element.

The child nodes of the new document node are constructed in a process that is very similar to that used for constructing the content of an element node, described under `<xsl:element>` on page 306. There are differences, however, because unlike an element node, a document node cannot have attribute or namespace nodes.

Although the XML specification requires a well-formed document to contain exactly one element node, optionally preceded or followed by comments and processing instructions, this restriction is not carried forward into the XDM data model. In XDM, a document node can contain any sequence of elements, text nodes, comments, and processing instructions (including an empty sequence) as its children. In fact, a document node can have any content that is allowed for an element node, except for the namespaces and attributes.

The process of forming the content of the document node is described below.

The first stage is to evaluate the sequence constructor contained in the `<xsl:document>` instruction (or in any other instruction that is being used to create a new document node, for example, `<xsl:copy>`, `<xsl:message>`, `<xsl:result-document>`, or `<xsl:variable>`). The sequence constructor is a sequence of instructions, and as its name implies, the result of evaluating these instructions is a sequence of items. Usually these values will all be newly constructed nodes but the sequence might also contain atomic values and/or references to existing nodes.

The way that the instructions in the sequence constructor are evaluated is described in the rules for each instruction; the items produced by each instruction are concatenated together (in the order in which the instructions appear in the stylesheet) to produce the final result sequence.

The second stage of the process is to use the result sequence delivered by evaluating the sequence constructor to create the content of the new document node. This process works as follows:

1. If there are any atomic values in the sequence, they are converted to strings using the XPath casting rules.

2. Any sequence of adjacent strings is converted to a single text node, using a single space as a separator between adjacent strings.

3. If there is a document node in the sequence, then it is replaced in the sequence by its children (this may produce an arbitrary sequence of elements, text nodes, comments, and processing instructions).

4. Adjacent text nodes within the sequence are combined into a single text node, *without* any space separator. Zero-length text nodes are removed completely.

It is an error if the resulting sequence contains an attribute or namespace node.

Finally, the nodes in the sequence are attached to the new document node as its children. Officially, this involves making a deep copy of each node: This is because nodes in the data model are immutable, so you cannot change the parent of an existing node. In practice, making a copy at this stage is very rarely necessary, because in most cases the node being attached has only just been created and will never be used independently of its new parent. The only case where it is necessary is where the result sequence contains references to existing nodes, which can be produced using the `<xsl:sequence>` instruction:

```
<xsl:document>
   <xsl:sequence select="//email[@date=current-date()]"/>
</xsl:document>
```

Even in this case, creating new nodes can be avoided if the result tree is to be immediately serialized.

Validating and Annotating the Document

The `validation` and `type` attributes control whether and how the new document is validated. They are available only if you are using a schema-aware processor. As usual, validation has two effects: it triggers a failure if the result document is invalid according to the schema, and it creates type annotations on the nodes in the tree.

The `validation` attribute has the same four values as on other elements: «strip», «preserve», «strict», and «lax». If the `validation` attribute is not specified, then the default is provided by the `default-validation` attribute on the `<xsl:stylesheet>` element, which in turn defaults to «strip».

- ❏ «strip» removes all type annotations, replacing them with `xs:untyped` for elements and `xs:untypedAtomic` for attributes.

- ❏ «preserve» leaves the type annotations as they are, determined by the `validation` and `type` attributes on the instructions that created individual elements and attributes.

- ❏ «strict» and «lax» firstly check that the tree represents a well-formed XML document, that is, that the children of the document node comprise exactly one element node, no text nodes, and any number of comments and processing instructions. If not, a failure is reported. Then the top-level element node (the document element) is validated against the schema definitions, with the difference being that «lax» validates an element only if a schema definition for that element can be found, while «strict» fails if no declaration of this element can be found.

- ❏ Validation of a document node works in the same way as validation of individual elements but with one important exception: ID/IDREF constraints defined in the schema are checked when validation is done at the document level but not when it is done at element level. This involves checking that `xs:ID` values are unique and that `xs:IDREF` and `xs:IDREFS` values reference an ID value somewhere in the document.

The «type» attribute gives the required type of the document element (not the document node). For example, if «type="mf:invoiceType"» is specified, then the single element child of the document node is validated against the schema type «mf:invoiceType».

Usage and Examples

The most likely reason for using `<xsl:document>` is to invoke validation of a temporary tree.

It is possible to perform element-level validation of the document element in a tree without using `<xsl:document>`, for example by writing:

```
<xsl:variable name="temp">
  <invoice xsl:type="mf:invoiceType">
    <xsl:call-template name="build-invoice"/>
  </invoice>
</xsl:variable>
```

However, this does not perform document-level validation: it doesn't check the ID and IDREF constraints defined in the schema, for example. To perform these extra checks, it is necessary to write the `<xsl:document>` instruction explicitly:

```
<xsl:variable name="temp">
  <xsl:document type="mf:invoiceType">
    <invoice>
      <xsl:call-template name="build-invoice"/>
```

```
      </invoice>
    </xsl:document>
  </xsl:variable>
```

There are certain other situations where `<xsl:document>` might be needed. For example, this is the only way of producing a sequence containing several new document nodes. It is also necessary if you want the value of a variable, or the default value of a parameter, to be a document node, and you also want to use the «as» attribute of `<xsl:variable>` or `<xsl:param>` to define the type of the variable, for example «as="document(element(*, mf:invoiceType))"».

See Also

`<xsl:result-document>` on page 445
`<xsl:message>` on page 386

xsl:element

The `<xsl:element>` instruction is used to create an element node and write it to the result sequence. It provides an alternative to using a literal result element and is useful especially when the element name or namespace is to be calculated at runtime.

Changes in 2.0

Two new attributes `validation` and `type` are available, to control whether and how the copied nodes are validated against a schema.

Format

```
<xsl:element
  name = { qname }
  namespace? = { uri-reference}
  use-attribute-sets? = qnames
  inherit-namespaces? = "yes" | "no"
  validation? = "strict" | "lax" | "preserve" | "strip"
  type? = qname>
  <!-- Content: sequence-constructor -->
</xsl:element>
```

Position

`<xsl:element>` is used as an instruction within a sequence constructor.

Attributes

Name	Value	Meaning
name mandatory	Attribute value template returning a lexical QName	The name of the element to be generated.
namespace optional	Attribute value template returning a URI	The namespace URI of the generated element.

continued

Name	Value	Meaning
use-attribute-sets optional	Whitespace-separated list of lexical QNames	List of named attribute sets containing attributes to be added to this output element.
inherit-namespaces optional	«yes» or «no». (Default is «yes»).	Indicates whether the namespaces of the constructed element will be inherited by its children.
validation optional	«strict», «lax», «preserve», or «skip»	Indicates whether and how the element should be subjected to schema validation, or whether existing type annotations on attributes and child elements should be retained or removed.
type optional	Lexical QName	Identifies a type declaration (either a built-in type, or a user-defined type imported from a schema) against which the new element is to be validated.

The `type` and `validation` attributes are mutually exclusive: if one is present, the other must be absent. These attributes are available only with a schema-aware XSLT processor.

Content

A sequence constructor.

Effect

The effect of this instruction is to create a new element node, and to return this node as the result of the instruction.

The name of the generated element node is determined using the `name` and `namespace` attributes. The way in which these attributes are used is described below in the section *The Name of the Element*.

The sequence constructor contained in the `<xsl:element>` instruction, together with the `use-attribute-sets` attribute, is used to form the content of the new element: that is, its namespaces, attributes, and child nodes. The way this works is described in the section *The Content of the Element*.

When a schema-aware XSLT processor is used, the new element (and its contained elements and attributes) may be validated to ensure that they conform to a type defined in a schema. This process results in the new element node having a type annotation. The type annotation affects the behavior of subsequent operations on this element node even though it is not visible when the result tree is serialized as raw XML. The validation and annotation of the new element node are controlled using the `type` and `validation` attributes. This is described in the section *Validating and Annotating the Element*.

The XSLT specification is written in terms instructions returning a value, which in this case is an element node. Sometimes it is convenient to think in terms of the start tag of the `<xsl:element>` element producing a start tag in the output XML file and the end tag of the `<xsl:element>` element producing the corresponding end tag, with the intervening sequence constructor producing the contents of the output element. However, this is a dangerous simplification, because writing the start tag and end tag are not separate operations that can be individually controlled, they are two things that happen together as a consequence of the `<xsl:element>` instruction being evaluated. This is explained in more detail in the section *Literal Result Elements* in Chapter 3, page 112.

6

XSLT Elements

The Name of the Element

The name of an element node has three parts: the prefix, the local name and the namespace URI. These are controlled using the `name` and the `namespace` attributes.

Both the `name` and the `namespace` attributes may be given as attribute value templates; that is, they may contain expressions nested within curly braces. One of the main reasons for using the `<xsl:element>` instruction in preference to a literal result element (described in the section *Literal Result Elements* in Chapter 3, page 112) is that `<xsl:element>` allows the name of the element to be decided at runtime, and this is achieved by using attribute value templates in these two attributes.

The result of expanding the `name` attribute value template must be a lexical QName; that is, a valid XML name with an optional namespace prefix, for example, «table» or «fo:block». If there is a prefix, it must correspond to a namespace declaration that is in scope at this point in the stylesheet, unless there is also a `namespace` attribute, in which case it is taken as referring to that namespace.

The local part of the name of the created element node will always be the same as the local part of the QName supplied as the value of the `name` attribute.

If the `<xsl:element>` instruction has a `namespace` attribute, it is evaluated (expanding the attribute value template if necessary) to determine the namespace URI part of the name of the created element node:

- ❏ If the value is a zero-length string, the element will have a null namespace URI.

- ❏ Otherwise, the value should be a URI identifying a namespace. This namespace does not need to be in scope at this point in the stylesheet, in fact it usually won't be. The processor may report an error if the value is not a legal URI.

If there is no `namespace` attribute:

- ❏ If the supplied QName includes a prefix, the prefix must be a namespace prefix that is in scope at this point in the stylesheet. In other words, there must be an «xmlns:prefix="uri"» declaration either on the `<xsl:element>` instruction itself or on some containing element. The namespace URI in the output will be that of the namespace associated with this prefix in the stylesheet.

- ❏ Otherwise, the default namespace is used. This is the namespace declared, in some containing element in the stylesheet, with an «xmlns="uri"» declaration. If there is no default namespace declaration in scope, then the element will have a null namespace URI. Note that this is one of the few places in XSLT where the default namespace is used to expand a `QName` having no prefix; in nearly all other cases, a null namespace URI is used. The reason is to ensure that the behavior is consistent with that of an element name used in the start tag of a literal result element.

The prefix part of the name of the new element node will normally be the same as the prefix part of the lexical QName supplied as the value of the `name` attribute (if that name has no prefix, then the new element node will have no prefix). In rare cases, however, the system may need to choose a different prefix to prevent conflicts: for example, if an attribute of the element uses the same prefix to refer to a different namespace.

The Content of the Element

The attributes, namespaces, and child nodes of the new element node are constructed in what is conceptually a four-stage process, though in practice most implementations are likely to collapse the four stages into one.

The first stage is to evaluate the sequence constructor contained in the `<xsl:element>` instruction. The sequence constructor is a sequence of instructions, and as its name implies, the result of evaluating these instructions is a sequence of items. Usually these values will all be newly constructed nodes but the sequence might also contain atomic values and/or references to existing nodes.

The way that the instructions in the sequence constructor are evaluated is described in the rules for each instruction; the items produced by each instruction are concatenated together (in the order in which the instructions appear in the stylesheet) to produce the final result sequence.

> *The instructions in a sequence constructor can be evaluated in any order, or in parallel, but their results must be assembled in the correct order on completion.*

If the `use-attribute-sets` attribute is present it must be a whitespace-separated list of lexical QNames that identify named `<xsl:attribute-set>` declarations in the stylesheet. The `<xsl:attribute>` instructions within these named attribute sets are evaluated, and the resulting sequence of attribute nodes is added to the start of the result sequence. For more details, see `<xsl:attribute-set>` on page 266.

The second stage of the process is to use the result sequence delivered by evaluating the sequence constructor (and the `use-attribute-sets` attribute if present) to create the content of the new element node. This process works as follows:

1. If there are any atomic values in the sequence, they are converted to strings using the XPath casting rules.

2. Any sequence of adjacent strings is converted to a single text node, using a single space as a separator between adjacent strings. This allows list-valued content to be constructed, for example where the schema for the result document requires the content of an element to be a sequence of integers.

3. If there is a document node in the sequence, then it is replaced in the sequence by its children (document nodes in the data model are not constrained to represent well-formed XML documents, so this may produce an arbitrary sequence of elements, text nodes, comments, and processing instructions).

4. Adjacent text nodes within the sequence are combined into a single text node, *without* any space separator, and zero-length text nodes are removed.

5. Duplicate attribute nodes are removed. If several attributes in the sequence have the same name, all but the last are discarded.

6. Duplicate namespace nodes are removed. If several namespace nodes in the sequence have the same name *and string-value* (that is, they bind the same namespace prefix to the same namespace URI), then all but one of them are discarded. It makes no difference which one is kept.

It is an error if the resulting sequence contains an attribute or namespace that is preceded by a node that is not an attribute or namespace node.

> *The reason for this rule is to allow the implementation the flexibility to generate the output as an XML file, without having to build the result tree in memory first. If attributes could be added at any time, the whole result tree would need to be kept in memory.*

It's also an error if there are conflicting namespace nodes at this point, that is, two namespace nodes that bind the same prefix to different namespace URIs, or a namespace node that declares a default namespace when the element itself is not in any namespace.

In the third stage of the process, the attribute nodes in the sequence are attached to the new element as its attributes, the namespace nodes are attached as its namespaces, and the other nodes are attached as its children. Officially, this involves making a deep copy of each node: this is because nodes in the data model are immutable, so you cannot change the parent of an existing node. In practice, making a copy at this stage is very rarely necessary, because in most cases the node being attached has only just been created and will never be used independently of its new parent. The only case where it is necessary is where the result sequence contains references to existing nodes, which can be produced using the `<xsl:sequence>` instruction:

```
<xsl:element name="digest">
   <xsl:sequence select="//email[@date=current-date()]"/>
</xsl:element>
```

In this situation, the result is exactly the same as if `<xsl:copy-of>` had been used instead of `<xsl:sequence>`.

When an element node appears in the result sequence and is copied to form a child of the newly constructed element, it also acquires copies of all the parent element's namespaces. Futhermore, these percolate down to all descendant elements, unless there's already a namespace present with a conflicting definition. This process is called namespace inheritance, and is discussed further on page 311. The process can be suppressed by setting «inherit-namespaces="no"» on the parent element.

The fourth and final stage of the process is called *namespace fixup*. Conceptually, this is done after all the nodes produced by the sequence constructor have been added to the new element. In practice all the information needed to do namespace fixup is available once all the attributes and namespaces have been added, and a processor that serializes the result tree "on the fly" is likely to perform this operation at that stage, so that the start tag of the serialized element can be output as early as possible. Namespace fixup is described in the next section.

Namespace Fixup

Namespace fixup is applied to any element node as soon as its content has been constructed, whether the node is created using the `<xsl:element>` instruction or using another mechanism such as a literal result element, `<xsl:copy>`, or `<xsl:copy-of>`. The process ensures that the new element node will automatically contain all the namespace nodes it needs to bind unique namespace prefixes to the namespaces used in the element name itself and on the names of all its attributes.

The namespace fixup process can do two things: it can add namespace nodes to the tree and it can change the prefixes allocated to element and attribute nodes. The specification isn't completely prescriptive, but it makes it fairly clear that the fixup process is expected to make the minimal changes necessary to ensure that all the consistency rules defined in XDM are satisfied. Typically, this will involve the following steps:

1. Examine the prefixes used on the element node and its attributes, and check that they are consistent with each other and with the element's existing namespace nodes. If there are any conflicts, allocate different prefixes to some or all of the nodes. Note that existing namespace nodes will never be changed by this process (this is because there might be namespace-sensitive content that relies on these namespaces).

2. For every prefix used on the element node or on one of its attributes, ensure that there is a namespace node that binds this prefix to the relevant namespace URI. This will only involve adding namespace nodes, never modifying or deleting them.

This process is described in conceptual terms and the real implementation might be very different. For example, a processor might not actually store real namespace nodes in respect of the namespaces used on the element and attribute names, but instead might create them only when they are actually referenced.

The processor does not attempt to create namespace nodes in respect of namespace-sensitive content appearing in element or attribute nodes. For example, if you write the attribute «xsi:type= "xs:integer"», namespace fixup will ensure that there is a namespace node for the «xsi» namespace, but not for the «xs» namespace. There are a number of reasons for this: one is that the processor often has no way of knowing that the content is namespace-sensitive, because it's not declared as such in a schema. Another is that namespace fixup happens before schema validation, because schema validation will fail if the right namespace bindings don't already exist. So in such cases it's your responsibility, when creating namespace-sensitive content, to ensure that the namespaces are declared. This can always be achieved using the <xsl:namespace> instruction, described on page 390.

Namespace fixup also ensures that every element has a namespace node that maps the prefix «xml» to the namespace URI http://www.w3.org/XML/1998/namespace. At any rate, this is what the specification says. In practice, implementations probably won't store a real node for this namespace; instead, they will simply behave as if it always existed.

Namespace Inheritance

It's worth observing one thing that namespace fixup *doesn't* do. When you create an element <b> as a child of <a>, namespace fixup does not try to give the <b> element a copy of every namespace node that is present for the <a> element. This is controlled instead by the [xsl:]inherit-namespaces attribute of the instruction that creates the <a> element.

XML Namespaces 1.1 introduces the ability to undeclare namespaces. It was always possible under XML Namespaces 1.0 to write:

```
<a xmlns="http://one.com/ns">
   <b xmlns=""/>
</a>
```

which has the effect that the http://one.com/ns namespace is in scope for <a> but not for <b>. This is represented in the data model by the fact that the <a> element has a namespace node that maps the empty prefix to the namespace URI http://one.com/ns, while the <b> element has no such namespace node. With XML Namespaces 1.1 it becomes possible to do the same thing with a nondefault namespace. You can now write:

```
<a xmlns:one="http://one.com/ns">
   <b xmlns:one=""/>
</a>
```

Again, this is represented in the data model by the fact that the <a> element has a namespace node that maps the prefix one to the namespace URI http://one.com/ns, while the <b> element has no such namespace node. However, if the above code appears in your stylesheet rather than your source document, then the <b/> element will acquire a copy of the namespace node «xmlns:one="http://one .com/ns"» as part of the process of element construction. This is because, by default, when an element is attached as a child to a new parent, it (and its descendants) acquire copies of all the namespace nodes that are present on the new parent, unless they actually bind the same prefix to a different namespace. This process is called *namespace inheritance*. If you want to disable this, you need to write:

```
<a xmlns:one="http://one.com/ns" xsl:inherit-namespaces="no">
   <b xmlns:one=""/>
</a>
```

You'll only really notice the difference if you put this structure in a variable and then use an instruction such as `<xsl:copy-of select="$temp//b"/>`. If namespace nodes are inherited, the result will be:

```
<b xmlns:one="http://one.com/ns"/>
```

But if namespace nodes are not inherited, the result will be:

```
<b/>
```

When you serialize the `<a>` element as an XML 1.0 document, it's not possible to represent the absence of the namespace, so the result will be the same either way, namely:

```
<?xml version="1.0"?>
<a xmlns:one="http://one.com/ns">
   <b/>
</a>
```

If you want a faithful representation of the tree, showing that the namespace is not in scope for the `<b>` element, you will need to serialize the result as an XML 1.1 document; moreover, you will have to explicitly say that you want to take advantage of this XML 1.1 feature by specifying the serialization parameter «undeclare-prefixes="yes"». If you do this, the output will be:

```
<?xml version="1.1"?>
<a xmlns:one="http://one.com/ns">
   <b xmlns:one=""/>
</a>
```

For more details of serialization options, see `<xsl:output>` on page 420, and Chapter 15.

Validating and Annotating the Element

This section is relevant only if you are using a schema-aware XSLT processor. With a non-schema-aware processor, you cannot use the `type` and `validation` attributes, and the type annotation on the new element will always be `xs:untyped`, which you can effectively ignore because it imposes no constraints.

With a schema-aware processor, you can validate the new element to ensure that it conforms with relevant definitions in a schema. If validation fails, a fatal error is reported. If it succeeds, the new element will have a type annotation that reflects the validation that was performed. This type annotation will not affect the way the element node is serialized, but if you want to do further processing on the element, the type annotation may affect the way this works. For example, if you sort a sequence of elements annotated with type `xs:integer`, you will get different results than if they are annotated as `xs:string`.

If you use the `type` attribute, the value of the attribute must be a lexical QName that identifies a known type definition. Generally, this means that it must either be a built-in type such as `xs:string` or `xs:dateTime`, or it must be the name of a global simple or complex type defined in a schema that has been imported using an `<xsl:import-schema>` declaration in the stylesheet. (That is, the local part of the QName must match the `name` attribute of a top-level `<xs:simpleType>` or `<xs:complexType>` element in a schema document whose target namespace matches the namespace URI part of the QName.)

> *The XSLT specification allows the implementation to provide other ways of accessing type definitions, perhaps through an API or a configuration file, and it also allows the type definition to originate from a source other than an XML Schema, but since it provides no details of how this might work, we won't explore the possibility further here.*

The processor validates that the constructed element conforms to the named type definition. If it does, the element is annotated with the name of this type. If it doesn't, processing fails.

Validating an element is a recursive process, which also involves validating all its attributes and child elements. So these contained elements and attributes may also acquire a different type annotation.

In general, it's likely that some of the contained elements and attributes will be validated against anonymous type definitions in the schema, that is, types defined inline as part of another type definition (or element or attribute declaration), rather than named global types. In this case, the XSLT processor invents a name for each such type definition and uses this invented name as the type annotation. The invented name is not visible to the application, though it might appear in diagnostics, but it is used during subsequent processing whenever there is a need to check that the element or attribute conforms to a particular type. (In practice, of course, the invented "name" might not really be a name at all, but a pointer to some data structure containing the type definition.)

There is potentially a lot of redundant processing if you validate every element that you add to the result tree, because elements at the bottom level of the tree will be validated repeatedly each time an ancestor element is validated. It's up to the XSLT processor to handle this sensibly; one approach that it might use is to mark the element as needing validation, but to defer the actual validation until it really needs to be done.

Validating the element may also have other effects; in particular, it may cause default values for elements and attributes within the element's content to be expanded. Default values can be defined in the schema using `<xs:element default="ABC">` or `<xs:attribute default="XYZ">`. So the element after validation may contain element and attribute values that were not put there explicitly by the stylesheet.

Validating an element using the `type` attribute places no constraints on the name of the element. It does not need to be an element name that is defined in any schema. The validation is concerned with the content of the element (including, of course, the names of its attributes and children) and not with its name.

In contrast, validation using the `validation` attribute is driven by the element's name.

There are two options for the `validation` attribute that cause schema validation to happen and two options that cause it not to happen. Let's take the last two first:

❑ «`validation="preserve"`» means that the new element will have a type annotation of `xs:anyType`, and the attributes and elements in its content will have their original type annotation. During the (formal) process of copying nodes from the sequence produced by evaluating the sequence constructor, the nodes are copied with their type annotations intact.

❑ «validation="strip"» means that the new element will have a type annotation of xs:untyped, and in this case the attributes and elements in its content (at any depth) will have their type annotation changed to xs:untypedAtomic or xs:untyped, respectively. (The type annotations are changed in the course of copying the nodes; the original nodes are, of course, unchanged).

The difference between xs:anyType and xs:untyped is rather subtle, and most applications won't notice the difference. However, the XSLT processor knows when it sees an xs:untyped element that all its descendants will also be xs:untyped, and this makes certain optimizations possible.

The other two options are «strict» and «lax»:

❑ «validation="strict"» causes the processor to look in the schema for an element declaration that matches the name of the element. That is, it looks for a top-level <xs:element> whose name attribute matches the local name of the element being validated, in a schema document whose target namespace matches the namespace URI of the element being validated. If it can't find such a definition, a fatal error is reported. Otherwise, the content of the element is validated against the schema-defined rules implied by this element declaration.

If the element declaration in the schema refers to a named type definition, then on successful validation, the element is annotated with this type name. If the element declaration contains an inline (and therefore unnamed) type definition, the XSLT processor invents a name for this implicit type, and uses this invented name as the type annotation, just as in the case described earlier for the type attribute.

If the element declaration requires it, then strict validation of an element proceeds recursively through the content of the element. It is possible, however, that the element declaration is liberal. It may, for example, define the permitted contents of the element using <xs:any>, with processContents set to «lax» or «skip». In this case, validation follows the schema rules. If «skip» is specified, for example, the relevant subtree is not validated. All nodes in such a subtree will be annotated as if «validation="strip"» were specified.

If an «xsi:type» attribute appears in the data being validated, then the system takes account of it according to the rules in the XML Schema specification. Elements validated against such an attribute will end up with this type as their type annotation.

❑ «validation="lax"» behaves in the same way as «validation="strict"», except that no failure occurs if the processor cannot locate a top-level schema declaration for the element. Instead of reporting an error, the element is annotated as xs:anyType, and validation continues recursively (again, in lax mode) with its attributes and child elements. Once an element is found that does have a schema definition, however, it is validated strictly against that definition, and if validation fails, a fatal error is reported.

I said that the processor looks in the schema for an appropriate element declaration, but where does it find the schema? It knows the namespace of the element name at this stage, so if a schema for this target namespace has been imported using <xsl:import-schema> (see page 368), then there is no problem. Otherwise, the specification leaves things rather open. It recognizes that some processors are likely to have some kind of catalog or repository that enables the schema for a given namespace to be found without difficulty, and it allows this to happen where the implementation supports it. You can also create an xsi:schemaLocation attribute node on the element being validated, to provide guidance on where a schema document might be found. In other cases, the implementation is allowed to report an error.

If neither the `type` nor `validation` attribute is present, then the system behaves as if the `validation` attribute were present and had the value given by the `default-validation` attribute of the containing `<xsl:stylesheet>` element. If no default is specified at that level, the effect is the same as «validation="strip"».

XSLT does not provide any way to request validation of an element against a local element or type definition in a schema. The way around this is to request validation only when you create an element for which there is a top-level definition in the schema. This will then implicitly validate the whole subtree contained by that element, including elements that have local definitions in the schema. Alternatively, many locally declared elements make use of a globally defined type, and you can then use the `type` attribute to validate against the type definition.

Usage and Examples

In most cases, elements in a result tree can be generated either using literal result elements in the stylesheet, or by copying a node from the source document using `<xsl:copy>`.

The only situations where `<xsl:element>` is absolutely needed are therefore where the element name in the result document is not fixed and is not the same as an element in the source document.

Using `<xsl:element>` rather than a literal result element can also be useful where different namespaces are in use. It allows the namespace URI of the generated element to be specified explicitly, rather than being referenced via a prefix. This means the namespace does not have to be present in the stylesheet itself, thus giving greater control over exactly which elements the namespace declarations are attached to. With a literal result element, all in-scope namespaces from the stylesheet are copied to the result document unless you exclude them using `[xsl:]exclude-result-prefixes`; this does not happen for `<xsl:element>`.

Example: Converting Attributes to Child Elements

This example illustrates how `<xsl:element>` can be used to create element nodes whose names and content are taken from the names and values of attributes in the source document.

Source

The source document `book.xml` contains a single `<book>` element with several attributes:

```
<?xml version="1.0"?>
<book title="Object-oriented Languages"
    author="Michel Beaudouin-Lafon"
    translator="Jack Howlett"
    publisher="Chapman &amp; Hall"
    isbn="0 412 55800 9"
    date="1994"/>
```

Stylesheet

The stylesheet `atts-to-elements.xsl` handles the book element by processing each of the attributes in turn (the expression «@*» selects all the attribute nodes). For each one, it outputs an element whose name is the same as the attribute name and whose content is the same as the attribute value.

The stylesheet is as follows:

```
<xsl:transform
 xmlns:xsl="http://www.w3.org/1999/XSL/Transform"
 version="2.0"
>
<xsl:output indent="yes"/>
<xsl:template match="book">
   <book>
       <xsl:for-each select="@*">
         <xsl:element name="{local-name()}" namespace="{namespace-uri()}">
           <xsl:value-of select="."/>
         </xsl:element>
       </xsl:for-each>
   </book>
</xsl:template>
</xsl:transform>
```

This selects all the attributes of the <book> element (using the expression «@*»), and for each one, it generates an element whose name is the same as the name of that attribute, and whose content is the value of that attribute.

Output

The XML output (on my system) is shown below. The stylesheet isn't guaranteed to produce exactly this output, because the order of attributes is undefined. This means that the <xsl:for-each> loop might process the attributes in any order, so the order of child elements in the output is also unpredictable. With Saxon, it actually depends on which XML parser you are using.

```
<book>
    <author>Michel Beaudouin-Lafon</author>
    <date>1994</date>
    <isbn>0 412 55800 9</isbn>
    <publisher>Chapman &amp; Hall</publisher>
    <title>Object-oriented Languages</title>
    <translator>Jack Howlett</translator>
</book>
```

See Also

<xsl:attribute> on page 254
<xsl:copy> on page 287

xsl:fallback

The <xsl:fallback> instruction is used to define processing that should occur if no implementation of its parent instruction is available.

Changes in 2.0

None.

Format

```
<xsl:fallback>
    <!-- Content: sequence-constructor -->
</xsl:fallback>
```

Position

`<xsl:fallback>` is an instruction. It is generally used within a sequence constructor. However, some new XSLT 2.0 instructions (`<xsl:analyze-string>`, `<xsl:next-match>`) allow an `<xsl:fallback>` element as a child even though they do not contain a sequence constructor. This is to allow fallback behavior to be defined for use when these instructions are encountered by an XSLT 1.0 processor.

Attributes

None.

Content

A sequence constructor.

Effect

There are two circumstances where `<xsl:fallback>` can be useful:

❑ In a stylesheet that uses XSLT features defined in version 2.0, to indicate what should happen if the stylesheet is used with an XSLT 1.0 processor. For example, the XSLT 2.0 specification introduces the new instruction `<xsl:result-document>`. If you want to use the `<xsl:result-document>` instruction in a stylesheet, and also want to specify what an XSLT 1.0 processor that doesn't understand this instruction should do, you can define the required behavior using `<xsl:fallback>`. XSLT 1.0 was carefully designed with extensibility in mind, so every XSLT 1.0 processor should implement this fallback behavior correctly even though the new XSLT 2.0 instructions were not defined at the time the processor was written.

❑ In a stylesheet that uses extension elements provided by a vendor, by the user, or by a third party, to indicate what should happen if the stylesheet is used with an XSLT processor that does not support these extensions.

If the `<xsl:fallback>` instruction is encountered in a sequence constructor that the processor can evaluate normally, it is ignored, along with its contents.

An instruction (as distinct from a literal result element) is an element that occurs in a sequence constructor and is either:

❑ in the XSLT namespace, or

❑ in a namespace designated as an extension namespace by its inclusion in the `[xsl:]extension-element-prefixes` attribute of the element itself or a containing element. This attribute must be in the XSLT namespace if its parent element is *not* in the XSLT namespace, and vice versa.

If an instruction is recognized by the XSLT processor, it is evaluated. The standard doesn't define exactly what "recognized by the XSLT processor" means. Typically, it means that either the instruction is a vendor-specific extension implemented by that vendor, or it is a user-defined extension that has been installed or configured according to the instructions given by the vendor. It is also quite permissible for one vendor, say Oracle, to recognize extensions defined by another vendor, say Microsoft.

If an instruction is *not* recognized by the XSLT processor, the action taken by an XSLT 2.0 processor is as follows:

❑ For an element in the XSLT namespace, if the effective version is «2.0» or less, an error is reported. If the effective version is higher than «2.0», fallback processing is invoked.

❑ For an extension element, fallback processing is invoked.

Similarly, an XSLT 1.0 processor invokes fallback processing when it sees an instruction in the XSLT namespace if the effective version is «2.0» (or indeed, any value other than «1.0»).

The effective version is the value of the [xsl:]version attribute on the nearest enclosing element that has such an attribute (the attribute must be in the XSLT namespace if the element is *not* in the XSLT namespace, and vice versa). The value is a decimal number (for example «2.3», «10.852», or «17»), and it is compared numerically. The idea is that a stylesheet, or a portion of a stylesheet, that uses facilities defined in some future XSLT version, 2.1 (say), should be given an effective version of «2.1».

Note that while XSLT 2.0 allows the version attribute to appear on any element in the XSLT namespace, XSLT 1.0 allowed it only on the <xsl:stylesheet> element. This means that if you want an XSLT 1.0 processor to invoke fallback behavior on a stylesheet that uses XSLT 2.0 features, you must either specify «version="2.0"» on the <xsl:stylesheet> element, or specify «xsl:version="2.0"» on a containing literal result element. In practice, it is a good idea to put the templates and other declarations that depend on XSLT 2.0 in a separate stylesheet module, and label that module with «version="2.0"» on the <xsl:stylesheet> element.

Fallback processing means that if the unknown instruction has an <xsl:fallback> child element, the <xsl:fallback> instruction is evaluated; otherwise, an error is reported. If there is more than one <xsl:fallback> instruction, they are all evaluated.

<xsl:fallback> is concerned only with fallback behavior for instructions within sequence constructors. Top-level declarations that the implementation doesn't recognize are simply ignored, as are unrecognized elements in another context (for example, an unrecognized child of an <xsl:choose> or <xsl:call-template> instruction).

Note that both the [xsl:]version attribute and the [xsl:]extension-element-prefixes attribute apply only within the stylesheet module in which they occur: they do not apply to stylesheet modules incorporated using <xsl:include> or <xsl:import>.

Usage

The <xsl:fallback> mechanism allows a stylesheet to be written that behaves sensibly with XSLT processors that handle different versions of XSLT. This is motivated by the experience of Web developers with HTML, and especially by the difficulty of writing Web pages that work correctly on different browsers. The design aimed to cater for a world in which some browsers would include an XSLT 2.0 processor and others would provide an XSLT 1.0 processor; in this situation, it would become necessary to write stylesheets that would work with either.

Similarly, it is very likely that each vendor of an XSLT processor (or each browser vendor) will add some bells and whistles of their own — indeed, this has already happened with XSLT 1.0. For server-side stylesheet processing you might be prepared to use such proprietary extensions and thus lock yourself into the products of one vendor, but more likely, you want to keep your stylesheets portable. The `<xsl:fallback>` mechanism allows you to do this by defining within any proprietary extension element what the XSLT processor should do if it doesn't understand it. This might be, for example:

❑ Do nothing, if the behavior is inessential, such as keeping statistics.

❑ Invoke an alternative implementation that achieves the same effect.

❑ Output fallback text to the user explaining that a particular facility cannot be offered and suggesting how they should upgrade.

An alternative way of defining fallback behavior when facilities are not available is to use the `element-available()` function, perhaps within an `[xsl:]use-when` attribute, and thus to avoid compiling or executing the relevant parts of a stylesheet. This function is described in Chapter 13, page 764. The two mechanisms have overlapping functionality, so use whichever you find most convenient.

Examples

The two examples that follow illustrate the principal use cases for `<xsl:fallback>`: creating stylesheets that are forward compatible across XSLT versions, and creating stylesheets that use vendor extensions while maintaining portability. The third example is not actually an example of `<xsl:fallback>` at all: it shows another method of achieving fallback behavior when `<xsl:fallback>` won't do the job.

Example 1: XSLT Forward Compatibility

The following example shows a stylesheet (`copy-to-output.xsl`) written to exploit a hypothetical new XSLT feature in version 6.1 of the standard that inserts a document identified by URI straight into the result tree. The stylesheet is written so that if this feature is not available, the same effect is achieved using existing facilities.

```
<xsl:template name="boilerplate" version="6.1">
   <div id="boilerplate">
      <xsl:copy-to-output href="boilerplate.xhtml">
         <xsl:fallback>
            <xsl:copy-of select="document('boilerplate.xhtml')"/>
         </xsl:fallback>
      </xsl:copy-to-output>
   </div>
</xsl:template>
```

Example 2: Vendor Portability

Writing a stylesheet that uses vendor extensions but is still portable is not particularly easy, but the mechanisms are there to achieve it, especially in the case where several vendors provide similar extensions but in slightly different ways.

For example, several XSLT 1.0 processors (certainly xt, Saxon 6, and Xalan) provide a feature to generate multiple output files from a single stylesheet. With XSLT 2.0 this popular facility has made it into the XSLT standard, but before that happened, each product had to invent its own syntax. If you want to write a stylesheet that uses the XSLT 2.0 facility when it is available, but with fallback implementations for these three products, you should in principle be able to do it like this (`multidoc.xsl`):

```
<xsl:template match="preface">
<a href="preface.html" xsl:version="2.0"
      xmlns:saxon6="http://icl.com/saxon"
      xmlns:xt="http://www.jclark.com/xt"
      xmlns:xalan="http://xml.apache.org/xalan/redirect"
      xsl:extension-element-prefixes="saxon6 xt xalan">
  <xsl:result-document href="preface.html">
   <xsl:call-template name="write-preface"/>
   <xsl:fallback>
      <saxon6:output href="preface.html">
         <xsl:call-template name="write-preface"/>
         <xsl:fallback/>
      </saxon6:output>
      <xt:document href="preface.html">
         <xsl:call-template name="write-preface"/>
         <xsl:fallback/>
      </xt:document>
      <xalan:write file="preface.html">
         <xsl:call-template name="write-preface"/>
         <xsl:fallback/>
      </xalan:write>
   </xsl:fallback>
  </xsl:result-document>
Preface</a>
</xsl:template>
```

This would work if all three 1.0 processors implemented the full XSLT 1.0 specification. Unfortunately, xt doesn't support forward-compatible processing and doesn't recognize `<xsl:fallback>`, so in practice the only way we could get this to work with xt was to use different overlay stylesheet modules for different processors. You'll find this solution in the subdirectory `ch06/fallback/xt`.

Hopefully, this little nightmare will disappear once XSLT 2.0 is widely implemented. However, by then the vendors, no doubt, will have thought of other good ideas to include as nonstandard extensions.

Example 3: Temporary Trees

This example doesn't actually use `<xsl:fallback>`; it's an example of where the same effect needs to be achieved by different means.

One of the most important new features introduced in XSLT 2.0 is the ability to process a tree-valued variable as a document in its own right, using facilities such as XPath path expressions and `<xsl:for-each>`. The following code, which is perfectly legal in XSLT 2.0, will be flagged as an error by a conforming XSLT 1.0 processor. The message will be something like "cannot convert result tree fragment to node-set":

```
<xsl:variable name="us-states">
  <state abbr="AZ" name="Arizona"/>
  <state abbr="CA" name="California"/>
  <state abbr="NY" name="New York"/>
</xsl:variable>
. . .
<xsl:value-of select="$us-states/state[@abbr='CA']/@name"/>
```

The change to make this legal in XSLT 2.0 involves no new instructions, so it isn't possible to write an `<xsl:fallback>` instruction to define what an XSLT 1.0 processor should do with this code: There's no suitable instruction to contain it. The only way of defining fallback behavior in this case is to test the XSLT version using the `system-property()` function. The following stylesheet (`lookup.xsl`) will work with both XSLT 1.0 and XSLT 2.0. This accesses a lookup table defined as a global variable in the stylesheet. With a 2.0 processor, it accesses the variable containing the lookup table directly. With a 1.0 processor, it does it by using the «`document('')`» construct to read the stylesheet as a secondary input document.

The code prevents an XSLT 2.0 processor executing the 1.0 code by means of the `use-when` attribute, which a 1.0 processor will ignore in forward-compatibility mode. The same technique can't be used to prevent a 1.0 processor executing the 2.0 code, so this uses a runtime check instead.

```
<xsl:stylesheet version="2.0"
    xmlns:xsl="http://www.w3.org/1999/XSL/Transform">

<xsl:variable name="us-states">
  <state abbr="AZ" name="Arizona"/>
  <state abbr="CA" name="California"/>
  <state abbr="NY" name="New York"/>
</xsl:variable>

<xsl:param name="state" select="'AZ'"/>

<xsl:variable name="lookup-table-1.0"
  select="document('')/*/xsl:variable[@name='us-states']"/>

<xsl:template match="/" name="main">
  <xsl:value-of select="$lookup-table-1.0/state[@abbr=$state]/@name"
                use-when="false()"/>
  <xsl:if test="system-property('xsl:version')!='1.0'">
    <xsl:value-of select="$us-states/state[@abbr=$state]/@name"/>
  </xsl:if>
</xsl:template>
</xsl:stylesheet>
```

In theory, an XSLT 1.0 processor could legitimately reject the above stylesheet at compile time, regardless of whether it specifies «`version="1.0"`» or «`version="2.0"`», but fortunately the XSLT 1.0 processors that I've tried accept it without quibble.

In this example I used the standard `document()` function to provide fallback processing that works with all XSLT 1.0 processors. In more complex examples, the fallback processing might need to use vendor extensions such as Microsoft's `msxml:node-set()` extension function. In this situation different fallback mechanisms would be needed for different processors.

See Also

Extensibility in Chapter 3, page 134
Literal Result Elements in Chapter 3, page 112
`element-available()` function in Chapter 7, page 764
`system-property()` function in Chapter 7, page 890
`use-when` attribute described under `<xsl:stylesheet>`, page 478

xsl:for-each

The `<xsl:for-each>` instruction selects a sequence of items using an XPath expression and performs the same processing for each item in the sequence.

Changes in 2.0

There are no changes to the syntax of this instruction in XSLT 2.0. However, the ability to process sequences of atomic values as well as sequences of nodes greatly increases its power.

Format

```
<xsl:for-each
  select = sequence-expression>
  <!-- Content: (xsl:sort*, sequence-constructor) -->
</xsl:for-each>
```

Position

`<xsl:for-each>` is an instruction, which is always used within a sequence constructor.

Attributes

Name	Value	Meaning
select mandatory	XPath Expression	The sequence of items to be processed

Content

Zero or more `<xsl:sort>` elements, followed by a sequence constructor.

Effect

The effect of the `<xsl:for-each>` instruction is to evaluate the sequence constructor that it contains once for each item in the selected sequence of items. The following sections describe how this is done.

The select Attribute

The `select` attribute is mandatory. The expression defines the items that will be processed. This may be any XPath expression, because every XPath expression returns a sequence. It is quite legitimate, and occasionally useful, to select a single item or an empty sequence.

The expression will often be a path expression, which may select nodes relative to the context node (the node currently being processed). Alternatively, it may make an absolute selection from the root node, or it may simply select the nodes by reference to a variable initialized earlier. By referencing a tree-valued variable, or by using the `document()` function (described in Chapter 13, page 754), it may also select the root node of another XML document.

The `<xsl:for-each>` instruction can also be used to process a sequence of atomic values. The following example causes five empty `<br>` elements to be output:

```
<xsl:for-each select="1 to 5"><br/></xsl:for-each>
```

The sequence constructor contained within the `<xsl:for-each>` element is evaluated once for each item in the `select` sequence. Within this sequence constructor, the context item is the item being processed (one of the selected items); the position() function gives the position of that item in order of processing (the first item processed has position()=1, and so on), and the last() function gives the number of items being processed.

Although there is a defined order of processing, each item in the sequence is processed independently of the others; there is no way that the processing of one item can influence the way other items are processed. This also means that you can't break out of the loop. Think of the items as being processed in parallel. If you need the processing of an item to depend in some way on previous items, there are two ways you can achieve this: you can look at earlier items in the input sequence (for example by using the preceding-sibling axis), or you can abandon use of <xsl:for-each>, and use recursion instead.

A common mistake is to forget that <xsl:for-each> changes the context item. For example, the following code will probably produce no output:

```
<xsl:for-each select="para">
  <p><xsl:value-of select="para"/></p>
</xsl:for-each>
```

Why? Because within the <xsl:for-each> element, the context node is a <para> element, so the <xsl:value-of> instruction is trying to display another <para> element that is a child of the first one. What the author probably intended was:

```
<xsl:for-each select="para">
  <p><xsl:value-of select="."/></p>
</xsl:for-each>
```

Sorting

If there are no child <xsl:sort> instructions, the selected items are processed in the order of the sequence produced by evaluating the select expression. If the select expression is a path expression, the nodes will be in *document order*. In the normal case where the nodes all come from the same input document, this means they will be processed in the order they are encountered in the original source document: for example, an element node is processed before its children. Attribute nodes belonging to the same element, however, may be processed in any order, because the order of attributes in XML is not considered significant. If there are nodes from several different documents in the sequence, which can happen when you use the doc() or document() functions (described in Chapter 13), the relative order of nodes from different documents is not defined, though it is consistent if the same set of nodes is processed more than once.

> *The direction of the axis used to select the nodes is irrelevant. (The direction of different axes is described in Chapter 9.) For example, «select="preceding-sibling::*"» will process the preceding siblings of the context node in document order (starting with the first sibling) even though the preceding-sibling axis is in reverse document order. The axis direction affects only the meaning of any positional qualifiers used within the select expression. So «select="preceding-sibling::*[1]"» will select the first preceding sibling element in the direction of the axis, which is the element immediately before the context node, if there is one.*

Although most XPath expressions return nodes in document order, not all do so. For example, the expression «title, author, publisher» returns a sequence containing first the child title elements, then the child author elements, and then the child publisher elements of the context node, regardless of the order that these nodes appear in the source document. The items returned by the XPath expression will be processed in the order of the sequence that is returned, not necessarily in document order.

If there are one or more `<xsl:sort>` instructions as children of the `<xsl:for-each>` instruction, the items are sorted before processing. Each `<xsl:sort>` instruction defines one component of the sort key. If the sort key contains several components, they apply in major-to-minor order. For example, if the first `<xsl:sort>` defines sorting by country and the second by state, then the nodes will be processed in order of state within country. If two items have equal sort keys (or if the same item is included more than once in the sequence), they will be processed in the order that they appeared in the original result of the `select` expression, unless the first `<xsl:sort>` element specifies «stable="no"», in which case there are no guarantees. For a more complete specification of how sorting works, see `<xsl:sort>` on page 455.

If you want to process the items in the reverse of their original order, specify:

```
<xsl:sort select="position()" order="descending">
```

Alternatively, call the `reverse()` function. The following instruction will process the preceding siblings of the context node in reverse document order (that is, starting with the sibling closest to the context node and working backward).

```
<xsl:for-each select="reverse(preceding-sibling::*)">
```

Usage and Examples

The main purpose of `<xsl:for-each>` is to iterate over a sequence of items. It can also be used, however, simply to change the context item. These two styles of use are illustrated in the following sections.

Iterating over a Sequence of Nodes

The most common use of `<xsl:for-each>` is to iterate over a sequence of nodes. As such it provides an alternative to `<xsl:apply-templates>`. Which you use is largely a matter of personal style; arguably `<xsl:apply-templates>` (*push* processing) ties the stylesheet less strongly to the detailed structure of the source document and makes it easier to write a stylesheet that can accommodate some flexibility in the structures that will be encountered, while `<xsl:for-each>` (*pull* processing) makes the logic clearer to the reader. It may even improve performance because it bypasses the need to identify template rules by pattern matching, though the effect is likely to be very small.

The following example processes all the attributes of the current element node, writing them out as elements to the result tree. This example is presented in greater detail under `<xsl:element>` on page 315.

```
<xsl:template match="book">
   <book>
      <xsl:for-each select="@*">
         <xsl:element name="{local-name()}"
                      namespace="{namespace-uri()}">
            <xsl:value-of select="."/>
         </xsl:element>
      </xsl:for-each>
   </book>
</xsl:template>
```

The next example is a general one that can be applied to any XML document.

Example: Showing the Ancestors of a Node

The following example stylesheet can be applied to any XML document. For each element it processes all its ancestor elements, in reverse document order (that is, starting with the parent node and ending with the document element), and outputs their names in a comment that shows the position of the current node.

Source

This stylesheet can be applied to any source document.

Stylesheet

This stylesheet is in the file nesting.xsl.

```
<xsl:transform xmlns:xsl="http://www.w3.org/1999/XSL/Transform"
 version="2.0"
>
<xsl:template match="*">
   <xsl:comment>
      <xsl:value-of select="name()"/>
      <xsl:for-each select="ancestor::*">
         <xsl:sort select="position()" order="descending"/>
         <xsl:text> within </xsl:text>
         <xsl:value-of select="name()"/>
      </xsl:for-each>
   </xsl:comment>
   <xsl:apply-templates/>
</xsl:template>
</xsl:transform>
```

Output

An example of the output this might produce is:

```
<!--BOOKS within BOOKLIST-->
   <!--ITEM within BOOKS within BOOKLIST-->
   <!--TITLE within ITEM within BOOKS within BOOKLIST-->Number, the
                                        Language of Science
   <!--AUTHOR within ITEM within BOOKS within BOOKLIST-->Danzig
   <!--PRICE within ITEM within BOOKS within BOOKLIST-->5.95
   <!--QUANTITY within ITEM within BOOKS within BOOKLIST-->3
```

Changing the Context Item

Another use of `<xsl:for-each>` is simply to change the context item. The need for this is reduced in XSLT 2.0, but it is still convenient on occasions. In XSLT 1.0, if you wanted to use the key() function (described in Chapter 13, page 812) to locate nodes in some ancillary document, it was necessary first to establish some node in that document (typically the root) as the context node, because the key() function will only find nodes in the same document as the context node.

For example, you might write:

```
<xsl:variable name="county">
   <xsl:for-each select="document('county-code.xml')">
      <xsl:value-of select="key('county-code', $code)/@name"/>
   </xsl:for-each>
</xsl:variable>
```

The effect is to assign to the variable the value of the name attribute of the first element whose county-code key matches the value of the $code variable.

In XSLT 2.0 this particular example becomes simpler, because the key() function now accepts a third argument identifying the document to be searched. You can now write:

```
<xsl:variable name="county"
       select="key('county-code', $code, document('county-code.xml'))/@name"/>
```

But there are other cases where the technique is still useful; for example, if you need to call a named template that is designed to operate on the context node.

In a stylesheet that handles multiple input documents, it is always a good idea to declare a global variable:

```
<xsl:variable name="root" select="/"/>
```

Then you can always return to the original source document by writing:

```
<xsl:for-each select="$root">
   ...
</xsl:for-each>
```

See Also

<xsl:apply-templates> on page 240
<xsl:sort> on page 455
document() function in Chapter 13, page 754
key() function in Chapter 13, page 812

xsl:for-each-group

The <xsl:for-each-group> instruction selects a set of items, arranges the items into groups based on common values or other criteria, and then processes each group in turn.

Changes in 2.0

This instruction is new in XSLT 2.0.

Format

```
<xsl:for-each-group
   select = expression
   group-by? = expression
   group-adjacent? = expression
```

```
        group-starting-with? = pattern
        group-ending-with? = pattern
        collation? = { uri } >
        <!-- Content: (xsl:sort*, sequence-constructor) -->
    </xsl:for-each-group>
```

Position

`<xsl:for-each-group>` is an instruction, which is always used within a sequence constructor.

Attributes

Name	Value	Meaning
select mandatory	XPath Expression	The sequence of items to be grouped, known as the population.
group-by optional	XPath Expression	Grouping key. Items with common values for the grouping key are to be allocated to the same group.
group-adjacent optional	XPath Expression	Grouping key. Items with common values for the grouping key are to be allocated to the same group if they are adjacent in the population.
group-starting-with optional	Pattern	A new group will be started for each item in the population that matches this pattern.
group-ending-with optional	Pattern	A new group will be started following an item that matches this pattern.
collation optional	Collation URI	Identifies a collation used to compare strings for equality when comparing group key values.

The attributes `group-by`, `group-adjacent`, `group-starting-with`, and `group-ending-with` are mutually exclusive. Exactly one of these four attributes must be present.

Content

Zero or more `<xsl:sort>` elements, followed by a sequence constructor.

Effect

Grouping takes as input a sequence of items (usually nodes) and organizes these items into groups. It then processes each of the groups in turn.

The effect of the `<xsl:for-each-group>` instruction is summarized as follows:

❑   The expression in the `select` attribute is evaluated. This can return any sequence (of nodes or atomic values). This sequence is known as the *population*, and the order of the items in the sequence is called *population order*.

❑   Each item in the population is allocated to zero or more groups. The way this is done depends on which of the four attributes `group-by`, `group-adjacent`, `group-starting-with`, and `group-ending-with` is specified and is described in detail below. When `group-by` is used, an item may have more than one grouping key and may therefore be allocated to any number of groups (zero or more). In all other cases, each item in the population is allocated to exactly one group. (For the benefit of mathematicians, the groups are then said to *partition* the population.)

❑ The initial item of each group is identified. This is the item in the group that is first in *population order*, as defined above. If one or more sort keys have been defined using <xsl:sort> elements within the <xsl:for-each-group> element, these sort keys are used to determine the processing order of the groups. Otherwise, the groups are processed in *order of first appearance*, that is, based on the position of their initial items in population order.

❑ There is a special rule covering what happens if an item is allocated to two groups and is the initial item in both of them. This can only happen if the item had several values for its grouping key, and the order of first appearance then relates to the order of these grouping keys in the result of the group-by expression. If the expression was «group-by="author"», and the value of this expression for the node in question was the sequence «("Gilbert", "Sullivan")», then the group for author Gilbert would be processed before the group for author Sullivan.

❑ The sequence constructor contained in the <xsl:for-each-group> element is evaluated once for each group. Within the sequence constructor, the function current-group() may be called to obtain the items that are members of this group (in population order), and if the groups were defined using group-by or group-adjacent, then the function current-grouping-key() may be called to obtain the value of the grouping key that characterizes this group of items.

❑ The sequences that result from evaluating the sequence constructor once for each group are concatenated (in processing order) to form the final result of the <xsl:for-each-group> instruction.

If the population is empty, then the number of groups will be zero. No group is ever empty. Whether the population contains nodes or atomic values, no attempt is made to remove duplicates. This means that if the same node appears twice in the population, it will generally appear twice in each group that it is allocated to.

The following sections describe the effect of each of the four attributes group-by, group-adjacent, group-starting-with, and group-ending-with in turn.

group-by

The most common way of using <xsl:for-each-group> is to group items based on common values for a grouping key, which is achieved using the group-by attribute.

The group-by attribute is an XPath expression, which is evaluated once for each item in the population. It is evaluated with this item as the context item, with the position of this item in the population as the context position, and with the size of the population as the context size.

The value of the group-by expression is in general a sequence. This sequence is first atomized (as described in Chapter 2, page 81), and duplicate values are then removed from the atomic sequence that results. For each distinct value that remains in the sequence, the item is allocated to a group identified by this value. The total number of groups is equal to the number of distinct values present in the grouping keys for all items in the population.

> *Duplicate nodes are not removed from the population, but duplicate grouping keys calculated for a single node are removed. So if the authors of a book are J. Smith and P. Smith, and your grouping key is «author/surname», then when you process the group for Smith, this book will be processed once, not twice.*

Grouping keys are compared based on their type. For example, numbers are compared as numbers, and dates are compared as dates. Two grouping keys are considered equal based on the rules of the XPath «eq» operator, which is explained in Chapter 8 on page 582. Strings are compared using the collation specified in the `collation` attribute if present (for more details on collations, see under `<xsl:sort>` on page 455). Two NaN (not-a-number) values are considered equal to each other even though they are not equal when compared using «eq». If two values cannot be compared (because they are of noncomparable types; for example, `xs:date` and `xs:integer`), then they are considered not equal, which means the items end up in different groups.

If the `group-by` expression for any item in the population evaluates to an empty sequence, then the item will not be allocated to any groups, which means it will not be processed at all.

group-adjacent

When the `group-adjacent` attribute is used to define the grouping criteria, items are assigned to groups on the following basis:

- ❑ The first item in the population starts a new group.
- ❑ Subsequent items in the population are allocated to the same group as the previous item in the population if and only if they share the same value for the grouping key defined by the `group-adjacent` attribute; otherwise, they are allocated to a new group.

The `group-adjacent` expression is evaluated once for each item in the population. During this evaluation, the context item is this item, the context position is the position of this item in population order, and the context size is the size of the population. The value that results from evaluating the `group-adjacent` expression is atomized (see page 81). Unlike the `group-by` attribute, the result of evaluating the `group-adjacent` expression, after atomization, must be a single value. A type error is reported if the value is an empty sequence, or if it is a sequence containing more than one atomic value.

Values of the grouping key are compared in the same way as for the `group-by` attribute. This means, for example, that strings are compared using the collation defined in the `collation` attribute if specified, and that NaN values compare equal.

There are two main reasons for using `group-adjacent` in preference to `group-by`:

- ❑ Firstly, when there is a genuine requirement not to group items with the same grouping key unless they are adjacent. For example, a sequence of temperature readings might be presented so that the only readings actually shown are those that differ from the previous reading. This can be achieved by grouping adjacent readings and only displaying the first reading in each group.
- ❑ Secondly, when it is known that the items with common grouping keys will always be adjacent in the population. In this case using `group-adjacent` might give the same result as `group-by`, but might be more efficient because the XSLT processor can perform the grouping in a single pass through the data.

group-starting-with

The `group-starting-with` attribute is an XSLT pattern (not an expression). Patterns are described in Chapter 12. Patterns apply only to nodes, so this attribute must be used only when the population consists entirely of nodes. The nodes in the population are assigned to groups on the following basis:

- ❑ The first node in the population starts a new group.
- ❑ Subsequent nodes in the population start a new group if they match the pattern, and are assigned to the same group as the previous node otherwise.

The result is that the initial node in each group (the one that comes first in population order) will always match the pattern, with the possible exception of the first group, which may contain no node that matches the pattern.

The `group-starting-with` attribute is useful where the population consists of a repeating group of nodes whose first member can be readily identified: for example, a `<header>` element followed by a sequence of `<para>` elements, then another `<header>`, and so on. In this case the grouping can easily be defined using «`group-starting-with="header"`».

group-ending-with

This attribute behaves in a very similar way to `group-starting-with`, except that the pattern identifies the last item in a group instead of the first. The nodes in the population are assigned to groups on the following basis:

❑ The first node in the population starts a new group.

❑ Subsequent nodes in the population start a new group if the previous node in the population matches the pattern, and they are assigned to the same group as the previous node otherwise.

The most common use case for this option is where input records contain a continuation marker of some kind. For example, the population might consist of elements that have the attribute «`continued="yes"`» or «`continued="no"`». A group can then be defined using the criterion «`group-ending-with= "*[@continued="no"]"`».

Sorting the Groups

If there are any `<xsl:sort>` elements as children of the `<xsl:for-each-group>`, these affect the order in which the groups are processed. They do not affect the order of the items within each group, nor which item in a group is considered to be the initial item.

The `select` expression in an `<xsl:sort>` element calculates a sort key that affects the group as a whole, but it is always evaluated with respect to the initial item in the group. The initial item in a group is the item within the group that was first in population order. The `select` expression is evaluated with this item as the context item, with the position of this item relative to the initial items of other groups as the context position, and with the number of groups as the context size.

If any of the attributes of the `<xsl:sort>` elements are attribute value templates, then the XPath expressions in these attribute value templates are evaluated with the same context item, position, and size as the `select` expression of the containing `<xsl:for-each-group>` element.

If there are no `<xsl:sort>` elements, or in cases where the initial items in two groups have the same values for their sort keys, the groups are processed in order of first appearance; that is, if the initial item of group G appeared in the population before the initial item of group H, then group G is processed before group H.

"Processed before" does not refer to the actual order of execution; the system can process the groups in any order, or in parallel. What it means is that the results of processing group G appear in the final result sequence ahead of the results of processing group H.

In practice, if the groups are sorted at all then they are nearly always sorted by the value of the grouping key: *group the addresses in each city, sorting the groups by city*. This can be conveniently coded as:

```
<xsl:for-each-group select="//address" group-by="city">
    <xsl:sort select="current-grouping-key()"/>
```

```
      <city-group>
        <xsl:copy-of select="current-group()"/>
      </city-group>
  </xsl:for-each-group>
```

The functions `current-group()` and `current-grouping-key()` are described on page 739 in Chapter 13.

An `<xsl:sort>` element within `<xsl:for-each-group>` is used to sort the groups. To sort the items within each group, use an `<xsl:sort>` element within the inner `<xsl:for-each>`, or write:

```
<xsl:perform-sort select="current-group()"/>
```

The `<xsl:perform-sort>` instruction is described on page 437.

You can also use the `<xsl:perform-sort>` instruction to sort the population before grouping starts.

Usage and Examples

The following sections give a number of examples of how `<xsl:for-each-group>` can be used to solve grouping problems. They are organized according to the four ways of defining the grouping criteria: `group-by`, `group-adjacent`, `group-starting-with`, and `group-ending-with`.

Using group-by

This is by far the most common kind of grouping. We'll start with a simple case.

Example: Single-Level Grouping by Value

This example groups a set of employees according to the department in which they work.

Source

We'll start with the following simple data file (`staff.xml`):

```
<staff>
  <employee name="John Jones" department="sales"/>
  <employee name="Barbara Jenkins" department="personnel"/>
  <employee name="Cormac O'Donovan" department="transport"/>
  <employee name="Wesley Thomas" department="personnel"/>
  <employee name="Maria Gomez" department="sales"/>
</staff>
```

Output

The requirement is to output an HTML document in which the staff are listed by department:

```
<h2>sales department</h2>
<p>John Jones</p>
<p>Maria Gomez</p>
<h2>personnel department</h2>
<p>Barbara Jenkins</p>
```

```
<p>Wesley Thomas</p>
<h2>transport department</h2>
<p>Cormac O'Donovan</p>
```

Stylesheet

This output is simple to achieve. The full stylesheet is in `group-by-dept.xsl`:

```
<xsl:template match="staff">
  <xsl:for-each-group select="employee" group-by="@department">
    <h2><xsl:value-of select="current-grouping-key()"/>
         <xsl:text> department</xsl:text></h2>
    <xsl:for-each select="current-group()">
      <p><xsl:value-of select="@name"/></p>
    </xsl:for-each>
  </xsl:for-each-group>
</xsl:template>
```

A number of variations are possible on this theme. To sort the deparments, use an `<xsl:sort>` element within the `<xsl:for-each-group>`. To sort the employees within each department, use an `<xsl:sort>` element within the `<xsl:for-each>`. The solution then becomes (`sorted-depts.xsl`):

```
<xsl:template match="staff">
<xsl:for-each-group select="employee" group-by="@department">
  <xsl:sort select="current-grouping-key()"/>
    <h2><xsl:value-of select="current-grouping-key()"/>
         <xsl:text> department</xsl:text></h2>
    <xsl:for-each select="current-group()">
      <xsl:sort select="@name"/>
      <p><xsl:value-of select="@name"/></p>
    </xsl:for-each>
  </xsl:for-each-group>
</xsl:template>
```

This general design pattern, where `<xsl:for-each-group>` is used at the outer level to iterate over the groups, and an inner `<xsl:for-each>` is used to iterate over the items within a group, is typical. But there are a number of useful variations:

❑ The inner loop is sometimes better done using `<xsl:apply-templates select="current-group()"/>`, especially if the group includes elements of different types.

❑ Sometimes the entire inner loop can be written as `<xsl:copy-of select="current-group()"/>`, especially when generating XML output.

❑ Sometimes the requirement is not to display the items in each group, but to calculate some aggregate function for these items: for example to list for each department, the name of the department, the number of employees, and the maximum salary. In this case, the inner loop might not be explicit. The number of employees in the group is easily computed as «`count(current-group())`». Our sample data doesn't show salary, but if this was available as an extra attribute on the `<employee>` element, then you could easily calculate the maximum salary as «`max(current-group()/@salary)`».

❑   If the requirement is to eliminate duplicates rather than to group all the items (in our example, to output a list of departments), then the inner loop can be omitted entirely. But in this case it may be simpler to use the `distinct-values()` function described on page 749.

❑   If you need to number the groups, or test whether you are processing the last group, then within the `<xsl:for-each-group>` element you can use `position()` and `last()` in the usual way. At this level, the context item is the initial item of the group being processed, and `position()` and `last()` refer to the position of this item in a list that contains the initial item of each group, in processing order.

The example above was expressed as a grouping problem ("list the employees grouped by department"), so it is easy to see that `<xsl:for-each-group>` can be used in the solution. Sometimes grouping problems are not so easy to recognize. This might be the case if the example above were expressed as "for each department, list the name of the department and the number of employees."

Example: Multilevel Grouping by Value

Sometimes there is a need to do multilevel grouping. For example, you might want to group the employees by department, and the departments by location. Assume that the `<employee>` element now has a location attribute as well as a department attribute. It doesn't really matter whether departments can span locations, the code will work either way.

Source

The data is now like this (`staff-locations.xml`):

```
<staff>
  <employee name="John Jones"
            department="sales"
            location="New York"/>
  <employee name="Barbara Jenkins"
            department="personnel"
            location="Los Angeles"/>
  <employee name="Cormac O'Donovan"
            department="transport"
            location="New York"/>
  <employee name="Wesley Thomas"
            department="personnel"
            location="Los Angeles"/>
  <employee name="Maria Gomez"
            department="sales"
            location="Seattle"/>
</staff>
```

Output

You might want the output presented like this:

```
Location: Los Angeles
    Department: Personnel
        Barbara Jenkins
        Wesley Thomas
Location: New York
    Department: Sales
        John Jones
```

```
      Department: Transport
          Cormac O'Donovan
  Location: Seattle
      Department: Sales
          Maria Gomez
```

Stylesheet

Assume that the indentation is achieved using CSS styles, so you can concentrate on getting the structure of the information right. To do this multilevel grouping, just use two levels of `<xsl:for-each-group>` elements (multi-level.xsl):

```
<xsl:template match="staff">
  <xsl:for-each-group select="employee" group-by="@location">
    <xsl:sort select="current-grouping-key()"/>
    <p class="indent0">
       <xsl:text>Location </xsl:text>
       <xsl:value-of select="current-grouping-key()"/>
    </p>
    <xsl:for-each-group select="current-group()" group-by="@department">
       <xsl:sort select="current-grouping-key()"/>
       <p class="indent1">
          <xsl:text>Location </xsl:text>
          <xsl:value-of select="current-grouping-key()"/>
       </p>
       <xsl:for-each select="current-group()">
         <xsl:sort select="@name"/>
         <p class="indent2">
            <xsl:text>Location </xsl:text>
            <xsl:value-of select="@name"/>
         </p>
       </xsl:for-each>
    </xsl:for-each-group>
  </xsl:for-each-group>
</xsl:template>
```

A similar requirement is where there is a composite grouping key ("group employees that have the same department and the same location"). There are two ways of handling this. You can either treat it as a single level of grouping, using the concatenation of the two values as the grouping key, or you can treat it as two nested groupings in which the outer level does nothing (composite.xsl):

```
<xsl:for-each-group select="employee" group-by="@location">
  <xsl:for-each-group select="current-group()" group-by="@department">
     .   .   .
  </xsl:for-each-group>
</xsl:for-each-group>
```

The two techniques are not completely identical. For example, with a single-level grouping using a concatenated key, the value of position() while processing a department will run continuously from 1 up to the total number of groups, but with a two-level grouping, position() will start again at 1 for each location.

The `group-by` option also allows an item to belong to more than one group. Suppose that an employee can work for several departments, and that the `department` attribute is extended to be a whitespace-separated list of department names. If you are using a schema-aware processor that annotates this attribute as belonging to a list-valued type, then all the examples we have written above will handle this situation without change. When you write «`group-by="@department"`», the value of the expression is atomized, and if the type is a list-valued type, this will return the sequence of atomic values contained in the attribute. The item with this grouping key is then allocated to one group for each department. I was careful to output the department name by referring to `<xsl:value-of select="current-grouping-key()"/>`; if I had written `<xsl:value-of select="@department"/>` the output would have been rather confusing, because instead of listing the name of the single department to which all the employees in this group belong, the code would list all the deparments to which the first employee in the group belongs.

Using group-adjacent

The `group-adjacent` option attaches significance not only to the value of the grouping key but also to the order of items in the population. So it shouldn't be a surprise to find that many of its applications come with document-oriented XML, where order is typically much more signicant than with data-oriented XML. However, I've also seen it used with great effect to analyze time-sequence data.

Here's a simple but common example: given a `<section>` consisting of `<para>` elements and `<bullet>` elements, you want to convert the `<para>` elements into `<p>` elements, and the `<bullet>` elements into `<li>` elements, with a `<ul>` element wrapped around a sequence of consecutive bullets. You can do this as follows:

```
<xsl:template match="section">
   <div>
      <xsl:for-each-group select="*"
                    group-adjacent="if (self::bullet) then 0 else position()">
         <xsl:apply-templates select="."/>
      </xsl:for-each-group>
   </div>
</xsl:template>
```

The grouping condition ensures that adjacent `<bullet>` elements go in a group together, while each `<para>` element goes in a group by itself (calling `position()` ensures each `<para>` element gets a unique grouping key — you could also have used `generate-id()`). We are only interested in the rule that processes the first bullet:

```
<xsl:template match="bullet">
  <ul>
    <xsl:apply-templates select="current-group()" mode="each-bullet"/>
  </ul>
</xsl:template>
```

This template rule processes the group of adjacent bullets by outputting the necessary `<ul>` element to the result tree, and inside this it creates the elements that represent each individual bullet, by calling another template rule (in a different mode) to process each one. The full stylesheet is in `bullets.xsl`, a sample source file in `bullets.xml`.

Now look at a more complex example, involving the formatting of a Shakespeare play. You can download the text of all Shakespeare's plays, marked up in XML by Jon Bosak, at `http://metalab.unc.edu/bosak/xml/eg/shaks200.zip`.

Example: Grouping Consecutive Elements by Name

This example shows how to tackle a problem in which the content of an element (in this case, a `<SPEECH>`) consists of a number of `<SPEAKER>` elements followed by a number of `<LINE>` elements.

Source

You can run this example on any of the Shakespeare plays. For convenience, the download directory contains the file `ado-scene1.xml`, containing the first scene from *Much Ado About Nothing*.

In this markup, a `<SCENE>` element consists of a sequence of `<SPEECH>` elements interleaved with stage directions. A `<SPEECH>` contains one or more `<SPEAKER>` elements indicating who is speaking, and one or more `<LINE>` elements indicating what they are saying. So in *Hamlet* you have speeches like this:

```
<SPEECH>
<SPEAKER>HAMLET</SPEAKER>
<LINE>My fate cries out,</LINE>
<LINE>And makes each petty artery in this body</LINE>
<LINE>As hardy as the Nemean lion's nerve.</LINE>
<LINE>Still am I call'd. Unhand me, gentlemen.</LINE>
<LINE>By heaven, I'll make a ghost of him that lets me!</LINE>
<LINE>I say, away! Go on; I'll follow thee.</LINE>
</SPEECH>
```

and also speeches with multiple speakers:

```
<SPEECH>
<SPEAKER>ROSENCRANTZ</SPEAKER>
<SPEAKER>GUILDENSTERN</SPEAKER>
<LINE>We'll wait upon you.</LINE>
</SPEECH>
```

There are very few occasions where Shakespeare allows two characters to speak together for more than a single line (the witches' speech in *Macbeth* is tagged as `<SPEAKER>ALL</SPEAKER>`), but here is an example from *Timon of Athens*:

```
<SPEECH>
<SPEAKER>PHRYNIA</SPEAKER>
<SPEAKER>TIMANDRA</SPEAKER>
<LINE>Well, more gold: what then?</LINE>
<LINE>Believe't, that we'll do any thing for gold.</LINE>
</SPEECH>
```

Output

Suppose that you want to output each speech as a row in a table, with the speakers listed in one column and the text in the other. It should look like this (you wouldn't normally make the table cells visible in this way, but it helps to be able to see the structure):

PHRYNIA TIMANDRA	More counsel with more money, bounteous Timon.
TIMON	More whore, more mischief first; I have given you earnest.
ALCIBIADES	Strike up the drum towards Athens! Farewell, Timon: If I thrive well, I'll visit thee again.
TIMON	If I hope well, I'll never see thee more.

Stylesheet

So what does the stylesheet look like?

The content of a <SPEECH> element consists of two groups: a group containing consecutive <SPEAKER> elements and a group containing consecutive <LINE> elements. So you could try to write it like this:

```
<xsl:template match="SPEECH">
  <tr>
  <xsl:for-each-group select="*" group-adjacent="name()">
    <td valign="top">
       <xsl:for-each select="current-group()">
          <xsl:apply-templates select="."/>
          <xsl:if test="position()!=last()"><br/></xsl:if>
       </xsl:for-each>
    </td>
  </xsl:for-each-group>
  </tr>
</xsl:template>
```

Here we are using the name of an element as its grouping key.

But I omitted one complication. Within the sequence of <LINE> elements, there can also be a <STAGEDIR> representing a stage direction, thus:

```
<SPEECH>
<SPEAKER>TIMON</SPEAKER>
<LINE>Long live so, and so die.</LINE>
<STAGEDIR>Exit APEMANTUS</STAGEDIR>
<LINE>I am quit.</LINE>
<LINE>More things like men! Eat, Timon, and abhor them.</LINE>
</SPEECH>
```

When this happens you would want to output it, in its proper place, in italics:

TIMON	Long live so, and so die.
	Exit APEMANTUS
	I am quit.
	More things like men! Eat, Timon, and abhor them.

What does this do to the stylesheet?

The second group, the one that comprises the right-hand column of the table, no longer shares a common element name. What you can do, however, is allocate <SPEAKER> elements to one group, and anything else to a different group.

```
<xsl:template match="SPEECH">
  <tr>
  <xsl:for-each-group select="*"
                      group-adjacent="if (self::SPEAKER) then 0 else 1">
    <td valign="top">
      <xsl:for-each select="current-group()">
        <xsl:apply-templates select="."/>
        <xsl:if test="position()!=last()"><br/></xsl:if>
      </xsl:for-each>
    </td>
  </xsl:for-each-group>
  </tr>
</xsl:template>
```

The fact that you output the content of the <SPEAKER> and <LINE> elements using <xsl:apply-templates> means that you don't have to change the body of this rule to handle <STAGEDIR> elements as well; all you need to do is add a template rule with «match="SPEECH/STAGEDIR"» to handle them.

To complete the stylesheet, you need to add template rules for the individual elements such as <STAGEDIR>. These are straightforward, so I will not list them here. You can find the complete stylesheet in speech.xsl.

You could actually have used a boolean grouping key, «group-adjacent="boolean (self:: SPEAKER) "», but that would be a little obscure for my taste.

All these examples so far would work equally well using group-by rather than group-adjacent, because there are no nonadjacent items that would have been put in the same group if you had used group-by. But it's still worth using group-adjacent, if only because it's likely to be more efficient — the system knows that it doesn't need to do any sorting or hashing, it just has to compare adjacent items.

Example: Handling Repeating Groups of Adjacent Elements

This example is a slightly more difficult variant of the previous example, in which the <SPEECH> elements have been omitted from the input markup.

Source

If the Shakespeare markup had been done by someone less capable than Jon Bosak, the <SPEECH> elements might have been left out. You would then see a structure like this:

```
<SPEAKER>PHRYNIA</SPEAKER>
<SPEAKER>TIMANDRA</SPEAKER>
<LINE>More counsel with more money, bounteous Timon.</LINE>
<SPEAKER>TIMON</SPEAKER>
<LINE>More whore, more mischief first; I have given you earnest.</LINE>
<SPEAKER>ALCIBIADES</SPEAKER>
<LINE>Strike up the drum towards Athens! Farewell, Timon:</LINE>
<LINE>If I thrive well, I'll visit thee again.</LINE>
```

I have modified the markup of this (very long) scene from *Timon of Athens* and included it as `timon-scene.xml`.

Output

The required output is the same as in the previous example: that is, a table, in which each row represents one speech, with the names of the speakers in one column and the lines spoken in the other.

Stylesheet

There are various ways of handling such a structure, none of them particularly easy. One approach is to do the grouping bottom-up: First, you put a group of consecutive speakers in a `<SPEAKERS>` element and a group of consecutive lines and stage directions in a `<LINES>` element, then you process the sequence of alternating `<LINES>` and `<SPEAKERS>` elements. Here's the logic, which is expanded into a full stylesheet in the download file `alternate-groups.xsl`:

```
<xsl:template match="SCENE">
<table>
  <xsl:variable name="sequence" as="element()*">
    <xsl:for-each-group select="*"
                        group-adjacent="if (self::SPEAKER)
                                        then 'SPEAKERS' else 'LINES'">
      <xsl:element name="{current-grouping-key()}">
        <xsl:copy-of select="current-group()"/>
      </xsl:element>
    </xsl:for-each-group>
  </xsl:variable>
  <xsl:for-each-group select="$sequence"
                      group-starting-with="SPEAKERS">
    <tr>
      <xsl:for-each select="current-group()">
        <td valign="top">
          <xsl:for-each select="*">
            <xsl:apply-templates select="."/>
            <xsl:if test="position() != last()"><br/></xsl:if>
          </xsl:for-each>
        </td>
      </xsl:for-each>
    </tr>
  </xsl:for-each-group>
<table>
</xsl:template>
```

This does the grouping in two phases. The first phase creates a sequence of alternating elements named `<SPEAKERS>` and `<LINES>`, which you constructed by choosing these as your grouping keys. This sequence is held in a variable. The second phase uses `group-starting-with` to recognize a group consisting of a `<SPEAKERS>` element followed by a `<LINES>` element. All that remains is to process each group, which of course consists of a `<SPEAKERS>` element holding one or more `<SPEAKER>` elements, followed by a `<LINES>` element holding one or more `<LINE>` and `<STAGEDIR>` elements.

If I had presented an example query "find all the speeches in Shakespeare involving two or more speakers and containing two or more lines," and had presented the solution as «collection ('shakes.xml')// SPEECH[SPEAKER[2] and LINES[2]]», you would probably have found the example rather implausible. But if you want to know how I found the Timon of Athens quote, you have your answer.

This stylesheet produced incorrect output when we tried it with AltovaXML 2008. It works correctly with Saxon and Gestalt.

Using group-starting-with

Like `group-adjacent`, the `group-starting-with` option selects groups of items that are adjacent in the population, and it therefore tends to be used with document-oriented XML. The difference is that with this option, there doesn't have to be any value that the adjacent nodes have in common: All that you need is a pattern that matches the first node in each group.

I could have used this technique for the previous Shakespeare example. In fact, given a scene consisting of alternating sequences of <SPEAKER> elements and <LINE> elements, with no <SPEECH> elements to mark the boundaries, I could have reconstructed the <SPEECH> elements by writing:

```
<xsl:template match="SCENE">
<xsl:copy>
  <xsl:for-each-group select="*" group-starting-with=
      "SPEAKER[not(preceding-sibling::*[1] [self::SPEAKER])]">
    <SPEECH>
       <xsl:copy-of select="current-group()"/>
    </SPEECH>
  </xsl:for-each-group>
</xsl:copy>
</xsl:template>
```

Here the pattern that marks out the first element in a new group is that it is a <SPEAKER> element whose immediately preceding sibling element (if it has one) is not another <SPEAKER> element.

A common use for `group-starting-with` is the implicit hierarchies one sees in XHTML. We will explore this in the next example.

Example: Handling Flat XHTML Documents

This example shows how to create a hierarchy to represent the underlying structure of an XHTML document in which headings and paragraphs are all represented as sibling elements.

Source

A typical XHTML document looks like this (`flat.xml`):

```
<html>
 <body>
  <h1>Title</h1>
  <p>We need to understand how hierarchies can be flat.</p>
  <h2>Subtitle</h2>
  <p>Let's get to the point.</p>
```

```
    <p>The second paragraph in a section often says very little.</p>
    <p>But the third gets to the heart of the matter.</p>
    <h2>Subtitle</h2>
    <p>To conclude, we are dealing with a flat hierarchy.</p>
  </body>
</html>
```

This fragment consists of a `<body>` element with eight child elements, all at the same level of the tree. Very often, if you want to process this text, you will need to understand the hierarchic structure even though it is not explicit in the markup. For example, you may want to number the last paragraph as «1.2.1».

Output

To manipulate this data, you need to transform it into a structure like the one below that reflects the true hierarchy:

```
<body>
  <div><head>Title</head>
    <p>We need to understand how hierarchies can be flat.</p>
    <div><head>Subtitle</head>
      <p>Let's get to the point.</p>
      <p>The second paragraph in a section often says very little.</p>
      <p>But the third gets to the heart of the matter.</p>
    </div>
    <div><head>Subtitle</head>
      <p>To conclude, we are dealing with a flat hierarchy.</p>
    </div>
  </div>
</body>
```

Stylesheet

The `group-starting-with` option is ideal for this purpose, because the `<h1>` and `<h2>` elements are easy to match. Here is the code (`unflatten.xsl`):

```
<xsl:template match="body">
<xsl:copy>
  <xsl:for-each-group select="*" group-starting-with="h1">
    <xsl:apply-templates select="." mode="group"/>
  </xsl:for-each-group>
</xsl:copy>
</xsl:template>

<xsl:template match="h1" mode="group">
<div><head><xsl:value-of select="."/></head>
  <xsl:for-each-group select="current-group() except ."
                      group-starting-with="h2">
    <xsl:apply-templates select="." mode="group"/>
  </xsl:for-each-group>
</div>
</xsl:template>
```

```
<xsl:template match="h2" mode="group">
<div><head><xsl:value-of select="."/></head>
  <xsl:for-each-group select="current-group() except ."
                      group-starting-with="h3">
    <xsl:apply-templates select="." mode="group"/>
  </xsl:for-each-group>
</div>
</xsl:template>

<xsl:template match="h3" mode="group">
<div><head><xsl:value-of select="."/></head>
  <xsl:copy-of select="current-group() except ."/>
</div>
</xsl:template>

<xsl:template match="p" mode="group">
  <xsl:copy-of select="current-group()"/>
</xsl:template>
```

I've shown this down to three levels; it should be obvious how it can be extended.

When an `<h1>` element is matched, it is processed as part of a group that starts with an `<h1>` element and then contains a number of `<p>` and `<h2>` elements interleaved. The template rule first outputs the contents of the `<h1>` element as a heading and then splits the contents of this group (excluding the first `<h1>` element, which is of no further interest) into subgroups. The first subgroup will typically start with an ordinary `<p>` element, and all subsequent subgroups will start with an `<h2>` element. Call `<xsl:apply-templates>` to process the first element in the subgroup, and this fires off either the «match = "p"» template (for the first group) or the «match = "h2"» template (for others). The «match = "p"» template simply copies the group of `<p>` elements to the result tree, while the «match = "h2"» template starts yet another level of grouping based on the `<h3>` elements, and so on.

If you wanted to be clever you could handle the `<h1>`, `<h2>`, `<h3>`,...,`<h8>` elements with a single generic rule. This could be done by writing the template rule as:

```
<xsl:template match="h1|h2|h3|h4|h5|h6|h7" mode="group">
  <xsl:variable name="this" select="name()"/>
  <xsl:variable name="next"
              select="translate($this, '12345678', '23456789')"/>
  <div><head><xsl:value-of select="."/></head>
    <xsl:for-each-group select="current-group() except ."
                      group-starting-with="*[name()=$next]">
      <xsl:apply-templates select="." mode="group"/>
    </xsl:for-each-group>
  </div>
</xsl:template>
```

Using group-ending-with

The `group-ending-with` option complements `group-starting-with` by matching the last item in a group instead of the first. This requirement is far less common, but it does arise. The classical example for it is where a large document has been broken up, for transmission reasons, into small arbitrary chunks, and the last chunk carries some distinguishing characteristic such as the absence of an attribute saying «continued="yes"». To reconstitute the documents from the sequence of chunks, group-ending-with is the answer:

```
<xsl:template match="sequence-of-chunks">
<xsl:for-each-group group-ending-with="*[not(@continued='yes')]">
   <doc>
       <xsl:copy-of select="current-group()/*"/>
   </doc>
</xsl:for-each-group>
</xsl:template>
```

I have also found group-ending-with useful on occasions when writing an up-conversion to XML from formats such as Excel spreadsheets, where the last line of a group can be detected by the presence of a word such as TOTAL or SUBTOTAL in a particular column.

Arranging Data in Tables

Arranging data in tables is a common requirement when generating HTML pages, and the <xsl:for-each-group> instruction can help with this in a number of ways. I will not present any detailed worked examples here, just a checklist of techniques. However, the examples are expanded in the download files: see towns.xml, towns-by-rows.xsl, and towns-by-columns.xsl.

If you need to arrange data in rows, like this:

Andover	Basingstoke	Crawley	Dorking
Egham	Farnham	Guildford	Horsham
Ironbridge	Jarrow	Kingston	Leatherhead

the simplest approach is this, where «$cols» is the number of columns required:

```
<xsl:for-each-group select="town"
                    group-adjacent="(position()-1) idiv $cols">
<tr>
   <xsl:for-each select="current-group()">
   <td>
      <xsl:value-of select="."/>
   </td>
   </xsl:for-each>
</tr>
</xsl:for-each-group>
```

If the data needs to be sorted first, use the <xsl:perform-sort> instruction. For example:

```
<xsl:variable name="sorted-towns" as="element()*">
  <xsl:perform-sort select="town">
     <xsl:sort/>
  </xsl:perform-sort>
</xsl:variable>
<xsl:for-each-group select="$sorted-towns"
                    group-adjacent="(position()-1) idiv $cols">
  . . .
</xsl:for-each-group>
```

The `<xsl:perform-sort>` instruction is described on page 437.

If you need to generate empty table cells to fill up the last row, one convenient way is to add them to the sequence before you start:

```
<xsl:variable name="gaps"
    select="(count(towns) idiv $cols)*$cols + $cols - count(towns)"/>
<xsl:variable name="padding" select="
  if ($gaps = $cols) then () else for $i in 1 to $gaps return ' '"/>
<xsl:variable name="cells" select="towns, $padding"/>
<xsl:for-each-group select="$cells">
    . . .
</xsl:for-each-group>
```

If you want to arrange the data in columns, like this:

Andover	Dorking	Guildford	Jarrow
Basingstoke	Egham	Horsham	Kingston
Crawley	Farnham	Ironbridge	Leatherhead

then it is probably simplest to use group-by. The grouping key (the things that the towns in a particular row have in common) is the value of «position() mod 3» where 3 is the number of rows, which you can calculate as «count($cells) idiv $cols»:

```
<xsl:for-each-group select="$cells"
                    group-by="position() mod (last() idiv $cols)">
<tr>
   <xsl:for-each select="current-group()">
   <td>
      <xsl:value-of select="."/>
   </td>
   </xsl:for-each>
</tr>
</xsl:for-each-group>
```

See Also

<xsl:perform-sort> on page 437
<xsl:sort> on page 455
Collations on page 459
current-group() function on page 739
current-grouping-key() function on page 740
distinct-values() function on page 749

xsl:function

The `<xsl:function>` declaration defines a stylesheet function that can be invoked using a function call from any XPath expression.

Changes in 2.0

This element is new in XSLT 2.0.

Format

```
<xsl:function
  name = qname
  as? = sequence-type
  override? = "yes" | "no">
  <!-- Content: (xsl:param*, sequence-constructor) -->
</xsl:function>
```

Position

`<xsl:function>` is a top-level declaration, which means that it always appears as a child of the `<xsl:stylesheet>` element.

Attributes

Name	Value	Meaning
name mandatory	Lexical QName	The name of the function.
as optional	SequenceType	The type of the value returned when this function is evaluated. A type error is reported if the result does not match this type.
override optional	«yes» or «no»	Indicates whether this function overrides any vendor-supplied function of the same name.

The construct `SequenceType` is described in Chapter 11.

Content

Zero or more `<xsl:param>` elements, followed by a sequence constructor.

Effect

User-written stylesheet functions can be called from XPath expressions in the same way as system-provided functions. The function defined by this `<xsl:function>` element is added to the static context for every XPath expression in the stylesheet, which means that the function will be invoked when evaluating a function call in an XPath expression that has a matching name and number of arguments (*arity*).

When a stylesheet function is called from an XPath expression, the parameters supplied in the function call are evaluated and bound to the variables defined in the `<xsl:param>` elements, the sequence constructor contained in the `<xsl:function>` element is evaluated, and the result of this evaluation is returned as the result of the XPath function call.

The name of the function is given as a lexical QName in the `name` attribute. This name must have a namespace prefix: This is to ensure that the name does not clash with the names of functions in the standard function library. The XSLT 2.0 specification defines several namespaces (all starting with «http://www.w3.org/») that are reserved — that is, they cannot be used for the names of user-defined functions, variables, or other stylesheet objects.

The stylesheet is allowed to contain two functions of the same name if they have different arity.

It is an error to have two functions in the stylesheet with the same name, arity, and import precedence, unless there is another with higher import precedence. When a function call in an XPath expression is evaluated, the function with highest import precedence is chosen.

The parameters to a function (which are defined using <xsl:param> elements as children to the <xsl:function> element) are mandatory parameters; it is not possible to use the required attribute to specify that a parameter is optional, or to specify a default value. The parameters are interpreted positionally: the first argument in the function call binds to the first <xsl:param> element, the second argument binds to the second <xsl:param>, and so on.

The values supplied as arguments to the function in the XPath function call are converted to the types defined by «as» attributes on the corresponding <xsl:param> elements if required, using the standard conversion rules described on page 505. If this conversion fails, a type error is reported. If an <xsl:param> element has no «as» attribute, then any value of any type is acceptable, and no checking or conversion takes place. This is equivalent to specifying «as="item()*"».

On entry to the function, the context item, position, and size are undefined. It is therefore an error to use the expression «.», or any relative path expression, or the functions position() and last(). Even a path expression beginning with «/» is not allowed, because such path expressions select from the root of the tree containing the context node. This means that all information needed by the function must either be passed explicitly as a parameter or be available in a global variable. Path expressions such as «$par/a/b/c» can be used to navigate from nodes that are supplied as parameters to other nodes in the same tree.

Other values in the dynamic context, such as the current template, current mode, current group, and current grouping key, are also either undefined or empty on entry to a stylesheet function.

The result of the function is obtained by evaluating the sequence constructor. This result may be a sequence consisting of nodes (either newly constructed nodes or references to existing nodes) or atomic values or both. If there is an «as» attribute on the <xsl:function> element, then the result of evaluating the sequence constructor is converted, if necessary, to the specified type. Once again, the standard conversion rules defined on page 505 are used. A type error is reported if this conversion fails. If the <xsl:function> element has no «as» attribute, then a result of any type may be returned, and no checking or conversion takes place.

The override Attribute

The override attribute controls what happens if a user-written function and a vendor-supplied function have the same name.

❏ «override="yes"» means that the user-written function wins. This is the default. This value maximizes portability: the same implementation of the function will be used on all XSLT processors.

❏ «override="no"» means that the vendor-supplied function wins. This setting is useful when the stylesheet function has been written as a fallback implementation of the function, for use in environments where no vendor-supplied implementation exists. For example, at http://www.exslt.org/ there is a definition of a mathematical function library, including the function math:sqrt(), which evaluates the square root of its argument. This function is likely to be available with a number of XSLT processors, but not all. By supplying an XSLT implementation of this function, and specifying «override="no"», the stylesheet author can ensure that a call to math:sqrt() will execute on any XSLT processor, and will take advantage of the vendor's native implementation when available.

You can find a square root function implemented in XSLT on Dimitre Novatchev's FXSL site at http://fxsl.sourceforge.net/. *It's faster than you might think. Nor is it a purely academic exercise. XSLT can be used to create graphical renditions of your data in SVG format, and this will often require such computations.*

Usage and Examples

In this section I will first outline a few ways in which stylesheet functions can be used. I will then look more specifically at the differences between stylesheet functions and named templates. Then I will discuss the use of recursive functions, which provide an extremely powerful programming tool.

Example: Calculating Annual Leave

Stylesheet functions can be used in many different ways. Here is a simple function, which can be applied to an `<employee>` element to calculate the employee's annual leave entitlement in days. In turn it calls another function, which calculates the duration in months between two dates. The full stylesheet is in `annual-leave.xsl`

Source

This example uses two very simple source documents `employees.xml` and `departments.xml`, both governed by a schema `employees.xsd`. The stylesheet is schema-aware. This means that to run it using AltovaXML 2008, you will need to modify the outermost element of the two source documents by adding the attributes:

```
xmlns:xsi="http://www.w3.org/2001/XMLSchema-instance"
xsi:schemaLocation="http://ns.megacorp.com/hr employee.xsd"
```

Stylesheet

```
<xsl:function name="pers:annual-leave" as="xs:integer"
              xpath-default-namespace="http://ns.megacorp.com/hr">
  <xsl:param name="emp" as="schema-element(employee)"/>
  <xsl:variable name="service"
                as="xs:yearMonthDuration"
                select="pers:monthDifference(
                          current-date(),
                          $emp/date-of-joining)"/>
  <xsl:choose>
    <xsl:when test="$service gt xs:yearMonthDuration('P10Y')">
      <xsl:sequence select="20"/>
    </xsl:when>
    <xsl:when test="$service gt xs:yearMonthDuration('P3Y')">
      <xsl:sequence select="17"/>
    </xsl:when>
    <xsl:otherwise>
      <xsl:sequence select="15"/>
    </xsl:otherwise>
  </xsl:choose>
</xsl:function>
```

```
<xsl:function name="pers:monthDifference" as="xs:yearMonthDuration">
  <xsl:param name="arg1" as="xs:date"/>
  <xsl:param name="arg2" as="xs:date"/>
  <xsl:variable name="m"
      select="(year-from-date($arg1) - year-from-date($arg2))*12
               + (month-from-date($arg1) - month-from-date($arg2))"/>
  <xsl:sequence select="$m * xs:yearMonthDuration('P1M')"/>
</xsl:function>
```

This function can now be called from any XPath expression. For example, you can process all the employees with more than 16 days' annual leave by writing:

```
<xsl:apply-templates select="//employee[pers:annual-leave(.) gt 16]"/>
```

Or you could process the employees sorted according to the number of days they are entitled to:

```
<xsl:apply-templates select="//employee">
  <xsl:sort select="pers:annual-leave(.)"/>
</xsl:apply-templates>
```

This function could be packaged in a library module with other similar functions, allowing reuse of the code, and allowing the algorithms to be changed in one place rather than having them scattered around many different stylesheets. For calculating properties of nodes, functions are much more flexible than named templates because of the way they can be called.

In the previous edition of this book, which was based on drafts of the XSLT 2.0 Recommendation, I was able to make use of a system function subtract-dates-yielding-yearMonth Duration, *thus avoiding the need to write the* pers:monthDifference *function myself. This function was dropped from the final specification, not because of its unwieldy name, but because no-one could quite agree on the specification: how many months are there, for example, between Feb 29, 2008 and Jan 31, 2008? In my version of the function, the answer is 1.*

As well as encapsulating properties of elements, functions can be used to encapsulate relationships. For example, the following function determines the responsible line manager for an employee:

```
<xsl:function name="pers:line-manager" as="schema-element(pers:employee)"
      xpath-default-namespace="http://ns.megacorp.com/hr">
  <xsl:param name="emp" as="schema-element(employee)"/>
  <xsl:variable name="mgr-nr"
                select="doc('departments.xml')
                          /departments
                          /department[@dept-nr = $emp/department]
                          /manager-nr"/>
  <xsl:sequence select="doc('employees.xml')
                          /key('emp', $mgr-nr)"/>
</xsl:function>
```

Users of this function do not need to know how the relationship between employees and their line manager is actually represented in the XML source documents, only that the information is obtainable. This function can then be used in a path expression, rather like a virtual axis:

```
<xsl:template match="pers:employee">
   <xsl:text>Manager: </xsl:text>
   <xsl:value-of select="pers:line-manager(.)/name"/>
</xsl:template>
```

In these examples I have declared the types of the parameters and the result by reference to types defined in a schema. This helps to document what the function is intended for, and it ensures that you will get an error message (rather than garbage output) if you call the function with incorrect parameters, for example a department rather than an employee element.

I have used the `xpath-default-namespace` attribute, which can be used on any XSLT element to define the namespace that is used for unprefixed element and type names occurring in XPath expressions. For details of this attribute, see the entry for `<xsl:stylesheet>` on page 465.

I also chose to put the functions in the same namespace as the elements that they operate on. This is not the only approach possible, but to my mind it establishes clearly that there is a close relationship between the types (such as `pers:employee`) and the functions designed to operate on those types — the functions act like methods on a class.

Functions versus Named Templates

XSLT offers two very similar constructs: named templates and stylesheet functions. This section discusses the differences between them and suggests when they might be used.

The main difference between named templates and stylesheet functions is the way they are called. Templates are called from the XSLT level using the `<xsl:call-template>` instruction, while stylesheet functions are called from XPath expressions using a function call. Another difference is that when a template is called, the caller's context is retained, which is not the case for a function call. The content model for the `<xsl:template>` and `<xsl:function>` elements is identical, and there is no difference in the way they are evaluated to produce a result, or in the kinds of result they can return. If you need to invoke the same functionality from both the XSLT and the XPath levels, it is very easy to define a named template as a wrapper for a stylesheet function:

```
<xsl:template name="my:func">
   <xsl:param name="p1" required="yes"/>
   <xsl:param name="p2" required="yes"/>
   <xsl:sequence select="my:func($p1, $p2)"/>
</xsl:template>
```

or to define a stylesheet function as a wrapper for a named template:

```
<xsl:function name="my:func">
   <xsl:param name="p1" />
   <xsl:param name="p2" />
    <xsl:call-template name="my:func">
      <xsl:with-param name="p1" select="$p1"/>
      <xsl:with-param name="p2" select="$p2"/>
   </xsl:call-template>
</xsl:function>
```

349

My own preference is to use stylesheet functions when I want to compute a value or to select exist-ing nodes, and to use a named template when I want to construct new nodes. This reflects the fact that, in general, the role of XSLT instructions is to construct nodes in the result tree, while the role of XPath expressions is to select nodes in the source tree and compute values derived from their content. It's dangerous to speculate about performance of products in general terms, but it seems to me quite likely that XPath engines will be optimized for navigating around source trees, while XSLT engines will be optimized for constructing result trees, and this difference may be reflected in the way the two call mechanisms work.

The fact that stylesheet functions do not have access to the context item may seem at first to be an inconve-nience. But I think that the fact that all parameters to the function are explicit greatly helps programming discipline, and produces code that is easier to maintain. It also makes life much easier for the optimizer, which brings another benefit in terms of faster execution.

Functions with side effects can cause some surprises at the XPath level, and creating a new node is a kind of a side effect. For example, one might expect that the result of the expression:

```
my:f($x) is my:f($x)
```

is always true. But if the function `my:f()` creates a new node, this is not the case. It is no longer a pure fun-ction, because it returns different results on different invocations. An optimizer has to recognize this pos-sibility when rearranging such an expression: it must make sure that the function is actually called twice.

Another example of this effect is the (admittedly rather perverse) expression:

```
count(//a/../my:f(.))
```

Normally when evaluating a path expression, the processor can first find all the nodes that the path expression locates, then sort them into document order and eliminate duplicates. But with the expression above, if «my:f()» creates new nodes then the result of the final count() depends critically on how many times the function «my:f()» is called, and the correct answer is that it must be called exactly once for each distinct parent of an <a> element in the source document.

> *This is the kind of expression that is used to sort out the sheep from the goats when doing XPath con-formance testing, and you'll find lots of cases like this in the W3C test suites for XSLT and XQuery. In practice, however, the issues rarely arise in real applications.*

Recursion

Stylesheet functions can be recursive: they can call themselves either directly or indirectly. Because XSLT is a functional programming language without side effects (at any rate, without updateable variables), recursion plays a key role in writing algorithms of any complexity.

In XSLT 1.0, such algorithms were written using recursive named templates. Apart from being rather long-winded, this had the drawback that it was difficult to return certain kinds of result: templates in XSLT 1.0 could only return results by constructing new nodes. In XSLT 2.0 both templates and functions offer much more flexibility in the types of result they can return, and stylesheet functions offer additional flexibility in the way they can be called (for example, they can be called from within a predicate used in a match pattern).

As it happens, many of the simple problems where recursion was needed in XSLT 1.0 can now be solved in other ways, because XPath 2.0 offers a wider range of aggregation functions, and functions such as tokenize() to break up a string into its parts. But there are still cases where recursion is needed, and even when it isn't, many people find the recursive solution more elegant than an iterative solution using `<xsl:for-each>` or the XPath «for» expression.

Here is a function that extracts the part of a string after the last «/» character:

```
<xsl:function name="str:suffix" as="xs:string">
   <xsl:param name="in" as="xs:string"/>
   <xsl:sequence select="
         if (contains($in, '/')
         then str:suffix(substring-after($in, '/'))
         else $in"/>
</xsl:function>
```

Note how all the logic is contained in a single XPath expression. I could have used `<xsl:choose>` to express the same logic, but with this kind of function I personally find it clearer to write the whole algorithm at the XPath level.

The function result is returned using an `<xsl:sequence>` instruction. It sometimes feels a little strange to use `<xsl:sequence>` when the value being computed is a single integer or string, but in the XDM model a single value is the same as a sequence of length 1, so it's worth getting used to the idea that everything is a sequence. When returning an atomic value, one could just as easily use `<xsl:copy-of>`, but I prefer `<xsl:sequence>` because it works in all cases; when you are returning nodes, you don't want to copy them unnecessarily. You might also be tempted to use `<xsl:value-of>`, and in this case it would work, but the semantics aren't quite what we want: `<xsl:value-of>` would convert the selected string into a text node, which would then be atomized back to a string by virtue of the function's declared return type. Even if the optimizer can sort this out, it's making unnecessary work.

Another observation about this function is that it is tail-recursive. This means that after calling itself, the function does nothing else before it returns to its caller. This property is important because tail-recursive functions can be optimized to save memory. Sometimes a problem with recursion is that if you recurse too deeply, say to 1000 levels or so, the system runs out of stack space and terminates with a fatal error. A good XSLT processor can optimize a tail-recursive function so that this doesn't happen. Basically the trick is that instead of making the recursive call and then unwinding the stack when it regains control, the function can unwind the stack first, and then make the recursive call. This is because the stack frame isn't needed once the recursive call returns.

I mentioned earlier that many functions can now be implemented easily without using recursion, and this one is no exception. It could also be written using regular expressions:

```
<xsl:function name="str:suffix" as="xs:string">
  <xsl:param name="in" as="xs:string"/>
  <xsl:sequence select="replace($in, '.*/([^/]*)', '$1')"/>
</xsl:function>
```

But this is a matter of personal style. It's a good idea to have more than one tool in your kitbag, and recursion is the most powerful one available.

One kind of problem where you will need recursion is when you need to analyze a graph (that is, a network of related objects). The next example shows the technique.

Example: Looking for Cycles among Attribute Sets

This example examines a stylesheet module (we'll stick to a single module for simplicity) and determines whether it contains any cycles among its attribute set definitions. Also to keep it simple, I'll assume that attribute sets have simple names and ignore the complications caused by namespace prefixes.

Source

The source document is any stylesheet module. But the example is only interesting if you run it on a stylesheet module that contains attribute sets that are (incorrectly) defined in terms of themselves. I've included such a sample as `cyclic-stylesheet.xsl`.

This example requires a schema-aware processor and assumes that the source document is validated against the schema for XSLT 2.0 stylesheets, which is included in the download as `schema-for-xslt20.xsd`.

The AltovaXML 2008 schema processor, unfortunately, rejects this schema as invalid.

Output

The stylesheet will report the name of any attribute set that is defined directly or indirectly in terms of itself.

Stylesheet

This stylesheet is available as `find-cycles.xsl`. We'll start with a function that returns the attribute sets that are directly referenced from a given attribute set:

```
<xsl:function name="cyc:direct" as="schema-element(xsl:attribute-set)*">
  <xsl:param name="in" as="schema-element(xsl:attribute-set)"/>
  <xsl:sequence select="$in/../xsl:attribute-set
                                [@name=$in/@use-attribute-sets]"/>
</xsl:function>
```

This returns any `attribute-set` in the containing document whose `name` attribute is equal to any of these strings. Notice what's going on: The schema for XSLT stylesheets tells us that the `use-attribute-sets` attribute is a sequence of strings. The «=» operator causes this attribute to be atomized, which returns the typed value of the attribute, namely this sequence of strings; it then returns true if any of the strings in this sequence is equal to the other operand. This will only work if the input document has been validated against its schema.

Now observe that an attribute set A references another attribute set B if either `cyc:direct(A)` includes B, or there is an attribute set in `cyc:direct(A)` that references B. This suggests the recursive function:

```
<xsl:function name="cyc:references" as="xs:boolean">
  <xsl:param name="A" as="schema-element(xsl:attribute-set)"/>
  <xsl:param name="B" as="schema-element(xsl:attribute-set)"/>
  <xsl:sequence select="
```

```
            (cyc:direct($A) intersect $B)
            or (some $X in cyc:direct($A) satisfies cyc:references($X, $B))"/>
  </xsl:function>
```

Unfortunately, this doesn't quite work: if we apply it to a node that doesn't participate in a cycle, but which references a node that does, then we'll go into an infinite loop. To protect against this we need to remember the route by which a node was reached and avoid processing it if it is reached again. The corrected function is:

```
<xsl:function name="cyc:references" as="xs:boolean">
  <xsl:param name="A" as="schema-element(xsl:attribute-set)"/>
  <xsl:param name="B" as="schema-element(xsl:attribute-set)"/>
  <xsl:param name="route" as="schema-element(xsl:attribute-set)*"/>
  <xsl:variable name="direct" select="cyc:direct($A)"/>
  <xsl:sequence select="exists($direct intersect $B) or
          (some $C in ($direct except $route)
                satisfies cyc:references($C, $B, ($route, $C)))"/>
  </xsl:function>
```

Now, finally, you can discover whether there are any cycles, that is, any attribute sets that reference themselves directly or indirectly:

```
<xsl:value-of select="some $X in /*/xsl:attribute-set
                      satisfies cyc:references($X, $X, ())"/>
```

This function isn't tail-recursive. The recursive call is inside a loop (the «some» expression). However, this is unlikely to matter in this case, because the chains of references from one attribute set to another are likely to be short.

An interesting observation about this function is that it is written entirely using constructs that are new in XSLT 2.0 and XPath 2.0: stylesheet functions, type checking based on schema-defined types, atomization of a list-valued attribute, the `<xsl:sequence>` instruction that allows XSLT instructions to return values other than nodes, the XPath `intersect` and `except` operators, and the XPath `some..satisfies` expression.

For a more generalized function that looks for cycles in any source data file, regardless how the relationships are represented, see the section *Simulating Higher Order Functions* under `<xsl:apply-templates>` on page 240.

See Also

`<xsl:template>` on page 483

xsl:if

The `<xsl:if>` instruction encloses a sequence constructor that will be evaluated only if a specified condition is true. If the condition is true, it returns the result of this evaluation; otherwise, it returns the empty sequence.

<xsl:if> is analogous to the *if* statement found in many programming languages.

Changes in 2.0

None.

Format

```
<xsl:if
  test = expression>
  <!-- Content: sequence-constructor ->
</xsl:if>
```

Position

<xsl:if> is an instruction. It is always used within a sequence constructor.

Attributes

Name	Value	Meaning
test mandatory	XPath Expression	The boolean condition to be tested

Content

A sequence constructor.

Effect

The test expression is evaluated. If the *effective boolean value* of the result is true, the contained sequence constructor is evaluated; otherwise, no action is taken (an empty sequence is returned).

Any XPath expression may be evaluated to obtain an effective boolean value. In brief, the rules are:

❑   If the value is an empty sequence, then the result is false.

❑   If the value is a sequence whose first item is a node, then the result is true.

❑   If the value is a singleton xs:boolean value, the result is that value.

❑   If the argument is a singleton numeric value, the result is false if the argument is NaN or zero; otherwise it is true.

❑   If the argument is a singleton instance of xs:string, xs:anyURI, or xs:untypedAtomic, the result is false if the string is zero length; otherwise, it is true.

❑   In all other cases, the result is an error.

These rules are the same as XPath itself uses in boolean contexts; for example, in «if» expressions and for the operands of the «and» and «or» operators. They are also the same as the rules used by the boolean() function, and they are designed to be fully compatible with XPath 1.0. Note that the effective boolean value of a sequence can be evaluated without looking beyond the second item in the sequence, which makes the rules very efficient.

Usage

The <xsl:if> instruction is useful where an action is to be performed conditionally. It performs the functions of the if-then construct found in other programming languages. If there are two or more alternative actions (the equivalent of an `if-then-else`, `switch`, or `Select Case` in other languages), use `<xsl:choose>` instead.

One common use of `<xsl:if>` is to test for error conditions. In this case it is often used with `<xsl:message>`.

Try to avoid using `<xsl:if>` as the entire content of a template rule. It's better to use a predicate instead, because this gives the processor more scope for optimization. For example:

```
<xsl:template match="para">
  <xsl:if test="@display='yes'">
    <p><xsl:apply-templates/></p>
  </xsl:if>
</xsl:template>
```

can be rewritten as:

```
<xsl:template match="para[@display='yes']">
  <p><xsl:apply-templates/></p>
</xsl:for-each>

<xsl:template match="para"/>
```

(Of course, it's always possible that the processor will perform this optimization anyway, but you can't rely on it.)

Examples

The following example outputs an `<hr>` element after processing the last of a sequence of `<para>` elements:

```
<xsl:template match="para">
  <p><xsl:apply-templates/></p>
  <xsl:if test="position()=last()">
    <hr/>
  </xsl:if>
</xsl:template>
```

The following example reports an error if the `percent` attribute of the current element is not a number between 0 and 100. The expression returns true if:

❑   the `percent` attribute does not exist,

❑   the value cannot be interpreted as a number (so that «`number(@percent)`» is NaN),

❑   the numeric value is less than zero, or

❑   the numeric value is greater than 100.

```
<xsl:if test="not(@percent) or
                  (string(number(@percent))='NaN') or
                  (number(@percent) lt 0) or
                  (number(@percent) gt 100)">
  <xsl:message>
     percent attribute must be a number between 0 and 100
  </xsl:message>
</xsl:if>
```

The next example shows the use of `<xsl:if>` in the context of a complete stylesheet.

Example: Formatting a List of Names

This example formats a list of names, using `<xsl:if>` to produce punctuation that depends on the position of each name in the list.

Source

The source file `authors.xml` contains a single `<book>` element with a list of authors:

```
<?xml version="1.0"?>
<book>
    <title>Design Patterns</title>
    <author>Erich Gamma</author>
    <author>Richard Helm</author>
    <author>Ralph Johnson</author>
    <author>John Vlissides</author>
</book>
```

Stylesheet

The stylesheet `authors.xsl` processes the list of authors, adding punctuation depending on the position of each author in the list:

```
<xsl:transform
 xmlns:xsl="http://www.w3.org/1999/XSL/Transform"
 version="2.0">
<xsl:output method="text"/>

<xsl:template match="book">
   <xsl:value-of select="title"/>
   by <xsl:for-each select="author">
      <xsl:value-of select="."/>
      <xsl:if test="position()!=last()">, </xsl:if>
      <xsl:if test="position()=last()-1">and </xsl:if>
</xsl:for-each>
</xsl:template>

</xsl:transform>
```

Output

```
Design Patterns
   by Erich Gamma, Richard Helm, Ralph Johnson, and John Vlissides
```

See Also

`<xsl:choose>` on page 282

xsl:import

`<xsl:import>` is a top-level element used to import the contents of one stylesheet module into another. The declarations in the importing stylesheet module have a higher *import precedence* than those in the imported module, which usually means that they will be used in preference, but the detailed rules vary for each type of declaration.

Changes in 2.0

There are no changes to the syntax of this instruction in XSLT 2.0. The rules for the `href` attribute have been reformulated to reflect current practice with XSLT 1.0: In effect, the way in which the URI is dereferenced to obtain a stylesheet module is now largely implementation defined. This allows for options such as catalogs or user-specified URI resolvers, as well as implementations that cache or precompile stylesheet modules.

Format

```
<xsl:import
  href = uri-reference />
```

Position

`<xsl:import>` is a top-level element, which means that it must appear as a child of the `<xsl:stylesheet>` element. Within an `<xsl:stylesheet>` element, the `<xsl:import>` child elements must come before any other children.

Attributes

Name	Value	Meaning
href mandatory	URI	The URI of the stylesheet to be imported

Like all other XSLT elements, the `<xsl:import>` declaration may also have a «use-when» attribute. This is described in Chapter 3 (see page 127).

Content

None; the element is always empty.

Effect

The `<xsl:import>` declaration loads the stylesheet module identified in its `href` attribute. First, we'll look at how this module is located and then at the question of import precedence, which determines how the declarations in the imported module are used.

Locating the Stylesheet Module

The URI contained in the `href` attribute may be an absolute URI or a relative URI reference. If relative, it is interpreted relative to the base URI of the XML document or external entity containing the `<xsl:import>` element. For example, if a file `main.xsl` contains the element `<xsl:import href="date.xsl"/>` then the system will, by default, look for `date.xsl` in the same directory as `main.xsl`. You can change this behavior by using the `xml:base` attribute, as described in Chapter 2 on page 54. This allows you to specify a different base URI for resolving the relative reference.

The URI, once resolved, must identify an XML document that is a valid XSLT stylesheet module. The declarations in the imported stylesheet are logically inserted into the importing stylesheet at the point where the `<xsl:import>` element appears. However:

❑ Imported declarations have lower import precedence than the declarations that appear directly in the importing stylesheet, or are incorporated into it using `<xsl:include>`. This is explained in more detail below.

❑ Imported elements retain their base URI, so anything that involves resolving a relative URI reference is done relative to the original URI of the imported stylesheet. This includes, for example, expansion of further `<xsl:import>` elements, or use of URIs as arguments to the `document()` function.

❑ When a namespace prefix is used (typically within a QName, but it also applies to freestanding prefixes such as those in the `xsl:exclude-result-prefixes` attribute of a literal result element), it is interpreted using only the namespace declarations in the original stylesheet module in which the QName occurred. An imported stylesheet module does not inherit namespace declarations from the module that imports it. This includes QNames constructed at execution time as the result of evaluating an expression; for example, an expression used within an attribute value template for the `name` or `namespace` attribute of `<xsl:element>`.

❑ The values of the `version`, `extension-element-prefixes`, `exclude-result-prefixes`, and `xpath-default-namespace` attributes that apply to an element in the imported stylesheet, as well as `xml:lang` and `xml:space`, are those that were defined in the `<xsl:stylesheet>` element of their own stylesheet module, not those on the `<xsl:stylesheet>` element of the importing module.

The imported stylesheet module may use the simplified stylesheet syntax described in Chapter 3. This allows an entire module to be defined as the content of an element such as `<HTML>`. It is then treated as if it were a stylesheet module containing a single template, whose match pattern is «/» and whose content is the literal result element.

The imported stylesheet module may contain `<xsl:include>` declarations to include further stylesheet modules, or `<xsl:import>` statements to import them. A stylesheet module must not directly or indirectly import itself.

It is not an error to import the same stylesheet module more than once, either directly or indirectly, but it is not usually a useful thing to do. The effect is that the same definitions or templates will be present with several different import precedences. The situation is exactly the same as if two stylesheet modules with different names but identical contents had been imported.

The `href` attribute must be a fixed value — it isn't possible to compute its value at runtime. This is because the first thing an XSLT processor does, long before any source document is available, is to assemble the stylesheet from all its constituent modules and compile it into some internal representation. However, there is a new facility in XSLT 2.0 that allows stylesheets to be tailored to different environments. The «use-when» attribute is allowed on `<xsl:import>` (and indeed on any other XSLT element) to define a compile-time condition defining whether this element should be included or ignored. For example, you can write:

```
<xsl:import href="altova-rules.xsl"
           use-when="system-property('xsl:product-name') = 'Altova XSLT Engine'"/>
<xsl:import href="gestalt-rules.xsl"
           use-when="system-property('xsl:product-name') = 'Gestalt'"/>
```

```
<xsl:import href="saxon-rules.xsl"
            use-when="system-property('xsl:product-name') = 'SAXON'"/>
```

to import different modules depending on whether you are running Saxon, Gestalt, or AltovaXML. (See `product-switch.xsl` in the downloaded code for a full version of the stylesheet).

If you use a relative URI reference in the `href` attribute, and the system can't resolve it, check that the base URI of the main stylesheet module is known. If you're using the JAXP API for invoking a transformation, a common mistake occurs when you supply the main stylesheet as a `StreamSource` object. If you do this, you need to call the `setSystemId()` method to ensure that the system knows where the input stream comes from. Similar problems often arise on the Microsoft platform if you supply the stylesheet in the form of a DOM Document.

Determining the Import Precedence

Each stylesheet module that is imported has an import precedence. The rules are:

❑ The precedence of a module that is imported is always lower than the precedence of the module importing it.

❑ If one module imports several others, then the one it imports first has lower precedence than the next, and so on.

This means that in the structure shown in Figure 6-3, the highest precedence module is A followed by C, F, B, E, and finally D. The numbers on the diagram illustrate this. The absolute values have no significance, it is only the relative order of import precedence that matters.

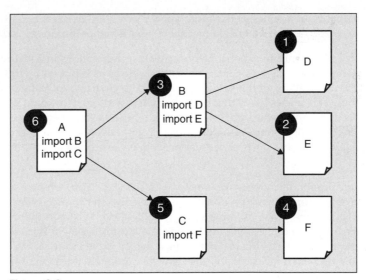

Figure 6-3

If one stylesheet module incorporates another using `<xsl:include>` rather than `<xsl:import>`, it has the same import precedence as the module that includes it (see Figure 6-4).

Here J is included in E, so it has the same import precedence as E, and similarly E has the same import precedence as C.

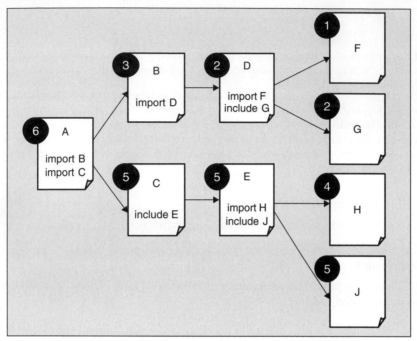

Figure 6-4

The import precedence of a stylesheet module applies to all the declarations in that module, so for example the <xsl:template> elements in module E have a higher import precedence than those in G.

As <xsl:import> statements must occur before any other declarations in a stylesheet module, the effect of these rules is that if each <xsl:import> statement were to be replaced by the content of the module it imports, the declarations in the resulting combined stylesheet would be in increasing order of import precedence. This makes life rather easier for implementors. However, it does not mean that <xsl:import> is a straightforward textual substitution process, because there is still a need to distinguish cases where two objects (for example template rules) have the same import precedence because they came originally from the same stylesheet or from stylesheets that were included rather than imported.

The XSLT 2.0 specification introduces the concept of a *stylesheet layer*, which is a group of stylesheet modules that have the same import precedence because they refer to each other using <xsl:include> rather than <xsl:import>. In the example above modules D and G are in the same layer; C, E, and J are in the same layer, and each of the other modules is in a layer of its own. Within a stylesheet layer the specification describes the concept of *declaration order*, which is the order that the declarations (top-level elements) would appear in if included stylesheets were expanded at the point of the <xsl:include> statement. The stylesheet layers (rather than modules) are considered to form a tree, with <xsl:import> elements acting as the links from a parent to a child in the tree.

The stylesheet tree for the example above is shown in Figure 6-5.

The concepts of stylesheet levels, declaration order, and the stylesheet tree have been used to tighten up the specification of how instructions such as <xsl:apply-imports> work. For example, an <xsl:apply-imports> instruction in module J can invoke a template in module H, because H is in a stylesheet layer that is a descendant of the layer that J is in.

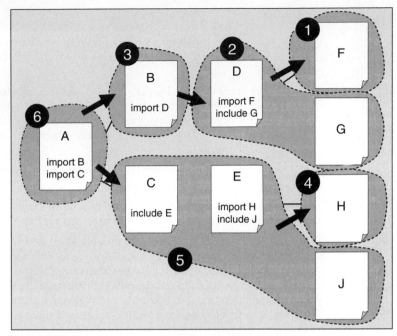

Figure 6-5

Effect of Import Precedence

The import precedence of a declaration affects its standing relative to other declarations of the same type, and may be used to resolve conflicts. The effect is as shown in the table below for each kind of declaration.

Element type	Rules
`<xsl:attribute-set>`	If there are two attribute sets with the same expanded name, they are merged. If there is an attribute that is present in both, then the one from the attribute set with higher import precedence wins. If there are two or more values for an attribute that have the same precedence, and this is the highest precedence, the XSLT processor chooses the one that was specified last (for a more precise definition of what ''last'' means, see `<xsl:attribute-set>` on page 266).
`<xsl:character-map>`	If there are several `<xsl:character-map>` declarations with the same name, then the one with highest import precedence wins. It is an error if this leaves no clear winner.
`<xsl:decimal-format>`	All the `<xsl:decimal-format>` elements in the stylesheet that share the same name are effectively merged. For each attribute, if the value is explicitly present on more than one `<xsl:decimal-format>` element, then the one with highest import precedence wins. It is an error if there is no clear winner.
`<xsl:function>`	If there are several `<xsl:function>` declarations with the same name and arity (number of arguments), then the one with highest import precedence wins. It is an error if this leaves no clear winner.

continued

Element type	Rules
`<xsl:import>` `<xsl:include>`	No conflicts arise; the import precedence of these elements is immaterial, except in determining the import precedence of the referenced stylesheet module.
`<xsl:import-schema>`	If there are several `<xsl:import-schema>` declarations for the same target namespace (or for no target namespace) then the one with highest import precedence wins. If this leaves more than one, then the rules are defined by reference to the XML Schema specifications, which give implementations a great deal of latitude.
`<xsl:key>`	All the key definitions are used, regardless of their import precedence. See `<xsl:key>` on page 376 for details.
`<xsl:namespace-alias>`	If several aliases for the same stylesheet prefix are defined, the one with the highest import precedence is used. It is an error if there is no clear winner.
`<xsl:output>`	All the `<xsl:output>` elements in the stylesheet that share the same name are effectively merged. In the case of the `cdata-section-elements` and `use-character-maps` attributes, the values from all the `<xsl:output>` elements are merged. For all the other attributes, if the value is explicitly present on more than one `<xsl:output>` element, then the one with highest import precedence wins. It is an error if there is no clear winner.
`<xsl:strip-space>` `<xsl:preserve-space>`	If there is more than one `<xsl:strip-space>` or `<xsl:preserve-space>` element that matches a particular element name in the source document, then the one with highest import precedence is used. If this still leaves several that match, each one is assigned a priority, using the same rules as for the `match` pattern in `<xsl:template>`. Specifically, an explicit QName has higher priority than the form «prefix:*», which in turn has higher priority than «*». The one with highest priority is then used. It is an error if this leaves more than one match, unless they all give the same answer.
`<xsl:template>`	When selecting a template rule for use with `<xsl:apply-templates>`, firstly all the template rules with a matching `mode` are taken. Of these, all those with a `match` pattern that matches the selected node are considered. If this leaves more than one, only those with the highest import precedence are considered. If this still leaves more than one, the one with highest priority is chosen: The rules for deciding the priority are given under `<xsl:template>` on page 483. It is an error if this still doesn't identify a clear winner. The XSLT processor has the choice of reporting the error or choosing the template rule that was specified last. (In practice, several processors output a warning message). In the case of named templates, if there are several `<xsl:template>` declarations with the same `name` attribute, then the one with highest import precedence wins. It is an error if this leaves no clear winner.
`<xsl:variable>` `<xsl:param>`	If there are several global `<xsl:variable>` or `<xsl:param>` declarations with the same name, then the one with highest import precedence wins. It is an error if this leaves no clear winner.

Usage

The rules for `<xsl:import>` are so pervasive that one would imagine the facility is central to the use of XSLT, rather in the way inheritance is central to writing in Java. In practice, many stylesheets never need to use `<xsl:import>`, but you will almost certainly need it once you start to develop a family of stylesheets to handle a wide range of source document types.

Like inheritance in object-oriented languages, `<xsl:import>` is designed to allow the creation of a library or reusable components, only in this case, the components are modules of stylesheets. And the mechanism works in a very similar way to inheritance. For example, you might have a stylesheet that simply defines your corporate color scheme, as a set of global variables defining color names. Another stylesheet might be defined to produce the basic framesets for your site, referring to these color names to supply the background detail. Now if you want to use this general structure but to vary some detail, for example to modify one of the colors because it clashes with an image you are displaying on a particular page, you can define a stylesheet for this particular page that does nothing apart from redefining that one color. This is illustrated in Figure 6-6.

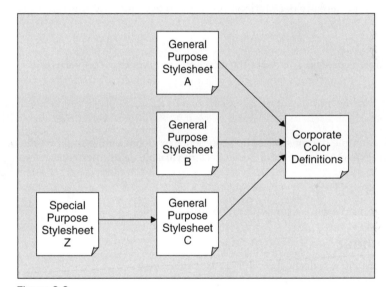

Figure 6-6

Suppose the stylesheet module for corporate color definitions looks like this:

```
<xsl:stylesheet xmlns:xsl="http://www.w3.org/1999/XSL/Transform"
      xmlns:color="http://acme.co.nz/colors"
      version="2.0">
<xsl:variable name="color:blue" select="'#0088ff'"/>
<xsl:variable name="color:pink" select="'#ff0088'"/>
<xsl:variable name="color:lilac" select="'#ff00ff'"/>
</xsl:stylesheet>
```

Now all the general-purpose stylesheets could `<xsl:include>` these definitions (without the need to `<xsl:import>` them unless they are being modified). This makes it easier to maintain the corporate brand image, because things are defined in one place only.

However, there are cases where you would want to depart from the general rule, and you can do so quite easily. If a particular document needs to use stylesheet C, but needs to vary the colors used, you can define stylesheet Z for it, as follows:

```
<xsl:stylesheet xmlns:xsl="http://www.w3.org/1999/XSL/Transform"
      xmlns:color="http://acme.co.nz/colors"
      version="1.0">
<xsl:import href="general-stylesheet-C.xsl"/>
<xsl:variable name="color:lilac" select="'#cc00cc'"/>
</xsl:stylesheet>
```

In fact, this might be the entire stylesheet. In common English, style Z is the same as style C but with a different shade of lilac. Note that all the references to variable «color:lilac» are interpreted as references to the definition in Z, even if the references occur in the same stylesheet module as a different definition of «color:lilac».

As a general principle, to incorporate standard content into a stylesheet without change, use <xsl:include>. If there are declarations you want to override, use <xsl:import>.

Examples

The first example is designed to show the effect of <xsl:import> on variables.

Example 1: Precedence of Variables

This example demonstrates the precedence of global variables when the principal stylesheet module and an imported module declare variables with the same name.

Source

This example can be run with any source XML file.

Stylesheet

The principal stylesheet module is variables.xsl.

```
<?xml version="1.0" encoding="iso-8859-1"?>
<xsl:stylesheet version="2.0"
    xmlns:xsl="http://www.w3.org/1999/XSL/Transform"
    xmlns:acme="http://acme.com/xslt"
    exclude-result-prefixes="acme">
<xsl:import href="boilerplate.xsl"/>
<xsl:output encoding="iso-8859-1" indent="yes"/>
<xsl:variable name="acme:company-name" select="'Acme Widgets Limited'"/>
<xsl:template match="/">
  <c><xsl:value-of select="$acme:copyright"/></c>
</xsl:template>

</xsl:stylesheet>
```

The imported stylesheet module is boilerplate.xsl.

```
<?xml version="1.0" encoding="iso-8859-1"?>
<xsl:stylesheet version="2.0"
    xmlns:xsl="http://www.w3.org/1999/XSL/Transform"
    xmlns:co="http://acme.com/xslt">
<xsl:variable name="co:company-name"
              select="'Acme Widgets Incorporated'"/>
<xsl:variable name="co:copyright"
              select="concat('Copyright © ', $co:company-name)"/>
</xsl:stylesheet>
```

Output

The output of this stylesheet will be:

```
<?xml version="1.0" encoding="iso-8859-1"?>
<c>Copyright © Acme Widgets Limited</c>
```

This is because in the variable declaration of «$co:copyright», the reference to variable «$co:company-name» matches the declaration of this variable in the principal stylesheet, because this has higher import precedence than the declaration in boilerplate.xsl.

The fact that different namespace prefixes are used in the two stylesheets is, of course, irrelevant: The prefix «acme» in the principal stylesheet maps to the same namespace URI as the prefix «co» in boilerplate.xsl, so the names are considered equivalent.

This example explicitly specifies encoding = "iso-8859-1" for both the stylesheet modules and the output. Most of my examples only use ASCII characters, and since the default character encoding UTF-8 is a superset of ASCII, this works fine. This time, though, I've used the copyright symbol «©», which is not an ASCII character, so it's important to specify the character encoding that my text editor uses, which is iso-8859-1.

The second example shows the effect of <xsl:import> on template rules.

Example 2: Precedence of Template Rules

In this example I shall define a complete stylesheet standard-style.xsl to display poems in HTML, and then override one of its rules in an importing stylesheet. The files required are all in the subdirectory import in the download file for this chapter.

Source

This example works with the poem that we used in Chapter 1. In the download file it's available as poem.xml. It starts like this:

```
<?xml version="1.0"?>
<poem>
<author>Rupert Brooke</author>
<date>1912</date>
```

```
<title>Song</title>
<stanza>
<line>And suddenly the wind comes soft,</line>
<line>And Spring is here again;</line>
<line>And the hawthorn quickens with buds of green</line>
<line>And my heart with buds of pain.</line>
</stanza>
etc.
</poem>
```

Stylesheet A

Here is `standard-style.xsl`:

```
<xsl:stylesheet version="2.0"
    xmlns:xsl="http://www.w3.org/1999/XSL/Transform">
<xsl:template match="/">
  <html>
    <head>
      <title><xsl:value-of select="//title"/></title>
    </head>
    <body>
      <xsl:apply-templates/>
    </body>
  </html>
</xsl:template>
<xsl:template match="title">
    <h1><xsl:apply-templates/></h1>
</xsl:template>
<xsl:template match="author">
    <div align="right"><i>by </i>
      <xsl:apply-templates/>
    </div>
</xsl:template>
<xsl:template match="stanza">
    <p><xsl:apply-templates/></p>
</xsl:template>
<xsl:template match="line">
    <xsl:apply-templates/><br/>
</xsl:template>
<xsl:template match="date"/>
</xsl:stylesheet>
```

Output A

When you run this stylesheet, the output starts like this (indented for clarity):

```
<html>
   <head>
     <meta http-equiv="Content-Type" content="text/html; charset=UTF-8">
     <title>Song</title>
   </head>
   <body>
     <div align="right">by Rupert Brooke</div>
```

```
<h1>Song</h1>
<p>
    And suddenly the wind comes soft,<br>
    And Spring is here again;<br>
    And the hawthorn quickens with buds of green<br>
    And my heart with buds of pain.<br>
</p>
```

Stylesheet B

Now we want to create a variant of this in which the lines of the poem are numbered. This will act as the principal stylesheet when you want this form of output. Here it is in `numbered-style.xsl`:

```
<xsl:stylesheet version="2.0"
    xmlns:xsl="http://www.w3.org/1999/XSL/Transform">
<xsl:import href="standard-style.xsl"/>
<xsl:template match="line">
    <xsl:number level="any" format="001"/>  
    <xsl:apply-imports/>
</xsl:template>
</xsl:stylesheet>
```

Note the use of the character reference « » to output a nonbreaking space. In HTML this is normally done by writing « ». You can use this entity reference in the stylesheet if you like (it's simply a symbolic name for the Unicode character XA0), but only if you declare it as an entity in the DTD. It's usually simpler just to use the numeric character reference.

Output B

This time the output starts like this. Again, the precise format depends on the processor (for example, some processors may output « », or « » instead of « »), but it should look the same when displayed in the browser:

```
<html>
    <head>
    <title>Song</title>
    </head>

    <body>
        <div align="right">by Rupert Brooke</div>
        <h1>Song</h1>
        <p>
            001  
            And suddenly the wind comes soft,<br>
            002  
            And Spring is here again;<br>
            003  
            And the hawthorn quickens with buds of green<br>
            004  
            And my heart with buds of pain.<br>
        </p>
```

All the template rules defined in standard-style.xsl are used as normal, except where the current node matches the pattern «line». In this situation there are two possible templates that match the node, so the one with higher import precedence is chosen. This is the one in the importing stylesheet module, namely numbered-style.xsl. As a result, the lines of the poem are output with a preceding line number, calculated using the <xsl:number> instruction, which is described on page 403. The use of <xsl:apply-imports> means that once the line number has been output, the line is displayed in the normal way, using the template rule from the standard-style.xsl stylesheet.

This use of <xsl:import> to customize the presentation produced by a stylesheet is very common. The rules in the importing stylesheet, which vary the standard presentation, are sometimes referred to as a *customization layer*. Another term used is *stylesheet overlay*. Sometimes the customization layer corresponds directly to an additional module in the schema or DTD: For example, if the schema that you use for press releases is an extended version of the schema used for general company documents, then you will want to write a customization layer over the general-purpose stylesheet to handle the additional features found in press releases.

See Also

<xsl:include> on page 372
<xsl:apply-imports> on page 237

xsl:import-schema

<xsl:import-schema> is a top-level declaration used to identify a schema containing definitions of types that are referred to in the stylesheet. This declaration is available only in a schema-aware processor.

Changes in 2.0

This element is new in XSLT 2.0.

Format

```
<xsl:import-schema
  namespace? = uri-reference
  schema-location? = uri-reference>
  <!-- Content: xs:schema? -->
</xsl:import-schema>
```

If the <xsl:import-schema> contains an inline schema (<xs:schema> element), then the schema-location attribute must be omitted.

Position

<xsl:import-schema> is a top-level declaration, which means that it must appear as a child of the <xsl:stylesheet> element. There are no constraints on its ordering relative to other declarations in the stylesheet.

Attributes

Name	Value	Meaning
namespace optional	URI	The namespace URI of the schema to be imported
schema-location optional	URI	A URI identifying the location of the schema to be imported

Content

The `<xsl:import-schema>` element may contain an inline schema document, represented by an `<xs:schema>` element (whose content in turn is as defined in the XML Schema specification).

Effect

If the stylesheet contains references to user-defined types, then the namespace in which these types are defined must be imported using an `<xsl:import-schema>` declaration. The same applies to user-defined element and attribute declarations.

Importing a schema makes the schema definitions available throughout the stylesheet, not only in the module where they are imported. (This differs from XQuery 1.0, where different modules may import different schemas.)

As with `<xs:import>`, the `<xsl:import-schema>` declaration states an intention to use schema components in a particular namespace, and it optionally gives a "hint" to the processor to indicate where definitions of those schema components may be found. You should explicitly import a schema document for every namespace that contains a definition that you want to refer to in the stylesheet. Importing a schema does not implicitly import other namespaces that are referenced from that schema using `<xs:import>`.

The XSLT specification defines the way that schema import works in terms of the way that the XML Schema specification defines `<xs:import>`. This leaves a great deal of discretion to the implementation. It is quite likely that an XSLT processor will want to cache schemas somewhere in a compiled form, to avoid analyzing them afresh every time a stylesheet is processed; many systems may also use catalogs or data dictionaries of some kind so that a local copy of a schema can be accessed rather than retrieving it over the Internet. The exact way in which the "hint" in the `schema-location` attribute is used is therefore very open-ended.

> *Although the terminology differs, this is not actually any different from the way the `href` attribute in `<xsl:include>` and `<xsl:import>` is handled. Reflecting common practice established with XSLT 1.0, the XSLT specification now recognizes that implementations can provide URI resolvers or catalogs to interpret these URIs, and that it is therefore impossible to be completely prescriptive about their interpretation.*

Using an inline schema document is exactly the same as putting the schema in a separate XML document and referencing it in the `schema-location` attribute. It's convenient to have the schema inline, however, if it contains definitions that are used only within this stylesheet, perhaps to define the structure of some working data or some constraints on a particular function parameter. If an `<xsl:import-schema>` declaration contains an inline schema document, then the `schema-location` attribute must be omitted. You can also omit the `namespace` attribute (if you don't, then it must match the `targetNamespace` of the inline schema).

In other cases, omitting the `namespace` attribute indicates that you want to import a schema that has no target namespace (that is, a schema for elements that are in no namespace). The `namespace` attribute should not be set to a zero-length string, since this is not a valid namespace URI.

If the `schema-location` attribute is omitted, and if there is no inline schema document, then it is assumed that the implementation will be able to locate a schema from knowledge of the target namespace alone.

It's not technically an error if no schema for the requested namespace can be found. But in practice this will usually trigger an error because the stylesheet will then contain references to schema definitions that haven't been imported.

It is a fatal error, however, if a schema can be found and it isn't valid according to the XML Schema specifications.

If there are multiple `<xsl:import-schema>` declarations for the same target namespace (or for the "null namespace"), then the one with highest import precedence is used. Import precedence is explained under `<xsl:import>` on page 357. If this leaves more than one, then the behavior is defined by reference to the XML Schema specification: it's defined to be the same as when a schema document contains more than one `<xs:import>` element for the same namespace. In practice, the schema specification leaves a lot of discretion to implementations on how to handle this. Some implementations may load multiple schema modules and check them for consistency; others (including Saxon) simply take the first one and assume that the others are equivalent.

Consistency rules for schemas extend beyond the question of multiple imports from a single stylesheet. The schema that's imported into the stylesheet must be consistent with the schema used to validate the source document. Since many systems will allow compiled schemas to be cached, probably sharing the cache between many different stylesheets, there is likely to be a more global consistency requirement. In general, it's probably not possible to have two different versions of the same schema (or to put it another way, two different schemas with the same target namespace, or with no target namespace) in use at the same time. Use of `<xs:redefine>` can potentially cause problems if you use the base definitions to compile the stylesheet and then use a redefined version to validate the source document. The details, however, are left to the implementation.

If a processor that is not schema-aware encounters an `<xsl:import-schema>` declaration, it will report an error. If you want to write stylesheets that work with both schema-aware and non-schema-aware processors, you can achieve this by attaching the attribute «use-when="system-property ('xsl:schema-aware')='yes')"» to any element that should be ignored by a non-schema-aware processor (that is, the `<xsl:import-schema>` declaration itself, and any element that uses a «type» or «validation» attribute, or references a schema-defined type). Of course, you will also have to provide an alternative element for use in this case.

Usage

It's not necessary to import every schema that has been used to validate an input document. You only need to import the schema if there is code in the stylesheet that actually references the names whose meaning is defined in the schema.

The places where such references may occur are as follows:

❑ In the `type` attribute of `<xsl:element>`, `<xsl:attribute>`, `<xsl:copy>`, `<xsl:copy-of>`, `<xsl:document>`, `<xsl:result-document>`, and the `xsl:type` attribute of literal result elements. This is always a `QName` identifying a top-level type definition, and unless it is one of the built-in types such as `xs:integer`, the schema in which the type is defined must be imported.

❑ In the «as» attribute of `<xsl:variable>`, `<xsl:param>`, `<xsl:with-param>`, `<xsl:function>`, and `<xsl:template>`. The value of this attribute is a description of an XPath type and is expressed using the `SequenceType` syntax defined in Chapter 11. If the `SequenceType` references the name of an atomic type, this will be a `QName` identifying either a built-in type such as `xs:date`, or a top-level simple type definition in a schema. If the latter is the case, the schema must be imported. If the `SequenceType` uses the constructs «element(N, T)» or «attribute (N, T)» then the rules are slightly more complicated, and are described below.

❑ In an XPath expression anywhere in the stylesheet that uses a `SequenceType`. This construct is used in expressions such as «$x instance of T» or «$x treat as T». The rules here are the same as for a `SequenceType` appearing in an «as» attribute, as described in the previous item.

❑ In an XPath expression that uses a constructor function for a user-defined atomic type (for example «mf:part-number('PXW5792')») or a cast to a user-defined atomic type (for example «'PXW5792' cast as mf:part-number»). In both these cases, the type name must be the name of a top-level simple type definition, and the schema containing this type definition must be imported.

❑ If you use the option «validation="strict"» or «validation="lax"», then you may be required to import the schema used to perform this validation, even if there are no explicit references in the stylesheet to the names defined in this schema. The XSLT specification leaves it open to the implementation to use other mechanisms to locate a schema at runtime to perform this validation, but if you import the schema explicitly, then you avoid any dependence on such mechanisms.

When the construct «schema-element(N)» or «schema-attribute(N)» is used in a `SequenceType`, then N must be the name of a global element or attribute declaration defined in an imported schema. Similarly, when the constructs «element(N, T)» or «attribute(N, T)» are used, then T must be the name of a simple or complex type defined in an imported schema, unless it is the name of a built-in type. But in these constructs the name N does not need to be present in the schema; this allows reference to local elements and attributes provided that they have a global type definition.

For example, if you create an element like this:

```
<temp xsl:type="xs:date">
  <xsl:value-of select="current-date()"/>
</temp>
```

you will later be able to match this using:

```
<xsl:if test="$p instance of element(temp, xs:date)">
```

even though there is no imported schema defining the element name «temp».

Examples

This example imports the schema for namespace «http://ns.megacorp.com/hr» from the location «http://schema.megacorp.com/hr/schema.xsd»:

```
<xsl:import-schema
    namespace = "http://ns.megacorp.com/hr"
    schema-location = "http://schema.megacorp.com/hr/schema.xsd"/>
```

The following example imports a no-namespace schema from the file «schema.xsd» in the same directory as the stylesheet:

```
<xsl:import-schema
    schema-location = "schema.xsd"/>
```

The following example imports the schema that defines the structure of XSLT stylesheets. (This import would be useful only in a stylesheet that is designed to process XSLT stylesheets as its input and/or result documents.).

```
<xsl:import-schema
    namespace = "http://www.w3.org/1999/XSL/Transform"
    schema-location="http://www.w3.org/2007/schema-for-xslt20.xsd"/>
```

The following example defines a union type for use locally within the stylesheet. This type allows either an xs:date, an xs:time, or an xs:dateTime:

```
<xsl:import-schema>
  <xs:schema targetNamespace="http://goliath.com/ns/local">
    <xs:simpleType name="dateOrTime">
      <xs:union memberTypes="xs:date xs:time xs:dateTime"/>
    </xs:simpleType>
  </xs:schema>
</xsl:import-schema>
```

This type might be used in the signature of a function that applies default formatting to the value, as follows:

```
<xsl:function name="local:format" as="xs:string">
  <xsl:param name="in" as="element(*, local:dateOrTime)"/>
  <xsl:variable name="data" select="data($in)"/>
  <xsl:choose>
    <xsl:when test="$data instance of xs:date">
      <xsl:sequence select="format-date($data, '[D] [MNn], [Y]')"/>
    </xsl:when>
    <xsl:when test="$data instance of xs:time">
      <xsl:sequence select="format-time($data, '[H]:[m]')"/>
    </xsl:when>
    <xsl:when test="$data instance of xs:dateTime">
      <xsl:sequence select="format-dateTime($data, '[H]:[m] on [D] [MNn], [Y]')"/>
    </xsl:when>
  </xsl:choose>
</xsl:function>
```

The full stylesheet is in file inline.xsl. Unfortunately it's not possible to use the union type directly as a parameter to the function («as="local:dateOrTime"») — although the meaning is intuitive, union types cannot appear directly in a SequenceType, only as a type annotation on element or attribute nodes.

xsl:include

<xsl:include> is a top-level element used to include the contents of one stylesheet module within another. The definitions in the included stylesheet module have the same *import precedence* as those in the including module, so the effect is as if these definitions were textually included at the point in the including module where the <xsl:include> element appears.

Changes in 2.0

There are no changes to the syntax of this instruction in XSLT 2.0. The rules for the `href` attribute have been reformulated to reflect current practice with XSLT 1.0: In effect, the way in which the URI is dereferenced to obtain a stylesheet module is now largely implementation defined. This allows for options such as catalogs or user-specified URI resolvers, as well as implementations that cache or precompile stylesheet modules.

Format

```
<xsl:include
  href = uri-reference />
```

Position

`<xsl:include>` is a top-level declaration, which means that it must appear as a child of the `<xsl:stylesheet>` element. There are no constraints on its ordering relative to other declarations in the stylesheet.

Attributes

Name	Value	Meaning
href mandatory	URI	The URI of the stylesheet to be included

Like all other XSLT elements, the `<xsl:include>` declaration may also have a «use-when» attribute. This is described in Chapter 3 (see page 127). This can be used in the same way as on `<xsl:import>`: see the example on page 358.

Content

None; the element is always empty.

Effect

The URI contained in the `href` attribute may be an absolute URI or a relative URI reference. If relative, it is interpreted relative to the base URI of the XML document or external entity containing the `<xsl:include>` element. For example, if a file `main.xsl` contains the element `<xsl:include href="date.xsl"/>`, then by default the system will look for `date.xsl` in the same directory as `main.xsl`. You can change this behavior by using the `xml:base` attribute to specify a base URI explicitly, as described in Chapter 2 on page 54.

The URI (once resolved) must identify an XML document that is a valid XSLT stylesheet. The top-level elements of this stylesheet are logically inserted into the including stylesheet module at the point where the `<xsl:include>` element appears. However:

❑   These elements retain their base URI, so anything that involves resolving a relative URI reference is done relative to the original URI of the included stylesheet. This rule applies, for example, when expanding further `<xsl:include>` and `<xsl:import>` elements, or when using relative URIs as arguments to the `document()` function.

❑   When a namespace prefix is used (typically within a QName, but it also applies to freestanding prefixes such as those in the `xsl:exclude-result-prefixes` attribute of a literal result element), it is interpreted using only the namespace declarations in the original stylesheet module in which the QName occurred. An included stylesheet module does not inherit namespace declarations from the module that includes it. This even applies to QNames constructed at execution time as the result of evaluating an expression, for example an expression used within an attribute value template for the name or namespace attribute of <xsl:element>.

❑ The values of the version, extension-element-prefixes, exclude-result-prefixes, and xpath-default-namespace attributes that apply to an element in the included stylesheet module, as well as xml:lang, xml:base, and xml:space, are those that were defined on their own <xsl:stylesheet> element, not those on the <xsl:stylesheet> element of the including stylesheet module.

The included stylesheet module may use the simplified stylesheet syntax, described in Chapter 3. This allows an entire stylesheet module to be defined as the content of an element such as <HTML>. It is then treated as if it were a module containing a single template, whose match pattern is «/» and whose content is the literal result element.

The included stylesheet module may contain <xsl:include> statements to include further stylesheets, or <xsl:import> statements to import them. A stylesheet must not directly or indirectly include itself.

It is not an error to include the same stylesheet module more than once, either directly or indirectly, but it is not a useful thing to do. It may well cause errors due to the presence of duplicate declarations; in fact, if the module contains definitions of global variables or named templates and is included more than once at the same import precedence, such errors are inevitable.

Usage and Examples

<xsl:include> provides a simple textual inclusion facility analogous to the #include directive in C. It provides a way of writing a stylesheet in a modular way so that commonly used definitions can be held in a library and used wherever they are needed.

If you are handling a wide range of different document types, the chances are they will have some elements in common, which are to be processed in the same way regardless of where they occur. For example, these might include standard definitions of toolbars, backgrounds, and navigation buttons to appear on your Web pages, as well as standard styles applied to data elements such as product names, e-mail contact addresses, or dates.

To incorporate such standard content into a stylesheet without change, use <xsl:include>. If there are definitions you want to override, use <xsl:import>.

<xsl:include> is a compile-time facility; it is used to assemble the complete stylesheet before you start executing it. People sometimes ask how to include other stylesheets conditionally at runtime, based on conditions found in the source document. The answer is simple: you can't. It would be like writing a program in Visual Basic that modifies itself as it executes. If you do want different sets of rules to be active at different times, consider using modes, or consider inverting the logic, so that instead of having an all-purpose stylesheet that tries to include different sets of rules on different occasions, you make your principal stylesheet module the one that is most closely tailored to the circumstances, and use <xsl:import> to import the all-purpose rules into it, at a lower import precedence than the specialized rules.

It can make a difference where in your stylesheet the <xsl:include> statement is placed. There are some kinds of objects — notably, template rules — where if there is no other way of deciding which one to use, the XSLT processor has the option of giving priority to the one that occurs last in the stylesheet. This isn't something you can easily take advantage of, because in all these cases the processor also has the option of reporting an error. As a general principle, it's probably best to place <xsl:include> statements near the beginning of the file, because then if there are any accidental overlaps in the definitions, the ones in your principal stylesheet will either override those included from elsewhere, or be reported as errors.

Example: Using <xsl:include> with Named Attribute Sets

This example shows the use of <xsl:include> to incorporate declarations (in this case of a named attribute set) from one stylesheet module into another.

Source

This example can be used with any source document, or with none, if you start execution with the named template main.

Stylesheet

Consider a principal stylesheet picture.xsl that includes a stylesheet attributes.xsl, as follows:

```
<xsl:stylesheet version="2.0"
   xmlns:xsl="http://www.w3.org/1999/XSL/Transform">
<xsl:include href="attributes.xsl"/>
<xsl:template match="/" name="main">
   <picture xsl:use-attribute-sets="picture-attributes">
      <xsl:attribute name="color">red</xsl:attribute>
   </picture>
</xsl:template>
</xsl:stylesheet>
```

This includes the module attributes.xsl:

```
<xsl:stylesheet version="2.0"
   xmlns:xsl="http://www.w3.org/1999/XSL/Transform">
<xsl:attribute-set name="picture-attributes">
   <xsl:attribute name="color">blue</xsl:attribute>
   <xsl:attribute name="transparency">100</xsl:attribute>
</xsl:attribute-set>
</xsl:stylesheet>
```

The named attribute set in the included stylesheet is used exactly as if it were defined in the principal stylesheet, at the point where the <xsl:include> statement appears.

Output

The resulting output is:

```
<picture transparency="100" color="red"/>
```

This is because attributes generated using <xsl:attribute> override those generated by using a named attribute set; it has nothing to do with the fact that the attribute set came from an included stylesheet.

See Also

<xsl:import> on page 357

xsl:key

The <xsl:key> element is a top-level declaration used to declare a named key, for use with the key() function in expressions and patterns.

Changes in 2.0

The restrictions on using global variables in the match and use attributes have been eased.

It is now possible to define keys of any type (for example numbers or dates) and to a specify a collation to be used when deciding whether two string-valued keys match.

The key values for a node can now be evaluated using a sequence constructor contained in the <xsl:key> element, as an alternative to using the use attribute. This allows the evaluation to invoke templates or other XSLT constructs such as <xsl:number>.

Format

```
<xsl:key
  name = qname
  match = pattern
  use? = expression
  collation? = uri>
  <!-- Content: sequence-constructor -->
</xsl:key>
```

Position

<xsl:key> is a top-level declaration, which means that it must be a child of the <xsl:stylesheet> element. It may appear any number of times in a stylesheet.

Attributes

Name	Value	Meaning
name mandatory	Lexical QName	The name of the key
match mandatory	Pattern	Defines the nodes to which this key is applicable
use optional	XPath Expression	The expression used to determine the value of the key for each of these nodes
collation optional	URI	The name of a collation used to compare string-valued keys

The syntax for a Pattern is defined in Chapter 12.

The use attribute and the sequence constructor are mutually exclusive: if the use attribute is present, the element must be empty, and if it is absent, then there must be a nonempty sequence constructor.

Content

A sequence constructor. This is used as an alternative to the `use` attribute to determine the value of the key.

Effect

The `name` attribute specifies the name of the key. It must be a valid lexical QName; if it contains a namespace prefix, the prefix must identify a namespace declaration that is in scope on the `<xsl:key>` element. The effective name of the key is the expanded name, consisting of the namespace URI and the local part of the name.

The `match` attribute specifies the nodes to which the key applies. The value is a `Pattern`, as described in Chapter 12. If a node doesn't match the pattern, then it will have no values for the named key. If a node does match the pattern, then the node will have zero or more values for the named key, as determined by the `use` attribute or the contained sequence constructor.

The simplest case is where each node has one key value, and the key values are unique. For example, consider the following source document:

```
<vehicles>
<vehicle reg="P427AGH" owner="Joe Karloff"/>
<vehicle reg="T788PHT" owner="Prunella Higgs"/>
<vehicle reg="V932TXQ" owner="William D. Abikombo"/>
</vehicles>
```

In the stylesheet you can define a key for the registration number of these vehicles, as follows:

```
<xsl:key name="vehicle-registration" match="vehicle" use="@reg"/>
```

The `use` attribute (or in its absense, the contained sequence constructor) specifies an expression used to determine the value or values of the key. This expression doesn't have to select an attribute, like «@reg» in the example above. For example, it could select a child element. It could also be a computed value, such as «count(*)» (the number of child elements that the node has). If the value is a sequence, the system creates an index entry for each item in the sequence, and the node can be found using any one of these values.

If the `use` expression returns nodes, the nodes will be atomized. The resulting values can be of any atomic type, or a mixture of different atomic types. When you use the `key()` function to search for a node, the value you supply is compared with the indexed values according to the rules of the XPath «eq» operator. Generally, this means you must supply a value of the right type: for example, if the indexed value is an integer, and you search for a string, then you won't find anything. However, the usual type conversions occur automatically: numbers such as integers and doubles can be compared with each other, and `xs:untypedAtomic` values can be compared to strings.

In backward-compatibility mode (when the stylesheet specifies «version="1.0"»), both the values returned by the `use` expression and the values supplied to the `key()` function are converted to strings and are compared as strings. This means you won't get a match between different representations of the same number, such as «1» and «001», but you will get a match between the number «1» and the string «"1"».

The `collation` attribute identifies a collation that will be used when the key value is a string. If no collation is specified, a default collation is used (this will usually be the Unicode Codepoint Collation, described below). Collations are discussed under `<xsl:sort>` on page 459. You need to decide whether you want to use a weak collation, in which strings such as «ASCII» and «ascii» are considered equivalent, or a strong collation, in which they are considered to be different. You might also need to consider what language should be used to define the matching rules. One of the options, which might be the best choice when you are comparing strings such as part numbers, is to use the Unicode Codepoint Collation, which considers two strings to be equal only if they use the same Unicode characters, as identified by their codepoint values. You can request this using the collation URI:

```
http://www.w3.org/2005/xpath-functions/collation/codepoint
```

XSLT 2.0 allows the pattern in the `match` attribute, and the expression in the `use` attribute, to reference global variables and to use the `key()` function to access other keys. But the definitions must not be circular; for example, if a key K makes use of the global variable V, then the value of V must not depend in any way on the key K.

There is no rule that stops two nodes having the same key value. For example, declaring a key for vehicle registration numbers in the example above does not mean that each registration number must be different. So a node can have more than one key value, and a key value can refer to more than one node.

To complicate things a bit further, there can be more than one `<xsl:key>` declaration in the stylesheet with the same name. The set of indexed values for the key is then the union of the sets produced by each `<xsl:key>` declaration independently. The import precedence of the key declarations makes no difference. All the `<xsl:key>` declarations with a given name must have the same values for the `collation` attribute, if present.

A key can be used to select nodes in any document, not just the principal source document. This includes a temporary document constructed within the stylesheet.

The effect of calling «key(K, V, R)», where K is a key name, V is a value, and R is a node, is to select every node N that satisfies all the following conditions:

❑ The node N must be in the subtree rooted at R, that is, it must have R on its `ancestor-or-self` axis.

❑ The node N must match the pattern defined in the `match` attribute of an `<xsl:key>` definition named K.

❑ One of the values in the sequence V must be equal to one of the values in the sequence obtained by evaluating the `use` attribute (or sequence constructor) of that key definition, with N as the context node. Values are compared using the XPath «eq» operator, with the specified collation.

If there are several nodes that satisfy these conditions, they are returned in document order, with duplicates eliminated.

If the third argument R is omitted, its effective value is «/», which means that the function searches the whole of the document containing the context node.

Usage and Examples

Declaring a key has two effects: it simplifies the code you need to write to find the nodes with given values, and it is likely to make access faster.

The performance effect, of course, depends entirely on the implementation. It would be quite legitimate for an implementation to conduct a full search of the document each time the `key()` function was called.

In practice, however, most implementations are likely to build an index or hash table, so there will be a one-time cost in building the index (for each document), but after this, access to nodes whose key value is known should be very fast.

The `<xsl:key>` element is usually used to index elements, but in principle it can be used to index any kind of node except namespace nodes.

Keys versus IDs

An alternative to using keys is to use XML-defined IDs. If you have attributes defined in a DTD or schema as being of type ID, you can find an element with a particular ID value using the `id()` function described in Chapter 13.

Why would you prefer to use keys, rather than relying on ID values? Keys have many advantages:

❑ ID values must be simple attributes of the elements they identify, they cannot be anything more complex.

❑ ID values must be unique.

❑ You cannot have two different sets of ID values in the same document, for example ISBNs and acquisition numbers; if you do, you have to be sure they will not clash with each other.

❑ ID values must take the form of XML names, for example they cannot contain characters such as «/» and «+».

❑ ID values are not recognized in a source document unless it is parsed with a validating XML parser or schema processor that reports attribute types to the XSLT processor. XML parsers are not required to behave in this way, so it is easy to end up with configuration problems that result in IDs not being recognized.

❑ Recognizing ID attributes in temporary trees is particularly troublesome, as it requires the temporary tree to be validated.

Using a Simple Key

The detailed rules for keys seem complicated, but most practical applications of keys are very simple. Consider the following key definition:

```
<xsl:key name="product-code" match="product" use="@code"/>
```

This defines a key whose name is «product-code», and which can be used to find `<product>` elements given the value of their `code` attribute. If a product has no `code` attribute, it won't be possible to find it using this key.

To find the product with code value «ABC-456», you can write, for example:

```
<xsl:apply-templates select="key('product-code', 'ABC-456')"/>
```

Note that you could just as well choose to index the attribute nodes:

```
<xsl:key name="product-code" match="product/@code" use="."/>
```

To find the relevant product you would then write:

```
<xsl:apply-templates select="key('product-code', 'ABC-456')/.."/>
```

I've used `<xsl:apply-templates>` here as an example. This will select all the `<product>` elements in the current document that have code «ABC-456» (I never said it had to be a unique identifier) and apply the matching template to each one in turn, processing them in document order, as usual. I could equally have used any other instruction that uses an XPath expression; for example, I could have assigned the node set to a variable, or used it in an `<xsl:value-of>` element.

The second argument to the key function should normally be a value of the same type as the use expression in the `<xsl:key>` declaration. It won't usually be a literal, as in my example, but is more likely to be a value obtained from somewhere else in the source document, or perhaps supplied as a parameter to the stylesheet. It may well have been passed as one of the parameters in the URL used to select this stylesheet in the first place; for example, a Web page might display a list of available products such as the one in Figure 6-7.

Figure 6-7

Clicking the Buy Now! button might cause a URL such as the following to be sent to the server:

```
http://www.naxos-breakfasts.com/servlet/buy?product="TK0372&quantity="1"
```

You then write a servlet (or an ASP.NET page if you prefer) on your Web server that extracts the query parameters `code` and `quantity` and fires off your favorite XSLT processor specifying `products.xml` as the source document, `show-product.xsl` as the stylesheet, and «TK0372» and «1» as the values to be supplied for the global stylesheet parameter called `prod-code` and `quantity`. Your stylesheet might then look like the one that follows.

```
<xsl:param name="prod-code" as="xs:string"/>
<xsl:param name="quantity" as="xs:integer"/>
<xsl:key name="product-code" match="product" use="@code"/>
<xsl:template match="/">
   <html>
   <body>
   <xsl:variable name="product" select="key('product-code', $prod-code)"/>
   <xsl:if test="not($product)">
      <p>There is no product with this code</p>
   </xsl:if>
   <xsl:apply-templates select="$product"/>
   </body>
   </html>
</xsl:template>
```

Multivalued Keys

A key can be multivalued, in that a single node can have several values, each of which can be used to find the node independently. For example, a book may have several authors, and each author's name can be used as a key value. This could be defined as follows:

```
<xsl:key name="book-author" match="book" use="author/name"/>
```

The use expression, «author/name», selects more than one node, so the typed value of each of its nodes (that is, the name of each author of the book) is used as one of the values in the set of node-value pairs that makes up the key.

In this particular example, as well as one book having several authors, each author may have written several books, so when you use an XPath expression such as:

```
<xsl:for-each select="key('book-author', 'Agatha Christie')">
```

you will be selecting all the books in which Agatha Christie was one of the authors. What if you want to find all the books in which Alex Homer and David Sussman are joint authors? You can do this using the intersect operator provided in XPath 2.0:

```
<xsl:variable name="set1"
    select="key('book-author', 'Alex Homer')"/>
<xsl:variable name="set2"
    select="key('book-author', 'David Sussman')"/>
<xsl:variable name="result"
    select="$set1 intersect $set2"/>
```

You can also supply a sequence of several values as the second argument to the key() function. For example, you might write:

```
<xsl:variable name="ac" select="key('book-author', 'Agatha Christie')">
<xsl:for-each select="key('book-author', $ac/author/name)">
```

The result of the select expression in the <xsl:for-each> instruction is the set of all books in which one of the authors is either Agatha Christie or a co-author of Agatha Christie. This is because $ac is the set of all books in which Agatha Christie is an author, so «$ac/author/name» is the set of all authors of these books, and using this set of named authors as the value of the key produces the set of books in which *any* of them is an author.

Example: Multivalued Nonunique Keys

This example shows how a node can have several values for one key, and a given key value can identify more than one node. It uses author name as a key to locate <book> elements.

Source

The source file is booklist.xml:

```
<booklist>
<book>
    <title>Design Patterns</title>
    <author>Erich Gamma</author>
```

```
        <author>Richard Helm</author>
        <author>Ralph Johnson</author>
        <author>John Vlissides</author>
    </book>
    <book>
        <title>Pattern Hatching</title>
        <author>John Vlissides</author>
    </book>
    <book>
        <title>Building Applications Frameworks</title>
        <author>Mohamed Fayad</author>
        <author>Douglas C. Schmidt</author>
        <author>Ralph Johnson</author>
    </book>
    <book>
        <title>Implementing Applications Frameworks</title>
        <author>Mohamed Fayad</author>
        <author>Douglas C. Schmidt</author>
        <author>Ralph Johnson</author>
    </book>
    </booklist>
```

Stylesheet

The stylesheet is `author-key.xsl`.

It declares the key and then simply copies the `<book>` elements that match the author name supplied as a parameter. You can run this stylesheet in Saxon with a call such as (all on one line):

```
java -jar c:\saxon\saxon9.jar -s:booklist.xml -xsl:author-key.xsl↵
     author="Ralph Johnson"
```

or in Altova (note the nested quotes):

```
AltovaXML -in booklist.xml -xslt2 author-key.xsl↵
     -param author="'John Vlissides'"
```

or in Gestalt:

```
gestalt author-key.xsl booklist.xml author="John Vlissides"
```

Note that parameters containing spaces have to be written in quotes on the command line. In Altova, two pairs of quotes are needed, because the value supplied for the parameter is an XPath expression rather than a string.

```
<xsl:transform
 xmlns:xsl="http://www.w3.org/1999/XSL/Transform"
 version="2.0"
>
<xsl:key name="author-name" match="book" use="author"/>
<xsl:param name="author" required="yes"/>
<xsl:template match="/">
```

```
        <xsl:copy-of select="key('author-name', $author)"/>
    </xsl:template>
    </xsl:transform>
```

Output

With the parameter set to the value «John Vlissides», the output is as follows:

```
<?xml version="1.0" encoding="utf-8"?>
<book>
    <title>Design Patterns</title>
    <author>Erich Gamma</author>
    <author>Richard Helm</author>
    <author>Ralph Johnson</author>
    <author>John Vlissides</author>
</book>
<book>
    <title>Pattern Hatching</title>
    <author>John Vlissides</author>
</book>
```

(In Altova, the result will not be indented, because the Altova processor discards whitespace text nodes from the input.)

Multiple Named Keys

There is nothing to stop you from defining several keys for the same nodes. For example:

```
<xsl:key name="book-isbn" match="book" use="isbn"/>
<xsl:key name="book-author" match="book" use="author/surname"/>
```

This allows you to find a book if either the author or the ISBN is known.

However, it's worth thinking twice before doing this. Assuming the XSLT processor implements the key by building an index or hash table, rather than by searching the whole document each time, you have to weigh the cost of building the index against the cost of finding the information by a search. If your transformation only needs to find a single book using its ISBN number, it might be simpler and faster to write:

```
<xsl:for-each select="//book[isbn='0-13-082676-6']"/>
```

and not use a key at all. Some products (Saxon-SA for example) will even decide for themselves whether to build an index to speed up such an expression.

Multiple Definitions for the Same Key

It's also possible to have several <xsl:key> declarations with the same name. For example:

```
<xsl:key name="artist-key" match="book" use="author/name"/>
<xsl:key name="artist-key" match="CD" use="composer"/>
<xsl:key name="artist-key" match="CD" use="performer"/>
```

Now you can use the key() function in an expression such as:

```
<xsl:apply-templates select="key('artist-key', 'Ringo Starr')"/>
```

The set of nodes this returns will be either <book> elements or <CD> elements or a mixture of the two; the only thing you know for certain is that each one will be either a book with Ringo Starr as one of the authors, or a CD with Ringo Starr listed either as the composer or as a performer.

If the use expression were the same in each case, you could simplify this. For example to find books and CDs with a particular publisher, you could write:

```
<xsl:key name="publisher-key" match="book | CD" use="publisher"/>
```

This example uses the union pattern «book | CD», which matches all <book> elements and all <CD> elements. Union patterns are described on page 690 in Chapter 12.

The different definitions do not all need to be in the same stylesheet module; all the key definitions in included and imported stylesheets are merged together regardless of their import precedence.

Composite Keys

Despite all the functionality we've been discussing, one thing that isn't available directly is support for composite or multi-part keys, that is, finding an employee using both the last name and first name in combination.

The simplest way to do this is by string concatenation. Define the key like this:

```
<xsl:key name="k" match="employee" use="concat(firstname, '#', lastname)"/>
```

and search for it like this:

```
key('k', concat($first, '#', $last))
```

I chose «#» here as a character that is unlikely to appear in the firstname or lastname values.

Using Keys for Grouping

In XSLT 2.0, the new <xsl:for-each-group> instruction (described on page 326) provides facilities for grouping nodes with common values for a grouping key, or for eliminating nodes with duplicate values for a grouping key. In XSLT 1.0, this was a much more difficult problem to solve, and you may well encounter XSLT 1.0 stylesheets that use the workaround for this problem known as Muenchian grouping, named after its inventor, Steve Muench of Oracle.

It shouldn't be necessary to use Muenchian grouping any more in XSLT 2.0. However, since it is widely used and you may have the job of converting stylesheets that use it, or of writing stylesheets that work under both XSLT 2.0 and XSLT 1.0, it's worth understanding how it works.

Say you want to group a list of employees according to their location. Typically, you want two nested loops, in pseudocode:

```
<xsl:for-each (distinct location)>
   <location name="...">
      <xsl:for-each (employee in that location)>
         <employee>
```

```
            (details)
          </employee>
        </xsl:for-each>
    </location>
  </xsl:for-each>
```

Muenchian grouping uses a key to identify the distinct locations and then to identify all the employees at a given location. The key is defined like this:

```
<xsl:key name="k" match="employee" use="location"/>
```

To find the distinct locations, scan all the employee elements, and select only those that are the first one in their location. In XSLT 2.0 you would write:

```
<xsl:for-each select="//employee[. is key('k', location)[1]]">
```

The «is» operator wasn't available in XPath 1.0, so this had to be written as:

```
<xsl:for-each select=
    "//employee[generate-id(.) = generate-id(key('k', location)[1])]">
```

The inner loop, which selects all the employees at the same location, is achieved by writing:

```
<xsl:for-each select="key('k', location)">
```

so the final code becomes:

```
<xsl:for-each select=
    "//employee[generate-id(.) = generate-id(key('k', location)[1])]">
    <location name="{location}">
      <xsl:for-each select="key('k', location)">
        <employee>
          <xsl:apply-templates/>
        </employee>
      </xsl:for-each>
    </location>
  </xsl:for-each>
```

In XSLT 2.0 this can be rewritten much more readably as:

```
<xsl:for-each-group select="//employee" group-by="location"
    <location name="{current-grouping-key()}">
      <xsl:for-each select="current-group()">
        <employee>
          <xsl:apply-templates/>
        </employee>
      </xsl:for-each>
    </location>
  </xsl:for-each>
```

See Also

key() function in Chapter 7, page 812
<xsl:for-each-group> on page 326

xsl:matching-substring

The `<xsl:matching-substring>` element is used within an `<xsl:analyze-string>` instruction to indicate the processing that should be applied to substrings of the input string that match the supplied regular expression.

Changes in 2.0

This element is new in XSLT 2.0.

Format

```
<xsl:matching-substring>
  <!-- Content: sequence-constructor -->
</xsl:matching-substring>
```

Position

`<xsl:matching-substring>` can only appear as a child of an `<xsl:analyze-string>` element, and it may not appear more than once.

Attributes

None.

Content

A sequence constructor.

Effect

The sequence constructor contained in the `<xsl:matching-substring>` element is evaluated once for each substring of the input string that matches the regular expression. The result of evaluating the sequence constructor is added to the result of the containing `<xsl:analyze-string>` instruction.

Usage and Examples

See `<xsl:analyze-string>` on page 230.

See Also

`<xsl:analyze-string>` on page 230
`<xsl:non-matching-substring>` on page 402

xsl:message

The `<xsl:message>` instruction outputs a message, and optionally terminates execution of the stylesheet.

Changes in 2.0

The `terminate` attribute may now be specified as an attribute value template.

The `select` attribute is new in XSLT 2.0.

Format

```
<xsl:message
   select? = expression
   terminate? = { "yes" | "no"} >
   <!-- Content: sequence-constructor -->
</xsl:message>
```

Position

`<xsl:message>` is an instruction. It is always used as part of a sequence constructor.

Attributes

Name	Value	Meaning
select optional	XPath Expression	The expression is evaluated to produce the content of the message.
terminate optional	Attribute value template returning «yes» or «no»	The value «yes» indicates that processing is terminated after the message is output. The default is «no».

Content

A sequence constructor. There is no requirement that this should only generate text nodes; it can produce any XML fragment. What happens to any markup, however, is not defined in the standard.

This means that writing `<xsl:message select="@status"/>` *could cause an error, on the grounds that you are trying to output an attribute node when there is no element to attach it to. It's safer to atomize the attribute node explicitly by calling* `data()` *or* `string()`.

Unlike other elements that allow a `select` attribute and a sequence constructor, in this case they are not mutually exclusive. The results of evaluating the `select` expression and the results of evaluating the sequence constructor are concatenated to form a single sequence.

Effect

The `<xsl:message>` instruction behaves in a similar way to `<xsl:result-document>` described on page 445; it uses the contained sequence constructor (in this case, with the results of evaluating any `select` expression added at the front) to construct a new document node, sends the constructed document to an implementation-defined destination, and returns an empty sequence.

Unlike `<xsl:result-document>`, the `<xsl:message>` element provides no direct control over the destination or format of the result. The intention is that it should be used to produce progress messages, errors and warnings, which are secondary to the purpose of the transformation.

If the `terminate` attribute is omitted, the value «no» is assumed.

The contents of the constructed document (which will often be a simple text node) are output where the user can be expected to see them. The XSLT specification does not actually say where it goes; this is implementation-dependent, and it might be determined by configuration options. The specification suggests an alert box on the screen and a log file as two possible destinations.

If the `terminate` attribute has the value «yes», execution of the stylesheet is abandoned immediately. In this situation (as indeed after any runtime error) the content of any output files is undefined.

6

XSLT Elements

Usage

The `<xsl:message>` instruction is generally used to report error conditions detected by the stylesheet logic. An example might be where an element such as `<sales>` is expected to have a numeric value, but is found to have a nonnumeric value:

❑ With «`terminate="no"`» (the default), the stylesheet can report the error and continue processing.

❑ With «`terminate="yes"`», the stylesheet can report the error and quit.

Before using `<xsl:message>` in a production environment, check what happens to the messages and whether they can be redirected. You need to be particularly clear about whether your messages are intended to be read by the source document author, the stylesheet author, or the end user: this will affect the way in which you write the text of the message.

The output produced by `<xsl:message>` can be unpredictable, because the sequence of execution of a stylesheet is not defined in the standard. For example, some products (including Saxon) defer evaluation of a variable until the variable is first used, which means that the order in which different variables are evaluated is difficult to predict. If evaluation of a variable triggers execution of `<xsl:message>`, the order of the messages may be surprising. Certainly, it can vary from one XSLT processor to another.

A common use of `<xsl:message>` is to generate diagnostic output so you can work out why your stylesheet isn't behaving as expected. This works well with products that have a fairly predictable sequence of execution, but it can be rather bewildering with a processor that does things in a different order from the one you would expect. Placing diagnostics as comments into the result tree (using `<xsl:comment>`) is probably a more flexible solution. Some products, of course, have vendor-defined debugging aids built-in, or available from third parties.

> The Microsoft MSXML parser ignores `<xsl:message terminate="no">`, so the message is not reported anywhere. If «`terminate="yes"`» is specified, it generates an error, which can be handled through the script on the HTML page that invoked the transformation.

Examples

The following example issues a message and quits if the value of the `<sales>` element is non-numeric:

```
<xsl:if test="string(number(sales))='NaN'">
   <xsl:message terminate="yes">
      <xsl:text>Sales value is not numeric</xsl:text>
   </xsl:message>
</xsl:if>
```

Unfortunately, there is no mechanism defined in the XSLT standard that allows the location of the error in the source document to be included in the message. In this example, validation against a schema would probably give better diagnostics.

The following example extends this by allowing several such errors to be reported in a single run, terminating the run only after all errors have been reported. It works by assigning a global variable to the set of nodes in error:

```
<xsl:variable name="bad-sales"
             select="//sales[not(. castable as xs:decimal)]"/>
<xsl:template match="/">
   <xsl:for-each select="$bad-sales">
      <xsl:message>Sales value <xsl:value-of select="."/>
         is not numeric
      </xsl:message>
   </xsl:for-each>
...
   <xsl:if test="$bad-sales">
      <xsl:message terminate="yes">
         <xsl:text>Processing abandoned</xsl:text>
      </xsl:message>
   </xsl:if>
</xsl:template>
```

Localized Messages

XSLT is designed very much with internationalization in mind, and no doubt the requirement to localize message text was discussed by the working group. They clearly decided that no special facilities were needed and instead included a detailed example in the XSLT 1.0 specification showing how the message text can be localized (output in the user's native language). The example is worth repeating because it shows a general technique.

Messages for a particular language are stored in a file whose name identifies the language, for example German messages might be stored in messages/de.xml. The message file might have the structure:

```
<messages>
   <message name="started">Angefangen</message>
   <message name="please-wait"/>Bitte warten!</message>
   <message name="finished"/>Fertig</message>
</messages>
```

A stylesheet that wishes to produce messages in the appropriate local language will need a parameter to identify this language. The stylesheet can then get access to the messages file for the appropriate language, and read the messages from there:

```
<xsl:param name="language" select="'en'" as="xs:string"/>
<xsl:template name="output-message">
   <xsl:param name="name"/>
   <xsl:variable name="message-file"
                select="concat('messages/', $language, '.xml')"/>
   <xsl:variable name="message-text"
                select="document($message-file)/messages"/>
```

```
   <xsl:message>
      <xsl:value-of select="$message-text/message[@name=$name]"/>
   </xsl:message>
</xsl:template>
```

The same technique can, of course, be used for producing localized text to include in the output of the transformation.

See Also

`<xsl:result-document>` on page 445

xsl:namespace

The `<xsl:namespace>` instruction constructs a namespace node that is written to the result sequence. Constructing namespace nodes in this way is not a frequent requirement, but there are situations where it is the only way of getting a required namespace declaration in the output.

Changes in 2.0

This instruction is new in XSLT 2.0.

Format

```
<xsl:namespace
  name = { string }
  select? = expression
  <!-- content: sequence-constructor -->
</xsl:namespace>
```

Position

`<xsl:namespace>` is an instruction. It is always used as part of a sequence constructor.

Attributes

Name	Value	Meaning
name mandatory	Attribute value template returning an NCName or a zero-length string	The name of the namespace node (which represents the namespace prefix)
select optional	XPath Expression	Expression to compute the string value of the namespace node (which represents the namespace URI)

Content

If the `select` attribute is present, the element must be empty. Otherwise, it must contain a nonempty sequence constructor.

Effect

The `name` attribute determines the name of the namespace node. This corresponds to the namespace prefix. If the value of the `name` attribute is a zero-length string, the namespace node defines the default namespace. Otherwise, the name must be an NCName (a valid XML name containing no colon). The `name` attribute can be written as an attribute value template, allowing the name to be computed dynamically.

The string value of the namespace node, which represents the namespace URI, is established using either the `select` attribute or the contained sequence constructor. For consistency, this instruction uses the results of evaluating the `select` attribute or sequence constructor in the same way as other instructions such as `<xsl:attribute>` and `<xsl:value-of>`. This means that the result may be a sequence. Adjacent text nodes are merged, the sequence is atomized, each item in the atomized sequence is converted to a string, and the resulting strings are concatenated, with an intervening space used as a separator in the case where the `select` attribute is used. Normally, however, the result of the `select` attribute should be a single string.

A zero-length string cannot be used as a namespace URI, so a runtime error occurs if the result of the computation just described is a zero-length string.

Note that a namespace node is not the same thing as a namespace declaration. An element has a namespace node for every namespace that is in scope. A namespace undeclaration, such as «xmlns=""» in XML Namespace 1.0, or «xmlns:z=""», which is allowed by XML Namespaces 1.1, is not represented by a namespace node. Rather, it is represented in the data model by the absence of a namespace node.

Usage and Examples

Although namespace declarations are a special kind of attribute in the surface XML syntax, they are represented quite differently in the XDM data model. This means that you cannot produce namespace declarations in the result document by using `<xsl:attribute>`, or by any other mechanism that produces attribute nodes.

The namespace declarations produced by the serializer are derived from the namespace nodes that are present in the result tree. However, there isn't a one-to-one mapping between namespace nodes and namespace declarations. An element in the result tree has a namespace node for every namespace prefix that is in scope for this element (even if it's also in scope for the element's parent).

In the vast majority of cases, the namespace nodes needed in a result tree are created automatically.

For namespaces used in the names of elements and attributes, this is guaranteed by the namespace fixup process described under `<xsl:element>` on page 310. This procedure is invoked whenever an element is created in a result tree, whether by `<xsl:element>`, a literal result element, or by `<xsl:copy>` or `<xsl:copy-of>`. It is the namespace fixup procedure that makes the final decision on what prefixes to use for these names.

> *Creating (or not creating) a namespace node will never change the name of an element or attribute. If you are outputting an element with local name `<table>` in no namespace, and you want it to be in namespace `http://garden-furniture.com/ns`, then you need to change the instruction that creates the element node. If you get the element names right (remembering that an element name includes the namespace URI as well as the local part), then the namespace nodes will usually look after themselves.*

The only difficulties arise therefore when you need namespaces to be declared in the result document that are not used in element and attribute names. I've come across three reasons for doing this:

1. You want the namespace to be declared once on an outer element of the document, whereas in the normal course of events it would be declared many times on inner elements. This is essentially cosmetic, but it can make a significant difference to the readability (and the size) of your output. In some cases this kind of declaration is necessary to make the output valid against a DTD, or simply against a written specification — the Locale Data Markup Language, for example, requires the element `<special>` to declare the namespace in which its children appear.

2. Your document uses namespace prefixes in the content (as distinct from in the names) of elements and attributes. This is the most common case and we'll devote the rest of the section to it.

3. The definition of the result document type uses namespace declarations as some kind of marker, where the mere presence of the namespace declaration carries information, whether or not the prefix that's being declared is ever used. This is a pretty weird way of using namespaces, but there's no law against it. In the case I saw, it was done because adding namespace declarations to a document can be done without changing the schema.

In the rest of this section we'll focus on the use of QNames in element and attribute content.

An example is if you want to output the following:

```
<price xsi:type="xs:decimal">23.50</price>
```

Your document must then contain a namespace declaration that binds the namespace prefix «xs» to the namespace URI «http://www.w3.org/2001/XMLSchema». The serializer will only produce such a declaration if it encounters a namespace node in the result tree that binds this prefix to this URI.

Here is one convenient way to output the above element:

```
<price xsi:type="xs:decimal">
    <xsl:namespace name="xs"
                   select="'http://www.w3.org/2001/XMLSchema'"/>
    <xsl:value-of select="23.50"/>
</price>
```

Note that there is no need to use `<xsl:namespace>` to produce a namespace declaration that binds the prefix «xsi» to the namespace http://www.w3.org/2001/XMLSchema-instance. Because this namespace is used in an attribute name, the namespace fixup process will ensure that it is declared. In fact, it would be declared in this case even without namespace fixup, because the rules for a literal result element ensure that all namespaces that are in scope for the literal result element in the stylesheet are copied to the result document, and the «xsi» namespace must be in scope here, or the stylesheet fragment would not be valid.

In fact there are five different ways that an element in the result tree can acquire namespace nodes:

❑   When an element is copied from a source tree using an `<xsl:copy>` or `<xsl:copy-of>` instruction, its namespace nodes are also copied, unless this is suppressed by writing «copy-namespaces="no"».

❑   When a literal result element is processed, all the namespace nodes that are in scope for this element in the stylesheet are copied to the result tree, unless this is suppressed using the `[xsl:]exclude-result-prefixes` attribute on some containing element. This attribute is described in the entry for `<xsl:stylesheet>` on page 471.

❑   Namespace nodes for namespaces used in element and attribute names are automatically created by the namespace fixup process.

❑   When an element is created in the result tree as a child of another element, whether by using `<xsl:element>`, `<xsl:copy>`, `<xsl:copy-of>`, or a literal result element, then unless the parent element was created using the option «[xsl:]inherit-namespaces="no"», the child element inherits (acquires a copy of) all the namespace nodes on its new parent element, provided they don't conflict with its existing namespace nodes.

❑ Namespace nodes can be created manually using the <xsl:namespace> instruction.

So the <xsl:namespace> instruction is needed only if none of the other mechanisms creates the required namespace declaration.

The namespace fixup process does not automatically create namespace nodes in respect of elements or attributes that have QName-valued content, even when there is a schema that describes the content as a QName. The reason for this is to allow namespace fixup and schema validation to operate as separate processes. Suppose that the schema defines the type of attribute start as being an xs:QName, and that you want to create the attribute «start="my:root"». Schema validation takes the string value of this attribute as input, checks that the namespace prefix «my» is declared, and generates firstly the typed value of this attribute (a QName consisting of the local name «root» and the namespace URI corresponding to prefix «my»), and secondly the type annotation of the attribute as an xs:QName. So the namespace node has to be created before schema validation takes place. This means it cannot be done by an automatic namespace fixup process, because at the time namespace fixup takes place, the attribute node has no type annotation, so you don't yet know that it's an xs:QName.

If you write a stylesheet that produces an XSLT stylesheet as its output, then it becomes very important to get the right namespace declarations into the output, because XSLT makes heavy use of attributes that contain namespace prefixes: they arise both in attributes such as the name attribute of <xsl:variable>, <xsl:template>, and <xsl:function>, and wherever the stylesheet contains XPath expressions. It's worth remarking that there is nothing in the schema for XSLT stylesheets that marks these attributes out as special. Even the name attributes that appear to have QName-valued content do not actually have a type of xs:QName. This is because although their lexical space is the same as xs:QName, they follow the convention "no prefix means no namespace", whereas the rule for the xs:QName type is "no prefix means default namespace". So these attributes are simply strings, which means it is the application that must choose a namespace prefix and then create a namespace node to bind this to the correct namespace URI.

The <xsl:namespace> instruction adds a namespace node to the result sequence produced by the sequence constructor that it is part of. Normally, this result sequence will immediately be used to create the content of an element node. In this case, the attribute and namespace nodes in the sequence need to come before any other nodes. It doesn't matter what order the attributes and namespace nodes are in relative to each other. It is an error if there are two namespace nodes that bind the same namespace prefix to different URIs; this could happen if you create a namespace node manually using <xsl:namespace> that clashes with one that is copied automatically from a source document by an <xsl:copy> or <xsl:copy-of> instruction, or from the stylesheet by a literal result element. This is only really likely to happen in the case of the default namespace. It is permissible to create a default namespace node using <xsl:namespace>, but it's probably not a good idea.

Namespace fixup happens after all the namespace nodes from this result sequence have been constructed, and it is constrained to generate prefixes that don't clash with these namespace nodes. If you have created a namespace node for the default namespace (that is, the empty prefix), then the system will have a problem if the element node itself is in the null namespace, because an element in the null namespace has to use the empty prefix, and it will no longer be available. This can cause a runtime failure.

See Also

<xsl:attribute> on page 254
<xsl:element> on page 306

xsl:namespace-alias

The `<xsl:namespace-alias>` element allows a namespace used in the stylesheet to be mapped to a different namespace used in the output. It is most commonly used when writing transformations that produce an XSLT stylesheet as their output.

Changes in 2.0

The rules for generating namespace prefixes have been made stricter. The "null namespace" is now treated in the same way as a real namespace (many XSLT 1.0 products did this, but the specification wasn't clear).

Format

```
<xsl:namespace-alias
   stylesheet-prefix = prefix | "#default"
   result-prefix = prefix | "#default"/>
```

Position

`<xsl:namespace-alias>` is a top-level declaration, which means it must be a child of the `<xsl:stylesheet>` element. It may be repeated any number of times in a stylesheet.

Attributes

Name	Value	Meaning
stylesheet-prefix mandatory	NCName or «#default»	A namespace prefix used in the stylesheet
result-prefix mandatory	NCName or «#default»	The prefix of the corresponding namespace to be used in the output

Content

None. The `<xsl:namespace-alias>` element is always empty.

Effect

The `<xsl:namespace-alias>` element affects the treatment of namespaces on literal result elements.

Normally, when an element node is output by processing a literal result element, the output element name will have the same local part, the same prefix, and the same namespace URI as those of the literal result element itself. The same applies to the attributes of the literal result element. The namespace nodes on the literal result element must be copied unchanged to the result tree, using the same prefix and namespace URI. (The XSLT specification states that when processing a literal result element, all the namespaces that are in scope for the element in the stylesheet, with certain defined exceptions, will also be present in the output, even if they aren't used. Redundant namespace nodes can be suppressed by using the `xsl:exclude-result-prefixes` attribute. For more details on this, see the section *Literal Result Elements*, on page 112 in Chapter 3.)

Suppose you want the output document to be an XSLT stylesheet. Then you need to create elements such as `<xsl:template>` that are in the XSLT namespace. However, you can't use `<xsl:template>` as a literal result element, because by definition, if an element uses the XSLT namespace, it is treated as an XSLT element.

The answer is to use a different namespace on the literal result element in the stylesheet, and include an `<xsl:namespace-alias>` declaration to cause this to be mapped to the XSLT namespace when the literal result element is output. So your literal result element might be `<out:template>`, and you could use an `<xsl:namespace-alias>` element to indicate that the stylesheet prefix «out» should be mapped to the result prefix «xsl».

The `<xsl:namespace-alias>` element declares that one namespace URI, the stylesheet URI, should be replaced by a different URI, the result URI, when literal result elements are output. The namespace URIs are not given directly, but are referred to by using prefixes that are bound to these namespace URIs as a result of namespace declarations that are currently in force. Either one of the namespace URIs may be the default namespace URI, which is referred to using the pseudoprefix «#default». If there is no default namespace defined, «#default» denotes the "null namespace URI", which for this purpose is treated as if it were an ordinary namespace.

The `<xsl:namespace-alias>` element describes the mapping in terms of prefixes, but it is primarily the namespace URI of the elements and attributes that it affects, rather than their prefixes. However, the way that the rules are drawn up means that in most cases (certainly when the same namespaces are in scope for the `<xsl:namespace-alias>` instruction and for the literal result element itself) the element in the result document will end up using the prefix defined in the `result-prefix` attribute (or no prefix, if this is specified as «#default»).

The substitution of one namespace URI for another affects the names of literal result elements themselves, and the names of all attributes of literal result elements. It also affects the URIs of namespace nodes copied into the result tree from a literal result element. It does not affect elements created using `<xsl:element>`, attributes created using `<xsl:attribute>`, or nodes copied using `<xsl:copy>`.

There was often confusion among XSLT 1.0 users about what namespaces they should expect to find declared in the result document, and different processors handled this differently. In XSLT 2.0, the rules have been clarified. Namespaces find their way from the stylesheet into the result document whenever a literal result element is evaluated. XSLT 2.0 states clearly that if the literal result element has a namespace node with the URI associated with the `stylesheet-prefix` of an `<xsl:namespace-alias>` instruction, it is not copied to the result tree as it normally would be; if it has a namespace node with the URI associated with the `result-prefix` of an `<xsl:namespace-alias>` instruction, then this namespace node is copied, even if the URI is one such as `http://www.w3.org/1999/XSL/Transform` that would normally not be copied. These rules are designed to produce the result that most users would expect: a literal result element `<out:template>` will produce an element in the result tree that will normally be serialized as `<xsl:template>`; the «xsl» namespace will be declared in the result document, and the «out» namespace will not be declared.

If there are several `<xsl:namespace-alias>` elements that specify the same `stylesheet-prefix`, the one with highest import precedence is used; a compile-time error is reported if there is more than one at the highest import precedence.

The aliasing of namespace URIs applies at the point when a literal result element in the stylesheet is evaluated to create an element node in a result sequence. It applies whether or not this element is written to a final result tree. This means that if you examine a temporary document into which literal result elements have been copied, the corresponding elements and attributes will use the namespace URI associated with the result prefix, not the stylesheet prefix.

Aliasing of namespaces happens before the namespace fixup process described under `<xsl:element>` on page 310.

Usage and Examples

The main justification for this facility is to enable stylesheets to be written that generate stylesheets as output. This is not as improbable a scenario as it sounds; there are many possible reasons for using such applications (sometimes referred to as *meta-stylesheets*), including the following:

❏ There are many proprietary template languages currently in use. Translating these templates into XSLT stylesheets creates an attractive migration route, and there is no reason why these translators should not be written in XSLT.

❏ There may be a continuing need for a template language, which is less complex and powerful than XSLT, for use by nonprogrammers. Again, these simple templates can easily be translated into XSLT stylesheets.

❏ There are some parts of an XSLT stylesheet that cannot easily be parameterized. For example, it is not possible to construct an XPath expression programmatically and then execute it (XSLT is not a reflexive language). The requirement to do this arises when visual tools are developed to define queries and reports interactively. One way of implementing such tools is to construct a customized stylesheet from a generic stylesheet, and again this is a transformation that can be assisted by using XSLT.

❏ You might have developed a large number of stylesheets that all have some common characteristic; for example, they might all generate HTML that uses the `<center>` tag. As the `<center>` tag is deprecated, you now want to modify these stylesheets to use `<div style="text-align: center">`. Why not write an XSLT transformation to convert them?

❏ There are tools that make it possible to generate XSLT stylesheets from a schema (see for example Schematron at `http://xml.ascc.net/resource/schematron/`). Because both the schema and the stylesheet are XML documents, this is an XML-to-XML transformation, so it should be possible to write it in XSLT.

In fact, having gone through all the trouble of defining XSLT stylesheets as well-formed XML documents, it would be very surprising if it were impossible to manipulate them using XSLT itself.

However, it is possible to create stylesheets as output without recourse to `<xsl:namespace-alias>`: just avoid using literal result elements, and use instructions such as `<xsl:element name = "xsl:template">` instead. I personally find this approach less confusing, although the stylesheet ends up being more verbose.

There may be other situations where `<xsl:namespace-alias>` is useful. The XSLT specification mentions one, the need to avoid using namespace URIs that have recognized security implications in the area of digital signatures. Another might arise if stylesheets and other documents are held in a configuration management system; there might be a need to ensure that namespaces recognized by the configuration management system, for example to describe the authorship and change history of a document, are not used directly in the stylesheet.

Aliasing the XML Namespace

It's possible to define an alias for the `xml` namespace. For example, the following stylesheet (`xml-space.xsl`):

```
<xsl:transform
   xmlns:xsl="http://www.w3.org/1999/XSL/Transform" version="2.0"
   xmlns:axml="alias">

<xsl:namespace-alias stylesheet-prefix="axml" result-prefix="xml"/>

<xsl:template name="main">
   <doc axml:space="preserve">text</doc>
</xsl:template>

</xsl:transform>
```

produces the following output:

```
<?xml version="1.0" encoding="UTF-8"?>
<doc xml:space="preserve">text</doc>
```

This is useful because it gets an «`xml:space="preserve"`» attribute into the result document without affecting the way that whitespace is handled in the stylesheet.

Choice of Prefixes in the Result Document

XSLT 2.0 has clarified the rules defining what prefixes are used in the result. This can be important; for example, if the target stylesheet contains an expression such as «`system-property("xslt:version")`», then this will only work if the prefix `xslt` has been declared. Follow through exactly what happens when you write the stylesheet:

```
<xsl:stylesheet version="2.0"
                xmlns:xsl="http://www.w3.org/1999/XSL/Transform"
                xmlns:oxsl="http://localhost/old.uri">

<xsl:namespace-alias stylesheet-prefix="oxsl" result-prefix="xsl"/>

<xsl:template match="/">
   <oxsl:stylesheet/>
</xsl:template>
</xsl:stylesheet>
```

This transformation executes just one instruction: the `<oxsl:stylesheet>` literal result element. Namespace aliasing causes this to generate an element with prefix `xsl`, local name `stylesheet`, and namespace URI `http://www.w3.org/1999/XSL/Transform`. The literal result element has two namespace nodes, representing the prefix bindings «`xmlns:xsl="http://www.w3.org/1999/XSL/Transform"`» and «`xmlns:oxsl="http://localhost/old.uri"`» (we will ignore the namespace node for the «`xml`» namespace). The first of these is copied to the result tree, because it matches the `result-prefix`, despite the fact that it would normally be an excluded namespace. The second namespace node is not copied, because its namespace URI («`http://localhost/old.uri`») is the one referred to by the `stylesheet-prefix` attribute. So the namespace node in the result tree will map the prefix «`xsl`» to the namespace URI «`http://www.w3.org/1999/XSL/Transform`».

Namespace fixup is then applied, but this doesn't need to do anything, because all the required prefixes are already declared.

When the time comes to serialize this result tree, namespace nodes are used to generate namespace declarations. So the output (ignoring the XML declaration) should be this:

```
<xsl:stylesheet xmlns:xsl="http://www.w3.org/1999/XSL/Transform"/>
```

XSLT 2.0 (unlike 1.0) really doesn't give the implementation any latitude to generate anything else in this situation. In 1.0, there was a general rule that the serializer could add any namespace declarations it chose, and by implication that it could give elements and attributes any prefix that it chose. In 2.0, the namespace fixup process is only allowed to add namespaces if they are actually needed to make the tree consistent, and in this case, they aren't.

Example of <xsl:namespace-alias>

The following example generates an XSLT stylesheet consisting of a single global variable declaration, whose name and default value are supplied as parameters. Although this is a trivial stylesheet, it could be useful when incorporated into another more useful stylesheet using <xsl:include> or <xsl:import>.

This example is available in the code download as alias.xsl.

Source

No source document is required. You can run this with Saxon using the command:

```
java -jar c:\saxon\saxon9.jar -it:main -xsl:alias.xsl
```

The «-it» option on the command line causes the transformation to start at the template named «main».

Stylesheet

```
<xsl:stylesheet version="2.0"
                xmlns:xsl="http://www.w3.org/1999/XSL/Transform"
                xmlns:oxsl="http://www.w3.org/local-alias">

<xsl:param name="variable-name">v</xsl:param>
<xsl:param name="default-value"/>
<xsl:output indent="yes"/>
<xsl:namespace-alias
                stylesheet-prefix="oxsl"
                result-prefix="xsl"/>

<xsl:template match="/" name="main">
   <oxsl:stylesheet version="1.0">
   <oxsl:variable name="{$variable-name}">
      <xsl:value-of select="$default-value"/>
   </oxsl:variable>
   </oxsl:stylesheet>
</xsl:template>
</xsl:stylesheet>
```

Output

If you default the values of the parameters «variable-name» and «default-value», the
output is as follows.

```
<?xml version="1.0" encoding="utf-8"?>
<xsl:stylesheet xmlns:xsl="http://www.w3.org/1999/XSL/Transform"
                version="1.0">
  <xsl:variable name="v"/>
</xsl:stylesheet>
```

See Also

Literal Result Elements in Chapter 3, on page 112.

xsl:next-match

The <xsl:next-match> instruction allows more than one template rule to be applied to the same node
in a source document. When <xsl:apply-templates> selects a node, it finds the best match template
rule to process this node. Within this template rule, you can use the <xsl:next-match> instruction to
invoke the next-best matching rule, and so on.

Changes in 2.0

This instruction is new in XSLT 2.0. It was introduced as an improved alternative to <xsl:apply-
imports>, though that instruction remains available for backward-compatibility reasons.

Format

```
<xsl:next-match>
    <!-- Content: (xsl:with-param | xsl:fallback)* -->
</xsl:next-match>
```

Position

<xsl:next-match> is an instruction, and is always used within a sequence constructor.

Attributes

None.

Content

The element may be empty, or it may contain one or more <xsl:with-param> and/or <xsl:fallback>
elements. An XSLT 2.0 processor will ignore the <xsl:fallback> instructions; they are allowed so that
fallback behavior can be defined for use when the stylesheet is processed using an XSLT 1.0 processor.
For details, see <xsl:fallback> on page 316.

Effect

<xsl:next-match> relies on the concept of a *current template rule*. A template rule becomes the
current template rule when it is invoked using <xsl:apply-templates>, <xsl:apply-imports>, or

`<xsl:next-match>`. Using `<xsl:call-template>` does not change the current template rule. However, using `<xsl:for-each>` makes the current template rule null, until such time as the `<xsl:for-each>` terminates, when the previous value is reinstated. The current template rule is also null while global variables and attribute sets are being evaluated.

Closely associated with this is the *current mode*. When a template rule is invoked using `<xsl:apply-templates>`, the mode specified on the `<xsl:apply-templates/>` instruction becomes the current mode (if no mode is named, then the default unnamed mode becomes the current mode). The current mode reverts to the default (unnamed) mode when a stylesheet function is called.

`<xsl:next-match>` searches for a template rule that matches the current node, using the same search rules as `<xsl:apply-templates>`, but considering only those template rules that (a) match the current mode, and (b) have lower import precedence or priority than the current template rule. For details of import precedence, see `<xsl:import>` on page 359. If no template rule is found, the built-in template rule is used (see page 243).

There is a clear analogy here with object-oriented programming. Writing a template rule that overrides another is like writing a method that overrides a method defined on the superclass. `<xsl:next-match>` behaves analogously to the `super()` function in object-oriented programming languages, allowing the new template rule to refine the behavior of the original template rule, rather than replacing it completely.

Within the stylesheet as a whole, there are potentially several template rules that match the context node. The rules for the `<xsl:apply-templates>` instruction define an ordering of these rules: They are considered first in decreasing order of import precedence, then within each import precedence in decreasing order of priority, and finally within each priority, by the order of the declarations in the stylesheet (it is actually an error to have two rules with the same priority, but the processor is allowed to ignore this error and select whichever comes last in the stylesheet). At the end of the list is the built-in template rule for the particular kind of node. What `<xsl:next-match>` does is choose the template rule that comes next in this pecking order, after the current template rule.

It is possible to specify parameters to be supplied to the called template, using `<xsl:with-param>` elements contained within the `<xsl:next-match>` element. These work in the same way as parameters for `<xsl:call-template>` and `<xsl:apply-templates>`; if the name of the supplied parameter matches the name of an `<xsl:param>` element within the called template, the parameter will take this value; otherwise, it will take the default value supplied in the `<xsl:param>` element. It is not an error to supply parameters that don't match any `<xsl:param>` element in the called template rule, they will simply be ignored. However, if the called template specifies a parameter with «required="yes"», then a runtime error occurs if no value is supplied for this parameter.

The effect of the `<xsl:next-match>` instruction is very similar to `<xsl:apply-imports>`. The main difference is that with `<xsl:apply-imports>`, the only template rules that can be invoked are those in imported stylesheet modules. By contrast, `<xsl:next-match>` can invoke other template rules of lower priority in the same stylesheet module and can also invoke template rules that have lower import precedence because they were imported into the parent stylesheet module earlier than the current template rule. Looking at Figure 6-4 on page 360, if the current template rule is in module C, then `<xsl:apply-imports>` will only consider template rules in module H, whereas `<xsl:next-match>` will also consider lower-priority rules in modules C, E, and J, as well as all rules in modules B, D, F, and G.

There is a special rule for the case where a template uses a union pattern and the two branches have different implicit priority, for example `<xsl:template match="* | foo">`. This is treated as if it were two separate template rules, which means that when you call `<xsl:next-match>`, the same template can be invoked more than once.

Usage and Examples

The intended usage pattern for `<xsl:next-match>` is illustrated by the following example.

One template rule might contain a general-purpose rule for formatting headings, as follows:

```
<xsl:template match="heading" priority="1">
   <xsl:number level="multiple" count="div1|div2|div3" format="1.1"/>
   <a name="{generate-id()}">
      <xsl:value-of select="."/>
   </a>
</xsl:template>
```

Another set of template rules contains specific rules for particular levels of headings:

```
<xsl:template match="div1/heading" priority="2">
   <h1><xsl:next-match/></h1>
</xsl:template>

<xsl:template match="div2/heading" priority="2">
   <h2><xsl:next-match/></h2>
</xsl:template>

<xsl:template match="div3/heading" priority="2">
   <h3><xsl:next-match/></h3>
</xsl:template>
```

These template rules each invoke the first rule using `<xsl:next-match>`, which avoids duplicating the common code in the template rule for each level of heading, and makes it easier to define changes later.

In this example I have made the priorities explicit, but in fact the default priorities could have been used. I always prefer to use explicit priorities when several rules match the same nodes, because it makes it clear to someone reading the stylesheet what your intentions were when you wrote it.

On this occasion there are three specialized rules, each invoking one generalized rule. But there are other problems where the structure can be inverted, so that the general rule invokes the special rule. For example, suppose you want to use a special color to render any inline text element that has the attribute «highlight="yes"». You might use a set of template rules like this:

```
<xsl:template match="term" priority="1">
   <i><xsl:apply-templates/></i>
</xsl:template>
<xsl:template match="emph" priority="1">
   <b><xsl:apply-templates/></b>
</xsl:template>
<xsl:template match="formula" priority="1">
   <code><xsl:apply-templates/></code>
</xsl:template>
```

and then process the highlight attribute in a higher priority template rule:

```
<xsl:template match="*[@highlight='yes']" priority="2">
   <span class="highlight"><xsl:next-match/></span>
</xsl:template>
```

Unlike `<xsl:apply-imports>`, where invoking multiple template rules is possible only by defining multiple stylesheet modules, `<xsl:next-match>` allows several rules to be defined within a single module, which is often preferable because it makes the logic more clear.

Note that both `<xsl:next-match>` and `<xsl:apply-imports>` impose the constraint that the two (or more) template rules that match a node in the source tree work on the source node completely independently of each other. Neither rule can see or modify the nodes that the other rule has written to the result tree. This also means that (as the examples above show) the second rule can only create nodes that are children or siblings of the nodes created by the first rule; it cannot create parent nodes.

In some situations, therefore, other solutions might work better. In particular, another design pattern (sometimes called a *micropipeline*) is to use a multipass transformation whereby one template rule creates a temporary tree, which it then processes using a second template rule (perhaps in a different mode). The code tends to look like this:

```
<xsl:template match="diagram">
   <xsl:variable name="temp">
     <div>
        <title><xsl:value-of select="caption"/></title>
        <body><xsl:copy-of select="content"/></body>
      </div>
   </xsl:variable>
   <xsl:apply-templates select="$temp/div"/>
</xsl:template>
```

This design pattern does not require use of `<xsl:next-match>` or `<xsl:apply-imports>`. One thing to watch out for when using this pattern is that the template rule for processing the `<div>` element might be expecting it to be part of a larger document; for example, it might expect its IDREF attributes to reference elements in the same tree. This won't be the case when you copy a `<div>` element into a temporary tree.

See Also

`<xsl:apply-imports>` on page 237
`<xsl:fallback>` on page 316
`<xsl:param>` on page 425
`<xsl:with-param>` on page 517

xsl:non-matching-substring

The `<xsl:non-matching-substring>` element is used within an `<xsl:analyze-string>` instruction to indicate the processing that should be applied to substrings of the input string that appear between the substrings that match the supplied regular expression.

Changes in 2.0

This element is new in XSLT 2.0.

Format

```
<xsl:non-matching-substring>
  <!-- Content: sequence-constructor -->
</xsl:non-matching-substring>
```

Position

`<xsl:non-matching-substring>` can only appear as a child of an `<xsl:analyze-string>` element, and it must not appear more than once.

Attributes

None.

Content

A sequence constructor.

Effect

The sequence constructor contained in the `<xsl:non-matching-substring>` element is evaluated once for each nonempty substring of the input string that appears between two substrings that match the regular expression. The result of evaluating the sequence constructor is added to the result of the containing `<xsl:analyze-string>` instruction.

If there is no `<xsl:non-matching-substring>` element, or if its sequence constructor is empty, then non-matching substrings are discarded.

Usage and Examples

See `<xsl:analyze-string>` on page 230.

See Also

`<xsl:analyze-string>` on page 230
`<xsl:matching-substring>` on page 386

xsl:number

The `<xsl:number>` element performs two functions. It can be used to allocate a sequential number to the current node, and it can be used to format a number for output. These functions are often performed together, but they can also be done separately.

Note that the facilities for number formatting in the `<xsl:number>` element are quite separate from those offered by the `format-number()` function and the `<xsl:decimal-format>` element.

Changes in 2.0

The `select` attribute has been added: This allows a node other than the context node to be numbered.

XSLT 2.0 defines error conditions that must be reported when incompatible attributes are used (for example, `level` and `value` cannot appear together). In XSLT 1.0, redundant attributes were silently ignored. XSLT 2.0 also defines the result of the instruction more precisely in corner cases, for example when there is no node that matches the `from` pattern.

New options have been added in XSLT 2.0 for formatting numbers as words (so you can output «Chapter Three») and as ordinal numbers (so you can output «Fit the First» or «3rd Act»).

Format

```
<xsl:number
  value? = expression
  select? = expression
  level? = "single" | "multiple" | "any"
  count? = pattern
  from? = pattern
  format? = { string }
  lang? = { nmtoken }
  letter-value? = { "alphabetic" | "traditional"}
  ordinal? = { string }
  grouping-separator? = { char }
  grouping-size? = { number }  />
```

Position

`<xsl:number>` is an instruction. It is always used within a sequence constructor.

Attributes

Name	Value	Meaning
value optional	XPath Expression	A user-supplied number to be formatted (instead of using a node sequence number).
select optional	XPath Expression	Selects the node whose sequence number is to be output (by default, the instruction numbers the context node).
level optional	«single», «multiple» or «any»	Controls the way in which a sequence number is allocated based on the position of the node in the tree.
count optional	Pattern	Determines which nodes are counted to determine a sequence number.
from optional	Pattern	Determines a cut-off point, a point in the document from which sequence numbering starts afresh.
format optional	Attribute value template returning a format string, as defined below	Determines the output format of the number.
lang optional	Attribute value template returning a language code, as defined in XML for the `xml:lang` attribute	Indicates a language whose conventions for number formatting should be used.
letter-value optional	Attribute value template returning «alphabetic» or «traditional»	Distinguishes between different numbering schemes used with the same language.

continued

Name	Value	Meaning
ordinal optional	Attribute value template returning a string	If the attribute is present and is not a zero-length string, it indicates that ordinal numbering is required. For English, a suitable value is «yes»; for inflected languages, it indicates the required ending; for example, «-o» or «-a» in Italian.
grouping-separator optional	Attribute value template returning a single character	A character to be used to separate groups of digits (for example, a comma as a thousand separator).
grouping-size optional	Attribute value template returning a number	The number of digits in each group, indicating where the grouping-separator should be inserted.

For the syntax of a pattern, see Chapter 12.

Content

None, the element is always empty.

Effect

The `<xsl:number>` instruction performs four tasks:

1. Determines a sequence number. This is actually a sequence of integers (to allow section numbers such as 1.16.2); since it is not necessarily a number in the XPath sense, the specification refers to it as the *place marker*.

2. Analyzes the format string into a sequence of format tokens.

3. Formats each part of the place marker using the appropriate format token.

4. Returns the resulting string as a text node.

These steps are considered individually in the following sections.

Determining a Sequence Number

If the `value` attribute is specified, the place marker is obtained by evaluating the expression in the `value` attribute and converting it to a sequence of integers. This is done by atomizing the sequence, calling the `number()` function for each value, applying the `round()` function and then casting to an integer. (This rather cumbersome procedure is chosen largely for backward-compatibility reasons.) If backward-compatibility mode is in effect (that is, if the `version` attribute on the `<xsl:stylesheet>` element or on some other enclosing element is «1.0»), then all items in the sequence after the first are discarded. This is to emulate the behavior of XSLT 1.0.

If the `value` attribute is specified, the `level`, `count`, and `from` attributes must not be specified.

It is a fatal error if the sequence is empty, or if any value in the sequence can't be converted to an integer, or produces an integer less than zero. (In backward-compatibility mode, however, the processor outputs «NaN» instead of reporting the error.) The <xsl:number> element is designed for handling the natural numbers that arise from counting nodes, so if you want to handle other cases, it's better to use the format-number() function described in Chapter 13, on page 788.

If no value attribute is specified, <xsl:number> determines a place marker based on the position of a node in a source document. When the select attribute is present, the node to be numbered is determined by evaluating the expression contained in this attribute; a type error is reported if the result is anything other than a single node. If the select attribute is omitted, the instruction operates on the context node. In this case, an error is reported if the context item is not a node. Either way, we will refer to this node as the *start node*.

The rules for determining the place marker (always a sequence of non-negative integers) depend on the value of the level, count, and from attributes. If any of these attributes is omitted, the default is as follows:

Attribute	Default value
level	«single»
count	A pattern that matches nodes of the same kind as the start node, and with the same name as the start node if it has a name. As always, names with namespace prefixes are matched using the relevant namespace URI rather than the prefix.
from	A pattern that matches the root node of the tree containing the selected node.

If the level attribute is «single» or «any» the place marker will normally contain a single integer; if it is «multiple» then it may contain several integers (for example «3.6.1»). It is also possible for the list to be empty.

The place marker is determined as follows:

level	Rules
single	This is designed for numbering peer nodes at the same level in the structure, for example the bullets in a list of bullets. First establish a target node. If the start node matches the count pattern, the target node is the start node (this is the normal case). Otherwise, the target node is the innermost ancestor of the start node that matches the count pattern. If there is no such node, the place marker is an empty sequence. Now establish a boundary node. If the from pattern is defaulted, this is the root of the tree (this is by far the most common case: the from attribute is rarely used with «level="single"»). Otherwise, the boundary node is the start node if it matches the from pattern, or else it is the innermost ancestor of the start node that matches the from pattern. If none of these nodes matches the pattern, then the boundary node is the root of the tree. If the boundary node is the target node, or is an ancestor of the target node, the place marker is the number of preceding siblings of the target node that match the count pattern plus one. For example, if the target node has six preceding siblings that match the count pattern, then the sequence number is 7. If no target node is found, or if the boundary node is not an ancestor-or-self of the target node, the place marker is an empty sequence.

continued

level	Rules
any	This is designed for numbering nodes that can appear at any level of the structure, for example the footnotes or equations in a chapter of a book. As a special case, if the start node is a document node, the place marker is an empty sequence. First form the set of countable nodes. This contains all nodes that match the count pattern and that can be reached from the start node using either the preceding axis or the ancestor-or-self axis. Now identify the boundary node. This is the last node (in document order) that matches the from pattern and that can be reached from the start node using either the preceding axis or the ancestor-or-self axis. If the from pattern was not specified, or if none of these nodes matches, use the root node of the tree. Exclude from the set of countable nodes all those that are before the boundary node in document order. If there are no countable nodes, the place marker is an empty sequence; otherwise, it is a single integer, equal to the number of countable nodes.
multiple	This is designed to produce a composite sequence number that reflects the hierarchic position of a node; for example, «2.17.1». First, form the set of countable nodes. This contains all nodes that match the count pattern and that can be reached from the start node using the ancestor-or-self axis. The boundary node is the same as with «level="single"». For each countable node (taking them in document order, that is, outermost first) that has the boundary node on its ancestor-or-self axis, count how many preceding siblings it has that also match the count pattern and add one for the node itself. The resulting sequence of integers makes up the composite place marker. It is possible for this sequence to be empty.

These rules appear complex but in practice most common cases are quite straightforward, as the examples given later in this section demonstrate.

Analyzing the Format String

Once the place marker has been determined, the next stage is to format it into a string.

The place marker, as you have seen, is a list of zero or more positive integers.

The formatting is controlled primarily using the format string supplied in the format attribute. If this is omitted, the default value is «1». The format string consists of a sequence of alternating formatting tokens and punctuation tokens. Any sequence of consecutive alphanumeric characters is taken as a formatting token, any other sequence is taken as a punctuation token. For example, if the format attribute is «1((a))», this is broken up into a formatting token «1», a punctuation token «((», a formatting token «a», and a punctuation token «))». The term *alphanumeric* is based on Unicode character categories, and it is defined to include letters and digits from any language (this means you can't decorate a number with characters such as «ª» and «º» that are classified as alphanumeric).

The punctuation token that precedes the first formatting token, if any, is called the prefix. The one that follows the last formatting token, if any, is called the suffix. The other punctuation tokens are referred to as separators.

In the most common case the place marker is a single number. In this situation, the output string consists of the prefix, followed by the result of formatting the number using the first formatting token, and then the suffix. So if the place marker is «42» and the format attribute is «[1]», then the final output is «[42]».

Where the place marker is a list of numbers, the rules are a little more complex but still have intuitive results; for example, if the list of numbers is «3, 1, 6» and the format attribute is «1.1(a)», then the final output is «3.1(f)» (because «f» is the sixth letter in the alphabet). The detailed rules are as follows:

❑   The prefix always appears at the start of the output string.

❑   The *n*th formatting token is used to format the *n*th number in the list where possible, using the rules in the following section.

❑   If there are more numbers in the list than formatting tokens, then the excess numbers are formatted using the last formatting token. For example, if the list is «3,1,2,5» and the format attribute is «A.1», then the output will be «C.1.2.5».

❑   If there are no formatting tokens, then a formatting token of «1» is used.

❑   If there are more formatting tokens than numbers in the list, the excess formatting tokens are ignored.

❑   The first number, after formatting, is added to the output string immediately after the prefix.

❑   Each subsequent number is preceded in the output by the separator that precedes the formatting token used to format this number, if there is one, or by «.» if there is no preceding separator.

❑   The suffix is added to the end of the output string.

Note that if the place marker is an empty sequence, the result will consist of the prefix and suffix only. For example, if the format string is «[1]», an empty sequence will be formatted as «[]». The most likely reason for an empty sequence is that no nodes matched the count pattern.

If there is no formatting token, then the same string is used for the prefix and the suffix. So if the format string is «$», then the number 20 will be formatted as «20».

Formatting the Numbers

This section describes how a single number is formatted using a single formatting token to construct a string that will form part of the final output string.

The XSLT specification defines this process only partially. There are some definitive rules, some guidance for the implementor, and many other cases that are left unspecified.

The definitive cases are listed in the table below.

Formatting token	Output sequence
1	1, 2, 3, 4, . . .
01	01, 02, 03, . . . , 10, 11, 12, . . . More generally, if the format token is «1» preceded by *n* zeros, the output numbers will be in decimal notation with a minimum of *n + 1* digits.
other Unicode digits	The above two rules also apply to any other Unicode digits equivalent to 0 and 1, for example Thai or Tamil digits. The number is output using the same family of digits as is used in the formatting token.
a	a, b, c, d, . . . , x, y, z, aa, ab, ac, ...
A	A, B, C, D, . . . , X, Y, Z, AA, AB, AC, ...

continued

Formatting token	Output sequence
i	i, ii, iii, iv, . . . , x, xi, xii, xiii, xiv, . . .
I	I, II, III, IV, . . . , X, XI, XII, XIII, XIV, . . .
w	one, two, three, . . . ten, eleven (in the chosen language)
W	ONE, TWO, THREE, . . . TEN, ELEVEN (in the chosen language)
Ww	One, Two, Three, . . . Ten, Eleven (in the chosen language)

The specification doesn't define these sequences in detail, for example it doesn't say whether "twenty-one" is hyphenated, or specify how to represent numbers above 1000 in Roman numerals (the Romans themselves had various conventions, such as putting horizontal lines above the letters, or boxes around them — effects that would be difficult to achieve in XML output). The specification does say, however, that if the number is too large to be formatted as requested, it should be output as if the formatting token were «1».

In the table above, the sequences are shown starting at one. However, many of the sequences also allow the number zero to be formatted. Zero will never appear in a place marker generated by counting nodes, but it can appear when the number is supplied using the «value» attribute.

The attributes grouping-separator and grouping-size can be used to control the separation of groups of digits. For example, setting «grouping-separator=" "» (a single space) and «grouping-size="2"» would cause the number 12345 to be output as «1 23 45». The groups will always be formed by counting digits from the right-hand side. If either of these attributes is specified, the other should also be specified.

The ordinal attribute allows you to request ordinal numbers rather than cardinal numbers. For example, with a formatting token of «1» and language set (explicitly or by default) to «en» (English), the value «ordinal="yes"» would produce «1st, 2nd, 3rd, 4th». With the formatting token «Ww», it would produce «First, Second, Third, Fourth». For languages other than English, the correct form of an ordinal number often depends on the noun it is qualifying. In the case of languages where this is simply done by changing the ending, the specification says that the value of the ordinal attribute should be the required ending, for example «ordinal="-e"» or «ordinal="-er"» in German. For other languages with more complicated rules, it's left to the implementor to sort out what to do. For formatting tokens that aren't included in the table above, the XSLT specification is not prescriptive. It indicates that any formatting token may be used to indicate a sequence starting with this token, provided the implementation supports such a sequence; if the implementation does not support such a sequence, it may format the number using the formatting token «1». So, for example, if an implementation supports the numbering sequence «α, β, γ, δ», you can invoke this sequence with a formatting token of «α».

In case the formatting token does not identify a numbering sequence unambiguously, two attributes are provided to give greater control:

❑   The lang attribute is intended to indicate the target language: for example, the sequence starting with a Cyrillic capital letter «А» (x0410 in Unicode) might be different for Russian («lang="ru"») and for Bulgarian («lang="bg"»). The language code is intended to take the same form as the xml:lang attribute defined in the XML specification.

❑   The most obvious case where this changes the output is for the formatting tokens such as «w». For example, if «lang="de"», the output for «w» would become «eins, zwei, drei».

409

❑ The `letter-value` attribute is intended for languages such as Hebrew that have several possible sequences starting with the same token (see http://www.i18nguy.com/unicode/hebrew-numbers.html). The two permitted values are «alphabetic» and «traditional».

The detailed effect of these attributes is left entirely to the implementor, so you can't expect different products necessarily to behave in the same way. There has been a great deal of discussion on Internet mailing lists about the exact details of certain numbering sequences. With those sequences such as Roman numerals and Hebrew numbering that have a long history, practices have certainly varied at different times and places, so there is no single answer.

All the attributes controlling formatting are attribute value templates, so they can be parameterized using expressions enclosed in curly braces. This is mainly useful if you want to select the values from a localization file based on the preferred language of the current user. To achieve this, you can use the same techniques as described for localizing messages: see `<xsl:message>` on page 389.

Outputting the Number

The final action of `<xsl:number>` is to write the generated string to the current result sequence, as a text node.

The reason it is a text node rather than a string is historical: In XSLT 1.0, instructions always produced nodes. Changing it to a string in XSLT 2.0 would under some circumstances have caused it to be separated from adjacent values by a space character, producing a backward-compatibility problem. In practice, text nodes and strings are usually interchangeable.

If you want to do something else with the number (perhaps to write it as an attribute or to copy it to every page heading), you can save it as the value of a variable, as follows:

```
<xsl:variable name="section-number" type="xs:string">
   <xsl:number/>
</xsl:variable>
```

Writing the value to a variable also allows you to perform further manipulation. For example, if you want to use the traditional numbering sequence for footnotes (*, †, ‡, §, ¶), you cannot do this directly in `<xsl:number>` because these characters are punctuation symbols rather than alphanumerics. What you can do, however, is use conventional decimal numbering and then convert, for example:

```
<xsl:template match="footnote">
  <xsl:variable name="footnote-number">
    <xsl:number level="any" from="section"/>
  </xsl:variable>
  <xsl:value-of select="translate($footnote-number, '12345', '*†‡§¶')"/>
</xsl:template>
```

The `translate()` function replaces characters in its second argument by the corresponding character in the third argument: It is described in Chapter 13. In practice it might be safer to use character references for these special characters to avoid them being mangled by a text editor that doesn't understand Unicode.

I have dodged a tricky question here, which is that if you want footnote numbers to start at 1 on each page, you can't allocate them until you have paginated the document. Some kinds of numbering are really the domain of XSL Formatting rather than XSL Transformations.

Usage and Examples

Although the rules for `<xsl:number>` are very general and sometimes complex, most common cases are quite straightforward.

The general rules allow for numbering any kind of node, but in practice the `<xsl:number>` instruction is almost invariably used for numbering elements. So in this section, I'll assume that the selected node is an element.

level = "single"

This option (the default) is used to number sibling elements.

The simplest way of using `<xsl:number>` is without any attributes:

```
<xsl:number/>
```

If the current element is the eighth `<item>` element owned by its parent element, say, this will write the text value «8» to the current output destination. Technically, the processor is counting all the elements that match the pattern in the `count` attribute, and the default for the `count` attribute in this case is a pattern that matches `<item>` elements.

For this simple kind of numbering, it is often better to use the `position()` function, particularly if there are many nodes to be numbered. This is because with a typical implementation, each node that is numbered using `<xsl:number>` will result in the preceding siblings being counted, which will take an increasingly long time as the number of siblings increases. With the `position()` function, it is much more likely that the system already knows the position and doesn't have to do any special walking around the tree and pattern matching. Of course, this is only possible where «position()» and `<xsl:number/>` produce the same answer, which will happen when the sequence of nodes being processed using `<xsl:apply-templates>` or `<xsl:for-each>` consists of all the sibling elements of a particular element type.

Another option for numbering is to use the `count()` function, for example «count(preceding-sibling::item)+1». This is often simpler if you want to use the number for further processing, rather than formatting it for output.

The `count` attribute of `<xsl:number>` can be used in two ways.

Firstly, it is useful if there are several different kinds of sibling elements that you want to count. There is an example of this in the entry for `<xsl:param>` on page 433, where we want to number the scenes, prologue and epilogue of a play in a single sequence. (The example actually uses «level="any"», but it applies equally well to «level="single"»):

```
<xsl:variable name="NR">
    <xsl:number count="SCENE|PROLOGUE|EPILOGUE" level="single"/>
</xsl:variable>
```

The number is then used to construct a hyperlink:

```
<A HREF="scene{$NR}.html">
    <xsl:value-of select="TITLE"/>
</A>
```

Without the count attribute, the PROLOGUE would be numbered 1, the first SCENE would also be numbered 1, and so would the EPILOGUE.

Another use of the count attribute is to specify that it is not the context node that should be counted, but an ancestor node. For example, in the template rule for a `<title>` element, you can use `<xsl:number>` to determine the number of the section that the title belongs to, by writing:

```
<xsl:template match="title">
   <xsl:number count="section"/>
. . .
</xsl:template>
```

This usage is less common, and with XSLT 2.0 the select attribute gives more flexibility, because its value is an expression rather than a pattern. The above example can be written as:

```
<xsl:template match="title">
   <xsl:number select="parent::section"/>
. . .
</xsl:template>
```

The select attribute is particularly handy when you want to construct a cross-reference to a node other than the context node. For example, if your document contains anchors with tags such as `<bookmark name="biog"/>`, and references to these anchors of the form `<ref name="biog"/>`, then your stylesheet might expand a reference as follows:

```
<xsl:key name="bm" match="bookmark" select="@name"/>

<xsl:template match="ref">
   <xsl:variable name="target" select="key('bm', @name)/ancestor::div"/>
   <xsl:text>(See section </xsl:text>
   <a href="{generate-id($target)}">
      <xsl:number select="$target"/>
   </a>
   <xsl:text>)</xsl:text>
. . .
</xsl:template>
```

The from attribute is rarely needed with «level="single"». In fact, it's difficult to construct an example that isn't completely artificial.

If you want numbering to start at a value other than 1, or perhaps to proceed in increments other than 1, you can capture the result of `<xsl:number>` in a variable and manipulate it using XPath expressions. For example, the following template rule numbers the items in a list starting at an offset passed in as a parameter:

```
<xsl:template match="item">
   <xsl:param name="first-number" select="1" as="xs:integer"/>
   <xsl:variable name="number"><xsl:number/></xsl:variable>
   <xsl:value-of select="$first-number + $number - 1"/>
. . .
</xsl:template>
```

Example: Identifying Location of Text within a Document

This example is adapted from the stylesheet used to produce the errata for the XSLT 2.0 and XPath 2.0 specifications. It searches the XSLT 2.0 specification for a given phrase (supplied as a the value of parameter $phrase) and outputs an HTML document listing all the places where the phrase occurs, with hyperlinks to the containing sections, and a description of the location of the text in terms such as "first numbered list, second item, third paragraph".

Source

This stylesheet takes no principal input. Execution starts with the template named main, and the code reads the XHTML version of the XSLT 2.0 specification directly from the Web.

Stylesheet

This stylesheet is xslt-search.xsl.

```
<?xml version='1.0'?>
<xsl:stylesheet version="2.0"
   xmlns:xsl="http://www.w3.org/1999/XSL/Transform"
   xmlns:xs="http://www.w3.org/2001/XMLSchema"
   xmlns:f="http://www.wrox.com/xslt-errata"
   xpath-default-namespace="http://www.w3.org/1999/xhtml">

<xsl:param name="spec" as="document-node()"
           select="doc('http://www.w3.org/TR/xslt20')"/>
<xsl:param name="phrase" as="xs:string" required="yes"/>
```

The main template searches the document for text nodes containing the required phrase. For each match, it finds the containing section in the specification and outputs a hyperlink to that section. Then it calls the f:location() function (which is the part we are interested in) to show the location of the text within the section:

```
<xsl:template name="main">
  <html>
    <head>
      <title>XSLT 2.0 Specification Search</title>
    </head>
    <body>
      <h1>XSLT 2.0 Specification Search</h1>
      <xsl:variable
          name="matches" select="$spec//text()[contains(.,$phrase)]"/>
      <xsl:choose>
        <xsl:when test="$matches">
          <h2>Matches for "<xsl:value-of select="$phrase"/>"</h2>
          <xsl:for-each select="$matches">
            <xsl:variable
                name="div" select="ancestor::div[(h1|h2|h3|h4)/a][1]"/>
            <h3>
             <a href="http://www.w3.org/TR/xslt20#{$div/(h1|h2|h3|h4)
               /a/@id}">
               <xsl:value-of select="$div/(h1|h2|h3|h4)"/>
             </a>
```

```
          </h3>
          <p>See <xsl:value-of select="f:location($div, ..)"/>:</p>
          <xsl:copy-of select="ancestor::p[1]"/>
        </xsl:for-each>
      </xsl:when>
      <xsl:otherwise>
        <h2>No matches found</h2>
      </xsl:otherwise>
    </xsl:choose>
    </body>
  </html>
</xsl:template>
```

The function `f:location()` does nothing for an element that is the only child of its parent. If the subsection is a direct child of the containing section, it outputs its position using `<xsl:number>`. If it is more deeply nested, it first makes a recursive call to display the position of its parent element, then appends its own position, again by calling `<xsl:number>`. The format used is «w», which displays the position in words, and this is followed by a friendly name of the type of element (for example, `<p>` becomes "paragraph") so with «ordinal="yes"» we get a string such as «first table, second row, third column, second paragraph».

```
<xsl:function name="f:location" as="xs:string">
  <xsl:param name="section" as="element()"/>
  <xsl:param name="subsection" as="element()"/>
  <xsl:choose>
    <xsl:when test="count($subsection/../*) = 1
                    or $subsection[self::span|self::a]">
      <xsl:value-of select="f:location($section, $subsection/..)"/>
    </xsl:when>
    <xsl:when test="$subsection/.. is $section">
      <xsl:value-of>
        <xsl:number select="$subsection" format="w" ordinal="yes"/>
        <xsl:text> </xsl:text>
        <xsl:apply-templates select="$subsection"
                             mode="user-element-name"/>
      </xsl:value-of>
    </xsl:when>
    <xsl:otherwise>
      <xsl:value-of>
        <xsl:value-of select="f:location($section, $subsection/..)"/>
        <xsl:text>, </xsl:text>
        <xsl:number select="$subsection" format="w" ordinal="yes"/>
        <xsl:text> </xsl:text>
        <xsl:apply-templates select="$subsection"
                             mode="user-element-name"/>
      </xsl:value-of>
    </xsl:otherwise>
  </xsl:choose>
</xsl:function>
```

Note the use of an `<xsl:value-of>` element to concatenate several text nodes into a single text node that can be converted to a string, as required by the function signature.

The stylesheet finishes with a list of template rules that convert the names of elements into user-friendly terms:

```
<xsl:template match="*" mode="user-element-name">
  <xsl:value-of select="name(.)"/>
</xsl:template>

<xsl:template match="p" mode="user-element-name">paragraph</xsl:template>
<xsl:template match="ul" mode="user-element-name"
>bulleted list</xsl:template>
<xsl:template match="ol" mode="user-element-name"
>numbered list</xsl:template>
... etc ...

</xsl:stylesheet>
```

Output

This output is produced by supplying "formatted result" as the search phrase. The `<xsl:number>` output is "first bulleted list, third list item".

See Figure 6-8, where the relevant text is highlighted.

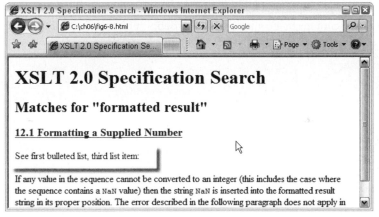

Figure 6-8

level = "any"

This option is useful when numbering objects within a document that have a numbering sequence of their own, independent of their position within the hierarchic structure. Examples are figures and illustrations, tables, equations, footnotes, and actions from a meeting.

The count attribute can usually be defaulted. For example, to number quotations within a document, you can write a template rule such as:

```
<xsl:template match="quotation">
  <table><tr>
```

```
        <td width="90%" valign="top">
          <i><xsl:value-of select="."/></i></td>
      <td><xsl:number level="any"/></td>
      </tr></table>
  </xsl:template>
```

Again, the `count` attribute is useful when several different element types are included in the same numbering sequence, for example there might be a single sequence that includes both diagrams and photographs.

Note that each evaluation of `<xsl:number>` is quite independent of any previous evaluations. The result depends only on the relative position of the selected element in the source document, and not on how many times the `<xsl:number>` element has been evaluated. So there is no guarantee that the numbers in the output document will be consecutive. In fact, if the output order is different from the input order then the numbers definitely won't be consecutive. If you want to number things based on their position in the output document, you can often achieve this by using the `position()` function. If this isn't adequate, the alternative is to perform a second pass, to add the sequence numbers. You can do this by writing the result of the first pass to a variable. The following example extracts all the `<glossary-item>` elements from a document, sorts them alphabetically, and numbers them in their output sequence. The variable `glossary` is used to hold the temporary results. Note that if you want to use `<xsl:number/>` for the numbering, this needs to be a tree rather than a flat sequence of parentless elements, because `<xsl:number/>` always numbers nodes in terms of their position in a tree.

Imagine a source document that contains glossary definitions scattered throughout the document, in the form:

```
<glossary-item>
    <term>XML</term>
    <definition>Extensible Markup Language</definition>
</glossary-item>
```

The relevant template looks like this:

```
<xsl:template name="make-glossary">
  <xsl:variable name="glossary">
    <xsl:perform-sort select="//glossary-item">
      <xsl:sort select="''term"/>
          </xsl:perform-sort>
  </xsl:variable>
  <table>
    <xsl:for-each select="$glossary/glossary-item">
      <tr>
        <td><xsl:number format="[1]"/></td>
        <td><xsl:value-of select="term"/></td>
        <td><xsl:value-of select="definition"/></td>
      </tr>
      </xsl:for-each>
  </table>
</xsl:template>
```

In this example, however, the numbers could have been generated equally well on the first pass using the `position()` function.

The `from` attribute is useful for indicating where numbering should restart:

```
<xsl:template match="footnote">
   <xsl:number level="any" from="chapter"/>
   <xsl:text> </xsl:text>
   <xsl:value-of select="."/>
</xsl:template>
```

The above code would number footnotes consecutively within a chapter, starting again at 1 for each chapter.

Example: Numbering the Lines of a Poem

The following example numbers the lines of a poem, showing the number to the right of every fourth line. Assume the input structure contains a `<poem>` element, a `<stanza>` element, and a `<line>` element: The lines are to be numbered within the poem as a whole, not within each stanza.

Source

This stylesheet can be used with the source file `theHill.xml`, shown in Chapter 4 on page 167.

Stylesheet

This stylesheet is `poem.xsl`. It uses `<xsl:number>` to get the number of every line but displays it only every fourth line, using the «mod» operator to get the remainder when the line number is divided by 4 (or some other number supplied as a parameter).

```
<xsl:stylesheet version="2.0"
     xmlns:xsl="http://www.w3.org/1999/XSL/Transform"
     xmlns:xs="http://www.w3.org/2001/XMLSchema"
     xpath-default-namespace="http://poetry.org/ns">

<xsl:param name="interval" select="4" as="xs:integer"/>

<xsl:template match="/">
<html>
  <head><title><xsl:value-of select="/poem/title"/></title></head>
  <body>
    <h1><xsl:value-of select="/poem/title"/></h1>
    <p><xsl:apply-templates select="/poem/stanza"/></p>
  </body>
</html>
</xsl:template>

<xsl:template match="stanza">
  <p><table><xsl:apply-templates/></table></p>
</xsl:template>

<xsl:template match="line">
  <tr>
    <td width="350"><xsl:value-of select="."/></td>
```

```
        <td width="50">
          <xsl:variable name="line-nr">
              <xsl:number level="any" from="poem"/>
          </xsl:variable>
          <xsl:if test="$line-nr mod $interval = 0">
              <xsl:value-of select="$line-nr"/>
          </xsl:if>
        </td>
      </tr>
    </xsl:template>
    </xsl:stylesheet>
```

Output

See Figure 6-9

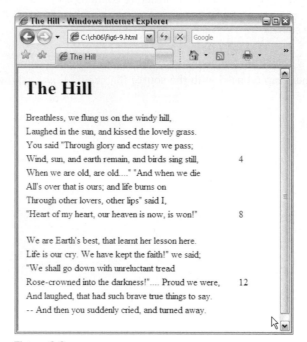

Figure 6-9

level = "multiple"

This option is typically used to produce the hierarchic sequence numbers often found in technical or legal documents; for example, 1.12.3, or A2(iii).

Note that an alternative way to produce such numbers is to use several calls on `<xsl:number>` with «level="single"» and different count attributes, for example:

```
<xsl:number count="chapter"/>.<xsl:number count="section"/>
    (<xsl:number count="clause"/>)
```

Another technique, which might be marginally faster, is to evaluate the chapter number once and pass it as a parameter to the template handling the section, and then pass both the chapter number and section number (or their concatenation) as parameters to the template handling each clause.

However, using «level="multiple"» is convenient, and in some cases — particularly with recursive structures, where <section> elements are contained within <section> elements — may be the only way of achieving the required effect.

The count attribute defines which ancestor elements should be included. Usually, this is expressed as a union pattern, as in the example below:

```
<xsl:template match="clause">
   <xsl:number
      format="1.1.1. "
      level="multiple"
      count="chapter | section | clause"/>
   <xsl:apply-templates/>
</xsl:template>
```

The effect of the rules is that a composite sequence number will be formed containing one component number for each ancestor (or the element itself) that is a <chapter>, <section>, or <clause>. If the structure is regular, so that chapters, sections, and clauses are neatly nested, each clause will be output preceded by a number such as 1.13.5, where 1 is the chapter number, 13 is the number of the section within the chapter, and 5 is the number of the clause within the section.

If the structure isn't regular, for example if there are sections that don't belong to a chapter, if there are clauses that have sections as siblings at the same level, or if there are sections nested within other sections, then the effects can be surprising, but a careful reading of the rules should explain what's going on.

A problem that sometimes occurs is that the numbering is context-sensitive. For example, within Chapter 1, clauses are numbered 1.2.3, but in Appendix A, they are numbered A.2.3. It's possible to achieve this effect by exploiting the fact that the format pattern is an attribute value template; for example, you could write:

```
<xsl:template match="clause">
   <xsl:variable name="format"
         select="if (ancestor::chapter)
                    then '1.1.1 '
                    else 'A.1.1 '"/>
   <xsl:number
      format="{$format}" level="multiple"
      count="appendix | chapter | section | clause"/>
   <xsl:apply-templates/>
</xsl:template>
```

This assumes that <chapter> elements are within a wrapper such as <chapters>, while <appendix> elements are similarly wrapped by <appendices>. If this isn't the case, for example, if the first <appendix> element has four <chapter> elements as its preceding siblings, then the first appendix will be numbered E. To solve this you will need to use two different <xsl:number> instructions for the two cases.

See Also

count() function in Chapter 13 on page 733
position() function in Chapter 13 on page 854

format-number() function, in Chapter 7 on page 788
<xsl:decimal-format> on page 298

xsl:otherwise

The <xsl:otherwise> element is used within an <xsl:choose> instruction to indicate the action that should be taken when none of the <xsl:when> conditions is satisfied.

Changes in 2.0

None.

Format

```
<xsl:otherwise>
  <!-- Content: sequence-constructor ->
</xsl:otherwise>
```

Position

<xsl:otherwise> can appear only as a child of an <xsl:choose> element. If it is present at all, it must be the last child of the <xsl:choose> element, and it must not appear more than once.

Attributes

None.

Content

A sequence constructor.

Effect

The sequence constructor of the <xsl:otherwise> element is evaluated if (and only if) none of the <xsl:when> elements in the containing <xsl:choose> element evaluates to true. If there is no <xsl:otherwise> element, then in this situation the <xsl:choose> produces no output.

Usage and Examples

See <xsl:choose> on page 282.

See Also

<xsl:choose> on page 282
<xsl:when> on page 515

xsl:output

The <xsl:output> element is a top-level declaration used to control the format of the serialized result document. An XSLT stylesheet is processed conceptually in two stages: the first stage is to build a result tree, and the second is to write out the result tree to a serial output file. The <xsl:output> element controls this second stage, which is often referred to as *serialization*. Serialization is described more fully in Chapter 15.

This second stage of processing, to serialize the tree as an output document, is not a mandatory requirement for an XSLT processor; the standard allows the processor to make the tree available in some other way; for example via the DOM API. A processor that does not write the tree to an output file is allowed to ignore this element. Processors that do provide serialization may also allow the definitions in this element to be overridden by parameters set in the API when the processor is invoked. See Appendix E for details of the JAXP API.

Changes in 2.0

An `<xsl:output>` declaration may be given a name, allowing a named output format to be defined that can be referenced in an `<xsl:result-document>` instruction.

An output method has been defined for XHTML.

Several new serialization parameters have been added: `byte-order-mark`, `escape-uri-attributes`, `include-content-type`, `normalization-form`, `undeclare-prefixes`, and `use-character-maps`.

The specification has become more prescriptive: in XSLT 1.0, implementations had more freedom to apply their own interpretation.

Format

```
<xsl:output
  name? = qname
  method? = "xml" | "html" | "xhtml" | "text" | qname-but-not-ncname
  byte-order-mark? = "yes" | "no"
  cdata-section-elements? = qnames
  doctype-public? = string
  doctype-system? = string
  encoding? = string
  escape-uri-attributes? = "yes" | "no"
  include-content-type? = "yes" | "no"
  indent? = "yes" | "no"
  media-type? = string
  normalization-form? = "yes" | "no"
  omit-xml-declaration? = "yes" | "no"
  standalone? = "yes" | "no" | "omit"
  undeclare-prefixes? = "yes" | "no"
  use-character-maps? = qnames
  version? = nmtoken />
```

Position

`<xsl:output>` is a declaration, which means it must be a child of the `<xsl:stylesheet>` element. It may appear any number of times in a stylesheet.

Attributes

Name	Value	Meaning
name optional	Lexical QName	Defines a name for this output format, so that it can be referenced in an `<xsl:result-document>` instruction.
method optional	«xml», «html», «xhtml», «text» or Lexical QName	Defines the required output format.

continued

Name	Value	Meaning
byte-order-mark optional	«yes» or «no»	Indicates whether a byte order mark should be written at the start of the output file.
cdata-section-elements optional	Whitespace-separated list of lexical QNames	Names those elements whose text content is to be output in the form of CDATA sections.
doctype-public optional	string	Indicates the public identifier to be used in the DOCTYPE declaration in the output file.
doctype-system optional	string	Indicates the system identifier to be used in the DOCTYPE declaration in the output file.
encoding optional	string	Defines the character encoding.
escape-uri-attributes optional	«yes» or «no»	Indicates whether URI-valued attributes in HTML and XHTML should be %HH encoded.
include-content-type optional	«yes» or «no»	Indicates whether a <meta> element should be added to the output to indicate the content type and encoding.
indent optional	«yes» or «no»	Indicates whether the output should be indented to indicate its hierarchic structure.
media-type optional	string	Indicates the media-type (often called MIME type) to be associated with the output file.
normalization-form optional	«NFC», «NFD», «NFKC», «NFKD», «fully-normalized», «none», or NMTOKEN	Indicates whether and how the Unicode characters in the serialized document should be normalized.
omit-xml-declaration optional	«yes» or «no»	Indicates whether an XML declaration is to be included in the output.
standalone optional	«yes», «no», or «omit»	Indicates that a standalone declaration is to be included in the output, and gives its value.
undeclare-prefixes optional	«yes» or «no»	Indicates whether (with XML 1.1 output) namespaces should be undeclared using «xmlns:p=""» when they go out of scope.
use-character-maps optional	Whitespace-separated list of lexical QNames	A list of the names of <xsl:character-map> elements that are to be used for character mapping.
version optional	NMTOKEN	Defines the version of the output format.

Content

None, the element is always empty.

Effect

A stylesheet can contain several output format definitions. This is useful if the stylesheet produces multiple result documents or if it produces different kinds of output on different occasions. One of the output format definitions can be unnamed, and the others are named using a QName in the same way as other stylesheet objects.

An output definition can be split over several <xsl:output> elements. All the <xsl:output> elements with the same name (as specified in the name attribute) constitute one output definition. In this case the attributes defined in these multiple elements are in effect combined into a single conceptual <xsl:output> element as follows:

❑ For the cdata-section-elements attribute, the lists of QNames supplied on the separate <xsl:output> elements are merged — if an element name is present in any of the lists, it will be treated as a CDATA section element.

❑ For the use-character-maps attribute, the lists of QNames on the separate <xsl:output> elements are concatenated. They are taken in order of the import precedence of the <xsl:output> declarations on which they appear, or where two declarations have the same import precedence, in declaration order.

❑ For all other attributes, an <xsl:output> element that specifies a value for the attribute takes precedence over one that leaves it defaulted. If several <xsl:output> elements specify a value for the attribute, the one with highest import precedence is used. It is an error if this leaves more than one value, unless they are all equal.

The concept of import precedence is explained under <xsl:import> on page 359.

The method attribute controls the format of the output, and this in turn affects the detailed meaning and the default values of the other attributes.

Four output methods are defined in the specification: «xml», «html», «xhtml», and «text». Alternatively, the output method may be given as a QName, which must include a non-null prefix that identifies a namespace that is currently in scope. This option is provided for vendor or user extensions, and the meaning is not defined in the standard. A vendor-defined output method can attach its own interpretations to the meanings of the other attributes on the <xsl:output> element, and it can also define additional attributes on the <xsl:output> element, provided they are in a namespace.

If the method attribute is omitted, the output will be in XML format, unless the result tree is recognizably HTML or XHTML. The result tree is recognized as HTML if:

❑ The root node has at least one element child, and

❑ The first element child of the root node is named <html>, in any combination of upper and lower case, and has a null namespace URI, and

❑ There are no text nodes before the <html> element, other than, optionally, a text node containing whitespace only.

The result tree is recognized as XHTML if:

❑ The root node has at least one element child, and

❑ The first element child of the root node is named <html>, in lower case, and has the namespace URI http://www.w3.org/1999/xhtml, and

❑ There are no text nodes before the `<html>` element, other than, optionally, a text node containing whitespace only, and

❑ Backward-compatibility mode is *not* in effect (specifically, if the `version` attribute of the `<xsl:stylesheet>` element in the principal stylesheet module is «2.0» or greater).

Examples

The following example requests XML output using iso-8859-1 encoding. The output will be indented for readability, and the contents of the `<script>` element, because it is expected to contain many special characters, will be output as a CDATA section. The output file will reference the DTD `booklist.dtd`; note that it is entirely the user's responsibility to ensure that the output of the stylesheet actually conforms to this DTD, and, indeed, that it is a well-formed XML document.

```
<xsl:output
    method="xml"
    indent="yes"
    encoding="iso-8859-1"
    cdata-section-elements="script"
    doctype-system="booklist.dtd" />
```

The following example might be used if the output of the stylesheet is a comma-separated-values file using US ASCII characters only:

```
<xsl:output
    method="text"
    encoding="us-ascii" />
```

See Also

`<xsl:character-map>` on page 280
`<xsl:result-document>` on page 445
Serialization, Chapter 15

xsl:output-character

The `<xsl:output-character>` element allows a character in the result tree to be mapped to a specific string used to represent this character in the serialized output.

Changes in 2.0

The element is new in XSLT 2.0.

Format

```
<xsl:output-character
    character = char
    string = string />
```

Position

`<xsl:output-character>` only appears as a child of the `<xsl:character-map>` element.

Attributes

Name	Value	Meaning
character mandatory	Character	A single XML character; the character that is to be replaced during serialization.
string mandatory	String	Any string; the string that is to replace the character during serialization.

Content

None. The `<xsl:output-character>` element is always empty.

Effect

The `<xsl:output-character>` element defines a mapping for a single character within a character map. The way character maps work is described in the entry for the `<xsl:character-map>` element on page 280, and in Chapter 15.

The character to be replaced, and the string that is to replace it, must consist entirely of valid XML characters; otherwise, it would not be possible to represent them in the stylesheet. Any special characters must be escaped in the usual way. For example, if you want the ampersand character to be mapped to the string «&ampersand;», write:

```
<xsl:output-character character="&amp;" string="&amp;ampersand;"/>
```

See Also

`<xsl:character-map>` on page 280
Serialization, Chapter 15

xsl:param

The `<xsl:param>` element is used either at the top level, to describe a global parameter, or immediately within an `<xsl:template>` or `<xsl:function>` element, to describe a local parameter to a template or function. It specifies a name for the parameter and a default value, which is used if the caller supplies no value for the parameter.

Changes in 2.0

An «as» attribute has been added to define the required type of the parameter.

A `required` attribute has been added to indicate whether the parameter is mandatory or optional.

A `tunnel` attribute has been added to support the new facility of tunnel parameters.

Format

Different subsets of the format are applicable to stylesheet parameters, template parameters, and function parameters.

Format for Stylesheet Parameters

```
<xsl:param
  name = qname
  select? = expression
  as? = sequence-type
  required? = "yes" | "no"
  <!-- Content: sequence-constructor -->
</xsl:param>
```

Format for Template Parameters

```
<xsl:param
  name = qname
  select? = expression
  as? = sequence-type
  required? = "yes" | "no"
  tunnel? = "yes" | "no">
  <!-- Content: sequence-constructor -->
</xsl:param>
```

Format for Function Parameters

```
<xsl:param
  name = qname
  as? = sequence-type
</xsl:param>
```

Position

`<xsl:param>` may appear as a top-level declaration (a child of the `<xsl:stylesheet>` element), or as an immediate child element of `<xsl:template>` or `<xsl:function>`. The three kinds of parameters are known as *stylesheet parameters*, *template parameters*, and *function parameters*. In the case of template parameters and function parameters, `<xsl:param>` elements must come before any other child elements.

Attributes

Name	Value	Meaning
name mandatory	Lexical QName	The name of the parameter
select optional	XPath Expression	The default value of the parameter if no explicit value is supplied by the caller
as optional	Sequence Type	The required type of the parameter value
required optional	«yes» or «no»	Indicates whether the parameter is optional or mandatory
tunnel optional	«yes» or «no»	Indicates whether the parameter is a tunnel parameter

The SequenceType construct is described in Chapter 4, on page 159, and more fully in Chapter 11, on page 668.

Content

An optional sequence constructor. If a `select` attribute is present, the element must be empty. For function parameters, the element must always be empty.

Effect

An `<xsl:param>` element at the top level of the stylesheet declares a global parameter; an `<xsl:param>` element appearing as a child of an `<xsl:template>` element declares a local parameter for that template, and an `<xsl:param>` element appearing as a child of an `<xsl:function>` element declares a local parameter for that function.

The `<xsl:param>` element defines the name of the parameter, and a default value. The default value is used only if no other value is explicitly supplied by the caller. Default values can be supplied for stylesheet parameters and template parameters, but not for function parameters, which must always be supplied in the function call.

An explicit value can be supplied for a template parameter by using the `<xsl:with-param>` element when the template is invoked using `<xsl:apply-templates>`, `<xsl:call-template>`, `<xsl:next-match>`, or `<xsl:apply-imports>`.

For function parameters, values are supplied in the function call. The syntax of function calls is defined in Chapter 7. Function calls pass parameters positionally rather than by name; the nth argument in the function call is evaluated to provide the value for the nth `<xsl:param>` element in the function definition.

The way in which explicit values are supplied for stylesheet parameters is implementation-defined (for example, they may be defined on the command line or through environment variables, or they may be supplied via a vendor-defined API). Microsoft APIs are described in Appendix D, and Java APIs in Appendix E.

The Type of the Parameter

The required type of the parameter can be specified using the «as» attribute. For example, «as="xs:integer"» indicates that a single integer is expected, «as="xs:string*"» indicates that a sequence of strings is expected, and «as="element()+"» indicates that the required type is a sequence of one or more element nodes. With a schema-aware processor it is also possible to supply schema-defined types, for example «as="abc:vehicle-registration"» indicates that the parameter must be an atomic value conforming to the user-defined atomic type abc:vehicle-registration, while «as="schema-element(EVENT)"» indicates that it must be an element node validated as being either an EVENT element or an element in the substitution group of EVENT.

If the «as» attribute is omitted, then the supplied value may be of any type.

The value that is actually supplied by the caller must be suitable for the required type. The value is converted if necessary using the standard conversion rules described on page 505, and it is a fatal error if this conversion fails. Because the ability to specify a type on `<xsl:param>` is new in XSLT 2.0, the 1.0 compatibility rules are never used even if the stylesheet version is set to «1.0». In summary, this means that the only conversions allowed are:

❑ Atomization (that is, extraction of the typed values of nodes, when the required type is an atomic value or a sequence of atomic values)

❑ Numeric promotion; for example, conversion of xs:integer to xs:double

427

❑ Promotion of `xs:anyURI` to `xs:string`

❑ Casting of `xs:untypedAtomic` values (which normally arise as a result of atomizing a node in a document that has not been schema-validated)

If the supplied parameter is the wrong type, then the error may be detected either at compile time or at runtime. With stylesheet parameters, however, the supplied value isn't known until runtime, so this is when the error will occur.

The «as» attribute on `<xsl:param>` also serves a second purpose. Like the «as» attribute on `<xsl:variable>`, it is used when the `<xsl:param>` element has a contained sequence constructor to distinguish whether the default value is the sequence obtained by evaluating the sequence constructor, or the result of building a temporary document using this sequence to provide the content. For example:

```
<xsl:param name="p">Madrid</xsl:param>
```

declares a parameter whose default value is a temporary tree consisting of a document node, which owns a text node whose string value is «Madrid»; while:

```
<xsl:param name="p" as="xs:string">Madrid</xsl:param>
```

declares a parameter whose required type is a single string, and whose default value is the string «Madrid». If you really need to say that the required type is a document node, and to supply a temporary document as the default value, then you can write it like this:

```
<xsl:param name="p" as="document-node()">
    <xsl:document>Madrid</xsl:document>
</xsl:param>
```

The Default Value of the Parameter

In the case of stylesheet parameters and template parameters, if no value for the parameter is supplied by the caller, a default value is used. The default value of the parameter may be given either by the XPath expression in the `select` attribute, or by the contents of the contained sequence constructor. If there is a `select` attribute, the `<xsl:param>` element must be empty.

The value is calculated in exactly the same way as the value of a variable in `<xsl:variable>`, and the rules are as given on page 503. Note that the default value need not be a constant; it can be computed in terms of the values of other parameters appearing earlier in the list and can also depend on information such as the context item and context size.

If there is no `select` attribute and the sequence constructor is empty, the default value of the parameter is a zero-length string, unless there is an «as» attribute, in which case the default value is an empty sequence. If the type given in the «as» attribute does not allow an empty sequence, then the parameter is mandatory.

If the `required` attribute has the value «yes», then the parameter is mandatory. In this case, it makes no sense to supply a default value, so the `select` attribute must be omitted and the element must be empty. Failing to supply a value for a mandatory parameter is a compile-time error in the case of `<xsl:call-template>`, but a runtime error in all other cases.

The Name of the Parameter

The name of the parameter is defined by the QName given in the `name` attribute. Normally, this will be a simple name (such as «num» or «list-of-names»), but it may be a name qualified with a prefix; for example «my:value». If it has a prefix, the prefix must correspond to a namespace that is in scope at that point in the stylesheet. As usual it is the namespace URI rather than the prefix that matters, so two variables «my:value» and «your:value» have the same name if the prefixes «my» and «your» refer to the same namespace URI. If the name has no prefix then it has a null namespace URI — it does not use the default namespace URI.

Parameter names are referenced in exactly the same way as variables, by prefixing the name with a dollar sign (for example, «$num») and all the rules for uniqueness and scope of names are exactly as if the <xsl:param> element was replaced by an <xsl:variable> element. The only difference between parameters and variables is the way they acquire an initial value.

Tunnel Parameters

Tunnel parameters are a new facility in XSLT 2.0. If a tunnel parameter is passed to a template when it is called, then it is automatically passed on to any further templates called from this template. For example, if template A creates a tunnel parameter and passes it on a call to template B, then when B calls C and C calls D, the tunnel parameter will be passed transparently through all these calls and will be accessible to template D, even if B and C were quite unaware of the parameter.

This feature is very useful when you are customizing a stylesheet. Suppose that D is a template rule that formats equation numbers in Roman numerals, and you want to use Greek letters instead. You can write a customization layer (an importing stylesheet) that overrides D with a template rule of your own. But suppose you want D sometimes to use Greek letters and sometimes Roman numerals, how do you pass it this information? Global variables only solve the problem if the choice is constant for all invocations of D during the course of a transformation. Adding parameters to every template en route from your top-level A template to the D template would require overriding lots of template rules in the base stylesheet, which you want to change as little as possible. So the answer is that you write a customized version of the A template that sets a tunnel parameter, and a customized version of D that reads the tunnel parameter, and the intermediate templates B and C don't need to be changed.

> *The theory behind tunnel parameters is the concept of dynamically scoped variables in functional programming languages such as Lisp.*

A tunnel parameter always starts life in an <xsl:with-param> element. This may be on any kind of template call that allows parameter passing: specifically, <xsl:apply-templates>, <xsl:call-template>, <xsl:apply-imports>, and <xsl:next-match>. For example:

```
<xsl:template match="/">
  <xsl:apply-templates select="body">
    <xsl:with-param name="mq:format-greek" tunnel="yes" select="true()"/>
  </xsl:apply-templates>
  <xsl:apply-templates select="back">
    <xsl:with-param name="mq:format-greek" tunnel="yes" select="false()"/>
  </xsl:apply-templates>
</xsl:template>
```

I've put the parameter name in a namespace here, to minimize the risk that it will clash with a parameter added by someone else.

This tunnel parameter will be passed silently up the call stack, through all calls of <xsl:apply-templates>, <xsl:call-template>, <xsl:apply-imports>, and <xsl:next-match>, until it reaches a template that is interested in it. This template can declare its interest by including the parameter declaration:

```
<xsl:param name="mq:format-greek" as="xs:boolean" required="yes" tunnel="yes"/>
```

and can then use the parameter value in the normal way, by referring to it as «$mq:format-greek» within an XPath expression.

Tunnel parameters are not passed through XPath function calls, so if the stylesheet evaluates an XPath expression which calls a stylesheet function, which in turn calls <xsl:apply-templates>, then the tunnel parameters will not be accessible in this call. Similarly, they are not available when an attribute set is expanded.

At the point where the parameter enters the tunnel (the <xsl:with-param> element), it must have a name that differs from all the other sibling <xsl:with-param> elements, whether these are tunnel parameters or not. Similarly, when it emerges from the tunnel (the <xsl:param> element), it must have a name that differs from other <xsl:param> elements in that template. But where it is being silently passed through intermediate templates, name clashes don't matter: silently passed tunnel parameters are in effect in a different symbol space from explicit parameters.

Tunnel parameters can be of any type. They can be optional or required parameters, and if optional, the receiving template can declare a default value. Reading the tunnel parameter in this way isn't destructive; it will still be passed on to further templates. Specifying a required type or a default value doesn't change the value that is passed on; for example, if the original value is a node, and the receiving template declares it as a string, then the node will be atomized for the purposes of the receiving template, but the value that's passed on will still be a node, unless a new <xsl:with-param> element is used to change the value.

Usage

The different kinds of parameters (stylesheet parameters, template parameters, and tunnel parameters) can be used in different ways. These are discussed in the following sections.

Using Stylesheet Parameters

Stylesheet parameters can be used in various ways to control the actions performed by the transformation. For example, they are particularly useful for selecting which part of the source document to process. A common scenario is that the XSLT processor will be running within a Web server. The user request will be accepted by an application: perhaps a Java Server Page, a Java servlet, or an ASP or PHP page. The request parameters will be read, and the stylesheet processing will be kicked off using an API defined by each vendor. Generally, this API will provide some way of passing the parameters that came from the HTTP request into the stylesheet as the initial values of global <xsl:param> elements.

If the stylesheet is running interactively in the browser, it will typically be invoked using a JavaScript API, which again will accept data from the user and pass it to the stylesheet in the form of parameter values.

If the API supports it, a global parameter may take a value of any type: not just a string, number, or boolean, but also a node or sequence of nodes. In some cases the API allows the parameter to be supplied in the form of an XPath expression, which is evaluated to generate the actual parameter value. Because the value can contain nodes, this provides another way of supplying secondary source documents for use by the stylesheet, as an alternative to the document() function. Many products allow such a parameter to be supplied as a DOM Document object.

Where a stylesheet needs to get system-dependent information (for example, the name of the user, or the operating system version number), it is often much easier to pass the information as a stylesheet parameter rather than writing extension functions to deliver the information on request.

Wherever you define a global variable, ask yourself whether it would be better to make it a stylesheet parameter instead. The default value of a stylesheet parameter can be used in exactly the same way as a global variable; the only difference is that you have added the ability for the user to change the value from outside. Also, remember that when one stylesheet module imports another, the importing module can override an `<xsl:param>` in the imported module with an `<xsl:variable>`, or vice versa.

The new facilities in XSLT 2.0 to declare a stylesheet parameter with «`required="yes"`», and to declare its required type, make stylesheet parameters a lot more robust than they were. There are still a few loopholes, however — there is no rule that prevents an importing module redefining a parameter by changing its type in arbitrary ways, or changing the setting to «`required="no"`».

Using Template Parameters

Template parameters are used more often with `<xsl:call-template>` than with `<xsl:apply-templates>`, though they are available to both, and in XSLT 2.0 they can also be used with `<xsl:apply-imports>` and `<xsl:next-match>`. The actual value of the parameter is set by the caller using an `<xsl:with-param>` element. Parameters are often needed by the recursive algorithms used in XSLT to handle lists of items: there are examples of such algorithms under `<xsl:call-template>` on page 271. In XSLT 2.0, however, it is often more convenient to implement such algorithms using `<xsl:function>`.

Declaring the expected type of a parameter, using the «`as`» attribute, is optional, but I would always recommend it. It provides useful documentation for anyone who has to debug the stylesheet later, as well as trapping errors when the caller provides incorrect parameter values. My experience is that it catches many coding errors that would otherwise have led to incorrect output being generated. In addition, the information is very useful to the XSLT processor itself, as it enables optimized code to be produced. For example, a test such as `<xsl:if test="$p= 3">` is very much simpler if it is known in advance that `$p` will always be an integer, than if the processor has to deal with the possibility of it being a node, a sequence of nodes, a sequence of doubles, or perhaps an `untypedAtomic` value.

Using Tunnel Parameters

Tunnel parameters provide a halfway house between global variables and local template parameters, combining the advantages of both and removing many of the problems of both. Compared with global variables, their great advantage is that their value can change in the course of the transformation. This doesn't mean that they introduce side effects, because only the caller of a template can set the value, not the callee. Compared with local parameters, their great advantage is that you don't have to change every template in the stylesheet to pass the values through.

I found a good use case for tunnel parameters in the stylesheet used to generate the XSLT working draft. The XML master version of this document includes entries describing each error condition that can arise. This is used both to generate inline descriptions of the errors in the document body and to generate a summary of errors in an appendix. Much of the code to handle the two cases is the same, but a few details differ; for example, the way that hyperlinks are generated. Traditionally, this problem is tackled using modes; however, even with the XSLT 2.0 ability to write a single template rule that works in more than one mode, using modes means that the intermediate template rules need to be aware of the fact that they can be invoked under two different circumstances. They shouldn't need to know this: only the code that produces different results in the two cases should need to know that there are two possible cases. A tunnel parameter indicating which phase of processing is active solves the problem neatly.

Examples

This section presents two examples showing the use of `<xsl:param>` to define template parameters. The first is a very simple demonstration of how parameters work with `<xsl:call-template>`. The second is a more complicated example, making use of tunnel parameters.

Example: Using `<xsl:param>` with a Default Value

This example shows a simple named template that defines a parameter and gives it a default value.

Source

This stylesheet works with any XML source file.

Stylesheet

The stylesheet is `call.xsl`.

It contains a named template that outputs the depth of a node (defined as the number of ancestors). The node may be supplied as a parameter; if it is not supplied, the parameter defaults to the current node.

The stylesheet includes a template rule for the document node that invokes this named template, defaulting the parameter, to display the name and depth of every element in the source document.

```
<xsl:transform
 xmlns:xsl="http://www.w3.org/1999/XSL/Transform"
 version="2.0"
>
<xsl:output method="text"/>

<xsl:template match="/">
<xsl:for-each select="//*">
    <xsl:value-of select="concat(name(), ' -- ')"/>
    <xsl:call-template name="depth"/>;
</xsl:for-each>
</xsl:template>

<xsl:template name="depth">
    <xsl:param name="node" as="node()" select="."/>
    <xsl:value-of select="count($node/ancestor::node())"/>
</xsl:template>
</xsl:transform>
```

Output

If the stylesheet is run using itself as the source document, the output is as follows:

```
xsl:transform -- 1;
xsl:output -- 2;
```

```
xsl:template -- 2;
xsl:for-each -- 3;
xsl:value-of -- 4;
xsl:call-template -- 4;
xsl:template -- 2;
xsl:param -- 3;
xsl:value-of -- 3;
```

Example: Tunnel Parameters

Realistic examples using tunnel parameters tend to involve customization of rather complex stylesheets, such as the DocBook stylesheet suite (http://docbook.sourceforge.net/) used for producing many technical manuals. Unfortunately, explaining such an example would take a full chapter of this book. So we'll make do with a simpler case.

Suppose that you start with the stylesheet play.xsl, which is designed to generate a set of linked HTML files containing the text of one of Shakespeare's plays as marked up by Jon Bosak. I won't present this stylesheet in full, because it's pretty standard, and most of it isn't relevant to the example: you can find it in the download files for this book. The challenge now is to customize this stylesheet so that instead of producing a single rendition of the play, it produces a script for each of the characters appearing in the play, with the lines spoken by the character highlighted. I have done this by producing another stylesheet module, scripts.xsl, which overrides selected template rules from the original.

Source

This stylesheet can be applied to any of the Shakespeare plays available from http://metalab.unc.edu/bosak/xml/eg/shaks200.zip. The examples use othello.xml, which is included in the download files for this book.

Output

The existing stylesheet, play.xsl, produces a set of HTML files: one file called play.html, which acts as a cover sheet and index, and one file for each scene in the play, with names such as sceneN.html. You can run it with a command like this:

```
java -jar c:\saxon\saxon9.jar othello.xml play.xsl dir=c:/temp/othello
```

The first page of the output, in the file play.html, is shown in Figure 6-10.

In the customized presentation, we want to create an index page that looks like the one shown in Figure 6-11.

This presents an index showing all the speaking parts in the play. Clicking on one of the names brings up a modified version of the front page shown before, in which the titles of the scenes are shown as active links if the character appears in these scenes, or as plain text otherwise. The actual text of the scene should also be modified so that the speaker's lines are highlighted.

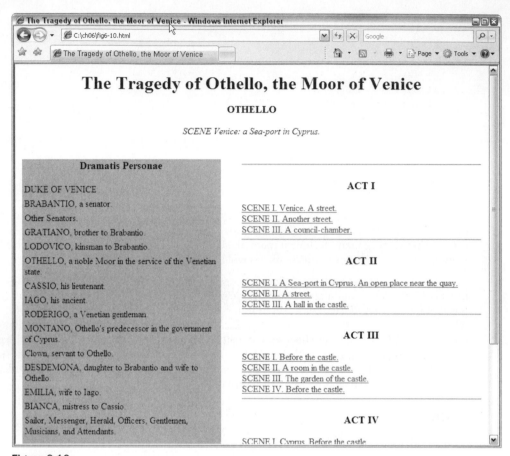

Figure 6-10

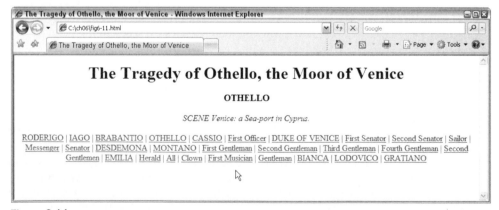

Figure 6-11

Stylesheet

The base stylesheet `play.xsl` is unmodified (it is one that has been included in the Saxon distribution for a while, to illustrate how a stylesheet can create multiple output files).

The customization layer is in the file `scripts.xsl`. This starts by importing `play.xsl`. It then contains a template rule providing the new control logic:

```
<xsl:template match="/">
  <xsl:variable name="play" select="PLAY"/>
  <xsl:result-document href="file:///{$dir}/index.html" format="play">
    <HTML>
    <HEAD><TITLE><xsl:apply-templates select="PLAY/TITLE"/></TITLE>
    </HEAD>
    <BODY BGCOLOR='{$backcolor}'>
        <CENTER>
            <xsl:value-of select="PLAY/TITLE"/></H1>
            <H3><xsl:apply-templates select="PLAY/PLAYSUBT"/></H3>
            <I><xsl:apply-templates select="PLAY/SCNDESCR"/></I>
        <BR/><BR/>
        <P>
          <xsl:for-each select="distinct-values(//SPEAKER)">
          <A HREF="{encode-for-uri(.)}/play.html">
            <xsl:value-of select="."/>
          </A>
          <xsl:if test="position() ne last()"> | </xsl:if>
          <xsl:apply-templates select="$play">
            <xsl:with-param name="speaker" select="." tunnel="yes"/>
          </xsl:apply-templates>
          </xsl:for-each>
        </P>
        </CENTER>
    </BODY>
    </HTML>
  </xsl:result-document>
</xsl:template>
```

This template creates the index page. It calls the `distinct-values()` function to get a list of speakers appearing in the play, and for each one, it firstly outputs a hyperlink to a `play.html` file in a subdirectory named after the speaker and then calls `<xsl:apply-templates>` to process the `<PLAY>` element, which is the outermost element in the source file. Crucially, it supplies the name of the speaker as a tunnel parameter to this template.

There are three template rules in the `play.xsl` stylesheet that need to be modified: these are the template for the `<PLAY>` element (because the `play.html` file now has to be placed in a subdirectory), the template for the `<SCENE>` element (which must now generate pages only for those scenes in which the selected speaker appears), and the template for the `<SPEECH>` element (to highlight the lines spoken by the selected speaker). Each of these contains a declaration of the tunnel parameter in an `<xsl:param>` element. Here is the modified template for the `<SCENE>` element:

```
<xsl:template match="SCENE|PROLOGUE|EPILOGUE">
    <xsl:param name="speaker" tunnel="yes" required="yes"/>

    <xsl:variable name="NR">
      <xsl:number count="SCENE|PROLOGUE|EPILOGUE" level="any"/>
    </xsl:variable>
    <xsl:variable name="play" select="ancestor::PLAY/TITLE"/>
    <xsl:variable name="act" select="ancestor::ACT/TITLE"/>
    <xsl:choose>
    <xsl:when test=".//SPEAKER = $speaker">
        <A HREF="scene{$NR}.html">
            <xsl:value-of select="TITLE" />
        </A><BR/>

        <xsl:result-document format="scene" href=
    "file:///{$dir}/{encode-for-uri($speaker, true())}/scene{$NR}.html">
            <HTML>
            <HEAD>
            <TITLE>
              <xsl:value-of select="concat($play, ' ', $act, ': ', TITLE)"/>
            </TITLE>
            </HEAD>
            <BODY BGCOLOR='{$backcolor}'>
            <P>
                <A HREF="play.html"><xsl:value-of select="$play"/>
                </A><BR/>
                <B><xsl:value-of select="$act"/></B><BR/>
            </P>
            <xsl:apply-templates/>
            </BODY>
            </HTML>
        </xsl:result-document>
    </xsl:when>
    <xsl:otherwise>
        <xsl:value-of select="TITLE"/><BR/>
    </xsl:otherwise>
    </xsl:choose>
</xsl:template>
```

The modifications here, apart from the addition of the `<xsl:param>` to declare the tunnel parameter, are the addition of the `<xsl:choose>` to generate the scene page conditionally, and the choice of file name produced by `<xsl:result-document>`.

The template rule for the `<SPEECH>` element becomes:

```
<xsl:template match="SPEECH">
    <xsl:param name="speaker" required="yes" tunnel="yes"/>
    <TABLE><TR>
    <TD WIDTH="160" VALIGN="TOP">
```

```
            <xsl:if test="SPEAKER = $speaker">
                <xsl:attribute name="BGCOLOR" select="'cyan'"/>
            </xsl:if>
            <xsl:apply-templates select="SPEAKER"/>
            </TD>
            <TD VALIGN="TOP">
            <xsl:apply-templates select="STAGEDIR|LINE"/>
            </TD>
            </TR></TABLE>
        </xsl:template>
```

The changes from the original are addition of the `<xsl:param>` declaring the tunnel parameter, and the addition of the `<xsl:if>` instruction that outputs an attribute changing the background color if the selected speaker participates in this `<SPEECH>` (a `<SPEECH>` can have more than one `<SPEAKER>`, the equality test succeeds if any of them match).

The key point about this example is that the original stylesheet has been customized and reused without changing it in any way. Without tunnel parameters, this would have required many more of its template rules to be changed, merely to pass the extra parameter through.

See Also

`<xsl:apply-templates>` on page 240
`<xsl:call-template>` on page 271
`<xsl:variable>` on page 500
`<xsl:with-param>` on page 517

xsl:perform-sort

The `<xsl:perform-sort>` instruction is used to sort a sequence. If you want to process the items in a sequence in sorted order, you can achieve this by adding `<xsl:sort>` elements to an `<xsl:apply-templates>` or `<xsl:for-each>` instruction. If you just want to sort the sequence, without processing the items individually, this can be done using `<xsl:perform-sort>`.

Changes in 2.0

This instruction is new in XSLT 2.0

Format

```
<xsl:perform-sort
  select? = {expression}
  <!-- Content: (xsl:sort+, sequence-constructor) ->
</xsl:perform-sort>
```

Position

`<xsl:perform-sort>` is an instruction, and may be used anywhere within a sequence constructor.

Attributes

Name	Value	Meaning
select optional	XPath Expression	Returns the input sequence to be sorted.

Content

The `<xsl:perform-sort>` instruction always contains one or more `<xsl:sort>` elements to specify the sort order.

In addition, it may contain a sequence constructor. This is an alternative to the `select` attribute: if the `select` attribute is present, then the `<xsl:perform-sort>` element must contain only `<xsl:sort>` elements. It can also contain `<xsl:fallback>` elements to define what an XSLT 1.0 processor should do when it encounters this instruction in forward-compatible mode.

Effect

The instruction forms an initial sequence by evaluating the expression in the `select` attribute or the contained sequence constructor, whichever is present. It then sorts this initial sequence to produce a sorted sequence, according to the rules for `<xsl:sort>`, which are given on page 458. The result of the `<xsl:perform-sort>` instruction is the sorted sequence.

Usage and Examples

The `<xsl:perform-sort>` instruction is useful when you want to create a sorted sequence in a variable, or as the result of a function. If you want to process items in sorted order you can achieve this using `<xsl:for-each>` or `<xsl:apply-templates>`, but these instructions do not deliver the sorted sequence directly as a value in its own right.

For example, you could define a global variable containing the speakers in a play, sorted alphabetically, by writing:

```
<xsl:variable name="sorted-speakers" as="xs:string*">
  <xsl:perform-sort select="distinct-values(//SPEAKER)">
    <xsl:sort select="."/>
  </xsl:perform-sort>
</xsl:variable>
```

The following function returns the earliest and latest date in a sequence of events, as a sequence of two `<event>` elements with `date` attributes:

```
<xsl:function name="f:first-and-last" as="schema-element(event)*">
   <xsl:param name="in" as=" schema-element(event)*"/>
   <xsl:variable name="sorted-events" as=" schema-lement(event)*">
      <xsl:perform-sort select="$in">
         <xsl:sort select="@date"/>
      </xsl:perform-sort>
   </xsl:variable>
   <xsl:sequence select="$sorted-dates[1], $sorted-dates[last()]"/>
</xsl:function>
```

See Also

`<xsl:apply-templates>` on page 240
`<xsl:for-each>` on page 322
`<xsl:sort>` on page 455

xsl:preserve-space

The `<xsl:preserve-space>` element, along with `<xsl:strip-space>`, is used to control the way in which whitespace nodes in the source document are handled.

Changes in 2.0

The syntax of a `NameTest` has been extended to allow the format «*:NCName», which matches all elements with a given local name, in any namespace.

Format

```
<xsl:preserve-space
  elements = tokens />
```

Position

`<xsl:preserve-space>` is a top-level declaration, which means that it must be a child of the `<xsl:stylesheet>` element. There are no constraints on its ordering relative to other declarations.

Attributes

Name	Value	Meaning
elements mandatory	Whitespace-separated list of `NameTests`	Defines the elements in the source document whose whitespace-only text nodes are to be preserved

The `NameTest` construct is defined in XPath, and is described in Chapter 9 on page 614.

Content

None, the element is always empty.

Effect

This declaration, together with `<xsl:strip-space>`, defines the way that whitespace-only text nodes in the source document are handled. Unless contradicted by an `<xsl:strip-space>` element, `<xsl:preserve-space>` indicates that whitespace-only text nodes occurring as children of a specified element are to be retained in the source tree.

Preserving whitespace-only text nodes is the default action, so this element only needs to be used where it is necessary to contradict an `<xsl:strip-space>` element. More specifically, a whitespace text node is stripped only if (a) it matches a `NameTest` specified in an `<xsl:strip-space>` element, and (b) it does not match a `NameTest` in an overriding `<xsl:preserve-space>` element.

The concept of whitespace-only text nodes is explained in Chapter 3 (see page 144). A whitespace-only text node is a text node whose text consists *entirely* of a sequence of whitespace characters, these being space, tab, carriage return, and linefeed (x20, x09, x0D, and x0A). The `<xsl:preserve-space>` element has no effect on whitespace contained in text nodes that also contain non-whitespace characters; such whitespace is always preserved and is part of the value of the text node.

This declaration also affects the handling of whitespace-only text nodes in any document loaded using functions such as `document()`, `doc()`, or `collection()`. It does not affect the handling of whitespace-only text nodes in the stylesheet, or in documents returned as the result of extension functions or passed to the stylesheet as the value of a stylesheet parameter. Also, the element does not affect anything that happens to the source document before the XSLT processor gets to see it, so if you create the source tree using an XML parser that strips whitespace nodes (as Microsoft's MSXML3 does, by default), then specifying `<xsl:preserve-space>` in the stylesheet will not get these nodes back — they are already gone.

Although an XML 1.1 parser will recognize the characters «x85» and «x2028» as representing line endings, the XSLT processor will not treat these characters as whitespace. It doesn't need to, because the XML parser will have converted them into regular newline characters.

Before a node is classified as a whitespace-only text node, the tree is normalized by concatenating all adjacent text nodes. This includes the merging of text that originated in different XML entities, and also text written within CDATA sections.

A whitespace-only text node may either be stripped or preserved. If it is stripped, it is removed from the tree. This means it will never be matched, it will never be copied to the output, and it will never be counted when nodes are numbered. If it is preserved, it is retained on the tree in its original form, subject only to the end-of-line normalization performed by the XML parser.

The `elements` attribute of `<xsl:preserve-space>` must contain a whitespace-separated list of NameTests. The form of a NameTest is defined in the XPath expression language; see Chapter 9, page 614. Each form of NameTest has an associated priority. The different forms of NameTest and their meanings are:

Syntax	Examples	Meaning	Priority
QName	title svg:width	Matches the full element name, including its namespace URI	0
NCName«:*»	svg:*	Matches all elements in the namespace whose URI corresponds to the given prefix	−0.25
«*:»NCName	*:address	Matches all elements with a given local-name, regardless of their namespace	−0.25
«*»	*	Matches all elements	−0.5

The priority is used when conflicts arise. For example, if the stylesheet specifies:

```
<xsl:strip-space elements="*"/>
<xsl:preserve-space elements="para clause"/>
```

then whitespace-only text nodes appearing within a `<para>` or `<clause>` will be preserved. Even though these elements match both the `<xsl:strip-space>` and the `<xsl:preserve-space>`, the NameTest in the latter has higher priority (0 as compared to −0.5).

If there is an `<xsl:strip-space>` element that matches the parent element, and also an `<xsl:preserve-space>` element that matches, then the decision depends on the import precedence and priority of the respective rules. Taking into consideration all the `<xsl:strip-space>` and `<xsl:preserve-space>` elements that match the parent element of the whitespace-only text node, the XSLT processor takes the one with highest import precedence (as defined in the rules for `<xsl:import>` on page 359). If there is more than one element with this import precedence, it takes the one with highest priority, as defined in the table above. If there is still more than one, and they are different (one preserve, one strip), the processor may either report an error, or choose the one that comes last in declaration order.

In deciding whether to strip or preserve a whitespace-only text node, only its immediate parent element is considered in the above rules. The rules for its other ancestors make no difference. The element itself, of course, is never removed from the tree: the stripping process will only remove text nodes.

Regardless of the `<xsl:strip-space>` and `<xsl:preserve-space>` declarations, if an individual element has the XML-defined attribute «xml:space="preserve"», then all descendant text nodes are preserved, unless this is cancelled by «xml:space="default"». If an `<xsl:strip-space>` doesn't seem to be having any effect, one possible reason is that the element type in question is declared in the DTD to have an `xml:space` attribute with a default value of «preserve». There is no way of overriding this in the stylesheet.

The `<xsl:strip-space>` and `<xsl:preserve-space>` declarations in the stylesheet are also ignored for a whitespace text node that forms the content of an element defined in the schema to have simple content. This is because changing the content of such an element could make it invalid. For example, if the schema defines the type as having `<xs:minLength value="1"/>`, then a value consisting of a single space is valid, but the element becomes invalid if the space is removed.

Usage

For many categories of source document, especially those used to represent data structures, whitespace-only text nodes are never significant, so it is useful to specify:

```
<xsl:strip-space elements="*"/>
```

which will remove them all from the tree. There are two main advantages in stripping these unwanted nodes:

❑ When `<xsl:apply-templates>` is used with a default `select` attribute, all child nodes will be processed. If whitespace-only text nodes are not stripped, they too will be processed, probably leading to the whitespace being copied to the output destination.

❑ When the `position()` function is used to determine the position of an element relative to its siblings, the whitespace-only text nodes are included in the count. This often leads to the significant nodes being numbered 2, 4, 6, 8, ...

Generally speaking, it is a good idea to strip whitespace-only text nodes belonging to elements that have element content, that is, elements declared in the DTD as containing child elements but no #PCDATA, or declared in a schema to have a complex type with «mixed="no"».

By contrast, stripping whitespace-only text nodes from elements with mixed content (elements declared in the DTD or schema to contain both child elements and #PCDATA) is often a bad idea. For example, consider the element below:

```
<quote>He went to <edu>Balliol College</edu> <city>Oxford</city> to read
<subject>Greats</subject></quote>
```

The space between the `<edu>` element and the `<city>` element is a whitespace-only text node, and it should be preserved, because otherwise when the tags are removed by an application that's only interested in the text, the words «College» and «Oxford» will run together.

It's worth noting that many XSLT processors do not physically remove whitespace text nodes from the tree; they only behave as if they did. Whether the nodes are physically removed or whether the processor creates a view of the tree in which these nodes are invisible, whitespace stripping can incur a significant cost. However, if whitespace is stripped while the tree is being built from serial XML input, the performance arguments are reversed: it then becomes cheaper to remove the whitespace nodes than to preserve them. Generally, if whitespace is insignificant, then it's best to get rid of it as early as possible.

Examples

To strip whitespace nodes from all elements of the source tree:

```
<xsl:strip-space elements="*"/>
```

To strip whitespace nodes from selected elements:

```
<xsl:strip-space elements="book author title price"/>
```

To strip whitespace nodes from all elements except the `<description>` element:

```
<xsl:strip-space elements="*"/>
<xsl:preserve-space elements="description"/>
```

To strip whitespace nodes from all elements except those in the namespace with URI `http://mednet.org/text`:

```
<xsl:strip-space elements="*"/>
<xsl:preserve-space elements="mednet:*"
                    xmlns:mednet="http://mednet.org/text" />
```

See Also

`<xsl:strip-space>` on page 465

xsl:processing-instruction

The `<xsl:processing-instruction>` instruction is used to write a processing instruction node to the result sequence.

Changes in 2.0

A `select` attribute has been added. Any leading spaces in the value of the processing instruction are now discarded.

Format

```
<xsl:processing-instruction
  name = { NCName }
  select? = expression>
```

```
        <!-- Content: sequence-constructor -->
    </xsl:processing-instruction>
```

Position

`<xsl:processing-instruction>` is an instruction. It is always used as part of a sequence constructor.

Attributes

Name	Value	Meaning
name mandatory	Attribute value template returning an NCName	The name (target) of the generated processing instruction
select optional	XPath Expression	Used to compute the string value (the data part) of the generated processing instruction

Content

If the `select` attribute is present, the element must be empty. If the `select` attribute is absent, the element may contain a sequence constructor.

Effect

The name of the generated processing instruction (in XML terms, the `PITarget`) is determined by the `name` attribute. This may be expressed as an attribute value template. The name must be valid as a `PITarget` as defined in the XML specification, and XSLT imposes the additional rule that it must be a valid `NCName`, as defined in the XML Namespaces Recommendation. This means it must be an XML `Name` that doesn't contain a colon (to make it an `NCName`) and that isn't the name «xml» in any mixture of upper and lower case (to make it a `PITarget`).

The specification is quite explicit that `<xsl:processing-instruction>` cannot be used to generate an XML declaration at the start of the output file. The XML declaration looks like a processing instruction, but technically it isn't one, and the ban on using the name «xml» makes this quite explicit. The XML declaration in the output file is generated automatically by the serializer and can be controlled using the `<xsl:output>` element.

The string value of the processing instruction (which corresponds to the `data` part of a processing instruction in XML terms) is generated using either the `select` attribute or the contained sequence constructor. If neither is present, the string value of the processing instruction node will be a zero-length string.

The space that separates the `PITarget` from the data is produced automatically when a processing instruction node is serialized. It is not present in the tree model.

The sequence produced by evaluating the `select` attribute or the contained sequence constructor is converted to a string in the same way as for `<xsl:attribute>` (see page 258), except that (a) the separator between adjacent values is always a single space, and (b) any leading whitespace in the value is discarded. The resulting string forms the string value of the new processing instruction.

If the resulting string contains the characters «?>», then a space is inserted between the characters to prevent it terminating the processing instruction.

The data part of a processing instruction cannot contain character references such as «₤», so an error occurs at serialization time if there are characters that can't be represented directly in the chosen character encoding of the output file. Some processing instructions may accept data that looks like a character reference, but this is an application-level convention, not something defined in the XML standard, so the XSLT processor will never generate such a reference automatically.

Usage

Use this instruction when you want to output a processing instruction.

Processing instructions are not widely used in most XML applications, so you will probably not need to use this instruction very often. They are used even less in HTML, though HTML 4.0 does recommend that any vendor-specific extensions should be implemented this way. In HTML the terminator for a processing instruction is «>» rather than «?>», and this difference is handled automatically during serialization by the HTML output method; see Chapter 15.

Note that you cannot generate a processing instruction in the output by writing a processing instruction in the stylesheet. Processing instructions in the stylesheet are ignored completely. You can, however, use `<xsl:copy>` or `<xsl:copy-of>` to copy processing instructions from the source tree to the result tree.

Examples

The following example outputs an `<?xml-stylesheet?>` processing instruction at the start of the output file:

```
<xsl:processing-instruction name="xml-stylesheet">
    <xsl:text>href="housestyle.css" type="text/css"</xsl:text>
</xsl:processing-instruction>
```

The generated output is:

```
<?xml-stylesheet href="housestyle.css" type="text/css"?>
```

Writing an XSLT stylesheet that produces an XML document that itself refers to a CSS stylesheet isn't such a crazy thing to do as it might seem. It often makes sense to do the first stage of processing of an XML file on the server, and the second stage in the browser. The first stage will extract the data that users want to see — and remove any information they are not allowed to see. The second stage applies the detailed rules for output formatting. The second stage can often be done just as easily with CSS as with XSLT, because anything CSS can't cope with, such as adding or reordering textual content, can be done in the first stage with XSLT.

One point to watch out for in generating an `<?xml-stylesheet?>` processing instruction, and which might well apply to other processing instructions, is the use of pseudo-attributes and pseudo-character and -entity references. The text «href="housestyle.css"» in the above example is designed to look like an XML attribute, but it is not actually an XML attribute; it is purely part of the processing instruction data. It is parsed by the application, not by the XML parser. As it is not a true XML attribute, you cannot generate it as an attribute node using the `<xsl:attribute>` instruction; rather, it is generated as text.

The rules for the `<?xml-stylesheet?>` processing instruction are defined in a short W3C Recommendation called *Associating Style Sheets with XML Documents*, available at http://www.w3.org/TR/xml-stylesheet. In addition to defining the data part of this processing instruction in the form of pseudo-attributes, the rules also allow the use of numeric character references such as «₤» and predefined entity references such as «>» and «&». Again, these are not true character references and entity references that the XML parser will recognize, and as a result they will not be generated by the

XSLT processor either. If you want to include «₤» as part of the data of the processing instruction, you can write, for example:

```
<xsl:processing-instruction name="xml-stylesheet">
  <xsl:text>href="housestyle.css" type="text/css" </xsl:text>
  <xsl:text>title="A title containing &amp;#x20A4;" </xsl:text>
</xsl:processing-instruction>
```

Another way of generating this processing instruction, which might be more suitable if the contents are highly variable, is to write a general template that takes the required information as a parameter. This parameter might be supplied in the form of an element:

```
<pi-data name="xml-stylesheet">
  <href>housestyle.css</href>
  <type>text/css</type>
  <title>a title</title>
</pi-data>
```

and the processing instruction might be generated by the template:

```
<xsl:template name="make-pi">
  <xsl:param name="pi-data" required="yes"/>
  <xsl:processing-instruction name="{$pi-data/@name}"
      select="for $att in $pi-data/* return
                concat(name($att), '=&quot;', string($att), '&quot;')"/>
</xsl:template>
```

This does not attempt to deal with the problems that arise if there are special characters in the data that need to be escaped. Note that the space that is needed between pseudo-attributes is generated automatically, because each pseudo-attribute is produced as one item in the result of the `select` attribute.

xsl:result-document

The `<xsl:result-document>` instruction is used to create a new result tree, and optionally to specify how the result tree should be serialized. The facility allows a transformation to produce multiple result documents, so you can write a stylesheet that splits a large XML file into smaller XML files, or into multiple HTML files, perhaps connected to each other by hyperlinks.

Changes in 2.0

This instruction is new in XSLT 2.0. Many XSLT 1.0 processors provided a similar capability as a proprietary extension, but there are likely to be differences in the detail. The abandoned working draft of XSLT 1.1 used the name `<xsl:document>` for a similar instruction, and it was implemented under this name in some products.

Format

```
<xsl:result-document
  format? = { qname }
  href? = { uri-reference }
  validation? = "strict" | "lax" | "preserve" | "strip"
  type? = qname
  method? = { "xml" | "html" | "xhtml" | "text" | qname-but-not-ncname }
```

```
    byte-order-mark? = { "yes" | "no" }
    cdata-section-elements? = { qnames }
    doctype-public? = { string }
    doctype-system? = { string }
    encoding? = { string }
    escape-uri-attributes? = { "yes" | "no" }
    include-content-type? = { "yes" | "no" }
    indent? = { "yes" | "no" }
    media-type? = { string }
    normalization-form? = {"NFC"|"NFD"|"NFKC"|"NFKD"|"fully-normalized"|nmtoken}
    omit-xml-declaration? = { "yes" | "no" }
    standalone? = { "yes" | "no" | "omit" }
    undeclare-prefixes? = { "yes" | "no" }
    use-character-maps? = qnames
    output-version? = { nmtoken }
>
    <!-- Content: {sequence-constructor} -->
</xsl:result-document>
```

Position

`<xsl:result-document>` is an instruction, which means it may occur anywhere in a sequence constructor.

Attributes

Name	Value	Meaning
format optional	Attribute value template returning a lexical QName	Defines the required output format.
href optional	Attribute value template returning a relative or absolute URI	Defines the location where the output document will be written after serialization.
validation optional	«strict», «lax», «preserve», or «strip»	Defines the validation to be applied to the result tree.
type optional	Lexical QName	Defines the schema type against which the document element should be validated.
method optional	Attribute value template returning «xml», «html», «xhtml», «text», or a prefixed lexical QName	Defines the serialization method to be used.
cdata-section-elements optional	Attribute value template returning a whitespace-separated list of lexical QNames	Names those elements whose text content is to be output in the form of CDATA sections.
doctype-public optional	Attribute value template returning a string	Indicates the public identifier to be used in the DOCTYPE declaration in the output file.

continued

Name	Value	Meaning
doctype-system optional	Attribute value template returning a string	Indicates the system identifier to be used in the DOCTYPE declaration in the output file.
encoding optional	Attribute value template returning a string	Defines the character encoding.
escape-uri-attributes optional	Attribute value template returning «yes» or «no»	Indicates whether URI-valued attributes in HTML and XHTML should be percent-encoded.
include-content-type optional	Attribute value template returning «yes» or «no»	Indicates whether a `<meta>` element should be added to the output to indicate the content type and encoding.
indent optional	Attribute value template returning «yes» or «no»	Indicates whether the output should be indented to indicate its hierarchic structure.
media-type optional	Attribute value template returning a string	Indicates the media-type (often called MIME type) to be associated with the output file.
normalization-form optional	Attribute value template returning «NFC», «NFD», «NFKC», «NFKD», «fully-normalized», «none», or an implementation-defined name in the form of an NMTOKEN.	Indicates whether and how the Unicode characters in the serialized document should be normalized.
omit-xml-declaration optional	Attribute value template returning «yes» or «no»	Indicates whether an XML declaration is to be included in the output.
standalone optional	Attribute value template returning «yes», «no», or «omit»	Indicates whether a `standalone` declaration is to be included in the output, and gives its value.
undeclare-prefixes optional	Attribute value template returning «yes» or «no»	Indicates whether (with XML 1.1 output) namespaces should be undeclared using «xmlns:p=""» when they go out of scope.
use-character-maps optional	Whitespace-separated list of lexical QNames	A list of the names of `<xsl:character-map>` elements that are to be used for character mapping.
output-version optional	Attribute value template returning an NMTOKEN	Defines the version of the output format (corresponds to the `version` attribute of `<xsl:output>`).

Content

The content of the `<xsl:result-document>` element is a sequence constructor.

The `<xsl:result-document>` element may contain an `<xsl:fallback>` element. If it does, the `<xsl:fallback>` element defines the action that an XSLT 1.0 processor will take when it encounters the `<xsl:result-document>` instruction. Note that the fallback processing only applies if the stylesheet is executing in forward-compatible mode, which will be the case if you set «version="2.0"» on the `<xsl:stylesheet>` element.

Effect

When the `<xsl:result-document>` instruction is evaluated, a new document node is created, in the same way as for the `<xsl:document>` instruction. The sequence constructor contained in the `<xsl:result-document>` is evaluated to produce a sequence of items, and this sequence is used to form the content of the document node as described under `<xsl:document>` in the section *The Content of the Document* on page 303. The tree rooted at this document node is referred to as a final result tree.

Validation of the result tree also follows the same rules as `<xsl:document>`: See *Validating and Annotating the Document* on page 305. Note that although the validation process (if requested) conceptually creates a result tree in which the elements and attributes are annotated with types, these type annotations will never be seen if the result tree is immediately serialized. But a very useful processing model is to run a series of transformations in a pipeline, where the output of one stylesheet provides the input to the next. The pipeline might also include non-XSLT applications. The new XProc specification from W3C (`www.w3.org/TR/XProc`) is designed to standardize the way such pipelines are written.

The difference between `<xsl:document>` and `<xsl:result-document>` is that `<xsl:document>` adds the new document node to the result sequence, making it available for further processing by the stylesheet, while `<xsl:result-document>` outputs the new document as a final result of the transformation.

What actually happens to a final result tree is to some degree system-dependent, and it is likely that vendors will provide a degree of control over this through the processor API.

Often, the result tree will be serialized (perhaps as XML or HTML) and written to a file on disk. The location of the file on disk is controlled using the `href` attribute, and the format in which it is serialized is controlled using the `format` attribute, supplemented by the serialization attributes (`method`, `byte-order-mark`, `cdata-section-elements`, `doctype-public`, `doctype-system`, `encoding`, `escape-uri-attributes`, `include-content-type`, `indent`, `media-type`, `normalization-form`, `omit-xml-declaration`, `standalone`, `undeclare-prefixes`, `use-character-maps`, and `output-version`).

If the `format` attribute is present then its value must be a lexical QName, which must match the `name` attribute of an `<xsl:output>` declaration in the stylesheet. The result tree will then be serialized as specified by that `<xsl:output>` declaration, except that any serialization attributes provided on the `<xsl:result-document>` override the corresponding attributes in the `<xsl:output>` declaration. All of the serialization attributes except `use-character-maps` are attribute value templates, which means that their values may be calculated at runtime, perhaps based on a stylesheet parameter or on data in the source document. If there is no `format` attribute, then the result tree (assuming it is serialized at all) will be serialized as specified by the unnamed `<xsl:output>` declaration if there is one, or the default serialization rules if not, except that again any serialization attributes provided on the `<xsl:result-document>` override the corresponding attributes in the `<xsl:output>` declaration. The effect of the serialization attributes is fully described in Chapter 15.

The way in which the `href` attribute is used is deliberately left a little vague in the specification, because the details are likely to be implementation-dependent. Its value is a relative or absolute URI. Details of the URI schemes that may be specified are left entirely to the implementation. The specification is also written in such a way that the URI can be interpreted as referring either to the result tree itself or to its serialized representation. The important thing that the specification says is that it is safe to use relative URIs as links from one output document to another: if you create one result document with «href="chap1.html"» and another with «href="chap2.html"», then the content of the first document can include an element such as `<a href="chap2.html">next chapter</a>` and expect the link to work, whether the result trees are actually serialized or not. The specification achieves this by saying that any relative URI used in the `href` attribute of an `<xsl:result-document>` element is interpreted relative to a *Base Output URI*, which in effect is supplied in the API that invokes the transformation.

> *We are used to thinking of URIs rather like filenames: as addresses of documents found somewhere on the disk. In fact, URIs are intended to be used as unique names for any kind of resource, hence their use for identifying namespaces and collations. Using URIs to identify final result trees (which might exist only as a data structure in memory) is no different. Implementations are expected to provide some kind of mechanism in their API to allow the application to process the result tree, given its URI.*
>
> *One way this might be done is to allow the application, when the transformation is complete, to use a method call such as* getResultDocument(URI) *to get a reference to the result tree with a given URI, perhaps returned in the form of a DOM document.*
>
> *Another possible mechanism is for the application to supply a resolver or listener object, which is notified whenever a result tree is created. This is the technique Saxon uses: if a user-written* OutputURIResolver *has been registered, then it is handed the result tree and the URI, and has free rein in deciding what to do with it.*

The specification of `<xsl:result-document>` is complicated by the fact that it is an instruction that has side effects. The instruction does not return a result (technically, it returns an empty sequence, which means it doesn't affect the result of evaluating the sequence constructor that it is part of). In a pure functional language, side effects are always problematical — though, of course, the only purpose of running any program is to change something in the environment in which it is run. Normally, if a compiler knows that a particular construct will return a particular result, then it can generate code that short cuts the evaluation of this construct. But it would destroy the purpose of `<xsl:result-document>` if it did nothing, just because the compiler already knows what result it will return.

To take an example of how this is a problem in practice, suppose that the stylesheet defined a variable as follows:

```
<xsl:variable name="dummy">
   <xsl:sequence select="3"/>
   <xsl:result-document href="hello.xml">
      <hello to="world"/>
   </xsl:result-document>
</xsl:variable>
```

Now suppose that this variable is never referenced, or is referenced only as «$dummy[1]». Is the result document produced, or not? Normally, an XSLT optimizer will avoid evaluating variables or parts of variables that aren't used, but this strategy causes problems if the evaluation of a variable has a side effect.

The way that the XSLT specification has dealt with this problem is essentially to say that you can only use `<xsl:result-document>` when the sequence constructor you are evaluating is destined to form the content of a final result tree. When the stylesheet starts executing, this condition is true for the sequence constructor contained in the first template to be evaluated, and it remains true except when you evaluate

`<xsl:variable>` or similar elements such as `<xsl:param>`, `<xsl:with-param>`, and `<xsl:message>`. You also can't use `<xsl:result-document>` while evaluating the result of a stylesheet function defined using `<xsl:function>`, or while computing the content of `<xsl:attribute>`, `<xsl:comment>`, `<xsl:value-of>`, `<xsl:namespace>`, `<xsl:processing-instruction>`, `<xsl:key>`, or `<xsl:sort>`. This restriction is a runtime rule rather than a compile-time rule; for example, you can use `<xsl:result-document>` within `<xsl:template>` if the template is called from within `<xsl:element>`, but not if it's called from within `<xsl:variable>`.

XSLT processors are allowed to evaluate instructions in any order. This means that you can't reliably predict the order in which final result trees get written. There is a rule preventing a stylesheet from writing two different result trees with the same URI, because if overwriting were allowed, the results would be nondeterministic. There is also a rule saying that it's an error to attempt to write a result tree and then read it back again using the `document()` function: this would be a sneaky way of exploiting side effects and making your stylesheet dependent on the order of execution. In practice, processors may have difficulty detecting this error, and you might get away with it, especially if you use different spellings of the URI, for example by writing to `file:///c:/temp.xml` and then reading from `FILE:///c:/temp.xml`.

The fact that order of execution is unpredictable has another consequence: if a transformation doesn't run to completion, because a runtime error occurred (or perhaps because `<xsl:message>` was used with «`terminate="yes"`»), then it's unpredictable as to whether a particular final result tree was output before the termination. In practice most processors only exploit the freedom to change the order of execution when evaluating variables or functions, so you are unlikely to run into this problem in practice.

Usage

There are two main reasons for using `<xsl:result-document>`. One reason is to generate multiple output files; the other is to exercise control over the validation or serialization of the principal output file.

Generating multiple output files is very common in publishing applications. The product documentation for Saxon, for example, consists of around 450 HTML files, which are generated by a single transformation from 20 input XML files. Sometimes it's better to do the transformation in two stages: First, split a large XML document into several small XML documents, and then convert each of these into HTML independently.

One common approach is to generate one principal output file and a whole family of secondary output files. The principal output file can then serve as an index. Usually a key part of the process will be the generation of hyperlinks that allow the user to navigate within the document family. This means you will need some mechanism for generating the filenames of the output files. Exactly how you do this depends on what's available in your input: one approach is to use the `generate-id()` function, which allocates a unique identifier to every node in your input documents.

Examples

The `<xsl:result-document>` instruction is often used to break up large documents into manageable chunks. In the section for `<xsl:param>` on page 433, there is an example of a stylesheet that breaks up one of Shakespeare's plays to produce a cover page together with one page per scene. But here we'll illustrate the principle with a much smaller document.

Example: Creating Multiple Output Files

This example takes a poem as input, and outputs each stanza to a separate file. A more realistic example would be to split a book into its chapters, but I wanted to keep the files small.

Source

The source file is `poem.xml`. It starts:

```
<poem>
<author>Rupert Brooke</author>
<date>1912</date>
<title>Song</title>
<stanza>
<line>And suddenly the wind comes soft,</line>
<line>And Spring is here again;</line>
<line>And the hawthorn quickens with buds of green</line>
<line>And my heart with buds of pain.</line>
</stanza>
<stanza>
<line>My heart all Winter lay so numb,</line>
<line>The earth so dead and frore,</line>
...
```

Stylesheet

The stylesheet is `split.xsl`.

We want to start a new output document for each stanza, so we use the `<xsl:result-document>` instruction in the template rule for the `<stanza>` element. Its effect is to switch all output produced by its sequence constructor to a different output file. In fact, it's very similar to the effect of an `<xsl:variable>` element that creates a tree, except that the tree, instead of being a temporary tree, is serialized directly to an output file of its own:

```
<?xml version="1.0"?>
<xsl:stylesheet xmlns:xsl="http://www.w3.org/1999/XSL/Transform"
                version="2.0">
<xsl:template match="poem">
   <poem>
      <xsl:copy-of select="title, author, date"/>
      <xsl:apply-templates select="stanza"/>
   </poem>
</xsl:template>
<xsl:template match="stanza">
   <xsl:variable name="file"
                 select="concat('verse', position(), '.xml')"/>
   <verse number="{position()}" href="{$file}"/>
   <xsl:result-document href="{$file}">
       <xsl:copy-of select="."/>
   </xsl:result-document>
</xsl:template>
</xsl:stylesheet>
```

To run this example under Saxon, you need to make sure that an output file is supplied for the principal output document. This determines the base output URI, and the other output documents will be written to locations that are relative to this base URI. For example:

```
java -jar c:\saxon\saxon9.jar -t -o:c:\temp\index.xml↵
-s:poem.xml -xsl:split.xsl
```

This will write the index document to `c:\temp\index.xml`, and the verses to files such as `c:\temp\verse2.xml`. The `-t` option is useful because it tells you exactly where the files have been written.

Output

The principal output file contains the skeletal poem below (indented for legibility):

```
<?xml version="1.0" encoding="utf-8"?>
<poem>
  <title>Song</title>
  <author>Rupert Brooke</author>
  <date>1912</date>
  <verse number="1" href="verse1.xml"/>
  <verse number="2" href="verse2.xml"/>
  <verse number="3" href="verse3.xml"/>
</poem>
```

Three further output files `verse1.xml`, `verse2.xml`, and `verse3.xml` are created in the same directory as the principal output file. Here is `verse1.xml`:

```
<?xml version="1.0" encoding="utf-8"?>
<stanza>
  <line>And suddenly the wind comes soft,</line>
  <line>And Spring is here again;</line>
  <line>And the hawthorn quickens with buds of green</line>
  <line>And my heart with buds of pain.</line>
</stanza>
```

For another version of this example, which uses the `element-available()` function to test whether the `<xsl:result-document>` instruction is implemented and takes fallback action if not, see the entry for `element-available()` on page 764 in Chapter 13.

See Also

`<xsl:output>` on page 420

xsl:sequence

The `<xsl:sequence>` instruction is used to deliver an arbitrary sequence, which may contain atomic values, nodes, or a combination of the two. It is the only XSLT instruction (with the exception of `<xsl:perform-sort>`) that can return references to existing nodes, as distinct from newly constructed nodes. Its most common use is to return the result of a stylesheet function.

Despite its name, `<xsl:sequence>` is often used to return a single item.

Changes in 2.0

This instruction is new in XSLT 2.0.

Format

```
<xsl:sequence
  select = {expression}
  <!-- Content: <xsl:fallback>* -->
</xsl:sequence>
```

Position

`<xsl:sequence>` is an instruction, and may be used anywhere within a sequence constructor. It is often used within `<xsl:function>`, to define the value that the function returns.

Attributes

Name	Value	Meaning
select mandatory	XPath Expression	Computes the value that the `<xsl:sequence>` instruction will return.

Content

The only content permitted is `<xsl:fallback>`. Any contained `<xsl:fallback>` instructions will be ignored by an XSLT 2.0 processor but can be used to define fallback action for an XSLT 1.0 processor.

Effect

The XPath expression contained in the `select` attribute is evaluated, and its result is returned unchanged as the result of the `<xsl:sequence>` instruction.

Usage and Examples

This innocent-looking instruction introduced in XSLT 2.0 has far-reaching effects on the capability of the XSLT language, because it means that XSLT instructions and sequence constructors (and hence functions and templates) become capable of returning any value allowed by the XPath data model. Without it, XSLT instructions could only be used to create new nodes in a result tree, but with it, they can also return atomic values and references to existing nodes.

To take an example, suppose you want to set a variable whose value is the numeric value of the `price` attribute of the context node, minus the value of the `discount` attribute if present. In XSLT 1.0 you might have written:

```
<xsl:variable name="discounted-price">
  <xsl:choose>
    <xsl:when test="@discount">
      <xsl:value-of select="@price - @discount"/>
    </xsl:when>
    <xsl:otherwise>
```

```
        <xsl:value-of select="@price"/>
      </xsl:otherwise>
    </xsl:choose>
  </xsl:variable>
```

This works, but the problem is that the result is not a number, but a document node (in XSLT 1.0 terminology, a result tree fragment) containing a text node that holds a string representation of the number. Not only is this an inefficient way of representing a number, it has also lost the type information, which means that if you use the value in operations that are type-sensitive, such as comparison or sorting, you might get an unexpected answer.

In XSLT 2.0, using the `<xsl:sequence>` instruction, you can rewrite this as:

```
<xsl:variable name="discounted-price" as="xs:double">
  <xsl:choose>
   <xsl:when test="@discount">
      <xsl:sequence select="@price - @discount"/>
   </xsl:when>
   <xsl:otherwise>
      <xsl:sequence select="@price"/>
   </xsl:otherwise>
  </xsl:choose>
</xsl:variable>
```

Within the `<xsl:when>` and `<xsl:otherwise>` branches, we now use `<xsl:sequence>` rather than `<xsl:value-of>`, to avoid creating a text node that we don't need. Look at the example carefully:

❑ The first `<xsl:sequence>` instruction contains an XPath arithmetic expression. If the source document has a schema, this assumes that the type of `@price` and `@discount` is numeric (typically, `xs:decimal`), and the result of the subtraction will be the same numeric type. If there is no schema, the nodes will be untyped, and the fact that they are used in an arithmetic expression will force the content of the attribute to be converted to an `xs:double`, which means that the result of the subtraction will also be an `xs:double`. The «as» attribute on the `<xsl:variable>` element ensures that whatever the numeric type of the result, it will be converted to an `xs:double`.

❑ The second `<xsl:sequence>` instruction simply returns the attribute node `@price` itself. The «as» attribute on the `<xsl:variable>` element causes the attribute node to be atomized, which extracts its typed value. If there is a schema, the node must be annotated with a numeric type for the conversion to `xs:double` to succeed. If there is no schema, then the untyped value of the attribute is converted to `xs:double` by casting.

❑ The «as="xs:double"» on the `<xsl:variable>` element ensures that a type error will be reported (typically at runtime) if there is no `@price` attribute, or if the content of the `@price` or `@discount` attribute is not numeric. Unlike the `number()` function, conversion to `xs:double` gives an error (rather than NaN) if the input is non-numeric.

❑ The first `<xsl:sequence>` instruction could be replaced by `<xsl:copy-of>` without any change in the meaning. When the select attribute returns atomic values, `<xsl:sequence>` and `<xsl:copy-of>` have exactly the same effect. If the second `<xsl:sequence>` instruction were replaced by `<xsl:copy-of>`, however, the effect would be subtly different. `<xsl:copy-of>` would create a copy of the attribute node, which is quite unnecessary in this case.

❑ Without the «as="xs:double"» on the <xsl:variable> element, all our efforts to return a numeric value rather than a temporary tree would be wasted; when <xsl:variable> has no «select» or «as» attribute, it automatically builds a temporary tree whose content is derived from the value returned by its contained sequence constructor.

It is possible to rewrite this whole construct as:

```
<xsl:variable name="discounted-price" as="xs:double"
    select="if (@discount)
            then @price - @discount
            else @price"/>
```

or if you really like brevity, as:

```
<xsl:variable name="discounted-price" as="xs:double"
              select="@price - (@discount, 0)[1]"/>
```

This illustrates that when you are calculating values, you often have a choice as to whether to do the work at the XPath level or at the XSLT level. My own preference with simple expressions such as this is to use the XPath approach, unless there is a need to use facilities that are only available at the XSLT level, such as the ability to create new nodes, or the more powerful instructions available in XSLT such as <xsl:number>, <xsl:analyze-string>, or <xsl:for-each-group>.

By far the most common use of <xsl:sequence> is the evaluation of the result of a stylesheet function, and there are examples of this under <xsl:function> on page 344.

The <xsl:sequence> instruction also enables template rules to return atomic values, or references to existing nodes. An example of the possibilities this opens up is shown in the section *Simulating Higher Order Functions* on page 250, which shows a generalized function for finding cycles in any XML data source, regardless of how the relationships are represented.

See Also

<xsl:function> on page 344
<xsl:copy-of> on page 292
<xsl:template> on page 433

xsl:sort

The <xsl:sort> element is used to define a component of a sort key. It is used within an <xsl:apply-templates>, <xsl:for-each>, <xsl:for-each-group>, or <xsl:perform-sort> instruction to define the order in which this instruction processes its data.

Changes in 2.0

The <xsl:sort> element may now be used within <xsl:for-each-group> and <xsl:perform-sort> as well as within <xsl:apply-templates> and <xsl:for-each>.

The value of the sort key may be calculated using an enclosed sequence constructor, as an alternative to using the select attribute.

In XSLT 1.0, `<xsl:sort>` was always used to sort a set of nodes. In 2.0 it is generalized so that it can sort any sequence.

A `collation` attribute has been added to allow the collating sequence for strings to be specified by means of a URI, and a `stable` attribute has been added to control how duplicates are handled.

Sorting is now sensitive to the types of the items being sorted. For example, if the sort key values are numeric, they will be compared as numbers rather than as strings.

Format

```
<xsl:sort
  select? = expression
  lang? = { nmtoken }
  order? = { "ascending" | "descending"}
  collation? = { uri }
  case-order? = { "upper-first" | "lower-first"}
  data-type? = { "text" | "number" | qname-but-not-ncname} >
  stable? = { "yes" | "no"}
  <!-- Content: {sequence-constructor} -->
</xsl:sort>
```

Position

`<xsl:sort>` is always a child of `<xsl:apply-templates>`, `<xsl:for-each>`, `<xsl:for-each-group>`, or `<xsl:perform-sort>`. Any number of sort keys may be specified, in major-to-minor order.

When used in `<xsl:for-each>`, `<xsl:for-each-group>`, or `<xsl:perform-sort>`, any `<xsl:sort>` elements must appear before the sequence constructor of the containing element.

When used in `<xsl:apply-templates>`, the `<xsl:sort>` elements can come before or after any `<xsl:with-param>` elements.

Attributes

Name	Value	Meaning
select optional	XPath Expression	Defines the sort key. The default is «.», the context item itself.
order optional	Attribute value template returning «ascending» or «descending»	Defines whether the nodes are processed in ascending or descending order of this key. The default is «ascending».
case-order optional	Attribute value template returning «upper-first» or «lower-first»	Defines whether upper-case letters are to be collated before or after lower-case letters. The default is language-dependent.
lang optional	Attribute value template returning a language code	Defines the language whose collating conventions are to be used. The default depends on the processing environment.
data-type optional	Attribute value template returning «text», «number» or Lexical QName	Defines whether the values are to be collated alphabetically or numerically, or using a user-defined type. The default is «text».

continued

Name	Value	Meaning
collation optional	Attribute value template returning collation URI	The collation URI identifies how strings are to be compared with each other.
stable optional	Attribute value template returning «yes» or «no»	This attribute is allowed only on the first `<xsl:sort>` element; if set to «no», it indicates that there is no requirement to retain the original order of items that have equal values for all the sort keys.

Except for `select`, all these attributes can be written as attribute value templates. The context item, context position, and context size for evaluating these attribute value templates are the same as the context for evaluating the `select` attribute of the containing instruction (that is `<xsl:for-each>`, `<xsl:apply-templates>`, `<xsl:for-each-group>`, or `<xsl:perform-sort>`).

Content

The element may contain a sequence constructor. This is used to compute the sort key value, as an alternative to using the `select` attribute. The two are mutually exclusive: if the `select` attribute is present, the element must be empty, and if it is not empty, the `select` attribute must be omitted. If neither is present, the default is «select=".">».

Effect

The list of `<xsl:sort>` elements appearing for example within an `<xsl:apply-templates>` or `<xsl:for-each>` element determines the order in which the selected items are processed. The items are sorted first by the first sort key; any group of items that have duplicate values for the first sort key are then sorted by the second sort key, and so on.

It's useful to start by establishing some clear terminology. There is a tendency to use the phrase *sort key* with several different meanings, often in the same sentence, so to avoid confusion I'll try to stick to the more precise terms that are used in the XSLT specification itself.

❑ A collection of `<xsl:sort>` elements, which together define all the criteria for performing a sort, is called a *sort key specification*.

❑ A single `<xsl:sort>` element within the sort key specification is called a *sort key component*. Often, of course, there will only be one component in a sort key specification.

❑ The result of evaluating a sort key component for one of the items to be sorted is called a *sort key value*.

So if you are sorting by last name and then first name, the sort key specification is "last name, then first name;" the sort key components are "last name" and "first name," and the sort key values are strings such as `"Kay"` and `"Michael"`.

It's also useful to be clear about how we describe the sorting process:

❑ The sequence that provides the input to the sort operation is called the *initial sequence*. In XSLT 1.0 the initial sequence was always a set of nodes in document order, but in 2.0 it can be any sequence of items (nodes or atomic values) in any order.

❑ The sequence that is produced as the output of the sort operation is called (naturally enough) the *sorted sequence*.

The overall rules for the sorting operation are fairly intuitive, but it's worth stating them for completeness:

❏ Given two items A and B in the initial sequence, their relative positions in the sorted sequence are determined by evaluating all their sort key values, one for each component in the sort key specification.

❏ The relative positions of A and B depend on the first pair of sort key values that is different for A and B; the second pair of sort key values needs to be considered only if the first sort key values for the two items are equal, and so on. For example, if you are sorting by last name and then first name, the system will only need to consider the first name for two individuals who have the same last name. I will explain later exactly what it means for one sort key value to be considered equal to another.

❏ Considering only this pair of sort key values, A comes before B in the sorted sequence if A's value for this sort key component is less than B's value, unless «order="descending"» is specified for this sort key component, in which case it comes after B. I will explain later what it means for one sort key value to be less than another.

❏ If all the sort key values for A and B are the same, then A and B appear in the sorted sequence in the same relative positions that they had in the initial sequence (the technical term for this is that the sort is *stable*). However, if «stable="no"» is specified on the first <xsl:sort> element, this requirement is waived, and the system can return duplicates in any order.

The sort key value for each item in the initial sequence is established by evaluating the expression given in the select attribute, or by evaluating the contained sequence constructor. This is evaluated for each item, with this item as the context item, with its position in the initial sequence as the context position, and with the number of items in the initial sequence as the context size.

This means that if you want to process a sequence in reverse order, you can specify a sort key as:

```
<xsl:sort select="position()" order="descending" />
```

You can also achieve other crafty effects: try, for example, sorting by «position() mod 3». This can be useful if you need to arrange data vertically in a table.

This just leaves the question of how the system decides whether one sort key value is equal to or less than another. The basic rule is that the result is decided using the XPath «eq» and «lt» operators. These are essentially the same as the «=» and «<» operators, except that they only compare a single atomic value to another single atomic value, and perform no type conversions other than numeric promotion (which means, for example, that if one operand is an integer and the other is a double, the integer will be converted to a double in order to perform the comparison).

There are several caveats to this general rule:

❏ The «lt» operator may raise an error when comparing values of different types (such as a number and a date) or when comparing two values of the same type for which no ordering relation is defined (for example, instances of the type xs:QName). This is treated as a fatal error.

❏ The <xsl:sort> element has an attribute data-type. This is only there for backward compatibility with XSLT 1.0, but you can still use it. If the value of the attribute is «text», then the sort key values are converted to strings (using the string() function) before being compared. If the value is «number», then they are converted to numbers using the number() function. The attribute also allows the value to be a prefixed QName, but the meaning of this depends entirely on the implementation. The feature was probably added to XSLT 1.0 to anticipate the use of schema-defined type names such as `xs:date`, and the implementation may allow this usage, but it's not defined in the standard. Instead, if you want to convert the sort key values to a particular type to do the comparison, you can achieve this using a cast or constructor function within the `select` attribute; for example, «`select="xs:date(@date-of-birth)"`».

❑ Another option that has been retained for backward compatibility with XSLT 1.0 is the ability to supply a sequence of values as the result of the `select` attribute, rather than a single value. If the `<xsl:sort>` element is in backward-compatibility mode (that is, if it's in the scope of an `[xsl:]version` attribute whose value is «`1.0`»), then all items in the sort key value after the first are ignored. Otherise, supplying a sequence of more than one item as the sort key value will cause an error.

❑ It is possible that evaluating a sort key value will return the empty sequence. XSLT specifies that for sorting purposes, the empty sequence is considered to be equal to itself and less than any other value.

❑ Another possibility is that when evaluating a numeric sort key value, the value will be the special value NaN (not a number). This would happen, for example, if you specify «`select=" number(@price)"`» and the element has no `price` attribute, or a `price` attribute whose value is «`$10.00`» (the «`$`» sign will cause the conversion to a number to fail). For sorting purposes, NaN is considered equal to itself, and less than any other numeric value (but greater than an empty sequence). This is different from the results of using the XPath comparison operators, where «`eq`» returns false if both operands are NaN.

❑ Last but not least, if the two values are strings, then they are compared using a collation. Collations are a broad subject so we will devote a separate section to them.

The `order` attribute specifies whether the order is ascending or descending. Descending order will produce the opposite result of ascending order. This means, for example, that NaN values will appear last rather than first, and also that the effect of the `case-order` attribute is reversed: If you specify «`case-order="upper-first"`» with «`order="descending"`», then *drall* will come before *Drall*.

The final sorted order of the items determines the sequence in which they are processed by the containing `<xsl:apply-templates>`, `<xsl:for-each>` , or `<xsl:for-each-group>` instruction, or the order in which they are returned by the containing `<xsl:perform-sort>` instruction. While the sorted sequence is being processed, the value of `position()` will reflect the position of the current item in the sorted sequence.

Collations

When the sort key values to be compared are strings, they are compared using a collation. A collation is essentially a mechanism for deciding whether two strings such as «`polish`» and «`Polish`» are considered equal, and if not, which of them should come first.

Choosing the right collation depends on the data that you are sorting, and on the expectations of the users. These expectations vary by country (in Germany, in most modern publications, «ä» is sorted along with «a», but in Sweden, it is sorted after «z») and also vary according to the application. Telephone directories, dictionaries, gazetteers, and back-of-book indexes each have their own rules.

XSLT 2.0 and XPath 2.0 share similar mechanisms for dealing with collations, because they are needed not only in sorting but also in defining what operators such as «eq» mean, and in functions such as `distinct-values()`. The assumption behind the design is that many computing environments (for example the Windows operating system, the Java virtual machine, or the Oracle database platform)

6

XSLT Elements

already include extensive mechanisms for defining and customizing collations, and that XSLT processors will be written to take advantage of these. As a result, sorting order will not be identical between different implementations.

The basic model is that a collation (a set of rules for determining string ordering) is identified by a URI. Like a namespace URI, this is an abstract identifier, not necessarily the location of a document somewhere on the Web. The form of the URI, and its meaning, is entirely up to the implementation. There is a proposal (RFC 4790) for IANA (the Internet Assigned Numbers Authority) to set up a register of collation names, but even if this comes to fruition, it will still be up to the implementation to decide whether to support these registered collations or not. Until such time, the best you can do to achieve interoperability is pass the collation URI to the stylesheet as a parameter; the API can then sort out the logic for choosing different collations according to which processor you are using.

The Unicode consortium has published an algorithm for collating strings called the Unicode Collation Algorithm (see `http://www.unicode.org/unicode/reports/tr10/index.html`). Although the XSLT specification refers to this document, it doesn't say that implementations have to support it. In practice, many of the facilities available in platforms such as Windows and Java are closely based on this algorithm. The Unicode Collation Algorithm is not itself a collation, because it can be parameterized. Rather, it is a framework for defining a collation with the particular properties that you are looking for.

You can specify the URI of the collation to be used in the `collation` attribute of the `<xsl:sort>` element. This is an attribute value template, so you can write `<xsl:sort collation="{$collation-uri}">` to use a collation that has been passed to the stylesheet as a parameter.

There is one collation URI that every implementation is required to support, called the *Unicode codepoint collation* (not to be confused with the Unicode Collation Algorithm mentioned earlier). This is selected using the URI

```
http://www.w3.org/2005/xpath-functions/collation/codepoint
```

Under the codepoint collation, strings are simply compared using the numeric code values of the characters in the string: if two characters have the same Unicode codepoint they are equal, and if one has a numerically lower Unicode codepoint, then it comes first. This isn't a very sophisticated or user-friendly algorithm, but it has the advantage of being fast. If you are sorting strings that use a limited alphabet, for example part numbers, then it is probably perfectly adequate.

Codepoint collation is subtly different from string comparisons in languages such as Java. Java represents Greek Zero Sign (x1018A) as a surrogate pair (xD800, xDD8A), and therefore sorts it before Wavy Overline (xFE4B). In XSLT, Wavy Overline comes first because its codepoint is lower.

If you specify a collation that the implementation doesn't recognize, then it raises an error. However, the word "recognize" is deliberately vague. An implementation could choose to recognize every possible collation URI that you might throw at it, and never raise this error at all. More probably, an implementation might decide to use parameterized URIs (for example, allowing a component such as «language=fr» to select the target language), and it's then an implementation decision whether to "recognize" a URI that contains invalid or missing parameters.

If you don't specify the collation attribute on `<xsl:sort>`, you can provide a hint as to what kind of collation you want by specifying the `lang` and/or `case-order` attributes. These are retained from XSLT 1.0, which didn't support explicit collation URIs, but they are still available for use in 2.0.

❑   The `lang` attribute specifies the language whose collation rules are to be used (this might be the language of the data, or the language of the target user). Its value is specified in the same way as the standard `xml:lang` attribute defined in the XML specification, for example «lang="en-US"» refers to U.S. English and «lang="fr-CA"» refers to Canadian French.

❑   Knowing the language doesn't help you decide whether upper-case or lower-case letters should come first (every dictionary in the world has its own rules on this), so XSLT makes this a separate attribute, `case-order`. Generally, case order will be used only to decide the ordering of two words that compare equal if case is ignored. For example, in German, where an initial upper-case letter can change the meaning of a word, some dictionaries list the adjective *drall* (meaning plump or buxom) before the unrelated noun *Drall* (a swerve, twist, or bias), while others reverse the order. Specifying «case-order="lower-first"» would place *drall* immediately before *Drall*, while «case-order="upper-first"» would have *Drall* immediately followed by *drall*.

If you say nothing at all about the collation you want, then the default is implementation-defined. For XPath operators and functions, the default is always the Unicode codepoint collation, but this is not necessarily the default for <xsl:sort>.

Usage

In this section we'll consider two specific aspects of sorting that tend to be troublesome. The first is the choice of a collation, and the second is how to achieve dynamic sorting — that is, sorting on a key chosen by the user at runtime, perhaps by clicking on a column heading.

Using Collations

XSLT is designed to be capable of handling serious professional publishing applications, and clearly this requires some fairly powerful sorting capabilities. In practice, however, the most demanding applications almost invariably have domain-specific collating rules; for instance, the rules for sorting personal names in a telephone directory are unlikely to work well for geographical names in a gazetteer. This is why the working groups decided to make the specification so open-ended in its support for collations.

Collations based on the Unicode collation algorithm (UCA) generally assign each character in the sort key value a set of weights. The primary weight distinguishes characters that are fundamentally different: «A» is different from «B». The secondary weight distinguishes secondary differences; for example, the distinction between «A» and «Ä». The tertiary weight is used to represent the difference between upper and lower case, for example «A» and «a». The way that weights are used varies a little in non-Latin scripts, but the principles are similar.

Rather than looking at each character separately, the Unicode collation algorithm compares two strings as a whole. First, it looks to see if there are two characters whose primary weights differ; if so, the first such character determines the ordering. If all the primary weights are the same, it looks at the secondary weights, and it only considers the tertiary weights if all the secondary weights are the same. This means for example that in French, «attache» sorts before «attaché», which in turn sorts before «attachement». The acute accent is taken into account when comparing «attache» with «attaché», because there is no primary difference between the strings, but it is ignored when comparing «attaché» with «attachement», because in this case there is a primary difference.

The *strength* of a collation determines what kind of differences it takes into account. For comparing equality between strings, it is often appropriate to use a collation with weak strength; for example, a collation with primary strength will treat «attache» as equal to «attaché». (In French this is not necessarily the right thing to do, as these two words have completely different meanings, but it would be appropriate if there is a high possibility that accents have been omitted from one of the strings.) When sorting, however, it is almost always best to use a collation with high strength, which will take secondary, and if necessary tertiary, differences into account when there are no primary differences.

Sometimes it is better, rather than defining two separate sort key components, to concatenate the sort key values into a single sort key component. For example, if you define a single sort key component as:

```
<xsl:sort select="concat(last-name, ' ', first-name)"/>
```

this might give better results than:

```
<xsl:sort select="last-name"/>
<xsl:sort select="first-name"/>
```

This is because in the second case above, a tertiary difference in the last name is considered more significant than a primary difference in the first name: so «MacMillan Tricia» will be sorted before «Macmillan Harold». When the sort key values are concatenated, the difference between «MacMillan» and «Macmillan» is only taken into account when the first names are the same. (To reproduce the order of entries found in a UK phone book, you would need a collation that interleaves the Macdonalds and McDonalds, but this is beyond the scope of the UCA.)

Dynamic Sort Keys

The select attribute contains an expression which is evaluated for each item in the initial sequence, with that item as the context item, to give the value that determines the item's position in the sequence. There's no direct way of specifying that you want to use different sort keys on different occasions. I've seen people try to write things like:

```
<xsl:param name="sort-key" >
. . .
    <xsl:for-each select="BOOK">
            <xsl:sort select="$sort-key"/>
```

hoping that if $sort-key is set to «TITLE», the elements will be sorted by title, and that if $sort-key is set to «AUTHOR», they will be sorted by author. This doesn't work: the variable $sort-key has the same value for every <BOOK> element, so the books will always be output in unsorted order. In this case, where the sort key is always a child element of the elements being sorted, you can achieve the required effect by writing:

```
<xsl:sort select="*[local-name()=$sort-key]">
```

Another way of making the sort conditional is to use a conditional expression as the sort key. This is much easier in XSLT 2.0 with the introduction of conditional expressions in XPath:

```
<xsl:sort select="if ($sort-key = 'title') then title
                     else if ($sort-key = 'author') then author
                     else if ($sort-key = 'isbn') then isbn
                     else publisher">
```

If the computation of the sort key is really complicated, you can do it in a sequence constructor rather than in the select attribute. This can even invoke templates or build temporary trees — there are no limits.

There are two other solutions to this problem that are worth mentioning, although both have their disadvantages:

❑ One is to generate or modify the stylesheet before compiling it, so that it includes the actual sort key required. This technique is popular when transformations are executed in the browser, typically under the control of JavaScript code in the HTML page. The stylesheet is then typically loaded from the server and parsed into a DOM document, which can be modified *in situ* before the transformation starts. The disadvantage is that this means recompiling the stylesheet each time it is run: this would probably be an unacceptable overhead if the transformation is running server-side within a Web server.

❑ Another is to use an extension function that permits the evaluation of XPath expressions that have been constructed dynamically, as strings. Such a function, `dyn:evaluate()`, is defined in the third-party function library at `http://www.exslt.org/`, and is available in this or a similar form with a number of XSLT processors including Saxon and Xalan.

Examples

I'll start with a couple of simple examples and then show a full working example that you can download and try yourself.

❑ Example 1: Process all the `<book>` children of the current node, sorting them by the value of the `isbn` attribute:

```
<xsl:apply-templates select="book">
  <xsl:sort select="@isbn"/>
</xsl:apply-templates>
```

❑ Example 2: Output the contents of all the `<city>` elements in the document, in alphabetical order, including each distinct city once only:

```
<ul>
<xsl:for-each select="distinct-values(//city)">
  <xsl:sort select="."/>
  <li><xsl:value-of select="."/></li>
</xsl:for-each>
</ul>
```

If «select="."» were omitted from the `<xsl:sort>` element, the effect would be the same, because this is the default, but I prefer to include it for clarity.

Example: Sorting on the Result of a Calculation

This example outputs a list of products, sorted by the total sales of each product, in descending order.

Source

This is the file `products.xml`:

```
<products>
<product name="strawberry jam">
   <region name="south" sales="20.00"/>
```

```
      <region name="north" sales="50.00"/>
   </product>
   <product name="raspberry jam">
      <region name="south" sales="205.16"/>
      <region name="north" sales="10.50"/>
   </product>
   <product name="plum jam">
      <region name="east" sales="320.20"/>
      <region name="north" sales="39.50"/>
   </product>
</products>
```

Stylesheet

`products.xsl` is a complete stylesheet written using the simplified stylesheet syntax, in which the entire stylesheet module is written as a single literal result element. Simplified stylesheets are described in Chapter 3, on page 125.

The `<xsl:sort>` element sorts the selected nodes (all the `<product>` elements) in descending order of the numerical total of the `sales` attribute over all their `<region>` child elements. The total is calculated using the `sum()` function (described on page 889) and displayed using the `format-number()` function (page 788).

```
<products xsl:version="2.0"
      xmlns:xsl="http://www.w3.org/1999/XSL/Transform">
<xsl:for-each select="products/product">
   <xsl:sort select="sum(region/@sales)" order="descending"/>
   <product name="{@name}"
            sales="{format-number(sum(region/@sales), '$####0.00')}"/>
</xsl:for-each>
</products>
```

For this to work correctly under XSLT 1.0, you need to add «`data-type="number"`» to the `<xsl:sort>` element. This is not needed with XSLT 2.0 because the type is recognized automatically.

Output

I have added line breaks for readability:

```
<products>
  <product name="plum jam" sales="$359.70"/>
  <product name="raspberry jam" sales="$215.66"/>
  <product name="strawberry jam" sales="$70.00"/>
</products>
```

See Also

`<xsl:apply-templates>` on page 240
`<xsl:for-each>` on page 322

`<xsl:for-each-group>` on page 326

`<xsl:perform-sort>` on page 437

xsl:strip-space

The `<xsl:strip-space>` declaration, along with `<xsl:preserve-space>`, is used to control the way in which whitespace nodes in the source document are handled. The `<xsl:strip-space>` declaration identifies elements in which whitespace-only text nodes are considered insignificant, so they can be removed from the source tree.

Changes in 2.0

The syntax of a `NameTest` has been extended to allow the format «`*:NCName`», which matches all elements with a given local name, in any namespace.

Format

```
<xsl:strip-space
  elements = tokens />
```

Position

`<xsl:strip-space>` is a top-level declaration, which means it is always a child of the `<xsl:stylesheet>` element. There are no constraints on where it appears relative to other declarations.

Attributes

Name	Value	Meaning
elements mandatory	Whitespace-separated list of `NameTests`	Defines elements in the source document whose whitespace-only text nodes are to be removed

The construct `NameTest` is defined in XPath, and is described in Chapter 9, on page 614.

Content

None, the element is always empty.

Effect, Usage, and Examples

See `<xsl:preserve-space>` on page 439. The two elements `<xsl:strip-space>` and `<xsl:preserve-space>` are closely related, so I have presented the rules and usage guidance in one place.

See Also

`<xsl:preserve-space>` on page 439

`<xsl:text>` on page 492

xsl:stylesheet

The `<xsl:stylesheet>` element is the outermost element of a stylesheet. The synonym `<xsl:transform>` can be used as an alternative.

Changes in 2.0

A number of new attributes have been added: xpath-default-namespace, default-collation, default-validation, input-type-annotation, and use-when. Several of these attributes, although usually used on the `<xsl:stylesheet>` element and described here for convenience, can actually be used on any XSLT element in the stylesheet.

Format

```
<xsl:stylesheet
  id? = id
  default-collation? = uri-list
  default-validation? = "preserve" | "strip"
  exclude-result-prefixes? = tokens
  extension-element-prefixes? = tokens
  input-type-annotations? = "preserve" | "strip" | "unspecified"
  use-when? = expression
  version = number
  xpath-default-namespace? = uri
  <!-- Content: (xsl:import*, other-declarations) -->
</xsl:stylesheet>
```

Position

`<xsl:stylesheet>` (or its synonym, `<xsl:transform>`) appears as the outermost element of every stylesheet module, except one that uses the *simplified–stylesheet* syntax described on page 125, in Chapter 3. It is used both on a principal stylesheet module and on one that is imported or included into another module.

As described in Chapter 3, a stylesheet can be embedded in another XML document. In this case the `<xsl:stylesheet>` element still forms the root of the stylesheet module, but it is no longer the outermost element of an XML document.

Namespace Declarations

There will always be at least one namespace declaration on the `<xsl:stylesheet>` element, typically:

```
xmlns:xsl="http://www.w3.org/1999/XSL/Transform"
```

This defines the *XSLT Namespace*, which is necessary to identify the document as an XSLT stylesheet. The URI part must be written exactly as shown. The prefix «xsl» is conventional and is used in all XSLT documentation, including this book and the standard itself, but you could choose a different prefix if you wanted; for example, «XSLT». You would then have to name the element `<XSLT:stylesheet>` instead of `<xsl:stylesheet>`.

You can also make this the default namespace by using the following declaration:

```
xmlns="http://www.w3.org/1999/XSL/Transform"
```

In this case the element name will simply be `<stylesheet>`, and other XSLT elements will similarly be unprefixed; for example, `<template>` rather than `<xsl:template>`. Although this works, it is not generally recommended, because the default namespace is then not available for literal result elements. The technique that works best is to reserve the default namespace for literal result elements that you want to go in the default namespace of the output document.

> You may come across a stylesheet that uses the namespace declaration:
> `xmlns:xsl="http://www.w3.org/TR/WD-xsl"`
>
> This is not an XSLT stylesheet at all, but one written in WD-xsl, the working-draft dialect of XSL that Microsoft shipped in 1998 with Internet Explorer 5. This is a very different language, and is not described in this book.

Many stylesheets also need to declare the XML Schema namespace, typically as:

```
xmlns:xs="http://www.w3.org/2001/XMLSchema"
```

This is needed to declare the types of variables or parameters, or to use conversions to types such as `xs:integer` and `xs:date`.

Attributes

Name	Value	Meaning
id optional	XML Name	An identifier used to identify the `<xsl:stylesheet>` element when it is embedded in another XML document.
default-collation optional	Whitespace-separated list of URIs	Defines the default collation to be used for XPath functions and operators.
default-validation optional	«preserve» or «strip»	Defines the validation applied to new element and attribute nodes when the instruction that creates them does not have an `[xsl:]validation` or `[xsl:]type` attribute. The default is «strip».
exclude-result-prefixes optional	Whitespace-separated list of NCNames	Defines any namespaces used in this stylesheet that should not be copied to the output destination, unless they are actually used in the result document.
extension-element-prefixes optional	Whitespace-separated list of NCNames	Defines any namespaces used in this stylesheet to identify extension elements.
input-type-annotations optional	«preserve», «strip», or «unspecified»	Defines how type annotations on input documents should be handled.
use-when optional	XPath expression, restricted to use information available at compile time	Defines a condition that must be true if the contents of this stylesheet module are to be included in the stylesheet. It must be possible to evaluate the condition statically, which means it will often consist of a test on the value of the `system-property()` function.

continued

467

Name	Value	Meaning
version mandatory	Number	Defines the version of XSLT required by this stylesheet. Use «2.0» for a stylesheet that requires XSLT 2.0 features, or «1.0» if you want the stylesheet to be portable between XSLT 1.0 and XSLT 2.0 processors.
xpath-default-namespace optional	Namespace URI	Defines the namespace URI that is assumed for unprefixed element names and type names occurring in XPath expressions, patterns, and certain other constructs such as the SequenceType in an `as` attribute.

The attributes `default-collation`, `exclude-result-prefixes`, `extension-element-prefixes`, `version`, `use-when`, and `xpath-default-namespace` can be specified on any element in the XSLT namespace. They can also be used on literal result elements, though in this case the attribute must be in the XSLT namespace, to distinguish it from user-defined attributes that are to be copied to the result tree. Collectively these attributes are referred to by names such as `[xsl:]version`, since they are sometimes namespace-prefixed.

These attributes are described here because they are usually used on the `<xsl:stylesheet>` element. They are not included in the proforma of other XSLT elements in order to save space.

The `[xsl:]use-when` attribute is more likely to appear on elements in a stylesheet other than the `<xsl:stylesheet>` or `<xsl:transform>` element. This attribute allows you to specify a compile-time conditional expression, and the element on which it appears will be included in the compiled stylesheet only if this condition is true. If the attribute is present on the `<xsl:stylesheet>` or `<xsl:transform>` element and takes the value `false`, the effect is as if the stylesheet module contained no top-level declarations. This attribute is described on page 127.

In the case of `default-collation`, `version` and `xpath-default-namespace`, the effective value of the attribute for a particular instruction in the stylesheet is the value on the nearest enclosing element, or the instruction itself, that has a value for this attribute. In the case of `extension-element-prefixes` and `exclude-result-prefixes`, the values are cumulative — a namespace is an extension namespace or excluded namespace if it is listed as such on some enclosing instruction.

In practice the most useful place to specify these attributes is often on the `<xsl:template>` or `<xsl:function>` declarations, in which case they apply to the body of a template or function.

The sections below (starting with *The id Attribute*) consider each of the attributes in turn, describing first the formal rules for the attribute, then advice on usage and examples where appropriate.

Content

The `<xsl:stylesheet>` element may contain XSLT elements referred to as *top-level declarations*. These elements are:

```
<xsl:attribute-set>
<xsl:character-map>
<xsl:decimal-format>
```

```
<xsl:function>
<xsl:import>
<xsl:import-schema>
<xsl:include>
<xsl:key>
<xsl:namespace-alias>
<xsl:output>
<xsl:param>
<xsl:preserve-space>
<xsl:strip-space>
<xsl:template>
<xsl:variable>
```

If there are any `<xsl:import>` elements, they must come before other top-level declarations.

The `<xsl:stylesheet>` element may also contain other elements provided they use a non-null namespace URI that is different from the XSLT namespace URI. If the namespace URI is recognized by the XSLT processor, it may interpret such elements in any way the vendor chooses, provided that the correct functioning of the stylesheet is not affected. If it does not recognize these elements, it should ignore them.

The id Attribute

This attribute allows an `<xsl:stylesheet>` element to be referenced when it is contained within another XML document.

Effect

The precise usage is not defined in the standard, but the expectation is that this id attribute will allow an embedded stylesheet to be referenced in an `<?xml-stylesheet?>` processing instruction. An example is given in Chapter 3 on page 102. The specification points out that for this to work, it may be necessary for the id attribute to be declared in a DTD or schema as having the attribute type ID. However, not all XSLT processors impose this restriction.

Usage

If the XSLT processor you are using supports embedding of stylesheets within the source document that they are to transform, then the typical layout will be like this:

```
<?xml version="1.0"?>
<?xml-stylesheet href="#style" type="text/xsl"?>
<!DOCTYPE data [
   <!ATTLIST xsl:stylesheet id ID #REQUIRED >
]>
<data>
...
...
   <xsl:stylesheet id="style" version="2.0"
      xmlns:xsl="http://www.w3.org/1999/XSL/Transform"
   >
   <xsl:include href="module1.xsl"/>
   <xsl:include href="module2.xsl"/>
   <xsl:template match="xsl:*"/>
   </xsl:stylesheet>
</data>
```

Note that when this structure is used, the stylesheet will be presented with the entire source document, including a copy of itself. The stylesheet therefore needs to be written to handle its own elements in an appropriate way, hence the empty template rule that matches all elements in the XSLT namespace.

XSLT 2.0 defines the media type (MIME type) «application/xslt+xml» for XSLT stylesheet modules, but the unofficial usage «text/xsl» is much more widely supported in today's products.

The default-collation Attribute

This attribute can be used at the `<xsl:stylesheet>` level to define the default collation used for all XPath expressions within the stylesheet module. It does not affect included or imported modules. The attribute can also appear on any other XSLT element (or, prefixed as `xsl:default-collation`, on a literal result element) to define a default with more local scope.

Effect

Collations are discussed under `<xsl:sort>` on page 459. However, collations are used not only when sorting but also whenever strings are compared. The default collation is used by operators such as «eq», «lt», «=», or «<», and by functions such as `min()`, `max()`, `distinct-values()`, and `index-of()` whenever no other collation is specified. As well as defining the collation used by these XPath operators and functions, the `[xsl:]default-collation` attribute also affects XSLT elements such `<xsl:key>` and `<xsl:for-each-group>`. One place that is not affected by this attribute, curiously, is `<xsl:sort>` itself.

Usage

To allow interoperability, the attribute can be specified as a list of collation URIs, separated by white-space. The processor will use as the default collation the first URI that it recognizes. This means that if you want to write a stylesheet that works under processors produced by Microsoft, IBM, and Oracle, and if each of these vendors supports different flavors of collation URI, then you can list your preferred collation for each of these vendors, and the product will pick the one that it understands. If the processor doesn't recognize any of the URIs, then it reports an error. You can avoid this error by including the Unicode codepoint collation, `http://www.w3.org/2005/xpath-functions/collation/codepoint`, as the last URI in the list.

It's permitted to use a relative URI, in which case it is resolved against the base URI of the element where it appears. This option is only likely to be useful in the case of a vendor who implements collation URIs as references to real documents, perhaps an XML document that contains a machine-readable specification of the collation rules.

The default-validation Attribute

Like most of the attributes on the `<xsl:stylesheet>` element, the `default-validation` attribute applies to everything that is textually within the stylesheet module. Unlike others, it can't be overridden with a different declaration on an inner element in the stylesheet. (I don't think there's any good reason for this restriction; it was put there simply to avoid adding unnecessary complexity).

Effect

This attribute applies to every instruction in the stylesheet that is allowed to take a `validation` or `type` attribute, provided neither of these attributes is actually present. It also affects literal result elements, which are allowed to take an `xsl:type` or `xsl:validation` attribute, in the same way. The effect is to supply a default value for the `[xsl:]validation` attribute on these instructions or literal result elements.

The possible values of the attribute are «preserve» and «strip», the default being «strip». (At one time the values «strict» and «lax» were also allowed, which explains the name of the attribute, but experience showed that these options were not useful.) The meanings of these values are explained under each instruction that takes a `validation` attribute, and vary slightly from one instruction to another, depending on whether it is dealing with single nodes or multiple nodes, elements or attributes.

Usage

This attribute affects every literal result element, and every `<xsl:element>`, `<xsl:copy>`, `<xsl:copy-of>` and `<xsl:result-document>` instruction within the stylesheet module, unless it has its own `validation` or `type` attribute.

Since the default is «`validation="strip"`», the only real question to consider is when to use «`validation="preserve"`». Given a schema-aware processor, and a stylesheet whose main job is to copy a selection of the nodes from the source document across to the result document with as few changes as possible, for further transformation by another stylesheet later on in the pipeline, it makes sense to preserve all the existing type annotations. However, check the specification of the individual instructions. `<xsl:copy validate="preserve">` probably doesn't do what you imagine. Since `<xsl:copy>` can completely change the content of an element, the type annotation on the element being copied is no longer reliable, so it isn't retained, even with this option. When a subtree is copied in its entirety, with no changes (typically using `<xsl:copy-of>`), it makes sense to retain type annotations. As soon as any changes are made, the result can only contain type annotations if you put it through schema validation.

The exclude-result-prefixes Attribute

This attribute defines a set of namespaces that are *not* to be copied into the result tree.

The XSLT processor is required to produce a correct tree that conforms with the XDM data model (as described on page 45, in Chapter 2) and with the XML Namespaces rules, so you will never find yourself with an output file using namespace prefixes that have not been declared. However, you can easily find yourself with a file containing unnecessary and unwanted namespace declarations; for example, declarations of namespaces that occur on nodes in your source document but are not used in the output document, or namespaces for extension functions that are used only in the stylesheet. These extra namespace declarations usually don't matter, because they don't affect the meaning of the output file, but they can clutter it up. They can also affect validation if you are trying to create a result document that conforms to a particular DTD. So this attribute is provided to help you get rid of them.

Effect

The XSLT specification requires that when a literal result element in the stylesheet is evaluated, the element is copied into the result tree along with all its namespace nodes, except for the XSLT namespace and any namespace that defines extension instructions. An element has a namespace node for every namespace that is in scope, including namespaces defined on ancestor elements as well as on the element itself, so the namespaces copied over include not only the namespaces defined on the literal result element, and those that are actually used on the literal result element, but even those that are merely *available* for use.

Very often, of course, one literal result element will be a child or descendant of another, and the namespace nodes on the child element will include copies of all the namespace nodes on the parent element. For example, consider the stylesheet below:

```
<xsl:stylesheet version="1.0"
                xmlns:xsl="http://www.w3.org/1999/XSL/Transform"/>

<xsl:template match="/">
```

```
        <acme:document xmlns:acme="http://acme.com/xslt">
          <acme:chapter>
             Once upon a time ...
          </acme:chapter>
        </acme:document>
    </xsl:template>

  </xsl:stylesheet>
```

This is represented by the tree shown in Figure 6-12, using the same notation as previously seen in Chapters 2 and 3. Although there are only two namespace declarations, these are propagated to all the descendant elements, so for example the `<acme:chapter>` element has two namespace nodes even though there are no namespace declarations on the element. (It also has a namespace node for the «xml» namespace, which is not shown in Figure 6-12.)

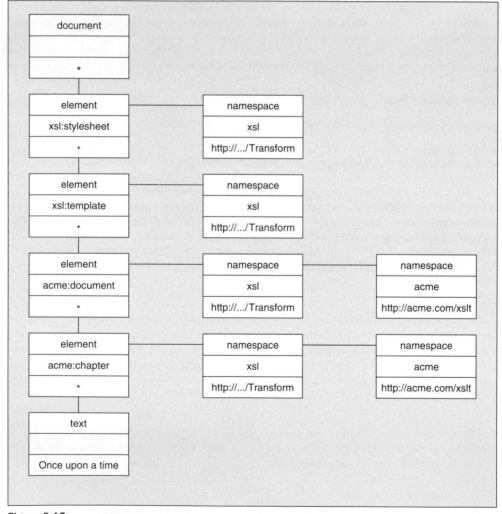

Figure 6-12

The specification says that each literal result element is copied with all its namespace nodes (but excluding the XSLT namespace), so the result tree will resemble Figure 6-13 (again, the «xml» namespace nodes are omitted).

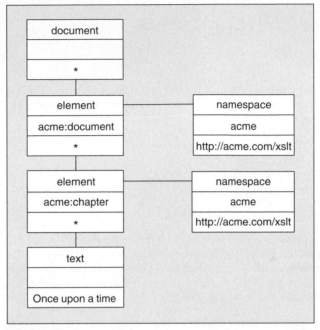

Figure 6-13

Both elements, `<acme:document>` and `<acme:chapter>`, have a namespace node for the «acme» namespace. However, this doesn't mean that the namespace declaration will be repeated unnecessarily in the output file: we're talking here about the abstract tree that is created, not the final serialized XML file. Avoiding duplicate namespace declarations is entirely the job of the XSLT serializer, and most serializers will produce the following output, shown indented for clarity:

```
<acme:document xmlns:acme="http://acme.com/xslt">
   <acme:chapter>
      Once upon a time ...
   </acme:chapter>
</acme:document>
```

What exclude-result-prefixes Does

The `exclude-result-prefixes` attribute isn't present to get rid of duplicate declarations, it's present to get rid of declarations that aren't wanted at all, which is a different matter entirely. For example suppose the stylesheet were like this:

```
<xsl:stylesheet version="1.0"
   xmlns:xsl="http://www.w3.org/1999/XSL/Transform"
   xmlns:var="http://another.org/xslt"
/>

<xsl:variable name="var:x" select="17"/>
```

```
<xsl:template match="/">
    <acme:document xmlns:acme="http://acme.com/xslt">
        <acme:chapter>
            Once upon a time ...
        </acme:chapter>
    </acme:document>
</xsl:template>

</xsl:stylesheet>
```

Then although the sequence constructor has not changed, the `<acme:document>` and `<acme:chapter>` elements each now have an extra namespace node, and this will be copied to the output file even though it is unused, resulting in the output:

```
<acme:document xmlns:acme="http://acme.com/xslt"
               xmlns:var="http://another.org/xslt">
    <acme:chapter>
        Once upon a time ...
    </acme:chapter>
</acme:document>
```

Why can't the XSLT processor simply include all the namespaces that are actually used in element and attribute names, and omit the rest? The reason is that many XML applications, like XSLT itself, will use the namespace mechanism to create unique values within their own data. For example, namespace prefixes might be used in attribute values as well as attribute names. The XSLT processor can't distinguish these from ordinary values, so it has to play safe.

So if there are namespaces you don't want in the output tree, you can specify them in the `exclude-result-prefixes` attribute of the `<xsl:stylesheet>` element. The attribute is a list of namespace prefixes, separated by whitespace, and with the option to exclude the default namespace under the pseudoprefix «#default». If you want more precise control (though it is rarely needed), you can also specify `[xsl:]exclude-result-prefixes` on any element in the stylesheet, remembering that the attribute must be prefixed when it appears on a literal result element, and unprefixed when it appears on an XSLT element. It affects all literal result elements that are textually within its scope.

The prefix, as always, is simply a way of referring to the associated namespace URI: it is the namespace URI that is really being excluded, not the prefix itself. So if the same namespace URI is declared again with a different prefix, it is still an excluded namespace.

What exclude-result-prefixes Doesn't Do

The `[xsl:]exclude-result-prefixes` attribute applies only to namespace nodes copied from the stylesheet using literal result elements. It does not affect namespace nodes copied from the source document using `<xsl:copy>` or `<xsl:copy-of>`; these can be suppressed by using the `copy-namespaces` attribute on the instruction itself.

Like the other attributes on the `<xsl:stylesheet>` element, the `exclude-result-prefixes` attribute applies only to elements actually within the stylesheet module, not to those brought in using `<xsl:include>` or `<xsl:import>`.

What happens if you try to exclude a namespace that is actually needed because it is used in the result tree? The XSLT processor is obliged to generate output that conforms to the Namespaces Recommendation, so it will ignore the request to exclude this namespace. Or more accurately, the evaluation of the literal result element will not cause the namespace node to be copied, but the namespace fixup process that comes into play when the element has been constructed will then generate namespace nodes for any namespaces that were missing. Namespace fixup is described under <xsl:element> on page 310.

Using exclude-result-prefixes will never move an element or attribute into a different namespace. People sometimes see an element such as <child xmlns=""> in the output, and ask how to get rid of the «xmlns=""». The answer is: look at the code that's generating the <child> element, and change it to put the element in the proper namespace. If the <child> element is in the same namespace as its parent, then the serializer won't need to generate the «xmlns=""» declaration.

Usage

The simplest way to decide which namespace prefixes to list here is by trial and error. Run the stylesheet, and if the output document contains namespace declarations that clearly serve no useful purpose, add them to the exclude-result-prefixes attribute and run the stylesheet again.

The XSLT namespace itself and namespaces used for extension elements will be excluded automatically. However, the stylesheet is also likely to contain references to the schema namespace, which you may not want in your result document. It will also contain any namespace you have used for defining your local stylesheet functions, which you almost certainly don't want in the result document.

A common cause of unwanted namespace declarations finding their way into the result document is where your stylesheet needs to refer to namespaces used in the source document; for example, in a template match pattern, but where none of these elements is copied into the destination document.

For example:

```
<xsl:stylesheet
        version="2.0"
        xmlns:xsl="http://www.w3.org/1999/XSL/Transform"
        xmlns:po="http://accounting.org/xslt"
        exclude-result-prefixes="po"
>
<xsl:template match="po:purchase-order">
   <order-details>
   ...
   </order-details>
</xsl:template>
</xsl:stylesheet>
```

Here the «po» namespace would be copied into the result document if it weren't for the exclude-result-prefixes attribute, because it is in scope when the literal result element <order-details> is evaluated.

As with the other <xsl:stylesheet> attributes, you don't have to apply the exclusion to the whole stylesheet if you don't want to, you can also apply it to any part of the stylesheet by using the xsl:exclude-result-prefixes attribute on any literal result element. It's probably a good idea in practice to keep the declaration of a namespace and the directive that excludes it from the result document together in one place.

The extension-element-prefixes Attribute

This attribute identifies a set of namespaces used for extension instructions. Extension instructions may be defined by an implementor, a user, or a third party. An example is the <sql:query> instruction in

Saxon, which allows data to be fetched from a relational database. They can be used anywhere an instruction can be used, that is, within a sequence constructor. If an element is found in a sequence constructor that is not in the XSLT namespace, then it must either be an extension instruction or a literal result element. If its namespace is the same as a namespace identified in the `[xsl:]extension-element-prefixes` attribute of the containing `<xsl:stylesheet>` element, of some other containing element, or of the element itself, then it will be treated as an extension instruction; otherwise, it will be treated as a literal result element.

Effect

The value of the attribute is a whitespace-separated list of prefixes; each of these prefixes must identify a namespace declaration present on the containing element. The default namespace (the namespace declared using the `xmlns` attribute) may be designated as an extension element namespace by using the pseudoprefix «#default».

The scope of the `extension-element-prefixes` attribute is the stylesheet module. It does not affect included or imported modules.

If a namespace is designated as an extension element namespace, then every XSLT processor will recognize that these elements are extension instructions. However, some XSLT processors may be unable to evaluate them. For example, if the namespace `http://saxon.sf.net/` is designated as an extension namespace, then both Saxon and AltovaXML will recognize that these elements are extensions, but the likelihood is that Saxon will know how to handle them and AltovaXML won't. If the processor knows how to evaluate the instruction, it does so; otherwise, it looks to see if the element contains an `<xsl:fallback>` instruction. If it does, the `<xsl:fallback>` instruction is evaluated; otherwise, an error is reported.

It is necessary to designate a namespace as an extension element namespace only to distinguish extension instructions from literal result elements. At the top level of the stylesheet, there is no risk of confusion. Any implementation can define its own top-level elements, using its own namespace, and other implementations will simply ignore these elements, treating them as data. So the `extension-element-prefixes` attribute is not needed to identify top-level elements used as vendor or user extensions. For example, you can use `<msxml:script>` as a top-level declaration, and processors other than Microsoft MSXML will probably ignore it (though there is nothing that says they have to).

Usage

This attribute should be set to a list of all the prefixes you are using for extension instructions in your stylesheet. The most common cases are either to omit it entirely or to include a single prefix for the namespace used by the vendor of your chosen XSLT processor for their own proprietary extensions. There will always be a namespace declaration for this namespace on the `<xsl:stylesheet>` element as well.

For example, if you are using Saxon:

```
<xsl:stylesheet
        version="2.0"
        xmlns:xsl="http://www.w3.org/1999/XSL/Transform"
        xmlns:saxon="http://saxon.sf.net/"
        extension-element-prefixes="saxon"
        >
```

Don't include the vendor's prefix unless you are actually using their proprietary extensions in the stylesheet. You don't need to include this attribute to use proprietary top-level elements such as `<msxml:script>`, or to use extension functions: You need it only if you want to use vendor-defined instructions within a sequence constructor, where they would otherwise be assumed to be literal result elements. An example of such an instruction in Saxon is `<saxon:doctype>`, which allows you to generate a DTD for the result document.

If your usage of vendor extensions is highly localized within the stylesheet, it is better to identify them using the `xsl:extension-element-prefixes` attribute of the extension element itself, or of a literal result element that surrounds the sequence constructor where the extensions are actually used. This aids portability and makes it easier to see which parts of the stylesheet are standard and which parts use proprietary extensions.

If you want to use extensions supplied by several different vendors, you can list them all in this attribute. An XSLT processor from one vendor won't object to finding another vendor's namespace in the list; it will only object if it is actually asked to evaluate a proprietary instruction that it doesn't understand, and even then if there is an `<xsl:fallback>` child element that defines the fallback behavior, it will carry on calmly executing that in place of the unrecognized instruction.

Although extension elements supplied by XSLT product vendors are likely to be the most common case, it's also possible in principle to install third-party extensions or to write your own (however, the APIs for doing so will be different for each vendor). So everything we've said about the vendor's extensions applies equally to your own extensions and those acquired from a third party.

For more information about the extensions provided by various vendors in their products, see the documentation for the relevant product.

An inventive way of using the `extension-element-prefixes` attribute is to flag elements that you want to reserve for debugging or annotation. For example, if you include the following element within a sequence constructor anywhere in the stylesheet, then the normal action will be to output an element to the result tree, showing the current values of the variables $var1 and $var2.

```
<debug:write var1="{$var1}" var2="{$var2}"><xsl:fallback/></debug:write>
```

When you no longer need to use this debugging instruction, you can disable it simply by declaring «debug» as an extension element prefix. This time the `<xsl:fallback/>` action will be taken, because the processor doesn't recognize the extension instruction.

The input-type-annotations Attribute

This attribute allows a processor to specify that it wants to treat input documents as untyped even if they have been schema-validated.

Effect

Specifying «input-type-annotations="strip"» causes all type annotations on input documents to be removed before any further processing. The term *input documents* here means the principal input document and any documents read using the functions `doc()`, `document()`, or `collection()`. The effect of stripping type annotations is that elements become marked as `xs:untyped`, and attributes as `xs:untypedAtomic`. The `nilled` flag on every element is set to false, but the flags that mark a node as an ID or IDREF are unaffected.

Unlike the other attributes, `input-type-annotations` does affect included and imported modules. The reason for the difference is that it takes effect at runtime, not at compile time. The rule is that if any module specifies «strip», then annotations will be stripped, unless there is also a module that specifies «preserve» in which case an error is reported. The value «unspecified» means what it says: it's the same as not including the attribute at all.

This attribute is a bit of an oddity because in other cases, it is left to the API to control what happens to the input document before a transformation starts. Although you can ask for type annotations to be removed from the input document, you can't ask for them to be added (by invoking validation) unless you're prepared to make a copy of the document.

Usage

In theory, the time to use this attribute is when (a) your stylesheet is relying on nodes being untyped (this might be the case, for example, if it wants to manipulate dates as strings using regular expressions), and (b) there is a possibility that it will be presented with typed input.

I haven't come across the need for this with Saxon, because the input will only be typed if you explicitly request it. But it might be handy when you want your stylesheet to work with other processors. AltovaXML validates the input document if it contains an `xsi:schemaLocation` attribute, which is something that the processing application may not be able to control.

The use-when Attribute

This attribute may be specified on any element in the stylesheet (if specified on a literal result element, it is named «xsl:use-when») and its value is an XPath expression. Although the full XPath syntax is allowed, the context for evaluation of the expression is severely restricted, which means that the expression cannot refer to anything in the source document or the stylesheet. In practice this means it is restricted to testing the results of functions such as `system-property()`, `function-available()`, and `element-available()`.

Effect

The expression is evaluated at compile time, and if its effective boolean value is false, the element on which it appears is effectively excluded from the stylesheet module at compile time. If the attribute is used on the `<xsl:stylesheet>` or `<xsl:transform>` element itself, the effect is slightly different: the element itself is not excluded (because this would make the stylesheet invalid); instead, all the top-level declarations are excluded, so the stylesheet module becomes empty. This is only useful, of course, for an included or imported module.

The `use-when` attribute is discussed more fully in Chapter 3, page 127.

Usage

This attribute is provided to allow you to write stylesheets that are portable across different XSLT processors. For example, you can specify «use-when="system-property('xsl:is-schema- aware')='yes'"» to mark a section of stylesheet code that should be ignored by a processor that is not schema-aware, or you can test the «xsl:vendor» system property to include sections of code that are specific to particular XSLT implementations. You can also use the `function-available()` function to conditionally include or exclude sections of code based on whether a particular extension function is available in the implementation you are running on.

There are more examples of the use of this attribute in Chapter 3 (see page 127). It can be used on any XSLT element, both declarations (notably `<xsl:include>`, `<xsl:import>`, and

<xsl:import- schema>), and instructions. Just remember that the expression cannot access the source document, and it cannot access any variables: it is designed only to test properties of the environment in which the stylesheet is compiled. Check the documentation of system-property() in your chosen implementation to see whether it gives you access to environment variables set at the operating system level.

The version Attribute

The version attribute defines the version of the XSLT specification that the stylesheet is relying on. At present there are two published versions of the XSLT Recommendation, namely versions 1.0 and 2.0, so this attribute should take one of these two values.

Effect

The version attribute may be used to switch the XSLT processor into forward- or backward-compatibility mode. The rules are different for an XSLT 1.0 processor and a 2.0 processor, as shown in the table below.

version	XSLT 1.0 Processor	XSLT 2.0 Processor
less than 1.0	forward-compatible mode	backward-compatible mode
1.0	1.0 mode	backward-compatible mode
between 1.0 and 2.0	forward-compatible mode	backward-compatible mode
2.0	forward-compatible mode	2.0 mode
greater than 2.0	forward-compatible mode	forward-compatible mode

Forward-compatible mode and backward-compatible mode are explained in Chapter 3. In essence:

❑ Forward-compatible mode means that the stylesheet doesn't fail if it contains constructs defined in a later version of the specification, provided that it avoids executing those constructs (for example, by using <xsl:fallback>).

❑ Backward-compatible mode, which applies only to 2.0, means that certain constructs behave in a different way to retain compatibility with 1.0. Most notably, using a sequence of items where a single item is expected does not cause an error, it causes all items after the first to be ignored.

The version attribute applies to the entire stylesheet module, except any parts contained within an XSLT element that has a version attribute, or a literal result element that has an xsl:version attribute. Its scope is the stylesheet module, not the full stylesheet tree constructed by applying <xsl:include> and <xsl:import> elements.

Note that in XSLT 1.0, the version attribute was allowed only on the <xsl:stylesheet> element, and xsl:version was allowed on literal result elements. In XSLT 2.0 this has been relaxed, so version can be specified on any element in the XSLT namespace. If your stylesheet is likely to be executed by an XSLT 1.0 processor, it is best to use it only in the places where it was allowed in XSLT 1.0.

Some products (XMLSpy is an example) use the version attribute to decide which processor to invoke. So if your stylesheet specifies «version="1.0"», it will run with a real XSLT 1.0 processor, not with a 2.0 processor in backward-compatibility mode. This means it will fail if it tries to use any 2.0 constructs.

Usage

If your stylesheet only uses features from XSLT 1.0, it is probably best to specify «version="1.0"» on the <xsl:stylesheet> element. Then it will work with any XSLT processor that conforms to XSLT 1.0 or a later version of the standard. (It will fail, however, on an XSLT 2.0 processor that doesn't support backward-compatibility mode. If such processors become common, this advice may need to change.)

If the stylesheet uses 2.0 features, you should specify «version="2.0"» on the <xsl:stylesheet> element. An XSLT 2.0 processor that encounters a stylesheet with «version="1.0"» at the start of the principal stylesheet module is supposed to give you a warning about possible incompatibilities and then process the stylesheet as if it were a 2.0 stylesheet, but with backward-compatibility mode switched on. (This doesn't guarantee 100% compatibility, but it's pretty close.)

If your stylesheet says «version="1.0"» this won't stop you from using XSLT 2.0 features; an XSLT 2.0 processor isn't expected to look at every construct you use and decide whether it would have been allowed in XSLT 1.0. But for certain specific features, it causes XSLT 2.0 and XPath 2.0 to behave differently. The main examples of this is the "first item" rule mentioned earlier, where XSLT 1.0 takes the first item of a sequence and ignores the rest. This is most commonly encountered with the <xsl:value-of> instruction, described on page 495. Other differences are more rarified, for example «10 div 0» gives you Infinity in backward-compatibility mode, but throws an error in 2.0 mode.

XSLT 2.0 allows you to put the version attribute on any element in the stylesheet, and at first sight a nice idea would be to flag any template rule that uses XSLT 2.0 features by labeling it with the attribute «version="2.0"». Unfortunately, however, XSLT 1.0 doesn't allow the version attribute to appear on the <xsl:template> element, so if you want your stylesheet to still work with 1.0, this won't work. A better idea is probably to put all the template rules that depend on XSLT 2.0 in a separate module, and label this module with «version="2.0"» at the <xsl:stylesheet> level. Of course, you will still need to provide 1.0 fallback behavior whenever you use a 2.0 construct.

The **xpath-default-namespace** Attribute

A common source of bewilderment for XSLT 1.0 users is when they see a source document that looks like this:

```
<para>Some text here</para>
```

and they try to match this with a template rule like this:

```
<xsl:template match="para">
```

or perhaps to output the value with an expression like this:

```
<xsl:value-of select="para"/>
```

and nothing happens. Only with experience do you learn to look near the top of the document for a tell-tale default namespace declaration:

```
<document xmlns="http://www.megacorp.com/ns">
```

Sometimes the default namespace declaration is even more carefully hidden, being placed as a default attribute value in the DTD. The XHTML specification is an example that uses this infuriating technique: hiding in its DTD is the snippet:

```
<!ELEMENT html (head, body)>
<!ATTLIST html
  %i18n;
  id ID #IMPLIED
  xmlns %URI; #FIXED 'http://www.w3.org/1999/xhtml'
>
```

which has the effect that every element you use in a document that invokes this DTD, an element written as `<br/>` perhaps, is actually in the namespace «http://www.w3.org/1999/xhtml» although you probably didn't know it.

When you write «match="br"» or «select="br"» in your stylesheet, you are asking for `<br>` elements in the null namespace, and you will not match `<br>` elements in any non-null namespace. To match elements in the namespace «http://www.w3.org/1999/xhtml», you first have to declare this namespace in your stylesheet (with a specific prefix):

```
<xsl:stylesheet . . .
    xmlns:xhtml="http://www.w3.org/1999/xhtml">
```

and then use this prefix whenever you refer to elements in this namespace: «match="xhtml:br"» and «select="xhtml:br"».

Effect

XSLT 2.0 hasn't found any way of eliminating the frustration of not realizing that the source elements were actually in a namespace, but it has eliminated the tedium of adding all the prefixes to your patterns and XPath expressions once you've realized what the problem is. You can now declare the namespace as being the default namespace for elements in XPath expressions by writing:

```
<xsl:stylesheet . . .
    xpath-default-namespace="http://www.w3.org/1999/xhtml">
```

and the names used in expressions and patterns can then remain unprefixed.

As with other attributes on the `<xsl:stylesheet>` element, this attribute can also be specified on other elements in the stylesheet, including literal result elements (as `xsl:xpath-default-namespace`). This allows you to define a different default XPath namespace in different regions of the stylesheet, which is useful if the stylesheet is processing different source documents. (But it might be simpler in this case to split the stylesheet into different modules.) The attribute affects everything that is textually within its scope, and doesn't extend to included or imported modules.

The value is a namespace URI rather than a prefix, which means that the stylesheet doesn't actually need to declare this namespace. This is convenient because it means the namespace won't be automatically copied into the result document. You can also set it to a zero-length string to restore the default setting, which is that unprefixed names are assumed to refer to elements that are in no namespace.

481

The XPath default namespace affects unprefixed names appearing in the following contexts:

❑ Element names (but not attribute names) appearing in path expressions: That is, an NCName used as a NameTest in an AxisStep, when the axis is one that selects elements.

❑ Element names used similarly in patterns.

❑ Element names and type names (but not attribute names) used in the SequenceType syntax for defining types, whether the SequenceType syntax is used within an XPath expression, or on its own within an «as» attribute in the stylesheet.

❑ Type names used in an XPath cast expression, for example «"MF00325Z" cast as part-number».

❑ Type names used in a «type» attribute in the stylesheet.

❑ Element names used in <xsl:strip-space> and <xsl:preserve-space>.

Note that although the namespace applies to unprefixed names appearing in a cast expression, it does not apply to the names of functions, including constructor functions such as «part-number ("MF00325Z")» where the function name is based on the name of a user-defined type in a schema. With constructor functions the namespace must always be given explicitly; an unprefixed function name can only be used for functions in the core library (that is, standard XSLT and XPath functions).

This means that if you import a schema with no target namespace, you cannot use constructor functions to create instances of the atomic types defined in that schema. Instead, you must use the more long-winded cast syntax. (In fact, this is the main reason that the cast syntax has been retained in the XPath language.)

> The XPath 2.0 specification refers to a concept called the default function namespace, which is the namespace in which unprefixed function names are located. Although XPath allows this to be defined as part of the evaluation context, XSLT does not pass this capability on to the user. When XPath expressions are used in XSLT stylesheets, the default function namespace is always the standard namespace http://www.w3.org/2005/xpath-functions. This means that calls on standard functions such as position() and last() never need to be prefixed in XSLT, though you can use a prefix that is bound to the standard namespace if you really want to.

Usage

I would recommend always using this attribute when your source documents use a default namespace declaration; the value should be the namespace URI of this default namespace declaration. Specifying an xpath-default-namespace will not stop existing code working that uses explicit prefixes to refer to names in this namespace.

One thing to watch out for is that if your stylesheet creates and uses temporary documents, the chances are that these don't use namespaces. Specifying an xpath-default-namespace makes it impossible to refer to names that are in the null namespace, for example elements in such a temporary document (you can't bind a namespace prefix to the null namespace, unfortunately). In this situation you can override the xpath-default-namespace in the relevant region of your stylesheet by writing «xpath-default-namespace="">».

If your stylesheet processes multiple source documents of different types, similar considerations apply. In this case it might be clearer to use explicit namespace prefixes for everything.

See Also

<xsl:transform> on page 495

xsl:template

The `<xsl:template>` element defines a template for producing output. It may be invoked either by matching nodes against a pattern, or explicitly by name.

Changes in 2.0

It is now possible to define a template rule that matches in multiple modes.

The new «as» attribute allows the type of the result to be defined. Moreover, the new `<xsl:sequence>` instruction means that a template can now return atomic values and references to existing nodes; it is no longer limited to constructing new nodes.

The syntax for patterns has been extended so that a template rule can now match nodes according to their schema-defined type. The match pattern may also now contain references to global variables or parameters.

Nonsensical combinations of attributes are now considered to be errors; for example, specifying `priority` or `mode` when there is no `match` attribute. In XSLT 1.0, such attributes were ignored.

Format

```
<xsl:template
  match? = pattern
  name? = qname
  priority? = number
  mode? = tokens
  as? = sequence-type>
  <!-- Content: (xsl:param*, sequence-constructor) -->
</xsl:template>
```

Position

`<xsl:template>` is a declaration, which means that it always appears as a child of the `<xsl:stylesheet>` element.

Attributes

Name	Value	Meaning
match optional	Pattern	A pattern that determines which nodes are eligible to be processed by this template. If this attribute is absent, there must be a `name` attribute.
name optional	Lexical QName	The name of the template. If this attribute is absent, there must be a `match` attribute.
priority optional	Number	A number (positive or negative, integer or decimal) that denotes the priority of this template and is used when several templates match the same node.

continued

6

XSLT Elements

Name	Value	Meaning
mode optional	Whitespace-separated list of mode names, or «#all»	The mode or modes to which this template rule applies. When `<xsl:apply-templates>` is used to process a set of nodes, the only templates considered are those with a matching mode.
as optional	SequenceType	The type of the sequence produced when this template is evaluated. A type error is reported if the result does not match this type.

The construct `Pattern` is defined in Chapter 12, while `SequenceType` is defined in Chapter 11.

The `mode` and `priority` attributes must not be specified unless the `match` attribute is also specified.

Content

Zero or more `<xsl:param>` elements, followed by a sequence constructor.

Effect

There must be either a `match` attribute or a `name` attribute, or both.

❑   If there is a `match` attribute, the `<xsl:template>` element defines a template rule that can be invoked using the `<xsl:apply-templates>` instruction.

❑   If there is a `name` attribute, the `<xsl:template>` element defines a named template that can be invoked using the `<xsl:call-template>` instruction.

❑   If both attributes are present, the template can be invoked in either of these ways.

The match Attribute

The match attribute is a `Pattern`, as defined in Chapter 12. The pattern is used to define which nodes this template rule applies to.

When `<xsl:apply-templates>` is used to process a selected set of nodes, each node is processed using the best-fit template rule for this node, as described under `<xsl:apply-templates>` on page 240.

A template is only considered a candidate if the node matches the pattern supplied in the `match` attribute and if the value of the `mode` attribute matches the `mode` attribute of the `<xsl:apply-templates>` instruction (as described on page 242).

If more than one template rule meets these criteria, they are first considered in order of import precedence (as described under `<xsl:import>` on page 359), and only templates with the highest import precedence are considered further.

If there is still more than one template rule (in other words, if two template rules that both match the node have the same import precedence), they are next considered in order of priority. The priority is either given by the value of the `priority` attribute, described below, or is a default priority that depends on the `match` pattern. The rules for determining the default priority of any pattern are given in Chapter 12, on page 686.

If this leaves one pattern with a numerically higher priority than all the others, this one is chosen. If there are several with the same priority, which is higher than all the others, the XSLT processor has the choice of reporting an error or choosing from the remaining templates the one that appears last in the stylesheet. Several processors in practice report a warning, which you can ignore if you wish. In my experience, however, this condition often indicates that the stylesheet author has overlooked something.

XSLT 2.0 allows the pattern to contain a reference to a global variable or parameter. This allows a pattern such as «match="part[@number=$param]"», which means that the same pattern will match different nodes on different runs of the stylesheet. But there are rules to prevent circular definitions: evaluating the variable must not invoke an <xsl:apply-templates> instruction, either directly or indirectly.

There are special rules concerning the handling of errors that occur when matching a node against a pattern. Theoretically, when you execute an <xsl:apply-templates/> instruction, the processor could evaluate every pattern against the selected nodes. This means that failures can occur if a pattern is inappropriate to the type of node: for example the pattern «B[.=3]» would give a type error when matching an element containing a date. The specification allows the processor to ignore this error and simply treat the pattern as not matching that particular node. This causes few problems in practice, but it creates the danger that real errors go unnoticed. It's best to keep patterns simple enough that runtime errors cannot occur while evaluating them.

The name Attribute

The name attribute is a lexical QName; that is, a name optionally qualified with a namespace prefix. If there is a prefix, it must correspond to a namespace declaration that is in scope on this element (which means it must be defined either on this element itself or on the <xsl:stylesheet> element). If there is no prefix, the namespace URI is null; the default namespace is not used.

This name is used when the template is invoked using <xsl:call-template>. The name attribute of the <xsl:call-template> element must match the name attribute of the <xsl:template> element. Two names match if they have the same local part and the same namespace URI, but the prefix can be different.

If there is more than one named template in the stylesheet with the same name, the one with higher import precedence is used; for details, see <xsl:import> on page 359. It is an error to have two templates in the stylesheet with the same name and the same import precedence, unless there is another one with the same name and a higher import precedence. This is an error even if the template is never called.

The priority Attribute

The priority attribute is a number, for example «17», «0.5», or «-3»: more specifically, an xs:decimal as defined in XML Schema, which allows an optional leading sign.

The priority attribute is used to decide which template to invoke when <xsl:apply-templates> is called and there are several possible candidates. For each node selected by the <xsl:apply-templates> instruction, a template rule is chosen using the following procedure:

- ❏ First select all the templates that have a match attribute.
- ❏ From these, select all the templates that match the mode that is used on the call of <xsl:apply-templates>. An <xsl:apply-templates> instruction uses either a specific mode (identified by a QName) or the default mode (which is unnamed) or it can specify «#current», in which case it uses whatever mode is the current mode at the time. An <xsl:template> element can specify a list of modes that it matches (which can include «#default» to indicate that it matches the default mode), or it can specify «#all» to indicate that it matches all modes; if it has no mode attribute, then it matches only the default mode.

❑   From these, select all those whose pattern matches the selected node.

❑   If there is more than one, select those that have the highest import precedence.

❑   If there is still more than one, select those that have the numerically highest priority.

If there are several matching templates left, and they all have the same import precedence and priority, the XSLT processor can either choose the one that occurs last in declaration order or report an error. Import precedence and declaration order are described under `<xsl:import>` on page 359.

If there are no templates that match the selected node, the built-in template for the relevant node kind is used. Built-in templates are described under `<xsl:apply-templates>` on page 243.

The rules for determining the default priority for a pattern are given in Chapter 12, on page 686.

Although the default priorities are carefully chosen, they do not guarantee that a highly selective pattern will always have higher priority than a less selective pattern. For example, the patterns «section/para» and «section/para[1]» both have priority +0.5. Similarly, the patterns «attribute(*, xs:integer)» and «attribute(*, xs:decimal)» have the same priority, even though the nodes that match the first pattern are a subset of those that match the second. Choosing your own priorities is therefore a more reliable approach.

The mode Attribute

If the `<xsl:template>` element has no mode attribute, then it applies only to the default (unnamed) mode, and it will be invoked only in response to an `<xsl:apply-templates>` instruction that uses the default mode. An `<xsl:apply-templates>` instruction uses the default mode if it has no mode attribute, if its mode attribute has the value «#default», or if its mode attribute has the value «#current» and the current mode is the default mode. The concept of the current mode is explained on page 238.

If the mode attribute is present and has the value «#all», then the template is applicable to all modes.

The mode attribute may also contain a list of modes to which the template is applicable. Each mode is written either as a lexical QName (the actual mode name) or as the token «#default» to indicate that the template is applicable to the default mode.

Mode names are compared using the usual rules for QNames — they match if the local name and namespace URI both match.

The mode specified on the `<xsl:template>` template is *not* automatically propagated to any `<xsl:apply-templates>` elements within its body. Although it is common practice to process an entire subtree in a single mode, and therefore for a template to continue using the mode it was called in, this is not the default behavior except in the case of built-in templates. However, the current mode can be propagated by explicitly calling `<xsl:apply-templates mode ="#current"/>`.

If you have a mode attribute on a template and there is no `<xsl:apply-templates>` element with a matching mode anywhere in the stylesheet, this is not an error, though it means the template will never be selected by any `<xsl:apply-templates>` call (it could however be invoked from the calling application if an initial mode is specified). This can be a handy way of commenting out a template rule.

Evaluating a Template

Once an `<xsl:template>` element is selected for processing, the following occurs:

❑   If it was called using `<xsl:apply-templates>`, the context node, context position, and context size are set up as required.

❑   A new stack frame is allocated, to hold a new instance of each local variable defined within the template.

❑   All parameters listed in `<xsl:param>` elements contained within the `<xsl:template>` element are evaluated. These `<xsl:param>` elements must come before any instructions in the content of the template. For each parameter, if a value was supplied by the caller (using an `<xsl:with-param>` element with matching name), this value is assigned to the parameter. If necessary, the supplied values are converted to the required type specified in the «as» attribute, using the standard conversion rules described on page 505. If the supplied value has the wrong type, an error is reported. If no value was supplied by the caller, then if the `<xsl:param>` element specifies «required="yes"» an error is reported; otherwise, the default value of the parameter is evaluated. This process is explained in more detail under `<xsl:param>` on page 425.

❑   The sequence constructor is evaluated. This means that the child instructions of the `<xsl:template>` element are evaluated to produce a result sequence. XSLT instructions and extension elements are processed using their individual rules; literal result elements and text nodes are written to the result sequence.

❑   The result of evaluating the sequence constructor is checked against the type given in the «as» attribute of the `<xsl:template>` element, if any. If necessary, the value is converted to the required type using the standard conversion rules given on page 505. If the value has the wrong type, a fatal error is reported.

When processing of the sequence constructor is complete, the stack frame containing its local variables is discarded, control returns to the calling template, and the context item, position, and size revert to their previous values. The value produced by evaluating the sequence constructor becomes the return value of the calling `<xsl:apply-templates>`, `<xsl:call-template>`, `<xsl:apply-imports>`, or `<xsl:next-match>` instruction. (If the calling instruction was `<xsl:apply-templates>`, the value is combined with the values delivered by the template rules for other selected nodes.)

The implementation, of course, is free to do things in a different order if it has the same effect. Some products use lazy evaluation, where the parameters are only evaluated when they are first used. Some products also use tail-call optimization, where a recursive template call is deferred until after the stack has been unwound; this reduces the risk of running out of stack space when calls are deeply nested. Such optimizations may show up if you use extension functions that have side effects, or if you use `<xsl:message>` to trace the sequence of execution.

Usage and Examples

We will look first at using template rules, and then I will give some advice on the use of modes. For examples of the use of named templates, see `<xsl:call-template>` on page 271.

Using Template Rules

A *template rule* is an `<xsl:template>` element with a `match` attribute, which can therefore be invoked using the `<xsl:apply-templates>` instruction.

This rule-based approach to processing is the characteristic way of writing XSLT stylesheets, though it is by no means the only way. Its biggest advantage is that the output for each element type can be defined independently of the context that the element appears in, which makes it very easy to reuse element types in different contexts or to add new element types to an existing document definition without rewriting the stylesheet templates for all the possible containing elements. A classic example of this approach to processing arises when converting semantic markup in a document to rendition markup, as the following example demonstrates.

Example: Template Rules

This example shows a typical use of template rules to handle narrative text with a free-form structure.

Source

The source file is `review.xml`.

This text contains the review of a concert performance, using both structured (data) and narrative (document) markup. Omitting some of the detail, it reads:

```
<review>
<event>
  <venue>Wigmore Hall</venue>
  <city>London</city>
  <date>2007-03-27</date>
  <artist>Carducci String Quartet</artist>
</event>
<text>
  <para>Back at the <venue>Wigmore Hall</venue> on <date iso=
"2007-03-27">27 March</date> another fine group, the <artist>Carducci
Quartet</artist>, was joined by pianist <artist>Nicola Eimer</artist>
for a programme of <composer>Mozart</composer>, <composer>Ravel
</composer> and <composer>Schumann</composer>. Following the current
fashion for the chamber versions of <composer>Mozart</composer>
concertos, the players opened with a lively and shapely performance of his
<work composer="Mozart" opus="K414">A major Concerto K414</work>. ....
  </para>
</text>
<byline>
  <author>Tim Homfray</author>
  <publication>The Strad</publication>
  <date iso="2007-06">June 2007</date>
</byline>
</review>
```

Stylesheet

The stylesheet file is `review.xsl`.

This stylesheet resists the temptation to use varied fonts for the names of composers and artists, but merely uses italics for names of musical works:

```
<xsl:stylesheet version="2.0"
    xmlns:xsl="http://www.w3.org/1999/XSL/Transform">

<xsl:template match="/">
<html>
```

```
    <head>
      <title><xsl:value-of select="review/event/artist"/></title>
      <style>
        body {
          font-family: Verdana, Arial, Helvetica, sans-serif;
          font-size: 10pt;
          font-style:normal;
          color: #3D5B96;
          line-height: 14pt;
        }v
      </style>
    </head>
    <body>
      <xsl:apply-templates/>
    </body>
  </html>
</xsl:template>

<xsl:template match="event">
<h1>
  <xsl:value-of select="artist, venue, format-date(date, '[D] [MNn,3] [Y]')"
                separator=" - "/>
</h1>
</xsl:template>

<xsl:template match="para">
   <p><xsl:apply-templates/></p>
</xsl:template>

<xsl:template match="para/*">
   <xsl:apply-templates/>
</xsl:template>

<xsl:template match="para/work" priority="2">
   <i><xsl:apply-templates/></i>
</xsl:template>

<xsl:template match="byline">
   <p style="font-weight: bold; font-style:italic">
     <xsl:value-of select="author, publication, date" separator=", "/>
   </p>
</xsl:template>

</xsl:stylesheet>
```

Note the use of CSS to achieve the styling, and the use of a priority attribute on the template for «match="para/work"» to ensure that it is selected in preference to the template for «match="para/*"». In fact, the template for «match="para/*"» (which handles all children of <para> other than <work>) does exactly what the built-in template would do — it outputs the text without any markup — but it does no harm to make it explicit.

Output

If the generated HTML is displayed in a browser, it will look like Figure 6-14.

489

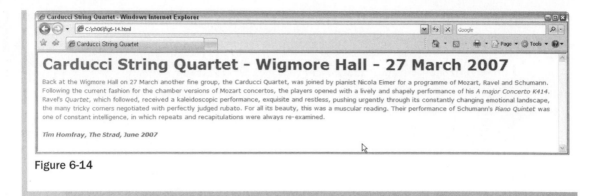

Figure 6-14

This stylesheet demonstrates a mixture of rigidly structured data processed using `<xsl:value-of>` instructions, sometimes called *pull* processing, and narrative markup processed using `<xsl:apply-templates>` instructions, referred to as *push* processing. The great advantage of the *push* approach is that the rules are written making no assumptions about the way the markup tags are nested in the source document. It is very easy to add new rules for new tags and to reuse rules if an existing tag is used in a new context.

Where the nesting of elements is more rigid, this very flexible rule-based style of processing has fewer benefits, so the *pull* programming style using `<xsl:value-of>` in conjunction with conventional flow-of-control constructs such as `<xsl:for-each>`, `<xsl:if>`, and `<xsl:call-template>` is often used. For further discussion of the different design approaches, see Chapter 17.

Using Modes

The classic reason for using modes is to enable the same content to be processed more than once in different ways; for example, the first pass through the document might generate the table of contents, the second pass the actual text, and the third pass an index.

Example: Using modes

The source document is a concert review in the same format as in the previous example. This time, however, the requirement is to produce at the end of the review a list of works mentioned in the text.

Source

The source file is `review.xml`. See previous example.

Stylesheet

The stylesheet file is `review + index.xsl`.

This stylesheet extends the previous one using `<xsl:import>`. After outputting the text as before, it now creates a table listing the works mentioned in the text. Note the use of an empty template rule with «`match="text()"`» to ensure that when the text is processed with «mode="index"», nothing is output. The only output comes from the template rule that matches <work> elements.

```
<xsl:stylesheet version="2.0"
    xmlns:xsl="http://www.w3.org/1999/XSL/Transform">

<xsl:import href="review.xsl"/>

<xsl:template match="review">
  <xsl:next-match/>
  <h2>Index of Works</h2>
  <table width="100%">
  <tr><th align="left">Composer</th><th align="left">Title</th>
      <th align="left">Opus</th></tr>
  <xsl:apply-templates select="text" mode="index"/>
  </table>
</xsl:template>

<xsl:template match="text()" mode="index"/>

<xsl:template match="para/work" mode="index">
    <tr>
    <td><xsl:value-of select="@composer"/></td>
    <td><xsl:value-of select="."/></td>
    <td><xsl:value-of select="@opus"/></td>
    </tr>
</xsl:template>

</xsl:stylesheet>
```

Output

The output is as shown in Figure 6-15.

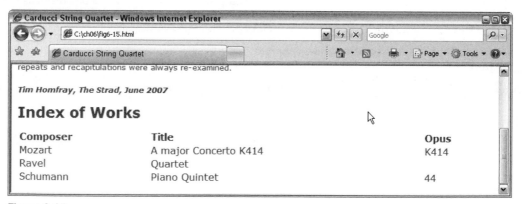

Figure 6-15

See Also

`<xsl:apply-templates>` on page 240
`<xsl:apply-imports>` on page 237
`<xsl:call-template>` on page 271
`generate-id()` function in Chapter 7, on page 797

xsl:text

The `<xsl:text>` instruction is used within a sequence constructor to output literal text to the result sequence. The main purpose of wrapping an `<xsl:text>` element around literal text is to control the output of whitespace.

Changes in 2.0

None.

Format

```
<xsl:text
  disable-output-escaping? = "yes" | "no">
  <!-- Content: character data -->
</xsl:text>
```

Position

`<xsl:text>` is an instruction. It is always used as part of a sequence constructor.

Attributes

Name	Value	Meaning
disable-output-escaping optional, deprecated	«yes» or «no»	The value «yes» indicates that special characters in the output (such as «<») should be output as is, rather than using an XML escape form such as «<». The default value is «no».

Content

A text node. The element may also be empty. It must not contain other elements such as `<xsl:value-of>`.

Effect

Text appearing within a sequence constructor in the stylesheet is copied to the result sequence (in the form of a new text node), whether it is enclosed by `<xsl:text>` or not. The only direct effect of enclosing text in an `<xsl:text>` element is that the handling of whitespace is different. A whitespace node appearing in the stylesheet (that is, a text node that consists only of whitespace) is copied to the result tree only if :

❑   it appears within an `<xsl:text>` element, or

❑   an enclosing element has the attribute «xml:space="preserve"», and this is not overridden by an inner enclosing element specifying «xml:space="default"»

The `disable-output-escaping` attribute controls whether special characters such as «<» should be escaped (that is, converted to a character reference or entity reference such as «<») if they appear in the text. The default value is «no». This attribute is deprecated but is retained for backward compatibility with XSLT 1.0; for further information, see page 945 in Chapter 15.

Usage

There are two main reasons for using `<xsl:text>`, which are to control the output of whitespace, and to disable the escaping of special characters by the serializer. The `disable-output-escaping` attribute is deprecated in XSLT 2.0, but there are still cases where it is useful; for details, see Chapter 15. The following section describes the more orthodox use of `<xsl:text>` to control whitespace.

Whitespace Control

The most obvious case where `<xsl:text>` is useful is to force output of whitespace. An example is given in the XSLT specification. If you write:

```
<xsl:value-of select="first-name"/> <xsl:value-of select="last-name"/>
```

the space between the first name and the last name will be lost, because it is part of a node that contains whitespace only (a single space character). To force a space to appear between the first name and the last name, write:

```
<xsl:value-of select="first-name"/>
<xsl:text> </xsl:text>
<xsl:value-of select="last-name"/>
```

The arrangement on three lines here is purely for readability, but it does not affect the output, because the newline characters are now in whitespace-only nodes that will not be output.

If you find this long-winded, another way of achieving the same effect is to write:

```
<xsl:value-of select="first-name, last-name" separator=" "/>
```

The other aspect of the problem is to prevent the output of unwanted whitespace. Fortunately in HTML output extra whitespace usually doesn't matter, because the browser will ignore it. For XML or text output, however, avoiding unwanted whitespace can be important.

If you are suffering from excess whitespace in your output, the first thing to establish is whether it comes from the source document or from the stylesheet. If the whitespace is adjacent to text copied from the source document, then it probably comes from the source document, but if it is adjacent to text that appears in the stylesheet, then this is the most likely source. Check also that the unwanted whitespace isn't coming from the serializer, by setting `<xsl:output indent="no"/>`.

If the unwanted whitespace comes from the source document, consider using `<xsl:strip-space>` to remove nodes consisting entirely of whitespace, or the `normalize-space()` function to remove leading and trailing spaces around visible text.

The `<xsl:text>` element can be used to suppress unwanted whitespace that originates in the stylesheet. For example, consider the following template:

```
<xsl:template match="stage-direction">
   [ <xsl:value-of select="."/> ]
</xsl:template>
```

The intention here is to output a stage direction enclosed in square brackets. But the text nodes containing the opening and closing square brackets also contain a newline character and several spaces, which will be written to the output destination along with the brackets themselves. To prevent this behavior, the simplest way is to wrap an `<xsl:text>` element around the text you want to output, thus:

```
<xsl:template match="stage-direction">
    <xsl:text>[ </xsl:text>
    <xsl:value-of select="."/>
    <xsl:text> ]<xsl:text/>
</xsl:template>
```

A variation on this, which works equally well, is to delimit the text with empty `<xsl:text>` elements:

```
<xsl:template match="stage-direction">
    <xsl:text/>[ <xsl:value-of select="."/> ]<xsl:text/>
</xsl:template>
```

The effect of this is that the extra newlines and spaces now belong to whitespace-only nodes, which are stripped from the stylesheet and ignored.

Examples

Here are two simple examples using `<xsl:text>` to control the output of whitespace:

1. Output first-name and last-name, separated by a space:

    ```
    <xsl:value-of select="first-name"/>
    <xsl:text> </xsl:text>
    <xsl:value-of select-"last-name"/>
    ```

    Another way to achieve the same effect is to use the `concat()` function:

    ```
    <xsl:value-of select="concat(first-name, ' ', last-name)"/>
    ```

2. Output a comma-separated list of values:

    ```
    <xsl:output method="text"/>
    <xsl:template match="book">
      <xsl:value-of select="title"/>,<xsl:text/>
      <xsl:value-of select="author"/>,<xsl:text/>
      <xsl:value-of select="price"/>,<xsl:text/>
      <xsl:value-of select="isbn"/><xsl:text>
    </xsl:text>
    </xsl:template>
    ```

    The purpose of the empty `<xsl:text/>` elements is to split the comma and the following newline character into separate text nodes; this ensures that the newline character becomes part of a whitespace-only node and is therefore not copied to the output. The final `<xsl:text>` element ensures that a newline is written at the end of each record.

    Another way to achieve this is with the separator attribute of `<xsl:value-of>`:

    ```
    <xsl:value-of select="title, author, price, isbn" separator=","/>
    ```

See Also

`<xsl:character-map>` on page 280
`<xsl:value-of>` on this page

xsl:transform

This is a synonym of `<xsl:stylesheet>`, described on page 465. The two element names may be used interchangeably.

Why is it useful to have two names for the same thing? Probably because it's the easiest way for a standards committee to keep all its members happy. More seriously, the existence of these two names is indicative of the fact that some people see XSLT as being primarily a language for transforming trees, while others see its main role as defining presentation styles. Take your pick.

Format

```
<xsl:transform
  id? = id
  default-collation? = uri-list
  default-validation? = "preserve" | "strip"
  exclude-result-prefixes? = tokens
  extension-element-prefixes? = tokens
  input-type-annotations? = "preserve" | "strip" | "unspecified"
  use-when? = expression
  version = number
  xpath-default-namespace? = uri

  <!-- Content: (xsl:import*, other-declarations) -->
</xsl:transform>
```

See Also

`<xsl:stylesheet>` on page 465

xsl:value-of

The `<xsl:value-of>` instruction constructs a text node, and writes it to the result sequence.

Changes in 2.0

In XSLT 2.0 the value to be output can be obtained by evaluating a contained sequence constructor as an alternative to using the `select` attribute.

A `separator` attribute has been added, allowing a sequence of values to be output separated by spaces, commas, or any other convenient string.

Format

```
<xsl:value-of
  select? = expression
  separator? = { string}
  disable-output-escaping? = "yes" | "no">
```

```
<!-- content: sequence-constructor -->
</xsl:value-of>
```

Position

`<xsl:value-of>` is an instruction. It is always used as part of a sequence constructor.

Attributes

Name	Value	Meaning
select optional	XPath Expression	The value to be output.
separator optional	Attribute value template returning a string	A string to be used to separate adjacent items in the output.
disable-output-escaping optional, deprecated	«yes» or «no»	The value «yes» indicates that special characters in the output (such as «<») should be output as is, rather than using an XML escape form such as «<». The default value is «no».

Content

If the `select` attribute is present, the element must be empty. Otherwise, it may contain a sequence constructor.

Effect

The most common use of `<xsl:value-of>` is to select a node, and output the value of that node as a string. For example, `<xsl:value-of select="@dept"/>` outputs the string value of the `dept` attribute of the context node. In the general case, however, the rules are more complicated.

The `select` expression or the contained *sequence-constructor* is evaluated. Adjacent text nodes in the resulting sequence are merged, and zero-length text nodes are removed. The sequence is then atomized, which causes any nodes in the sequence to be replaced by their typed values.

If the atomized sequence is empty, the result of the `<xsl:value-of>` instruction is a text node containing a zero-length string. Text nodes are allowed to be zero-length so long as they have no parent. But if you try to use a zero-length text node to form the content of an element, the text node disappears in the process.

If the atomized sequence contains a single value, this is converted to a string (by applying the XPath 2.0 casting rules). A new text node is constructed with this string as its value, and the text node is returned as the result of the `<xsl:value-of>` instruction (which usually means it will be written to a result tree). If the sequence contains more than one item, then the effect depends on whether backward-compatibility mode is enabled. This depends on the nearest `version` or `xsl:version` attribute found on a containing element, known as the effective version. If the effective version is less than «2.0», then backward-compatibility mode is in force. However, if there is a `separator` attribute, then the instruction behaves according to the XSLT 2.0 rules regardless of the effective version.

Under the backward-compatibility rules, any item after the first in the sequence is discarded, and the instruction behaves as if the sequence only contained one item.

Under the 2.0 rules, each value in the atomized sequence is converted to a string by applying the XPath casting rules, and these strings are concatenated, with the chosen separator inserted between adjacent strings. A new text node is constructed that contains this string as its value, and the text node is returned as the result of the instruction. The default separator (under the 2.0 rules) is a single space when the `select` attribute is used, or a zero-length string when a sequence constructor is used. This means that

```
<a><xsl:value-of select="1 to 5"/></a>
```

will output:

```
<a>1 2 3 4 5</a>
```

but:

```
<a>
  <xsl:value-of>[<xsl:sequence select="1 to 5"/>]</xsl:value-of>
</a>
```

will output:

```
<a>[12345]</a>
```

The deprecated `disable-output-escaping` attribute has the same effect as it has with `<xsl:text>`. Special characters such as «<» in the string value of the select expression will be escaped just as if they occurred in literal text, and the `disable-output-escaping` attribute can be used to suppress this in the same way. For details, see Chapter 15 on page 945.

Usage

The `<xsl:value-of>` element is the most common way of writing text to a result tree.

Because the instruction is so common, it is often used unthinkingly when other constructs might be more appropriate. For example, it is very common to encounter code such as:

```
<xsl:variable name="x">
    <xsl:value-of select="a/b/c/d"/>
</xsl:variable>
```

when it would be much more appropriate to write:

```
<xsl:variable name="x" select="a/b/c/d"/>
```

The difference is that the first variable creates a new temporary tree containing a document node and a text node, with the text node being a copy of data selected from the input document; the second variable is simply a reference to the selected node in the source. So the second construct is not only shorter and more readable, it is also likely to be much more efficient. The optimizer can't simply treat the two constructs as equivalent, because they are not. For example, if «a/b/c/d» selects nothing, then «empty($x)» will return false in the first case, true in the second.

Similarly, when a function returns a string result, people sometimes write code like this:

```
<xsl:function name="f:string-function" as="xs:string">
  <xsl:param name="p"/>
  <xsl:value-of select="upper-case($p)"/>
</xsl:function>
```

Here «upper-case($p)» returns a string. The <xsl:value-of> instruction creates a text node with this string as its value. Because the function is declared to return xs:string, the text node is then atomized to extract the original string. The system would have to do a lot less work if these multiple conversions were avoided, which can be achieved simply by replacing <xsl:value-of> with <xsl:sequence>.

Nevertheless, the <xsl:value-of> instruction has a useful role to play. If you really do want to create a text node — in particular, if you are creating the content of an element — then <xsl:value-of> is the right way to do it.

The following example shows the correct use of <xsl:value-of> to create the content of new element nodes:

```
<xsl:template match="book">
   <book>
      <publisher><xsl:value-of select="../@name"/></publisher>
      <title><xsl:value-of select="@title"/></title>
      <author><xsl:value-of select="@author"/></author>
      <isbn><xsl:value-of select="@isbn"/></isbn>
   </book>
</xsl:template>
```

The new XSLT 2.0 option to use the sequence constructor to obtain the value, rather than the select attribute, is provided mainly to make <xsl:value-of> compatible with other instructions such as <xsl:attribute> and <xsl:comment>. But there are some cases where it can be very useful. Consider the following:

```
<xsl:function name="f:section-title" as="xs:string">
   <xsl:param name="section" as="element()"/>
   <xsl:value-of>
      <xsl:number select="$section" format="I"/>
      <xsl:text> </xsl:text>
      <xsl:value-of select="$section/title"/>
   </xsl:value-of>
</xsl:section>
```

Without the outer <xsl:value-of> element, the body of this function would create three text nodes, and this would cause a type error, because a sequence of three text nodes cannot be converted to the declared return type of the function, xs:string. The effect of the outer <xsl:value-of> instruction is to concatenate the three text nodes into one, and a single text node can be converted to a string, so the function succeeds. In effect, the <xsl:value-of> instruction is doing the same thing at the XSLT level as the concat() function does at the XPath level.

Avoiding Surprises

There are two situations in which <xsl:value-of> might not give the result you expect.

The first should be less common with XSLT 2.0 than it was with 1.0, but it will still happen in stylesheets that specify «version="1.0"» and thus invoke backward-compatibility mode. The surprise is that only the first item in a sequence is actually output. For example, if the context node is a <book> element and you specify <xsl:value-of select="author"/>, only the first author (in document order) will actually be output. This changes when you specify «version="2.0"»: all the authors are now output, using a single space as the default separator.

Of course, if you have become accustomed to the 1.0 behavior, then the surprise might be the other way around. If your stylesheet specifies <xsl:value-of select="following-sibling::para"/>, then when you change it to say «version="2.0"», the output will contain all the following sibling paragraphs rather than just the first. You can easily correct this by changing it to <xsl:value-of select="following-sibling::para[1]"/>.

The second situation that sometimes causes surprise is typified by the question "Why have all the tags disappeared?" If you use <xsl:value-of> to output an element such as a <para> element that contains complex or mixed content, then it will extract the value of this element as a string. If there are nested elements, for example elements marked up by tags such as <i> or <b>, then these are lost in the course of converting to a string. If you want these tags to appear in the output, then use <xsl:copy-of> to copy the element, not <xsl:value-of>.

This situation may also change in XSLT 2.0 if you use a schema-aware processor. If the select expression selects an element, and the element is described in the schema as having complex element-only content, then atomization will raise a runtime error. For example if the source document contains the element:

```
<book>
    <title>XSLT 2.0 Programmer's Reference</title>
    <author>Michael Kay</author>
    <publisher>Wiley</publisher>
</book>
```

then with a processor that is not schema-aware (or an XSLT 1.0 processor), the instruction <xsl:value-of select="book"/> will produce the output:

```
XSLT 2.0 Programmer's ReferenceMichael KayWiley
```

But with a schema-aware processor, assuming the schema declaration is:

```
<xs:element name="book">
    <xs:complexType>
        <xs:sequence>
            <xs:element name="title" type="xs:string"/>
            <xs:element name="author" type="xs:string"/>
            <xs:element name="publisher" type="xs:string"/>
        </xs:sequence>
    </xs:complexType>
</xs:element>
```

the result will be a runtime error. If you want to concatenate the text nodes within the <book> element, then you can still do so, by writing <xsl:value-of select="string(book)"/>, but it's not something that atomization will do automatically for you. This is because, for data-oriented XML, it doesn't usually make sense.

With mixed content, however (where text and marked-up elements can be freely mixed in the content), it does make sense to extract the textual content without the markup, and <xsl:value-of> will do this whether or not there is a schema. Mixed content is described in the schema using <xs:complexType mixed="true">.

Examples

The table below shows some common ways in which `<xsl:value-of>` is used.

Instruction	Effect
`<xsl:value-of select="."/>`	Create a text node containing the string value of the context item.
`<xsl:value-of select="title"/>`	Create a text node containing the string values of the child `<title>` elements of the context node, space separated. (In 1.0 mode, discard all but the first `<title>`.)
`<xsl:value-of select="sum(@*)"/>`	Create a text node containing the sum of the values of the attributes of the current node, converted to a string. If there is any non-numeric attribute, the result will be NaN or, if a schema is in use, a type error.
`<xsl:value-of select="$x"/>`	Create a text node containing the value of variable $x, after converting it to a string.

See Also

`<xsl:copy-of>` on page 292
`<xsl:text>` on page 492

xsl:variable

The `<xsl:variable>` element is used to declare a local or global variable in a stylesheet, and to give it a value.

Changes in 2.0

A new attribute, «as», has been introduced. This allows the type of the variable to be declared; it also determines whether an `<xsl:variable>` element containing a sequence constructor will use the value of the sequence to construct a temporary document or will simply set the value of the variable to be this sequence.

Format

```
<xsl:variable
  name = qname
  select? = expression
  as? = sequence-type>
  <!-- Content: sequence-constructor -->
</xsl:variable>
```

Position

The `<xsl:variable>` element may appear either as a top-level declaration (that is, as a child of the `<xsl:stylesheet>` element), or as an instruction within a sequence constructor.

Attributes

Name	Value	Meaning
name mandatory	Lexical QName	The name of the variable.
select optional	Expression	An expression that is evaluated to give the value of the variable. If omitted, the value is determined from the contents of the `<xsl:variable>` element.
as optional	SequenceType	Declares the type of the variable. A type error occurs if the value of the expression cannot be converted to this type using the standard type conversions defined below (page 505). In addition, the presence of this attribute on an `<xsl:variable>` element with nonempty content indicates that the result of evaluating the contained sequence constructor is to be used directly as the value of the variable, rather than being used to construct a temporary document.

The `SequenceType` construct is described in Chapter 11.

Content

An optional sequence constructor. If a `select` attribute is present, the `<xsl:variable>` element must be empty.

Effect

An `<xsl:variable>` element may appear either at the top level of the stylesheet (in which case it declares a global variable) or as an instruction within a sequence constructor (in which case it declares a local variable).

The Name of the Variable

The name of the variable is defined by a lexical QName. Normally, this will be a simple name such as «city» or «total-sales», but it may be a name qualified with a prefix, for example «my:value». If it has a prefix, the prefix must correspond to a namespace that is in scope at that point in the stylesheet. Two variables, «my:value» and «your:value», have matching names if the prefixes «my» and «your» refer to the same namespace URI. If the name has no prefix, it has a null namespace URI — it does not use the default namespace URI.

The scope of a global variable is the entire stylesheet, including any stylesheets that are included or imported. A global variable may even be referenced before it is declared. The only constraint is that circular definitions are not allowed; if variable x is defined in terms of y, then y may not be defined directly or indirectly in terms of x.

The scope of a local variable is block-structured; it may be referenced in any following sibling element or in a descendant of a following sibling. This is illustrated in Figure 6-16.

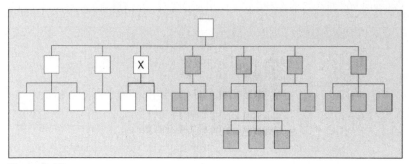

Figure 6-16

The diagram shows, for a variable X, the elements that may contain a reference to X; the shaded elements may refer to X, and the unshaded elements may not. Specifically, a local variable may be referenced in any following sibling element, or in a descendant of a following sibling. It cannot be referenced within its own descendants, and it goes out of scope when the end tag for its parent element is encountered. Unlike global variables, a forward reference to a local variable is not allowed. If you think of XSLT instructions as being like the statements in a block-structured language such as C, Java, or JavaScript, and the enclosing element as being like a block enclosed in these languages by curly braces, the scope rules will seem very familiar.

Two global variables may have the same name only if they have different *import precedence*; in other words, if one of them was in an imported stylesheet (for further details, see <xsl:import> on page 357). In this case, the definition with higher import precedence wins. Note that the higher precedence definition applies everywhere, even within the imported stylesheet that contains the lower precedence definition. This means it is not a good idea to rely on precedence to resolve accidental name clashes between independently developed modules, it's better to use namespaces.

XSLT 1.0 did not allow a local variable to be defined with the same name as another local variable already in scope. This restriction was there as a way of detecting user errors. The restriction has gone in XSLT 2.0, although there is still a warning in the specification advising that this isn't good practice. In fact, not all XSLT 1.0 processors actually enforced this rule. If a variable reference is used when two or more variables with the matching name are in scope, then the reference is taken to refer to the one whose scope is smallest.

This principle extends to variables declared within an XPath expression. To take an extreme example, it is legal to write:

```
<xsl:variable name="x" select="'A'"/>

<xsl:template match="para">
  <xsl:variable name="x" select="$x, 'B'"/>
  <xsl:variable name="x" select="$x, 'C'"/>
  <xsl:value-of select="for $x in ($x, 'D') return ($x, '+')"/>
</xsl:template>
```

The output of the template will be «A + B + C + D +».

These rules on uniqueness and scope of names apply equally to parameters declared using <xsl:param>; the <xsl:param> instruction is effectively just another way of declaring a variable.

The Value of the Variable

The value of the variable may be given either by the XPath expression in the `select` attribute, or by the contents of the contained sequence constructor. If there is a `select` attribute, the `<xsl:variable>` element must be empty. If there is no `select` attribute and the sequence constructor is empty, the value of the variable is a zero-length string, unless there is an `as` attribute, in which case the value is an empty sequence (assuming that the `as` attribute permits an empty sequence).

Figure 6-17 summarizes the different ways of specifying the value. The numbers in brackets refer to the numbered paragraphs below that explain the option in more detail.

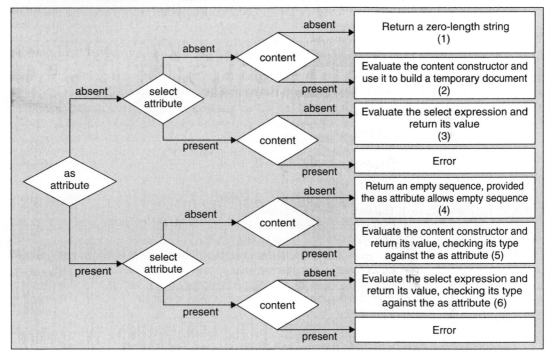

Figure 6-17

1. The following example declares a parameter whose default value is a zero-length string:

```
<xsl:param name="input"/>
```

Again, this option is not useful for variables, but it can be useful with `<xsl:param>`, which follows exactly the same rules.

2. If a sequence constructor is used with no `as` attribute, a temporary document is constructed. This is done by creating a new document node and using the value of the result sequence to form the children of the document node. The detailed rules for constructing the content of the document node are the same as those for the `<xsl:document>` instruction and are given on page 303. The value of the variable will be the document node at the root of the tree. For example:

```
<xsl:variable name="tree">
  <data>
    <country code="de">Germany</country>
```

```
          <country code="fr">France</country>
          <country code="gb">United Kingdom</country>
          <country code="us">United States</country>
        </data>
      </xsl:variable>
```

Here the value of the variable is a document node, whose only child is a `<data>` element, which in turn has four `<country>` elements as its children. Temporary documents are described in more detail on page 510.

3. If the `select` attribute is provided without an `as` attribute, the effect is the same as if «`as="item()*"`» were specified: no type checking or conversion takes place, and the value may be of any type. For example:

```
   <xsl:variable name="pi" select="3.14159e0"/>
```

Here the value of the `select` attribute is again of type `xs:double`, but for a different reason: it was written as a double literal, and no conversion has taken place.

4. The following example declares a parameter whose default value is an empty sequence:

```
   <xsl:param name="codes" as="xs:integer*"/>
```

This option is not very useful for variables, but it can be useful with `<xsl:param>`, which follows exactly the same rules.

5. If a sequence constructor is used with an «`as`» attribute, the instructions in the sequence constructor are evaluated. The result sequence is checked against the type specified in the «`as`» attribute and is converted if necessary using the standard conversion rules described on page 505. An error is reported if the conversion is not possible. The processor may report this as a compile-time error if it can tell at compile time that the value of the expression will never be convertible to the required type. For example:

```
   <xsl:variable name="n" as="xs:integer">
     <xsl:number/>
   </xsl:variable>
```

Here the sequence constructor returns a single text node. The contents of this text node are converted to an integer, which becomes the value of the variable.

6. If the `select` attribute is provided, its value must be an XPath expression. This expression is evaluated. The value is checked against the type specified in the «`as`» attribute and, if necessary, is converted to this type using the standard conversion rules described on page 505. An error occurs if this conversion is not possible. Otherwise, the error will be reported at runtime. For example:

```
   <xsl:variable name="pi" select="3.14159" as="xs:double"/>
```

Here the value of the `select` expression is of type `xs:decimal`, but the final value of the variable is an `xs:double`, because the «`as`» attribute forces a conversion.

Note that if an expression is used to assign a literal string value to a variable, the string literal must be enclosed in quotes, and these quotes are additional to the quotes used around the XML attribute.

So to assign the string value «London» to the variable named «city», you can write either of the following:

```
<xsl:variable name="city" select="'London'"/>
<xsl:variable name="city" select='"London"'/>
```

You can also write:

```
<xsl:variable name="city" as="xs:string">London</xsl:variable>
```

A common mistake is to write:

```
<xsl:variable name="city" select="London"/> <!-- WRONG -->
```

This sets the value of «$city» to a sequence containing all the element children of the context node that have element name <London>. This will probably be an empty sequence. If you get into the habit of using the «as» attribute, (in this case «as="xs:string"»), the compiler will tell you about this mistake. A schema-aware processor might also warn you that there is no <London> element defined in the schema. But in other cases, you won't get any error message, because it's a perfectly valid thing to write; it will just cause your stylesheet to produce the wrong output.

You won't be alone if you make this mistake; there's an example of it in the original XSLT 1.0 specification, which had to be fixed in a subsequent erratum.

You don't need the extra quotes if you want the value to be a number:

```
<xsl:variable name="max-size" select="255"/>
```

Standard Conversion Rules

This section provides the detailed conversion rules used when converting the supplied value of a variable (the result of evaluating its select attribute or its sequence constructor) to the type required by the «as» attribute. The same conversion rules are used under a number of other circumstances, such as when values are supplied for stylesheet parameters. They are the same as the *function conversion rules* defined in XPath 2.0, which define what happens when the supplied arguments in a function call differ from the declared types of the parameters, with the exception that the rules described here never use XPath 1.0 backward-compatibility mode. The reason for this is that they are always invoked in contexts where backward compatibility issues do not arise.

The rules take as input a *supplied value* and a *required type*, and they produce as output a *result value*. The required type has two parts: the *required item type* (for example, integer or element) and the *required cardinality*. The required cardinality may be *exactly-one* (when there is no occurrence indicator in the SequenceType as written) or *zero-or-one*, *zero-or-more*, or *one-or-more*, corresponding to the occurrence indicators «?», «*», and «+».

Instead of returning a result value, the rules may also result in a type error, if the supplied value cannot be converted to the required type.

The rules are as follows:

1. If the supplied value is an instance of the required type, return it unchanged as the result value. This includes the case where the supplied value belongs to a subtype of the required type.

2. If the required item type is an atomic type, the supplied value is atomized. Atomization causes each node in the supplied sequence to be replaced by its typed value, while leaving any atomic values in the sequence unchanged. Note that the typed value of a node can be a sequence of zero or more atomic values. Elements declared in the schema to have element-only content have no typed value, so this operation can result in an error.

3. Any item in the atomized sequence that is of type `xs:untypedAtomic` is cast to the required item type. Such items are most likely to arise as the result of atomizing a node in a schema-less document. This means, for example, that an attribute such as `@date-of-birth` will be acceptable where the required type is `xs:date`, provided that either (a) the attribute is annotated as an `xs:date` as a result of schema validation, or (b) the attribute is unvalidated and its textual form is acceptable as an `xs:date`.

4. If the required item type is a numeric type (one of `xs:double`, `xs:float`, `xs:decimal`, or `xs:integer`, or a type derived from these by restricting the range of values), then any numeric value in the atomized sequence is promoted to the required numeric type where possible. An integer can be promoted to any other numeric type, a decimal can be promoted to `xs:float` or `xs:double`, and an `xs:float` can be converted to an `xs:double`. However, other conversions are not possible; for example if the required item type is `xs:integer` but the supplied value is `xs:double`, a type error will be reported.

5. If the required item type is `xs:string` and the supplied value is of type `xs:anyURI`, then the URI is converted to a string (XDM effectively treats `xs:anyURI` as a subtype of `xs:string`, even though XML Schema does not define it that way).

If, after these conversions, the sequence conforms to the required type, then it is returned as the result value. If not, the system reports a type error. Type errors may be reported at runtime, but if the system can tell in advance that the expression will return a value of the wrong type, then they can also be reported at compile time.

These rules are not as liberal as the rules that were used in XPath 1.0 for type conversions, where, for example, a boolean could be supplied when a string was expected, and it would be treated as the string `"true"` or `"false"`. Because the type system in XSLT 2.0 is so much richer, you have to get used to the idea of thinking about what type of value you are handling, and of doing any necessary conversions yourself, using explicit casts or calls on constructor functions.

Usage

Variables are useful, as in any programming language, to avoid calculating the same result more than once.

Global variables are useful for defining constants, such as a color value, that will be used in many places throughout the stylesheet. They can also be used to extract values from the principal source document.

Unlike variables in many programming languages, *XSLT variables cannot be updated*. Once they are given an initial value, they retain this value until they go out of scope. This feature has a profound effect on the programming style used when a stylesheet needs to do calculations. The subject of *programming without assignment statements* is discussed in detail in Chapter 17.

Examples

Most XSLT variables fall into one of the three categories:

❑ Variables used to avoid repeating a common expression in more than one place. This might be simply to make the code more readable or to ensure that you only have to make a change in one place if the value changes or perhaps because it gives a performance benefit.

❑ Variables used to capture context-sensitive information, allowing the variable to be used after the context has changed.

❑ Variables holding intermediate results, allowing a transformation to be carried out as a series of separate steps.

In each case the variable might be local or global. I'll show some examples of each kind.

Convenience Variables

Consider this example, which calculates the number of goals scored by, and against, a soccer team.

```
<xsl:variable name="for"
              select="sum($matches/team[.=$this]/@score)"/>
<xsl:variable name="against"
              select="sum($matches[team=$this]/team/@score) - $for"/>
. . .
<td><xsl:value-of select="$for"/></td>
<td><xsl:value-of select="$against"/></td>
```

This uses two rather complex expressions to construct the variables «for» and «against», which calculate the number of goals scored by, and against, the team identified by the variable «$team». It would be quite possible in this case to avoid using the variable «against». The expression that calculates its value could equally be written at the point where the variable is used, in the second `<xsl:value-of>` instruction. The same is true of the «for» variable, though this time the expression would need to be written twice, in both places where the variable is used, and this might give a performance penalty. However, these variables are really being used only for clarity; it would be quite possible to write the stylesheet without them.

This is true because nothing can change between the variables being defined and being used. The source document can't change, and the values of the variables `$this` and `$matches` can't change. The context (for example the current position in the source document) can change, but in this example (a) it doesn't, and (b) the expressions don't depend on the context anyway.

I call these *convenience variables* because you could get by without them if you had to (though there might be a performance hit). They can be used either as global variables or as local variables. Creating global convenience variables that refer to sets of nodes in the source document is often a useful programming technique; for example:

```
<xsl:variable name="group-A-matches" select="//match[@group='A']"/>
```

These act rather like views in an SQL database.

Variables to Capture Context-Sensitive Values

These variables are most often useful in conjunction with `<xsl:for-each>`, which changes the context item. Consider the following example.

Example: Using a Variable for Context-Sensitive Values

This example shows how a variable can be used to hold on to information that depends on the context, for use when the context has changed.

Source

The source file is `opera.xml`. It contains a list of operas and details of their composers.

```xml
<?xml version="1.0"?>
<programme>
   <opera>
      <title>The Magic Flute</title>
      <composer>Mozart</composer>
      <date>1791</date>
   </opera>
   <opera>
      <title>Don Giovanni</title>
      <composer>Mozart</composer>
      <date>1787</date>
   </opera>
<opera>
      <title>Ernani</title>
      <composer>Verdi</composer>
      <date>1843</date>
   </opera>
   <opera>
      <title>Rigoletto</title>
      <composer>Verdi</composer>
      <date>1850</date>
   </opera>
   <opera>
      <title>Tosca</title>
      <composer>Puccini</composer>
      <date>1897</date>
   </opera>
<composer name="Mozart">
      <fullname>Wolfgang Amadeus Mozart</fullname>
      <born>1756</born>
      <died>1791</died>
   </composer>
   <composer name="Verdi">
      <fullname>Guiseppe Verdi</fullname>
      <born>1813</born>
      <died>1901</died>
   </composer>
   <composer name="Puccini">
      <fullname>Giacomo Puccini</fullname>
      <born>1858</born>
      <died>1924</died>
   </composer>
</programme>
```

Stylesheet

The stylesheet is the file `opera.xsl`. This is a complete stylesheet: It uses the simplified stylesheet syntax described on page 125, in Chapter 3.

The stylesheet contains two nested `<xsl:for-each>` loops. In the outer loop, it sets a variable «c» to the context node (the current composer). In the expression controlling the inner loop, this variable is used. It would not be correct to use «.» in place of «$c», because the `<composer>` element is no longer the context node. In this example it would be possible to use the `current()` function here (this function is described on page 734, in Chapter 13), but there are other cases where a variable is necessary.

```
<html
    xmlns:xsl="http://www.w3.org/1999/XSL/Transform"
    xsl:version="2.0">

<body><center>
    <h1>Programme</h1>
    <xsl:for-each select="/programme/composer">
        <h2><xsl:value-of
            select="concat(fullname, ' (', born, '-', died, ')')"/></h2>
        <xsl:variable name="c" select="."/>
        <xsl:for-each select="/programme/opera[composer=$c/@name]">
            <p><xsl:value-of select="title"/></p>
        </xsl:for-each>
    </xsl:for-each>
</center></body>
</html>
```

Output

See Figure 6-18.

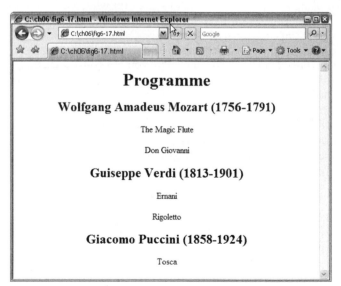

Figure 6-18

One case where context variables are very useful is when handling multiple source documents.

In any stylesheet that handles multiple source documents, it is useful to include a global variable that refers to the document node of the principal source document, thus:

```
<xsl:variable name="root" select="/"/>
```

This means it is always possible to refer to the source document by using this variable. Without this, when the context node is in a secondary document, there is no way of accessing data from the principal document.

For example, the expression «//item» refers to all <item> elements in the same document as the context node. If you actually want all <item> elements in the principal source document, then (provided you have included the global variable declaration above) you can use the expression «$root//item».

If there is a document referenced from the stylesheet, for example to hold look-up data such as messages or tax rates, it is also useful to define this in a global variable, for example:

```
<xsl:variable name="tax-rates" select="document('tax-rates.xml')"/>
```

Variables to Hold Intermediate Results

When a complex transformation task is undertaken, it is often useful to split it into a sequence of steps. The output of one step can be held in a variable, which is then used as the input to the next step.

Any kind of value can be used as an intermediate result, but most commonly it will either be a sequence of items, or a temporary document.

The value of a variable will be a temporary document (or a result tree fragment as it was known in XSLT 1.0) if it is defined using the content of the <xsl:variable> element rather than the select attribute, and if there is no as attribute.

Variables evaluated using a sequence constructor are useful when you use <xsl:call-template> or <xsl:apply-templates> to calculate a value that you then want to manipulate further. If such a value is complex, it will generally take the form of a temporary document. Such documents are needed whenever you require working data that is too complex to hold in a simple sequence. With XSLT 2.0, it is possible to perform any operation on a temporary document that you can perform on the principal source document, or on a document loaded using the document() function. This greatly increases their usefulness. There are two main categories:

❑   Intermediate results of a multiphase transformation.

It's often useful to break up a transformation into a sequence of steps (often referred to as a *pipeline*), to simplify the logic. A temporary tree can be used as the output of the first phase and the input to the next.

❑   Working data passed as a parameter through template or function calls.

For example, if you need to create a data structure such as a list of keyword/value pairs, and pass this as a parameter to a function or template, then the best way to construct this data structure is as a tree.

The next example shows a multiphase transformation.

Example: A Multiphase Transformation

This example performs a transformation in two phases. The first phase starts with a list containing the results of a series of soccer matches, and computes a league table showing the standing of the various teams. The second phase renders this league table in HTML. These are quite separate operations and it's best to keep them separate. In fact, we'll keep them completely separate by using different stylesheet modules and different modes.

Source

The source document is soccer.xml. It contains the results of individual matches. Here are the first few:

```
<results group="A">
<match>
<date>10-Jun-98</date>
<team score="2">Brazil</team>
<team score="1">Scotland</team>
</match>
<match>
<date>10-Jun-98</date>
<team score="2">Morocco</team>
<team score="2">Norway</team>
</match>
<match>
<date>16-Jun-98</date>
<team score="1">Scotland</team>
<team score="1">Norway</team>
</match>
. . .
</results>
```

Stylesheet

The first phase of the transformation calculates a league table. This is in module league.xsl, shown below:

```
<xsl:transform
 xmlns:xsl="http://www.w3.org/1999/XSL/Transform"
 version="2.0"
>


<xsl:variable name="teams" select="distinct-values(//team)"/>
<xsl:variable name="matches" select="//match"/>

<xsl:template match="results">
<league>
  <xsl:for-each select="$teams">
    <xsl:variable name="this" select="."/>
    <xsl:variable name="played" select="count($matches[team=$this])"/>
    <xsl:variable name="won"
          select="count($matches[team[.=$this]/@score gt
                                  team[.!=$this]/@score])"/>
```

```
        <xsl:variable name="lost"
            select="count($matches[team[.=$this]/@score lt
                                    team[.!=$this]/@score])"/>
        <xsl:variable name="drawn"
            select="count($matches[team[.=$this]/@score eq
                                   team[.!=$this]/@score])"/>
        <xsl:variable name="for"
            select="sum($matches/team[.=current()]/@score)"/>
        <xsl:variable name="against"
            select="sum($matches[team=current()]/team/@score) - $for"/>

        <team name="{ . }" played="{$played}" won="{$won}" drawn="{$drawn}"
            lost="{$lost}" for="{$for}" against="{$against}"/>

    </xsl:for-each>
</league>
</xsl:template>

</xsl:transform>
```

Since we're talking about usage of <xsl:variable> here, it's worth drawing attention to the way this example uses variables. There are a couple of global variables to define the list of teams and the list of matches. The stylesheet only contains one template, so these variables could equally well have been local, but making them global reflects the fact that they are potentially reusable. Within the template, the variable $this is set to the context item so that it can be used within predicates, where the context item will have changed. Then the computation is done entirely within a sequence of local variable declarations. This is a very characteristic programming style. Finally, the template outputs one <team> element for each team, with attributes indicating the number of matches won and lost, the goals scored, and so on.

The second stylesheet show-league.xsl renders the league table into HTML. It's quite straightforward:

```
<xsl:transform
 xmlns:xsl="http://www.w3.org/1999/XSL/Transform"
 version="2.0"
>

<xsl:import href="league.xsl"/>

<xsl:variable name="league">
  <xsl:apply-templates select="results"/>
</xsl:variable>
```

Note the variable here to capture the result of the first phase of processing. The value of this variable will be a document node containing the <league> element created by the previous stylesheet.

```
<xsl:template match="/">
<html>
  <head><title>League Table</title></head>
```

```
    <body>
      <h1>League Table</h1>
      <xsl:copy-of select="$league"/>
      <table border="2" cellpadding="5">
        <thead>
          <th>Team</th>
          <th>Played</th>
          <th>Won</th>
          <th>Lost</th>
          <th>Drawn</th>
          <th>For</th>
          <th>Against</th>
        </thead>
        <tbody>
        <xsl:for-each select="$league/league/team">
          <tr>
            <td><xsl:value-of select="@name"/></td>
            <td><xsl:value-of select="@played"/></td>
            <td><xsl:value-of select="@won"/></td>
            <td><xsl:value-of select="@lost"/></td>
            <td><xsl:value-of select="@drawn"/></td>
            <td><xsl:value-of select="@for"/></td>
            <td><xsl:value-of select="@against"/></td>
          </tr>
        </xsl:for-each>
        </tbody>
      </table>
    </body>
  </html>
</xsl:template>

</xsl:transform>
```

Output

The output of the stylesheet is shown in Figure 6-19.

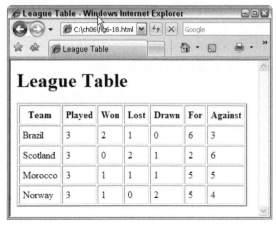

Figure 6-19

Avoiding Trivial Documents

There is a tendency to create temporary documents when they aren't needed. One often sees constructs like this:

```
<xsl:variable name="played">
    <xsl:value-of select="count($matches[team=$this])"/>
</xsl:variable>
```

This first calculates a number (the result of the count() function). It then converts this number to a string, wraps the string into a text node, creates a document node with the text node as its only child, and sets the value of the variable to be this document node. The chances are that the variable will then be used in an expression such as «$played>5», in which a number is required: so the system has to atomize the document node, extract its string value by reading all its text node descendants, and then convert the resulting string to a number. You can save yourself two lines of code, and the system a lot of unnecessary work, by writing instead:

```
<xsl:variable name="played" select="count($matches[team=$this])"/>
```

Here the value of the variable is a number. No need to create the temporary document, and no need to atomize it later to extract the value.

I call this kind of variable a trivial document. A trivial document behaves almost exactly like an untypedAtomic value. Here is a slightly more complicated example:

```
<xsl:variable name="width">
   <xsl:choose>
      <xsl:when test="@width">
         <xsl:value-of select="@width"/>
      </xsl:when>
      <xsl:otherwise>0</xsl:otherwise>
   </xsl:choose>
</xsl:variable>
```

In XSLT 2.0 it is almost always possible to avoid this kind of construct and the overheads that go with it. Write this instead as:

```
<xsl:variable name="width" as="xs:integer"
   select="if (@width) then @width else 0"/>
```

Or more concisely:

```
<xsl:variable name="width" as="xs:integer" select="(@width, 0)[1]"/>
```

There are several benefits in declaring the type. Firstly, it's good documentation for anyone reading the stylesheet. Secondly, it causes the system to do some error checking for you: if the width isn't an integer, you''ll get an appropriate error message. Finally, it's likely to be more efficient. A document node is a very heavyweight object compared with an integer.

The important change here was adding the «as» attribute to declare the type. It's this that eliminates the need to create the document node. You can retain the use of <xsl:choose> in the body of the <xsl:variable> if you prefer, writing it as:

```
<xsl:variable name="width" as="xs:integer">
   <xsl:choose>
      <xsl:when test="@width">
         <xsl:sequence select="@width"/>
      </xsl:when>
      <xsl:otherwise>
         <xsl:sequence select="0"/>
      </xsl:otherwise>
   </xsl:choose>
</xsl:variable>
```

In this example above I have substituted `<xsl:sequence>` for `<xsl:value-of>`. In fact, either instruction would work. But using `<xsl:value-of>` creates a text node, only to extract its value and convert this to an integer, which is unnecessarily inefficient.

Beginners sometimes try to write this as:

```
<xsl:choose>
    <xsl:when test="@width">
        <xsl:variable name="width" select="@width"/>
    </xsl:when>
    <xsl:otherwise>
        <xsl:variable name="width" select="0"/>
    </xsl:otherwise>
</xsl:choose>
```

This won't work, because when you get to the end tag of the `<xsl:choose>` element, both variable declarations will have gone out of scope!

See Also

`<xsl:param>` on page 425

xsl:when

The `<xsl:when>` element always appears as a child of `<xsl:choose>`. It defines a condition to be tested and the action to be performed if the condition is true.

Changes in 2.0

None.

Format

```
<xsl:when
  test = expression>
  <!-- Content: sequence-constructor -->
</xsl:when>
```

Position

`<xsl:when>` is always a child element of `<xsl:choose>`. There must be at least one `<xsl:when>` element within an `<xsl:choose>` element.

Attributes

Name	Value	Meaning
test mandatory	XPath Expression	The boolean condition to be tested

Content

A sequence constructor.

Effect

The `<xsl:choose>` element is evaluated as follows:

❏ The first `<xsl:when>` element whose `test` expression has an effective boolean value of `true` is selected; subsequent `<xsl:when>` elements are ignored regardless of the value of their `test` expression.

❏ If none of the `<xsl:when>` elements has a `test` expression that is `true`, the `<xsl:otherwise>` element is selected. If there is no `<xsl:otherwise>` instruction, no element is selected.

❏ The sequence constructor contained in the selected child element (if any) is evaluated in the current context: that is, the effect is as if the relevant sequence constructor appeared in place of the `<xsl:choose>` instruction.

Any XPath expression may be evaluated to obtain an effective boolean value. The rules are given in the section for `<xsl:if>` on page 353.

The `test` expression in a `<xsl:when>` element after the selected one is not evaluated. This means it is safe to write code such as this:

```
<xsl:choose>
  <xsl:when test="not($x castable as xs:integer)">
    <xsl:sequence select="-1"/>
  </xsl:when>
  <xsl:when test="xs:integer($x) lt 0">
    <xsl:sequence select="-1"/>
  </xsl:when>
  <xsl:otherwise>
    <xsl:sequence select="xs:integer($x)"/>
  </xsl:otherwise>
</xsl:choose>
```

The conversion to an integer will not be attempted, and cannot therefore cause a failure, if the condition in the first `<xsl:when>` is true.

Usage and Examples

See `<xsl:choose>` on page 282

See Also

`<xsl:choose>` on page 282
`<xsl:otherwise>` on page 420
`<xsl:if>` on page 353

xsl:with-param

The `<xsl:with-param>` element is used to set the values of parameters when calling a template, either when using `<xsl:call-template>` or when using `<xsl:apply-templates>`. It can also be used with `<xsl:apply-imports>` and with `<xsl:next-match>`.

Changes in 2.0

The `<xsl:with-param>` element can now be used as a child of `<xsl:apply-imports>` or `<xsl:next-match>`.

The `as` and `tunnel` attributes have been added.

When used with `<xsl:call-template>`, XSLT 2.0 defines compile-time errors if there is mismatch between the parameters supplied in the call and the parameters declared for the target `<xsl:template>` element.

Format

```
<xsl:with-param
  name = qname
  select? = expression
  as? = sequence-type
  tunnel? = "yes" | "no">
  <!-- Content: sequence-constructor -->
</xsl:with-param>
```

Position

`<xsl:with-param>` is always a child of `<xsl:apply-templates>`, `<xsl:call-template>`, `<xsl:apply-imports>`, or `<xsl:next-match>`.

Attributes

Name	Value	Meaning
name mandatory	Lexical QName	The name of the parameter.
select optional	XPath Expression	The value of the parameter to be supplied to the called template.
as optional	SequenceType	Defines the type of the value.
tunnel optional	«yes» or «no»	Indicates whether this is a tunnel parameter.

Content

An optional sequence constructor. If a `select` attribute is present, the `<xsl:with-param>` element must be empty.

Effect

The `<xsl:with-param>` element assigns a value to a parameter. The value of the parameter can be used within the called template.

517

The value of the parameter is established in exactly the same way as for the `<xsl:variable>` element. That is, the value is obtained by evaluating the `select` expression if present, or the contained sequence constructor if not.

Except for tunnel parameters (those where «`tunnel="yes"`» is specified), the parameter value is available only to the immediately called template. If the called template has an `<xsl:param>` element whose name matches that of the `<xsl:with-param>` element, then the value assigned to the `<xsl:with-param>` element is available within the template. If the called template has no such parameter, the value is ignored, except when using `<xsl:call-template>`, when this is an error. In the case of `<xsl:apply-templates>`, the parameter value is available in each of the templates that is called (one per selected node). The parameter is effectively evaluated once only — it will have the same value for each of these templates.

The name of the parameter is defined by a lexical QName. Normally, this will be a simple name such as «`city`» or «`total-sales`», but it may be a name qualified with a prefix, for example «`my:value`». If it has a prefix, the prefix must correspond to a namespace that is in scope at that point in the stylesheet. The true name of the parameter is determined not by the prefix but by the namespace URI; so the name «`my:value`» will match a parameter declared as «`your:value`» if the prefixes «`my`» and «`your`» refer to the same namespace. If the name has no prefix, it has a null namespace URI — it does not use the default namespace.

It is an error for two sibling `<xsl:with-param>` elements to have the same name, after namespace prefixes are replaced with namespace URIs. In other words, you can't supply two values for the same parameter. This applies even if one is a tunnel parameter and the other is not.

The `<xsl:with-param>` element does not actually declare a variable, so there is no problem if the name is the same as that of a variable that is currently in scope. In fact, it is quite normal to pass a parameter in the form:

```
<xsl:with-param name="current-user" select="$current-user"/>
```

This is used to ensure that the variable «`$current-user`» in the called template has the same value as the variable «`$current-user`» in the calling template.

If the «`as`» attribute is present, then the supplied value of the parameter is converted to the specified type using the same rules as for `<xsl:variable>`. There is no requirement that this type must be identical to the declared type of the corresponding `<xsl:param>`: For example the `<xsl:with-param>` might specify «`as="xs:byte"`» when the `<xsl:param>` specifies «`as="xs:integer"`». This means that potentially two conversions may take place, from the type of the supplied value as calculated by the select expression, to the type declared in the «`as`» attribute of `<xsl:with-param>`, to the type declared in the «`as`» attribute of the corresponding `<xsl:param>`. In each case the standard conversion rules are used, as described in the entry for `<xsl:variable>` on page 505.

The option «`tunnel="yes"`» allows the parameter to be set up as a tunnel parameter. Tunnel parameters are described in the entry for `<xsl:param>` on page 429, with a worked example on page 433.

Usage and Examples

Parameters to templates take on considerable significance in XSLT because variables cannot be updated. This means that many tasks that in conventional programming languages are done by updating variables in a loop are done instead in XSLT using recursive calls and parameters. The consequences of this are explained in Chapter 17, and there are some detailed examples of the technique in Chapters 19 and 20.

Examples of recursive calls are also included in this chapter under `<xsl:call-template>` on page 274.

See Also

`<xsl:apply-imports>` on page 237
`<xsl:apply-templates>` on page 240
`<xsl:call-template>` on page 271
`<xsl:param>` on page 425

Summary

This was a long chapter, but I hope you agree that every page was worth it! We have examined all of the XSLT elements in detail and have provided working examples to bolster your understanding of how they are used.

Many of the XSLT instructions described in this chapter contain embedded XPath expressions to compute their input. The next four chapters present a detailed description of the syntax and semantics of XPath expressions.

XPath Fundamentals

This chapter defines some fundamental features of the XPath language. The first half of the chapter describes the basic syntactic and lexical conventions of the language, and the second half describes the important notion of context: this establishes the way in which XPath expressions interact with the environment in which they are used, which for our purposes primarily means the containing XSLT stylesheet.

The complete grammar of the language is summarized in Appendix A, and for convenience I have split the constructs of the language across five chapters, as follows:

Chapter	Scope
7	Notation used for describing the grammar
	Overall structure of the language
	Lexical rules (including comments and whitespace handling)
	Literals
	Variable references
	Parenthesized subexpressions
	Context item expression «.»
	Function calls
	Conditional expressions: «if»
8	Arithmetic operators: «+», «-», . . .
	Value comparison operators: «eq», «lt», . . .
	General comparison operators: «=», «<», . . .
	Node identity and ordering operators: «is», «<<», «>>»
	Boolean operators: «and», «or»

continued

Chapter	Scope
9	Path expressions: «/», «//»
	Steps and axes
	Union, intersect, and except operators
10	Sequence concatenation operator: «,»
	Numeric range operator: «to»
	Filter expressions «a[b]»
	Mapping expressions: «for»
	Quantified expressions: «some» and «every»
11	SequenceType production
	«instance of»
	«castable as»
	«cast as»
	«treat as»

As with other programming languages, the syntax is defined in a set of *production rules*. Each rule defines the structure of a particular construct as a set of choices, sequences, or repetitions.

I took the formal production rules directly from the XPath specification document (http://www.w3.org/TR/xpath20), but reordered them for ease of explanation, and I made minor changes to the typography and to some of the production names for ease of reading. I also pulled in those rules from the XML and XML Namespaces standards that the XPath syntax references. I've tried to do this in a way that leaves the original rule clearly recognizable, so you can relate it to the original specification if you need to. However, I have tried in this book to include all the information you need from the XPath specification, so this should only be necessary if you need to see the precise wording of the standard.

Notation

The XPath specification, by and large, uses the same syntax notation as the rest of the family of XML specifications. This is often referred to as extended BNF, though the number of variations you find on the BNF theme can be a little bewildering. I have stuck fairly closely to the notation used in the XPath 2.0 specification, though I have allowed myself a little typographic license in the hope that this adds clarity.

As in the rest of the book, I used French quotation marks «thus» (also known as chevrons or guillemets) to surround pieces of XPath text that you write: I chose this convention partly because these marks stand out more clearly, but more importantly to distinguish these quotation marks unambiguously from quotation marks that are actually part of the expression. So if I say, for example, that literals can be enclosed either in «"» or «'» marks, then it's clear that you don't actually write the chevrons. XPath syntax doesn't use chevrons with any special meaning (though like any other Unicode character, you can use them in string literals and comments), so you can be sure that any chevron you see is not to be included in the expression.

The notations used in production rules are as follows:

Construct	Meaning
«abc»	The literal characters abc
xyz	A construct that matches the production rule named xyz
P|Q	A choice of P or Q
P?	Either P, or nothing
P*	Zero or more repetitions of P
P+	One or more repetitions of P
[i-n]	One of the characters in the range «i» to «n» inclusive
(P)	A subexpression

The production rules in XPath implicitly define the precedence of the different operators. For example, the rule for OrExpr defines it as a sequence of AndExpr operands separated by «or» operators. This is a convenient way of defining that the «and» operator binds more tightly than «or». The precedence order of all the operators is summarized in Appendix A.

One consequence of this style of definition is that the simplest OrExpr consists of a single AndExpr with no «or» operator present at all. This leads to all sorts of surprises. For example, because of the way the grammar is written, «3» is not just an IntegerLiteral, it is also a FilterExpr, a RelativePathExpr, a MultiplicativeExpr, a TreatExpr, and quite a few other things besides. This means that I can't use the term OrExpr when I want to refer specifically to an expression that uses an «or» operator. Instead, I'll refer to this as "an «or» expression." This distinction works quite well in most cases, and if there's any risk of confusion, then I'll try to spell out exactly what construct I'm talking about.

Although the production rules in XPath define the operator precedence, they do not impose any type checking. This follows the practice of most modern language specifications, where rules for type checking are regarded as being enforced in a second phase of processing, after the raw parsing of the syntax. It would be hard to define all the type checking rules in the grammar, because many of them operate at a distance. Since the type-checking rules can't all be defined in the grammar, the language designers decided to go to the other extreme, and define none of them in the grammar.

This means that the grammar allows many kinds of expression that are completely nonsensical, such as «3 | 'bread'» (where «|» is the set union operator). It's left to the type-checking rules to throw this out: the rules for the «|» operator say that its operands must be of type «node()*», that is, sequences of nodes. Think of an analogy with English — there are sentences that are perfectly correct grammatically but still nonsense: "An easy apple only trumpets yesterday."

Where to Start

Some people prefer to present the syntax of a language bottom-up, starting with the simplest constructs such as numbers and names, while others prefer to start at the top, with a construct like Program or Expression.

What I've chosen to do is to start at the top, with the section *Expressions*, which is really just an opportunity to provide an overview of the grammar, and then work bottom-up, starting with the basic building blocks of the language in this chapter and progressing through the other operators in the next four chapters. Each of these chapters describes a reasonably self-contained set of expressions that you can write in XPath. There's no obviously logical order to these, but I decided to present the simpler operators and expressions first, to make life as easy as possible if you decide to read the chapters sequentially. This also corresponds broadly with the order in which material is presented in the XPath specification itself.

> *If you want to find where in the book a particular construct is described, you might find the syntax summary in Appendix A helpful.*

Many languages distinguish the lexical rules, which define the format of basic tokens such as names, numbers, and operators, from the syntactic rules, which define how these tokens are combined to form expressions and other higher-level constructs. The XPath specification includes both syntactic and lexical production rules, but they are not quite as cleanly separated as in some languages. The main distinction between the two kinds of rule is that whitespace can be freely used between lexical tokens but not within a lexical token. I will try to distinguish carefully between syntax rules and lexical rules as we come across them in the grammar. The main difference is that when something is described as a syntax rule you can use whitespace and comments freely between the symbols, which is not the case for a lexical rule.

Expressions

The top-level construct in XPath (the entry point to the list of productions) is called `Expr`. This is described with the following syntax:

Expression	Syntax
Expr	ExprSingle («,» ExprSingle)*
ExprSingle	ForExpr
	| QuantifiedExpr
	| IfExpr
	| OrExpr

These rules indicate that an `Expr` is a list of `ExprSingle` expressions separated by commas, and an `ExprSingle` is either a `ForExpr`, a `QuantifiedExpr`, an `IfExpr`, or an `OrExpr`.

Here are some examples of the constructs mentioned in these rules:

Construct	Example
Expr	1 to 3, 5, 7, 11, 13
ExprSingle	*any of the examples below*
ForExpr	for $i in 1 to 10 return $i * $i
QuantifiedExpr	some $i in //item satisfies exists($i/*)
IfExpr	if (exists(@price)) then @price else 0
OrExpr	@price > 3 or @cost < 2

I'll cover the «,» operator (which concatenates two sequences), together with the ForExpr and the QuantifiedExpr in Chapter 10, which is all about expressions on sequences. The IfExpr (which allows you to write conditional «if..then..else» expressions) is covered in this chapter, on page 551, and the OrExpr, which allows you to use the boolean «or» operator, and provides the entry point to most of the rest of the XPath syntax, is described in Chapter 8.

The ExprSingle construct has a special role in the grammar. Because the «,» symbol is overloaded (it's used both as an operator for concatenating two lists and also as a syntactic delimiter in constructs such as a function call), there are places where you might expect the grammar to allow any Expr to appear but where, in fact, only an ExprSingle is allowed. This means that if you want to use a «,» operator in such contexts, you have to enclose the expression in parentheses.

The constructs IfExpr, ForExpr, and QuantifiedExpr are syntactically unusual in the XPath grammar because they start with keywords and contain multiple subexpressions. In a conventional language, they would probably be called statements rather than expressions. Nevertheless, they are true expressions, in the sense that they can be evaluated to produce a result, and they can appear anywhere in the grammar where an expression is required.

The OrExpr starts a list of productions that contains all the conventional expressions of the language, as follows:

Expression	Syntax
OrExpr	AndExpr («or» AndExpr)*
AndExpr	ComparisonExpr («and» ComparisonExpr)*
ComparisonExpr	RangeExpr ((ValueComp | GeneralComp | NodeComp) RangeExpr)?
RangeExpr	AdditiveExpr («to» AdditiveExpr)?
AdditiveExpr	MultiplicativeExpr ((«+» | «−») MultiplicativeExpr)*

continued

7

XPath Fundamentals

Expression	Syntax
MultiplicativeExpr	UnionExpr ((«*» | «div» | «idiv» | «mod») UnionExpr)*
UnionExpr	IntersectExceptExpr ((«union» | «|») IntersectExceptExpr)*
IntersectExceptExpr	InstanceOfExpr ((«intersect» | «except») InstanceOfExpr)*
InstanceofExpr	TreatExpr («instance» «of» SequenceType)?
TreatExpr	CastableExpr («treat» «as» SequenceType)?
CastableExpr	CastExpr («castable» «as» SingleType)?
CastExpr	UnaryExpr («cast» «as» SingleType)?
UnaryExpr	(«—» | «+»)* PathExpr

These expressions all have a similar form: each defines an expression in terms of expression in the row below combined with particular infix or prefix operators. These operators are all described in the following chapters, according to the role that they play.

At the level of PathExpr, the syntax starts to become rather more specialized again, which shouldn't be surprising because path expressions are the characteristic feature of the XPath language that gives it its special flavor. Chapter 9 is devoted to path expressions, where you will find the full syntax.

Below the level of path expressions, the most primitive expressions in the language are referred to as primary expressions. At that level we will pick up the story again in this chapter, on page 539.

As explained in Chapter 1, XPath is a read-only expression language. It's a general principle of XPath that expression evaluation is free of side effects: evaluating an expression isn't going to change the values of any variables, write information to log files, or prompt the user for their credit card number. Therefore evaluating the same expression more than once, in the same context, shouldn't make any difference to the answer or to the final output, and equally it shouldn't make any difference in which order expressions are evaluated. As a result, the XSLT and XPath specifications generally say nothing about order of evaluation.

The only way side effects can occur from evaluating an expression is if the expression calls user-written (or vendor-written) extension functions, because the XPath specification doesn't constrain what an extension function can do. Equally, it makes no guarantees about when, and in what order, extension functions are called.

Examples

Examples of expressions occur throughout this book. Here is a selection, brought together to indicate the variety of constructs that fall under this heading. Like many of the examples of XPath expressions in this section of the book, these have been collected together into XSLT stylesheets, complete with sample data, so that you can see for yourself how they work and experiment with your own changes. You'll find these particular examples in a file called ch07/expressions.xsl in the download for this book. Make a note of what else is available in the downloads, because I won't always be mentioning the file names explicitly.

Expression	Description
`$x + ($y * 2)`	Returns the result of multiplying `$y` by two and adding the value of `$x`.
`//book | //magazine`	Returns a sequence of nodes containing all of the `<book>` and `<magazine>` elements in the same document as the context node. (This could also be written, perhaps more efficiently, as «//(book|magazine)».)
`substring-before (author, ' ')`	Finds the value of the first `<author>` child of the context node and returns that part of the value that precedes the first space character.
`chapter and verse`	Returns the `xs:boolean` value `true` if the context node has a child `<chapter>` element and also a child `<verse>` element.
`93.7`	Returns the decimal value `93.7`.
`sum(//product/ (price * qty))`	Returns the result of multiplying the values of `<price>` and `<qty>` for every `<product>` element in the document, and summing the results.
`avg((//product)[position() le 5])/price)`	Returns the average `<price>` of the first five `<product>` elements in the document.

Lexical Constructs

An XPath 2.0 expression is written as a sequence of Unicode characters. Every character that's available in XML 1.0 can be used in an XPath expression, and possibly characters that are available in XML 1.1 as well, though that's been left up to the implementation to decide.

XPath itself isn't concerned with how these characters are encoded. XPath expressions will often be embedded in other languages such as XSLT, or they may be constructed as runtime character strings using a programming language such as Java or JavaScript. Any escape conventions local to the host language will be applied before the XPath parser gets to see the expression, and the syntax described in the XPath Recommendation (and in the XPath chapters of this book) is the syntax after such escapes have been expanded. For example:

❑   When XPath expressions are written in an XSLT stylesheet, the escaping conventions of XML apply. This means, for example, that a «<» character must be escaped as «<» and an ampersand as «&». Since XPath expressions are invariably written inside an attribute value in the stylesheet, the delimiting quotation marks of the attribute value (usually «"», but you can choose «'» if you prefer) must also be escaped, typically as «"» or «'», respectively. It's also worth remembering that the XML parser normalizes whitespace in an attribute value, so if you want to write an expression that tests whether some element in your source document contains a tab character, you should write this as `<xsl:if test = "contains(x, '&#x09;')">`. As far as XPath is concerned, an XPath expression can contain a tab character inside a string literal (and indeed, that's what it sees in this example), but to get the tab character past the XML parser, you need to escape it.

❑ Similarly, when XPath expressions are written within character strings in a host language such as Java, you will need to use the escaping conventions of that language: for example, a backslash needs to be written as «\\» and a quotation mark as «\"».

XPath is an unusual language in that it has no reserved words. Unembellished names in an XPath expression, such as «table» and «author», refer to elements or attributes in the source document that have these names. Since there are no restrictions on what you can call the elements in your source document (other than the characters that can be used), XPath has been designed so there are no restrictions on the names that can appear in the XPath expression. The result is that other names (for example, the names of variables and functions, as well as language keywords) have to be either embellished in some way, or recognized by the context in which they appear. There are several ways the grammar achieves this:

❑ Names of variables are always preceded by a «$» sign, for example «$x» (whitespace is allowed between the «$» and the «x», though it is rarely used in practice).

❑ Names of functions are always followed by a left parenthesis; for example, «not(». Again, whitespace is allowed before the «(». Some syntactic keywords use the same convention. For example, «if» in a conditional expression is always followed by «(», and node tests such as «element()» are also written with parentheses. (This node test matches any element node; if you leave out the parentheses, then it matches only elements that have the name «element».)

❑ Some operators, such as «and», «or», and «div», are written as keywords, but they are recognized as keywords only if they appear in a context where an operator is expected. The language is carefully arranged so that there is no ambiguity, and you can happily write constructs such as «and or or» to test whether there is an element called `<and>` or an element called `<or>` in your source document.

❑ Some operator names consist of doubled keywords, such as «instance» «of» or «castable» «as». These are recognized only if they appear as a pair. You can use whatever whitespace and comments you wish between the keywords.

❑ The keywords «for», «some», and «every», which introduce expressions described in Chapter 10, are recognized by virtue of the fact that they are always followed by a «$» sign (which in turn introduces the name of a variable).

As with most languages, the first stage in processing an XPath expression is lexical analysis, also known as tokenizing. The first stage of identifying the tokens is done fairly mechanically, and does not depend in any way on the syntactic context. At each stage, the longest sequence of characters that could comprise a single token is read. There are a few places where this can lead to surprises; for example, «x+1» is read as three tokens, whereas «x -1» is read as a single token. This is because XML names can contain a «-» character but not a «+» character. To ensure that «x -1» is read as a subtraction rather than as a single name, you need a space before the «-» for example «x -1». You also need to be careful with the humble «.» character, which can appear in several different roles in XPath: as a decimal point within a number, as a separator character within a name, and as a symbol in its own right, representing the context item. So, for example if you write «$a is .» (which tests whether variable $a refers to the context node), then you need a space between the «is» and the «.».

Once the text has been split into tokens, the tokens are classified. It is at this stage that the decision is made whether a name such as «div» is being used as an element name in a path expression, as a function name, as a variable name, or as an operator or keyword. As we have seen, the decision on how to classify a token may depend on the tokens that precede and follow it. It's likely that many parsers will also group together compound symbols such as «cast» «as» at this stage, though the details of how this is done are left entirely to the implementation.

The following sections present the basic lexical constructs found within an XPath expression.

Comments

Comments may appear in an XPath expression anywhere that whitespace may appear. Comments begin with «(:» and end with «:)», which feels slightly comical until you get used to it. But it means that comments are quite distinctive visually, and they read well because they look parenthetical.

Here is an example of a comment within an XPath expression:

```
if (string(@x))
then (: attribute x exists and is non-empty :) @x
else "none"
```

Was it really necessary for XPath to invent a completely new syntax for comments? Well, none of the obvious candidates would work. The C/Java convention is heavily reliant on symbols such as «/» and «», which are already overloaded in XPath. The SQL convention of «--» doesn't work because it's perfectly legal to have two adjacent hyphens in an XML name. The XML syntax of <!--x--> doesn't work in an expression that's embedded in an XML attribute in a stylesheet. Because of XML attribute normalization, anything that attaches significance to line endings is ruled out. Curly braces were tried at one stage, but they are easily confused with the delimiters for attribute value templates in XSLT, or the equivalent embedded expressions in XQuery (and they were a new invention anyway). So smileys it is....*

XPath 2.0 comments can be nested. This allows you to comment out a section of code even if it already contains comments. So, for example, the following expression is legal, and evaluates to 3:

```
3 (: + if (number(@x))
   then (: attribute x exists and is non-zero :) @x
   else 0
:)
```

To achieve this, the production rules for comments are given as follows:

Symbol	Lexical Rules
Comment	«(:» (CommentContents | Comment)* «:)»
CommentContents	Char

The way this rule works is that within a comment, you can have a sequence of things, each of which is either a character or a comment. Since the system always looks for the longest matching construct, if it sees «(:» within a comment then it will interpret this as the start of a nested comment, rather than as two ordinary characters.

Changes in XPath 2.0

XPath 1.0 provided no way of writing comments within an expression. The facility has become necessary because with the introduction of conditional expressions, «for» expressions, and the like, XPath 2.0 expressions can be much longer and more complex.

Numeric Literals

Numeric literals represent constant numbers. There are three types of number that can be written as constants within an XPath 2.0 expression; these correspond to the types xs:integer, xs:decimal, and xs:double. The type of the value is inferred from the way it is written. The rules are shown in the table below.

Symbol	Lexical Rules
IntegerLiteral	Digit+
DecimalLiteral	(«.» Digit+) | (Digit+«.» Digit*)
DoubleLiteral	((«.» Digit+) | (Digit+(«.» Digit*)?)) («e» | «E») («+» | «−»)? Digit+
Digit	[0-9]

That is to say:

❏ A sequence of one or more digits, with no decimal point or «e» or «E», is interpreted as an integer literal. For example, «0», «23», and «0034» are all integer literals.

❏ A sequence of one or more digits, with a decimal point among the digits or at the beginning or end, is interpreted as a decimal literal. Examples are «1.50», «.001», and «3.».

❏ A literal in scientific notation (or to be pedantic, in Fortran notation) is interpreted as an xs:double value. It starts with the mantissa, which may take the same form as either an integer or a decimal literal, followed by the letter «E» in upper or lower case (there is no distinction between the two, though upper case «E» is always used on output), followed by an exponent expressed as an integer, optionally preceded by a plus or minus sign. Examples are «0e0», «0.314159e+001», and «1.E-6».

The production rule for Digit is written as a *regular expression* and means that Digit is a sequence of one or more characters, each in the range 0 to 9. The square brackets do not mean that the construct is optional, as in some other syntax notations; rather they indicate a range of characters.

You may be wondering why a leading minus sign is not allowed at the front of a numeric literal. The answer is that it is allowed, but it's not part of the literal, so it's not included in these rules. You can write «-1», but this is technically not a numeric literal; it is an arithmetic expression using a unary minus operator. This operator is described in Chapter 8.

The actual value of the literal is defined in a way that guarantees consistency with the interpretation of values of type `xs:integer`, `xs:decimal`, or `xs:double` by XML Schema. These rules aren't as clear-cut as you might imagine; for example, if you specify a decimal value with more decimal places than your implementation supports, the processor has the option of either rounding the value (in any way it chooses) or reporting an error.

There's a significant change in this area from XPath 1.0, where all numeric values were treated as double-precision floating point. In XPath 1.0, the literal «1.5» represented an `xs:double`; in XPath 2.0, it is an `xs:decimal`. This can affect the precision of numerical calculations. The chances are that the only applications that will notice the change are those that are numerically fairly sophisticated (for example, an XSLT stylesheet that does trigonometrical calculations to produce SVG output). If you have such an application, it may be worth replacing any literals of the form «1.5» by «1.5e0» when you migrate to XPath 2.0.

It's worth mentioning here that the rules for output of numbers are not the same as the rules for input. When a number is converted to a string, the results are determined by the casting rules given in Chapter 11. To summarize these:

❏   An `xs:integer` value is output as an integer, for example, «42» or «-315»

❏   An `xs:decimal` value with no fractional part is output as if it were an integer, with no decimal point. If it has a fractional part, it is output with at least one digit before and after the decimal point, and no other insignificant leading or trailing zeros. Examples of `xs:decimal` output are «42», «-315», «18.6», «-0.0015».

❏   An `xs:double` or `xs:float` value that's within the range 1e-6 to 1e+6 (one millionth to one million, positive or negative) is output in the same way as a decimal. Outside this range, exponential notation is used, with one significant digit before the decimal point. Examples of `xs:double` output are «42», «-315», «18.6», «-0.0015», «1.003e-12», «-8.752943e13».

These rules have the effect that you often don't need to know whether the numbers you are dealing with are integers, decimals, or doubles. For example, if @width is an attribute in a schema-less document whose value is «width="17"», then the value of «string(@width+1)» is «18»; you never need to know that the result of the addition was actually an `xs:double` (the rules for arithmetic involving mixed types are in Chapter 8).

If you want more control over the formatting of numeric output, XSLT has a function `format-number()`, which offers detailed control. There's nothing comparable in XPath itself, but you can get rid of surplus decimal digits by using the `round-half-to-even()` function described in Chapter 13.

Examples

Expression	Description
86	The `xs:integer` value eighty-six
3.14159	An `xs:decimal` value representing π to five decimal places
1.0E-6	The `xs:double` value one-millionth

Changes in XPath 2.0

XPath 1.0 supported the lexical forms now used for integer literals and decimal literals, but interpreted the values as double-precision floating point. There was no support in XPath 1.0 for scientific notation.

String Literals

A `StringLiteral` represents a constant string.

Symbol	Lexical Rules
StringLiteral	(«"» ([^"])* «"»)+
	| («'» ([^'])* «'»)+

Unless you are familiar with regular expressions you may find this production rule difficult to read. The original in the XPath Recommendation is even more cryptic, and I have replaced it with a form that I find simpler to explain.

What it is saying is actually quite simple; a `StringLiteral` is either a sequence of any characters other than double quotes, enclosed between double quotes, or a sequence of any characters other than single quotes, enclosed between single quotes. For example, «"John"», or «'Jane'», or «"don't"» or «'I said "go"!'».

In both cases you can put several of these sequences together end to end (the «+» sign indicates repetition). This has the effect of doubling the delimiting quote character, which provides an escaping mechanism, allowing you to use the delimiter within the string. For example, you can write «'O''Connor'» to represent the string «O'Connor».

A `StringLiteral` is a lexical token. Whitespace within a `StringLiteral` is allowed and is significant (whitespace characters are part of the value).

If you are using XPath expressions within an XSLT stylesheet, or any other XML document, then there are two special considerations to bear in mind. Firstly, within an XML attribute delimited by «"» signs, any «"» sign needs to be written as «"», while if «'» signs are used as the attribute delimiter, any «'» characters in the value must appear as «'». Secondly, some care is needed when using tab, carriage-return, and newline characters within a literal, because the XML parser is required to replace these by space characters before the XPath expression parser ever gets to see them, as part of the process of *attribute value normalization*. You can use character references such as «	», «
», and «» to prevent this happening. However, character references such as this are recognized only if the XPath expression is preprocessed by an XML parser. They are not recognized when the expression is written as a string in a Java or C# program.

Examples

The following examples assume XPath is being used in a freestanding environment with no need to escape special characters:

Expression	Description
`"John's"`	The string «John's»
`'"'`	A string consisting of a single character, the double quotation mark
`'O''Reilly'`	The string «O'Reilly»

The following examples assume that XPath expressions are contained in an attribute within an XML document; for example, an XSLT stylesheet:

XSLT Attribute	Description
`select="'John''s'"`	The string «John's». The character used as the string delimiter can be escaped by doubling it.
`select="'&quot;'"`	A string consisting of a single character, the double quotation mark. The character used as the XML attribute delimiter can be escaped by using an XML entity or character reference.
`select="'Don''t say &quot;yes&quot;'"`	The string «Don't say "yes"». This combines the two escaping techniques from the previous examples.

Changes in XPath 2.0

The ability to include the string-delimiter character within the string by doubling it is new in XPath 2.0. The convention has been adopted from SQL and has the advantage of being backward-compatible with XPath 1.0.

XSLT Usage

Handling the two kinds of quotation marks in XPath expressions written within stylesheets can be tricky, even with the new escape convention introduced in XPath 2.0. You can often circumvent the problems (and produce clearer code) by using variables. For example, instead of writing:

```
<xsl:if test="@input = 'Don''t say &quot;yes&quot;'">
   ...
</xsl:if>
```

write instead:

```
<xsl:variable name="s" as="xs:string">
  <xsl:text>Don't say "yes"</xsl:text>
</xsl:variable>
<xsl:if test="@input = $s">
   ...
</xsl:if>
```

Within XML text nodes, apostrophes and quotation marks can be written literally without escaping — there is no need to use the entity references «'» and «"».

I find it quite useful to have two global variables available in a stylesheet, as follows:

```
<xsl:variable name="apos" as="xs:string">'</xsl:variable>
<xsl:variable name="quot" as="xs:string">"</xsl:variable>
```

This makes it possible to use the variables «$apos» and «$quot» to construct strings using the `concat()` function, for example:

```
<xsl:value-of select="concat($quot, @input, $quot)"/>
```

Names

Names are used within an XPath expression to refer to elements and attributes in a source document, and to refer to objects such as variables, functions, and types.

Expression	Lexical Rules
QName	(Prefix «:»)? LocalPart
Prefix	NCName
LocalPart	NCName
NCName	(Letter | «_») (NCNameChar) *
NCNameChar	Letter | Digit | «.» | «-» | «_» | CombiningChar | Extender

The productions QName and NCName are actually defined in the XML Namespaces Recommendation, not in XPath itself. This ensures that any name that can be used for an element or attribute in a source document can also be used in an XPath expression. These are lexical rules, rather than syntax rules, which means that no whitespace is allowed between the symbols.

Informally, an NCName starts with a letter or underscore, and continues with zero or more NCNameChars, which may be letters, digits, or the three punctuation characters dot, hyphen, and underscore. The «Letter» and «Digit» categories include a wide variety of characters and ideographs in non-Latin scripts as well as accented Latin letters, while the «CombiningChar» and «Extender» categories cover accents and diacritics in many different languages.

The rules for Letter, Digit, CombiningChar, and Extender are given in the XML specification. The definitions are in the form of long lists of Unicode characters, and little would be gained by repeating them here. The basic principle is that if a name is valid in XML, then it is also valid in XPath.

In nearly all contexts, the kind of name that is allowed in XPath is a QName. This means a lexical QName as defined in the XML Namespaces Recommendation, which either takes the form «prefix:local-name», where both the prefix and the local-name are NCNames (no-colon names), or the simpler form «local-name» in which the prefix is omitted. If a prefix is present, then it must always be one that has been declared in the static namespace context for the XPath expression, as described later in this chapter. If no prefix is present, then the interpretation depends on what kind of name it is. If it is used where an element name is expected, then it is taken to refer to the default namespace for elements, which is also defined in the static context of the expression. If it is used where an attribute name is expected, then the local-name is assumed to be a name that is not in any namespace.

As in XML, names are case-sensitive, and names are only considered to match when they consist of exactly the same sequence of characters (or more strictly, the same Unicode code-points). This is true even when the Unicode standards describe characters as equivalent; for example, different ways of writing accented letters.

Examples

The following are examples of valid NCNames:

```
A

alpha

Π

א

_system-id

iso-8859-1

billing.address

Straßenüberführung

ΕΛΛΑΣ

_···_‾‾‾_···_
```

I have seen an example of an XML document that used «_» on its own as an element name, but it is not something I would recommend.

XSLT Usage

QNames are also used in XSLT stylesheets in a number of other contexts, outside the scope of XPath expressions. They are used both to refer to elements in the source document (for example, in `<xsl:preserve-space>` and `<xsl:strip-space>`) and to name and refer to objects within the stylesheet itself, including variables, templates, modes, and attribute sets.

There are also some situations where QNames can be constructed dynamically as a result of evaluating an expression. They are used, for example, in `<xsl:element>` and `<xsl:attribute>` to generate names in the result document, and in the `key()` and `format-number()` functions to refer to objects (keys and decimal-formats, respectively) defined in the stylesheet. QNames constructed at runtime are never used to match names in the source document, and they are never used to match template names, variable names, mode names, or attribute set names in the stylesheet; these references must all be fixed names.

Whether the QName is written statically in the stylesheet, or whether it is constructed dynamically, if the name has a prefix then the prefix must be declared by a namespace declaration on some surrounding element in the stylesheet module. For example:

```
<xsl:apply-templates select="math:formula" xmlns:math="http://math.org/"/>
```

Here the namespace is declared on the actual element that uses the prefix, but it could equally be any ancestor element.

The actual element in the source document does not need to have the tag «math:formula», it can use any prefix it likes (or even the default namespace) provided that in the source document the element name is in the namespace URI «http://math.org/».

If the QName does not have a prefix, then the rules are more complicated, and there are three possibilities:

❏ In the case of a name used as the name of a literal result element in the stylesheet, or in a small number of other places, the namespace that's used is the one declared using a default namespace declaration in the stylesheet, in the form «xmlns = "some.uri"». If there is no such declaration, the name is assumed to be in no namespace.

❏ In the case of a name used as an element name or type name in an XPath expression, or in certain other contexts such as:

  ❏ an XSLT pattern

  ❏ the elements attribute of <xsl:strip-space> or <xsl:preserve-space>

  ❏ the as attribute of elements such as <xsl:function> and <xsl:variable>

  ❏ the type attribute of instructions such as <xsl:element>

  the name is assumed to be in the namespace declared using the xpath-default-namespace attribute on the <xsl:stylesheet> element. This can also be overridden on any other element in the stylesheet. If there's no such declaration, the name is assumed to be in no namespace.

❏ A name is being "used as an element name" if it appears in an axis step (see Chapter 9) whose axis is anything other than the attribute or namespace axis. Some names appearing in the SequenceType production used to describe types also fall into this category.

❏ Names used to refer to attribute and namespace nodes, as well as the names of variables, functions, and stylesheet objects such as modes, keys, and named templates, are always considered to be in no namespace when they are unprefixed.

The reasoning behind these rules is that names of elements in the stylesheet use the standard XML default namespace «xmlns=" "»; names of elements in the source document use the special default xpath-default-namespace, and names of objects other than elements never use a default namespace.

A QName with no prefix appearing in an XPath expression never uses the default namespace defined in the source document.

It's a common mistake to forget this. Your source document starts as follows:

```
<html xmlns="http://www.w3.org/1999/xhtml">
```

and your stylesheet starts:

```
<?xml version="1.0"?>
<xsl:stylesheet xmlns:xsl="http://www.w3.org/1999/XSL/Transform"
    xmlns="http://www.w3.org/1999/xhtml"
    version="2.0">
<xsl:template match="html">
```

Why doesn't the template rule for «match="html"» fire when the <html> element is encountered? The answer is that the default namespace (declared with «xmlns="..."») applies to unprefixed QNames in the source document, but it doesn't apply to unprefixed QNames appearing in expressions and match patterns in the stylesheet. You either need to write:

```
<?xml version="1.0"?>
<xsl:stylesheet xmlns:xsl="http://www.w3.org/1999/XSL/Transform"
    xmlns:xhtml="http://www.w3.org/1999/xhtml"
    version="2.0">
<xsl:template match="xhtml:html">
```

or you need to define an xpath-default-namespace:

```
<?xml version="1.0"?>
<xsl:stylesheet xmlns:xsl="http://www.w3.org/1999/XSL/Transform"
    xpath-default-namespace="http://www.w3.org/1999/xhtml"
    version="2.0">
<xsl:template match="html">
```

What's worse, your source document might actually not start with:

```
<html xmlns="http://www.w3.org/1999/xhtml">
```

but rather with:

```
<!DOCTYPE html SYSTEM "http://www.w3.org/TR/xhtml1/DTD/xhtml1-strict.dtd">
<html>
```

Here it's not obvious that the <html> element is actually in a namespace. But it is, because hidden away inside the DTD is the sneaky little definition:

```
<!ELEMENT html (head, body)>
<!ATTLIST html
  %i18n;
  id       ID       #IMPLIED
  xmlns    %URI;    #FIXED 'http://www.w3.org/1999/xhtml'
>
```

which has the effect of adding the namespace declaration «xmlns="http://www.w3.org/1999/ xhtml"» to the <html> element whether you asked for it or not. This means that a bare «match="html"» in your stylesheet won't match this element; you need to match the namespace as well.

Operators

There is no hard-and-fast rule about exactly what constitutes an operator in the XPath language; but this is a good place to provide a general overview of the different kinds of operator.

We can classify as first-order operators all the operators that take one or more expressions as their operands, and produce a result that is obtained by evaluating the operands, and combining the values of the operands in some way. The first-order operators are listed in the table below, in precedence order. Operators listed on the same row of the table have the same precedence.

Operator	Effect
,	Sequence concatenation
or	Boolean disjunction (A or B)

continued

537

Operator	Effect
and	Boolean conjunction (A and B)
eq ne lt le gt ge	Ordering comparison between single values
= != < <= > >=	Ordering comparison between sequences
<< is >>	Ordering/identity comparison between nodes
to	Constructs a sequence of consecutive integers
+ −	Addition, subtraction
* div idiv mod	Multiplication, division, modulus
| union	Union of two sequences considered as sets of nodes
intersect except	Intersection and difference of sequences considered as sets of nodes

Some of these operators are written as symbols, some as words. Where words are used, they are not reserved words: they are recognized as operators by virtue of where they appear in an expression. This means that it is quite legitimate to write an expression such as «div div div» in which the first and final words represent names of elements in the source document, and the middle word is a «div» operator.

The symbols «*» and «/» double as operators and as expressions in their own right. In an operator context, «*» means multiplication, but in an expression context, it selects all the child elements of the context node. If the context node is the element `<a><b>2</b></a>`, then the expression «*∗*» evaluates to «4». In fact, «*» also has a third role, as an occurrence indicator after a type name, as in «xs:integer*».

As operators are tokens, they may always be preceded and followed by whitespace, and must not include any embedded whitespace. In some cases it is necessary to precede or follow an operator by whitespace to ensure it is recognized. This applies not only to the named operators (such as «and» and «or») but also to the minus sign «-», which could be mistaken for a hyphen if written with no preceding space.

The numeric comparison operators are written here as XPath sees them; when they appear in an XSLT stylesheet, the special characters «<» and «>» should be written «<» and «>», respectively.

The second group of operators can be classified as type operators. These take two operands, one of which is a value, the other a type. The operators in this category are:

- ❏ instance of
- ❏ cast as
- ❏ castable as
- ❏ treat as

Again, none of these words are reserved in any way. All these operators, together with the syntax for describing a type, are fully described in Chapter 11.

The final group of operators are best described as higher-order operators. These are characterized by the fact that they don't simply evaluate their operands and combine the resulting values: each has its own rules for how the different subexpressions contribute to the final result. These operators have custom syntax that doesn't always look like a conventional operator at all. They are shown in the following table.

Expression	Meaning
`for $x in E1 return E2`	Evaluates E2 once for every value in E1, concatenating the resulting sequences.
`some $x in E1 satisfies E2`	Returns `true` if E2 is `true` for any item in E1.
`every $x in E1 satisfies E2`	Returns `true` if E2 is `true` for every item in E1.
`if (E1) then E2 else E3`	Evaluates E2 or E3 depending on the value of E1.
`E1 / E2`	Evaluates E2 once for every value in E1, returning a sequence of nodes in document order.
`E1 [ E2 ]`	Returns those items in the sequence E1 for which E2 evaluates to `true`.

This concludes our survey of the lexical constructs in an XPath expression. We will now look at the basic syntactic building blocks, which are referred to as primary expressions.

Primary Expressions

Primary expressions are the most basic kinds of expression in XPath, and ultimately, all XPath expressions are constructed by combining primary expressions using various operators. The following sections in this chapter describe each kind of primary expression. These are described by the syntax:

Expression	Syntax

`PrimaryExpr`	`Literal |`
	`VariableReference |`
	`ParenthesizedExpr |`
	`ContextItemExpr |`
	`FunctionCall`

`Literal`	`NumericLiteral |` `StringLiteral`

`NumericLiteral`	`IntegerLiteral |`
	`DecimalLiteral |`
	`DoubleLiteral`

We have already covered numeric and string literals earlier in the chapter. The rest of the chapter therefore concentrates on the four other kinds of primary expressions: variable references, parenthesized expressions, the context item expression, and function calls.

The only real thing that these different kinds of `PrimaryExpr` have in common is the context in which they can be used.

According to the syntax rules, any `PrimaryExpr` can be followed by a predicate to form a `FilterExpr`, so for example «17[1]» and «'Berlin'[3]» are both legal. And in fact, in XPath 2.0 these expressions are not only syntactically legal, they also make sense semantically: a single item such as «17» or

«'Berlin'» is a sequence of length one, and applying a predicate to it can return either that item or an empty sequence. Filter expressions are described in Chapter 8.

Examples

Expression	Description
23.5	A NumericLiteral is a PrimaryExpr
'Columbus'	A StringLiteral is a PrimaryExpr
$var	A VariableReference is a PrimaryExpr
contains(@name, '#')	A FunctionCall is a PrimaryExpr
(position() + 1)	A parenthesized expression is a PrimaryExpr

The notable omission from the list of primary expressions is AxisStep: an axis step such as «child::node()» is not a PrimaryExpr, even though it contains no other expressions. This ensures that an expression such as «para[1]» is unambiguously a PathExpr, with the predicate «[1]» taken as part of the Step, rather than it being a FilterExpr consisting of a PrimaryExpr «para» followed by a Predicate «[1]». It is possible to turn an AxisStep into a PrimaryExpr by putting it in parentheses, so «(para)[1]» is a FilterExpr. In this case the meaning is the same, but this will not always be the case.

Variable References

A VariableReference is a reference to a variable. The variable may be declared in an enclosing «for», «some», or «every» expression, as described in Chapter 10, or it may be defined outside the XPath expression. In the case of XSLT, this means that it may be declared in an <xsl:variable> or <xsl:param> element in the stylesheet.

Expression	Syntax
VariableReference	«$» QName

The use of a «$» sign is necessary to distinguish a variable reference from a reference to an element in the source document: «para» selects a child <para> element in the source, while «$para» is a reference to a variable.

Whitespace is allowed between the $ sign and the QName, though it is rarely used (it was not permitted in XPath 1.0).

Usage

The QName must match the name of a variable that is in scope at the point where the expression containing the variable name appears. A variable can be declared either within a containing «for», «some», or «every» expression, or (in XSLT) in an <xsl:variable> or <xsl:param> element; note that if the name contains a namespace prefix, it is the namespace URI that must match, not necessarily the prefix. The XPath expression must be within the scope of this <xsl:variable> or <xsl:param> element — the scope rules are given in Chapter 6 on page 502.

The value of the variable reference is whatever value has been assigned to it by the matching «for», «some», or «every» expression, or (with XSLT) the matching <xsl:variable> or <xsl:param> declaration. The value may be of any type: any sequence containing nodes, atomic values, or a mixture of both.

A variable reference can be used anywhere in an XPath expression where a value is required. It cannot be used to represent concepts of the language other than values; for example, you can't use a variable in place of a name, a node type, or an axis. Nor can you use a variable to hold an entire expression.

A common misunderstanding about variables is to write a path expression such as:

```
/booklist/book/$property
```

thinking that if the value of $property is the string "title", then this is equivalent to writing:

```
/booklist/book/title
```

You can do this sort of thing in a shell scripting language, where variables work by textual substitution: in that kind of language the content of a variable can hold any part of an expression. But in XPath, variables hold values, not pieces of an expression. The actual meaning of the above expression is:

```
/booklist/book/"title"
```

which will return the string "title" once for each book element.

The way to achieve the desired effect is to write:

```
/booklist/book/*[local-name() eq $property]
```

Some processors (including Saxon) offer an evaluate() extension function, which allows you to construct an XPath expression at runtime, from a string which might be held in a variable. But this capability is not present in the standard.

It's relatively unusual to see variables whose name includes a namespace prefix. It can be useful, though, if you want to write a general-purpose reusable library module in XSLT or XQuery; you can then define global variables to hold constants visible to users of the library, and putting these in a specific namespace will help to ensure that there are no naming conflicts. In fact, XQuery requires that global variables exported from a module are declared in the namespace associated with that module.

Examples

```
$x

$lowest-common-denominator

$ALPHA

$my-ns-prefix:param1

$ Π

$ (: you can have a comment here :) x
```

Parenthesized Expressions

A `ParenthesizedExpr` either consists of an expression enclosed in parentheses, or it consists of an empty pair of parentheses, used to represent the empty sequence.

Expression	Syntax
ParenthesizedExpr	«(» Expr? «)»

When the contained `Expr` is present, parentheses have the same effect in XPath as in most other languages; they change the order of evaluation, so that the enclosed expression is evaluated first, regardless of the normal operator precedence.

Parentheses are sometimes needed around an expression that uses the «,» operator (which denotes list concatenation), to avoid the «,» being interpreted as a separator between the arguments in a function call or the clauses of a «for» expression. For example, to find the maximum of two numbers $i and $j, you need to write «max(($i, $j))», to make it clear that the function is being called with one argument (a sequence) and not with two. The «,» operator is described in detail in Chapter 10. Because «,» has the lowest precedence of any operator, it is generally necessary to use parentheses with it. However, if it is used at the top level of an XPath expression, the parentheses are not needed. For example, one can write in XSLT:

```
<xsl:apply-templates select="title, author, abstract, body"/>
```

to process the four selected elements in the order indicated.

If there is no contained expression, that is, if the `ParenthesizedExpr` is written as «()», then its value is the empty sequence. For example, the expression «$a union ()» returns the union of the sequence $a and the empty sequence; this has the effect of returning all the nodes in $a, in document order and with duplicates removed. The «union» operator (which can also be written «|») is described in Chapter 9.

One special case where the meaning of parentheses may not be immediately apparent is in conjunction with predicates. Predicates are used to filter the items in a sequence; for example, «$seq[.>= 0]» selects all the items in the sequence $seq whose value is greater than zero. As explained in Chapter 9, the meaning of a predicate is subtly different when it appears as part of an axis step. The result of this distinction is that:

❑ «ancestor::node()[1]» selects the innermost ancestor of the context node (that is, its parent)

❑ «(ancestor::node())[1]» selects the outermost ancestor of the context node (that is, the root of the tree).

For a more complete explanation of this distinction, see the sections on *Axis Steps* in Chapter 9 and *Filter Expressions* in Chapter 10.

Another rather specialized use for parentheses is to remove syntactic ambiguities when using the «/» symbol as an expression referring to the document node at the root of the current tree. When «/» is followed by a name, or by the symbol «*», then it is assumed to be the start of a rooted path expression.

This means that if you want to follow «/» with a named operator, you need to enclose it in parentheses, for example:

```
if ((/) instance of document(schema-element(mf:invoice))) then ...
```

or

```
if ((/) intersect $nodes) then ...
```

Another way of disambiguating «/» in such expressions is to write it as «/.».

Changes in XPath 2.0

The syntax «()» to represent an empty sequence, and the use of the «,» operator to perform sequence concatenation, are new in XPath 2.0.

Because a `Step` in a path expression is now a general expression (see Chapter 9), it becomes possible in XPath 2.0 to use parentheses in a path expression such as «book/(chapter|appendix)/title».

Context Item Expressions

The `ContextItemExpr` is simply the expression «.»:

Expression	Syntax
ContextItemExpr	«.»

The context item may either be a node or an atomic value, or its value may be undefined. If the value is undefined, then evaluating the expression «.» causes an error.

At the outermost level of an XPath expression, the value of the context item is established by the calling environment. For example, in XSLT it is determined by the innermost <xsl:for-each> or <xsl:apply-templates> iteration. Where XPath expressions are evaluated from a host language such as Java or C#, the calling API often provides the application with a way to set the initial context item.

Internally within an XPath expression, there are two constructs that change the context item. Within a predicate P of an expression such as «$SEQ[P]», the predicate is evaluated for each item in $SEQ in turn, with that item as the context item, and on the right-hand side of the «/» operator, in a path expression such as «E1/E2», the context item for evaluating E2 is set to each item in E1 in turn.

The value of the context item is not changed in the body of a «for» expression (described in Chapter 10). It is therefore wrong to write something like:

```
sum(for $x in //item return ./@price * ./@qty)
```

Instead, you need to write:

```
sum(for $x in //item return $x/@price * $x/@qty)
```

Changes in XPath 2.0

In XPath 1.0, the «.» symbol was an abbreviation for the Step «self::node()». This restricted its value to being a reference to a node (never an atomic value), and it also imposed certain other restrictions; for example, it was not possible to apply a predicate to «.». In XPath 2.0 you can use constructs such as «.[*]» which returns the context item only if it is a node that has a child element.

In XPath 1.0, «.» was never undefined — it always had a value, and the value was always a single node. In XPath 2.0, there are many situations in which it can be undefined; for example, it is undefined on entry to a function body written in XSLT or XQuery.

Usage

The two places where «.» is commonly used are:

❑   With the operator «//» in a relative path expression such as «.//A», which (loosely speaking) selects all the descendant <A> elements of the context node. The «.» is necessary here because if the expression started with «//», it would select all descendants of the root node.

❑   On its own, to perform operations on the value of the context item. This usually arises in expressions such as «.=3» or «string-length(.)» where we want to test the value of the context node, or in the XSLT instruction <xsl:value-of select="."/>, which outputs the atomized value of the context item to the result tree.

Some people also like to use «.» for clarity at the start of a relative path expression such as «./TITLE», but in fact this is precisely equivalent to «TITLE» on its own.

In XPath 2.0, if you want to remove duplicates from a sequence of nodes $seq, and sort them into document order, you can write «$seq/.», or equivalently, «./$seq». The sorting and deduplication is part of the defined behavior of the «/» operator.

Function Calls

A FunctionCall invokes a function. This may be one of the system-defined functions described in Chapter 13, or it may be a vendor- or user-supplied function.

Each built-in or user-defined atomic type also has a corresponding constructor function available for constructing values of that type (for example, «xs:date('2008-02-29')» constructs a date).

There may also be additional functions described in a host language in which XPath is embedded — for example, the XForms standard defines a number of additional XPath functions. Some of these duplicate functionality that is now in the standard XPath 2.0 library, but others define functionality specific to the XForms environment; for example, the instance() function, which provides access to an XML document that holds the data collected using an interactive form.

Expression	Syntax
FunctionCall	QName «(» (ExprSingle («,» ExprSingle)*)? «)»

continued

Expression	Syntax
ExprSingle	ForExpr |
	QuantifiedExpr |
	IfExpr |
	OrExpr

The syntax of a function call consists of the function name, which is in general a QName, followed by the list of zero or more supplied arguments, in the usual way.

Each argument must be an ExprSingle. This basically means any XPath expression, as long as it does not contain a top-level «,» operator. If you want to supply a list of values separated by commas as a single argument, you must enclose it in parentheses. Note the difference between:

```
concat("A", " nice", " cup", " of", " tea")
```

which calls the concat() function with five separate arguments, each one a single string, and:

```
string-join(("A", "nice", "cup", "of", "tea"), " ")
```

which calls the string-join() function with two arguments, the first one being a sequence of five strings, and the second a string containing a single space character. These two function calls are both legal, and as it happens they both have the same effect. Both the functions are described in Chapter 13. The concat() function is exceptional in that it allows an arbitrary number of arguments to be supplied.

The arguments themselves can be expressions such as «/», «.», or «@*», which may look a bit strange at first encounter. For example, the function call «exists(/*)» returns true if the context node is in a tree whose root is a document node that has an element node as a child.

Identifying the Function to Be Called

The set of functions that is available for calling is defined in the static context for the XPath expression, as described later in this chapter. This means that it is known at compile time whether a particular function name is valid or not. You can therefore expect a compile time error if you call a function that does not exist.

The function name is a QName. Like other QNames, it is written as a lexical QName (with an optional prefix and a local name, separated by a colon), and this lexical QName is expanded using the namespace declarations that are in scope for the XPath expression. So the expanded name of the function consists of a namespace URI and a local-name. The XPath static context includes a default namespace URI for function names, which will usually be quite separate from the default namespace URI for other kinds of name. Throughout this book I have assumed that the default namespace URI for functions will be http://www.w3.org/2005/xpath-functions, which contains the standard library of functions listed in Chapter 13. When this is the case, functions such as count() and exists() may be called with unprefixed names. XSLT requires that this is always the default namespace for function names, though other XPath environments may define a different default. You will often see function calls like count() written with a prefix as fn:count(), but this is never necessary in XSLT.

7

XPath Fundamentals

545

The function name is recognized in the XPath syntax by virtue of the fact that it is followed by a left parenthesis. This means that certain unprefixed names used as keywords in the language are not available for use as function names, specifically `attribute()`, `comment()`, `document-node()`, `element()`, `empty-sequence()`, `if()`, `item()`, `node()`, `processing-instruction()`, `schema-attribute()`, `schema-element()`, `text()`, `type()`, and `typeswitch()`. The name `typeswitch()` is not actually used as a keyword in XPath but is reserved for compatibility with XQuery.

The set of functions that are available for calling will generally include the following:

❑ The core library of XPath functions described in Chapter 13.

❑ Additional functions defined by the host language in which XPath is embedded, for example, the XSLT functions which are also described in Chapter 13.

❑ Constructor functions corresponding to the built-in atomic types in XML Schema, for example, `xs:date()` and `xs:float()`. For details of these functions, see Chapter 11.

❑ Constructor functions corresponding to user-defined atomic types in any imported schema. These are also described in Chapter 11.

❑ Additional functions made available by the vendor of the XPath processor. These should be in a namespace controlled by that vendor. An example is the function `saxon:evaluate()` offered by the Saxon product. For details, see the documentation supplied by the vendor.

❑ User-written functions, written in XSLT or XQuery.

❑ User-written functions (known as extension functions in XSLT, external functions in XQuery) written in an unrelated programming language, such as Java, C#, or JavaScript. The mechanisms for linking to such functions, and for converting values between the XPath data types and those of the target language, have been left to implementors to define.

It is not possible to write functions in XPath itself. For this, you need XSLT 2.0, XQuery 1.0, or potentially some other language that supports the capability. XPath only provides the ability to call such functions, not to define them.

A number of useful third-party function libraries have become available for XSLT 1.0 processors (see for example `http://www.exslt.org` and `http://fxsl.sf.net/`), and the same is starting to happen for XSLT 2.0 and XQuery 1.0. An example is Priscilla Walmsley's library at `http://www.functx.com`, which is available in both XSLT and XQuery versions.

Functions, at least in theory, are uniquely identified by their expanded QName (that is, namespace URI and local name) and their *arity* — that is, the number of arguments. The idea is that the static context contains a list of functions that are available to be called, and it cannot contain two functions with the same name and the same arity. There is no overloading of functions, so you can't have two functions with the same name and the same number of arguments, distinguished only by the types of the arguments.

> *Products that allow you to call Java methods are quite likely to provide some kind of overloading in practice, if one can extrapolate from what XSLT 1.0 processors do. The specification leaves enough latitude to allow this: all aspects of external calls are essentially implementation-defined. Conceptually, a product can satisfy the letter of the law by claiming that for each possible Java method name and number of arguments, there is a single function in the static context, and it is this notional function that decides which of several Java methods to call, based on the types of the arguments supplied.*

Converting the Arguments and the Result

At compile time, every function in the static context has a known signature defining the types of the arguments and the type of the result. For example, consider a function that calculates the total sales of a product (the actual logic isn't important).

Here is the XSLT 2.0 implementation:

```
<xsl:function name="mf:product-sales" as="xs:decimal">
  <xsl:param name="product" as="schema-element(mf:product)"/>
  <xsl:sequence select="sum($product//sale[@product-code eq $product/code])"/>
</xsl:function>
```

And here is the equivalent in XQuery 1.0:

```
declare function mf:product-sales ($product as schema-element(mf:product))
        as xs:decimal {
    sum($product//sale[@product-code eq $product/code])
};
```

In both cases, we have defined the function name as `mf:product-sales` (we'll assume that the namespaces have been declared properly), and we have defined it to take a single argument, which is an element conforming to the schema-defined element declaration `mf:product`. This means the element will be either a valid `mf:product` or a member of its substitution group; the detailed meaning of the syntax «`schema-element(mf:product)`» is given in Chapter 11. The return type of the function is declared to be an `xs:decimal`.

> There's no formal link between the namespaces used for functions and the namespaces used for elements, attributes, and schema-defined types. But with functions which, like this one, are very specific to a particular element type, I think it's a useful convention to put the function in the same namespace as the element type.

An XPath expression that invokes this function might look like this:

```
//mf:product[mf:product-sales(.) gt 100000]
```

This expression returns a sequence containing all the `<mf:product>` elements that have total sales in excess of 100,000.

In this example, the required type of the argument was a single node, and the result type of the function was a single atomic value. It is also possible, of course, for functions to take sequences as their arguments, or to return sequences as their result. In general, the required type of an argument has two parts: the required cardinality and the required item type. The required cardinality is shown by an occurrence indicator after the type and may be one of:

Occurrence Indicator	Meaning
(none)	Exactly one item
*	Any number of items
+	One or more items
?	Either one item, or none

The required item type defines a type that each item in the supplied value must conform to. This may be a very generic type, such as «node()», or a very specific type, such as «element(mf:product)» or «xs:unsignedByte». If no required type is specified for an argument, the implicit default is «item()*». This allows any sequence of items, in other words any value at all.

The XPath processor is required to check that the arguments supplied in the function call are of the right type, and it can also apply a very limited number of conversions to make them the right type. These rules are referred to as the *function conversion rules*. The rules are as follows:

1. First, at compile time, the name of the function and the number of arguments are used to locate the signature of the function to be called. An error occurs if no suitable function can be located. Once the signature has been located, the processor may do some compile-time checking of arguments, but the only guarantee is that each argument in the function call will be checked against the declared type of the corresponding parameter in the signature at runtime, using the rules below.

2. Each supplied argument is evaluated, to produce a value. This in general is a sequence that may contain atomic values, nodes, or a mixture of the two. (Note, however, that the processor isn't obliged to evaluate an argument that isn't used — this means that errors may go undetected.)

3. If the required item type is xs:anyAtomicType or a subtype of this (that is, if the function expects atomic values for this argument, rather than nodes), then the following steps are carried out:

   ❏ The supplied sequence is atomized. Atomization replaces each node in the supplied sequence by its typed value (which may itself be a sequence) and leaves any atomic values in the sequence unchanged.

   ❏ If any of the values in the atomized sequence are of type xs:untypedAtomic (which will normally be the case when the values are extracted from elements and attributes that have not been validated against any schema), then the system attempts to convert them to the required type by casting. The rules showing what casts are possible are given in Chapter 11, but they essentially follow the rules defined in XML Schema — if the required type is xs:date, for example, then the xs:untypedAtomic value must have the form of a valid lexical xs:date value. If the cast isn't possible, the error is fatal.

   ❏ If the required type is a numeric type (xs:double, xs:float, xs:decimal, or a type derived from any of these by restricting the allowed set of values), and if the supplied value is also numeric, then type promotion is attempted. For example, it is acceptable to supply an xs:integer value where an xs:double is expected. Numeric type promotion is described in detail in Chapter 8, because it plays an important role for arithmetic operators.

   ❏ If the required type is xs:string and the supplied value is an instance of xs:anyURI, the URI is converted to a string. In effect, XPath treats xs:anyURI as a subtype of xs:string even though XML Schema does not define it that way.

4. At this stage, a final check is made that the argument value is now a valid instance of the required type. For this to be true, each item in the sequence must be an instance of the required item type, and the number of items in the sequence must match the required cardinality. The detailed rules are the same as those for the «instance of» operator, which is described in Chapter 11. If the value doesn't conform as required, a type error is reported.

5. If all is well, the function is called, and the result of the function call expression (as you would expect) is the value returned by the function, which will always conform to the type given in the function signature.

Changes in XPath 2.0

The rules given in the previous section impose much stricter type checking than XPath 1.0, which always attempted to convert the supplied arguments to the required type. XPath 2.0 effectively retains this behavior in two cases: firstly, when the value you supply is a node in a document that has not been schema-validated, and secondly, when you run in backward-compatibility mode, which in XSLT is activated by setting «version="1.0"» in the <xsl:stylesheet> element..

So there are cases where function calls would have succeeded in XPath 1.0, but will fail under 2.0. An example is an expression such as «string-length(position())=2». The argument to the string-length() function must be of type xs:string, but the result returned by the position() function is of type xs:integer. XPath 1.0 would cheerfully convert the integer to a string, but XPath 2.0 is stricter — if you intend a conversion to take place, you must invoke it explicitly, for example by calling the string() function.

Backward-compatibility mode changes the function calling rules by adding an extra rule before rule 3 in the list above. This rule is in two parts:

❑   If the required cardinality of the parameter is zero or one (that is, if the parameter doesn't permit a sequence of more than one item), then all items in the supplied value after the first are discarded.

❑   If the required item type is a string or number type, then the supplied value is converted to a string or number using the string() or number() function as appropriate.

These rules apply only where the required type of the parameter fits into the XPath 1.0 type system. For example, if the required type is xs:date, no extra conversions are performed. More specifically, the first rule (which discards all but the first item in a sequence) applies only where the required item type is «item()», «node()», xs:string, or a numeric type such as xs:double. The second rule applies only if the required item type is xs:string or a numeric type.

Although the XPath 1.0 type system also included a boolean data type, there is no special treatment of xs:boolean in the backward-compatibility rules. That's because the only XPath 1.0 function that actually expected a boolean argument was the not() function, and this function in XPath 2.0 has been defined in a way that is fully backward compatible.

XPath 1.0 never defined any rules for calling external user-defined functions, so backward compatibility in that area is entirely a matter for implementors.

Side Effects

None of the standard functions have side effects; they don't change the values of variables, they don't produce any output, and they don't change any settings in the browser or the operating system. They don't even create any new nodes, though both XSLT and XQuery allow you to write functions that can be called from XPath to create new nodes.

There is nothing to stop an extension function from having side effects; for example, an extension function could print a message or increment a counter, or even do something more radical such as modify the source document or the stylesheet itself. However, extension functions with side effects are likely to be rather unpredictable, since there is nothing to say in which order things happen. For example, you can't assume that global variables in XSLT are evaluated in any particular order or that they are evaluated only once, and a global variable that is never accessed might never be evaluated at all.

Functions can have side effects even if you think of them as read-only. You might imagine that if you write an extension function `ext:read()` that reads a line of input from the console, then the expression «(ext:read(), ext:read())» will read two lines, and return them in order. You could be in for a surprise. The system might read two lines, and return them out of order; or it might read a single line, and return two copies of it. This happens because calling the `ext:read()` function has the side effect of changing the current reading position in a file connection. Implementations might try to be more helpful than this, but you can't rely on it.

The closest that the standard library comes to a function with side effects is the `trace()` function, which is supposed to produce diagnostic output. Like other functions in the standard library, this is described in Chapter 13. However, the specification gives so much latitude in terms of the way this is implemented that it would be quite legitimate for an implementation to do nothing when it encounters this function call. You might well find that with an optimizing processor, the output produced by multiple calls on the `trace()` function bears very little relationship to the expected order of execution.

The formal semantics of the language does try to deal with functions that create new nodes in a sanitary way. XPath itself, when confined to the standard function library, is a read-only language, but both XSLT and XQuery do allow functions that create and return new nodes. For example, in XSLT:

```
<xsl:function name="f:make" as="element()">
  <e/>
</xsl:function>
```

or in XQuery:

```
declare function f:make() as element() {
  <e/>
};
```

These functions create all sorts of complexities in the language semantics: for example, it is no longer possible to take a function call out of a loop and execute it once only. It also means that the expression «f:make() is f:make()» is false. Frankly, in XSLT stylesheets I would advise against writing such functions — I think it's good coding practice in XSLT to use XSLT instructions and templates when creating nodes in the result tree, and to use XPath expressions and functions when reading information from the source tree. XQuery doesn't have this distinction between instructions and expressions, so the same function mechanism has to serve both purposes. But you need to use it with care.

Examples

These examples are in the file `function-calls.xsl`, but you will probably need to edit the file before running it, as it uses an extension function that is available only in James Clark's xt processor.

Expression	Description
`true()`	A call on a standard function that always returns the `xs:boolean` value `true`.
`string-length($x)`	A call on a standard function that expects a string, and returns the number of characters it contains. The actual value supplied can be a node, provided its type is either `xs:string` or `xs:untypedAtomic`. If $x is a non-string value, such as an `xs:anyURI`, a type error occurs, unless you are running in backward-compatibility mode.

continued

Expression	Description
count(*)	A call on a standard function that evaluates the path expression «*» (which returns all element children of the context node) and returns a number indicating how many nodes there are in this sequence.
xt:intersection ($x,$y)	A call on an extension function. It is identified as an extension function by the presence of a prefix «xt:», which must correspond to a namespace declaration that is in scope. The rules for locating an implementation of this extension function are implementor-defined.

Conditional Expressions

A conditional expression corresponds to the «if..then..else» construct found in almost every programming language. A condition is evaluated, and based on the result, the expression returns the result of evaluating either the «then» or the «else» branch.

Expression	Syntax
IfExpr	«if» «(» Expr «)» «then» ExprSingle «else» ExprSingle

The «else» branch is constrained to be an ExprSingle (an expression containing no top-level comma) because a trailing comma would be ambiguous when the expression appears, for example, as an argument in a function call. The «then» branch is constrained to be an ExprSingle purely for symmetry. Any expression can be used as the condition, and although it would be unusual for this expression to use the «,» operator, there is no reason to disallow it.

Note that both branches (the «then» and the «else») must be present. It's quite common to write «else ()» to return nothing (an empty sequence) when the condition is false, but you have to write this explicitly.

The expression used as the condition to be tested (inside the parentheses) is evaluated to give its *effective boolean value*. Unusually, XPath 2.0 doesn't apply strict type checking to this expression, rather it defines a set of rules allowing a wide range of values to be converted to the xs:boolean values true or false. The rules are the same as for the boolean() function described on page 721, in summary:

❑ If the condition is an empty sequence, its effective boolean value is false.

❑ If the condition is a sequence whose first item is a node, its effective boolean value is true.

❑ If the condition is a singleton xs:boolean value, the result is this value.

❑ If the condition is a singleton numeric value, the result is false if the argument is NaN or zero; otherwise, it is true.

❑ If the condition is a singleton instance of xs:string, xs:anyURI, or xs:untypedAtomic, the result is false if the string is zero length; otherwise, it is true.

❑ In all other cases, an error is reported.

There is no atomization applied to any nodes in the sequence. This means that if the value includes one or more nodes, the result is true, regardless of the contents of the node. Even if «@married» is an attribute whose typed value is the xs:boolean value false, the result of the expression «if (@married) then "yes" else "no"» is the string «yes». If you want to test the contents of the node, rather than testing for its existence, use the data() function to atomize it explicitly, or write the test in the form «if (@married = true()) then ..».

Note that the effective boolean value of a sequence doesn't simply test whether the sequence is empty, because of the special cases for a singleton sequence. If you want to test whether a sequence is empty, use the empty() or exists() functions described in Chapter 13.

These rules for forming the effective boolean value are consistent with the rules used in other XPath contexts where a true/false value is required. These include:

❑ The operands of «and» and «or» (see Chapter 8)

❑ The argument of the functions boolean() and not() (see Chapter 13)

❑ The expression used as a predicate within square brackets in an axis step or filter expression, so long as the value is not numeric (see Chapters 9 and 10)

❑ The expression in the «satisfies» clause of «some» and «every» expressions (see Chapter 10)

The same rules are also used in XSLT 2.0, in evaluating the <xsl:if> and <xsl:choose> instructions.

A significant feature of these rules is that the processor can determine the effective boolean value of any sequence without looking further than the second item in the sequence. This makes the algorithm very efficient.

However, the rules are not the same as the rules in XML Schema for converting a string to an xs:boolean value. In XML Schema, the valid lexical representations of the xs:boolean value false are «0» and «false», while the valid lexical representations of true are «1» and «true». The XML Schema rules are used in XPath 2.0 in the following circumstances:

❑ By the expression «$S cast as xs:boolean»

❑ By the xs:boolean() constructor function (note the difference from the boolean() function in the core library, sometimes written as fn:boolean() to emphasize the difference)

❑ When an xs:untypedAtomic value is implicitly converted to an xs:boolean value in the course of a function call, where one of the function arguments has a required type of xs:boolean

Conditional expressions are one of the few places in the XPath language where you get a guarantee that an expression will or will not be evaluated. Specifically, if the condition is true then the «else» branch will not be evaluated, while if it is false, the «then» branch will not be evaluated. This means you can safely use expressions that could otherwise cause errors, for example:

```
if ($cols ne 0) then (count($items) idiv $cols) else ()
```

I personally prefer putting in the explicit test «$cols ne 0» rather than writing «if ($cols)..» and relying on the fact that zero is treated as false.

Changes in XPath 2.0

Conditional expressions are new in XPath 2.0. In the context of an XSLT stylesheet, they often make it possible to replace a cumbersome <xsl:choose> instruction. For example, the following:

```
<xsl:variable name="color">
  <xsl:choose>
    <xsl:when test="$day='Sunday'">white</xsl:when>
    <xsl:otherwise>red</xsl:otherwise>
  </xsl:choose>
</xsl:variable>
```

can now be replaced with:

```
<xsl:variable name="color"
              select="if ($day eq 'Sunday') then 'white' else 'red'"/>
```

The rules for calculating the effective boolean value of an expression have been carefully chosen to be compatible with the rules for converting strings, numbers, or node-sets to booleans in XPath 1.0, while at the same time generalizing them to handle an arbitrary sequence. If they seem arbitrary, blame history.

Examples

Expression	Description

`if (@x)`
`then @x`
`else 0`
	Returns the attribute node `@x` if it exists, or the `xs:integer` value zero otherwise. (This can also be expressed as «(@x,0)[1]».)

`if ($area/sales)`
`then avg($area/sales/@value)`
`else number('NaN')`
	Returns the average sales value for the selected area if there were any sales, or the not-a-number value `NaN` otherwise.

`if (normalize-space(.))`
`then string(.)`
`else ()`
	Returns the context item converted to a string if it contains any non-whitespace characters; otherwise, returns the empty sequence. This relies on the fact that `normalize-space()` returns a zero-length string (which is treated as `false`) if all the characters in the string are whitespace.

The XPath Evaluation Context

XPath was designed as an expression language that could be embedded in other languages. The first such language was XSLT, but it was always envisaged that this would only be one of many host languages. Subsequent experience has shown that this did indeed happen: XPath (sometimes in the form of a restricted subset) has been used not only within XSLT and XPointer but also within a variety of programming languages such as Java and Perl, and also as a sublanguage for expressing constraints within XForms and XML Schema.

To make XPath suitable for this role as a sublanguage, there needs to be a clear interface between XPath and the host language. This interface specifies what information is provided by the host environment to the XPath environment, and the sum total of this information is referred to as the *evaluation context*.

The evaluation context can be split into two halves: information that is available at compile time (while the XPath expression is being parsed and checked for static errors) and information that is available only at runtime. These two parts are called the static context and the dynamic context, and they are described in the next two sections of this chapter.

An XPath host language such as XSLT should always specify how the static and dynamic context for XPath expressions are set up. Some aspects of the context may be under user control, some may have fixed values, and other parts may be completely implementation defined. This will vary from one host language to another. As far as XPath is concerned, it doesn't matter whether the information is fixed in the host language specification or whether it is provided by the vendor or by the user: the information is there somehow, and it is available for use.

As I describe each part of the evaluation context in the following sections, I will explain both how things work when you use XPath from XSLT, and the more general rules that apply in other environments.

The Static Context

The static context contains information that's needed while performing the analysis or compilation phase on an XPath expression.

In many environments, XPath is a "load and go" technology: you submit an expression as a string, and it is compiled and executed straight away. In this case, the distinction between the static context and the dynamic context isn't all that important. In other environments, however, there is a distinction. XSLT stylesheets are often compiled once and then executed many times, and the XPath expressions within the stylesheet will typically be compiled when the stylesheet is compiled (usually not into machine code, but into some intermediate form that a runtime interpreter can later process). So it's worth making the distinction between the two phases even if they are often combined.

The various parts of the static context are described in the sections that follow.

XPath 1.0 Compatibility Mode

We've generally referred to this as *backward-compatibility mode*, which is what XSLT calls it. This value is a boolean: compatibility mode is either on or off. Compatibility mode will be switched on when users want the effect of an XPath expression to be as close as possible to the effect that the same expression would have had under XPath 1.0.

In XSLT, compatibility mode for XPath expressions in a stylesheet is switched on by setting the «version» attribute to «1.0», either on the <xsl:stylesheet> element or on an inner element in the stylesheet if it is required only for certain expressions and not for others. If the stylesheet specifies «version="2.0"», then 1.0 compatibility mode will be off.

XPath processors (and XSLT processors) are not obliged to offer XPath 1.0 compatibility mode. It's seen as a transition aid rather than as a permanent feature of the language.

Setting XPath 1.0 compatibility mode does not mean that everything in the language is 100% backward compatible, though it gets close. Appendix C contains a list of the incompatibilities that remain; most of them are corner cases that few users are likely to encounter, but one or two are more significant.

So what exactly changes if you set 1.0 compatibility mode? The following rules are applied only when in this mode:

❑ We have already seen, earlier in this chapter (page 549), how the function calling rules are affected. In summary, a supplied sequence may be truncated to its first value, and arguments of any type may be converted to strings or numbers if that is what the function expects.

❑ Similar rules apply to arithmetic operators such as «+» and «div». These are described in Chapter 8. They are treated in the same way as a function that expects two xs:double arguments — the supplied operands are converted to xs:double using the number() function, and the arithmetic is performed in double-precision floating point.

❑ In an expression using one of the operators «=», «!=», if one of the operands is numeric, then the other operand is converted to an xs:double value by applying the number() function. If the operator is one of «<», «<=», «>», «>=», then both operands are converted to xs:double values. There are also special rules when one of the arguments is an xs:boolean value.

What lies behind these rules is that XPath 1.0 was a weakly typed language, in which the arguments of function calls and operators were implicitly converted to the required type. XPath 2.0 has a much richer type system, in which such implicit conversion would often give unexpected results. So with XPath 2.0, you have to do the conversions you want explicitly. But this creates a backward-compatibility problem. The rules given above are designed to minimize this problem by catering for all the cases that could actually arise with a 1.0 expression. The reason that strings and numbers are treated differently from other types is that they are the only atomic types that were supported in XPath 1.0 — except for booleans. And in the case of booleans, weak typing continues to apply in XPath 2.0: every value can be converted to a boolean when it is used in a context such as the condition of an «if» expression, by taking its *effective boolean value*. The rules for this are described on page 551.

The following table illustrates some expressions whose results differ when running in backward-compatibility mode.

Expression	XPath 1.0 Compatibility Mode	
	On	Off
contains(3.14, ".")	true	type error
"apple"+"pear"	NaN	type error
"apple"< 3	false	type error
@a < "42" where @a has the untyped value "7"	true (numeric comparison)	false (string comparison)

In-Scope Namespaces

Many XPath expressions contain prefixed QNames. The names of elements and attributes can be prefixed, as can the names of variables, functions, and types. A prefix in such a name means nothing by itself: to know what type the name «xs:integer» refers to, you have to know what namespace URI is bound to the prefix «xs». It isn't possible to define the binding of a prefix to a namespace URI within the XPath expression itself, so instead it has to be part of the context. It's part of the static context so that the XPath processor can work out at compile time what all names appearing in the expression are actually referring to.

This part of the static context is modeled as a set of (prefix, URI) pairs. No prefix may appear more than once. It's an error if the XPath expression contains a QName whose prefix isn't present in this list.

In XSLT, because a stylesheet is an XML document, the in-scope namespaces for an XPath expression are defined by writing namespace declarations such as «xmlns:xs="http://www.w3.org/2001/XMLSchema"» in a containing element (often, but not necessarily, the <xsl:stylesheet> element). The namespace prefixes you can use within an XPath expression are precisely those that you could use in an element name or attribute name appearing in the same place in the stylesheet.

Each stylesheet module has its own static context, so a global variable declared in one module as:

```
<xsl:variable name="this:color" select="'red'" xmlns:this="http://module1/ns"/>
```

might be referenced in another module as:

```
<xsl:attribute name="bgcolor" select="$that:color" xmlns:that="http://module1/ns"/>
```

For other host languages, a different way of establishing the namespace context might be used. XQuery, for example has its own syntax for declaring namespaces, as does XPointer. In XQuery some namespaces (such as the XML Schema namespace) are hardwired, and others can be declared in the query prolog using syntax such as:

```
declare namespace saxon = "http://saxon.sf.net/";
```

In XPointer the syntax is:

```
xmlns(xs=http://www.w3.org/2001/XMLSchema)
```

When XPath is used from a programming language such as Java, there will generally be some method in the API that allows a namespace to be declared. In some APIs it is possible to declare namespaces implicitly by nominating a node in a source document, indicating that all the namespaces that are in scope for that node should be considered to be in scope for the XPath expression.

Default Namespaces

When a QName that has no namespace prefix is used, default namespaces come into play.

In XPath 1.0, the rule was simple: no prefix means no namespace. That is, unprefixed names always referred to objects whose namespace URI was null. In XPath 2.0 there is more flexibility. The static context potentially contains two defaults, for use with different kinds of names:

❑   The default namespace for elements and types, as the name implies, is used to qualify any name within the XPath expression that is recognized as an element name or a type name. In path expressions, it is always possible to distinguish element names by means of the axis on which they appear: if the axis is the attribute or namespace axis, then unprefixed names are considered to be in no namespace, whereas on any other axis, the namespace URI for an unprefixed name is taken from this default. The default is also used for element names appearing in a test such as «element(invoice, *)», and for the names of types, in constructs such as «attribute (*, part-number)».

In XSLT 2.0, the default namespace for elements and types can be set or unset using the [xsl:]xpath-default-namespace attribute on any element in the stylesheet. This is described on page 480.

❑   The default namespace for functions is used to qualify unprefixed names used in function calls, for example «f()». In XSLT this is always the standard namespace http://www.w3.org/2005/xpath-functions, which contains the functions listed in Chapter 13. Other host languages or APIs might define a different default.

For other kinds of name, for example attribute names and variable names, there is no default namespace. For these names, no prefix always means no namespace.

In-Scope Schema Definitions

This part of the static context represents the schema information that is available at the time an XPath expression is compiled. Technically, it consists of:

- ❑ A set of named top-level type definitions (simple and complex types)
- ❑ A set of named top-level element declarations
- ❑ A set of named top-level attribute declarations

Type definitions, element declarations, and attribute declarations are referred to collectively as schema components (there is apparently a good reason why types are "defined", whereas elements and attributes are "declared", but the explanation I was given was pretty tortuous).

The specifications don't say exactly what information can be extracted from these definitions; this is left to the implementation to sort out. In theory XPath itself, because it doesn't actually validate elements against the schema, doesn't need to know very much about them at all. All it needs to be able to do is to look at the type annotation on a node and decide whether the node is or is not an instance of a given type in the schema, which it can do by knowing the names of the types and the type hierarchy. In practice of course, XPath implementations can use a lot more information than this for optimization purposes.

XPath itself isn't concerned with where these definitions come from. It's the job of the host language to decide which types are made available in the context. In practice there's a minimum set of types that must be available, because the XPath functions and operators need them: this set corresponds roughly to the set of types that a basic XSLT processor will make available, but it's XSLT that defines this set, not XPath itself.

In XSLT, the schema components provided in the static context include:

- ❑ Some or all of the built-in types of XML Schema. In the case of a schema-aware processor, this includes all the built-in types, but in the case of a basic (non-schema-aware) processor it is a smaller subset (see page 548).
- ❑ Schema components from schemas imported using the `<xsl:import-schema>` declaration in the stylesheet. This declaration can only be used if the XSLT processor is schema-aware.
- ❑ Other implementation-defined types needed to support vendor extensions; for example, the ability to call external Java methods.

For example, if you want to reference components from the OpenGIS schema for geographical coordinate systems, you might write in your stylesheet:

```
<xsl:import-schema namespace="http://www.opengis.net/gml" schema-location=
          "http://schemas.opengis.net/gml/3.1.1/base/coordinateSystems.xsd"/>
```

You will probably want to bind a prefix to this namespace:

```
<xsl:stylesheet .... xmlns:gml="http://www.opengis.net/gml">
```

You can then use XPath expressions that reference components in this schema, for example:

```
<xsl:if test=". instance of element(*, gml:CoordinateSystemAxisType)">
```

7

XPath Fundamentals

557

A different host language, however, could make schema components available in a different way entirely. There is no obligation on the host language to put this under user control.

An XPath expression cannot make explicit reference to types (for example, in an «instance of» expression, described in Chapter 11) unless those types are present in the static context. This also applies to element declarations named in a «schema-element(N)» test, and to attribute declarations named in a «schema-attribute(N)» test. (These constructs are all defined in Chapter 11.) Elements and attributes that are named in the ordinary way within a path expression, however, do not need to have a declaration present in the static context.

The set of schema components that are present in the static context may be a subset of those available at runtime. This is an issue that caused the working groups a great deal of grief: what happens if the XPath expression calls the doc() function to load a document, and that document is validated using a schema (perhaps the schema named in its xsi:schemaLocation attribute) that wasn't supplied as part of the static context for the XPath expression? The problem arises when you write an XPath expression such as «doc('abc.xml')/a/b instance of xs:integer». To evaluate this, the XPath processor needs to look at the type annotation on the <b> element and determine whether this type is a subtype of xs:integer. How is it supposed to know?

In fact, it's not just expressions like this that need the type information. A simple comparison such as «if (doc('abc.xml')/a/b=$x) then ...» uses the typed value of the <b> element, and to determine how to do the comparison, the processor needs to know the type.

The answer the working group came up with is to invoke magic (or, in the phrase that was used at the time, a "winged horse"). The practical reality is that in many cases the XPath processor will have a fairly intimate relationship with the XML parser and/or the XML schema validator. In such cases, the XPath processor probably has access to all the schema information that was used when validating the document. It would be very difficult to formalize all this information as part of the evaluation context, so all that the specification says is that if such information is available, the XPath processor can use it to evaluate expressions like this. If the information isn't available, then the document must be rejected.

There are very many different scenarios for how documents are parsed, validated, and queried. In a typical XSLT environment, the parsing and validation usually happen just before the transformation starts. In an XML database, however, parsing and validation happen when the document is loaded into the database, which may be months or years before the query is executed. The XPath specification tries to cope with this variety of different usage scenarios, but in doing so, it inevitably leaves some aspects of the language implementation-defined.

You can avoid these problems by explicitly importing all the schemas that are used to validate documents used by your XPath expressions.

In-Scope Variables

The static context for an XPath expression includes a list of the variables that can be referenced. The information available at this time includes the name of the variable and its type, but not the actual value. It's up to the host language how these variables are declared: in XSLT, for example, they are declared using <xsl:variable> and <xsl:param> elements in the stylesheet. The scoping rules are also defined by the host language; for example, XSLT specifies that global variables are available to any XPath expression anywhere in the stylesheet (in any module), while local variables are available only within XPath expressions contained in an attribute of an element that is a following-sibling of the variable declaration, or a descendant of a following-sibling. So the stylesheet parameter:

```
<xsl:param name="start" as="xs:integer?" required="no"/>
```

adds a variable with name «start» and type «xs:integer?» to the static context of every XPath expression in the stylesheet.

The name of a variable is a QName: that is, it contains a namespace URI and a local name. In practice, it's quite unusual to put variables in a namespace, but it is permitted. It's more common to see this with XQuery, which associates namespaces with modules, so that variables exported by a module will carry the namespace of that module.

It is an error for the XPath expression to refer to variables that aren't present in the static context. In a system that does static type checking, it's also a static error to use a variable in a way that is inconsistent with its type. In systems that do dynamic type checking (which will usually be the case for XSLT), such errors are reported only if they occur when the XPath expression is evaluated.

This aspect of the static context differs from all the other aspects in that it can vary for different parts of a single XPath expression. The static context for a nested subexpression may include variables declared in containing «for», «some», or «every» expressions, as well as the variables made available by the host language. The XPath expressions that declare new variables are all listed in Chapter 8.

In-Scope Functions

The static context for an XPath expression also includes a list of the functions that can be called from within the expression. Each function is identified uniquely by its name (a QName, containing a namespace URI and local name) together with its *arity*, which is an integer indicating how many parameters the function has. Two functions with the same name but different numbers of parameters are regarded as being completely distinct functions.

The information that's needed about each function at compile time, apart from the name and arity, is the function signature. The function signature defines the type of each of the function's parameters, as well as the type of its result. This information enables the XPath processor to decide at compile time whether a function call is legitimate: it can check, firstly, that a function with the right name and number of arguments actually exists, and secondly, (if the processor does static type checking) that the arguments are each of the correct type. Even when the processor doesn't do static type checking, the signature is useful for optimization, because it enables the processor to generate code to convert the supplied values to the required type.

Like other aspects of the static context, the way in which the in-scope functions are populated is defined by the host language. In most host languages, the function library is likely to include at least:

❑   The functions defined in the core library; that is, the functions listed in Chapter 13 of this book.

❑   A constructor function corresponding to each atomic type in the in-scope schema definitions. These functions are used to construct an instance of the corresponding atomic type; for example, the function «xs:date('2004-06-01')» can be used to construct a date.

However, if a host language wanted to restrict the function library, it could choose to do so. For example, a host language might choose to support the whole function library with the exception of the doc() and collection() functions.

In XSLT, the in-scope functions include the two categories above, together with:

❑ A number of standard functions defined within the XSLT specification; for example, `format-number()`, `format-date()`, and `generate-id()`. These are described along with the XPath functions in Chapter 13.

❑ User-defined functions written in the stylesheet using the `<xsl:function>` declaration.

❑ Extension functions; for example, functions written as Java methods. The way in which extension functions are made available in the static context depends on the implementation. For example, XSLT processors written in Java generally provide an implicit binding to Java methods, in which the namespace URI of the function identifies a Java class name, and the local name identifies the method name within a class. In such cases the set of in-scope functions for the XPath processor effectively includes every public method in every class on the Java classpath. Other XSLT processors require an explicit binding of extension functions in the stylesheet, for example, through a vendor-defined declaration such as `<msxsl:script>`. In these cases, the functions added to the static context are those that are explicitly declared. (Extension functions are fully described in Chapter 16).

In principle, it's a static error if the XPath expression contains a call on a function that isn't present in the static context. However, this rule doesn't apply when XSLT backward-compability mode is in effect. This is to allow you to write conditional code that calls different extension functions depending on which XSLT processor you are using. Under these circumstances, the error won't actually be reported until the function call is executed at runtime.

As we saw above, function names contain a namespace URI and a local name. In an actual function call, the function name is written using an optional namespace prefix and a local name. If the prefix is absent, then the function is assumed to belong to the default namespace for functions, which we described earlier in this chapter on page 556. Usually (and always in XSLT), the default namespace for functions will be the namespace for the core function library, that is, `http://www.w3.org/2005/xpath-functions`. The XPath specification allows any namespace URI to be chosen as the default, but the host language doesn't have to pass this flexibility on to the user.

If there is a default namespace for functions (and as we've seen, there usually will be), then it becomes impossible to refer to functions that aren't in any namespace, because there is no way of associating a namespace prefix with names in the null namespace. The practical consequence of this is that if you import a schema with no target namespace, you will not be able to call constructor functions for the atomic types defined in that schema. Instead, you will have to use the more verbose «cast as» syntax, which is described in Chapter 9. For example, if you have an atomic type called «percentage», you will have to write «98 cast as percentage» rather than «percentage(98)».

Although constructor functions are named after atomic types, they use the default namespace for functions, not the default namespace for elements and types. For example, if the default namespace for elements and types is «http://ns.acme.com/», and there is an atomic type «part-number» defined in the schema for this namespace, then you will be able to refer to the type without using a prefix; for example, «"AXZ98532" cast as part-number». But when you use the constructor function, the default namespace for functions applies, so you will typically need to use a namespace prefix, in this case: «acme:part-number("AXZ98532")».

Collations

The static context for XPath expressions includes a set of collations, one of which is marked as the default collation. A collation is essentially a set of rules for comparing and sorting strings. One collation might decide that «pass» and «Paß» are equal, another that they are distinct.

As far as XPath is concerned, collations are defined outside the system, and a collation is treated as a black box. The XPath processor knows which collations exist (because they are listed in the static context), but it doesn't know anything about their characteristics, beyond the fact that it can use the collation to compare two strings.

Collations are identified by URIs. These are like namespace URIs, in that they don't necessarily identify real resources on the Web: they are just globally unique names, ensuring that collations defined by one vendor can't be confused with those defined by a different vendor. There is only one collation whose name has been standardized, namely:

```
http://www.w3.org/2005/xpath-functions/collation/codepoint
```

This collation, called the Unicode Codepoint Collation, compares strings character by character, using the numeric values assigned to each character in the Unicode standard. So, for example, «"Z" < "a"» is true when using this collation, because the numeric code for «Z» is 90, and the code for «a» is 97.

As with other aspects of the static context, it's up to the host language to say what collations are available and how they are defined. In this area, however, XSLT as a host language has nothing to say: it leaves it entirely up to the implementation. Many implementations are likely to devise a scheme whereby URIs identify collations provided by the programming language environment, by a database system, or by the operating system.

In Java, for example, you can define a collator by creating an object of class `java.text.Collator`. You can obtain a collator for a particular Locale, which will give you the basic rules for a language (for example, «ä» collates after «z» in Swedish, but not in German). You can then parameterize the collator: for example you can set its strength, which determines whether or not it ignores accents and case, and you can control whether it applies Unicode normalization to the characters before comparison: this process recognizes that there are alternative ways of coding the same character in Unicode, either as combined characters (one codepoint representing lower-case-c-with-cedilla) or as separate characters (separate codepoints for the «c» and the cedilla). Saxon allows you to specify a collation URI that specifies these parameters explicitly, for example the URI:

```
http://saxon.sf.net/collation?lang=de;strength=secondary;
```

requests a collation suitable for German («lang=de») in which secondary differences between characters (in practice this means case) are considered significant, but tertiary differences (in practice, accents) are not. So «"A"="a"» is false but «"a"="ä"» is true. However, this way of constructing a collation URI is peculiar to Saxon, and other products will have their own conventions.

If you want to write XPath expressions that are portable between products, it's a good idea to assign your chosen collation URI to a variable in the host language, and to reference it using the variable within the XPath expression itself.

The default collation is the one that's used in simple comparisons, such as «@a = "potato"». It's worth thinking carefully about your choice of default collation. Generally speaking, if you're searching for text then you want to cast the net wide, which means you want a weak collation (one that treats «A» and «ä» as equal). But if you're sorting, you want to make fine distinctions, which means you need a strong collation. Sorting algorithms look first for primary differences between words («a» versus «b»), then for secondary differences («a» versus «A») and then for tertiary differences («a» versus «ä»). So you will usually want the sort algorithm to take all these differences into account.

Having said this, it's worth noting that XPath doesn't actually do sorting. If you want to sort data, you need XSLT or XQuery. XPath provides many functions for comparing strings, including comparing whether one string is less than another, but it can't actually sort a collection of strings into order.

It's also interesting to note that although XPath defines the set of collations as part of the static context, there's nothing in the XPath language definition that uses this information at compile time. Collations are used only at runtime, and requesting a collation that doesn't exist is defined as a dynamic error rather than a static error. The reason collations are in the static context is a carryover from XQuery. XQuery defines sorting of sequences using an «order by» clause in which the collation must be known at compile time. The reason for this restriction is that XQuery systems running on large databases need to make compile-time decisions about which indexes can be used to access the data, and this can only be done by comparing the sort order requested in the query against the collation that was used when constructing the index.

Base URI

When an XPath expression calls the doc() function to load a document, the argument is a URI identifying the document. This may either be an absolute URI (for example, «http://www.w3.org/TR/doc.xml») or a relative URI such as «index.xml». If it is a relative URI, the question arises, what is it relative to? And the answer is: it is relative to the base URI defined in the static context.

Where XPath expressions are contained within an XML document, as happens with XSLT, it's fairly obvious what the base URI should be: it's essentially the URI of the document containing the XPath expression. (This isn't a completely clear-cut concept, because a document might be reachable by more than one URI. The thinking comes from the way URLs are used in a Web browser, where any relative URL in an HTML page is interpreted relative to the URL that was used to fetch the page that it contains. Generalizing this model has proved a fairly tortuous business.)

Where XPath expressions arise in other contexts, for example, if they are generated on the fly within a C++ program, it's far less clear what the base URI should be. So XPath delegates the problem: the base URI is whatever the host language says it is. The context dependency is made explicit by identifying the base URI as part of the static context, and as far as XPath is concerned, the problem disappears.

It's again worth noting that there is nothing in the XPath language semantics that causes the base URI to have any effect at compile time. It is used only at runtime, and then only when certain functions are used (including not only doc() but also collection() and static-base-uri()). The reason it's defined as part of the static context is the expectation that it will be a property of the document containing the text of the XPath expression.

Statically Known Documents and Collections

Later in the chapter (see page 567) we'll be looking at how the available documents and collections form part of the dynamic context of an XPath expression. Normally, one might expect that nothing is known at compile time about the documents that the query might access when the time comes to execute it.

However, this isn't always the case, especially in a database environment. This information in the static context acknowledges that in some environments, an XPath expression might be compiled specifically to execute against a particular source document or collection of source documents and that the system might be able to use this knowledge at the time it compiles the expression.

This is especially the case in a system that does static type checking. One of the difficulties with static type checking arises when the XPath expression contains a construct such as:

```
doc("invoice.xml")/invoice/line-item[value > 10.00]
```

To perform strict static type checking on this expression, the system needs to know what the data type of «value» is. If «value» were a date, for example, then the expression would be in error (you can't compare a date with a number), and the type checker would have to report this. But how can we know what the type of «value» is, if we don't know in advance what type of document «invoice.xml» is?

The specification makes provision for some documents and/or collections to be recognized by the system at compile time. For example, you might compile an XPath expression against a particular database, and you might know that all the documents in that database, or in some part of that database, have been validated against a particular schema. This knowledge might allow the system to know that the example expression above is type-safe. Without this knowledge, to get this query past a system that does static type checking you would need to change it to:

```
doc("invoice.xml")/invoice/line-item
        [(value treat as xs:decimal) > 10.00]
```

This is obviously very inconvenient. It's no surprise that most of the vendors who are planning to implement static type checking in their products are running in a database environment, where the schemas are all known in advance.

This discussion probably affects XQuery much more than it does XPath. Most vendors of XML databases are using XQuery rather than XPath as the query language (though some offered XPath as a stop-gap). There's nothing intrinsic to the argument, however, that makes it only relevant to XQuery, and that's why this information is also part of the static context in XPath.

The Dynamic Context

We've now finished our tour of the static context, which contains all the information available at compile time about the environment in which an XPath expression will run. We'll now look at the information that's available at execution time.

In principle, all the information that was available in the static context remains available to the XPath processor when evaluating the query. The dynamic context supplements this with additional information. In practice, however, the XPath processor is free to discard information that it will not need at runtime. For example, it doesn't need to know the names of variables at runtime, it only needs to know where the values of the variables will be held.

The following sections look at the different parts of the dynamic context in turn.

The Focus

The *focus* is a collective term used to describe three important pieces of information in the dynamic context: the context item, the context position, and the context size.

The most important of these is the context item. Consider the simple path expression «@code». This selects an attribute named «code». But an attribute of what? This expression only makes sense if the context item identifies an element node. The expression then selects the «code» attribute of that element. When an XPath expression like this is embedded in some host language, it is the job of the host language to define how the context item is initialized.

The term *context node* is often used to mean "the context item, assuming it is a node". Very often the context item will be a node, but it can also be an atomic value such as a string or a number.

In an XSLT template rule, for example, the context node is the node that was matched by the template rule. So if you write:

```
<xsl:template match="product">
  <xsl:value-of select="@code"/>
</xsl:template>
```

then the XPath expression «@code» is evaluated with the matched `<product>` element as the context node.

To see the effect of the context position and size, it's probably easiest to look at an `<xsl:for-each>` instruction; for example:

```
<xsl:for-each select="author">
  <xsl:value-of select="."/>
  <xsl:if test="position() != last()">, </xsl:if>
</xsl:for-each>
```

The XPath expression «.», used in the `<xsl:value-of>` instruction, simply selects the context item. The instruction then writes a text node containing the value of this item converted to a string.

The function `position()` returns the value of the context position, and the function `last()` returns the value of the context size. In an `<xsl:for-each>` instruction, each item in the selected sequence (here, each `<author>` element) is processed in turn. While each item is being processed, it becomes the context item, and its position in the sequence of items being processed becomes the context position. Positions are always numbered starting at one. The context size is the number of items in the sequence, which of course is the same for each of the items. So the test `<xsl:if test="position() != last()">, </xsl:if>` outputs a comma after every item except the last.

XSLT also initializes the context position and size when a sequence of nodes is processed using `<xsl:apply-templates>`.

In other host languages, for example, in APIs for invoking XPath, it's quite common that there is no provision for setting the context position and size, only the context item. There is no obligation on the host language to provide this capability. It can choose always to set the context position and size to one, or to leave them undefined (in which case it's an error to use the functions `position()` or `last()`).

The context item will very often be a node, but in principle it can be any kind of item, that is, a node or an atomic value. In XSLT 2.0, for example, you can use the `<xsl:for-each>` instruction to process a sequence of strings, and within such an instruction the context item will be a string. If you then use a path expression that relies on the context item being a node (for example, a path expression such as «@code»), it will fail with an error.

The focus is initialized by the host language on entry to an XPath expression, but the focus can change when evaluating a subexpression. There are two constructs in XPath that change the focus: the path expression «A/B», and the filter expression «S[P]». Path expressions are described in full detail in Chapter 9 of this book, and filter expressions in Chapter 10. Let's take the filter expressions first.

> *In fact there are two very similar constructs of the form S[P] that use predicates in square brackets, and we'll explain the difference between them in Chapters 9 and 10. For the purpose of this discussion, there is no distinction — they both handle the focus in the same way.*

In this construct, «S» is a sequence (that is, it's some expression whose value is a sequence — and as every expression evaluates to a sequence, this actually means it can be any expression whatsoever). «P» is a predicate, which filters the sequence by selecting only those items that match a given condition. So if we write «author[@surname="Smith"]» we are selecting those <author> elements that have a «surname» attribute whose value is «Smith».

Within the predicate, just as within an <xsl:for-each> instruction in XSLT, the context item is the item from the sequence that's being tested; the context position is the position of that item in the sequence being filtered (counting from one); and the context size is the number of items in the sequence. This means, for example, that you can select the first half of the sequence by writing:

```
$sequence[position() * 2 <= last()]
```

There is a special rule for predicates, namely that if the value of the predicate is a number *N*, then it is treated as a shorthand for the condition «[position()=*N*]», which selects the *N*th item in the sequence.

For path expressions of the form «A/B», the rules are the same as the rules for predicates. The expression B is evaluated once for each node in the sequence produced by evaluating A, and while B is being evaluated, that node is the context item, the position of that node in the sequence is the context position, and the number of items in the sequence is the context size. However, it's very hard to construct a useful path expression that actually uses position() or last() on the right-hand side of the «/» operator. Using them inside a predicate such as «A/B[last()]» doesn't count, of course, because the focus changes again once you're inside the predicate.

It's also important to be aware that certain expressions *don't* change the focus. Specifically, the focus is not changed within a «for», «some», or «every» expression (these expressions are described in Chapter 10). So the expression:

```
«every $i in //item satisfies @price lt 100)»
```

is incorrect (at any rate, it doesn't do what you probably intended), because the context item doesn't change within this expression, which means that the relative path expression «@price» is not evaluated relative to each item in turn. The way you should write this is:

```
«every $i in //item satisfies $i/@price lt 100)»
```

It's easy to forget that a path expression such as «//item» requires a context node. This expression selects nodes starting from the document node at the root of the tree containing the context node. So when the context item changes, if it selects a node in a different document, then the result of «//item» changes too. This also means (which can come as a surprise) that when the context item isn't a node, an expression such as «//item» gives you an error. For example, this means you can't write:

```
«tokenize(sentence, "\s+")[not(. = //stopword)]»
```

because by the time you're in the predicate, the context item is one of the strings produced by the tokenize() function, which means there is no context node, and therefore no root for «//stopword» to select from. The solution to this problem is to assign the result of the expression «//stopword» (or perhaps the root node from which it navigates) to a variable.

Variable Values

The dynamic context of an XPath expression also holds the values of all the variables that are defined in the static context. Each of these variables must have a value by the time the expression is evaluated, it is not possible for a variable to be "null" or "uninitialized". The closest thing to a null value is the value «()», the empty sequence.

The value of each variable will always conform to its declared type. If the type of the variable is «xs:decimal», for example, the value can be an instance of «xs:decimal» or an instance of «xs:integer» (which is a subtype of «xs:decimal»), but it cannot be an «xs:string» or an «xs:float».

The way that the variable acquires its value is up to the host language. In many languages there will not be a meaningful distinction between declaring a variable (in the static context) and giving it a value (in the dynamic context). In XSLT there is no distinction in the case of <xsl:variable>, but there is in the case of <xsl:param>. In the example on page 559, we showed a stylesheet parameter declared as:

```
<xsl:param name="start" as="xs:integer?" required="no"/>
```

The value supplied to this parameter when the stylesheet is invoked becomes part of the dynamic context for every XPath expression in the stylesheet. If no value is supplied, the dynamic context contains the default value, which in this case is the empty sequence, «()».

Function Implementations

For every function defined in the static context of the expression, there must be an implementation available so that the function can be called and can return a result.

I don't think this is saying anything very profound, so I will move on. It does make the point that although the signatures of the in-scope functions must be known when the XPath expression is compiled, there is scope for substituting different implementations of the function at runtime.

Current dateTime

The specification tries to ensure that all the information that an XPath expression can depend on is included formally as part of the context. An XPath expression that uses the functions current-date(), current-time(), or current-dateTime() depends on the current date and time, so this is modeled as part of the dynamic context.

XPath is designed on the basis that functions are always pure functions, and a characteristic feature of a pure function is that when you call it repeatedly, it returns the same result each time. The current date and time in the dynamic context are therefore defined not to change during the execution of an XPath expression. In fact, in XSLT, they are defined not to change during the execution of an entire stylesheet. This means that the functions are not useful for applications such as performance instrumentation; they are intended rather for recording the approximate time at which a stylesheet or query was executed, and for use in business logic calculations such as displaying a date three days from today.

Implicit Timezone

XML Schema allows values to be specified without a timezone, for example, as «2008-01-31 T22:00:00». This can be interpreted as meaning that the timezone is unknown, but this interpretation makes life very complicated when dates and times are compared with each other: it means, for example, that «2008-01-31» is definitely earlier than «2008-02-05», but it's uncertain whether «2008-01-31» is earlier than «2008-02-01», because if the first date is used in a part of the world whose timezone is «-12:00», it refers to the same period of 24 hours as the second date in a place whose timezone is «+12:00». Such uncertainty causes havoc with query languages, and so XPath took a different approach. Instead of interpreting the absence of a timezone as meaning that the timezone is unknown, it interprets it as meaning that an implicit timezone should be assumed. Where possible, this will be the timezone in the place where the user is located, or failing that, the timezone in the place where the computer is located. However, XPath doesn't worry itself with how the implicit timezone is set up: it simply says that there is one, leaves it to the host environment to initialize it, and goes on to specify how it is used when performing operations on dates and times.

Some host languages might choose to specify how the implicit timezone is initialized: in Java, for example, it could have a defined relationship to the current locale. XSLT, however, chooses to pass the buck to the implementation. It's likely that many implementations will use the timezone setting from the computer on which the XSLT processor is running, which may or may not give useful results.

The implicit timezone is used behind the scenes by a number of operators that manipulate dates and times, but it is also available explicitly to the XPath user through the function implicit-timezone(), which is included in Chapter 13.

Available Documents and Collections

One of the aims in defining the evaluation context for XPath is to list all the things in the environment that can affect the result of an XPath expression. Two of the most environment-dependent constructs in the language are the doc() function (and its XSLT precursor, document()), which loads a document using a URI, and the collection() function, which similarly identifies a collection of documents using a URI.

In the XSLT 1.0 specification there was a fairly detailed description of how the document() function was supposed to work. It described in some detail the process of URI resolution, the way in which the URI was dereferenced to fetch a resource from the Web, the requirement for this resource to contain well-formed XML, and the way that the media type of the resource affected the interpretation of any fragment identifier in the URI.

But at the same time, the specification said that the input to the XSLT processor was a tree, following the rules in the data model, and that nothing in the specification should constrain the way in which the tree was constructed.

There's clearly a tension between these two definitions, and this revealed itself, during the life of the specification, in some practical problems. Notoriously, the Microsoft XSLT processor took the second statement at face value, and stripped spaces from the source document by default, which meant that it often produced different results from other XSLT processors. Another XSLT processor decided to expand XInclude directives in the source document by default. Both of these decisions were entirely conformant according to the specification, and yet they led to practical interoperability problems.

Even more extreme effects can be achieved by exploiting the URIResolver interface in the Java JAXP API (which Microsoft has emulated in the System.Xml framework classes under the name XmlResolver). This allows the user to nominate a routine that will intercept all requests for a URI from the doc() function, and take over the job of delivering a document in response to the request. This means, for example, that you can call the `doc()` function with the URI «`special://prime/100`» and return a document containing the first 100 prime numbers, constructed algorithmically. This mechanism is undoubtedly useful, but it rather makes a mockery of any detailed description in the language specification of how the `doc()` function is supposed to work.

Rather than try and tighten up the specs to force interoperability, the working groups decided that this was a place where allowing implementations some freedom was actually in users' best interests. The way that this is reflected in the spec may seem a little confusing. It simply says that the dynamic context of an XPath expression provides a mapping from URIs onto document nodes. The easiest way to read this is by thinking of the mapping as being an external function rather like the Java `URIResolver`: if you give it a URI, it comes back with a document node. This function might go out to the Web, retrieve an XML document, parse it, validate it, and turn it into a tree in the data model. Or, it might return a document node that represents a virtual document, which is actually a collection of data in a relational database. Or, it might construct an XML document containing the first 100 prime numbers. Quite simply, anything goes.

So you can't be sure that the same call on the `doc()` function will produce the same results on two different implementations. The hope is that market forces will ensure that most products support the obvious mappings from URIs to documents, even though these mappings are no longer mandatory, and might not be provided by XPath processors designed to operate in specialized environments.

As well as the `doc()` function which returns a document node corresponding to a URI, XPath 2.0 also provides the `collection()` function which returns a collection of documents (actually, a sequence). While there is a great deal of precedent and user expectation for the way in which URIs will map to individual documents, there is very little precedent for the concept of a document collection identified by URI, and it's likely therefore that different processors will interpret this concept in very different ways. There is a tendency, however, for good ideas to be copied from one implementation to another, so perhaps conventions will start to appear. However, the concept of collections is really intended as an abstraction of an XML database, or part of an XML database, and since the system architecture of different XML databases is highly variable, there might well remain radical differences in the way that the concept of a collection is realized.

As with other aspects of the context, the host language gets a say in the matter. For example, a host language could say that the set of available documents and collections is always empty, and thus constrain XPath expressions to operate on a single document, or on documents accessible through variables. Indeed, the current draft of XML Schema 1.1, which uses XPath expressions to define assertions, does just this. But in the case of XSLT, little more is said on the subject. The only thing that XSLT adds is a specification of the `document()` function, which continues to be available in XSLT and is now defined in terms of the simpler XPath 2.0 `doc()` function.

Summary

XPath expressions are used in XSLT to select data from the source document and to manipulate it to generate data to place in the result document. XPath expressions play the same role for XML as the SQL `SELECT` statement plays for relational databases — they allow us to select specific parts of the document for transformation, so that we can achieve the required output. Their use is not restricted to XSLT stylesheets — they can also be used with XPointers to define hyperlinks between documents, and many DOM implementations allow XPath expressions to be used to find nodes within the DOM.

This chapter provided an introduction to the basic constructs in XPath expression: an overview of the grammar and the lexical rules, and explanation of some of the basic constructs such as literals, variable references, function calls, and conditional expressions.

In this chapter we also described all the contents of the XPath evaluation context, including both the static and the dynamic context. The context is important because it establishes the interface between XPath and a host language such as XSLT, and it identifies all the external information that may affect the result of an XPath expression.

The next four chapters explore the XPath language in more depth. Chapter 8 looks at the basic operators for arithmetic, boolean comparisons, and testing identity and ordering of nodes. Chapter 9 describes path expressions and the operations for combining sets of nodes to form their union, intersection, or difference. Chapter 10 examines expressions on sequences, notably the «for» expression, which provides a general mapping capability to construct one sequence by applying an expression to each item of an input sequence. Then, Chapter 11 discusses operations on types.

After a return to XSLT to describe match patterns in Chapter 12, Chapter 13 provides a catalog of all the functions in the core library, and Chapter 14 gives the syntax for regular expressions, which are used in three of these functions.

7

XPath Fundamentals

XPath: Operators on Items

This chapter defines the simple operators available for use in XPath expressions. This is inevitably a rather arbitrary category, but these operators seem to have enough in common to justify putting them together in one chapter. All these operators return single items (as distinct from sequences) — in fact, all of them except the arithmetic operators in the first section return a boolean result.

More specifically, this chapter describes the following families of operators:

- ❑ Arithmetic operators, «+», «-», «*», «div», and «mod»
- ❑ Value comparison operators «eq», «ne», «lt», «le», «gt», «ge»
- ❑ General comparison operators «=», «!=», «<», «<=», «>», «>=»
- ❑ Node comparison operators «<<», «is», and «>>»
- ❑ Boolean operators «and» and «or»

Many of these operators behave in much the same way as similar operators in other languages. There are some surprises, though, because of the way XPath handles sequences, and because of the way it mixes typed and untyped data. So don't skip this chapter just because you imagine that everything about these operators can be guessed.

Arithmetic Operators

These operators are normally used to perform calculations on numbers, which may be of any of the numeric types: xs:integer, xs:decimal, xs:float, or xs:double. They are also overloaded to perform calculations on dates and durations.

Note that this section only describes arithmetic operators built in to the XPath syntax. These operators are complemented by a range of arithmetic functions in the standard function library, described in Chapter 13. The functions in this library include abs(), ceiling(), floor(), round(), round-half-to-even(), sum(), max(), min(), and avg().

Syntax

The syntax of expressions using the arithmetic operators is defined by the following syntax productions in the XPath grammar.

Expression	Syntax
AdditiveExpr	MultiplicativeExpr ((«+»| «-») MultiplicativeExpr)*
MultiplicativeExpr	UnionExpr ((«*»| «div» | «idiv» | «mod») UnionExpr)*
UnaryExpr	(«-» | «+»)* PathExpr

The priority of operators is indicated by the grammar. Unary «+» and «-» have a higher priority (bind more tightly) that the multiplicative operators «*», «div», «idiv», and «mod», which in turn have higher priority than the binary forms of «+» and «-». In between union operators and unary operators, there is a long list of operators with intermediate priority, such as «intersect» and «cast as». A full list of operator priorities, showing how these operators relate to others, is given in Appendix A.

There are two division operators: «div» for exact division, and «idiv» for integer division. The precise rules for these are described below. The «mod» operator gives the remainder when one number is divided by another. The reason that the «/» symbol isn't used for division is that this would conflict with its use in path expressions, which are described in Chapter 9.

When using the minus operator, take care that it does not get confused with a hyphen within a name. If it immediately follows a name, use a space to separate it. Note that «price-discount» (without spaces) is a single hyphenated name, whereas «price − discount» (with spaces) performs a subtraction. If in doubt, use spaces to separate an operator from the surrounding tokens: it never does any harm.

If there are several operators with the same priority, they are evaluated from left to right. For example «5-2-2» means «(5-2)-2», which evaluates to «1».

Type Promotion

There are special rules for arithmetic operators to determine the type of the result of the expression, based on the types of the operands.

If the operands have the same type, then in general the result is the same type as the operands. So, for example, the sum of two xs:integer values is an xs:integer, while the result of multiplying two xs:double values is an xs:double. The exception to this rule is the «div» operator, when the operands are xs:integer values: in this case, the result is an xs:decimal. For example, the result of «5 div 2» is the xs:decimal value «2.5».

The phrase "the same type" in this rule means the underlying numeric type: one of xs:integer, xs:decimal, xs:float, or xs:double. If you add two xs:short values, the result will be an xs:integer, not an xs:short. (At any rate, it's not guaranteed to be an xs:short; the only requirement on the implementation is that the result must be an xs:integer, and returning an xs:short would satisfy that requirement, as long as the result of the operation is in the range of values that xs:short can handle.)

If you use these operators to combine two values that are of different types, type promotion kicks in. This defines a pecking order among the four numeric types: xs:double wins over xs:float, xs:float over xs:decimal, and xs:decimal over xs:integer. If you mix two types, then the loser in this pecking order is first converted to the type of the winner, and the result has the same type as the winner. So, for example, the result of the expression «2.5 + 1» is the xs:decimal value «3.5», because «2.5» is an xs:decimal and «1» is an xs:integer, and xs:decimal is higher in the pecking order.

Changes in XPath 2.0

The main change affecting arithmetic operators is the increased range of data types they can handle. In XPath 1.0, all numbers were handled as double-precision floating point, and the operators were not overloaded to handle any other data types.

In XPath 1.0, the arguments supplied to the function were automatically converted to numbers, using the rules for the number() function (which is described in Chapter 13). This means, for example, that the result of «1 + true()» would be 2 (true() converts to 1), and the result of «"apple"+"pear"» would be NaN (any non-numeric string converts to the special not-a-number value NaN, and adding two NaNs gives NaN). These conversions are still carried out in XPath 2.0 if you run with backward compatibility enabled, which is what happens in an XSLT stylesheet that specifies «version = "1.0"». The main advantage of this behavior is that you never get a runtime error (only NaN results), and if this is important to you, you can achieve the same effect in XPath 2.0 by using the number() function explicitly, even without backward compatibility enabled.

The «idiv» operator is new in XPath 2.0. It does integer division and is particularly useful when calculating how many rows and columns you need for a table; for example, if you have $N items to arrange in three columns, then the number of rows needed is «($N + 2) idiv 3». Although the result is always an integer, the operands don't have to be integers: for example, the result of «3.6 idiv 1.5» is «2». Another handy use of this operator is to convert any number $x to an integer by writing «$x idiv 1».

Unary plus has been added to the language largely so that any value accepted as the lexical value of a number by XML Schema is also accepted as a valid constant value in an XPath expression. XML Schema accepts «+1.0» as a legal representation of a number, so XPath 2.0 accepts it too.

The relative precedence of the union operator «|» and unary minus has changed since XPath 1.0. In 1.0, the expression «-@price|@cost» was interpreted as «-(@price|@cost)», whereas it now means «(-@price) | (@cost)». Usually this will give a type error on the grounds that the operands of «|» must be nodes, but in the case where there is no @price attribute and @cost has the value 12, the expression will return -12 in XPath 1.0 but + 12 in XPath 2.0.

Effect

The detailed rules for these operators are as follows. The rules are given here on the assumption that the special rules for XPath 1.0 backward compatibility are not in force; the changes that apply under backward-compatibility mode are described later.

1. The operands are atomized, as described on page 220 in Chapter 5. This means that nodes are replaced by their typed values; for example, if one of the operands is the attribute node «@price», then the typed value of this attribute is extracted.

2. If, after atomization, either operand is an empty sequence, then the result of the operation is also an empty sequence. For example, if the context node has no price attribute, then the result of «@price * 0.8» is the empty sequence, «()».

3. If either operand after atomization is a sequence of more than one item, a type error is raised. For example, if you write the expression «price * 0.8» and the context node has more than one child element called <price>, a type error ensues. The significance of it being a type error is that it may be reported either at compile time or at runtime, as discussed in the section on *Static and Dynamic Type Checking* in Chapter 5 (page 221).

4. If either operand is an xs:untypedAtomic value, then it is converted (using the casting rules) to an xs:double. This situation will normally occur when the operand as written is a node in a schema-less document. For example, suppose the expression is «@price * 0.8», and there is no schema, and the price attribute in the source document is written as «price = "129.99"». Then the attribute value will be converted to the xs:double value 1.2999e2, and the result of the multiplication will also be an xs:double. Note the difference with numeric literals, described on page 530 in Chapter 7 — in the case of a value contained in an untyped node, it is always converted to an xs:double when used as an operand of «*», regardless of whether it is written in exponential notation or not.

    The conversion to an xs:double uses the casting rules (described in Chapter 11), not the rules of the number() function. This means that if the value isn't a valid number, the expression will fail with a runtime error, rather than returning the value NaN.

5. If the operands are now of an acceptable type for the operator, the calculation is carried out. In the case of numeric operands, all combinations of numeric values are acceptable, and the values are first promoted to a common type as described in the section *Type Promotion* above. The only other kinds of operands that are acceptable are certain combinations of dates, times, and durations, which are described in the section *Arithmetic using Durations* below. The calculation may succeed or fail (the most obvious example of a failure is division by zero); if it fails, a runtime error is reported.

6. If the operands are of the wrong type, then a type error is raised. For example, this will happen if one of the operands is an xs:boolean or xs:string value.

There are two differences to these rules when backward compatibility is in force. Firstly, in step 3, instead of reporting an error when there is more than one item in the sequence, all items except the first are discarded. Secondly, after step 4, any operand of type xs:untypedAtomic, xs:string, xs:boolean, xs:decimal (including xs:integer), or xs:float is converted to an xs:double value, using the number() function. This means that the result will also be of type xs:double. If the value of an operand can't be converted, the answer comes out as NaN rather than an error. This rule is written in such a way that arithmetic on dates, times, and durations is unaffected by backward-compatibility mode — it follows the normal 2.0 rules.

Arithmetic Using Numbers

This section describes some of the corner cases that can arise when doing numeric arithmetic.

Integer Arithmetic

With integer operands, there are few surprises.

❏   Division by zero is a fatal error. This can arise with any of the operators «div», «idiv», or «mod».

❏   The language spec doesn't define the maximum size of an integer, though it does say it must be at least 18 decimal digits, which should be enough for most purposes. Every conforming implementation is required to provide an option to detect integer overflow and report it as a fatal error. It's also permissible to provide a mode where arithmetic wraps around (as it does in many programming languages like Java and C). If both options are available, the spec doesn't say which should be the default. The thinking is that some users will want to pay the cost of the runtime error detection, whereas others will prefer raw speed.

The result of dividing two integers using the «div» operator is an xs:decimal value, but the spec doesn't say what the precision of the result should be. For example, if you write «10 div 3», then one system might produce the answer «3.333», while another produces «3.3333333333333333».

The «mod» operator, which gives the remainder from an integer division, can be confusing when negative numbers are involved. I find the following rules of thumb helpful:

❑ The result is positive if the first operand is positive, negative if it is negative.

❑ The result depends only on the absolute value of the second operand, not on its sign.

It's also useful to think of the «mod» operator in conjunction with «idiv». Thus:

Expression	Result	Expression	Result
20 mod 3	2	20 idiv 3	6
20 mod −3	2	20 idiv −3	−6
−20 mod 3	−2	−20 idiv 3	−6
−20 mod −3	−2	−20 idiv −3	6

In all cases (except where $y is zero) the result of «($x idiv $y)*$y + ($x mod $y)» is $x.

Decimal Arithmetic

Decimal arithmetic is useful because it avoids the rounding errors that arise with floating-point calculations. This is particularly true when handling values that are discrete rather than continuous, of which the most obvious example is money.

Again, the language spec doesn't define the maximum precision that can be held in an xs:decimal value. This is more likely to be a problem with xs:decimal than with xs:integer, and it means that different products are likely to give different answers to the same calculation (though hopefully, only a little bit different!).

The main problem is with division. Even systems that support indefinite-precision xs:decimal values (as Saxon does, for example) have to make a decision as to how many digits to retain in the result of «10 div 3», and the spec offers no clues.

As with integer arithmetic, division by zero is a fatal error.

The rules for handling overflow are subtly different from the rules for integers. In the case of xs:decimal, overflow (that is, calculation of a result that is too big for the system to handle, whatever this limit might be) must be reported as an error. So unlike the situation with integers, there is no prospect of the system giving you a spurious result by wrapping around.

Arithmetic with xs:decimal values can also cause *underflow*. This happens when the result of a computation is smaller than the smallest value that can be recorded, but greater than zero. Equally, of course, it could be a very small negative number. For example, if you multiply 0.00000001 by itself, and the system can only handle 10 decimal places after the decimal point, you will get an underflow. The rule in this case is that the result returned must be the xs:decimal value 0.0.

Floating-Point Arithmetic

Floating-point arithmetic (whether using single precision xs:float, or double-precision xs:double) is defined by the rules of the IEEE 754 specification. These rules were summarized in Chapter 5.

The XPath 1.0 specification tied the definition of floating-point arithmetic pretty closely to the same rules as were adopted in Java. But in fact, the IEEE 754 specification offers a number of options, and XPath 2.0 gives implementors a bit more freedom to select which options to provide. In particular, the specification allows for errors to be raised on overflow or underflow conditions, whereas the XPath 1.0 profile always returned positive or negative infinity in the overflow case, and positive or negative zero for underflow. So in corner cases, the behavior may not be exactly the same as with XPath 1.0, and not quite so consistent across different processors.

The unary minus operator is defined to change the sign of the operand. This is subtly different from subtracting the operand from zero, because it means that «-0e0» represents negative zero rather than positive zero. There's very little difference between the two: about the only way of telling them apart is by a test such as «1 div $x > 0», which returns true if $x is positive zero (the division gives positive infinity), but false if $x is negative zero. For practical purposes, the distinction between the two values is rarely important, and it is lost once you write the results away to an XML document. Its only significance is that it preserves a useful difference in the intermediate results of complex calculations.

Floating-point arithmetic can always give you rounding errors, because there are values that can be written accurately in decimal notation that can't be expressed accurately in binary. So, for example, the result of the expression «1.0E-3 * 1.0E-4» might not be displayed as «1.0E-7» as you would expect, but as «1.0000000000000001E-7». You can round it to the number of decimal places required using the round-half-to-even() function, or in XSLT, by using the format-number() function. Both are described in Chapter 13.

Examples of Numeric Arithmetic

Expression	Description
$X + 1	The result of adding 1 to the value of the variable $X.
last()-1	One less than the position of the last node in the context list.
@margin*2	Twice the value of the margin attribute of the context node. This will work only if the margin attribute either has a numeric type, or is untyped and has a value that can be interpreted as a number.
ceiling(count (item) div 3)	One-third of the number of child <item> elements of the context node, rounded upwards. (Useful if you are arranging the items in three columns).
$seq[position() <= last() idiv 2]	Selects the first half of the items in the sequence $seq, rounded down. For example, if there are 11 items in the sequence, it selects the first five.
item[position() mod 2 = 0]	Selects the even-numbered child <item> elements of the context node. (Again, this can be useful if you are arranging items in a table).
count($list) mod 5 + 1	The number of items in the sequence $list modulo 5, plus one. The result will be a number in the range 1 to 5.

continued

Expression	Description
-@credit	The negated numeric value of the credit attribute of the context element node. If the context node has no credit attribute, or if its value is not numeric, the result of the expression is «()» (the empty sequence), unless backward-compatibility mode is set, in which case it is NaN (not a number).
+@credit	The plus sign here is not a no-op; it forces conversion of the attribute node to a number. It also tells the compiler that the result will be a number, which can be useful when doing static typing and optimization.
1---1	A not very useful but perfectly legal way of writing the value zero. The first minus sign is a binary subtraction operator; the next two are unary minus signs.

Arithmetic Using Durations

As well as being used for conventional arithmetic with numbers, the arithmetic operators are used to perform certain operations on dates, times, and durations. Not all combinations make sense; for example, it's sensible to add 3 days to a date, but it isn't sensible to add two dates.

There's a table in the XPath 2.0 specification that lists all the combinations of operators and operands that are permitted, and the number that involve dates, times, and durations is alarmingly large. But appearances are deceptive: on closer examination, it turns out that these are all permutations on a small number of themes. The number of permutations is large because it involves:

- **Three date/time types:** xs:date, xs:dateTime, and xs:time
- **Two duration types:** xs:yearMonthDuration and xs:dayTimeDuration
- Symmetric operations, for example (duration + date) as well as (date + duration)

In fact, all the options boil down to five basic categories:

Expression	Meaning
date/time +|- duration	Returns a date/time that is a given duration after or before the supplied date/time. For example, 2008-12-31 plus three days is 2009-01-03.
duration +|- duration	Adds or subtracts two durations to give another duration. For example, one hour plus two hours is three hours.
duration *|div number	Multiplies a duration by a numeric factor, or divides it by a numeric factor, to give another duration. For example, one month times 3 is three months.
date/time - date/time	Determines the interval between two dates/times, as a duration. For example, 2009-01-03 minus 2008-12-31 is three days.
duration div duration	Determines the ratio between two durations, as a number. For example PT12H divided by PT10M is 72.

In each of these cases the following rules hold:

❑ If the operator is «+» or «*» (but not if it is «-» or «div») then the operands may be written in either order.

❑ Subtracting a positive duration is the same as adding a negative duration (a negative duration is written, for example, as «-P3D» to represent minus three days).

❑ The duration must be either an xs:dayTimeDuration or an xs:yearMonthDuration. The first kind is equivalent to an exact number of seconds, the second to an exact number of months. The primitive type xs:duration can't be used for arithmetic, because the variation in the length of a month creates too many uncertainties.

❑ Multiplying a duration by a number such as 0.5 is the same as dividing it by 2.0.

The following sections examine each of the four cases in a bit more detail.

Date/Time Plus Duration

This section covers the following combinations of operands:

Operand 1	Operand 2	Result
xs:date	xs:yearMonthDuration	xs:date
xs:date	xs:dayTimeDuration	xs:date
xs:dateTime	xs:yearMonthDuration	xs:dateTime
xs:dateTime	xs:dayTimeDuration	xs:dateTime
xs:time	xs:dayTimeDuration	xs:time

The allowed operators are «+» and «-». If the operator is «+», then the operands may appear in either order; if it is «-», then the date/time must be the first operand and the duration the second. Subtracting a positive duration has the same effect as adding a negative duration, and vice versa.

The decision to allow arithmetic using the two subtypes xs:yearMonthDuration and xs:dayTimeDuration, while not allowing it using the parent type xs:duration, is slightly perverse, since any xs:duration value can be decomposed into an xs:yearMonthDuration and an xs:dayTimeDuration. But by now, you should be used to the idea that the handling of durations in XML Schema and XPath has a few rough edges.

Let's start by seeing how to add an xs:dayTimeDuration to an xs:dateTime. This is reasonably straight-forward. An xs:dayTimeDuration represents an exact number of seconds. When you add this to an xs:dateTime you get the value that represents the instant in time that is this number of seconds later (or earlier, if the duration is negative) than the original, in the same timezone. (The algorithm ignores the leap seconds that can be inserted arbitrarily into the calendar to handle variations in the earth's speed of rotation.)

If you're adding an xs:dayTimeDuration to an xs:date, rather than to an xs:dateTime, you can get the right answer by considering the xs:dateTime at 00:00:00 on the date in question and then ignoring the time part of the result.

If you're adding the duration to an xs:time, the result is taken modulo 24 hours. For example, 03:00:00 plus P1D is 03:00:00, and 03:00:00 plus PT36H is 15:00:00.

If you're adding an `xs:yearMonthDuration` to an `xs:date`, the rules are slightly more complicated. What is 31st January plus one month? The answer given by the specification is that it is 28th February, or 29th February if it's a leap year.

Adding an `xs:yearMonthDuration` to an `xs:dateTime` is the same as adding it to the date part of the `xs:dateTime`, and returning the time portion unchanged. Adding an `xs:yearMonthDuration` to an `xs:time` is not allowed, because it would always return the value unchanged.

Duration Plus Duration

You can only add or subtract two durations of the same type. The allowed combinations of operands are:

Operand 1	Operand 2	Result
`xs:yearMonthDuration`	`xs:yearMonthDuration`	`xs:yearMonthDuration`
`xs:dayTimeDuration`	`xs:dayTimeDuration`	`xs:dayTimeDuration`

The operator can be either «+» or «-».

The rules are reasonably obvious (at any rate, they appear to be obvious to the writer of the specification, which simply says that the result is the sum or difference of the two durations). Remember that an `xs:yearMonthDuration` is equivalent to an `xs:integer` number of months, and an `xs:dayTimeDuration` is equivalent to an `xs:decimal` number of seconds. The addition and subtraction of two durations, whether they are positive or negative in sign, thus reduces to simple arithmetic on numbers.

For example, subtracting `PT6H` (6 hours) from `P1D` (one day) gives `PT18H` (18 hours).

Only binary «+» and «-» can be used with durations: the unary «+» and «-» operators, for no particularly good reason, are constrained to work only with numbers. The easiest way to turn a positive duration into an equivalent negative duration is to multiply it by «-1», as described in the next section.

Duration Times Number

An `xs:dayTimeDuration` or `xs:yearMonthDuration` can be multiplied or divided by a number, to give another duration of the same type. The operand combinations are:

Operand 1	Operand 2	Result

`xs:yearMonthDuration`	`xs:double`
	`xs:float`
	`xs:decimal`
		`xs:yearMonthDuration`

`xs:dayTimeDuration`	`xs:double`
	`xs:float`
	`xs:decimal`
		`xs:dayTimeDuration`

The operator can be «*» (multiply) or «div» (divide). If the operator is «*», the operands can appear in either order; if it is «div», then the numeric operand must be the second operand.

The effect of the operation is equivalent to converting the duration to a number of months or seconds, performing a numeric multiplication or division, and then converting the result back to a duration.

Date/Time Minus Date/Time

The problem of comparing dates and times is illustrated nicely by the following letter published in *The Times* of London, which we will return to later:

This week the wives of two of my nephews have given birth to sons. The first was born at 12.11 am on July 10 in Melbourne; the second arrived at 9.40 pm on July 9 in London. I am confused as to which is the older.   *(John Wayman, Sudbury, Suffolk. 13 July 2007)*

The subtraction operator «-» can be used to subtract date/time values to give a duration, provided the operands match one of the rows in the following table:

Operand 1	Operand 2	Result
xs:date	xs:date	xs:dayTimeDuration
xs:dateTime	xs:dateTime	xs:dayTimeDuration
xs:time	xs:time	xs:dayTimeDuration

If the first operand represents an instant in time later than the second operand, then the result will be a positive duration; if it represents an earlier instant in time, then the result will be a negative duration.

If the date/time was supplied without a timezone, then it is assumed to represent a date/time in the implicit timezone defined by the evaluation context (see Chapter 7).

For operands of type xs:dateTime, the result is the duration corresponding to the number of seconds that separate the two instants in time, taking timezone into account. For example, the difference between the ages of John Wayman's two great-nephews is

```
xs:dateTime('2007-07-09T21:40:00+01:00') -
        xs:dateTime('2007-07-10T00:11:00+10:00')
```

which makes the British child 6 hours and 29 minutes younger than his Australian cousin, despite having an earlier date on his birth certificate.

For operands of type xs:date, the result is the difference between the starting instants of the two dates. Since the dates can be in different timezones, the result is not necessarily an integer number of days.

For operands of type xs:time, the values are assumed to represent two times occurring on the same date. If the times are in the same timezone (or both in no timezone), this gives results that are reasonably intuitive — except that 01:00:00 minus 22:00:00 is not 3 hours, but −21 hours. With different timezones, the answers can be quite surprising. For example the difference between 22:00:00-05:00 (10 p.m in New York) and 01:00:00Z (1 a.m in London) is the same as the difference between 2008-01-01T22:00:00-05:00 and 2008-01-01T01:00:00Z, namely 26 hours.

A working draft of the XPath 2.0 specification included functions to compute the difference between two dates in months. These functions were dropped because of difficulties in defining exactly what they should return. What's the difference in months, for example, between 29 Feb 2008 and 31 Jan 2008?

Duration Divided by Duration

It is possible to divide an xs:dayTimeDuration by another xs:dayTimeDuration, or an xs:yearMonthDuration by another xs:yearMonthDuration, to obtain an xs:double. The division operator must be «div» («idiv» is not supported). The result is equivalent to converting both the durations into a number of months or seconds and performing a numeric division.

Here are some examples:

Expression	Result
xs:dayTimeDuration("P10D") div xs:dayTimeDuration("PT6H")	40
xs:dayTimeDuration("-P1D") div xs:dayTimeDuration("PT1S")	−86400
xs:yearMonthDuration("P1M") div xs:yearMonthDuration("P1Y")	0.083333333...

This operation provides the easiest way to convert a duration into a number of months, days, or seconds. To convert an xs:dayTimeDuration to seconds, for example, just divide it by xs:dayTimeDuration("PT1S"). This is useful when you need to perform calculations that are not directly supported by the operations available on durations. Examples include:

❑ Dividing a distance by a duration to obtain an average speed.

❑ Multiplying the number of hours worked by the hourly rate to obtain the amount of money due.

❑ Determining the day of the week for a given date.

The following code illustrates how to display the day of the week, supplied in the variable $date:

```
("Sunday", "Monday", "Tuesday", "Wednesday", "Thursday", "Friday", "Saturday")
  [1 + (($date - xs:date("1901-01-06")) div xs:dayTimeDuration("P1D") mod 7)]
```

In XSLT 2.0, however, you can display the day of the week using the format-date() function, described in Chapter 13.

Value Comparisons

XPath 2.0 has introduced a completely new set of operators for comparing single atomic values. These are shown in the table below.

Operator	Meaning
eq	equals
ne	not equals
lt	less than
le	less than or equal to
gt	greater than
ge	greater than or equal to

These were introduced primarily because they have much cleaner and more predictable behavior than the XPath 1.0 operators «=», «!=», «<», «<=», «>», and «>=». The XPath 1.0 operators are still available, and they are described later in this chapter under the heading *General Comparisons* on page 588.

The real driver for introducing these new operators was not really the requirements of XSLT users, but the needs of XQuery, which is a superset of XPath 2.0. XQuery needs to be able to search large databases, and if you want to search a terabyte of data then you need to take advantages of indexes. This means you need to be able to rearrange the query as written by the user into a form that can take advantage of the indexes known to be available, and this rewriting of an expression into a different form is only possible if the operators have very clean mathematical properties. For example, a very useful property that makes rearranging expressions possible is called *transitivity*, which means that if «A=B» and «B=C» are both true, then you know that «A=C» will also be true. Unfortunately, this isn't the case for the «=» operator in XPath 1.0. For example, in XPath 1.0, «1=true()» and «true()="true"» are both true, but «1="true"» is false.

But although these operators were introduced specifically to enable XQuery optimization, I think it's a good idea to get into the habit of using them for most routine comparisons. You probably won't see any very visible performance benefit for the average XSLT stylesheet, but you may find that you make fewer errors because the behavior of the operators is simpler and more predictable. As a bonus, it's easier to write «le» than «<=».

In the XPath syntax, the two kinds of comparison operator, as well as the three operators «is», «<<», and «>>», which we will meet later in this chapter (see page 594), are presented like this:

Expression	Syntax
ComparisonExpr	RangeExpr ((ValueComp | GeneralComp |NodeComp) RangeExpr)?
ValueComp	«eq» | «ne» | «lt» | «le» | «gt» | «ge»
GeneralComp	«=» | «!=» | «<» | «<=» | «>» | «>=»
NodeComp	«is» | «<<» | «>>»

This means that all 15 operators listed here have the same priority. For all these operators the result of the expression is always an xs:boolean value. The reference to RangeExpr in the syntax can be ignored for now: it just refers to the next kind of expression in operator precedence order, which happens to be the range expression (of the form «1 to 10») described in Chapter 10.

The biggest difference between the value comparison operators and the general comparison operators described on page 588 is that the value comparison operators always compare two atomic values with each other, whereas the general comparison operators can be used to compare sequences.

Permitted Operand Types

The detailed effect of the comparison depends on the types of the two operands. These must be compatible with each other. There are some data types that can be compared using the «eq» and «ne» operators but not the «lt», «le», «gt», or «ge» operators. An example is xs:QName — you can test whether two xs:QName values are equal to each other but not whether one is less than the other.

The permitted operand types for value comparisons are summarized in the two tables that follow. Both operands must have the same type (as defined by a row in the table). Comparing two values whose types don't match (for example comparing an integer to a string) doesn't give you a result of false; it is a type error. This means the error may be reported either at compile time or at runtime, as discussed in Chapter 3. (As we'll see later, xs:untypedAtomic values are treated as strings.)

The first table is for «eq» and «ne», and shows for each data type how the comparison is done.

Data type	Definition of eq
xs:string or xs:anyURI	An anyURI value is treated as a string. The two strings are compared using the default collation established in the static context for the expression. Collations are described in detail on page 459. In consequence, the results may be quite different in different environments, for example, in one context the strings «Strasse» and «Straße» may be equal; in another context, they may be unequal.
numeric	Any two numeric values can be compared (xs:integer, xs:decimal, xs:float, or xs:double). If they are of different types, one value is first promoted to the type of the other in the same way as for arithmetic operators (see page 571). They are then tested for numeric equality (this means, for example, that «1.00» and «01» will compare as equal). There are a couple of special cases with floating point numbers: positive and negative zero are considered equal to each other, but NaN (not a number) is not equal to any other number; in fact, it is not even equal to itself.
xs:boolean	Two xs:boolean values are equal if they are both true, or both false.
xs:dateTime	Two xs:dateTime values are equal if they represent the same instant in time. This means that if both include a timezone, they are adjusted so that they are in the same timezone (conventionally UTC, but any timezone would do). Although the XPath data model retains the original timezone attached to the value, it plays no part in the comparison: the two xs:dateTime values «2008-01-01T02:00:00Z» and «2007-12-31T21:00:00-05:00» (2 a.m. in London and 9 p.m. the previous day in New York) are considered equal. If either or both of the values have no timezone, they are considered to represent times in the implicit timezone defined by the XPath evaluation context, as described in Chapter 7. If implicit timezones are set depending on the locale or preferences of the individual user, this means that two xs:dateTime values that appear equal for one user might appear not equal for another — but this can only happen in the situation where one of the values has an explicit timezone and the other does not.
xs:date	In most cases it is likely that xs:date values will be stored without a timezone, in which case the test whether two dates are equal is straightforward. If a date does have a timezone, then it is a significant part of the value. Dates are equal if their starting instants are simultaneous, which will normally happen only if they have the same timezone (the exception occurs near the International Date Line — today's date in timezone −12:00 compares equal with tomorrow's date in timezone +12:00). If one date has a timezone and the other does not, the implicit timezone is used in the comparison in the same way as for xs:dateTime values. This happens whenever you compare the result of current-date() with a simple date such as «2008-01-01» — the implicit timezone is used for the simple date, and this is always the same as the timezone used by the current-date() function.
xs:time	Values of type xs:time are considered to represent times on the same day, and are then compared in the same way as xs:dateTime values. This means, for example, that «02:00:00Z» and «21:00:00-05:00» (2 a.m. in London and 9 p.m. in New York) are considered not equal — they are 24 hours apart.

continued

Data type	Definition of eq
xs:gYear xs:gYearMonth xs:gMonth xs:gMonthDay xs:gDay	Values of these types are comparable only with other values of the same type. Since all of these types allow an optional timezone, they follow the same rules as xs:date. In fact, one way of defining equality is by converting the values to xs:date values by supplying arbitrary values for the missing components and then comparing the resulting dates.
xs:QName	Two xs:QName values are equal if they have the same namespace URI (or if both have no namespace URI) and if they have the same local name. Both the URI and the local name are compared in terms of Unicode codepoints, no collation is used. The prefix part, if any, is ignored.
xs:base64Binary xs:hexBinary	Although these two types share the same value space, it is not possible to compare one with the other directly: you have to cast the value first. For each of the types, values are equal if they consist of the same sequence of octets.
xs:NOTATION	The value space of xs:NOTATION is the same as the value space of xs:QName and xs:NOTATION values are compared in the same way as xs:QName values. However, you cannot compare an xs:QName to an xs:NOTATION.
xs:duration	An xs:duration value is considered to comprise an integer number of months plus a decimal number of seconds. Two durations are considered equal if the months parts are equal and the seconds parts are equal. This means, for example, that PT1H equals PT60M. It also means that the zero-length xs:yearMonthDuration is equal to the zero-length xs:dayTimeDuration.

The «ne» operator is the exact inverse of «eq»: if an «eq» comparison raises an error, then «ne» also raises an error; if «eq» returns true, then «ne» returns false, and if «eq» returns false, then «ne» returns true. This applies even for peculiar cases like NaN: if the value of $x is NaN, then «$x eq $x» is false, while «$x ne $x» is true. Another reassuring feature of these operators is that if «$a eq $b» is true, then «$b eq $a» is also true. (It's worth mentioning these things because as we'll see later in the chapter, when it comes to the «=» and «!=» operators it's best not to make any assumptions).

The other four operators in this group, «lt», «le», «gt», and «ge», work only for data types that are ordered. The data types that have an ordering, and the way the ordering works, are defined in the table below.

Data type	Definition of ordering
xs:string or xs:anyURI	An xs:anyURI value is treated as a string. The ordering of strings is determined by a collation, in the same way as equality comparison. These operators use the default collation established in the XPath evaluation context, as described in Chapter 7. There's a tension between equality comparison and ordering comparisons: for testing equality, you often want a *weak* collation; for example, one that compares «yes» and «YES» as equal. But for ordering, you often want to put the strings in some kind of order, even if it's fairly arbitrary, so you want «yes» either to be less than «YES», or greater than it (that is, you want a *strong* collation). If you want to use different collations for different operations, you can achieve this by using the compare() function described in Chapter 13, but for the «eq» and «lt» family of operators, you have to choose a single collation that may be a compromise.

continued

Data type	Definition of ordering
Numeric	Any two numeric values can be compared (xs:integer, xs:decimal, xs:float, or xs:double). If they are of different types, one value is first promoted to the type of the other in the same way as arithmetic operators (see page 571). They are then tested for numeric order (this means, for example, that «10» is greater than «2»).
xs:boolean	The value false is considered, quite arbitrarily, to be less than true.
xs:dateTime	One xs:dateTime value is considered less than another if it represents an earlier instant in time. As with equality testing, the two values are adjusted to a common timezone using the implicit timezone from the evaluation context if the value does not have its own timezone. The effect is, for example, that «2008-01-01T01:00:00Z» is less than «2007-12-31T23:00:00-05:00».
xs:date	In XML Schema, xs:date values are described as being partially ordered. This means that for some pairs of dates, one of them is clearly earlier than the other, but for other pairs (in particular, a pair of dates in which one has a timezone and the other does not) it's impossible to decide. Putting such a rule into a query language would have been impossibly complex, so instead the decision is made by interpreting all dates without a timezone as being in the implicit timezone defined by the evaluation context. The rule is that one date is less than another if it starts earlier than the other one starts, even if the two dates overlap: for example, «2008-01-01+10:00» is less than «2008-01-01Z» because the New Year starts earlier in Sydney than it does in London.
xs:time	Values of type xs:time present a particular problem for ordering, because the values are cyclic. Converting both values to the UTC timezone would produce some strange results; for example, it would make «18:00:00-05:00» greater than «20:00:00-05:00», because the equivalent UTC times are «23:00:00Z» and «01:00:00Z», respectively. So instead, the two times are considered to be on the same date (it doesn't matter what date you choose) and are expanded to xs:dateTime values by using that date. They are then compared in the same way as xs:dateTime values. This doesn't remove all anomalies, but it does make the results reasonably intuitive whenever the two times are in the same timezone.
xs:gYear xs:gYearMonth xs:gMonth xs:gMonthDay xs:gDay xs:QName xs:base64Binary xs:hexBinary xs:NOTATION	These types have no ordering defined. Using any of the operators «lt», «le», «gt», «ge» with values of these types is a type error. There's no particular reason for this restriction — in most of these cases it would have been quite possible to define a useful ordering — but the working groups decided it wasn't needed.
xs:duration	xs:duration values themselves are not considered to be ordered, so the operators «lt», «le», «gt», and «ge» are not available. This removes the problem of deciding whether 30 days is less than, equal to, or greater than one month. The two XPath subtypes of xs:duration, namely xs:yearMonth-Duration and xs:dayTimeDuration, are much more well behaved. The effect of comparing them is the same as converting the value to a number of months, or a number of seconds, and comparing the two numbers. This means, for example, that «PT36H» (36 hours) is greater than «P1D» (one day).

8

XPath: Operators on Items

In nearly all cases the four operators have the obvious relationship to each other; for example, if «$a lt $b» is true, then «$a le $b» is also true, as is «$b gt $a». The one exception is the xs:double (and xs:float) value NaN. If NaN appears as either operand of any of these four operators, or as both operands, then the result is always false.

Type Checking for Value Comparisons

The operands in a value comparison are processed according to the following rules. These rules apply to all six operators. Note that there are no special backward-compatibility rules here, because these operators were not available in XPath 1.0.

1. Each of the operands is atomized, as described on page 220 in Chapter 5. This means that when you supply a node as the argument, the typed value of the node is extracted.

2. If either operand (after atomizing) is a sequence containing more than one value, then a type error occurs.

3. If either operand (after atomizing) is an empty sequence, the result is an empty sequence.

4. If either of the operands (after atomizing) is of type xs:untypedAtomic (which will generally be the case if the value has been extracted from an element or attribute in a schema-less document), then it is converted to a string (a value of type xs:string). This is true even if the other operand is a number.

5. If the two values are not comparable then a type error occurs. This can happen because their types are incompatible with each other (for example one is an xs:string and the other an xs:decimal), or it can happen because both values belong to a type for which ordering is not defined, such as xs:QName.

6. Otherwise, the values are compared according to the ordering rules for their data type, as described in the table in the previous section.

There are a couple of controversial decisions reflected in these rules.

The first is that either operand is allowed to be an empty sequence. The specification vacillated on this question in early drafts.

The main argument in favor of allowing an empty sequence is that the empty sequence should behave like a null value in SQL — any operator or function that has «()» as an argument should return «()» as a result. This also makes it easier to handle optional elements and attributes. This principle has not been followed systematically throughout the language, but it is followed by most of the operators. At one stage the language design also included SQL-like three-valued logic, but this was dropped, largely because it was incompatible with XPath 1.0. In most cases, XPath 1.0 and now also XPath 2.0 treat absent data in almost exactly the same way as SQL, but without relying on three-valued logic. For example, in an expression such as «//item[@code eq 3]», items that have no code attribute will not be selected. Equally, if you write «//item[@code ne 3]», items that have no code attribute will not be selected. (In both cases, the value of the predicate is an empty sequence, and the effective boolean value of an empty sequence is false). But unlike SQL, the XPath expression «//item[not(@code=3)]» does select items with no code attribute. The SQL rule that «not(null)» returns «null» has no parallel in XPath.

The argument in favor of disallowing an empty sequence was to maximize the freedom of the optimizer to rearrange predicates, so as to make use of indexes. Although the current rules do not compromise transitivity, they do make other rewrites impossible; for example, the expressions «A ne B» and «not(A eq B)» are no longer equivalent.

The other controversial decision is that `xs:untypedAtomic` values are converted to strings regardless of the type of the other operand. Taking again the example «@code eq 3», this means you will get a type error if the source document has no schema, because you can't compare a string to a number. This rule was introduced in order to make equality transitive. For example, suppose @code is an untyped attribute whose string value is «4.00». Then «@code eq "4.0"» and «@code eq 4.0e0» would both be `true` (one is a string comparison and the other a numeric comparison), and since «4.0 eq 4.0e0» is true, transitivity would then require that the string comparison «"4.0" eq "4.0e0"» is also true. This clearly isn't feasible; as strings, these values are not the same thing.

Despite all the efforts to make the `eq` *operator transitive, it turns out that in corner cases, it isn't. This problem arises because of the numeric promotion rules. Given three numbers* `xs:float('1.0')`, `xs:decimal('1.0000000000100000000001')`, `xs:double('1.00000000001')`, *the float and the double are both equal to the decimal, but they are not equal to each other. This turns out to create quite a problem for operations that rely on transitivity, notably the* `distinct-values()` *function and the* `<xsl:for-each-group>` *instruction.*

Examples of Value Comparisons

Expression	Description
`$x eq 2`	This is true if $x is a sequence of exactly one item, and that item is an instance of `xs:double`, `xs:float`, or `xs:decimal` (or a type derived from these by restriction) that is numerically equal to 2. It is also true if the single item in $x is a node whose typed value is one of these numeric types and is numerically equal to 2. The result is false if the item in $x is a different numeric value, and it is effectively false if $x is empty. If $x contains more than one item, or contains a non-numeric value, or if it is an untyped node, the result is an error.
`count($x) gt 2`	This is true if the number of items in the sequence $x is 3 or more, and it is false otherwise. No type error can occur in this case, because the value returned by the `count()` function will always be an integer, and `count()` accepts any type of value as its argument.
`@x eq "yes"`	This is true if the context node has an attribute named x, and the type of that attribute is either `xs:string` or `xs:untypedAtomic` or a type derived from `xs:string` by restriction, and the value of the attribute compares equal to the string «yes» under the rules of the default collation (which is context-dependent). If the attribute doesn't exist, then the effective value is false. If the attribute has a different type, the result is a type error.
`@retirement-date ge current-date()`	This is true if the context node has an attribute named `retirement-date`, and the type of that attribute is `xs:date` or a user-defined type defined as a restriction of `xs:date`, and the value of the attribute is the same as or after the current date. In the unlikely event that the `retirement-date` attribute has a timezone associated with it, this will be taken into account in the comparison; if not, the implicit timezone is used, which will always be the same as the timezone used in the result of the `current-date()` function. If the `retirement-date` attribute does not exist the effective result is false. If the attribute has any type other than `xs:date`, including the case where it has type `xs:untypedAtomic`, a type error occurs.

General Comparisons

The term *general comparisons* is used for expressions involving the six operators «=», «!=», «<», «<=», «>», and «>=». These operators are retained and generalized from XPath 1.0. As we shall see, they are considerably more powerful than their counterparts used in value comparisons, but this also means that they may be rather more expensive, and they can also lead to a few surprises — they don't always give the answer you expect.

The syntax for these operators has already been given, because they are combined into the same production rules as the simpler operators «eq», «ne», «lt», «le», «gt», and «ge», which are given on page 582.

General comparisons are more powerful than value comparisons in two ways:

❑   General comparisons allow either or both operands to be sequences (of zero, one, or many items), whereas value comparisons require the operands to be single items.

❑   General comparisons are more flexible in the way they handle untyped atomic values (that is, data from schema-less documents). In particular, the way an untyped value is handled depends on the type of the value that it is being compared with.

In addition, general comparisons have special rules for use when backward-compatibility mode is selected (in XSLT, this applies when the version attribute is set to «1.0»).

Remember that if you are embedding your XPath expressions in an XML document — for example, an XSLT stylesheet or an XML Schema — then the «<» character must be escaped as «<». Many people also like to escape «>» as «>», though this is not strictly necessary.

Changes in XPath 2.0

Despite the special rules for handling backward-compatibility mode, the general comparison operators are probably the area where incompatibilities between XPath 1.0 and XPath 2.0 are most likely to be encountered. This is mainly because of the generalization of the data model to handle sequences, and also because of the increased range of data types. XPath 1.0 only supported four data types (string, number, boolean, and node-set). Given two operands, and allowing for symmetry, there were therefore 10 possible combinations of operand types, and each of these was described separately. Because there was little consistency to the XPath 1.0 rules, generalizing them to handle a much richer set of data types proved difficult.

The incompatibility that you are most likely to hit is when comparing strings, or untyped nodes. In XPath 1.0, an equality comparison («=») between two nodes (all nodes were untyped in those days) treated both values as strings, while an ordering comparison («<») treated them as numbers. This led to oddities such as the fact that «"2"="2.0"» was false, while «"2"<="2.0"» and «"2">="2.0"» were both true. This has been swept away in XPath 2.0; if you compare two strings, or untyped values, using any of these operators, then they are compared as strings, using the default collation defined in the XPath evaluation context. So if you have an expression such as «@discount < @max-discount», and the element in question is <e discount="5" max-discount="10"/>, then XPath 1.0 would return true, while XPath 2.0 returns false. The solution is to make sure that if you want a numeric comparison, you force it by converting the values explicitly to numbers, for example, by using the number() function (which is described in Chapter 13).

(Note that this problem only occurs if both values are strings. It's much more common to see expressions in which one value is a string and the other is a number; for example, «@price>10.00», and these continue to work as before.)

Another incompatibility occurs when comparing a sequence of nodes to a boolean value. In XPath 1.0, «$node-set=true()» was true if the node-set was nonempty. In XPath 2.0, a sequence compares equal to true() if, after atomization, it contains an item that is equal to true(). This is a pretty radical change in meaning, but fortunately this kind of expression occurs very rarely in practice.

In both the above cases, the XPath 1.0 behavior is retained when you run in backward-compatibility mode. The new behavior occurs only when you change the version attribute in your stylesheet to say «version="2.0"».

Rules for General Comparisons

I will present the rules first and then discuss their consequences.

1. In backward-compatibility mode, if one of the operands is a singleton boolean value, then the other operand is replaced by its effective boolean value. The comparison then proceeds by applying the rest of the rules, although both operands are now singletons. This rather strange rule made more sense in XPath 1.0, and it is therefore retained in compatibility mode, but it very rarely affects the outcome. For the rules on effective boolean value, see the description of the boolean() function on page 721.

2. Each of the operands is atomized. This means that if the operand starts out as a sequence of nodes, the process turns it into a sequence of atomic values. There may be more atomic values than nodes (if some of the nodes are defined in the schema to contain a list), or fewer (if some of them contain empty lists). The original operand may contain atomic values as well as nodes, and the atomization process leaves these atomic values alone.

3. The remaining rules are applied to compare each pair of items from the two sequences, taking one value in the pair from the first sequence and the other value from the second sequence. This means that if one sequence contains four items, and the other contains five, then each item in the first sequence must be compared with each item in the second, giving 20 comparisons to be done in total. If any of these comparisons is true, the result of the general comparison is true. If they are all false, the result is false. If any of the comparisons fails with an error, the general comparison as a whole fails. However, it's not defined in what order the comparisons are done, so if there's a pair of items for which the comparison is true, and another pair for which it raises an error, then the final result might be either true or an error.

4. Considering each pair of items from the two sequences in turn, if one item of the pair is an xs:untypedAtomic value (typically, a value extracted from a node in a schema-less document), then it is converted to a more specific type. If both items in the pair are xs:untypedAtomic values, then they are both converted to xs:string values. If only one item is an xs:untypedAtomic value, then it is converted to the type of the other item. There is a special rule when the second item is numeric: in this situation the xs:untypedAtomic value is always converted to an xs:double value. This caters for a situation such as comparing the untyped value «2.1» with the xs:integer value «2»; it would be unreasonable to convert the value «2.1» to an integer before doing the comparison.

5. There is now a further rule that comes into play only when backward-compatibility mode is enabled. This is that if one of the items in the pair is numeric, and the other is not, then the non-numeric item is converted to an xs:double using the number() function. If the value isn't numeric, this returns NaN, and the comparison will be false. But a comparison such as «"23"=23» is allowed, and will succeed, under the backward compatibility rules. In pure XPath 2.0 mode, comparison of a string to a number is not allowed; you have to convert one of the operands explicitly to the type of the other, to make it clear whether a string comparison or a numeric comparison is intended.

589

6. Finally, after any conversions defined in steps 4 and 5, the two items are compared using the rules for the corresponding value comparison operator: that is, one of «eq», «ne», «lt», «le», «gt», and «ge», depending on whether the original operator was «=», «!=», «<», «<=», «>», or «>=». If the result of this comparison is true, then no further work is needed, and the result of the whole general comparison expression is true. If the result is false, however, the process moves on to the next pair of values.

Fortunately, it's quite rare in practice for both operands to be sequences of more than one item. This case can get very expensive, though there are plenty of ways an XPath processor can avoid actually doing M × N comparisons. It's made more complicated by the fact that the conversion rules apply separately to each pair of items. This means that if you have the comparison «@a = (12, "pineapple")», where the node «@a» is untyped, then the untyped value has to be converted to a number to be compared with the number 12, and to a string to be compared with the string "pineapple". In the general case, it isn't possible to do all the conversions upfront, before starting the pairwise comparison.

The more type information you can supply at compile time, the more likely it is that the XPath processor will actually know in advance that it doesn't have to deal with these complications, because they can't actually arise. For example, if you are writing a function in XSLT that has a parameter $p, and the function contains the test «if ($p=3) then ...», then declaring the parameter as an xs:integer (if that's what it is) can make a world of difference — if you don't declare its type, then the processor is going to have to assume the worst, which is that it might be an arbitrary mixture of typed nodes, untyped nodes, integers, strings, dates, and anything else the caller of the function cares to throw at it. But if you declare it as an xs:integer then the compiler can quietly replace the complex «=» operator with the much simpler and presumably faster «eq» operator. Alternatively, if you know that $p will be an integer, you can write the expression using the «eq» operator directly.

Existential Comparison

The peculiar property of these operators, namely that A = B is true if there is an item in A that is equal to an item in B, is sometimes called *existential semantics* — the operator is testing for the existence of a matching pair of items. This section explores the consequences of this rule..

Where a sequence $N is compared with a string "Mary", the test «$N="Mary"» is effectively a shorthand for "if there is an item $n in $N such that $n eq "Mary"". Similarly, the test «$N!="Mary"» is effectively a shorthand for "if there is an item $n in $N such that $n ne 'Mary'". If $N contains two items, whose values are "Mary" and "John", then «$N='Mary'» and «$N!='Mary'» will both be true, because there is an item that is equal to 'Mary' and another that is not. If $N is an empty sequence, then «$N='Mary'» and «$N!='Mary'» will both be false, because there is no item that is equal to 'Mary', but there is also no item that is not equal to 'Mary'.

Note that when the operand is a sequence of nodes, we are only concerned with the nodes that are members of the sequence in their own right. The children of these nodes are not members of the sequence. So if $N is the element:

```
<people>
  <person>Mary</person>
  <person>John</person>
</people>
```

then «$N="Mary"» will not return true. In this case $N is a singleton sequence. Its only item is the
<people> element, and that element is not equal to "Mary". In fact, with a schema-aware processor
this comparison might well throw an error, on the grounds that the <people> node cannot be atomized.
To perform an existential comparison for this example, you should write «$N/person="Mary"». In this
expression, $N/person is a sequence of two <person> nodes, and one of them is equal to "Mary".

So, these examples show some of the surprises in store:

❑ You can't assume that «$X=$X» is true. It usually will be, but if «$X» is an empty sequence, it will
be false, because there is no item in the first sequence that is equal to an item from
the second.

❑ You can't assume that «$X!=3» means the same as «not($X=3)». When «$X» is a
sequence, the first expression is true if any item in the sequence is not equal to 3, while the second is true if no item in the sequence is equal to 3. Generally speaking, it is best to steer clear
of the «!=» operator unless you know exactly what you are doing. Use «not(x=y)» instead; it is
more likely to match the intuitive meaning.

❑ You can't assume that if «$X=$Y and $Y=$Z», then «$X=$Z». Again, sequences are the culprit. Two
sequences are considered equal if there is a value that both have in common, so
«(2,3)=(3,4)» is true, and «(3,4)=(4,5)» is true, but «(2,3)=(4,5)» is false.

In this strange Orwellian world where some values seem to be more equal than others, the one consola-
tion is that «$X=$Y» always means the same as «$Y=$X».

Although «!=» is often best avoided, it can be useful to test whether all items in a sequence have the
same value. For example, writing <xsl:if test="not($documents//version!=1.0)"> tests whether
there is any node in the sequence «$documents//version» whose numeric value is not 1.0. However, it
is probably less confusing to write the above test as:

```
<xsl:if test="every $d in $documents//version
              satisfies $d eq 1.0">
```

The «some» and «every» expressions are described in Chapter 10.

It is important to remember that an equality test compares the typed values of the nodes, not their identity. For example, «..=/» might seem to be a natural way of testing whether the parent of the context
node is the root of the tree. In fact this test will also return true if the parent node is the outermost element, because in a well-formed (and schema-less) tree the typed value of the outermost element is the
same as the typed value of the document node. Not only is the test wrong, it could also be very expensive:
the value of the root contains all the text in the document, so you might be constructing two strings each
a million characters long and then comparing them. XPath 2.0 provides an operator for comparing nodes
by identity: you can write this test as «.. is /». The «is» operator is described under *Node Comparisons*
on page 593.

The rules for comparing two sequences using «=» apply equally when comparing two sequences using an
operator such as «<»: the comparison in this case is true if there is some value in the first sequence that is
less than some value in the second sequence, under the rules for the «lt» operator. If all the values in the
two sequences have the same data type, then the result actually follows the rules in the following table,
where max() and min() represent the maximum and minimum numeric values of items in the sequence,
ignoring any NaN values.

Expression	Result
M<N	True when min(M) < max(N)
M<=N	True when min(M) <= max(N)
M>N	True when max(M) > min(N)
M>=N	True when max(M) >= min(N)

Examples of General Comparisons

Expression	Description
@width=3	Tests whether the width attribute of the context node, after converting to a number, has the numeric value 3. If there is no width attribute, the result will be false.
	If the width attribute exists and is typed as numeric, the result will be true if and only if the numeric value is equal to 3. If the width attribute exists and is untyped, the result will be true if the width attribute can be converted to a number equal to 3; for example, if it is «3» or «3.00». If the width attribute is defined in the schema as a list-valued attribute, then the result is true if any of the values in this list is equal to 3.
@width=(10, 20, 30)	Tests whether the width attribute has the value 10, 20, or 30.
	If the attribute is untyped, it is compared as a number. If the attribute is defined in the schema as being list-valued, then the comparison is true if any item in the list is equal to 10, 20, or 30.
@width !=$x	If there is no width attribute the result will be false.
	If the attribute width is untyped, then if the variable $x holds a numeric value, a numeric comparison is performed; if it holds a string value, a string comparison is performed. The result will be true if the values are different.
	If the attribute width is typed, then an error will occur if the type is incompatible with the type of $x.
	If $x holds a sequence, the result will be true if there is any item in the sequence whose typed value is not equal to the width attribute, using string comparison; it will be false if the sequence is empty. If the schema-defined type of the width attribute is a list type, then the comparison is performed with each item in that list considered individually.
count(*)>10	Returns true if the context node has more than ten element children.
sum(SALES)<10000	Returns true if the sum of the numeric values of the <SALES> children of the context node is less than 10,000.
position()< last() div 2	Returns true if the context position is less than half the context size, that is, if the position of this node is less than half way down the list of nodes being processed.
not(//@temp<=0.0)	Returns true if all values of the temp attribute in the document are numeric, and greater than zero.

Node Comparisons

This section describes the three operators «<<», «is», and «>>», which are used to compare nodes. The «is» operator tests whether the two operands evaluate to the same node; the operators «<<» and «>>» test whether one node is before or after another in document order.

The syntax has already been covered under *Value Comparisons* on page 581: these operators are defined by the same production rule that defines the value comparison operators (the «eq» family) and the general comparison operators («=» and friends).

For all three operators, each operand must be either a single node or an empty sequence. If either operand is an empty sequence, the result is an empty sequence (which will be treated as false if it is used in a boolean test such as a predicate). If either operand is a sequence containing more than one item, or an item other than a node, then a type error is reported.

The «is» Operator

The «is» operator tests whether both operands evaluate to the same node. The nodes must be identical; it's not enough to have the same name or the same value, they must actually be the same node.

> *Terminology here can get messy. If two nodes are identical, then they are one node, not two. Better perhaps to say that two values are references to the same node (but that's not the language of the W3C specs). Identity causes other problems: it doesn't fit well into a language that in most other respects is purely functional. For example, if you write a function f() in XSLT or XQuery that creates and returns a new element node, then the expression «f() is f()» returns false, because each time f() is called, it creates a node with distinct identity. This breaks the rule that applies to all other XPath function calls, namely that calling the same function repeatedly with the same arguments and the same evaluation context always returns the same result.*

Here's an example of how the «is» operator can be used. Sometimes you have a sequence of elements such as:

```
<H1/><p/><p/><p/><H1/><p/><p/><H1/><p/><p/>
```

and you need to select all the <p/> elements that follow a particular <H1> element, up to the next <H1> element. (I have shown all the elements as empty because we're not interested in their content for this example.) Let's suppose that the variable $H identifies the <H1> element where you want to start. The expression «$H/following-sibling::p» selects all the <p> elements after the start element, but it doesn't stop when it reaches the next <H1>. You want to select only the <p> elements whose immediately preceding <H1> element is $H. Here is the expression to do this:

```
$H/following-sibling::p[preceding-sibling::H1[1] is $H]
```

Another way of solving this problem would be to write:

```
$H/following-sibling::p except $H/following-sibling::H1/following-sibling::p
```

but I think the solution using the «is» operator is likely to be more efficient. (The «except» operator is described in Chapter 9, on page 628.)

> *In XSLT 2.0, problems like this can also be tackled using the construct <xsl:for-each-group group-starting-with="H1">. See Chapter 6, page 340.*

The operators «<<» and «>>»

The operators «<<» and «>>» test whether one node is before or after another in document order. For example, «$A << $B» is true if and only if $A precedes $B in document order. The concept of document order is described in Chapter 2, on page 57.

There is no requirement that the two nodes should be in the same document. Document order is defined as an ordering of all the nodes encountered, across all documents. If nodes are in different documents, then you can't predict which one will be first in document order, but although the answer is arbitrary, it will be consistent within a single run.

Consider again the problem given in the previous section, where the input has the form:

```
<H1/><p/><p/><p/><H1/><p/><p/><H1/><p/><p/>
```

Another way of finding all the <p> elements that follow an <H1> element identified by the variable $H is:

```
$H/following-sibling::p[not($H/following-sibling::H1[1] << .)]
```

This selects those <p> elements that are before the next <H1> element. Note the careful construction of the predicate, which is designed to work even when $H does not have a «following-sibling::H1». It works because when one of the operands of «<<» is an empty sequence, the result of the comparison is an empty sequence, which is treated as false. If the expression were written:

```
$H/following-sibling::p[$H/following-sibling::H1[1] >> .]
```

then it would not select any <p> elements after the last <H1> element.

Changes in XPath 2.0

These three operators are new in XPath 2.0.

In XPath 1.0 the only way to test whether two variables $A and $B referred to the same node was to write something like «count($A|$B) = 1». This relies on the fact that the union operator «|» removes duplicate nodes. If you see this construct when upgrading existing code to XPath 2.0, using the «is» operator will almost certainly be more efficient.

In an XSLT 1.0 stylesheet, nodes could also be compared for identity using the expression «generate-id($A) = generate-id($B)». Again the «is» operator is more direct and more likely to be efficient.

Boolean Expressions

This section concludes the chapter with a description of the operators «and» and «or».

There is no «not» operator in XPath, it's provided as a function instead, and is described in Chapter 13, on page 850.

Expression	Syntax
OrExpr	AndExpr («or» AndExpr)*
AndExpr	ComparisonExpr («and» ComparisonExpr)*

The syntax shows that the «and» operator binds more tightly than «or», so that «A and B or C and D» means «(A and B) or (C and D)». Personally, I prefer to use parentheses to avoid any doubt.

The fact that an AndExpr is defined in terms of a ComparisonExpr just means that the family of operators including «=» and «eq» are next in precedence order after «and». These operators were described earlier in this chapter.

An «or» expression returns true if either of its operands is true, while an «and» expression returns true if both of its operands are true.

The operands of «and» and «or» are converted to xs:boolean values by taking their effective boolean value. This applies the same rules as for the conditional («if») expression described in Chapter 7, and the boolean() function, described in Chapter 13. For example, a string is false if it is zero-length, and a sequence is false if it is empty.

Shortcut Semantics

XPath 1.0 defined that the right-hand operand of «and» or «or» wasn't evaluated if the result could be established by evaluating the first operand (that is, if the first operand was false in the case of «and», or true in the case of «or»). The reason for this rule was to give clearly defined behavior in the event of errors occurring. In XPath 2.0, the language designers have decided to sacrifice some of this predictability in favor of giving the implementation maximum freedom to rearrange expressions so that indexes can be used. For example, suppose you write an expression like this, to select all the male employees who are retiring today:

```
//employee[@sex='M' and @retirement-date=current-date()]
```

The XPath 1.0 rules say that you can't look at the retirement date until you've established that the employee is male. But if you have a hundred thousand employees, and they are indexed on their date of retirement, then the most efficient strategy would be to use the index, find the employees who are retiring today, and then select those among them who are male. The reason the rules were changed in XPath 2.0 is to allow systems to use this more efficient strategy.

Suppose you know that for female employees only (for some reason) the value of the retirement-date attribute might not be a date at all, but the string value «standard». A schema can be defined using a union type that allows the value to hold either a date, or this special value. The XPath 1.0 rules guaranteed that you would never look at the retirement-date attribute of female employees while evaluating the expression, which would mean that you can never get the error that occurs when comparing the string «standard» to a date. The XPath 2.0 rules don't give you this guarantee. To protect yourself against the failure, you could write:

```
//employee[if (@sex='M')
           then @retirement-date = current-date()
           else false()]
```

Unlike the «and» and «or» operators, the «if» expression does give you a guarantee: if the condition is false, the «then» branch will not be executed. Similarly, if the condition is true, the «else» branch will not be executed.

Another situation where these rules matter is if one branch contains a call on an external function that has side effects. Writing such functions is something that's been left very much implementation-defined, but many XPath implementations will allow calls to external routines, and once they allow that, it's impossible to prevent such functions having arbitrary side effects. If you want to prevent a subexpression being evaluated because it has side effects, the only reliable way to ensure this is with an «if» expression; don't rely on «and» and «or».

Note that there are no null values in XPath, as there are for example in SQL, and there is therefore no need for three-valued logic to handle unknown or absent data. Instead, you may need to test explicitly for absent values, as shown in some of the examples below.

Examples

Expression	Description
$x>3 and $x<8	Returns true if the value of variable $x is greater than 3 and less than 8.
@name and @address	Returns true if the context node has both a name and an address attribute. (Both the operands are sequences of nodes, which are converted to the xs:boolean true if they contain at least one node, and to false if they are empty).
string(@name) and string(@address)	Returns true if the context node has both a name and an address attribute and if neither is a zero-length string. (Both the operands are strings, which are converted to the xs:boolean true if their length is non-zero. If an attribute is absent, the sequence will be empty, and its string value will therefore be the empty string).
true()	A trivial AndExpr consisting of a single function call.
$x=5 or $x=10	Returns true if the variable $x has the value 5 or 10. This could also be written as «$x = (5, 10)».
@name or @id	Returns true if the context node has a name attribute, an id attribute, or both.
not(@id) or @id=""	Returns true if the context node has no id attribute or if it has an id attribute and the value is an empty string.
//para[position()=1 or position()=last()]	Selects the <para> elements that are either the first or the last (or the only) <para> children of their parent node.

Summary

This chapter described the following groups of XPath operators:

❑   Arithmetic operators, «+», «-», «*», «div», and «mod»

❑   Value comparison operators «eq», «ne», «lt», «le», «gt», «ge»

❑   General comparison operators «=», «!=», «<», «<=», «>», «>=»

❑   Node comparison operators «<<», «is», and «>>»

❑   Boolean operators «and» and «or».

Many of these operators behave in a way that is likely to be familiar from other languages, though there are differences because of the different data model, in particular, the fact that everything in XPath is a sequence.

The next chapter describes the most distinctive feature of the XPath language, namely path expressions. Unlike the operators in this chapter, these are quite unique to XPath.

Looking further ahead, Chapter 10 is devoted to operations used to process sequences. The tour of the language syntax finishes in Chapter 11, which describes operations on types. Chapter 12 returns specifically to XSLT with a description of match patterns, which use a subset of the XPath syntax. The standard functions available in XPath and XSLT are described in Chapter 13.

8

XPath: Operators on Items

9

XPath: Path Expressions

This chapter defines the syntax and meaning of *path expressions*. Path expressions are the most distinctive feature of the XPath language, the construct that gives the language its name. The chapter also describes other constructs in the language that are closely associated with path expressions, in particular *steps* and *axes* and the «union», «intersect», and «except» operators.

Path expressions are used to select nodes in a tree, by means of a series of steps. Each step takes as its starting point a node, and from this starting point, selects other nodes.

Each step is defined in terms of:

❑ An *axis*, which defines the relationship to be followed in the tree (for example, it can select child nodes, ancestor nodes, or attributes)

❑ A *node test*, which defines what kind of nodes are required, and can also specify the name or schema-defined type of the nodes

❑ Zero or more *predicates*, which provide the ability to filter the nodes according to arbitrary selection criteria

Because they are closely associated with processing the results of path expressions, this chapter also describes the operators used to combine two sets of nodes by taking their union, intersection, or difference.

Although I've chosen *Path Expressions* as the title for this chapter, the term is actually a slippery one. Because of the way W3C defines the XPath grammar, all sorts of unlikely constructs such as «2» or «count($x)» are technically path expressions. The things I will actually cover in this chapter are:

❑ The binary «/» operator as applied to nodes. This is used in expressions like «$chap/title». There's another use of the «/» operator that applies to atomic values, in what I call a *simple mapping expression*, and I will cover that in Chapter 10.

❑ Axis steps, for example «ancestor::x» or «following-sibling::y[1]», including abbreviated axis steps such as «x» (short for «child::x») and «@y» (short for «attribute::y»). Axis steps are expressions in their own right, but they are often used before or after the «/» operator.

❑ Variants on the «/» operator that can be used to write abbreviated path expressions, notably «/» as a freestanding expression, «/» at the start of a path expression, and the «//» pseudo-operator.

❑ What I call the Venn operators: union, intersect, and except. These are often used to combine the results of several path expressions, or to form a step of a path expression.

Examples of Path Expressions

Before describing the different kinds of path expression in more detail, it may be helpful to look at some examples.

Expression	Description
`para`	Selects all the `<para>` element children of the context node.
`@title`	Selects all the `title` attributes of the context node. The result will either be empty or contain a single attribute node.
`book/author/first-name`	Selects the `<first-name>` elements that are children of the `<author>` elements that are children of the `<book>` elements that are children of the context node.
`para[@id]`	Selects all the `<para>` element children of the context node that have an `id` attribute.
`para/@id`	Selects the `id` attributes of all the `<para>` element children of the context node. This differs from the previous example in that the result is a sequence of attribute nodes rather than a sequence of element nodes.
`/*/para`	Selects all the `<para>` element children of the containing document element (that is, of the outermost element of the document containing the context node). The «*» is a wildcard that selects all elements on the chosen axis.
`$sections/body`	Selects all `<body>` element children of nodes in the sequence identified by the variable `$sections`. A type error occurs if `$sections` contains an item that isn't a node. The results will be in document order even if the original sequence `$sections` isn't in document order.
`$sections[3]/body`	Selects all `<body>` element children of the third node in the sequence identified by the variable `$sections`.
`$sections/.`	Selects all the nodes that are present in the value of the variable `$sections`, but with duplicates removed, and sorted into document order. The only effect of the «/.» in this case is to force the reordering and deduplication.
`/contract/clause[3]/ subclause[2]`	Selects the second `<subclause>` of the third `<clause>` of the `<contract>` that is the document element. If the document element is not a `<contract>`, or if any of the other components are missing, it produces an empty sequence.
`//figure`	Selects all the `<figure>` elements in the document.
`city[not(@name = preceding-sibling:: city/@name)]`	Selects all the child `<city>` elements of the context node that do not have a `name` attribute that is the same as the `name` attribute of a preceding `<city>` element with the same parent. It thus selects a set of child `<city>` elements with unique names.

continued

Expression	Description
`*/name()`	Selects the names of the children of the context node. The path expressions given above all select nodes in a tree. However, the «/» operator can also be used as a simple mapping operator to compute atomic values for each node in a sequence; this example returns a sequence of strings, each being the name of a child element of the context node. I refer to this kind of expression as a *simple mapping expression*, and because this chapter is all about expressions that operate on nodes, I will cover simple mapping expressions in Chapter 10.

The `PathExpr` construct is probably the most complex construct in the XPath language. The actual production rules are quite complicated and hard to follow, but they are there to make path expressions easy to write, especially if you are familiar with Unix-style path names for directories and files. Most of the syntactic complications arise from the range of abbreviations that are permitted, so we will cover the basic constructs and operators first, and introduce the syntactic abbreviations later.

Changes in XPath 2.0

In XPath 2.0, the syntax of path expressions has been generalized so that any expression can be used as a step in a path. For example, «doc('a.xml')/id('Z123')» is now a valid path expression. This makes «/» behave in a similar way to other binary operators. An expression used on the left-hand side of the «/» operator can be any expression that returns a sequence of nodes; the expression used on the right of «/» (in effect, the last step in a simple mapping expression) can also return atomic values.

In XPath 1.0, path expressions were defined to return a node-set, that is, a set of nodes with no duplicates, in no particular order. XSLT 1.0, however, always processed the resulting nodes in document order. The XPath 2.0 data model does not support node-sets as such, but by redefining path expressions to return a sequence of nodes in document order with no duplicates, the result is effectively the same.

There are new facilities in XPath 2.0 to select nodes according to their schema-defined type, rather than selecting them only by name. These facilities are described in detail in Chapter 11.

The constructs «.» and «..» can now be followed by predicates.

The axes are unchanged from XPath 1.0, with one exception: the namespace axis has been deprecated. This means that XPath 2.0 implementations may or may not make this axis available. All the information that was available by using the namespace axis in XPath 1.0 (that is, the ability to find all the namespaces declared for any given element) can now be obtained through two new functions: `in-scope-prefixes()` and `namespace-uri-for-prefix()`. These functions are described in Chapter 13. The reason for replacing the namespace axis with these functions is to allow implementations more flexibility to implement namespaces efficiently. Modeling the information using namespace nodes imposed burdens on the implementation that offered no real benefit to users; for example, the ability to do union and intersection operations on sets of namespace nodes, and the ability to get back from a namespace node to its parent element.

It is now possible to select nodes with a given local-name, regardless of their namespace. This is done using the syntax «*:local-name», which mirrors the syntax «prefix:*» that is used to select all nodes in a given namespace, regardless of their local-name.

The operators «except» and «intersect» are new in XPath 2.0, and the keyword «union» has been introduced as a synonym for «|». The alternative spelling «union» has been added because it is familiar from SQL, and because the operator «|» can get rather lost visually when it is used to combine the results of two complex «for» expressions. This applies especially to XQuery, where the operator may often be used to combine the results of two FLWOR expressions that might each be a dozen lines long (FLWOR expressions are XQuery's equivalent to the SELECT statement of SQL).

Document Order and Duplicates

There are three kinds of expression in XPath 2.0 whose result is always guaranteed to be a sequence of nodes in document order, with no duplicates. They are all covered in this chapter. Specifically, they are:

❑ Any expression using the unary or binary path operator «/», or the pseudo-operator «//», unless the expression on the right-hand-side of the operator returns atomic values rather than nodes

❑ Any axis step (even an axis step like «preceding-sibling::*» that uses a reverse axis delivers its results in forwards document order)

❑ Any expression using one of the binary operators «union», «intersect», and «except».

The elimination of duplicates is always based on node identity, not value.

Many simple path expressions naturally return results in document order anyway and would never select duplicates. In these cases, the system doesn't have to do any extra work to satisfy this rule. For example, any path expression that does downward selection using the child axis will naturally retrieve the nodes in document order. But it's easy to come up with path expressions that don't have this property; for example, «following-sibling::*/..» selects the parents of all the following siblings, and of course they all have the same parent, so after eliminating duplicates this expression returns at most a single node.

Generally, the automatic sort into document order is a choice that avoids surprises, especially when processing loosely structured text: if an expression selects a number of text nodes in a document, then document order is the order that is most likely to retain the meaning. The only situation that can sometimes be confusing is when you write an expression such as «$sorted-employees/name» where the sequence in $sorted-employees has been carefully sorted into some logical order (for example, sorting employees by length of service). You can't do this kind of sorting in XPath alone, but it's easily done in XSLT or XQuery. In this situation, the «/» operator destroys the ordering and gives you the names of the employees in document order. The solution in this case is to use a «for» expression instead of a path expression, as described in Chapter 10.

There is no specific function in XPath to take an existing sequence and reorder it in document order, but you can achieve this easily by writing the dummy path expression «$seq/.», or if you prefer, by taking the union with an empty sequence: «$seq|()».

The Binary « / » Operator

Informally, we could say that a path expression is a sequence of steps separated by «/» or «//». This is reflected in the syntax rule:

Syntax

Expression	Syntax
RelativePathExpr	StepExpr ((«/» | «//») StepExpr)*
StepExpr	AxisStep | FilterExpr

We will come back to the pseudo-operator «//» later in the the chapter; for the moment, we will discuss the meaning of «/». Moreover, we will confine ourselves for the moment to the case where the expression on the right hand side of «/» selects nodes (we will see in Chapter 10 that the operator can also be overloaded to select atomic values). Understanding this operator is the key to understanding path expressions.

An arithmetic expression such as «A+B+C» can be decomposed into the form «(A+B)+C», and defined in terms of a binary «+» operator that takes two operands. Similarly, a path expression of the form «A/B/C» can be decomposed into «(A/B)/C», which means that the result of a path expression is defined entirely in terms of the meaning of the binary «/» operator. There is a difference, however: The «/» operator is a higher-order operator, because the expression used as its right-hand operand is evaluated repeatedly, once for every item in the sequence selected by the first operand.

Effect

So what exactly does the «/» operator do?

I will explain this in terms of an expression «E1/E2», where E1 and E2 are arbitrary expressions. This expression is evaluated as follows:

- ❑ E1 is evaluated to produce a sequence of nodes; let's call this S1. If the result of E1 contains an atomic value, a type error is reported.

- ❑ For each node in S1, the expression E2 is evaluated. The context for evaluating E2 has this node from S1 as the context node. It also has the position of this node in the sequence S1 as the context position, and the number of nodes in S1 as the context size, but in practice it's very rare to write an expression on the right-hand side of «/» that depends on the context position or size.

- ❑ Each time E2 is evaluated, it produces a sequence which must either consist entirely of nodes, or entirely of atomic values (if it doesn't, a type error is reported). For the moment, we're only interested in the case where it delivers nodes; the other case is described in Chapter 10 (page 644). All the nodes produced when E2 has been evaluated once for every node in S1 are bundled together into a single sequence. Duplicate nodes are then removed, and the remaining nodes are sorted into document order.

- ❑ The resulting sequence of nodes forms the result of the path expression «E1/E2».

The most common kind of expression to use on the right hand side of «/» is an *axis step*. We'll describe axis steps in detail later in this chapter, on page 606. The syntax also allows a FilterExpr, which in effect means any expression, except that if it contains operators that bind less tightly than «/» (an obvious example is «|») then it must be written in parentheses.

Let's look at a simple example where both operands are axis steps: the expression «child::book/attribute::isbn». (I'm deliberately using the verbose syntax here, the abbreviated form is «book/@isbn».) So E1 in this example is the expression «child::book», which selects all the elements that are children of the context node and have the name «book». It's possible that the context node doesn't have any <book> children, of course, in which case this will give you an empty sequence, and when that happens, the result of «E1/E2» is also an empty sequence. But let's suppose it selects three books. For each one of these <book> elements, the E2 expression (in our case «attribute::isbn») is evaluated, with that <book> as the context node. The step expression «attribute::isbn» selects the attribute node whose name is isbn and whose parent node is the context node. So assuming that each <book> element actually has an isbn attribute, the final result contains three attribute nodes, one for each of the three books. In this case there won't be any duplicate nodes to get rid of, and the final result will be the sequence of three attribute nodes in document order.

As we've already noted, in XPath 2.0 «/» is a regular operator in the sense that there are no syntactic restrictions on its operands, but it is a little unusual because it evaluates the expression on the right repeatedly. Operators and functions that work like this are often called higher-order operators, and if you've used functional programming languages before, you will recognize «/» as behaving like a *map* or *apply* operator in such languages; it maps the sequence that's the result of the first expression by applying the second expression to each item in that sequence.

Another interesting thing about the «/» operator is that there's very little point using an expression on the right-hand side if its result doesn't depend in some way on the context node. However, there is no rule that enforces this as a constraint. You can write an expression such as «$N/$M» if you like, as long as $N is a sequence of nodes. If you follow through the rules given above, you'll see that the result contains all the nodes in $M, in document order, except in the case where $N is empty, in which case the final result is empty. During the design stage, some reviewers wanted to disallow such expressions. But on the whole, it's not a good principle in language design to disallow things just because they aren't useful. On that basis, you would stop people writing «$X+0», or «$X*1». There's even a case that makes sense: «./$M» selects all the nodes in $M, in document order and with duplicates removed.

> *Don't make the mistake of thinking that if $n holds the string* "title", *say, then* «./$n» *means the same as* «./title». *Variables in XPath represent values, not parts of an expression. To select the child elements whose name is in $n, use* «*[name()=$n]».*

Examples of the Binary «/» Operator

The following examples illustrate that although axis steps are often used as operands of «/», any kind of expression is legal:

Expression	Description
descendant::para/@style	In this example both operands are axis steps. The first step selects the descendants of the context node that are <para> elements; the second step uses the abbreviated syntax «@style», which is short for «attribute::style», and selects the style attributes of these elements.
section[1]/clause[3]	In this example each of the operands includes a positional predicate. The first step selects the first <section> element that is a child of the context node, the second Step selects the third <clause> element that is a child of the selected <section>.
chapter/section/para/ sentence	This path expression selects every <sentence> element that is a child of a <para> element that is a child of a <section> element that is a child of a <chapter> element that is a child of the context node. The expression can be decomposed into a nested set of expressions each of which uses a binary «/» operator: «((chapter/section)/para)/sentence».
doc('a.xml')/id('Z123')	This example illustrates that the operands of the «/» operator do not have to be AxisStep expressions. This example selects the document with a particular relative URI, and using the resulting document node as the context node, then selects the element with a particular ID value.

continued

Expression	Description
book/(chapter|appendix)	This is another example that uses an operand that is not an AxisStep. For each selected \<book\> element, it evaluates the expression «(chapter|appendix)», which selects all the child \<chapter\> and \<appendix\> elements of the book, in document order.
$chap/title	Using a variable reference on the left-hand side of «/» is very common in «for» expressions, which we will examine in Chapter 10. A typical example is «for $chap in //chapter return string-length($chap/title)». This kind of construct is even more common in XQuery.
./title	This expression means exactly the same as «title» on its own: it selects the children of the context node that are named \<title\>. Some people feel that the leading «./» adds clarity: it makes it clear to the reader that the expression depends on the context node, and distinguishes it more clearly from a variable reference «$title».

Associativity of the «/» Operator

In the vast majority of cases the «/» operator is associative, which means that «(A/B)/C» returns the same result as «A/(B/C)». For those with insatiable curiosity, there are only three situations that I know of where this is not the case:

❑ The expression is not associative if one of the steps creates new nodes. There is no expression in XPath itself that creates new nodes, but an XPath expression can contain a call to a function written in XSLT that creates such nodes. In XQuery, steps in a path expression can even construct nodes directly, for example, you can write « \<p q="2"/\>/@q». If we use the XQuery syntax for illustration, we can see that «$A/../\<B/\>» eliminates duplicate nodes in the result of «$A/..», and therefore the number of \<B\> elements in the result is equal to the number of distinct nodes that are parents of nodes in $A. But the expression «$A/(../\<B/\>)» creates one \<B/\> element for every node in $A that has a parent. So the number of \<B/\> elements returned in the two cases is different.

❑ The expression is not associative if one of the steps uses the position() or last() functions. For example, consider the expression «A/remove($S, position())». The remove() function, described in Chapter 13, returns the sequence of items supplied in its first argument, except for the item whose position is given in the second argument. This means that if A contains exactly one node, then the result is all the nodes in $S except the first. But if A contains two nodes, then the result is the union of «remove($S, 1)» and «remove($S, 2)», which (think about it carefully) contains all the nodes in $S. Now if we extend this to the expression «A/B/remove($S, position())» we can see that the result should contain all the nodes in $S except when «A/B» contains exactly one node, because the expression should be evaluated as «(A/B)/remove($S, position())». But if it were written the other way, as «A/(B/remove($S, position))», the first node in $S would be dropped only if every A has exactly one B child.

❑ Finally, «/» is not associative when one step selects nodes and another selects atomic values. For example, «(A/..)/name()» selects one node (the parent of all the A children, that is, the node you started from) and then selects its name. However, «A/(../name())» repeats the name of the parent node as many times as there are «A» nodes.

These examples are fairly pathological, but you might like to try them out on your chosen XPath processor to see how well it handles them. There may well be much simpler path expressions in which «/» is not associative, but I haven't discovered them yet!

Axis Steps

This section discusses the expressions called axis steps. Axis steps are often used as operands of the «/» operator in a path expression, which is how they got their name (a path consists of many steps). But an axis step is an expression in its own right, and it can be used on its own without any need for a «/» operator. We've also seen that XPath 2.0 allows the operands of «/» to be any kind of expression, they are no longer constrained to be axis steps. So the «/» operator and axis steps have become quite decoupled in the semantics of the language. However, they are so often used together that it makes sense to retain the term *path expression* to describe any expression that uses either a «/» operator or an axis step or both.

An axis step selects a set of nodes that are related in some way to the context node: for example, the children, the parent, or the following siblings of the context node. The relationship in question is called an axis. An axis is essentially a one-to-many relationship between nodes. If you prefer, you can think of it as a function which takes a single node as input, and produces a sequence of related nodes (for example, the children, the attributes, or the ancestors of that node) as output. Because axes are used so frequently and could be said to be the core feature of the XPath language, we don't use the standard function call syntax, but the underlying theory can be expressed in purely functional terms.

An axis step has three parts: the axis, the node test, and the predicates. The axis and the predicates can be defaulted, but the node test is always present. These three parts are discussed in more detail in the sections that follow: axes on page 609, node tests on page 613, and predicates on page 617. In this section, we'll start with an overview.

A step is based on a particular axis, and it can also choose to filter the nodes that are present on the axis. There are two kinds of filter that can be used, alone or in combination:

❑ A node test allows nodes to be selected according to the kind of node, the name and namespace of the node, and (as we shall see in Chapter 11) the type annotation of the node, as determined by schema validation.

❑ The step can also include general-purpose predicates, which can specify an arbitrary boolean condition that a node must satisfy, or can select nodes at particular positions in the sequence returned by the axis.

The next section gives the syntax of axis steps.

Syntax of Axis Steps

Expression	Syntax
AxisStep	(ForwardStep | ReverseStep) PredicateList
PredicateList	Predicate *
Predicate	«[» Expr «]»
ForwardStep	(ForwardAxis NodeTest) | AbbrevForwardStep

continued

Expression	Syntax
ReverseStep	(ReverseAxis NodeTest) | AbbreReverseStep
ForwardAxis	«child ::» | «descendant ::» | «attribute ::» | «self ::» | «descendant-or-self ::» | «following-sibling ::» | «following ::» | «namespace ::»
ReverseAxis	«parent ::» | «ancestor ::» | «preceding-sibling ::» | «preceding ::» | «ancestor-or-self ::» |

The split between forward and reverse axes in this grammar is cosmetic. It's presented this way because there are semantic distinctions in the way predicates are evaluated in the two cases, and it's nice when semantic distinctions can be related clearly to syntactic distinctions.

The abbreviations for steps will be covered later (see page 621). For the moment, we'll concentrate on the unabbreviated syntax in which the axis names are spelt out in full.

Effect

A step can be used to follow any axis and to find any kind of node.

Each axis returns a set of nodes relative to a specific origin node, for example, its previous siblings or its ancestors. The axis step returns a subset of the nodes on this axis, selected by the kind of node, the name of the node, the schema-defined type of the node, and the predicate expressions.

The NodeTest supplies any restrictions on the node kind, name, and type of the selected nodes, while the predicate expressions provide arbitrary boolean conditions that the nodes must satisfy, or positional filters that constrain their relative position.

The result of an axis step is always a sequence of nodes (possibly an empty sequence) with no duplicates, in document order. This is true even if the axis is one of the reverse axes, such as preceding-sibling, that selects nodes that are before the context node in document order.

For example, the step «ancestor::node()», given any starting node, finds all the ancestors of that node. When the step is used in a path expression such as «$n/ancestor::node()», it returns a sequence containing all the ancestors of all the nodes in $n. The sequence will be in document order, which means that the outermost ancestor (the root of the tree) will appear first in the result.

To understand the meaning of positional predicates in the step (for example «[3]») it is often useful to think of an axis as retrieving nodes in a particular order, but the formal definition doesn't require this. Instead these predicates are defined in terms of a number assigned to each node. For a forward axis (as shown in the syntax above), the nodes are numbered to show their relative position in document order, while for a reverse axis, they are numbered in reverse document order. The effect of positional predicates (such as «booklist/book[3]») is to select those nodes whose number matches the value of the predicate. This means that if the axis is a forward axis, the positional predicate «[3]» will return the node that is third in document order; if it is a reverse axis, the same predicate will return the node that is third in reverse document order.

So the evaluation of the axis step, for a given context node, proceeds as follows:

1. All the nodes on the selected axis are found, starting at the context node.

2. Those that satisfy the node test (that is, those of the required node kind, name, and type) are selected.

607

3. The remaining nodes are numbered from 1 to N in document order if the axis is a forward axis, or in reverse document order if it is a reverse axis.

4. The first (leftmost) predicate is applied to each node in turn. When evaluating the predicate, the context node (that is, the result of the «.» expression) is that node, the context position (the result of the position() function) is the number assigned to the node in stage 3, and the context size (the result of the last() function) is the largest number allocated in stage 3. A numeric predicate such as «[2]» or «[last()-1]» is interpreted as a shorthand for «[position() = 2]» or «[position() = last()-1]», respectively. The node is selected if the predicate is true, and it is discarded if the predicate is false.

5. Stages 3 and 4 are repeated for any further predicates. For each predicate, the nodes that survive to this stage are renumbered 1 to N, in document order for a forwards axis, or reverse document order for a reverse axis.

Examples of Axis Steps

Expression	Description
child::title	Selects child elements of the context node named <title>.
title	Short form of «child::title».
attribute::title	Selects attributes of the context node named title.
@title	Short form of «attribute::title».
ancestor::xyz:*	Selects ancestor elements of the context node whose names are in the namespace with prefix «xyz».
*[@width]	Selects all child elements of the context node that have a width attribute.
text()[starts-with(.,'The')]	Selects every text node that is a child of the context node and whose text content starts with the characters «The».
*[@code][position() < 10]	Selects the first nine child elements of the context node that have a code attribute.
*[position() < 10][@code]	Selects from the first nine child elements of the context node those that have a code attribute.
self::*[not(@code = preceding-sibling:: */@code)]	Selects the current element node provided that it does not have a code attribute with the same value as the code attribute of any preceding sibling element.
namespace::*	Selects all the namespace nodes that are in scope for the context node. If the context node is not an element, the result will be empty.
self::item	Selects the context node if it is an <item> element, or an empty sequence otherwise. This is usually used in a predicate, for example «*[not(self::item)]» selects all the children of the context node except those that are <item> elements. This relies on the rules for *effective boolean value*, whereby an empty sequence is treated as false.

continued

Expression	Description
comment()	Selects all comment nodes that are children of the context node.
@comment()	Short for «attribute::comment()», this selects all comment nodes on the attribute axis. The attribute axis can only contain attribute nodes, so this will always return an empty sequence; nevertheless it is a legal step.

Axes

An *axis* is a path through the document tree, starting at a particular node (which I'll call the origin) and following a particular relationship between nodes. There are 13 axes defined in XPath, as follows:

- ❑ ancestor
- ❑ ancestor-or-self
- ❑ attribute
- ❑ child
- ❑ descendant
- ❑ descendant-or-self
- ❑ following
- ❑ following-sibling
- ❑ namespace
- ❑ parent
- ❑ preceding
- ❑ preceding-sibling
- ❑ self

This section explains the meaning of each of the axes, giving both a textual definition and a diagram.

The diagram shows the origin node in dark shading, while the nodes on the axis are numbered in the sequence they appear on the axis. The diagram does not show attribute and namespace nodes.

Description	Diagram

ancestor

Selects all the nodes that are ancestors of the origin node. The first node on the axis is the parent of the origin node, the second is its grandparent, and so on; the last node on the axis is the root of the tree.

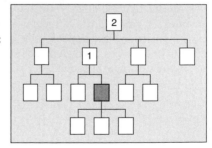

continued

9

XPath: Path Expressions

XPath: Path Expressions

Description	Diagram

ancestor-or-self
Selects the same nodes as the ancestor axis, but starting with the origin node rather than with its parent.

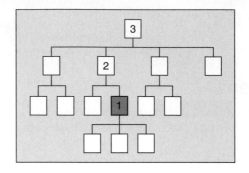

attribute
If the origin node is an element, this axis selects all its attribute nodes. Otherwise, it selects nothing (an empty sequence). The result is in document order; however, document order for attributes is arbitrary and unpredictable. The attributes won't necessarily be in the order in which they appeared in the original lexical XML, and the order may vary from one XSLT processor to another. Note also that namespace declarations are not treated as attribute nodes and will never be selected by the attribute axis.

child
Selects all the children of the origin node, in document order. For any node except a document node or element node, this selects nothing. Note that the children of an element node do not include its attributes or namespace nodes, only the text nodes, element nodes, processing instructions, and comments that make up its content.

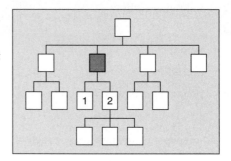

descendant
Selects all the children of the origin node, and their children, and so on recursively. The resulting nodes are in document order. If the origin is an element, this effectively means that the descendant axis contains all the text nodes, element nodes, comments and processing instructions that appear in the original source document between that element's start and end tags, in their original sequence.

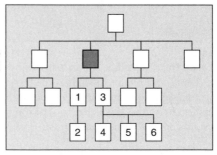

continued

Description	Diagram

descendant-or-self

This is the same as the descendant axis, except that the first node selected is the origin node itself.

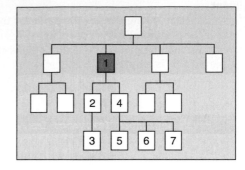

following

This selects all the nodes that appear after the origin node in document order, excluding the descendants of the origin node. If the origin is an element node, for example, this effectively means that it contains all the text nodes, element nodes, comments and processing instructions in the document that start after the end tag of the origin element. The following axis will never contain attribute or namespace nodes.

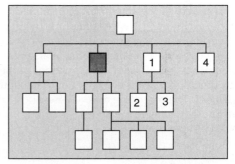

following-sibling

This selects all the nodes that follow the origin node in document order, and that are children of the same parent node. If the origin is a document node, an attribute node, or a namespace node, then the following-sibling axis will always be empty.

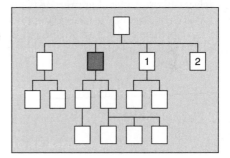

namespace

If the origin node is an element, this axis selects all the namespace nodes that are in scope for that element; otherwise, it is empty. The order of the namespace nodes is undefined. The namespace nodes correspond to namespace declarations (xmlns="x" or xmlns:y="z") on the element itself or on one of its ancestor elements, but excluding any namespace declaration that cannot be used on this element because it is masked by another declaration of the same namespace prefix, or because it is undeclared (XML 1.1 only). For more information about namespace nodes see Chapter 2.

continued

Description	Diagram

parent

This axis selects a single node, the parent of the origin node. If the origin node is a document element node, or any other node that happens to be the root of a tree, then the parent axis is empty.

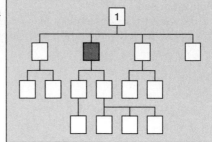

preceding

This selects all the nodes that appear before the origin node, excluding the ancestors of the origin node. If the origin is an element node, this effectively means that it contains all the text nodes, element nodes, comments and processing instructions in the document that finish before the start tag of the origin element. The preceding axis will never contain attribute or namespace nodes.

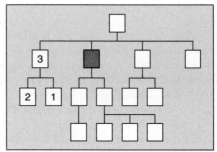

preceding-sibling

This selects all the nodes that precede the origin node, and that are children of the same parent node. If the origin is a document node, an attribute node, or a namespace node, then the preceding-sibling axis will always be empty.

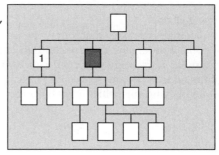

self

This selects a single node, the origin node itself. This axis will never be empty. The self axis is generally used with a node test as a way of testing whether the context node conforms to that node test: for example, the filter expression «$nodes[self::para]» selects items in $nodes that are <para> elements. This could equally be written «$nodes/self::para».

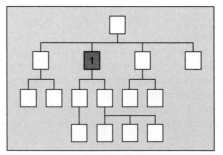

Node Tests

An axis step always includes a node test. This tests whether a node satisfies specified constraints on the kind of node or the name of the node.

Expression	Syntax
NodeTest	NameTest | KindTest

A `NodeTest` is either a `NameTest` or a `KindTest`. A `NameTest` selects nodes by name, while a `KindTest` allows selection based on the kind of node (for example, elements, text nodes, or comments) and also (in the case of elements and attributes) its schema-defined type.

Specifying a `NameTest` implicitly causes selection of a particular kind of node: attributes for the attribute axis, namespaces for the namespace axis, and elements in all other cases.

Usage

A `NodeTest` is used in an `AxisStep` to specify the name and/or kind of the nodes to be selected by the `Step`.

In general, you specify either the name of the nodes or their kind. If you specify a `NameTest`, this implicitly selects nodes of the principal node kind for the axis used in the `AxisStep`. For the attribute axis, this selects attribute nodes; for the namespace axis, it selects namespace nodes, and for all other axes, it selects element nodes.

Specifying `node()` as the `KindTest` selects all nodes on the axis. You must specify `node()` if you want the `AxisStep` to select nodes of more than one kind.

Specifying `processing-instruction()` or `comment()` or `text()` as the `KindTest` selects nodes of the specified kind. It doesn't make sense to specify any of these on the attribute or namespace axes, because they can't occur there. These nodes are unnamed, except for processing instructions, which is why there is an option in this single case to specify both the node kind and the node name required.

Examples of Node Tests

Expression	Description
TITLE	This `NameTest` selects all `<TITLE>` elements, unless it is used with the attribute axis (in the form «attribute::TITLE» or «@TITLE»), when it selects the TITLE attribute, or with the namespace axis (as «namespace::TITLE»), when it selects the namespace node whose prefix is TITLE.
news:article	This `NameTest` selects all nodes with local name «article» within the «news» namespace. These may be attribute nodes or element nodes, depending on the axis. There must be an enclosing element in the style sheet that declares the «news» prefix, by having an attribute of the form: «xmlns:news = "urn:newsml:iptc.org:20001006: NewsMLv1.0:1"». The node in the source document must have a name that uses this namespace URI, but it does not need to use the same prefix.

continued

9

XPath: Path Expressions

Expression	Description
MathML:*	This `NameTest` selects all nodes whose names are in the MathML namespace. These may be attribute nodes or element nodes, depending on the axis. There must be an enclosing element in the stylesheet that declares this prefix, by having an attribute of the form: «xmlns:MathML = "http://www.w3.org/1998/Math/MathML"».
*	This `NameTest` selects all elements, unless it is used with the attribute axis (in the form «attribute::*» or «@*») when it selects all attributes, or with the namespace axis (as «namespace::*»), when it selects all namespaces.
text()	This `NodeTest` selects all text nodes on the relevant axis.
processing-instruction()	This `NodeTest` selects all processing instructions on the relevant axis. Note that the XML declaration at the start of the document is *not* a processing instruction, even though it looks like one.
processing-instruction ('ckpt')	This `NodeTest` selects all processing instructions with the name (or `PITarget` as the XML specification calls it) «ckpt»: for example, the processing instruction <?ckpt frequency = daily?>.
node()	This `NodeTest` selects all nodes on the relevant axis.

Name Tests

As we have seen, a `NodeTest` is either a `NameTest` or a `KindTest`. This section describes `NameTests`. A `NameTest` is either a name, or a generic name specified using wildcards.

Syntax

Expression	Syntax
NameTest	QName | Wildcard
Wildcard	«*» | NCName«:*» | «*:»NCName

Note that a `NameTest` cannot contain embedded whitespace.

Usage

In general, a `NameTest` will match some names and will not match others.

The `NameTest` «*» matches any name. (But when used as an expression on its own, «*» is short for «child::*», which selects all child elements of the context node. The fact that the result is restricted to element nodes only is because «*», when used in an `AxisStep`, selects only nodes of the principal node kind for the axis, and for all axes except the attribute and namespace axes, the principal node kind is element nodes.)

> **A surprising effect of this rule is that you can't write:**
>
> ```
> <xsl:copy-of select="@*[not(self::title)]"/>
> ```
> **to copy all attributes of an element except the title attribute. Why? Because the**

> principal node kind for the self axis is element nodes, so if the context node is an
> attribute named title, «self::title» won't select it. Instead, write:
>
> `<xsl:copy-of select="@*[not(self::attribute(title))]"/>`

The NameTest «xyz:*» matches any name whose namespace is the one currently bound to the namespace prefix «xyz». The name being tested doesn't need to use the same prefix, so long as it refers to the same namespace URI.

A NameTest of the form «*:code» matches any node whose local-name is code, regardless of its namespace (it will match names in any namespace, as well as names that are in no namespace).

The NameTest «xyz:code» matches any name whose namespace is the one currently bound to the namespace prefix «xyz» and whose local part is «code». Again, the name being tested doesn't need to use the same prefix, provided it refers to the same namespace URI.

The interpretation of a NameTest such as «code» (with no namespace prefix) depends on the context:

- ❑ If it is used with any axis other than the attribute or namespace axes, then it selects elements whose name is in the namespace identified in the XPath context (see Chapter 7) as the default namespace for element and type names. In XSLT, this is established using the `[xsl:]xpath-default-namespace` attribute, typically on the `<xsl:stylesheet>` element. It is not affected by a default namespace declaration of the form «xmlns="some.uri"».

- ❑ If it is used with the attribute or namespace axis, then it selects nodes whose namespace URI is null.

> If your source document uses a default namespace declaration such as «xmlns =
> "some.uri"», then a `<code>` element in the source document will not be selected by
> an XPath expression such as «//code», even if the stylesheet contains the same
> namespace declaration «xmlns="some.uri"». This is because in the XPath
> expression, the default namespace is ignored. You will either need to specify an
> explicit namespace declaration such as «xmlns:x="some.uri"» and refer to the
> element as «//x:item», or to declare an xpath-default-namespace in the stylesheet.

Note that if a default namespace for elements has been set up, then the only way to select those elements whose namespace URI is null is to include a predicate that tests the result of the namespace-uri() function.

Examples of Name Tests

Expression	Description
*	Matches any name. If «*» is used on its own, it represents the step «child::*», which selects all child elements of the context node, regardless of their name.
xt:*	Matches any name in the namespace bound to the prefix «xt». If «xt:*» is used on its own, it represents the step «child::xt:*», which selects all child elements of the context node that are in the namespace bound to the prefix «xt».

continued

Expression	Description
title	Matches a node whose local name is name «title» and whose namespace URI is null, unless a default namespace for elements has been established in the context (and then, only when the axis is not the attribute or namespace axis).
wrox:title	Matches the name that has local part «title» and whose namespace is the namespace currently bound to the prefix «wrox».
*:title	Matches any name whose local part is «title», whether or not it is in a namespace.

Kind Tests

As we have seen, a `NodeTest` is either a `NameTest` or a `KindTest`. `NameTests` were described in the previous section; this section describes `KindTests`. A `KindTest` represents a constraint on the kind of nodes that are selected by an `AxisStep`.

Expression	Syntax
KindTest	DocumentTest | ElementTest | AttributeTest | PITest | CommentTest | TextTest | AnyKindTest
PITest	«processing-instruction» «(» (NCName | StringLiteral)? «)»
DocumentTest	«document-node» «(» ElementTest? «)»
CommentTest	«comment» «(» «)»
TextTest	«text» «(» «)»
AnyKindTest	«node» «(» «)»

The constructs `ElementTest` and `AttributeTest` are used primarily to test the schema-defined type of a node. These constructs are explained together with other type-related constructs on page 672 in Chapter 11.

Note that the names «comment», «text», and so on cannot be used as function names, but apart from this, they are not reserved words. It is quite possible to have elements or attributes called «text» or «node» in your source XML document, and therefore you can use «text» or «node» as ordinary names in XPath. This is why the names are flagged in a `KindTest` by the following parentheses, for example, «text()». The syntax rules are written so that the keyword and the following left parenthesis are treated as a compound symbol by the XPath parser, which in effect means that the parser does a look-ahead for the «(» before deciding whether a keyword such as «text» is to be interpreted as a `NameTest` or as a `KindTest`.

There are three ways you can select processing instructions. The simple test is «processing-instruction()», which selects any processing instruction node regardless of its name. If you want to select processing instructions named «xml-stylesheet», say, then you can write either «processing-instruction("xml-stylesheet")» or «processing-instruction(xml-stylesheet)». The two are equivalent: the syntax with quotes is retained for compatibility with XPath 1.0, while the syntax without quotes is introduced for symmetry with the «element(...)» and «attribute(...)» tests described in Chapter 11.

Usage

A `KindTest` can be used within an `AxisStep` to restrict the `Step` to return nodes of a particular kind. The keywords «comment», «text», and «processing-instruction» are self-explanatory: they restrict the

616

selection to nodes of that particular kind. The keyword «node» selects nodes of any kind and is useful because an AxisStep has to include some kind of NodeTest, so if you want all the nodes on the axis, you can specify node(). For example, if you want all child nodes, specify «child::node()». Remember that although «node()» as a NodeTest selects any kind of node, «node()» as an AxisStep means «child::node()» and therefore selects only children of the context node. If you want to select attributes as well, write «@*|node()».

If you want to select all elements, you can use the KindTest element(), and if you want to select all attributes, you can use attribute(). However, it is more usual in these cases simply to use the NodeTest «*». Specifying «*» selects the nodes of the principal node kind for the selected axis, which will always be elements in the case of an axis that can contain elements, and attributes in the case of an axis that can contain attributes. The KindTests element() and attribute() are generally used with parameters that specify the schema-defined type of the required elements or attributes, as described in Chapter 11.

Similarly, the KindTest document-node() can be used without parameters to select all document nodes. But you won't see this used much in practice, because the document node can be selected using the simpler syntax «/», discussed later in this chapter on page 623. With parameters, the document-node() KindTest can be used to test for the document node containing an element of a particular schema-defined type — again, this is described in Chapter 11.

There is no specific KindTest for namespace nodes. But all the nodes on the namespace axis are namespace nodes, so the expressions «namespace::*» and «namespace::node()» both work fine, provided that your implementation supports use of the namespace axis.

Examples of Kind Tests

These examples show some different KindTests, used in the context of a containing path expression.

Expression	Description
parent::node()	Selects the parent of the context node, whether this is an element node or the root node. This differs from «parent::*», which selects the parent node only if it is an element. The expression «parent::node()» is usually abbreviated to «..».
//comment()	Selects all comment nodes in the document.
child::text()	Selects all text node children of the context node. This is usually abbreviated to «text()».
@comment()	A strange but legal way of getting an empty node-set: it looks for all comment nodes on the attribute axis, and of course finds none.
self::attribute(title)	Selects the context node if it is an attribute named «title».

Predicates

We saw earlier that a step has three parts: an axis, a NodeTest (which is either a NameTest or a KindTest), and optionally a list of predicates. We've examined the first two parts in the preceding sections; now it's time to look at predicates.

A predicate is a qualifying expression used to select a subset of the nodes in a sequence. The predicate may be any XPath expression, and it is written in square brackets.

Expression	Syntax
PredicateList	Predicate *
Predicate	«[» Expr «]»

There are two very similar constructs in XPath that use predicates. They can be used in an AxisStep, to qualify the nodes selected by the axis, and they can be used in a FilterExpr, to filter any sequence. We will talk about the more general filter expressions in Chapter 10 and concentrate here on the use of predicates with an AxisStep. The meaning of the two cases is very similar, and it's easy to use them without always being aware of the difference.

For example:

Expression	Description
para[position() > 1]	Here the predicate «[position() > 1]» is being applied to the AxisStep «para», which is short for «./child::para». It selects all the <para> element children of the context node except the first. Because the expression is an AxisStep, the results are guaranteed to be in document order and to contain no duplicates.
$para[position() > 1]	Here the predicate «[position() > 1]» is being applied to the value of the variable-reference «$para». The expression selects all items in the sequence except the first. The result does not have to be in document order (it can contain atomic values as well as nodes, so document order would not make sense), and it can contain duplicates. The items in the result are returned in their original order.

In both cases the effect of a predicate is to select a subset of the items in a sequence. There's a significant difference when a predicate is used with a path expression of more than one step. For example:

Expression	Description
chapter/para[1]	Here the predicate «[1]» is being applied to the Step «para», which is short for «./child::para». It selects the first child <para> element of each child <chapter> element of the context node.
(chapter/para)[1]	This is a FilterStep where the predicate «[1]» is being applied to the sequence of nodes selected by the path expression «chapter/para». The expression selects a single <para> element, the first child <para> of a <chapter> that is a child of the context node.

In effect, the predicate operator «[]» has higher precedence (it binds more tightly) than the path operator «/».

Another distinction between the two cases is that in the case of a FilterExpr, the items are always considered in their original order when evaluating the predicate. In the case of an AxisStep, the nodes are considered in the order of the relevant axis. This is explained in more detail below.

A predicate may be either a boolean expression or a numeric expression. These are not distinguishable syntactically; for example, the predicate «[$p]» could be either. The distinction is only made at runtime. (That's the official rule, anyway. If an optimizer can work out in advance whether the value is numeric or boolean, then it will. It's a good idea to declare the types of your variables and parameters, which will make the optimizer's job easier.)

The following table shows some examples of boolean predicates:

Expression	Description
`section[@title = 'Introduction']`	Here the predicate is a conventional boolean expression. This example selects every child `<section>` element that has a `title` attribute with the value «Introduction».
`section[title]`	The predicate is true if the relevant section has at least one child `<title>` element.
`title[substring-before(.,':')]`	The `PredicateExpr` evaluates to true if the string-value of the title has one or more characters before its first colon: that is, if the `substring-before()` function returns a nonempty string.
`book[not(author = preceding-sibling::author)]`	The `PredicateExpr` here is true if the author of the book is not the same as the author of some preceding book within the same parent element. The effect of this expression is to select the first book by each author.

If the value of the predicate is a number (that is, if its type label is `xs:decimal`, `xs:integer`, `xs:float`, or `xs:double`, or some subtype of these), it is treated as a numeric predicate. If it is of any other type, it is converted to an `xs:boolean` value using the effective boolean value rules described in Chapter 7 (these are the same as the rules for the `boolean()` function). So for example, the predicate «[@sequence-number]» is true if the context node has a `sequence-number` attribute, and is false otherwise. The actual numeric value of the attribute `sequence-number` is immaterial: the value of «@sequence-number» is a sequence of nodes, so it is treated as «[boolean(@sequence-number)]». If you want to use the sequence number attribute as a numeric predicate, write «[number(@sequence-number)]». Or, if you prefer brevity, write «[+@sequence-number]».

A numeric predicate «[P]» is simply a shorthand for the boolean predicate «[position() = P]», so you could also achieve the required effect by writing «[position() = @sequence-number]».

Note that the rules for recognizing a predicate as a number are very strict. For example, a string written as «"20"» is not considered to be a number: it's the type label on the value that matters, not the format of the value itself. Equally, the XSLT variable declared in the example below is not a number, it is the document node at the root of a temporary tree (see the `<xsl:variable>` topic in Chapter 6):

```
<xsl:variable name="index">3</xsl:variable>
```

If you want to use this value as a predicate, either write it so the value of the variable is a number:

```
<xsl:variable name="index" select="3"/>
```

(but don't write «select = "'3'"», because that would make it a string) or force it to a number in the predicate. Any of the following will work:

```
<xsl:value-of select="item[number($index)]"/>
<xsl:value-of select="item[+$index]"/>
<xsl:value-of select="item[position()=$index]"/>
```

As explained in Chapter 7, every expression is evaluated with a particular focus. The focus for evaluating the predicate is not the same as the focus for the expression that it forms part of. The predicate is applied separately to each node selected by the axis, and each time it is evaluated:

❑   The context item (the item selected by «.») is the node to which the predicate is being applied.

❑   The context position (the result of the position() function) is the number assigned to that node within the sequence of nodes.

❑   The context size (the result of the last() function) is the number of nodes in the sequence.

As we saw earlier the number assigned to a node selected by an AxisStep depends on the direction of the axis used in that AxisStep. Some axes (child, descendant, descendant-or-self, following, following-sibling) are forward axes, so the position() function numbers the nodes in document order. Other axes (ancestor, ancestor-or-self, preceding, preceding-sibling) are reverse axes, so position() numbers them in reverse document order. The self and parent axes return a single node, so the order is irrelevant. The ordering of nodes on the attribute and namespace axes is undefined, so positional predicates on these axes don't make much sense, though they are permitted.

The following table shows some examples of positional predicates.

Expression	Description
para[1]	Selects the first <para> child element of the context node.
para[last()]	Selects the last <para> child element of the context node.
para[position()!=1]	Selects all <para> child elements of the context node, other than the first.
para[position() = 1 to 5]	Selects the first five <para> elements. This works because the «=» operator returns true if the left-hand operand (position()) contains a value that is equal to one of the items in the right-hand operand (1 to 5), which is true if position() is in the range 1 to 5.
para[last()-1]	Returns the last but one <para> child of the context node.
para[3.2]	Returns an empty sequence. The value 3.2 is treated as a numeric predicate. The value of position() will never be equal to 3.2, so no elements are selected.
para[position()]	Selects all child <para> elements. The predicate expands to «[position()= position()]», which is always true.
para[position()-1]	Returns an empty sequence. The predicate expands to «[position() = position()-1]», which is always false.
para[number(@nr)]	Returns every child <para> element that has a nr attribute whose numeric value is equal to the position of the <para> element in the sequence. This rather perverse example illustrates that specifying a numeric predicate gives no guarantee that at most one node will be selected.

An AxisStep can contain a sequence of zero or more predicates. Specifying two separate predicates is not the same thing as combining the two predicates into one with an «and» operator. The reason is that the context for the second predicate is different from the context for the first. Specifically, in the second predicate, the context position (the value of the position() function) and the context size (the value of the `last()` function) consider only those nodes that successfully passed through the previous predicate. What this means in practice is shown in the examples below:

Expression	Description
`book[author = "P. D. James"][1]`	The first book that was written by P. D. James.
`book[1][author = "P. D. James"]`	The first book, provided that it was written by P. D. James.
`book[position() = 1 and author = "P. D. James"]`	The first book, provided that it was written by P. D. James. This is the same as the previous example, because in that example the second predicate is not dependant on the context position.

Abbreviated Axis Steps

Logically, an axis step has three parts, which we have examined in the previous sections: the axis, the node test, and the predicates. However, the most commonly used axis steps can be written in an abbreviated notation, and in this section we will look at these abbreviations.

In XPath 1.0, the expression «.» was considered to be an abbreviation for the step «self::node()». In XPath 2.0 this is no longer the case, because «.» can also be used when the context item is an atomic value rather than a node. For this reason, «.» is now classified as a primary expression in its own right, and was therefore covered with the other kinds of primary expression in Chapter 7.

Syntax

Expression	Syntax
AbbrevForwardStep	«@»? NodeTest
AbbrevReverseStep	«..»

This syntax describes three abbreviations for axis steps: the defaulted child axis, the use of «@» to represent the attribute axis, and the use of «..» to represent the parent axis. We will consider these in the next three sections; we will then examine the freestanding «/» expression and see that it can be treated as an abbreviation for a more complex expression involving axis steps.

Note that because of the way these constructs are used in the definition of an axis step, any of them can be followed by predicates in square brackets.

Defaulting the Axis Name in a Step

A full step is written in the form:

```
axis-name :: NodeTest Predicates?
```

Since the most common axis is the child axis, it is possible to omit the «child::» part and write the step in the abbreviated form:

```
NodeTest Predicates?
```

For example, the path expression «employee/name/first-name» consists of three steps, each of which has been abbreviated in this way. It is short for «child::employee/child::name/ child::first-name».

9

XPath: Path Expressions

Most people writing XPath expressions use this abbreviation all the time without really thinking about it. In fact, it's rare to see «child::» spelled out explicitly. But I do sometimes like to write the full form to alert the reader to what's going on. For example, the expression «record[*]» selects all <record> elements that have one or more child elements. I sometimes write this as «record[child::*]» so that anyone reading the code can see more clearly what it means. The full syntax for the expression, of course, is «child::record[child::*]», and you could spell it out even more explicitly by writing «child::record[exists(child::*)]». (The exists() function is in Chapter 13).

There's one exception to the general rule that if you don't specify an axis, you get the child axis. This is when you use a NodeTest of the form «attribute(...)» or «schema-attribute(...)». This kind of NodeTest is used when testing the schema-defined type of an attribute node; it is described in detail in Chapter 11. Because the NodeTest makes it clear that you are looking for attributes rather than child elements, the system in this case chooses the attribute axis as the default. This avoids your having to write «attribute::attribute(*)» or «@attribute(X)», both of which read rather oddly, though they are both legal and logical.

The «@» Abbreviation

When the «@» sign appears in front of a NodeTest, it indicates that you are selecting nodes using the attribute axis. It is short for «attribute::».

What this means in practice is that in a path expression «A/@B», B is referring to an attribute of A, while in the path expression «A/B», B is referring to a child element of A.

Again, this abbreviation is ubiquitous among XPath developers, and it's rare to see «attribute::» written out in full. In fact, the «@» in front of an attribute name has become so familiar that people often think of it as being almost part of the name. I'm probably not the only one who has found myself typing <person @id = "B123"> in an XML document (which, of course, will be thrown out by an XML parser).

> Take care when using the «self::» axis. You can write «self::title» to test whether the context node is a <title> element, but you can't write «self::@title» to test whether it is a title attribute. This is because «@» is short for «attribute::», and «self::attribute::title» doesn't make sense: you can either look on the self axis or the attribute axis, but not both at once. Write «self::attribute(title)» instead.

Examples

Expression	Description
@category	Abbreviation for «attribute::category».
@xml:space	Abbreviation for «attribute::xml:space».
@*	Abbreviation for «attribute::*» (selects all attributes of the context node).
@xsl:*	Abbreviation for «attribute::xsl:*» (selects all attributes in the namespace bound to the prefix xsl).

The «..» Abbreviation

The construct «..» appearing as an abbreviated step is short for «parent::node()». As such, it selects the parent of the context node. If the context node has no parent (that is, if it is the root of a tree), then it selects an empty sequence.

This notation is found most commonly at the start of a relative path expression. For example, «../@name» selects the name attribute of the parent of the context node. It is possible to use «..» anywhere in a path expression, though the need rarely arises. For example, «//title/..» selects all elements in the document that have a child element called <title>. The same result could be achieved, perhaps more naturally, by writing «//*[title]».

Document nodes never have a parent, so «/..» is always an empty sequence. In XPath 1.0, there was no direct way of representing an empty sequence, and so you may see this notation used when an empty sequence is needed, perhaps as the default value of a parameter in an XSLT template rule. In XPath 2.0 it's more natural to write this as «()». Indeed, an XPath 2.0 processor that implements the static typing feature (see Chapter 3) may well give you an error if you write «/..», kindly pointing out to you that it will never select anything.

Writing «not(..)» is a simple way of testing whether the context node is the root.

As explained in Chapter 2, the element containing an attribute is considered to be the parent of the attribute, even though the attribute is not a child of the element. Unlike biological relationships, in XPath the parent and child relationships are not the inverse of each other. This allows you to use an expression such as «idref('abc')/..» to select the elements that have an IDREF attribute with the value «abc» (the idref() function is described in Chapter 13; it is one of the few constructs that make it natural to select an attribute node without going via its parent element.)

In XPath 1.0 the expression «..» could not be followed by a predicate: you could not write <xsl:if test = "..[@color = 'black']">. This was probably an oversight by the language designers, and the restriction has been lifted in XPath 2.0. As you would expect, this expression tests whether the parent element node has a color attribute whose value is «black».

Examples in Context

Expression	Effect
exists(..)	Tests whether the context node has a parent (in other words, whether it is the root of a tree).
../@name	Selects the name attribute of the parent of the context node.

The Root Expression «/»

I've invented the term *root expression* to refer to the expression «/», when used on its own (that is, when used as an expression, rather than as an operator). This doesn't actually have a name in the XPath syntax, and I feel it's important enough to give it one.

The meaning of this expression is: the node that is the root of the tree containing the context node, provided that this is a document node.

The symbol «/» is unusual because it is used both as an operator and as an expression in its own right. This can lead to some syntactic ambiguities; for example, the expression «/ union /*» looks as if it is trying to find the union of the two node sequences «/» and «/*», but actually it is an absolute path expression whose first step is «child::union» («union» is a legitimate element name) and whose second step is «child::*». If «/» is followed by something that could be a legitimate step in a path expression, then that's the interpretation that's chosen. Adding whitespace after the «/» doesn't make any difference. What you need to do if you want the other interpretation is to put the «/» in parentheses, thus: «(/) union /*».

This ambiguity was actually present, and unremarked upon, in XPath 1.0, though, it arose less frequently because there weren't many operators in XPath 1.0 that could sensibly be applied to «/» as an operand. The «|» operator does not cause any ambiguities because it cannot be confused with an element name.

I've classified the root expression as an abbreviated axis step because for most purposes it can be regarded as equivalent to the expression «ancestor-or-self::document-node()». However, there's a significant difference: if the context item doesn't have an ancestor that is a document node, you get a runtime error rather than an empty sequence as the result.

Technically, therefore, the expression «/» is defined in the language specification as being equivalent to:

```
root(self::node()) treat as document-node()
```

This means that it selects the same node as the `root()` function described in Chapter 13, when given the context node «self::node()» as an argument, but raises an error if this node isn't a document node (the «treat as» expression is covered in Chapter 11).

Various errors can arise if you use the «/» expression inappropriately:

❑ It's an error if there is no context item. This happens, for example, at the outer level of an XSLT function body.

❑ It's an error if there is a context item but the context item isn't a node. This can easily happen in XSLT within the `<xsl:analyze-string>` instruction, which always sets the context item to a string, or it can happen if you are using the `<xsl:for-each>` instruction to process a result of a function such as `tokenize()` or `distinct-values()`, which both return a sequence of atomic values.

❑ It's an error if the context item is in a tree whose root is something other than a document node. In XPath 1.0, every tree had a document node at its root, in fact, it was called a root node rather than a document node because there was no distinction. But the XPath 2.0 data model allows you to have orphaned trees with no document node. Commonly these will have an element as their root. They can also have other kinds of node as the root; for example, an attribute or text node, but in this case the tree can only contain one node.

The language could have been designed so that «/» was a synonym of the axis step «ancestor-or-self::node()[last()]», which selects the root of the tree whatever kind of node it is. The designers decided not to do this to avoid the surprises that can otherwise occur if you find yourself at a different kind of node from the one you were expecting. This decision also has the advantage that the type of the expression «/» is known more precisely: it always returns a document node, which means that it is always safe to use it in contexts (such as a call to a user-defined function) where a document node is the required type.

Although I have classified the root expression as an abbreviated axis step, it's unusual to use it explicitly as an operand of the «/» operator. Unusual, but not illegal. You will usually need to put it in parentheses if you try it; for example, «$x/(/)» selects the document node at the root of the tree containing the node

$x. A unary «/» operator appearing in an expression such as «/book/chap/title» can be seen as an abbreviation for «(/)/book/chap/title», so the root expression is being used as an implicit axis step whenever you write a path expression starting with «/». Which forms the subject of the next section. . . .

Rooted Path Expressions

I will use the term *rooted path expression* to mean a path expression that starts with «/» or «//». In XPath 1.0 these were called absolute path expressions; there is no specific name for them in the 2.0 specification, but I have avoided the word *absolute* because it conceals the fact that the value of these expressions does, in fact, depend on the context node.

The full syntax for path expressions is shown below. We already saw the production RelativePathExpr at the beginning of this chapter.

Syntax

Expression	Syntax
PathExpr	(«/» RelativePathExpr?) | («//» RelativePathExpr) | RelativePathExpr
RelativePathExpr	StepExpr ((«/» | «//») StepExpr)*

This production indicates that there are four forms a path expression can take, namely:

- ❏ «/» (a *root expression*, already discussed on page 623)
- ❏ «/» RelativePathExpr(the subject of this section)
- ❏ «//» RelativePathExpr (discussed later on page 626)
- ❏ RelativePathExpr (a sequence of steps separated by the binary «/» operator, which we examined at the start of this chapter)

A rooted path represents a path starting at the root node of the tree that contains the context node.

The syntax «/A/B/C» is familiar to anyone who has used Unix filenames, though it is not actually very logical. I find it helpful to think of the «/» at the start of a rooted path expression as being a unary version of the binary «/» operator. This means that a rooted path «/X» can be considered as an abbreviation for the expression «(/)/X», in the same way as «-3» is an abbreviation for «(0)-3». That is, the «/» is really just a binary operator with a defaulted first operand. The implicit first operand in this case is the node selected by the root expression «/». After this expansion, a rooted path behaves in exactly the same way as a relative path, which was described at the start of this chapter.

A consequence of these rules is that a rooted path such as «/X» will throw an error in all the cases where the root expression «/» throws an error. Specifically:

- ❏ It's an error if there is no context item.
- ❏ It's an error if there is a context item but the context item isn't a node.
- ❏ It's an error if the context item is in a tree whose root is something other than a document node.

There's a good reason for the restriction that a rooted path expression can only be used to select within a tree that's rooted at a document node. If it were allowed to start from any kind of node, there would be

625

some strange surprises. For example, if the root of the tree were an element node named `<A>`, then the expression «`/A`» would not select that element. This expression is an abbreviation for «`(/)/child::A`», so it would select all elements named A that are children of the root element, but not the root element itself. Rather than allow such surprises to occur, the working group decided to make this an error. If you want to select relative to the root of a non-document tree, you can always do this with a relative path expression whose first step is a call to the `root()` function, described in Chapter 13. For example, you can select all the A elements in a tree, even an A element that is the root of the tree, with the expression «`root(.)/descendant-or-self::A`».

If you want to start from the root of a different document than the one containing the context node, the simplest approach is to write a path expression whose first component is a variable reference identifying the root of the tree you want to make your selection from. This happens frequently in XSLT. If you are writing a stylesheet that loads several source documents using the `doc()` function, there is no direct way of selecting the root of the principal source document when the context node is in a different one. To solve this problem, it is useful to include in your stylesheet a global variable declaration of the form `<xsl:variable name = "input" select = "/"/>`. You can then refer to the root of the principal document at any time as «`$input`», and you can select other nodes in this tree with relative path expressions of the form «`$input/A/B`».

Examples of Rooted Paths

Expression	Description
`/price-list`	Selects the document element within the current document, provided its name is `<price-list>`. (*Current document* here and in the other examples means the tree containing the context node, assuming that the tree is rooted at a document node).
`/*`	Selects the document element within the current document, whatever its name.
`/child::node()`	Selects all nodes that are immediate children of the document root, that is, the document element plus any comments or processing instructions that come before or after the document element. (However, note that the `<?xml version = "1.0"?>` at the start of a document is *not* a processing instruction; in fact, it is not a node at all and is not accessible using XPath).
`/*/xsl:*`	Selects all element nodes with names in the namespace associated with the «`xsl:`» namespace prefix that are immediate children of the document element. (If applied to an XSLT stylesheet, this would select all the top-level XSLT declarations).
`//figure`	This path expression selects all the `<figure>` elements in the current document.

The «`//`» Abbreviation

Colloquially, «`//`» in a path expression means "find all descendants". More formally, whether it appears at the start of a path expression or as a binary operator, it is equivalent to writing «`/descendant-or-self::node()/`».

I refer to «`//`» as a pseudo-operator because its semantics are described by means of a textual expansion into a different expression; this differs from a proper operator whose effect is described in terms of evaluating the operands and combining the results.

The expression «`//A`» is often used to select all `<A>` elements in the document.

How does this work? The expression «//» is equivalent to the rooted path «/descendant-or-self::node()/child::A», which in turn (as we saw in the previous section) expands to «(/)/descendant-or-self::node()/child::A». This selects all <A> elements whose parent is either the document node or a descendant of the document node, looking as always within the tree that contains the context node. Since every element has a parent that meets these criteria, it selects all <A> elements. Similarly, «//@B» means «/descendant-or-self::node()/attribute::B», which selects all B attributes in the current document.

In most cases «//A» gives the same answer as «/descendant::A», but the significance of the formal expansion becomes apparent when positional predicates are involved. The expression «//para[1]» expands to «/descendant-or-self::node()/child::para[1]», which selects every <para> element that is the first child of its parent. This isn't the same as «/descendant::para[1]», which selects the first <para> element in the entire document.

The «//» abbreviation can also be used as an infix operator anywhere that «/» can appear. For example, «.//A» selects all <A> elements that are descendants of the context node. Again, the official meaning is «./descendant-or-self::node()/child::A». The «./» in this expanded expression is redundant: people often write path expressions such as «./A/B», but the «./» in most cases is pure noise. But with «//», the leading «.» becomes necessary to indicate that you want to start the selection at the context node, not at the root document node.

Expressions using «//» can be expensive to evaluate, because the XPath processor will often have to search the whole document to find the selected nodes. If you can specify a more restricted search, it is generally a good idea to do so — for example, if you know that all the <book> elements are children of the document element, then specifying «/*/book» will generally be much more efficient than writing «//book». Of course, actual performance characteristics of different products may vary. In some XML database products, elements are indexed in such a way that «//book» becomes very fast.

Examples Using «//»

Expression	Description
//figure	Selects all <figure> elements in the document.
//book[@category = 'fiction']	Selects all <book> elements in the document that have a category attribute with the value «fiction».
//*/*	Selects all element nodes that have an element as a parent, in other words all elements except those that are immediate children of the root node. Here «*» is a NameTest that matches any element.
//book/title	Selects all <title> elements that have a <book> element as their parent.
chapter//footnote	Selects all <footnote> elements that are descendants of a <chapter> element that itself is a child of the context node.
.//footnote	Selects all <footnote> elements that are descendants of the context node.
doc('lookup.xml')//entry	Selects all <entry> elements within the document identified by the relative URI lookup.xml. The doc() function is described in Chapter 13, page 750.
$winners//*/@name	Selects the name attribute of all elements that are descendants of a node that belongs to the node-set identified by the variable $winners.

continued

627

Expression	Description
`.//..`	This strange but perfectly legal expression combines «`//`», which finds the descendants of a node, and «`..`», which finds its parent. The effect is to find all nodes that are the parent of a descendant of the context node, plus the parent of the context node itself.
`chapter//footnote`	Selects all `<footnote>` elements that are descendants of a `<chapter>` element that itself is a child of the context node.

Comparing «`//`» with «`/descendant::`»

Consider the two expressions «`$chapters//diagram[1]`» and «`$chapters/descendant::diagram[1]`»:

«`$chapters//diagram[1]`» means «`$chapters/descendant-or-self::node()/child::diagram[1]`», that is, every `<diagram>` element that is the first `<diagram>` child of its parent element and that is a descendant of a node in `$chapters`.

«`$chapters/descendant::diagram[1]`» means the first `<diagram>` element (taking them in document order) that is a descendant of a node in `$chapters`. Another way of writing this is «`($chapters//diagram)[1]`».

To see the difference, consider the following source document:

```
<chapter>
   <section>
       <diagram nr="12"/>
       <diagram nr="13"/>
   </section>
   <diagram nr="14"/>
   <section>
       <diagram nr="15"/>
       <diagram nr="16"/>
   </section>
</chapter>
```

With this document, if the variable `$chapters` contains only the outer `<chapter>` element, «`$chapters//diagram[1]`» will select diagrams 12, 14, and 15, while both «`$chapters/descendant::diagram[1]`» and «`($chapters//diagram)[1]`» will select diagram 12 only.

Combining Sets of Nodes

Until now this chapter has been all about path expressions. This section describes operators that combine two sets of nodes. Although these aren't technically path expressions, they are invariably used in conjunction with path expressions, so it's useful to deal with them at the same time. The operators are:

- ❑ Union, written «`union`» or «`|`», which includes a node in the result if it is present in either of the two supplied sets, eliminating any duplicates.

- ❑ Intersection, written «`intersect`», which includes a node in the result if it is in both the two sets.

- ❑ Difference, written «`except`», which includes a node in the result if it is in the first set and is not in the second.

These are sometimes called set operators, but the word "set" is so overloaded that I prefer the term *Venn operators*, after the nineteenth-century English mathematician who popularized the diagrams used to explain them.

The XDM data model does not actually support sets (that is, collections with no intrinsic order and with duplicates disallowed). Instead, sets of nodes are simulated using sequences. The actual type of the operands for the `union`, `intersect` and `except` operators is «node()*», which allows any sequence of nodes. This is also the type of the result. But semantically, these operators ignore any duplicates in the input sequence, and they ignore the order of the nodes in the input sequence. The result sequence will never contain any duplicates, and the results will always be in document order. The effect of the three operators is illustrated in Figure 9-1.

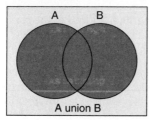 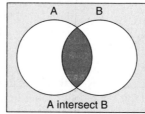 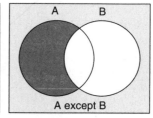

Figure 9-1

As with path expressions, when we talk about duplicate nodes in this section, we are always talking about multiple references to the same node, that is, we are concerned with node identity, not with the values contained in the nodes. Unfortunately, XDM talks about sequences containing nodes, when it really means that sequences contain references to nodes. I personally feel uncomfortable talking about a sequence containing two nodes that have the same identity, or containing the same node more than once: I find it much more natural to talk about a sequence containing two references to the same node.

> *Users often questioned whether the node-sets of XPath 1.0 were true sets, given that (in XSLT at any rate) the nodes were always processed in document order. The answer is that they were indeed true sets, because it was not possible to have distinct collections such as (A, B), (B, A), and (A, B, B, A). There was only one collection in the XPath 1.0 model that could contain the nodes A and B, and the fact that the nodes were always processed in a canonical order doesn't change this.*

> *In XPath 2.0, it is possible to have distinct sequences such as (A, B), (B, A), and (A, B, B, A). However, the operators described in this section treat these sequences as if they were identical. So these operators are using sequences to simulate node-sets, and I shall therefore use the term node-sets to describe these values.*

Syntax

Expression	Syntax
UnionExpr	IntersectExceptExpr ((«union» | «|») IntersectExceptExpr)*
IntersectExceptExpr	PathExpr ((«intersect» | «except») PathExpr)*

This syntax shows that the «union» operator (which has «|» as a synonym) binds less tightly than the «intersect» and «except» operators. So the expression «A union B intersect C» means «A union (B `intersect C)`». As always, there is no shame in adding extra parentheses if you're not sure about the rules (or even if you are).

Both operands to the union, intersect, and except operators must be sequences of zero or more nodes. A type error will occur if this isn't the case. The input sequences don't have to be in any particular order, and they are allowed to contain duplicates; the original order and the duplicates will have no effect on the result.

Examples

Expression	Description
`*/figure	*/table`	Returns a node-set containing all the grandchildren of the context node that are `<figure>` or `<table>` elements. This can also be written «`*/(figure|table)`».
`book[not(@publisher)]	book[@publisher = 'Wrox']`	Returns all the `<book>` children of the context node that either have no publisher attribute or that have a publisher attribute equal to "Wrox". Note that the same result could be achieved, perhaps more efficiently, by using the «or» operator in the predicate.
`(.|..)/title`	Returns all the `<title>` elements that are immediate children of either the context node or the parent of the context node.
`sum((book|magazine)/ @sales)`	Returns the total of the sales attribute values for all the `<book>` and `<magazine>` children of the context node.
`(//* | //@*)[. = 'nimbus2000']`	Returns a node-set containing all the element and attribute nodes in the document whose string value is «nimbus2000».
`following::para intersect $chap//*`	Returns all `<para>` nodes that are after the context node in document order, provided that they are descendants of the node in variable $chap.
`key('a', 'Gilbert') intersect key('a', 'Sullivan')`	The XSLT key() function selects nodes using a defined index. This expression selects nodes that are indexed both under «Gilbert» and under «Sullivan».
`exists(. intersect $arg)`	Returns true if the context node is included in the sequence $arg.
`@* except @note`	Selects all the attributes of the context node except the note attribute.

Usage

The «intersect» operator is also useful for testing whether one node is a member of a given set of nodes. For example, the following expression tests whether node $N is a descendant of node $A:

```
if ($N intersect $A/descendant::node()) then ...
```

This works because if $N is among the descendants of $A, the intersection will contain $N, and the effective boolean value of a sequence containing one node is true. If $N is not among the descendants of $A, the intersection will be empty, and the effective boolean value of an empty sequence is false.

The «except» operator is useful when there is a need to process all the child elements of a node, or all its attributes, except for certain specific exclusions. For example, the XSLT instruction:

```
<xsl:copy-of select="@* except @last-changed"/>
```

copies all the attributes of the context node to the result document except for the `last-changed` attribute (if there is one).

Set Intersection and Difference in XPath 1.0

XPath 1.0 provided no equivalent to the «intersect» and «except» operators. In XPath 1.0, if you want to form the intersection between two node-sets $p and $q, the following rather tortuous expression achieves it:

```
$p [ count( . | $q ) = count( $q ) ]
```

This selects the nodes in $p that are also in $q. They must be in $q, because their union with $q has the same number of nodes as $q itself.

Similarly, the following XPath 1.0 expression finds the nodes that are in $p and not in $q:

```
$p [ count( . | $q ) != count( $q ) ]
```

If you see these constructs when you are upgrading XPath 1.0 code, you can confidently replace them with the XPath 2.0 constructs:

```
$p intersect $q
$p except $q
```

which are not only a lot easier to understand, but will probably be much more efficient as well.

Some XSLT 1.0 processors also provided extension functions to implement set intersection and difference; for example, the functions defined in the EXSLT library (http://www.exslt.org). These have been superseded by the new operators.

Sets of Atomic Values

The operators `union`, `intersect`, and `except` work only on sets of nodes. There are no equivalent operators in XPath 2.0 to handle sets of atomic values. However, it's easy to achieve the same effect for yourself, as follows:

Operator	Expression
Union	`distinct-values($A, $B)`
Intersect	`distinct-values($A[. = $B])`
Except	`distinct-values($A[not(. = $B)])`

Summary

XPath expressions are used to select data from the source document and to manipulate it to generate data to place in the result document. Path expressions play the same role for XML as the SQL SELECT statement plays for relational databases — they allow us to select specific parts of the document for transformation, so that we can achieve the required output.

This chapter has provided a full description of the meaning of path expressions, the «/» operator as it applies to nodes, steps, axes, node tests, and predicates, and it also covered the other operations defined on sequences of nodes, namely the union, intersect, and except operators.

The next chapter will describe constructs in the XPath language that operate on any kind of sequence, whether it contains nodes, atomic values, or a mixture of the two.

XPath: Sequence Expressions

One of the most notable innovations in XPath 2.0 is the ability to construct and manipulate sequences. This chapter is devoted to an explanation of the constructs in the language that help achieve this.

Sequences can consist either of nodes, or of atomic values, or of a mixture of the two. Sequences containing nodes only are a generalization of the node-sets offered by XPath 1.0. In the previous chapter we looked at the XPath 2.0 operators for manipulating sets of nodes, in particular, path expressions, and the operators «union», «intersect», and «except».

In this chapter we look at constructs that can manipulate any sequence, whether it contains nodes, atomic values, or both. Specifically, the chapter covers the following constructs:

❑   *Sequence concatenation operator*: «,»

❑   *Numeric range operator*: «to»

❑   *Filter expressions*: «a[b]»

❑   *Mapping expressions*: «for»

❑   *Simple mapping expressions*: «/» applied to atomic values

❑   *Quantified expressions*: «some» and «every»

First, some general remarks about sequences.

Sequences (unlike nodes) do not have any concept of identity. Given two values that are both sequences, you can ask (in various ways) whether they have the same contents, but you cannot ask whether they are the same sequence.

Sequences are immutable. This is part of what it means for a language to be free of side effects. You can write expressions that take sequences as input and produce new sequences as output, but you can never modify an existing sequence in place.

Sequences cannot be nested. If you want to construct trees, build them as XML trees using nodes rather than atomic values.

A single item is a sequence of length one, so any operation that applies to sequences also applies to single items.

Sequences do not have any kind of type label that is separate from the type labels attached to the items in the sequence. As we will see in Chapter 11, you can ask whether a sequence is an instance of a particular sequence type, but the question can be answered simply by looking at the number of items in the sequence, and at the type labels attached to each item. It follows that there is no such thing as (say) an "empty sequence of integers" as distinct from an "empty sequence of strings". If the sequence has no items in it, then it also carries no type label. This has some real practical consequences, for example, the sum() function, when applied to an expression that can only ever return a sequence of xs:duration values, will return the integer 0 (not the zero-length duration) when the sequence is empty, because there is no way at runtime of knowing that if the sequence hadn't been empty, its items would have been durations.

Functions and operators that attach position numbers to the items in a sequence always identify the first item as number 1 (one), not zero. (Although programming with a base of zero tends to be more convenient, Joe Public has not yet been educated into thinking of the first paragraph in a chapter as paragraph zero, and the numbering convention was chosen with this in mind.)

This chapter covers the language constructs that handle general sequences, but there are also a number of useful functions available for manipulating sequences, and these are described in Chapter 13. Relevant functions include: count(), deep-equal(), distinct-values(), empty(), exists(), index-of(), insert-before(), remove(), subsequence(), and unordered().

The Comma Operator

The comma operator can be used to construct a sequence by concatenating items or sequences. We already saw the syntax in Chapter 7, because it appears right at the top level of the XPath grammar:

Expression	Syntax
Expr	ExprSingle («,» ExprSingle)*
ExprSingle	ForExpr | QuantifiedExpr | IfExpr | OrExpr

Although the production rule ExprSingle lists four specific kinds of expression that can appear as an operand of the «,» operator, these actually cover any XPath expression whatsoever, provided it does not contain a top-level «,».

Because the «,» symbol also has other uses in XPath (for example, it is used to separate the arguments in a function call, and also to separate clauses in «for», «some», and «every» expressions, which we will meet later in this chapter), there are many places in the grammar where use of a general Expr is restricted, and only an ExprSingle is allowed. In fact, the only places where a general Expr (one that contains a top-level comma) is allowed are:

❏　As the top-level XPath expression

❏　Within a parenthesized expression

❏　Within the parentheses of an «if» expression

❏　Within square brackets as a predicate

Neither of the last two is remotely useful, so in practice the rule is: if you want to use the comma operator to construct a list, then either it must be at the outermost level of the XPath expression or it must be written in parentheses.

For example, the `max()` function expects a single argument, which is a sequence. If you want to find the maximum of three values $a, $b, and $c, you can write:

```
max(($a, $b, $c))
```

The outer parentheses are part of the function call syntax; the inner parentheses are needed because the expression «max($a, $b, $c)» would be a function call with three parameters rather than one, which would be an error.

> *XPath does not use the JavaScript convention whereby a function call with three separate parameters is the same as a function call whose single parameter is a sequence containing three items.*

The operands of the «,» operator can be any two sequences. Of course, a single item is itself a sequence, so the operands can also be single items. Either of the sequences can be empty, in which case the result of the expression is the value of the other operand.

The comma operator is often used to construct a list, as in:

```
if ($status = ('current', 'pending', 'deleted', 'closed')) then ...
```

which tests whether the variable $status has one of the given four values (recall from Chapter 8 that the «=» operator compares each item in the sequence on the left with each item in the sequence on the right, and returns true if any of these pairs match). In this construct, you probably aren't thinking of «,» as being a binary operator that combines two operands to produce a result, but that's technically what it is. The expression «A,B,C,D» technically means «(((A,B),C),D)», but because list concatenation is associative, you don't need to think of it this way.

The order of the items in the two sequences is retained in the result. This is true even if the operands are nodes: there is no sorting into document order. This means that in XSLT you can use a construct such as:

```
<xsl:apply-templates select="title, author, abstract"/>
```

to process the selected elements in a specified order, regardless of the order in which they appear in the source document. This example is not necessarily processing exactly three elements: there might, for example, be five authors and no abstract. Because the path expression «author» selects the five authors in document order, they will be processed in this order, but they will be processed after the `<title>` element whether they precede or follow the title in the source document.

Examples

Here are some examples of expressions that make use of the «,» operator to construct sequences.

Expression	Effect
`max(($net, $gross))`	Selects whichever of $net and $gross is larger, comparing them according to their actual type (and using the default collation if they are strings).
`for $i in (1 to 4, 8, 13)` `return $seq[$i]`	Selects the items at positions 1, 2, 3, 4, 8, and 13 of the sequence $seq. For the meaning of the «to» operator, see the next section.

continued

Expression	Effect
`string-join((@a, @b, @c), "-")`	Creates a string containing the values of the attributes @a, @b, and @c of the context node (in that order), separated by hyphens.
`(@code,"N/A")[1]`	Returns the `code` attribute of the context node if it has such an attribute, or the string «N/A» otherwise. This expression makes use of the fact that when the `code` attribute is absent, the value of `@code` is an empty sequence, and concatenating an empty sequence with another sequence returns the other sequence (in this case the singleton string «N/A») unchanged. The predicate in square brackets makes this a filter expression: filter expressions are described later in this chapter, on page 637.
`book/(author,title,isbn)`	Returns a sequence containing the `<author>`, `<title>`, and `<isbn>` children of a `<book>` element, *in document order*. Although the «,» operator retains the order as specified, the «/» operator causes the nodes to be sorted into document order. So in this case the «,» operator is exactly equivalent to the union operator «|».
`<xsl:value-of select = "first, middle, last"/>`	This XSLT instruction outputs the values of the child elements `<first>`, `<middle>`, and `<last>` (not necessarily exactly one of each), in that order, space-separated.

Numeric Ranges: The «to» Operator

A range expression has the syntax:

Expression	Syntax
RangeExpr	AdditiveExpr («to» AdditiveExpr)?

The effect is to return a sequence of consecutive integers in ascending order. For example, the expression «1 to 5» returns the sequence «1,2,3,4,5».

The operands do not have to be constants, of course. A common idiom is to use an expression such as «1 to count($seq)» to return the position number of each item in the sequence $seq. If the second operand is less than the first (which it will be in this example if $seq is an empty sequence), then the range expression returns an empty sequence. If the second operand is equal to the first, the expression returns a single integer, equal to the value of the first operand.

The two operands must both evaluate to single integers. You can use an untyped value provided it is capable of being converted to an integer; for example, you can write «1 to @width» if width is an attribute in a schema-less document containing the value «34». However, you can't use a decimal or a double value without converting it explicitly to an integer. If you write «1 to @width + 1», you will get a type error, because the value of «@width + 1» is the double value 35.0e0. Instead, write «1 to xs:integer(@width) + 1» or «1 to 1 + @width idiv 1».

If either operand is an empty sequence, the result is an empty sequence. For example, this would happen if you ran any of the examples above when the context node did not have a width attribute. Supplying a sequence that contains more than one item, however, is an error.

If you want a sequence of integers in reverse order, you can use the `reverse()` function described in Chapter 13. For example, «`reverse(1 to 5)`» gives you the sequence «`5,4,3,2,1`». In an earlier draft of the specification you could achieve this by writing «`5 to 1`», but the rules were changed because this caused anomalies for the common usage «`1 to count($seq)`» in the case where `$seq` is empty.

Although the semantics of this operator are expressed in terms of constructing a sequence, a respectable implementation will evaluate the sequence lazily, which means that when you write «`1 to 1000000`» it won't actually allocate space in memory to hold a million integers. Depending on how you actually use the range expression, in most cases an implementation will be able to iterate over the values without laying them out end-to-end as a list in memory.

Examples

Here are some examples of expressions that make use of the «`to`» operator to construct sequences.

Expression	Effect
`for $n in 1 to 10` `return $seq[$n]`	Returns the first 10 items of the sequence `$seq`. The «`for`» expression is described later in this chapter, on page 640.
`$seq[position() = 1 to 10]`	Returns the first 10 items of the sequence `$seq`. This achieves the same effect as the previous example, but this time using a filter expression alone. It works because the «`=`» operator compares each item in the first operand (there is only one, the value of `position()`) with each item in the second operand (that is, each of the integers 1 to 10) and returns `true` if any of them matches. It's reasonable to expect that XPath processors will optimize this construct so that this doesn't actually involve 10 separate comparisons for each item in the sequence.

Note that you can't simply write «`$seq[1 to 10]`». If the predicate isn't a single number, it is evaluated as a boolean, and attempting to get the effective boolean value of a sequence of numbers is an error. |
`string-join( for $i in 1 to $N` `return " "," ")`	Returns a string containing `$N` space characters.
`for $i in 1 to 5 return $i*2`	Returns the sequence «`2, 4, 6, 8, 10`».
`for $i in 1 to count($S) return` `concat($S[$i], $T[$i])`	Returns a sequence that contains pairs of corresponding values from the two input sequences `$S` and `$T`. For example, if `$S` is the sequence `("a","b","c")` and `$T` is the sequence `("x","y","z")`, the result will be the sequence `("ax","by","cz")`.
`<xsl:for-each` `    select = "1 to 5">` `    </xsl:for-each>`	This XSLT example shows how to output a sequence of five empty ` ` elements.

Filter Expressions

A filter expression is used to apply one or more `Predicates` to a sequence, selecting those items in the sequence that satisfy some condition.

Expression	Syntax
FilterExpr	PrimaryExpr Predicate*
Predicate	«[» Expr «]»

A `FilterExpr` consists of a `PrimaryExpr` whose value is a sequence, followed by zero or more `Predicates` that select a subset of the items in the sequence. Each predicate consists of an expression enclosed in square brackets, for example «[@name = 'London']» or «[position() = 1]».

Since in XPath 2.0 every value is a sequence, it is possible to apply predicates to any value whatsoever. For example, the expression «concat($n, " error", "s"[$n!=1])» outputs a string such as "0 errors", "1 error", or "5 errors". In the case where $n is 1, the third argument to concat() is an empty sequence, which contributes nothing to the output.

Recall from Chapter 7 that a `PrimaryExpr` is a literal, a variable reference, «.», a function call, or a parenthesized expression. This means that if you want to filter the result of any expression other than the first four in this list, you will have to write it in parentheses.

Each predicate is applied to the sequence in turn; only those items in the sequence for which the predicate is true pass through to the next stage. The final result consists of those items in the original sequence that satisfy each of the predicates, retaining their original order.

A predicate may be either a numeric predicate (for example «[1]» or «[last()-1]»), or a boolean predicate (for example «[count(*) gt 5]» or «[@name and @address]»). If the value of the expression is a single number, it is treated as a numeric predicate; otherwise, it is converted, if necessary, to an xs:boolean and is treated as a boolean predicate. The conversion is done using the rules for computing the *effective boolean value*, which are the same rules as are used for the condition in an «if» expression (described in Chapter 7 on page 551) or for the operand of the boolean() function (described in Chapter 13 on page 721), except that if the value is a single number — which might be an integer, decimal, float, or double — then the predicate is treated as a numeric predicate rather than a boolean predicate.

If the value of the predicate contains nodes, there is no automatic atomization of the nodes (that is, the values of the nodes are not extracted). In fact, if the value of the predicate contains one or more nodes, then its effective boolean value is always true. This means, for example, that «person[@isMarried]» selects any <person> element that has an isMarried attribute, irrespective of the value of that attribute. If you want to test the value of the attribute, you can atomize it explicity using the data() function, or you can use a comparison such as «person[@isMarried = true()]». (But beware, if backward-compatibility mode is switched on, then «person[@isMarried = true()]» means the same as «person[@isMarried]».)

A numeric predicate whose value is N is equivalent to the boolean predicate «[position() eq N]». So, for example, the numeric predicate «[1]» means «[position() eq 1]», and the numeric predicate «[last()]» means «[position() eq last()]».

It's important to remember that this implicit testing of position() happens only when the predicate expression actually evaluates to a single number. For example, «$paras[1 or last()]» does not mean «$paras[position() = 1 or position() = last()]», because the result of evaluating «1 or last()» is a boolean, not a number (and as it happens, it will always be true). Similarly, «book[../@book-nr]» does not mean «book[position() = ../@book-nr]», because the result of «../@book-nr» is a node, not a number.

A neat way to force the node to be atomized in such cases is to use the unary «+» operator: write «book[+../@book-nr]».

A consequence of the rule is that if the predicate is a number that is not equal to an integer, the result will be an empty sequence. For example, «$S[last() div 2]» will select nothing when the value of last() is an odd number. If you want to select a single item close to the middle of the sequence, use «$S[last() idiv 2]», because the idiv operator always returns an integer.

In nearly all practical cases, a numeric predicate selects either a single item from the sequence or no items at all. But this is not part of the definition. To give a counter-example, «$x[count(*)]» selects every node whose position is the same as the number of children it has.

As discussed in Chapter 7, every XPath expression is evaluated in some context. For an expression used as a predicate, the context is different from the context of the containing expression. While evaluating each predicate, the context is established as follows:

- ❏ The *context item* (the item referenced as «.») is the item being tested.

- ❏ The *context position* (the value of the position() function) is the position of that item within the sequence of items surviving from the previous stage.

- ❏ The *context size* (the value of the last() function) is the number of items surviving from the previous stage.

To see how this works, consider the filter expression «$headings[self::h1][last()]». This starts with the sequence of nodes that is the value of the variable «$headings» (if this sequence contains items that are not nodes, then evaluating the predicate «self::h1» will raise an error). The first predicate is «[self::h1]». This is applied to each node in «$headings» in turn. While it is being applied, the context node is that particular node. The expression «self::h1» is a path expression consisting of a single AxisStep: it selects a sequence of nodes. If the context node is an <h1> element this sequence will contain a single node — the context node. Otherwise, the sequence will be empty. When this value is converted to a boolean, it will be true if it contains a node, and false if it is empty. So the first predicate is actually filtering through those nodes in «$headings» that are <h1> elements.

The second predicate is now applied to each node in this sequence of <h1> elements. In each case the predicate «[last()]» returns the same value: a number indicating how many <h1> elements there are in the sequence. As this is a numeric predicate, a node passes the test when «[position() = last()]», that is, when the position of the node in the sequence (taken in its original order) is equal to the number of nodes in the sequence. So the meaning of «$headings[self::h1][last()]» is "the last <h3> element in the sequence $headings."

Note that this isn't the same as «$headings[last()][self::h1]», which means "the last item in $headings, provided that it is an <h1> element."

The operation of a Predicate in a FilterExpr is very similar to the application of a Predicate in an AxisStep (which we studied in Chapter 9, on page 618), and although they are not directly related in the XPath grammar rules, you can often use predicates without being fully aware of which of these two constructs you are using. For example, «$para[1]» is a FilterExpr, while «para[1]» is an AxisStep. The main differences to watch out for are, firstly, that in a path expression the predicates apply only to the most recent Step (for example, in «book/author[1]» the «[1]» means the first author within each book), and secondly, that in a filter expression the items are always considered in the order of the supplied sequence, whereas in an `AxisStep` they can be in forward or reverse document order, depending on the direction of the axis.

Examples

Expression	Description
`$paragraphs[23]`	Selects the 23rd item in the sequence that is the value of variable `$paragraphs`, taking them in the order of that sequence. If there is no 23rd item, the expression returns an empty sequence.
`key('empname', 'John Smith')[@loc = 'Sydney']`	Assuming that the key «empname» has been defined in the containing stylesheet to select employees by name, this selects all employees named `John Smith` who are located in Sydney. The `key()` function is available only in XSLT.
`(//section|//subsection) [title = 'Introduction']`	Selects all `<section>` and `<subsection>` elements that have a child `<title>` element with the content «Introduction».
`(//@href/doc(.)) [pricelist][1]`	This first selects all documents referenced by URLs contained in `href` attributes anywhere in the source document, by applying the `doc()` function to the value of each of these attributes. The «/» operator causes any duplicates to be removed, as described in Chapter 9. From this set of documents it selects those whose outermost element is named `<pricelist>`, and from these it selects the first. The order of nodes that are in different documents is not defined, so if there are several price lists referenced, it is unpredictable which will be selected.

Where a predicate is used as part of a `FilterExpr` (as distinct from an `AxisStep`), the items are considered in their original sequence for the purpose of evaluating the `position()` function within the predicate. There are some cases where the order of the sequence is not predictable, but it is still possible to use positional predicates. For example, the result of the `distinct-values()` function is in an undefined order, but you can still write «`distinct-values($in)[1]`» to obtain one item in the sequence, chosen arbitrarily.

The «for» Expression

The «`for`» expression is one of the most powerful new features in XPath 2.0 and is closely related to the extension to the data model to handle sequences. Its effect is to apply an expression to every item in an input sequence and to return the concatenated results of these expressions.

The syntax also allows several sequences to be provided as input, in which case the effect is to apply an expression to every combination of values taken one from each sequence.

Expression	Syntax
ForExpr	«for» «$» VarName «in» ExprSingle («,» «$» VarName «in» ExprSingle)* «return» ExprSingle
VarName	QName

An `ExprSingle` is any XPath expression that does not contain a top-level «,» operator. If you want to use an expression containing a «,» operator, write it in parentheses. For example, the expression «for $i in (1,5,10) return $i + 1» returns the sequence «2,6,11».

We'll look first at «for» expressions that operate on a single sequence and then move on to the more general case where there are multiple input sequences.

Mapping a Sequence

When used with a single sequence, the «for» expression applies the expression in the «return» clause to each item in the input sequence. The relevant item in the input sequence is accessed not as the context item but as the value of the variable declared in the «for» clause.

These variables are referred to as range variables, to distinguish them from variables supplied from outside the XPath expression, such as variables declared in an XSLT stylesheet. The term comes originally from the branch of mathematical logic called predicate calculus.

In most cases the expression in the «return» clause will depend in some way on the range variable. In other words, the «return» value is a function of the range variable, which means we can rewrite the «for» expression in the abstract form:

```
for $x in $SEQ return F($x)
```

where «F($x)» represents any expression that depends on $x (it doesn't have to depend on $x, but it usually will).

What this does is to evaluate the expression «F($x)» once for each item in the input sequence $SEQ and then to concatenate the results, respecting the original order of the items in $SEQ.

In the simplest case, the return expression «F($x)» returns one item each time it is called. This is illustrated in Figure 10-1, where the function «F($x)» in this example is actually the expression «string-length($x)».

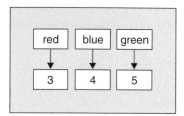

Figure 10-1

We say that the expression «for $x in $SEQ return string-length($x)» *maps* the sequence «"red", "blue","green"» to the sequence «3,4,5».

In this case, the number of items in the result will be the same as the number of items in the input sequence.

However, the return expression isn't constrained to return a single item; it can return any sequence of zero or more items. For example, you could write:

```
for $s in ("red", "blue", "green") return string-to-codepoints($s)
```

The function `string-to-codepoints()`, which is part of the standard library defined in Chapter 13, returns for a given string, the Unicode code values of the characters that make up the string. For example, «`string-to-codepoints("red")`» returns the sequence «114, 101, 100». The result of the above expression is a sequence of 12 integers, as illustrated in Figure 10-2.

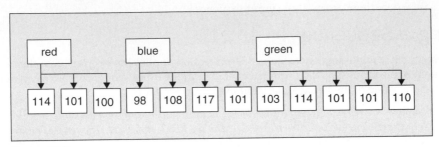

Figure 10-2

The integers are returned in the order shown, because unlike a path expression, there is nothing in the rules for a «for» expression that causes the result sequence to be sorted into document order. Indeed, document order is not a meaningful concept when we are dealing with atomic values rather than nodes.

Examples

Expression	Description
`for $i in 1 to 5` `return $i*$i`	Returns the sequence «1,4,9,16,25». This example is a one-to-one mapping.
`for $i in 0 to 4` `return 1 to $i`	Returns the sequence «1,1,2,1,2,3,1,2,3,4». This example is a one-to-many mapping. Note that for the first item in the input sequence (0), the mapping function returns an empty sequence, so this item contributes nothing to the result.

The Context Item in a «for» Expression

A common mistake is to forget that «for» expressions don't set the context node. The following example is wrong (it's not an error, but it doesn't do what the writer probably intended):

```
(:wrong:) sum(for $i in item return @price * @qty)
```

The correct way of writing this is:

```
(:correct:) sum(for $i in item return $i/@price * $i/@qty)
```

Generally speaking, there is usually something amiss if the range variable is not used in the «return» expression. However, there are exceptions to this rule. For example, it's quite reasonable to write:

```
string-join(for $i in 1 to $n return "-", "")
```

which returns a string containing $n hyphens.

It's also often (but not invariably) a sign of trouble if the value of the return expression depends on the context item. But it's not actually an error: the context item inside the return expression is exactly the same as the context item for the «for» expression as a whole. So it's legal to write an expression such as:

```
chapter/(for $i in 1 to 10 return section[$i])
```

which returns the first 10 sections of each chapter.

Combining Multiple Sequences

The «for» expression allows multiple input sequences to be defined, each with its own range variable. For example, you can write:

```
for $c in //customer,
    $o in $c/orders,
    $ol in $o/line
return $ol/cost
```

The simplest way to think about this is as a nested loop. You can regard the «,» as a shorthand for writing the keywords «return for», so the above expression is equivalent to:

```
for $c in //customer
return
   for $o in $c/orders
   return
       for $ol in $o/line
       return $ol/cost
```

Note that each of the range variables can be referenced in the expression that defines the input sequence for the next range variable.

In the example above, each iteration is rather like a step in a path expression; it selects nodes starting from the node selected in the containing loop. But it doesn't have to be this way. For example, you could equally write an expression such as:

```
for $c in doc('customers.xml')//customer,
    $p in doc('products.xml')//product [$c/orders/product-code = $p/code]
    return $c/line/cost
```

It's still true that this is equivalent to a nested-loop expression:

```
for $c in doc('customers.xml')//customer
return
   for $p in doc('products.xml')//product [$c/orders/product-code = $p/code]
   return $c/line/cost
```

The other way to think about this, particularly if you are familiar with SQL, is as a relational join. The system isn't actually obliged to evaluate the «for» expression using nested loops (this applies whether you write it in the abbreviated form using multiple range variables separated with commas, or whether you use the expanded form shown above). Instead, the optimizer can use any of the mechanisms developed over the years in relational database technology to evaluate the join more rapidly. There's no guarantee that it will do so, so you need to use potentially expensive constructs like this with some care.

One of the differences between the open-source Saxon-B product and its commercial cousin Saxon-SA, is that Saxon-SA optimizes joins. Both products will try to move subexpressions out of a loop if they don't depend on the range variable. So the expression «doc('products.xml')//product» will probably only be evaluated once, and the expression «$c/orders/product-code» will only be evaluated once for each customer. But after this, Saxon-B will compare every product code in the customer file with every product code in the product file, while Saxon-SA will create an index (in effect, doing a hash join). The bigger the data file, the more of a difference this makes.

In XSLT, you can "hand-optimize" a join by using keys: see the description of the <xsl:key> declaration in Chapter 6 (page 376).

Example

Expression	Description

count(for $i in 1 to 8,
        $j in 1 to 8
     return f:square($i,$j))
	Assuming that «f:square(row,column)» returns an integer identifying the piece that occupies a square on a chessboard, or an empty sequence if the square is unoccupied, this expression returns all the pieces on the board.

Simple Mapping Expressions

You may have noticed that there are some strong similarities between «for» expressions and path expressions. The expression:

```
for $c in chapter return $c/section
```

returns exactly the same result as the path expression:

```
chapter/section
```

However, there are some significant differences between «for» expressions and path expressions:

❑ In a path expression, both the input sequence and the step expression are required to return nodes exclusively. A «for» expression can work on any sequence, whether it contains nodes or atomic values or both, and it can also return any sequence.

❑ Path expressions always sort the resulting nodes into document order, and eliminate duplicates. A «for» expression returns the result sequence in the order that reflects the order of the input items.

❑ In a path expression, the context item for evaluating a step is set to each item in the input sequence in turn. In a «for» expression, the range variable fulfils this function. The context item is not changed. Nor are the context position and size (position() and last()) available to test the position of the item in the input sequence.

Simple mapping expressions use the convenient syntax of path expressions (that is, the «/» operator), but they work on atomic values rather than nodes. Specifically, the expression on the right-hand side of «/» must return a sequence that consists entirely of atomic values. For example, the expression «*/name()» returns a sequence of strings — the names of the child elements of the context node. There is no sorting into document order here, because document order doesn't mean anything for atomic values. The result is exactly the same as the expression «for $x in * return name($x)», just with a more compact syntax.

Here are some other examples of simple mapping expressions at work:

Expression	Description
`sum(order/(@price*@quantity))`	Returns the result of calculating `@price` times `@quantity` for each child `<order>` and summing the results.
`string-join(` `  ancestor::*/name(), '/')`	Returns a string such as «book/chapter/section/para» giving the names of the ancestors of the context node, separated by «/» characters.
`avg(product/number(` `  substring-after(@price, '$')))`	Returns the result of taking the `@price` attributes of all the child `<product>` elements, stripping off the leading «$» sign, converting to a number, and then averaging.

In most cases the system will be able to distinguish a path expression from a simple mapping expression by the way it is written. In some cases, however — for example, if the expression calls a user-written function whose return type is not declared — the two cases can't be distinguished until runtime. The initial processing in both cases is the same: for each item in the sequence returned by the first expression, evaluate the second expression and concatenate the results. The rule is then:

❑ If all the items in the result are nodes, we have a path expression. Duplicate nodes are eliminated, and those that remain are sorted into document order.

❑ If all the items in the result are atomic values, we have a simple mapping expression, and we are done.

❑ If there's a mixture of nodes and atomic values, an error is reported.

A simple mapping expression always maps from nodes to atomic values. You can't have atomic values on the left-hand side of the «/» operator. For example, you can't write «avg(*/name()/string-length())» to get the average length of the names of the child elements. Only the last step in the path can return atomic values, so you have to write this as «avg(*/string-length(name()))». Why the restriction? Possibly because some people didn't like the consequence that the value of «1/10» would be 10.

The following table compares simple mapping expressions with «for» expressions and path expressions:

Feature	For Expression	Path Expression	Simple Mapping Expression
Syntax	`for $x in E1 return E2`	`E1/E2`	`E1/E2`
Returns items of type:	nodes or atomic values	nodes	atomic values
Iterates using:	range variable	context item	context item
Results are in document order with duplicates eliminated?	no	yes	no

The «some» and «every» Expressions

These expressions are used to test whether some item in a sequence satisfies a condition, or whether all values in a sequence satisfy a condition.

The syntax is:

Expression	Syntax
QuantifiedExpr	(«some» | «every») «$» VarName «in» ExprSingle («,» «$» VarName «in» ExprSingle)* «satisfies» ExprSingle
VarName	QName

The name *quantified expression* comes from the mathematics on which these expressions are based: the «some» expression is known in formal logic as an existential quantifier, while the «every» expression is known as a universal quantifier.

As with the «for» expression, these two expressions bind a range variable to every item in a sequence in turn, and evaluate an expression (the «satisfies» expression) for each of these items. Instead of returning the results, however, a quanitified expression evaluates the effective boolean value of the «satisfies» expression. In the case of «some», it returns true if at least one of these values is true, while in the case of «every», it returns true if all of the values are true. The range variables can be referenced anywhere in the expression following the «satisfies» keyword, and the expression following the «in» keyword can use all variables declared in previous clauses of the expression (but not the variable ranging over that expression itself).

For example:

```
some $p in //price satisfies $p > 10000
```

is true if there is a <price> element in the document whose typed value is a number greater than 10,000, while:

```
every $p in //price satisfies $p > 10000
```

is true if every <price> element in the document has a typed value greater than 10,000.

The result of the expression (unless some error occurs) is always a single xs:boolean value.

The «satisfies» expression is evaluated to return a boolean value. This evaluation returns the *effective boolean value* of the expression, using the same rules as for the boolean() function and the condition in an «if» expression. For example, if the result of the expression is a string, the effective boolean value is true if the string is not zero-length. The expression will almost invariably reference each one of the range variables, although the results are still well defined if it doesn't.

> As with «for» expressions, «some» and «every» expressions do not change the context item. This means that the following is wrong (it's not an error, but it doesn't produce the intended answer):
>
> ```
> (:wrong:) some $i in //item satisfies price > 200
> ```

> **It should be written instead:**
>
> ```
> (:correct:) some $i in //item satisfies $i/price > 200
> ```

Note that if the input sequence is empty, the «some» expression will always be `false`, while the «every» expression will always be `true`. This may not be intuitive to everyone, but it is logical — the «every» expression is true if there are no counter-examples; for example, it's true that every unicorn has one horn, because there are no unicorns that don't have one horn. Equally, and this is where the surprise comes, it is also true that every unicorn has two horns.

You can exploit this. I was experimenting recently with the new feature in XML Schema 1.1 to write XPath assertions in a schema, and I wanted to express the rule "if this element has a `<simpleContent>` child which itself has a `<restriction>` child, then the `<restriction>` in turn must have a `<simpleType>` child". I found I could write this as:

```
every $r in simpleContent/restriction satisfies $r/simpleType
```

If there isn't a «simpleContent/restriction», this assertion is automatically true.

It is always possible to rewrite an «every» expression as a «some» expression, and vice versa. The expression:

```
every $s in $S satisfies C
```

is equivalent to:

```
not(some $s in $S satisfies not(C))
```

and of course:

```
some $s in $S satisfies C
```

is equivalent to:

```
not(every $s in $S satisfies not(C))
```

Alternatively, if there is only a single range variable, you can usually rewrite the expression:

```
some $s in $S satisfies $s/C
```

as:

```
exists($S[C])
```

which some people prefer, as it is more concise. If the sequence $S consists of nodes, you can also leave out the call on the `exists()` function; for example, you can rewrite:

```
if (some $i in //item satisfies $i/price * $i/quantity > 1000) ...
```

as:

```
if (//item[price*quantity > 1000]) ...
```

10

XPath: Sequence Expressions

647

The difference is a matter of taste. The «some» expression, however, is more powerful than a simple predicate because (like the «for» expression) it can handle joins, using multiple range variables.

The XPath 2.0 specification describes the semantics of the «some» and «every» expressions in a rather complicated way, using a concept of "tuples of variable bindings". This happened because the XPath 2.0 specification is generated by subsetting XQuery 1.0, whose core construct, the FLWOR expression, makes use of this concept already. It would have been possible to specify «some» and «every» in a much simpler way for XPath users. In fact, the expression:

```
some $s in $S, $t in $T, $u in $U satisfies CONDITION
```

has exactly the same effect as the expression:

```
exists(for $s in $S, $t in $T, $u in $U return boolean(CONDITION)[.])
```

while the expression:

```
every $s in $S, $t in $T, $u in $U satisfies CONDITION
```

has exactly the same effect as the expression:

```
empty(for $s in $S, $t in $T, $u in $U return not(CONDITION)[.])
```

The rather unusual predicate «[.]» selects all the items in a sequence whose effective boolean value is true. In the first case, the result is true if the result of the «for» expression contains at least one value that is true, while in the second case, the result is true if the result of the «for» expression contains no value that is false.

(The functions exists() and empty() are described in Chapter 13. The exists() function returns true if the supplied sequence contains one or more items, while empty() returns true if the sequence contains no items.)

Examples

Expression	Description
some $i in //item satisfies $i/price gt 200	Returns true if the current document contains an <item> element with a <price> child whose typed value exceeds 200.
some $n in 1 to count($S)-1 satisfies $S[$n] eq $S[$n + 1]	Returns true if there are two adjacent values in the input sequence $S that are equal.
every $p in //person satisfies $p/@dob castable as xs:date	Returns true if every <person> element in the current document has a dob attribute that represents a valid date, according to the XML Schema format YYYY-MM-DD.
some $k in //keyword, $p in //para satisfies contains($p, $k)	Returns true if there is at least one <keyword< in the document that is present in at least one<para> element of the document.
every $d in //termdef/@id satisfies some $r in //termref satisfies $d eq $r/@def	Returns true if every <termdef> element with an id attribute is referenced by at least one <termref> element with a matching def attribute.

Quantification and the «=» Operator

An alternative to using the «some» expression (and sometimes also the «every» expression) is to rely on the implicit semantics of the «=» operator, and other operators in the same family, when they are used to compare sequences. As we saw in Chapter 8, these operators can be used to compare two sequences, and return `true` if any pair of items (one from each sequence) satisfies the equality condition.

For example, the expression:

```
//book[author="Kay"]
```

means the same as:

```
//book[some $a in author satisfies $a eq "Kay"]
```

Similarly, the expression:

```
//book[author=("Kay", "Tennison", "Carlisle")]
```

means the same as:

```
//book[some $a in author,
          $s in ("Kay", "Tennison", "Carlisle")
       satisfies $a eq $s]
```

It's a matter of personal style which one you choose in these cases. However, if the operator is something more complex than straight equality — for example, if you are comparing the two values using the `compare()` function with a non-default collation — then the only way to achieve the effect within XPath is to use a «some» or «every» expression.

Errors in «some» and «every» Expressions

Dynamic (runtime) errors can occur in «some» and «every» expressions just as in any other kind of XPath expression, and the rules are the same. But for these expressions the rules have some interesting consequences that are worth exploring.

Let's summarize the rules here:

❑   If a dynamic error occurs when evaluating the «satisfies» expression, then the «some» or «every» expression as a whole fails with an error.

❑   As soon as the system finds an item in the sequence for which the «satisfies» expression is true (in the case of «some») or false (in the case of «every»), it can stop the evaluation. It doesn't need to look any further. This means that it might not notice errors that would be found if it carried on to the bitter end.

❑   The system can process the input sequence in any order that it likes. This means that if there is one item for which evaluating the «satisfies» expression returns `true`, and another for which it raises an error, then you can't tell whether the «some» expression will return `true` or raise the error.

Some systems might deliberately choose to exploit these rules by evaluating the error cases last (or pretending to do so) so as to minimize the chance of the expression failing, but you can't rely on this.

What does this mean in practice? Suppose you have an attribute defined in the schema as follows:

```
<xs:attribute name="readings">
   <xs:simpleType>
    <xs:list>
       <xs:simpleType>
         <xs:union>
           <xs:simpleType>
             <xs:restriction base="xs:decimal"/>
           </xs:simpleType>
           <xs:simpleType>
             <xs:restriction base="xs:string">
               <xs:enumeration value="n/a"/>
             </xs:restriction>
           </xs:simpleType>
         </xs:union>
       </xs:simpleType>
    </xs:list>
   </xs:simpleType>
</xs:attribute>
```

Or to put it more simply, the attribute's typed value is a list of atomic values, each of which is either a decimal number or the string value «n/a». For example, the attribute might be written «readings = "12.2 -8.4 5.6 n/a 13.1"».

Now suppose you want to test whether the set of readings includes a negative value. You could write:

```
if (some $a in data(@readings) satisfies $a lt 0) then ...
```

The chances are you will get away with this. Most processors will probably evaluate the condition «$a lt 0» against each value in turn, find that the condition is true for the second item in the list, and return true. However, a processor that decided to evaluate the items in reverse order would encounter the value «n/a», compare this with zero, and hit a type error: you can't compare a string with a number. So one processor will give you the answer true, while another gives you an error.

You can protect yourself against this error by writing the expression as:

```
if (some $a in data(@readings)[. instance of xs:decimal]
     satisfies $a lt 0)
then ...
```

Or in this case, you can mask the error by writing:

```
if (some $a in data(@readings) satisfies number($a) lt 0) then ...
```

This works because «number('n/a')» returns NaN (not-a-number), and «NaN lt 0» returns false.

Summary

This chapter covered all the various kinds of expressions in the XPath language that are designed to manipulate general sequences, specifically:

- ❑   The «,» operator, which appends two sequences

- ❑   The «to» operator, which forms a sequence of ascending integers

- ❑   Filter expressions, which are used to find those items in a sequence that satisfy some predicate

- ❑   The «for» expression, which applies an expression to every item in a sequence and returns the results, as a new sequence

- ❑   Simple mapping expressions, which apply the «/» operator to atomic values

- ❑   The «some» and «every» expressions, which test whether a condition is true for some value (or every value) in an input sequence, returning a boolean result

Don't forget that these are not the only constructs available for manipulating sequences. For sequences of nodes, path expressions can be used, as well as the «union», «intersect», and «except» operators, as discussed in Chapter 9. And in Chapter 13 you will find descriptions of all the functions in the standard XPath library, including many functions that are useful for operating on sequences, for example, count(), deep-equal(), distinct-values(), empty(), exists(), index-of(), insert-before(), remove(), sub-sequence(), and unordered().

The next chapter deals with operations involving types: operations that convert a value of one type into a value of another type, and operations that test the type of a value.

10

XPath: Sequence Expressions

11

XPath: Type Expressions

This chapter is concerned with XPath expressions that involve types. This includes operations to convert a value of one type to a value of another type (which is called casting), and operations to test whether a value belongs to a particular type.

The type system for XPath was fully explained in Chapter 5. Recall in particular that there are two separate but related sets of types we are concerned with:

❑ Every value in XPath (that is, the result of every expression) is an instance of a *sequence type*. This reflects the fact that every XPath value is a sequence. A sequence type in general defines an *item type* that each of the items in the sequence must conform to, and a *cardinality* that constrains the number of items in the sequence. The items may be either nodes or atomic values, so item types divide into those that permit nodes and those that permit atomic values. There are also two special item types, the type `item()`, which permits anything, and the type `empty-sequence()`, which permits nothing.

❑ Every element and attribute node conforms to a type definition contained in a schema, or a built-in type definition that is implicit in every schema. To distinguish these clearly from sequence types, I will refer to these types as *schema types*. A schema type may be either a simple type or (for elements only) a complex type. A simple type may be either a list type, a union type, or an atomic type. A type definition constrains the contents of a node (that is, the value of an attribute, or the attributes and children of an element); it does not constrain the name of the node.

We need to use careful language to avoid confusing these two views of the type system. When we have an XPath value that is a node, we will speak of the node being an *instance of* a sequence type — for example, every element is an instance of the sequence type `element()`. At the same time, the node is *annotated with* a schema type — for example, an element node may be annotated as an `mf:invoice` (which will be the name of a complex type defined in some schema).

These two sets of types (sequence types and schema types) overlap: in particular, atomic types such as `xs:integer` belong to both sets. However, list types, union types, and complex types are never used as item types or sequence types; they are used only to annotate nodes. Equally, item types such as `comment()` are only used in sequence types; they are never used to annotate nodes. This idea is illustrated in Figure 11-1.

The first part of this chapter is concerned with conversion of values from one type to another. These types are always atomic types; no conversions are defined for any types other than atomic types. The process of atomization, which extracts the typed value of a node, could be regarded as a conversion, but we won't treat it as such for our present purposes.

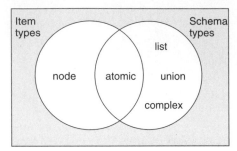

Figure 11-1

Atomic types can be referred to by the name given to them in the schema. A schema can define anonymous atomic types, but because these have no name, they can't be referenced in an XPath expression. Named atomic types are always defined by a top-level `<xs:simpleType>` element in a schema (more specifically, by an `<xs:simpleType>` element that is a child of either an `<xs:schema>` element or an `<xs:redefine>` element), and these elements always have a `name` attribute.

The final part of this chapter deals with two operators («`instance of`» and «`treat as`») that take as their "operands" an arbitrary XPath value (that is, a sequence), and a sequence type. (I've written "operands" in quotes, because a true operand is always a value, and in the XPath view of the world, types are not values). These two constructs require a special syntax for describing sequence types. For example, «`attribute(*, xs:date)?`» describes a sequence type whose item type matches any attribute node annotated as an `xs:date`, and whose cardinality allows the sequence to contain zero or one values. I will refer to such a construct as a *sequence type descriptor*, because the construct seems to need a name, and the XPath specification doesn't give it one.

Converting Atomic Values

The operation of converting an atomic value of one type into an atomic value of another type is called casting.

> *The word* casting *is used with the meaning that it has in SQL, which is subtly different from the usage in many other programming languages. In Java, casts perform a dual role: casting an Object is more like the «`treat as`» operator described later in this chapter, which doesn't actually change the value from one type to another. But casts in Java are also used for conversions among the primitive types, which is analogous to casting in XPath.*

As well as an operator to perform a cast, XPath also provides a second operator to test whether a cast is possible. This has been provided because there is no way of recovering from the error that occurs when a cast fails (if, for example, you convert a string to a date and the string does not contain a valid date). Instead of attempting the cast and then dealing with the error when it fails, XPath encourages you first to test whether it will succeed and then to perform the conversion only if this is the case. So if `$p` is a user-supplied parameter that is supposed to contain a valid date, you can write:

```
if ($p castable as xs:date) then xs:date($p) else ()
```

The syntax for the «`cast as`» and «`castable as`» operators is shown below. Both operators are written as compound tokens.

Expression	Syntax
CastableExpr	CastExpr («castable» «as» SingleType)?
CastExpr	UnaryExpr («cast» «as» SingleType)?
SingleType	AtomicType «?»?
AtomicType	QName

The rule for `SingleType` is confusing at first sight. It means that the `AtomicType` may optionally be followed by a question mark.

In all these cases, the `AtomicType` must correspond to the name of an atomic type (that is, a simple type that is not a list type or a union type) that is present in the static context for the XPath expression. Most commonly, this will be one of the built-in types such as `xs:integer` or `xs:date`, but it can also be a user-defined type. The type name is written as a `QName`, and its namespace prefix must therefore have been declared to reference the `targetNamespace` of the schema in which the type is defined. If the name has no prefix, the default namespace for elements is used; in XSLT, this will be the null namespace, unless the `xpath-default-namespace` attribute has been set to identify a different namespace.

> *The concept of the static context was described in Chapter 7. An atomic type will be present in the static context either if it is a built-in type such as* `xs:date`, *or if it is defined in a schema that has been explicitly imported using the* `<xsl:import-schema>` *declaration in XSLT, or its equivalent in a different XPath host language.*

A question mark after the type name means that an empty sequence is allowed as the value. For example, the expression «@A cast as xs:integer» will fail if the attribute A does not exist, but the expression «@A cast as xs:integer?» will succeed, returning an empty sequence.

The «castable as» expression returns `true` if the corresponding «cast as» expression would succeed, and `false` if the corresponding «cast as» expression would fail. For example, the string «2009-02-29» is not a valid date, so the expression «"2009-02-29" castable as xs:date» returns `false`.

Both the «cast as» and «castable as» operators perform atomization on the supplied value. This means that if the supplied value is a node, its typed value is first extracted. If the operand (after atomization) is a sequence of more than one item, then a type error occurs in the case of «cast as», or the value `false` is returned in the case of «castable as».

There is a shorthand for a «cast as» expression, which is to use a constructor function. For example, the expression «@A cast as xs:integer?» can be rewritten as a function call, «xs:integer(@A)». There is a constructor function available for every built-in atomic type, and for every named atomic type in an imported schema, and its effect is identical to using the «cast as» expression with the «?» option (that is, if an empty sequence is supplied to a constructor function, it returns an empty sequence). The only cases where you need to use the full «cast as» expression are:

❏   When you want to indicate that an empty sequence is *not* allowed.

❏   When the type name is defined in a schema with no target namespace (unless the default function namespace is the null namespace, which would be unusual, and cannot arise in XSLT). When your type names are unprefixed, you have to use the more verbose «cast as» syntax.

The sections that follow describe all the rules for converting a supplied value to a target type. We'll start by considering the rules for converting from a primitive type to another primitive type and then go on to consider how derived types are handled.

11

XPath: Type Expressions

655

Converting between Primitive Types

The type conversions described in this section start with an atomic value that is labeled with a primitive type. For these purposes we consider a primitive type to be either one of the primitive types defined in Part 2 of the XML Schema specification, or the XPath-defined atomic type `xs:untypedAtomic`.. Although in XPath the types `xs:integer`, `xs:dayTimeDuration` and `xs:yearMonthDuration` are sometimes treated as primitive, in this chapter we will treat them as derived types, which is what they actually are.

For reasons of space, few examples of conversions are given in this chapter. However, in the download files for this book there is a stylesheet, `cast.xsl`, which exercises all the conversions between primitive types. It requires a schema-aware XSLT processor.

We couldn't get this stylesheet to run with our version of AltovaXML 2008.

The following table lists for each source type, the permitted destination types. The detailed rules for these conversions are then given in the subsequent sections, which for ease of reference are arranged alphabetically according to the type of the source value for the conversion.

Source Type	Permitted Result Types
anyURI	anyURI, string, untypedAtomic
base64Binary	base64Binary, hexBinary, string, untypedAtomic
boolean	boolean, decimal, double, float, string, untypedAtomic
date	date, dateTime, gDay, gMonth, gMonthDay, gYear, gYearMonth, string, untypedAtomic
dateTime	date, dateTime, gDay, gMonth, gMonthDay, gYear, gYearMonth, string, time, untypedAtomic
decimal	boolean, decimal, double, float, string, untypedAtomic
double	boolean, decimal, double, float, string, untypedAtomic
duration	duration, string, untypedAtomic
float	boolean, decimal, double, float, string, untypedAtomic
gDay	gDay, string, untypedAtomic
gMonth	gMonth, string, untypedAtomic
gMonthDay	gMonthDay, string, untypedAtomic
gYear	gYear, string, untypedAtomic
gYearMonth	gYearMonth, string, untypedAtomic
hexBinary	base64Binary, hexBinary, string, untypedAtomic
NOTATION	NOTATION, string, untypedAtomic
QName	QName, string, untypedAtomic
string	anyURI, base64Binary, boolean, date, dateTime, decimal, double, duration, float, gDay, gMonth, gMonthDay, gYear, gYearMonth, hexBinary, NOTATION (note 1), QName (note 2), string, time, untypedAtomic

continued

Source Type	Permitted Result Types
time	time, string, untypedAtomic
untypedAtomic	anyURI, base64Binary, boolean, date, dateTime, decimal, double, duration, float, gDay, gMonth, gMonthDay, gYear, gYearMonth, hexBinary, string, time, untypedAtomic

Note 1: Casting from a string to xs:NOTATION *itself is not allowed, because* xs:NOTATION *is an abstract type. Casting to a user-defined subtype of* xs:NOTATION *is permitted, but only if the string is written as a string literal.*

Note 2: Casting from a string to xs:QName *is allowed only if the string is written as a string literal. This means that the cast can always be done at compile time, which avoids problems in deciding the appropriate namespace context to use for the conversion.*

Converting from anyURI

Destination Type	Rules
anyURI	The value is returned unchanged.
string	The value is returned as a string containing exactly the same characters as the supplied anyURI value. No percent-encoding or -decoding of special characters is performed.
untypedAtomic	Returns the same result as converting to a string, but the result is labeled as untypedAtomic.

Converting from base64Binary

Destination Type	Rules
base64Binary	The value is returned unchanged.
hexBinary	A hexBinary value is constructed containing the same octets as the original base64Binary value.
string	The canonical lexical representation of the base64Binary value is returned, as a string. This representation is defined in Part 2 of the XML Schema specification (be sure to read the latest version, the original has been corrected). It outputs the value with no whitespace.
untypedAtomic	Returns the same result as converting to a string, but the result is labeled as untypedAtomic.

Converting from boolean

Destination Type	Rules
boolean	The value is returned unchanged.
decimal	true is converted to 1.0, false to 0.0.

continued

11

XPath: Type Expressions

Destination Type	Rules
double	`true` is converted to `1.0e0`, `false` to `0.0e0`.
float	`true` is converted to `xs:float(1.0e0)`, `false` to `xs:float(0.0e0)`.
string	Returns the string `"true"` or `"false"`.
untypedAtomic	Returns the same result as converting to a string, but the result is labeled as `untypedAtomic`.

Converting from date

Destination Type	Rules
date	The value is returned unchanged.
dateTime	Returns the `dateTime` representing the instant in time at which the relevant date starts. The timezone (or the absence of a timezone) is retained unchanged. For example, the date `2008-04-04` becomes the `dateTime 2008-04-04T00:00:00`.
gDay	Returns a `gDay` value containing the same day component and timezone (or absence of a timezone) as the original date.
gMonth	Returns a `gMonth` value containing the same month component and timezone (or absence of a timezone) as the original date.
gMonthDay	Returns a `gMonthDay` value containing the same month and day components and timezone (or absence of a timezone) as the original date.
gYear	Returns a `gYear` value containing the same year component and timezone (or absence of a timezone) as the original date.
gYearMonth	Returns a `gYearMonth` value containing the same year and month components and timezone (or absence of a timezone) as the original date.
string	Returns the canonical lexical representation of the date, retaining the original timezone. For example, a date with no timezone might be converted to the string «2008-06-19», while a date in the Pacific timezone might become «2008-06-19-08:00». The timezone is represented as «±hh:mm», except for UTC which is represented by the single letter «Z».
untypedAtomic	Returns the same result as converting to a string, but the result is labeled as `untypedAtomic`.

Converting from dateTime

Destination Type	Rules
date	The date component of the `dateTime` value is returned, including the original timezone (or absence of a timezone).
dateTime	The value is returned unchanged.
gDay	Returns a `gDay` value containing the same day component and timezone (or absence of a timezone) as the original localized `dateTime`.

continued

Destination Type	Rules
gMonth	Returns a `gMonth` value containing the same month component and timezone (or absence of a timezone) as the original localized `dateTime`.
gMonthDay	Returns a `gMonthDay` value containing the same month and day components and timezone (or absence of a timezone) as the original localized `dateTime`.
gYear	Returns a `gYear` value containing the same year component and timezone (or absence of a timezone) as the original localized `dateTime`.
gYearMonth	Returns a `gYearMonth` value containing the same year and month components and timezone (or absence of a timezone) as the original localized `dateTime`.
string	Returns the lexical representation of the `dateTime`, retaining the original timezone. The timezone is represented as «±hh:mm», except for UTC, which is represented by the single letter «Z». This is not the same as the canonical lexical representation defined in XML Schema, which always normalizes the timezone to UTC.
time	Returns the time component of the original localized `dateTime`, retaining its timezone.
untypedAtomic	Returns the same result as converting to a string, but the result is labeled as `untypedAtomic`.

Converting from decimal

Destination Type	Rules
boolean	The value 0.0 is converted to `false`, and any other value is converted to `true`.
decimal	The value is returned unchanged.
double	The result is the closest `double` value to the supplied `decimal`. This may involve some loss of precision, because `decimal` values cannot usually be represented exactly in binary. The detailed rules are defined by saying that the result is equivalent to converting the `decimal` to a string and then converting the `string` to a `double`. If the value exceeds the largest possible `double` value this is treated as a numeric overflow, which gives three options: raising an error, returning Infinity, or returning the largest non-infinite double value.
float	As with conversion from `decimal` to `double`, the rules are defined by saying that the `decimal` is converted to a `string`, and the `string` is then converted to a `float`. The same considerations apply.
string	If the decimal represents a whole number (whether or not it is actually an instance of `xs:integer`), then it is represented on output as a string of decimal digits with no trailing zero and no decimal point. There is no truncation or rounding of significant digits, but insignificant leading or trailing zeroes are omitted. However, if the absolute value is less than one, a zero digit is included before the decimal point. The string starts with a «-» sign if the value is negative, but it never contains a «+» sign.
untypedAtomic	Returns the same result as converting to a string, but the result is labeled as `untypedAtomic`.

Converting from double

Destination Type	Rules
boolean	The values positive zero, negative zero, and NaN are converted to false, and any other value is converted to true.
decimal	The result is the decimal value, within the range of decimal values that the implementation can handle, whose value is numerically closest to the value of the supplied double; if two values are equally close, the value is rounded toward zero. The range and precision of the decimal type is left to the implementor's discretion, so results may vary from one system to another. If the double is too large to be represented as a decimal, or if it is infinity or NaN, an error occurs.
double	The value is returned unchanged.
float	The special values NaN and infinity are converted to their float equivalents. Otherwise, binary digits are removed from the least significant end of the value to make the value fit within the precision supported by the float type. If the exponent is larger than the largest exponent allowed by a float, the result is positive or negative infinity. If the exponent is smaller than the smallest exponent allowed by a float, the result is positive or negative zero.
string	If the value is NaN (not-a-number), it is output as the string «NaN». Positive and negative infinity are represented as «INF» and «-INF». Numbers whose absolute value is greater than or equal to 1.0e–6, and less than 1.0e+6, are represented in conventional decimal notation; for example, «17.523» or «42» (never «42.0»). Numbers outside this range are output in "scientific" notation, in a form such as «1.56003E-5». There are constraints on the precise form of this value; for example, it includes no plus sign and no insignificant leading or trailing zeros except adjacent to the decimal point, and the «E» must be a capital «E». Apart from these constraints, the system can choose any string that preserves the original value when converted back to a double. If you want a more user-friendly representation of the number, XSLT allows you to control the formatting using the format-number() function. Outside the XSLT environment, you can trim unwanted digits using the function round-half-to-even(), which is described in Chapter 13.
untypedAtomic	Returns the same result as converting to a string, but the result is labeled as untypedAtomic.

Converting from duration

Destination Type	Rules
duration	The value is returned unchanged.
string	The duration is output in a normalized form in which the number of months will be less than 12, the number of hours less than 24, the number of minutes and seconds less than 60. Zero-valued components are omitted. A zero-length duration is output as «PT0S», unless it is an instance of xs:yearMonthDuration, in which case it is output as «P0M».
untypedAtomic	Returns the same result as converting to a string, but the result is labeled as untypedAtomic.

Converting from float

Destination Type	Rules
boolean	The values positive zero, negative zero, and NaN are converted to false, and any other value is converted to true.
decimal	The result is the decimal value, within the range of decimal values that the implementation can handle, whose value is numerically closest to the value of the supplied float; if two values are equally close, the value is rounded toward zero. Overflow is handled in the same way as for double-to-decimal conversion: See page 660.
double	The value space for float is a strict subset of that for double, so it is possible to convert every float value to a double without loss. The specification achieves this by stating that the conversion returns the double that has the same exponent and mantissa as the supplied float, with zero, NaN and infinity being treated specially.
float	The value is returned unchanged.
string	The rules are the same as those for double-to-string conversion: see page 660.
untypedAtomic	Returns the same result as converting to a string, but the result is labeled as untypedAtomic.

Converting from gDay

Destination Type	Rules
gDay	The value is returned unchanged.
string	The output will be in the form ---DD, followed by a timezone if the value includes one, formatted as for xs:date.
untypedAtomic	Returns the same result as converting to a string, but the result is labeled as untypedAtomic.

Converting from gMonth

Destination Type	Rules
gMonth	The value is returned unchanged.
string	The output will be in the form --MM, followed by a timezone if the value includes one, formatted as for xs:date. (There was an error in the XML Schema Recommendation, corrected in later editions, which gave the format as --MM--).
untypedAtomic	Returns the same result as converting to a string, but the result is labeled as untypedAtomic.

11

XPath: Type Expressions

Converting from gMonthDay

Destination Type	Rules
gMonthDay	The value is returned unchanged.
String	The output will be in the form --MM-DD, followed by a timezone if the value includes one, formatted as for xs:date.
untypedAtomic	Returns the same result as converting to a string, but the result is labeled as untypedAtomic.

Converting from gYear

Destination Type	Rules
gYear	The value is returned unchanged.
string	The output will be in the form YYYY, followed by a timezone if the value includes one, formatted as for xs:date. Negative years are preceded by «-».
untypedAtomic	Returns the same result as converting to a string, but the result is labeled as untypedAtomic.

Converting from gYearMonth

Destination Type	Rules
gYearMonth	The value is returned unchanged.
string	The output will be in the form YYYY-MM, followed by a timezone if the value includes one, formatted as for xs:date. Negative years are preceded by «-».
untypedAtomic	Returns the same result as converting to a string, but the result is labeled as untypedAtomic.

Converting from hexBinary

Destination Type	Rules
base64Binary	A base64Binary value is constructed containing the same octets (bytes) as the original hexBinary value.
hexBinary	The value is returned unchanged.
string	The canonical lexical representation of the hexBinary value is returned, as a string. This representation uses two hexadecimal digits to represent each octet in the value. The digits used are 0–9 and A–F (uppercase).
untypedAtomic	Returns the same result as converting to a string, but the result is labeled as untypedAtomic.

Converting from NOTATION

Destination Type	Rules
NOTATION	Casting to xs:NOTATION itself is not permitted, because xs:NOTATION is an abstract type. When casting to a type derived from xs:NOTATION, the value is returned unchanged, provided that it meets the rules for the subtype.
string	If the value contains a prefix, the result is in the form «prefix:localName»; otherwise, the result is the local name.
untypedAtomic	Returns the same result as converting to a string, but the result is labeled as untypedAtomic.

Converting from QName

Destination Type	Rules
QName	The value is returned unchanged.
string	If the value contains a prefix, the result is in the form «prefix:localName»; otherwise, the result is the local name.
untypedAtomic	Returns the same result as converting to a string, but the result is labeled as untypedAtomic.

Converting from string

Destination Type	Rules
anyURI base64Binary boolean date dateTime decimal double duration float gDay gMonth gMonthDay gYear gYearMonth hexBinary string time	The string is converted to the destination type using the same rules as are applied during schema validation of an element or attribute declared with this type. Firstly, whitespace is normalized or collapsed as determined by the whiteSpace facet of the target type. (Except for the trivial conversion from string to string, this means that leading and trailing whitespace is removed). Then the resulting value is tested to check that it is a valid lexical representation for the specified atomic type, and the corresponding value of that type is returned. The rules are refined in the case of the date and time types to allow the timezone information to be retained (in XML Schema, these are lost during the process of validation).
NOTATION	Conversion to xs:NOTATION itself is not allowed, because xs:NOTATION is an abstract type. Conversion to a type derived from xs:NOTATION follows the same rules as conversion to a QName — the value must be supplied as a string literal.

continued

11

XPath: Type Expressions

Destination Type	Rules
QName	Casting from a string to a QName is allowed only if the value is supplied as a string literal. The namespace context is taken from the static context of the XPath expression. If the QName contains no prefix, then the default namespace for elements and types is used (in XSLT, this is the namespace declared using the `xpath-default-namespace` attribute).
untypedAtomic	The returned value contains the same characters as the original string, but the result is labeled as untypedAtomic.

Converting from time

Destination Type	Rules
string	Returns the canonical lexical representation of the time, retaining the original timezone. For example, the value might be output as «13:20:05.012+01:00». The timezone is represented as «±hh:mm», except for UTC, which is represented by the single letter «Z».
time	The value is returned unchanged.
untypedAtomic	Returns the same result as converting to a string, but the result is labeled as untypedAtomic.

Converting from untypedAtomic

The rules for conversion from an untypedAtomic value to any other type are exactly the same as the rules for converting from an equivalent string. See page 663.

Converting between Derived Types

The previous section listed all the permitted conversions between primitive atomic types. Now we need to consider what happens if the supplied value belongs to a derived type, or if the destination type is a derived type. Note that we are still only concerned with atomic types. The destination type of a cast cannot be a list or union type. It may however be a type that is derived by restriction. This includes both built-in derived types such as xs:integer, xs:short, and xs:Name, and also user-defined derived types, provided that they are named types in a schema that has been imported in the static context of the XPath expression.

The case where the supplied value belongs to a derived type is easy. As always, the principle of substitutability holds: a value of a subtype may always be used as input to an operation that accepts values belonging to its supertype. This means that conversion from a derived type to its base type is always successful. However, there is one minor caveat. In the tables in the previous section, conversion of a value to its own primitive type is always described with the rule "The value is returned unchanged." However, if the source value belongs to a subtype of the primitive type (that is, a type derived by restriction from the primitive type), this rule should be amended to read "The value is returned unchanged, but with the type label set to the destination type". For example, if you cast the value xs:short(2) to the type xs:decimal, the type label on the result will be xs:decimal. In fact, it is always a rule for casting operations that the type label on the result value is the type that you were casting to.

For the second case, casting to a derived type, there are a number of different rules that come into play, and we will consider them in the following sections.

❑ If the supplied value is of type `xs:string` or `xs:untypedAtomic`, then casting is designed to follow the same rules as schema validation. This is described in the next section: *Casting from xs:string to a Derived Type*.

❑ The general rule when casting from types other than `xs:string` or `xs:untypedAtomic` is the "up, across, down" rule. This is described in *Casting Non-string Values to a Derived Type* on page 666.

❑ There are some special rules that apply when casting to one of the three built-in derived types `xs:integer`, `xs:dayTimeDuration`, and `xs:yearMonthDuration`. These are described in the sections *Casting to an xs:integer* on page 667, and *Casting to xs:yearMonthDuration and xs:dayTimeDuration* on page 668.

Certain derived schema types, notably `xs:ID`, `xs:IDREF`, `xs:NOTATION`, and `xs:ENTITY` have associated constraints that a schema validator will check at the level of the document as a whole: for example `xs:ID` values must be unique, `xs:IDREF` values must match an `xs:ID` somewhere in the document, `xs:NOTATION` and `xs:ENTITY` values must refer to a notation or entity declared in the DTD. These rules are not enforced when casting, because there is no containing document to provide context.

Casting from xs:string to a Derived Type

This section describes what happens when the source value of a cast is an instance of `xs:string` or a type derived from `xs:string`, or when it is an instance of `xs:untypedAtomic`, and when the target type is a derived type. This includes the case where the target type is itself a subtype of `xs:string`. (Casting from `xs:string` to another primitive type was described on page 663).

The design is intended to imitate what happens when a string making up the content of an element or attribute in raw lexical XML is put through schema validation, when the type defined for the element or attribute is the same as the atomic type used as the target of the cast operation.

The stages are as follows:

1. The supplied value is converted to an instance of `xs:string`. This always succeeds.

2. Whitespace normalization is applied, as defined by the `whiteSpace` facet for the target type. This takes one of the values `preserve`, `replace`, or `collapse`. If the value is `replace`, then any occurrence of the characters tab (x09), newline (x0A), or carriage return (x0D) is replaced by a single space character. If the value is `collapse`, then whitespace is processed using the rules of the `normalize-space()` function described on page 845.
   Most types, including most subtypes of `xs:string`, have a `whiteSpace` facet of `collapse`. The `xs:string` type itself uses the value `preserve`, and the built-in type `xs:normalizedString` (despite its name) uses `replace`.

3. The lexical value obtained after whitespace normalization is checked against the pattern facets of the target type (which include the pattern facets of its supertypes). The cast fails if the string does not match these regular expressions. Note that multiple patterns specified in the same simple type definition are alternatives (the string must match one of the patterns), while patterns on different levels are cumulative (the string must match them all).

4. The value is then converted to the primitive supertype of the target type, using the rules for converting a string to another primitive type given on page 663.

5. The resulting value is checked to ensure that it is in the value space of the derived target type, that is, to ensure that it conforms to all the other facets defined on that type.

6. Finally, the result is constructed by taking the value determined in step 4 and attaching the name of the target type as the type label.

Converting Non-string Values to a Derived Type

This section describes the rules for casting any value other than an xs:string or xs:untypedAtomic to a derived type, including a type derived from xs:string. There are some exceptions to these rules when the target type is xs:integer, xs:dayTimeDuration, or xs:yearMonthDuration; these are covered in subsequent sections.

The general rule is "go up, then across, then down". For example, if you are converting from a subtype of xs:decimal to a subtype of xs:string, you first convert the supplied value *up* to an xs:decimal, then you convert the xs:decimal *across* to an xs:string, and then you convert the xs:string *down* to the final destination type. Of course, any of the three stages in this journey may be omitted where it isn't needed. See Figure 11-2, which shows casting from xs:long to xs:token.

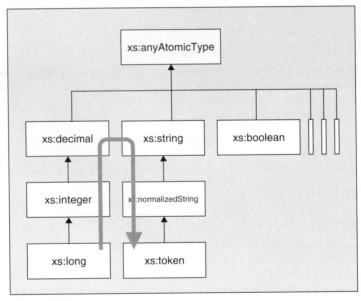

Figure 11-2

The last leg of this journey, the *down* part, now needs to be explained.

The rule here is (in general) that the value is not changed, but it is validated against the restrictions that apply to the subtype. These restrictions are defined by facets in the schema definition of the type. If the value satisfies the facets, then the cast succeeds and the result has the same value as the source, but with a new type label. If the value does not satisfy the facets, then the cast fails. For example, the expression «xs:positiveInteger(-5)» will cause an error, because the value -5 does not satisfy the minInclusive facet for the type (which says that the lowest permitted value is zero).

There is a slight complication with the pattern facet. This facet defines a regular expression that the value must conform to. The pattern facet, unlike all the others, is applied to the lexical value rather than the internal value. To check whether a value conforms to the pattern facet, the system must first convert the value to a string. This is bad news if the pattern facet has been used to constrain input XML documents to use a form other than the canonical representation; for example, to constrain an xs:boolean attribute to the values «0» and «1». The conversion to a string will produce the value «true» or «false» and will therefore fail the pattern validation. Generally speaking, using the pattern facet with types other than string (or string-like types such as xs:anyURI) is best avoided.

The actual string that is checked against the pattern facet is as follows:

❑ When converting from xs:string or xs:untypedAtomic, the value being converted.

❑ In other cases, a lexical representation of the result of converting the value to the primitive base type of the target type, where the primitive types are considered to include xs:integer, xs:dayTimeDuration, and xs:yearMonthDuration. The lexical representation chosen is generally the same as the result of casting the value to xs:string using the rules in this chapter, except in cases where XML Schema defines a canonical lexical representation that is different from the result of XPath casting. This affects the following cases:

   ❑ For xs:decimal, a whole number is represented as (say) «12.0» rather than «12».

   ❑ For xs:double and xs:float, the value is always in exponential notation with a single non-zero digit before the decimal point; for example, «1.2E1» rather than «12».

   ❑ For xs:time and xs:dateTime, the value (if it has a timezone) is adjusted to UTC, so «12:00:00-05:00» is represented as «17:00:00Z».

   ❑ For xs:date, the timezone is adjusted to be in the range -11:59 to +12:00, adding or subtracting a day as necessary.

Suppose, for example, that the schema defines a my:utcTime type as a restriction of xs:time, with <xs:pattern value=".*Z"/>. This constrains the value to end with «Z». The cast «my:utcTime ("12:00:00+01:00")» will therefore fail. However, «my:utcTime(xs:time("12:00:00+01:00"))» will succeed. The cast to xs:time succeeds because the value is a valid time, and the cast to my:utcTime succeeds because the canonical lexical representation of the value is «11:00:00Z», which matches the pattern, despite the fact that the actual value is not in UTC. As I said before, the best advice one can give is to avoid this area.

Casting to an xs:integer

Generally, casting to a derived type fails if the facets of the derived type are not satisfied. The type xs:integer is derived by restriction from xs:decimal, with a facet indicating that there must not be a fractional part. Normally, this would mean that casting 12.3 to an xs:integer would fail.

However, there is a special rule for casting numeric values to integers, or to subtypes derived from xs:integer. The value is first cast to the primitive type, xs:decimal, in the usual way, and then the value is truncated toward zero. This means that «xs:integer(10 div 3)» is 3, and «xs:integer (3.5 - 8.7)» is -5.

This special rule does not apply when casting from a string to an integer. In this case xs:integer is treated like any other derived type, which means that a cast such as «xs:integer("2.5")» will fail.

Casting to xs:yearMonthDuration and xs:dayTimeDuration

When an xs:duration is cast to an xs:yearMonthDuration or to an xs:dayTimeDuration, the components of the supplied value that are not applicable to the target type are discarded. This ensures that the cast will always succeed. For example, if the supplied value is xs:duration('P1Y1D') (one year and a day, a duration found in insurance policies and fairy tales), casting to xs:yearMonthDuration produces P1Y, while casting to xs:dayTimeDuration produces P1D.

This rule applies only when the supplied value is an instance of xs:duration or one of its subtypes (either one of the built-in subtypes, or a user-defined subtype). It does not apply, for example, when casting from xs:string. Furthermore, it applies only to these built-in duration subtypes, and any user-defined types derived from them. It does not apply to a user-defined type derived directly from xs:duration, even one whose definition is identical to that of the built-in type.

Sequence Type Descriptors

The operators described in the previous section work only on atomic types, which can always be referenced by a simple QName (unless they are anonymous types, in which case they can't be referenced at all). Later in this chapter, we will be defining two important operators «instance of» and «treat as». These can be applied to any sequence type (that is, any type in the XPath type system). Sequence types cannot always be represented by a simple name; instead, XPath defines a syntactic construct for describing these types. The production rule for this is called SequenceType. I find it useful to have a name for the actual description of a type written according to this syntax, so I've coined the name *sequence type descriptor* for this.

Sequence type descriptors are used in XPath itself only in expressions involving these two operators «instance of» and «treat as». However, they are used much more widely in XSLT, notably to declare the types of variables, functions, and parameters in the «as» attribute of <xsl:variable>, <xsl:param>, <xsl:function>, <xsl:template>, and other similar places. They also arise in XQuery.

The syntax is quite complicated, so we'll take it in stages, explaining the semantics as we go along.

Expression	Syntax
SequenceType	(ItemType OccurrenceIndicator?) | «empty-sequence» «(» «)»
OccurrenceIndicator	«?» | «*» | «+»
ItemType	AtomicType | KindTest | «item» «(» «)»
AtomicType	QName
KindTest	DocumentTest | ElementTest | AttributeTest | PITest | CommentTest | TextTest | AnyKindTest

The first rule tells us that a sequence type descriptor is either an ItemType followed optionally by an OccurrenceIndicator, or it is the compound symbol «empty-sequence()».

The «empty-sequence()» construct is used very rarely in practice. The only value that conforms to this type is the empty sequence. This is why no occurrence indicator is allowed in this case. The only practical example I have seen where «empty-sequence()» is useful is in an XQuery «typeswitch» expression. You can use it in XPath, but «$x instance of empty-sequence()» means the same as «empty($x)», so it's not a vital feature. It's really there only for completeness, so that every type used in expressing the formal semantics of the language is also accessible to users of the language.

Apart from «empty-sequence()», every other sequence type descriptor consists of an ItemType followed optionally by an OccurrenceIndicator. The ItemType defines what kind of items can appear in a sequence, and the OccurrenceIndicator says how many of them are allowed. The three occurrence indicators (which in computer science theory are often called Kleene operators) will be familiar from their use in regular expressions and DTDs. They are:

Occurrence Indicator	Meaning
*	Zero or more occurrences allowed
+	One or more occurrences allowed
?	Zero or one occurrence allowed

If no OccurrenceIndicator is present, then a sequence will only conform to the type if it contains exactly one item.

The rest of the syntax provides different ways of expressing an ItemType.

First of all, the compound symbol «item()» allows any kind of item, that is, any atomic value, or any node. (As with other compound symbols, you can use spaces before, between, or after the parentheses, but it's usually written without spaces so that's how I shall do it here.) You can combine «item()» with an occurrence indicator, so «item()» matches a single item, «item()?» matches a sequence that is either empty or contains a single item, «item()+» matches any non-empty sequence, and «item()*» matches any sequence whatsoever.

Every other way of writing the ItemType matches either atomic values, or nodes, but not both.

Matching Atomic Values

Matching atomic values is easy, because atomic types have names. (You can have anonymous atomic types in a schema, but there is no way to refer to them in a sequence type descriptor). If you use a QName as the ItemType, then it must be the name of a type that is known in the static context of the XPath expression, as described in Chapter 7, and this type must be an atomic type. In XSLT 2.0 this means it must either be one of the built-in types such as xs:integer, or a user-defined atomic type in a schema that has been imported using the <xsl:import-schema> declaration.

The XSLT 2.0 specification defines a minimum set of atomic types that every processor (even one that does not support schema import) must provide, namely:

```
xs:anyAtomicType, xs:anyURI, xs:base64Binary, xs:boolean, xs:date, xs:dateTime,
xs:dayTimeDuration, xs:decimal, xs:double, xs:duration, xs:float, xs:gDay,
xs:gDayMonth, xs:gMonth, xs:gMonthDay, xs:gYear, xs:gYearMonth, xs:hexBinary,
xs:integer, xs:QName, xs:string, xs:time, xs:untypedAtomic, xs:yearMonthDuration
```

11

XPath: Type Expressions

This set was chosen because it is sufficient to allow all the functions in the core function library (that is, the functions listed in Chapter 13) to be used. Schema-aware processors, however, will support the full set of built-in types defined in XML Schema as well as user-defined types declared using `<xs:simpleType>` declarations in an imported schema.

Most of these types were described fully in Chapter 5, but two are worth a special mention.

❑ `xs:untypedAtomic` is the type of the atomic value that results from atomizing a node that has not been annotated (as a result of schema validation) with any more specific type. It is possible to create an `xs:untypedAtomic` value by casting (and it is sometimes convenient to do so), but the most common way of getting these values is by atomizing an unvalidated node.

❑ `xs:anyAtomicType` is a supertype for all atomic types. Used as an item type, this will match any atomic value (for example, a string, an integer, or a boolean), and will not match a node. It's an abstract type, so something that is an instance of `xs:anyAtomicType` will always be an instance of some other more specific type in addition. (The name is rather poorly chosen, I feel. One might expect the instances of this type to be types, just as in Java the instances of `Class` are classes. But the name follows the tradition set by `xs:anyType` and `xs:anySimpleType`.)

Note that the QName must be the name of an atomic type, not merely a simple type. Simple types, in the XML schema classification, also include list types and union types. Atomic values contained in an XPath sequence always belong to an atomic type, not a list or union type, and a sequence type descriptor is therefore constrained to use atomic types. This rules out types such as `xs:NMTOKENS`, `xs:IDREFS`, and `xs:ENTITIES`, which are list types, as well as `xs:anyType`, which is a complex type.

Matching Nodes

All other sorts of `ItemType` are used to match nodes. These all come under the umbrella of the `KindTest` construct.

I'll dispose of the simple kinds of node first, and then move on to elements and attributes, which is where the real complexity comes.

Expression	Syntax
KindTest	AnyKindTest | DocumentTest | ElementTest | AttributeTest | CommentTest | TextTest | PITest
AnyKindTest	«node» «(» «)»
DocumentTest	«document-node» «(» ElementTest? «)»
CommentTest	«comment» «(» «)»
TextTest	«text» «(» «)»
PITest	«processing-instruction» «(» (NCName | StringLiteral)? «)»

If you're reading the book sequentially, you may have a sense of *déjà vu* about these rules. We met them before in Chapter 9, on page 616, where they appear as part of the syntax for a `NodeTest` in a path expression. Conveniently, the syntax for testing the type of a node in an «instance of» or «treat as» expression is exactly the same as the syntax for saying what kinds of node you want to select in a step of a path expression. What's more, because the syntax of XSLT match patterns is defined in terms of path expressions, you can use the same constructs when defining an XSLT template rule.

The construct «node()» is the most general item type here: it matches any item that is a node.

Note, however, that if you use «node()» on its own as a step in a path expression or as an XSLT match pattern, it is short for «child::node()» and will only match nodes that are found on the child axis. The only nodes that can be found on the child axis are elements, text nodes, comments, and processing instructions.

The constructs «comment()» and «text()» are straightforward: they match comment nodes and text nodes, respectively.

For matching document nodes, you can write the test «document-node()», which matches any document node, or you can be more specific. If you include an ElementTest within the parentheses, then this ItemType will only match a document node that satisfies the following two conditions:

❑   The document node must be the root of a tree that corresponds to a well-formed XML document. Specifically this means that the document node must have exactly one element node, and no text nodes, among its children. It is allowed to have comments and processing instructions before or after the element node.

❑   The element node that is a child of this document node must match the ElementTest given within the parentheses. The syntax for ElementTest is given in the next section.

This construct allows you to test what can be loosely called the "document type", for example, you can test whether an input document returned by the doc() function is an invoice, by writing:

```
if (doc("inv.xml") instance of document-node(schema-element(mf:invoice))) ...
```

This construct tests whether the document node is labeled as an invoice, as the result of previous validation. If the document has not been validated, the result will be false, whether or not validation would succeed if attempted. The way you control whether doc() invokes validation depends on the XSLT processor you are using. With Saxon, you can control it using the options -val:lax or -val:strict on the command line, or on a per-document basis using parameters appended to the URI. With AltovaXML, the document will be validated if it has an xsi:schemaLocation attribute.

Because the same syntax is used in XSLT patterns (described in the next chapter), you can also use it in template rules:

```
<xsl:template match="document-node(schema-element(mf:invoice))">
```

The «processing-instruction()» construct can also be written with empty parentheses, in which case it will match any processing instruction. As an alternative, you can provide a name within the parentheses, in which case it will only match processing instructions with that name. For compatibility with XPath 1.0, the name can optionally be written in quotes, as a string literal. This means you can match an <?xml-stylesheet?> processing instruction using either of the constructs:

```
processing-instruction(xml-stylesheet)
processing-instruction("xml-stylesheet")
```

The two forms are precisely equivalent, except that using an invalid name is an error in the first case but not the second (you just won't select anything).

Matching Elements and Attributes

The syntax for matching elements and attributes is more complex, because it allows you to take advantage of the type information attached to these nodes as a result of schema validation. The type annotation of an element or attribute node may be any type defined in an XML Schema, or a built-in. In the case of attributes, it must be a simple type, for elements it can be either a simple or a complex type. All simple types are allowed, including list types and union types. However, although any type defined in a schema can appear as a node annotation, the only types you can refer to directly are those that:

❑ have a name (that is, they are not anonymous types, which means they must be defined in top-level type definitions in the schema), and

❑ are declared in a schema that has been imported in the static context of the XPath expression. In XSLT this is achieved using the `<xsl:import-schema>` declaration.

Here's the basic syntax for element and attribute tests (it is organized slightly differently from the official W3C grammar):

Expression	Syntax
ElementTest	BasicElementTest | SchemaElementTest
AttributeTest	BasicAttributeTest | SchemaAttributeTest
BasicElementTest	«element» «(» (ElementNameOrWildCard («,» TypeName «?»?) ?) ? «)»
BasicAttributeTest	«attribute» «(» (AttribNameOrWildcard («,» TypeName)?) ? «)»
ElementNameOrWildcard	ElementName | «*»
AttribNameOrWildcard	AttributeName | «*»
ElementName	QName
AttributeName	QName
TypeName	QName

We will come back to the `SchemaElementTest` and `SchemaAttributeTest` later. The meaning of this syntax doesn't leap out from the page, so it's best to explain it by listing all the possible cases. The general form is «element (*NAME*, *TYPE*)», where *NAME* defines conditions on the name of the element, and *TYPE* defines conditions on its type annotation.

Here are the rules for matching elements:

Test	Matches
element()	Any element node.
element(*)	Any element node.
element(N)	Any element node whose name is N. In a path expression this is equivalent to just writing the element name N on its own, but in contexts where a SequenceType is required, it provides a way of saying that a value must be an element with a particular name, whether or not this name is defined in any schema.
element(*,T)	Any element node whose type annotation shows it to be valid according to the rules of schema type T. The type T can be a simple type or a complex type, but it must be a named type that is defined in an imported schema (this allows a built-in type, of course). If the element has the attribute «xsi:nil = "true"», then it matches only if the type name T in the sequence type descriptor is followed by a question mark.
element(N,T)	Any element node whose name is N and that is annotated as an instance of schema type T. This combines the previous two options into a single condition.

The rules for matching attributes are very similar, but they are simpler because attributes cannot be marked as nillable:

Test	Matches
attribute()	Any attribute node.
attribute(*)	Any attribute node.
attribute(N)	Any attribute node whose name is N.
attribute(*,T)	Any attribute node whose type annotation shows it to be valid according to the rules of schema type T. The type T must always be a named simple type that is defined in an imported schema (this allows a built-in type, of course).
attribute(N,T)	Any attribute node whose name is N and that is annotated as an instance of the schema type T.

Using Global Element and Attribute Declarations

The basic element and attribute tests described in the previous section allow you to test an element or attribute node according to its name and its type annotation, provided that the type annotation is a named simple or complex type in the schema. It's very common, however, to find that elements are declared in a schema using global element declarations and with an anonymous type: to take an example from the schema for XSLT 2.0 stylesheets:

```
<xs:element name="apply-imports" substitutionGroup="xsl:instruction">
  <xs:complexType>
    <xs:complexContent>
      <xs:extension base="xsl:versioned-element-type">
```

11

XPath: Type Expressions

```
                <xs:sequence>
                    <xs:element ref="xsl:with-param" minOccurs="0" maxOccurs="unbounded"/>
                </xs:sequence>
            </xs:extension>
        </xs:complexContent>
    </xs:complexType>
</xs:element>
```

The syntax «element(E, T)» doesn't work in this case, because the type is anonymous. Instead, the construct «schema-element(S)» can be used. This matches any element that has been validated against the global element declaration named «S» in the schema. It's not necessary that the name of the element should be «S»; it can also be an element in the substitution group of «S».

The official rule for «schema-element(S)» is that the element must satisfy two conditions: its element name must be present in the substitution group of S, and its type annotation must be either the type of S or one of its subtypes. There is a slight loophole in that this will match an element that was actually validated against a local element declaration that just happened to match the name and type of something in the substitution group. This loophole does little harm and was left in because preventing it would require additional information to be retained in the data model, namely an extra annotation indicating the element declaration that was used to validate an element.

It's much less common to encounter global attribute declarations, but they are also supported in the same way, for symmetry.

The full syntax for this form of ElementTest and AttributeTest is shown below.

Expression	Syntax
SchemaElementTest	«schema-element» «(» ElementName «)»
SchemaAttributeTest	«schema-attribute» «(» AttributeName «)»

Examples

Let's try to put these different forms into context by seeing how they can be used with a real schema. I'll use as my example the schema for XSLT 2.0 stylesheets, which is published in an appendix of the XSLT 2.0 specification at http://www.w3.org/TR/xslt20. This example is therefore relevant if you are using XPath expressions to access an XSLT 2.0 stylesheet (which is not as esoteric a requirement as you might think), and it also assumes that the XSLT 2.0 stylesheet has been validated against this schema.

The schema starts with a couple of complex type definitions like this:

```
<xs:complexType name="generic-element-type">
    <xs:attribute name="extension-element-prefixes" type="xsl:prefixes"/>
    <xs:attribute name="exclude-result-prefixes" type="xsl:prefixes"/>
    <xs:attribute name="xpath-default-namespace" type="xs:anyURI"/>
    <attribute ref="xml:space">
    <attribute ref="xml:lang">
    <xs:anyAttribute namespace="##other" processContents="skip"/>
</xs:complexType>
<xs:complexType name="versioned-element-type">
    <xs:complexContent>
        <xs:extension base="xsl:generic-element-type">
```

```
                <xs:attribute name="version" type="xs:decimal" use="optional"/>
            </xs:extension>
        </xs:complexContent>
    </xs:complexType>
```

Every element in the XSLT namespace has a type that is derived ultimately from «generic-element-type», and most of them are also derived from «versioned-element-type». If we want to use a sequence type descriptor (perhaps to declare a variable or a function argument in XSLT) that accepts any element in the XSLT namespace that is valid against this schema, we could declare this as:

```
<xsl:param name="p" as="element(*, xsl:generic-element-type)"/>
```

If we wanted to exclude those elements that don't allow a version attribute (there is only one, <xsl:output>, which in fact does allow a version attribute, but defines it differently), then we could write the sequence type descriptor as:

```
<xsl:param name="p" as="element(*, xsl:versioned-element-type)"/>
```

The schema goes on to provide two abstract element declarations, like this:

```
<xs:element name="declaration" type="xsl:generic-element-type" abstract="true"/>

<xs:element name="instruction" type="xsl:versioned-element-type" abstract="true"/>
```

These are declared as abstract because you can't actually include an element in a stylesheet whose name is <xsl:declaration> or <xsl:instruction>. The reason these two element declarations exist is so that they can act as the heads of substitution groups. This greatly simplifies the definition of other types. For example, there are many places in XSLT where you can use a construct called a *sequence constructor*. A sequence constructor is a sequence of elements in the stylesheet that may include variable definitions, instructions, and literal result elements, and its format is defined in the schema like this:

```
<xs:group name="sequence-constructor-group">
    <xs:choice>
        <xs:element ref="xsl:variable"/>
        <xs:element ref="xsl:instruction"/>
        <xs:group ref="xsl:result-elements"/>
    </xs:choice>
</xs:group>
```

Elements that allow a sequence constructor as their content, such as <xsl:if> and <xsl:sequence>, make use of a complex type definition that refers to this structure:

```
<xs:complexType name="sequence-constructor">
    <xs:complexContent mixed="true">
        <xs:extension base="xsl:versioned-element-type">
            <xs:group ref="xsl:sequence-constructor-group"
                      minOccurs="0" maxOccurs="unbounded"/>
        </xs:extension>
    </xs:complexContent>
</xs:complexType>
```

The abstract element <xsl:instruction> was introduced for convenience in defining the schema, but it is equally convenient for describing types in XPath, because we can now write:

```
schema-element(xsl:instruction)
```

to match any element that is an XSLT instruction: that is, an element that is in the substitution group of `<xsl:instruction>`. An example of such an element is `<xsl:apply-imports>`, which as we have already seen is defined like this:

```
<xs:element name="apply-imports" substitutionGroup="xsl:instruction">
  <xs:complexType>
    <xs:complexContent>
      <xs:extension base="xsl:versioned-element-type">
        <xs:sequence>
          <xs:element ref="xsl:with-param" minOccurs="0" maxOccurs="unbounded"/>
        </xs:sequence>
      </xs:extension>
    </xs:complexContent>
  </xs:complexType>
</xs:element>
```

The schema for XSLT 2.0 stylesheets does not include any global attribute declarations, so you will never see a sequence type descriptor of the form «schema-attribute(xsl:xxxx)». This is fairly typical: attributes are most commonly declared either as part of the element declaration to which they belong, or in constructs such as `xs:attributeGroup`. For example, the set of «xsl:» prefixed attributes that can appear on literal result elements is defined in the schema for XSLT 2.0 in an attribute group:

```
<xs:attributeGroup name="literal-result-element-attributes">
  <xs:attribute name="extension-element-prefixes" form="qualified"
                type="xsl:prefixes"/>
  <xs:attribute name="exclude-result-prefixes" form="qualified"
                type="xsl:prefixes"/>
  <xs:attribute name="xpath-default-namespace" form="qualified"
                type="xs:anyURI"/>
  <xs:attribute name="use-attribute-sets" form="qualified"
                type="xsl:QNames" default=""/>
  <xs:attribute name="version" form="qualified"
                type="xs:decimal"/>
  <xs:attribute name="type" form="qualified"
                type="xsl:QName"/>
  <xs:attribute name="validation" form="qualified"
                type="xsl:validation-type"/>
</xs:attributeGroup>
```

This means that even these attributes (which are unusual because their names are in the target namespace of the schema) are not declared globally and therefore not available for use in sequence type descriptors. It would be possible to change the schema to the following form (selecting just three of the attributes for brevity):

```
<xs:attribute name="version" form="qualified" type="xs:decimal"/>
<xs:attribute name="type" form="qualified" type="xsl:QName"/>
<xs:attribute name="validation" form="qualified" type="xsl:validation-type"/>

<xs:attributeGroup name="literal-result-element-attributes">
   <xs:attribute ref="version" form="qualified" type="xs:decimal"/>
   <xs:attribute ref="type" form="qualified" type="xsl:QName"/>
   <xs:attribute ref="validation" form="qualified" type="xsl:validation-type"/>
</xs:attributeGroup>
```

and you could then use «schema-attribute(xsl:version)» as a sequence type descriptor.

Much more common, I think, is to use the form «attribute(*, T)» which matches attributes that have a particular type annotation. For example, many attributes in XSLT have the type xsl:QName. An example is the name attribute of <xsl:function>, allowing you to write, for example, <xsl:function name="math:sqrt">. This type is a variant of the built-in type xs:QName. It has the same lexical form as an xs:QName but is not derived from it because the validation rules are subtly different: in XML Schema, an xs:QName with no prefix is assumed to be in the default namespace, but in XSLT, an xsl:QName with no prefix is assumed to be in no namespace.

If you wanted to write a stylesheet to process all the attributes of type xsl:QName, perhaps to standardize the namespace prefixes that are used, you could define an XSLT template rule of the form:

```
<xsl:template match="attribute(*, xsl:QName)">
  . . .
</xsl:template>
```

There is no way of writing a sequence type descriptor that matches a local element or attribute definition in a schema. In many cases local element and attributes in a schema are defined by reference to a global type, and in this case you can use the syntax «element(E, T)» or «attribute(A, T)». With this syntax, the name E or A can be any element or attribute name you choose; it doesn't have to be the name of a global element or attribute defined in the schema.

We've now finished our survey of the SequenceType syntax, and the next two sections describe the two XPath constructs («instance of» and «treat as») in which this syntax is used.

The «instance of» Operator

The «instance of» operator is used to test whether a given value conforms to a particular type. Unlike Java, the two words must be separated by whitespace.

Expression	Syntax
InstanceOfExpr	TreatExpr («instance» «of» SequenceType) ?

As usual, the fact that the first operand is listed as a TreatExpr is simply a way of indicating the operator priorities; these are summarized in Appendix A.

The «instance of» expression always returns a boolean result. The first operand is evaluated, and if it conforms to the specified sequence type (as defined by the rules in the previous section) the answer is true; otherwise, it is false.

It's important to remember, whether you are testing atomic values or nodes, that the «instance of» operator is testing whether the value has a label that identifies it as a member of the specified type. It isn't testing whether the value would be a valid member of that type if the label were changed. For example:

```
5 instance of xs:positiveInteger
```

returns false (surprisingly), because although 5 satisfies all the conditions for a positive integer, it is not labeled as such: the type label for a numeric literal of this kind is simply xs:integer. Similarly, given an element <price>13.50</price> as the context item, the expression:

```
price instance of element(*, xs:decimal)
```

will return `false` unless the element has actually been validated and given a type annotation of `xs:decimal`, or some type derived from `xs:decimal`. The fact that validation against this type would succeed is not enough; the validation must actually have been done, so that the required type annotation is present on the node.

The «instance of» operator does not atomize its operand, so an expression such as «@code instance of xs:decimal» is always going to return `false`. You need either to atomize the value explicitly, by writing «data(@code) instance of xs:decimal», or to test the type annotation of the node, by writing «@code instance of attribute(*, xs:decimal)».

If an element or attribute is list-valued, then the type annotation on the node may be a list type, for example, «attribute(*, xs:IDREFS)». But when you extract the typed value of this node using the `data()` function, the result is a sequence of xs:IDREF values, which you can test using the sequence type descriptor «xs:IDREF*». You cannot write «data(@x) instance of xs:IDREFS», because xs:IDREFS is not an atomic type.

Similarly, when the schema defines an element or attribute as having a union type, then the type annotation on the node will be the union type, but the atomic values that result from atomization will belong to one or another of the members of the union type.

The «instance of» expression tests the dynamic type of a value, that is, the actual type of the value after the operand expression has been evaluated. This may or may not be the same as the static type of the operand expression. The static type of an expression will always be a supertype of the dynamic type of any possible value of the expression (or the same type, of course).

Here are some examples of «instance of» expressions used in context:

Expression	Effect
`$seq[. instance of node()]`	Selects the items in `$seq` that are nodes, discarding any that are atomic values.

`if (some $s in $seq`
`  satisfies $s`
`  instance of node())`
`then ...`
	Tests whether the sequence `$seq` contains at least one node.

`if (not($seq instance of`
`    xs:anyAtomicType*))`
`then ...`
	This has exactly the same effect as the previous example. If a sequence is not an instance of «xs:anyAtomicType*», then it must contain at least one node.

`$p instance of item() +`	This tests whether `$p` is a non-empty sequence. The result is the same as calling «exists($p)».

The «treat as» Operator

The «treat as» operator can be regarded as an assertion; the programmer is asserting that at runtime, the value of an expression will conform to a given type. If the assertion turns out to be wrong, evaluation of the expression will fail with a runtime error.

This is the syntax:

Expression	Syntax
TreatExpr	CastableExpr («treat» «as» SequenceType)?

The «treat as» operator is extremely important if you are using an XPath processor that does strict static type checking (or if you want to write code that is portable between processors that do such checking and those that don't). However, if you want to write robust code, there is no harm in using «treat as» to make explicit any assumptions you are making about types even in a system that does all its type checking dynamically, which will generally be the case when XPath is used within XSLT stylesheets.

Suppose that you are using a schema that defines a union type, an attribute quantity, say, whose value can be either an integer or one of the two strings «out-of-stock» or «unknown». It might look reasonable to write:

```
if (@quantity = "out-of-stock")
    then -2
else if (@quantity = "unknown")
    then -1
else @quantity + 2
```

Unfortunately, it's not as easy as that. The three places where @quantity is used all do atomization, which will produce either a string or an integer, but at compile time it's not known which. The «=» comparison in the condition of the «if» will fail if the value turns out to be an integer, because you can't compare an integer to a string. The «+» operator would similarly fail if the value turned out to be a string. You and I can see that this will never happen, but the XPath processor is not so clever. All it knows at compile time is that the value might be either an integer or a string.

A processor that does strict static typing will throw this out with compile time errors, because it detects that the code is unsafe (meaning, it could throw type errors at runtime). How do you get round this?

Firstly, you could try rewriting the expression like this:

```
if (data(@quantity) instance of xs:string)
then
    if (@quantity = "out-of-stock")
        then -2
    else if (@quantity = "unknown")
        then -1
    else error()
else @quantity + 2
```

For a system that does dynamic type checking, this is good enough. It avoids the error that would otherwise occur at runtime when you try to compare an integer to a string.

But unfortunately this still won't persuade a static type checker that all is well, because it can't follow through the logic of this code to work out that when you take one path, the value of @quantity must be a string, and when you take a different path, it must be an integer. So you need to use «treat as», like this:

```
if (data(@quantity) instance of xs:string) then
  if ((data(@quantity) treat as xs:string) = "out-of-stock")
    then -2
  else if ((data(@quantity) treat as xs:string) = "unknown"))
    then -1
  else error()
else (data(@quantity) treat as xs:integer) + 2
```

This code will work both on systems that do strict static typing, and on those that don't. The «treat as» operator is essentially telling the system that you know what the runtime type is going to be, and you want any checking to be deferred until runtime, because you're confident that your code is correct.

I rather suspect that few XPath 2.0 implementations will decide to implement strict static typing, so this might all turn out to be slightly irrelevant. The enthusiasm among implementors for strict static typing is far stronger in XQuery circles, where the need for optimization is so much greater. XQuery has an additional construct, the «typeswitch» expression, which makes code like that shown above much less painful to write.

There is another workaround to this problem, which is add type conversions which you know are unnecessary, but which placate the type checker. So you could write the above expression instead as:

```
if (string(@quantity) = "out-of-stock")
    then -2
else if (string(@quantity) = "unknown")
    then -1
else xs:integer(@quantity) + 2
```

Summary

This chapter provided details of all the type-related constructs and expressions in the XPath 2.0 language.

At the beginning of the chapter we described the «cast» and «castable» operators, and constructor functions, which are used to convert an atomic value of one type to an atomic value of a different type. We provided detailed tables showing all the type conversions that are allowed by the language.

Then, moving beyond atomic types, we examined the syntax for describing sequence types. This syntax is used only in two places in XPath, the «instance of» and «treat as» expressions, but XQuery and XSLT users will use the same syntax much more widely, for example, whenever the types of variables or functions are declared.

Finally, we explained how these two expressions, «instance of» and «treat as», actually work.

We've now finished our tour of the XPath language syntax. The next chapter returns to XSLT with an explanation of the syntax used in match patterns, which is based on XPath syntax but is not actually part of the XPath language. Then in Chapter 13 we will look at the built-in function library — this chapter provides an alphabetical listing of all the functions in this library, including all the functions provided by every conformant XPath 2.0 processor, together with some additional functions available when XPath is used within an XSLT stylesheet.

12

XSLT Patterns

A pattern is used in XSLT to define a condition that a node must satisfy in order to be selected. The most common use of patterns is in the `match` attribute of `<xsl:template>`, where the pattern says which nodes the template rule applies to. For example, `<xsl:template match ="abstract"` introduces a template rule that matches every `<abstract>` element. This chapter defines the syntax and meaning of XSLT patterns.

Patterns (sometimes called *match patterns*) are used in just six places in an XSLT stylesheet:

- ❏ In the `match` attribute of `<xsl:template>`, to define the nodes in a source document to which a template applies

- ❏ In the `match` attribute of `<xsl:key>`, to define the nodes in a source document to which a key definition applies

- ❏ In the `count` and `from` attributes of `<xsl:number>`, to define which nodes are counted when generating numbers

- ❏ In the `group-starting-with` and `group-ending-with` attributes of `<xsl:for-each-group>`, to identify a node that acts as the initial or final node in a group of related nodes

Patterns and Expressions

Most of the patterns found in stylesheets are simple and intuitive. For example:

Pattern	Meaning
`title`	Matches any `<title>` element
`chapter/title`	Matches any `<title>` element whose parent is a `<chapter>` element
`speech[speaker = "Hamlet"]`	Matches any `<speech>` element that has a child `<speaker>` element whose value is «Hamlet»
`section/para[1]`	Matches any `<para>` element that is the first `<para>` child of a `<section>` element

The rules for the more complex patterns, however, are quite technical — so I'm afraid some of the explanations in this chapter are not going to be easy reading.

Patterns are defined in terms of the name, type, and content of a node, and its position relative to other nodes in the tree. To understand how patterns work, you therefore need to understand the tree model (described in Chapter 2) and the different kinds of node.

Patterns look very similar to XPath expressions, and it turns out that they are closely related. However, patterns and expressions are not quite the same thing. In terms of its syntax, every pattern is a valid XPath expression, but not every XPath expression is a valid pattern. It wouldn't make any sense to use the expression «2+2» as a pattern, for example — which nodes would it match?

> *Expressions are defined in the XPath 2.0 Recommendation, which allows them to be used in contexts other than XSLT stylesheets. For example, XPath expressions are used in the XPointer specification to define hyperlinks between documents, and they are used in some Document Object Model (DOM) implementations as a way for applications to navigate around the DOM data structure. XML Schema 1.1 will allow XPath expressions to be used in a schema to define assertions. Patterns are local to the XSLT Recommendation, and they are found only in stylesheets, though the draft XProc pipeline language also uses them.*

It would have been quite possible for XSLT to define both the syntax and the meaning of patterns quite independently of the XPath rules for expressions, but this would risk unnecessary inconsistency. What the XSLT language designers chose to do instead was to define the syntax of patterns in such a way that every pattern was sure to be a valid expression, and then to define the formal meaning of the pattern in terms of the meaning of the expression.

Look at the simplest pattern in the earlier examples, «title». If «title» is used as an expression, it's an abbreviation for «./child::title», and it means "select all the <title> children of the context node." How do we get from that to a definition of the pattern «title» as something that matches all <title> elements?

The next section *The Formal Definition* gives the formal definition of patterns in terms of expressions. In practice, it's easier to think of most patterns as following their own rules — rather like the intuitive examples listed earlier — and referring to the formal definition only to resolve difficult cases. So I'll follow the formal explanation with an informal definition that's not only more intuitive, but also closer to the way most implementations are likely to work.

When patterns are used in template rules, we need to consider what happens if the same node is matched by more than one pattern. This situation is discussed in the section *Conflict Resolution* on page 686 in this chapter.

A new feature of the XPath 2.0 data model is that it is possible to create nodes in a tree whose root node is not a document node. Such trees cause additional complications for the semantics of pattern matching. The section *Matching Parentless Nodes* on page 688 explains how these nodes are handled.

The bulk of the chapter is then devoted to an explanation of the syntax of patterns, and the usage of each syntactic construct that can appear in a pattern.

Changes in XSLT 2.0

The syntax of patterns is probably the area of the specification that has changed least between XSLT 1.0 and XSLT 2.0. However, because many capabilities of patterns are picked up implicitly by virtue of the way they are defined in terms of expressions, they benefit automatically from many of the new features in XPath 2.0.

The most notable facility this introduces is the ability to match nodes according to their schema-defined type. For example, you can match all date-valued attributes with the pattern «match="attribute(*, xs:date)"», and you can match all elements in the substitution group of the event element with the pattern «match = "schema-element(event)"».

There are also some changes in the semantics of patterns, designed to cope with the complications introduced by parentless element and attribute nodes.

In XSLT 1.0 there were three restrictions on the content of a predicate used in a pattern. All three restrictions have been removed in XSLT 2.0.

❑   When a pattern was used in the match attribute of <xsl:template> or <xsl:key>, the predicate was not allowed to contain any references to variables. This was to prevent circular definitions. XSLT 2.0 allows variable references, provided that they do not introduce a circular definition.

❑   For the same reasons, when a pattern was used in the match attribute of <xsl:template> or <xsl:key>, XSLT 1.0 did not allow the predicate to use the key() function. Again, this rule has been replaced with a more permissive rule that says you can use the key() function provided it doesn't introduce a circularity.

❑   In XSLT 1.0, patterns were not allowed to use the current() function (described on page 734 in Chapter 13) within a predicate. XSLT 2.0 allows this and defines that, within a pattern, current() refers to the node that is being tested against the pattern.

The Formal Definition

The XSLT specification defines the way patterns are evaluated in terms of the XPath expression that is equivalent to the pattern. We've already seen that every pattern is a valid XPath expression. In fact, the rules are written so that the only XPath expressions that can be used as patterns are those that return a sequence of nodes. The idea is that you should be able to decide whether a node matches a pattern by seeing whether the node is in the sequence returned by the corresponding expression.

This then raises the question of context. The result of the XPath expression «title» is all the <title> children of the context node. Does that include the particular <title> element we are trying to match, or not? It obviously depends on the context. Because we want the pattern «title» to match every <title> element, we could express the rule by saying that the node we are testing (let's call it N) matches the pattern «title» if we can find a node (A, say) anywhere in the document, which has the property that when we take A as the context node and evaluate the expression «title» the node N will be selected as part of the result. In this example, we don't have to look very far to find node A: in fact, only as far as the parent node of N.

So the reason that a <title> element matches the pattern «title» is that it has a parent node, which when used as the context node for the expression «./child::title» returns a sequence that includes that <title> element. The pattern might be intuitive but, as you can see, the formal explanation is starting to get quite complex.

In an early draft of the XSLT 1.0 specification, the rules allowed almost any path expression to be used as a pattern. For example, you could define a pattern «ancestor::*[3]», which would match any node that was the great grandparent of some other node in the document. It turned out that this level of generality was neither needed nor possible to implement efficiently, and so a further restriction was imposed, that the only axes you could use in a pattern were the child and attribute axes (the various axes were

12

XSLT Patterns

explained in Chapter 9). A consequence of this is that the only place where the XSLT processor has to look for node *A* (the one to use as a context node for evaluating the expression) is among the ancestors of the node being matched (*N*), including *N* itself.

This brings us to the formal definition of the meaning of a pattern. For the moment let's ignore the complications caused by parentless nodes; I return to these later on page 688.

> **The node $N matches a pattern PAT if $N is a member of the sequence selected by the expression «root($N)//(PAT)».**

The way this rule is expressed has changed since XSLT 1.0, but the effect is the same. It has become possible to simplify the rule as a result of the generalization of path expressions that has happened in XPath 2.0. In XPath 1.0, XPath expressions such as «//(a|b)» or «//(/a)» were not allowed, so this rule would have made many patterns illegal.

Let's see what this rule means. We start with a node $N that we want to test against the pattern. First we find the root node of the tree containing $N. Then we look for all the descendant-or-self nodes of this root node, which means all the nodes in the tree except for attributes and namespaces. For each one of these nodes, we evaluate the pattern as if it were an XPath expression, using that node as the context node. If the result includes the original node $N, we have a match.

Applying the Definition in Practice

Let's see how this rule works by testing it against some common cases:

❑ If the pattern is «title» then a node matches the pattern if the node is included in the result of the expression «root(.)//(title)» which is the same as «//title». This expression selects all <title> elements in the document, so a node matches the pattern if and only if it is a <title> element.

❑ If the pattern is «chapter|appendix» then a node matches the pattern if it is selected by the expression «root(.)//(chapter|appendix)» This expression is equivalent to «//chapter | //appendix» and matches all <chapter> and <appendix> elements in the document.

❑ If the pattern is «/» then a node matches if it is selected by the expression «root(.)//(/)» This rather strange XPath expression selects the root node of every descendant of the root node, and then eliminates duplicates: so it is actually equivalent to the expression «/» which selects the root node only. (There are complications if the root node is not a document node, for example if it is a parentless element. I will cover these complications later in the chapter: see page 688.)

❑ If the pattern is «chapter/title», then a node matches if it is selected by the expression «root(.)//(chapter/title)», which selects all <title> elements that are children of <chapter> elements.

❑ If the pattern is «para[1]», then a node matches if it is selected by the expression «root(.)//(para[1])», which selects any <para> element that is the first <para> child of its parent.

❑ If the pattern is «id('S123')», then a node matches if it is selected by the expression «root(.)//(id('S123'))», which is equivalent to the expression «id('S123')» and selects the element with an ID value of «S123».

An Algorithm for Matching Patterns

This means there is a theoretical algorithm for testing whether a given node N matches a pattern P, as follows: for each node, starting from N and working through its ancestors up to the root node, evaluate P as an XPath expression with that node as the context node. If the result is a sequence of nodes containing N, the pattern matches; otherwise, keep trying until you get to the root.

XSLT processors don't usually use this algorithm, it's there only as a way of stating the formal rules. The processor will usually be able to find a faster way of doing the test — which is just as well, since pattern matching would otherwise be prohibitively expensive.

Although the formal rules usually give the answer you would expect intuitively, there can be surprises. For example, you might expect the pattern «node()» to match any node; but it doesn't. The equivalent expression, «//(node())» is short for «root(.)/descendant-or-self::node()/child:: node()», and the only nodes that this can select are nodes that are children of something. Because document nodes, attribute nodes, and namespace nodes are never children of another node (see the description of the tree model on page 45 in Chapter 2), they will never be matched by the pattern «node()».

Patterns Containing Predicates

The formal equivalence of patterns and expressions becomes critical when considering the meaning of predicates (conditions in square brackets), especially predicates that explicitly or implicitly use the position() and last() functions.

For example, the pattern «para[1]» corresponds to the expression «root(.)//(para [position() = 1])». This expression takes all the <para> children of the context node, and then filters this sequence to remove all but the first (in document order). So the pattern «para[1]» matches any <para> element that is the first <para> child of its parent. Similarly, the pattern «*[1][self::para]» matches any element that is the first child of its parent and that is also a <para> element, while «para[last()! = 1]» matches any <para> element that is a child of an element with two or more <para> children.

An Informal Definition

Because they are written in terms of expressions, the formal rules for a pattern such as «book//para», encourage you to think of the pattern as being evaluated from left to right, which means finding a <book> element and searching for all its <para> descendants to see if one of them is the one you are looking for.

An alternative way of looking at the meaning of this expression, and the way in which most XSLT processors are likely to implement the pattern-matching algorithm, is to start from the right. The actual logic for testing a node against the pattern «book//para» is likely to be along the lines:

- ❑ Test whether this is a <para> element. If not, then it doesn't match.
- ❑ Test whether there is a <book> ancestor. If not, then it doesn't match.
- ❑ Otherwise, it matches.

If there are predicates, these can be tested en route, for example to evaluate the pattern «speech [speaker = 'Hamlet']», the logic is likely to be the following:

- ❑ Test whether this is a <speech> element. If not, then it doesn't match.

❑ Test whether this element has a `<speaker>` child whose typed value is «Hamlet» If not, then it doesn't match.

❑ Otherwise, it matches.

Most patterns can thus be tested by looking only at the node itself and possibly its ancestors, its attributes, and its children. The patterns that are likely to be the most expensive to test are those that involve looking further afield.

For example, consider the pattern «para[last()-1]», which matches any `<para>` element that is the last but one `<para>` child of its parent. Most XSLT processors, unless they have an exceptionally good optimizer, are going to test whether a particular `<para>` element matches this pattern by counting how many children the parent element has, counting how many preceding `<para>` siblings the test `<para>` has, and comparing the two numbers. Doing this for every `<para>` element that is processed could get a little expensive, especially if there are hundreds of them with the same parent. With the patterns «para[1]» or «para[last()]» you've a slightly better chance that the processor will figure out a quicker way of doing the test, but it would be unwise to rely on it.

If you write a stylesheet with a lot of template rules, then the time taken to find the particular rule to apply to a given node can make a significant difference. The exact way in which different XSLT processors do the matching may vary, but one thing you can be sure of is that patterns containing complex predicates will add to the cost.

Conflict Resolution

When a pattern is used in the definition of a template rule, it is possible that several patterns may match the same node. There are rules for resolving this conflict, which are described in the section *Choosing a Template Rule* in the entry for `<xsl:apply-templates>` in Chapter 6, page 242. One of the factors these rules take into account is the *default priority* of the pattern, which is determined from the way it is written.

The default priority is decided according to the following rules. A numerically higher value indicates a higher priority. Note that some of the priorities are fractional, and some are negative.

If the pattern is a union of two or more patterns («P1|P2»), then the processor treats it as if there were two completely separate template rules specified, one for P1 and one for P2, and it calculates the default priority of P1 and P2 independently, using the rules in the table.

If the pattern starts with an axis specifier («child::», «attribute::» or «@»), this does not affect the priority.

Pattern Syntax	Default Priority

`document-node(schema-element(QName))`
`document-node(element(QName, QName))`
`schema-element(QName)`
`element(QName, QName)`
`schema-attribute(QName)`
`attribute(QName, QName)`
	+0.25

`QName`
`document-node(element(QName))`
`document-node(element(*, QName))`
	0.0

continued

Pattern Syntax	Default Priority

`element(QName)`
`element(*, QName)`
`attribute(QName)`
`attribute(*, QName)`
`processing-instruction(Literal)`
`processing-instruction(NCName)`	

`NCName:*` `*:NCName`	−0.25

`/`
`document-node()`
`document-node(element())`
`document-node(element(*))`
`* element()`
`element(*)`
`attribute()`
`attribute(*)`
`text()`
`comment()`
`processing-instruction()`
`node()`
	−0.5

Otherwise	+0.5

These default priorities are carefully chosen to reflect the selectivity of the pattern:

❑ The patterns «node()» and «text()» and «*» are not very selective at all; they match any node of the right node kind, so they have a low priority of -0.5.

❑ Patterns of the form «abc:*» or «@xyz.*» are more selective; they will match element or attribute nodes belonging to a particular namespace only, so they have a higher priority than the previous category. Patterns such as «*:abc» are also placed in this category, because they are less specific than a pattern that fully specifies the node name but more specific than one that specifies only the kind of node.

❑ Patterns such as «title» or «@isbn» are the ones most commonly encountered; their default priority of 0.0 reflects the fact that in terms of selectivity, they are typical. Other patterns that specify the kind of node as well as its name fall into the same group. Patterns that specify the schema type of the node without specifying its name; for example, «element(*, pers:employee)» are placed at the same level because they might be more or less specific than a pattern specifying the node name.

❑ Patterns that specify both the node name and its schema type, for example «attribute(@code, mf:part-number)», are more specific than those that specify only the name or the type, so they get a priority of +0.25.

❑ Patterns that provide a more specific context, for example «book[@isbn]» or «chapter/title» or «para[1]», have a higher priority, so they will be chosen in preference to templates whose patterns are respectively «book», «title» or «para». Note, however, that this category can also include patterns that turn out not to be very selective at all; for example, «//node()».

All these values are chosen to leave you free to allocate your own priorities as natural numbers, for example «1» «2» «3», and such templates will always be chosen ahead of those with a system-allocated default priority.

12

XSLT Patterns

You may find that stylesheets are easier to understand and less error prone if you avoid relying on default priorities, and use explicit priorities whenever you have more than one template rule that can match the same node.

Although the default priorities are carefully chosen, they do not guarantee that a highly selective pattern will always have higher priority than a less selective pattern. For example, the patterns «section/para» and «section/para[1]» both have priority +0.5. Similarly, the patterns «attribute(*, xs:integer)» and «attribute(*, xs:decimal)» have the same priority, even though the nodes that match the first pattern are a subset of those that match the second. Choosing your own priorities is therefore a more reliable approach.

A complete description of the conflict resolution rules, including the role played by the default priority of the pattern, is described under <xsl:apply-templates> on page 242 in Chapter 6.

Matching Parentless Nodes

In XSLT 1.0, every node belonged to a tree with a document node at its root. In fact, because the root was always the same kind of node, this kind of node was known as a root node rather than a document node. This has changed in XSLT 2.0: you can now have elements, or even attributes and text nodes, that have no parent. For example, if you write:

```
<xsl:variable name="seq" as="element()*">
  <e>2</e>
  <f>5</f>
  <g>9</g>
</xsl:variable>
```

then the value of the variable $seq is a sequence of three element nodes. These element nodes have no parent, and they are therefore not siblings of each other. The XPath expression «$seq/e» will not select anything, because none of the three nodes in $seq has a child element whose name is «e». If you want to select the «e» element, you should write «$seq[self::e]» (or, if you prefer, «$seq/self::e»).

A tree may thus be rooted at an element node rather than a document node, and this affects the rules for pattern matching. Two consequences of parentless elements complicate the rules.

The first consequence has to do with error handling. In XPath, using an expression such as «/» or «//book» is an error if the context item is in a tree whose root is not a document node. The same applies to the id() and key() functions. This could mean that if you wrote <xsl:apply-templates select = "$seq"/>, where $seq is a sequence of parentless elements, then as soon as the system tried to match it against a template rule specifying <xsl:template match = "/">, a runtime error would occur. This would happen, of course, only if the processor took the naive approach of matching every node against every pattern in the stylesheet, and even then only if it took the formal approach of evaluating the equivalent XPath expression. In practice, neither the user nor the implementor would be very happy if this was defined to be an error, so the specification includes a (very ad hoc) rule saying that the system never attempts to match a parentless node against a pattern starting with «/» or key() or id(), and therefore never hits this error condition.

More generally, runtime errors can also occur when evaluating a predicate in a pattern. For example, matching the pattern «//book[@price div 0 = 0]» could cause a runtime error (division by zero). The spec is open ended about these; it makes it clear that whether or not a particular error is ever reported will depend on the order in which the processor chooses to test the different patterns, and even then, on its evaluation strategy for a particular pattern. It also allows processors to ignore such errors, simply behaving as if the pattern does not match.

The other problem that occurs with parentless nodes is that using the definition as we have it so far, the pattern «match = "ex"» means «match = "child::e"» and would match an <e> element only if it is a child of something. The working group decided that this would be just too confusing, and resolved that the pattern «e» should match every <e> element whether or not it has a parent. Similarly, «chapter / para» should match every <para> whose parent is a <chapter>, whether or not the <chapter> has a parent.

The way that the formal definition of patterns has been bent to meet this requirement is somewhat tortuous. It is done by introducing two new axes, child-or-top, and attribute-or-top, and using these axes in the first step of a RelativePathPattern in place of the usual child and attribute axes. The child-or-top axis selects the children of the context node, unless the context node is a parentless element, text node, comment, or processing instruction, in which case it selects the parentless context node itself. Similarly, the attribute-or-top axis selects the context node itself if it is a parentless attribute node. Given these two extra axes, the equivalence between patterns and XPath expressions continues to hold. (These axes, of course, are purely notional. You can't use them explicitly either in an XPath expression or in a pattern.)

Note that this refinement does not apply to patterns starting with «/». The pattern «//book», which in XSLT 1.0 matched exactly the same nodes as the pattern «book», now has a slightly different meaning: it selects only <book> elements that are descendants of a document node. It will not select a parentless <book> element, or a <book> element in a tree whose root is a parentless element. This, incidentally, means that «match = "//book"» is quite likely to be less efficient than «match = "book"» because the system now has to check what kind of node is at the root of the tree.

The Syntax of Patterns

The rest of this chapter gives the detailed syntax rules for patterns.

The indented hierarchy that follows shows the overall structure of the rules. Constructs marked with the symbol § are defined in the XPath grammar, specifically in Chapter 7.

```
Pattern
    PathPattern
        RelativePathPattern
            PatternStep
                PatternAxis
                NodeTest
                Predicates
                    Expr §
        IdKeyPattern
            Literal §
            VariableReference §
```

The rules are presented in top-down order, starting with the Pattern construct itself.

The production rules use the same syntax notation that is used to define the syntax of XPath expressions as described in Chapter 7. The entry for each construct defines the syntax using a BNF notation, it describes the meaning of the construct in a section headed *Effect* and then includes sections relating to the *Usage* of the construct, followed by *Examples*. The BNF uses chevrons to enclose literal symbols but is otherwise conventional: alternatives are indicated using «|», repetition by «*», and optional constructs by «?»

Pattern

This is the top-level construct for the XSLT Pattern syntax. A pattern defines a condition that is either true or false for any given node in a document. The syntax for a `Pattern` is a subset of the syntax for a `UnionExpr` (and therefore for an `Expr`) in the XPath expression syntax.

Syntax

Expression	Syntax
Pattern	PathPattern | Pattern «|» PathPattern

A `Pattern` is either a `PathPattern` or a sequence of `PathPatterns` separated by the union operator «\|».

The syntax of a `PathPattern` is given in the next section.

Effect

A node matches a `Pattern` if it matches any of the `PathPatterns` contained in the `Pattern`.

Usage

Although «\|» is technically a union operator, it is simpler to read it as «or» — a node matches the pattern «A\|B» if it matches either A or B or both.

In patterns, the «\|» operator can be used only at the top level. XPath 2.0 allows expressions such as «(chap\|appendix)/title», but this is not a valid pattern. The required effect can be achieved by writing «chap/title\|appendix/title» or, if you prefer, «title[parent::chap\|parent:: appendix]».

Examples

Construct	Meaning
TITLE	«TITLE» is a PathPattern, so it is also a Pattern.
preface|chapter| appendix	A node matches this pattern if it is a `<preface>` element, a `<chapter>` element, or an `<appendix>` element.
/|*	A node matches this pattern if it is either a document node or an element node.

PathPattern

A `PathPattern` states conditions that a node must satisfy based on its name, its node kind, its position relative to other nodes, and/or its ID and key values.

This construct is a subset of the `PathExpr` construct in the XPath grammar.

Syntax

Expression	Syntax
PathPattern	RelativePathPattern | «/» RelativePathPattern? | «//» RelativePathPattern | IdKeyPattern ((«/»|«//»)RelativePathPattern) ?

This production rule is the way the syntax is defined in the XSLT specification. However, the following equivalent production rule may be easier to understand, and it corresponds more closely with the description in the *Usage* section discussed later.

Expression	Syntax
PathPattern	«/»| RelativePathPattern | «/» RelativePathPattern | «//» RelativePathPattern | IdKeyPattern| IdKeyPattern «/» RelativePathPattern| IdKeyPattern «//»RelativePathPattern

The syntax of a RelativePathPattern (page 693) and that of an IdKeyPattern (page 704) are described later.

Effect

The syntax rule reproduced earlier from the XSLT specification can be better understood by listing the seven different kinds of PathPattern, as follows:

Construct	Meaning
«/»	Matches a document node.
RelativePathPattern	Matches a node that can appear anywhere in the document. Example: «book/chapter/title» matches any <title> element whose parent is a <chapter> element that is a child of a <book> element.
«/» RelativePathPattern	Matches a node via a defined path from a document node. Example: «/book/title» matches a <title> element that is a child of a <book> element whose parent is a document node.
«//» RelativePathPattern	Matches a node that can appear anywhere in the document. The inclusion of the leading «//» rules out nodes in trees that don't have a document node at their root. It also affects the default priority of a template rule that uses this pattern. The default priority of a pattern comes into play when two template rules match the same node: for details, see the description of <xsl:template> in Chapter 6, page 483. Example: «//title» matches any <title> element within a tree that is rooted at a document node.
IdKeyPattern	Matches a node with a given ID attribute or key value. For example, «id('A001')» matches an element with an ID attribute whose value is «A001».
IdKeyPattern «/» RelativePathPattern	Matches a pattern defined relative to the children of a node with a given ID attribute or key value. For example, «id('A001')/title» matches the <title> child of an element with an ID attribute whose value is «A001».
IdKeyPattern «//» RelativePathPattern	Matches a pattern defined relative to the descendants of a node with a given ID attribute or key value. For example, «id('A001')//title» matches any <title> element that is a descendant of an element with an ID attribute whose value is «A001».

Usage

The pattern «/» matches any document node. This means that if you have several trees (which will be the case in a stylesheet that uses the document() or doc() functions described in Chapter 13), the pattern «/» will match the document nodes of each one. This makes it difficult to write different template rules to match the document nodes of different trees. There are a few ways around this problem:

❑ If your documents are of different types (that is, if they use different schemas, or different top-level elements in the same schema), then you can distinguish them using a pattern such as «document-node(schema-element(invoice))» or «document-node(schema-element (purchase-order))» These constructs are described on page 700 later in the chapter.

❑ You can use different modes to process each tree (see the section *Modes* on page 247 in Chapter 6).

❑ You can start the processing of secondary documents at the element node immediately below the root. A pattern such as «/item» will match an item element that is an immediate child of the document node. This kind of pattern is often useful when your stylesheet is dealing with multiple source documents, because it allows you to distinguish them by the name of the document element.

The pattern «/@width» is legal but meaningless; it would match a width attribute of the document node, but as the document node cannot have attributes, there is no such node.

To match every <para> element, use the pattern «para» in preference to «//para» The latter will work (except in non-document trees), but its default priority is different, and it may be less efficient. For the other kinds of PathPattern, see RelativePathPattern (on this page) and IdKeyPattern (page 704) discussed later.

Examples

Construct	Meaning
/	Matches a document node.
/*	Matches the outermost element node in a document (the document element). In the case of a tree that is not well formed (see page 48 in Chapter 2), it matches any element whose parent is a document node.
/booklist	Matches any <booklist> element whose parent is a document node.
//book	Matches any <book> element that has a document node as an ancestor.
book	Matches any <book> element.
element(*, mfg:invoice)	Matches any element annotated as conforming to the schema-defined type mfg:invoice.
attribute(*, xs:date)	Matches any attribute annotated as an xs:date, including subtypes of xs:date.
id('figure-1')	Matches an element with an ID attribute having the value 'figure-1'.
id('figure-1')//*	Matches any descendant element of an element with an ID attribute having the value 'figure-1'.
key('empnr', '624381') /@dob	Matches the dob attribute of an element having a value '624381' for the key named empnr.

RelativePathPattern

A `RelativePathPattern` consists of a `PatternStep` defining conditions that a node must satisfy, optionally preceded by a `RelativePathPattern` that a parent or ancestor node must satisfy (the syntax puts it the other way around, but the effect is the same, and it's easier to think of it from right to left). The syntax for a `RelativePathPattern` is a subset of the syntax for a `RelativePathExpr` in the XPath Expression language.

Syntax

Expression	Syntax
RelativePathPattern	PatternStep | PatternStep «/» RelativePathPattern | PatternStep «//» RelativePathPattern

A `RelativePathPattern` is thus a sequence of one or more `PatternSteps` separated by either of the operators «/» (is-parent-of) or «//» (is-ancestor-of).

The syntax of a `PatternStep` is described on the next page.

Effect

Because in practice patterns are likely to be evaluated from right to left, it's easier to explain the semantics if we rearrange the syntax, as follows.

Expression	Syntax
RelativePathPattern	PatternStep | RelativePathPattern «/» PatternStep | RelativePathPattern «//» PatternStep

With the first form, `PatternStep`, a node matches the pattern if it satisfies the conditions (node name, node kind, and predicates) defined in the `PatternStep`. The simplest and most common form of `PatternStep` is simply an element name, for example «title».

With the second form, `RelativePathPattern` «/» `PatternStep`, a node matches the pattern if it satisfies the conditions (node name, node kind, and predicates) defined in the `PatternStep`, and if its parent node matches the `RelativePathPattern`. This `RelativePathPattern` may in turn include conditions that the parent node's parent or ancestor nodes must satisfy.

With the third form, `RelativePathPattern` «//» `PatternStep`, a node matches the pattern if it satisfies the conditions (node name, node kind, and predicates) defined in the `PatternStep`, and if it has an ancestor that matches the `RelativePathPattern`. This `RelativePathPattern` may in turn include conditions that the ancestor node's parent or ancestor nodes must satisfy.

Usage

Notice that although there is an equivalence between `RelativePathPattern` in the pattern language and `RelativePathExpr` in the expression language, the meaning of a `RelativePathPattern` is most easily explained by examining the `PatternSteps` from right to left, starting at the node being tested and working up through its ancestors, if necessary; this is despite the fact that the meaning of a `RelativePathExpr` is explained by considering the Steps from left to right, starting at the context node. It's likely that most implementations will adopt a strategy similar to the algorithm as I've explained it here.

Generally speaking, there is no point in making patterns any more selective than is necessary. For example, if a <row> element always appears as a child of <table>, then there is no point in specifying the pattern as «table/row» — you might just as well use the simpler pattern «row».

In theory, everything you can do in a RelativePathPattern could be done in a single PatternStep, because the pattern «A/B» means exactly the same as «B[parent::A]» and the pattern «A//B» means exactly the same as «B[ancestor::A]». However, where several steps are present, the form using «/» and «//» operators is a lot easier to read.

Examples

Construct	Meaning
title	This is a PatternStep, and therefore the simplest form of RelativePathPattern. It selects any <title> element.
section/title	This is a RelativePathPattern consisting of two PatternSteps joined by the «/» (is-parent-of) operator. It matches a <title> element whose parent is a <section> element.
chapter//footnote	This is a RelativePathPattern consisting of two PatternSteps joined by the «//» (is-ancestor-of) operator. It matches a <footnote> element that is a descendant of a <chapter> element.
chapter/section//footnote	A more complex RelativePathPattern that matches any <footnote> element that is a descendant of a <section> element that is a child of a <chapter> element.
chapter[1]//footnote	This pattern matches every <footnote> element in the first chapter (more strictly, in a <chapter> that is the first child <chapter> of its parent).

PatternStep

A PatternStep defines conditions that an individual node must satisfy: typically some combination of the node name, node kind, schema type, and a set of boolean or numeric predicates. The syntax for a PatternStep is a subset of the syntax for an AxisStep in the XPath expression language.

Syntax

Expression	Syntax
PatternStep	PatternAxis? NodeTest Predicates
PatternAxis	«child» «::» | «attribute» «::» | «@»

continued

Expression	Syntax
NodeTest	NameTest | KindTest
NameTest	QName |
	«*» |
	NCName «:*» |
	«*:» NCName
Predicates	(«[» Expr «]»)*

The syntax of KindTest is given later on page 697. The constructs QName, NCName, and Expr are all defined in the XPath 2.0 grammar, and are described in Chapter 7.

Effect

To describe the effect of a PatternStep we'll look at each of its components separately: first the Pattern-Axis, then the two kinds of NodeTest, that is, NameTests and KindTests, and finally the Predicates.

The PatternAxis

The PatternAxis may take the form «attribute::» (abbreviated «@») or «child::» (abbreviated to nothing: «») In general, if no PatternAxis is specified, the child axis is assumed; the only exception is that when the NodeTest is an AttributeTest (for example, «attribute(*)») the attribute axis is assumed.

In the formal rules for evaluating a pattern, the steps in a RelativePathPattern are evaluated from left to right, and the choice of axis determines whether this step looks at the children or the attributes of the nodes found in the previous step.

Looking at it informally, it is simplest to think of the axis specifier as simply a way of saying what kind of node is required.

❑   If the child axis is used and the NodeTest is a NameTest (for example, «title», «*», or «svg:*») then we are looking for an element node.

❑   If the child axis is used and the NodeTest is a KindTest (for example, «comment()» or «text()»), then we are looking for that kind of node. If the NodeTest is «node()», then we are looking for any node on the child axis: specifically, elements, text nodes, comments, or processing instructions. Note that the pattern «node()», which is short for «child::node()», will not match document nodes, attributes, or namespace nodes, because these nodes never appear as the child of another node.

❑   If the attribute axis is used and the NodeTest is a NameTest (for example, «@title», «@*», or «@svg:*»), then we are looking for an attribute node.

❑   If the attribute axis is used and the NodeTest is a KindTest (for example, «@schema-attribute (xml:space)»), then we are looking for nodes on the attribute axis. Of course, the only nodes found on the attribute axis are attribute nodes. The patterns «@comment()» and «@text()» are not illegal, but they are pointless, because the attribute axis cannot contain comments or text nodes. However, the NodeTest «@node()» looks for any node on the attribute axis, so it is equivalent to «@*».

If the PatternStep is the first PatternStep in a top-level RelativePathPattern, then it matches parentless nodes as if they had a parent. For example, the PatternStep «child::title» or «title» will match a `<title>` element that has no parent node, and the `PatternStep` «schema-attribute (xml:space)» will match an `xml:space` attribute that has no parent element.

The only two axes that are available directly in a pattern are the child and attribute axes. However, testing for the presence of related nodes on a different axis can be done in the predicate of the `PatternStep`. Any expression can be used in the predicate, and so all axes are available. For example:

```
caption[preceding-sibling::*[1][self::figure]]
```

matches a `<caption>` element whose immediately preceding sibling element is a `<figure>` element.

The NameTest

A `NameTest` such as «*» or «prefix:*» is purely testing the name of the node. This works whether or not there is a schema. There are four forms:

❑ A lexical QName such as «title» or «mfg:invoice» must match both the local name and the namespace URI of the node. If the QName has a prefix, then it is expanded using the namespace declarations on surrounding elements in the stylesheet; if not, the XPath default namespace is used. The XPath default namespace can be set using the `[xsl:]xpath-default-namespace` attribute, which is described in the entry for `<xsl:stylesheet>` in Chapter 6, page 480.

❑ The `NameTest` «*» matches any node of the principal node kind for the axis.

❑ The `NameTest` «prefix:*» matches any node whose name is in a particular namespace. There must be a declaration for this namespace (of the form «xmlns:prefix = "uri"») on some enclosing element in the style-sheet module, and the namespace is the one with the corresponding URI.

❑ The `NameTest` «*:local-name» matches any node with the specified local name, regardless of its namespace. This includes nodes whose name is not in any namespace.

In all these cases, a `NameTest` matches nodes only of the principal node kind for the selected axis. This means that if the `PatternAxis` is «@» or «attribute::», the `NameTest` selects attribute nodes with the given name; otherwise, it matches element nodes only.

Patterns that match nodes by name are extremely common and work well with many kinds of document. If you find yourself writing a pattern with many alternatives, for example:

```
match="b | i | u | sub | sup | s"
```

then (if you are using a schema-aware processor) it may be worth asking yourself what these elements have in common. One possibility is that they are all members of the same substitution group defined in the schema: in this case, you may be able to replace the pattern with one such as «match = "schema-element(inline)"». Another possibility is that the elements all have the same internal structure. In this case they are likely to conform to the same type definition in the schema, so you can replace the list of elements by a pattern of the form «match = "element(*, inline-type)"».

If the list includes most of the members of a substitution group, or most elements conforming to a given type, then you could consider excluding the unwanted ones with a predicate, for example: «match = "schema-element(inline)[not(self::schema-element(span))]"». Alternatively, if the pattern is being used to define a template rule, simply define another template rule with higher priority to catch the exceptions.

A pattern of the form «prefix:*», which matches all the elements (or attributes) in a particular namespace, is often useful if all that you want to do is exclude such elements from the result tree. An empty template rule takes the form:

```
<xsl:template match="svg:*" xmlns:svg="http://www.w3.org/2000/svg"/>
```

This example causes all subtrees rooted at an element in the namespace http://www.w3.org/2000/svg to be excluded from the result. (This is the namespace for the W3C Scalable Vector Graphics specification: see http://www.w3.org/TR/SVG11/).

«*:local-name» patterns are new in XSLT 2.0. They should be used with care, because in principle the names in one namespace bear no relationship to names in a different namespace; for example, the «xsl:sequence» element in the XSLT namespace is quite unrelated to the «xs:sequence» element in the XML Schema namespace. However, there are cases where you might need to write a stylesheet that handles several namespaces that are variants of each other, in which many of the elements are common to more than one namespace. This can occur when matching (X)HTML, which may or may not use the XHTML namespace, or when matching RSS, which also exists in both namespace and no-namespace variants.

The KindTest

Whereas a NameTest is designed to match nodes primarily by their name, a KindTest matches specific kinds of nodes. In the case of element and attribute nodes, it also allows matching against the type annotation attached to the node as a consequence of schema validation.

The syntax of a KindTest, copied from the XPath specification, is as follows:

Expression	Syntax
KindTest	DocumentTest | ElementTest | AttributeTest | TextTest | PITest | CommentTest | AnyKindTest
DocumentTest	«document-node» «(» ElementTest? «)»
ElementTest	BasicElementTest | SchemaElementTest
BasicElementTest	«element» «(» (ElementNameOrWildCard («,» TypeName «?»?) ?) ? «)»
SchemaElementTest	«schema-element» «(» QName «)»
AttributeTest	BasicAttributeTest | SchemaAttributeTest

continued

Expression	Syntax
BasicAttributeTest	«attribute» «(» (AttributeNameOrWildcard («,» TypeName)?)? «)»
SchemaAttributeTest	«schema-attribute» «(» QName «)»
TextTest	«text» «(» «)»
PITest	«processing-instruction» «(» (NCName| StringLiteral)? «)»
CommentTest	«comment» «(» «)»
AnyKindTest	«node» «(» «)»
NodeName	QName| «*»
TypeName	QName

A KindTest is used to define the kind of node that is required and, optionally, information about its schema-defined type.

Let's take the simple cases first:

❑ «text()» matches any text node.

❑ «comment()» matches any comment node.

❑ «node()» matches any node whatsoever (but remember that on its own, it means «child::node()», which searches only for nodes that are children of something).

❑ «processing-instruction()» matches any processing instruction node.

❑ «processing-instruction(NCName)» matches any processing instruction node with the given name (the name of a processing instruction is referred to in the XML Specification as the *PITarget*). For compatibility with XPath 1.0, the NCName may be written in quotes as a StringLiteral.

❑ «document-node()» matches any document node.

❑ «element()» matches any element node. This can also be written as «element(*)».

❑ «attribute()» matches any attribute node. This can also be written as «attribute(*)».

Now things start to get more complicated, because the other kinds of KindTest are concerned with testing for specific types of node as defined in a schema. In general, you will use these KindTests only to match nodes in documents that have been validated against a schema.

KindTests for Element Nodes

Let's look first at the options for matching element nodes:

❑ «element(QName)» matches any element node whose name is the given QName. As a pattern, this is exactly the same as writing the QName on its own. (The reason for providing this syntax is that a KindTest is allowed in contexts other than patterns; for example, in the «as» attribute of an <xsl:param> element.)

❏ «`schema-element(QName)`» is used to test for an element that matches a top-level element declaration in the schema identified by the given `QName`. It's an error to use this form unless you have imported a schema containing this top-level element declaration. For example, if you write «`schema-element(mfg:invoice)`», then the schema for the «`mfg`» namespace must have been imported, and must include a top-level element declaration of the form «`xs:element name="invoice"`».

The element is considered to match if two conditions are satisfied:

❏ Its name is either the same as the `QName`, or the name of an element defined in the schema to be a member of the substitution group with the named element as its head.

❏ The type of the element node, identified from its type annotation, matches the type defined for this element declaration in the schema. This rule is there because a schema can allow the same name to be used in different contexts with different type definitions.

❏ «`element(*, QName)`» is used to test for an element whose type annotation indicates that it has been successfully validated against the schema-defined type definition identified by the `QName`. The `QName` can identify a built-in type such as «`xs:dateTime`», or a type (which may be a simple type or a complex type) that is the subject of a named type definition in an imported schema. The test will match any element that has a type annotation that refers to the named type, or a type derived from the named type by restriction or by extension.

If the element includes the attribute «`xsi:nil = "true"`», then it will match this `KindTest` only if the `QName` is followed by the symbol «`?`». This extra test is necessary because without it, the system would not be able to make any assumptions about the contents of the element, since `xsi:nil` essentially allows an element to have no content even when the schema would otherwise require it.

❏ The KindTest «`element(QName, QName)`» tests both the name of the node and its type: the name must match the first `QName`, or the name of one of the elements in its substitution group, and the type annotation must match the second `QName` (which must be the name of a top-level type definition in an imported schema). Again, if the element includes the attribute «`xsi:nil = "true"`», then it will match this `KindTest` only if the second `QName` is followed by the symbol «`?`».

KindTests for Attribute Nodes

`KindTests` for attribute nodes follow the same format as those for element nodes, with minor variations. The same options are available, though in practice they are likely to be used rather differently. In particular, global attribute declarations are not used very often in XML Schema, and matching against the names of a top-level simple type definition is probably a more likely scenario.

❏ «`attribute(QName)`» matches any attribute whose name matches the given `QName`: as a pattern, this means exactly the same as `@QName` or `attribute::QName`.

❏ «`schema-attribute(QName)`» is used to test for an attribute that matches a top-level attribute declaration in the schema identified by the given `QName`. It's an error to use this form unless you have imported a schema containing this top-level attribute declaration. The attribute is considered to match if two conditions are satisfied:

❏ Its name is the same as the QName.

❏ The type of the attribute node, identified from its type annotation, matches the type defined for this attribute declaration in the schema.

❑ «attribute(*, QName)» is used to test for an attribute whose type annotation indicates that it has been successfully validated against the schema-defined simple type definition identified by the QName. The QName can identify a built-in type such as «xs:dateTime», or a type (it will always be a simple type) that is the subject of a named type definition in an imported schema. The test will match any attribute that has a type annotation that refers to the named type, or a type derived from the named type by restriction. For example, the KindTest «attribute(*, xs:date)» matches any attribute whose type (as established by schema validation) is xs:date.

❑ The KindTest «attribute(QName, QName)» is essentially a combination of «attribute (QName)» and «attribute(*, QName)». This tests both the name of the node and its type: the name must match the first QName, and the type annotation must match the second QName (which must be the name of a top-level simple type definition in an imported schema).

KindTests for Document Nodes

The document-node() KindTest can take an argument that is an element() or schema-element() KindTest; it then matches any document node that has the specified kind of element as its only element child. For this KindTest to work, the document must be a well-formed document in the sense that the document node has exactly one element node as a child, and no text node children, and the element node must have been validated against a schema. Here are two examples:

Construct	Meaning
document-node(schema-element(mfg:invoice))	Matches the document node at the root of a well-formed document whose outermost element has been validated against the top-level element declaration named «invoice» in the schema for the namespace associated with the prefix «mfg», or an element in the substitution group headed by the «invoice» element. This schema must have been imported into the stylesheet.
document-node(element(*, fin:movement))	Matches the document node at the root of a well-formed document whose outermost element has the type annotation «fin:movement», or a type derived from this by restriction or extension. The schema for the namespace associated with the prefix «fin» must have been imported into the stylesheet.

Using KindTests

The simple KindTests comment(), processing-instruction(), and text() are used whenever you want to match one of these kinds of node. These are used comparatively rarely. For example, it's unusual to define a template rule that matches text nodes: usually a stylesheet will either copy text nodes unchanged, or suppress them from the output, and the choice is usually controlled from the template rule for the containing element node.

The default template rule for comment nodes causes them to be discarded; if you want to copy comment nodes to the output, you can achieve this by adding the template rule.

```
<xsl:template match="comment()"><xsl:copy/></xsl:template>
```

However, this will work only if the template rule used to process the containing element issues the instruction <apply-templates/> to process all its children.

The [schema-]element() and [schema-]attribute() KindTests are most useful when you a processing a source document that has been validated against a schema, especially when the schema is fairly complex. It allows you to define a generic rule for a whole class of elements or attributes. There are a number of ways such a class can be identified, and the approach you use will depend on the design of your schema:

❑ Identifying the elements or attributes by type, using the syntax «element(*, QName)» or «attribute(*, QName)» is useful for processing elements and attributes that have simple content. For example, if all elements containing monetary amounts are identified as being of type «money», then you can define a template rule with the pattern «match = "element(*, money)"» that contains the formatting logic for values of this type. This will also work if the schema defines subtypes derived by restricting the money type; for example, a subtype that restricts the values to be positive sums of money.

❑ Where the schema defines many elements that share the same complex type, the syntax «element(*, QName)» can again be useful to define generic logic that applies to all elements of this type. For example, a schema for retail banking might define a generic type «movement» that represents all movements of money from one account to another. A template rule declared with «match = "element(*, QName)"» will match all elements declared with this type, or with a type derived from it.

❑ You need to be aware that in choosing a template rule, the system takes no account of the type hierarchy in the schema. If direct-debit is defined as a subtype of movement, this does not mean that the template rule defined with «match = "element(*, direct-debit)"» takes priority over the rule with «match = "element(*, movement)"» You need to allocate explicit priorities in the stylesheet to make sure that the right rule is invoked.

❑ If subtypes have been defined by extending the base type, then it can often be useful to invoke processing of the extensions by using the <xsl:next-match> instruction, described in Chapter 6. The template rule for the base type can process all the contents that are common to all instances of the type, while the template rule for an extended type needs to process only those contents that are included in the extension.

❑ Sometimes substitution groups are used to define a collection of similar elements. Whereas types identify elements or attributes with common content, substitution groups identify elements that are interchangeable in terms of where they can appear in a document. But XML Schema also imposes a rule that an element in a substitution group must have a content model that is either a restriction or an extension of the content model of the substitution group head. This means that the elements in a substitution group will generally have some content in common, for example all elements in the substitution group of <event> might have attributes time and place. In this case a pattern such as «schema-element(event)» can be used to process this common content.

❑ Patterns that match all elements in a substitution group can also be useful in contexts other than <xsl:template>. For example, suppose a genealogy database allows a <person> element to contain any number of <event> elements among its children, and that elements such as <birth>, <death>, <baptism>, and <burial> are defined as elements within the substitution group for <event>. In this case, if you want to number the events for a particular person you can use <xsl:number count="schema-element(event)"/>.

Predicates

The form of a Predicate is defined in the XPath expression language: it is any expression enclosed in square brackets. For example «[speaker='Hamlet']», or «[@width> 100]» or «[*]», or «[1]». A PatternStep may include any number of predicates. These are additive — a node must satisfy all the predicates if it is to match.

There are two kinds of predicate: those that depend on the node's position relative to its siblings, and those that don't. A positional predicate is one whose value is a number, or one that uses the functions `position()` or `last()`; all others are nonpositional. For example, the predicates «[1]», «[position() !=1]», and «[last()-1]» are all positional predicates, whereas «[@name = 'Tokyo']» and «[*]» are nonpositional.

For a nonpositional predicate, its meaning is that the `PatternStep` matches a node only if the *effective boolean value* of the predicate is true. The concept of effective boolean value is defined in XPath, and is summarized in the entry for `<xsl:if>` on page 353 in Chapter 6. For example, the predicate «[@security = 'secret']» is true when the node has a `security` attribute whose value is 'secret', so any `PatternStep` that uses this predicate will fail if the node has no `security` attribute or if the `security` attribute has any value other than 'secret'.

For a positional predicate, the meaning of the predicate can be deduced from the formal rules given at the start of this chapter. However, it is easier to understand their meaning by using informal rules. A numeric predicate such as «[1]» or «[last()-1]» is equivalent to the boolean predicate «[position() = 1]» or «[position() = last()-1]». So to evaluate a positional predicate, we need to know what `position()` and `last()` are.

The use of positional predicates with the attribute axis doesn't make much sense, because the order of attributes is undefined (though I did see one stylesheet that was using «@*[1]» to match the first attribute, and «@*» — which has lower priority — to match the others, which is perfectly legitimate so long as you realize that it's unpredictable which of the attributes will be the first). In the following description, I'll assume that you're using the child axis.

If there is only one predicate in the `PatternStep`, or if this predicate is the first, then:

❑   `last()` is the number of siblings of the node being tested that satisfy the `NodeTest` (including the node itself). For example, if we are testing a `<para>` element against the pattern «para[last() = 1]», then `last()` is the number of `<para>` elements that are children of the parent of the `<para>` element being tested. This pattern will match any `<para>` element that is the only `<para>` child of its parent.

❑   `position()` is the position of the node being tested among these siblings, taking them in document order and counting from one. So «para[1]», which means «para[position() = 1]», will match any `<para>` element that is the first `<para>` child of its parent element, in document order.

Note that it is the position of the node relative to its siblings that counts, not the position in the sequence you are processing the nodes. For example, suppose you want to process all the `<glossary-entry>` elements in a document, in alphabetical order. You can write:

```
<xsl:apply-templates select="//glossary-entry">
    <xsl:sort/>
<xsl:apply-templates>
```

Then suppose you have the following two template rules:

```
<xsl:template match="glossary-entry[1]">
. . .
</xsl:template>
<xsl:template match="glossary-entry">
. . .
</xsl:template>
```

The first template rule will be used for any `<glossary-entry>` that is the first `<glossary-entry>` child of its parent. Not, as you might expect, the first `<glossary-entry>` in alphabetical order, nor even the first `<glossary-entry>` element in the document. If you want to apply different processing to the `<glossary-entry>` that is first in alphabetical order, the way to do it is as follows:

```
<xsl:template match="glossary-entry">
  <xsl:choose>
    <xsl:when test="position()=1">
      . . .
    </xsl:when>
    <xsl:otherwise>
      . . .
    </xsl:otherwise>
  </xsl:choose>
</xsl:template>
```

This is because the context position within the body of the template rule is the position of the node in the list of nodes being processed, whereas the result for deciding whether a node matches a pattern is the same regardless of the processing context.

If there are several predicates in the PatternStep, then position() and last() in predicates after the first apply to the nodes that survived the previous predicates. So «speech[speaker= 'Hamlet'] [1]» matches a `<speech>` element that is the first `<speech>` element among its siblings, counting only those `<speech>` elements in which one of the `<speaker>`s is Hamlet.

The position() and last() functions relate to children of the same parent even when the «//» operator is used. For example, «chapter//footnote[1]» matches any footnote element that is a descendant of a `<chapter>` element and that is the first footnote child of its parent. There is no simple way to write a pattern that matches the first footnote element in a `<chapter>`, because the relevant expression «(chapter//footnote)[1]» is not a valid pattern. (Why not? No good reason, it's just that the spec doesn't allow it.)

If you do need to write a template rule for the first `<footenote>` element in a `<chapter>`, the cleanest solution is probably to write your own function. You can invoke this in a predicate within the pattern, for example «match="footnote[test:position-in-chapter(.) = 1]"». The definition of the function might look like this.

```
<xsl:function name="test:position-in-chapter" as="xs:integer">
  <xsl:param name="in" as="element()"/>
  <xsl:number level="any" from="chapter"/>
</xsl:function>
```

Examples

The following table provides some examples of PatternSteps.

Construct	Meaning
child::title	Matches elements named `<title>`.
title	Short form of «child::title».
attribute::title	Matches attributes named `<title>`.

continued

Construct	Meaning
`@title`	Short form of «attribute::title».
`*[@width]`	Matches an element node that has an attribute named `width`.
`text()[starts-with(.,'The')]`	Matches a text node whose text content starts with the characters «The».
`p[@code][position() lt 10]`	Matches a `<p>` element that is among the first nine `<p>` elements of its parent that have a `code` attribute.
`p[position() lt 10][@code]`	Matches a `<p>` element that is among the first nine `<p>` elements of its parent and that has a `code` attribute.
`*[not(@code = preceding-sibling::*/@code)]`	Matches an element node provided that it does not have a `code` attribute with the same value as the `code` attribute of any preceding sibling element.
`comment()`	Matches any comment node.
`@comment()`	Matches comment nodes that are found on the attribute axis of their parent node. Because the attribute axis contains attribute nodes only, this condition can never be satisfied; nevertheless, it is a legal `PatternStep`.

IdKeyPattern

This construct allows a pattern to be matched only if the node being tested (or one of its ancestors) has a specified ID attribute or key value.

This construct is a subset of the `FunctionCall` construct in an Expression, described in Chapter 7. The only function calls that can be used in a pattern (except within predicates) are the `id()` and `key()` functions, and these can be used only with arguments that are literals or variable references.

The `id()` function is an XPath function, while the `key()` function is exclusive to XSLT. Both are described in Chapter 13.

Syntax

Expression	Syntax
`IdKeyPattern`	«id» «(» Value «)» | «key» «(» StringLiteral «,» Value «)»
`Value`	Literal|VariableReference

For both the `id()` and `key()` functions, the required value of the ID or key can be specified as either a literal or a variable reference (in the form «$» QName). For the `id()` function, the only kind of literal that makes sense is a string literal (for example, «"E-102"»). For the key function, numeric literals also make sense if the key values are numeric. It is not possible to supply literals for other data types such as `xs:date` values.

With the `key()` function, the first argument is the name of the key. This must be specified as a string literal, and it must match the name of a key defined in the stylesheet.

Usage

This facility provides an equivalent to the ability in Cascading Style Sheets (CSS) to define a style for a specific node in the source document. Here are some ways it can be used:

❏ If for a particular source document you want to use a general-purpose stylesheet, but want to override its behavior for certain selected nodes, you can write a stylesheet that imports the general-purpose one and then write the overriding rules in the form of templates that match specific identified elements in the source document.

❏ Sometimes the source document is generated dynamically from a database. Perhaps there is something in the source document you want to highlight, say the search term that was used to locate this record. You could flag this item while generating the source document by giving it a special ID attribute value known to the stylesheet.

In practice, this construct isn't as useful as it might seem. Even though XSLT 2.0 has made it a lot more flexible by allowing the value to be specified as a variable (which in general is likely to be a stylesheet parameter), this form of pattern still achieves nothing that can't be achieved just as easily with a predicate, and it is unlikely to be any more efficient.

For example, if `<book>` elements are keyed on their ISBN property, which is implemented as a child element, then the following declarations are equivalent:

Using a direct pattern match:

```
<xsl:template match="book[isbn='1-861002-68-8']">
```

Using a key definition:

```
<xsl:key name="isbn-key" match="book" use="isbn"/>
<xsl:template match="key('isbn-key', '1-861002-68-8')>
```

Of course, there may be a performance difference between the two, but this depends on how the XSLT processor is implemented. There is certainly no intrinsic reason why the predicate should be less efficient.

Examples

`id('figure1')`	Matches a node with an ID attribute equal to the string `'figure1'`. An attribute is an ID attribute if it is defined in the Document Type Definition (DTD) or schema as having type `ID` (the name of the attribute is irrelevant).
`key('empnr',$ pers)`	Matches a node having a value of `$pers` for the key named «empnr», where `$pers` is typically a stylesheet parameter.

The following example shows how this feature can be used in a stylesheet.

Example: Using the key() Pattern to Format a Specific Node

This example shows how to use the `key()` pattern to format one selected node differently from the others. The selected node will be specified by a stylesheet parameter.

Source

The source document, `itinerary.xml`, is a tour itinerary.

```
<itinerary>
<day number="1">Arrive in Cairo</day>
<day number="2">Visit the Pyramids at Gaza</day>
<day number="3">Archaelogical Museum at Cairo</day>
<day number="4">Flight to Luxor; coach to Aswan</day>
<day number="5">Visit Temple at Philae and Aswan High Dam</day>
<day number="6">Cruise to Edfu</day>
<day number="7">Cruise to Luxor; visit Temple at Karnak</day>
<day number="8">Valley of the Kings</day>
<day number="9">Return flight from Luxor</day>
</itinerary>
```

Stylesheet

Let's start with a straightforward stylesheet, `itinerary.xsl`, to display this itinerary.

```
<?xml version="1.0" encoding="iso-8859-1"?>
<xsl:stylesheet version="2.0"
      xmlns:xsl="http://www.w3.org/1999/XSL/Transform">
<xsl:template match="/">
  <html>
    <head>
      <title>Itinerary</title>
    </head>
    <body><center>
      <xsl:apply-templates select="//day"/>
    </center></body>
  </html>
</xsl:template>
<xsl:template match="day">
  <h3>Day <xsl:value-of select="@number"/></h3>
  <p><xsl:apply-templates/></p>
</xsl:template>
</xsl:stylesheet>
```

Now let's specialize this by importing it into another stylesheet, `today.xsl`, which displays the activities for a selected day in red.

```
<?xml version="1.0" encoding="iso-8859-1"?>
<xsl:stylesheet version="2.0"
      xmlns:xsl="http://www.w3.org/1999/XSL/Transform"
      xmlns:xs="http://www.w3.org/2001/XMLSchema"
```

```
        exclude-result-prefixes="xs">
<xsl:import href="itinerary.xsl"/>
<xsl:param name="highlight-day" as="xs:integer" required="yes"/>
<xsl:key name="day-number" match="day" use="xs:integer(@number)"/>
<xsl:template match="key('day-number', $highlight-day)//text()">
    <font color="red"><xsl:value-of select="."/></font>
</xsl:template>
</xsl:stylesheet>
```

To run this stylesheet using Saxon, enter the command line:

```
java net.sf.saxon.Transform -t itinerary.xml today.xsl highlight-day=5
```

Output

The resulting output is as follows, when the $highlight-day parameter is set to 5:

```
<html>
   <head>
      <META http-equiv="Content-Type" content="text/html; charset=utf-8">
      <title>Itinerary</title>
   </head>
   <body>
      <center>
         <h3>Day 1</h3>
         <p>Arrive in Cairo</p>
         <h3>Day 2</h3>
         <p>Visit the Pyramids at Gaza</p>
         <h3>Day 3</h3>
         <p>Archaelogical Museum at Cairo</p>
         <h3>Day 4</h3>
         <p>Flight to Luxor; coach to Aswan</p>
         <h3>Day 5</h3>
         <p><font color="red">
            Visit Temple at Philae and Aswan High Dam</font></p>
         <h3>Day 6</h3>
         <p>Cruise to Edfu</p>
         <h3>Day 7</h3>
         <p>Cruise to Luxor; visit Temple at Karnak</p>
         <h3>Day 8</h3>
         <p>Valley of the Kings</p>
         <h3>Day 9</h3>
         <p>Return flight from Luxor</p>
      </center>
   </body>
</html>
```

While this example shows one way of using this feature, I have to admit that it's not very convincing. You could achieve the same effect by writing the relevant pattern as «day[@number = 5]», without the need to introduce a key at all.

Summary

This chapter described the syntax and meanings of patterns, whose main use in an XSLT stylesheet is to define which template rules apply to which nodes in the source document, but which are also used in the `<xsl:key>`, `<xsl:number>`, and `<xsl:for-each-group>` elements.

Patterns, although their syntax is a subset of that for XPath expressions, are evaluated in a different way from expressions, though we saw that the formal rules express the meaning of a pattern in terms of the corresponding expression.

The next chapter describes the library of standard functions that can be used within XPath expressions in a stylesheet.

13

The Function Library

This chapter describes all the standard functions included in the XSLT 2.0 and XPath 2.0 specifications for use in XPath expressions. Most of these functions are defined in the W3C specification *XPath 2.0 and XQuery 1.0 Functions and Operators*, and these should be available in all XPath 2.0 implementations. Others, marked as XSLT-only, are defined in the XSLT 2.0 specification, and are available only in XPath expressions used within an XSLT stylesheet.

For each function, I give its name, a brief description of its purpose, a list of the arguments it expects and the value it returns, the formal rules defining what the function does, and finally usage advice and examples.

These are not the only functions you can call from an XPath expression:

❑ So-called *constructor functions* are available, corresponding to built-in and user-defined atomic types. For example, there is a function called xs:float() to create values of type xs:float, xs:date() to create values of type xs:date, and so on. These functions are also available for user-defined atomic types. They are described in Chapter 11.

❑ User-defined functions can be created using the XSLT <xsl:function> declaration; these functions are available for calling from XPath expressions in the stylesheet.

❑ Vendor-defined functions may be available. These will be in a namespace controlled by the vendor of the particular product.

❑ It may be possible to call functions written in external languages such as Java, JavaScript, or C#. See Chapter 16 for details.

❑ When XPath is used within another host language, additional functions may be defined. For example, the XForms specification uses XPath and defines a number of XForms-specific functions for use in that environment.

The syntax of a function call is described in Chapter 7. This defines where a function call can be used in an expression, and where it can't. You can use a function call anywhere that an expression or value can be used, provided that the type of value it returns is appropriate to the context where it used. (Unlike XPath 1.0, this includes the ability to use a function call as a step in a path expression.) Within a function call, the values supplied as arguments can be any XPath expression, subject only to the rules on types (for example, some functions require an argument that is a sequence of nodes). So a function call such as «count(..)», though it looks strange, is perfectly legal: «..» is a valid XPath expression that returns the parent of the context node (it's described in Chapter 9, on page 623).

I've arranged the functions in alphabetical order (combining the XPath-defined and XSLT-defined functions into a single sequence), so you can find a function quickly if you know what you're looking for. However, in case you only know the general area you are interested in, you may find the classification that follows in the section *Functions by Category* useful. This is followed by a section called *Notation*, which describes the notation used for function specifications in this chapter. The rest of the chapter is taken up with the functions themselves, in alphabetical order.

A Word about Naming

Function names such as `current-dateTime()` seem very strange when you first come across them. Why the mixture of camelCasing and hyphenation? The reason they arise is that XPath 1.0 decided to use hyphenated lower-case names for all functions, while XML Schema decided to use camelCase for the names of built-in types. Wherever the XPath 2.0 function library uses a schema-defined type name as part of a function name, it therefore uses the camelCase type name as a single word within the hyphenated function name.

So it may be madness, but there is method in it!

Throughout this book, I write these function names without a namespace prefix. In fact the functions are defined to be within the namespace `http://www.w3.org/2005/xpath-functions`, which is often referred to using the namespace prefix «fn». (Earlier drafts of the specification used different namespaces, which you may still encounter). In XSLT this is the default namespace for function names, so you will never need to write them with a namespace prefix. I have therefore omitted the prefix when referring to the names in this book. In the W3C specifications, however, you will often see the functions referred to by names such as `fn:position()` or `fn:count()`.

Functions by Category

Any attempt to classify functions is bound to be arbitrary, but I'll attempt it anyway. A few functions appear in more than one category. The number after each function is a page reference to the entry where the function is described. Functions marked † are available in XSLT only (that is, they are not available when executing freestanding XPath expressions or in XQuery).

Boolean Functions

`boolean()` 721, `false()` 779, `not()` 850, `true()` 899.

Numeric Functions

`abs()` 714, `avg()` 718, `ceiling()` 723, `floor()` 779, †`format-number()` 788, `max()` 830, `min()` 830, `number()` 851, `round()` 870, `round-half-to-even()` 872, `sum()` 889.

String Functions

`codepoints-to-string()` 725, `compare()` 727, `concat()` 729, `contains()` 730, `ends-with()` 773, `lower-case()` 827, `matches()` 828, `normalize-space()` 845, `normalize-unicode()` 847, `replace()` 862, `starts-with()` 875, `string()` 877, `string-join()` 879, `string-length()` 880, `string-to-codepoints()` 881, `substring()` 883, `substring-after()` 885, `substring-before()` 887, `tokenize()` 894, `upper-case()` 910.

Date and Time Functions

adjust-date-to-timezone() 715, adjust-dateTime-to-timezone() 715, adjust-time-to-timezone() 715, current-date() 738, current-dateTime() 738, current-time() 738, day-from-date() 744, day-from-dateTime() 744, †format-date() 781, †format-dateTime() 781, †format-time() 781, hours-from-dateTime() 800, hours-from-time() 800, implicit-timezone() 806, minutes-from-dateTime() 832, minutes-from-time() 832, month-from-date() 833, month-from-dateTime() 833, seconds-from-dateTime() 873, seconds-from-time() 873, timezone-from-date() 893, timezone-from-dateTime() 893, timezone-from-time() 893, year-from-date() 911, year-from-dateTime() 911.

Duration Functions

days-from-duration() 745, hours-from-duration() 801, minutes-from-duration() 832, months-from-duration() 834, seconds-from-duration() 874, years-from-duration() 911.

Aggregation Functions

avg() 718, count() 733, max() 830, min() 830, sum() 889.

Functions on URIs

base-uri() 719, collection() 726, doc() 750, doc-available() 750, document-uri() 764, encode-for-uri() 771, escape-html-uri() 775, iri-to-uri() 811, resolve-uri() 867, static-base-uri() 876, †unparsed-text() 904, †unparsed-text-available() 904.

Functions on QNames

local-name-from-QName()826, namespace-uri-from-QName()841, node-name() 843, prefix-from-QName() 857, QName() 858, resolve-QName() 864.

Functions on Sequences

count() 733, deep-equal() 745, distinct-values() 749, empty() 770, exists() 778, index-of() 807, insert-before() 810, remove() 861, subsequence() 882, unordered() 901.

Functions That Return Properties of Nodes

base-uri() 719, data() 741, document-uri() 764, †generate-id() 797, in-scope-prefixes() 808, lang() 819, local-name() 824, name() 835, namespace-uri() 837, namespace-uri-for-prefix() 839, nilled() 842, node-name() 843, root() 870, string() 877, †unparsed-entity-public-id() 902, †unparsed-entity-uri() 902.

Functions That Find Nodes

collection() 726, doc() 750, †document() 754, id() 802, idref() 804, †key() 812, root() 870.

Functions That Return Context Information

base-uri() 719, collection() 726, †current() 734, current-date() 738, current-dateTime() 738, †current-group() 739, †current-grouping-key() 740, current-time() 738, default-collation() 748, doc() 750, implicit-timezone() 806, last() 820, position() 854, †regex-group() 860.

Diagnostic Functions

`error()` 774, `trace()` 896.

Functions That Return Information about the XSLT Environment

†`element-available()` 764, †`function-available()` 792, †`system-property()`890, †`type-available()`899

Functions That Assert a Static Type

`exactly-one()` 777, `one-or-more()` 853, `zero-or-one()` 912.

Notation

For each function (or for a closely related group of functions) there is an alphabetical entry in this chapter containing the following information:

- ❑ The name of the function

- ❑ A summary of the purpose of the function, often with a quick example

- ❑ *Changes in 2.0.* In cases where a function was present in XSLT 1.0 or XPath 1.0, the entry for the function in this chapter contains a section that describes any changes in behavior introduced in the 2.0 version of the specs. If there are no changes, this section will say so. In cases where the function is new in XPath 2.0 or XSLT 2.0, this section is omitted.

- ❑ The function signature, described below

- ❑ A section entitled *Effect*, which describes in fairly formal terms what the function does

- ❑ Where appropriate, a section entitled *Usage*, which give advice on how to make best use of the function

- ❑ A set of simple examples showing the function in action

- ❑ Cross-references to other related information in this book

Technically, a function in XPath is identified by its name and arity (number of arguments). This means that there is no formal relationship between the function `substring()` with two arguments and the function `substring()` with three arguments. However, the standard function library has been designed so that in cases like this where there are two functions with different arity, the functions in practice have a close relationship, and it is generally easier to think of them as representing one function with one or more of the arguments being optional. So this is how I have presented them.

The signatures of functions are defined with a table like the one that follows:

Argument	Type	Meaning
input	`xs:string?`	The containing string
start	`xs:double`	The position in the containing string of . . .
length (optional)	`xs:double`	The number of characters to be included . . .
Result	*xs:string*	*The required substring . . .*

The first column here gives a conventional name for the argument (or "Result" to label the row that describes the result of the function). Arguments to XPath functions are supplied by position, not by name, so the name given here is arbitrary; it is provided only to allow the argument to be referred to within the descriptive text. The text "(optional)" after the name of an argument indicates that this argument does not need to be supplied; in this case, this means that there is one version of the function with two arguments, and another version with three.

The second column gives the required type of the argument. The notation is that of the `SequenceType` syntax in XPath, introduced in Chapter 11. This consists of an item type followed optionally by an occurrence indicator («?», «*», or «+»). The item type is either the name of a built-in atomic type such as `xs:integer` or `xs:string`, or one of the following:

Item type	Meaning
`item()`	Any item (either a node or an atomic value)
`node()`	Any node
`element()`	Any element node
`xs:anyAtomicType`	Any atomic value
`Numeric`	An `xs:double`, `xs:float`, `xs:decimal`, or `xs:integer`

The occurrence indicator, if it is present, is either «?» to indicate that the supplied argument can contain zero or one items of the specified item type, or «*» to indicate that it can be a sequence of zero or more items of the specified item type. (The occurrence indicator «+», meaning one or more, is not used in any of the standard functions.)

Note the difference between an argument that is optional, and an argument that has an occurrence indicator of «?». When the argument is optional, it can be omitted from the function call. When the occurrence indicator is «?», the value must be supplied, but the empty sequence «()» is an acceptable value for the argument.

Many functions follow the convention of allowing an empty sequence for the first argument, or for subsequent arguments that play a similar role to the first argument, and returning an empty sequence if any of these arguments is an empty sequence. This is designed to make these functions easier to use in predicates. However, this is only a convention, and it is not followed universally. Most of the string functions instead treat an empty sequence the same way as a zero-length string.

When these functions are called, the supplied arguments are converted to the required type in the standard way defined by the XPath 2.0 function calling mechanism. The details of this depend on whether XPath 1.0 backward compatibility is activated or not. In XSLT this depends on the value of the `[xsl:]version` attribute in the stylesheet, as follows:

❑ In 2.0 mode, the standard conversion rules apply. These rules appear in Chapter 6 on page 505, under the heading *Converting the Arguments and the Result*. They permit only the following kinds of conversion:

    ❑ Atomization of nodes to extract their numeric values

    ❑ Promotion of numeric values to a different numeric type; for example, `xs:integer` to `xs:double`

    ❑ Promotion of `xs:anyURI` values to `xs:string`

13

The Function Library

❑   Casting of a value of type `xs:untypedAtomic` to the required type. Such values generally arise by extracting the content of a node that has not been schema-validated. The rules for casting from `xs:untypedAtomic` values to values of other types are essentially the rules defined in XML Schema for conversion from the lexical space of the type to the value space: more details are given in Chapter 11 (see *Converting from string* on page 663).

❑   In 1.0 mode, two additional conversions are allowed:

      ❑   If the required type is `xs:string` or `xs:double` (perhaps with an occurrence indicator of «?»), then the first value in the supplied sequence is converted to the required type using the `string()` or `number()` function as appropriate, and other values in the sequence are discarded.

      ❑   If the required type is `node()` or `item()` (perhaps with an occurrence indicator of «?»), then if the supplied value contains more than one item, all items except the first are ignored.

The effect of these rules is that even though the function signature might give the expected type of an argument as `xs:string`, say, the value you supply can be a node containing a string, or a node whose value is untyped (because it has not been validated using a schema), or an `xs:anyURI` value. With 1.0 compatibility mode on, you can also supply values of other types; for example, an `xs:integer` or an `xs:date`; but when compatibility mode is off, you will need to convert such values to an `xs:string` yourself, which you can achieve most simply by calling the `string()` function.

Code Samples

Most of the examples for this chapter are single XPath expressions. In the download file for this book, these code snippets are gathered into stylesheets, which in turn are organized according to the name of the function they exercise. In many cases the examples use no source document, in which case the stylesheet generally has a single template named `main`, which should be used as the entry point. In other cases the source document is generally named `source.xml`, and it should be used as the principal input to the stylesheet. Any stylesheets that require a schema-aware processor have names of the form `xxx-sa.xsl`.

Function Definitions

The remainder of this chapter gives the definitions of all the functions, in alphabetical order.

abs

The `abs()` function returns the absolute value of a number. For example, «`abs(-3)`» returns 3.

Signature

Argument	Type	Meaning
input	Numeric?	The supplied number.
Result	*Numeric?*	*The absolute value of the supplied number. The result has the same type as the input.*

Effect

If the supplied number is positive, then it is returned unchanged. If it is negative, then the result is «`-$input`».

Negative zero and negative infinity become positive zero and positive infinity. Positive zero, positive infinity, and NaN are returned unchanged. If the argument is an empty sequence, the result is an empty sequence.

The result has the same primitive numeric type as the input. For example, if the input value is an xs:integer, the result will be an xs:integer, and if the input is an xs:double, the result will be an xs:double.

> *Primitive here means one of the four types* xs:double, xs:float, xs:decimal, *and* xs:integer. *Clearly, if the input is an* xs:negativeInteger, *the result cannot also be an* xs:negativeInteger — *it will actually be an* xs:integer. *If the input is an* xs:positiveInteger, *you have a guarantee that the result will be an* xs:integer, *but this doesn't prevent the system returning something that is actually a subtype of* xs:integer — *for example, it would be legitimate to return the original* xs:positiveInteger *unchanged.*

Examples

Expression	Result
abs(2)	2
abs(-2)	2
abs(-3.7)	3.7
abs(-1.0e-7)	1.0e-7
abs(number('NaN'))	NaN

adjust-date-to-timezone, adjust-dateTime-to-timezone, adjust-time-to-timezone

This entry describes a collection of three closely related functions. These functions have the effect of returning a date, time, or dateTime based on a supplied date, time, or dateTime, modified by adding, removing, or altering the timezone component of the value.

Signature

Argument	Type	Meaning
input	xs:date?, xs:dateTime?, or xs:time?	The date, time, or dateTime value whose timezone is to be adjusted. The type of this value must correspond to the name of the function invoked. For example, in the case of adjust-time-to-timezone() it must be an xs:time value.
timezone (optional)	xs:dayTimeDuration?	Specifies the new timezone value. If this argument is omitted, the effect is the same as setting it to the result of the function implicit-timezone().
Result	*xs:date?, xs:dateTime?, or xs:time?*	*The adjusted date, dateTime, or time value.*

Effect

If the input is an empty sequence, the result is an empty sequence.

If there is no `timezone` argument (that is, if the function is called with a single argument), the effect is the same as calling the function with a second argument of «`implicit-timezone()`». This adjusts the value to the timezone supplied in the dynamic context, which ideally will be the timezone where the user is located.

If the `timezone` argument is supplied, and is not an empty sequence, then it must be a duration between −50400 seconds and +50400 seconds, that is ±14 hours. To specify a timezone one hour ahead of UTC, write «`xs:dayTimeDuration("PT1H")`».

These functions can be used to remove a timezone from a value that has a timezone, to add a timezone to a value that lacks a timezone, or to return the value that is equivalent to the supplied value, but in a different timezone. These effects are summarized in the table below.

Existing timezone	timezone argument is ()	timezone argument is not ()
Absent	returns the input value unchanged	result has the same components as input, with the addition of the specified timezone
Present	result is the localized value of the input, with the timezone removed	result represents the same instant as the input value, but in a different timezone

The only complex case here is the one in the bottom-right cell of the table, where the supplied value already has a timezone and this is to be replaced with a new timezone. The effect varies slightly depending on which if the three functions is used:

❑ For an `xs:dateTime`, the result is an `xs:dateTime` that represents the same instant in time as the input value, but in the new timezone.

❑ For an `xs:time`, the result is an `xs:time` that represents the time in the new timezone that is simultaneous with the time provided as the input value.

❑ For an `xs:date`, the date is converted to an `xs:dateTime` representing 00:00:00 on the specified date; the requested adjustment is applied to this `xs:dateTime` value, and the result is the date part of the adjusted `xs:dateTime`.

Examples

Assume that `$CET` is set to the timezone value +01:00, represented by the `xs:dayTimeDuration` PT1H. Assume that `$EST` is set to the timezone value -05:00, represented by the `xs:dayTimeDuration` -PT5H. Assume also that the implicit timezone is the timezone value -08:00, represented by the `xs:dayTimeDuration` -PT8H.

Here are some examples using `xs:time` values:

Expression	Result
`adjust-time-to-timezone( xs:time("15:00:00+01:00"), $EST)`	`09:00:00-05:00`
`adjust-time-to-timezone( xs:time("15:00:00"), $EST)`	`15:00:00-05:00`
`adjust-time-to-timezone( xs:time("15:00:00+01:00"))`	`06:00:00-08:00`
`adjust-time-to-timezone( xs:time("15:00:00+01:00"), ())`	`15:00:00`
`adjust-time-to-timezone( xs:time("15:00:00"), ())`	`15:00:00`

The corresponding examples using xs:dateTime values are:

Expression	Result
adjust-dateTime-to-timezone(xs:dateTime("2008-03-01T15:00:00+01:00"), $EST)	2008-03-01T09:00:00-05:00
adjust-dateTime-to-timezone (xs: dateTime("2008-03-01T15:00:00"), $EST)	2008-03-01T15:00:00-05:00
adjust-dateTime-to-timezone (xs: dateTime("2008-03-01T15:00:00+01:00"))	2008-03-01T06:00:00-08:00
adjust-dateTime-to-timezone (xs:dateTime("2008-03-01T15:00:00+01:00"), ())	2008-03-01T15:00:00
adjust-dateTime-to-timezone (xs: dateTime("2008-03-01T15:00:00"), ())	2008-03-01T15:00:00

Adjusting the timezone component of a date is a less intuitive operation, but is still well defined:

Expression	Result
adjust-date-to-timezone(xs:date("2008-03-01+01:00"), $EST)	2008-02-29-05:00
adjust-date-to-timezone(xs:date("2008-03-01"), $EST)	2008-03-01-05:00
adjust-date-to-timezone(xs:date("2008-03-01+01:00"))	2008-02-29-08:00
adjust-date-to-timezone(xs:date("2008-03-01+01:00"), ())	2008-03-01
adjust-date-to-timezone(xs:date("2008-03-01"), ())	2008-03-01

Usage

Values of types xs:dateTime, xs:time, and xs:date() either have a timezone component, or have no timezone. If they have a timezone component, it is useful to think in terms of two properties of the value, which we can call the local value and the absolute value. For example suppose you call current-time() and the implicit timezone is the timezone for Germany, +01:00. The value returned might be 14:54:06+01:00. The absolute value of this is the equivalent time in UTC (or "Zulu time", popularly Greenwich Mean Time or GMT). This is 13:54:06. The local value is the time in its original timezone, 14:54:06.

Converting the value to a string always gives you the local value: 14:54:06+01:00. Getting the components of the value also returns a component of the local value: hours-from-time() applied to this value returns 14. But comparisons between two values, or calculations such as adding a duration, use the absolute value.

You can in effect freeze a value in its current timezone by calling adjust-X-to-timezone() with an empty sequence «()» as the second argument. Applied to this value, the result will be the time 14:54:06, with no timezone component. Calling hours-from-time() on this value will still return 14.

You can also determine the equivalent time in a different timezone by calling adjust-X-to-timezone() specifying the new timezone. If the input value is 14:54:06+01:00, and the new timezone is +00:00, the result will be a time value whose absolute value and local value are both 13:54:06. When you convert this to a string, the value is «13:54:06Z», and when you call hours-from-time(), the result is «13». Similarly, if you adjust this value to the timezone −05:00 (New York time), the absolute value will still be 13:54:06, but the local value will be 08:54:06.

13

The Function Library

If you have a value with no timezone component, you can set a timezone, either by supplying the required timezone in the second argument or by omitting the second argument, which sets the timezone to the implicit timezone taken from the evaluation context. When you do this, the local value of the result will be the same as the timezoneless input value. For example, if the input is 14:54:06, and you set the timezone to −08:00, then the local value of the result will be 14:54:06, which means that its absolute value will be 22:54:06. When you convert the result to a string, the result will be «14:54:06-08:00», and when you extract the hours component, the result will be «14».

The functions work slightly differently for the three types:

- ❑ For xs:dateTime, an adjustment to the time may also cause the date to change. For example, if the input time is 2008:02:29T22:00:00Z, then adjusting the timezone to +10:00 will produce the local value 2008:03:01T08:00:00+10:00.

- ❑ For xs:time, all adjustments are made modulo 24 hours.

- ❑ For xs:date, the value is treated as if it were an xs:dateTimerepresenting 00:00:00 on the specified date. The adjustment is made to this xs:dateTime, and the time component is then removed. For example, if the input date is 2004:03:31+00:00, then adjusting the timezone to −05:00 will return the date 2004:02:29−05:00. This involves an inevitable loss of information. You can read the semantics of the function as being "tell me what the date is in a place in timezone X, at the time when the day represented by a given date has just started in timezone Y".

See Also

implicit-timezone() on page 806

avg

The avg() function returns the average of a sequence of numbers or durations.

Signature

Argument	Type	Meaning
sequence	xs:anyAtomicType*	The input sequence. Any untyped atomic values in the input are converted to xs:double values. The resulting sequence must consist entirely of numbers, or entirely of durations of the same kind.
Result	xs:anyAtomicType?	*The average of the values in the input sequence. This will be a value of the same primitive type as the values in the input sequence. If the input values are xs:integer values, the result will be an xs:decimal.*

Effect

If the input sequence is empty, the result is an empty sequence. This is not an error, even though a literal interpretation of the rules would involve dividing by zero.

In all other cases the result is the same as «sum($sequence) div count($sequence)». Note that $sequence here is the atomized sequence generated by the function calling mechanism. If the sequence supplied in the call was a sequence of nodes, the number of atomic values is not necessarily the same as the number of nodes. For example, if «avg(@a)» is called to process a single attribute that is defined in the schema to contain a list of integers, then it will return the average of these integers.

The sequence of operations is as follows:

1. The sequence supplied in the argument is atomized (this is a standard action of the function calling rules when the required type only allows atomic values).

2. Any untyped atomic values in the resulting sequence (typically, values extracted from nodes in a schemaless document) are converted to xs:double values. If this conversion fails, a runtime error is reported.

3. If the sequence now contains any NaN (not-a-number) values, the result of the avg() function is NaN.

4. If the values are all numeric, they are summed according to the rules for the numeric «+» operator, which means that the result will depend on the types that are present in the sequence. If there is at least one xs:double, the sum will be an xs:double; otherwise, if there is an xs:float it will be an xs:float, otherwise xs:decimal or xs:integer.

5. If the values are all durations, they are similarly summed according to the rules of the «+» operator. In consequence, it is not possible to mix the two duration types, xs:dayTimeDuration and xs:yearMonthDuration.

6. Finally, the total is divided by the number of items using the «div» operator. In the case of a numeric total, this means that the average will be the same numeric type as the sum, unless the sum is an xs:integer in which case the average will be an xs:decimal. If the items are durations, the result will be a duration of the same type as the items.

The processor is allowed to use a different algorithm which might behave differently in the event of arithmetic overflow.

Examples

Expression	Result
avg((1.0, 2.6, 3.0))	xs:decimal('2.2')
avg(())	()
avg((1, xs:float('3.5'), 5.5))	xs:float('3.3333333')
avg((1, 2, 3))	xs:decimal('2.0')
avg((xs:dayTimeDuration('P1D'), xs:dayTimeDuration ('PT12H')))	xs:dayTimeDuration ('PT18H')

See Also

count() on page 733
max() on page 830
min() on page 830
sum() on page 889

base-uri

The base-uri() function returns the base URI of a specific node in a document.

Signature

Argument	Type	Meaning
input-node (optional)	`node()?`	The node whose base URI is required
Result	`xs:string`	*The base URI of the node specified in the first argument, or the context node if there are no arguments*

Effect

When the function is called with no arguments, the effect is the same as supplying the argument «.» — that is, it returns the base URI of the context node. If there is no context node, an error is reported.

When the first argument is present, the function returns the base URI of the input node supplied. This is a property of the node, defined in the data model. If the node was created by parsing raw XML, then the base URI is typically the URI of the resource containing the raw XML used to create the node. If the input XML used external entities, or if it was assembled from multiple source documents using XInclude, then the base URI will identify the original external entity or source document. The base URI of a node may also be altered by using the `xml:base` attribute in the XML. This attribute is defined in the W3C Recommendation *XML Base* (`www.w3.org/TR/XMLBase`).

The base URI of a node is typically used when resolving a relative URI contained in the value of that node. By definition, relative URIs refer to files (or to be more general, resources) relative to the base URI of the file containing the relative URI.

When nodes are not created directly by parsing raw XML, the concept of base URI is not so clear-cut. XSLT defines that a node in a temporary tree derives its base URI from the base URI of the stylesheet.

If the first argument is supplied, but its value is an empty sequence, the function returns an empty sequence. An empty sequence is also returned if the function is applied to a node that does not have a base URI (for example, a parentless attribute or text node), or if the base URI of the node is unknown.

Usage and Examples

The `base-uri()` function is useful mainly in conjunction with `resolve-uri()`: it gives you a base URI against which a relative URI can be resolved. For example, if you want to locate the document identified by a relative URI held in an `href` attribute in a source document, the following code should be used:

```
doc(resolve-uri(@href, base-uri(.)))
```

Where input documents are assembled from multiple external entities, the `base-uri()` function can also be useful for diagnostics, to report where an error or anomaly was found during processing. In one data cleansing application, I was able to create a report in which such anomalies were grouped according to the base URI of the element where they occured, and then sorted according to the document order of those elements, thus simplifying the job of manually correcting the errors.

See Also

boolean

The `boolean()` function calculates the *effective boolean value* of the supplied argument.

Changes in 2.0

The function has been generalized in XPath 2.0, so it accommodates a wider range of possible arguments.

Signature

Argument	Type	Meaning
value	item()*	The value whose effective boolean value is required
Result	xs:boolean	*The effective boolean value of the argument*

Effect

Many XPath 2.0 values have an effective boolean value. The `boolean()` function is used to calculate the effective boolean value explicitly, but it is also calculated implicitly in a number of contexts where a boolean value is required: see the *Usage* section below. The rules are as follows:

❏ If the argument is an empty sequence, then the effective boolean value is `false`.

❏ If the argument is a sequence whose first item is a node, then the effective boolean value is `true`.

❏ If the argument is a singleton `xs:boolean` value, the result is the value of the argument.

❏ If the argument is a singleton numeric value, the result is `false` if the argument is NaN or zero; otherwise, it is `true`.

❏ If the argument is a singleton instance of `xs:string`, `xs:anyURI`, or `xs:untypedAtomic`, the result is `false` if the string is zero length; otherwise, it is `true`.

❏ In all other cases, the function reports an error.

Examples

Assume the source document:

```
<doc>
  <emp name="John" age="53"/>
  <emp name="Mary"/>
</doc>
```

with the variable $John bound to the first `<emp>` element, and $Mary bound to the second.

Expression	Result
boolean(//emp[@age=21])	false
boolean(//emp[@age=53])	true
boolean(number($John/@age))	true
boolean(number($Mary/@age))	false
boolean(count($John/*))	false

continued

Expression	Result
`boolean(string($John/@surname))`	`false`
`boolean(string($John/@name))`	`true`
`boolean("true")`	`true`
`boolean("false")`	`true`

Usage

In most cases conversion to an `xs:boolean` occurs automatically when the context requires it; it is only necessary to call the `boolean()` function explicitly in order to force a conversion. For example, these rules are invoked automatically when an expression is used as the condition in an «if» expression, in the «satisfies» clause of the «some» and «every» expressions, and for the operands of «and» and «or». They are also invoked in XSLT stylesheets for expressions used in `<xsl:if>` and `<xsl:when>` instructions.

The detailed rules for establishing the effective boolean value may appear somewhat arbitrary. They were defined this way in large measure for backward compatibility with XPath 1.0, which allowed sequences of nodes but did not allow sequences of strings, booleans, or numbers. The rules will probably come naturally if you are familiar with weakly typed languages such as Perl or Python, but there are a few traps to beware of. For example, if you convert the boolean value `false` to a string, you get the string `"false"`, but the effective boolean value of this string is `true`.

The `boolean()` function does not always return the same result as the `xs:boolean()` constructor. `xs:boolean()` (like «cast as xs:boolean») follows the rules in XML Schema that define the lexical representations of the `xs:boolean` type. This treats the strings `"1"` and `"true"` as `true`, and `"0"` and `"false"` as `false`; anything else is an error.

XSLT Examples

The following example prints a message if the source document contains a `<header>` element and no `<footer>`, or if it contains a `<footer>` and no `<header>`.

```
<xsl:if test="boolean(//header) != boolean(//footer)">
   <xsl:message>Document must contain headers and footers,
                            or neither</xsl:message>
</xsl:if>
```

The conversion of the two node sequences «//header» (true if there are any `<header>` elements in the document) and «//footer» (true if there are any `<footer>` elements) needs to be explicit here, because we want to do a boolean comparison, not a comparison of two node sequences.

The following example sets a variable to the `xs:boolean` value `true` or `false`, depending on whether the document contains footnotes. In this case the explicit conversion is probably not necessary, since it could be done later when the variable is used, but it is probably more efficient to retain only an `xs:boolean` value in the variable rather than retaining the full set of footnote nodes. An intelligent XSLT processor will recognize that the expression «//footnote» occurs in a context where a boolean is required, and scan the document only until the first footnote is found, rather than retrieving all of them. (In this example, however, using the function `exists()` would achieve the same effect.)

```
<xsl:variable name="uses-footnotes" select="boolean(//footnote)"/>
```

See Also

exists() on page 778
false() on page 779
true() on page 899

ceiling

The ceiling() function rounds a supplied number up to the nearest whole number. For example, the expression «ceiling(33.9)» returns 34.

Changes in 2.0

The function has been generalized to work on all numeric types.

Signature

Argument	Type	Meaning
value	Numeric	The supplied value.
Result	Numeric	*The result of rounding $value up to the next highest integer. The result has the same primitive type as the supplied value.*

Effect

If the number is an xs:integer, or is equal to an xs:integer, then it is returned unchanged.

Otherwise, it is rounded up to the next highest whole number. If the supplied value is an xs:decimal, the result will be an xs:decimal, if it is an xs:double, the result will be an xs:double, and if it is an xs:float, the result will be an xs:float.

The xs:double and xs:float types in XPath support special values such as infinity, negative zero and NaN (not-a-number), which are described on page 199 in Chapter 5. If the argument is NaN, the result will be NaN. Similarly, when the argument is positive or negative infinity, the function will return the value of the argument unchanged.

If the argument value is an xs:double or xs:float greater than -1.0 but less than zero it will be rounded up to negative zero. For most practical purposes, negative zero and positive zero are indistinguishable, but dividing a number by negative zero produces negative infinity, while dividing by positive zero produces positive infinity.

Examples

Expression	Result
ceiling(1.0)	xs:decimal 1.0, displayed as «1»
ceiling(1.6)	xs:decimal 2.0, displayed as «2»
ceiling(17 div 3)	xs:decimal 6.0, displayed as «6»
ceiling(-3.0)	xs:decimal −3.0, displayed as «-3»
ceiling(-8.2e0)	xs:double −8.0e0, displayed as «-8»
ceiling(number('xxx'))	xs:double NaN, displayed as «NaN»
ceiling(-0.5e0)	xs:double −0.0e0, displayed as «-0»

13

The Function Library

Usage

One situation where this function is useful is when calculating the size of a table. If you have a sequence $ns and you want to arrange the values in three columns, then the number of rows needed is: «ceiling(count($ns) div 3)».

Although the result is numerically equal to an integer, it does not necessarily have the type xs:integer. You can force it to an integer by using the xs:integer() constructor function, for example, «xs:integer(ceiling(count($ns) div 3))».

See Also

floor() on page 779
round() on page 870
«idiv» operator on page 574 in Chapter 8

codepoint-equal

The codepoint-equal() function compares two strings character by character: the strings are equal if they contain the same sequence of characters, regardless of the default collation in force.

Signature

Argument	Type	Meaning
value-1	xs:string?	The first string to be compared
value-2	xs:string?	The second string to be compared
Result	*xs:boolean?*	*true if the two strings contain the same characters*

Effect

The function compares the two strings character by character, and returns true only if the strings are identical in terms of Unicode codepoints.

If either value-1 or value-2 is an empty sequence, the result is an empty sequence. This is an exception to the usual rule that string-handling functions treat an empty sequence as a zero-length string.

If the default collation is the Unicode codepoint collation, the result is exactly the same as comparing the strings using the XPath eq operator. The difference is that this function does not depend on how the default collation has been set up in the context. It is therefore useful when comparing strings such as filenames or purchase order numbers, where use of natural-language collations is inappropriate.

Although the function signature requires the arguments to be strings, the function calling rules ensure that it will also accept xs:anyURI values. In fact, it is particularly appropriate for comparing URIs and was added to the function library for that reason.

Examples

Expression	Result
codepoint-equal("http://www.w3.org/", "http://www.w3.org/")	true
codepoint-equal("http://www.w3.org/", "HTTP://www.w3.org/")	false
codepoint-equal("", "")	true
codepoint-equal((), "banana")	()

See Also

compare() on page 727
eq operator in Chapter 8 on page 582

codepoints-to-string

The codepoints-to-string() function takes as input a sequence of integers representing the Unicode codepoint values of the characters in a string, and returns the corresponding string. For example, «codepoints-to-string((65,66,67))» returns the string "ABC".

Signature

Argument	Type	Meaning
codepoints	xs:integer*	The sequence of codepoints. These must represent characters that are valid in XML 1.0 or XML 1.1, depending on the version that the processor supports.
Result	xs:string	*The string consisting of characters with the given codepoint values.*

Effect

The function returns a string whose characters correspond to the Unicode codepoints in the supplied sequence.

A character whose codepoint is above xFFFF must be supplied as a single integer value, not as two code values forming a surrogate pair.

If the supplied sequence is empty, the result will be a zero-length string.

A common case, of course, is where the sequence of codepoints contains a single integer, in which case the resulting string will be of length one.

Integers that do not represent valid codepoints cause a runtime error. This includes the case of codepoints that are valid in Unicode, but not in XML (for example the integer zero).

Examples

Expression	Result
codepoints-to-string((65, 83, 67, 73, 73))	"ASCII"
codepoints-to-string(48 to 57)	"0123456789"
codepoints-to-string(())	The zero-length string ("")
codepoints-to-string(64+$n)	The nth letter of the English alphabet

Usage

There are two main ways of using this function: as a way of constructing a string algorithmically, and as a complement to the function string-to-codepoints().

As an example of the first kind of application, suppose you need to construct the hexadecimal representation of an integer. This might make use of an expression to return a single hex digit representing a value in the range 0–15. Here is a possible way of writing this expression:

```
codepoints-to-string(if ($d<10) then (48+$d) else (87+$d))
```

13

The Function Library

725

Personally, I prefer to code this as:

```
substring("0123456789abcdef", $d+1, 1)
```

As an example of the second kind of application, suppose that you want to reverse the order of the characters in a string. One way of doing this is:

```
codepoints-to-string(reverse(string-to-codepoints($s)))
```

In this example, the two functions `string-to-codepoints()` and `codepoints-to-string()` are being used simply as a way of breaking the string into a sequence of characters, and reassembling the characters into a string; the fact that the characters are represented by Unicode codepoints has no relevance.

See Also

`string-to-codepoints()` on page 881

collection

The `collection()` function returns a sequence of documents, or more generally a sequence of nodes, identified by a URI. The way in which a URI can be used to locate a collection of documents is entirely implementation-defined.

Signature

Argument	Type	Meaning
uri (optional)	xs:string?	A URI that identifies a collection of documents, or nodes within documents. If the argument is omitted, or is supplied as an empty sequence, the function returns the default collection of documents, established as part of the context by the calling application.
Result	node()*	*The sequence of documents, or nodes within documents, identified by the URI.*

Effect

This function is specified in very abstract terms, and it's likely that its detailed behavior will vary considerably from one implementation to the next.

Many XML databases have the concept of a collection as a container for documents, and the containers generally have a name, which can be mapped into some kind of URI. Beyond that, there are many variations; for example, some systems might allow collections to be nested hierarchically, some systems might use a collection to store all the documents that are validated against one particular schema, and so on. Some implementations map the concept of a collection onto a simple directory containing the documents (perhaps with a filter applied to the document names), or onto an XML catalog file that holds a list of the documents within the collection.

All that the spec really says about this function is that the supplied URI argument is resolved against the base URI from the static context, and the resulting absolute URI is used to identify a collection of documents; the result is a sequence containing the document nodes of these documents. In fact it isn't constrained to return document nodes, there might be collections that return other kinds of nodes.

The specification also says that the function is *stable*, which means that if you call it twice in the same expression (or, in the case of XSLT, in the same transformation), then you get the same answer back each time. In other words, a collection at least gives the appearance of being immutable for the duration of a query or transformation.

There's one other provision: if you call the `document-uri()` function on a document that was returned as part of the collection, then this will either return nothing, or it will return a URI that can be used as input to the `doc()` function to retrieve the original document. This rule gives you a useful guarantee if you want to follow hyperlinks between different documents in the collection.

Beyond this, it's not really possible to say what the `collection()` function does, without going into the details of individual implementations. The following table gives a summary of its behavior in the main XSLT 2.0 implementations available at the time of writing:

Product	Action
Altova	If the URI identifies a catalog file (see below), then the files listed in the catalog are loaded and returned as the result of the `collection()` function. Alternatively the argument may specify a directory and/or a filename pattern. For example, `collection("*.xml")` selects all files with extension `.xml` in the same directory as the stylesheet.
Gestalt	Gestalt allows you to supply a URI that references a directory, for example «`file:///c:/input-dir/*`». The collection that is returned contains a document node for each well-formed XML file in that directory.
Saxon	Saxon allows you to set up your own `CollectionURIResolver`, which can interpret the collection URI any way it likes. By default, it provides two options: the collection URI can resolve to a catalog file (see below), which lists the documents to be loaded; or it can be a URI referring to a directory, in which case all the XML files in that directory are loaded. It is also possible to specify query parameters in the URI that define a filename pattern that restricts the files selected, together with details such as whether the directory contents are scanned recursively, whether parsing errors are fatal, and whether schema or DTD validation is to be attempted. Further details at `http://www.saxonica.com/documentation/sourcedocs/collections.html`.

The format of the catalog file used by Saxon and Altova is not defined in any standard, but it is similar for both products. Here is an example:

```
<collection>
  <doc href="dir/chap1.xml"/>
  <doc href="dir/chap2.xml"/>
  <doc href="dir/chap3.xml"/>
  <doc href="dir/chap4.xml"/>
</collection>
```

Saxon also allows an attribute «`stable="no"`» on the `<collection>` element to override the normal requirement for the collection to be immutable. It can save the processor a lot of work (and memory) to omit this check.

See Also

`doc()` on page 750

compare

The `compare()` function is used to compare two strings, and to decide whether they are equal, or if not, which one sorts before the other.

For example, under most collations «`compare("ALPHA", "BETA")`» returns -1.

Signature

Argument	Type	Meaning
value-1	xs:string?	The first string to be compared
value-2	xs:string?	The second string to be compared
collation (optional)	xs:string	A URI identifying the collation to be used to perform the comparison
Result	xs:integer?	*−1 if* value-1 *is considered less than* value-2 *, zero if they are considered equal, +1 if* value-1 *is considered greater than* value-2

Effect

If either value-1 or value-2 is an empty sequence, the result is an empty sequence.

If value-1 is less than value-2, the function returns -1; if they are equal, it returns 0; and if value-1 is greater than value-2, it returns +1. The string comparison is done using the supplied collation if specified; if the collation argument is omitted, the comparison is done using the default collation. For more information on collations, see the section *Collations* in Chapter 6, page 459.

Examples

These examples assume the availability of two collation URIs: $strong, which considers first the character value, then accents, then case (with upper case first); and $weak, which considers only the character value.

Expression	Result	Explanation
compare("espace", "espacer")	−1	The shorter string comes first.
compare("espace", "espacé", $strong)	−1	The unaccented string comes first.
compare("espace", "Espacé", $strong)	−1	Accent differences are more significant than case differences.
compare("espace", "espacé", $weak)	0	Accents make no difference.
compare("espacer", "espacé", $strong)	+1	The base characters are examined before the accents.

Usage

Often compare() is followed by a three-way branch. Because XPath has no switch or case expression, it is best to assign the result of the function to a variable to avoid doing the comparison twice. For example, in XSLT:

```
<xsl:variable name="c" select="compare(A, B)" as="xs:integer"/>
<xsl:choose>
   <xsl:when test="$c eq -1"> ... </xsl:when>
   <xsl:when test="$c eq 0"> ... </xsl:when>
   <xsl:when test="$c eq +1"> ... </xsl:when>
</xsl:choose>
```

Or, in XQuery 1.0:

```
let $c := compare(A, B) return
    if ($c = -1) then ...
```

```
        else if ($c = 0) then ...
        else ...
```

In pure XPath 2.0, you can do this rather awkwardly with a «for» expression:

```
    for $c in compare(A, B) return
        if ($c = -1) then ...
        else if ($c = 0) then ...
        else ...
```

See Also

Collations on page 459 in Chapter 6
Value Comparisons on page 581 in Chapter 8

concat

The concat() function takes two or more arguments. Each of the arguments is converted to a string, and the resulting strings are joined together end-to-end.

For example, the expression «concat('Jane', ' ', 'Brown')» returns the string «Jane Brown».

Changes in 2.0

None.

Signature

This function is unique in that it can take any number of arguments (two or more).

Argument	Type	Meaning
value (repeated)	xs:anyAtomicType	A string to be included in the result
Result	xs:string	*The result of concatenating each of the arguments in turn*

Effect

Each of the supplied strings is appended to the result string, in the order they appear.

Any argument that is an empty sequence is ignored. If all the arguments are empty sequences, the result is a zero-length string.

Note that all the arguments will automatically be cast to strings.

Examples

Expression	Result
concat("a", "b", "c")	The string «abc»
concat("chap", 3)	The string «chap3»
concat("a", (), (), "b")	The string «ab»
concat("a", ("b", "c"))	In 1.0 mode: the string «ab» (when a sequence is converted to a string in backward-compatibility mode, all items after the first are discarded). In 2.0 mode: error. The argument must be a single string, not a sequence of strings. Use the string-join() function instead.

13

The Function Library

Usage in XSLT

The `concat()` function is often a convenient alternative to using multiple `<xsl:value-of>` elements to construct an output string. For example, the following expression creates a text node containing a concatenation of three strings:

```
<xsl:value-of select="concat(first-name, ' ', last-name)"/>
```

This is equivalent to:

```
<xsl:value-of>
  <xsl:value-of select="first-name"/>
  <xsl:text> </xsl:text>
  <xsl:value-of select="last-name"/>
</xsl:value-of>
```

(Note the need for the outer `<xsl:value-of>` instruction — without this, the result would be a sequence of three text nodes rather than a single text node.) However, with XSLT 2.0 it is even simpler to write:

```
<xsl:value-of select="first-name, last-name" separator=" "/>
```

Another situation where `concat()` is useful is in defining a key, including look-up keys (`<xsl:key>`), sort keys (`<xsl:sort>`), and grouping keys (`<xsl:for-each-group>`). XSLT keys cannot be multipart values, but you can get round this restriction by concatenating the parts of the key with an appropriate separator. For example:

```
<xsl:key name="full-name" match="person"
                          use="concat(first-name, ' ', last-name)"/>
```

This key can then be used to retrieve the person (or persons) with a given name using an expression such as:

```
<xsl:for-each select="key('full-name', 'Peter Jones')">...</xsl:for-each>
```

See Also

`contains()` in the following section
`string-join()` on page 879
`substring()` on page 883

contains

The `contains()` function tests whether one string contains another as a substring. For example, the expression «`contains('Santorini', 'ant')`» returns true.

Changes in 2.0

An optional `collation` argument has been added.

Signature

Argument	Type	Meaning
input	xs:string?	The containing string
test	xs:string?	The test string

continued

Argument	Type	Meaning
collation (optional)	`xs:string`	The collation to be used
Result	`xs:boolean`	*true if the containing string has a substring that is equal to the test string, otherwise false*

Effect

If the Unicode codepoint collation is used (this is the default), then the result is `true` if the first string (`input`) contains a consecutive sequence of characters where each character has the same Unicode value as the corresponding character of the second string (`test`).

If `test` is zero-length, the result is always `true`.

If `input` is zero-length, the result is `false` except when `test` is also zero-length.

If either of the first two arguments is an empty sequence, the effect is the same as if it were a zero-length string.

If no collation is specified, then the default collation from the static context is used. When a collation is used, it is used to break both of the strings into a sequence of collation units, and the function returns `true` if the collation units generated for `test` form a subsequence of the collation units generated for `input`.

Because this function compares substrings, rather than just performing an equality match or ordering on two strings as a whole, it imposes particular constraints on the way the collation works — it only makes sense to use a collation that considers the string character by character. For a function such as `compare()`, it would be quite viable to use a collation that sorts «January» before «February», or «5 Oak Street» before «10 Maple Drive». But a collation that does this isn't also going to be able to look for substrings of characters in a meaningful way.

This doesn't mean that each character must be considered in isolation. The collation can still consider characters in groups, as with the traditional rule in Spanish that «ch» collates as if it were a single character following «c», and «ll» as a single letter after «l». But where characters are grouped in this way, it is likely to affect the way substrings are matched, as we will see.

The XPath specification isn't completely prescriptive about how substring matching using a collation should work, and there are several possible approaches that an implementation could use. I'll describe the way the Saxon processor does it, which makes heavy use of the collation support in Java: other Java-based processors are therefore quite likely to be similar.

Firstly, let's look at a case where Java treats one character as two collation units. With a primary strength collation for German, the string «Straße» generates a sequence of seven collation units, which are exactly the same as the collation units generated for the string «strasse». This means that «contains ("Straße", $t)» returns true when $t is any one of «ß», «aß», «ße», «ss», «as», «ass», or «se» (among others). Few surprises here.

Java also allows a collation to perform decomposition of combined characters. For example, the character «ç» can be decomposed into two characters, the letter «c» and a nonspacing cedilla. The advantage of doing this is that Unicode allows two ways of representing a word such as «garçon», using either six codepoints or seven, and normalizing the text so it only uses one of these forms gives better results when matching strings. For collating, Java chooses to use the decomposed form in which the accents are represented separately. (For more information on normalization, see the entry for the `normalize-unicode()` function on page 847.)

Under such a collation, the string «garçon» is represented as seven collation units, the same as the collation units for the string «garc,on», in which the cedilla is represented by a separate nonspacing character. The effect of this is that the result of «contains("garçon", $t)» is true when $t is any of «ç», «rç», or «ço», and also when it is «c» or «rc», but not (and here's the surprise) when it is «co».

> *I've written «garc,on» to illustrate that the «c» and the cedilla are two separate Unicode codepoints. But of course the cedilla is actually a nonspacing character, so in real life this string of seven codepoints would appear on the page as «garçon».*

Java could instead have standardized on the composed form of the character, but the accent-blind matching would then not work: «contains("garçon", "c")» would be false.

Now let's look at a case where a pair of characters represents a single collation unit. Here we turn back to Spanish, where in older publications «ch» collates after «c» and «ll» collates after «l». We can set this up in Java by defining a RuleBaseCollator using a rule that defines «c < ch < d» and «l < ll < m». (Modern Spanish practice follows the English collating rules, so I had to set up these rules myself.)

When you do this, you find that «contains("chello", $t)» returns true if $t is «ch» or «che» or «ello», but is false if it is «c» or «h» or «l» or «hello». What is happening is that because «ch» and «ll» are being treated as single characters for collation purposes, they are also treated as single characters for the purpose of substring matching.

These rules for substring matching using a collation apply not only to the contains() function, but also to ends-with(), starts-with(), substring-before(), and substring-after().

Examples

These examples assume that the default collation is the Unicode codepoint collation, which compares strings codepoint by codepoint.

Expression	Result
contains("Shakespeare", "spear")	true
contains("", "a")	false
contains("Shakespeare", "")	true
contains("", "")	true
contains((), "a")	false

Usage

The contains() function is useful mainly for very simple matching; for example, testing whether a string contains a space. For more complex matching of strings, the matches() function is available in XPath 2.0 with full support for regular expressions.

See Also

ends-with() on page 773
matches() on page 828
starts-with() on page 875
substring() on page 883
substring-after() on page 885
substring-before() on page 887

count

The count() function takes a sequence as its argument, and returns the number of items in the sequence. For example, the expression «count((4,5,6))» returns 3.

Changes in 2.0

The function is generalized in XPath 2.0 so that it can return the number of items in any sequence.

Signature

Argument	Type	Meaning
sequence	item()*	The sequence whose items are to be counted
Result	*xs:integer*	*The number of items in the supplied sequence*

Effect

The count() function takes any sequence as its argument, and returns the number of items present in the sequence.

If the sequence contains nodes, each node counts as one item. The function does not count the number of atomic values contained in the node's typed value, and it does not count the children or descendants of the node.

Examples

Consider the source document:

```
<doc>
  <obs at="10:42:06" colors="red green"/>
  <obs at="11:43:12" colors="green blue orange"/>
</doc>
```

and assume that this has been validated using a schema that defines the colors attribute as a sequence of strings.

Expression	Result
count(//obs)	2
count(//obs/@colors)	2
count(data(//obs/@colors))	5
count(//@*)	4
count(//obs/@date)	0
count((5 to 10))	6

Usage

Avoid using count() to test whether a sequence of nodes is empty; for example, by writing:

```
if (count(book[author='Hemingway']) != 0) then . . .
```

This can be better expressed as:

```
if (book[author='Hemingway']) then . . .
```

or, if you prefer:

```
if (exists(book[author='Hemingway'])) then . . .
```

A good processor will optimize the first expression so as to avoid counting all the books (it can stop counting books and take the then path as soon as it finds the first one that matches), but it's always best to avoid relying on such optimizations if you can.

The count() function is a useful way of finding the position of a node within a source document. In XSLT it can provide an effective alternative to using <xsl:number>, and in non-XSLT environments, it may be the only way of doing numbering. For example, if the context node is a <bullet> element, then «count(preceding-sibling::bullet)+1» returns the number of this <bullet> within the sequence of <bullet> elements. The advantages of using count() over <xsl:number>, apart from the fact that it's available in non-XSLT environments, are that it is rather more flexible in defining what you want to count, and it can be used directly in expressions. However, <xsl:number> gives a simple way of obtaining the sequence number, formatting it, and inserting it in the result tree in a single operation; it may also in some cases be easier for the processor to optimize.

Avoid using count() where last() would do the job just as well. This situation arises in XSLT when you are processing a sequence of nodes using <xsl:apply-templates> or <xsl:for-each>; the number of nodes in that sequence is then available from the last() function. For example, it is probably inefficient to write:

```
<xsl:for-each select="book[author='Hemingway']">
   <h2>Book <xsl:value-of select="position()"/> of
           <xsl:value-of select="count(../book[author='Hemingway'])"/>
   </h2>
   . . .
</xsl:for-each>
```

because — unless the XSLT processor is rather clever — it will have to reevaluate the expression «../book[author='Hemingway']» each time round the loop.

Instead, write:

```
<xsl:for-each select="book[author='Hemingway']">
   <h2>Book <xsl:value-of select="position()"/> of
           <xsl:value-of select="last()"/>
   </h2>
   . . .
</xsl:for-each>
```

An alternative is to assign the sequence of nodes to a variable, so it is only evaluated once.

See Also

sum() on page 889
last() on page 820

current

This function is available in XSLT only.

The current() function returns a single item, the item that is the context item at the point in the stylesheet where the XPath expression containing this function call is called.

Changes in 2.0

The function has been generalized so that it may return any item (a node or an atomic value), not only a node. The function may now be used within an XSLT pattern.

Signature

There are no arguments.

	Type	Meaning
Result	*item()*	*The item that is the context item at the outermost level of the XPath expression containing the function call*

Effect

At any point in the processing of a stylesheet, there is generally a context item. The XPath expression «.», if it is used as a standalone expression within a stylesheet, will always select the context item and will return the same result as the expression current(). Within an XPath expression, the context item may change; for example, within a predicate, the context item is the item being tested using the predicate. The result of the current() function, however, is the same wherever it is used within an expression. This makes it useful within predicates, as a way of referring to the item that would have been the context item at the outermost level.

This is best explained by example. The following example processes all <part> elements that have a code attribute whose value is the same as the code attribute of the element that is the context item at the point where the instruction is evaluated.

```
<xsl:apply-templates select="//part[@code = current()/@code]"/>
```

Another way of writing this would be:

```
<xsl:apply-templates select="for $c in . return //part[@code = $c/@code]"/>
```

and in fact this substitution is completely general; any complete XPath expression that references the current() function could be replaced by one in which a variable is bound to the value of «.» at the outermost level of the expression, and the call on current() is replaced by a reference to that variable.

The context item in a stylesheet is established as follows:

❑ When evaluating a global variable, the context item is the initial context item, supplied by the calling application (it may be undefined if no initial context item has been supplied). Usually, this will be the document node of the main input document.

❑ When <xsl:apply-templates> is used to process a selected set of nodes, each selected node in turn becomes the context item. So when a template rule is invoked, the context item is always the node that caused that template rule to be selected. On return from <xsl:apply-templates>, the context item reverts to its previous value.

❑ When <xsl:for-each> is used to process a selected sequence of items, each selected item in turn becomes the context item. When the <xsl:for-each> loop completes, the context item reverts to its previous value.

❑ When a stylesheet function is called from within an XPath expression, the context item is undefined. This means that any attempt to reference «.» or current() will raise an error.

❑ The <xsl:for-each-group> and <xsl:analyze-string> instructions also change the context item; for details, see the description of these instructions in Chapter 6.

❑ All other instructions, including <xsl:call-template> and <xsl:apply-imports>, leave the context item unchanged.

When the current() function is used in a pattern, it refers to the node that is being matched against the pattern. For example, the pattern «part[ancestor::*/@code !=current()/@code]» matches all part elements that have an ancestor with a code attribute that differs from the code attribute on the element itself.

Usage

The reason the current() function is provided is to allow you to determine the XSLT context item when it is different from the XPath context item — specifically, inside a predicate. The XPath context item can always be determined using the expression «.».

The most common situation where current() is useful is when you want to follow a cross-reference from the context node to some other node. For example, the expression «//department[deptNr=current()/@dept]» finds a <department> element referenced from the dept attribute of the context item (which might be an <employee> element).

Example

The following example shows the use of current() in a predicate.

Example: current()

This example lists the books in a catalog; in the description of each book, it also lists other books in the same category.

Source

The source document is booklist.xml.

```
<booklist>
<book category="S">
    <title>Number, the Language of Science</title>
    <author>Danzig</author>
</book>
<book category="FC">
    <title>The Young Visiters</title>
    <author>Daisy Ashford</author>
</book>
<book category="FC">
    <title>When We Were Very Young</title>
    <author>A. A. Milne</author>
</book>
```

```
<book category="CS">
    <title>Design Patterns</title>
    <author>Erich Gamma</author>
    <author>Richard Helm</author>
    <author>Ralph Johnson</author>
    <author>John Vlissides</author>
</book>
</booklist>
```

Stylesheet

The stylesheet is `list-books.xsl`. It processes all the books in an `<xsl:for-each>` loop, and for each one it displays the title and the first author. Then it looks for other books in the same category. Here it uses the predicate «`[./@category=current()/@category]`», which is true if the `category` attribute of the context element is the same as the `category` attribute of the current element. The context element is the one being tested; the element returned by `current()` is the one whose entry is being displayed. It also tests that these two elements are distinct elements, using the condition «`not(. is current())`». In this case, you could also get away with writing «`.!=current()`», which tests whether the two nodes have a different string value, but it can be a more expensive test, and it doesn't mean quite the same thing.

```
<xsl:transform
    xmlns:xsl="http://www.w3.org/1999/XSL/Transform"
    version="2.0"
    xmlns:book="books.uri"
    exclude-result-prefixes="book"
>
<xsl:template match="/">
  <html><body>
    <xsl:for-each select="//book">
        <h1><xsl:value-of select="title"/></h1>
        <p>Category: <xsl:value-of
                 select="$categories/category
                 [@code=current()/@category]/@desc"/>
        </p>
    </xsl:for-each>
  </body></html>
</xsl:template>
<xsl:variable name="categories">
  <category code="S" desc="Science"/>
  <category code="CS" desc="Computing"/>
  <category code="FC" desc="Children's Fiction"/>
</xsl:variable>
</xsl:transform>
```

Output

The output of the transformation is as follows.

```
<html>
    <body>
        <h1>Number, the Language of Science</h1>
```

```
            <p>Category: Science</p>
            <h1>The Young Visiters</h1>
            <p>Category: Children's Fiction</p>
            <h1>When We Were Very Young</h1>
            <p>Category: Children's Fiction</p>
            <h1>Design Patterns</h1>
            <p>Category: Computing</p>
        </body>
    </html>
```

current-date, current-dateTime, current-time

These three functions are used to obtain the current date, the current time, or both.

Signature

These functions take no arguments.

	Type	Meaning
Result	xs:date, xs:dateTime, or xs:time	*The current date, dateTime, or time*

Effect

The current date and time forms part of the runtime context of an XPath expression. It will normally be taken from the system clock.

The resulting value will always have an explicit timezone component. The timezone will be taken from the implicit timezone provided by the evaluation context. In practice, this means it will probably be derived from the system default timezone for the machine on which the XSLT processor is running, or from the profile of the particular user.

In XSLT 2.0 it is defined that multiple calls on current-dateTime() and the other two functions will return the same result every time they are called within a single transformation. This means you can't call the function at the beginning and the end of the transformation to measure the elapsed time. The reason for this rule is that XSLT is rather purist about being a strictly functional language, and in a strictly functional language, calling the same function twice with the same arguments always returns the same result. This property makes life much simpler for optimizers.

In XQuery 1.0, the same rule applies to multiple calls within a single query.

Examples

Expression	Possible Result
current-date()	An xs:date, say 2008-06-02Z
current-dateTime()	An xs:dateTime, say 2008-06-02T12:35:02-05:00
current-time()	An xs:time, say 12:35:02Z

Usage

Standalone XPath 2.0 does not provide any facilities for formatting the date and time for display. You can do this in XSLT 2.0 using the functions `format-date()`, `format-dateTime()`, and `format-time()`.

See Also

`adjust-date/time-to-timezone()` functions described on page 738
`format-date/time/dateTime()` on page 781
`X-from-date/time/dateTime()` functions described in their alphabetical position in this chapter, where X is one of `year`, `month`, `day`, `hours`, `minutes`, `seconds`, or `timezone`.

current-group

This function is available in XSLT only.

The `current-group()` function returns the set of items making up the group that is currently being processed using the `<xsl:for-each-group>` instruction.

Signature

There are no arguments.

	Type	Meaning
Result	`item()*`	*A sequence of items, specifically the sequence that is being processed in the current iteration of an* `<xsl:for-each-group>` *instruction*

Effect

When the stylesheet starts executing, there is no current group; the `current-group()` function then returns an empty sequence.

The `<xsl:for-each-group>` instruction, described in Chapter 6, page 326, takes as input a sequence of items (called the population) and a grouping expression or pattern. It allocates each item in the population to zero or more groups of items, and then processes each group in turn. While it is processing each group, the `current-group()` function returns the sequence of items that participate in that group.

The `current-group()` function does not need to be called textually within the `<xsl:for-each-group>` instruction. Its scope is dynamic, and the current group remains available in called templates unless another nested `<xsl:for-each-group>` instruction is evaluated. On completion of an `<xsl:for-each-group>` instruction, it reverts to its previous value.

The `current-group()` function can also be called while evaluating the sort key in an `<xsl:sort>` element contained within the `<xsl:for-each-group>` instruction. This affects the order in which groups are processed. In this context, `current-group()` refers to the group whose sort key is being calculated. For example, to sort groups in order of decreasing size, write `<xsl:sort select="count(current-group())" order="descending"/>`.

On entry to a stylesheet function, the current group is an empty sequence.

Usage and Examples

See `<xsl:for-each-group>` on page 326 in Chapter 6

13

The Function Library

See Also

`<xsl:for-each-group>` on page 326 in Chapter 6
`current-grouping-key()` in the following section

current-grouping-key

This function is available in XSLT only.

The `current-grouping-key()` function returns the value of the grouping key that defines the group currently being processed using the `<xsl:for-each-group>` instruction. The grouping key is the value of the expression in the `group-by` or `group-adjacent` attribute. When grouping is done using patterns, there is no current grouping key.

Signature

There are no arguments.

	Type	Meaning
Result	`xs:anyAtomicType?`	*This is the value of the `group-by` or `group-adjacent` expression that is shared by all the items in the current group.*
		The return type indicates that the grouping key can be of any atomic type; for example, `xs:string`, `xs:decimal`, or `xs:date`.
		When there is no current group, the function returns an empty sequence.

Effect

When the stylesheet starts executing, there is no current grouping key; the `current-grouping-key()` function then returns an empty sequence.

The `<xsl:for-each-group>` instruction, described in Chapter 6, page 326, takes as input a sequence of items called the population and a grouping expression or pattern. If the grouping criteria are defined using the `group-by` or `group-adjacent` attributes, then while each group is being processed, the `current-grouping-key()` function returns the grouping key value that characterizes that group.

If the grouping criteria are defined using the `group-starting-with` or `group-ending-with` attributes of `<xsl:for-each-group>`, the current grouping key is an empty sequence.

The `current-grouping-key()` function does not need to be called textually within the `<xsl:for-each-group>` instruction. Its scope is dynamic, and the current grouping key remains available in called templates unless another nested `<xsl:for-each-group>` instruction is evaluated. On completion of an `<xsl:for-each-group>` instruction, it reverts to its previous value.

The `current-grouping-key()` function can also be called while evaluating the sort key in an `<xsl:sort>` element contained within the `<xsl:for-each-group>` instruction. This affects the order in which groups are processed. In this context, `current-grouping-key()` refers to the group whose sort key is being calculated. For example, to sort groups in descending order of their grouping key, write `<xsl:sort select="current-grouping-key()" order="descending"/>`.

On entry to a stylesheet function, the current grouping key is an empty sequence.

Usage and Examples

The following example groups a set of books by the name of the author. For each author, a section heading is displayed giving the name of the author, followed by a list of the books written by this author. The authors are sorted by name. A book that has several authors will be listed more than once.

```
<xsl:for-each-group select="//book" group-by="author">
  <xsl:sort select="current-grouping-key()"/>
  <h2><xsl:value-of select="current-grouping-key()"/></h2>
  <xsl:apply-templates select="current-group()"/>
</xsl:for-each-group>
```

See Also

current-group() on page 739
<xsl:for-each-group>, page 326 in Chapter 6

current-time

See current-date() on page 738

data

The data() function returns the atomized value of a sequence. This means that any nodes in the input sequence are replaced by their typed values.

Signature

Argument	Type	Meaning
sequence	item()*	The input sequence
Result	xs:anyAtomicType*	*A sequence based on the input sequence, in which all nodes have been replaced by their typed values*

Effect

Atomization is a process that is invoked implicitly when a sequence containing nodes is used in a context where atomic values are expected. For example, if you write «@a+42», the attribute node represented by the expression «@a» is atomized to obtain a number, which is then added to 42. The data() function invokes atomization explicitly, and is used either in a context where implicit atomization does not occur (for example, the argument to the count() function is not atomized), or in cases where you want to make it clear to the reader what is going on.

Atomization applies the following process to each item in the input sequence. The results are concatenated together retaining the original sequence order:

- ❏ If the input sequence contains an atomic value, the atomic value is added to the result sequence unchanged.

- ❏ If the input sequence contains a node, the typed value of the node is added to the result sequence.

The typed value of a node depends on its type annotation. In the absence of a schema, or when the type annotation is xs:untypedAtomic or xs:untyped, the typed value is the same as the string value, but the resulting atomic value remains an xs:untypedAtomic value rather than a string, which allows it to be used in contexts (for example, as an operand of «+») where a string would not be allowed.

If the node is annotated with some other type annotation, which generally will happen only as a result of schema validation, the typed value reflects the type definition in the schema:

❑ If the schema type is a simple type, the result is, in general, a sequence of zero or more atomic values. For example, if the type is xs:NMTOKENS, the result is a sequence of atomic values of type xs:NMTOKEN. If the type is a user-defined type defined as a list of xs:unsignedInteger values, then the typed value is a sequence of atomic values of type xs:unsignedInteger. If the schema type is a union type allowing a choice of xs:integer or xs:string, then the typed value will be either an xs:integer or an xs:string.

❑ If the schema type is a complex type (which implies that the node is an element), there are four cases to consider:

  ❑ The type may be a complex type with simple content. This means that the type allows attributes but does not allow child elements. In this case the element content is processed exactly as for a simple type, as described above. The attributes are ignored.

  ❑ The type may allow mixed content (defined using «mixed="true"» on the type definition in the schema). In this case the typed value is the same as the string value, which is the concatenation of all the text node descendants of the element. For example, the typed value of the element <chem>H₂O</chem> is the string «H2O». The result is labeled as an untyped atomic value.

  ❑ The type may define that the element is always empty. In this case, the typed value is an empty sequence.

  ❑ If the type allows element content only, then atomizing the element is an error. A system that does static type checking may report this as a compile-time error; otherwise, it will be reported at runtime. You can avoid this error by using the string value of the element instead of its typed value; for example, by writing «string($emp)» instead of «data($emp)».

Examples

Suppose that the variable $x is bound to the following element, which has been validated using a schema that defines the content model of <rows> as zero or more <row> elements, and the content model of the <row> element to contain a number attribute of type xs:integer and a colors attribute whose type is xs:NMTOKENS.

```
<rows>
  <row number="1" colors="red green"/>
  <row number="2" colors="yellow purple"/>
</rows>
```

Expression	Result
data($x/row/@number)	(1, 2)
data($x/row/@colors)	("red", "green", "yellow", "purple")
data($x)	Error. An element with element-only content does not have a typed value.
data($x/row)	()

Note that the above examples could equally well be written in the style «$x/row/@number/data(.)».

Usage

Atomization is normally carried out automatically when an operation that expects atomic values is applied to a sequence. For example, if the argument to the sum() function is a set of nodes, then the typed values of those nodes will be extracted and totaled.

The data() function is provided so that atomization can be done explicitly in situations where it is not automatic. For example, the count() function does not automatically atomize its argument: it counts the nodes in the sequence, not the atomic values that result from atomization. The result is not the same, because if an element or attribute is declared in the schema to have a type such as list-of-integers, then atomizing the element or attribute may produce zero, one, or more atomic values.

Similarly, when testing the value of an element or attribute whose type is xs:boolean, be careful to make sure that the value is atomized: write «if (data(@married))...» rather than «if(@married)...». This is because the value of «@married» is a sequence of zero or one attribute nodes, and the effective boolean value of a sequence of nodes (which is what the «if» expression tests) is true if there is at least one node in the sequence, regardless of its contents. If the attribute exists and has the value «married="false"», the test «if(@married)...» will return true. Another way of forcing atomization is to write this as «if (@married=true())...».

See Also

The Type Matching Rules on page 219 in Chapter 5

dateTime

This function constructs an xs:dateTime value from a supplied xs:date and xs:time.

Signature

Argument	Type	Meaning
date	xs:date?	A supplied date
time	xs:time?	A supplied time
Result	*xs:dateTime?*	*The* xs:dateTime *formed by combining the supplied date and time*

Effect

If either of the arguments is an empty sequence, the result is an empty sequence.

Otherwise, the result is formed by combining the supplied date and time.

If neither of the arguments includes a timezone, the result will not include a timezone. If one of the arguments includes a timezone and the other does not, or if both include the same timezone, the result will have this timezone. If the two arguments both contain timezones and they are different, then an error occurs.

Note that the time value «24:00:00» is considered to represent exactly the same value as «00:00:00» (that is, midnight), and this is treated as the start of the day rather than the end.

13

The Function Library

Examples

Expression	Result
dateTime(xs:date('2008-01-01'), xs:time('12:00:00'))	2008-01-01T12:00:00
dateTime(xs:date('2008-01-01'), xs:time('12:00:00Z'))	2008-01-01T12:00:00Z
dateTime(xs:date('2008-01-01Z'), xs:time('12:00:00Z'))	2008-01-01T12:00:00Z
dateTime(xs:date('2008-01-01+02:00'), xs:time('12:00:00Z'))	Error (different timezones)
dateTime(xs:date('2008-01-01+02:00'), xs:time('24:00:00'))	2008-01-01T00:00:00+02:00

See Also

current-date(), -dateTime(), -time() on page 738
format-date(), -dateTime(), -time() on page 781

day-from-date, day-from-dateTime

These two functions extract the day-of-the-month component from an xs:date or xs:dateTime value. For example, on Christmas Day «day-from-date(current-date())» returns 25.

Signature

Argument	Type	Meaning
input	xs:date? or xs:dateTime?	The value from which a component is to be extracted. The type of the supplied argument must correspond to the type implied by the function name.
Result	xs:integer?	The day, in the range 1-31.

Effect

The function returns the day component of the supplied xs:date or xs:dateTime. The value is used in its local timezone (not normalized to UTC). If the argument is an empty sequence, the result is an empty sequence.

Examples

Expression	Result
day-from-date(xs:date("2008-02-28"))	28
day-from-dateTime(xs:dateTime("2008-02-28T13:00:00"))	28
day-from-date(xs:date("2008-07-31+01:00"))	31
day-from-dateTime(xs:dateTime("2008-07-31T23:00:00-05:00"))	31

See Also

current-date(),-dateTime(),-time() on page 738
format-date(),-dateTime(),-time() on page 781
month-from-date(),-dateTime() on page 833
year-from-date(),-dateTime() on page 911

days-from-duration

This function extracts the value of the days component from a normalized xs:duration value.

Signature

Argument	Type	Meaning
input	xs:duration?	The duration whose days component is to be extracted. If an empty sequence is supplied, an empty sequence is returned.
Result	xs:integer?	*The days component.*

Effect

The function returns the days component of the supplied xs:duration. The duration value is first normalized so that the number of hours is less than 24, the number of minutes is less than 60, and so on. However, there is never any conversion of days to months or vice versa. The result will be negative if the duration is negative.

Examples

Expression	Result
days-from-duration(xs:duration("P5DT12H"))	5
days-from-duration(xs:dayTimeDuration("PT72H"))	3
days-from-duration(xs:dayTimeDuration("-P1D"))	-1
days-from-duration(xs:yearMonthDuration("P1M"))	0

See Also

hours-from-duration on page 801
minutes-from-duration on page 832
seconds-from-duration on page 874

deep-equal

The deep-equal() function performs a deep comparison between two sequences:

❑ The items in corresponding positions in each sequence must be deep-equal to each other.

❑ If the items are nodes, they are compared by examining their children and attributes recursively.

Signature

Argument	Type	Meaning
sequence-1	`item()*`	The first operand of the comparison
sequence-2	`item()*`	The second operand of the comparison
collation (optional)	`xs:string`	The collation to be used for comparing strings (at any depth)
Result	`xs:boolean`	*True if the sequences are deep-equal; otherwise, false*

Effect

This function may be used to compare:

❑ Two nodes, to see whether the subtrees rooted at those nodes have identical content at every level

❑ Two sequences, to see whether the items they contain are pairwise deep-equal

The function is therefore defined to operate on sequences, though in many cases it will be used to compare two singleton element or document nodes.

At the top level, two sequences are deep-equal if they have the same number of items, and if each item in the first sequence is deep-equal to the item in the corresponding position of the other sequence. A consequence of this rule is that an empty sequence is deep-equal to another empty sequence.

Where the item in a sequence is an atomic value, the corresponding item in the other sequence must also be an atomic value, and they must compare as equal using the «eq» operator, using the specified `collation` if they are strings, URIs, or untyped atomic values. If two items in corresponding positions are not comparable (for example, if one is an integer and the other is a string, or if one is a date and the other is an element node), then the function returns false; it does not report an error. Nodes are not atomized. NaN is considered to be equal to itself.

If two items in corresponding positions are nodes, then to be deep-equal they must satisfy a number of conditions:

❑ They must be the same kind of node (for example, both elements or both text nodes).

❑ They must have the same name, that is, the same namespace URI and the same local name, or they must both be unnamed nodes such as text nodes.

❑ In the case of document nodes, and element nodes whose type allows one or more element children, the sequences of children for the two nodes must be deep-equal to each other, after discarding any comments and processing instructions.

❑ In the case of element nodes, there must be a one-to-one correspondence between the attributes of the two elements (same attribute name, and typed values that are deep-equal).

❑ In the case of attribute nodes and element nodes whose type does not allow element children, the typed values must be deep-equal to each other.

❑ In the case of text nodes, comments, processing instructions, and namespace nodes, they must have the same string value, compared using the selected collation. Note however that comments, processing instructions, and namespace nodes are only taken into account if they occur directly as items in the sequences supplied as arguments to the `deep-equal()` function. When they occur within the content of an element node, they are not considered.

Nodes can be deep-equal even if they differ in certain respects:

❑ When comparing elements, the namespace nodes of the elements do not need to be the same, and contained comments and processing instructions are not taken into consideration. (The fact that the namespace nodes can be different also means that one element can pass validation while the other fails validation, if they happen to contain `xs:QName` values in their content.)

❑ Type annotations are not taken into account; for example, two attributes can be equal if one is annotated as an `xs:decimal` with value 3.0, and the other is annotated as `xs:integer` with value 3.

❑ The order of attributes within an element can vary. (But the order of attribute nodes in the top-level sequence is significant.)

❑ The base URI can vary.

❑ When comparing document nodes, the document URI is ignored, as are unparsed entities.

Surprisingly, however, whitespace text nodes are taken into account even within an element that has an element-only content model. Furthermore, although comments and processing instructions appearing as children of an element are not compared directly, their presence can affect the result because they split a text node into two: so `<e>123<?pi?>456</e>` and `<e>123456</e>` are not deep-equal.

Examples

Expression	Result
`deep-equal((1,2,3), (1,2,3))`	true
`deep-equal((1,2,3), (3,2,1))`	false
`deep-equal((1,2), (1.0, 2.0))`	true
`deep-equal((), ())`	true

In the following examples, assume that `$doc` refers to the following document:

```
<doc>
    <e att1="a" att2="b" att3="c"><f/><g/></e>
    <e att3="C" att1="a" att2="b"><f/></e>
    <e att3="C" att1="a" att2="b"><f/><g/></e>
</doc>
```

and assume that `$weak` refers to a collation under which «c» and «C» compare as equal. Then:

Expression	Result
`deep-equal($doc/e[1], $doc/e[2])`	false
`deep-equal($doc/e[1], $doc/e[3], $weak)`	true
`deep-equal($doc/e[1]/@*, $doc/e[2]/@*, $weak)`	*Undefined (the result depends on the order of attribute nodes, which is unpredictable)*

Usage

The `deep-equal()` function represents one particular way of deciding whether two nodes or sequences are equal to each other. In practice there are probably two common ways it is likely to be used:

❑ To compare two sequences of atomic values: the result is true if the two sequences are the same length, and the sequences are pairwise equal to each other.

❑ To compare two element or document nodes to see if they have the same content at every level of the hierarchy.

Note that comparing two element nodes using the «=» or «eq» operators fails if the elements are defined in the schema to have a complex type, unless this is a complex type allowing mixed content, in which case the elements are compared by comparing their string values.

The definition of deep equality for nodes is one that will suit some tastes and not others. For example, it treats comments and processing instructions within an element as insignificant, but whitespace between elements as significant. It also treats the order of child elements (but not attributes) as significant. If you don't like this definition, the answer is simple: define your own function, and use that instead.

Saxon provides a function `saxon:deep-equal()` *which is modeled on the standard* `deep-equal()` *function, but provides an extra argument allowing user control over the way in which the comparison is performed. Details are at* `http://www.saxonica.com/documentation/extensions/functions/deepequal.html`.

default-collation

The `default-collation()` function returns the URI of the default collation, that is, the collation that is used when no collation is explicitly specified in a function such as `compare()`.

Signature

This function takes no arguments.

	Type	Meaning
Result	`xs:string`	*The URI of the default collation from the runtime context*

Usage

The `default-collation()` function is useful when you want to assign a collation conditionally, for example:

```
compare($x, $y, if ($param-uri) then $param-uri else default-collation())
```

When you call a function that expects a collation, you can always omit the argument to request the default collation, but you cannot supply a value such as an empty sequence or a zero-length string: if the argument is present, then it must be a valid collation.

See Also

max() on page 830
min() on page 830
Value Comparisons on page 581 in Chapter 8

distinct-values

The `distinct-values()` function eliminates duplicate values from a sequence.

For example, «`distinct-values((3, 5, 3, 6))`» might return «`(5, 6, 3)`».

Signature

Argument	Type	Meaning
sequence	`xs:anyAtomicType*`	The input sequence
collation (optional)	`xs:string`	The collation to be used when comparing values that are strings
Result	`xs:anyAtomicType*`	*The input sequence, with duplicate values removed*

Effect

If a sequence containing nodes is supplied as the argument, the nodes are first atomized as part of the standard function calling rules.

An untyped atomic value in the sequence is treated as a string.

If two or more values in the sequence are equal to each other (according to the rules of the «eq» operator, using the specified collation when comparing strings), then only one of them is included in the result sequence. It is not defined which of them will be retained (for example, if the input sequence contains the `xs:integer` 3 and the `xs:decimal` 3.0, then it is unpredictable which of these two values will be present in the result). In addition, the order of the values in the result sequence is undefined.

If the sequence contains two values that are not comparable using the «eq» operator (for example, an integer and a string), then these values are treated as distinct; no error is reported.

For the purpose of this function, NaN is considered equal to itself, and distinct from any other value.

Examples

Assume that the default collation is case-blind, that is, that it treats the strings «A» and «a» as equal. The table below gives one possible result for each expression; a particular XPath processor might return some permutation of this result, or might include different items from a set that are equal to each other (such as «A» and «a»).

Expression	Possible Result
`distinct-values((1, 2, 3, 3.5, 2.0, 1.0))`	`3.5, 2.0, 1, 3`
`distinct-values(("A", "B", "C", "a", "b", "c"))`	`"B", "c", "a"`
`distinct-values((xs:time("12:20:02Z"), xs:time("13:20:02+01:00")))`	`xs:time("13:20:02+01:00")`
`distinct-values((1, "a", current-date()))`	`"a", 1, 2008-05-08Z`

Usage

The `distinct-values()` function provides the only direct way of eliminating duplicate values in XPath 2.0 and in XQuery 1.0. In XSLT 2.0, however, richer functionality is available in the form of the `<xsl:for-each-group>` instruction.

If you apply the function to a sequence of nodes, the result will be the distinct values present in those nodes, not the nodes themselves. To process the nodes, you will have to find the nodes having each value. The typical logic is the following, which returns a sequence of integers representing the number of employees in each department:

```
for $x in distinct-values(//employee/@dept)
   return count(//employee[@dept = $x])
```

In practice the processing of the result will probably be done in XSLT, XQuery, or some other host language, because it will usually involve generating nodes in the output, which XPath cannot do on its own.

Having found the distinct values that appear in a sequence, it is possible to determine the positions of each of these values using the `index-of()` function. For example, if you are using XQuery, then you can sort the distinct values in order of their first appearance in the sequence by writing:

```
(: XQUERY 1.0 EXAMPLE :)
 for $d in distinct-values($sequence)
 order by index-of($sequence, $d)[1]
 return $d
```

Alternatively, you could sort them in order of their frequency of occurrence by writing:

```
(: XQUERY 1.0 EXAMPLE :)
 for $d in distinct-values($sequence)
 order by count(index-of($sequence, $d))
 return $d
```

XPath 2.0 has no sorting capability, so this operation can only be done in the host language. In XSLT, it is usually more convenient to use the `<xsl:for-each-group>` instruction.

See Also

`index-of()` on page 807
`<xsl:for-each-group>` in Chapter 6 on page 326

doc, doc-available

The `doc()` function retrieves an external XML document by means of a URI, and returns the document node at the root of the tree representation of that XML document. Its companion function `doc-available()` determines whether an equivalent call on the `doc()` function would succeed in locating a document.

Changes in 2.0

These functions are new in XPath 2.0. The `doc()` function is a simplified version of the `document()` function that was provided in XSLT 1.0 and which remains available in XSLT 2.0 (see page 754). When combined with functions such as `resolve-uri()` and `base-uri()`, the `doc()` function provides most of the capability of the XSLT 2.0 `document()` function, but with a much simpler interface.

Signatures

The doc() function

Argument	Type	Meaning
uri	xs:string?	The URI of the document to be loaded
Result	*document-node()?*	*The document node of the document identified by this URI*

The doc-available() function

Argument	Type	Meaning
uri	xs:string?	The URI of the document to be loaded
Result	*xs:boolean*	*True if a call on the* doc() *function with the same argument would succeed; false if it would fail*

Effect

The doc() function gives XPath a window on the outside world, by allowing it to retrieve documents identified by a URI. Potentially this makes any XML document anywhere on the Web available for processing.

However, because the doc() function is an interface between the XPath processor and the world outside, many aspects of its behavior depend on the implementation, or on the way that the implementation is configured. XPath 2.0 is expected to be used in a great variety of environments (for example, some XPath processors might only work with XML documents that have been preloaded into a purpose-designed database) and the spec therefore gives a great deal of freedom to implementors. In fact, the formal specification of this function simply says that the evaluation context for processing an XPath expression provides a mapping of URIs to document nodes; if you specify a URI for which a mapping exists, then you get back the corresponding document node, and if you specify a URI for which no mapping exists, you get an error.

The term *mapping* here is deliberately abstract. It actually allows the implementation to do anything it likes to get from the URI you specify to the tree that comes back. Many implementations will allow users to control the process, either by implementing user hooks like the URIResolver in Java's JAXP interface and the XmlResolver in .NET, or by setting options in configuration files or command line parameters.

Before the URI is used, it is first resolved into an absolute URI. You can resolve the URI yourself using the resolve-uri() function, in which case you have a free choice of the base URI to use, but if you pass a relative URI to the doc() function then it will always be resolved against the base URI from the static context of the XPath expression. In XSLT 2.0 this generally means the URI of the containing stylesheet module; in XQuery it means the base URI given in the query prolog. If the relative URI was read from a source document, then it should normally be resolved against the base URI of the document from where it was read, but this is left to the application to do.

One rule that the implementation must enforce is that if you call doc() twice with the same absolute URI, you get the same document node back each time. In XSLT, this rule applies for the duration of a transformation, not just for a single XPath expression evaluation.

What is likely to happen in a typical implementation is this:

❑ The URI (once resolved into an absolute URI) is checked against a list of documents that are already loaded. If the URI is in the list, the same document node is returned again.

❑ Otherwise, the absolute URI is used to identify and fetch an XML document, for example, by using the `file` or `http` URI schemes.

❑ The XML document is parsed, and optionally validated using a DTD validator or schema processor.

❑ A tree representation of the document is built in memory, and the document node at the root of this tree is returned as the result of the function.

Many processors are likely to allow users to control aspects of this process, including:

❑ Locating the physical resource containing the source XML (if indeed it is source XML). Mechanisms such as catalogs or user hooks (like the JAXP `URIResolver`) might be used to provide an indirection between the URI and the location of the resource.

❑ Selecting an XML parser, and setting options to determine whether it performs DTD and/or schema validation.

❑ Setting options that define whether `XInclude` directives in the source document are expanded, and whether any information in the source document (such as insignificant whitespace, comments, processing-instructions, or unused namespaces) is to be excluded from the tree representation.

❑ Setting tuning options; for example, parameters that control space/time tradeoffs in the way the tree is built.

❑ Setting error-handling options; for example, whether a parsing error is to be treated as fatal, or whether an empty sequence (or perhaps a fallback document) should be returned in such cases.

If a schema is used to validate the document, then it must be compatible with any schema that was used when compiling the XPath expression. Here again, the detailed rules have been left to the implementation. The processor may require that the input document is validated against a schema that was known at compile time, or it may allow validation using a different schema, provided that the tree that comes back contains enough information to allow the type definitions to be located at runtime. The processor is supposed to ensure that there is no version incompatibility between the compile time and runtime schemas, but it wouldn't be surprising to come across a processor that simply passes this responsibility back to the user.

The `doc-available()` function works exactly the same way as the `doc()` function, except that instead of returning a document node when a document can be loaded and throwing an error when it can't, `doc-available()` returns true in the first case and false in the second. In the absence of any try/catch capability either in XSLT or XPath, this allows you to test for errors before they occur, so that processing can continue when the required document does not exist or has invalid content.

Usage and Examples

There are three main ways an XPath expression can access nodes in input documents.

❑ The input document (or a node within it) can be supplied as the context node.

❑ A node can be included in the value of a variable available in the context.

❑ The XPath expression can invoke the `doc()` function (or the `collection()` function) to access the document by URI.

Which of these three approaches is used is a matter of application convenience, and may be influenced by the facilities available in the host language or the processor API for configuring the behavior of the different options.

The following example shows an expression that uses a look-up table in an external document. The look-up table might have the form shown below and be held in a document called «countries.xml»:

```
<countries>
    <country name="Andorra" code="ad"/>
    <country name="United Arab Emirates" code="ae"/>
    <country name="Afghanistan" code="af"/>
    <country name="Antigua and Barbuda" code="ag"/>
    ...
  </countries>
```

A query that uses this table to display the number of employees located in each country might look like this:

```
string-join(
    for $c in doc("countries.xml")/country return
      concat($c/@name, ": ",
             count(//employee[location/country = $c/@code]))
    "&#x0a;")
```

This will return a string of the form:

```
Andorra: 0
United Arab Emirates: 12
Afghanistan: 1
Antigua and Barbuda: 25
...
```

If you want to process a document if and only if it actually exists, you can use logic of the form

```
<xsl:variable name="doc" select="if (doc-available($uri)) then doc($uri) else ()"/>
```

You should be aware of a few points:

❑   It's reasonable to expect that the document will actually be read and parsed only once

❑   If the document can't be read, or if it exists but can't be parsed as XML or validated, then you won't get any explanation as to why.

❑   If the URI is invalid, or if a runtime error occurs in computing the value of the URI, then doc-available() will throw an error rather than returning false. To avoid this failure (for example, when reading the URI from an input document), add the test «if ($uri castable as xs:anyURI)...».

❑   Once a document URI has been reported as unavailable, it remains unavailable for the rest of the transformation. In theory at least, you can't use doc-available() repeatedly to see whether the document has been created yet, and you can't use it to test for the existence of files created during the transformation by the <xsl:result-document> instruction.

See Also

base-uri() on page 719
collection() on page 726

`document-uri()` on page 764
`resolve-uri()` on page 867
`document()` in the next entry

document

This function is available in XSLT only.

The `document()` function finds an external XML document by resolving a URI reference, parses the XML into a tree structure, and returns its root node. It may also be used to find a set of external documents, and it may be used to find a node other than the root by using a fragment identifier in the URI.

For example, the expression «`document('data.xml')`» looks for the file `data.xml` in the same directory as the stylesheet, parses it, and returns the root node of the resulting tree.

Changes in 2.0

This function is retained largely for backward compatibility with XSLT 1.0; a simplified version is now available in XPath 2.0 as the `doc()` function described on page 750.

The specification of the function has been generalized to allow the first argument to be an arbitrary sequence of URIs, and it has also become less prescriptive, to allow greater freedom to configure the way in which the URI is interpreted and the way in which the retrieved documents are parsed.

Signature

Argument	Type	Meaning
href	`item()*`	A sequence, which may contain values of type `xs:string` or `xs:anyURI`, or nodes containing such values. These URIs are used to locate the documents to be loaded.
base (optional)	`node()`	If the argument is present, it must be a node. The base URI of this node is used for resolving any relative URIs found in the first argument.
Result	`node()*`	*A sequence of nodes, in document order. In the common case where a single URI is specified, and this URI contains no fragment identifier, the result will normally be a single document node.*

Effect

In brief, the `document()` function locates an XML document, using a URI. The resulting XML document is parsed and a tree is constructed. On completion, the result of the `document()` function is the document node of the new document.

If a sequence of URIs is provided, rather than a single URI, then the result is a sequence of document nodes. If a URI contains a fragment identifier, then the result may be an element node rather than a document node. The details are described in the following sections.

I will describe the effect of the function by considering the different ways of determining a base URI to use for resolving relative URIs. However, first a word about URIs and URLs, which are terms I use rather freely throughout this section.

Resolving the URI

The XSLT specification always uses the term URI: Uniform Resource Identifier. The concept of a URI is a generalization of the URLs (Uniform Resource Locators) that are widely used on the Web today and displayed on every cornflakes packet. The URI extends the URL mechanism, which is based on the established Domain Name System (with its hierarchic names such as `www.ibm.com` and `www.cam.ac.uk`), to allow other global naming and numbering schemes, including established ones such as ISBN book numbers and international telephone numbers. While URIs are a nice idea, the only ones that really enable you to retrieve resources on the Web are the familiar URLs. This is why the terms URI and URL seem to be used rather interchangeably in this section and indeed throughout the book. If you read carefully, though, you'll see that I've tried to use both terms correctly.

The way URIs are used to locate XML documents, and the way these XML documents are parsed to create a tree representation, are not defined in detail. In fact, the XSLT `document()` function defines this process in terms of the XPath `doc()` function, and the XPath `doc()` function essentially says that it's a piece of magic performed by the context of the XPath expression, not by the XPath processor itself. This reflects the reality that when you are using an application programming interface (API) such as the Java JAXP interface or the `System.Xml.Xsl` class in Microsoft's .NET, you can supply your own code that maps URIs to document nodes in any way you like. (The relevant class is called `URIResolver` in JAXP, `XmlResolver` in .NET.) This might not even involve any parsing of a real XML file; for example, the `URIResolver` might actually retrieve data from a relational database, and return an XML document that encapsulates the results of the query.

There's an expectation, though, that most XSLT processors — unless running in some kind of secure environment — will allow you to specify a URL (typically one that starts «http:» or «file:») that can be dereferenced in the usual way to locate a source XML document, which is then parsed. The details of how it is parsed, for example whether schema or Document Type Definition (DTD) validation is attempted and whether XInclude processing is performed, are likely to depend on configuration settings (perhaps options on the command line, or properties set via the processor's API). The language specification leaves this open-ended.

A URI used as input to the `document()` function should generally identify an XML document. If the URI is invalid, or if it doesn't identify any resource, or if that resource is not an XML document, the specification leaves it up to the implementation to decide what to do: it can either report the error, or ignore that particular URI. Implementations may go beyond this; for example, if the URI identifies an HTML document, they may attempt to convert the HTML to XML — this is all outside the scope of the W3C specifications.

A URI can be relative rather than absolute. A typical example of a relative URI is `data.xml`. Such a URI is resolved (converted to an absolute, globally unique URI) by interpreting it as relative to some base URI. By default, a relative URI that appears in the text of an XML document is interpreted relative to the URI of the document (or more precisely, the XML entity) that contains it, which in the case of the `document()` function is usually either the source document or the stylesheet. So if the relative URI `data.xml` appears in the source document, the system will try to find the file in the same directory as the source document, while if it appears in the stylesheet, the system will look in the directory containing the stylesheet. The base URI of a node in an XML document can be changed using the `xml:base` attribute, and this will be taken into account. In addition, the `document()` function provides a second argument so that the base URI can be specified explicitly, if required.

The actual rule is that the `href` argument may be a sequence of nodes or atomic values. In the case of a node in this sequence, the node may contain a URI (or indeed, a sequence of URIs), and if such a URI is relative then it is expanded against the base URI of the node from which it came. In the case of an atomic value in the sequence, this must be an xs:string or xs:anyURI value, and it is expanded using the base URI of the stylesheet.

The expansion of relative URIs exploits the fact that in the XPath data model, described on page 45 in Chapter 2, every node has a base URI. (Don't confuse this with the namespace URI, which is quite unrelated.) By default, the base URI of a node in the source document or the stylesheet will be the URI of the XML document or entity from which the node was constructed. In some cases, for example when the input comes from a Document Object Model (DOM) document or from a relational database, it may be difficult for the processor to determine the base URI (the concept does not exist in the DOM standard). What happens in this situation is implementation-defined. Microsoft, whose MSXML3 processor is built around its DOM implementation, has extended its DOM so it retains knowledge of the URI from which the document was loaded.

With XSLT 2.0, you can override the default rules for establishing the base URI of a node by using the xml:base attribute of an element. This attribute is defined in a W3C Recommendation called *XML Base* (http://www.w3.org/TR/xmlbase/); it is intended to fulfill the same function as the <base> element in HTML. If an element has an xml:base attribute, the value of the attribute must be a URI, and this URI defines the base URI for the element itself and for all descendants of the element node, unless overridden by another xml:base attribute.

The URI specified in xml:base may itself be a relative URI, in which case it is resolved relative to the base URI of the parent of the element containing the xml:base attribute (that is, the URI that would have been the base URI of the element if it hadn't had an xml:base attribute).

With XSLT 2.0, it is also possible that the node used to establish the base URI for the document() function will be a node in a temporary tree created as the value of a variable. Normally, the base URI for such a node will be the base URI of the <xsl:variable> (or <xsl:param>, or <xsl:with-param>) element that defines the temporary tree. But if an element in the stylesheet has an xml:base attribute, that defines the base URI in the same way as for a source document.

If several calls on the document() function use the same URI (after expansion of a relative URI into an absolute URI), then the same document node is returned each time. You can tell that it's the same node because the «is» operator returns true: «document('a.xml') is document('a.xml')» will always be true. If you use a different URI in two calls, then you may or may not get the same document node back: «document('a.xml') is document('A.XML')» might be either true or false.

A fragment identifier identifies a part of a resource: for example, in the URL http://www.wrox.com/booklist#april2008, the fragment identifier is april2008. In principle, a fragment identifier allows the URI to reference a node or set of nodes other than the root node of the target document; for example, the fragment identifier could be an XPointer expression containing a complex expression to select nodes within the target document. In practice though, this is all implementation defined. The interpretation of a fragment identifier depends on the media type (often called MIME type) of the returned document. Implementations are not required to support any particular media types (which means they are not required to support fragment identifiers at all). Many products support a simple fragment identifier consisting of a name that must be the value of an ID attribute in the target document, and support for XPointer fragment identifiers is likely to become increasingly common now that a usable XPointer specification has finally been ratified.

Parsing the Document

Once the URI has been resolved against a base URI, the next steps are to fetch the XML document found at that URI, and then to parse it into a tree representation. The specification says very little about these processes, which allows the implementation considerable freedom to configure what kind of URLs are acceptable, and how the parsing is done. It is not even required that the resource starts life as XML: an implementation could quite legitimately return a document node that represents an HTML document, or the results of a database query. If the URL does refer to an XML file, there are still variations allowed in how it is parsed; for example, whether DTD or schema validation takes place, and whether XInclude references are expanded. A vendor might provide additional options such as the ability to strip comments, processing instructions, and unreferenced namespaces. You need to check the documentation for your product to see how such factors can be controlled.

The specification does say that whitespace-only nodes are stripped following the same rules as for the source document, based on the `<xsl:strip-space>` and `<xsl:preserve-space>` declarations in force. This is true even if the document happens to be a stylesheet.

URIs Held in Nodes

For a simple case such as «document(@href)», the result is a single node, namely the root node of the document referenced by the `href` attribute of the context node.

More generally, the argument may be a sequence of nodes, each of which contains a sequence of URIs. The result is then the sequence obtained by processing each of these in turn. For example, «document(//@href)» returns the sequence of documents located by dereferencing the URIs in all the `href` attributes in the original context document. The result is returned in document order of the returned nodes (a somewhat academic concept since they will usually be different documents). The result is not necessarily in the order of the `href` attributes, and duplicates will be eliminated.

If any of the nodes contains a relative URI, it will be resolved relative to the base URI of that node. The base URI of a node is established using the rules given on page 45. In fact, each node in the supplied sequence could potentially have a different base URI.

This all sounds terribly complicated, but all it really means is that if the source document contains the link «data.xml», then the system will look for the file `data.xml` in the same directory as the source document.

These rules also cover the case where the argument is a reference to a variable containing a temporary tree, for example:

```
<xsl:variable name="index">index.xml</xsl:variable>
<xsl:for-each select="document($index)">
 . . .
</xsl:for-each>
```

In this case relative URI «index.xml» is resolved relative to the base URI of the `<xsl:variable>` element in the stylesheet, which is generally the URI of the stylesheet module itself.

Usage: document() Applied to Nodes

A common use of the `document()` function is to access a document referenced from the source document, typically in an attribute such as `href`. For example, a book catalog might include links to reviews of each book, in a format such as:

```
<book>
    <review date="1999-12-28" publication="New York Times"
                    text="reviews/NYT/19991228/rev3.xml"/>
```

```
            <review date="2000-01-06" publication="Washington Post"
                                text="reviews/WPost/20000106/rev12.xml"/>
    </book>
```

If you want to incorporate the text of these reviews in your output document, you can achieve this using the `document()` function. For example:

```
<xsl:template match="book">
    <xsl:for-each select="review">
        <h2>Review in <xsl:value-of select="@publication"/></h2>
        <xsl:apply-templates select="document(@text)"/>
    </xsl:for-each>
</xsl:template>
```

As the argument `@text` is a node, the result will be the root node of the document whose URI is the value of the `text` attribute, interpreted relative to the base URI of the `<review>` element, which (unless it comes from an external XML entity or is affected by an `xml:base` attribute on some ancestor node) will be the same as the URI of the source document itself.

Note that in processing the review document, exactly the same template rules are used as we used for the source document itself. There is no concept of particular template rules being tied to particular document types. If the review document uses the same element tags as the book catalog, but with different meanings, this can potentially create problems. There are two possible ways round this:

❑ *Namespaces*: use a different namespace for the book catalog and for the review documents.

❑ *Modes*: use a different mode to process nodes in the review document, so that the `<xsl:apply-templates>` instruction in the example would become:

```
<xsl:apply-templates select="document(@text)" mode="review"/>
```

You might find that even if the element names are distinct, the use of modes is a good discipline for maintaining readability of your stylesheet. For more detail on modes, see `<xsl:apply-templates>` (page 240) and `<xsl:template>` (page 483) in Chapter 6.

Another useful approach, which helps to keep your stylesheet modular, is to include the templates for processing the review document in a separate stylesheet incorporated using `<xsl:include>`.

Example: Using the document() Function to Analyze a Stylesheet

A stylesheet is an XML document, so it can be used as the input to another stylesheet. This makes it very easy to write little tools that manipulate stylesheets. This example shows such a tool, designed to report on the hierarchic structure of the modules that make up a stylesheet.

This example uses the `document()` function to examine a stylesheet and see which stylesheet modules it incorporates using `<xsl:include>` or `<xsl:import>`. The modules referenced by `<xsl:include>` or `<xsl:import>` are fetched and processed recursively.

Source

The source is any stylesheet, preferably one that uses `<xsl:include>` or `<xsl:import>`. A file `dummy.xsl` is provided in the code download for the book for you to use as a sample.

Stylesheet

The stylesheet `list-includes.xsl` uses the `document()` function to access the document referenced in the `href` attribute of `<xsl:include>` or `<xsl:import>`. It then applies the same template rules to this document, recursively. Note that the root template is applied only to the initial source document, to create the HTML skeleton page.

```
<xsl:transform
 xmlns:xsl="http://www.w3.org/1999/XSL/Transform"
 version="1.0"
>
<xsl:template match="/">
  <html>
  <head><title><xsl:value-of select="static-base-uri()"/></title></head>
  <body>
    <h1>Stylesheet Module Structure</h1>
    <p><xsl:value-of select="static-base-uri()"/></p>
    <ul>
      <xsl:apply-templates select="*/xsl:include | */xsl:import"/>
    </ul>
  </body></html>
</xsl:template>
<xsl:template match="xsl:include | xsl:import">
 <li><xsl:value-of select="concat(local-name(), 's ' ,@href)"/>
  <xsl:variable name="module" select="document(@href)"/>
  <ul>
   <xsl:apply-templates
        select="$module/*/xsl:include | $module/*/xsl:import"/>
  </ul>
 </li>
</xsl:template>
</xsl:transform>
```

Output

The output for the `dummy.xsl` stylesheet is as shown in Figure 13-1.

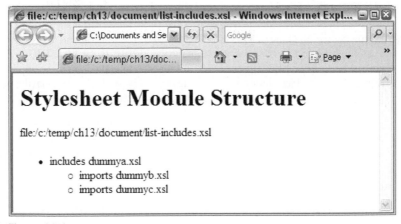

Figure 13-1

URIs as Atomic Values

As an alternative to supplying a URI that is held in the content of a node, the first argument may supply a URI as an atomic string. For convenience, the function accepts both `xs:string` and `xs:anyURI` types, as well as untyped atomic values. (Untyped atomic values are unlikely to arise in practice, since they normally arise only from atomizing a node in a schemaless document, and if you supply a node as an argument to the `document()` function, then the rules that apply are those in the previous section, *URIs Held in Nodes*.)

The first argument may be evaluated to produce a single atomic value containing a URI or a sequence of them. It is even possible to mix atomic values and nodes in the input sequence; nodes are processed as described in the previous section, and atomic values as described here.

The most common case is a URL hard-coded in the stylesheet, for example «`document ('tax-rates.xml')`».

Another common case is «`document('')`», which refers to the stylesheet itself. This construct was often used with XSLT 1.0, where it provided a convenient way to maintain look-up tables in the stylesheet itself. It is likely to be less common with XSLT 2.0, since the ability to hold a temporary tree in a global variable is usually much more convenient. The URI may be supplied as an `xs:string`, an `xs:anyURI`, or an untyped atomic value, and in each case is converted to a string. (XSLT 1.0 also allowed it to be supplied as a boolean or an integer, which creates a theoretical backward incompatibility — but since converting a boolean or number is unlikely to yield a useful URL, the point is rather academic.)

The string is treated as a URI reference; that is, a URI optionally followed by a fragment identifier separated from the URI proper by a «#» character. If it is a relative URI, it is treated as being relative to the base URI of the stylesheet element that contains the expression in which the function call was encountered. This will normally be the URI of the principal stylesheet document, but it may be different if `<xsl:include>` or `<xsl:import>` was used, or if pieces of the stylesheet are contained in external XML entities, or if the base URI of any relevant element in the stylesheet has been set explicitly by using the `xml:base` attribute.

Again, all this really means is that relative URLs are handled just like relative URLs in HTML. If you write «`document('tax-rates.xml')`» in a particular stylesheet module, then the system looks for the file `tax-rates.xml` in the same directory as that stylesheet module.

If the string is an empty string, then the document referenced by the base URI is used. The XSLT specification states that «`document("")`» will return the root node of the stylesheet. Strictly speaking, however, this is true only if the base URI of the XSL element containing the call to the `document()` function is the same as the system identifier of the stylesheet module. If the base URI is different, perhaps because the stylesheet has been built up from a number of external entities, or because the `xml:base` attribute has been used, the object loaded by «`document("")`» will not necessarily be the current stylesheet module; in fact, it might not be a well-formed document at all, in which case an error will be reported.

If the call is contained in a stylesheet brought in using `<xsl:include>` or `<xsl:import>`, it returns the root node of the included or imported stylesheet, not that of the principal stylesheet document.

Usage: document() Applied to Atomic Values

With XSLT 1.0, this form of the `document()` function was very useful for handling data used by the stylesheet for reference information; for example, look-up tables to expand abbreviations, message files in different languages, or the text of the message of the day, to be displayed to users on the login screen.

Such data can either be in the stylesheet itself (referenced as «document("")») or be in a separate file held in the same directory as the stylesheet (referenced as «document("messages.xml")») or a related directory (for example «document("../data/messages.xml")»).

With XSLT 2.0, it is no longer necessary to use a secondary document for these purposes, because the data can be held in a tree-valued variable in the stylesheet and accessed directly. However, it may in some cases be more convenient to maintain the data in a separate file (for example, it makes it easier to generate the data periodically from a database), and in any case you may still want to write stylesheets that work with XSLT 1.0 processors, especially if you want the transformation to happen client-side. So I'll show the XSLT 1.0 technique first and then show how the same problem can be tackled in XSLT 2.0.

XSLT allows data such as look-up tables to appear within any top-level stylesheet element, provided it belongs to a non-default namespace.

Example: A Look-Up Table in the Stylesheet

This example uses data in a look-up table to expand abbreviations of book categories. Two techniques are shown: in the first example the look-up table is held in the stylesheet; in the second example it is held in a separate XML document.

Source

This is the `booklist.xml` file we saw earlier:

```
<booklist>
<book category="S">
    <title>Number, the Language of Science</title>
    <author>Danzig</author>
</book>
<book category="FC">
    <title>The Young Visiters</title>
    <author>Daisy Ashford</author>
</book>
<book category="FC">
    <title>When We Were Very Young</title>
    <author>A. A. Milne</author>
</book>
<book category="CS">
    <title>Design Patterns</title>
    <author>Erich Gamma</author>
    <author>Richard Helm</author>
    <author>Ralph Johnson</author>
    <author>John Vlissides</author>
</book>
</booklist>
```

Stylesheet

The stylesheet is `list-categories.xsl`. It processes each of the `<book>` elements in the source file and, for each one, finds the `<book:category>` element in the stylesheet whose `code` attribute matches the `category` attribute of the `<book>`. Note the use of `current()` to refer to the current book; it would be wrong to use «.» here, because «.» refers to the context node, which is the `<book:category>` element being tested.

```
<xsl:transform
 xmlns:xsl="http://www.w3.org/1999/XSL/Transform"
 version="1.0"
 xmlns:book="http://ns.wrox.com/books.uri"
 exclude-result-prefixes="book"
>
<xsl:template match="/">
  <html><body>
    <xsl:for-each select="//book">
       <h1><xsl:value-of select="title"/></h1>
       <p>Category: <xsl:value-of
                     select="document('')/*/book:category
                     [@code=current()/@category]/@desc"/>
       </p>
    </xsl:for-each>
  </body></html>
</xsl:template>
<book:category code="S" desc="Science"/>
<book:category code="CS" desc="Computing"/>
<book:category code="FC" desc="Children's Fiction"/>
</xsl:transform>
```

Output

The output of this stylesheet is as follows:

```
<html>
   <body>
      <h1>Number, the Language of Science</h1>
      <p>Category: Science</p>
      <h1>The Young Visiters</h1>
      <p>Category: Children's Fiction</p>
      <h1>When We Were Very Young</h1>
      <p>Category: Children's Fiction</p>
      <h1>Design Patterns</h1>
      <p>Category: Computing</p>
   </body>
</html>
```

XSLT 2.0 Stylesheet

Now, let's modify this stylesheet to take advantage of XSLT 2.0 facilities. It's renamed `list-categories2-0.xsl`. It isn't a big change; the lines that are different are shown with a shaded background.

```
<xsl:transform
 xmlns:xsl="http://www.w3.org/1999/XSL/Transform"
 version="2.0"
```

```
    >
    <xsl:template match="/">
      <html><body>
        <xsl:for-each select="//book">
           <h1><xsl:value-of select="title"/></h1>
             <p>Category: <xsl:value-of
                          select="$categories[@code=current()/@category]/@desc"/>
           </p>
        </xsl:for-each>
      </body></html>
    </xsl:template>
      <xsl:variable name="categories" as="element(category)*">
      <category code="S" desc="Science"/>
      <category code="CS" desc="Computing"/>
      <category code="FC" desc="Children's Fiction"/>
      </xsl:variable>
    </xsl:transform>
```

Supplying an Explicit Base URI

This section discusses what happens when the second argument to the document() function is supplied. In this instance, instead of using the containing node or the stylesheet as the base for resolving a relative reference, the base URI of the node supplied as the second argument is used. In other words, if a node in href contains a relative reference such as «data.xml», the system will look for the file data.xml in the directory containing the XML document from which the node in $base was derived.

The value of the second argument must be a single node. For example, the call «document(@href, /)» will use the root node of the source document as the base URI, even if the element containing the href attribute was found in an external entity with a different URI.

This option is not one that you will need to use very often, but it is there for completeness. If you want to interpret a link relative to the stylesheet, you can write, for example:

```
document(@href, document(""))
```

This works because the second argument returns the root node of the stylesheet, which is then used as the base URI for the relative reference contained in the href attribute.

With the extended function library that XPath 2.0 makes available, an alternative is to resolve the relative reference yourself by calling the resolve-uri() function, which is described on page 867. This allows you to resolve against any base URI, which does not have to be the base URI of any particular node. I have used this in a situation where the base URI for resolving references was passed as a parameter to the stylesheet.

See Also

id() on page 802
key() on page 812
resolve-uri() on page 867

763

document-uri

The `document-uri()` function returns a URI associated with a document node.

Signature

Argument	Type	Meaning
input	`node()?`	The document node whose URI is required. If the node is not a document node, or if an empty sequence is supplied, the empty sequence is returned.
Result	`xs:string?`	*The URI of the document node.*

Effect

The URI that is returned is always an absolute URI, and it has the property that if you passed it as an argument to the `doc()` function, you would get the input node back.

If no absolute URI is known for the supplied document node, the empty sequence is returned.

Usage

This function is provided to allow a reference to a particular document to be constructed, either in the result document of an XSLT transformation, or simply in error messages. It is particularly useful where the transformation is processing a large batch of similar input documents, accessed perhaps using the `collection()` function, or perhaps supplied as a parameter to the transformation or query in a global variable.

To take an XSLT example, you might be producing a result document that acts as an index to a collection of input documents. This might include code such as:

```
<xsl:for-each select="collection('documents')">
   <xsl:sort select="/doc/title"/>
   <p><a href="{document-uri(.)}">
        <xsl:value-of select="/doc/title"/>
      </a>
   </p>
</xsl:for-each>
```

See Also

base-uri() on page 719
collection() on page 726
doc() on page 750

element-available

This function is available in XSLT only.

This function is used to test whether a particular XSLT instruction or extension element is available for use.

For example, the expression «element-available('xsl:text')» returns `true`.

Changes in 2.0

None.

Signature

Argument	Type	Meaning
name	xs:string	The name of the element being tested. The string must take the form of a lexical QName.
Result	*xs:boolean*	*true if the named element is available for use as an instruction, false otherwise.*

Effect

The first argument must take the form of a lexical QName: that is, an XML name with an optional namespace prefix that corresponds to a namespace declaration that is in scope at the point in the stylesheet where the element-available() function is called.

If this namespace declaration identifies the XSLT namespace http://www.w3.org/1999/XSL/Transform, then the function returns true if the name is the name of an XSLT-defined *instruction*, and false otherwise.

The instructions defined in XSLT 1.0 were as follows.

```
<xsl:apply-imports>
<xsl:apply-templates>
<xsl:attribute>
<xsl:call-template>
<xsl:choose>
<xsl:comment>
<xsl:copy>
<xsl:copy-of>
<xsl:element>
<xsl:fallback>
<xsl:for-each>
<xsl:if>
<xsl:message>
<xsl:number>
<xsl:processing-instruction>
<xsl:text>
<xsl:value-of>
<xsl:variable>
```

In the XSLT 2.0 specification, several new instructions have been added to this list.

```
<xsl:analyze-string>
<xsl:document>
<xsl:for-each-group>
<xsl:next-match>
<xsl:perform-sort>
<xsl:namespace>
<xsl:result-document>
<xsl:sequence>
```

13

The Function Library

765

Instructions are XSLT elements that can appear directly within a sequence constructor. Top-level XSLT declarations such as <xsl:template> and <xsl:key> are not instructions, so in theory they should return false (but don't rely on it: at least one popular processor, Microsoft MSXML3, returns true for all XSLT elements). Similarly, elements such as <xsl:param>, <xsl:with-param>, <xsl:sort>, <xsl:when>, and <xsl:otherwise> are not instructions, because they can appear only in specific contexts and not anywhere in a sequence constructor.

If the prefix of the QName identifies any namespace other than the XSLT namespace, then the function returns true if and only if the XSLT processor has an implementation available for the named instruction: that is, if this element can be used as an extension instruction in a sequence constructor, rather than being treated simply as a literal result element.

Note that the result of the element-available() function does not depend on whether the namespace has been designated as an extension namespace by using the [xsl:]extension-element-prefixes attribute. If the XSLT processor has an implementation of the instruction available, the function should return true whether or not it is currently in a designated extension namespace.

If the QName has no prefix, the default namespace (declared using «xmlns="some.uri"») is used. This is one of the few cases where this happens, and the reason is that the name is always an element name: the default namespace applies only to elements.

However, if the QName expands to a name with a null namespace URI, the result of the function will always be false. This is because both XSLT instructions and extension elements will always have a non-null namespace URI.

In principle, you can construct the value of the argument as a runtime expression, rather than supplying it as a string literal. I can't think of any possible reason why it might be useful to do this, but implementors have to allow for the possibility.

Usage and Examples

There are two ways to use this function: it can be used to test for XSLT elements introduced in a later version of XSLT, and it can be used to test for the presence of vendor or third-party extensions.

Testing for Features Available in Later XSLT Versions

This function was introduced in XSLT 1.0, but it becomes useful only now that version 2.0 of the specification is available. As we've seen, the XSLT 2.0 specification introduces several new instructions. If you want to use an instruction such as <xsl:next-match> that became available only in a particular version of XSLT, then you can test to see whether it is available with your chosen XSLT processor before using it. If it is not available, you can either use <xsl:if> or the use-when attribute to avoid executing it, or use the <xsl:fallback> mechanism to cope with its absence.

So why was the function specified as part of version 1.0? The answer is obvious when you think about it: you want to write a stylesheet that uses version 2.0 features, so you call element-available() in order to fail gracefully if you're running with an XSLT processor that supports version 1.0 features only. However, this will work only if the version 1.0 XSLT processor supports the element-available() function, which is why it was specified from the start. This is an unusually thoughtful piece of forward planning: the XSLT designers didn't want to get into the same kind of forward-compatibility problems that have bedeviled HTML. Of course, it still means that if you want your stylesheet to run with XSLT processors that support different levels of the language, you will have to write and test conditional code in your stylesheet, but at least the capability is there.

In principle, you can test whether a version 1.0 instruction is available on the basis that there may be subset implementations around; unfortunately, this will work only if the subset implementation includes the element-available() function, which is not guaranteed; it tends to be one of the things that implementors leave till last.

> *It's tempting to use the* use-when *attribute to mask XSLT 2.0 code from XSLT 1.0 processors. This doesn't work, unfortunately, as* use-when *is a 2.0 facility, and 1.0 processors won't recognize it.*

Note that if you write a stylesheet that uses features defined in XSLT version 2.0, and if you want to run it with an XSLT 1.0 processor, then you must specify «version="2.0"» on the <xsl:stylesheet> element, or «xsl:version="2.0"» on some literal result element, even if you write an <xsl:if> test using element-available() to avoid executing the relevant code. If you specify «version="1.0"», then any use of new XSLT 2.0 elements is flagged as an error even if the code is never executed.

Here is an example that tests to see whether the new XSLT 2.0 facility to produce multiple output documents is available by testing element-available('xsl:result-document'). If it isn't available, you can use an alternative approach; for example, you can use the proprietary syntax for this functionality offered by your chosen XSLT 1.0 processor.

Example: Creating Multiple Output Files

This example takes a poem as input, and outputs each stanza to a separate file. A more realistic example would be to split a book into its chapters, but I wanted to keep the files small. The example is written to work with Saxon version 6.x (which implements XSLT 1.0) and also with any processor that conforms to the XSLT 2.0 specification.

Source

The source file is poem.xml. It starts:

```
<poem>
<author>Rupert Brooke</author>
<date>1912</date>
<title>Song</title>
<stanza>
<line>And suddenly the wind comes soft,</line>
<line>And Spring is here again;</line>
<line>And the hawthorn quickens with buds of green</line>
<line>And my heart with buds of pain.</line>
</stanza>
<stanza>
<line>My heart all Winter lay so numb,</line>
<line>The earth so dead and frore,</line>
. . .
```

Stylesheet

The stylesheet is in file split.xsl. The part to look at is the <xsl:choose> instruction, where each branch calls element-available() to test whether a particular instruction is available, before calling that instruction.

13

The Function Library

Note that «saxon» is defined as an extension element prefix, so the `<saxon:output>` element is recognized as an instruction. The `<xsl:stylesheet>` element specifies «version="2.0"» so that an XSLT 1.0 processor will not reject `<xsl:result-document>` as an error.

```xml
<?xml version="1.0"?>
<xsl:stylesheet xmlns:xsl="http://www.w3.org/1999/XSL/Transform"
    version="2.0">
<xsl:template match="poem">
    <poem>
        <xsl:copy-of select="title"/>
        <xsl:copy-of select="author"/>
        <xsl:copy-of select="date"/>
        <xsl:apply-templates select="stanza"/>
    </poem>
</xsl:template>
<xsl:template match="stanza">
    <xsl:variable name="file"
                  select="concat('verse', string(position()), '.xml')"/>
    <verse number="{position()}" href="{$file}"/>
    <xsl:choose>
    <xsl:when test="element-available('xsl:result-document')">
        <xsl:result-document href="{$file}">
            <xsl:copy-of select="."/>
        </xsl:result-document>
    </xsl:when>
    <xsl:when test="element-available('saxon:output')"
              xmlns:saxon="http://icl.com/saxon">
        <saxon:output file="{$file}"
                      xsl:extension-element-prefixes="saxon">
            <xsl:copy-of select="."/>
        </saxon:output>
    </xsl:when>
    <xsl:otherwise>
        <xsl:message terminate="yes"
            >Cannot write to multiple output files</xsl:message>
    </xsl:otherwise>
    </xsl:choose>
</xsl:template>
</xsl:stylesheet>
```

Output

Provided the stylesheet is run with one of the processors that support the required capability, the principal output file will contain the following skeletal poem (new lines added for legibility).

```xml
<?xml version="1.0" encoding="utf-8" ?>
<poem>
<title>Song</title>
<author>Rupert Brooke</author>
<date>1912</date>
<verse number="1" href="verse1.xml"/>
```

```
<verse number="2" href="verse2.xml"/>
<verse number="3" href="verse3.xml"/>
</poem>
```

Three further output files verse1.xml, verse2.xml, and verse3.xml are created in the same directory as this outline. Here is verse1.xml:

```
<?xml version="1.0" encoding="utf-8" ?>
<stanza>
<line>And suddenly the wind comes soft,</line>
<line>And Spring is here again;</line>
<line>And the hawthorn quickens with buds of green</line>
<line>And my heart with buds of pain.</line>
</stanza>
```

To run this using Saxon 9.x (which implements XSLT 2.0), use a command line of the form:

```
java -jar c:\MyJava\saxon9.jar -t -o:c:\temp\outline.xml poem.xml split.xsl
```

With this command line, the output files will all be written to the directory c:\temp. The `<saxon:output>` instruction in Saxon 6.x works slightly differently: it will write the files verseN.xml to the current directory, not necessarily to the directory containing the outline.xml file.

Note that in this stylesheet, all the information needed to evaluate the `<xsl:when>` conditions is available at compile time. A good XSLT processor will generate code only for the path that is actually going to be executed.

You can't use element-available() to test whether the XSLT 2.0 element `<xsl:import-schema>` is available, because this is a declaration rather than an instruction, and a conformant XSLT 2.0 processor should therefore return false (the same result as an XSLT 1.0 processor). If you use this element in an XSLT 1.0 stylesheet, an error will be reported if you specify «version="1.0"» on the `<xsl:stylesheet>` element, but if you specify «version="2.0"», then an XSLT 1.0 processor will ignore the `<xsl:import-schema>` element, under the rules for forward-compatible processing. Instead you can test whether the XSLT processor you are using is schema-aware using the system-property() function (described on page 890 in this chapter) together with the use-when attribute described in the entry for `<xsl:stylesheet>` in Chapter 6.

Testing for Vendor Extensions

The previous example also demonstrates a second way of using the function, namely to test for vendor or third-party extensions. If you know that a particular extension instruction is present in some implementations and not others, you can use the element-available() test to see whether it is present, and again use either `<xsl:if>` or `<xsl:fallback>` to handle the situation when it isn't. The example split.xsl used this technique to test whether the `<saxon:output>` instruction was available.

An alternative to using the element-available() function is to use the `<xsl:fallback>` mechanism described in Chapter 3, page 141. An `<xsl:fallback>` element allows you to define what processing should occur if its containing instruction isn't available. The two mechanisms are essentially equivalent. A possible limitation of `<xsl:fallback>` is that it can only be used within an element that permits element children: it could not be used, for example, within <xsl:copy-of> as currently defined. However, all the new instructions in XSLT 2.0 have been designed so that <xsl:fallback> can be used as a child element.

See Also

function-available() on page 792
system-property() on page 890
type-available() on page 899
<xsl:fallback> in Chapter 6, page 316

empty

The empty() function returns true if and only if the argument is an empty sequence.

For example, the expression «empty(//a)» returns true if the context document contains no <a> elements.

Signature

Argument	Type	Meaning
sequence	item()*	The input sequence
Result	xs:boolean	true if the input sequence is empty, otherwise false

Effect

The function returns true if and only if the supplied sequence is empty.

Examples

Assume the source document:

```
<para>See also <a ref="elsewhere.xml" style=""/>.</para>
```

Expression	Result
empty(/para)	false
empty(/para/a)	false
empty(/para/a/@style)	false
empty(/para/b)	true
empty(/para/a[2])	true

Usage

Note that empty() is used only to test whether the number of items in a sequence is zero. As the examples above illustrate, it is *not* used to test whether a node is empty, in the sense of an element that has no children, or an attribute whose string value is a zero-length string.

To test whether an element $E has no element or text node children (or comments or processing instructions), you can write «if (empty($E/node()) ...».

To test whether the string value of a node $N is the zero-length string, you can write «if (string($N) eq "") ...».

Remember also that a test on any value in the condition of an «if» expression is done by taking the effective boolean value of the expression, as defined under the boolean() function on page 721. For example, if the expression is a path expression then the condition is true if the path expression selects one or more nodes; if it is a string, then the condition is true if the string is not zero-length. So, for example:

```
if (not(*)) then X else Y
```

has the same effect as:

```
if (empty(*)) then X else Y
```

and similarly, if @a refers to a list-valued attribute, then:

```
if (normalize-space(@a)) then X else Y
```

is equivalent to:

```
if (empty(data(@a))) then Y else X
```

See Also

boolean() on page 721
exists() on page 778
not() on page 850

encode-for-uri

The encode-for-uri() function is used to apply percent-encoding to special characters in a string when the string is intended to be used as part of a URI.

For example, «concat('http://www.wikipedia.org/', encode-for-uri('Gerhard Schröder'))» returns «http://www.wikipedia.org/Gerhard%20Schr%C3%B6der».

Signature

Argument	Type	Meaning
value	xs:string	The input string, to which percent-encoding is to be applied
Result	*xs:string*	*The percent-encoded string*

Effect

The result string is formed from the input string by escaping special characters according to the rules defined in RFC 3986, (http://www.ietf.org/rfc/rfc3986.txt). Special characters are escaped by first encoding them in UTF-8, then representing each byte of the UTF-8 encoding in the form %HH where HH represents the byte as two hexadecimal digits. The digits A–F are always in upper case.

All characters are escaped except the following:

❑   A-Z a-z 0-9

❑   hyphen «-», underscore «_», period «.», and tilde «~»

Examples

Expression	Result
encode-for-uri("simple.xml")	"simple.xml"
encode-for-uri("my doc.xml")	"my%20doc.xml"
encode-for-uri("f+o.pdf")	"f%2Bo.pdf"
encode-for-uri("Grüße.html")	"Gr%C3%BC%C3%9Fe.html"

Usage

This function is designed for use by applications that need to construct URIs.

The rules for URIs (given in RFC3986, http://www.ietf.org/rfc/rfc3986.txt) make it clear that a string in which special characters have not been escaped is not a valid URI. In many contexts where URIs are required, both in XPath functions such as the doc() function and in places such as the href attribute of the <a> element in HTML, the URI should in theory be fully escaped according to these rules. In practice, software is very often tolerant and accepts unescaped URIs, but applications shouldn't rely on this.

The rules for escaping special characters (officially called *percent-encoding*) are rather peculiar. To escape a character, it is first encoded in UTF-8, which in general represents a character as one or more octets (bytes). Each of these bytes is then substituted into the string using the notation «%HH», where HH is the value of the byte in hexadecimal. For example, the space character is represented as «%20», and the euro symbol as «%E2%82%AC». Although RFC 3986 allows the hexadecimal digits «A-F» to be in either upper or lower case, the encode-for-uri() function mandates upper case, to ensure that escaped URIs can be compared as strings.

Historically, the same algorithm has been used to escape URLs and URIs using character encodings other than UTF-8. However, in most environments where XPath is used UTF-8 is the recommended encoding for URIs, and this is therefore the only encoding that the encode-for-uri() function supports.

Which characters need to be escaped? The answer to this depends on context. Essentially, characters fall into three categories: those that can be used freely anywhere in a URI, those that cannot be used anywhere and must always be escaped, and those that have a special meaning in a URI and must be escaped if they are to be used without this special meaning. This function escapes everything except the first category (referred to in the RFC as *unreserved* characters).

Because this function applies escaping to characters that have special meaning in a URI, such as «/» and «:», it should never be used to escape a URI as a whole, only to escape the strings that make up the components of a URI while it is being constructed. In theory, this is always the right way to construct a URI: each of its components should be escaped individually (for example, the URI scheme, the authority, the path components, the query parameters, and the fragment identifier), and the components should then be assembled by adding the appropriate delimiters. This is the only way of ensuring, for example, that an «=» sign is escaped if it appears as an ordinary character in a path component, but not if it appears between a keyword and a value in the query part.

But often in practice the unescaped URI (if I may call it that — technically, if it isn't escaped then it isn't a URI) arrives in one piece and escaping needs to be applied to the whole string. In this case an alternative approach is to use the iri-to-uri() function described on page 811, or, if the URI appears in the context of an HTML document, the escape-html-uri() function described on page 775.

See Also

escape-html-uri() on page 775
iri-to-uri() on page 811
escape-uri-attributes serialization option in <xsl:output>: Chapter 15 page 938

ends-with

The ends-with() function tests whether one string ends with another string. For example, the expression
«ends-with('17 cm', 'cm')» returns true.

Signature

Argument	Type	Meaning
input	xs:string?	The containing string
test	xs:string?	The test string
collation (optional)	xs:string	A collation URI
Result	*xs:string?*	*True if the input string ends with the test string; otherwise, false*

Effect

If the Unicode codepoint collation is used (this is the default), then the system tests to see whether the last *N* characters of the input string match the characters in the test string (where *N* is the length of the test string). If so, the result is true; otherwise, it is false. Characters match if they have the same Unicode value.

If the test string is zero-length, the result is always true. If the input string is zero-length, the result is true only if the test string is also zero-length. If the test string is longer than the input, the result is always false.

If either the input or the test argument is an empty sequence, it is treated in the same way as a zero-length string.

If no collation is specified, then the default collation from the static context is used. If a collation is used, this collation is used to test whether the strings match. See the description of the contains() function on page 730 for an account of how substring matching works with a collation.

Examples

These examples assume that the default collation is the Unicode codepoint collation, which compares strings codepoint by codepoint.

Expression	Result
ends-with("a.xml", ".xml")	true
ends-with("a.xml", ".xsl")	false
ends-with("a.xml", "")	true
ends-with("", "")	true
ends-with((), ())	true

13

Usage

The `ends-with()` function is useful when the content of text values, or attributes, has some internal structure. For example, the following code can be used to strip an unwanted «/» at the end of an `href` attribute:

```
doc(if (ends-with(@href, '/')
    then substring(@href, 1, string-length(@href)-1)
    else @href)
```

Many string manipulations that can be done using `ends-with()` (but not those that rely on collations) can also be achieved using the `matches()` function, which allows regular expressions to be used. The above example could also be coded using `replace()`:

```
doc(replace(@href, '/$', ''))
```

See Also

`contains()` on page 730
`matches()` on page 828
`starts-with()` on page 875
`string-length()` on page 880
`substring()` on page 883

error

The `error()` function can be called when the application detects an error condition; it causes evaluation of the XPath expression as a whole to fail. In XSLT, this will cause the entire transformation to fail.

Signature

Argument	Type	Meaning
code (optional)	xs:QName?	An error code
description (optional)	xs:string	A description of the error
object (optional)	item()?	A value associated with the error
Result	*None*	*This function does not return a result; it always raises an error*

The `error()` function in fact has four signatures:

- ❑   `error()`
- ❑   `error(code)`
- ❑   `error(code, description)`
- ❑   `error(code, description, object)`

The `code` argument can be an empty sequence if the `description` is present, but not otherwise.

Effect

The `error()` function always reports an error, it never returns a result.

Calling the `error()` function causes the XPath expression as a whole to fail, since XPath provides no try/catch mechanism for catching errors.

Under XSLT, calling the error function causes the whole transformation to fail: the effect is the same as `<xsl:message terminate="yes"/>`.

The various arguments can be used to provide information about the error. The exact way in which this information is used depends on the implementation.

Error codes are defined as QNames. The error codes defined by the system (such as `XPTY0004` for the type error that occurs when calling a function with incorrect arguments) are technically local names associated with the namespace `http://www.w3.org/2005/xqt-errors`. User-defined error codes should be in a user-owned namespace. There is an assumption that a calling application will have access to these error codes, either as a QName, or as a URI with a fragment identifier (for example `http://www.w3.org/2005/xqt-errors#XPTY0004`). However, the details depend on the API design.

Examples

Expression	Result
`error()`	Causes termination, with no explanation
`error(xs:QName("docbook: invalid-page-ref"))`	Causes termination, with an error code «invalid-page-ref» in the namespace associated with the «docbook» prefix
`error((), "Invalid parameter value")`	Causes termination, with a specified message, but no specified error code

Usage

The `error()` function is useful when the application encounters a condition that it is not designed to handle, for example, invalid arguments passed to a function.

Every runtime error defined by the XSLT and XPath suite of specifications itself has a short code, such as FORG0001. These codes (which are listed in Appendix B) are all to be regarded as the local part of a QName, whose namespace URI is `http://www.w3.org/2005/xqt-errors`. The specification suggests that this code might be made available to applications via the API of the XPath processor, though there is nothing prescriptive about this. It makes sense for vendor-defined and user-defined error codes to fit into the same scheme of things by using `xs:QName` values as error values, with an explicit namespace. An implementation that allows error messages to be localized will typically provide some way of using the `xs:QName` as a code to look up a message in a file of message texts appropriate to the user's language.

This error-handling scheme is fine for product-quality applications that need to be delivered to a large number of users, localized to different languages, and so on. If you're just writing a simple stylesheet that's going to be used once and thrown away, it's all rather over the top. In this case, you can just pass a message that says what's gone wrong in the form of a string.

See Also

`trace()` on page 896
`<xsl:message>` in Chapter 6 on page 386
Error codes: Appendix B

escape-html-uri

The `escape-html-uri()` function applies the URI escaping conventions defined in the HTML 4.0 specification to an input string.

For example, «escape-html-uri('http://www.wikipedia.org/Gerhard Schröder')» returns «http://www.wikipedia.org/Gerhard Schr%C3%B6der».

Signature

Argument	Type	Meaning
value	xs:string?	The input string, to which URI escaping is to be applied. An empty sequence is treated as a zero-length string.
Result	xs:string	The URI in its escaped form, as a string.

Effect

The result string is formed from the input string by escaping non-ASCII characters according to the rules defined in the HTML 4.0 specification. Non-ASCII characters are escaped by first encoding them in UTF-8, then representing each byte of the UTF-8 encoding in the form %HH where HH represents the byte as two hexadecimal digits. The digits A–F are always in upper case.

The term "non-ASCII" here means any Unicode character outside the codepoint range x20 to x7E inclusive. Note in particular that a space character is *not* escaped.

Examples

Expression	Result
escape-html-uri("http://mhk.me.uk/~index.html")	"http://mhk.me.uk/~index.html"
escape-html-uri("my doc.xml")	"my doc.xml"
escape-html-uri("Grüße.html")	"Gr%C3%BC%C3%9Fe.html"

Usage

This function is designed for use by applications that generate HTML.

By default, when the HTML or XHTML serialization methods are used (see Chapter 15), all attributes that are defined in the HTML/XHTML specification as containing URIs will be escaped by the serializer, using the rules defined for this function. In principle, therefore, the necessary escaping is done automatically.

There are two situations where escaping sometimes needs to be done manually, that is, by means of explicit calls on this function:

❑ When the output contains URIs in attributes that are not defined as URI attributes in the HTML and XHTML specifications. This can arise because there are many extensions of HTML in popular use, and because XHTML allows embedding of other XML vocabularies such as SVG and MathML that may themselves make use of URIs.

❑ When the automatic action of the serializer has been disabled by setting the serialization property «escape-uri-attributes» to the value «no». This is sometimes necessary to prevent unwanted escaping, especially of URI attributes that are interpreted locally within the browser. Although the HTML specification states that all URI attributes should be escaped, the reality is that in today's browsers this can sometimes cause problems; for example, when a "URI" is actually JavaScript code, or when a fragment identifier in a hyperlink contains a same-document reference to an anchor whose name contains non-ASCII characters. If automatic URI escaping in the serializer is causing such problems, it can be switched off, and the stylesheet can then perform manual escaping of selected URIs using the `escape-html-uri()` function.

See Also

`encode-for-uri()` on page 771
`iri-to-uri()` on page 811
`escape-uri-attributes` option in `<xsl:output>`: Chapter 15

exactly-one

The `exactly-one()` function returns its argument unchanged, provided that it is a sequence containing exactly one item. In other cases, it reports an error.

Signature

Argument	Type	Meaning
value	`item()*`	The input value. Although the function signature says that any sequence of items is allowed, a runtime error will occur if the number of items is not exactly one.
Result	`item()`	*The same as the supplied value, after checking to ensure that it contains a single item.*

Effect

The `exactly-one()` function returns its argument unchanged, provided that it is a sequence containing exactly one item. In other cases, it reports an error.

This function is useful with XPath processors that perform pessimistic static type checking, as described in Chapter 5. As such, it is unlikely to be needed in XSLT. Calling this function acts as a promise by the programmer that the argument will be a sequence containing exactly one item. This allows the expression to be used in contexts that require a single value (for example, the operands of the «is» operator) when the processor might otherwise have reported a static type error. The XPath expression is still type-safe, because the check that the sequence does indeed contain a single item will be done at runtime, just as it would with a processor that does not enforce static type checking.

Examples

Assume the source document:

```
<list separator=";"/>
```

with a schema that defines the `separator` attribute to be optional.

Expression	Result
`string-join(("a", "b", "c"), /list/@separator)`	Succeeds unless the processor is doing static type checking, in which case it gives a compile-time error because the second argument of `string-join()` must not be an empty sequence.
`string-join(("a", "b", "c"), exactly-one (/list/@separator))`	Succeeds whether the processor is doing static type checking or not, because the check that the typed value of `@separator` contains a single item is deferred until runtime.

Usage

This function is never needed unless you are using a processor that does static type checking.

However, you may still find it useful as a way of inserting runtime checks into your XPath expressions, and documenting the assumptions you are making about the input data.

See Also

one-or-more() on page 853
zero-or-one() on page 912
«treat as» expression on page 678 in Chapter 11

exists

The exists() function returns true if and only if a supplied sequence contains at least one item.

Signature

Argument	Type	Meaning
sequence	item()*	The input sequence
Result	*xs:boolean*	true *if the input sequence is non-empty; otherwise,* false

Effect

The function returns true if and only if the supplied sequence contains at least one item.

Examples

Assume the source document:

```
<para>See also <a ref="elsewhere.xml" style=""/>.</para>
```

Expression	Result
exists(/para)	true
exists(/para/a)	true
exists(/para/a/@style)	true
exists(/para/b)	false
exists(/para/a[2])	false

Usage

This function is largely cosmetic: when testing to see if nodes exist, some people prefer to write an expression such as «author[exists(child::element())]» over the more cryptic «author[*]». But they have the same meaning.

Writing exists() explicitly is good practice when you are testing to see whether a sequence of atomic values (rather than nodes) is non-empty. This is because the effective boolean value of an atomic sequence is false not only when the sequence is empty, but also when it contains a single numeric zero, zero-length string, or boolean false value.

Writing «exists(X)» is precisely equivalent to writing «not(empty(X))».

See Also

boolean() on page 721
empty() on page 770
not() on page 850

false

This function returns the boolean value false.

Changes in 2.0

None.

Signature

There are no arguments.

	Type	Meaning
Result	*xs:boolean*	*The xs:boolean value false*

Usage

There are no boolean constants available in XPath expressions, so the functions true() and false() can be used where a constant boolean value is required.

The most common usage is when passing an argument to a function that expects a boolean value.

XSLT Example

The following code calls a named template, setting the parameter «verbose» to false:

```
<xsl:call-template name="do-the-work">
    <xsl:with-param name="verbose" select="false()"/>
</xsl:call-template>
```

See Also

true() on page 899

floor

The floor() function returns the largest integer value that is less than or equal to the numeric value of the argument. The result has the same type as the supplied value. For example, if the supplied value is an xs:double, then the result is returned as an xs:double.

For example, the expression «floor(11.3)» returns 11.0 (this is displayed as "11", but it is actually a decimal value).

Changes in 2.0

The function has been generalized to work with all numeric types.

Signature

Argument	Type	Meaning
value	Numeric?	The supplied number. If an empty sequence is supplied, an empty sequence is returned.
Result	Numeric?	*The result of rounding down the supplied number to the integer below. The result has the same type as the supplied value.*

Effect

If the number is an xs:integer, or is equal to an xs:integer, then it is returned unchanged.

Otherwise, it is rounded down to the next lowest whole number. If the supplied value is an xs:decimal, the result will be an xs:decimal, if it is an xs:double, the result will be an xs:double, and if it is an xs:float, the result will be an xs:float. In the case of negative numbers, the rounding is away from zero.

The xs:double and xs:float types in XPath support special values such as infinity, negative zero and NaN (not-a-number), which are described on page 199 in Chapter 5.

If the argument is NaN (not-a-number), the result will be NaN. Similarly, when the argument is positive or negative infinity, the function will return the value of the argument unchanged.

Examples

Expression	Result
floor(1.0)	xs:decimal 1.0, displayed as «1»
floor(1.6e0)	xs:double 1.0e0, displayed as «1»
floor(17 div 3)	xs:decimal 5.0, displayed as «5»
floor(-3.0)	xs:decimal −3.0, displayed as «-3»
floor(-8.2e0)	xs:double −9.0e0, displayed as «-9»
floor(number('NaN'))	xs:double NaN

Usage

Like round() and ceiling(), this function is useful when calculating sizes of HTML tables.

Two alternatives you may want to consider are:

❏ Using the xs:integer() constructor function. This differs from floor() in that it always truncates (rounds toward zero); also, it returns an actual integer, rather than returning a value of the same type as the argument.

❏ Using the expression «$x idiv 1». This produces the same result as the xs:integer() constructor function, but saves you from having to declare the XML Schema namespace.

See Also

ceiling() on page 723
round() on page 870

Converting to an xs:integer in Chapter 9, page 667
The «idiv» operator, under *Arithmetic Operators* in Chapter 8, page 574

format-date, format-dateTime, format-time

These three functions are available in XSLT only.

The three functions format-date(), format-dateTime(), and format-time() return a formatted representation of a date and/or time, as a string. For example, «format-date(current-date(), '[MNn] [D], [Y]')» might return the string «December 31, 2009».

Signature

Argument	Type	Meaning
value	xs:date? xs:dateTime? xs:time?	The date, dateTime, or time to be formatted. The type of value is determined by the name of the function.
picture	xs:string	A picture string identifying the components to be output and the format in which they are output.
language (optional)	xs:string?	A string following the same rules as the xml:lang attribute in XML, to indicate the language to be used for formatting the date/time. For example, «en» indicates English, «de» German, and «es» Spanish.
calendar (optional)	xs:string?	A string giving a code for the calendar to be used for formatting the date/time.
country (optional)	xs:string?	A code identifying the country associated with the date/time, for example the country in which the dated event took place.
Result	xs:string?	*The formatted date/time.*

The last three arguments are optional, but they must either all be supplied or all be omitted. That is, the function must be called either with two arguments or with five. Calling it with two arguments is equivalent to supplying an empty sequence «()» for each of the last three arguments; an empty sequence for any of these arguments invokes the default value.

Effect

If the value argument is an empty sequence, then the result is an empty sequence.

The Picture Argument

The picture argument consists of a string containing so-called variable markers enclosed in square brackets. Characters outside the square brackets are literal characters to be copied to the result; variable markers within the square brackets indicate components of the date and time to be added to the output string, and the format in which they are to be displayed.

If square brackets are needed as literal characters in the result they should be doubled.

For example, if the picture is given as «[D1]/[M1]/[Y1,4]» then the date 1 February 2008 will be displayed as «1/2/2008».

Each variable marker consists of a *component specifier* identifying which component of the date or time is to be displayed; an optional *formatting token*; an optional *presentation modifier*; and finally, an optional *width modifier*, preceded by a comma if it is present.

The components of the date and time are identified by the following letters:

Letter	Component	Default Format
Y	Year	Four digits
M	Month of year	Numeric 1–12
D	Day of month	Numeric 1–31
d	Day of year	Numeric 1–366
F	Day of week	Name of day (language dependent)
W	Week of year	Numeric 1–53
w	Week of month	Numeric 1–5
H	Hour (24 hours)	Numeric 00–23
h	Hour (12 hours)	Numeric 1–12
P	A.M. or P.M.	Alphabetic (language dependent)
m	Minutes in hour	Numeric 00–59
s	Seconds in minute	Numeric 00–59
f	Fractional seconds	Numeric, one decimal place
Z	Timezone	Numeric, for example +08:00
z	Timezone	GMT+n
C	Calendar	Name of calendar, for example «Old Style»
E	Era	Text or abbreviation describing the baseline from which the year is calculated, for example A.D. or the name of a monarch

The formatting token consists of one or more additional letters or digits. The value can be either a formatting token recognized by the <xsl:number> instruction (see page 403 in Chapter 6), or one of the values «N» «n», or «Nn» indicating that the component is to be output by name. Ignoring values such as «a» and «A» that are unlikely to be useful, at least in English, this leaves the following as examples of the possibilities.

Character	Resulting Format	Example
1	Decimal numeric format with no leading zeroes: 1, 2, 3, . . .	1, 2, 3
01	Decimal format, two digits: 01, 02, 03, . . .	01, 02, 03
Other Unicode digit	Decimal numeric format, using the set of Unicode digits in which the given digit represents the value one.	١,٢,٣,٤,٥
i	Lower-case Roman numerals.	i, ii, iii, iv

continued

Character	Resulting Format	Example
I	Upper-case Roman numerals.	I, II, III, IV
N	Name of component, in upper case.	MONDAY, TUESDAY
n	Name of component, in lower case.	monday, tuesday
Nn	Name of component, in title case.	Monday, Tuesday
W	Number expressed in upper case words.	ONE, TWO, THREE
w	Number expressed in lower case words.	one, two, three
Ww	Number expressed in title case words.	One, Two, Three
t	Indicates so-called traditional numbering. The meaning of this depends on the language; it is intended to produce the same effect as «letter-value="traditional"» in <xsl:number>. The requirement most often cited is for Hebrew numbering.	
o	Indicates ordinal numbering. For example, «1o» gives 1st, 2nd, 3rd ..., while «wo» gives first, second, third, and «Wwo» gives First, Second, Third. All these examples are of course language dependent: the language is controlled using the language argument.	

Not all combinations of these make sense, but the specification leaves it very open to implementations how to interpret combinations other than the obvious ones. The golden rule for this function is that so long as the syntax of the picture is correct, it is never supposed to raise an error — if the processor doesn't understand the format that you asked for, it should output the date in some fallback format.

The width modifier, if present, indicates how many digits or letters should be included in the result. It takes the form «,m» or «,m-n», where m is a number giving the minimum width, or «*» to indicate no minimum, and n is the maximum width, or «*» to indicate no maximum. If n is omitted, it is assumed to be equal to m.

Specifying leading zeros in the formatting token is regarded as a shorthand for the width modifier: for example, «01» is a shorthand for «1,2-2». For most numeric fields, the width specified controls whether leading zeroes are output: if the minimum width is 2, then the value 8 will be output as 08. The year field is treated specially: a maximum width of 2 indicates that the century should be omitted. The fractional seconds are also handled differently: the minimum and maximum width indicate the minimum and maximum number of decimal places to be output.

For named fields, such as the name of the month and the day of the week, the width modifier controls the choice of abbreviations. For example, specifying «3-3» requests abbreviations that are exactly three characters long. The specification doesn't say exactly how the abbreviations should be chosen; some systems might use a dictionary of abbreviated forms (for example JLY for July), while others might use simple truncation of the full name. Names should be padded to the minimum length if they are shorter.

It's an error to request output of a field that isn't applicable to the type of input value; for example, component «H» for a date, or «Y» for a time. (It's alright, however, to ask for the timezone to be displayed when the value contains no timezone: the relevant component will simply be omitted.)

13

The Function Library

The Language Argument

The `language` argument defines the language to be used for those parts of the output date that are language dependent. The most obvious examples are the names of the days of the week and the months of the year: for example, if the value is «en» then a date might be output as «Sunday 13 December 1987», while with «de» (the code for German) the same date would be «Sonntag 13 Dezember 1987». The choice of language is also likely to affect the way the ordinal numbers are represented («4th» in English, «4.» in German, and «4éme» in French), and the choice of words or abbreviations equivalent to the English «p.m.» and «A.D.».

Since the variety of calendars and numbering schemes that implementations might support is completely open ended, it's quite possible that the `language` attribute might be used in other ways than these, for example to decide between «IV» and «IIII» as the representation of the number 4 in Roman numerals.

Implementations are not required to support any particular languages, and the set of languages that are supported is likely to depend on the choice of calendar.

The Calendar Argument

The World Wide Web Consortium takes its name very seriously, and bends over backward to ensure that it caters to every society on the planet. While most of the Western world, and much of the Eastern world, now uses the Gregorian calendar first introduced in the sixteenth century, there are many other calendars still in use. The XSLT specification defines the following codes that you can use to represent different calendars.

Code	Calendar
AD	Anno Domini (Christian Era)
AH	Anno Hegirae (Muhammedan Era)
AME	Mauludi Era (solar years since Mohammed's birth)
AM	Anno Mundi (Jewish Calendar)
AP	Anno Persici
AS	Aji Saka Era (Java)
BE	Buddhist Era
CB	Cooch Behar Era
CE	Common Era
CL	Chinese Lunar Era
CS	Chula Sakarat Era
EE	Ethiopian Era
FE	Fasli Era
ISO	ISO 8601 calendar
JE	Japanese Calendar
KE	Khalsa Era (Sikh calendar)

continued

Code	Calendar
KY	Kali Yuga
ME	Malabar Era
MS	Monarchic Solar Era
NS	Nepal Samwat Era
OS	Old Style (Julian Calendar)
RS	Rattanakosin (Bangkok) Era
SE	Saka Era
SH	Mohammedan Solar Era (Iran)
SS	Saka Samvat
TE	Tripurabda Era
VE	Vikrama Era
VS	Vikrama Samvat Era

This looks like a pretty impressive list, but before you get too excited that your favorite calendar is in the list, you should be aware that there is no requirement for implementations to support all these. And even if a calendar is supported, there are snags that you need to be aware of.

The date-formatting functions assume that the date and/or time will be represented using the types defined in XML Schema, which are based on the ISO 8601 specification. This doesn't mean that you have to be using a schema to take advantage of them, because you can always construct an instance of one of these types using a call to a constructor function; for example, «xs:date("1999-11-16")». It does mean, however, that you have to ensure that your dates and times are in ISO format before you can use these functions. If your XML documents contain dates in nonstandard formats such as «16 NOV 99» or «11/16/1999», then you are going to have to convert them first to the ISO format. And the same is true if your dates are in a different calendar.

> *A very common use of these functions is simply to output the current date; for example, {«format-dateTime(current-dateTime(), ...)» . In this case you don't have to worry about whether the supplied date is in the correct ISO format and calendar: it always will be.*

If the calendar argument selects a calendar other than the Gregorian calendar, then the date is translated into that calendar before extracting the relevant component. Not all calendars include concepts directly equivalent to months and weeks (for example, some calendars use lunar months), but most have concepts that are sufficiently similar for this to work. In practice, the handling of non-Gregorian calendars is likely to vary depending on your implementation and is only very loosely described in the XSLT specification.

The numbering of days of the week and weeks of the year may vary from one country or language to another. If you want predictable results, select the «ISO» calendar in the calendar argument. The results will then follow the rules in ISO 8601:

❑ Days of the week are numbered from 1 (Monday) to 7 (Sunday).

❑ Weeks of the year are numbered so that week 1 is the Monday-to-Sunday week that includes the first Thursday of the year. The days before week 1 fall in week 52 or 53 of the previous year.

❏ ISO 8601 does not define a numbering for weeks within a month. You will have to see what your implementation returns.

It's important to understand the distinction in XML Schema between the value space of a type and the lexical space. The value space for xs:date simply contains one data point for every day in the history of the world, past, present, and future (within limits, but they need not concern us). It's not meaningful to ask whether these data points are represented as integers or strings or to ask what format they are in — or to get to the point, it's not meaningful to ask what calendar they are in. There is a data point representing the day when the Great Fire of London started, and you can represent this data point using any calendar you like. So the value space of dates in XML Schema is calendar neutral.

The same is not true of the lexical space. The lexical representation of dates in XML Schema uses the Gregorian calendar. In fact, it uses the Gregorian calendar even to represent dates that occurred long before the Gregorian calendar was invented: this is referred to as the *proleptic* Gregorian calendar (ISO 8601 calls it ''prolaptic,'' but that appears to be an error). This simply projects the Gregorian calendar backward in time. This is really no different from our use of ''B.C.'' dates: we are using a representation of dates that is unrelated to the way those same dates were represented in contemporary records.

This means that if you want to use a non-Gregorian calendar, you have to be very careful. For example, if you are storing a historical document that records that the Great Fire of London broke out on September 2, 1666, then if you want to represent this correctly using the xs:date type you need to know how to convert it into a Gregorian date. In fact, the correct lexical representation of this date is «1666-09-12», as there was then a 10-day difference between the Julian and Gregorian calendars. (Although the Gregorian calendar was introduced in 1585, Britain has always been slow to pick up European ideas, and did not adopt it until 1752.)

If you now want to format this date using the Julian calendar, you can do so by specifying «OS» in the calendar argument. This will produce the correct output («Sunday 2nd Sept 1666») only if you represented the date correctly in the value space. If you were careless, and created the date by writing «xs:date("1666-09-02")», then the formatted output will be «Thursday 23rd Aug 1666».

I suspect what this means in practice is that if you need to use non-Gregorian calendars, the support provided in XSLT 2.0 may not actually be sufficient for your needs; it allows you to convert dates from the Gregorian calendar to a different calendar, but does not provide a conversion in the reverse direction. There are software utilities available to do that, which could be integrated as extension functions, but if you use them then you may well find that they also offer date formatting capability that is better than that offered by your XSLT processor.

If you ask for a date to be formatted using a calendar that hasn't been implemented, the system will output the date using a calendar of its own choosing (you can be fairly certain this will be the Gregorian calendar) but adding to the output a tag indicating that it is a different calendar from the one that was requested.

The inclusion of «ISO» as a calendar name in this list has a special purpose. Sometimes, you want to format the date not in order to present the information to a human reader, but to pass information to other software. The format-date() function, for example, is the only way available in standard XSLT of finding out the day of the week or the week number in the year. If you want to determine whether a given date is a Sunday, then it would be unfortunate if you had to test the result against a language-dependent string. If you choose ISO as the calendar, then you can do this test as:

```
<xsl:variable name="is-Sunday" as="xs:boolean"
        select="format-date(current-date(), 'F1', (), 'ISO', ()) = '7'"/>
```

This is because the ISO 8601 standard specifies numeric representations of the days of the week from Monday (1) to Sunday (7). Similarly, you can get the ISO week number by writing:

```
<xsl:value-of select="format-date(current-date(), 'W', (), 'ISO', ())"/>
```

ISO week numbers (which in some countries are widely used in project planning and similar applications) are chosen so that week 1 is the Monday-to-Sunday week that includes 4th January. Week 1 may thus start before or after 1st January, but always starts on a Monday.

The Country Argument

The country argument allows you to indicate the country associated with the date and time being formatted. For example, if the date and time refer to the death of Erasmus, which took place on July 12, 1536 in Basel, Switzerland, then you can set the country argument to «ch», which is the ISO country code for Switzerland. The system can use this information to assist in converting Gregorian dates to a date in the chosen calendar, since with many non-Gregorian calendars, different variants of the calendar were in use in different places at different times. For example, although in the old Julian calendar the day and the month were synchronized across much of Europe, New Year's day varied in different countries, so the year number might be different from one country to another.

In some cases, such as the Islamic calendar, the start of a day is tied to sunrise or sunset, so accurate conversion of a date into another calendar requires not only knowledge of the time of day, but also knowledge of where the event took place.

More prosaically, the country code might be used to determine the abbreviated names of timezones. Names such as EST and PST are recognized in the US, but not necessarily in other English-speaking countries. It's probably not a good idea to ask for time zone names, however. The xs:dateTime type simply doesn't have this information. Within a limited range of dates and countries, the system might be able to work out that the time zone displacement -04:00 refers to US Eastern Daylight Time; but this doesn't work if the time is supplied without a date, if the country is unknown, or if the date is in the future (as many US citizens discovered in 2007, the dates for daylight savings time changes are set by governments as they see fit).

The value of the country argument is expected to be an ISO country code, but the use that the system makes of the information is entirely implementation defined. You can always supply an empty sequence as the value of this argument.

Usage and Examples

Here are some examples showing how the date 2008-11-03 might be formatted using various values of the picture argument, assuming the use of the English language and the Gregorian calendar.

Picture	Output
[D]/[M]/[Y]	3/11/2008
[M]/[D]/[Y]	11/3/2008
[MNn] [Do], [Y] [E]	November 3rd, 2008 A.D
[Y]-[M,2]-[D,2]	2003-11-08
[MN] [YI]	NOVEMBER MMVIII
[Y][[week [W]:[FNn]]]	2008[week 45:Monday]

13

The Function Library

787

The following examples show how the time 09:30:02.26-05:00 might be formatted, under the same assumptions. It is possible, of course, to output date and time components at the same time, using a single picture.

Picture	Output
`[H01].[m01]`	09.30
`[h].[m01] [P]`	9.30 A.M
`[H01]:[m01]:[s01].[f001] [ZN]`	09:30:02.260 EST

See Also

`day-from-date()`, `day-from-dateTime()` on page 744
`month-from-date()`, `month-from-dateTime()` on page 833
`year-from-date()`, `year-from-dateTime()` on page 911
`hours-from-time()`, `hours-from-dateTime()` on page 800
`minutes-from-time()`, `minutes-from-dateTime()` on page 832
`seconds-from-time()`, `seconds-from-dateTime()` on page 873
`timezone-from-date()`, `timezone-from-dateTime`, `timezone-from-time()` on page 893

format-number

This function is available in XSLT only.

The `format-number()` function is used to convert numbers into strings for display to a human user. It is also useful when converting to legacy formats that require a number to occupy a fixed number of character positions. The format of the result is controlled using the `<xsl:decimal-format>` declaration in an XSLT stylesheet.

For example, the expression «`format-number(12.5, '$#0.00')`» returns the string «`$12.50`».

Changes in 2.0

In XSLT 1.0, the effect of the function was defined by reference to the Java JDK 1.1 specifications. This created problems because the JDK 1.1 description left many details underspecified, and later versions of the JDK not only clarified the specification, but also added new features. It was therefore decided in XSLT 2.0 to provide a freestanding definition of this function. This is largely compatible with the old JDK 1.1 specification, but the rules are now much more precise, and in corner cases they will not necessarily give the same results as implementations based on the JDK, let alone non-Java implementations. For example, the JDK 1.1 specification did not say how rounding was done. The actual JDK 1.1 implementation used the rule of rounding a final 5 to the nearest even number, and this is the rule that XSLT 2.0 has adopted, but XSLT 1.0 processors might well do rounding differently.

Signature

Argument	Type	Meaning
value	`Numeric?`	The number to be formatted
picture	`xs:string`	A picture string identifying the way in which the number is to be formatted

continued

Argument	Type	Meaning
format (optional)	xs:string	A string in the form of a lexical QName, that identifies an <xsl:decimal-format> declaration in the stylesheet, giving further information about the required formatting options
Result	xs:string?	*The formatted number*

Effect

The function returns a string value; this is the result of formatting the given value using the format picture supplied in picture, while applying the rules defined in the decimal format named in format if present, or using the default decimal format otherwise.

The decimal-format Name

The format argument, if it is present, must take the form of a lexical QName; that is, an XML name optionally prefixed with a namespace prefix that corresponds to a namespace declaration that is in scope at the point in the stylesheet where the format-number() function is called. There must be an <xsl:decimal-format> element in the stylesheet with the same expanded name, using the namespace URIs rather than prefixes in the comparison.

If the format argument is omitted, the default decimal format is used. A default decimal format can be established for a stylesheet by including an <xsl:decimal-format> element with no name. If there is no unnamed <xsl:decimal-format> element in the stylesheet, the system uses a built-in default format, which is the same as specifying an <xsl:decimal-format> with no attributes.

The Picture String

The structure of the picture string is as follows. Here, and in the text that follows, I will use the default characters for each role: for example «;» as the pattern separator, «.» as the decimal point, «0» as the zero digit, «#» as the optional digit placemarker, and so on. Remember, though, that you can change the characters that are used in each of these roles using the <xsl:decimal-format> declaration.

Construct	Content
picture	subpicture («;»subpicture)?
subpicture	prefix? integer («.»fraction)? suffix?
prefix	Any characters except special characters
suffix	Any characters except special characters
integer	«#»* «0»* (but also allowing «,» to appear)
fraction	«0»* «#»* (but also allowing «,» to appear)

The first subpicture is used for formatting positive numbers. The second (optional) subpicture is used for negative numbers. If only one subpicture is specified, then the subpicture used for negative numbers is the same as the positive subpicture, but with a minus sign added before the prefix. The actual character used for the minus sign depends on the <xsl:decimal-format> declaration.

The prefix and suffix are just literal characters that are output at the start and end of the number. The only real reason to use them, other than simple convenience, is when they are different for positive and negative numbers. For example, you can use this mechanism to implement the accounting convention of displaying negative numbers in parentheses.

If the prefix or suffix includes a «%» sign, the percent sign will be displayed in the place where it appears in the prefix or suffix, and the number will be multiplied by 100. Similarly, you can also use a per-mille sign «‰» in which case the number will be multipled by 1000.

If the number is one of the special values positive or negative infinity or NaN, then it is displayed using the representation defined in the `<xsl:decimal-format>` declaration. The positive subpicture (including its prefix and suffix) is used for displaying positive zero and positive infinity, while the negative subpicture (perhaps with a different prefix and suffix) is used for negative zero and negative infinity. No prefix and suffix are used when NaN is formatted.

The special characters used are as follows.

Special Character	Default Value	Meaning
zero-digit	«0»	A digit will always appear at this point in the result string
digit	«#»	A digit will appear at this point in the result string unless it is a redundant leading or trailing zero
decimal-point	«.»	Separates the integer and the fraction part of the number
grouping-separator	«,»	Separates groups of digits
pattern-separator	«;»	Separates the positive and negative subpictures
minus-sign	«-»	Minus sign
percent-sign	«%»	Multiplies the number by 100 and shows it as a percentage
per-mille	«‰»	Multiplies by 1000 and shows it as per mille

The original JDK 1.1 implementation had the feature (I use the term politely) that if there was an explicit negative subpicture, it served to specify the negative prefix and suffix only; the number of digits, grouping separators, and other characteristics were all taken from the positive subpicture, and any specification to the contrary in the negative subpicture was ignored. This curiosity was not actually documented in the JDK 1.1 specification, though it was retained (and documented) in JDK 1.2. Since XSLT 1.0 referred explicitly to the JDK 1.1 specification (but not to the JDK 1.1 implementation), it's likely that some XSLT 1.0 processors share this behavior and others do not. XSLT 2.0 does away with it: all aspects of formatting for a negative number depend on the negative subpicture alone.

In the fractional part of the number, a «0» means you will get a digit in that position whatever its value, while a «#» means you will get a digit only if it is non-zero. You will never get more digits displayed than there are «0» and «#» signs. For example, «.00##» displays a minimum of two and a maximum of four digits after the decimal point. If there are more significant digits in the number than you have asked to be displayed, then the number is rounded. It is rounded to the nearest value that can be displayed, and if it is midway between two such values, it is rounded to the one whose last digit is even. For example, with a picture of «0.00», the value 0.125 is shown as «0.12», while 0.875 is shown as «0.88». This is different from the rounding rule that many of us were taught at school, which always rounds 0.5 upward, but it is preferred by many statisticians and accountants because it means that numbers are equally likely to be rounded up or down, which avoids introducing bias. If you prefer a different rounding rule, you can always round the number yourself before formatting it.

If no digits are displayed to the right of the decimal point, then the decimal point itself will not be displayed.

In the integer part of the picture, that is, on the left of the decimal point if there is one, the rules are different, because the value will never be truncated: if you don't define enough digit positions to accommodate the number, the system will display the full integer part of the value anyway. There will always be at least as many digits as there are «0» digits in the picture, but it makes little difference how many «#» signs appear to the left of the decimal separator: their only real function is to space out any grouping separator characters.

The `format-number()` function doesn't provide any direct way of space-padding the number so that numbers can be vertically aligned in a column. With HTML output this is best achieved using the CSS property «text-align:right». With text output, the simplest way to achieve this effect is to format the number, use the `string-length()` function to determine the length of the result, and then add the requisite number of spaces to the front.

The grouping separator («,» by default) is commonly used for thousands, but in some countries for ten thousands. You can specify grouping separators either at regular intervals or at irregular intervals, and they can appear in either the integer part or the fractional part of the number. For example, if you write «#,##0.00», then you will get a grouping separator every three digits to the left of the decimal point, while if you specify «#,##,###,###0.00», then you will get separators at the specified positions only. The rule is that if all your explicit grouping separators are regularly spaced, then the system will add implicit grouping separators when it extends the picture on the left, but if the explicit separators are at irregular intervals, then no implicit separators will be added.

If the picture string is invalid, then the implementation is required to report an error.

Usage

Note that this facility for formatting numbers is completely separate from the facilities available through the <xsl:number> element. There is some overlapping functionality, but the syntax of the pictures is quite unrelated. The `format-number()` function formats a single number, which need not be an integer. <xsl:number> is primarily designed to format a list of positive integers. For formatting a single positive integer, either facility can be used.

Examples

The following example shows the result of `format-number()` using the default decimal format. Examples with non-default decimal formats are shown under the <xsl:decimal-format> element in Chapter 6, page 298.

Number	Picture String	Result
1234.5	#,##0.00	1,234.50
123.456	#,##0.00	123.46
1000000	#,##0.00	1,000,000.00
-59	#,##0.00	-59.00
1 div 0.0e0	#,##0.00	Infinity
1234	###0.0###	1234.0

continued

Number	Picture String	Result
1234.5	###0.0###	1234.5
.00025	###0.0###	0.0002
.00035	###0.0###	0.0004
0.25	#00%	25%
0.736	#00%	74%
1	#00%	100%
-42	#00%	-4200%
-3.12	#.00;(#.00)	(3.12)
-3.12	#.00;#.00CR	3.12CR

See Also

`<xsl:decimal-format>` page 298 in Chapter 6
`<xsl:number>` page 403 in Chapter 6

format-time

See `format-date()` on page 781

function-available

This function is available in XSLT only.

You can call `function-available()` to test whether a particular function is available for use. It can be used to test the availability both of standard system functions and of user-written functions, including both XSLT stylesheet functions and extension functions.

For example, the expression «`function-available('concat')`» returns `true`.

Changes in 2.0

An optional second argument has been added, giving the arity of the required function.

In XSLT 2.0, except when running in backward-compatibility mode, it is a static error if an XPath expression contains a call on a function that is not available. Therefore, the way in which `function-available()` is used needs to change: instead of calling it using a normal runtime conditional instruction (`<xsl:choose>` or `<xsl:if>`), it should be called in a compile-time conditional expression, using the `[xsl:]use-when` attribute.

Signature

Argument	Type	Meaning
name	`xs:string`	The name of the function being tested. The string must take the form of a lexical QName.
arity (optional)	`xs:integer`	The arity (number of arguments) of the function being tested.
Result	`xs:boolean`	`true` *if the named function is available to be called,* `false` *otherwise.*

Effect

The first argument must take the form of a lexical QName: that is, an XML name, with an optional namespace prefix that corresponds to a namespace declaration that is in scope at the point in the stylesheet where the `function-available()` function is called.

If there is no prefix, or if the namespace URI is the standard function namespace http://www.w3.org/ 2005/xpath-functions, the call tests whether there is a system function with the specified name. The system functions are those defined in the XPath and XSLT Recommendations; vendors are not allowed to supply additional functions in this namespace, nor are they allowed to omit any. So an XSLT processor that conforms to XSLT version 2.0 will return `true` if the name is one of the function names in this chapter (for example «current» , «position» , or «regex-group»). This means you can test whether a new XPath 2.0 or XSLT 2.0 function is supported in your XSLT processor by writing, for example:

```
use-when="function-available('matches')"
use-when="function-available('regex-group')"
```

If the QName includes a non-null namespace (other than the standard function namespace), the XSLT processor returns `true` if there is a stylesheet function, constructor function, or extension function available with the given name. In general, if `function-available()` returns `false`, then you are safe in assuming that a call on the function would fail, and if it returns `true`, then there will be some way of calling the function successfully.

If the second argument to the function is supplied, then `function-available()` returns `true` only if there is a function available with the specified name and the specified number of arguments. When the second argument is omitted, the result is true if there is some function with the required name, regardless of the number of arguments.

There is no way of finding out at runtime what the types of the arguments should be, which means that knowing a function is available is not enough to ensure that any given call on the function will be successful.

The functions that are considered to be available are those in the static context of the XPath expression containing the call on `function-available()`. If `function-available()` is evaluated from the `use-when` attribute, this includes core XPath and XSLT functions, constructor functions for built-in types, and extension functions. If `function-available()` is evaluated during stylesheet execution, it also includes stylesheet functions (defined using `<xsl:function>`) and constructor functions for types imported from a schema.

Usage

There are two ways of using `function-available()`: it can be used to achieve backward compatibility when using standard functions defined after version 1.0 of the specification, and it can be used to test for the presence of vendor or third-party extensions.

The ability to test for the existence of stylesheet functions is not particularly useful, especially as this cannot be done within a `use-when` attribute (it will always return false, because stylesheet functions are not present in the static context for evaluating `use-when`).

Testing for the Existence of System-Defined Functions

The ability to test whether a particular system-defined function is available was not especially useful with version 1.0 of the specification. It was designed to come into its own when later versions of the specification were published. If you want to use a function that is newly defined in version 2.0, then you can test to see whether it is available with a particular XSLT processor, before using it. If it is not

13

The Function Library

available, you can use `<xsl:if>` to avoid executing it. Provided that you enable *forward-compatible mode* by setting the `version` attribute on the `<xsl:stylesheet>` element to `"2.0"`, a conformant XSLT 1.0 processor should not object to the presence of an expression in your stylesheet that calls an unknown function, unless the expression is actually executed.

For example, the function `current-date()` becomes available in XPath 2.0. You can test for its existence by writing:

```
<xsl:if test="function-available('current-date')">
```

For a fuller example, see the end of this section.

In theory, you could test whether a function such as `current-date()` is available by calling «system-property('xsl-version')» and testing whether the result is equal to «2.0». But the reality is that there will be processors that have implemented some of the XPath 2.0 functions but not yet all of them. A processor isn't supposed to return «2.0» as the value of «system-property('xsl:version')» unless it is a fully conformant XSLT 2.0 processor; but if it isn't a fully conformant processor, then by definition you can't be sure whether it follows the rules. So it's better to use the finer-grained check offered by `function-available()`.

Testing for Vendor or Third-Party Extensions

The second way of using `function-available()` is to test for vendor or third-party extensions. If you know that a particular extension function is present in some implementations and not others, you can use the `function-available()` test to see whether it is present, and use the new `use-when` attribute to handle the situation when it isn't.

The `use-when` attribute provides a way of conditionally including or excluding parts of a stylesheet at compile time, based on a compile-time condition. There are more details of this feature on page 127 in Chapter 3. The compile-time condition is an XPath expression, restricted to operate with a very limited context, which means that it can only access information known at compile time. It cannot, for example, access a source document, or refer to variables. But the context does include the set of extension functions that are available. This is illustrated in the example that follows.

Example 1: Testing for xx:node-set() Extensions

The XSLT 2.0 working draft allows you to use a temporary tree (the value constructed when an `<xsl:variable>` element is not empty) in any context where a node can be used. This feature was not available in XSLT 1.0, which handled temporary trees as a distinct type, known as a result tree fragment. Many vendors filled the gap by allowing a temporary tree to be converted to a node-set using an extension function (for example, `xt:node-set()` or `msxml:node-set()`). If you want to write a stylesheet that is as portable as possible, you need to write code that discovers which of these facilities is available.

Stylesheet

The following stylesheet (`node-set-available.xsl`) contains a named template that takes a temporary tree as a parameter and calls `<xsl:apply-templates>` to process its root node in a particular mode. When running with an XSLT 2.0 processor, it does this simply by passing the tree to `<xsl:apply-templates>` directly; in other cases, it tries to determine whether one of the proprietary `node-set()` extension functions is available, and uses that.

```
<xsl:stylesheet
        xmlns:xsl="http://www.w3.org/1999/XSL/Transform"
        version="2.0">
<xsl:template name="process-tree-fragment"
        xmlns:msxml="urn:schemas-microsoft-com:xslt"
        xmlns:xt="http://www.jclark.com/xt"
        xmlns:saxon6=" http://icl.com/saxon">
  <xsl:param name="fragment"/>
  <xsl:choose>
    <xsl:when test="number(system-property('xsl:version')) &gt; 1.0">
      <xsl:apply-templates mode="process-fragment"
                           select="$fragment"/>
    </xsl:when>
    <xsl:otherwise use-when="system-property('xsl:version') eq '1.0'">
      <xsl:choose>
        <xsl:when test="function-available('msxml:node-set')">
          <xsl:apply-templates mode="process-fragment'
                               select="msxml:node-set($fragment)"/>
        </xsl:when>
        <xsl:when test="function-available('xt:node-set')">
          <xsl:apply-templates mode="process-fragment"
                               select="xt:node-set($fragment)"/>
        </xsl:when>
        <xsl:when test="function-available('saxon6:node-set')">
          <xsl:apply-templates mode="process-fragment"
                               select="saxon6:node-set($fragment)"/>
        </xsl:when>
        <xsl:otherwise>
          <xsl:message terminate="yes">
            Cannot convert result tree fragment to node-set
          </xsl:message>
        </xsl:otherwise>
      </xsl:choose>
    </xsl:otherwise>
  </xsl:choose>
</xsl:template>
</xsl:stylesheet>
```

This named template can be called as follows, to process all the nodes in the result tree fragment.

```
<xsl:call-template name="process-tree-fragment">
  <xsl:with-param name="fragment" select="$supplied-fragment"/>
</xsl:call-template>
```

The logic here is slightly tortuous. You need to look at it in two different ways: as an XSLT 1.0 stylesheet, and as a 2.0 stylesheet.

As a 1.0 stylesheet, the outer `<xsl:choose>` takes the `<xsl:otherwise>` branch, because the processor version is 1.0. The use-when attribute on the `<xsl:otherwise>` element is ignored: the XSLT 1.0 processor will be operating in forward-compatible mode, because the stylesheet specifies «version="2.0"», and in forward-compatible mode, unknown attributes on XSLT elements are ignored. The 1.0 processor then takes one of the branches of the inner `<xsl:choose>`, depending on which of the `xx:node-set()` extension functions is available.

As an XSLT 2.0 stylesheet, the outer `<xsl:choose>` takes the `<xsl:when>` branch. It completely ignores the `<xsl:otherwise>` branch, by virtue of the `use-when` condition. The `use-when` condition is necessary, because an XSLT 2.0 processor would otherwise report a static (compile time) error when it sees an XPath expression that calls an unknown function such as `saxon6:node-set()`, even though the function is not actually evaluated at runtime.

When this example is run with an XSLT 2.0 processor, it doesn't actually invoke the `function- available()` function — which arguably makes it a poor choice of example for this section. The next example attempts to remedy this.

The next example is similar — but this time, instead of looking for a vendor-supplied extension function, we will be looking for a user-supplied function implemented as a Java method.

Example 2: Testing Availability of a Java Method

In this example, we'll assume that the stylesheet (`charset-available.xsl`) is always going to run under a particular XSLT 2.0 processor, but that it might run under different Java VMs. We'll suppose the existence of an XSLT 2.0 processor that can run under both JDK 1.3 and JDK 1.4, and we'll suppose that we want to use the Java method «`Charset.isSupported()`» in the `java.nio.charset` package, which was new in JDK 1.4. Under JDK 1.3, we'll behave as if the extension function returned `false`.

Stylesheet

We achieve this by writing two versions of a variable declaration. Only one of them is compiled, based on the value of the `use-when` attribute.

```
<xsl:template match="/">
  <xsl:variable name='charset-ok'
      as='xs:boolean'
      select='Charset:isSupported("EUC-JP")'
      xmlns:Charset='java:java.nio.charset.Charset'
      use-when='function-available("Charset:isSupported", 1)'/>
  <xsl:variable name='charset-ok'
      as='xs:boolean'
      select='false()'
      xmlns:Charset='java:java.nio.charset.Charset'
      use-when='not(function-available("Charset:isSupported", 1))'/>
  <xsl:result-document
      encoding="{if ($charset-ok) then 'EUC-JP' else 'UTF-8'}">
    <xsl:apply-templates/>
  </xsl:result-document>
</xsl:template>
```

generate-id

This function is available in XSLT only.

The generate-id() function generates a string, in the form of an XML Name, that uniquely identifies a node. The result is guaranteed to be different for every node that participates in a given transformation.

For example, the expression «generate-id(..)» might return the string «N015732» when using one XSLT processor, and «b23a1c79» when using another.

Changes in 2.0

None.

Signature

Argument	Type	Meaning
node (optional)	node()?	The input node. If the argument is omitted, the context node is used. If an empty sequence is supplied, the zero-length string is returned.
Result	xs:string	*A string value that uniquely identifies the node. This will consist only of ASCII alphanumeric characters, and the first character will be alphabetic. This makes the identifier suitable for use in many contexts, for example as an ID value in an XML document or an HTML anchor.*

Effect

If the node argument is omitted, it defaults to «.», the context item. A type error occurs if this is not a node.

If the node argument is an empty sequence, the function returns a zero-length string.

The function returns an arbitrary string. Within a given transformation, the function will always return the same string for the same node, and it will always return different strings for different nodes: in other words, «generate-id($A)=generate-id($B)» is true if and only if «$A is $B» is true, and this includes the case where the nodes are in different documents.

The generated identifiers are unique within a single execution of the stylesheet. If the same stylesheet is used several times, with the same or different source documents, the function may generate the same identifiers in each run but is under no obligation to do so.

Usage and Examples

In XSLT 1.0, the generate-id() function was often used to determine whether two expressions represented the same node, that is, to compare nodes by identity. XPath 2.0 offers the «is» operator for this purpose, so this usage can be expected to dwindle.

The main intended purpose of the generate-id() function is to create hyperlinks in the output document. For example, it can be used to generate ID and IDREF attributes in an output XML document, or <a name="X"> and <a href="#X"> pairs in an output HTML document.

13

The Function Library

797

Example: Using generate-id() to Create Links

This example takes as input a file `resorts.xml` containing details of a collection of holiday resorts, each of which includes a list of hotels.

Source

```
<resorts>
   <resort>
      <name>Amsterdam</name>
      <details>A wordy description of Amsterdam</details>
      <hotel>
         <name>Grand Hotel</name>
         <stars>5</stars>
         <address> . . . </address>
      </hotel>
      <hotel>
         <name>Less Grand Hotel</name>
         <stars>2</stars>
         <address> . . . </address>
      </hotel>
   </resort>
   <resort>
      <name>Bruges</name>
      <details>An eloquent description of Bruges</details>
      <hotel>
         <name>Central Hotel</name>
         <stars>5</stars>
         <address> . . . </address>
      </hotel>
      <hotel>
         <name>Peripheral Hotel</name>
         <stars>2</stars>
         <address> . . . </address>
      </hotel>
   </resort>
</resorts>
```

Stylesheet

The stylesheet `resorts.xsl` constructs an output HTML page in which the hotels are listed first, followed by information about the resorts. Each hotel entry contains a hyperlink to the relevant resort details. The links for the resorts are generated using `generate-id()` applied to the `<resort>` element.

This is a complete stylesheet that uses the *Simplified Stylesheet* syntax introduced on page 125, in Chapter 3.

```
<html xmlns:xsl="http://www.w3.org/1999/XSL/Transform" xsl:version="2.0">
<body>
   <h1>Hotels</h1>
   <xsl:for-each select="//hotel">
```

```
  <xsl:sort select="number(stars)" order="descending" data-type="number"/>
     <h2><xsl:value-of select="name"/></h2>
      <p>Address: <xsl:value-of select="address"/></p>
      <p>Stars: <xsl:value-of select="stars"/></p>
      <p>Resort: <a href="#{generate-id(parent::resort)}">
             <xsl:value-of select="parent::resort/name"/></a></p>
  </xsl:for-each>
  <h1>Resorts</h1>
  <xsl:for-each select="//resort">
     <h2>
        <a name="{generate-id()}"><xsl:value-of select="name"/></a>
     </h2>
      <p><xsl:value-of select="details"/></p>
  </xsl:for-each>
</body>
</html>
```

Notice how generate-id() is used twice, once to generate the identifier of the resort, the next time to generate a link from the hotel.

Output

The following output was obtained using Saxon. I have added some extra indentation to show the structure. A different product will generate different identifiers in the <a> elements, but the links will work just as well.

```
<html>
   <body>
      <h1>Hotels</h1>
        <h2>Grand Hotel</h2>
          <p>Address:  . . . </p>
          <p>Stars: 5</p>
          <p>Resort: <a href="#d2e3">Amsterdam</a></p>
        <h2>Central Hotel</h2>
          <p>Address:  . . . </p>
          <p>Stars: 5</p>
          <p>Resort: <a href="#d2e36">Bruges</a></p>
        <h2>Less Grand Hotel</h2>
        <p>Address:  . . . </p>
         <p>Stars: 2</p>
          <p>Resort: <a href="#d2e3">Amsterdam</a></p>
       <h2>Peripheral Hotel</h2>
          <p>Address:  . . . </p>
          <p>Stars: 2</p>
          <p>Resort: <a href="#d2e36">Bruges</a></p>
     <h1>Resorts</h1>
        <h2><a name="d2e3">Amsterdam</a></h2>
          <p>A wordy description of Amsterdam</p>
        <h2><a name="d2e36">Bruges</a></h2>
          <p>An eloquent description of Bruges</p>
   </body>
</html>
```

There is no inverse function to `generate-id()`: specifically, there is no direct way to find a node if its generated id is known, other than the potentially inefficient:

```
//node()[generate-id()=$X]
```

If you need to do this, however, you can set up a key definition as follows.

```
<xsl:key name="gid-key" match="*" use="generate-id()"/>
```

Then find the element with a given id value using the expression:

```
key('gid-key', $X)
```

It is important to appreciate that the generated identifiers bear no resemblance to any ID attribute values in the source document, so the nodes cannot be found using the `id()` function.

Also, the ID values generated in one run of the processor may be different from those generated in a subsequent run. You need to bear this in mind if you are using the ID values as hyperlinks. If the transformation is likely to be run more than once, then it isn't safe to reference these ID values from another document, or even to save them as a bookmark in a browser.

See Also

id() on page 802
key() on page 812
«is» operator in Chapter 8 on page 593

hours-from-dateTime, hours-from-time

These two functions extract the hour component from an `xs:dateTime` or `xs:time` value. For example, at noon local time both these functions return 12.

Signature

Argument	Type	Meaning
input	`xs:dateTime?` or `xs:time?`	The value from which the hour component is to be extracted. The type of the supplied argument must correspond to the type implied by the function name.
Result	`xs:integer`	*The hour, in the range 0 to 23 (midnight is represented as 0).*

Effect

The function returns the hour component of the supplied `xs:dateTime` or `xs:time`. The value is from the time as expressed in its local timezone (not normalized to UTC). This means that if the time (or dateTime) has a timezone, the value is the time in that timezone; if it has no timezone, it is the value as written.

If an empty sequence is supplied, an empty sequence is returned.

Examples

Expression	Result
hours-from-time(xs:time("12:35:03.142"))	12
hours-from-dateTime(xs:dateTime("2008-02-28T13:55:30"))	13
hours-from-time(xs:time("23:59:59+01:00"))	23
hours-from-dateTime(xs:dateTime("2008-07-31T22:10:00-05:00"))	22
hours-from-dateTime(xs:dateTime("2008-07-31T24:00:00"))	0

See Also

current-date(),-dateTime(),-time() on page 738
format-date(),-dateTime(),-time() on page 781
minutes-from-dateTime(),-time() on page 832
seconds-from-dateTime(),-time() on page 873

hours-from-duration

This function extracts the value of the hours component from a normalized xs:duration value.

Signature

Argument	Type	Meaning
input	xs:duration?	The value from which the component is to be extracted. If an empty sequence is supplied, an empty sequence is returned.
Result	xs:integer?	The hours component, in the range −23 to +23.

Effect

The function returns the hours component of the supplied xs:duration. The duration value is first normalized so that the number of hours is less than 24, the number of minutes is less than 60, and so on. The result will be negative if the duration is negative. The result will therefore be in the range −23 to +23.

Examples

Expression	Result
hours-from-duration(xs:dayTimeDuration("P5DT12H30M"))	12
hours-from-duration(xs:dayTimeDuration("PT72H"))	0
hours-from-duration(xs:duration("-PT36H15M"))	-12
hours-from-duration(xs:yearMonthDuration("P12M"))	0

13

The Function Library

See Also

days-from-duration() on page 745
minutes-from-duration() on page 832
seconds-from-duration() on page 874

id

The id() function returns a sequence containing all the elements in a given document with given ID attribute values.

For example, if the code attribute is defined as an ID attribute, then the expression «id('A321-780')» might return the single element <product code="A321-780">.

Changes in 2.0

A second optional argument has been added, to define which document is to be searched. The semantics of the function have been redefined in terms of the XPath 2.0 type system.

Signature

Argument	Type	Meaning
values	xs:string*	Specifies the required ID values
node (optional)	node()	Identifies the document to be searched
Result	element()*	*A sequence of nodes, in document order, containing the nodes with the required ID values*

Effect

The function is designed to make it easy to find all the elements referenced in an element or attribute of type xs:IDREF or xs:IDREFS, but there is no requirement that it should be used this way. The rules are defined so that the supplied argument can be any of the following:

❑ A string containing an ID value

❑ A string containing a space-separated list of ID values

❑ A node containing an ID value

❑ A node containing a space-separated list of ID values

❑ A sequence of any of the above

Any nodes in the sequence are atomized as part of the function calling mechanism. The resulting strings are then tokenized by splitting their contents on whitespace boundaries. Each token is used as a candidate ID value. If there is a node in the selected document that has an ID attribute or ID content equal to this candidate ID value then this node is included in the result of the function.

The rules for this function say that the nodes that are selected must have the is-id property. There are various ways a node might acquire this property:

❑ With a schema-aware processor, an element or attribute acquires the is-id property if it is declared as having type xs:ID, or a type derived by restriction from xs:ID, or a complex type with simple content where the simple content is `xs:ID` or derived from `xs:ID`. (There's some ambiguity about list or union types constructed from `xs:ID`.)

❑ If the input document has a DTD, an attribute declared in the DTD as having type `ID` will normally acquire the `is-id` property. However this isn't 100% reliable; it may depend on how the XML parser has been configured, and some parsers don't report this information at all

❑ An attribute named `xml:id` will always have the `is-id` property.

By contrast, it is not necessary for the candidate `ID`s to be declared as type `IDREF` or `IDREFS`, though the function is designed to produce the expected result when they are, that is, it finds the nodes referenced by the `IDREF` or `IDREFS` values in the argument sequence.

It is not an error if there is no element with an `ID` equal to one of the candidate `ID` values. In this situation, there will simply be no node in the resulting sequence corresponding to this value. In the simplest case, where there is only one candidate `ID` value supplied, the resulting sequence will be empty if the `ID` is not present.

The second argument, if supplied, identifies the document to be searched. This does not have to be the document node, it can be any node within the target document. This argument defaults to the context node. Whether the argument is explicit or implicit, it must be a node in a tree whose root is a document node. If the argument is omitted, then a runtime error is reported if the context item is undefined, or if it is not a node. The nodes in the supplied `values` argument will often come from the same document, but this is not required.

IDs and Validation

`ID` values only really work properly if the source document is valid (in the XML sense: meaning, loosely, that it obeys the rules in its own DTD or Schema). However, XPath is designed to allow invalid documents as well as valid ones to be processed. One possible kind of validity error is that `ID` values are not unique within the document. This is explicitly covered in the specification: the first node with that `ID` value is located. Other validity errors may also be present, for example an `ID` attribute may contain embedded spaces. In this case it will not be retrieved.

When no schema is used, a non-validating XML parser isn't required to read attribute definitions from an external DTD. In this situation the XSLT processor will assume there are no `ID` attributes present, and the `id()` function will always return an empty result. If this appears to be happening, check what options are available for configuring the XML parser, or try a different parser. Most good parsers will report the attribute type, even though it isn't absolutely required by the XML standard.

XML Schema introduces the ability for elements as well as attributes to be used as IDs, and the function supports this. There's a slight oddity, however. If the source document has an element of the form `<employee nr="e12345">...</employee>`, where nr is an `ID` attribute, then `id('e12345')` will return the `<employee>` element. However, if the source is `<employee><nr>e12345</nr>....</employee>`, where nr is of type `xs:ID`, then `id('e12345')` will return the `<nr>` element, not the `<employee>`.

Usage and Examples

The `id()` function provides an efficient means of locating nodes given the value of an `ID` attribute.

In a sense it is a convenience function, because if the attribute named `id` is always an `ID` attribute, then the expression:

```
id('B1234')
```

is equivalent to the path expression:

```
//*[@id='B1234']
```

However, the chances are that in most implementations, the `id()` function will be much more efficient than the straightforward path expression with a predicate, because the processor is likely to build an index rather than doing a sequential search.

In XSLT it is also possible to use `key()` in place of `id()`. The main advantage of the `id()` function over using `key()` is that it handles a whitespace-separated list of IDs in one go. The `key()` function cannot do this, because there is nothing to stop a key value containing a space.

The `id()` function when used with a single argument locates elements in the same document as the context node. XPath 2.0 provides two ways to locate elements in a different document. You can either use the `id()` function on the right-hand side of the «/» operator, for example «doc("lookup.xml")/id($param)», or you can supply a second argument, like this: «id($param, doc("lookup.xml"))».

Where the source document includes an IDREFS attribute, it is possible to locate all the referenced elements at once. For example, if the `<book>` element has an attribute `authors` which is an IDREFS attribute containing a whitespace-separated list of author ids, the relevant `<author>` elements can be retrieved and processed using a construct such as:

```
string-join(id(@authors)/surname), ', ')
```

See Also

key() on page 812
idref() in the following section

idref

The `idref()` function performs the inverse operation to the `id()` function: it locates all the nodes in a document that contain IDREF or IDREFS values referencing a given ID value.

Signature

Argument	Type	Meaning
target	xs:string*	A sequence of ID values. The function finds all element and attribute nodes of type IDREF or IDREFS that contain a reference to at least one of the ID values in this argument.
node (optional)	node()	Identifies the document to be searched.
Result	node()*	*The element and attribute nodes that were found, in document order, without duplicates.*

Effect

If the `idrefs` argument is supplied as a node, or a sequence of nodes, then the values of the nodes are automatically atomized by the function calling mechanism. The argument can thus be supplied as any of the following:

❑   A string containing an ID value

❑   A node containing an ID value

❑   A sequence of either of the above

The function locates element and attribute nodes that have the `is-idref` property and that contain an ID value equal to one of the supplied strings. Note that when an attribute node is matched, it is the attribute node that is returned by the function, not the containing element.

In a schema-aware processor, both elements and attributes can have the `is-idref` property: they will be given this property if they have a content type that is either `xs:IDREF` or `xs:IDREFS`, or a type derived from these types. In a non-schema-aware processor, only attribute values can be recognized as `IDREF` or `IDREFS` attributes, and they are recognized as a consequence of validation using a DTD.

It is not an error if there is no node that references one of the target `ID` values (or even if there is no node that has this `ID` value). In this situation, there will simply be no node in the resulting sequence corresponding to this value. In the simplest case, where there is only one candidate `ID` value supplied, the resulting sequence will be empty if the document contains no reference to this `ID` value.

If the second argument is supplied, the nodes that are returned will come from the same document as the node supplied in this argument. This must be a node in a tree whose root is a document node. The default for this argument is the context node: a runtime error is then reported if the context item is undefined or if it is not a node. The nodes in the supplied `target` argument will often come from the same document, but this is not required.

IDs and Validation

`ID` and `IDREF` values only really work properly if the source document is valid (in the XML sense: meaning, loosely, that it obeys the rules in its own DTD or Schema). However, XPath is designed to allow invalid documents as well as valid ones to be processed. One possible kind of validity error is that an attribute of type `IDREF` or `IDREFS` may contain a value that is not a legal `ID` value. This situation is not an error as far as XPath is concerned; it just means that this function will never retrieve that node.

When no schema is used, a non-validating XML parser isn't required to read attribute definitions from an external DTD. In this situation the XSLT processor will assume there are no `IDREF` or `IDREFS` attributes present, and the `idref()` function will always return an empty result. If this appears to be happening, check what options are available for configuring the XML parser, or try a different parser. Most good parsers will report the attribute type, even though it isn't absolutely required by the XML standard.

Example

Consider the following data, representing part of a family tree (`idref/source.xml`):

```
<person id="I001">
  <name="Queen Elizabeth II"/>
  <spouse ref="I002"/>
</person>
<person id="I003">
  <name="Prince Charles"/>
  <mother ref="I001"/>
  <father ref="I002"/>
</person>
```

Given a `<person>` element as the context node, and assuming that the `ref` attributes have type `xs:IDREF`, it is possible to find the children of a person as:

```
idref(@id)/(parent::father|parent::mother)/parent::person
```

Note the need to check the names of the parent and grandparent elements. Without this check, one would find relatives other than the children, for example the spouse. This is because an `IDREF` in XML doesn't capture any information about which relationship is being modeled; that is implicit in the context in which the `IDREF` appears.

Sorry about the confusion here between family trees and XML trees. A family tree is of course not a tree at all in the computer science sense, because people (unlike nodes) have two parents. This means that the parent-child relationship in the family tree cannot be represented by a parent-child relationship in the XML tree; instead, it is represented here by an `ID`/`IDREF` relationship. Of course, it could have been modeled in either direction, or redundantly in both directions, but the representation chosen above works well because it is in relational third normal form.

See Also

`id()` on page 802

implicit-timezone

The `implicit-timezone()` function returns the value of the implicit timezone from the runtime context. The implicit timezone is used when comparing dates, times, and dateTimes that have no explicit timezone.

Signature

This function takes no arguments.

	Type	Meaning
Result	xs:dayTimeDuration	*The value of the implicit timezone*

Effect

Timezones are represented as values of type `xs:dayTimeDuration`, in the range `-PT14H` to `+PT14H`. This function simply returns the value of the implicit timezone from the runtime XPath context. The way that the value is initialized is determined by the implementation; it might be set using an API, or it might simply be taken from the system clock. The idea is that the implicit timezone should be the timezone in which the user is located, but when users are scattered around the world it is not always possible to achieve this.

There are a number of operators and functions that make use of the implicit timezone. The most obvious is when comparing an `xs:dateTime` that has a timezone to one that does not; in this case, the `xs:dateTime` without an explicit timezone is assumed to represent a time in the implicit timezone. This means that an expression such as:

```
if (current-time() gt xs:time('12:00:00')) then . . .
```

can be read as "if the current time in the user's timezone is after midday...." (The result of the `current-time()` function will always be in the implicit timezone.)

In the world of XML Schema types, timezone simply means a time shift from UTC. Don't confuse it with a geographical concept which is sometimes also called timezone; for example, the Eastern time area of the United States. The US Eastern time area has different displacements from UTC at different times of the year. Knowing that the timezone is −05:00 doesn't tell you that you're in the US Eastern time area; you might be in the US Central time area in summer, or in Peru at any time of year.

Example

If the system is correctly configured for a user situated in New York, with no daylight savings time in operation, the function `implicit-timezone()` will return «`-PT05:00`».

See Also

`adjust-date/time/dateTime-to-timezone()` family of functions on page 715
`current-date/time/dateTime()` family of functions on page 738
`timezone-from-date/time/dateTime()` family of functions on page 893

index-of

The `index-of()` function returns a sequence of integers indicating the positions within a particular sequence where items equal to a specified value occur.

For example, «`index-of(("a","b","c"), "b")`» returns 2.

Signature

Argument	Type	Meaning
sequence	`xs:anyAtomicType*`	The sequence to be searched
value	`xs:anyAtomicType`	The value to be found
collation (optional)	`xs:string`	The collation to be used when comparing strings
Result	`xs:integer*`	*A list containing the positions within the supplied* sequence *where items that are equal to the specified* value *have been found*

Effect

If either the `sequence` or the `value` is supplied as a node, the nodes are atomized (to extract their values) as part of the function calling rules. This function therefore operates on a sequence of atomic values. It finds all the items in the atomized `sequence` that compare as equal to the supplied `value` under the rules of the «`eq`» operator, using the specified collation when comparing strings, or the default collation if none is specified. It then returns the positions of these items in ascending numeric order, using the usual convention of numbering positions starting at 1.

This means that if a sequence of nodes is supplied, and the nodes are list-valued (for example, a node whose type is `xs:NMTOKENS`), then the positions returned are the positions in the atomized sequence, which may not be the same as the positions of the nodes in the original sequence.

Untyped atomic values are compared as strings. Values that cannot be compared are treated as not equal. This means that if you search for an integer in a sequence of strings, the result is an empty sequence, not an error.

If no matching items are found, the result is an empty sequence.

Another way of writing this function, assuming that the default collation is used and that the values have already been atomized, would be:

```
for $i in 1 to count($sequence) return
    if ($sequence[$i] eq $value) then $i else ()
```

13

The Function Library

Examples

Consider the source document:

```
<doc>
  <obs at="10:42:06" colors="red green"/>
  <obs at="11:43:12" colors="green blue orange"/>
</doc>
```

and assume that this has been validated using a schema that defines the `colors` attribute as a sequence of strings.

Expression	Result
`index-of(//@colors, "red")`	1
`index-of(//@colors, "green")`	(2, 3)
`index-of(//@colors, "pink")`	()
`index-of(//@colors, 23)`	()

You can take advantage of the fact that `index-of()` throws no error when comparing values that can never be equal. For example, if you have a list-of-union type that allows a sequence containing a mixture of strings and dates, testing «$sequence=current-date()» could throw an error if one of the items in the sequence is a string rather than a date. Rewriting the expression as «exists(index-of($sequence, current-date()))» solves the problem.

in-scope-prefixes

The `in-scope-prefixes()` function returns a sequence of strings, representing all the namespace prefixes that are in scope for a given element.

Changes in 2.0

This function is new in XPath 2.0. It is provided as a replacement for the namespace axis, which is now deprecated.

Signature

Argument	Type	Meaning
element	`element()`	The element whose in-scope namespaces are to be returned
Result	`xs:string*`	*The prefixes of the in-scope namespaces*

Effect

In the XPath data model, the namespaces that apply to a particular element are modeled as a set of namespace nodes: the name of the namespace node represents a namespace prefix, and the string value of the namespace node represents the namespace URI.

In XPath 1.0 it was possible to find the namespace nodes for a given element using the namespace axis. In XPath 2.0 the namespace axis has been deprecated. This was done because many implementations did not physically represent namespaces as nodes in memory, for efficiency reasons, and presenting the information as "virtual nodes" could be expensive, because of the overhead that nodes carry to maintain information about their identity, their parentage, their base URI, and so on. XPath 2.0 has therefore provided a new mechanism to allow applications to obtain the namespace information when it is needed.

The `in-scope-prefixes()` function returns all the prefixes of the in-scope namespaces for an element, or to express it in terms of the data model, the names of all the namespace nodes for that element. The order in which the names appear is unpredictable. The list will always include the name «xml», since the XML namespace is in scope for every element. If there is a default namespace in force for the element, the list will also include the zero-length string to represent the default namespace. Any string in the result other than the zero-length string will be returned as an instance of `xs:NCName`.

The namespace URIs corresponding to each of these prefixes can be determined using the function `namespace-uri-for-prefix()` described on page 839.

Examples

Consider the source document below. Note that this includes a namespace undeclaration for the «soap» namespace, as permitted by XML Namespaces 1.1:

```
<?xml version="1.1"?>
<soap:Envelope
        xmlns:soap="http://schemas.xmlsoap.org/soap/envelope/"
        xmlns:xs="http://www.w3.org/2001/XMLSchema">
  <soap:Body>
    <echoString xmlns="http://example.com/soapdemo"
               xmlns:xsi="http://www.w3.org/2001/XMLSchema-instance"
               xmlns:soap="">
      <inputString xsi:type="xs:string">Hello</inputString>
    </echoString>
  </soap:Body>
</soap:Envelope>
```

Expression	Result
`in-scope-prefixes(/soap:Envelope)`	`("xs", "soap", "xml")` *(in any order)*
`in-scope-prefixes(//*:inputString)`	`("xs", "", "xsi", "xml")` *(in any order)*

Usage

Like the namespace axis that it replaces, this function is unlikely to be needed every day of the week. It is generally needed only when dealing with documents that use namespace prefixes as part of the content of elements and attributes (and not only in forming the names of elements and attributes). I have also seen situations where it is necessary simply to detect whether a particular namespace is declared, regardless whether or not it is actually used. For example, you might want to find all your stylesheets that declare the namespace `http://icl.com/saxon` because you have decided to migrate from Saxon 6.5 (which uses this namespace) to Saxon 9.x (which does not). You could find these using the query:

```
collection("stylesheets")[//*["http://icl.com/saxon" =
                              for $p in in-scope-prefixes(.)
                              return namespace-uri-for-prefix($p, .)]]
```

See Also

`namespace-uri-for-prefix()` on page 839
`resolve-QName()` on page 864

insert-before

The `insert-before()` function returns a sequence constructed by inserting an item, or a sequence of items, at a given position within another sequence.

For example, «`insert-before(("a","b","c"), 2, "X")`» returns «`("a", "X", "b", "c")`».

Signature

Argument	Type	Meaning
sequence-1	`item()*`	The original sequence
position	`xs:integer`	The position in the original sequence where the new items are to be inserted
sequence-2	`item()*`	The items that are to be inserted
Result	`item()*`	*The constructed sequence*

Effect

Remember that sequences are immutable: despite its name, this function doesn't modify the supplied sequence; it constructs a new sequence containing items copied from the two input sequences.

The returned sequence consists of all items in `sequence-1` whose position is less than the specified `position`, followed by all items in `sequence-2`, followed by all remaining items in `sequence-1`. Positions, as always, are numbered starting at one. It's not an error if `position` is outside the actual range of positions in the sequence.

In other words, the result is the same as the value of the expression:

```
$sequence-1[position() lt $position],
$sequence-2,
$sequence-1[position() ge $position]
```

Examples

Expression	Result
`insert-before(1 to 5, 4, (99, 100))`	`(1, 2, 3, 99, 100, 4, 5)`
`insert-before(1 to 5, 0, 99)`	`(99, 1, 2, 3, 4, 5)`
`insert-before(1 to 5, 10, 99)`	`(1, 2, 3, 4, 5, 99)`

Usage

Although functions are provided to insert items into and remove items from a sequence, there is no function to replace the item at a given position $p. To achieve this, you can write:

```
insert-before(remove($seq, $p), $p, $new-item)
```

or perhaps more simply:

```
$seq[position() lt $position],
$new-item,
$seq[position() gt $position]
```

See Also
remove() on page 861
«,» operator on page 634 in Chapter 10

iri-to-uri

iri-to-uri() converts an IRI (Internationalized Resource Identifier) into a URI by percent-encoding special characters according to the rules of RFC 3986 and RFC 3987.

For example, «iri-to-uri('http://www.wikipedia.org/Gerhard Schröder')» returns «http://www.wikipedia.org/Gerhard%20Schr%C3%B6der».

Signature

Argument	Type	Meaning
value	xs:string?	The input string, to which URI escaping is to be applied. An empty sequence is treated as a zero-length string.
Result	xs:string	*The URI in its escaped form, as a string.*

Effect

As the name of the function suggests, its purpose is to take an IRI as input and produce a valid URI by escaping those characters that are allowed in an IRI but not in a URI. For completeness, it also escapes those characters that are not allowed in an IRI.

An IRI is essentially a URI in which non-ASCII characters are permitted; for example, the string «http://www.münchen.de/» is a valid IRI, but it is not a valid URI. Applying this function would convert this IRI to «http://www.m%C3%BCnchen.de/». (Whether this is actually a useful thing to do is a separate matter — current browsers accept this IRI with the «ü», but reject it after percent-encoding.)

The result string is formed from the input string by escaping special characters according to the rules defined in RFC 3986. Special characters are escaped by first encoding them in UTF-8, then representing each byte of the UTF-8 encoding in the form %HH, where HH represents the byte as two hexadecimal digits. The digits A–F are always in upper case.

The characters that are considered "special" in this definition are characters outside the range x21 to x7E, together with «<», «>», «"», «{», «}», «|», «\», «^», and «'». Note that this includes the space character, which will be encoded as %20.

If a «%» character occurs in the input string, it will *not* be escaped as «%25».

Examples

Expression	Result
iri-to-uri("simple.xml")	"simple.xml"
iri-to-uri("http://w3.org/simple.xml")	"http://w3.org/simple.xml"
iri-to-uri("my doc.xml")	"my%20doc.xml"
iri-to-uri("Grüße.html")	"Gr%C3%BC%C3%9Fe.html"
iri-to-uri("100% Java.html")	"100%%20Java.html"

13

The Function Library

Usage

Although IRIs (Internationalized Resource Identifiers) are not very often mentioned, an increasing number of interfaces and protocols actually accept them even though they may still use the term URI. Technically, a URI does not allow non-ASCII characters. This function allows you to bridge from an environment where IRIs are allowed (whether officially or unofficially) to a world where they are not recognized.

The handling of percent signs can cause problems, because two different IRIs, for example «My Documents» and «My%20Documents», will be converted to the same URI, which means that the conversion cannot be accurately reversed. If you know that any percent signs in the input string genuinely represent a percent character rather than signalling an escape sequence, then it is a good idea to convert them to «%25» before calling this function. This can be done by calling «replace($in, '%', '%25')».

See Also

escape-uri-attributes serialization option on page 938 in Chapter 15.
encode-for-uri() on page 771
escape-html-uri() on page 775

key

This function is available in XSLT only.

The key() function is used to find the nodes with a given value for a named key. It is used in conjunction with the <xsl:key> element described on page 376 in Chapter 6.

For example, if there is a key definition:

```
<xsl:key name="vreg" match="vehicle" use="@reg"/>
```

then the expression «key('vreg', 'N498PAA')» might return the single element <vehicle reg="N498PAA">.

Changes in 2.0

The key value can now be of any type and is compared according to the rules for that type. The key definitions in <xsl:key> can also now specify a collation to be used for comparing strings.

An optional third argument has been added to identify the document to be searched.

Signature

Argument	Type	Meaning
name	xs:string	Specifies the name of the key. The value of the string must be a lexical QName that identifies a key declared using an <xsl:key> element in the stylesheet.
value	xs:anyAtomicType*	Specifies the required value of the key, in a way that depends on the type. See below.

continued

Argument	Type	Meaning
top (optional)	node()	Identifies the tree to be searched. If this argument is omitted, the document containing the context node is searched.
Result	node()*	*The nodes with the required key values, returned without duplicates, and in document order.*

Effect

The first argument must take the form of a lexical QName, that is, an XML name optionally prefixed with a namespace prefix that corresponds to a namespace declaration that is in scope at the point in the stylesheet where the key() function is called. If there is no namespace prefix, the relevant namespace URI is null; the default namespace is not used. There must be an <xsl:key> element in the stylesheet with the same expanded QName, using the namespace URIs rather than prefixes in the comparison. If there is more than one <xsl:key> element with this name, they are all used: a node is considered to match the key if it matches any of the key definitions with this name.

The second argument is a sequence of atomic values (usually a single atomic value, but this is treated as a sequence of length one). If the value actually supplied in the function call includes nodes, the nodes are atomized to create a sequence of atomic values. The result of the key() function contains every node in the same document as the context node that has at least one key value that is equal to one of the values supplied in this sequence.

The key values can be of any type. The values of the keys as indexed using <xsl:key> will be compared with the keys supplied in the key() function, using the rules of the XPath «eq» operator without any special type conversion; this means, for example, that if the indexed value is the xs:integer value 23, it will not be retrieved by the call «key('k', '23')», because the integer 23 and the string '23' do not compare as equal. Untyped atomic values (values extracted from unvalidated nodes) are treated as strings and can only be compared with strings. If a collation is specified in the <xsl:key> declaration, it will be used when comparing strings; otherwise, the default collation will be used.

The optional top argument identifies the tree to be searched. The value can be any node, not necessarily a document node. The default value is the document node of the tree containing the context node. The function searches the subtree rooted at this node, so you can either search a whole document, or a subtree rooted at a particular element (this differs from the id() and idref() functions). A node will be selected by the function only if it has top as an ancestor-or-self node. When the third argument is omitted, it's an error if there is no context item, or if the context item isn't a node. It's also an error to search in a tree that doesn't have a document node as its root (this rule is for the convenience of implementors, to allow indexes to be maintained at the level of a document).

Usage and Examples

The key() function is provided to make associative access to nodes (finding the nodes given their content) more convenient and more efficient. Efficiency of course depends entirely on the implementation, but it is likely that most implementations will use some kind of index or hash-table data structure to make the key() function faster than the equivalent path expression using predicates to select the required value.

Another use for keys is that they provide an efficient way of grouping related nodes together. This usage is needed far less under XSLT 2.0, because of the introduction of the <xsl:for-each-group> instruction, but it is still worth your while to understand it.

We will examine these two ways of using keys in turn.

Using Keys to Find Nodes by Value

To locate the `<book>` elements having J. B. Priestley as the content of one of their `<author>` child elements, you could write:

```
<xsl:for-each select="//book[author='J. B. Priestley']">
```

However, it is probably more efficient, if this is done frequently in the stylesheet, to define the author name as a key.

```
<xsl:key name="book-author" match="book" use="author"/>
. . .
<xsl:for-each select="key('book-author', 'J. B. Priestley')"/>
```

The `key()` function normally locates elements in the same document as the context node. When you need to locate elements in a different document, you can identify this in the third argument, for example:

```
<xsl:copy-of select="key('book-author', 'J. B. Priestley', document('a.xml'))"/>
```

The key value is usually supplied as a string, or as an expression that returns a string. In XSLT 2.0 it can also be a value of another atomic type; for example, you can use a number or a date as a key. It does not have to be a single value; you can supply a sequence of strings (or numbers or dates, if that is how the key is defined), and the function will return all the nodes that match any one of the values.

Keys are particularly useful for following cross-references. If you supply the key value as a node, or a sequence of nodes, then the values held in those nodes will be used as the key values. The next example explores this in more detail.

Example: Using Keys as Cross-References

This example uses two source files: the principal source document is a file containing a list of books, and the secondary one (accessed using the `document()` function) contains biographies of authors. The author name held in the first file acts as a cross-reference to the author's biography in the second file, rather like a join in SQL.

Source

The principal source document is an abbreviated version of the `booklist.xml` file:

```
<booklist>
<book category="FC">
    <title>The Young Visiters</title>
    <author>Daisy Ashford</author>
</book>
<book category="FC">
    <title>When We Were Very Young</title>
    <author>A. A. Milne</author>
</book>
</booklist>
```

The secondary source document, `authors.xml`, reads like this. I've included only two authors to keep it short, but the `key()` function would really come into its own if there were hundreds of entries.

```
<authors>
<author name="A. A. Milne">
<born>1852</born>
<died>1956</died>
<biog>Alan Alexander Milne, educated at Westminster School and Trinity Col-
lege Cambridge, became a prolific author of plays, novels, poetry, short
stories, and essays, all of which have been overshadowed by his children's
books. </biog>
</author>
<author name="Daisy Ashford">
<born>1881</born>
<died>1972</died>
<biog>Daisy Ashford (Mrs George Norman) wrote The Young Visiters, a small
comic masterpiece, while still a young child in Lewes. It was found in a
drawer in 1919 and sent to Chatto and Windus, who published it in the same
year with an introduction by J. M. Barrie, who had first insisted on meeting
the author in order to check that she was genuine.
</biog>
</author>
</authors>
```

Stylesheet

The stylesheet is in the file author-biogs.xsl. It declares a key to match <author> elements by their name attribute. This is intended for use with the authors.xml file, though there is nothing in the key definition to say so.

Note the use of a global variable to reference the secondary source file. It would be possible to use the document() function each time the file is accessed, and any XSLT processor worthy of the name would actually read and parse the file only once, but using a variable in my view makes it easier to see what is going on.

The actual call on the key() function is in the path expression «$biogs/key('biog', $name)». The purpose of the first step, $biogs, is to switch the context node to the authors.xml document, because the key() function (when used with two arguments) always looks in the document containing the context node. The expression could equally have been written «key('biog', name, $biogs)».

```
<xsl:transform xmlns:xsl="http://www.w3.org/1999/XSL/Transform"
  version="2.0"
>
<xsl:key name="biog" match="author" use="@name"/>
<xsl:variable name="biogs" select="document('authors.xml')"/>
<xsl:template match="/">
  <html><body>
  <xsl:variable name="all-books" select="//book"/>
    <xsl:for-each select="$all-books">
                <!-- for each book in the booklist file -->
      <h1><xsl:value-of select="title"/></h1>
      <h2>Author<xsl:if test="count(author)!=1">s</xsl:if></h2>
      <xsl:for-each select="author">
                <!-- for each author of this book -->
        <xsl:variable name="name" select="."/>
        <h3><xsl:value-of select="$name"/></h3>
```

```
                         <!--locate the biography by key lookup -->
             <xsl:variable name="auth"
                           select="$biogs/key('biog', $name)"/>
             <p>
               <xsl:value-of select="concat($auth/born, ' - ', $auth/died)"/>
             </p>
             <p><xsl:value-of select="$auth/biog"/></p>
        </xsl:for-each>
      </xsl:for-each>
    </body></html>
  </xsl:template>
</xsl:transform>
```

Output

The output obtained if you run this stylesheet with the subset of the booklist.xml file shown earlier is as follows.

```
<html>
   <body>
      <h1>The Young Visiters</h1>
      <h2>Author</h2>
      <h3>Daisy Ashford</h3>
      <p>1881 - 1972</p>
      <p>Daisy Ashford (Mrs George Norman) wrote The Young Visiters, a small
comic masterpiece, while still a young child in Lewes. It was found in a
drawer in 1919 and sent to Chatto and Windus, who published it in the
same year with an introduction by J. M. Barrie, who had first insisted on
meeting the author in order to check that she was genuine.
</p>
      <h1>When We Were Very Young</h1>
      <h2>Author</h2>
      <h3>A. A. Milne</h3>
      <p>1852 - 1956</p>
       <p>Alan Alexander Milne, educated at Westminster School and Trinity
College Cambridge, became a prolific author of plays, novels, poetry,
short stories, and essays, all of which have been overshadowed by his chil-
dren's books.</p>
      </body>
   </html>
```

Using Keys for Grouping

Because keys provide an efficient way of retrieving all the nodes that share a common value, they are useful when you need to group nodes with common values in the output.

This technique is sometimes called the Muenchian grouping method, after Steve Muench of Oracle who introduced it. In XSLT 1.0, it was the only way of performing grouping efficiently. In XSLT 2.0, the `<xsl:for-each-group>` construct will usually provide a more convenient solution; however, you will still encounter the Muenchian method used in old stylesheets, and there is no reason why you should not continue to use it.

To solve any grouping problem, you need two nested loops. The outer loop selects one node to act as a representative of each group, typically the first node in document order that is a member of the group. The processing associated with this node outputs information about the group as a whole, typically the common value used to group the nodes together, perhaps with counts or subtotals calculated over the members of the group, plus any necessary formatting. The inner loop then processes each member of the group in turn.

With the Muenchian method, a key is defined on the common value that determines group membership. For example, if all the cities in a country compose one group, then the key definition will be as follows.

```
<xsl:key name="country-group" match="city" use="@country"/>
```

The outer loop selects one city for each country. The way of doing this is to select all the cities, and then filter out those that are not the first in their country. You can tell that a city is the first one for its country by comparing it with the first node in the sequence returned by the key() function for that country.

```
<xsl:for-each select="//city[. is key('country-group', @country)[1]]">
```

The «is» operator is new in XPath 2.0. In an XSLT 1.0 stylesheet, the equivalent expression would apply generate-id() to both operands, and compare the results using the «=» operator.

Within this loop the code can output any heading it needs, such as the name of the country. It can then start an inner loop to process all the cities in this country, which it can find by using the key once again.

```
<xsl:for-each select="key('country-group', @country)">
```

The following shows a complete example of this technique.

Example: Using Keys for Grouping

This example creates a list of cities, grouped by country.

Source

The source cities.xml is a list of cities.

```
<cities>
    <city name="Paris" country="France"/>
    <city name="Roma" country="Italia"/>
    <city name="Nice" country="France"/>
    <city name="Madrid" country="Espana"/>
    <city name="Milano" country="Italia"/>
    <city name="Firenze" country="Italia"/>
    <city name="Napoli" country="Italia"/>
    <city name="Lyon" country="France"/>
    <city name="Barcelona" country="Espana"/>
</cities>
```

Stylesheet

The stylesheet citygroups.xsl is as follows:

```
<xsl:transform
 xmlns:xsl="http://www.w3.org/1999/XSL/Transform"
 version="2.0"
>
<xsl:key name="country-group" match="city" use="@country"/>
<xsl:template match="/">
  <html><body>
   <xsl:for-each select="//city[. is key('country-group', @country)[1]]">
      <xsl:value-of select="@country"/></h1>
      <xsl:for-each select="key('country-group', @country)">
         <xsl:value-of select="@name"/><br/>
      </xsl:for-each>
   </xsl:for-each>
  </body></html>
</xsl:template>
</xsl:transform>
```

Output

Viewed in a browser, the output is as shown in Figure 13-2.

Figure 13-2

See Also

<xsl:key> on page 376 in Chapter 6
id() on page 802

lang

The lang() function tests whether the language of a given node, as defined by the xml:lang attribute, corresponds to the language supplied as an argument.

For example, if the context node is the element <para lang="fr-CA"> (indicating Canadian French), then the expression «lang('fr')» would return true.

Changes in 2.0

An optional second argument has been added to allow nodes other than the context node to be tested.

Signature

Argument	Type	Meaning
language	xs:string	The language being tested
node (optional)	node()	The node being tested. If omitted, the context node is tested.
Result	*xs:boolean*	true *if the language of the selected node is the same as, or a sublanguage of, the language being tested.*

Effect

The function tests the node identified by the second argument if present, or the context node if it is omitted. When the second argument is absent, a runtime error occurs if there is no context item, or if the context item is not a node.

The language of the selected node is determined by the value of its xml:lang attribute, or if it has no such attribute, by the value of the xml:lang attribute on its nearest ancestor node that does have such an attribute. If there is no xml:lang attribute on any of these nodes, the lang() function returns false.

The xml:lang attribute is one of the small number of attributes that are given a predefined meaning in the XML specification (in fact, you could argue that it is the only thing in the XML specification that has anything to say about what the contents of the document might mean to its readers). The value of the attribute is a language identifier as defined in RFC 3066; this takes one of the following four forms:

❑ A two- or three-letter language code defined in the international standard ISO 639. For example, English is «en» and French is «fr». This can be given in either upper case or lower case, though lower case is usual.

❑ A language code as above, followed by one or more subcodes: each subcode is preceded by a hyphen «-». For example, US English is "en-US"; Canadian French is "fr-CA". The first subcode, if present, must be either a two-letter country code from the international standard ISO 3166 or a subcode for the language registered with IANA (Internet Assigned Numbers Authority). The ISO 3166 country codes are generally the same as Internet top-level domains; for example, "DE" for Germany or "CZ" for the Czech Republic, but with the notable exception of the United Kingdom, whose ISO 3166 code (for some reason) is "GB" rather than "UK". These codes are generally written in upper case. The meaning of any subcodes after the first is

13

The Function Library

generally not defined (though a few have been registered with IANA), but they must contain ASCII letters (a–z, A–Z) only.

❏ A language code registered with IANA (see `http://www.isi.edu/in-notes/iana/assign-ments/languages/`), prefixed "i-", for example, "i-Navajo".

❏ A user-defined language code, prefixed "x-", for example, "x-Java" if the element contains a Java program.

The `xml:lang` attribute defines the language of all text contained within the element it appears on, unless it is overridden by another `xml:lang` attribute in an inner element. So if a document is written in English but contains quotations in German, the `xml:lang` language code on the document element might say «xml:lang="en"», while an element containing a quotation specifies «xml:lang="de"».

The `lang()` function allows you to test whether the language for the context node is the one you are expecting. For example «lang('en')» returns `true` if the language is English, while «lang ('jp')» returns `true` if it is Japanese.

Specifically, the rules are as follows:

❏ If the value of `xml:lang` for the selected node is equal to the string supplied in the argument, ignoring differences of case, the function returns `true`.

❏ If the leading part of the value of `xml:lang` for the selected node, up to some hyphen «-», is equal to the string supplied in the argument, again ignoring differences of case, the function returns `true`.

❏ Otherwise, the function returns `false`.

Examples

Expression	Result
`boolean(//*[lang('de')])`	`true()` if the document contains any elements marked as being in German
`/*/msg[@code=$p][lang('fr')]`	The `<msg>` element with a required code value that is marked as being in French

Usage

This function provides a convenient way of testing the language used in a source document. Assuming that the source document has been properly marked up using the `xml:lang` attribute as defined in the XML specification, the `lang()` function allows you to do language-dependent processing of the data.

The `lang()` function only allows you to test whether the language is one of the languages you are expecting; if you want to find out the actual language, you will need to read the `xml:lang` attribute directly. You can find the relevant attribute using the expression «(ancestor-or-self::*/ @xml:lang)[last()]».

last

The `last()` function returns the value of the context size. When processing a sequence of items, if the items are numbered from one, `last()` gives the number assigned to the last item in the sequence.

Changes in 2.0

None.

Signature

This function takes no arguments.

	Type	Meaning
Result	`xs:integer`	*A number, the value of the context size. As the name implies, this is context dependent.*

Effect

The XPath specification defines the value of the `last()` function in terms of the *context size*.

The context size is part of the *focus*, which is described in the spec as having three components: the context item, the context position, and the context size. However, it may be easier to think of the focus as being a bit like an `Iterator` object in a language such as Java. Behind the iterator is a list of items that are processed individually (though not necessarily in any particular order). The context item, position, and size can be thought of as three methods provided by this iterator object: the context position is a number that ranges from 1 to the size of the list, the context item is the item found at the context position, and the context size is the number of items in the list.

When a top-level XPath expression is evaluated (that is, an XPath expression that is not part of another expression), the context size is set by the host language. In XSLT, it is set from the XSLT context. For example:

- ❑ When a global `<xsl:variable>` declaration is being evaluated, or in certain other contexts such as evaluating the `use` expression in `<xsl:key>`, or evaluating the initial template that matches the root node, it is normally set to 1 (one).
- ❑ When `<xsl:apply-templates>` is called to process a sequence of nodes, the context size is the number of nodes selected in the call of `<xsl:apply-templates>`.
- ❑ When `<xsl:for-each>` is called to process a sequence of items, the context size is the number of items selected in the call of `<xsl:for-each>`.

This means that within an `<xsl:for-each>` iteration, the test `<xsl:if test="position()=last()">` succeeds when the last item in the sequence is being processed.

Many APIs that enable XPath expressions to be executed from languages like Java or JavaScript allow the caller to set the context item, but not the context position or size. In such cases, the context position and size on entry to the XPath expression will normally both be one.

Within an XPath expression, the context size changes within a predicate and on the right-hand side of the «/» operator.

- ❑ In a predicate, `last()` refers to the number of items in the sequence that is being filtered using the predicate. For example, «$seq[last()]» selects the last item in a sequence (this is short for «$seq[position()=last()]»), while «$seq[ceiling(last() div 2)]» selects the item at the midway position of the list (the fourth item in a list of eight, the fifth item in a list of nine).
- ❑ It's less common to find `last()` being used on the right-hand side of a «/» operator. It refers to the number of items in the sequence selected by the left-hand operand of the «/». I can't find a

very plausible way of using this, but it can be done. For example, «$a/(if (last()=2) then .
else ())» returns all items from $a if there are exactly two items, and in all other cases returns
nothing. But there are simpler ways of writing this!

Usage

When `last()` is used within a predicate in a filter expression, the focus refers to the sequence of items
being filtered. If the filter is used within a step of a path expression, then the context size is the number
of nodes selected by the current step of the expression, after applying any previous filters. For example,
suppose the source document is as follows:

```
<countries>
  <country name="France" capital="Paris" continent="Europe"/>
  <country name="Germany" capital="Berlin" continent="Europe"/>
  <country name="Spain" capital="Madrid" continent="Europe"/>
  <country name="Italy" capital="Rome" continent="Europe"/>
  <country name="Poland" capital="Warsaw" continent="Europe"/>
  <country name="Egypt" capital="Cairo" continent="Africa"/>
  <country name="Libya" capital="Tripoli" continent="Africa"/>
  <country name="Nigeria" capital="Lagos" continent="Africa"/>
</countries>
```

Then:

❑   The expression «countries/country[last()]» returns the <country> element for Nigeria.

❑   The expression «countries/country[@continent='Europe'][last()]» returns the
    <country> element for Poland.

❑   The expression «countries/country[@continent='Europe'][last()-1]» returns the
    <country> element for Italy.

❑   The expression «countries/country[@continent='Africa'] [position() !=last()]»
    returns the <country> elements for Egypt and Libya.

An easy mistake is to think that **last()** returns a boolean value. You can use **last()**
in a predicate to match the last node, for example «**para[last()]**». This is a
shorthand for the predicate «**[position()=last()]**», because in a predicate, a
numeric value X is equivalent to a test for the condition « **position()=X**». However,
this doesn't extend to other contexts, for example if you write:

if (last()) then ...

then the numeric value of the **last()** function is simply converted to a boolean as if
the **boolean()** function were used. The result will always be true, because **last()**
can never be zero.

Usage in XSLT

The `last()` function can be called in XSLT as a freestanding XPath expression, or in simple tests such
as `<xsl:if test="position()=last()">`. This kind of usage is frequent in XSLT, because XSLT makes
heavy use of the focus. To understand the effect of calling `last()`, you need to know how different XSLT
instructions set the focus.

When `last()` is used as a top-level expression within an `<xsl:template>` (and not within `<xsl:
for-each>`), it returns the number of nodes selected by the relevant `<xsl:apply-templates>` select

expression. This is because `<xsl:apply-templates>` sets the focus to refer to the sequence of nodes selected by the `select` expression, after sorting them into the order in which they are processed.

For example, the following code can be used to number all the figures in a document. The `last()` function prints the number of figure elements in the document.

```
<xsl:apply-templates select="//figure"/>
. . .
<xsl:template match="figure" version="2.0">
   <div align="center">
   <img src="{@href}"/>
   <p>Figure <xsl:value-of select="position(), 'of', last()"/></p>
   </div>
</xsl:template>
```

(The «version="2.0"» setting is used to ensure that `<xsl:value-of>` displays the whole sequence in its `select` attribute, not just the first item.)

Similarly, when `last()` is used as a top-level expression within `<xsl:for-each>`, it returns the number of items selected by the relevant `<xsl:for-each>` select expression. Again, this is because `<xsl:for-each>` sets the focus to refer to the sequence of items selected by the `select` expression, after sorting into the correct order.

If the `last()` function is used within the `select` expression of an `<xsl:sort>` element, then it refers to the number of items being sorted. For example, specifying the following sort key:

```
<xsl:sort select="position() mod (ceiling(last() div 3))"/>
```

will sort the nodes A, B, C, D, E, F, G, H into the sequence A, D, G, B, E, H, C, F, which might be useful if you want to arrange them in a table with three columns.

The `last()` function can be used as a qualifier in a pattern when the last child of a given element is to be treated differently from the others. For example:

```
<xsl:template name="normal-p" match="p">
   <xsl:copy>
      <xsl:apply-templates/>
   </xsl:copy>
</xsl:template>
<xsl:template match="p[last()]">
   <xsl:call-template name="normal-p"/>
   <hr/>
</xsl:template>
```

However, this may not perform well on all processors, because in principle each `<p>` element needs to be tested to see if it is the last one, which may involve looking at all the children of the parent of the `<p>` element. Some processors may optimize this construct, but it's best not to assume it will (in Saxon, as it happens, «match="p[last()]"» is quite efficient, but «match="p[last()-1]"» is rather expensive).

Using `<xsl:if>` will often achieve the same effect more economically:

```
<xsl:template match="p">
   <xsl:copy>
      <xsl:apply-templates/>
   </xsl:copy>
```

```
      <xsl:if test="position()=last()">
         <hr/>
      </xsl:if>
   </xsl:template>
```

However, note that these two examples are not strictly equivalent. If the <p> elements are processed by a call on <xsl:apply-templates> with no <xsl:sort> specification, they will have the same effect; but if a sort key is specified, then the second template will output an <hr/> element after the last <p> element in the order of the output, whereas the first will output the <hr/> element after the last <p> element in document order.

See Also

count() on page 733
position() on page 854
<xsl:number> in Chapter 6, page 403

local-name

The local-name() function returns the local part of the name of a node, that is, the part of the name after the colon if there is one, or the full name otherwise.

For example, if the context node is an element named <title> then the expression «local-name()» returns «title»; for an element named <ms:schema>, it returns «schema».

Changes in 2.0

Under XPath 2.0 it is an error to supply a sequence containing more than one node, except when running in backward-compatibility mode.

Signature

Argument	Type	Meaning
node (optional)	node()?	Identifies the node whose local name is required. If the argument is an empty sequence, the function returns a zero-length string. If the argument is omitted, the target node is the context node. It is then an error if there is no context item, or if the context item is not a node
Result	xs:string	*A string value: the local part of the name of the target node.*

Effect

The local name of a node depends on the kind of node, as follows:

Node kind	Local name
document	None, a zero-length string is returned
element	The element name, after any colon
attribute	The attribute name, after any colon
text	None, a zero-length string is returned

continued

Node kind	Local name
processing instruction	The *target* used in the processing instruction to identify the application for which it is intended
comment	None, a zero-length string is returned
namespace	The namespace prefix; or the zero-length string if this is the default namespace

Examples

Consider the source document:

```
<my:doc xmlns:my="http://mhk.me.uk/some.uri" security="high" xml:id="A23"/>
```

Expression	Result
`local-name(/)`	`" "`
`local-name(/*)`	`"doc"`
`local-name(/*/@*[.='high'])`	`"security"`
`local-name(/*/@*[.='A23'])`	`"id"`

Usage

This function can be useful if you need to test the local name without also testing the namespace URI. For example, if you want to select both `<title>` and `<html:title>` elements, you could do this by writing:

```
*[local-name()='title']
```

However, XPath 2.0 allows you to achieve this more directly by writing:

```
*:title
```

In some ways this can be seen as a misuse of the XML Namespaces facility. The names in one namespace are supposed to bear no relation to the names in another, so any similarity between the names `<title>` and `<html:title>` is a pure coincidence.

In practice, this isn't always true. What often happens is that one namespace is adapted from another. For example, the US Post Office might devise a schema (and associated namespace) for representing US names and addresses, and the Canadian Post Office might then create a variant of this, with a different namespace URI, for Canadian names and addresses. The two schemas will have many elements in common, and it's quite reasonable to try to write a stylesheet that can handle either. If you want to write template rules that match on both a `<us:address>` and a `<canada:address>`, there are two ways of doing it:

Either list both possibilities:

```
<xsl:template match="us:address | canada:address">
```

or match on the local name only:

```
<xsl:template match="*[local-name()='address']">
```

or equivalently:

```
<xsl:template match="*:address">
```

It's not a good idea to use this construct simply to avoid the hassle of declaring the namespace prefix. Your code will almost certainly be less efficient, and it runs the risk of producing incorrect results because it can match elements in namespaces you weren't expecting.

XSLT Example

The following stylesheet fragment outputs an HTML table listing the attributes of the current element, sorted first by namespace and then by local name:

```
<xsl:template match="*" mode="tabulate">
   <table>
      <xsl:for-each select="attribute::node()">
      <xsl:sort select="namespace-uri()"/>
      <xsl:sort select="local-name()"/>
         <tr>
         <td><xsl:value-of select="namespace-uri()"/></td>
         <td><xsl:value-of select="local-name()"/></td>
         <td><xsl:value-of select="."/></td>
         </tr>
      </xsl:for-each>
   </table>
</xsl:template>
```

See Also

name() on page 835
namespace-uri() on page 837

local-name-from-QName

The function local-name-from-QName() returns the local-name part of an xs:QName value.

Signature

Argument	Type	Meaning
value	xs:QName?	The xs:QName value whose local-name part is required. If the supplied value is an empty sequence, an empty sequence is returned.
Result	*xs:NCName?*	The local-name part of the xs:QName.

Effect

Given an expanded QName (that is, an instance of type xs:QName), this function returns the local-name part of the value.

The result is an xs:NCName. This is a type derived by restriction from xs:string, so the return value can be used anywhere that a string can be used. In a basic XSLT processor, which does not recognize the xs:NCName type directly, the value can still be used as a string.

Examples

Expression	Result
local-name-from-QName(QName('http://mhk.me.uk/some.uri', 'my:invoice'))	"invoice"
local-name-from-QName(node-name(@xml:space))	"space"

The second example assumes that the context node has an attribute called xml:space.

See Also

QName() on page 858
namespace-uri-from-QName() on page 841

lower-case

The lower-case() function converts upper-case characters in a string to lower case.

For example, «lower-case("McAndrew")» returns "mcandrew".

Signature

Argument	Type	Meaning
value	xs:string?	The string to be converted
Result	*xs:string*	*The string with upper-case letters converted to lower case.*

Effect

For those whose only language is English, the matter of converting characters between upper case and lower case is straightforward: there is a direct one-to-one mapping between the 26 upper-case letters A–Z and the 26 lower-case letters a–z. In other languages, the relationship is not always so simple. In many Oriental scripts there is no concept of case at all. Even with Western languages there are many complications. To take a few examples:

❑ The upper-case equivalent of the German «ß» character is the character pair «SS».

❑ In most languages, the lower-case equivalent of «I» is «i», but in Turkish, it is «ı» (known as "dotless I").

❑ Some characters have multiple lower-case forms, depending on context; for example, the lower-case version of the Greek «Σ» (sigma) is «σ» or «ς» depending on where in the word it appears.

❑ Some accented characters exist in both upper-case and lower-case forms, but the upper-case form is usually written without accents when it appears in running text.

Fortunately, the Unicode consortium has defined a mapping from upper-case to lower-case characters, and the XPath specification refers to this mapping. An outline of the principles can be found in Unicode Technical Report #21 (http://www.unicode.org/unicode/reports/tr21/). This material has been merged into Unicode 4.0, but in my view the original technical report is easier to read. The actual

13

The Function Library

character mappings can be extracted from the database of Unicode characters found on the Unicode Web site.

The effect of the function is as follows:

❑ If the input is an empty sequence, the result is the zero-length string.

❑ Otherwise, every character in the input string is replaced by its corresponding lower-case character (or sequence of characters) if there is one, or it is included unchanged in the result string if it does not.

The function does not implement case mappings that Unicode defines as being locale-sensitive (such as the Turkish dotless I). A good implementation will support the mappings that are context-sensitive (such as the choice between the two lower-case sigma characters), but it would be unwise to rely on it.

Examples

Expression	Result
lower-case("Sunday")	"sunday"
lower-case("2+2")	"2+2"
lower-case("CÉSAR")	"césar"
lower-case("ΕΛΛΑΣ")	"ελλας"

Usage

With simple ASCII keywords, it's safe to use the lower-case() or upper-case() functions to do a case-blind comparison, for example:

```
if (lower-case($param) = "yes") then ...
```

With a more extensive alphabet, it's better to use a specific collation for this purpose. The reason is that converting two strings to lower case for comparison doesn't always work («STRASSE» will be mapped to «strasse», while «Straße» will be mapped to «straße»). Converting both to upper case is better, though there are still a few problems that can crop up.

So it's best to use this function only if you genuinely need to convert a string to lower case, not just in order to perform comparisons.

Note also that the «i» flag can be used to achieve case-blind matching in regular expressions used by the matches(), replace(), and tokenize() functions.

See Also

translate() on page 897
upper-case() on page 910

matches

The matches() function tests whether a supplied string matches a regular expression.

Signature

Argument	Type	Meaning
input	xs:string?	The string to be tested against the regular expression. If an empty sequence is supplied, it is treated as a zero-length string.
regex	xs:string	The regular expression.
flags (optional)	xs:string	One or more letters indicating options on how the matching is to be performed. If this argument is omitted, the effect is the same as supplying a zero-length string, which defaults all the option settings.
Result	xs:boolean?	*True if the input string matches the regular expression, false if not.*

Effect

Regular expressions provide a powerful pattern-matching capability for strings.

The syntax of regular expressions supported by this function is described in Chapter 14. The syntax is based on the regular expression syntax defined for the pattern facet in XML Schema, which, in turn, is based on the established conventions used in languages such as Perl. The meaning of the flags argument is also described in Chapter 14, on page 925.

Note that whereas the pattern facet in XML Schema uses a match that is implicitly anchored to the ends of the string, this function does not. A pattern specified in XML Schema must match the entire string to be successful; the regex specified in this function only needs to match some substring. For example, «#[0-9]+» will match a string if it contains as a substring a «#» character followed by one or more digits. If you want to test whether the entire string takes the form of a «#» character followed by one or more digits, use the regex «^#[0-9]+$».

If the regular expression or the flags argument does not conform to the specified syntax, a fatal error is reported at runtime (or at compile time, if it can be detected then).

Examples

Assume that $e is the following element:

```
<verse>A grand little lad was young Albert
All dressed in his best, quite a swell
With a stick with an horse's head handle
The finest that Woolworth's could sell.</verse>
```

Expression	Result
matches($e, "grand")	true
matches($e, "^The finest", "m")	true
matches($e, "(^.*$)*", "m")	true
matches($e, "Albert.*Woolworth's", "s")	true
matches($e, "woolworth's", "i")	true

continued

13

The Function Library

Expression	Result
matches("banana", "^(.a)+$")	true
matches("23 May 2008", "^[0-9]+\s[A-Z][a-z]+\s[0-9]+$")	true
matches("", "a*")	true

In XSLT, the fourth example might be written:

```
<xsl:if test="matches($e, 'Albert.*Woolworth''s', 's')">. . .</xsl:if>
```

Note the use of two apostrophes to represent a single apostrophe within a string literal.

Usage

The `matches()` function provides a powerful alternative to the `contains()`, `starts-with()`, and `ends-with()` functions. It might be more expensive, but this is only likely to make a difference if searching a large amount of text, or when using an unusually complex regular expression.

See Also

Regular Expression Syntax, Chapter 14
contains() on page 730
ends-with() on page 773
replace() on page 862
starts-with() on page 875
tokenize() on page 894

max, min

The `max()` and `min()` functions returns the maximum or minimum value in a sequence. The input sequence may contain any items that can be compared using the «lt» and «gt» operators.

Signature

Argument	Type	Meaning
sequence	xs:anyAtomicType*	The input sequence
collation (optional)	xs:string	Collation used for comparing strings
Result	*xs:anyAtomicType?*	*The maximum/minimum value found in the input sequence*

Effect

If the sequence supplied in the function call contains nodes, then the nodes will automatically be atomized (to extract their typed values) as part of the function call mechanism.

Any untyped atomic values in the atomized sequence (which will typically result from atomizing a node in a schema-less document) are converted to xs:double values. A runtime error is reported if there are values that cannot be converted. If there are NaN (not-a-number) values in the sequence, which might happen if you do the conversion to numbers yourself using the number() function, then the result of the function is NaN. If the input sequence is empty, the result is an empty sequence.

If the sequence contains numeric values of different types, then they are all converted to the *least common type*. This means that if the sequence contains an xs:double, all the values will be converted to xs:double; otherwise, if it contains an xs:float, all the values will be converted to xs:float. Similarly, if the sequence contains a mixture of xs:string and xs:anyURI values, then the xs:anyURI values will be converted to xs:string.

In the resulting sequence, all the values must be comparable using the «lt» operator. This rules out values of types such as xs:QName and xs:hexBinary for which no ordering is defined, and it rules out sequences that mix values such as integers and strings. The max() function then returns a value that is greater than or equal to every other value in the sequence, while the min() function returns a value that is less than or equal to every other value in the sequence. This will always be a value after any conversion: for example «max((10, 1.5e0))» is the xs:double value 10e0.

If there are two values that both satisfy this condition (for example two xs:dateTime values in different timezones) then it is not predictable which of them will be returned.

If the collation argument is supplied, then it is used when comparing strings. If the sequence contains strings and no collation is supplied, then the default collation is used.

Examples

Expression	Result
max((10, 20, xs:float(-5), 13))	20 as an xs:float value
max(("a", "x", "b"))	"x" (assuming a typical collation)
max(2)	2
max(())	()
min((xs:dayTimeDuration('PT10S'), xs:dayTimeDuration('PT1M')))	PT10S as an xs:dayTimeDuration
min((xs:date('2000-01-01'), current-date()))	2000-01-01 as an xs:date

Usage

Note that max() and min() return an atomic value. If you supply a sequence of nodes, the nodes are atomized, and the highest (or lowest) atomic value is returned. If you actually want to know which node contained the highest or lowest value, you will have to search for it, using a predicate. For example:

```
$nodes[size=max($nodes/size)]
```

Because of this limitation, it may sometimes be better to use the technique of sorting the nodes and selecting the first or last. For example:

```
<xsl:for-each select="$nodes">
  <xsl:sort select="size"/>
  <xsl:if test="position() = last()">
    <xsl:sequence select="."/>
  </xsl:if>
</xsl:for-each>
```

A common usage is to find the larger or smaller of two values. Remember in this case that you need to construct a sequence containing the two values: «max((0, $amount-due))». If you forget the second pair of parentheses, you are calling the two-argument form of the function, which is likely to result in the rather cryptic message "Unknown collation".

min

See max() on page 830

minutes-from-dateTime, minutes-from-time

The two functions minutes-from-dateTime() and minutes-from-time() extract the minutes component from an xs:date or xs:dateTime value. For example, at 16:30 local time both these functions return 30.

Signature

Argument	Type	Meaning
input	xs:time or xs:dateTime?	The value from which the minutes component is to be extracted. The type of the supplied argument must correspond to the type implied by the function name.
Result	xs:integer	The minutes component, in the range 0 to 59.

Effect

The function returns the minutes component of the supplied xs:time or xs:dateTime. The value is from the time as expressed in its local timezone (which will be the same as the minutes component of the time in UTC except in the case where the timezone offset is not a multiple of one hour).

Examples

Expression	Result
minutes-from-time(xs:time("12:35:03.142"))	35
minutes-from-dateTime(xs:dateTime("2008-02-28T13:55:30"))	55
minutes-from-time(xs:time("00:30:02+01:00"))	30
minutes-from-dateTime(xs:dateTime("2008-07-31T03:10:00+08:30"))	10

See Also

current-date(), -dateTime(), -time() on page 738
format-date(), -dateTime(), -time() on page 781
day-from-date(), -dateTime() on page 744
year-from-date(), -dateTime() on page 911

minutes-from-duration

This function extracts the value of the minutes component from a normalized xs:duration value.

Signature

Argument	Type	Meaning
input	xs:duration?	The value from which the component is to be extracted. If an empty sequence is supplied, an empty sequence is returned.
Result	*xs:integer?*	*The minutes component, in the range −59 to +59.*

Effect

The function returns the minutes component of the supplied xs:duration. The duration value is first normalized so that the number of hours is less than 24, the number of minutes is less than 60, and so on. The result will be negative if the duration is negative.

Examples

Expression	Result
minutes-from-duration(xs:dayTimeDuration("PT12H20M"))	20
minutes-from-duration(xs:duration("PT210S"))	3
minutes-from-duration(xs:duration("-PT75M"))	-15
minutes-from-duration(xs:yearMonthDuration("P1Y"))	0

See Also

days-from-duration() on page 745
hours-from-duration() on page 801
seconds-from-duration() on page 874

minutes-from-time

See minutes-from-dateTime() on page 832.

month-from-date, month-from-dateTime

These two functions extract the month component from an xs:date or xs:dateTime value. For example, on Christmas Day «month-from-date(current-date())» returns 12.

Signature

Argument	Type	Meaning
input	xs:date? or xs:dateTime?	The value whose month component is to be extracted. The type of the supplied argument must correspond to the type implied by the function name. If an empty sequence is supplied, an empty sequence is returned.
Result	*xs:integer?*	*The month, in the range 1 (January) to 12 (December).*

13

The Function Library

833

Effect

The function returns the month component of the supplied `xs:date` or `xs:dateTime`. The value is used in its local timezone (not normalized to UTC).

Examples

Expression	Result
month-from-date(xs:date("2008-02-28"))	2
month-from-dateTime(xs:dateTime("2008-02-28T13:00:00"))	2
month-from-date(xs:date("2008-07-31+01:00"))	7
month-from-dateTime(xs:dateTime("2008-07-31T23:00:00-05:00"))	7

See Also

current-date(), -dateTime(), -time() on page 738
format-date(), -dateTime(), -time() on page 781
day-from-date(), -dateTime() on page 744
year-from-date(), -dateTime() on page 911

months-from-duration

This function extracts the value of the months component from a normalized `xs:duration` value.

Signature

Argument	Type	Meaning
input	xs:duration?	The value from which the component is to be extracted. If an empty sequence is supplied, an empty sequence is returned.
Result	xs:integer?	*The months component, in the range −11 to +11.*

Effect

The function returns the months component of the supplied `xs:duration`. The duration value is first normalized so that the number of months is less than 12. The result will be negative if the duration is negative.

Examples

Expression	Result
months-from-duration(xs:yearMonthDuration('P1Y3 M'))	3
months-from-duration(xs:yearMonthDuration('P15 M'))	3
months-from-duration(xs:duration('-P1Y3 M'))	−3
months-from-duration(xs:dayTimeDuration('P365D'))	0

See Also

years-from-duration on page 911

name

The name() function returns a string in the form of a lexical QName that represents the name of a node. For example, if the context node is an element named <ms:schema>, then the expression «name()» will return the string «ms:schema».

Changes in 2.0

Under XPath 2.0 it is an error to supply a sequence containing more than one node, unless running in backward-compatibility mode.

The data model now retains the namespace prefix, so the prefix returned by this function is more predictable.

Signature

Argument	Type	Meaning
node (optional)	node()?	Identifies the node whose name is required. If the argument is an empty sequence, the function returns a zero-length string. If the argument is omitted, the target node is the context node. It is then an error if there is no context item, or if the context item is not a node.
Result	xs:string	*A string value: a QName representing the name of the target node.*

Effect

The name of a node depends on the kind of node, as follows:

Node kind	Name
document	None, a zero-length string is returned.
element	The element name (a lexical QName), as it appears in the source XML.
attribute	The attribute name (a lexical QName), as it appears in the source XML.
text	None, a zero-length string is returned.
processing instruction	The *target* used in the processing instruction to identify the application for which it is intended.
comment	None, a zero-length string is returned.
namespace	The namespace prefix; or the zero-length string if this is the default namespace. (This is *not* prefixed with «xmlns:».)

Except for element and attribute nodes, name() returns the same value as local-name().

For elements and attributes, the name() function is the only XPath construct whose result depends directly on the namespace prefixes used in the node name, as distinct from the local name and the namespace URI.

13

The Function Library

Where the node is an element or attribute from a source document, the QName returned will normally use the same prefix as appeared in the original XML source. However, it is good practice not to rely on a particular prefix being used, because originators of XML documents generally assume that they have a free choice of namespace prefixes, and any preprocessing applied to the document before the transformation starts could change the prefixes. When the node was constructed during the course of the transformation, for example by an <xsl:element> or <xsl:attribute> instruction, the XSLT language specification in most cases mandates the prefix that will be used. There are a few cases, however, where the system may need to choose a different prefix in order to avoid conflicts, and in these cases the result of the name() function becomes unpredictable.

Usage

The name() function is useful when you want to display the element name, perhaps in an error message, because the form it takes is the same as the way in which users will generally write the element name.

So, for example, you could use name() in the output of the diagnostic trace() function:

```
for $e in child::* return
  trace(string(.), concat("contents of element ", name()))
```

You can also use the name() function to test the name of a node against a string, for example, «doc:title[name(..)='doc:section']». However, it's best to avoid this if you can:

❏ Firstly, this fails if the document uses a different prefix to refer to the namespace. There's nothing here to tell the system to treat «doc:section» as a QName, so if the writer of a particular document chose to use the prefix «DOC» instead of «doc» for this namespace, the test would fail, even though the names are equivalent.

❏ Secondly, there is usually a better way of doing it: this particular example can be written as «doc:title[parent::doc:section]». In fact, in most cases where you want to test whether a node has a particular name, you can do it using a predicate of this form. The «self» axis is particularly useful. For example, to test whether the current node is a figure element, write «if (self::figure) then ...». This doesn't work for attribute nodes (because the principal node kind of the self axis is element nodes; see *Name Tests* in Chapter 9, page 614). Instead you can write «if (self::attribute(figure)) then...».

One common requirement is to sort data on the value of a sort key that is supplied as a runtime parameter (this might be because the user has asked interactively for a table to be sorted on a particular column). XSLT does not allow the expression that defines the sort criteria to be completely dynamic. But very often the possible sort keys are all element children of the elements that represent the rows being sorted. In this situation it is possible to define the sort key like this:

```
<xsl:for-each select="row">
   <xsl:sort select="*[name()=$sortkey]"/>
```

If you are using namespaces it is safer to do such tests using the node-name() function, which gives you an xs:QName as its result: an xs:QName represents an expanded name (namespace URI plus local name) and is not sensitive to the choice of prefix. Alternatively, use the namespace-uri() and local-name() functions to test the two components of the expanded name separately.

If you want to select all attributes except the description attribute, you can write:

```
@*[name() != 'description']
```

This is namespace-safe, because an unprefixed attribute name always represents a name in no namespace. But in XPath 2.0, I prefer:

```
@* except @description
```

In XSLT, avoid using `name()` to generate a name in the result document, for example, by writing `<xsl:element name="{name()}"/>`. The problem is that any prefix in `name()` is interpreted in the light of namespace declarations appearing in the stylesheet, not namespace declarations in the original source document. The correct tool for this job is `<xsl:copy>`. There are cases where `<xsl:copy>` won't do the job; for example, you may want to use the name of an attribute in the input document to generate the name of an element in the output document. In this case, use `local-name()` and `namespace-uri()` separately, for example:

```
<xsl:element name="{local-name()}" namespace="{namespace-uri()}">
```

Examples

Consider the source document:

```
<my:doc xmlns:my="some.uri" security="high" xml:id="A23">
   <!-- comment --> text <?action when="now"?>
</my:doc>
```

Expression	Result
`name(/)`	`""`
`name(/*)`	`"my:doc"`
`name(/*/@*[.='high'])`	`"security"`
`name(/*/@*[.='A23'])`	`"xml:id"`
`name(//comment())`	`""`
`name((//text())[1])`	`""`
`name(//processing-instruction())`	`"action"`
`name(//namespace::my)`	`"my"`

See Also

`local-name()` on page 824
`namespace-uri()` in the following section
`node-name()` on page 843

namespace-uri

The `namespace-uri()` function returns a string that represents the URI of the namespace in the expanded name of a node. Typically, this will be a URI used in a namespace declaration, that is, the value of an `xmlns` or `xmlns:*` attribute in the source XML.

For example, if you apply this function to the outermost element of an XSLT stylesheet by writing the expression «`namespace-uri(doc('')/*)`», the result will be the string «`http://www.w3.org/1999/XSL/Transform`».

13

The Function Library

Changes in 2.0

The result is an `xs:anyURI` value rather than a string. This makes very little difference in practice.

Signature

Argument	Type	Meaning
node (optional)	`node()?`	Identifies the node whose namespace URI is required. If the argument is an empty sequence, the function returns a zero-length string. If the argument is omitted, the target node is the context node. It is then an error if there is no context item, or if the context item is not a node.
Result	`xs:anyURI`	*The namespace URI of the expanded name of the target node.*

Effect

The namespace URI of a node depends on the kind of node, as follows:

Node kind	Namespace URI
document	None, a zero-length URI is returned.
element	If the element name as given in the source XML contained a colon, the value will be the URI from the namespace declaration corresponding to the element's prefix. Otherwise, the value will be the URI of the default namespace. If this is null, the result will be a zero-length URI.
attribute	If the attribute name as given in the source XML contained a colon, the value will be the URI from the namespace declaration corresponding to the attribute's prefix. Otherwise, the result will be a zero-length URI.
text	None, a zero-length URI is returned.
processing instruction	None, a zero-length URI is returned.
comment	None, a zero-length URI is returned.
namespace	None, a zero-length URI is returned.

Except for element and attribute nodes, `namespace-uri()` returns an empty string.

The result of the function is an `xs:anyURI` value rather than an `xs:string`. However, the type promotion rules ensure that an `xs:anyURI` can be used almost anywhere that an `xs:string` is allowed. There are one or two exceptions, for example the casting rules are different, but unless you choose strings such as «true» and «false» as namespace URIs and then attempt to cast them to `xs:boolean` the differences are unlikely to be noticed.

Examples

Consider the source document:

```
<my:doc xmlns:my="http://ibm.com/ebiz" security="high" xml:id="A23"/>
```

Expression	Result
namespace-uri(/)	""
namespace-uri(/*)	"http://ibm.com/ebiz"
namespace-uri(/*/@security)	""
namespace-uri(/*/@xml:id)	"http://www.w3.org/XML/1998/namespace"
namespace-uri(/*/namespace::my)	""

Usage

Let's start with some situations where you *don't* need this function.

If you want to test whether the context node belongs to a particular namespace, the best way to achieve this is using a NameTest of the form «prefix:*». For example, to test (in XSLT) whether the current element belongs to the «http://ibm.com/ebiz» namespace, write:

```
<xsl:if test="self::ebiz:*" xmlns:ebiz="http://ibm.com/ebiz">
```

If you want to find the namespace URI corresponding to a given prefix the best solution is to use namespace nodes. You might need to do this if namespace prefixes are used in attribute values: the XSLT standard itself uses this technique in attributes such as extension-element-prefixes, and there is no reason why other XML document types should not do the same. If you have an attribute «@value», which you know takes the form of a namespace-qualified name (a QName), you can get the associated namespace URI using the expression:

```
namespace-uri-for-prefix(substring-before(@value, ':'), .)
```

The namespace-uri() function, by contrast, is useful in display contexts, where you just want to display the namespace URI of the current node, and also if you want to do more elaborate tests. For example, you may know that there is a whole family of namespaces whose URIs all begin with urn:schemas.biztalk, and you may want to test whether a particular element is in any one of these. You can achieve this by writing:

```
if (starts-with(namespace-uri(), 'urn:schemas.biztalk')) then ...
```

See Also

local-name() on page 824
name() on page 835

namespace-uri-for-prefix

The function namespace-uri-for-prefix() returns the namespace URI corresponding to a given namespace prefix in the in-scope namespaces of a particular element node.

Changes in 2.0

This function is new in XPath 2.0. Together with in-scope-prefixes(), it provides a replacement for the namespace axis, which is deprecated in XPath 2.0.

Signature

Argument	Type	Meaning
prefix	`xs:string?`	The namespace prefix whose corresponding namespace URI is required, or the zero-length string to get the default namespace URI. If the argument is an empty sequence, it is treated as a zero-length string.
element	`element()`	The element node to be examined to find an in-scope namespace declaration for this prefix.
Result	`xs:anyURI?`	*The namespace URI corresponding to the given prefix.*

Effect

The in-scope namespaces for an element are represented in the data model as namespace nodes, and the behavior of this function is therefore described in terms of a search of the namespace nodes.

This function searches the namespace nodes of the given element. If it finds a namespace node whose name matches the given prefix, then it returns the string value of this namespace node, as an `xs:anyURI` value. If it doesn't find one, then it returns the empty sequence.

Example

The following example shows the in-scope namespace URIs for every element in a source document.

Source

Note that this includes a namespace undeclaration for the «soap» namespace, as permitted by XML Namespaces 1.1.

```
<?xml version="1.1" encoding="iso-8859-1"?>
<soap:Envelope
      xmlns:soap="http://schemas.xmlsoap.org/soap/envelope/"
      xmlns:xs="http://www.w3.org/2001/XMLSchema">
  <soap:Body>
    <echoString xmlns="http://example.com/soapdemo"
                xmlns:xsi="http://www.w3.org/2001/XMLSchema-instance"
                xmlns:soap="">
      <inputString xsi:type="xs:string">Hello</inputString>
    </echoString>
  </soap:Body>
</soap:Envelope>
```

Stylesheet

```
<xsl:template match="*">
  <element name="{name()}"
           namespaces="{for $n in in-scope-prefixes(.)
                                 return namespace-uri-for-prefix($n, .)}"/>
  <xsl:apply-templates/>
</xsl:template>
```

Output

(Reformatted for legibility.) Note the absence of the SOAP namespace from the inner elements.

```
<element name="soap:Envelope"
         namespaces="http://www.w3.org/XML/1998/namespace
                     http://schemas.xmlsoap.org/soap/envelope/
                     http://www.w3.org/2001/XMLSchema"/>
<element name="soap:Body"
         namespaces="http://www.w3.org/XML/1998/namespace
                     http://schemas.xmlsoap.org/soap/envelope/
                     http://www.w3.org/2001/XMLSchema"/>
<element name="echoString"
         namespaces="http://www.w3.org/XML/1998/namespace
                     http://www.w3.org/2001/XMLSchema
                     http://www.w3.org/2001/XMLSchema-instance
                     http://example.com/soapdemo"/>
<element name="inputString"
         namespaces="http://www.w3.org/XML/1998/namespace
                     http://www.w3.org/2001/XMLSchema
                     http://www.w3.org/2001/XMLSchema-instance
                     http://example.com/soapdemo"/>
```

Usage

This function is often used in conjunction with `in-scope-prefixes()`, which finds the prefixes of all the in-scope namespaces for an element as a sequence of strings.

Note that if the requirement is to resolve a lexical QName to obtain an `xs:QName` value, the `resolve-QName()` function provides an easier way of doing this.

See Also

`in-scope-prefixes()` on page 808
`resolve-QName()` on page 804

namespace-uri-from-QName

The function `namespace-uri-from-QName()` returns the namespace URI part of an `xs:QName` value.

Signature

Argument	Type	Meaning
value	xs:QName?	The xs:QName value whose namespace URI part is required. If the supplied value is an empty sequence, an empty sequence is returned.
Result	xs:anyURI?	The namespace URI part of the xs:QName.

Effect

Given an expanded QName (that is, an instance of type `xs:QName`), this function returns the namespace URI part of the value. If the `xs:QName` is in no namespace, it returns a zero-length URI.

Examples

Expression	Result
`namespace-uri-from-QName(QName ('http://mhk.me.uk/some.uri','invoice'))`	`"http://mhk.me.uk/some.uri"`
`namespace-uri-from-QName (node-name(@xml:space))`	`"http://www.w3.org/XML/1998/namespace"`

The second example assumes that the context node has an attribute called `xml:space`.

See Also

`QName()` on page 858
`local-name-from-QName()` on page 826

nilled

The `nilled()` function returns true if applied to an element that (a) specifies «`xsi:nil="true"`», and (b) has been successfully validated against a schema.

Signature

Argument	Type	Meaning
input	`node()?`	The node being tested
Result	`xs:boolean?`	*True for an element that has the nilled property*

Effect

If the input is an element node that has the attribute «`xsi:nil="true"`» and that has been subjected to schema validation, the function returns true.

If the input is an element node that does not have an «`xsl:nil`» attribute, or that has the value «`xsi:nil="false"`», or if it is an element node that has not been assessed against a schema, the function returns false.

The function returns the empty sequence if it is applied to a node other than an element, or if the argument is an empty sequence.

Examples

Assume the context node is the following element:

```
<person xmlns:xsi="http://www.w3.org/2001/XMLSchema-instance">
  <title xsi:nil="true"/>
  <first>Samuel</first>
```

```
    <middle xsi:nil="false">W</middle>
    <last>Johnson</last>
</person>
```

and that it is validated against the following schema:

```
<xs:schema xmlns:xs="http://www.w3.org/2001/XMLSchema"
           xmlns:xsi="http://www.w3.org/2001/XMLSchema-instance">
  <xs:element name="person">
    <xs:complexType>
      <xs:sequence>
        <xs:element ref="title"/>
        <xs:element ref="first"/>
        <xs:element ref="middle"/>
        <xs:element ref="last"/>
      </xs:sequence>
    </xs:complexType>
  </xs:element>
  <xs:element name="title" nillable="true" type="xs:NCName"/>
  <xs:element name="first"  nillable="true" type="xs:NCName"/>
  <xs:element name="middle" nillable="true" type="xs:NCName"/>
  <xs:element name="last"  nillable="true" type="xs:NCName"/>
</xs:schema>
```

Expression	Result
nilled(title)	true
nilled(first)	false
nilled(middle)	false
nilled(last)	false

Usage

The xsi:nil attribute is an explicit way of saying that a value is absent. Although its meaning is entirely up to the application, the intended purpose is to distinguish unknown data (a person's title is unknown) from data known to be empty (a person is known to have no middle name). When an element that has xsi:nil set to true is validated, it is given the *nilled* property in the data model, and this function allows this property to be tested. For most practical purposes, using the nilled() function achieves the same as testing the xsi:nil attribute directly, so long as you are sure that the element has been validated.

The *nilled* property is present in the data model primarily to support the rules for type matching: a *nilled* element will not match a type of the form «element(N, T)», but it will match «element(N, T?)». These rules are given in Chapter 11, in the section *Matching Elements and Attributes* on page 672. This function is provided to allow direct access to this property.

node-name

The node-name() function returns a value of type xs:QName containing the expanded name of a node, that is, the namespace URI and local name.

13

The Function Library

843

Signature

Argument	Type	Meaning
input	node()?	The node whose name is required
Result	*xs:QName?*	*The name of the node if it has a name, or an empty sequence if it has no name*

Effect

If the node is an element or attribute, then the function returns an xs:QName whose components are the namespace URI, local name, and prefix of this node. If the node is not in a namespace, then the namespace URI component of the xs:QName will be absent (the function namespace-uri-from-QName() will return the empty sequence).

If the node is a processing instruction, the function returns an xs:QName whose local name is the name of the processing instruction, and whose namespace URI and prefix are absent.

If the node is a text node, comment, or document node, or if an empty sequence is supplied, then the function returns an empty sequence.

If the node is a namespace node, then the function returns an xs:QName whose local name represents the namespace prefix and whose namespace URI and prefix are absent; except when the namespace node represents the default namespace, in which case the function returns an empty sequence.

Examples

It's difficult to illustrate function calls that return xs:QName values, because displaying an xs:QName as a string loses information about the namespace URI. In these examples I'll display the value in so-called Clark notation (after James Clark, the editor of the XSLT 1.0 and XPath 1.0 specifications), which uses the format «{uri}local-name».

Assume the following source document:

```
<soap:Envelope xmlns:soap="http://schemas.xmlsoap.org/soap/envelope/"
      xmlns:xs="http://www.w3.org/2001/XMLSchema">
  <soap:Body>
    <echoString xmlns="http://example.com/soapdemo"
                xmlns:xsi="http://www.w3.org/2001/XMLSchema-instance"
                xmlns:soap="">
      <inputString xsi:type="xs:string">Hello</inputString>
    </echoString>
  </soap:Body>
</soap:Envelope>
```

Expression	Result (in Clark notation)
node-name(/*)	{http://schemas.xmlsoap.org/soap/envelope/}Envelope
node-name(/*/*/*)	{http://example.com/soapdemo}echoString
node-name(//@*:type)	{http://www.w3.org/2001/XMLSchema-instance}type

Usage

To access the components of the xs:QName returned by the node-name() function, you can use the functions local-name-from-QName() and namespace-uri-from-QName(). Alternatively, if you don't like long function names, you can use the `local-name()` and `namespace-uri()` functions to get these two components directly from the node itself.

See Also

`local-name-from-QName()` on page 826
`namespace-uri-from-QName()` on page 841
`local-name()` on page 824
`name()` on page 835
`namespace-uri()` on page 837

normalize-space

The `normalize-space()` function removes leading and trailing whitespace from a string, and replaces internal sequences of whitespace with a single space character.

For example, the expression «`normalize-space('x&#x9;y')`» returns the string «x y».

Changes in 2.0

None.

Signature

Argument	Type	Meaning
value (optional)	xs:string?	The input string. If the argument is omitted, it defaults to `string(.)`. If an empty sequence is supplied, the function returns a zero-length string.
Result	xs:string	*A string obtained by removing leading and trailing whitespace from the input string, and replacing internal sequences of whitespace by a single space character.*

Effect

When the function is called with no arguments, the argument defaults to the result of applying the `string()` function to the context item; an error is reported if there is no context item.

Whitespace is defined, as in the XML specification, as a sequence of space, tab, newline, and carriage return characters (#x9, #xA, #xD, and #x20).

Examples

Expression	Result
`normalize-space(" the quick &#x9; brown fox ")`	`"the quick brown fox"`
`normalize-space(" ")`	`""`
`normalize-space("piano")`	`"piano"`
`normalize-space(())`	`""`

Usage

It is often a good idea to apply the `normalize-space()` function to any string read from the source document before testing its contents, as many users will assume that leading and trailing whitespace has no significance and that within the string, multiple spaces or tabs are equivalent to a single space.

13

The Function Library

845

Don't imagine that the XSLT `<xsl:strip-space>` declaration does this for you. The only thing it does is to remove text nodes that contain whitespace only.

Using `normalize-space()` shouldn't be necessary when accessing structured information in a schema-validated document. The schema should specify for each type (in the `xs:whiteSpace` facet) how whitespace is to be treated, and this will normally ensure that redundant whitespace is removed automatically when nodes are atomized. Note that the action of the `normalize-space()` function is equivalent to the option `<xs:whiteSpace value="collapse"/>` in XML Schema. This removes whitespace more vigorously than the schema type `xs:normalizedString`, which uses the option `<xs:whiteSpace value="replace"/>` (this doesn't replace runs of spaces with a single space, it only replaces individual newlines, carriage returns or tabs with single space characters.)

However, if you access the string value of an element with a mixed content type (typically by calling the `string()` function explicitly, or by accessing the text nodes of an element explicitly), then schema-defined whitespace normalization will not be applied, so using `normalize-space()` is a good idea.

The `normalize-space()` function can be particularly useful when processing a whitespace-separated list of values. Such lists are used in some document designs. With a schema processor, the system can deliver the value as a sequence of strings, but in the absence of a schema you have to tokenize the sequence yourself. You can call `normalize-space()` to ensure that there is a single space between each string, and it is then possible to use `substring-before()` to get the next token. To make this easier still, I usually add a space at the end of the string after normalization, so that every token is followed by a single space.

One situation where it isn't safe to use `normalize-space()` is where you are processing mixed element content containing character-level formatting attributes. For example, if you process the nodes that result from the element:

```
<p>Some <i>very</i> traditional HTML</p>
```

then the spaces after «Some» and before «traditional» are significant, even though they appear respectively at the end and the beginning of a text node.

XSLT Example

The following key declaration indexes the titles of books with whitespace normalized:

```
<xsl:key name="book-title" match="book" use="normalize-space(title)"/>
```

This may then be used to locate books by title as follows:

```
<xsl:for-each select="key('book-title', normalize-space($title))">
```

The effect is that it will be possible, without knowing how many spaces and newlines there are, to retrieve a book appearing in the source document as:

```
<book>
    <title>Object Oriented Languages -
                Basic Principles and Programming Techniques</title>
</book>
```

See Also

`concat()` on page 729
`substring-after()` on page 885
`substring-before()` on page 887

normalize-unicode

The `normalize-unicode()` function returns a canonical representation of a string in which different ways of representing the same Unicode character have been reduced to a common representation. This makes it possible to compare two strings accurately.

Signature

Argument	Type	Meaning
input	`xs:string?`	The string to be normalized. If an empty sequence is supplied, the function returns a zero-length string.
normalization-form (optional)	`xs:string`	The normalization algorithm to be used.
Result	*`xs:string`*	*The result of normalizing the string.*

Effect

The function applies a Unicode normalization algorithm to the input string, and returns the normalized string as its result. If the `normalization-form` argument is omitted, the default is NFC. The only normalization form that all implementations must support is NFC. Other normalization forms can be requested (including but not limited to «NFC», «NFD», «NFKC», «NFKD», «FULLY-NORMALIZED») using the `normalization-form` argument; a runtime error is reported if the requested normalization form is not supported by the implementation. For the meanings of these normalization forms, see the *Usage* section below.

Example: Unicode Normalization

This example shows the effect of normalizing the string «garçon» first to NFC, then to NFD, and then back to NFC. Note that 231 (xE7) is the Unicode codepoint for lower-case C with cedilla, while 807 (x0327) is the codepoint for a combining cedilla.

Stylesheet

```
<xsl:variable name="initial" select="'garcon'"/>
<xsl:variable name="nfc" select="normalize-unicode($initial)"/>
<xsl:variable name="nfd" select="normalize-unicode($initial, 'NFD')"/>
<xsl:variable name="nfc2" select="normalize-unicode($initial, 'NFC')"/>
<ex><xsl:value-of select="string-to-codepoints($initial)"/></ex>
<ex><xsl:value-of select="string-to-codepoints($nfc)"/></ex>
<ex><xsl:value-of select="string-to-codepoints($nfd)"/></ex>
<ex><xsl:value-of select="string-to-codepoints($nfc2)"/></ex>
```

Output

```
<ex>103 97 114 231 111 110</ex>
<ex>103 97 114 231 111 110</ex>
<ex>103 97 114 99 807 111 110</ex>
<ex>103 97 114 231 111 110</ex>
```

13

The Function Library

The value supplied for the `normalization-form` argument is converted to upper case, and leading and trailing spaces are removed.

Usage

The subject of character normalization has a long, tortured history. There have always been two interest groups concerned with character encoding: those primarily interested in data processing have favored fixed-length encodings of each character, with composite characters treated as a single unit, while those more concerned with publishing and printing have favored variable-length encodings in which the separate parts of a composite character (for example, a base letter and a diacritical mark) were encoded separately. Inevitably, the only way both communities could be satisfied was by a standard that allowed both, and that is exactly what Unicode does. The letter «Å» for example (which is widely used in Swedish) can be encoded either using the single codepoint x00 C5 (called LATIN CAPITAL A WITH RING ABOVE) or by the two codepoints x0041 (LATIN CAPITAL LETTER A) followed by x030A (COMBINING RING ABOVE). To make matters even worse, there is also a separate code x212B (ANGSTROM SIGN), which is visually indistinguishable from the letter «Å» but has a separate code because it is considered to have its own meaning.

This means that unless special precautions are taken, when you search for text containing the character «Å», you will not find it unless you choose the same representation as is used in the text you are searching. This applies not only to the textual content, but also to the markup: all three representations of this character are acceptable in XML names, and if you use one representation in the source XML, and a different representation in a path expression, then they won't match.

Unicode normalization is an algorithm that can be applied to Unicode strings to remove these arbitrary differences.

The W3 C Working Draft *Character Model for the World Wide Web 1.0: Normalization* (`http://www.w3.org/TR/charmod-norm/`), specifies that documents on the Web should be subject to "early normalization": that is, they should be normalized at the time they are created, and it advocates the use of a particular normalization algorithm called NFC (further details below). If everyone followed this advice, there would be no need for a `normalize-unicode()` function in XPath. But unfortunately, there is little chance of this happening.

The normalization algorithms have been published in Unicode Technical Report #15 (`http://www.unicode.org/unicode/reports/tr15`). There are several, notably normalization forms C, D, KC, and KD, and "fully normalized". (Why have one standard when you can have five?) The default used by the `normalize-unicode()` function is NFC (normalization form C), but the other forms can be requested using the second parameter to the function, provided that the implementation supports them — they aren't mandatory.

Normalization forms C and KC replace decomposed characters by composed characters; in our example using «Å», they choose the single-codepoint representation x00 C5 in preference to the two-codepoint representation x0041x030A. Normalization forms D and KD prefer the decomposed representation, that is x0041x030A.

As a general rule, most software that produces Unicode text (for example, text editors) will produce NFC output most of the time. This is useful, and explains why you don't hear of many people having real-world XPath expressions that fail because of normalization issues. But it's certainly a possibility, and one of the concerns is that it is also a security risk — using the "wrong" representation of characters could be a way of getting round validation software.

The K variants (NFKC and NFKD) differ from NFC and NFD in that they normalize further; specifically, they normalize away distinctions between "compatibility variants" of characters. These compatibility variants exist because Unicode was created as the union of many different preexisting character sets. The designers had to make the decision whether two characters in different character sets were really representations of the same character. The problem in merging two characters into one is that it would lose information when data is converted into Unicode and then back again — the original data stream could not necessarily be reconstituted. So Unicode adopted the approach of allowing multiple representations of a character as *compatibility variants*. The distinction between the letter «Å» and the Ångstrom symbol is an example of this phenomenon; normalization forms NFKC and NFKD eliminate the distinction between these two characters. Another example is the distinction between the two characters «f» «i» and the single character «fi» (really just a graphical visualization of the two separate characters, but recognized as a single character for the benefit of typesetting applications). Another one (and here the "loss of information" argument starts to become significant) is the distinction between the superscript digits «²» and «³» and the ordinary digits «2» and «3».

When you take a substring of a normalized string, the substring will always be normalized, and this is true for all the normalization forms discussed here. Splitting a string between a letter «c» and a non-spacing cedilla that follows it may not produce a very meaningful result, but the result is normalized, in the sense that the normalization algorithm will not change it. However, concatenating two normalized strings is not guaranteed to produce a normalized string. This is true whether you choose a composed form (NFC) or a decomposed form (NFD):

❏ With NFC, concatenating a string that ends with letter «c» and a string that starts with a non-spacing cedilla produces a string that is not in normalized form NFC.

❏ With NFD, concatenating a string that ends with a non-spacing modifier and a string that starts with a non-spacing modifier may produce a string that is not in normalized form NFD, because this normalization form requires multiple non-spacing modifiers applying to the same letter to be in a standard order.

This means that the concat() function, and other XPath functions that concatenate strings such as string-join(), as well as node construction instructions in XSLT and XQuery, are not guaranteed to produce normalized output even if they are given normalized input. Another place where string concatenation occurs implicitly is in forming the string value of an element with mixed content. The W3C policy of early normalization means that this problem should be corrected as soon as possible. One way of doing this is to call the normalize-unicode() function on the results of the string concatenation; another is to do the normalization at the time the result of a transformation or query is serialized (see the normaliation-form option of <xsl:output>, described in Chapter 15).

The term fully-normalized refers to an additional normalization format defined by W3C (see *Character Model for the World Wide Web: Normalization*, http://www.w3.org/TR/charmod-norm/). A string is defined to be fully normalized if it is in NFC and if it doesn't start with a combining character. The significance of this is that if you concatenate two fully normalized strings the result is guaranteed to be fully normalized as well. The specification isn't very explicit about how you get a string into fully-normalized form, but the idea is apparently that if it starts with a combining character, you add a space in front of it.

See Also

Serialization, Chapter 15

not

The not() function returns `true` if the effective boolean value of the argument is `false`, and vice versa.

For example, the expression «not(2+2=4)» returns `false`.

Changes in 2.0

This function has been generalized to accept a wider range of types.

Signature

Argument	Type	Meaning
value	item()*	The input value
Result	xs:boolean	true *if the effective boolean value of the argument is false, otherwise* false

Effect

In effect, the argument is converted to a boolean using the rules of the `boolean()` function, and the return value is then `true` if this is `false`, `false` if it is `true`.

The rules for determining the effective boolean value are described under the `boolean()` function on page 721. If the value is one that does not have an effective boolean value (for example, a sequence of three integers), then an error is reported.

Examples

Expression	Result
not(*)	true if the context node has no child elements
not(normalize-space(@a))	true if attribute @a is absent, is zero-length, or consists entirely of whitespace
not(author="Kay")	true if the context node does not have an author child element whose typed value is "Kay"

Usage

Note that writing «not($A=2)» is not the same thing as writing «$A!=2». The difference arises when $A is a sequence: «not($A=2)» will be `true` if $A does not contain an item that is equal to 2, while «$A!=2» is `true` only if A *does* contain an item that is *not* equal to 2. For example, if $A is an empty sequence, «not($A=2)» will be `true`, while «$A!=2» will be `false`.

It is easy to forget this when testing attribute values; for example, the following two examples behave the same way if the attribute go is present (they output «go» if the value is anything other than «no»), but they behave differently if the attribute is absent (the second one outputs «go», but the first one outputs nothing).

```
1: if (@go!='no') then "go" else ""
2: if (not(@go='no')) then "go" else ""
```

When used with sequences, the comparison operators such as «=» and «!=» are subject to an implicit *if there exists* qualifier: «$X=$Y» is true *if there exists an item* x *in* $X *and an item* y *in* $Y *such that* x eq y. If you want to achieve an *if all* qualifier, for example, *if all nodes in* N *have a* size *attribute equal to 0*, then you can achieve this by negating both the condition and the expression as a whole: «not($N/@size!=0)». But in XPath 2.0, it is probably clearer to write this out explicitly:

```
if (every $s in $N/@size satisfies $s eq 0) . . .
```

XSLT Examples

The following test succeeds if the context node has no children:

```
<xsl:if test="not(node())">
```

The following test succeeds if the context node has no parent (that is, if it is a root node):

```
<xsl:if test="not(parent::node())">
```

The following <xsl:for-each> statement processes all the child elements of the context node except the <notes> elements:

```
<xsl:for-each select="*[not(self::notes)]">
```

The following test succeeds if the string-value of the context node is zero-length (assuming that the context item is a node):

```
<xsl:if test="not(string(.))">
```

The following test succeeds if the name attribute of the context node is absent or is a zero-length string:

```
<xsl:if test="not(string(@name))">
```

The following test succeeds if the name attribute of the first node in node-set $ns is different from the name attribute of each subsequent node in the node-set (we assume that this attribute is present on all nodes in the node-set):

```
<xsl:if test="not($ns[1]/@name = $ns[position()!=1]/@name)">
```

See Also

boolean() on page 721
false() on page 779
true() on page 899

number

The number() function converts its argument to a value of type xs:double.

For example, the expression «number('-17.3')» returns the xs:double value –17.3e0.

Changes in 2.0

A leading «+» sign is allowed in the number, and exponential notation is permitted, to align the rules with XML Schema.

Signature

Argument	Type	Meaning
value (optional)	item()?	The value to be converted. If the argument is omitted, the context item is used. If an empty sequence is supplied, the result is NaN.
Result	xs:double	*A double-precision floating-point number: the result of converting the given* value. *If the argument cannot be converted to a number, the function returns NaN (not-a-number).*

Effect

The conversion rules used are the same as the rules for casting to an xs:double (and therefore, the same as the xs:double() constructor function), with the exception that if the value is not convertible to a number, the result is NaN (not-a-number) rather than an error.

If the value supplied is a node, then the node is first atomized in the usual way.

The only atomic types that can be converted to a number are booleans, strings, and other numbers. The conversion is as follows:

Supplied type	Conversion rules
xs:boolean	false becomes zero; true becomes one.
xs:string	The rules are the same as the rules for writing an xs:double value in XML Schema.
xs:integer, xs:decimal, xs:float	*The result is the same as converting the value to a string, and then converting the resulting string back to an* xs:double.

Examples

Expression	Result
number(12.3)	xs:double 12.3e0, displayed as "12.3"
number("12.3")	xs:double 12.3e0, displayed as "12.3"
number(true())	xs:double 1.0e0, displayed as "1"
number("xyz")	xs:double NaN
number("")	xs:double NaN

Usage

In XPath 1.0, conversion to a number was generally implicit so it was rarely necessary to use the number() function explicitly. This remains the case if XPath 1.0 backward-compatibility mode is used. When this mode is not enabled, however, type errors will be reported when strings or booleans are supplied in contexts where a number is expected; for example, as operands to numeric operators such as «+». You still get implicit conversion when you supply an untyped node as the operand (for example, «@code+1» is okay), but not when the value is explicitly typed. For example, if the date-of-birth attribute is an untyped string in the format of an ISO 8601 date, the following is an error under XPath 2.0 rules:

```
substring(@date-of-birth, 1, 4) < 1970
```

This is because `substring()` returns a string, and you cannot compare a string to a number. Instead, write:

```
number(substring(@date-of-birth, 1, 4)) < 1970
```

There is one important situation where conversion needs to be explicit: this is in a `predicate`. The meaning of a predicate depends on the type of the value, in particular, a numeric predicate is interpreted as a comparison with the context position. If the value is not numeric, it is converted to a boolean.

So for example, if a value held in an attribute or in a temporary tree is to be used as a numeric predicate, you should convert it explicitly to a number, thus:

```
$sales-figures[number(@month)]
```

To test whether a value (for example, in an attribute) is numeric, use `number()` to convert it to a number and test the result against NaN (not-a-number). The most direct way to do this is:

```
if (string(number(@value))='NaN') then ...
```

Alternatively, use the «castable as» operator described in on page 655 in Chapter 11.

See Also

`boolean()` on page 721
`string()` on page 877
`cast` expression in Chapter 11 on page 655

one-or-more

The `one-or-more()` function returns its argument unchanged, provided that it is a sequence containing one or more items. If the input is an empty sequence, it reports an error.

Signature

Argument	Type	Meaning
value	`item()*`	The input value. Although the function signature says that any sequence of items is allowed, a runtime error will occur if the number of items is zero.
Result	*item()*	*The same as the supplied value, after checking to ensure that it is not an empty sequence.*

Effect

The `one-or-more()` function returns its argument unchanged, provided that it is a sequence containing at least one item. If an empty sequence is supplied, it reports an error.

This function is useful with XPath processors that perform static type checking, as described in Chapter 5. Calling this function acts as a promise by the programmer that the argument will be a sequence containing at least one item. This allows the expression to be used in contexts that require a single value (for example, a call to a function that has a parameter with the required type «item()+») when the processor might otherwise have reported a static type error. The XPath expression is still type-safe, because the check that the sequence does indeed contain at least one item will be done at runtime, just as it would with a processor that does not enforce static type checking.

Examples

Expression	Result
one-or-more(1)	1
one-or-more((1,2,3))	1,2,3
one-or-more(())	Error

Usage

As it happens, functions in the core library do not generally have a required type such as «item()+», even in cases like min(), max() and avg() where there is no meaningful result that can be returned for an empty sequence. This is because the designers decided that rather than reporting an error for these functions when the argument is an empty sequence, it made more sense to return an empty sequence as the result. However, if you do want to make a runtime check that a sequence is not empty before calling a function such as avg(), then calling one-or-more() is a simple way to do the check.

See Also

exactly-one() on page 777
zero-or-one() on page 912
«treat as» expression on page 678 in Chapter 11

position

The position() function returns the value of the context position. When processing a list of items, position() gives the number assigned to the current item in the list, with the first item being numbered as 1.

Changes in 2.0

None.

Signature

This function takes no arguments.

	Type	Meaning
Result	xs:integer	A number, the value of the context position. As the name implies, this is context-dependent.

Effect

The XPath specification defines the value of the position() function in terms of the *context position*.

The context position is part of the *focus*, which is described in the spec as having three components: the context item, the context position, and the context size. However, it may be easier to think of the focus as being a bit like an Iterator object in a language such as Java. Behind the iterator is a list of items that are processed individually (though not necessarily in any particular order). The context item, position, and size can be thought of as three methods provided by this iterator object: the context position is a number that ranges from 1 to the size of the list, the context item is the item found at the context position, and the context size is the number of items in the list.

When a top-level XPath expression is evaluated (that is, an XPath expression that is not part of another expression), the context position is set by the host language. In XSLT, it is set from the XSLT context. For example:

❑ When a global `<xsl:variable>` declaration is being evaluated, or in certain other contexts such as evaluating the `use` expression in `<xsl:key>`, or evaluating the initial template that matches the root node, it is normally set to 1 (one).

❑ When `<xsl:apply-templates>` or `<xsl:for-each>` is called to process a sequence of nodes, the nodes are numbered 1 to N in their sorted order, and while each node is being processed the context position is the number assigned to that node. (There is no implication that node 1 is processed before node 2, incidentally.)

This means that within an `<xsl:for-each>` iteration, the test `<xsl:if test="position()=last()">` succeeds when the last item in the sequence is being processed.

Many APIs that enable XPath expressions to be executed from languages like Java or JavaScript allow the caller to set the context item, but not the context position or size. In such cases, the context position and size on entry to the XPath expression will both be one.

Within an XPath expression, the context size changes within a predicate and on the right-hand side of the «/» operator.

❑ In a predicate, `position()` refers to the position of the item that is being filtered using the predicate within the sequence of items being filtered. For example, «$seq[position()!=1]» selects all items except the first in a sequence, because the first item is the only one for which the predicate is false.

❑ It's less common to find `position()` being used on the right-hand-side of a «/» operator. It refers to the position of the context item in the sequence selected by the left-hand operand of the «/». So «$x/position()» is another way of writing «1 to count($x)». A more interesting example is:

```
<xsl:value-of select="$sequence/(if (position() mod 10 = 0)
                    then concat(., '&#xa;')
                          else string(.))"/>
```

which outputs the items in $sequence with a newline after every 10 items.

Remember that the focus is not changed within a «for» expression. If you need to know within the body of a «for» expression what the position of the item being processed is, you need to rewrite it. Instead of doing:

```
for $s in $sequence
return EXPR
```

write:

```
for $i in 1 to count($sequence),
    $s in $sequence[$i]
return EXPR
```

You can then use $i within EXPR to refer to the position of $s within the sequence.

Usage in XSLT

The `position()` function is often used as a complete XPath expression within an XSLT stylesheet. The function has particular significance in XSLT because it gives the position of the item currently being processed by an `<xsl:for-each>` instruction (as well as other instructions such as `<xsl:apply-templates>` and `<xsl:for-each-group>`). The two main uses of the `position()` function in XSLT are to *display* the current position, and to *test* the current position.

Displaying the Current Position

In this role the `position()` function can be used for simple numbering of paragraphs, sections, or figures.

In XSLT this provides an alternative to the use of `<xsl:number>`. There is much less flexibility to control how the numbering is done than when using `<xsl:number>`, but the `position()` function has two important advantages:

❑   It is generally faster.

❑   It numbers items in the order they are output, whereas `<xsl:number>` can only allocate a number based on the position of a node in the source document. This means `<xsl:number>` is of little use when a list has been sorted using `<xsl:sort>`.

If you use `position()`, you can still exploit the formatting capabilities of `<xsl:number>` by writing, for example:

```
<xsl:number value="position()" format="(a)"/>
```

This determines the position of the node and formats the result according to the given format pattern; the resulting sequence will be «(a)», «(b)», «(c)», and so on.

Testing the Current Position

It is possible to test the position of the current item either in a boolean expression in an `<xsl:if>` or `<xsl:when>` element, or in a predicate within a filter expression or pattern.

A common requirement is to treat the first or last item in a list differently from the rest. For example, to insert a horizontal rule after every item except the last, the following logic might be used:

```
<xsl:for-each select="item">
<xsl:sort select="@name"/>
   <p><xsl:value-of select="@name"/>:
      <xsl:value-of select="description"/></p>
   <xsl:if test="position() != last()">
      <hr/>
   </xsl:if>
</xsl:for-each>
```

Within a predicate in an expression or pattern, a numeric value represents an implicit test against the result of `position()`: for example, «item[1]» is equivalent to «item[position()=1]», and «item[last()]» is equivalent to «item[position()=last()]».

> You can only use this shorthand in a predicate; that is, within square brackets. If you use a numeric value in other contexts where a Boolean is expected, the number is converted to a boolean on the basis that 0 is false; everything else is true. So **<xsl:if test="1">** does *not* mean **<xsl:if test="position()=1">**; it means the same as **<xsl:if test="true()">**.

See Also

last() on page 820
<xsl:number> in Chapter 6 page 403

prefix-from-QName

The `prefix-from-QName()` function extracts the prefix from an expanded QName. For example, «`prefix-from-QName(node-name(@xml:space))`» returns the string «xml».

Signature

Argument	Type	Meaning
value	xs:QName?	The supplied QName
Result	xs:NCName	*The prefix of the QName if there is one, or the empty sequence otherwise*

Effect

If the first argument is an empty sequence, the function returns an empty sequence.

If the supplied QName includes a prefix, the prefix is returned as an instance of xs:NCName. This is derived from xs:string, so the value can be used anywhere that a string can be used. If the QName is unprefixed, the function returns an empty sequence.

Usage

In the XML Schema specifications, it is stated that the value space for the type xs:QName contains two parts: the local name and the namespace URI. The XPath data model (XDM), however, modifies this to say that it also retains a third part, the namespace prefix. The main reason for this difference is to ensure that every value in XDM can be converted to a string; without this rule, a great number of special exceptions were needed to cater for the fact that not all values could be serialized successfully. Retaining the prefix also gives usability benefits, because although in theory the choice of namespace prefixes is arbitrary, in practice choosing familiar prefixes greatly aids human readability of XML documents. There is also software around that attaches more significance to namespace prefixes than it probably should — which is excusable, since the base XML specification itself describes DTD-based validation in a way that treats namespace prefixes, rather than the associated URIs, as significant.

QNames arise most often as the names of elements and attributes. If XDM documents are constructed in the normal way by parsing source XML (with or without schema validation), then the original prefixes from the source document will be retained in the tree, and will be accessible by calling «`prefix-from-QName(node-name($node))`». If there was no prefix, this returns an empty sequence. When nodes are constructed using instructions such as <xsl:element> and <xsl:attribute>, then the namespace prefixes are usually predictable from the rules for those instructions, and can be accessed in the same way. In unusual cases, however, where the same prefix is used for more than one purpose, the system may need to invent a different prefix from the one requested (this process is called *namespace fixup*).

A QName can also arise as the typed value of a node (an example is the attribute «xsi:type= "xs:integer"», where both the name and the value of the attribute are QNames). In this case, assuming a schema-aware processor, the expression «`prefix-from-QName(@xsi:type)`» will return the string «xs».

Although this function makes the prefix of a QName available to applications, it should be used with care. It is good practice to allow document originators to choose arbitrary prefixes, and applications should attach significance only to the namespace URI, not to the prefix.

13

The Function Library

Examples

Consider this source document, validated using a schema-aware processor:

```
<?xml version="1.0"?>
<my:doc xmlns:my="http://mhk.me.uk/some.uri" security="high"
        xmlns:xsi="http://www.w3.org/2001/XMLSchema-instance"
        xsi:type="my:dateType">2008-01-01</my:doc>
```

Expression	Result
prefix-from-QName(node-name(my:doc))	"my"
prefix-from-QName(node-name(my:doc/@xsi:type))	"xsi"
prefix-from-QName(node-name(my:doc/@security))	()
prefix-from-QName(my:doc/@xsi:type)	"my"
prefix-from-QName(node-name(my:doc/@missing))	()

See Also

local-name-from-QName() on page 826
namespace-uri-from-QName() on page 841

QName

The QName() function returns a value of type xs:QName, given a namespace URI and the lexical form of the name. For example, «QName("http://www.w3.org/1999/xhtml", "html")» returns the name «html» in the XHTML namespace.

Signature

Argument	Type	Meaning
namespace	xs:string?	The namespace URI part of the xs:QName. To construct a QName that is in no namespace, supply either a zero-length string or an empty sequence.
lexical-qname	xs:string	The lexical form of the QName, with or without a prefix. It must conform to the syntax of a QName as defined in the XML Namespaces specification (which is the same as the lexical space for an xs:QName defined in XML Schema).
Result	*xs:QName*	*The newly constructed* xs:QName.

Effect

A value of type xs:QName has two significant parts (a namespace URI, and a local name), and it also retains information about the namespace prefix. This function constructs an xs:QName value from these components.

XPath uses the term *lexical QName* to refer to a QName in the form local-name or prefix:local-name, and *expanded QName* to refer to the underlying value of the QName, in which the prefix has been resolved to a namespace URI by reference to some set of namespace declarations. This function creates an expanded QName directly, without going through the stage of resolving the prefix. The namespace URI of the QName is taken from the `namespace` argument. The local-name part is taken from the `lexical-name` after stripping off any prefix; and the prefix part is taken from the prefix in the `lexical-name` if there is one.

It's an error to supply a prefix without also supplying a namespace URI.

Examples

Expression	Result
`QName("http://www.w3.org/XML/1998/namespace", "xml:space")`	The `xs:QName` usually written as «`xml:space`»
`QName("http://www.w3.org/2001/XMLSchema-instance", "xsi:type")`	The `xs:QName` usually written as «`xsi:type`»
`QName("", "html")`	An `xs:QName` with local name «`html`» in no namespace
`QName("http://www.w3.org/1999/xhtml", "html")`	An `xs:QName` with local name «`html`» in the XHTML namespace, with no prefix

Usage

The `QName()` function is useful when you want to compare node names against a specified name, especially one determined at runtime. This is done by using it in conjunction with the `node-name()` function.

For example, suppose that you are dealing with source documents for which several variants of the schema exist, all using different namespace URIs, and suppose that the actual namespace URI to be used in a particular run is passed in as a parameter. This makes it difficult to use path expressions in the natural way, because path expressions can only refer to names that are fully known (that is, both the namespace URI and local name are known) at compile time.

You can define a set of global variables like this:

```
<xsl:variable name="address" select="QName($ns, 'address')"/>
<xsl:variable name="postalcode" select="QName($ns, 'postalcode') "/>
```

and so on.

It is then possible to use path expressions such as:

```
select="*[node-name()=$address]/*[node-name()=$postalcode]"
```

to locate nodes.

See Also

`local-name-from-QName()` on page 826
`namespace-uri-from-QName()` on page 841
`node-name()` on page 843

regex-group

This function is available in XSLT only.

The `regex-group()` function returns a captured substring resulting from matching a regular expression using the `<xsl:analyze-string>` instruction.

Signature

Argument	Type	Meaning
group	xs:integer	Identifies the captured subgroup that is required. The *n*th captured subgroup provides the string that was matched by the part of the regular expression enclosed by the *n*th left parenthesis.
Result	xs:string	*The string that was matched by the nth subexpression of the regular expression.*

Effect

When the `<xsl:analyze-string>` instruction is used to match a string against a regular expression (regex), its `<xsl:matching-substring>` child element is invoked once for each substring of the input string that matches the regular expression. The substring that matched the regex can be referred to within this element as «.», because it becomes the context item, and for consistency with other regex languages it is also available as the value of «regex-group(0)». Sometimes, however, you need to know not only what the substring that matched the regex was, but which parts of that substring matched particular parts of the regex. The group of characters that matches a particular parenthesized subexpression within the regex is referred to as a *captured group*; and the captured group that matches the *n*th parenthesized subexpression is accessible as the value of «regex-group(n)».

The substrings matched by `<xsl:analyze-string>` are available during the execution of the sequence constructor within the `<xsl:matching-substring>` element, including any templates called from instructions within this sequence constructor, that is, the scope is dynamic rather than static.

Note that it is only the `<xsl:analyze-string>` instruction that makes captured groups available. They are not made available by the regex functions `matches()`, `replace()`, and `tokenize()`.

Usage and Examples

The `regex-group()` function is always used together with the `<xsl:analyze-string>` instruction, described in Chapter 6, page 230.

For example, suppose you are analyzing a comma-separated-values file containing lines like this.

```
423,"Barbara Smith","General Motors",1996-03-12
```

Given this line as the content of variable $in, you might analyze it using the code:

```
<xsl:analyze-string select="$in" regex='("([^"]*?)")|([^,]+?),'>
  <xsl:matching-substring>
    <cell>
      <xsl:value-of select="regex-group(2)"/>
      <xsl:value-of select="regex-group(3)"/>
    </cell>
```

```
      </xsl:matching-substring>
    </xsl:analyze-string>
```

The regex here has two alternatives. The first alternative, «(" ([^"]*?) ")», matches a string enclosed in quotes. The second alternative, «([^,]+?),», matches a sequence of non-comma characters followed by a comma. If a string within quotes is matched, then the characters between the quotes are matched by the «[^"]*?» part of the regex. This appears after the second «(» in the regex, so the string that it matches is available as «regex-group(2)». If a nonquoted string is matched, it is matched by the «[^,]+?» part, which appears after the third «(» in the regex, and is therefore available as «regex-group(3)». Rather than work out whether group 2 or group 3 was matched, the XSLT code simply outputs both: the one that was not matched will be a zero-length string, so it is simpler to copy it to the output than to write the conditional code to find out whether it was actually matched.

A full stylesheet containing this example is shown under the unparsed-text() function (page 907).

See Also

<xsl:analyze-string> on page 230 in Chapter 6

remove

The remove() function returns a sequence that contains all the items in an input sequence except the one at a specified position.

Signature

Argument	Type	Meaning
sequence	item()*	The input sequence
position	xs:integer	The position of the item to be removed
Result	item()*	*A sequence containing all the items in the input sequence except the item at the specified position*

Effect

The effect is the same as the expression:

```
$sequence[position() ne $position]
```

This means that if the position parameter is less than one or greater than the number of items in the input sequence, the input sequence is returned unchanged.

Examples

Expression	Result
remove((1 to 5), 4)	1, 2, 3, 5
remove((1 to 5), 10)	1, 2, 3, 4, 5
remove((), 1)	()

Usage

A common requirement, especially in recursive functions, is to get the *tail* of a sequence, that is, all items except the first. There are several ways of doing this in XPath 2.0, all equivalent. Take your pick:

- ❏ `$sequence[position() ne 1]`
- ❏ `subsequence($sequence, 2)`
- ❏ `remove($sequence, 1)`

There's no intrinsic reason why any of these should perform better or worse than the others — it all depends on the implementation. In Saxon, all three generate the same runtime code.

See Also

`insert-before()` on page 810
`subsequence()` on page 882

replace

The `replace()` function constructs an output string from an input string by replacing all occurrences of substrings that match a supplied regular expression with a given replacement string. The replacement string may include references to captured groups within the input string.

Signature

Argument	Type	Meaning
input	xs:string?	The input string. If an empty sequence is supplied, an empty sequence is returned.
regex	xs:string	The regular expression, written according to the rules given in Chapter 14.
replacement	xs:string	The replacement string.
flags (optional)	xs:string	One or more letters indicating options on how the matching is to be performed. If this argument is omitted, the effect is the same as supplying a zero-length string, which defaults all the option settings.
Result	*xs:string?*	*The string produced by replacing substrings of the input string that match the regular expression.*

Effect

The rules for the syntax of regular expressions and for the flags argument are given in Chapter 14.

The input string is processed from left to right, looking for substrings that match the regular expression supplied in the regex argument. Characters that don't participate in a match are copied unchanged to the output string. When a substring is found that does match the regex, the substring is not copied to the output, but the replacement string is copied instead. The search then resumes at the character position following the matched substring. For example, the result of «`replace("banana", "a", "A")`» is «bAnAnA».

It can happen that two substrings starting at the same position both match the regex. There are two ways this situation can arise.

Firstly, it happens when part of the regex is looking for repeated occurrences of a substring. For example, if the regex is «(an)*a» then immediately after the «b» of «banana», there are three possible matches, the matched substrings being «a», «ana», and «anana». The rule here is that «*» is a greedy quantifier: it matches as long a substring as it can. So the result of the expression «replace("banana", "(an)*a", "#")» is «b#». If you want to match the shortest possible substring, add a «?» after the quantifier to make it non-greedy: «replace("banana", "(an)+?a", "#")» is «b#na». Note that the final three characters of «banana» don't result in a replacement, because two matches never overlap: the middle «a» cannot participate in two different matching substrings.

Another situation that can cause two different substrings to match at the same position is where the regex contains two alternatives that both match. For example, the regex «a|ana» could match the second character of «banana», or it could match characters 2 to 4. The rule here is that the first (leftmost) alternative wins. So the result of «replace("banana", "a|ana", "#")» is «b#n#n#», whereas the result of «replace("banana", "ana|a", "#")» is «b#n#».

The replacement string supplied in the replace argument can contain the variables «$1», «$2», . . . to refer to parts of the input string that were matched by parts of the regular expression. If you want to include a «$» sign in the replacement string, you must write it as «\$», and if you want to include a «\» character, you must write it as «\\». (These rules might seem bizarre. But it was done this way for compatibility with other languages, and to allow other features to be added in the future.)

The variable $N refers to the substring of the input that was matched by the Nth parenthesized subexpression of the regex. You can find out which the Nth subexpression is by simply counting «(» characters from the first character of the regex. For example, in the regex «([0-9]+)([A-Z]+)([0-9]+)», $1 refers to the digits at the start of the string, $2 to the group of letters in the middle, and $3 to the digits at the end. So if you want to insert a hyphen between the groups of letters and digits, you can write:

```
replace($input, "^([0-9]+)([A-Z]+)([0-9]+)$", "$1-$2-$3")
```

If you run this with the input string «23MAR2008», the result will be «23-MAR-2008». (Note the use of an anchored regex here to match and replace the entire string.)

If the «$» sign is followed by more than one digit, for example «($823)», the system will try to locate the 823rd matching subexpression. If the regex doesn't contain that many subexpressions, it will assume that the «3» is an ordinary character and will look for the 82nd subexpression. If that still fails, it will look for the 8th subexpression. If that fails yet again, it will replace the «$8» by a zero-length string, so the final output will be «(23)».

A «$0» in the replacement string refers to the entire matched string.

If the replacement string contains a variable that hasn't been matched, perhaps because the relevant parenthesized subexpression was in a branch that wasn't used, then a zero-length string is substituted for the variable. If the subexpression was matched more than once, then it's the last one that is used.

If the regex does not match the input string, the replace() function will return the input string unchanged. If this is not the effect you are looking for, use the matches() function first to see if there is a match.

If the regex is one that matches a zero-length string, that is, if «matches("", $regex)» is true, the system reports an error. An example of such a regex is «a*». Although various interpretations of such a construct are possible, the Working Group decided that the results were too confusing and decided not to allow it.

Examples

Expression	Result
replace("banana", "a", "o")	"bonono"
replace("banana", "(ana|na)", "[$1]")	"b[ana][na]"
replace("banana", "(an)+", "**")	"b**a"
replace("banana", "(an)+?", "**")	"b****a"
replace("facetiously", "[aeiouy]", "[$0]")	"f[a]c[e]t[i][o][u]sl[y]"

Usage

The replace() function provides a much-needed string replacement capability for XPath. In XPath 1.0 it was possible to do simple one-for-one character replacement using the translate() function, but anything more complex required the use of cumbersome recursive templates in XSLT.

One limitation of the replace() function, however, is that the result is always a string: this function cannot be used directly for so-called *up-conversion* applications where the aim is to generate markup within the string (a typical example of such a conversion is the requirement to replace newlines in a string by empty <br> elements). For such applications, the XSLT <xsl:analyze-string> instruction is more powerful.

See Also

<xsl:analyze-string> in Chapter 6, page 230
matches() on page 828
tokenize() on page 894
translate() on page 897
Regular Expressions, Chapter 14

resolve-QName

The resolve-QName() function returns a value of type xs:QName (that is, an expanded QName consisting of a namespace URI and a local name), taking as input a lexical QName (a string in the form «prefix:local-name» or simply «local-name»), by resolving the prefix used in the lexical QName against the in-scope namespaces of a given element node.

Signature

Argument	Type	Meaning
lexical-qname	xs:string?	The lexical QName whose prefix is to be resolved. It must conform to the syntax of a QName as defined in the XML Namespaces specification (which is the same as the lexical space for an xs:QName defined in XML Schema).
element	element()	An element node whose in-scope namespaces are to be used to resolve the namespace prefix used in the lexical QName.
Result	*xs:QName?*	*The expanded xs:QName, containing the namespace URI corresponding to the prefix supplied in the lexical QName.*

Effect

If the first argument is an empty sequence, the function returns an empty sequence.

The local-name part of the resulting xs:QName value will always be the same as the local-name part of the supplied lexical QName: that is, the part after the colon, if there is a colon, or the whole string otherwise. The constructed xs:QName will also retain any prefix that was present in the supplied lexical QName.

If the lexical QName has no prefix, then the default namespace for the given element will be used. More precisely, the system looks for an unnamed namespace node of the given element. If it finds one, then the namespace URI component of the result is taken from the string value of this namespace node. If there is no unnamed namespace node, then the namespace URI component of the resulting xs:QName value will be null.

If the lexical QName does have a prefix, then the system looks for a namespace node of the given element whose name matches this prefix. If it finds one, then the namespace URI component of the result is taken from the string value of this namespace node. If there is no matching namespace node, then the function reports an error.

Examples

Consider the source document:

```
<doc xmlns:one="http://mhk.me.uk/one.uri" xmlns="http://mhk.me.uk/default.uri">
   <data-zero>title</data-zero>
   <chap xmlns="" att-one="text">
    <data-one>one:value</data-one>
    <data-two>value</data-two>
  </chap>
</doc>
```

And suppose that the following variables are bound:

```
<xsl:variable name="doc" select="/top:doc"
              xmlns:top=" http://mhk.me.uk/default.uri"/>
<xsl:variable name="chap" select="$doc/chap"/>
<xsl:variable name="data1" select="$doc/chap/data-one"/>
<xsl:variable name="data2" select="$doc/chap/data-two"/>
```

Expression	Result (in Clark notation)
resolve-QName($doc/*[1], $doc)	{http://mhk.me.uk/default.uri}title
resolve-QName($chap/@att-one, $chap)	{}text
resolve-QName(string($data1), $data1)	{http://mhk.me.uk/one.uri} value
resolve-QName(string($data2), $data2)	{} value

In these examples I have shown the resulting URI in *Clark notation*, named after James Clark, the lead designer of XSLT 1.0 and XPath 1.0. This notation represents an expanded QName in the form «{namespace-uri}local-name».

Note that all these examples resolve a lexical QName found in the content of the document against the element node that contains the value. This is the normal and probably the only sensible way to use this function, since the prefix of a QName only has meaning in the context of the element where it is used.

Usage

The purpose of this function, as the examples show, is to resolve QName values found in the content of elements or attributes within a document.

It's never necessary to use this function to resolve QNames used as element and attribute names, because the system does that for you.

It's also unnecessary to use this function if you have a schema-aware processor, and a schema that declares the relevant elements and attributes as having type `xs:QName`. In this case the schema processor will do the work for you, and you can access the expanded QName as the typed value of the element or attribute, using the `data()` function.

The function is needed when you have lexical QNames in the document content and they aren't declared as such in the schema. This can happen for a number of reasons:

❑ You are using a processor that isn't schema-aware, or a source document for which no schema has been written.

❑ The lexical QName doesn't make up the whole of the element or attribute value, for example, it might be buried inside an XPath expression.

❑ The value of the attribute isn't always a QName (an example is the `default` attribute of the `<xs:element>` element in XML Schema itself, whose type depends on the type of the element being defined).

❑ You don't want to use the rules that XML Schema uses for handling the default namespace (an example is the `name` attribute of the `<xsl:variable>` element in XSLT, where an unprefixed name uses the null namespace rather than the default namespace).

Let's look at this last example more closely. If your source documents are XSLT stylesheets (it is actually quite common to process stylesheets using XSLT), then there are many lexical QNames used within the content of the document (for example, in the `name` attribute of templates, keys, and functions, the `mode` attribute of `<xsl:apply-templates>`, and myriad other places). These aren't declared as `xs:QName` values in the schema for XSLT, however. The reason is subtle: although an XML Schema would do the correct validation if these attributes had type `xs:QName`, it would not do the conversion from the lexical space to the value space correctly. This is because XSLT specifies that when there is no prefix, these names are in the null namespace, regardless of any default namespace declaration, while XML Schema when it processes `xs:QName` values decides that the absence of a prefix implies use of the default namespace (I don't think this rule is in the spec, but it seems to be the way that XML Schema processors are expected to behave).

This means that you can only use this function for names found in XSLT stylesheets if you handle the unprefixed case yourself. Fortunately, this is easy enough:

```
if (contains(@name, ':'))
then resolve-QName(@name, .)
else QName("", @name)
```

Rather surprisingly, it's also possible to come across QNames that aren't declared as such when you run XPath expressions against an XML Schema document. This is because values of any type can appear in places such as the `xs:enumeration` facet of a simple type, or the `default` attribute of an element or attribute declaration. Because these constructs might contain values of any type, their declared type in the schema for schemas is simply `xs:string`. The only way you can work out that one of these strings needs to be treated as a QName is by rather complex analysis of the schema.

See Also

QName() on page 858
in-scope-prefixes() on page 808

resolve-uri

The resolve-uri() function converts a URI reference into an absolute URI by resolving it against a specified base URI.

Signature

Argument	Type	Meaning
reference	xs:string?	The URI reference to be resolved. If this argument is an empty sequence, an empty sequence is returned.
base-uri (optional)	xs:string	The base URI against which the relative reference is to be resolved. If this argument is omitted, the base URI from the static context is used. This must be an absolute URI.
Result	*xs:string*	*The resulting absolute URI.*

Effect

It's worth starting by establishing the correct terminology. A *URI Reference* is either a *URI* or a relative reference. A *URI* is an *absolute URI* optionally followed by «#fragment». An absolute URI starts with a scheme-name and a colon (for example «http:»).

> *A relative reference is often referred to as a* relative URI. *Technically, this is incorrect: if it's not absolute, then it's not a URI. But it's common usage, and you'll find it elsewhere in this book.*

The arguments are defined as xs:string rather than xs:anyURI because this allows the supplied argument to be either an xs:string or an xs:anyURI, under the XPath function calling rules.

If the value supplied as reference is a URI (as distinct from a relative reference) then no resolution is needed, and the value is returned unchanged. Otherwise, it must be a relative reference, and it will be resolved against the absolute URI supplied in the second argument, or against the base URI from the static context if the second argument is omitted.

The process of URI resolution takes a relative reference such as «details.html» and resolves it against an absolute URI such as «http://example.com/index.html» to produce an absolute URI such as «http://example.com/details.html». Note that this process is done purely by analyzing the two character strings, it doesn't require any access to the network to find out whether these files actually exist. This means that it is quite legitimate to apply the operation to things like collation URIs that don't necessarily represent real resources on the Web.

The actual algorithm for URI resolution is described in section 5 of Internet RFC 3986 (http://www.ietf.org/rfc/rfc3986.txt). In essence, the relative reference is appended after the last «/» in the path component of the base URI, and some tidying up is then done to remove redundant «/./» and «/../» components.The resolve-uri() specification leaves some latitude for implementations in deciding how to handle edge cases. It says that the implementation must use "an algorithm such as the ones described in RFC 2396 or RFC 3986". There are several reasons for this apparent vagueness. Firstly, the working group wanted to allow implementors to take advantage of existing library code. Secondly, the RFCs themselves leave some corner cases open; in particular, they aren't very prescriptive about what happens when the input strings are not strictly valid according to the RFC rules. RFC 3986, for example, says that the base URI must be an absolute URI (which means it mustn't contain a fragment identifier), but it hints that you can turn it into an absolute URI by stripping off the fragment identifier before you start. Another example: there's a popular URI scheme used in the Java world for addressing files within a JAR archive. These URIs attach special meaning to «!» as a separator, and as such they don't follow the syntax in the RFCs. It's convenient for users if these almost-URIs can be resolved in the same way as true URIs, and the spec deliberately leaves enough wriggle-room to permit this.

If the second argument of `resolve-uri()` is omitted, the effect is the same as using the function call «`resolve-uri($relative, static-base-uri())`»: this means that the base URI is taken from the static context of the XPath expression. The way this is set up is (as the name implies) very context-dependent.

❑ In the case of XPath expressions within an XSLT stylesheet the base URI is reasonably well-defined: the base URI of the stylesheet module is used, unless the stylesheet contains `xml:base` attributes, or is split into multiple XML external entities. But the base URI of the stylesheet module may be unknown; this might happen if the XSLT code was read from a string constructed in memory rather than from a file.

❑ In the case of XPath expressions constructed programmatically, for example, by a Java or JavaScript application, all bets are off. Your XPath API may provide a way of setting the base URI, but it's more likely in my experience that it won't. In this situation relative URI references are rather meaningless, and it's best to avoid them.

Examples

Most of these examples are taken from Appendix C of RFC 2396, and assume a static base URI of «`http://a/b/c/d;p?q`». The RFC includes other more complex examples that are worth consulting.

Expression	Result
`resolve-uri("g")`	`"http://a/b/c/g"`
`resolve-uri("./g")`	`"http://a/b/c/g"`
`resolve-uri("g/")`	`"http://a/b/c/g/"`
`resolve-uri("/g")`	`"http://a/g"`
`resolve-uri("?y")`	`"http://a/b/c/?y"`
`resolve-uri("g?y")`	`"http://a/b/c/g?y"`
`resolve-uri("")`	`"http://a/b/c/d;p?q"` (but see Note)
`resolve-uri("#s")`	`"http://a/b/c/d;p"?q#s"` (but see Note)
`resolve-uri("../g")`	`"http://a/b/g"`

> *RFC 2396 is rather coy in its description of how a relative reference of `""` (the zero-length string) is supposed to behave, giving a description that only really makes sense in the context of a web browser. RFC 3986 clears this up.*

Usage

The most likely place you will need to use the `resolve-uri()` function is in conjunction with the `doc()` function, described on page 750. By default, a relative reference passed to the `doc()` function is resolved relative to the base URI from the static context of the XPath expression. If the relative URI was read from a source document, it makes much more sense to resolve it against the base URI of the node that contained it. The code usually looks something like this:

```
doc(resolve-uri(@href, base-uri(.)))
```

See Also

base-uri() on page 719
doc() on page 750
escape-uri() on page 811
static-base-uri() on page 876

reverse

The reverse() function returns a sequence in reverse order. For example, «reverse(1 to 5)» returns the sequence «5, 4, 3, 2, 1».

Signature

Argument	Type	Meaning
sequence	item()*	The input sequence
Result	item()*	*A sequence containing the same items as the input sequence, but in reverse order*

Effect

The result of the function contains exactly the same items as the input sequence, but the order is reversed. The effect is the same as the expression:

```
for $i in 1 to count($sequence) return
    $sequence[count($sequence) - $i + 1]
```

or if you prefer a recursive formulation:

```
if (empty($sequence))
  then ()
  else (reverse(remove($sequence, 1)), $sequence[1])
```

Examples

Expression	Result
reverse(1 to 5)	5, 4, 3, 2, 1
reverse(1)	1
reverse(())	()
reverse(ancestor::*)	A list of ancestor elements, in reverse document order (that is, innermost first)

See Also

unordered() on page 901

13

The Function Library

root

The root() function returns the root node of the tree containing a specified start node, or the root of the tree containing the context node.

Signature

Argument	Type	Meaning
start-node (optional)	node()?	A node in the tree whose root is required. If the argument is omitted, it defaults to the context node. It is then an error if the context item is not a node (for example, if it is an atomic value, or if it is undefined).
Result	node()?	*The root of the tree containing the start node.*

Effect

If the start-node argument is supplied and its value is an empty sequence, then the result of the function is an empty sequence.

In other cases, the function returns the root node of the tree containing the start-node. The result is the same as the path expression «(ancestor-or-self::node())[1]». This node is not necessarily a document node, since it is possible in the XPath 2.0 data model to have elements or other nodes that are parentless. The system follows the parent axis until it finds a node that has no parent, and then it returns that node. If the start node has no parent, then the start node itself is returned as the result of the function.

Examples

Expression	Result
root()	The root node of the tree containing the context node
root($x)	The root node of the tree containing the node $x
$seq/root()	A sequence containing the root nodes of all the trees containing nodes in $seq, in document order with duplicates removed

Usage

The effect of the root() function, when called with no argument, is very similar to the effect of the expression «/». However, «/» will return the root node of the tree containing the context node only if the root is a document node; in other cases, it reports a runtime error.

See Also

The Root Expression «/» on page 623 in Chapter 9.

round

The round() function returns the closest integer to the numeric value of the argument, as an instance of the same type as the argument.

For example, the expression «round(4.6)» returns the xs:decimal value 5.0.

Changes in 2.0

The function has been generalized to accept arguments of any numeric type.

Signature

Argument	Type	Meaning
value	`Numeric?`	The input value. If an empty sequence is supplied, an empty sequence is returned.
Result	*`Numeric?`*	*The result of rounding the first argument to the nearest integer, but expressed as a value of the same type as the input value.*

Effect

The XPath specification is very precise about the results of `round()`. The rules are given in the tables below. The first table applies regardless of the type:

If the argument is...	Then the result is...
Equal to an integer N	N
Between N and N+ 0.5	N
Exactly N + 0.5	N + 1
Between N + 0.5 and N + 1	N + 1

Note that this rounds +3.5 to +4.0, but −3.5 to −3.0.

For values of type `xs:float` and `xs:double`, there are additional rules to cover the special IEEE values. The concepts of positive and negative zero, positive and negative infinity, and NaN are explained in the section on the `xs:double` type in Chapter 5, page 198.

If the argument is...	Then the result is...
Between −0.5 and zero	Negative zero
Positive zero	Positive zero
Negative zero	Negative zero
Positive infinity	Positive infinity
Negative infinity	Negative infinity
NaN (not-a-number)	NaN

Examples

Expression	Result
`round(3.2)`	`xs:decimal 3.2`, displayed as `"3.2"`
`round(4.6e0)`	`xs:double 5.0e0`, displayed as `"5"`

continued

Expression	Result
round(7.5)	xs:decimal 8.0, displayed as "8"
round(-7.5)	xs:decimal -7.0, displayed as "-7"
round(-0.0e0)	xs:double negative zero, displayed as "0"

Usage

The round() function is useful when you want the nearest integer, for example, when calculating an average, or when deciding the geometric coordinates for an object to be displayed. If you want to convert the result to a value of type xs:integer, use the xs:integer() constructor function, or the construct «round($x) idiv 1».

See Also

ceiling() on page 723
floor() on page 779
round-half-to-even() in the next entry
«idiv» operator on page 574 in Chapter 8

round-half-to-even

The round-half-to-even() function performs rounding to a specified number of decimal places. The rounding algorithm used is to round to the nearest value that has the required precision, choosing an even value if two values are equally close.

Signature

Argument	Type	Meaning
input	Numeric?	The number to be rounded. If an empty sequence is supplied, an empty sequence is returned.
precision (optional)	xs:integer	If positive, the number of significant digits required after the decimal point. If negative, the number of zeroes required at the end of the integer part of the result. The default is zero.
Result	Numeric?	*The rounded number. This will have the same type as the supplied number.*

Effect

The precision argument indicates the number of decimal digits required after the decimal point. More generally, the function rounds the supplied number to a multiple of 10^{-p} where p is the requested precision. So if the requested precision is 2, the value is rounded to a multiple of 0.01; if it is zero, the value is rounded to a multiple of 1 (in other words, to an integer), and if it is −2, the value is rounded to a multiple of 100.

If the precision argument is not supplied, the effect is the same as supplying the value zero, which means the value is rounded to an integer.

The value is rounded up or down to whichever value is closest: for example, if the required precision is 2, then 0.123 is rounded to 0.12 and 0.567 is rounded to 0.57. If two values are equally close then the half-to-even rule comes into play: 0.125 is rounded to 0.12, while 0.875 is rounded to 0.88.

This function is designed primarily for rounding of `xs:decimal` values, but it is also available for other numeric types. For `xs:integer`, the behavior is exactly the same as if the value were an `xs:decimal` (which, in fact, it is). For `xs:double` and `xs:float` it may not work so well. The specification states that the floating-point value is first cast to an `xs:decimal` value; the rounding is then applied to this decimal number, and the result is then converted back to the original type. This process may introduce rounding errors, and may fail completely if the implemetation supports a range of values for `xs:decimal` which is less than the range allowed for `xs:double`.

Examples

Expression	Result
`round-half-to-even(1.1742, 2)`	1.17
`round-half-to-even(1.175, 2)`	1.18
`round-half-to-even(2.5, 0)`	2.0
`round-half-to-even(273, -1)`	270
`round-half-to-even(-8500, -3)`	-8000

Usage

Most of us were probably taught at school that when numbers are rounded, 0.5 should be rounded upward. Professional accountants and statisticians, however, often prefer the "half-to-even" rule because it avoids creating bias: it means that on average, the total of a large set of numbers will remain roughly the same when all the numbers are rounded.

This function is useful when you want to display the results of a numerical calculation to a certain number of decimal places. Floating-point arithmetic often produces rounding errors because decimal values cannot be represented exactly in binary; for example, the result of «0.3e0 div 3» is «0.09999999999999999» rather than «0.1». Rounding the result say to six decimal places by writing «round-half-to-even(0.3e0 div 3,6)» corrects this error, and produces the result «0.1».

In XSLT, you can also achieve this rounding by using the `format-number()` *function, described on page 788.*

See Also

`ceiling()` on page 723
`floor()` on page 779
`format-number()` on page 788
`round()` on page 870

seconds-from-dateTime, seconds-from-time

The two functions `seconds-from-dateTime()` and `seconds-from-time()` extract the seconds component (including fractional seconds) from an `xs:dateTime` or `xs:time` value.

Signature

Argument	Type	Meaning
input	xs:time? or xs:dateTime?	The value from which the seconds component is to be extracted. The type of the supplied argument must correspond to the type implied by the function name. If an empty sequence is supplied, an empty sequence is returned.
Result	xs:decimal?	*The seconds component, in the range 0 to 59.999 . . .*

Effect

The function returns the seconds component of the supplied xs:time or xs:dateTime. The value is from the time as expressed in its local timezone (not normalized to UTC).

Examples

Expression	Result
seconds-from-time(xs:time("12:35:03.142"))	3.142
seconds-from-dateTime(xs:dateTime("2008-02-28T13:55:30-01:00"))	30

See Also

current-date(), -dateTime(), -time() on page 738
format-date(), -dateTime(), -time() on page 781
hours-from-dateTime(), -time() on page 800
minutes-from-dateTime(), -time() on page 832
timezone-from-dateTime(), -time() on page 893

seconds-from-duration

This function extracts the value of the seconds component (including fractional seconds) from a normalized xs:duration value.

Signature

Argument	Type	Meaning
input	xs:duration?	The value whose seconds component is to be extracted. If an empty sequence is supplied, an empty sequence is returned.
Result	xs:decimal?	*The seconds component, including any fractional seconds.*

Effect

The function returns the seconds component of the supplied xs:duration. The duration value is first normalized so that the number of hours is less than 24, the number of minutes is less than 60, and so on. However, months are never converted to days, or vice-versa. The result will be negative if the duration is negative. The result is therefore a decimal number in the range −60.0 to +60.0, exclusive.

XPath processors are required to maintain duration values to a precision of three decimal places (one millisecond). Some processors may maintain a finer precision than this, but it is optional.

Examples

Expression	Result
seconds-from-duration(xs:dayTimeDuration("PT1M30.5S"))	30.5
seconds-from-duration(xs:duration("P1MT150S"))	30
seconds-from-duration(xs:dayTimeDuration("-PT0.0055S"))	-0.0055
seconds-from-duration(xs:yearMonthDuration("P1M"))	0

See Also

days-from-duration on page 745
hours-from-duration on page 801
minutes-from-duration on page 832

seconds-from-time

see seconds-from-dateTime() on page 873

starts-with

The starts-with() function tests whether one string starts with another string.

For example, the expression «starts-with('$17.30', '$')» returns true.

Changes in 2.0

An optional collation argument has been added.

Signature

Argument	Type	Meaning
input	xs:string?	The containing string
test	xs:string?	The test string
collation (optional)	xs:string	A collation URI
Result	*xs:boolean*	*True if the containing string starts with the test string, otherwise false*

Effect

If there is no collation argument, then the system tests to see whether the first N characters of the input string match the characters in the test string (where N is the length of the test string). If so, the result is true; otherwise, it is false. Characters match if they have the same Unicode value.

If the test string is empty, the result is always true. If the input string is empty, the result is true only if the test string is also empty. If the test string is longer than the input, the result is always false.

If either the input or the test argument is an empty sequence, it is treated in the same way as a zero-length string.

If a collation is specified, this collation is used to test whether the strings match. See the description of the contains() function on page 730 for an account of how substring matching works with a collation. If the collation argument is omitted, the function uses the default collation from the static context.

Examples

Expression	Result
starts-with("#note", "#")	true
starts-with("yes", "yes")	true
starts-with("YES", "yes")	false
starts-with("yes", "")	true

Usage

For more sophisticated string matching, use the matches() function, which provides the ability to match against a regular expression. However, the matches() function does not give the ability to use a collation.

See Also

contains() on page 730
ends-with() on page 773
matches() on page 808
string-length() on page 880

static-base-uri

The static-base-uri() function returns the base URI from the static context of the XPath expression. In XSLT this will be the base URI of the element in the stylesheet containing the expression.

Signature

	Type	Meaning
Result	xs:anyURI	*The base URI from the static context of the XPath expression*

Effect

The function returns the base URI from the static context. This is determined by the host language in which the expression appears. For an XPath expression used in an XSLT stylesheet, the base URI is the URI of the stylesheet module, unless this is modified with an xml:base attribute.

The base URI is used when resolving a relative URI contained in the expression, for example as an argument of the doc() or document() function.

It is possible that the base URI is unknown. This can happen in XSLT if the stylesheet is supplied as a DOM, or as a character string or input stream with no associated URI. In this case this function returns an empty sequence.

Usage

In XSLT 2.0 and XQuery 1.0 it is well defined how the base URI in the static context is established. If you invoke XPath expressions via an API from a programming language (for example, a Java or

.NET API) then there may be no explicit way of setting the base URI, especially if the API was originally designed for XPath 1.0. In this case the `static-base-uri()` function is defined to return an empty sequence.

See Also

base-uri() on page 719
doc() on page 750
document() on page 754
resolve-uri() on page 867

string

The `string()` function converts its argument to a string. When the argument is a node, it extracts the string value of the node; when the argument is an atomic value, it converts the atomic value to a string in a similar way to the `xs:string()` constructor function.

For example, the expression «`string(4.00)`» returns the string `"4"`.

Changes in 2.0

The function has been generalized to take a wider range of types as its input.

In XPath 1.0, when a sequence containing several nodes was supplied, the `string()` function returned the string value of the first node, and ignored the rest. This behavior is retained in XPath 2.0 when running in 1.0 backward-compatibility mode; but in 2.0 mode, supplying more than one item in the argument is an error.

Signature

Argument	Type	Meaning
value (optional)	item()?	The value to be converted. If the argument is omitted, it defaults to the context item.
Result	xs:string	*The result of converting the argument to a string.*

Effect

Values of most types can be converted to a string.

If the function is called with no arguments, the effect is the same as supplying «.» (the context item) as the first argument.

If the supplied value is an empty sequence, the result is a zero-length string. (Don't confuse supplying an argument whose value is «()» with not supplying an argument — the effect is different.)

If the supplied value is a single node, the result is the string value of that node. The string value of a node is defined as follows:

❑ For a document node or element node, the string value is the concatenation of all the descendant text nodes.

❑ For an attribute, the string value is the attribute value.

❑ For a text node, the string value is the textual content.

13

The Function Library

❑ For a comment, the string value is the text of the comment.

❑ For a processing instruction, the string value is the *data* part of the processing instruction, that is, the part after the name that forms the *target* of the processing instruction.

❑ For a namespace node, the string value is the namespace URI.

If the supplied value is a single atomic value the result is the same as the result of casting the atomic value to a string. Every atomic value can be cast to a string — the rules are given in Chapter 11.

Note that taking the string value of a node is not the same as taking the typed value and converting it to a string. For example, the typed value might be a sequence of integers, but no conversion is defined from a sequence of integers to a string. In some cases a node has no typed value, notably in the case where the schema defines it as having element-only content (as distinct from mixed or empty content). Such an element has no typed value, but it still has a string value that is the concatenation of the descendant text nodes.

The type signature does not allow a sequence of more than one item to be supplied. However, if XPath 1.0 compatibility mode is enabled, any items in the sequence after the first are ignored.

Examples

Assume that the context node is the element:

```
<e example="yes"><first>17</first><second>blue</second></e>
```

Expression	Result
string()	"17blue"
string(first)	"17"
string(second)	"blue"
string(@example)	"yes"
string(+47.20)	"47.2"
string(2=2)	"true"
string(*)	In 1.0 mode: "17" In 2.0 mode: error

Usage

When converting atomic values to strings, there isn't really anything to choose between using the string() function and using the xs:string() constructor function.

When the argument is a node, the two functions behave differently. The string() function extracts the string value of the node, while xs:string() extracts the typed value and converts it to a string. In the absence of a schema, they do exactly the same thing. But with a schema, here are two cases where they can give different results:

❑ Where the node has a list-valued simple type (for example, a list of integers), string() will give the textual content of the node (a space-separated list of numbers), whereas xs:string() will fail if the list contains more than one item, or is empty.

❑ Where the node is an element with an element-only content model, string() will give the concatenation of the descendant text nodes of the element, while xs:string() will fail.

See Also

boolean() on page 721
number() on page 851
Converting Atomic Values on page 654 in Chapter 11

string-join

The `string-join()` function returns a string constructed by concatenating all the strings in a supplied sequence, with an optional separator between adjacent strings.

For example, «`string-join(("a","b","c"), "|")`» returns «a|b|c».

Signature

Argument	Type	Meaning
sequence	xs:string*	The supplied sequence of strings.
separator	xs:string	The separator to be used between adjacent strings. If no separator is required, supply a zero-length string for this argument.
Result	*xs:string*	*The result of concatenating the supplied strings and inserting separators.*

Effect

Each of the strings in the supplied sequence is appended to the result string, retaining the order in which the strings appear in the sequence. Each string except the last is followed by the requested `separator` string.

If the supplied sequence is empty, the result is always a zero-length string.

Examples

Expression	Result
string-join(("a", "b", "c"), ", ")	"a, b, c"
string-join(("A", "B", "C"), "")	"ABC"
string-join("Z", "+")	"Z"
string-join((), "~")	""

Usage

The expression:

```
string-join(ancestor-or-self::*/name(), "/")
```

will return a path such as:

```
book/chapter/section/title
```

Note that there is no implicit conversion of the items in the sequence to strings, even in XPath 1.0 compatibility mode. If the items are not strings, you need to convert them explicitly. For example, given a sequence of numbers, you can write:

```
string-join($seq/string(), ", ")
```

The `string-join()` function is often a handy alternative to `concat()`, because you can in effect give it a sequence of sequences to output. For example:

```
string-join(("debits:", $debits, "credits:", $credits), " ")
```

might produce the string:

```
debits: 23.40 18.50 67.00 credits: 17.00 5.00 4.32
```

In XSLT, functionality very similar to the `string-join()` function is invoked implicitly by the `<xsl:value-of>` instruction, and also in attribute value templates. For example, the instruction `<e a="{1 to 4}"/>` produces the result `<e a="1 2 3 4"/>`. The `<xsl:value-of>` instruction has a `separator` attribute to allow user control over the choice of separator, while attribute value templates always use a single space.

See Also

`concat()` on page 729

string-length

The `string-length()` function returns the number of characters in a string value.

For example, the expression «`string-length('Beethoven')`» returns 9.

Changes in 2.0

None.

Signature

Argument	Type	Meaning
value (optional)	xs:string?	The string whose length is required. If the argument is an empty sequence, the result of the function is 0 (zero).
Result	*xs:integer*	*A number: the number of characters in the value of the argument.*

Effect

When the argument is omitted, the function gives the string length of the value obtained by applying the `string()` function to the context item. It's an error if there is no context item.

Characters are counted as instances of the XML `Char` production. This means that a Unicode surrogate pair (a pair of 16-bit values used to represent a Unicode character in the range `#x10000` to `#x10FFFF`) is treated as a single character.

It is the number of characters in the string that matters, not the way they are written in the source document. A character written using a character reference such as «`&#255;`» or an entity reference such as «`&amp;`» is still one character.

Unicode combining and non-spacing characters are counted individually, unless the implementation has normalized them. The implementation is allowed to turn strings into normalized form, but is not required to do so. In normalized form NFC, accents and diacriticals will frequently be merged with the letter that they modify into a single character. To assure yourself of consistent answers in such cases, the `normalize-unicode()` function should be called to force the string into normalized form.

Examples

These examples assume that the XPath expression is used in a host language that expands XML entity references and numeric character references; for example, XSLT or XQuery.

Expression	Result
`string-length("abc")`	3
`string-length("&lt;&gt;")`	2
`string-length("""")`	1
`string-length("")`	0
`string-length('&#xFFFD;')`	1
`string-length('&#x20000;')`	1

Usage

The `string-length()` function can be useful when deciding how to allocate space on the output medium. For example, if a list is displayed in multiple columns then the number of columns may be determined by some algorithm based on the maximum length of the strings to be displayed.

It is *not* necessary to call `string-length()` to determine whether a string is zero-length, because converting the string to an `xs:boolean`, either explicitly using the `boolean()` function, or implicitly by using it in a boolean context, returns `true` only if the string has a length of one or more. For the same reason, it is not usually necessary to call `string-length()` when processing the characters in a string using a recursive iteration, since the terminating condition when the string is empty can be tested by converting it to a boolean.

See Also

`normalize-unicode()` on page 847
`substring()` on page 883

string-to-codepoints

The `string-to-codepoints()` function returns a sequence of integers representing the Unicode codepoints of the characters in a string. For example, «`string-to-codepoints("A")`» returns 65.

Signature

Argument	Type	Meaning
input	`·xs:string?`	The input string
Result	`xs:integer*`	*The codepoints of the characters in the input string*

Effect

If an empty sequence or a zero-length string is supplied as the input, the result is an empty sequence.

In other cases, the result contains a sequence of integers, one for each character in the input string. Characters here are as defined in Unicode and XML: a character above xFFFF that is represented as a surrogate pair counts as one character, not two. The integers that are returned will therefore be in the range 1 to x10FFFF (decimal 1114111).

Examples

Expression	Result
string-to-codepoints("ASCII")	65, 83, 67, 73, 73
string-to-codepoints("𘚠")	100000
string-to-codepoints("")	()

See Also

codepoints-to-string() on page 725

subsequence

The subsequence() function returns part of an input sequence, identified by the start position and length of the subsequence required.

For example the expression «subsequence(("a", "b", "c", "d"), 2, 2)» returns «("b", "c")».

Signature

Argument	Type	Meaning
sequence	item()*	The input sequence.
start	xs:double	The position of the first item to be included in the result.
length (optional)	xs:double	The number of items to be included in the result. If this argument is omitted, all items after the start position are included.
Result	*xs:string*	*The sequence of items starting at the start position*

Effect

The two-argument version of the function is equivalent to:

```
$sequence[position()>= round($start)]
```

The three-argument version is equivalent to:

```
$sequence[position()>= round($start)
           and position() < (round($start) + round($length))]
```

A consequence of these rules is that there is no error if the start or length arguments are out of range. Another consequence is that if the start or length arguments are NaN, the result is an empty sequence.

The arguments are defined with type xs:double for symmetry with the substring() function, which itself uses xs:double arguments for backward compatibility with XPath 1.0, which did not support any numeric type other than double. If you supply an integer, it will automatically be converted to a double.

The fact that they are doubles rather than integers is occasionally convenient because the result of a calculation involving untyped values is a double. For example:

```
subsequence($seq, 1, @limit + 1)
```

works even when the limit attribute is untyped, in which case the value of «@limit+1» is an xs:double.

Examples

Expression	Result
subsequence(3 to 10, 2)	4, 5, 6, 7, 8, 9, 10
subsequence(3 to 10, 5, 2)	7, 8
subsequence(1 to 5, 10)	()
subsequence(1 to 10, 2.3, 4.6)	2, 3, 4, 5, 6

See Also

insert-before() on page 810
remove() on page 861
Filter Expressions on page 637 in Chapter 10

substring

The substring() function returns part of a string value, determined by character positions within the string. Character positions are counted from one.

For example, the expression «substring('Goldfarb', 5, 3)» returns the string «far».

Changes in 2.0

None.

Signature

Argument	Type	Meaning
input	xs:string?	The containing string. If an empty sequence is supplied, the result is a zero-length string.
start	xs:double	The position in the containing string of the first character to be included in the result string.
length (optional)	xs:double	The number of characters to be included in the result string. If the argument is omitted, characters are taken from the start position up to the end of the containing string.
Result	xs:string	The required substring of the containing string.

Effect

Informally, the function returns a string consisting of the characters in the input string starting at position start; if a length is given, the returned string contains this many characters; otherwise, it contains all characters up to the end of the value.

Characters within a string are numbered 1, 2, 3..., n. This will be familiar to Visual Basic programmers but not to those accustomed to C or Java, where numbering starts at zero.

Characters are counted as instances of the XML `Char` production. This means that a Unicode surrogate pair (a pair of 16-bit values used to represent a Unicode character in the range #x10000 to #x10FFFF) is treated as a single character.

Combining and non-spacing characters are counted individually, unless the implementation has normalized them into a single combined character. The implementation is allowed to turn strings into Unicode normalized form, but is not required to do so. In normalized form NFC, accents and diacritics will typically be merged with the letter that they modify into a single character.

It is possible to define this function in terms of the `subsequence()` function. With two arguments, the function has the same result as:

```
codepoints-to-string(
        subsequence(string-to-codepoints($input), $start)))
```

With three arguments, the definition becomes:

```
codepoints-to-string(
        subsequence(string-to-codepoints($input), $start, $length)))
```

These rules cover conditions such as the start or length being negative, NaN, fractional, or infinite. The comparisons and arithmetic are done using IEEE 754 arithmetic, which has some interesting consequences if values such as infinity and NaN, or indeed any non-integer values are used. The rules for IEEE 754 arithmetic are summarized in Chapter 2.

The equivalence tells us that if the `start` argument is less than one, the result always starts at the first character of the supplied string, while if it is greater than the length of the string, the result will always be an empty string. If the `length` argument is less than zero, it is treated as zero, and again an empty string is returned. If the `length` argument is greater than the number of available characters, and the start position is within the string, then characters will be returned up to the end of the containing string.

Examples

Expression	Result
`substring("abcde", 2)`	`"bcde"`
`substring("abcde", 2, 2)`	`"bc"`
`substring("abcde", 10, 2)`	`""`
`substring("abcde", 1, 20)`	`"abcde"`

Usage

The `substring()` function is useful when processing a string character-by-character. One common usage is to determine the first character of a string:

```
substring($filename, 1, 1)
```

Or when manipulating personal names in the conventional American format of first name, middle initial, last name:

```
string-join((first-name, substring(middle-name, 1, 1), last-name), " ")
```

The following example extracts the last four characters in a string:

```
substring($s, string-length($s)-3)
```

Using substring() as a Conditional Expression

The technique outlined in this section is thankfully obsolete, now that XPath 2.0 offers «if» expressions, as described in Chapter 7. But you may encounter it in XSLT 1.0 stylesheets, and you may still have to use it if you write code that has to run under both XPath 1.0 and XPath 2.0, so it's worth a mention here.

Suppose that $b is an xs:boolean value, and consider the following expression:

```
substring("xyz", 1, $b * string-length("xyz"))
```

Under XPath 1.0 rules, the xs:boolean $b when used in an arithmetic expression is converted to a number: 0 for false, 1 for true. So the value of the third argument is 0 if $b is false, 3 if $b is true. The final result of the substring() function is therefore a zero-length string if $b is false, or the string "xyz" if $b is true. The expression is equivalent to «if ($b) then "xyz" else ""» in XPath 2.0.

In fact the third argument doesn't need to be exactly equal to the string length for this to work, it can be any value greater than the string length. So you could equally well write:

```
substring("xyz", 1, $b * (1 div 0))
```

exploiting the fact that «1 div 0» under XPath 1.0 is infinity, and zero times infinity is NaN. This obscure construct provided XPath 1.0 programmers with a substitute for a conditional expression.

If you try to run this code under XPath 2.0, it will fail: «1 div 0» is an xs:decimal division rather than an xs:double division, and the xs:decimal type has no infinity value. If you need to rewrite this so that it works under both XPath 1.0 and XPath 2.0, the simplest way is to replace the «1 div 0» by a very large but finite number. In XSLT, you can define this as a global variable. Remember, though, that exponential notation for numbers is not available in XPath 1.0.

See Also

substring-after() in the following section
substring-before() on page 887
string-length() on page 880
contains() on page 730

substring-after

The substring-after() function returns that part of a string value that occurs after the first occurrence of some specified substring.

For example, the expression «substring-after('print=yes', '=')» returns «yes».

Changes in 2.0

An optional collation argument has been added.

Signature

Argument	Type	Meaning
value	xs:string?	The containing string
test	xs:string?	The test string
collation (optional)	xs:string	Identifies the collation to be used for comparing strings.
Result	xs:string	*A string containing those characters that follow the first occurrence of the test substring within the containing string*

Effect

If the containing string (value) does not contain the test substring, the function returns a zero-length string. Note that this could also mean that the containing string ends with the test substring; the two cases can be distinguished by calling the ends-with() function.

If the value does contain the test substring, the function returns a string made up of all the characters that appear in value after the first occurrence of the test substring.

If either of the first two arguments is an empty sequence, it is treated as if it were a zero-length string.

If the test substring is zero-length, the function returns value.

If value is zero-length, the function returns a zero-length string.

If a collation is specified, this collation is used to test whether the strings match. See the description of the contains() function on page 730 for an account of how substring matching works with a collation. If the collation argument is omitted, the function uses the default collation.

> *Things get complicated if the collation classifies characters such as space or hyphen as ignorable for sorting purposes. If hyphen is ignorable, then «substring-after("a-b-c", "b-")» returns «-c». That's because the match chosen for «b-» is the minimal matching substring, which is «b».*

Examples

Expression	Result
substring-after("my.xml", ".")	"xml"
substring-after("my.xml", "m")	"y.xml"
substring-after("my.xml", "xml")	" "
substring-after("my.xml", "#")	" "
substring-after("", "#")	" "
substring-after("my.xml", "")	"my.xml"

Usage

The substring-after() function was often used in XPath 1.0 to analyze a string that contains delimiter characters. For example, when the string is a whitespace-separated list of tokens, the first token can be obtained using:

```
substring-before($s, ' ')
```

and the rest of the string using

```
substring-after($s, ' ')
```

With XPath 2.0, this can be done more robustly using the `tokenize()` function. However, there are still many cases where it is more convenient to use `substring-after()`. For example, to extract the local part of a lexical QName, you can write:

```
substring-after($qname, ':')
```

XSLT Example

The following example shows a recursive template that takes a whitespace-separated list as input, and outputs each token separated by an empty `<br/>` element.

```
<xsl:template name="output-tokens">
    <xsl:param name="list" as="xs:string" required="yes"/>
    <xsl:variable name="nlist"
        select="concat(normalize-space($list),' ')"/>
    <xsl:variable name="first" select="substring-before($nlist, ' ')"/>
    <xsl:variable name="rest" select="substring-after($nlist, ' ')"/>
    <xsl:value-of select="$first"/>
    <xsl:if test="$rest">
        <br/>
        <xsl:call-template name="output-tokens">
            <xsl:with-param name="list" select="$rest"/>
        </xsl:call-template>
    </xsl:if>
</xsl:template>
```

See Also

`contains()` on page 730
`substring()` on page 883
`substring-before()` in the next section

substring-before

The `substring-before()` function returns that part of a string value that occurs before the first occurrence of some specified substring.

For example, the value of «`substring-before('print=yes', '=')`» is the string «print».

Changes in 2.0

An optional `collation` argument has been added.

Signature

Argument	Type	Meaning
value	xs:string?	The containing string
test	xs:string?	The test string

continued

13

The Function Library

Argument	Type	Meaning
collation (optional)	xs:string	Identifies the collation to be used for comparing strings
Result	xs:string	*A string containing those characters that precede the first occurrence of the test substring within the containing string*

Effect

If the containing string (value) does not contain the test substring, the function returns a zero-length string. Note that this could also mean that the value starts with the test string; the two cases can be distinguished by calling the starts-with() function.

If the value does contain the test substring, the function returns a string made up of all the characters that appear in the value before the first occurrence of the test substring.

If either of the strings is an empty sequence or a zero-length string, the function returns a zero-length string.

If a collation is specified, this collation is used to test whether the strings match. See the description of the contains() function on page 730 for an account of how substring matching works with a collation. If the collation argument is omitted, the function uses the default collation.

Things get complicated if the collation classifies characters such as space or hyphen as ignorable for sorting purposes. If hyphen is ignorable, then «substring-before("a-b-c", "-b")» returns «a-». That's because the match chosen for «-b» is the minimal matching substring, which is «b».

Examples

Expression	Result
substring-before("my.xml", ".")	"my"
substring-before("my-xml.xml", "xml")	"my-"
substring-before("my.xml", "")	" "
substring-before("my.xml", "#")	" "

Usage and Examples

An example of the use of substring-after() and substring-before() to process a whitespace-separated list of tokens is given under substring-after() on page 887.

If the only reason for using substring-before() is to test whether the string has a given prefix, use starts-with() instead. You could write:

```
if (substring-before($url, ':')='https') then ...
```

but the following is simpler:

```
if (starts-with($url, 'https:')) then ...
```

In XPath 1.0, the substring-before() and substring-after() functions were often used in conjunction to find and replace portions of a string. In XPath 2.0, this kind of string manipulation is much easier using regular expressions, as offered by the replace() function.

See Also

sum

The sum() function calculates the total of a sequence of numeric values or durations.

For example, if the context node is the element <rect x="20" y="30"/>, then the expression «sum(@*)» returns 50. (The expression «@*» is a sequence containing all the attributes of the context node.)

Changes in 2.0

This function is generalized in XPath 2.0 so that it can sum over all the numeric types, and also over durations.

In XPath 1.0 the function returned NaN if the sequence contained a value that could not be converted to a number. In XPath 2.0 (even under backward-compatibility mode) this situation causes a failure.

Signature

Argument	Type	Meaning
sequence	xs:anyAtomicType*	The set of items to be totaled
zero-value (optional)	xs:anyAtomicType	The value to be returned when the sequence is empty
Result	*xs:anyAtomicType*	*The total of the values in the sequence*

Effect

Although the function signature states that the input sequence must consist of atomic values, the function calling rules ensure that the actual argument can be a sequence of nodes — the nodes in this sequence will be atomized, which extracts their typed values. If the source document has been validated using a schema, then the type of the resulting values depends on the schema, while if it has not been validated, the result of atomization will be untyped atomic values.

Any untyped atomic values in the sequence are converted to xs:double values. A runtime error is reported if this conversion fails. If the sequence contains any NaN (not-a-number) values, which might happen if you do the conversion yourself by calling the number() function, then the result of the function is NaN.

The values in the sequence are added using the «+» operator. An error is reported if there are values that cannot be added using the «+» operator. This will happen if the sequence contains values of types other than the numeric types, the duration types, and xs:untypedAtomic, or if it contains a mixture of durations and other types. If you are totaling durations, all the durations must either be of type xs:dayTimeDuration or they must all be of type xs:yearMonthDuration — you cannot mix the two, and you cannot use duration values unless they match one of these subtypes.

If the input sequence is empty, then the value returned is the value specified in the zero-value argument. If this argument is omitted, the return value for an empty sequence is the xs:integer value 0.

The purpose of this argument is to allow a return value to be specified that has the appropriate type, for example, an `xs:double` 0.0e0 for use when totaling doubles, or the value `PT0 S` when totaling `xs:dayTimeDuration` values. This is needed because there is no runtime type information associated with an empty sequence — an empty sequence of `xs:double` values does not look any different from an empty sequence of `xs:dayTimeDuration` values.

Examples

Expression	Result
sum((1, 2, 3, 4))	10 (xs:integer)
sum((1, 2, 3, 4.5))	10.5 (xs:decimal)
sum((1, 2, 3.5e0, 4.5))	11.0e0 (xs:double)
sum(())	0 (xs:integer)
sum((), 0.0e0)	0.0e0 (xs:double)
sum((xs:dayTimeDuration("P3D"), xs:dayTimeDuration("PT36H")))	xs:dayTimeDuration("P4DT12H")
sum((), xs:dayTimeDuration("PT0 S"))	xs:dayTimeDuration("PT0 S")

Usage

The `sum()` function can be used to create totals and subtotals in a report. It is also useful for calculating geometric dimensions on the output page.

A problem that sometimes arises is how to get a total over a set of values that aren't present directly in the source file, but are calculated from it. For example, if the source document contains `<book>` elements with attributes `price` and `sales`, how would you calculate the total sales revenue, which is obtained by multiplying `price` by `sales` for each book, and totaling the result over all books? Or, how would you total a set of numbers if each one has a leading «$» sign, which you need to strip off first? In XPath 1.0 this was difficult to achieve, but the solution in XPath 2.0 is simple:

In the first case:

```
sum(//book/(price * sales))
```

In the second case:

```
sum(//price/number(substring-after(., '$')))
```

See Also

avg() on page 718
count() on page 733

system-property

This function is available in XSLT only.

The `system-property()` function returns information about the processing environment.

For example, with a processor that implements XSLT version 2.0, the expression «system-property ('xsl:version')» returns 2.0.

Changes in 2.0

Several new system properties have been defined in XSLT 2.0.

The result of the function is now always a string. In XSLT 1.0 (although the spec was not a hundred percent clear on the point) the «xsl:version» system property was returned as a number.

Signature

Argument	Type	Meaning
name	xs:string	Specifies the name of the system property required. The value of the string should be in the form of a lexical QName that identifies a system property. If there is no system property with this name, the function returns a zero-length string.
Result	*xs:string*	*The value of the requested system property.*

Effect

The supplied argument is converted into an expanded name using the namespace declarations in scope for the stylesheet element that contains the call on system-property().

There are several system properties that every implementation must support. These are all in the XSLT namespace, and are listed as follows. The first three were available in XSLT 1.0, the others are new in XSLT 2.0.

System Property	Value
xsl:version	A number giving the version of XSLT implemented by the processor. For conformant XSLT processors, this will be 1.0 or 2.0. For processors that provide a partial implementation, or an implementation of intermediate working drafts, other versions may be returned. It's a good idea to write your stylesheet on the assumption that new XSLT versions may be introduced in the future.
xsl:vendor	A string identifying the vendor of the XSLT processor. In practice it will sometimes also identify the product name, but the actual value is implementation defined. For Microsoft's MSXML3 product, the value is simply «Microsoft».
xsl:vendor-url	A string: the URL of the vendor's Web site. For example, MSXML3 returns «http://www.microsoft.com».
xsl:product-name	This property is new in XSLT 2.0. It is intended to identify the product name of the XSLT processor; for example, «Xalan» or «Saxon».
xsl:product-version	This property is new in XSLT 2.0. It is intended to identify which version of the XSLT processor is being used; for example, «7.6.5». If there are several variants of a product (for example, Xalan-C and Xalan-J), it is up to the implementor whether the variant is returned as part of the product name or as part of the product version.
xsl:is-schema-aware	This property returns the string «yes» or «no», depending on whether the XSLT 2.0 processor is schema-aware or not.

13

The Function Library

continued

System Property	Value
`xsl:supports-serialization`	This property returns the string «yes» or «no», depending on whether the XSLT 2.0 processor supports serialization or not.
`xsl:supports-backwards-compatibility`	This property returns the string «yes» or «no», depending on whether the XSLT 2.0 processor supports running in backward-compatibility mode. A processor that does not support this mode will report an error if «version="1.0"» is specified.
`xsl:supports-namespace-axis`	This property was introduced to the specification by means of an erratum, so not all processors will support it. It returns «yes» if the implementation recognizes the namespace axis, or «no» if it does not. An implementation that has not been updated to recognize this property will return a zero-length string.

Any additional system properties returned by this function are implementation-defined. Such properties should either be in a namespace specific to the vendor, or in no namespace. Some products provide access to environment variables or Java system properties using this mechanism; this can be particularly useful as a way of parameterizing the `use-when` construct.

Usage

The `system-property()` function can be used to determine details about the processor running the stylesheet, either for display purposes (for example, to produce a comment in the generated output), or to apply conditional logic.

The function is especially useful when used in conjunction with the `use-when` attribute. For example, you can import a schema only if the processor is schema-aware by writing

```
<xsl:import-schema schema-location="..."
            use-when="system-property('xsl:is-schema-aware') eq 'yes'"/>
```

You can use the same approach on `<xsl:include>` and `<xsl:import>` to include entire stylesheet modules conditionally. If the processor allows you to access environment variables set from the operating system shell, this provides a powerful way of maintaining different variants of your stylesheet for different processing scenarios, rather like `#ifdef` directives in C.

Generally, it is best to avoid testing the system version to see whether particular features are available, unless there is no other way of doing so. The functions `function-available()` and `element-available()` and the `<xsl:fallback>` instruction often serve this need better, and the forward- compatibility features described on page 130 in Chapter 3 can be used to ensure that a stylesheet can work with processors that implement an older dialect of XSLT.

However, there are some cases where testing «system-property('xsl:version')» is the only practical way of discovering whether a feature is available. For example, the XSLT 2.0 working draft introduces the ability to use a tree-valued variable (or a result tree fragment, as it is known in XSLT 1.0) as a document node, in contexts such as `<xsl:for-each>` and `<xsl:apply-templates>`. Since this feature does not introduce any new functions or XSLT elements, the only practical way to test whether it is available is to check the XSLT version supported.

Examples

The following code outputs a documentary comment into the generated HTML.

```
<HTML>
  <xsl:comment>
    Generated with XSLT stylesheet <xsl:value-of select="static-base-uri()"/>
    using <xsl:value-of select="system-property('xsl:product-name')"/>
    version <xsl:value-of select="system-property('xsl:product-version')"/>
  </xsl:comment>
  . . .
```

See Also

element-available() page 764
function-available() on page 792
<xsl:fallback> on page 316 in Chapter 6

timezone-from-date, timezone-from-dateTime, timezone-from-time

These three functions extract the timezone component from an xs:date, xs:time, or xs:dateTime value. For example, for a user in California, «timezone-from-dateTime(current-dateTime())» typically returns the dayTimeDuration «-PT8H».

Signature

Argument	Type	Meaning
input	xs:date?, xs:time?, or xs:dateTime?	The value from which the timezone component is to be extracted. The type of the supplied argument must correspond to the type implied by the function name.
Result	*xs:dayTimeDuration?*	*The timezone, expressed as a duration.*

Effect

The function returns the timezone component of the supplied xs:date, xs:time, or xs:dateTime.

If the argument is an empty sequence, or if it is a date, time, or dateTime containing no timezone, then the result is an empty sequence. Otherwise, the function returns the timezone from the specified value. The timezone is returned in the form of an xs:dayTimeDuration value giving the offset from UTC (or Greenwich Mean Time, in common language).

If you want the timezone as a numeric value in hours, divide it by «xs:dayTimeDuration("PT1H")».

Examples

Expression	Result
timezone-from-date(xs:date("2008-02-28"))	()
timezone-from-dateTime(xs:dateTime("2008-02-28T13:00:00-06:00"))	-PT6H
timezone-from-time(xs:time("13:00:00+01:00"))	PT1H
timezone-from-dateTime(xs:dateTime("2008-07-31T23:00:00Z"))	PT0S

13

The Function Library

893

See Also

```
adjust-date/time-to-timezone on page 715
current-date(), -dateTime(), -time() on page 738
format-date(), -dateTime(), -time() on page 781
implicit-timezone() on page 806
```

tokenize

The tokenize() function splits a string into a sequence of substrings, by looking for separators that match a given regular expression.

For example, «tokenize("12, 16, 2", ",\s*")» returns the sequence «("12", "16", "2")».

Signature

Argument	Type	Meaning
input	xs:string?	The input string. If an empty sequence or zero-length string is supplied, the function returns an empty sequence.
regex	xs:string	The regular expression used to match separators, written according to the rules given in Chapter 14.
flags (optional)	xs:string	One or more letters indicating options on how the matching is to be performed. If this argument is omitted, the effect is the same as supplying a zero-length string, which defaults all the option settings.
Result	xs:string*	*A sequence whose items are substrings of the input string.*

Effect

The rules for the syntax of regular expressions and the flags argument are given in Chapter 14.

The input string is processed from left to right, looking for substrings that match the regular expression supplied in the regex argument. A consecutive sequence of characters that doesn't participate in a match is copied as a string to form one item in the output sequence. A sequence of characters that does match the regex is deemed to be a separator and is discarded. The search then resumes at the character position following the matched substring.

It can happen that two substrings starting at the same position both match the regex. There are two ways this situation can arise.

Firstly, it happens when part of the regex is looking for repeated occurrences of a substring. For example, suppose the regex is «\n+», indicating that any sequence of one or more consecutive newlines acts as a separator. Then clearly, if two adjacent newline characters are found, the regex could match on the first one alone, or on the pair. The rule here is that «+» is a greedy quantifier: it matches as long a substring as it can, in this case, both newline characters. In this example, this is what you want to happen. But if you were trying to remove comments in square brackets by using a regex such as «\[.*\]», this would have the wrong effect — given the input «Doolittle [1] and Dalley [2]», the first separator identified would be «[1] and Dalley [2]». If you want to match the shortest possible substring, add a «?» after the quantifier to make it non-greedy, thus: «\[.*?\]».

Another situation that can cause two different substrings to match at the same position is where the regex contains two alternatives that both match. For example, when the regex «#|##» is applied to a string that contains two consecutive «#» characters, both branches will match. The rule here is that the first (leftmost) alternative wins. In this case, this is almost certainly not what was intended: rewrite the expression as «##|#», or as «##?».

If the input string starts with a separator, then the output sequence will start with a zero-length string representing what was found before the first separator. If the input string ends with a separator, there will similarly be a zero-length string at the end of the sequence. If there are two adjacent separators in the middle of the string, you will get a zero-length string in the middle of the result sequence. In all cases the number of items in the result sequence is the number of separators in the input string plus one.

If the regex does not match the input string, the `tokenize()` function will return the input string unchanged, as a singleton sequence. If this is not the effect you are looking for, use the `matches()` function first to see if there is a match.

If the regex is one that matches a zero-length string, that is, if «matches("", $regex)» is true, the system reports an error. An example of such a regex is «\s*». Although various interpretations of such a construct are possible, the Working Group decided that the results were too confusing and decided not to allow it.

Examples

Expression	Result
`tokenize("Go home, Jack!", "\W+")`	`("Go", "home", "Jack", "")`
`tokenize("abc[NL]def[XY]", "\[.*?\]")`	`("abc", "def", "")`

Usage

A limitation of this function is that it is not possible to do anything with the separator substrings. This means, for example, that you can't treat a number differently depending on whether it was separated from the next number by a comma or a semicolon. One solution to this problem is to process the string in two passes: first, do a `replace()` call in which the separators «,» and «;» are replaced by (say) «,#» and «;#»; then use `tokenize()` to split the string at the «#» characters, and the original «,» or «;» will be retained as the last character of each substring in the tokenized sequence. Another approach, if you are using XSLT, is to use the `<xsl:analyze-string>` instruction.

A similar technique is possible when there are no separators available. Suppose that the input is alphanumeric, and you want to break it into a sequence of alternating alphabetic and numeric tokens, so that the input «W151TBH» is split into the three strings «("W", "151", "TBH")». Here's how to do this:

```
tokenize(replace($input, "([0-9]+|[A-Za-z]+)", "$1#"), "#")[.]
```

The predicate «[.]» at the end of this expression causes zero-length strings in the result to be filtered out (there will be a zero-length string at the end of the sequence).

See Also

<xsl:analyze-string> in Chapter 6, page 230
matches() on page 828
replace() on page 862
Regular Expressions: Chapter 14

13

The Function Library

trace

The `trace()` function is used to produce diagnostic output. The format and destination of the output is implementation-defined.

Signature

Argument	Type	Meaning
value	`item()*`	*A value that is to be displayed in the diagnostic output*
message	`xs:string`	*A message that is to be output along with the displayed value*
Result	`item()*`	*The function returns the displayed* `value`, *unchanged*

Effect

The detailed effect of this instruction depends on the implementation; some implementations might ignore it entirely. The idea of the function is that when it is evaluated, a message should be produced to some diagnostic output stream (perhaps a log file or perhaps an interactive console) showing the message string and the contents of the supplied value. The function then returns this value, and execution continues normally.

Note that since the order of execution of different expressions is undefined, the trace output will not necessarily be strictly sequential, and it may be difficult to see what is going on when the same `trace()` expression is evaluated repeatedly. This problem can be reduced if the message, rather than being a simple literal string, is constructed from variables that provide some context.

The specification doesn't say whether the presence of the `trace()` function should or should not affect the optimizer's evaluation strategy. Some implementors may decide that to make the trace output intelligible, certain optimizations should be suppressed; others may decide that the execution strategy with tracing should be as close as possible to the execution strategy without tracing, to reduce the risk of so-called Heisenbugs, in which the behavior of the expression changes when debugging is switched on.

Usage and Examples

Suppose you are having problems understanding why the function call «sum(//@price)» is returning NaN. Try changing it to:

```
«sum(//trace(@price, "price value"))»
```

to see the price values that are being used in the computation.

> *In the Saxon implementation, when you trace a sequence, you get one message for each item in the sequence. Saxon pipelines the evaluation of sequences, and tracing doesn't change the pipeline, so you might find that the evaluation of different sequences is interleaved. This can be confusing, but it gives you a faithful picture of what is happening internally. Other implementations might give you one message for the entire sequence, and might break the evaluation pipeline in order to output the message.*

Sometimes you might just want to output a value that is not actually used in the computation. In this case, you can usually use an empty sequence as the value, and put the required value into the message — just remember that the `trace()` function will then return an empty sequence. For example, you could write:

```
«sum(//(trace((),concat("reading price for ", string(@code)), @price) »
```

In an XSLT environment, I usually find that tracing is best performed using the `<xsl:message>` instruction, and I typically use `trace()` only in XQuery. For detailed inspection of values as they are computed, there are a number of good XSLT debuggers available. But occasionally, `trace()` is a useful tool to take out of the kitbag.

See Also

`<xsl:message>` in Chapter 6 on page 386

translate

The `translate()` function substitutes characters in a supplied string with nominated replacement characters. It can also be used to remove nominated characters from a string.

For example, the result of «`translate('ABC-123', '-', '/')`» is the string «`ABC/123`».

Changes in 2.0

An empty sequence is not accepted for the second and third arguments, except in backward-compatibility mode.

Signature

Argument	Type	Meaning
value	`xs:string?`	The supplied string
from	`xs:string`	The list of characters to be replaced, written as a string
to	`xs:string`	The list of replacement characters, written as a string
Result	`xs:string?`	*A string derived from the supplied string, but with those characters that appear in the second argument replaced by the corresponding characters from the third argument, or removed if there is no corresponding character*

Effect

For each character in the supplied string, one of three possible actions is taken:

❑ If the character is not present in the list of characters to be replaced, the character is copied to the result string unchanged.

❑ If the character is present at position P in the list of characters to be replaced, and the list of replacement characters is of length P or greater, then the character at position P in the list of replacement characters is copied to the result string.

❑ If the character is present at position P in the list of characters to be replaced, and the list of replacement characters is shorter than P, then no character is copied to the result string.

Note that the third argument must be present, but it can be a zero-length string. In this case, any character present in the second argument is removed from the supplied string.

If a character appears more than once in the list of characters to be replaced, the second and subsequent occurrences are ignored, as are the characters in the corresponding position in the third argument.

If the third argument is longer than the second, excess characters are ignored.

In these rules a *character* means an XML character, not a 16-bit Unicode code. This means that a Unicode surrogate pair (a pair of 16-bit values used to represent a Unicode character in the range #x10000 to #x10FFFF) is treated as a single character, whichever of the three strings it appears in.

Examples

Expression	Result
translate("aba12", "abcd", "ABCD")	"ABA12"
translate("aba121", "12", "")	"aba"
translate("a\b\c.xml", "\", "/")	"a/b/c.xml"
translate("5,000.00", ".,", ",.")	"5.000,00"

Usage and Examples

Many of the XPath 1.0 use cases for the translate() function can now be achieved more conveniently in XPath 2.0 by other more powerful functions, such as matches() and replace().

In an XSLT stylesheet you might see the translate() function being used to perform simple case conversion, for example:

```
translate($X,
        'abcdefghijklmnopqrstuvwxyz',
        'ABCDEFGHIJKLMNOPQRSTUVWXYZ')
```

This can now be done much better using the upper-case() and lower-case() functions.

The translate() function is useful to remove extraneous punctuation or whitespace; for example, to remove all whitespace, hyphens, and parentheses from a telephone number, write:

```
translate($X, '&#x20;&#x9;&#xA;&#xD;()-', '')
```

Another use for translate() is to test for the presence of a particular character or range of characters. For example, to test whether a string contains a sequence of three or more ASCII digits, write:

```
contains(translate($X, '0123456789', '9999999999'), '999')
```

Of course, you could do this equally well using «matches($X, '[0-9]{3}')».

The translate() function can be surprisingly powerful. For example, to remove all characters other than digits from a string, you can write:

```
translate($X, translate($X, '0123456789', ''), '')
```

The inner call on translate() strips the digits from $X, thus building a list of characters that appear in $X and are not digits. The outer call processes $X again, this time removing the non-digit characters.

See Also

contains() on page 730
matches() on page 828

replace() on page 862
substring() on page 883
substring-after() on page 885
substring-before() on page 887

true

This function returns the boolean value `true`.

Changes in 2.0

None.

Signature

This function takes no arguments.

	Type	Meaning
Result	`xs:boolean`	*The `xs:boolean` value `true`*

Effect

There are no boolean constants available in XPath expressions, so the functions `true()` and `false()` can be used where a constant boolean value is required.

Usage

The most common occasion where constant boolean values are required is when supplying an argument to a function or to an XSLT template. See the example below.

XSLT Example

The following code calls a named template, setting the parameter «verbose» to `true`:

```
<xsl:call-template name="do-the-work">
   <xsl:with-param name="verbose" select="true()"/>
</xsl:call-template>
```

See Also

false() on page 779

type-available

This function is available in XSLT only.

This function is used to test whether a particular schema type is available in the static context.

For example, the expression «type-available('xs:integer')» returns `true`.

13

The Function Library

899

Signature

Argument	Type	Meaning
name	xs:string	The name of the type being tested. The string must take the form of a lexical QName.
Result	xs:boolean	true *if the named type is available in the static context,* false *otherwise.*

Effect

The first argument must take the form of a lexical QName; that is, an XML name with an optional name-space prefix that corresponds to a namespace declaration that is in scope at the point in the stylesheet where the type-available() function is called. If the name is unprefixed, then the default namespace from the stylesheet (defined by «xmlns="some.uri"») is assumed.

With a basic XSLT processor (the minimal conformance level), the function returns true if the name is one of the following:

❑ One of the schema primitive types available in every XSLT processor: xs:string, xs:boolean, xs:decimal, xs:double, xs:float, xs:date, xs:time, xs:dateTime, xs:duration, xs:QName, xs:anyURI, xs:gDay, xs:gMonthDay, xs:gMonth, xs:gYearMonth, xs:gYear, xs:base64Binary, or xs:hexBinary

❑ One of the derived built-in types available in every XSLT processor: xs:integer, xs:yearMonth-Duration, xs:dayTimeDuration

❑ One of the special types xs:anyType, xs:anySimpleType, xs:anyAtomicType, xs:untyped, xs:untypedAtomic

With a schema-aware XSLT processor the function will also return true if the type is one of:

❑ The abstract primitive type xs:NOTATION

❑ One of the derived built-in numeric types xs:nonPositiveInteger, xs:negativeInteger, xs:long, xs:int, xs:short, xs:byte, xs:nonNegativeInteger, xs:unsignedLong, xs:unsignedInt, xs:unsignedShort, xs:unsignedByte, xs:positiveInteger

❑ One of the derived built-in string types xs:normalizedString, xs:token, xs:language, xs:NMTOKEN, xs:Name, xs:NCName, xs:ID, xs:IDREF, xs:ENTITY

❑ One of the built-in list types xs:ENTITIES, xs:IDREFS, xs:NMTOKENS

❑ A user-defined simple type or complex type defined in a schema that has been imported using an <xsl:import-schema> declaration

Vendors are allowed to define additional types in their own namespace, and type-available() can also be used to test for these types.

Usage

The stated purpose of this function is to allow you to test whether a particular type is available for use, so that you can conditionally exclude code that refers to a type if it is not available. However, its practical usefuless is limited by the fact that types imported using <xsl:import-schema> are not available in the static context for an [xsl:]use-when expression, which means that testing for the availability of a user-defined type in [xsl:]use-when will always return false.

In practice, therefore, this function is only likely to be useful when testing for vendor-defined types which might be imported implicitly.

See Also

`element-available()` on page 764
`function-available()` on page 792
`system-property()` on page 890
`<xsl:fallback>` in Chapter 6, page 316

unordered

The formal definition of the `unordered()` function is that it returns a sequence that is an arbitrary reordering of the sequence provided as its argument. In practice, this is really a pseudo-function — wrapping an expression in a call of `unordered()` tells the XPath processor that you don't care what order the results of that expression are in, which means that the processor might be able to avoid the cost of sorting them into the right order.

For example, «`unordered(ancestor::*)`» returns the ancestor elements in whatever order the system finds most convenient. (In Saxon, it currently returns them in reverse document order, that is, innermost ancestor first.)

Signature

Argument	Type	Meaning
sequence	`item()*`	The supplied sequence
Result	`item()*`	*A sequence that contains the same items as the supplied sequence, but in an arbitrary order*

Effect

The ordering of the items in the result is arbitrary, which means the processor can choose any order it likes. This doesn't mean it has to be a randomized order; on the contrary, the system might well choose to return the original order unchanged. In fact, it would be completely conformant with the specification for this function to be implemented as a no-operation. It's really best to think of it as an optimization hint.

Note that although the `unordered()` function allows the system to return the results of the argument expression in any order, it doesn't absolve it from the need to eliminate duplicates. In practice this reduces the possibilities available to an optimizer considerably; for example, in forming a union between two sequences of nodes «`$A|$B`», the system is required both to sort the result in document order and to remove duplicates. Writing it as «`unordered($A|$B)`» removes the requirement to sort the results, but not the requirement to eliminate duplicates. Since the system is very likely to eliminate duplicates as a by-product of sorting, this might not result in any changes to the execution strategy chosen by the optimizer.

Usage and Examples

Because the XPath data model is defined in terms of sequences rather than sets, the ordering of the results of an expression is usually well defined. For example, the results of a path expression are always in document order, and the results of the `index-of()` function are defined to be in ascending numeric order. By enclosing such expressions in a call of `unordered()`, you can tell the system that you don't care

13

about the order. For example, «unordered(preceding-sibling::*)» returns the preceding siblings of the context node in an arbitrary order, rather than in document order as usual. In the current version of Saxon, the preceding siblings will be returned in reverse document order, because that is the fastest way of finding them, but you should not rely on this behavior as it may vary from one product to another and might depend on other circumstances.

Some functions take a sequence as an argument and produce a result that doesn't depend on the order of the items in the sequence. Obvious examples are count() and sum(). In such cases, it's reasonable to assume that the optimizer will insert a call on unordered() automatically, and that you don't need to do it yourself: «count(unordered(X))» gives the same result as «count(X)», and removes the need to sort the items in X into the right order.

The place where the unordered() function really comes into its own is in handling joins, for example:

```
//customer/order[@prod-code = //product[supplier=$s]/@code]
```

or equivalently:

```
for $o in //customer/order,
    $p in //product[supplier=$s][@code=$o/@prod-code]
return
    $o
```

There are many different ways of writing join expressions in XPath, just as there are in SQL, and it's often the case that you are only interested in knowing which elements are selected, not in getting them back in a particular order. If you make it clear that you don't care about the order, by wrapping the join expression in a call on the unordered() function, then the system can select from a wider choice of possible access paths to retrieve the data. This is particularly true if there are indexes to the data, which is likely if it is stored in an XML database.

unparsed-entity-public-id, unparsed-entity-uri

These two functions are available in XSLT only.

These functions give access to the public identifier and system identifier of unparsed entities declared in the DTD of the source document.

Changes in 2.0

The unparsed-entity-public-id() function is new in XSLT 2.0.

Signatures

The unparsed-entity-public-id() function

Argument	Type	Meaning
name	xs:string	Specifies the name of the unparsed entity required. The value of the string should be an XML *Name*.
Result	xs:string	*The public identifier of the unparsed entity with the given name, if there is one. Otherwise, a zero-length string.*

The unparsed-entity-uri() function

Argument	Type	Meaning
name	xs:string	Specifies the name of the unparsed entity required. The value of the string should be an XML *Name*.
Result	xs:anyURI	*The URI (system identifier) of the unparsed entity with the given name, if there is one. Otherwise, a zero-length string.*

Effect

These two functions operate on the document containing the context node. An error is reported if the context item is undefined, or if it is not a node, or if it is a node in a tree whose root is not a document node.

If the document containing the context node includes an unparsed entity whose name is equal to the supplied string, then the unparsed-entity-public-id() function will return the public identifier of the entity if it has one (signaled by the PUBLIC keyword in XML), while the unparsed-entity-uri() function will return its system identifier. In all other cases, the functions return a zero-length string.

If the system identifier is given in the source XML as a relative URI reference, the XSLT processor should expand it into an absolute URI before returning it.

Usage

An unparsed entity is an entity defined in the DTD using a declaration of the form:

```
<!ENTITY weather-map SYSTEM "weather.jpeg" NDATA JPEG>
```

It's the NDATA (meaning "not XML data") that makes it an unparsed entity; and because it is an unparsed entity, it can't be referenced using a normal entity reference of the form «&weather-map;» but must instead be referenced by name in an attribute of type ENTITY or ENTITIES; for example, <forecast map="weather-map">.

If you're using a schema-aware XSLT processor, and the document has been validated against a schema that defines the map attribute as being of type xs:ENTITY, then you can process the attribute using a rule such as:

```
<xsl:template match="attribute(*, xs:ENTITY)">
    <img src="{unparsed-entity-uri(.)}"/>
</xsl:template>
```

Without a schema, you are simply expected to know that the map attribute is of type xs:ENTITY, and expected to pick up the attribute value in a call such as «unparsed-entity-uri(@map)». This call returns the absolute URI of the actual resource, that is, something like «file:///c:/documents/forecasts/weather.jpeg».

Unparsed entities are one of the more rarely used features of XML; they derive from SGML, and this explains why people who use unparsed entities are also inclined to use public identifiers to refer to them. Public identifiers were designed to tackle the same problem as URNs, namely to provide a way of giving unique names to objects, without becoming locked in to the location where the object can be found. They are often used in conjunction with Oasis catalogs.

13

The Function Library

903

Note that it is the public and system identifier of the unparsed entity that is returned, not the public and system identifier of the notation named in its NDATA clause. XSLT provides no way of finding out the notation name («JPEG» in our example) or the URI for the notation, so even if you have a schema that flags the attribute as one that contains an unparsed entity reference, you still have to know what kind of reference you are expecting.

This is not exactly in the spirit of section 4.4.6 of the XML specification, which states: "When the name of an unparsed entity appears as a token in an attribute of declared type ENTITY or ENTITIES, a validating processor must inform the application of the system and public (if any) identifiers for both the entity and its associated notation." However, unparsed entities are hardly XML's most widely used feature, so it is unsurprising that XSLT support for them should be incomplete.

The rules in the XSLT specification don't explicitly state this, but in practice, if you use a nonvalidating XML parser to process the source document, the parser isn't obliged to pass information to the XSLT processor about unparsed entities declared in the external subset of the DTD, and the unparsed-entity-public-id() and unparsed-entity-uri() functions are therefore likely to return a zero-length string. If this happens, try using a validating XML parser — assuming of course that the source document is valid.

Examples

If the DTD contains the declaration:

```
<!ENTITY weather-map SYSTEM "weather.jpeg"
    PUBLIC "-//MEGACORP//WEATHER/" NDATA JPEG>
```

then the expression «unparsed-entity-public-id('weather-map')» returns the public identifier «-//MEGACORP//WEATHER/».

Given the entity definition:

```
<!ENTITY weather-map SYSTEM "weather.jpeg" NDATA JPEG>
```

and the entity reference:

```
<FORECAST MAP="weather-map"/>
```

the following code will insert an <IMG> element into the HTML output:

```
<xsl:template match="FORECAST">
    <IMG HREF="{unparsed-entity-uri(@MAP)}"/>
</xsl:template>
```

See Also

Trees, Not Documents, in Chapter 2, page 42.

unparsed-text, unparsed-text-available

These two functions are available in XSLT only.

The unparsed-text() function returns the content of an external file in the form of a string. Its companion function, unparsed-text-available(), tests whether a call on unparsed-text() would succeed.

Signatures

The unparsed-text() function

Argument	Type	Meaning
href	xs:string?	The URI of the external text file to be loaded. If an empty sequence is supplied, the result is an empty sequence.
encoding (optional)	xs:string	The character encoding of the text in the file.
Result	xs:string?	*The textual content of the file.*

The unparsed-text-available() function

Argument	Type	Meaning
href	xs:string?	The URI of the external text file to be loaded. If an empty sequence is supplied, the result is false.
encoding (optional)	xs:string?	The character encoding of the text in the file. If an empty sequence is supplied, the function behaves as if the argument were omitted.
Result	xs:boolean	*True if a call on* unparsed-text() *with the same arguments would succeed; false if it would fail.*

Effect

This pair of functions is analogous to the doc()/doc-available() pair described on page 750, except that the file referenced by the URI is treated as text rather than as XML. The file is located and its textual content is returned as the result of the unparsed-text() function, in the form of a string.

The value of the href argument is a URI. It mustn't contain a fragment identifier (the part marked with a «#» sign). It may be an absolute URI or a relative URI reference; if it is relative, it is resolved against the base URI of the stylesheet. This is true even if the relative reference is contained in a node in a source document. In this situation it is a good idea to resolve the URI yourself before calling this function. For example, if the reference is in an attribute called src then the call might be «unparsed-text(resolve-uri(@src, base-uri(@src)))». The resolve-uri() function is described on page 867; its first argument is the relative reference, and the second argument is the base URI used to resolve it.

The optional encoding argument specifies the character encoding of the file. This can be any character encoding supported by the implementation; the only encodings that an implementation must support are UTF-8 and UTF-16. The system will not necessarily use this encoding: the rules for deciding an encoding are as follows and are based on the rules given in the XLink recommendation:

❏　First, the processor looks for so-called external encoding information. This typically means information supplied in an HTTP header, but the term is general and could apply to any metadata associated with the file, for example WebDAV properties.

❏　Next, it looks at the media type (MIME type), and if this identifies the file as XML, then it determines the encoding using the same rules as an XML parser (for example, it looks for an XML declaration, and if there is none, it looks for a byte order mark).

Why would you use this function, rather than doc()*, to access an XML document? The thinking is that it is quite common for one XML document to act as an envelope for another XML document that*

13

The Function Library

is carried transparently in a CDATA section, and if you want to create such a composite document, you will want to read the payload document without parsing it.

❑   Next, it uses the encoding argument if this has been supplied.

❑   If there is no encoding argument, the XSLT processor can use "implementation-defined heuristics" to guess the encoding; if that fails, then it tries to use UTF-8 encoding. The term "implementation-defined heuristics" could cover a wide range of strategies, such as recognizing known document types like HTML from the first few bytes of the file, or treating the file as Windows codepage 1252 if it cannot be decoded as UTF-8.

Various errors can occur in this process, and they are generally fatal. This is why the auxiliary function unparsed-text-available() is provided: if any failure is going to occur when reading the file, then calling unparsed-text-available() will in effect catch the error before it occurs.

One limitation is that it is not possible to process a file if it contains characters that are invalid in XML (this applies to most control characters in the range x00 to x1F under XML 1.0, but only to the null character x00 under XML 1.1).

Usage and Examples

There are a number of ways this function can be used, and I will show three. These are as follows:

❑   Up-conversion: that is, loading text that lacks markup in order to generate the XML markup

❑   XML envelope/payload applications

❑   HTML boilerplate generation

Up-Conversion

Up-conversion is the name often given to the process of analyzing input data for structure that is implicit in the textual content, and producing as output an XML document in which this structure is revealed by explicit markup. I have used this process, for example, to analyze HTML pages containing census data, in order to clean the data to make it suitable for adding to a structured genealogy database. It can also be used to process data that arrives in non-XML formats such as comma-separated values or EDI syntax.

The unparsed-text() function is not the only way of supplying non-XML data as input to a stylesheet; it can also be done simply by passing a string as the value of a stylesheet parameter. But the unparsed-text() function is particularly useful because the data is referenced by URI, and accessed under the control of the stylesheet.

XSLT 2.0 is much more suitable for use in up-conversion applications than XSLT 1.0. The most important tools are the <xsl:analyze-string> instruction, which enables the stylesheet to make use of structure that is implicit in the text, and the <xsl:for-each-group> instruction, which makes it much easier to analyze poorly structured markup. These can often be used in tandem: in the first stage in processing, <xsl:analyze-string> is used to recognize patterns in the text and mark these patterns using elements in a temporary tree, and in the second stage, <xsl:for-each-group> is used to turn flat markup structures into hierarchic structures that reflect the true data model.

Here is an example of a stylesheet that reads a comma-separated-values file and turns it into structured markup.

Example: Processing a Comma-Separated-Values File

This example is a stylesheet that reads a comma-separated-values file, given the URI of the file as a stylesheet parameter. It outputs an XML representation of this file, placing the rows in a `<row>` element and each value in a `<cell>` element. It does not attempt to process a header row containing field names, but this would be a simple extension.

Input

This stylesheet does not use any source XML document. Instead, it expects the URI of an ordinary text file to be supplied as a parameter to the stylesheet.

This is what the input file `names.csv` looks like.

```
123,"Mary Jones","IBM","USA",1997-05-14
423,"Barbara Smith","General Motors","USA",1996-03-12
6721,"Martin McDougall","British Airways","UK",2001-01-15
830,"Jonathan Perkins","Springer Verlag","Germany",2000-11-17
```

Stylesheet

This stylesheet `analyze-names.xsl` uses a named template `main` as its entry point: a new feature in XSLT 2.0.

The command for running the stylesheet under Saxon 9.0 looks like this.

```
java -jar saxon9.jar -it:main -xsl:analyze-names.xsl input-uri=names.csv
```

The `-it` option here indicates that processing should start without an XML source document, at the named template `main`.

The stylesheet first reads the input file using the `unparsed-text()` function, and then uses two levels of processing using `<xsl:analyze-string>` to identify the structure. The first level (using the regex «\n») splits the input into lines. The second level is explained more fully under the description of the `regex-group()` function on page 860: it extracts either the contents of a quoted string, or any value terminated by a comma, and copies this to a `<cell>` element.

```
<?xml version="1.0"?>
<xsl:stylesheet xmlns:xsl="http://www.w3.org/1999/XSL/Transform"
    xmlns:xs="http://www.w3.org/2001/XMLSchema"
    version="2.0">
<xsl:param name="input-uri" as="xs:string"/>
<xsl:output indent="yes"/>
<xsl:template name="main">
  <xsl:variable name="in"
              select="unparsed-text($input-uri, 'iso-8859-1')"/>
  <table>
  <xsl:analyze-string select="$in" regex="\n">
    <xsl:non-matching-substring>
```

13

The Function Library

907

```
        <row>
        <xsl:analyze-string select="." regex='("([^"]*?)")|([^,]+?),'>
          <xsl:matching-substring>
            <cell>
                <xsl:value-of select="regex-group(2)"/>
                <xsl:value-of select="regex-group(3)"/>
            </cell>
          </xsl:matching-substring>
        </xsl:analyze-string>
        </row>
      </xsl:non-matching-substring>
    </xsl:analyze-string>
    </table>
</xsl:template>
</xsl:stylesheet>
```

Output

The output is as follows:

```
<?xml version="1.0" encoding="UTF-8"?>
<table xmlns:xs="http://www.w3.org/2001/XMLSchema">
   <row>
      <cell>123</cell>
      <cell>Mary Jones</cell>
      <cell>IBM</cell>
      <cell>USA</cell>
   </row>
   <row>
      <cell>423</cell>
      <cell>Barbara Smith</cell>
      <cell>General Motors</cell>
      <cell>USA</cell>
   </row>
   <row>
      <cell>6721</cell>
      <cell>Martin McDougall</cell>
      <cell>British Airways</cell>
      <cell>UK</cell>
   </row>
   <row>
      <cell>830</cell>
      <cell>Jonathan Perkins</cell>
      <cell>Springer Verlag</cell>
      <cell>Germany</cell>
   </row>
</table>
```

XML Envelope/Payload Applications

It is not uncommon to find structures in which one XML document is wrapped in a CDATA section inside another. For example:

```
<envelope>
  <header>... </header>
  <payload>
     <![CDATA[<target-document>...</target-document>]]>
  </payload>
</envelope>
```

I don't normally recommend this as a good way of designing nested structures. In general, it is usually better to nest the structure directly, without using CDATA. That is, to use:

```
<envelope>
  <header>... </header>
  <payload>
     <target-document>...</target-document>
  </payload>
</envelope>
```

But sometimes you don't get to design the documents yourself; and there are some advantages for the CDATA approach, such as the ability for the payload document to include a DOCTYPE declaration.

Handling such structures in XSLT is not easy: the payload document is presented as a single text node, not as a tree of element nodes. However, the unparsed-text() function makes it much easier to output such structures. All you need to do is:

```
<xsl:output cdata-section-elements="payload"/>
<xsl:template match="/">
<envelope>
  <header>... </header>
  <payload>
     <xsl:value-of select="unparsed-text('payload.xml')"/>
  </payload>
</envelope>
```

HTML Boilerplate Generation

Generally, it is best to think of HTML in terms of a tree of element and text nodes, and to manipulate it as such in the stylesheet. Occasionally, you may need to process HTML that is not well formed, and cannot easily be converted into a well-formed structure. For example, you may be dealing with a syndicated news feed that arrives in HTML, whose format is sufficiently unpredictable that you don't want to rely on tools that automatically turn the HTML into structured XHTML. You might want to output the HTML news stories embedded in your own XSLT-generated pages.

An option in such cases is to treat the HTML as unparsed text rather than as a tree of nodes. You can read the HTML news feed using the unparsed-text() function, and you can output it to the serialized result, using the disable-output-escaping option, provided your processor supports this.

```
<xsl:value-of select="unparsed-text('news.html')"
               disable-output-escaping="yes"/>
```

Remember when you use `disable-output-escaping` that not all processors support the feature and that it works only if the output of the stylesheet is serialized. You can't always tell whether the output is going to be serialized or not; for example, if you run a transformation in Internet Explorer, the output HTML is serialized and then reparsed before being displayed, but if you run the same transformation in the Firefox browser, the result tree is passed directly to the rendering engine, bypassing the serialization stage. This means that `disable-output-escaping` doesn't work with a client-side transformation in Firefox.

See Also

`<xsl:analyze-string>` on page 230 in Chapter 6

upper-case

The `upper-case()` function converts lower-case characters in a string to upper case.

Signature

Argument	Type	Meaning
value	xs:string?	The string to be converted
Result	xs:string	*The string with lower-case letters converted to upper case*

Effect

See the entry for `lower-case()` on page 827 for a description of how this function is defined in terms of Unicode case mappings.

The effect of the function is as follows:

❑ If the input is an empty sequence, the result is the zero-length string.

❑ Otherwise, every character in the input string is replaced by its corresponding upper-case character (or sequence of characters) if there is one, or is included unchanged in the result string if not.

The function does not implement case mappings that Unicode defines as being locale-sensitive (such as the Turkish dotless I).

Examples

Expression	Result
upper-case("Sunday")	"SUNDAY"
upper-case("2+2")	"2+2"
upper-case("césar")	"CÉSAR"
upper-case("ελλας")	"ΕΛΛΑΣ"

Usage

See `lower-case()` on page 827

See Also

lower-case() on page 827
translate() on page 897

year-from-date, year-from-dateTime

These two functions extract the year component from an xs:date or xs:dateTime value. For example, «year-from-date(current-date())» might return 2008.

Signature

Argument	Type	Meaning
input	xs:date? or xs:dateTime?	The value from which the year component is to be extracted. The type of the supplied argument must correspond to the type implied by the function name. If an empty sequence is supplied, an empty sequence is returned.
Result	xs:integer	*The year. The range of values is implementation-defined; negative years (representing BC dates) are allowed.*

Effect

The function returns the year component of the supplied xs:date or xs:dateTime. The value is used in its local timezone (not normalized to UTC).

Examples

Expression	Result
year-from-date(xs:date("2008-02-28"))	2008
year-from-dateTime(xs:dateTime("1969-07-20T16:17:00-04:00"))	1969

See Also

current-date(), -dateTime(), -time() on page 738
format-date(), -dateTime(), -time() on page 781
day-from-date(), -dateTime() on page 744
month-from-date(), -dateTime() on page 833

years-from-duration

This function extracts the value of the years component from a normalized xs:duration value.

Signature

Argument	Type	Meaning
input	xs:duration	The value from which the component is to be extracted
Result	xs:integer	*The years component*

Effect

The function returns the years component of the supplied `xs:duration`. The duration value is first normalized so that the number of months is less than 12. The result will be negative if the duration is negative.

Examples

Expression	Result
`years-from-duration(xs:yearMonthDuration("P1200Y"))`	1200
`years-from-duration(xs:duration("P18M"))`	1
`years-from-duration(xs:duration("-P3Y6M"))`	-3
`years-from-duration(xs:dayTimeDuration('P8000D'))`	0

See Also

`months-from-duration` on page 834

zero-or-one

The `zero-or-one()` function returns its argument unchanged, provided that it is a sequence containing no more than one item. In other cases, it reports an error.

Signature

Argument	Type	Meaning
value	`item()*`	The input value. Although the function signature says that any sequence of items is allowed, a runtime error will occur if the number of items is not zero or one.
Result	`item()`	*The same as the supplied value, after checking to ensure that it is either an empty sequence or contains a single item.*

Effect

The `zero-or-one()` function returns its argument unchanged, provided that it is a sequence containing no more than one item. In other cases, it reports an error.

This function is useful with XPath processors that perform static type-checking, as described in Chapter 5. Calling this function acts as a promise by the programmer that the argument will be a sequence that is either empty, or contains exactly one item. This allows the expression to be used in contexts that require an optional single value (for example, the argument of a function such as `root()`) when the processor might otherwise have reported a static type error. The XPath expression is still type-safe, because the check that the sequence does indeed contain a single item will be done at runtime, just as it would with a processor that does not enforce static type checking.

Examples

Assume the source document:

```
<paint colors="red"/>
```

with a schema that defines the colors attribute with type xs:NMTOKENS (that is, it allows a list of colors to be specified, but our sample document only specifies one).

Expression	Result
string(@colors)	Succeeds unless the processor is doing static type checking, in which case it gives a compile-time error because the argument to string() must be a sequence of zero or one items
string(zero-or- one(@colors))	Succeeds whether the processor is doing static type checking or not, because the check that the typed value of @colors contains at most one item is deferred until runtime

Usage

This function is never needed unless you are using a processor that does static type checking.

However, you may still find it useful as a way of inserting runtime checks into your XPath expressions, and documenting the assumptions you are making about the input data.

See Also

exactly-one() on page 777
one-or-more() on page 853

Summary

Much of the power of any programming language comes from its function library, which is why this chapter explaining the function library is one of the longest in the book. The size of the function library has grown greatly since XSLT and XPath 1.0, largely because of the richer set of types supported.

The next chapter defines the syntax of the regular expressions accepted by the three functions matches(), replace(), and tokenize(), and by the XSLT instruction <xsl:analyze-string>.

13

The Function Library

14

Regular Expressions

This chapter defines the regular expression syntax accepted by the XPath functions `matches()`, `replace()`, and `tokenize()`, which were described in the previous chapter, as well as the `<xsl:analyze-string>` instruction described in Chapter 6.

This regular expression syntax is based on the definition in XML Schema, which in turn is based on the definition in the Perl language, which is generally taken as the definitive reference for regular expressions. However, all dialects of regular expression syntax have minor variations. Within Perl itself there are features that are deprecated, there are features that differ between Perl versions, and there are features that don't apply when all characters are Unicode.

XML Schema defines a subset of the Perl regular expression syntax; it chose this subset based on the requirements of a language that only does validation (that is, testing whether or not a string matches the pattern) and that only deals with Unicode strings. The requirements of the `matches()` function in XPath are similar, but XPath also uses regular expressions for tokenizing strings and for replacing substrings. These are more complex requirements, so some of Perl's regular expression constructs that XML Schema left out have been added back in for XPath.

In the grammar productions in this chapter, as elsewhere in the book, I generally enclose characters of the target language (that is, the regex language) in chevrons, for example «|». I have avoided using the more concise notation «[abcd]» because I think it is confusing to use regular expressions when defining regular expressions. If a character is not enclosed in chevrons, then it is either the name of another non-terminal symbol in the grammar, or a symbol that has a special meaning in the grammar.

The description of the syntax of regular expressions closely follows the description given in the XML Schema Recommendation. You can find this in Appendix F of Schema Part 2. The second edition corrects numerous errors in the original. The latest version of the Recommendation can be found at http://www.w3.org/TR/xmlschema-2.

Remember that the syntax rules given here apply to the regular expression after it has been preprocessed by the host language.

❑   If a regular expression is used within an XML document (for example, an XSLT stylesheet), then special characters such as «&» must be escaped using XML entity or character references such as «&». If it appears within an XSLT attribute value template (for example, in the regex attribute of `<xsl:analyze-string>`), then curly braces must be doubled. If it appears within an XPath string literal, then any apostrophe or quotation mark that matches the string delimiters must be doubled.

❑ On the other hand, if your XPath expression is written as a string literal within a host language such as Java or C#, then a backslash will need to be written as «\\» (which means that a regular expression to match a single backslash character becomes «\\\\»).

Branches and Pieces

The top-level syntax of a regular expression (regex) is described by the following rules:

Construct	Syntax
regex	branch («|» branch)*
branch	piece*
piece	atom quantifier?

A regular expression consists of one or more *branches*, separated by «\|» characters. For example, «abc\|def» matches either of the strings «abc» or «def». A regex matches a string if any of the branches matches the string. If more than one branch leads to a match, then the one that is chosen is the first one that matches (starting from the left).

A *branch* consists of one or more *pieces*, concatenated together. A branch consisting of two pieces A and B matches a string if the string can be split into two substrings, with the first substring matching A and the second matching B. For example, «def» is the concatenation of three pieces, «d», «e», and «f», and it matches a string consisting of a «d» followed by an «e» followed by an «f». The regex «[a-z][0-9]» consists of two pieces, «[a-z]» and «[0-9]», and it matches any string that consists of a letter in the range «[a-z]» followed by a digit in the range «[0-9]».

A *piece* is an *atom*, optionally followed by a *quantifier*. Quantifiers are described in the next section.

Unlike content models in XML Schema, there are no rules preventing ambiguities or backtracking in a regular expression. It is perfectly legal to have a regex with two branches that both match the same string, or to have two branches that start with the same characters, for example «abc\|abd».

Quantifiers

Quantifiers indicate whether, and how often, a construct may be repeated. The syntax is as follows:

Construct	Syntax
quantifier	indicator «?»?
indicator	«?» | «*» | «+» | («{» quantity «}»)
quantity	quantRange | quantMin | quantExact
quantRange	quantExact «,» quantExact
quantMin	quantExact «,»
quantExact	Digit+
Digit	«0»|«1»|«2»|«3»|«4»|«5»|«6»|«7»|«8»|«9»

A quantifier is either one of the symbols «?», «*», or «+», or a quantity enclosed between curly braces. A quantifier may be followed by «?» to indicate that it is a non-greedy quantifier.

A quantity is either a number, or a number followed by a comma, or two numbers separated by a comma: *number* here means a sequence of one or more digits.

The piece «A?» matches a single «A» or a zero-length string; «A*» matches a sequence of zero or more «A»s, while «A+» matches a sequence of one or more «A»s.

The piece «A{3}» matches a sequence of exactly three «A»s; «A{3,}» matches a sequence of three or more «A»s, and «A{3,5}» matches a sequence of at least three and at most five «A»s.

By default, quantifiers are greedy — they match as many occurrences of the relevant characters as they can, subject to the regex as a whole succeeding. For example, given the input string «17(c)(ii)», the regular expression «\(.*\)$» will match the substring «(c)(ii)». Adding a «?» after the quantifier makes it non-greedy, so the regex «\(.*?\)$» will match the substring «(c)». This doesn't affect the matches() function, which is only concerned with knowing whether or not there is a match, but it does affect replace() and tokenize(), and XSLT's <xsl:analyze-string>, which also need to know which particular characters matched the regex.

Atoms

Atoms are the parts of a regular expression that match specified characters. The various options are defined by the syntax below.

Construct	Syntax
atom	Char | charClass | backReference | («(» regex «)»)
Char	*Any XML character except* . \ ? * + | ^ $ { } ( ) [ ]
charClass	charClassEsc | charClassExpr | «.» | «^» | «$»
charClassExpr	«[» charGroup «]»
backReference	«\» [1-9] [0-9]*

An atom is either a *normal character*, a *character class*, a *back-reference*, or a regex enclosed in parentheses.

A *normal character* (Char) is any character except «.», «\», «?», «*», «+», «|», «^», «$», «{», «}», «(», «)», «[» and «]». A normal character matches itself, and if the «i» flag is used, it also matches upper- and lower-case variants of itself (for a more precise definition see *Flags* on page 925).

A *character class* (charClass) is either a *character class escape* or a *character class expression*, or one of the metacharacters «.», «^», or «$». We will see what a *character class escape* is later, on page 920.

The metacharacter «.» in a regex matches any single character except a newline character (x0A), except when the «s» (dot-all) flag is set, in which case it matches any character including a newline.

The metacharacters «^» and «$» match the beginning and end of the input string, respectively, except when the «m» (multiline) flag is set, in which case they match the beginning and end of each line.

The beginning of a line is either the start of the entire string or the position immediately after a newline (x0A) character; the end of a line is either the end of the entire string or the position immediately before a newline character. So (with multiline mode off) the regex «^The» matches a string that begins with the characters «The», while the regex «\.xml$» matches a string that ends with the characters «.xml».

A *character class expression* is a *character group* enclosed in square brackets, for example «[A-Z]». Character groups are described on page 919. A character group defines a set of permitted characters; it matches a single character from the input if the character is a member of this set.

Subexpressions

An atom written in the form of a regular expression within parentheses is referred to as a subexpression (or group). Subexpressions serve two main purposes:

❑   They allow a sequence of characters to be defined as repeated or optional. For example, the regex «([0-9],)*[0-9]» matches strings such as «1,2,3» or «8,0».

❑   They allow the application to determine which parts of the input string were matched by particular parts of the regular expression. For example, when the string «12 September 2008» is matched by the regex «([0-9]+)\s([A-Za-z]+)\s([0-9]+)», three groups are captured, corresponding to the three parenthesized subexpressions: group 1 is the string «12», group 2 is the string «September», and group 3 is the string «2008». Note that when a parenthesized subexpression has a quantifier, or when it is within an enclosing construct that allows repetition, it is the last matching substring that is accessible as the content of the corresponding group.

Subexpressions can be nested. They are numbered according to the position of the opening parenthesis, counting from the left. For example, when the string «12 September 2008» is matched by the regex «([0-9]+)\s(([A-Z])([a-z]+))\s([0-9]*)», group 2 will be «September», group 3 will be «S», and group 4 will be «eptember».

In the replace() function, groups can be referenced within the replacement string using a character sequence such as «$1» or «$2». For example, the result of «replace('12 September 2008', '([0-9]+)\s([A-Za-z]+)\s([0-9]+)', '$2 $1, $3')» will be «September 12, 2008».

Within the <xsl:analyze-string> instruction, the contents of matched groups of characters can be referenced using the regex-group() function, described on page 860 in Chapter 13.

Back-References

A back-reference can be used to refer to a captured group from within the regular expression itself. A back-reference is written as a backslash followed by a positive number. Back-references are often used to match opening and closing quotes; for example, the regex «(['"]).*\1» matches the strings «"Hello"» and «'Hello'» but not «"Hello'».

A single digit following a «\» is always recognized as part of the back-reference; subsequent digits are recognized as part of the back-reference only if there are sufficiently many parenthesized subexpressions earlier in the regex. For example, «\15» is recognized as a back-reference only if there are at least 15 parenthesized subexpressions preceding it in the regular expression; if this is not the case, then it is interpreted as a back-reference «\1» followed by the digit «5».

Character Groups

A *character group* always appears within square brackets; it defines a set of permitted characters, and matches a single character from the input string if it is a member of that set. There are various ways the set of permitted characters can be defined, using the following syntax:

Construct	Syntax
charGroup	posCharGroup | negCharGroup | charClassSub
posCharGroup	(charRange | charClassEsc)+
negCharGroup	«^» posCharGroup
charClassSub	(posCharGroup | negCharGroup) «-» charClassExpr

A character group is either a *positive group*, a *negative group*, or a *subtraction*. Examples of the three kinds are «[a-z]», «[^0-9]», and «[a-z-[pqr]]».

A *positive group* (posCharGroup) consists of a sequence of one or more parts, each of which is either a *character range* or a *character class escape*. A positive group matches a character if any one of its parts matches the character. For example, «[a-zA-Z0-9%#]» matches any character that falls in one of the ranges «a» to «z», «A» to «Z», or «0» to «9», as well as the «%» and «#» characters.

A *negative group* (negCharGroup) consists of a circumflex «^» followed by a *positive group*. A negative group matches any character that is not matched by the corresponding positive group. For example, the negative group «[^abc]» matches any character except «a», «b», or «c».

A *subtraction* (charClassSub) consists of either a positive group or a negative group, followed by the «-» symbol, followed by a character class expression (which, as we saw earlier, is a character group enclosed in square brackets). A subtraction matches any character that matches the group preceding the «-» operator, provided it does not also match the character class expression following the «-» operator. For example, «[0-9-[5]]» matches any digit except «5».

Character Ranges

A *character range* (which is always part of a *character group*) defines a set of permitted characters that contains either a single character or a range of characters occupying adjacent Unicode codepoints.

> *If you are comparing these rules with the ones in XML Schema Part 2, be sure to look at the second edition; the original XML Schema Recommendation got this syntax badly wrong. In fact, there are still a couple of errors in the second edition.*

Construct	Syntax
charRange	codepointRange | XmlCharIncDash
codepointRange	charOrEsc «-» charOrEsc
charOrEsc	XmlChar | SingleCharEsc
XmlChar	Any XML character except «[» «]» «\» «-»
XmlCharIncDash	Any XML character except «[» «]» «\»

A *character range* is either a *codepoint range* or a *single character* (XMLCharIncDash).

A *codepoint range*, for example, «a-z», consists of two characters, or *single character escapes*, separated by a «-» character. The Unicode codepoint for the second character must be greater than or equal to the codepoint for the first. Specifying a codepoint range is equivalent to listing all the Unicode characters with codepoints in that range, for example «[0-9]» is equivalent to «[0123456789]».

A *single character* is any character permitted by the XML specification, other than the three characters listed: «[», «]», and «\». There is an additional rule not shown in the grammar: if «^» appears at the start of a character group, then it is taken to indicate that the group is a negative character group. This means that it can't appear at the start of a positive character group, except in the case where the positive character group is part of a negative character group. (You can't have a double negative, so «[^^]» matches any character except a circumflex.)

> *There has been a lot of confusion about whether and where hyphens are allowed within square brackets, other than their two special meanings to indicate a codepoint range such as* [0-9] *and a subtraction such as* [A-Z-[IO]]. *At one stage an erratum was issued making any usage such as* [+-] *invalid, but this was subsequently withdrawn. In the second edition of XML Schema Part 2, the grammar and the textual narrative are inconsistent. If you want to be safe, escape any hyphen that is intended to represent the hyphen character itself, for example* [+\-].

Single character escapes are described in the following section.

Character Class Escapes

The next table describes various constructs introduced with a backslash («\»). These constructs are known collectively as *character class escapes* (charClassEsc); each character class escape defines a subset of the Unicode character set, and it can appear either at the top level of a regular expression (as an atom), or within square brackets. Within this category, a *single character escape* (SingleCharEsc) represents a single Unicode character; these can also appear as the start or end of a character range, as we saw in the previous section.

Construct	Syntax
charClassEsc	SingleCharEsc | MultiCharEsc | catEsc | complEsc
SingleCharEsc	«\» («n» | «r» | «t» | «\» | «|» | «.» | «?» | «*» | «+» | «(» | «)» | «{» | «}» | «-» | «[» | «]» | «^» | «$»)
MultiCharEsc	«\» («s» | «S» | «i» | «I» | «c» | «C» | «d» | «D» | «w» | «W»)
catEsc	«\p {» charProp «}»
complEsc	«\P {» charProp «}»
charProp	Category | IsBlock
Category	One of the two-character codes listed in the section *Character Categories* on page 924
IsBlock	«Is» BlockName
	where BlockName is the name of one of the Unicode code blocks listed in the section Character Blocks on page 922

A *character class escape* defines a set of characters, and matches any single character from this set.

There are four kinds of character class escapes: *single character escapes, multicharacter escapes, category escapes,* and *complementary escapes.*

The published XPath Functions and Operators Recommendation defines a back-reference as a fifth kind of character class escape. This is incorrect, because a back-reference matches a sequence of characters rather than a single character, which means that it makes no sense within square brackets. This is fixed by an erratum to the spec.

A *single character escape* (SingleCharEsc) consists of a backslash followed by one of the characters shown below. The single character escape matches a single character, as shown in the table.

Single character escape	Matches
«\n»	newline (x0A)
«\r»	carriage return (x0D)
«\t»	tab (x09)
«\\» «|» «\.» «\?» «*» «\+» «\(» «\)» «\{» «\}» «\-» «\[» «\]» «\^» «\$»	The character following the backslash, for example, «\?» matches a question mark

A *multicharacter escape* (MultiCharEsc) is a «\» followed by one of the characters shown below. Each multicharacter escape matches one of a number of different characters (but it only matches one character at a time).

Multicharacter escape	Matches
«\s»	space (x20), tab (x09), newline (x0A), or carriage return (x0D)
«\i»	An initial name character: specifically, a character classified in the XML specification as a Letter, or «:» or «_»
«\c»	A name character, as defined by the NameChar production in the XML specification
«\d»	A decimal digit: anything that matches «\p{Nd}»
«\w»	A character considered to form part of a word, as distinct from a separator between words: specifically a character that does not match «\p{P}» or «\p{Z}» or «\p{C}»
«\S»	Any character that does not match «\s»
«\I»	Any character that does not match «\i»
«\C»	Any character that does not match «\c»
«\D»	Any character that does not match «\d»
«\W»	Any character that does not match «\w»

The two constructs «\i» and «\c» are defined by reference to the XML specification. The definitions in question have changed slightly between XML 1.0 and XML 1.1. The XPath specification leaves it to the implementor to decide whether to use the XML 1.0 or XML 1.1 definitions. Some products (Saxon is an example) might give you the choice, as a configuration option.

14

Regular Expressions

A *category escape* «\p{prop}» matches any character with the property *prop*, as defined in the Unicode character database. A *complementary escape* «\P{prop}» matches any character that does not have the property *prop*. The *prop* may either represent the block of characters being matched or a character category. The next two sections define the character blocks and categories.

Character Blocks

Character blocks are simply names for ranges of characters in Unicode. For example, «\p{IsHebrew}» matches any character in the range x0590 to x05FF, while «\P{IsHebrew}» matches any character that is not in this range.

The names of the blocks are listed in the table below. The name of the block is preceded by «Is» in the regular expression, which then matches any character in the block. Note that some of the blocks (such as PrivateUse) map to several ranges of codes.

Range	Name	Range	Name
x0000-x007F	BasicLatin	x0D00-x0D7F	Malayalam
x0080-x00FF	Latin-1Supplement	x0D80-x0DFF	Sinhala
x0100-x017F	LatinExtended-A	x0E00-x0E7F	Thai
x0180-x024F	LatinExtended-B	x0E80-x0EFF	Lao
x0250-x02AF	IPAExtensions	x0F00-x0FFF	Tibetan
x02B0-x02FF	SpacingModifierLetters	x1000-x109F	Myanmar
x0300-x036F	CombiningDiacriticalMarks	x10A0-x10FF	Georgian
x0370-x03FF	Greek	x1100-x11FF	HangulJamo
x0400-x04FF	Cyrillic	x1200-x137F	Ethiopic
x0530-x058F	Armenian	x13A0-x13FF	Cherokee
x0590-x05FF	Hebrew	x1400-x167F	UnifiedCanadianAboriginal-Syllabics
x0600-x06FF	Arabic	x1680-x169F	Ogham
x0700-x074F	Syriac	x16A0-x16FF	Runic
x0780-x07BF	Thaana	x1780-x17FF	Khmer
x0900-x097F	Devanagari	x1800-x18AF	Mongolian
x0980-x09FF	Bengali	x1E00-x1EFF	LatinExtendedAdditional
x0A00-x0A7F	Gurmukhi	x1F00-x1FFF	GreekExtended
x0A80-x0AFF	Gujarati	x2000-x206F	GeneralPunctuation
x0B00-x0B7F	Oriya	x2070-x209F	SuperscriptsandSubscripts
x0B80-x0BFF	Tamil	x20A0-x20CF	CurrencySymbols
x0C00-x0C7F	Telugu	x20D0-x20FF	CombiningMarksforSymbols
x0C80-x0CFF	Kannada	x2100-x214F	LetterlikeSymbols

continued

Range	Name	Range	Name
x2150-x218F	NumberForms	x3190-x319F	Kanbun
x2190-x21FF	Arrows	x31A0-x31BF	BopomofoExtended
x2200-x22FF	MathematicalOperators	x3200-x32FF	EnclosedCJKLettersand-Months
x2300-x23FF	MiscellaneousTechnical	x3300-x33FF	CJKCompatibility
x2400-x243F	ControlPictures	x3400-x4 DB5	CJKUnifiedIdeographs-ExtensionA
x2440-x245F	OpticalCharacterRecognition	x4E00-x9FFF	CJKUnifiedIdeographs
x2460-x24FF	EnclosedAlphanumerics	xA000-xA48F	YiSyllables
x2500-x257F	BoxDrawing	xA490-xA4CF	YiRadicals
x2580-x259F	BlockElements	xAC00-xD7A3	HangulSyllables
x25A0-x25FF	GeometricShapes	xE000-xF8FF	PrivateUse
x2600-x26FF	MiscellaneousSymbols	xF900-xFAFF	CJKCompatibilityIdeographs
x2700-x27BF	Dingbats	xFB00-xFB4F	AlphabeticPresentationForms
x2800-x28FF	BraillePatterns	xFB50-xFDFF	ArabicPresentationForms-A
x2E80-x2EFF	CJKRadicalsSupplement	xFE20-xFE2F	CombiningHalfMarks
x2F00-x2FDF	KangxiRadicals	xFE30-xFE4F	CJKCompatibilityForms
x2FF0-x2FFF	IdeographicDescription-Characters	xFE50-xFE6F	SmallFormVariants
x3000-x303F	CJKSymbolsandPunctuation	xFE70-xFEFE	ArabicPresentationForms-B
x3040-x309F	Hiragana	xFEFF-xFEFF	Specials
x30A0-x30FF	Katakana	xFF00-xFFEF	HalfwidthandFullwidthForms
x3100-x312F	Bopomofo	xFFF0-xFFFD	Specials
x3130-x318F	HangulCompatibilityJamo		

The list above corresponds to XML Schema 1.0 second edition. This removed some blocks that were defined in the first edition, notably for characters above xFFFF. XML Schema 1.1 reinstates most of these, sometimes under slightly different names, and also adds additional blocks corresponding to characters in more recent versions of Unicode. The blocks listed in the table should be supported by all XSLT 2.0 and XPath 2.0 processors; other blocks (such as x1D100-x1D1FF, MusicalSymbols) may be supported in some processors and not in others.

14

Regular Expressions

Character Categories

Characters in the Unicode character database are assigned to a category and subcategory. For example, category «L» denotes letters, and within this «Lu» denotes upper-case letters. Within a regular expression, «\p{L}» matches any letter, and «\p{Lu}» matches any upper-case letter. The complementary sets can also be selected: «\P{L}» matches any character that is not a letter, and «\P{Lu}» matches any character that is not an upper-case letter.

The list of categories, with a few examples of characters found in each, is listed in the table below.

Category	Description	Examples
L	**Letters**	
Lu	Upper case	A, B, Φ, Φ
Ll	Lower case	a, b, ö, λ
Lt	Title case	Dz (x01C5)
Lm	Modifier	Arabic TATWEEL (x0640)
Lo	Other	Hebrew ALEF (x05D0)
M	**Marks**	
Mn	Non-spacing	Combining acute accent (x0301)
Mc	Spacing	Gujarati vowel sign AA (x0ABE)
Me	Enclosing	Combining enclosing circle (x20DD)
N	**Numbers**	
Nd	Decimal digits	1, 2, 3, 4, ١, ٢, ٣, ٤
Nl	Numeric letters	Roman numeral ten thousand (x2182)
No	Other	Superscript ^{2} ^{3} (x00B2, x00B3)
P	**Punctuation**	
Pc	Connector	_ (x005F)
Pd	Dash	em dash (x2014)
Ps	Open	([{
Pe	Close	)]}
Pi	Initial quote	« (x00AB)
Pf	Final quote	» (x00BB)
Po	Other	! ? ¿(x00BF)
Z	**Separators**	
Zs	Space	space (x0020), non-breaking space (x00A0)
Zl	Line	line separator (x2028)

continued

Category	Description	Examples
Zp	Paragraph	paragraph separator (x2029)
S	**Symbols**	
Sm	Mathematical	+<=>| ~ ¬ ±
Sc	Currency	$ ¢ £ ¥ €
Sk	Modifier	acute accent « ´ », cedilla « ¸ »
So	Other	¦ § © °
C	**Others**	
Cc	Control	tab (x0009), newline (X000A)
Cf	Format	soft hyphen (x00AD)
Co	Private use	
Cn	Not assigned	

Flags

The effect of a regular expression can be modified by setting one or more flags. These are supplied in a separate argument of the XPath function matches(), replace(), or tokenize(), or in a separate attribute of the XSLT instruction <xsl:analyze-string>. The flags are expressed as a string containing one or more of the four characters «i», «m», «s», and «x» (they can be written in any order, and no harm is done if a character is repeated). This section explains the meanings of the flags.

The «i» flag

This flag causes the regular expression to use case-insensitive mode. In this mode, a letter used in the regular expression matches characters in the input string regardless of their case; for example, the regex «Monday» matches the strings «Monday» or «monday» or «MONDAY». Without this flag, characters must match exactly. Note that collations are not used for regex comparisons.

Case-insensitive mode affects constructs in the regular expression as follows:

❑ When a character is used as an atom it represents that character and all its case variants. For example, the regex «abc» matches «abc» or «ABC» or «Abc», among others.

❑ When a character is used as an XmlCharIncDash within square brackets, it represents that character and all its case variants. For example, the regex «[ab]» matches «a», «A», «b», or «B». This applies even if the character appears as part of a negative character group or a subtraction; for example, «[^ab]» matches any character except «a», «A», «b», or «B», while [A-Z-[IO]] matches any upper- or lower-case ASCII alphabetic character except «i», «I», «o», or «O».

❑ When a character range is used, the expression matches the characters in the range together with their case variants. For example, «[P-U]» has the same effect as «[PQRSTU]»: it matches all characters that are case variants of any of these six letters. As it happens, this includes the six letters «pqrstu» together with «ſ» (x017F, *long S*, an archaic form of the letter «s»).

❑ Back-references are matched using case-blind comparison; for example, «([A-Z]).*\1» matches «Ohio» and «Atlanta» as well as «OHIO», «ohio», «ATLANTA», and «atlanta».

In most cases it's fairly obvious what counts as a *case variant* of a character. Officially it's defined in terms of the `upper-case()` and `lower-case()` functions described in Chapter 13: `$C` is a case variant of `$D` if `upper-case($C)` equals `upper-case($D)`, or `lower-case($C)` equals `lower-case($D)`, or both. Occasionally, this gives slightly unexpected results; for example, the letter «I» has four case variants: «I», «i», «İ», and «ı». This oddity arises because some languages (English) drop the dot over the «i» when translating from lower case to upper case, whereas other languages (Turkish) keep it.

The «i» flag does not affect constructs other than those listed above. For example, it does not affect the meaning of «\p{Lu}», which matches upper-case letters only, whether or not the flag is set.

The «m» flag

The «m» flag switches on multiline mode. In the default mode (called string mode) the meta-characters «^» and «$» match the beginning and end of the input string. In multiline mode, the input string is treated as a sequence of individual lines separated by a newline (x0A) character. The meta-characters «^» and «$» then match the beginning and end of any line.

The spec, as published, isn't clear as to what happens when the last character of the string is a newline character. An erratum has been issued to make XPath behave in the same way as other languages that support multiline mode: there is no zero-length line at the end.

The «s» flag

The «s» flag switches on dot-all mode. By default, the meta-character «.» in a regular expression matches any character in the input except a newline (x0A) character. In dot-all mode, «.» matches any character, including a newline.

The «x» flag

The «x» flag causes whitespace in the regular expression to be ignored, except within square brackets. By default, whitespace characters in a regular expression represent themselves, for example, the regex «*» matches a sequence of zero or more spaces. If the «x» flag is set, whitespace in the regex is ignored and can be used to make the layout more readable. Whitespace characters can always be matched using character escapes such as «\s» and «\n».

In some other regular expression languages (for example, Perl), the «x» flag also allows comments to be included in a regular expression, starting with «#» and ending with a newline. This feature wasn't included in the XPath dialect because newline is an inappropriate choice of delimiter, given that XML parsers are expected to replace newlines with spaces when processing an attribute value. If you want to include a comment in a regular expression within an XSLT stylesheet, use XML comments:

```
<xsl:variable name="date-regex" as="xs:string">
  ([0-9]+)      <!-- day number: one or more digits (group 1)-->
  \s+           <!-- whitespace -->
  ([A-Za-z]+)   <!-- month name (group 2) -->
  \s+           <!-- whitespace -->
  ([0-9]{4})    <!-- year number: exactly four digits (group 3) -->
</xsl:variable>
<xsl:analyze-string select="date" regex="{$date-regex}" flags="x">
   ...
</xsl:analyze-string>
```

Perl treats an escaped space (a space preceded by a backslash) as a significant space, despite the presence of this flag. The XPath rules don't follow this precedent — spaces are ignored even if preceded by a backslash.

Disallowed Constructs

Finally, here are some examples of constructs that might be familiar from other regular expression dialects that have not been included in the XPath 2.0 definition. A conformant XPath 2.0 processor is expected to reject any attempt to use constructs that aren't allowed by the grammar presented in this chapter. A few of these constructs are shown in the following table.

Disallowed Construct	Meaning in other languages
[a-z&&[^oi]]	Intersection: any character in the range «a» to «z», except for «o» and «i»
[a-z[A-Z]]	Union: same as «[a-zA-Z]»
\0nn, \xnn, \unnnn	Character identified by Unicode codepoint in octal or hexadecimal
\a, \e, \f, \cN	Various control characters not allowed in XML 1.0
\p{Alpha}, \P{Alpha}	Character classes defined in POSIX
\b, \B	Word boundary
\A, \Z, \z	Beginning and end of input string
\g, \G	End of the previous match
X*+	Non-backtracking or possessive quantifiers (in Java, these force the matching engine down this path even if this results in the match as a whole failing)
(?...)	Expressions that set various special options; non-capturing subexpressions; comments

Summary

This chapter provided a rather technical definition of the regular expression syntax provided for use in the XPath functions `matches()`, `replace()`, and `tokenize()`, and in the XSLT `<xsl:analyze-string>` instruction.

Having given this very detailed definition of the regex grammar, it's worth including a warning that some processors may cut corners by exposing whatever regex dialect is supported by their existing libraries. Microsoft's XML Schema processor, for example, uses the .NET regex dialect rather than the one defined by W3C.

Caveat emptor!

14

Regular Expressions

15

Serialization

Serialization in an XSLT context means the process of taking a result tree (the output of a transformation) and converting it into lexical XML, usually as a file in filestore. XSLT also allows serialization into other formats, including HTML and text files.

As mentioned in Chapter 2, although serialization is not part of the core function of an XSLT processor, the language provides constructs such as `<xsl:output>` that enable you to control the process from within a stylesheet. Many products may also allow you to invoke the serializer as a separate component. With XSLT 2.0, the specification of serialization has been moved into a separate W3C Recommendation, to allow reuse of the facilities from within other XML processing languages such as XQuery and XProc. You can find the W3C specification at `http://www.w3.org/TR/xslt-xquery-serialization/`.

Serialization is controlled by a set of parameters, each of which has a name and a value. The most important parameter is «method», which takes one of the values «xml», «html», «xhtml», or «text». This determines which serialization method is used (user-defined or vendor-defined serialization methods are also allowed, but are outside the scope of this book). When serialization is invoked from XSLT, the serialization parameters are generally controlled using the attributes of the `<xsl:output>` or `<xsl:result-document>` instructions described in Chapter 6. It is often possible, however, to set further parameters from the invoking application, or as options on the command line.

In this chapter, we will start by examining each of the four output methods in turn: XML, HTML, XHTML, and TEXT. Then we'll look at other serialization capabilities in the XSLT specification, notably character maps and `disable-output-escaping`.

Details of the syntax of elements such as `<xsl:output>`, `<xsl:result-document>`, and `<xsl:character-map>` are found in the appropriate alphabetical sections in Chapter 6.

The XML Output Method

When the output method is «xml», the output file will usually be a well-formed XML document, but the actual requirement is that it should be either a well-formed XML external general parsed entity or a well-formed XML document entity, or both.

An external general parsed entity is something that could be incorporated into an XML document by using an entity reference such as «&doc;». The following example shows a well-formed external general parsed entity that is not a well-formed document:

```
A <b>bold</b> and <emph>emphatic</emph> statement
```

An example of a well-formed document that is not a well-formed external general parsed entity (because it contains a standalone attribute) is:

```
<?xml version="1.0" encoding="utf-8" standalone="yes"?>
<p>A <b><bold></b> and <emph>emphatic</emph> statement</p>
```

The rules for document entities and external general parsed entities overlap, as shown in Figure 15-1.

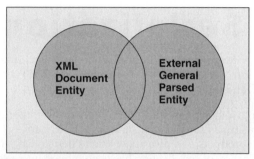

Figure 15-1

Essentially, an XSLT stylesheet can output anything that fits in either of the two shaded circles, which means anything that is a well-formed XML document entity, a well-formed external general parsed entity, or both.

Well, almost anything:

❑ It must also conform to the XML Namespaces Recommendation.

❑ There is no explicit provision for generating an internal DTD subset, although it can be achieved, with difficulty, by using character maps.

❑ Similarly, there is no explicit provision for generating entity references, though this can also be achieved by means of character maps.

In the XML standard, the rules for an external parsed entity are given as:

```
extParsedEnt ⇨  TextDecl? content
```

where content is a sequence of components including child elements, character data, entity references, CDATA sections, processing instructions, and comments, each of which may appear any number of times and in any order.

The corresponding rule for a document entity is effectively:

```
document ⇨  XMLDecl? Misc* doctypedecl? Misc* element Misc*
```

where Misc permits whitespace, comments, and processing instructions.

So the principal differences between the two cases are:

❏ A `TextDecl` (text declaration) is not quite the same thing as an `XMLDecl` (XML declaration), as discussed below.

❏ A document may contain a `doctypedecl` (document type declaration), but an external parsed entity must not. A document type declaration is the `<!DOCTYPE ...>` header identifying the DTD and possibly including an internal DTD subset.

❏ The body of a document is an `element`, while the body of an external parsed entity is `content`. Here `content` is effectively the contents of an element but without the start and end tags.

❏ In a document, any whitespace that immediately follows the XML declaration is insignificant. In an external general parsed entity, however, such whitespace is significant. This means that the serializer cannot add whitespace here unless it is explicitly requested.

The `TextDecl` (text declaration) looks at first sight very much like an XML declaration; for example, `<?xml version="1.0" encoding="utf-8"s?>` could be used either as an XML declaration or as a text declaration. There are differences, however:

❏ In an XML declaration, the `version` attribute is mandatory, but in a text declaration it is optional.

❏ In an XML declaration, the `encoding` attribute is optional, but in a text declaration it is mandatory.

❏ An XML declaration may include a `standalone` attribute, but a text declaration must not.

So the following are all examples of well-formed external general parsed entities:

```
1: <quote>Hello!</quote>
2: <quote>Hello!</quote><quote>Goodbye!</quote>
3: Hello!
4: <?xml version="1.0" encoding="utf-8"?>Hello!
```

The following is a well-formed XML document, but it is *not* a well-formed external general parsed entity, because of both the `standalone` attribute and the document type declaration. This is also legitimate output:

```
<?xml version="1.0" encoding="utf-8" standalone="no"?>
<!DOCTYPE quote SYSTEM "hello.dtd">
<quote>Hello!</quote>
```

The following is neither a well-formed XML document nor a well-formed external general parsed entity.

```
<?xml version="1.0" encoding="utf-8" standalone="no"?>
<!DOCTYPE quote SYSTEM "hello.dtd">
<quote>Hello!</quote>
<quote>Goodbye!</quote>
```

It cannot be an XML document because it has more than one top-level element, and it cannot be an external general parsed entity because it has a `<!DOCTYPE>` declaration. A stylesheet attempting to produce this output is in error. The XSLT specification also places two other constraints on the form of the output, although these are rules for the implementor to follow rather than rules that directly affect the stylesheet author. These rules are:

❏ The output must conform to the rules of the XML Namespaces Recommendation. If the output is XML 1.0, then it must conform to XML Namespaces 1.0, and if it is XML 1.1, then it must conform to XML Namespaces 1.1.

If the output is an XML document, the meaning of this is clear enough, but if it is merely an external entity, some further explanation is needed. The standard provides this by saying that when the entity is pulled into a document by adding an element tag around its content, the resulting document must conform with the XML Namespaces rules.

❏ The output file must faithfully reflect the result tree. This requirement is easy to state informally, but the specification includes a more formal statement of the requirement, which is surprisingly complex.

The rule is expressed by describing what may change when the data model is serialized to XML and then parsed again to create a new data model. Things that may change include the order of attributes and namespace nodes and the base URI. If the parsing stage does DTD or schema validation, then this may cause new attribute or element values to appear, as specified by the DTD or schema. Perhaps the most significant change is that type annotations on element and attribute nodes will not be preserved. Any type annotations in the data model after such a round trip will be based on revalidation of the textual XML document; the type annotations in the original result tree are lost during serialization.

Serialization never adds attributes such as `xml:base` or `xsi:type`. If you want these present in the output, you must put them in the result tree, just like any other attribute.

Between XSLT 1.0 and XSLT 2.0, there is a change in the way the rules concerning namespace declarations are described. In XSLT 1.0, it was the job of the serializer to generate namespace declarations, not only for namespace nodes explicitly present on the result tree, but also for any namespaces used in the result document, but not represented by namespace nodes. This situation can happen because there is nothing in the rules for `<xsl:element>` and `<xsl:attribute>`, for example, that requires namespace nodes to be created for the namespace URI used in the names of these nodes. In XSLT 2.0, however, the specification describes a process called namespace fixup, which ensures that an element in a result tree always has a namespace node for every namespace that is used either in the element name or in the name of any of its attributes. This means that it is no longer the responsibility of the serializer to create these namespace declarations. The reason for this change is that with XSLT 2.0, the content of temporary trees (including their namespace nodes) becomes visible to the stylesheet, and the namespace nodes need to be present in the tree to make it usable for further processing. Namespace fixup is described in Chapter 6 under `<xsl:element>` on page 306.

Although the output is required to be well-formed XML, it is not the job of the serializer to ensure that the XML is valid against either a DTD or a schema. Just because you generate a document type declaration that refers to a specific DTD, or a reference to a schema, don't expect the XSLT processor to check that the output document actually conforms to that DTD or schema. Instead, XSLT 2.0 provides facilities to validate the result tree against a schema before it is serialized, by using the `validation` or `type` attribute on `<xsl:result-document>`.

With the «xml» output method, the other attributes of `<xsl:output>` or `<xsl:result-document>` are interpreted as follows. Attributes that are not applicable to this output method are not included in the table, and they are ignored if you specify them.

The W3C serialization specification speaks of `doctype-system`, `doctype-public` and so on as serialization parameters. This is because the specification is designed to be used independently of XSLT, and therefore abstracts away from the actual XSLT syntax used. In this book we're concerned with how to control serialization from XSLT, so we'll refer to these things as attributes, which is how they appear in XSLT's concrete syntax.

Attribute	Interpretation
cdata-section-elements	This is a list of element names, each expressed as a lexical QName, separated by whitespace. Any prefix in a QName is treated as a reference to the corresponding namespace URI in the normal way, using the namespace declarations in effect on the actual `<xsl:output>` or `<xsl:result-document>` element where the `cdata-section-elements` attribute appears. Because these are element names, the default namespace is assumed where the name has no prefix. When a text node is output, if the parent element of the text node is identified by a name in this list, then the text node is output as a CDATA section. For example, the text value «James» is output as «`<![CDATA[James]]>`», and the text value «AT&T» is output as «`<![CDATA[AT&T]]>`». Otherwise, this value would probably be output as «`AT&amp;T`». The XSLT processor is free to choose other equivalent representations if it wishes, for example a character reference, but the standard says that it should not use CDATA unless it is explicitly requested. The CDATA section may be split into parts if necessary, perhaps when the terminator sequence «`]]>`» appears in the data, or when there is a character that can only be output using a character reference because it is not supported directly in the chosen encoding.
doctype-system	If this attribute is specified, the output file will include a document type declaration (that is, `<!DOCTYPE>`) after the XML declaration and before the first element start tag. The name of the document type will be the same as the name of the first element. The value of this attribute will be used as the system identifier in the document type declaration. This attribute should not be used unless the output is a well-formed XML document.
doctype-public	This attribute is ignored unless the `doctype-system` attribute is also specified. It defines the value of the public identifier to go in the document type declaration. If no public identifier is specified, none is included in the document type declaration.
encoding	This specifies the preferred character encoding for the output document. All XSLT processors are required to support the values «UTF-8» and «UTF-16» (which are also the only values that XML parsers are required to support). This encoding name will be used in the encoding attribute of the XML or Text declaration at the start of the output file, and all characters in the file will be encoded using these conventions. The standard encoding names are not case-sensitive. If the encoding is one that does not allow all XML characters to be represented directly, for example «iso-8859-1», then characters outside this subset will be represented where possible using XML character references (such as «`&#x20A4;`»). It is an error if such characters appear in contexts where character references are not recognized (for example within a processing instruction or comment, or in an element or attribute name). If the result tree is serialized to a destination that expects a stream of Unicode characters rather than a stream of bytes, then the `encoding` attribute is ignored. This happens, for example, if you send the output to a Java `Writer`. It often causes confusion when you use the `transformNode()` method in Microsoft's MSXML API, which returns the serialized result of the transformation as a string: This is a value of type `BSTR`, which is encoded in UTF-16 regardless of the encoding you requested in the stylesheet.

15

Serialization

continued

Attribute	Interpretation
indent	If this attribute has the value «yes», the idea is that the XML output should be indented to show its hierarchic structure. The XSLT processor is not obliged to respect this request, and if it does so, the precise form of the output is not defined. There are some constraints on how indentation should be achieved. In effect, it can only be done by adding whitespace-only text nodes to the tree, and these cannot be added adjacent to an existing non-whitespace text node. XSLT 2.0 has introduced a rule that the added text node must be adjacent to an element node, that is, immediately before a start tag or after an end tag (in 1.0, it could be added as a child of an empty element). Note that even with these restrictions, adding whitespace nodes to the output may affect the way the recipient interprets it. This is particularly true with mixed content models, where an element can have both elements and text nodes as its children. The serializer is not allowed to add whitespace text nodes to the content of an element that has the attribute «xml:space="preserve"», and the spec advises against adding whitespace to an element that is known to have mixed content.
media-type	This parameter defines the media type of the output file (often referred to as its MIME type). The default value is «text/xml». The specification doesn't say what use is made of this information: it doesn't affect the contents of the output file, but it may affect the way it is named, stored, or transmitted, depending on the environment. For example, the information might find its way into an HTTP protocol header.
normalization-form	One of the controversial features of Unicode has always been that it allows the same character to be represented in more than one way. For example, the letter «ç» (lower-case «c» with cedilla) can be represented either as a single character (with codepoint xE7), or as the two codepoints: «c» (x63) and «,» (xB8). This fact causes considerable problems for software that performs comparison, search, and indexing operations on Unicode text. There have been long debates about whether XML should require such characters to be normalized (that is, to require one of these representations and disallow the other). The result of the debate is a compromise: XML 1.1 strongly encourages the use of normalized encodings. It encourages applications to output normalized text, and encourages parsers to provide an option that checks for normalized text, but it does not go so far as to say that non-normalized documents are not well formed. XSLT 2.0 responds to this by providing an option to serialize the document in Unicode-normalized form. Specify «NFC» for composed normal form, «NFD» for decomposed normal form, any other supported normalization form, or «none» (the default) for no normalization. An alternative approach is to make sure that individual text nodes, attribute nodes, and so on are already normalized in the result tree. You can do this by calling the normalize-unicode() function, described in Chapter 13, whenever you construct a character string that might not already be normalized.

continued

Attribute	Interpretation
omit-xml-declaration	If this attribute has the value «yes», the serializer will not output an XML declaration (or, by implication, a text declaration; recall that XML declarations are used at the start of the document entity, and text declarations are used at the start of an external general parsed entity). If the attribute is omitted, or has the value «no», then a declaration will be output. The declaration will include both the `version` and `encoding` attributes (to ensure that it is valid both as an XML declaration and as a text declaration). It will include a `standalone` attribute only if `standalone` is set to «yes» or «no». If you select an encoding such as «iso-8859-1» and omit the XML declaration, the output may be unintelligible to an XML parser. Nevertheless, the specification allows you to omit it, because there are sometimes alternative ways for an XML parser to determine the encoding. (Also, you might want to serialize several chunks of XML separately and then combine them using a text editor.)
standalone	If this attribute is set to «yes», then the XML declaration will specify «standalone="yes"». If it is set to «no», then the XML declaration will specify «standalone="no"». If the attribute is omitted, or is set to the value «omit», then the XML declaration will not include a `standalone` attribute. This will make it a valid text declaration, enabling its use in an external general parsed entity. This attribute should not be used unless the output is a well-formed XML document.
undeclare-prefixes	This attribute only comes into effect when you specify «version="1.1"». XML Namespaces 1.1 introduces the ability to *undeclare* a namespace. It's always been possible to undeclare the default namespace, using the syntax «xmlns=""», but now you can also undeclare a namespace with a specific prefix, using the syntax «xmlns:pfx=""». The result tree created by an XSLT 2.0 processor may have a namespace that is in scope for a particular element, but not in scope for its children. This is most likely to happen if you create the element using the option «inherit-namespaces="no"». The strict way to serialize such a tree is to generate namespace undeclarations on the child elements. However, the serializer does not do this by default, because these undeclarations may cause a lot of unwanted clutter in the output document. Instead, you have to request them explicitly by setting this attribute to «yes».
use-character-maps	The value of this attribute is a list of character map names; these character maps must be defined in the stylesheet. The serializer will use the named character maps to translate specific characters into the strings given in the character map. For further details, see page 941.
version	This attribute indicates the version of XML to be used in the output document. This can be «1.0» or «1.1». The XSLT specification requires only one of these versions to be supported: The thinking was that early in the life of XSLT 2.0, many implementations would only support XML 1.0, but in five years' time, there might be vendors who wanted only to support XML 1.1. As already mentioned, support for a particular version of XML also implies support for the corresponding version of XML Namespaces.

15

Serialization

continued

Attribute	Interpretation
	The XPath data model, and therefore the result tree, is not tied to a particular version of XML. It supports the union of what can be represented in XML 1.0 and XML 1.1. This creates the possibility that the result tree uses features that cannot be represented faithfully (or at all) in XML 1.0. If such features are used, the serializer may need to fall back to a 1.0 representation, or if all else fails, report an error.

Do remember that the <xsl:output> element will only be effective if you actually use the XSLT processor to serialize the XML. If you write the output of the transformation to a DOM, and then use a serializer that comes with your DOM implementation (for example by using the save method or the xml property in the case of the Microsoft DOM implementation), then the <xsl:output> specifications will have no effect.

The HTML Output Method

When the method attribute is set to «html», or when it is defaulted and the result tree is recognized as representing HTML, the output will be an HTML file. By default, it will follow the rules of HTML 4.0.

Requesting HTML serialization gives no guarantee that the result will be valid HTML. You can use any elements and attributes you like in the result tree, and the serializer will output them, following the HTML conventions where appropriate, but without enforcing any rules as to which elements can be used where.

HTML is output in the same way as XML, except where specific differences are noted. These differences are:

❑ Certain elements are recognized as empty elements. They are recognized in any combination of upper and lower case, but they must not be in a namespace. These elements are output with a start tag and no end tag. For HTML 4.0 these elements are:

`<area>`	`<frame>`	`<isindex>`
`<base>`	`<hr>`	`<link>`
`<basefont>`	`<img>`	`<meta>`
` `	`<input>`	`<param>`
`<col>`		

❑ The `<script>` and `<style>` elements (again in any combination of upper and lower case) do not require escaping of special characters. In the text content of these elements, a «<» character will be output as «<», not as «<».

❑ HTML attributes whose value is a URI (for example, the href attribute of the `<a>` element, or the src attribute of the `<img>` element) are recognized, and special characters within the URI are escaped as defined in the HTML specification. Specifically, non-ASCII characters in the URI will be represented by converting each byte of the UTF-8 representation of the character to «%HH» where HH represents the byte value in hexadecimal. This feature may be suppressed by setting «escape-uri-attributes="no"».

❑ Special characters may be output using entity references such as «é» where these are defined in the relevant version of HTML. This is at the discretion of the XSLT processor; it doesn't have to use these entity names.

❑ Processing instructions are terminated with «>» rather than «?>». Processing instructions are not often used in HTML, but the HTML 4.0 standard recommends that any vendor extensions should be implemented this way, rather than by adding element tags to the language. So it is possible they will be seen more frequently in the future.

❑ Attributes that are conventionally written with a keyword only, and no value, will be recognized and output in this form. Common examples are <TEXTAREA READONLY> and <OPTION SELECTED>. This is shorthand, permitted in SGML but not in XML, for an attribute that has only one permitted value, which is the same as the attribute name. In XML, these tags must be written as <TABLE BORDER="BORDER"> and <OPTION SELECTED="SELECTED">. The HTML output method will normally use the abbreviated form, as this is the only form that older HTML browsers will recognize.

❑ The special use of the ampersand character in dynamic HTML attributes is recognized. For example, the tag <TD WIDTH="&{width};"> is correct HTML, though it would not be correct in XML, because of the ampersand character. To produce this output from a literal result element, the tag in the stylesheet would need to be written as <TD WIDTH="&{{width}};">: note the double curly braces, to prevent them being interpreted with their special meaning in attribute value templates.

A common source of anxiety with HTML output is the use of ampersands in URLs. For example, suppose you want to generate the output:

```
<a href="http://www.acme.com/search.asp?product=widgets&country=spain">
Spanish Widgets
</a>
```

However you try to produce this using standard XSLT, the ampersand will always come out as «&». The reason for this is simple: «&», although commonly used and widely accepted, is not actually correct HTML, and according to the standard it must be escaped as «&». All respectable browsers accept the correct escaped form, so the answer is: don't worry about it.

Although the serializer won't generally check that the result tree is valid HTML, there is one exception: it must not use characters that are allowed in XML but not in HTML, notably Unicode characters in the range x80 to x9F. If these characters appear in your XML, the chances are that they got there by accident. Microsoft's cp1252 character set (sometimes called *ANSI*) is generally similar to iso-8859-1 but uses codes in this range to refer to special characters such as the Euro currency symbol, dagger, em-dash, middle dot, and the trademark sign. If a document that uses these characters is correctly labeled, then these characters will be translated into their Unicode equivalents (for example the Euro sign will become x20AC), and all will be well. If, however, the document is wrongly labeled with «encoding="iso-8859-1"», then these characters will be represented in the XML with codes in the range x80 to x9F, which will cause an error when you try to serialize as HTML, because HTML does not allow characters in that range. The remedy is to change the XML declaration of the source document from «encoding="iso-8859-1"» to «encoding="cp1252"».

The other serialization attributes are interpreted as follows when HTML output is selected. Attributes not listed are not applicable to HTML, and are ignored.

15

Serialization

937

Attribute	Interpretation
doctype-system	If this attribute is specified, the output file will include a document type declaration immediately before the first element start tag. The name of the document type will be «HTML» or «html». The value of the parameter will be used as the system identifier in the document type declaration.
doctype-public	If this attribute is specified, the output file will include a document type declaration immediately before the first element start tag. The name of the document type will be «HTML» or «html». The value of the parameter will be used as the public identifier in the document type declaration.
encoding	This specifies the preferred character encoding for the output document. If the encoding is one that does not allow all XML characters to be represented directly, for example «iso-8859-1», then characters outside this subset will be represented where possible using either entity references or numeric character references. The processor is encouraged not to use such references for characters that are within the encoding, except in special cases such as the nonbreaking space character, which may be output either as itself (it looks just like an ordinary space) or as « », «&#a0;», or « ». It is an error if characters that can't be represented directly appear in contexts where character references are not recognized (for example within a script element, within a comment, or in an element or attribute name).
escape-uri-attributes	This attribute determines whether non-ASCII characters appearing in URI-valued attributes should be escaped using the %HH convention. The default is «yes». Although HTML requires URIs to be escaped in this way, there are several reasons why you might choose to suppress this. Firstly, the URIs might already be in escaped form: you can do the escaping from within the stylesheet, with much greater control, using the escape-html-uri() function described in Chapter 13. Secondly, browsers do not always handle escaped URIs correctly. This is especially true when the URI is handled on the client side; for example, when it invokes JavaScript functions, or when it contains a fragment identifier.
include-content-type	If this attribute is set to «yes» (or if it is omitted), the serializer will add a `<meta>` element as a child of the HTML `<head>` element, provided that the result tree contains a `<head>` element. This `<meta>` element contains details of the media type and encoding of the document. Any existing `<meta>` element containing this information will be replaced. You may want to suppress this by specifying the value «no», for example if the stylesheet is copying a document that already includes such an element.
indent	If this attribute has the value `<yes>`, the idea is that the HTML output should be indented to show its hierarchic structure. The XSLT processor is not obliged to respect this request, and if it does so, the precise form of the output is not defined. When producing indented output, the processor has much more freedom to add or remove whitespace than in the XML case, because of the way whitespace is handled in HTML. The processor can add or remove whitespace anywhere it likes so long as it doesn't change the way a browser would display the HTML.

continued

Attribute	Interpretation
media-type	This attribute defines the media type of the output file (often referred to as its MIME type). The default value is «text/html». The specification doesn't say what use is made of this information; it doesn't affect the contents of the output file, but it may affect the way it is named, stored, or transmitted, depending on the environment. For example, the information might find its way into an HTTP protocol header.
normalization-form	This attribute is used in the same way as for the XML output method, described on page 934.
use-character-maps	This attribute is used in the same way as for the XML output method, described on page 935.
version	This attribute determines the version of HTML used in the output document. It is up to the implementation to decide which versions of HTML should be supported, though all implementations can be expected to support the default version, namely version 4.0.

The XHTML Output Method

An XHTML document is an XML document, so when you specify «method="XHTML"», most of the rules for the XML output method are inherited without change. However, there are special guidelines for serializing XHTML so that it is rendered correctly in browsers that were designed originally to handle HTML, and in addition some of the features of HTML serialization, such as URI escaping and addition of <meta> elements, are also applicable to XHTML. So the XHTML output method is essentially a blend of features from the XML and HTML methods.

> It's worth asking yourself whether you really need to use this method. If the browser understands XHTML, then serializing the result tree as XML will work fine. If the browser doesn't understand XHTML, and is going to handle it as if it were HTML, then why not serialize the tree as HTML to start with?

In fact, the XHTML output method works in the same way as the XML output method (and uses all the serialization parameters that control the XML method) with specific exceptions. These exceptions are:

❑ The way that empty elements are output depends on the way the element is declared in the XHTML DTD. For an element whose content model is empty, such as <hr> or <br> or <img>, the serializer should use an XML empty-element tag, taking care to include a space before the final «/>», so that the tag looks like <hr/> or <img src="a.jpeg"/>. For an element that is empty but allowed to have content, such as a <p> element, the serializer should use a start tag followed by an end tag, thus: <p></p>.

❑ The entity reference «'» is not recognized by all browsers, so the serializer will probably use «&#27;» instead.

❑ The serializer needs to take care with whitespace (for example newlines) appearing in attribute values. The specification doesn't say exactly how this should be handled, but it's probably safest, if there is any whitespace other than a single space character, to represent it using numeric character references.

15

Serialization

❑ The serializer must not output redundant namespace declarations, since these would violate the XHTML DTD. (At one time this rule was wider and encouraged the serializer to put XHTML elements in the default namespace. However, the serializer has no discretion in this area — namespace prefixes are chosen by the user, not by the serializer.) Because DTDs are not namespace-aware, it's always the case that if you choose the wrong prefix, the result document of a transformation may be invalid against the DTD.

The XHTML output method also inherits two specific features of the HTML output method:

❑ Non-ASCII characters in URI-valued attributes are escaped using the %HH convention, unless you suppress this by specifying «escape-uri-attributes="no"».

❑ A <meta> element is added as the child of the <head> element, unless you suppress this using «include-content-type="no"».

You can control whether an XML declaration is output using the «omit-xml-declaration» attribute. The XHTML 1.0 specification advises against using an XML declaration, but points out that under the XML rules, it may be omitted only if the encoding is UTF-8 or UTF-16.

The Text Output Method

When you specify «method="text"», the result tree is output as a plain text file. The values of the text nodes of the tree are copied to the output, and all other nodes are ignored. Within text nodes, all character values are output using the relevant encoding as determined by the encoding attribute; there are no special characters such as «&» to be escaped.

The way in which line endings are output (for example LF or CRLF) is not defined; the implementation might choose to use the default line-ending conventions of the platform on which it is running.

The attributes that are relevant to text output are listed below. All other attributes are ignored.

Attribute	Interpretation
encoding	This specifies the preferred character encoding for the output document. The default value is implementation-defined, and may depend on the platform on which it is running. If the encoding is one that does not allow all XML characters to be represented directly, for example «iso-8859-1», then any character outside this subset will be reported as an error.
media-type	This parameter defines the media type of the output file (often referred to as its MIME type). The default value is «text/plain». The specification doesn't say what use is made of this information: It doesn't affect the contents of the output file, but it may affect the way it is named, stored, or transmitted, depending on the environment. For example, the information might find its way into an HTTP protocol header.

Using the <xsl:output> declaration

The defaulting mechanisms ensure that it is usually not necessary to include an <xsl:output> element in the stylesheet. By default, the XML output method is used unless the first thing output is an <HTML> element, in which case either the HTML or the XHTML output method is used, depending on the namespace.

The `<xsl:output>` element is concerned with how your result tree is turned into an output file. If the XSLT processor allows you to do something else with the result tree, for example passing it to the application as a DOM Document or as a stream of SAX events, then the `<xsl:output>` element is irrelevant.

The `encoding` attribute can be very useful to ensure that the output file can be easily viewed and edited. Unfortunately, though, the set of possible values varies from one XSLT implementation to another, and may also depend on the environment. For example, many XSLT processors are written in Java and use the Java facilities for encoding the output stream, but the set of encodings supported by each Java VM is different. However, support for iso-8859-1 encoding is fairly universal, so if you have trouble viewing the output file because it contains UTF-8 Unicode characters, setting the encoding to iso-8859-1 is often a good remedy, at least if your document is written in a Western European language.

> **If your stylesheet generates accented letters or other special characters, and it looks as if they have come out incorrectly in the output, chances are they are correctly represented in UTF-8, but you are looking at them with a text editor that doesn't understand UTF-8. Either select a different output encoding (such as iso-8859-1), or get a text editor such as jEdit (`www.jedit.org`) that can work with UTF-8. If the problem occurs when you view the file in a browser, the most likely explanation is that the `<meta>` element gives the wrong `charset`.**

The `encoding` attribute determines how the XSLT processor serializes the output as a stream of bytes, but it says nothing about what happens to the bytes later. If the processor writes to a file, the file will probably be written in the chosen encoding. But if the output is accessed as a character string through an API, or is written to a character field in a database, the encoding of the characters may be changed before you get to see them. A classic example of this effect is the Microsoft `transformNode()` interface (see Appendix D), which returns the result of the transformation as a `BSTR` string. Because this is a `BSTR`, it will always be encoded in UTF-16, regardless of the encoding you request. The same thing will happen with the JAXP interface (see Appendix E); if you supply a `StreamResult` based on a `Writer`, the encoding then depends on how the particular `Writer` encodes Unicode characters, and the XSLT processor has no control over the matter.

Character Maps

A character map is used during serialization when it is named in the `use-character-maps` serialization attribute. This is a list of named character maps; these character maps are concatenated in the order that they are listed, and any conflicts are resolved by choosing the mapping for a character that is last in the list.

During serialization, character mapping is applied to characters appearing in the content of text nodes and attribute nodes. It is not applied to other content (such as comments and processing instructions), nor to element and attribute names. It is not applied to characters for which `disable-output-escaping` has been specified, nor to characters in CDATA sections (that is, characters in the content of elements listed in the `cdata-section-elements` serialization parameter). In the case of the HTML and XHTML output methods, character mapping is applied to characters in URI-valued attributes after they have been subjected to URI escaping under the rules of the HTML and XHTML output methods, and it is also applied to attributes in a generated `<meta>` element.

If a character is included in the character map, this bypasses the normal XML/HTML escaping, as well as Unicode normalization. For example, if a character map causes the character «∧» to be replaced by «&&», then it will be output as «&&», not as «&&», even though the result is invalid XML.

The final stage of serialization is character encoding (as determined by the encoding parameter). This converts logical Unicode characters into actual bytes or octets; for example, if the encoding is UTF-8 then the character «ç» will be represented by the two octets «x3c xA7». You cannot use character maps to alter the effect of the character encoding process.

Usage

Character maps are useful in many situations where you need precise control over the serialization of the result tree.

In general, if you are producing XML output that is to be used by another application, or if you are producing HTML output that is destined to be displayed in a browser, then the standard serialized output should be perfectly adequate. The situations where you need a finer level of control are typically:

❑   If the output is designed to be edited by humans rather than processed by a machine. In this case, you may want, for example, to control the use of entity references in the output.

❑   If you need XML output containing an internal DTD subset within the document. Generate the DTD as text, using characters such x2039 and x2040 (left/right-pointing angle bracket) as substitutes for «<» and «>».

❑   If the output format is not standard HTML or XML, but some proprietary extension with its own rules. Such dialects are commonly encountered with HTML, though fortunately they are very rare in the case of XML. A similar requirement arises where the required output format is SGML.

❑   If the application that processes the HTML or XML that you produce is buggy. You live in the real world and life isn't perfect. For example, it is rumored that some very old browsers will not accept an «&» in a URL that has been escaped as «&», even though the HTML standard requires the escaped form. If you encounter such bugs, you may need to work around them.

❑   If the required output format uses what I call *double markup*. By this I mean the use of XML tags in places where tags are not recognized by an XML parser, generally within CDATA sections or comments. I don't think that this is a particularly good design pattern for XML, because it is not possible to model the structure correctly as a tree using the XPath data model, but document structures such as this exist and you may be obliged to produce them. You can solve this problem using character maps by choosing two characters to map to the CDATA start and end delimiters («<![CDATA[» and «]]>») or the comment start and end delimiters («<!--» and «-->»). An example is shown on page 943.

❑   Finally, there are some transformations where generating the correct result tree is really difficult, or really slow. An example might be where the document structure uses interleaved markup. This is used where there are two parallel hierarchies running through the same document; for example, one for the chapter/section/paragraph structure and one for the paginated layout. An expert will know when it's time to give up and cheat — which in this case means producing markup in the result document by direct intervention at the serialization stage, rather than generating the correct result tree and having the markup produced automatically by the serializer. The problem, of course, is that beginners are inclined to give up and cheat far too soon, which leads to code that is difficult to extend and maintain.

Choosing Characters to Map

Applications for character maps probably fall into two categories: those where you want to choose a nonstandard string representation of a character that occurs naturally in the data, and those where you want to choose some otherwise unused character to trigger some special effect in the output.

An example in the first category would be the example shown earlier:

```
<xsl:character-map name="NBSP">
   <xsl:output-character character=" " string=" "/>
</xsl:character-map>
```

This forces the nonbreaking space character to be output as an entity reference. If the document is to be edited, many people will find the entity reference easier to manipulate because it shows up as a visible character, whereas the nonbreaking space character itself appears on the screen just like an ordinary space.

An example in the second category is choosing two characters to represent the start and end of a comment. Suppose that the requirement is to transform an input document by "commenting out" any element that has the attribute «delete="yes"». By commenting out, I mean outputting something like:

```
<!--
  <para delete="yes">
     This paragraph has been deleted
  </para>
-->
```

This is tricky, because the result cannot be modeled naturally as a result tree — comment nodes cannot have element nodes as children. So we'll choose instead to output the <para> element to the result tree unchanged, but preceded and followed by special characters, which we will map during serialization to comment start and end delimiters.

The best characters to choose for such purposes are the characters in the Unicode Private Use Area, for example the characters from xE000 to xF8FF. These characters have no defined meaning in Unicode, and are intended to be used for communications where there is a private agreement between the sender and the recipient as to what they mean. In this case, the sender is the stylesheet and the recipient is the serializer.

If you assign private use characters in information that is passed between applications, especially applications owned by different organizations, you should make sure that your use of the characters is well documented.

Here is a stylesheet that performs the required transformation:

Example: Using a Character Map to Comment-Out Elements

This example copies the input unchanged to the output, except that any element in the input that has the attribute «delete="yes"» is output within a comment.

Stylesheet

The stylesheet is comment-out.xsl:

```
<?xml version="1.0"?>
<!DOCTYPE xsl:stylesheet [
  <!ENTITY start-comment "&#xE501;">
  <!ENTITY end-comment "&#xE502;">
]>
```

```
<xsl:stylesheet version="2.0"
      xmlns:xsl="http://www.w3.org/1999/XSL/Transform">

<xsl:output use-character-maps="comment-delimiters"/>

<xsl:character-map name="comment-delimiters">
  <xsl:output-character character="&start-comment;" string="&lt;!--"/>
  <xsl:output-character character="&end-comment;" string="--&gt;"/>
</xsl:character-map>

<xsl:template match="*">
  <xsl:copy>
    <xsl:copy-of select="@*"/>
    <xsl:apply-templates/>
  </xsl:copy>
</xsl:template>

<xsl:template match="*[@delete='yes']">
  <xsl:text>&start-comment;</xsl:text>
  <xsl:copy-of select="."/>
  <xsl:text>&end-comment;</xsl:text>
</xsl:template>

</xsl:stylesheet>
```

Source

One of the paragraphs in the source file `resume.xml` is:

```
<p delete="yes">Aidan is also in demand as a consort singer,
performing with groups including the Oxford Camerata and the Sarum
Consort, with whom he has made several acclaimed recordings on the
ASV label of motets by Bach and Peter Philips sung by solo voices.</p>
```

Output

When the stylesheet is applied to the source file `resume.xml`, the above paragraph appears as:

```
<!--<p delete="yes">Aidan is also in demand as a consort singer,
performing with groups including the Oxford Camerata and the Sarum
Consort, with whom he has made several acclaimed recordings on the
ASV label of motets by Bach and Peter Philips sung by solo voices.</p>-->
```

Limitations of Character Maps

A character map applies to a whole result document; you cannot switch character mapping on and off at will.

The character map must be fixed at compile time. You cannot compute the output string at runtime, and there is no way the process can be parameterized. (You can, however, substitute a different character map by having different definitions of the same character map in different stylesheet modules, and deciding which one to import using `<xsl:import>`.)

Character mapping may impose a performance penalty, especially if a large number of characters are mapped.

Character mapping has no effect unless the result of the transformation is actually serialized. If the result tree is passed straight to another application that doesn't understand the special characters, it is unlikely to have the desired effect.

Character mapping only affects the content of text and attribute nodes. It doesn't affect characters in element and attribute names, or markup characters such as the quotes around an attribute value.

The character to be mapped, and all the characters in the replacement string, must be valid XML characters. This is because there is no way of representing invalid characters in the `<xsl:output-character>` element in the stylesheet. This means that character maps cannot be used to generate text files containing characters not allowed in XML, such as the NUL character (x00).

Disable Output Escaping

XSLT 1.0 provided an alternative way of getting fine-grained control over the serializer, namely the `disable-output-escaping` attribute of the `<xsl:value-of>` and `<xsl:text>` instructions. This has been deprecated in XSLT 2.0, but it is still likely to be supported in many processors because it is so widely used (and abused) in XSLT 1.0 stylesheets.

Reasons to Disable Output Escaping

Normally, when you try to output a special character such as «<» or «&» in a text node, the special character will be escaped in the output file using the normal XML escaping mechanisms. The escaping is done by the serializer: the text node written in the result tree contains a «<» or «&» character, and the serializer translates this into «<» or «&». The serializer is free to represent the special characters any way it wants; for example, it can write «<» as «<», «<», or «<![CDATA[<]]>», because these are all equivalent according to the XML standard. The one thing it will not write is «<». So, it doesn't matter how you write the «<» in your input: the serializer sees a «<» and escapes it in the output.

There are several valid reasons why you might not want this behavior. For example:

❑   The output is not XML or HTML at all; it is (say) a data file in comma-separated-values format.

❑   The output is HTML and you want to exploit one of the many HTML quirks where special characters are needed without escaping; for example, a «<» sign in a piece of client-side JavaScript on your HTML page.

❑   The output is XML and you want to achieve some special effect that the XSLT processor doesn't allow; for example, outputting an entity reference such as «&current-date;» or an internal DTD subset containing an entity declaration.

❑   The output is some format that uses angle-bracket syntax but is not pure XML or HTML; for example, ASP.NET pages or Java Server Pages, which both use «<%» and «%>» as delimiters, or XQuery, in which an unescaped «<» can be used as an operator symbol. (If you are generating Java Server Pages, note that these have an alternative syntax that is pure XML; however, this is not widely used.)

If the output is not XML or HTML at all, then rather than using `disable-output-escaping`, it is better to set «`method="text"`» on the `<xsl:output>` element. In this case, special characters will never be escaped (which also means that disabling output escaping has no effect).

Why disable-output-escaping Is Deprecated

The use of `disable-output-escaping` is often discouraged; indeed it is officially deprecated in XSLT 2.0.

The first reason for this is that it works only if the result tree is being serialized. If the result tree is fed directly into another application, then `disable-output-escaping` has no effect. This happens, for example, in the Firefox browser, where the HTML-structured result tree is used directly by the rendering engine, without first serializing it as text and then re-parsing it. So a stylesheet that depends on `disable-output-escaping` won't always work.

The second reason that the facility is discouraged is that it's often a symptom of careless programming: Its use reveals that the stylesheet author is thinking too much in terms of creating tags in a serialized file, not in terms of creating nodes in a result tree.

Here's an example of a misuse of disabling output escaping that you will often encounter (only in other people's stylesheets, of course). The author wanted to get markup tags into the output document, and they couldn't see how to achieve this with the regular facilities of `<xsl:element>` or literal result elements. For example, the author might have been thinking along these lines:

```
<!-- WRONG -->
<xsl:template match="bullet"/>
    <xsl:if test='not(preceding::*[1][self::bullet])'>
        <ul>
    </xsl:if>
    <li><xsl:value-of select="."/></li>
    <xsl:if test='not(following::*[1][self::bullet])'>
        </ul>
    </xsl:if>
</xsl:template>
<!-- WRONG -->
```

The intended effect here is to output a `<ul>` tag if the preceding element is not a bullet element, and to output a `</ul>` tag when the following element is not a bullet element. Of course, it doesn't work, because the `<ul>` and `</ul>` tags are not properly nested; this template will be thrown out by the XML parser before the XSLT processor even gets to look at it.

So their next thought might be to write the tags as text, as follows:

```
<xsl:template match="bullet"/>
    <xsl:if test='not(preceding::*[self::list-item])'>
        <xsl:text disable-output-escaping="yes">&lt;ul&gt;</xsl:text>
    </xsl:if>
    <li><xsl:value-of select="."/></li>
    <xsl:if test='not(following::*[self::list-item])'>
        <xsl:text disable-output-escaping="yes">/&lt;ul&gt;</xsl:text>
    </xsl:if>
</xsl:template>
```

You now have something that is legal XML and indeed legal XSLT, but it's not guaranteed to work under all circumstances. And even if it does work, it's badly written code, because it's cutting against the grain of the language.

With a bit of thought you can usually find a way to achieve the output you want without resorting to such devices.

The first thing is to think in terms of outputting a result tree containing nodes, not a text file containing tags. Don't try to generate the `<ul>` start tag and the `</ul>` end tag as two separate actions; try to generate a `<ul>` element node as a single action, and then generate its children.

In fact, when you see this kind of logic, you can be pretty sure that the problem being tackled is a grouping problem. The solution to a grouping problem always involves two nested loops: In this case, an outer loop to generate the `<ul>` element and an inner loop to generate the `<li>` elements. The solution to this particular grouping problem is shown as the first example of how to use the `group-adjacent` attribute of `<xsl:for-each-group>`, on page 335 in Chapter 6.

Using disable-output-escaping to Wrap HTML in CDATA

One technique used quite often is to wrap HTML inside an XML document, for example:

```
<message>
  <header>
    <sent-by>Dept 178</sent-by>
    <recipient>App 263</recipient>
  </header>
  <content type="text/html">
    <![CDATA[
      <html>
        <head><title>An HTML page with unmatched tags</title></head>
        <body>HTML authors are often lazy!<p></body>
      </html>
    ]]>
  </content>
</message>
```

One way you can include the HTML within the XML message is to put it through a program such as Dave Raggett's *html tidy* utility (available from `http://www.w3.org/`), which converts it to well-formed XHTML. But you may not want to risk changing it, so using a CDATA section as shown here is the only alternative. When you do this, however, the «<» and «>» characters are no longer treated as markup characters; they are now ordinary text. If you try to run an XSLT transformation that outputs the HTML enclosed in this message, these characters will therefore be escaped, typically by writing them as «<» and «>». This isn't what you want; so you can solve the problem by writing:

```
<xsl:template match="content[@type='text/html']">
  <xsl:value-of select="." disable-output-escaping="yes"/>
</xsl:template>
```

But remember that this is likely to work only if the output is serialized by the XSLT processor; it won't work if you write the result to a DOM.

15

Serialization

947

Character Maps as a Substitute
for disable-output-escaping

Character maps are less powerful than `disable-output-escaping`, because you can't switch them on and off for different parts of the result tree. But this is also their strength. The problem with `disable-output-escaping` is that it requires some extra information to pass between the transformation engine and the serializer, in addition to the information that's defined in the data model. (As evidence for this, look at the clumsy way that `disable-output-escaping` requests are encoded in a `SAXResult` stream in the Java JAXP interface.) This information is generally lost if you want to pass the result tree to another application before serializing it. The problem gets worse in XSLT 2.0, which allows temporary trees and parentless text nodes to be created and processed within the course of a transformation. One of the difficulties in designing this feature was whether a request to disable output escaping should be meaningful when the data being written was not being passed straight to the serializer, but was being written to a temporary tree or a parentless text node.

Most of the things that can be done with `disable-output-escaping`, including the bad things, can also be done with character maps. The big advantage of character maps is that they don't distort the data model, which means that they don't impact your ability to use a stylesheet-based transformation as a component in an application with clean interfaces to other components.

If you want to convert code that was written to use `disable-output-escaping` to use character maps instead, the most direct approach is to define substitutes for the characters that are changed by XML escaping:

```xml
<?xml version="1.0"?>
<!DOCTYPE xsl:stylesheet [
  <!ENTITY doe-lt "&#xE801;">
  <!ENTITY doe-amp "&#xE802;">
  <!ENTITY doe-gt "&#xE803;">
  <!ENTITY doe-apos "&#xE804;">
  <!ENTITY doe-quot "&#xE805;">
]>

<xsl:stylesheet version="2.0"
    xmlns:xsl="http://www.w3.org/1999/XSL/Transform"
    xmlns:doe="http://www.wrox.com/xslt/ch15/doe">

<xsl:output use-character-maps="disable-escaping"/>

<xsl:character-map name="disable-escaping">
  <xsl:output-character character="&doe-lt;" string="&lt;"/>
  <xsl:output-character character="&doe-amp;" string="&amp;"/>
  <xsl:output-character character="&doe-gt;" string="&gt;"/>
  <xsl:output-character character="&doe-apos;" string="&apos;"/>
  <xsl:output-character character="&doe-quot;" string="&quot;"/>
</xsl:character-map>

<xsl:function name="doe:disable-escaping" as="xs:string">
  <xsl:param name="in" as="xs:string"/>
  <xsl:sequence select="translate($in, '&lt;&amp;&gt;&apos;&quot;',
                '&doe-lt;&doe-amp;&doe-gt;&doe-apos;&doe-quot;')"/>
</xsl:function>
```

Then, wherever the existing code uses `<xsl:value-of select="XXX" disable-output-escaping ="yes"/>`, change it to say `<xsl:value-of select="doe:disable-escaping(XXX)"/>`. This will replace the characters that are normally escaped by their substitutes, and the substitutes will be turned back into the unescaped original characters during serialization, by virtue of the character map.

Although this mechanical replacement of `disable-output-escaping` by character maps will always work, there may often be better ways of doing it in particular circumstances.

Remember that if you expose the unserialized result tree to another application, it will see the private-use characters such as xE801 in text and attribute nodes.

Summary

This chapter has described the four serialization methods XML, HTML, XHTML, and TEXT, which can be invoked to process the XSLT result tree. It also explained the new XSLT 2.0 facility of character maps, and the XSLT 1.0 `disable-output-escaping` capability which it replaces, both of which are there to get you out of sticky corners when the standard serialization mechanisms prove inadequate.

This provides a nice link into the next chapter, which describes the range of techniques that allow vendors and users to extend the capability of XSLT when there is a need to do things that are outside the scope of the standard.

15

Serialization

Part III
Exploitation

16

Extensibility

Previous chapters have discussed standard features of the XSLT language. This chapter discusses what happens when you need to stray beyond the XSLT 2.0 language specification. It's concerned with questions such as:

❑ What extensions are vendors allowed to provide?

❑ How much are implementations allowed to vary from each other?

❑ How can you write your own extensions?

❑ How can you write stylesheets that will run on more than one vendor's XSLT processor?

There is some interesting history here. XSLT 1.0 allowed stylesheets to call user-written extension functions but provided no standard way of writing them. The draft XSLT 1.1 specification defined a general mechanism for creating extension functions written in any language and then defined detailed interfaces for Java and JavaScript (or ECMAScript, to give it its vendor-neutral name). This specification was published as a working draft but was subsequently withdrawn. There were a number of reasons for this, one of which was simply that events were overtaken by the more ambitious XSLT 2.0 initiative. But part of the reason was that the proposals for standardizing extension function interfaces attracted heavy public criticism (see http://xml.coverpages.org/withdraw-xslScript.html). It's difficult in retrospect to summarize the arguments that were waged against the idea, but they probably fell into three categories: some people thought extension functions were a bad idea in principle and should not be encouraged, some people disapproved of singling out two languages (Java and JavaScript) for special treatment, and some people felt that the W3C shouldn't be putting language bindings into the core XSLT specification, the job should be done in separate specifications preferably produced by a different organization.

The result of this minor furor is that there is no defined interface for writing extension functions, either in XSLT 1.0 or in XSLT 2.0. However, conventions have emerged at least for XSLT 1.0 (the draft 1.1 specification was influenced by these conventions, and in turn exerted its own influence on the products, despite being abandoned), and it is worth giving these some space.

At the time of writing this edition, only a limited number of XSLT 2.0 processors are available, and it is difficult to see trends emerging as to what capabilities vendors will choose to provide. However, there's no reason to believe that this will be significantly different from the capabilities often found in XSLT 1.0 processors. Some of the examples in this chapter therefore relate to XSLT 1.0 processors such as MSXML from Microsoft and Xalan-J from Apache.

What Vendor Extensions Are Allowed?

The XSLT 2.0 language specification makes no distinction between what vendors are allowed to do, and what users and third parties are allowed to do. For example, it says that the set of languages supported by the `format-date()` function is implementation-defined. This can be interpreted in two ways:

❏ Vendors can support as many or as few languages as they think their target market requires.

❏ Vendors are allowed (but not required) to provide localization mechanisms that enable users or third parties to extend the set of supported languages.

Nowhere in the XSLT specification does it say that implementors must provide facilities for users to define their own extensions. Many implementations will choose to do so, but to find out what extensibility is permitted by the language, we need to look at two things: firstly, the information that is defined to be part of the context or environment, and secondly, the features of the language whose behavior is implementation-defined. There are detailed lists of these features in the W3C specification, but they fall into a few broad categories.

❏ Some features of the language are optional, in the sense that conformant processors are not required to provide them. For example, a processor can choose not to implement schema-aware processing, and it can choose not to implement the `disable-output-escaping` attribute or the namespace axis.

❏ Interfaces between the XSLT processor and the outside world are generally implementation-defined. This includes the mechanisms for invoking the XSLT processor and delivering its results, the mechanism for reporting errors, and the details of how URIs are interpreted in constructs such as `<xsl:include>`, `<xsl:import>`, `<xsl:import-schema>`, and the `document()` and `doc()` functions.

❏ The XSLT vocabulary is extensible in five key areas. In each of these cases, the vendor can extend the vocabulary and, if they wish, they can also enable users or third parties to extend it:

  ❏ **Extension functions:** The set of functions that can be called from XPath expressions, and any mechanisms for adding additional functions, are implementation-defined, as long as any functions outside the language-defined core are in a separate namespace.

  ❏ **Extension instructions:** The set of instructions that can appear in a sequence constructor is extensible, as long as the namespace used for any extension instructions is declared in the stylesheet in an «extension-element-prefixes» attribute.

  ❏ **Extension attributes:** Additional attributes can be added to any XSLT element, as long as they are in a separate namespace. There are rules limiting the effect that such attributes may have: essentially, they must not change the result of the transformation except to the extent that the W3C specification leaves the result explicitly implementation-defined.

  ❏ **Extension declarations:** Additional top-level declarations can be defined in the stylesheet, provided that the element name is in a separate namespace. These are subject to the same constraints as extension attributes.

  ❏ **Extension types:** Additional types can be made available. This feature is defined primarily so that extension functions can return application-oriented objects (for example, a `sql:connect()` function might return an object of type `sql:DatabaseConnection`), but there are no limits on how the facility might be used.

❏ The set of collations that can be used for sorting and comparing strings is implementation-defined.

❏ Many localization attributes, for example those used to control the formatting of dates and numbers, have an implementation-defined range of possible values.

When the specification says that the behavior of a particular feature is *implementation-defined*, this places an onus on the vendor of a conformant product to describe in the product documentation what choices they have made. There are also some features of the language that are *implementation-dependent*: the difference here is that vendors are not expected to document the exact behavior of the product. An example of an implementation-dependent feature is the maximum depth of recursion that is permitted. This will depend on a great many factors outside the software vendor's direct control, so it's not reasonable to expect a definitive statement.

Extension Functions

Extending the library of functions that can be called from XPath expressions has proved to be by far the most important way in which vendors extend the capability of the language, and so we will concentrate most of our attention on this particular extensibility mechanism.

When Are Extension Functions Needed?

There are a number of reasons you might want to call an extension function from your stylesheet:

❑   You might want to get data held externally, perhaps in a database or in an application.

❑   You may need to access system services that are not directly available in XSLT or XPath. For example, you might want to use a random number generator, or append a record to a log file.

❑   You might want to perform a complex calculation that is cumbersome to express in XSLT, or that performs poorly. For example, if you are generating SVG graphics, you might need to use trigonometric functions such as `sin()` and `cos()`. This situation arises far less with XSLT 2.0 than it did in 1.0, because the core function library is so much richer, especially in its ability to do string manipulation and date/time arithmetic. But if the function you need is out there in some Java library, it's no crime to call it.

❑   A more questionable use of external functions is to get around the "no side effects" rule in XSLT, for example to update a counter. Avoid this if you can; if you need such facilities, then you haven't yet learned to think about solving problems in the way that is natural for XSLT. More on this in the next chapter.

There are two ways of using extension functions in XSLT. You can write your own extension functions, or you can call extension functions that already exist. These functions might be provided by your XSLT vendor, or they might come from a third-party library such as:

❑   Dimitre Novatchev's FXSL library at `http://fxsl.sourceforge.net/`. This library concentrates on providing the primitives needed for higher-order programming, and uses them to provide a basic set of operations equivalent to those found in languages such as Haskell. There are some interesting demonstrations of how these can be used to solve practical programming problems.

❑   Priscilla Walmsley's FunctX library at `http://www.xsltfunctions.com`. This library, available in both XSLT and XQuery forms, provides a remarkably extensive collection of utility functions for manipulating strings, numbers, dates, node sequences, and more.

❑   The EXSLT library found at `http://www.exslt.org/` (many EXSLT functions provide capabilities that are no longer needed in 2.0, but some of them, such as the mathematical functions, are still very relevant).

Actually some of these libraries are implemented in XSLT, which means that the functions they contain are not, strictly speaking, extensions at all. But the way you write your code to call them is the same either way, so the distinction isn't really important.

16

Extensibility

Many XSLT vendors designed their interfaces for Java and JavaScript so that the extensive class libraries available in both these languages would be directly accessible to the stylesheet, with no further coding required. This is certainly true for mathematical functions, string manipulation, and date handling. Which language you choose to use to write extension functions is a matter of personal choice, though it will be heavily constrained by the XSLT processor you are using. With a Java-based processor such as Saxon or Xalan-J, the natural choice is to write extension functions in Java. With Microsoft processors, the natural choice is a .NET language such as C#. If you are using the Gestalt processor, it is probably because your favorite language is Eiffel. Processors written in C or C++ tend to require a more complex procedure for linking extension functions, if they are supported at all.

When Are Extension Functions Not Needed?

There is probably a tendency for newcomers to XSLT to write extension functions simply because they haven't worked out how to code the logic in an XSLT stylesheet function. Slipping back into a programming language you have used for years, rather than battling with an unfamiliar one, is always going to be tempting when you have deadlines to meet. It's understandable, but it's not the right thing to do.

There are other wrong reasons for using extension functions. These include:

❑ *Believing that an XSLT implementation of the logic is bound to be slower*: Don't believe this until you have proved it by measurement — and don't let it influence you unless you need the extra performance. I did a quick test to compare the FXSL code for calculating square roots (to four decimal places) using pure XSLT with a call to Java. This is a worst-case scenario because it's very computation-intensive. Using FXSL took around 1900µs per call, while calling Java took 12µs. So there's a significant difference, but the question is, does it matter? Is that 1900µs going to be noticeable on the bottom line, and is it worth the cost of making your stylesheet processor-dependent?

❑ *Supplying external data to the stylesheet*: The best way to supply information to the stylesheet is in the form of a stylesheet parameter. Another good way is to provide the data in the form of an XML document, in response to a call on the document() function (many processors allow you to write logic that intercepts the URI supplied to the document() function, or you could use a URI that invokes a servlet or a Web service).

❑ *Achieving side effects*: There are some side effects that are reasonably acceptable, for example writing messages to a log file — these are basically actions that do not affect the subsequent processing of the stylesheet, so the order of events is not critically important. But trying to get round the no-side-effects rule in other ways is nearly always the wrong thing to do, though it can be very tempting. Sooner or later, the optimizer will rearrange your code in a way that stops your extension function from working.

❑ *Using XSLT as a job control language*: I have seen stylesheets that consist entirely of calls to external services, effectively using XSLT as a scripting language to invoke a sequence of external tasks. XSLT wasn't designed for this role, and the fact that order of execution in XSLT is undefined makes it a poor choice of tool for this job. Use an XML pipeline processor (XProc), a shell script language, or the ant utility.

Calling Extension Functions

Extension functions are always called from within an XPath expression. A typical function call looks like this:

```
my:function($arg1, 23, string(title))
```

The name of an extension function will always contain a namespace prefix and a colon. The prefix («my» in this example) must be declared in a namespace declaration on some containing element in the stylesheet, in the usual way. The function may take any number of arguments (zero or more), and the parentheses are needed even if there are no arguments. The arguments can be any XPath expressions; in our example, the first argument is a variable reference, the second is a number, and the third is a function call. The arguments are passed to the function by value, which means that the function can never modify the values of the arguments (though if you pass nodes, the function may be able to modify the contents of the nodes). The function always returns a result.

We'll have more to say about the types of the arguments, and the type of the result, in due course.

What Language Is Best?

Many processors offer only one language for writing extension functions (if indeed they allow extension functions at all), so the choice may already be made for you. Some processors offer a choice; for example Xalan-J supports both Java and JavaScript. Microsoft's MSXML supports any of the usual scripting languages, for example JScript and VBScript, and the `System.Xml.Xsl` processor in .NET allows any .NET language (C#, C++, ASP.NET, VB.NET, and so on).

Generally, I'd suggest using the native language for your chosen processor; for example, Java for Oracle, Saxon on Java, and Xalan-J; JScript for MSXML; Python for 4XSLT; Eiffel for Gestalt; and C# for Saxon on .NET. If you want to use your stylesheet with more than one processor, write one version of the extension function for each language.

Client-Side Script

If you are generating HTML pages, your stylesheet can put anything it likes in the HTML page that it is generating. This includes `<script>` elements containing JavaScript code to be executed when the HTML page is displayed.

Don't get confused between script that you generate in the output HTML, and script that is executed in your stylesheet during the course of the transformation. It's especially easy to get the two confused when the transformation itself is running within the browser. Remember that stylesheet extension functions are always called using function calls in XPath expressions, while you are generating the HTML to be displayed. HTML `<script>` is always called in response to browser events such as the user clicking on a button.

Binding Extension Functions

When you call «my:function()» from within an XPath expression, the XSLT processor needs to find a suitable function to call. This process is called *binding*. The XSLT specification does not define how the binding is done, and a variety of approaches can be found in popular products. In this section, I will present a selection of these, if only to illustrate the variety of approaches in use.

Binding in MSXML

MSXML uses a special top-level element `<msxsl:script>` to define extension functions, which may be written in a variety of languages, though JavaScript is the most popular. The JavaScript code is written inline within the `<msxsl:script>` element.

The Microsoft .NET processor (`System.Xml.Xsl`) also supports this mechanism, but its use is discouraged, and can lead to problems with memory usage.

Here is an example stylesheet that uses an extension written in VBScript, just to be different. The implementation of the function is written inline within the `<msxsl:script>` element.

Example: Using VBScript in an MSXML3 Stylesheet

This example shows a stylesheet that converts dimensions in inches to the equivalent in millimeters.

Source

The source file is `inches.xml`. Double-click on it in Windows Explorer to invoke the stylesheet.

```
<?xml version="1.0" encoding="iso-8859-1"?>
<?xml-stylesheet type="text/xsl" href="to-mm.xsl"?>
<dimensions>
The size of the picture is <inches>5</inches> by <inches>12</inches>.
</dimensions>
```

Stylesheet

The stylesheet is `to-mm.xsl`.

It contains a simple VBScript function within an `<msxsl:script>` element, and invokes this as an extension function from the template rule for the `<inches>` element.

```
<xsl:stylesheet
     xmlns:xsl="http://www.w3.org/1999/XSL/Transform"
     version="1.0"
     xmlns:extra="urn:extra-functions"
>
<msxsl:script xmlns:msxsl="urn:schemas-microsoft-com:xslt"
       language="VBScript"
       implements-prefix="extra"
>
Function ToMillimetres(inches)
   ToMillimetres = inches * 25.4
End Function
</msxsl:script>
<xsl:output method="html"/>
<xsl:template match="/" >
<html><body><p>
   <xsl:apply-templates/>
</p></body></html>
</xsl:template>
<xsl:template match="inches">
   <xsl:text> </xsl:text>
   <xsl:value-of select="format-number(extra:ToMillimetres(number(.)),
                                       '0.00')"/>
   <xsl:text>mm </xsl:text>
</xsl:template>
</xsl:stylesheet>
```

Output

The following text is displayed in the browser:

```
The size of the picture is 127.00mm by 304.80mm.
```

Note that this doesn't work in Firefox, which doesn't recognize the `<msxsl:script>` element.

These scripts can call COM objects located via the system registry in the usual way. However, if the stylesheet is running in the browser, the user's security settings may prevent your script from instantiating a client-side object.

Of course, this example uses an extension function to do something that could be trivially done within an XSLT 2.0 stylesheet function.

JavaScript and VBScript are both dynamically typed languages, which made them a good fit with XSLT 1.0 and XPath 1.0. However, it's easy to get tripped up by the fact that the function calling conventions aren't always what you expect. For example, both in XPath 1.0 and in 2.0, if a function in the core library such as `starts-with()` expects a string, then you can supply an attribute node, and the value of the attribute will be extracted automatically (in XPath 2.0 this process is called *atomization*). JavaScript doesn't declare the types of function parameters, which means that no such conversion is possible: if you supply an attribute node, that's what the JavaScript code will see, and if it was expecting a string, it will probably fail.

The Xalan-J product also supports JavaScript extension functions using a similar mechanism, but this time the binding element is `<xalan:script>`, where the «xalan» prefix represents the URI `http://xml.apache.org/xslt`. Several `<xalan:script>` elements can be grouped together in a `<xalan:component>` element. Note that this mechanism only works with the interpreted XSLT processor, not with the XSLTC compiler which is also part of the Xalan-J bundle.

There's nothing to stop you having an `<msxsl:script>` declaration and a `<xalan:script>` declaration in the same stylesheet. An XSLT processor is required to ignore top-level declarations in an unknown namespace, so each processor will ignore the declaration that's intended for the other. This means you can have two implementations of the same extension function in your stylesheet, one for use when you're running MSXML, another for use when running Xalan.

Binding by Namespace in Java Processors

Most of the Java XSLT processors (Saxon, Xalan, jd.xslt, Oracle, xt) support an implicit binding of extension functions to Java methods, based on the idea that the namespace URI used in the function identifies the Java class, and the local name of the function corresponds to the method name. Xalan-J (which refers to this approach as the "abbreviated syntax" for extension binding) also allows the namespace URI to represent a Java package, leaving the local name of the function to represent both the class name and the method name.

For example, the following stylesheet can be used in Saxon to calculate a square root.

Example: An Extension Function to Calculate a Square Root

This example shows a stylesheet that returns the square root of a number in the source document.

16

Extensibility

Source

The source document is `sqrt.xml`:

```
<number>2.0</number>
```

Stylesheet

The stylesheet is `sqrt.xsl`.

This stylesheet calls an external function `Math:sqrt()`, where the namespace prefix «Math» is bound to the namespace URI «java:java.lang.Math». Saxon recognizes namespace URIs beginning with «java:» as special — the part of the URI after the «java:» is interpreted as a Java class name. The processor loads this Java class (which must be on the classpath) and looks to see whether it contains a static method called «sqrt» that can take an argument that is a double. It does, so this method is called, and the result is taken as the return value from the function call.

```
<xsl:transform
 xmlns:xsl="http://www.w3.org/1999/XSL/Transform"
 xmlns:xs="http://www.w3.org/2001/XMLSchema"
 exclude-result-prefixes="xs"
 version="2.0">

<xsl:template match="number">
  <result>
    <xsl:value-of select="Math:sqrt(xs:double(.))"
                  xmlns:Math="java:java.lang.Math"/>
  </result>
</xsl:template>
</xsl:transform>
```

Output

```
<?xml version="1.0" encoding="UTF-8"?>
<result>1.4142135623730951</result>
```

Although each of the Java XSLT processors supports implicit bindings of Java methods to extension functions in much this kind of way, the details vary from one processor to another, and it may be difficult to write code that is completely portable across processors. In particular, processors are likely to vary in how they map between the XPath types and Java types. This is especially true if the Java class contains several methods of the same name, but with different argument types (method overloading). To find out the detail of how each processor handles this, you will need to consult the documentation for your specific product.

Most of what I've said so far about extension functions applies equally to XSLT 1.0 and XSLT 2.0. In fact, most of the processors mentioned do not yet have an XSLT 2.0 version. So it remains to be seen how vendors will tackle the challenge of mapping the much richer type system in XSLT 2.0 to Java classes.

Most of these processors allow a call on a Java method to return a wrapped Java object, which can then be supplied as an argument to another extension function. For example, you might have a function `sql:connect()` that returns an object of type "SQL connection," and another function `sql:query()` that accepts a SQL connection as its first argument. In XSLT 1.0, with its limited type system, this object is generally modeled using a single extra type "external object." With XSLT 2.0, it is possible to go further than this and implicitly import any number of user-defined types into the stylesheet. Saxon takes this to its logical extreme, and implicitly imports the whole of the Java class hierarchy, mapping class names into the namespace `http://saxon.sf.net/java-type`. The result is that (assuming the prefix «class» is bound to this namespace) you can declare a variable such as:

```
<xsl:variable name="connection" as="class:java.sql.Connection"
              select="sql:connect(...)"/>
```

This means that these external objects can be used with complete type safety, because the Java class hierarchy has been mapped to the XSLT/XPath type hierarchy.

Generally, processors map the common types into their obvious equivalent in the external programming language. For example, in Java, an `xs:double` maps to a Java `double`, an `xs:string` to a `String`, an `xs:boolean` to a Java `boolean`, and so on. The `xs:integer` type is a little tricky because XML Schema doesn't define its maximum range; Saxon maps it to a Java `long`, but other products may make a different choice; for example «java.math.BigInteger». Bindings for the more common types are defined in the Java Architecture for XML Binding (JAXB, see `http://java.sun.com/xml/downloads/jaxb.html`). The same bindings are used in the draft XQuery API for Java (`www.xquery.com/tutorials/xqj_tutorial/`), and it's quite likely that they will also be adopted by XSLT vendors. The more complex date, time, and duration types, which have no direct equivalent in Java, have been mapped to new classes introduced in JDK 1.5 for the purpose: `Duration` and `XMLGregorianCalendar`, both in package `javax.xml.datatypes`.

With XSLT 1.0 most XSLT processors naturally followed the *weak typing* approach of implicitly converting the supplied parameters in the XPath function call to the required type declared in the Java method. However, with XSLT 2.0 it is more logical to switch to a stricter model aligned with the XPath 2.0 function calling rules, where only very limited conversions between the supplied value and the required type are supported. For backward-compatibility reasons, however, Saxon still supports many implicit conversions, for example allowing a boolean to be supplied where an integer is expected.

When the values passed to an extension function are nodes, rather than atomic values, the data mapping issues become more complicated. The accepted standard for manipulating XML trees in most languages is the DOM, and it's likely that many processors will offer extension functions the ability to manipulate nodes using the DOM interface, even though the DOM does not match the XSLT/XPath data model particularly well. This is discussed in the section *XPath Trees and the DOM* on page 963.

Binding Using External Objects in the Microsoft .NET Processor

With the Microsoft `System.Xml.Xsl` processor, extension function calls are treated as calls to methods on external objects, and the objects themselves must be supplied by the calling application. A detailed explanation of the mechanism is given at `http://support.microsoft.com/kb/323370/EN-US/`. For example, suppose you want to call the method `GetPrice()` on an object of class `Product` in the .NET namespace `Inventory`. You need to choose a namespace URI to refer to this extension object, say `urn:Product`. Then in the calling application, before invoking the XSLT processor, you can do:

```
Inventory.Product product = catalog.GetProduct('12345');
XsltArgumentList args = new XsltArgumentList();
args.AddExtensionObject('urn:Product', product);
```

The argument list is supplied as a parameter to the `Transform` method that runs the transformation:

```
xslt.Transform(xmlDoc, args, Response.OutputStream);
```

Extensibility

In the stylesheet you can then call methods on this object using a call of the form:

```
<xsl:value-of select="product:GetPrice()" xmlns:product="urn:Product"/>
```

One benefit of this design is that it does not depend on dynamic loading of classes, which means it is likely to be fairly efficient.

Binding to Assemblies in Saxon on .NET

Saxon runs both on Java and on .NET. The .NET version of the product uses a similar approach to the Java product, where the namespace URI part of the extension function name is used to identify the class, and the local part is used to identify the method within that class. The namespace URI, however, is rather more elaborate than that used in the Java case, reflecting the complexity (and power) of the mechanisms for controlling dynamic loading of assemblies in .NET.

Extension functions can be written in any .NET language (C# is most common). To call a method `GetPrice()` in class `Product` in namespace `Inventory`, the general format is:

```
<xsl:value-of select="product:GetPrice()"
              xmlns:product="clitype:Inventory.Product"/>
```

If the assembly containing the code is a system assembly, or if it has been preloaded by the application, this is all that is needed. If the assembly needs to be dynamically loaded then additional information can be supplied in the form of query parameters. For example, to load an assembly that is stored with a strong name in the global assembly cache, you can specify the assembly name, version, and public key token as follows:

```
<xsl:value-of select="product:GetPrice()" xmlns:product=
  "clitype:Inventory.Product?asm=InvApp;ver=5.0.0.1;sn="b03e5f7e11c50a4b"/>
```

Saxon on .NET allows both static and instance-level methods to be invoked, in the same way as the Java product, and with similar conventions for mapping the argument types. It also allows property values to be accessed as if the property were a zero-argument method (the name is used as is, no "Get" prefix is added.)

Binding to Extension Functions in Gestalt

The Gestalt XSLT 2.0 processor written by Colin Adams illustrates yet another approach to extension function binding.

Extension functions must be written in Eiffel, and each extension function is implemented as a subclass of `XM_XPATH_SYSTEM_FUNCTION`. The class needs to implement as a minimum a method `evaluate_item()` (for functions with singleton results) or `create_iterator()` (if the result is a sequence), and methods that tell the system what the types of the arguments and result are. The class can also override other methods such as `optimize()` that are called at compile time. For example, this would allow a function that accepts a regular expression as an argument to do some preprocessing of the regular expression at compile time if it is supplied as a string literal.

You then need to create an object representing your library of extension functions as a subclass of `XM_XPATH_FUNCTION_LIBRARY`, and you must register this function library with the XSLT processor via an API call `add_extension_function_library()` before running a transformation.

This approach to binding of extension functions puts a lot more burden on the developer, but it also gives the ability for close integration and high performance. Essentially, it means that extension functions written by users have exactly the same status as functions built into the system by the vendor.

XPath Trees and the DOM

We haven't got space in this book for a detailed description of the DOM interface, but most readers will already have come across it in some form, and it is described in detail in most good books on XML. The DOM provides an object model (and therefore an API) for navigating and manipulating XML data in tree form. Many XSLT processors allow extension functions to access nodes by using the methods defined in the DOM API.

If you want extension functions to access the XSLT source tree, or a secondary input tree that was loaded using the `document()` function, or even a temporary tree constructed during the course of the XSLT transformation, then you can generally do this by passing a node as one of the function arguments. The extension function can then manipulate this node, and other related nodes such as its children and parent, as objects in a DOM structure. It may also be possible for an extension function to construct a new tree, and return it (typically as a DOM Document object) to the calling XPath expression, where it can be manipulated as a secondary input tree in the same way as the result of the XSLT `document()` function. Some products may also allow a DOM that's passed to an extension function to be modified in situ — this is definitely a dubious practice, because it creates a dependency on order of execution, but it's not absolutely prohibited.

The only problem with using the DOM in this way is that there are many small but significant differences between the tree model used by XSLT and XPath, and the tree model defined in the DOM specification. For example, the DOM exposes entity references and CDATA sections, the XPath model doesn't.

This is exacerbated by the fact that there are two different implementation approaches adopted by XSLT vendors: both are perfectly valid and both need to be catered for. Some products, such as Microsoft MSXML3, are DOM-oriented. This processor uses a DOM as its internal tree model, and provides the XPath model as a virtual data structure (a view or wrapper) on top of this. This means, for example, that CDATA sections will be physically present on the tree, and XPath operations such as `following-sibling::node()` will dynamically merge the CDATA contents with the surrounding text nodes. When an extension function is called, such a product will present the native underlying DOM to the called function, CDATA nodes and all. Other products (Saxon is an example, as is the XSLT processor in Microsoft .NET) use an internal data structure that is closely aligned to the XPath model described in Chapter 2. This data structure will have discarded any information that is not needed for XPath processing, such as CDATA sections and entity references. When an external function is called, the situation is now reversed; such a product will provide the DOM interface as a wrapper on top of the native XPath model.

It's impossible to hide all the differences between these two approaches. For example, where the XSLT specifications dictate that whitespace nodes must be stripped from the tree, a DOM-oriented product will probably not remove these nodes physically from the tree, but will simply hide them from XPath view. A product that uses a native XPath tree is likely to remove the unwanted whitespace nodes from the tree while building the tree. This means that with one approach, the stripped whitespace nodes will be present in the DOM as seen by extension functions, and with the other, they will be absent.

Another difference is that with a native XPath tree, adjacent text nodes will be merged (or normalized) into a single node, whereas with a native DOM tree, they may be unnormalized. (Actually, MSXML3 doesn't always normalize text nodes correctly even in the XPath tree view.)

What all this means is that if you want your extension functions to be fully portable between different processors, you have to be aware of these possible differences, and work around them. The following table lists the areas of potential differences between the DOM view and the XPath view.

16

Extensibility

XPath Node	DOM Node	Correspondence
Document	Document	One to one.
Element	Element	One to one.
Attribute	Attr	The XPath tree never represents namespace declarations as attributes named `xmlns` or `xmlns:*`. The DOM might or might not have such `Attr` nodes. If the source document used entity references within the attribute value, these might or might not be preserved in the DOM. The value of the `getSpecified` property in the DOM is unpredictable.
Text	Text	The DOM text nodes might or might not be normalized. If CDATA sections were used in the original document, CDATA nodes might or might not be present in the DOM. If the source document used entity references within the text value, these might or might not be preserved in the DOM. Whitespace nodes that have been stripped as far as XSLT processing is concerned might or might not be present as text nodes in the DOM.
Processing instruction	Processing instruction	One to one.
Comment	Comment	One to one.
Namespace	N/A	There is no direct equivalent in the DOM to XPath's namespace nodes. It is possible in a DOM for elements and attributes to use namespace URIs that are not declared anywhere on the tree.
N/A	CDATA section	CDATA section nodes may be present on the DOM tree if this is the native data structure used by the processor, but they are unlikely to be present if the processor constructs a DOM from the XPath tree.
N/A	Entity reference	Entity reference nodes may be present on the DOM tree if this is the native data structure used by the processor, but they are unlikely to be present if the processor constructs a DOM from the XPath tree.

When you call methods defined in the DOM, the result will follow the DOM rules, not the XPath rules. For example, in XPath the string value of an element node is the concatenation of all the text content within that element; but in the DOM, the apparently similar `nodeValue()` method returns `null`.

It's not a good idea to attempt to update a DOM that is passed to an extension function. Three things might happen, depending on the implementation:

❑ The attempt to update the DOM may cause an exception.

❑ If the DOM was constructed as a copy of the XPath tree, the updates may succeed, but have no effect on the tree as seen subsequently within the stylesheet.

❑ If the DOM and the XPath tree are different views of the same data, then updates may affect the subsequent XSLT processing. This might cause subsequent failures, for example, if nodes have been deleted while the XSLT processor holds references to them.

Constructing a new tree, in the form of a DOM, and returning this to the stylesheet as the result of the extension function, is perfectly OK if the implementation allows it.

These rules for the mapping of XPath trees probably seem rather complicated, and there are certainly lots of potential pitfalls. My own advice would be to steer clear of this area if you possibly can. Navigating around the tree is something you can do perfectly well within XSLT and XPath; you don't need to escape into a different language for this. It's simpler, and usually quite adequate, to pass simple strings and numbers to your extension functions.

If you want to write an extension function that constructs and returns a new tree, you might well find that a simpler alternative is to call the `document()` function and implement a `URIResolver` (or in .NET, an `XmlResolver`) that takes the URI provided in this call, and returns the relevant data source. The JAXP URIResolver interface is described in Appendix E, and an overview of the .NET transformation API is provided in Appendix D.

Calling External Functions within a Loop

I wanted to show an example that includes a reasonably realistic stylesheet with multiple calls on extension functions. It turns out that all the examples I used for this in XSLT 1.0 are things that can be done quite straightforwardly with standard facilities in XSLT 2.0. However, with this caveat, I've decided to retain this example to show the principles.

This example is specific to the Saxon processor. It can be made to work with any processor that supports Java extension functions, but it will need minor alterations.

Example: Calling External Functions within a Loop

In this example, we will use a Java `BufferedReader` object to read an external file, copying it to the output one line at a time, each line being followed by an empty `<br/>` element. (The alternative way of doing this would be to read the file using the `unparsed-text()` function described in Chapter 13, and then to break it into its lines using `<xsl:analyze-string>`.)

Source

This stylesheet doesn't need a primary source document.

The real input is a serial file, which can be any text file. For example, the following `hiawatha.txt`:

```
Take your bow, O Hiawatha,
Take your arrows, jasper-headed,
Take your war-club, Puggawaugun,
And your mittens, Minjekahwan,
And your birch-canoe for sailing,
And the oil of Mishe-Nama.
```

Stylesheet

The stylesheet can be downloaded as `reader.xsl`.

First, we declare the namespaces we will need. It's often easiest to declare these namespaces on the `<xsl:stylesheet>` element itself. I shall stick to the convention of using the «java:*» URI to identify the name of the Java class, and I will also use the abbreviated class name as the namespace prefix. You won't usually want these namespaces appearing in the result document, so you can suppress them using `exclude-result-prefixes`.

```
<xsl:stylesheet
    xmlns:xsl="http://www.w3.org/1999/XSL/Transform"
    version="2.0"
    xmlns:xs="http://www.w3.org/2001/XMLSchema"
    xmlns:FileReader="java:java.io.FileReader"
    xmlns:BufferedReader="java:java.io.BufferedReader"
    exclude-result-prefixes="FileReader BufferedReader">
```

The name of the file we want to read from will be supplied as a parameter to the stylesheet. We need to declare the type of the parameter, because the Java class has three constructors that take a single argument, and Saxon needs to know (at compile time) which of them to call.

```
<xsl:param name="filename" as="xs:string"/>
```

When we are ready to read the file, we create the `BufferedReader` in a variable. Then we call a template to read the file, line by line.

```
<xsl:template name="main">
<out>
    <xsl:variable name="reader"
            select="BufferedReader:new(FileReader:new($filename))"/>
    <xsl:call-template name="read-lines">
        <xsl:with-param name="reader" select="$reader"/>
    </xsl:call-template>
</out>
</xsl:template>
```

The `read-lines` template reads and outputs the first line of the file, and then calls itself recursively to process the remainder. The `readLine()` method of the `BufferedReader` class returns `null` to indicate that the end of file has been reached, and in Saxon, a Java null is translated to a return value of an empty sequence. So we test whether to continue the recursion using the test «`exists($line)`», which returns `false` when the return value was null.

```
<xsl:template name="read-lines">
    <xsl:param name="reader"/>
    <xsl:variable name="line"
                select="BufferedReader:readLine($reader)"/>
    <xsl:if test="exists($line)">
        <xsl:value-of select="$line"/><br/>
        <xsl:call-template name="read-lines">
            <xsl:with-param name="reader" select="$reader"/>
        </xsl:call-template>
    </xsl:if>
</xsl:template>
</xsl:stylesheet>
```

Note that this template is tail-recursive: it does no further work after calling itself. This means that a processor that provides tail-call optimization should be able to handle arbitrary long input files. A processor without this feature may fail with a stack overflow, perhaps after reading 500 or 1000 lines of text.

Output

When you run this stylesheet, you need to supply a value for the filename parameter. For example:

```
java net.sf.saxon.Transform -it:main -xsl:reader.xsl filename=hiawatha.txt
```

This command line invokes Saxon without a source document, specifying «main» as the name of the first template to be executed, and «hiawatha.txt» as the value of the «filename» parameter.

The output looks like this, adding newlines for clarity.

```
<?xml version="1.0" encoding="UTF-8"?>
<out>
Take your bow, O Hiawatha,<br/>
Take your arrows, jasper-headed,<br/>
Take your war-club, Puggawaugun,<br/>
And your mittens, Minjekahwan,<br/>
And your birch-canoe for sailing,<br/>
And the oil of Mishe-Nama.<br/>
</out>
```

In this example, the function call does have side effects, because the reader variable is an external Java object that holds information about the current position in the file being read, and advances this position each time a line is read from the file. In general, function calls with side effects are dangerous, because XSLT does not define the order in which statements are executed. But in this case, the logic of the stylesheet is such that an XSLT processor would have to be very devious indeed to execute the statements in any order other than the obvious one. The fact that the recursive call on the read-lines template is within an <xsl:if> instruction that tests the $line variable means that the processor is forced to read a line, test the result, and then, if necessary, make the recursive call to read further lines.

The next example uses side effects in a much less controlled way, and in this case causes results that will vary from one XSLT processor to another.

Functions with Uncontrolled Side Effects

Just to illustrate the dangers of using functions with side effects, we'll include an example where the effects are not predictable.

Example: A Function with Uncontrolled Side Effects

This example shows how a processor can call extension functions in an unpredictable order, causing incorrect results if the functions have side effects. This can apply even when the extension function is apparently read-only.

Source

Like the previous example, this stylesheet doesn't use a source document.

In this example we'll read an input file containing names and addresses; for example, `addresses.txt`. We'll assume this file is created by a legacy application and consists of groups of five lines. Each group contains a customer number on the first line, the customer's name on the second, an address on lines three and four, and a telephone number on line five. Because that's the way legacy data files often work, we'll assume that the last line of the file contains the string «****».

```
15668
Mary Cousens
15 Birch Drive
Wigan
01367-844355
17796
John Templeton
17 Spring Gardens
Wolverhampton
01666-932865
19433
Jane Arbuthnot
92 Mountain Avenue
Swansea
01775-952266
****
```

Stylesheet

We might be tempted to write the stylesheet as follows (`addresses.xsl`), modifying the previous example:

```
<xsl:stylesheet
    xmlns:xsl="http://www.w3.org/1999/XSL/Transform" version="2.0"
    xmlns:xs="http://www.w3.org/2001/XMLSchema"
    xmlns:FileReader="java:java.io.FileReader"
    xmlns:BufferedReader="java:java.io.BufferedReader"
    exclude-result-prefixes="FileReader BufferedReader">
<xsl:output indent="yes"/>
<xsl:param name="filename" as="xs:string"/>
<xsl:template name="main">
    <xsl:variable name="reader"
               select="BufferedReader:new(FileReader:new($filename))"/>
    <xsl:call-template name="read-addresses">
        <xsl:with-param name="reader" select="$reader"/>
    </xsl:call-template>
</xsl:template>
<xsl:template name="read-addresses">
    <xsl:param name="reader"/>
    <xsl:variable name="line1"
                select="BufferedReader:readLine ($reader)"/>
```

```
      <xsl:if test="$line1 != '****'">
        <xsl:variable name="line2"
                       select="BufferedReader:readLine($reader)"/>
        <xsl:variable name="line3"
                       select="BufferedReader:readLine($reader)"/>
        <xsl:variable name="line4"
                       select="BufferedReader:readLine($reader)"/>
        <xsl:variable name="line5"
                       select="BufferedReader:readLine($reader)"/>
        <label>
          <address>
            <xsl:value-of select="$line3"/><br/>
            <xsl:value-of select="$line4"/><br/>
          </address>
          <recipient>Attn: <xsl:value-of select="$line2"/></recipient>
        </label>
        <xsl:call-template name="read-addresses">
            <xsl:with-param name="reader" select="$reader"/>
        </xsl:call-template>
      </xsl:if>
  </xsl:template>
</xsl:stylesheet>
```

What's the difference? This time we are making an assumption that the four variables $line2, $line3, line4, and $line5 will be evaluated in the order we've written them. *There is no guarantee of this*. The processor is quite at liberty not to evaluate a variable until it is used, and if this happens then $line3 will be evaluated *before* $line2, and worse still, $line5 (because it is never used) might not be evaluated at all, meaning that instead of reading a group of five lines from the file, the template will only read four lines each time it is invoked.

Output

The result, in the case of Saxon, is a disaster.

```
<?xml version="1.0" encoding="UTF-8"?>
<label>
   <address>15 Birch Drive<br/>Wigan<br/>
   </address>
   <recipient>Attn: Mary Cousens</recipient></label>
<label>
   <address>John Templeton<br/>17 Spring Gardens<br/>
   </address>
   <recipient>Attn: 17796</recipient>
</label>
<label>
   <address>19433<br/>Jane Arbuthnot<br/>
   </address>
   <recipient>Attn: 01666-932865</recipient>
</label>
```

```
<label>
    <address>01775-952266<br/>****<br/>
    </address>
    <recipient>Attn: Swansea</recipient>
</label>
```

Saxon doesn't evaluate a variable until you refer to it, and it doesn't evaluate the variable at all if you never refer to it. This becomes painfully visible in the output, which reveals that it's simply not safe for an XSLT stylesheet to make assumptions about the order of execution of different instructions.

This stylesheet might work on some XSLT processors, but it certainly won't work on all.

The correct way to tackle this stylesheet in XSLT 2.0 is to read the whole text using the `unparsed-text()` function, then to split it into lines using either `<xsl:analyze-string>` or the `tokenize()` function, and then to use grouping facilities to split it into groups of five lines each. There is no need for extension functions at all.

This example raises the question of whether there is any way you can write a call to an extension function and be sure that the call will actually be executed, given that the function is one that returns no result. It's hard to give a categorical answer to this because there is no limit on the ingenuity of optimizers to avoid doing work that makes no contribution to the result tree. However, with Saxon today a function that returns no result is treated in the same way as one that returns `null`, which is interpreted in XPath as an empty sequence. So you can call a void method using:

```
<xsl:sequence select="class:voidMethod()"/>
```

and provided the `<xsl:sequence>` instruction itself is evaluated, the method will always be called.

Keeping Extensions Portable

As soon as your stylesheet uses extension functions, or other permitted extensions such as extension instructions or extension attributes, keeping it portable across different XSLT processors becomes a challenge. Fortunately, the design of the XSLT language anticipated this problem, and offers some help.

There are a number of interrogative functions that you can use to find out about the environment that your stylesheet is running in. The most important are as follows:

❑ The `system-property()` function, which allows you to determine the XSLT version supported and the name and version of the XSLT processor itself.

❑ The `function-available()` function, which allows you to determine whether a particular extension function is available. This is particularly useful when you are using a third-party library such as EXSLT, where the same functions may be available under a number of different XSLT processors.

Use these functions to test whether particular vendor extensions are available before calling them. The best way to do this is using the new «use-when» attribute described in Chapter 3, which allows a section of the stylesheet (perhaps a whole template, perhaps a single `<xsl:value-of>` instruction) to be conditionally included or excluded from the stylesheet at compile time. For example, the following code sets a variable to the result of the `random:random-sequence()` function (defined in EXSLT) if it is available, or to the fractional seconds value from the current time if not.

```
<xsl:variable name="random-number"
              select="seconds-from-time(current-time()) mod 1.0e0"
              use-when="not(function-available('random:random-sequence', 2))"
              xmlns:random="http://exslt.org/random"/>
<xsl:variable name="random-number"
              select="random:random-sequence(1, ())"
              use-when="function-available('random:random-sequence', 2)"
              xmlns:random="http://exslt.org/random"/>
```

(In fact, the «use-when» attribute on the first `<xsl:variable>` declaration is not strictly needed, assuming these are local variables. If the «use-when» attribute on the second variable evaluates to true, this variable will shadow the first variable, and it does no harm for both variables to be present.)

Note that the rules for the «use-when» attribute require it to be a condition that can be evaluated at compile time. It's therefore not permitted in this expression to reference the values of variables or stylesheet parameters, or to access the contents of a source document.

You can use similar techniques to make a stylesheet portable between different XSLT versions. In this case there are additional facilities available, notably the `[xsl:]version` attribute, which can be attached to any element in the stylesheet. Version compatibility is fully discussed in Chapter 3, on page 128.

Summary

Extension functions are useful to extend the capabilities of XSLT stylesheets. They allow stylesheets to access external system services and to perform calculations that are difficult or inefficient to achieve in "pure" XSLT and XPath.

There are other extensibility mechanisms in XSLT, including extension instructions, extension declarations, and extension attributes, but extension functions are by far the most widely used, so that's what we concentrated on in this chapter.

In the next chapter, we move away from detailed specifications of interfaces and look at using the facilities of XSLT to create well-designed stylesheets.

16

Extensibility

17

Stylesheet Design Patterns

This chapter looks at four common design patterns for XSLT stylesheets.

The concept of design patterns was introduced by Erich Gamma, Richard Helm, Ralph Johnson, and John Vlissides in their classic book *Design Patterns: Elements of Reusable Object-Oriented Software* (Addison-Wesley Publishing, 1995). Their idea was that there was a repertoire of techniques that were useful again and again. They presented 23 different design patterns for object-oriented programming, claiming not that this was a complete list but that the vast majority of programs written by experienced designers fell into one or more of these patterns.

For XSLT stylesheets, the vast majority of stylesheets I have seen fall into one of four design patterns. These are as follows:

- ❏ Fill-in-the-blanks stylesheets
- ❏ Navigational stylesheets
- ❏ Rule-based stylesheets
- ❏ Computational stylesheets

Again, this doesn't mean that these are the only ways you can write stylesheets, nor does it mean that any stylesheet you write must follow one of these four patterns to the exclusion of the other three. It just means that a great many stylesheets actually written by experienced people follow one of these four patterns, and if you become familiar with these patterns, you will have a good repertoire of techniques that you can apply to solving any given problem.

I describe the first three design patterns rather briefly, because they are not really very difficult. The fourth, the computational design pattern, is explored in much greater depth — not because it is encountered more often, but because it requires a different way of thinking about algorithms than you use with conventional procedural programming languages.

Fill-in-the-Blanks Stylesheets

Many proprietary templating languages have been built up around HTML. The template looks largely like a standard HTML file but with the addition of extra tags used to retrieve variable data and insert it at a particular point in the HTML data page. The designers of XSLT took care to ensure that, in spite of the power of XSLT as a full transformation language, it would still be possible to use it in this simple way, bringing it within the reach of nonprogrammers with HTML authoring skills.

Example: A "Fill-in-the-Blanks" Stylesheet

Here's an example of such a stylesheet. It uses the *simplified stylesheet* syntax, so the `<xsl:stylesheet>` element and the `<xsl:template match="/">` element are implicit.

Input

This XML document, `orgchart.xml`, represents an organization chart showing the senior management of a certain company at a particular date. It is organized as a recursive structure that directly reflects the management hierarchy. You may recognize the names, but the roles are entirely fictitious.

```xml
<?xml version="1.0" encoding="iso-8859-1"?>
<orgchart date="2004-03-31">
<person>
    <name>Tim Berners-Lee</name>
    <title>Chief Executive Officer</title>
    <reports>
        <person>
            <name>Sharon Adler</name>
            <title>Technical Director</title>
            <reports>
                <person>
                    <name>Tim Bray</name>
                    <title>Chief Engineer</title>
                </person>
                <person>
                    <name>James Clark</name>
                    <title>Director of Research</title>
                </person>
            </reports>
        </person>
        <person>
            <name>Henry Thompson</name>
            <title>Operations and Finance</title>
        </person>
        <person>
            <name>David Megginson</name>
            <title>Human Resources</title>
        </person>
        <person>
            <name>Steve Muench</name>
            <title>Marketing</title>
        </person>
        <person>
```

```
            <name>Scott Boag</name>
            <title>International</title>
        </person>
    </reports>
</person>
```

Stylesheet

There are many creative ways to display this data; for example, you could use SVG graphics, Explorer-style trees implemented in client-side JavaScript, or just indented lists. I'm not trying to teach you any clever HTML tricks, so in this stylesheet (`orgchart.xsl`) I'll show the data instead, as a rather boring table, with one row per person and three columns for the person's name, their title, and the name of their boss.

```
<html xmlns:xsl="http://www.w3.org/1999/XSL/Transform"
      xsl:version="2.0">
<head>
      <title>Management Structure</title>
</head>
<body>
   <h1>Management Structure</h1>
   <p>The following responsibilities were announced on
      <xsl:value-of select="format-date(/orgchart/@date,
                                  '[D1] [MNn] [Y1]')"/>:</p>
   <table border="2" cellpadding="5">
   <tr>
     <th>Name</th><th>Role</th><th>Reporting to</th>
   </tr>
   <xsl:for-each select="//person">
     <tr>
        <td><xsl:value-of select="name"/></td>
        <td><xsl:value-of select="title"/></td>
        <td><xsl:value-of select="ancestor::person[1]/name"/></td>
     </tr>
   </xsl:for-each>
   </table>
   <hr/>
</body>
</html>
```

The key to this design pattern is that the stylesheet has the same structure as the desired output. Fixed content is included directly in the stylesheet as text or as literal result elements, while variable content is included by means of `<xsl:value-of>` instructions that extract the relevant data from the source document. Repeated sections of output, typically rows in a table or items in a list, can be enclosed by `<xsl:for-each>`, and conditional sections by `<xsl:if>` or `<xsl:choose>`.

Output

The output of this stylesheet is shown in Figure 17-1.

Figure 17-1

This kind of stylesheet makes very limited use of XSLT's power, but it is very similar to a wide variety of proprietary templating languages currently in use. Experience has shown that this kind of stylesheet is easy for experienced HTML authors to write, even if they have no programming training. This is an important consideration, because on many larger Web sites there is a constant need to introduce new page templates at very short notice, and this becomes much easier to achieve if content authors and editors can do the work themselves.

One restriction, of course, is that the input has to come from an XML document. This contrasts with most of the proprietary languages, where the input often comes directly from a relational database. Fortunately, all popular relational databases now provide convenient ways to extract data from a database in XML form. Ideally, this doesn't even need to be a serial XML document that has to be re-parsed by the XSLT processor. It will often be possible to transfer the data directly from the database to the XSLT processor in a structured form; for example, as a DOM tree in memory or as a SAX event stream. The details of how to do this depend on the database product you are using and are beyond the scope of this book.

Another approach is to use the document() function (described in Chapter 13, page 754) with a URI that addresses a servlet with parameters to retrieve the required data.

Navigational Stylesheets

Navigational stylesheets are a natural progression from simple fill-in-the-blanks stylesheets.

Like fill-in-the-blanks stylesheets, a navigational stylesheet is still essentially output-oriented. However, it is now likely to use named templates or stylesheet functions as subroutines to perform commonly needed tasks; it may use variables to calculate values needed in more than one place, and it may use constructs such as keys, parameters, and sorting.

Whereas a fill-in-the-blanks stylesheet looks like HTML sprinkled with a few extra control statements, a navigational stylesheet (once you look beyond the angle-bracket syntax) has a rather similar structure to a conventional procedural program with variables, conditional statements, for loops, and subroutine calls.

Navigational stylesheets are often used to produce reports on data-oriented XML documents, where the structure of the source document is regular and predictable.

Example: A Navigational Stylesheet

This example shows the use of a navigational stylesheet to produce a very simple sales report.

Input

Suppose the source document, `booklist.xml`, looks like this:

```xml
<?xml version="1.0" encoding="iso-8859-1"?>
<booklist>
   <book>
      <title>Angela's Ashes</title>
      <author>Frank McCourt</author>
      <publisher>HarperCollins</publisher>
      <isbn>0 00 649840 X</isbn>
      <price>6.99</price>
      <sales>235</sales>
   </book>
   <book>
      <title>Sword of Honour</title>
      <author>Evelyn Waugh</author>
      <publisher>Penguin Books</publisher>
      <isbn>0 14 018967 X</isbn>
      <price>12.99</price>
      <sales>12</sales>
   </book>
</booklist>
```

Stylesheet

The following navigational stylesheet (`booksales.xsl`) produces a report on the total number of sales for each publisher.

```xml
<xsl:stylesheet xmlns:xsl="http://www.w3.org/1999/XSL/Transform"
   xmlns:xs="http://www.w3.org/2001/XMLSchema"
   exclude-result-prefixes="xs"
   version="2.0">

<xsl:key name="pub" match="book" use="publisher"/>
```

We need to declare a variable that refers to the input document, for later use in a named template that has no context node.

```
<xsl:variable name="in" select="/" as="document-node()"/>
```

The global variable «$publishers» is a sequence of strings containing one string for each distinct publisher found in the source file. This uses the new distinct-values() function introduced in XPath 2.0.

```
<xsl:variable name="publishers" as="xs:string*"
   select="distinct-values(/booklist/book/publisher)"/>
```

The main template iterates over the distinct publishers using <xsl:for-each>.

```
<xsl:template match="/">
<html>
<head>
   <title>Sales volume by publisher</title>
</head>
<body>
   <h1>Sales volume by publisher</h1>
   <table>
      <tr>
         <th>Publisher</th><th>Total Sales Value</th>
      </tr>
      <xsl:for-each select="$publishers">
         <tr>
            <td><xsl:value-of select="."/></td>
            <td><xsl:call-template name="total-sales"/></td>
         </tr>
      </xsl:for-each>
   </table>
</body>
</html>
</xsl:template>
```

Finally, a named template that calculates the total sales for the publisher. The name of the publisher is supplied as an implicit parameter in the context node; however, to make the template more reusable a parameter is declared with this as the default.

```
<xsl:template name="total-sales">
   <xsl:param name="publisher" select="."/>
   <xsl:value-of select="sum($in/key('pub', $publisher)/sales)"/>
</xsl:template>
</xsl:stylesheet>
```

This stylesheet is not very far removed from the fill-in-the-blanks example earlier in the chapter. But because it uses some top-level elements such as <xsl:key> and a named template, it now needs to use the full syntax with an <xsl:stylesheet> element.

Output

The output is shown in Figure 17-2.

Figure 17-2

The obvious difference between a fill-in-the-blanks stylesheet and this navigational stylesheet is that the `<xsl:stylesheet>` and `<xsl:template>` elements are now explicit, which makes it possible to introduce other top-level elements, such as `<xsl:key>` and global `<xsl:variable>` elements. More subtly, the range of XSLT features used means that this stylesheet has crossed the boundary from being an HTML document with added control instructions, to being a real program. The boundary, though, is a rather fuzzy one, with no visa required to cross it, so many people who have learned to write simple fill-in-the-blanks stylesheets should be able, as they expand their knowledge, to progress to writing navigational stylesheets of this kind.

Although the use of flow-of-control instructions like `<xsl:if>`, `<xsl:call-template>`, and `<xsl:for-each>` gives such a stylesheet a procedural feel, it does not violate the original concept that XSLT should be a declarative language. This is because the instructions do not have to be executed in the order they are written — variables can't be updated, so the result of one instruction can't affect the next one. For example, it's easy to think of the `<xsl:for-each>` instruction in this example processing the selected nodes in document order and adding them one by one to the result tree, but it would be equally valid for an XSLT processor to process them in reverse order, or in parallel, as long as the nodes are added to the result tree in the right place. That's why I was careful to call this design pattern *navigational* rather than *procedural*. It's navigational in that you say exactly where to find the nodes in the source tree that you want to visit, but it's not procedural, because you don't define the order in which you will visit them.

New features available in XSLT 2.0 and XPath 1.0 greatly increase the scope of what can be achieved with a navigational stylesheet. Many problems that in XSLT 1.0 required complex programming (using the computational design pattern described later in this chapter) can now be tacked within the navigational approach. Examples include grouping problems, and problems that require splitting up of text fields, using delimiters such as commas or newlines, as well as many arithmetic operations such as summing the total value of an invoice. The features that provide this capability include the following:

❑ The availability of sequences in the data model, together with the «for» expression in XPath, to manipulate them.

❑ Grouping constructs, including the `<xsl:for-each-group>` instruction in XSLT 2.0 and the `distinct-values()` function in XPath 2.0.

❑ Text manipulation facilities, notably the `<xsl:analyze-string>` instruction in XSLT 2.0 and the `replace()` and `tokenize()` functions in XPath 2.0.

❑ Aggregation functions such as `avg()`, `min()`, and `max()`.

The ability to write chunks of reusable code in the form of stylesheet functions that can be invoked from XPath expressions, rather than only as templates to be called using XSLT instructions, also helps to make navigational stylesheets much easier to write.

You will often see this kind of code criticized by experts because it doesn't take advantage of XSLT's most powerful feature, the ability to write template rules. The criticism is justified when you use this design pattern inappropriately, in a situation where a rule-based stylesheet would be better. But there are many simple problems where, in my view, this pattern works perfectly well. It produces code that is readable and efficient.

Rule-Based Stylesheets

A rule-based stylesheet consists primarily of rules describing how different features of the source document should be processed, such as "if you find a `<species>` element, display it in italic."

Some would say that this rule-based approach is the essence of the XSLT language, the principal way that it is intended to be used. I would say that it's one way of writing stylesheets, often the best way, but not the only way, and not necessarily the best answer in every situation. It's often strongly recommended in books for beginners, but I think that the main reason for this is that for many beginners the navigational pattern is what comes naturally, because it has a very similar feel to programs written in procedural languages. It's important that every XSLT programmer be comfortable with writing rule-based stylesheets, so it makes sense to teach this approach early on.

Unlike navigational stylesheets, a rule-based stylesheet is not structured according to the desired output layout. In fact, it makes minimal assumptions about the structure of either the source document or the result document. Rather, the structure reads like an inventory of components that might be encountered in the source document, arranged in arbitrary order.

Rule-based stylesheets are therefore most useful when processing source documents whose structure is flexible or unpredictable, or which may change a lot in the future. It is very useful when the same repertoire of elements can appear in many different document structures, so a rule like "display dates in the format *23 March 2008*" can be reused in many different contexts.

Rule-based stylesheets are a natural evolution of CSS. In CSS, you can define rules of the form "for this class of elements, use this display rendition." In XSLT, the rules become much more flexible, in two directions: the pattern language for defining which elements you are talking about is much richer, and the actions you can define when the rule is fired are vastly more wide-ranging.

A simple rule-based stylesheet consists of one rule for each element name. The typical rule matches a particular element name, outputs an HTML tag to define the rendition of that element, and calls `<xsl:apply-templates>` to process the child nodes of the element. This causes text nodes within the element to be copied to the output and nested child elements to be processed each according to its own template rule. In its simplest form, a rule-based stylesheet often contains many rules of the form:

```
<xsl:template match="para">
   <p><xsl:apply-templates/></p>
</xsl:template>
```

This simple rule does a direct replacement of `<para>` tags by `<p>` tags. Most real stylesheets do something a bit more elaborate with some of the tags, but they may still contain many rules that are as simple as this one.

XSLT 2.0 introduces the ability to define rules that match elements and attributes by their type, as defined in a schema, rather than simply by their name or context. This makes the technique even more powerful when handling document structures that are highly complex or extensible. For example, you can match all the elements in a particular substitution group with a single template rule, which means that the stylesheet doesn't need to change when new elements are added to the substitution group later. Similarly, you can define a template rule that formats all elements containing part numbers or dates, irrespective of the element or attribute name.

Example: A Rule-Based Stylesheet

Rule-based stylesheets are often used to process narrative documents, where most of the processing consists in replacing XML tags by HTML tags. This example illustrates this by showing how a Shakespeare play can be rendered in HTML.

Input

The input `scene2.xml` is a scene from a play; Act I, Scene 2 of Shakespeare's *Othello*. It starts like this:

```
<?xml version="1.0" encoding="iso-8859-1" ?>
<SCENE>
    <TITLE>SCENE II. Another street.</TITLE>
    <STAGEDIR>Enter OTHELLO, IAGO, and Attendants with
                 torches</STAGEDIR>
    <SPEECH>
       <SPEAKER>IAGO</SPEAKER>
       <LINE>Though in the trade of war I have slain men,</LINE>
       <LINE>Yet do I hold it very stuff o' the conscience</LINE>
       <LINE>To do no contrived murder: I lack iniquity</LINE>
       <LINE>Sometimes to do me service: nine or ten times</LINE>
       <LINE>I had thought to have yerk'd him here under the ribs.</LINE>
    </SPEECH>
    <SPEECH>
       <SPEAKER>OTHELLO</SPEAKER>
       <LINE>'Tis better as it is.</LINE>
    </SPEECH>
</SCENE>
```

There are some complications that aren't shown in this sample, but which the stylesheet needs to take account of.

The top-level element is not always a `<SCENE>`; it might also be a `<PROLOGUE>` or `<EPILOGUE>`. The `<STAGEDIR>` element (representing a stage direction) can appear at any level of nesting; for example, a stage directive can appear between two speeches, between two lines of a speech, or in the middle of a line.

Several people can speak at the same time. In this case a single `<SPEECH>` element has more than one `<SPEAKER>`. In general, a `<SPEECH>` consists of one or more `<SPEAKER>` elements followed by any number of `<LINE>` and `<STAGEDIR>` elements in any order.

Stylesheet

The stylesheet `scene.xsl` consists of a number of template rules. It starts by declaring a global variable (used simply as a constant) and a rule for the document element.

```
<xsl:stylesheet
    xmlns:xsl="http://www.w3.org/1999/XSL/Transform"
    version="1.0">

<xsl:variable name="backcolor" select="'#FFFFCC'" />

<xsl:template match="SCENE|PROLOGUE|EPILOGUE">
  <html>
  <head>
    <title><xsl:value-of select="TITLE"/></title>
    <style type="text/css">
      h1 {text-align:center}
      h2 {text-align:center; font-size:120%; margin-top:12; margin-bottom:12}
      body {background-color: <xsl:value-of select="$backcolor"/>}
      div.speech {float:left; width:100%; padding:0; margin-top:6}
      div.speaker {float:left; width:160;}
      div.text {float:left}
    </style>
  </head>
  <body>
      <xsl:apply-templates/>
  </body>
  </html>
</xsl:template>
```

Note the use of CSS to achieve the detailed styling. There's nothing inconsistent about using XSLT and CSS in combination in this way. You can also generate a reference to an external CSS stylesheet, but the advantage of generating it inline is that the content can be parameterized.

The appearance of `<xsl:value-of>` is a rare departure from the purely rule-based pattern, just to prove that none of the patterns has to be used to the exclusion of the others.

The template rule for the `<SPEECH>` element outputs the names of the speakers on the left, and the lines of the speech, plus any stage directives, on the right. Rather than using HTML tables, which is often discouraged for accessibility reasons, we use CSS classes for the actual positioning as follows:

```
<xsl:template match="SPEECH">
  <div class="speech">
```

```
        <div class="speaker">
          <xsl:apply-templates select="SPEAKER"/>
        </div>
        <div class="text">
          <xsl:apply-templates select="STAGEDIR|LINE"/>
        </div>
      </div>
    </xsl:template>
```

The remaining template rules are straightforward. Each of them simply outputs the text of the element, using an appropriate HTML rendition. The only complication, which doesn't actually occur in this particular scene, is that for some elements (<STAGEDIR> and <SUBHEAD>) the HTML rendition is different, depending on the element's context, and so there is more than one rule defined for these elements.

```
<xsl:template match="TITLE">
  <h1><xsl:apply-templates/></h1>
  <hr/>
</xsl:template>

<xsl:template match="SPEAKER">
    <b>
      <xsl:apply-templates/>
      <xsl:if test="not(position()=last())"><br/></xsl:if>
    </b>
</xsl:template>

<xsl:template match="SCENE/STAGEDIR">
  <h2>
    <xsl:apply-templates/>
  </h2>
</xsl:template>

<xsl:template match="SPEECH/STAGEDIR">
  <p>
    <i><xsl:apply-templates/></i>
  </p>
</xsl:template>

<xsl:template match="LINE/STAGEDIR">
  <xsl:text>[ </xsl:text>
  <i><xsl:apply-templates/></i>
  <xsl:text> ]</xsl:text>
</xsl:template>

<xsl:template match="SCENE/SUBHEAD">
  <h2><xsl:apply-templates/></h2>
</xsl:template>

<xsl:template match="SPEECH/SUBHEAD">
  <p><b><xsl:apply-templates/></b></p>
</xsl:template>
```

```
<xsl:template match="LINE">
  <xsl:apply-templates/>
  <br/>
</xsl:template>
</xsl:stylesheet>
```

This particular stylesheet doesn't use any XSLT 2.0 features, so I left the version number as «1.0».

Output

The output obtained is shown in Figure 17-3.

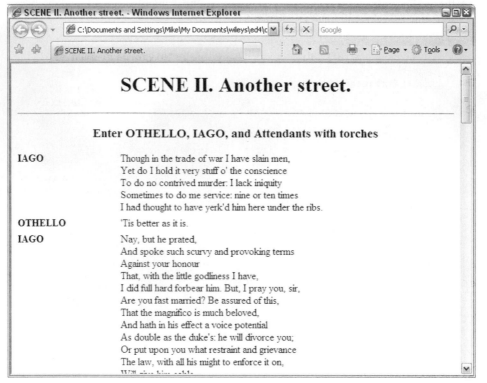

Figure 17-3

Most of the time, a rule-based stylesheet creates a result tree with a structure similar to the source tree — with most of the source text appearing in the same order in the result document, usually with different tags. The closer this describes the transformation you want to do, the closer your stylesheet will be to the example shown above. However, this doesn't mean that the processing has to be purely sequential. You can process chunks of the tree more than once using modes, you can reorder the nodes of the tree, and you can grab data from ancestor nodes, all without deviating from the rule-based design pattern.

The characteristic feature of a rule-based stylesheet is that there is generally one template rule for each class of object found in the source document. I use the term *class* very loosely here: the "classes of object" might correspond to types in a schema, or to element names, or perhaps to element names qualified by their context or content.

Of course, it's possible to mix design patterns, particularly if your source document contains a mixture of "data-oriented" and "text-oriented" structures (an example might be a job application form). Then it's quite appropriate to use a navigational pattern for the regular structures and a rule-based pattern for the less regular. For example, I created a Web site that provides information about concert soloists. This contains a mixture of structured data (their name, instrument or voice, photo, and contact details), semi-structured data about the performances they have taken part in, and unstructured text. The stylesheet to display the data contains a corresponding mixture of coding styles. The larger and more complex your stylesheet, the more likely it is to contain examples of each of the design patterns.

Computational Stylesheets

Computational stylesheets are the most complex of the four design patterns. They arise when there is a need to generate nodes in the result tree that do not correspond directly to nodes in the source tree. With XSLT 1.0, this happened most commonly when dealing with structure in the source document that is not explicit in its markup. For example:

❑ A text field in the source might consist of a comma-separated list of items that is to be displayed as a bulleted list in the output.

❑ There might be a need to generate <section> elements in the output where a section is not explicit in the source but is defined as comprising an <h1> element and all its following sibling elements up to the next <h1> element.

With XSLT 2.0, many of these problems can be tackled using new facilities built into the language: the first of these examples can be handled using <xsl:analyze-string>, and the second using <xsl:for-each-group>. However, sooner or later you will exhaust the capabilities of these constructs and need to write a stylesheet in the form of a general-purpose program. Examples of such problems include the following:

❑ Starting a new page (or other unit) when a running total has reached some threshold value

❑ Analyzing a parts explosion to see if it contains any cycles

❑ Creating graphical representations of numeric data using the vector graphics standard SVG as the output format

When you write computational stylesheets, you invariably run up against the fact that XSLT does not have an assignment statement, and that it is therefore not possible to write loops in the way you are probably used to in other languages. So you need to understand some of the concepts of *functional programming*, which the following section tries to explain.

Programming without Assignment Statements

Back in 1968, the renowned computer scientist Edsger Dijkstra published a paper under the title *GoTo Statement Considered Harmful*. His thesis, suggesting that programs should be written without goto statements, shattered the world as most programmers saw it. Until then they had been familiar with early dialects of FORTRAN and COBOL in which the vast majority of decisions in a program were implemented by using a construct that mapped directly to the conditional jump instruction in the hardware: «if *condition* `goto` *label*». Even the design notation of the day, the ubiquitous flowchart drawn in pencil using a clear plastic template, represented control flow in this way.

Dijkstra argued that structured programs, written using `if-then-else` and `while-do` constructs instead of `goto` statements, were far less likely to contain bugs and were far more readable and therefore maintainable. The ideas were fiercely controversial at the time, especially among practicing programmers, and for years afterwards the opponents of the idea would challenge the structured programming enthusiasts with arguments of the form, "OK, so how do you do *this* without a `goto` statement?"

Today, however, the battle is won, and the `goto` statement has been consigned to history. Modern languages like Java don't provide a `goto` statement, and we no longer miss it.

But for just as long, there has been another group of enthusiasts telling us that assignment statements are considered harmful. Unlike Dijkstra, these evangelists have yet to convince a skeptical world that they are right, though there has always been a significant band of disciples who have seen the benefits of the approach.

This style of coding, without assignment statements, is called *Functional Programming*. The earliest and most famous functional programming language was Lisp (sometimes ridiculed as "Lots of Irritating Superfluous Parentheses"), while more modern examples include ML, Haskell, and Scheme. (See, for example, *Simply Scheme: Introducing Computer Science* by Brian Harvey and Matthew Wright, MIT Press, 1999.)

XSLT is a language without assignment statements, and although its syntax is very different from these languages, its philosophy is based on the concepts of functional programming. It is not a full-fledged functional programming language because you cannot manipulate functions in the same way as data, but in most other respects, it fits into this category of language. If you want to do anything complicated, you must get used to programming without assignment statements. At first, it probably won't be easy: just as early FORTRAN and COBOL programmers instinctively reached for the `goto` statement as the solution to every problem, if your background is in languages like C or Visual Basic, or even Java, you will just as naturally cherish the assignment statement as your favorite all-purpose tool.

So what's wrong with assignment statements, and why aren't they available in XSLT?

The crux of the argument is that it's the assignment statements that impose a particular order of execution on a program. Without assignment statements, we can do things in any order, because the result of one statement can no longer depend on what state the system was left in by the previous statement. Just as the `goto` statement mirrors the `jump` instruction in the hardware, so the assignment statement mirrors the `store` instruction, and the reason we have assignment statements in our programming languages today is that they were designed to take advantage of sequential von Neumann computers with jump and store instructions. If we want to free ourselves from sequential thinking modeled on sequential hardware architecture, we should find a way of describing what effect we want to achieve, rather than saying what sequence of steps the machine should take in order to achieve it.

The idea of a functional program is to describe the output as a function of the input. XSLT is a transformation language; it is designed to transform an input document into an output document. So, we can regard a stylesheet as a function that defines this transformation: a stylesheet is a function $O=S(I)$ where I is the input document, S is the stylesheet, and O is the output document. Recall the statement made by James Clark at the 1995 Paris workshop, which I quoted in Chapter 1, page 28:

> A DSSSL stylesheet very precisely describes a function from SGML to a flow object tree.

This concept clearly remained a key part of the XSLT vision throughout the development of the language. (And, indeed, the flow objects of DSSSL [Document Style Semantics and Specification Language] eventually became the Formatting Objects of XSL-FO.)

We're using the word *function* here in something close to its mathematical sense. Languages like FORTRAN and Visual Basic have borrowed the word to mean a subroutine that returns a result, but the mathematical concept of a function is not that of an algorithm or sequence of steps to be performed, rather it is a statement of a relationship. The square-root function defines a relationship between 3 and 9, namely `3=sqrt(9)`. The essence of a function is that it is a fixed, constant, reliable relationship, and evaluating it doesn't change the world. When you ask me "what's the square root of 9 if you work it out?" I can honestly reply "exactly the same as if I don't." I can say this because square root is a *pure* function; it gives the same answer whoever calls it and however often they call it, and calling it once doesn't change the answer it gives next time; in fact, it doesn't change anything.

The nice property of pure functions is that they can be called any number of times, in any order, and produce the same result every time. If I want to calculate the square root of every integer between zero and a thousand, it doesn't matter whether I start at zero and work up, or start at a thousand and work down, or whether I buy a thousand and one computers and do them all at the same time; I know I will get the same answer. Pure functions have no side effects.

An assignment statement isn't like that. The effect of an assignment statement "if you work it out" is *not* the same as if you don't. When you write «x=x+1;» (a construct, incidentally, which most of us found completely absurd when we were first introduced to programming), the effect depends very much on how often the statement is executed. When you write several assignment statements, for example:

```
temp = x;
x = y;
y = temp;
```

then the effect depends on executing them in the right order.

This means, of course, that a pure function can't update external variables. As soon as we allow assignment, we become dependent on doing things in sequence, one step at a time in the right order.

Don't object-oriented languages achieve the same thing by preventing one object from updating data held in another? No, because although they prevent direct writing to private data, they allow the same effect to be achieved by `get()` and `set()` methods. An update to a variable achieved indirectly through a defined interface creates exactly the same dependence on sequence of execution as an update done directly with an assignment statement. A pure function must have no side effects; its only output is the result it returns.

The main reason that functional languages are considered ideal for a stylesheet language (or a tree transformation language, if you prefer) is not so much the ability to do things in parallel or in any order, but rather the ability to do them incrementally. We want to get away from static pages; if you're showing a map of the traffic congestion hotspots in your area, then when the data for a particular road junction changes, you want the map updated in real time, and it should be possible to do this without recalculating and redrawing the whole map. This is only possible if there's a direct relationship — a function — between what's shown at a particular place on the map display and a particular data item in the underlying database. So if we can decompose our top-level stylesheet function, `O=S(I)`, into a set of smaller, independent functions, each relating one piece of the output to one piece of the input, then we have the potential to do this on-the-fly updating.

Another benefit of this incremental approach is that when a large page of XML is downloaded from the network, the browser can start displaying parts of the output as soon as the relevant parts of the input are available. Some XSLT processors already do this: Xalan, for example, runs the transformation in parallel with the XML parsing process. If the stylesheet were a conventional program with side effects, this wouldn't be possible, because the last bit of input to arrive could change everything.

The actual "functions" in XSLT take several forms. The most obvious functions in XSLT 2.0 are the stylesheet functions written using an `<xsl:function>` element. However, templates (both named templates and template rules) also act as functions: the only real difference between an `<xsl:function>` and an `<xsl:template>` is that the former is called from an XPath expression, and the latter from an XSLT instruction.

XSLT template rules and stylesheet functions act as small, independent functions relating one piece of the output to one piece of the input. Functions and template rules in XSLT have no side effects; their output is a pure function of their input. Stylesheet functions follow this model more strictly than templates, because the only input they have is the values of the parameters to the function (plus global variables and the results of functions such as `document()`, which access parts of the context that cannot vary from one function call to another within a given transformation). Templates are less pure, because they also take the current position in the input document, and other context information, as implicit input parameters. But the principle is the same.

> *Technically, functions in XSLT are not completely pure, because they can create nodes with distinct identity. If a function creates and returns a new node `<a/>`, then calling the function twice with the same arguments produces two elements with the same content but with different identity, which means that the expression «f() is f() » will return* `false`. *Fortunately, it's not too difficult for an optimizer to detect when a function has this characteristic.*

It doesn't matter in what order the template rules are executed, so long as we assemble their individual outputs together in the right way to form the result tree. If part of the input changes, then we need to reevaluate only those template rules that depend on that part of the input, slotting their outputs into the appropriate place in the output tree. In practice, of course, it's not as easy as that, and no one has yet implemented an incremental stylesheet processor that works like this. However, many XSLT processors do take advantage of the freedom to change the order of evaluation, by using a technique known as *lazy evaluation*.

Lazy evaluation means, in general, that expressions are not evaluated until their values are actually needed. This provides two benefits: firstly, it avoids allocating memory to hold the results. (Although modern machines have vast amounts of memory, processing large XSLT documents can be very memory-intensive, and the overhead of allocating and deallocating memory dynamically accounts for a lot of the cost of XSLT processing.) Secondly, lazy evaluation sometimes means that an expression doesn't need to be evaluated at all. To take a simple example, in a function call such as «string-join($sequence, $separator)», there is no need to evaluate the second argument unless the first argument is a sequence containing two or more items.

Meanwhile, while the researchers and product developers work out how to optimize XSLT execution using incremental and parallel evaluation, you, as a user, are left with a different problem: learning how to program without assignment statements. After this rather lengthy digression into computer science theory, in the next section I shall get my feet back on the ground and show you some examples of how to do this.

However, first let's try and separate this from another programming challenge that arose with XSLT 1.0, namely the limited number of types available. This restriction has been greatly eased in XSLT 2.0, now that arbitrary sequences are available in the data model. In terms of language design principles, the lack of assignment statements and the absence of a rich type system are quite separate matters. With XSLT 1.0, you often hit the two issues together:

❑ The only effect a template could have was via the output it produced (because of the ban on side effects).

❑ And the only output it could produce, if you wanted to process it further, was a character string (because of the limited range of types available).

However, in XSLT 2.0 it becomes possible for a template to construct an arbitrary sequence or a tree, which can be used as input to further stages of processing. It is also possible for a template to return references to existing nodes in the source tree, without making a new copy. The introduction of temporary trees and sequences in XSLT 2.0 greatly reduces the contortions that are necessary to implement complex algorithms in your transformations.

So Why Are They Called Variables?

XSLT, as we have seen, does have variables that can hold values. You can initialize a variable to a value, but what you can't do is change the value of an existing variable once it has been initialized.

People sometimes ask, why call it a variable if you can't vary it? The answer lies in the traditional mathematical use of the word *variable*: a variable is a symbol that can be used to denote different values on different occasions. When I say "area = length × breadth," then *area*, *length*, and *breadth* are names or symbols used to denote values: here, they denote properties of a rectangle. They are variables because these values are different every time I apply the formula, not because a given rectangle is changing size as I watch.

Avoiding Assignment Statements

In the following sections I'll look at some of the common situations where assignment statements appear to be needed, and show how to achieve the required effect without them.

Conditional Initialization

This problem has an easy solution, so I shall get it out of the way quickly.

In conventional languages you might want to initialize a variable to zero in some circumstances and to a value of one in others. You might write:

```
int x;
if (zeroBased) {
    x=0;
} else {
    x=1;
}
```

How can you do the equivalent in XSLT without an assignment statement? The answer is simple. Think of the equivalent:

```
int x = (zeroBased ? 0 : 1 );
```

which has its parallel in XSLT 2.0 as:

```
<xsl:variable name="x" select="if ($zeroBased) then 0 else 1">
```

Another useful expression when initializing variables is:

```
<xsl:variable name="d" select="(@discount, 0)[1]" as="xs:decimal"/>
```

which selects the value of the discount attribute if there is one, or zero otherwise.

Neither of these constructs was available in XSLT 1.0.

Avoid Doing Two Things at Once

Another common requirement for variables arises when you are trying to do two things at once. For example, you are trying to copy text to the output destination, and at the same time to keep a note of how much text you have copied. You might feel that the natural way of doing this is to keep the running total in a variable and update it as a side effect of the template that does the copying. Similarly, you might want to maintain a counter as you output nodes, so that you can start a new table row after every ten nodes.

Or perhaps you want to scan a set of numbers calculating both the minimum and the maximum value; or while outputting a list of employees, to set a flag for later use if any salary greater than $100,000 was found.

You have to think differently about these problems in XSLT. Think about each part of the output you want to produce separately and write a function (or template rule) that generates this piece of the output from the input data it needs. Don't think about calculating other things at the same time.

So you need to write one function to produce the output and another to calculate the total. Write one template to find the minimum and another to find the maximum.

This might mean writing a little more code, and it might take a little longer because work is being repeated — but it is usually the right approach. The problem of repeated processing can often be solved by using variables for the sequences used as input to both calculations: if you need to use a particular set of nodes as input to more than one process, save that sequence in a variable, which can then be supplied as a parameter to the two separate templates or functions.

One problem I encountered where multiple results were needed involved processing a tree, making small changes if particular situations were encountered. At the end I wanted both the new tree and a flag telling me whether any changes had been made. It turned out that the best way to solve this was first to search the tree looking for the nodes that needed to change and then to process it again, making the changes. Although this incurs an extra cost in processing the tree twice when changes are needed, it achieves a significant saving when no changes are needed, because it avoids making an unnecessary copy of the tree.

An approach that may sometimes give better performance is to write a template or function that returns a composite result. With XSLT 2.0, it is possible to return a composite result structured either as a sequence or as a tree. The calling code is then able to access the individual items of this sequence, or the individual nodes of the tree, using an XPath expression. For example, the following recursive template, when supplied with a sequence of nodes as a parameter, constructs a tree containing two elements, <min> and <max>, set to the minimum and maximum value of the nodes, respectively. A working stylesheet based on this example can be found in the download file as minimax.xsl; it can be used with a source document such as booklist.xml.

```
<xsl:template name="get-min-and-max" as="document-node()">
  <xsl:param name="nodes" as="node()*"/>
  <xsl:param name="min-so-far" select="number('INF')" as="xs:double"/>
  <xsl:param name="max-so-far" select="number('-INF')" as="xs:double"/>
  <xsl:choose>
    <xsl:when test="$nodes">
      <xsl:call-template name="get-min-and-max">
        <xsl:with-param name="nodes" select="remove($nodes, 1)"/>
        <xsl:with-param name="min-so-far"
                        select="if (number($nodes[1]) lt $min-so-far)
                                   then $nodes[1]
                                   else $min-so-far"/>
        <xsl:with-param name="max-so-far"
                        select="if (number($nodes[1]) gt $max-so-far)
                                   then $nodes[1]
                                   else $max-so-far"/>
      </xsl:call-template>
    </xsl:when>
    <xsl:otherwise>
      <xsl:document>
         <min><xsl:value-of select="$min-so-far"/></min>
         <max><xsl:value-of select="$max-so-far"/></max>
      </xsl:document>
    </xsl:otherwise>
  </xsl:choose>
</xsl:template>
```

When you call this template, you can let the second and third parameters take their default values:

```
<xsl:variable name="min-and-max">
  <xsl:call-template name="get-min-and-max">
    <xsl:with-param name="nodes" select="//item/price"/>
  </xsl:call-template>
</xsl:variable>
Minimum price is: <xsl:value-of select="$min-and-max/min"/>.
Maximum price is: <xsl:value-of select="$min-and-max/max"/>.
```

One particular situation where it is a good idea to save intermediate results in a variable, and then use them as input to more than one process, is where the intermediate results are sorted. If you've got a large set of nodes to sort, the last thing you want to do is to sort it more than once. The answer to this is to do the transformation in two passes: the first pass creates a sorted sequence, and the second does a transformation on this sorted sequence. If the first pass does nothing other than sorting, then the data passed between the two phases can simply be a sequence of nodes in sorted order. If it does other tasks as well as sorting (perhaps numbering or grouping), then it might be more appropriate for the first phase to construct a temporary tree.

There are actually two ways you can achieve a multistage transformation in XSLT:

❑   Create a temporary tree in which the nodes appear in sorted order. Then use `<xsl:for-each>` or `<xsl:apply-templates>` to process the nodes on this tree in their sorted order. This is similar to the min-and-max example above; it relies on having either XSLT 2.0 or an XSLT 1.0 processor with the `exslt:node-set()` extension function.

❑   Use a sequence of stylesheets (often called a *pipeline*): the first stylesheet creates a document in which the nodes are sorted in the right order, and subsequent stylesheets take this document as their input. Such a chain of stylesheets can be conveniently constructed using an XProc pipeline processor (http://www.w3.org/XML/Processing/) or if you prefer to write your own Java code, by using the JAXP interface described in Appendix E. The advantage of this approach compared with a single stylesheet is that the individual stylesheets in the chain are easier to split apart and reuse in different combinations for different applications.

Note that neither of these techniques violates the XSLT design principle of "no side effects."

Don't Iterate, Recurse

One of the most common uses of variables in conventional programming is to keep track of where you are in a loop. Whether this is done using an integer counter in a «for» loop, or using an Iterator object to process a list, the principle is the same: we have a variable that represents how far we have got and that tells us when we are finished.

In a functional program, you can't do this, because you can't update variables. So instead of writing a loop, you need to write a recursive function.

In a conventional program a common way to process a list of items is as follows:

```
iterator = list.iterator();
while (iterator.hasNext()) {
    Item item = iterator.next();
    item.doSomething();
}
```

There's no assignment statement here (the «item» variable is declared repeatedly within the loop and never changes its value once initialized). However, the code relies on the iterator containing some sort of updateable variable that keeps track of where it is, and the «iterator.next()» call implicitly changes the state of this internal variable.

In a functional program we handle this by recursion rather than iteration. The pseudocode becomes:

```
function process(list) {
    if (!isEmpty(list)) {
        doSomething(getFirst(list));
        process(getRemainder(list));
    }
}
```

This function is called to process a list of objects. It does whatever is necessary with the first object in the list, and then calls itself to handle the rest of the list. (I'm assuming that getFirst() gets the first item in the list and getRemainder() gets a list containing all items except the first). The list gets smaller each time the function is called, and when it finally becomes empty, the function exits, and unwinds through all the recursive calls.

> It's important to make sure there is a terminating condition such as the list becoming empty. Otherwise, the function will keep calling itself forever — the recursive equivalent of an infinite loop.

So, the first lesson in programming without variables is to use recursion rather than iteration to process a list. With XSLT, this technique isn't necessary to handle every kind of loop, because XSLT and XPath collectively provide built-in facilities, such as <xsl:apply-templates> and <xsl:for-each> and the «for» expression, that process all the members of a sequence, as well as functions like sum() and count()

to do some common operations on sequences; but whenever you need to process a set of things that can't be handled with these constructs, you need to use recursion.

Is recursion expensive? The answer is, not necessarily. Generally, a recursive scan of a sequence using the head/tail method illustrated above has O(n) performance, which means that the time it takes is directly proportional to the size of the list — exactly the same as with a conventional loop. In fact, it's quite possible for a reasonably smart compiler to generate exactly the same code for a recursive procedure as for an iterative one. A common compilation technique with functional programming languages is that of *tail call optimization*, which recognizes that when a function calls itself as the last thing it does (as in the proforma code above) there's no need to allocate a new stack frame or new variables; you can just loop back to the beginning.

Unfortunately, not all XSLT processors implement tail call optimization, which means that a recursive scan of a list can run out of memory, typically after processing 500 or 1000 items. Among the currently available XSLT 2.0 processors, Saxon and Gestalt implement tail call optimization, while Altova apparently does not. A programming technique that is often useful in such cases is called *divide-and-conquer* recursion. With head-tail recursion, the function processes one item, and then calls itself to process the rest of the sequence, which means that the maximum depth of recursive calls is equal to the number of items in the sequence. With divide-and-conquer recursion, by contrast, the function calls itself to process the first half of the sequence, and then calls itself again to process the second half. Although the number of function calls is the same, the maximum depth of recursion is now the logarithm of the size of the sequence: for example, to process a sequence of 1000 items the maximum depth of recursion will be 10. With a little ingenuity, many recursive algorithms that process a sequence of items can be written using this divide-and-conquer approach.

Time for some coding: the next example shows head-tail recursion in practice.

Example: Aggregating a List of Numbers

The following example uses a recursive template to process a whitespace-separated list of numbers.

Input

Suppose you have a string that holds a white-space-separated list of numbers, for example (12, 34.5, 18.2, 5), and you want to replace this with a cumulative sequence (12, 46.5, 64.7, 69.7) in which each number is the sum of the previous values. An example of an application that might need to do this is a billing application, where the input sequence contains the values of individual transactions, and the output sequence shows a running balance.

This could be done with an XPath expression such as follows:

```
for $i in 1 to count($seq)
    return sum($seq[position() = 1 to $i])
```

However, this involves $n^2/2$ additions, which gets more and more expensive as the size of the sequence increases. It's reasonable to look for a solution that is more scalable than this.

For the sake of an example, this is the entire content of the document, `number-list.xml`.

```
<numbers>12 34.5 18.2 5</numbers>
```

We'll suppose that there is a schema that validates this as a sequence of `xs:decimal` values, so we don't need to be concerned with the parsing of the string; we can simply access the typed value of the element as a sequence.

To make this work in AltovaXML 2008, we added an «xsi:noNamespaceSchemaLocation» attribute to the source file. Altova uses this as a signal that validation is required.

Schema

The schema used to validate this trivial source document is `number-list.xsd`.

```
<xs:schema xmlns:xs="http://www.w3.org/2001/XMLSchema">

<xs:element name="numbers" type="number-list"/>

<xs:simpleType name="number-list">
  <xs:list itemType="xs:decimal"/>
</xs:simpleType>

</xs:schema>
```

Stylesheet

Here's the recursive stylesheet (in file `number-total.xsl`):

```
<xsl:stylesheet xmlns:xsl="http://www.w3.org/1999/XSL/Transform"
    xmlns:xs="http://www.w3.org/2001/XMLSchema"
    xmlns:f="local-functions.uri"
    exclude-result-prefixes="xs f"
    version="2.0">

<xsl:import-schema schema-location="number-list.xsd"/>
<xsl:function name="f:total-numbers" as="xs:decimal*">
    <xsl:param name="input" as="xs:decimal*"/>
    <xsl:param name="total" as="xs:decimal"/>
    <xsl:if test="exists($input)">
      <xsl:variable name="x" as="xs:decimal"
                    select="$input[1] + $total"/>
      <xsl:sequence select="$x"/>
      <xsl:sequence select="f:total-numbers(subsequence($input,2),$x)"/>
    </xsl:if>
</xsl:function>

<xsl:template match="/">
  <total values="{f:total-numbers(numbers, 0)}"/>
</xsl:template>
</xsl:stylesheet>
```

To run this, you need a schema-aware XSLT2.0 processor, such as Altova or Saxon-SA. (With Saxon-SA, remember to set `-val:strict` on the command line. With Altova, the source document needs to contain a reference to the schema.)

Notice how closely the function `f:total-numbers` mirrors the pseudocode structure given earlier.

If the supplied list is empty, the function returns nothing (an empty sequence).

The first time the function is called, it returns the value of the first item in the sequence (obtained by adding the value of this item to the running total, which is initialized to zero). It then calls itself to process the rest of the list and returns the result of this processing.

Each subsequent time the function is called, it processes the first value in what's left of the input sequence, adds this to the running total that was supplied as a parameter, outputs this value, and then calls itself to process the tail of the sequence.

Eventually, the function will call itself with an empty sequence as the argument, at which point it returns, unwinding the entire stack of function calls.

At first sight this function looks tail-recursive: the recursive call is the last thing it does. But this is a false impression; on return from the recursive call, it has to append the result of that call with the first item in the sequence, to construct a new result. So tail-call optimization might not apply here. However, there are ways that a clever processor can get round this problem.

Output

```
<?xml version="1.0" encoding="UTF-8"?>
<total values="12 46.5 64.7 69.7"/>
```

Here's another example, this time processing a sequence of nodes. XPath provides built-in functions for counting nodes and for totaling their values, but they aren't always flexible enough; sometimes you need to walk round the nodes yourself.

Example: Using Interleaved Structures

XML makes it very easy to represent hierarchic structures, such as the chapters, sections, and paragraphs of a book. But what do you do when there are structures that are nonhierarchic? An example is the text of a play: one way of splitting the text is according to who is speaking, and another way is to follow the meter of the verse. The problem is that lines of verse aren't neatly nested inside speeches, and speeches aren't nested inside lines of verse: the two structures are interleaved. The usual solution to this problem is to use the hierarchic XML tagging to represent one of the structures (say the speeches) and to use empty element tags to mark the boundaries in the other structure.

(Another design approach is referred to as *standoff markup*: the markup for either or both of the structures is held separately from the text itself, using XPointer references to identify

17

Stylesheet Design Patterns

the text to which it relates. Markup of parallel structures is a complicated subject, of great concern to linguistics scholars, and many academic papers are devoted to the topic.)

Input

This example (`scene4-3.xml`) is an extract from Shakespeare's *Othello*, Act IV, Scene 3. I have departed from Jon Bosak's markup to show the line endings as they are given in the Arden Shakespeare edition.

```
<?xml version="1.0" encoding="iso-8859-1"?>
<SCENE REF="4.3">
<STAGEDIR>Enter OTHELLO, LODOVICO, DESDEMONA, EMILIA and
attendants</STAGEDIR>

<SPEECH>
<SPEAKER>LODOVICO</SPEAKER>
I do beseech you, sir, trouble yourself no further.<NL/>
</SPEECH>

<SPEECH>
<SPEAKER>OTHELLO</SPEAKER>
O, pardon me: 'twill do me good to walk.<NL/>
</SPEECH>

<SPEECH>
<SPEAKER>LODOVICO</SPEAKER>
Madam, good night; I humbly thank your ladyship.<NL/>
</SPEECH>

<SPEECH>
<SPEAKER>DESDEMONA</SPEAKER>
Your honour is most welcome.
</SPEECH>

<SPEECH>
<SPEAKER>OTHELLO</SPEAKER>
Will you walk, sir?<NL/>
O, Desdemona, -
</SPEECH>

<SPEECH>
<SPEAKER>DESDEMONA</SPEAKER>
My lord?
</SPEECH>

<SPEECH>
<SPEAKER>OTHELLO</SPEAKER>
Get you to bed<NL/> on th' instant; I will be returned forthwith<NL/>
dismiss your attendant there: look't be done.<NL/>
</SPEECH>

<SPEECH>
<SPEAKER>DESDEMONA</SPEAKER>
I will, my lord.<NL/>
```

```
</SPEECH>
<STAGEDIR>Exeunt Othello, Lodovico, and attendants</STAGEDIR>
</SCENE>
```

Output

Typically, a printed edition of this play is formatted with the kind of layout shown in Figure 17-4, in which lines that are split across multiple speeches are indented to show their relationship.

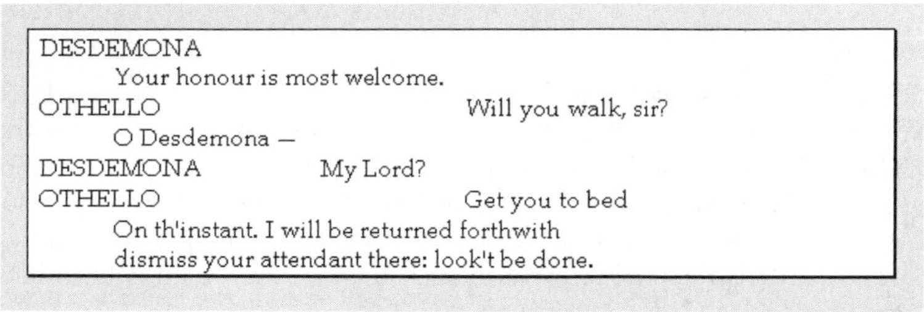

```
DESDEMONA
        Your honour is most welcome.
OTHELLO                              Will you walk, sir?
        O Desdemona —
DESDEMONA            My Lord?
OTHELLO                           Get you to bed
        On th'instant. I will be returned forthwith
        dismiss your attendant there: look't be done.
```

Figure 17-4

Achieving this format is not easy (especially details such as the omission of a new line if the indented text fits on the same line as the speaker's name), and it certainly requires a computational stylesheet to achieve it. Rather than attempt this, I will tackle a simpler problem, which is to invert the structure so that the primary XML hierarchy shows the lines, and the start of each speech is tagged by an empty element.

```
<?xml version="1.0" encoding="UTF-8"?>
<scene><title>SCENE III. Another room In the castle.</title>
<stagedir>Enter OTHELLO, LODOVICO, DESDEMONA, EMILIA and
attendants</stagedir>

<speech speaker="LODOVICO"/>
<line>I do beseech you, sir, trouble yourself no further.</line>

<speech speaker="OTHELLO"/>
<line>O, pardon me: 'twill do me good to walk.</line>

<speech speaker="LODOVICO"/>
<line>Madam, good night; I humbly thank your ladyship.</line>

<speech speaker="DESDEMONA"/>
<line>Your honour is most welcome.

<speech speaker="OTHELLO"/>
Will you walk, sir?</line>
<line>O, Desdemona, -

<speech speaker="DESDEMONA"/>
My lord?
```

```
  <speech speaker="OTHELLO"/>
  Get you to bed</line> <line>on th' instant; I will be returned
   forthwith</line>
  <line>dismiss your attendant there: look't be done.</line>

  <speech speaker="DESDEMONA"/>
  <line>I will, my lord.</line>

  <stagedir>Exeunt Othello, Lodovico, and attendants</stagedir>
  </scene>
```

Stylesheet

I tackle this by processing the text sequentially, using a recursive template. The structure I have followed below is a two-phase approach. The first phase flattens the structure so that both the speech boundaries and the line boundaries are represented by empty elements, appearing as siblings of the text nodes. The result of the first phase is held in the variable $flat. This variable holds a sequence of (parentless) element and text nodes. The second phase then adds the hierarchic structure of <line> elements containing the text and <speech> nodes.

Here is the top-level logic of the stylesheet invert.xsl. Note how the second phase starts by processing only the first node in the sequence $flat. after the initial <NL/>.

```
<xsl:stylesheet
   xmlns:xsl="http://www.w3.org/1999/XSL/Transform"
   version="2.0">

<xsl:template match="SCENE">
   <xsl:variable name="flat">
      <NL/>
      <xsl:apply-templates mode="phase1"/>
   </xsl:variable>
   <xsl:apply-templates select="$flat/NL[following-sibling::node()]"
                        mode="phase2"/>
</xsl:template>
```

Now the template rules for the first phase, the flattening phase. This is handled by a single rule which processes a <SPEECH> by first creating a <speaker> element containing the name of the speaker and then copying all the nodes from the original except for the <SPEAKER> element. We are assuming here that each speech has only one speaker.

```
<xsl:template match="SPEECH" mode="phase1">
   <speaker><xsl:value-of select="SPEAKER"/></speaker>
   <xsl:copy-of select="node() except SPEAKER"/>
</xsl:template>
```

We now have a flat structure containing <speaker> elements, empty <NL> elements, text nodes, and <stagedir> elements. Phase 2 is structured so a template rule is called once for each node in the sequence $flat. In each case, this template rule calls <xsl:apply-templates> to process the next node in the sequence (and thus, by implication, the rest of the sequence beyond). I refer to this style of processing as *sibling recursion*. When an <NL>

element is encountered, a new `<line>` element is written to the result tree, and the following elements generate children of this `<line>` element. When any other kind of node is encountered, it is simply copied to the result tree at the current level.

```
<xsl:template match="NL" mode="phase2">
  <line>
    <xsl:apply-templates
        select="following-sibling::node()[1][not(self::NL)]"/>
        mode="phase2"/>
  </line>
  <xsl:apply-templates select="following-sibling::node()[1]"/>
</xsl:template>

<xsl:template match="node()" mode="phase2">
  <xsl:copy-of select="."/>
  <xsl:apply-templates
        select="following-sibling::node()[1][not(self::NL)]"
        mode="phase2"/>
</xsl:template>
</xsl:stylesheet>
```

The expression «`following-sibling::node()[1][not(self::NL)]`» selects the next sibling node, provided it is not an `<NL>` element; if the next sibling is an `<NL>` element, it selects an empty sequence.

There is very little that is specific to XSLT 2.0 in this stylesheet, with the exception of the sequence of nodes used as an intermediate variable. The second phase could have been written without explicit recursion, using `<xsl:for-each-group>`, but in my view the recursive solution in this case is not really any more difficult.

This stylesheet also demonstrates that recursive processing of a sequence can often be carried out very elegantly, using `<xsl:apply-templates>`. I find that there is a tendency when writing recursive code to reach straight for `<xsl:call-template>` (or, in XSLT 2.0, `<xsl:function>`) when `<xsl:apply-templates>` can often do the job far better.

Superficially, the logic of this stylesheet doesn't bear much resemblance to the prototypical head/tail recursive structure described earlier. But in fact, this is precisely the underlying structure. The «`match="SCENE"`» template selects all the `<NL>` elements, each one implicitly identifying a sequence that starts with that `<NL>` and continues up to the next `<NL>`. The processing of this sequence is split between the two «`mode="phase2"`» template rules, each of which has the structure "handle this node, then recursively process the next sibling". Processing the next sibling here is effectively processing the remainder of the list. The test for the terminating condition is implicit, because `<xsl:apply-templates>` does nothing when the selected node sequence is empty.

Recursion: Summary

By now the principle should be clear. Whenever you need to find something out by processing a sequence of items, write a recursive template that is given the sequence as a parameter. If the sequence isn't empty, deal with the first item, and make a recursive call to deal with the rest of the sequence that follows the first item.

As I mentioned, with XSLT 1.0 there was another problem when doing this, which had nothing to do with the lack of an assignment statement, but was a consequence of the limited range of types available. The result of a template in XSLT 1.0 was always a temporary tree, and with XSLT 1.0 (without the widely implemented `exslt:node-set()` extension) there were only two things you could do with the tree: you could copy it to the final result tree, or you could convert it to a string.

With XSLT 2.0, this becomes much easier because a template (or a function) can return an arbitrary sequence, which you can manipulate in any way you like. You can also choose to construct a temporary tree, which can now be manipulated just like an original source document. Furthermore, you can take advantage of the fact that in XSLT 2.0 a template rule or function can return references to existing nodes, by using the `<xsl:sequence>` instruction, so constructing a new tree is often unnecessary.

For another example that takes advantage of this, see the Knight's Tour in Chapter 20.

Summary

This chapter described four design patterns for writing XSLT stylesheets:

- ❑ Fill-in-the-blanks
- ❑ Navigational
- ❑ Rule-based
- ❑ Computational

The approach to problems in the computational stylesheets may seem unfamiliar, because XSLT is a pure functional programming language, with no assignment statements or other side effects that constrain the order of execution. The result of this is that many of the more complex algorithms need to be written using recursive functions or templates.

18

Case Study: XMLSpec

This is the first of a group of three chapters that aim to show how all the facilities of the XSLT language can work together to solve real XML processing problems of significant complexity. Most of the code is presented in these chapters, but the complete stylesheets, and specimen data files, can be downloaded from the Wrox Web site at http://www.wrox.com/.

As I described in the previous chapter, XSLT has a broad range of applications, and in these three chapters I have tried to cover a representative selection of problems. The three examples I have chosen are as follows:

❏   The first example is a stylesheet for rendering sequential documents: specifically, the stylesheet used for rendering W3C specifications such as the XML and XSLT Recommendations. This is a classic example of the *rule-based* design pattern described on page 980 in Chapter 17.

❏   The second example, in Chapter 19, is concerned with presenting structured data. I chose a complex data structure with many cross-references to illustrate how a navigational stylesheet can find its way around the source tree: the chosen example is a data file containing the family tree of the Kennedys. This example is particularly suitable for demonstrating how stylesheets and schemas can work together.

❏   The final example stylesheet, in Chapter 20, is quite unrealistic but fun. It shows how XSLT can be used to calculate a knight's tour of the chessboard, in which the knight visits every square without ever landing on the same square twice. This is not the sort of problem XSLT was designed to solve, but by showing that it can be done I hope it will convince you that XSLT has the computational power and flexibility to deal with the many more modest algorithmic challenges that arise in routine day-to-day formatting applications. New features in XSLT 2.0 make this kind of application much easier to write, which means that the stylesheet is almost a total rewrite of the XSLT 1.0 version.

The stylesheet presented in this chapter was written for a practical purpose, not to serve as an example of good programming practice. I wrote in an earlier edition of this book that the stylesheet was originally written by Eduardo Gutentag and subsequently modified by James Clark. The stylesheet at that time was around 750 lines long. The current version has grown to over 3000 lines in three different stylesheet modules, and claims as its authors Norman Walsh, Chris Maden, Ben Trafford, Eve Maler, and Henry S. Thompson. No doubt others have contributed too, and I am grateful to W3C and to these individuals for placing the stylesheet in the public domain. Because the stylesheet has grown so much, and because many of the template rules are quite repetitive, I have omitted much of the detail from this chapter, selecting only those rules where there is something useful to say. But I haven't tried to polish the code for publication — I am presenting the stylesheet as it actually is, warts and all, because this provides many opportunities to discuss the realities of XSLT programming. It gives the opportunity to analyze the code as written and to consider possible ways in which it can be improved. To the individuals whose code I am criticizing, I apologize if this causes them any embarrassment. I do it because I know that all good software engineers value criticism, and these people are all top-class software engineers.

Before embarking on this chapter, I did wonder whether there was any value in presenting in a book about XSLT 2.0 a stylesheet that is written almost entirely using XSLT 1.0. As the chapter progressed, I found that it actually provided a good opportunity to identify those places where XSLT 2.0 can simplify the code that needs to be written. I hope that it will therefore serve not only as a case study in the use of XSLT 1.0 but also as an introduction to the opportunities offered by the new features in 2.0.

Formatting the XML Specification

In this worked example, we'll study the stylesheet used for formatting the XML specifications themselves. You may have noticed that on the W3C Web site, you can get the specifications for standards such as XML, XSLT, and XPath either in XML format or in HTML. We'll look at a stylesheet for converting the XML Recommendation from its XML form to its HTML form, shown in Figure 18-1.

Figure 18-1

The DTDs and stylesheets used for the XSLT, XQuery, and XPath specifications are adapted from the version used for the XML specification, and we'll take a look at the adaptations too.

The download file for this chapter on `http://www.wrox.com/` contains the versions of the stylesheet modules that were actually used to publish the final XSLT 2.0 Recommendation on January 23, 2007. These may differ slightly from the version presented in the text.

This stylesheet is a classic example of the *rule-based* design pattern, which was introduced on page 980 in Chapter 17. It makes minimal assumptions about where all the different elements in the XML source document appear relative to each other, and it allows new rules to be added freely as the document structure evolves.

You'll probably find it helpful while reading this stylesheet to have the XML source document readily accessible. The official version of XML 1.0 Fourth Edition (the document shown above) is located on the Web at `http://www.w3.org/TR/REC-xml/REC-xml-20060816.xml`.

There is also a DTD called `xmlspec.dtd`. You can view the source either in a text editor or in an XML editor, such as XML Spy, or by using the default XML viewer in Internet Explorer or Firefox. Because there is an `<?xml-stylesheet?>` reference to an XSLT stylesheet (specifically, the stylesheet presented in this chapter), the browser will automatically apply the stylesheet and show you the generated HTML.

You might imagine that XML parsers these days are pretty reliable, and that XML published by W3C is likely to be problem-free. However, I get an error trying to display this XML in Internet Explorer. It chokes on the DTD, with the message "The character '>' was expected. Error processing resource `'http://www.w3.org/TR/REC-xml/xmlspec.dtd'`. Line 218, Position 53", showing a sample of text that suggests some kind of buffer corruption. The local copy of the document, which is included in the download file for this book, is supposedly identical, but displays in IE without problems. Well, almost without problems. On my configuration, to get the non-ASCII characters to display correctly, I have to change the stylesheet to say `<xsl:output encoding="iso-8859-1"/>`.

There's another separate problem with the XML (also in the DTD) that causes the Microsoft .NET parser to reject it. You can see this problem if you try to apply the stylesheets using Saxon on .NET. This time the message is: "'xlink' is an undeclared namespace. Line 380, position 9." The element in question is a `<label>` element, and there's no sign of an xlink namespace anywhere nearby. The DTD, however, adds attributes in the XLink namespace to a number of elements, and also attempts to declare the namespace at the same time. Since the DTD in this area is littered with comments saying "compensate for IE bug", it looks as if the authors have stretched the use of advanced DTD features to the point where it breaks widely used XML parsers. The lesson seems to be: keep things simple.

If you want to avoid these problems, just delete the text «SYSTEM "xmlspec.dtd"» from the second line of the XML document.

As often happens in publishing organizations, the W3C has struggled with the problem of improving its processes while also retaining backwards compatibility and a recognizable house style. It also has the classic conflict between the desire of the organization to maintain consistency of approach and the desire of editors to experiment and innovate. The stylesheet we are looking at was used to produce the fourth edition of the XML 1.0 specification, over 8 years after the original, and in that time it has been adapted to be able to handle many other specifications as well. Some of these changes have found their way into the original stylesheets, and some have resulted in "forking" of the code, as we will see when we look at the versions used to produce the XSLT specification.

The stylesheet used to publish XML 1.0 Fourth Edition consists of three modules: `REC-xml.xsl`, which imports `diffspec.xsl`, which imports `xmlspec.xsl.`, as shown in Figure 18-2. While the role of `diffspec.xsl` is clearly to enable highlighting of changes between document versions, the functional split between the first and third of these modules is less clear. However, most of the work is done in `xmlspec.xsl`, and it is on this module that we shall focus our attention.

Figure 18-2

Preface

Let's start at the beginning:

```
<?xml version="1.0"?>
<!--This file was created automatically by html2xhtml-->
<!--from the HTML stylesheets. Do not edit this file.-->
```

The stylesheet is an XML document, so it starts with an XML declaration. There's no encoding declaration; actually, all the characters are ASCII, which means that any XML parser should be able to load this document without difficulty.

The comment is rather interesting. Earlier versions of the spec were published in HTML, not in XHTML. It's not easy to maintain two versions of a stylesheet, one to generate HTML and one for XHTML, because all the result elements are in different namespaces in the two cases. It seems that the production team solved this problem by writing a stylesheet that generated the XHTML stylesheet from the HTML version, by changing namespaces where necessary. As I have remarked elsewhere in this book, stylesheets that modify stylesheets seem to crop up very often in real-world XSLT-based applications.

The conversion means that the XHTML namespace is present on many elements in the stylesheet, but I've left it out in presenting the code because it adds a lot of clutter.

```
<xsl:transform xmlns:xsl="http://www.w3.org/1999/XSL/Transform"
               xmlns:saxon="http://icl.com/saxon"
               exclude-result-prefixes="saxon"
               version="1.0">
```

Note that the `<xsl:transform>` element (which is of course a synonym for `<xsl:stylesheet>`) specifies «version="1.0"». This doesn't guarantee that the stylesheet makes no use of XSLT 2.0 features, but it's a good clue: it means that when the stylesheet is run on an XSLT 2.0 processor, it will run in backward-compatibility mode, and when run on an XSLT 1.0 processor, errors will be reported at compile time if any XSLT 2.0 constructs are found. This stylesheet is widely used to produce a whole range of documents, and like most other organizations, W3C wouldn't want its business-critical publishing operation to rely on software that isn't yet widely implemented. So the main stylesheet does indeed stick to XSLT 1.0. As we'll see later, some of the "overlays" to the stylesheet do take advantage of 2.0.

The reference to the Saxon namespace (in fact the old Saxon 6.5 namespace) in the header turns out to be a red herring. There is no use of this namespace within the body of the document, and the stylesheet has no dependencies on features specific to Saxon or any other XSLT processor. Someone put this in to do some experiments and forgot to take it out. It does no harm, apart from raising a false alarm about the portability of the stylesheet.

```
<!-- ========================================================= -->
<!-- xmlspec.xsl: An HTML XSL[1] Stylesheet for XML Spec V2.1[2] markup

     Version: $Id: xmlspec.xsl,v 1.1 2006/08/15 19:18:25 plehegar Exp $

     URI:     http://dev.w3.org/cvsweb/spec-prod/html/xmlspec.xsl

     Authors: Norman Walsh (norman.walsh@sun.com)
              Chris Maden (crism@lexica.net)
```

```
                    Ben Trafford (ben@legendary.org)
                    Eve Maler (eve.maler@sun.com)
                    Henry S. Thompson (ht@cogsci.ed.ac.uk)

      Date:         Created 07 September 1999
                    Last updated $Date: 2006/08/15 19:18:25 $ by $Author: plehegar $
-->
```

A fairly standard control header. There's then some legal stuff, without which we would not be able to reproduce the code in this book. There's a lot of change history as well, which I'll leave out.

```
<xsl:preserve-space elements="*"/>

<xsl:strip-space elements="
    abstract arg attribute authlist author back bibref blist body case col
    colgroup component constant constraint constraintnote copyright def
    definitions descr div div1 div2 div3 div4 div5 ednote enum enumerator
    example exception footnote front gitem glist graphic group header
    htable htbody inform-div1 interface issue item itemizedlist langusage
    listitem member method module note notice ol olist orderedlist orglist
    param parameters prod prodgroup prodrecap proto pubdate pubstmt raises
    reference resolution returns revisiondesc scrap sequence slist
    sourcedesc spec specref status struct table tbody tfoot thead tr
    typedef ul ulist union vc vcnote wfc wfcnote"/>
```

These two elements together indicate that boundary whitespace (whitespace that appears in whitespace-only text nodes) is to be retained for all elements except the long list of elements whose whitespace is to be stripped. The `<xsl:preserve-space>` element here is actually redundant, because the default is to preserve whitespace anyway. The elements listed for stripping are essentially those that do not allow mixed content in the DTD. It would be nice if there were an easier way of achieving this, but sadly there isn't, not even in XSLT 2.0.

Some processors, notably those from Microsoft and Altova, strip whitespace text nodes unconditionally before XSLT processing starts. This stripping can cause problems when the source document contains nodes in which whitespace is significant. You can see the consequence of this in Figure 18-3, which shows an extract from section 1.2 of the XML Recommendation, as rendered in Internet Explorer.

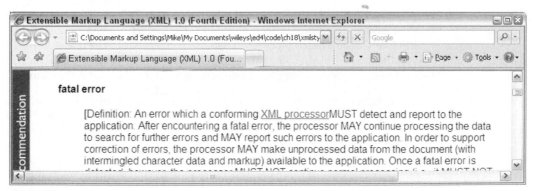

Figure 18-3

Note the absence of any space between the hyperlinked phrase "XML processor" and the word "MUST". In the XML source, the relevant markup is:

```
<termdef id="dt-fatal" term="Fatal Error">An error which a conforming <termref ↵
def="dt-xml-proc">XML processor</termref>

    <rfc2119>MUST</rfc2119> detect and report to the application.
```

Between the `<termref>` element and the `<rfc2119>` element there is whitespace (lots of it), which should be displayed in HTML as a single space; but the Microsoft XML parser has stripped the space, so the words run together on the screen. The only real way to avoid this, when transformations are invoked using the `<?xml-stylesheet?>` processing instruction, is to add an «xml:space="preserve"» attribute to some containing element in the XML source.

Let's move on. The next thing in the stylesheet is a set of parameter declarations:

```
<xsl:param name="validity.hacks" select="1"/>
<xsl:param name="show.diff.markup" select="0"/>
<xsl:param name="additional.css"/>
<xsl:param name="additional.title"/>
<xsl:param name="called.by.diffspec" select="0"/>
<xsl:param name="show.ednotes" select="1"/>
<xsl:param name="tabular.examples" select="0"/>
<xsl:param name="toc.level" select="5"/>
```

These global parameters allow the behavior of the stylesheet to be customized. Like many publishing organizations, W3C tries hard to maintain a consistent house style for its publications, and the use of a common DTD and stylesheet goes a long way toward achieving this. However, different publications do have different requirements, so there is a need to manage variety. Sometimes, the authors needed to introduce a new feature in the stylesheet but didn't want to change the way existing documents were rendered, so they put in a parameter to control the new feature. Sometimes, the parameters reflect the needs of different stages in the publication cycle; for example, the parameter «show.ednotes» controls whether editorial notes should be displayed.

In a previous version of the stylesheet some of these parameters were declared using the syntax.

```
<xsl:param name="validity.hacks">1</xsl:param>
```

It's good to see that this has been fixed. Placing the value in the content of the element means that the value is not a simple number or string, but rather a temporary tree, which however much the XSLT processor optimizes it is likely to be a much more heavyweight data structure. The use of «0» and «1» as parameter values, rather than the more obvious `true()` and `false()`, can be justified by the fact that with many XSLT processors, there is no way of supplying boolean parameter values from the command line.

There are two ways these parameters can be set. Either the values can be supplied from the calling application (typically, from the command line) or the parameters can be overridden in an overlay stylesheet. An overlay stylesheet (we'll see examples later) is a stylesheet that imports the main `xmlspec.xsl` stylesheet and makes modifications or extensions to it. If the parameters were designed to be set in this way only, they could have been defined using `<xsl:variable>` rather than `<xsl:param>`, but using `<xsl:param>` is more versatile because it allows either mechanism to be used.

```
<xsl:key name="ids" match="*[@id]" use="@id"/>
<xsl:key name="specrefs" match="specref" use="@ref"/>
```

The stylesheet uses two key definitions. These are designed to make hyperlinks within the document easier to follow. The first key matches any attribute named «id», on any element, making it easy to find an element with a given «id» attribute. The DTD allows an «id» attribute on any element whatsoever. In fact, it defines the type of the attribute to be «ID», so these elements could also be located using the id() function. (Sorry for the overloading of this term!) In fact, the stylesheet avoids the use of the id() function altogether, probably because id() isn't guaranteed to work correctly unless the document is processed using a validating parser.

The second key definition is a little surprising. A <specref> is a cross-reference: it is used wherever the text says something like "See section 8.2." I wouldn't expect to see any code that needs to locate all the cross-references; a more natural usage would be to index the elements that act as the target of a cross-reference. But on examination, it turns out that this key definition is not used. No doubt it is the result of another experiment, and someone forgot to delete it. Again, it does no harm — the chances are that an XSLT processor will completely ignore a key definition if the key is never used.

```
<xsl:output method="xml"
       encoding="UTF-8"
       doctype-public="-//W3C//DTD XHTML 1.0 Transitional//EN"
       indent="no"
       doctype-system="http://www.w3.org/TR/xhtml1/DTD/xhtml1-transitional.dtd"/>
```

The <xsl:output> declaration indicates how the result tree should be serialized. Although the stylesheet is designed to generate XHTML, it uses the XML output method because the XHTML method was introduced only in XSLT 2.0. The main difference is that XHTML serialization is more careful to avoid XML constructs that older HTML browsers might not handle correctly; for example, an empty paragraph represented as <p></p>. Setting «indent="no"» is sensible on a production stylesheet, because the output is much smaller. The definitions can always be changed in an overlay stylesheet, or in some cases from the command line (with Saxon, for example, by specifying «!indent=yes»).

```
<!-- Output a warning for unhandled elements! -->
<xsl:template match="*">
  <xsl:message>
    <xsl:text>No template matches </xsl:text>
    <xsl:value-of select="name(.)"/>
    <xsl:text>.</xsl:text>
  </xsl:message>

  <font color="red">
    <xsl:text>&lt;</xsl:text>
    <xsl:value-of select="name(.)"/>
    <xsl:text>&gt;</xsl:text>
    <xsl:apply-templates/>
    <xsl:text>&lt;/</xsl:text>
    <xsl:value-of select="name(.)"/>
    <xsl:text>&gt;</xsl:text>
  </font>
</xsl:template>
```

This is a useful catchall template rule to make sure that the source document and the stylesheet are consistent with each other. In principle, validating the source document against a DTD should ensure that it contains no surprises. But in practice, DTDs change over time, and there's no way to be sure which version of the DTD was used — indeed, there's no way to be sure that the document was validated at all. So this template rule matches any element for which there is no other more specific template rule in the

18

Case Study: XMLSpec

stylesheet. It produces a message (typically on the console) to indicate that an unexpected element was encountered, and it then copies the offending data to the result document in such a way that the start and end tags will show up visibly in the HTML (in red). This is a good way of helping document authors to notice and correct the error.

The `<font>` element is deprecated in XHTML 1.0. Perhaps the stylesheet author used it deliberately so that it would not only show up visually but would also be flagged by an XHTML validator, thus forcing the document author to fix the problem before publication.

```
<!-- Template for the root node. Creation of <html> element could
          go here, but that doesn't feel right. -->
  <xsl:template match="/">
    <xsl:if test="//prod[@num] and //prod[not(@num)]">
      <xsl:message terminate="yes">
        <xsl:text>Manually and automatically numbered productions </xsl:text>
        <xsl:text>cannot coexist.</xsl:text>
      </xsl:message>
    </xsl:if>
    <xsl:apply-templates/>
  </xsl:template>
```

I don't know why the stylesheet author felt uneasy about including the code to generate the `<html>` element in this template rule. Perhaps it was because the template rule for a document node is invoked when processing the root of any document tree, not only the principal source document. If the logic for creating the skeleton of the output HTML goes in the template rule for the outermost element (which in this case is called `<spec>`), then it's less likely to be invoked by accident when temporary trees or secondary input documents are processed.

The `<xsl:if>` in this rule is an example of a common technique, using the stylesheet to detect validity problems in the source document that cannot be enforced by a schema or DTD. I don't think there's any harm in using XSLT to do such validation, but my inclination would be to put it in a separate processing stage from the HTML formatting. It's best to write XML applications as a pipeline in which individual steps perform separate functions. (With XML Schema 1.1, it should become possible to enforce contraints like this one as assertions in the schema.)

The remaining rules in the stylesheet are presented in alphabetical order, by element. This is a good way of making sure that any rule can be found quickly. Unfortunately, it also has a drawback, which is that rules that work closely together (for example, the rules for formatting the front matter, or the rules for outputting syntax productions) can be widely separated in the source file. For the purposes of exposition, I've therefore regrouped them according to their logical function. The first group I will consider are the template rules that handle the general outline of the HTML output.

Creating the HTML Outline

The main template rule is evaluated when the `<spec>` element in the source document is encountered. This is always the outermost element of the XML document. It's fairly lengthy, so we'll take it piece by piece.

```
<!-- spec: the specification itself -->
<xsl:template match="spec">
  <html xmlns="http://www.w3.org/1999/xhtml">
```

```
    <xsl:if test="header/langusage/language">
      <xsl:attribute name="lang">
        <xsl:value-of select="header/langusage/language/@id"/>
      </xsl:attribute>
    </xsl:if>
```

The code starts by generating the <html> element, giving it a «lang» attribute if and only if the source document defines its language in the form <langusage><language id="en"/></langusage>. This is useful because W3C specifications are often translated into languages other than English. Documenting which language is used can help search engines and browsers designed to make web pages more accessible; for example, with audio rendition. Exceptionally, I have shown the XHTML namespace declaration on this occasion; it actually appears on the outermost literal result element in every template rule.

```
<head>
  <title>
    <xsl:apply-templates select="header/title"/>
    <xsl:if test="header/version">
      <xsl:text> </xsl:text>
      <xsl:apply-templates select="header/version"/>
    </xsl:if>
    <xsl:if test="$additional.title != ''">
      <xsl:text> -- </xsl:text>
      <xsl:value-of select="$additional.title"/>
    </xsl:if>
  </title>
  <xsl:call-template name="css"/>
</head>
```

The next stage is to output the <head> element. Most of the above section is concerned with generating the document title (as it appears in the title bar of the browser window). This is a concatenation of the <title> and <version> elements in the source <header> element. Given that the HTML title can't contain any markup, I would probably have kept this code simpler. In XSLT 2.0 it can be abbreviated to:

```
<title>
  <xsl:value-of select="header/title, header/version,
                ('--', $additional.title)[$additional.title]"/>
</title>
```

Note the call on the named template «css», which we'll look at in a moment:

```
    <body>
      <xsl:apply-templates/>
      <xsl:if test="//footnote[not(ancestor::table)]">
        <hr/>
        <div class="endnotes">
          <xsl:text>&#10;</xsl:text>
          <h3>
            <xsl:call-template name="anchor">
              <xsl:with-param name="conditional" select="0"/>
              <xsl:with-param name="default.id" select="'endnotes'"/>
            </xsl:call-template>
            <xsl:text>End Notes</xsl:text>
          </h3>
```

```
            <dl>
              <xsl:apply-templates select="//footnote[not(ancestor::table)]"
                                    mode="notes"/>
            </dl>
          </div>
        </xsl:if>
      </body>
    </html>
  </xsl:template>
```

The main content of the document is produced by the `<xsl:apply-templates/>` call that immediately follows the `<body>` start tag. This processes the children of the `<spec>` element, using their respective template rules, and generates the output of each of these children independently. There are generally three children: `<header>`, `<body>`, and `<back>`. The header contains front material such as the status section and abstract, the body contains the numbered sections of the document, and the `<back>` element contains the appendices.

I haven't come across a W3C document that uses footnotes or endnotes, which is what the rest of this rule is dealing with. It displays all `<footnote>` elements, other than those found within a `<table>`, as endnotes at the end of the document. A couple of comments on this code:

❑ The XPath expression «`//footnote[not(ancestor::table)]`» is probably fairly expensive to evaluate, as it involves a scan of the whole document. Because the expression is used twice, it's a natural candidate for a variable.

❑ It's possible that the author imagined that `<xsl:text>&#10;</xsl:text>` would cause the following text to be displayed on a new line. In fact, HTML browsers treat a newline character exactly the same as a space. Alternatively, it's possible that the author simply wanted to create some breaks in the HTML to make it usable in a text editor, without having to switch to `<xsl:output indent="yes"/>`. Either way, it does no harm. (Actually, I've shown the code from the original HTML stylesheet here. The conversion to XHTML has caused the numeric character reference «`&#10;`» to be replaced by a real newline, which upsets the indentation, though it doesn't change the meaning.)

The named template css, which is called from the above template rule, looks like this:

```
  <xsl:template name="css">
    <style type="text/css">
      <xsl:text>
code            { font-family: monospace; }

div.constraint,
div.issue,
div.note,
div.notice      { margin-left: 2em; }

ol.enumar       { list-style-type: decimal; }
ol.enumla       { list-style-type: lower-alpha; }
ol.enumlr       { list-style-type: lower-roman; }
ol.enumua       { list-style-type: upper-alpha; }
ol.enumur       { list-style-type: upper-roman; }

</xsl:text>
      <xsl:if test="$tabular.examples = 0">
```

```
            <xsl:text>
    div.exampleInner pre { margin-left: 1em;
                           margin-top: 0em; margin-bottom: 0em}
    div.exampleOuter {border: 4px double gray;
                      margin: 0em; padding: 0em}
    div.exampleInner { background-color: #d5dee3;
                       border-top-width: 4px;
                       border-top-style: double;
                       border-top-color: #d3d3d3;
                       border-bottom-width: 4px;
                       border-bottom-style: double;
                       border-bottom-color: #d3d3d3;
                       padding: 4px; margin: 0em }
    div.exampleWrapper    { margin: 4px }
    div.exampleHeader { font-weight: bold;
                        margin: 4px}
    </xsl:text>
        </xsl:if>
        <xsl:value-of select="$additional.css"/>
      </style>
      <link rel="stylesheet" type="text/css">
        <xsl:attribute name="href">
        <xsl:text>http://www.w3.org/StyleSheets/TR/</xsl:text>

        <xsl:choose>
          <xsl:when test="/spec/@role='editors-copy'">base</xsl:when>
          <xsl:otherwise>
            <xsl:choose>
              <xsl:when test="/spec/@w3c-doctype='wd'">W3C-WD</xsl:when>
              <xsl:when test="/spec/@w3c-doctype='rec'">W3C-REC</xsl:when>
              <xsl:when test="/spec/@w3c-doctype='pr'">W3C-PR</xsl:when>
              <xsl:when test="/spec/@w3c-doctype='cr'">W3C-CR</xsl:when>
              <xsl:when test="/spec/@w3c-doctype='note'">W3C-NOTE</xsl:when>
              <xsl:otherwise>base</xsl:otherwise>
            </xsl:choose>
          </xsl:otherwise>
        </xsl:choose>
        <xsl:text>.css</xsl:text>
      </xsl:attribute>
    </link>
  </xsl:template>
```

This code generates two elements within the HTML `<head>` element: a `<style>` element and a `<link>` element. Together, these define the CSS stylesheet that is used by the browser to render the HTML. This combined use of XSLT and CSS is one that I would very much recommend. It means that the XSLT stylesheet can be concerned with getting the structure of the HTML correct and can leave the fine detail of fonts and margins to the CSS stylesheet.

Why use both a `<link>` and a `<style>`? The `<link>` contains a reference to a CSS stylesheet stored on the W3C Web server, while the `<style>` contains local modifications and additions. I suspect that the reason for the split is to do with change control. Changing a CSS stylesheet on the Web server, when there are many documents that refer to it, is a risky thing to do, especially when many of these documents are supposed to be stable specifications. Making minor improvements to the formatting is safer if the modifications affect only new documents, not old. This could be achieved, of course, by introducing a new version of the CSS stylesheet on the server. Perhaps, W3C (like many organizations) has change control processes that made it easier for the XSLT stylesheet authors to introduce the changes locally.

Note how both the `<link>` and the `<style>` can be customized. The `<link>` generates a reference to a CSS stylesheet conditionally, depending on the type of document. The various CSS stylesheets are identical except for the choice of a background image: the stylesheet for Working Drafts, for example, specifies:

```
body {
   background-image: url(http://www.w3.org/StyleSheets/TR/logo-WD);
}
```

while that for Recommendations has:

```
body {
   background-image: url(http://www.w3.org/StyleSheets/TR/logo-REC);
}
```

This image contains the vertical text shown on the top left-hand corner of the displayed page.

The CSS definitions generated within the `<style>` element include any definitions present in the content of the variable `$additional.css`. By default, this holds an empty string. However, the variable can be overridden in an overlay stylesheet to define additional CSS display classes, and this is commonly done; for example, the XSLT specification uses extra classes for displaying proforma XSLT element definitions.

There's a bit of redundant coding in this template: the `<xsl:when>` conditions in the inner `<xsl:choose>` could simply be added to the outer `<xsl:choose>`. But it's not wrong.

Formatting the Document Header

The stylesheet generates the title of the HTML document by accessing the `<title>` element within the `<header>` element of the source XML file. To understand such expressions, you need to take a look at the structure of the `<header>` element in the source document. The actual file contains a lot of material that isn't actually rendered in the HTML; some of this is in the form of XML comments, some in a more structured `<revisiondesc>` element. Earlier editions of the XML specification contained fascinating snippets such as:

```
<sitem>1997-03-21 : TB : massive changes on plane flight from Chicago
to Vancouver</sitem>
```

but sadly, these are no longer present. (They were fascinating for two reasons: first, because I'm sure that Tim Bray would have written that comment differently if he was intending it for a wide audience; second, because it shows that even the authors of the XML specification committed the faux pas of using a private microsyntax within the XML elements, rather than marking up the structure of the entry in the form of three subelements: date, author, and details. This is one of the reasons that regular expression handling in XSLT 2.0 is so valuable. Try sorting these comments first by author, then by date, using XSLT 1.0 alone.)

In abbreviated form, the structure of the XML specification starts like this:

```
<spec w3c-doctype="rec">
   <header>
      <title>Extensible Markup Language (XML) 1.0</title>
```

```
        <version>&versionOfXML; (Fourth Edition)</version>
        <w3c-designation>&doc.ident;</w3c-designation>
        <w3c-doctype>W3C Recommendation</w3c-doctype>
        <pubdate>
            <day>&draft.day;</day>
            <month>&draft.month.name;</month>
            <year>&draft.year;</year>
        </pubdate>

        <publoc>
            <loc href="url">url</loc>
            (<loc href="url">XHTML</loc>, <loc href="url">XML</loc>, . . .
        </publoc>
        <latestloc>
            <loc href="url">url</loc>
        </latestloc>
        <prevlocs>
            <loc href="url">url</loc>
        </prevlocs>

        <authlist>
            <author role="le">
                <name>Tim Bray</name>
                <affiliation>Textuality and Netscape</affiliation>
                <email href="mailto:tbray@textuality.com">
                            tbray@textuality.com</email>
            </author>

              more authors
        </authlist>
        <errataloc href="&errataloc;"/>
        <preverrataloc href="&preverrataloc;"/>
        <translationloc href="&translationloc;"/>
        <abstract>
            <p>The Extensible Markup Language (XML) is a subset of SGML
               that is completely described in this document . . .
            </p>
        </abstract>

        <status>
        <p>This section describes the status . . .</p>

        <p>This document specifies a syntax. . . It is a product of the
<loc  href='url'>XML Core Working Group</loc>.
<phrase diff="add"><loc role="erratumref"
href="http://www.w3.org/XML/xml-19980210-errata#E100">[E100]</loc>
 A list of current W3C Recommendations . . . can be found at
<loc href='url'>url</loc>.</p>

        <p>This specification uses the term URI, which is defined by
<bibref ref="Berners-Lee"/>, a work in progress expected to update
<bibref ref="RFC1738"/> and <bibref ref="RFC1808"/>. </p>
        </status>
    </header>
```

```
      <body>
        main section of document
      </body>
      <back>
        appendices
      </back>
  </spec>
```

Note that some of the tags are structural elements with predictable nesting, while others such as `<loc>` can appear in all sorts of places, including inline within the text.

The next few template rules are all concerned with processing this header:

```
<!-- header: metadata about the spec -->
<!-- pull out information into standard W3C layout -->

<xsl:template match="header">
  <div class="head">
    <xsl:if test="not(/spec/@role='editors-copy')">
      <p>
        <a href="http://www.w3.org/">
          <img src="http://www.w3.org/Icons/w3c_home"
               alt="W3C" height="48" width="72"/>
        </a>
        <xsl:choose>
          <xsl:when test="/spec/@w3c-doctype='memsub'">
            <a href="http://www.w3.org/Submission/">
              <img alt="Member Submission"
                   src="http://www.w3.org/Icons/member_subm"/>
            </a>
          </xsl:when>
          <xsl:when test="/spec/@w3c-doctype='teamsub'">
            <a href="http://www.w3.org/2003/06/TeamSubmission">
              <img alt="Team Submission" src="http://www.w3.org/Icons/team_subm"/>
            </a>
          </xsl:when>
        </xsl:choose>
      </p>
    </xsl:if>

    <xsl:text>&#10;</xsl:text>
    <h1>
      <xsl:call-template name="anchor">
        <xsl:with-param name="node" select="title[1]"/>
        <xsl:with-param name="conditional" select="0"/>
        <xsl:with-param name="default.id" select="'title'"/>
      </xsl:call-template>

      <xsl:apply-templates select="title"/>

      <xsl:if test="version">
      <xsl:text> </xsl:text>
      <xsl:apply-templates select="version"/>
    </xsl:if>
```

```
    </h1>
    <xsl:if test="subtitle">
      <xsl:text>&#10;</xsl:text>
      <h2>
        <xsl:call-template name="anchor">
          <xsl:with-param name="node" select="subtitle[1]"/>
          <xsl:with-param name="conditional" select="0"/>
          <xsl:with-param name="default.id" select="'subtitle'"/>
        </xsl:call-template>
        <xsl:apply-templates select="subtitle"/>
      </h2>
    </xsl:if>
    <xsl:text>&#10;</xsl:text>

    <h2>
      <xsl:call-template name="anchor">
        <xsl:with-param name="node" select="w3c-doctype[1]"/>
        <xsl:with-param name="conditional" select="0"/>
        <xsl:with-param name="default.id" select="'w3c-doctype'"/>
      </xsl:call-template>

      <xsl:choose>
        <xsl:when test="/spec/@w3c-doctype = 'review'">
          <xsl:text>Editor's Draft</xsl:text>
        </xsl:when>
        <xsl:otherwise>
          <xsl:value-of select="w3c-doctype[1]"/>
        </xsl:otherwise>
      </xsl:choose>
      <xsl:text> </xsl:text>

      <xsl:if test="pubdate/day">
        <xsl:apply-templates select="pubdate/day"/>
        <xsl:text> </xsl:text>
      </xsl:if>
      <xsl:apply-templates select="pubdate/month"/>
      <xsl:text> </xsl:text>
      <xsl:apply-templates select="pubdate/year"/>
    </h2>

    <dl>
      <xsl:apply-templates select="publoc"/>
      <xsl:apply-templates select="latestloc"/>
      <xsl:apply-templates select="prevlocs"/>
      <xsl:apply-templates select="authlist"/>
    </dl>

    <!-- output the errataloc and altlocs -->
    <xsl:apply-templates select="errataloc"/>

    <xsl:apply-templates select="preverrataloc"/>
    <xsl:apply-templates select="translationloc"/>
    <xsl:apply-templates select="altlocs"/>
```

Case Study: XMLSpec

```
<xsl:choose>
  <xsl:when test="copyright">
    <xsl:apply-templates select="copyright"/>
  </xsl:when>
  <xsl:otherwise>

    <p class="copyright">
      <a href="http://www.w3.org/Consortium/Legal/ipr-notice#Copyright">
        <xsl:text>Copyright</xsl:text>
      </a>

      <xsl:text> &#xa9; </xsl:text>
      <xsl:apply-templates select="pubdate/year"/>
      <xsl:text> </xsl:text>
      <a href="http://www.w3.org/">

        <acronym title="World Wide Web Consortium">W3C</acronym>
      </a>
      <sup>&#xae;</sup>
      <xsl:text> (</xsl:text>
      <a href="http://www.lcs.mit.edu/">
        <acronym title="Massachusetts Institute of Technology">
                MIT</acronym>
      </a>

      <xsl:text>, </xsl:text>
      <a href="http://www.ercim.org/">
        <acronym title="European Research Consortium
                        for Informatics and Mathematics">ERCIM</acronym>
      </a>
      <xsl:text>, </xsl:text>
      <a href="http://www.keio.ac.jp/">Keio</a>
      <xsl:text>), All Rights Reserved. W3C </xsl:text>

        <a href="http://www.w3.org/Consortium/Legal/ipr-notice#Legal_Disclaimer">
liability</a>
          <xsl:text>, </xsl:text>
          <a href="http://www.w3.org/Consortium/Legal/ipr-notice#W3C_Trademarks">
trademark</a>
          <xsl:text>, </xsl:text>
          <a href="http://www.w3.org/Consortium/Legal/copyright-documents">
document use</a>
          <xsl:text> and </xsl:text>

          <a href="http://www.w3.org/Consortium/Legal/copyright-software">
software licensing</a>

          <xsl:text> rules apply.</xsl:text>
        </p>
      </xsl:otherwise>
    </xsl:choose>
  </div>
  <hr/>
```

```
            <xsl:apply-templates select="notice"/>
            <xsl:apply-templates select="abstract"/>
            <xsl:apply-templates select="status"/>
            <xsl:apply-templates select="revisiondesc"/>
    </xsl:template>
```

There's a lot of code here, though nothing especially complicated. One general criticism is that this template rule has grown far too big, which makes it difficult for overlay stylesheets to make modifications; it would be better restructured to use one named template for each of the main output elements. Note that the template rule controls the ordering of items in the result document (for example, the abstract will always precede the status section, regardless of which comes first in the source XML). However, the formatting of each subsection is delegated to a template rule for that particular element. This is therefore a blend of the *navigational* and *rule-based* design patterns. The generation of HTML anchors is also delegated, this time to a named template with parameters. The template looks like this:

```
<xsl:template name="anchor">
  <xsl:param name="node" select="."/>
  <xsl:param name="conditional" select="1"/>
  <xsl:param name="default.id" select="''"/>
  <xsl:variable name="id">
    <xsl:call-template name="object.id">
      <xsl:with-param name="node" select="$node"/>
      <xsl:with-param name="default.id" select="$default.id"/>
    </xsl:call-template>
  </xsl:variable>
  <xsl:if test="$conditional = 0 or $node/@id">
    <a name="{$id}" id="{$id}"/>
  </xsl:if>
</xsl:template>
```

which in turn calls:

```
<xsl:template name="object.id">
  <xsl:param name="node" select="."/>
  <xsl:param name="default.id" select="''"/>

  <xsl:choose>
    <!-- can't use the default ID if it's used somewhere else in the document! -->
    <xsl:when test="$default.id != '' and not(key('ids', $default.id))">
      <xsl:value-of select="$default.id"/>
    </xsl:when>

    <xsl:when test="$node/@id">
      <xsl:value-of select="$node/@id"/>
    </xsl:when>
    <xsl:otherwise>
      <xsl:value-of select="generate-id($node)"/>
    </xsl:otherwise>
  </xsl:choose>
</xsl:template>
```

The anchor template generates an element of the form `<a name="NNN" id="NNN">`. Generating both attributes helps to ensure maximum portability across different browser versions. If the parameter `$conditional` is set to «1», the template does nothing (actually, it computes an ID value and then ignores it: an example where lazy evaluation will produce performance savings). The actual ID value is taken either from the @id attribute of the node passed as a parameter (which defaults to the context node), or from the $default-id parameter. Surprisingly, the $default-id parameter overrides the @id attribute, provided that it is indeed a unique identifier within the source document.

It's instructive to see how much easier this would all be with XSLT 2.0. We could start by rewriting the object.id template as a function:

```
<xsl:function name="f:object.id" as="xs:string">
  <xsl:param name="node" as="node()"/>
  <xsl:param name="default.id" as="xs:string"/>
  <xsl:sequence select="
        if ($default.id != '' and not($node/key('ids', $default.id))
          then $default.id
        else if ($node/@id)
          then $node/@id"/>
        else generate-id($node)"/>
</xsl:function>
```

If you prefer, the conditional expression in `<xsl:sequence>` could be written more concisely as:

```
select="($default.id[. != '' and not($node/key('ids',.))],
        $node/@id,
        generate-id($node))[1]"
```

The anchor template could also be turned into a function:

```
<xsl:function name="f:anchor">
  <xsl:param name="node" as="node()"/>
  <xsl:param name="conditional" as="xs:boolean"/>
  <xsl:param name="default.id" as="xs:string"/>

  <xsl:variable name="id" select="f:object.id($node, $default-id)"/>
  <xsl:if test="$conditional = 0 or $node/@id">
    <a name="{$id}" id="{$id}"/>
  </xsl:if>
</xsl:function>
```

and a call on this template, previously written as:

```
<xsl:call-template name="anchor">
   <xsl:with-param name="node" select="w3c-doctype[1]"/>
   <xsl:with-param name="conditional" select="0"/>
   <xsl:with-param name="default.id" select="'w3c-doctype'"/>
</xsl:call-template>
```

can now be rewritten as:

```
<xsl:sequence select="f:anchor(w3c-doctype[1], false(), 'w3c-doctype')"/>
```

Apart from reducing the size of the two templates from 14/15 lines to 10 lines or less, the size of the call is reduced from 5 lines to 1, and because the anchor template is called 21 times in the stylesheet, this reduces the total size of the stylesheet by 94 lines. (I hope your productivity is not measured by the number of lines of XSLT code that you produce.) Some people argue that verbosity is not a problem in itself, but in my view, if you can see the whole of a template or function on the screen at one time, you are likely to understand its logic more quickly and to make fewer mistakes when you modify it.

The only thing you lose by doing this conversion is the ability of the templates to have default parameters. But I'm not entirely sure this is a great loss: certainly, it's a feature that many languages don't provide.

Creating the Table of Contents

Immediately after the header, the first part of the body of the document is the table of contents. This is generated from within the template rule for the `<body>` element, and it is controlled by a parameter `$toc.level` that defines the number of levels in the table of contents; for example, if this is set to «2», then first- and second-level headings will be listed. HTML cannot produce page numbers, so the table of contents instead contains hyperlinks to the headings of the actual sections.

```
<xsl:template match="body">
  <xsl:if test="$toc.level &gt; 0">
    <div class="toc">
      <xsl:text>&#10;</xsl:text>
      <h2>
        <xsl:call-template name="anchor">
          <xsl:with-param name="conditional" select="0"/>
          <xsl:with-param name="default.id" select="'contents'"/>
        </xsl:call-template>
        <xsl:text>Table of Contents</xsl:text>
      </h2>
      <p class="toc">
        <xsl:apply-templates select="div1" mode="toc"/>
      </p>
      <xsl:if test="../back">
        <xsl:text>&#10;</xsl:text>
        <h3>
          <xsl:call-template name="anchor">
            <xsl:with-param name="conditional" select="0"/>
            <xsl:with-param name="default.id" select="'appendices'"/>
          </xsl:call-template>
          <xsl:text>Appendi</xsl:text>
          <xsl:choose>
            <xsl:when test="count(../back/div1 | ../back/inform-div1) > 1">
              <xsl:text>ces</xsl:text>
            </xsl:when>
            <xsl:otherwise>
              <xsl:text>x</xsl:text>
            </xsl:otherwise>
          </xsl:choose>
        </h3>

        <p class="toc">
          <xsl:apply-templates mode="toc"
                               select="../back/div1 | ../back/inform-div1"/>
          <xsl:call-template name="autogenerated-appendices-toc"/>
        </p>
      </xsl:if>
      <xsl:if test="//footnote[not(ancestor::table)]">
        <p class="toc">
          <a href="#endnotes">
            <xsl:text>End Notes</xsl:text>
          </a>
```

1019

```
            </p>
          </xsl:if>
        </div>
        <hr/>
      </xsl:if>
      <div class="body">
        <xsl:apply-templates/>
      </div>
    </xsl:template>
```

The `<body>` template rule generates the table of contents, and then it uses `<xsl:apply-templates>` to process its own children. The table of contents is produced by applying templates to all the top-level (`<div1>`) sections and appendices in a special mode «toc», and by generating the headings «Table of Contents», «Appendix» or «Appendices», and «End Notes», as required. There is also provision for referencing appendices that are automatically generated by the stylesheet, for example a glossary or index of error codes.

Nine lines of code to generate "Appendix" or "Appendices"! In XSLT 2.0, that becomes

```
<xsl:value-of select="if (count(../back/(div1|inform-div1)) = 1)
                      then 'Appendix' else 'Appendices'"/>
```

Let's see how the table of contents is produced. The structure of the `<body>` element, and also of `<back>`, consists of a sequence of `<div1>` elements representing top-level sections, like this:

```
<div1>
    <head>First-level heading</head>
    <p>Some text</p>
    <div2>
        <head>Second-level heading</head>
        <p>Some more text</p>
        <div3>
            <head>Third-level heading</head>
            <p>Lots more text</p>
        </div3>
    </div2>
</div1>
```

Each `<div1>` element contains a `<head>` element giving its section title, paragraphs of immediate content, and zero or more `<div2>` elements containing level-2 subsections. The `<div2>` elements similarly contain a `<head>` and zero or more `<div3>` elements for level-3 subsections, and so on.

In the `<back>` section, a non-normative appendix is represented by an `<inform-div1>` element instead of the usual `<div1>`, but otherwise the structure is the same.

Non-normative is jargon meaning "for information only, not officially part of the specification."

The template rule that generates an entry for a top-level section in the table of contents looks like this:

```
<!-- mode: toc -->
<xsl:template mode="toc" match="div1">
  <xsl:apply-templates select="." mode="divnum"/>
  <a>
```

```
        <xsl:attribute name="href">
          <xsl:call-template name="href.target">
            <xsl:with-param name="target" select="."/>
          </xsl:call-template>
        </xsl:attribute>
        <xsl:apply-templates select="head" mode="text"/>
      </a>
      <br/>

      <xsl:text>&#10;</xsl:text>
      <xsl:if test="$toc.level &gt; 1">
        <xsl:apply-templates select="div2" mode="toc"/>
      </xsl:if>
    </xsl:template>
```

This starts by applying templates to itself with mode `divnum`; this invokes a template to calculate the section number. We'll take a look at this template rule shortly. The rule then generates an HTML `<a>` element to produce a hyperlink. The `href` attribute is generated by calling a named template `href.target`, with the current node (the `<div1>` element) as a parameter. The content of the `<a>` element (the displayed text that the user clicks on) is produced by applying templates to the `<head>` element, with the special mode `text`. The stylesheet doesn't actually contain a template rule for this mode; it is used simply to invoke the built-in template rule, which returns the textual content of the `<head>` element, minus any markup.

The «`href.target`» template looks like this:

```
<xsl:template name="href.target">
  <xsl:param name="target" select="."/>
  <xsl:text>#</xsl:text>
  <xsl:choose>
    <xsl:when test="$target/@id">
      <xsl:value-of select="$target/@id"/>
    </xsl:when>
    <xsl:otherwise>
      <xsl:value-of select="generate-id($target)"/>
    </xsl:otherwise>
  </xsl:choose>
</xsl:template>
```

To my mind this is crying out to be replaced by an XSLT 2.0 function, something like:

```
<xsl:function name="f:href.target" as="xs:string">
  <xsl:param name="target" as="node()"/>
  <xsl:sequence select="concat('#', ($target/@id, generate-id ($target))[1]"/>
</xsl:function>
```

This would allow the code:

```
<a>
    <xsl:attribute name="href">
        <xsl:call-template name="href.target">
            <xsl:with-param name="target" select="."/>
        </xsl:call-template>
    </xsl:attribute>
    <xsl:apply-templates select="head" mode="text"/>
</a>
```

to be rewritten as:

```
<a href="{f:href.target(.)}">
  <xsl:apply-templates select="head" mode="text"/>
</a>
```

If the global parameter $toc.level is greater than one, then the <div2> elements that are children of this <div1> are processed in mode «toc» to generate another level in the table of contents.

The template rule for <div2> elements in mode «toc» and the template rules for further levels, such as <div3>, are very similar to the <div1> rule. They differ only in that they apply templates to the next level down (the <div2> template processes the <div3> children, and so on) and in the amount of indentation added before the section number — this is added crudely in the form of four nonbreaking spaces per level, using the instruction:

```
<xsl:text>    </xsl:text>
```

Hexadecimal «a0» (decimal 160) is the Unicode code for the nonbreaking space character, better known to HTML authors as the entity reference « ». This is not available as a built-in entity in XML. It is possible to define it as an entity in the DTD, but the authors of this stylesheet chose to write it explicitly as a numeric character reference.

It wouldn't be difficult to write a parameterized template that handled all the <divN> elements in one rule, but the alternative approach of writing five separate rules is perfectly defensible.

The templates to calculate section numbers have one variant for each level of heading, and also vary depending on whether the section is in the <body> (a main section) or in the <back> matter (an appendix). Here are some of them:

```
<!-- mode: divnum -->
<xsl:template mode="divnum" match="div1">
  <xsl:number format="1 "/>
</xsl:template>

<xsl:template mode="divnum" match="back/div1 | inform-div1">
  <xsl:number count="div1 | inform-div1" format="A "/>
</xsl:template>

<xsl:template mode="divnum" match="div2">
  <xsl:number level="multiple" count="div1 | div2" format="1.1 "/>
</xsl:template>

<xsl:template mode="divnum" match="back//div2">
  <xsl:number level="multiple" count="div1 | div2 | inform-div1" format="A.1 "/>
</xsl:template>

<xsl:template mode="divnum" match="div3">
  <xsl:number level="multiple" count="div1 | div2 | div3" format="1.1.1 "/>
</xsl:template>

<xsl:template mode="divnum" match="back//div3">
  <xsl:number level="multiple"
    count="div1 | div2 | div3 | inform-div1" format="A.1.1 "/>
</xsl:template>
```

All these templates work by calling `<xsl:number>` with appropriate parameters. The default «level="single"» is used for the top-level headings, and «level="multiple"» for all other levels, with a «count» attribute that matches that level and all ancestor levels. The format of the numbering is adjusted for appendices (sections with `<back>` as an ancestor) to use alphabetic identifiers (A, B, C, . . .) for the first component of the number.

Giving a list of alternatives in the `count` attribute is a common way of doing multilevel numbering. It means, in effect, outputting a sequence number for each ancestor element that is either an `<inform-div1>` or a `<div1>` or a `<div2>` and so on. Like most template rules in a rule-based stylesheet, it doesn't attempt to do any validation: if the input structure is wrong, it will produce some sort of output nevertheless, and it's up to the document author to work out what the problem is. This raises an interesting question that you need to consider when designing your own stylesheets: Is it the job of the stylesheet to detect and report on errors in the source document?

The use of `<inform-div1>` as a separate tag for non-normative appendices was a pretty clumsy design decision, and the stylesheet author has to pay the price here. It would have been much cleaner to give the `<div1>` element an attribute «normative="no"». Sadly, it is often the case that stylesheet authors have to cope with XML structures that could have been designed better. In XSLT 2.0, if this stylesheet were schema aware, it's likely that `<inform-div1>` would be in the substitution group of `<div1>`, and it would then be possible to replace all references to «div1» in these template rules by «schema-element(div1)», which would pick up the `<inform-div1>` elements automatically.

It would again be possible to make these template rules generic across levels. In fact, the template rule shown above for `<div3>` elements would produce exactly the right output if it were applied to a `<div1>` or `<div2>` element, because of the way that `<xsl:number>` is defined. The «format» attribute of `<xsl:number>` can also be parameterized using an attribute value template: in XSLT 2.0 one could write:

```
<xsl:template mode="divnum" match="div3">
   <xsl:number level="multiple"
      count="div1 | div2 | div3 | inform-div1"
      format="{if (ancestor::back) then 'A.1.1' else '1.1.1'}"/>
</xsl:template>
```

However, it does no harm for the stylesheet author to spell things out more explicitly.

The templates for producing section numbers in the table of contents are reused, of course, when producing the section numbers in the body of the document. I'll describe how this is done in the next section.

Creating Section Headers

We'll now look at the template rules used to format the section headers. These all have the same structure, and they reuse components we have already seen: the named `anchor` template that generates the target of a hyperlink, and the `divnum` mode that produces the section number for any given section. Here are the first two:

```
<xsl:template match="div1/head">
  <h2>
    <xsl:call-template name="anchor">
      <xsl:with-param name="conditional" select="0"/>
      <xsl:with-param name="node" select=".."/>
    </xsl:call-template>
    <xsl:apply-templates select=".." mode="divnum"/>
```

```
      <xsl:apply-templates/>
    </h2>
  </xsl:template>

  <xsl:template match="div2/head">
    <h3>
      <xsl:call-template name="anchor">
        <xsl:with-param name="conditional" select="0"/>
        <xsl:with-param name="node" select=".."/>
      </xsl:call-template>
      <xsl:apply-templates select=".." mode="divnum"/>
      <xsl:apply-templates/>
    </h3>
  </xsl:template>
```

It would be entirely possible to use a single generic template by replacing the literal result element <h*N*> with the construct:

```
<xsl:element name="{replace(name(..), 'div', 'h')}">
```

This uses the XPath 2.0 `replace()` function, but the same logic could be written almost as easily by using XPath 1.0 functions such as `concat()` and `substring-after()`. Another way to avoid repetition of code between these templates would be to write separate template rules at the top level and call a common component to produce the inner content:

```
<xsl:template match="div1/head">
    <h2>
        <xsl:apply-templates select="." mode="head"/>
    </h2>
</xsl:template>

<xsl:template match="div2/head">
    <h3>
        <xsl:apply-templates select="." mode="head"/>
    </h3>
</xsl:template>

<xsl:template match="head" mode="head">
    <xsl:call-template name="anchor">
        <xsl:with-param name="conditional" select="0"/>
        <xsl:with-param name="node" select=".."/>
    </xsl:call-template>
    <xsl:apply-templates select=".." mode="divnum"/>
    <xsl:apply-templates/>
</xsl:template>
```

Yet another approach would be for the common template rule to be invoked using <xsl:next-match/> rather than by using a separate mode.

Formatting the Text

The bulk of the stylesheet is taken up with template rules to process simple textual markup within the body of the document. Most of these are very straightforward, and to avoid tedious repetition I will show only a small sample of them.

Probably the most common element is the <p> element, which marks a paragraph, as in HTML:

```
<xsl:template match="p">
  <p>
    <xsl:if test="@id">
      <xsl:attribute name="id">
        <xsl:value-of select="@id"/>
      </xsl:attribute>
    </xsl:if>
    <xsl:if test="@role">
      <xsl:attribute name="class">
        <xsl:value-of select="@role"/>
      </xsl:attribute>
    </xsl:if>
    <xsl:apply-templates/>
  </p>
</xsl:template>
```

You've probably got the message by now that I don't much like unnecessary verbosity. The first thing I notice about this template rule is that the five lines:

```
<xsl:if test="@id">
    <xsl:attribute name="id">
      <xsl:value-of select="@id"/>
    </xsl:attribute>
</xsl:if>
```

are equivalent to the single line:

```
<xsl:copy-of select="@id">
```

The next is that <xsl:if> renames the «role» attribute as «class», so it's less easy to simplify, though with XSLT 2.0 you can reduce it to:

```
<xsl:if test="@role">
  <xsl:attribute name="class" select="@role"/>
</xsl:if>
```

But the essential structure of this template rule is typical of many others: it translates one element in the source document into one element in the result document, making minor adjustments to the attributes, and then calls <xsl:apply-templates/> to process the content of the element. This is the typical style of a rule-based stylesheet. Here are some other simple examples of such rules:

```
<!-- sub: subscript -->
<xsl:template match="sub">
  <sub>
    <xsl:apply-templates/>
  </sub>
</xsl:template>

<!-- term: the actual mention of a term within a termdef -->
<xsl:template match="term">
  <b><xsl:apply-templates/></b>
</xsl:template>
```

```
<!-- emph: in-line emphasis -->
<xsl:template match="emph">
  <em><xsl:apply-templates/></em>
</xsl:template>

<!-- rfc2119: identifies RFC 2119 keywords -->
<xsl:template match="rfc2119">
  <strong><xsl:apply-templates/></strong>
</xsl:template>

<!-- item: generic list item -->
<xsl:template match="item">
  <li><xsl:apply-templates/></li>
</xsl:template>

<!-- quote: a quoted string or phrase -->
<!-- it would be nice to use HTML <q> elements, but browser support is abysmal-->
<xsl:template match="quote">
  <xsl:text>"</xsl:text>
  <xsl:apply-templates/>
  <xsl:text>"</xsl:text>
</xsl:template>
<!-- affiliation: follows a name in author and member -->
<xsl:template match="affiliation">
  <xsl:text>, </xsl:text>
  <xsl:apply-templates/>
</xsl:template>
```

There are some elements in the XML that are not rendered in the HTML at all, for example:

```
<xsl:template match="revisiondesc">
  <!-- suppressed by default -->
</xsl:template>
```

I generally write empty template rules using the shorter style:

```
<xsl:template match="revisiondesc"/>
```

but one can't criticize this writer for adding a comment to make the intention clear.

The XML specification represents tables in exactly the same way as HTML, except that some additional attributes are permitted. So the template rule's job is essentially to copy the element while adjusting those attributes:

```
<!-- table: the HTML table model adopted wholesale; note however that we -->
<!-- do this such that the XHTML stylesheet will do the right thing. -->
<xsl:template match="caption|col|colgroup|tfoot|thead|tr|tbody">
  <xsl:element name="{local-name(.)}">
    <xsl:for-each select="@*">
      <!-- Wait: some of these aren't HTML attributes after all. . . -->

      <xsl:choose>
        <xsl:when test="local-name(.) = 'role'">
          <xsl:attribute name="class">
            <xsl:value-of select="."/>
```

```
          </xsl:attribute>
        </xsl:when>
        <xsl:when test="local-name(.) = 'diff'">
          <!-- nop -->
        </xsl:when>

        <xsl:otherwise>
          <xsl:copy>
            <xsl:apply-templates/>
          </xsl:copy>
        </xsl:otherwise>
      </xsl:choose>
    </xsl:for-each>
    <xsl:apply-templates/>
  </xsl:element>

</xsl:template>
```

I think I would have been inclined to handle these attributes using template rules, especially as we've already seen the same code to rename a `role` attribute as a `class` attribute, elsewhere in the stylesheet. Instead of `<xsl:for-each select="@*">` and the big `<xsl:choose>` instruction, I would write `<xsl:apply-templates select="@*" mode="table-att"/>`, with the three template rules:

```
<xsl:template match="@role" mode="table-att">
  <xsl:attribute name="class" select="."/>
</xsl:template>

<xsl:template match="@diff" mode="table-att"/>

<xsl:template match="@*" mode="table-att">
  <xsl:copy/>
</xsl:template>
```

In a previous version of the stylesheet, the above rule was also used to handle `<td>` and `<th>` elements. These have now been extracted into a separate rule:

```
<xsl:template match="td|th">
    <xsl:element name="{local-name(.)}" namespace="http://www.w3.org/1999/xhtml">
      <xsl:for-each select="@*">
        <!-- Wait: some of these aren't HTML attributes after all... -->
        <xsl:choose>
          <xsl:when test="local-name(.) = 'role'">
            <xsl:attribute name="class">
              <xsl:value-of select="."/>
            </xsl:attribute>
          </xsl:when>
          <xsl:when test="local-name(.) = 'diff'"/>
          <xsl:when test="local-name(.) = 'colspan' and . = 1"/>
          <xsl:when test="local-name(.) = 'rowspan' and . = 1"/>
          <xsl:otherwise>
            <xsl:copy-of select="."/>
          </xsl:otherwise>
        </xsl:choose>
      </xsl:for-each>
```

```
                <xsl:apply-templates/>
            </xsl:element>
        </xsl:template>
```

Careful inspection reveals that the only difference is the handling of the `colspan` and `rowspan` attributes; if the original template had been restructured to apply templates to the attributes, this modification could have been handled without duplicating the logic by defining a few new rules:

```
<xsl:template match="th/@colspan[.=1]"/>
<xsl:template match="th/@rowspan[.=1]"/>
<xsl:template match="td/@colspan[.=1]"/>
<xsl:template match="td/@rowspan[.=1]"/>
```

This is a good demonstration of how the "push" style of processing using `<xsl:apply-templates>` can give stylesheets greater potential for change than the "pull" style using `<xsl:for-each>`.

Producing Lists

The DTD for these documents provides a number of ways of defining lists. For example, an ordered list looks like this:

```
<p>The design goals for XML are:</p>
<olist>
<item><p>XML shall be straightforwardly usable over the
        Internet.</p></item>
<item><p>XML shall support a wide variety of applications.</p></item>
<item><p>XML shall be compatible with SGML.</p></item>
<item><p>It shall be easy to write programs which process XML
        documents.</p></item>
<item><p>The number of optional features in XML is to be kept
            to the absolute minimum, ideally zero.</p></item>
<item><p>XML documents should be human-legible and reasonably
        clear.</p></item>
<item><p>The XML design should be prepared quickly.</p></item>
<item><p>The design of XML shall be formal and concise.</p></item>
<item><p>XML documents shall be easy to create.</p></item>
<item><p>Terseness in XML markup is of minimal importance.</p></item>
</olist>
```

The rule for ordered lists aims to decide automatically what kind of numbering to apply to nested levels of list: «1,2,3» for the outermost level, «a,b,c» for the second level, «i,ii,iii» for the third level, and so on.

```
<!-- olist: an ordered list -->
<xsl:template match="olist">
  <xsl:variable name="numeration">
    <xsl:call-template name="list.numeration"/>
  </xsl:variable>
  <ol class="enum{$numeration}">
    <xsl:apply-templates/>
  </ol>
</xsl:template>
```

```
<xsl:template name="list.numeration">
    <xsl:variable name="depth" select="count(ancestor::olist)"/>
    <xsl:choose>
      <xsl:when test="$depth mod 5 = 0">ar</xsl:when>
      <xsl:when test="$depth mod 5 = 1">la</xsl:when>
      <xsl:when test="$depth mod 5 = 2">lr</xsl:when>
      <xsl:when test="$depth mod 5 = 3">ua</xsl:when>
      <xsl:when test="$depth mod 5 = 4">ur</xsl:when>
    </xsl:choose>
</xsl:template>
```

Previous versions of the stylesheet used an incredibly verbose recursive template to achieve the same effect; it would be nice to think that my criticism in earlier editions of the book influenced the rewrite! It could still be made simpler in XSLT 2.0. Given that `list.numeration` is only called from one place, the template rule could be written as:

```
<!-- olist: an ordered list -->
<xsl:template match="olist">
  <xsl:variable name="depth" select="count(ancestor::olist)"/>
  <xsl:variable name="numeration"
                select="('ar', 'la', 'lr', 'ua', 'ur')[$depth mod 5 + 1]"/>
  <ol class="enum{$numeration}">
    <xsl:apply-templates/>
  </ol>
</xsl:template>
```

Making Cross-References

If you read W3C working drafts and recommendations online, you'll notice that they are very heavily hyperlinked. Terms with special meanings are linked to their definitions; cross-references from one section of the specification to another are represented by hyperlinks; references to other documents are represented first by a link to the bibliography and then from the bibliography to the external document on the Web if it is available; there are references from a document to previous versions of the document, and so on. In the XML specification, every use of a grammar symbol such as «elementdecl» is linked to the grammar rule where it is defined. Similarly, in the XSLT specification, every use of an XSLT element name such as «xsl:sequence» is linked to its definition. In this section, we will look at the rules that are used to create these links. There are many of these, and I'll pick a selection that illustrates the techniques used.

Let's take the linking of term references to term definitions. Here is an example of a term definition from the XML specification that defines one term and contains two references to terms defined elsewhere in the specification:

```
<p><termdef id="dt-xml-doc" term="XML Document">A data object is an
<term>XML document</term> if it is <termref def="dt-wellformed">well-
formed</termref>, as defined in this specification. A well-formed XML document
may in addition be <termref def="dt-valid">valid</termref> if it meets certain
further constraints.</termdef></p>
```

(A curious definition, because having said that all XML documents are well-formed, it seems rather odd to use the phrase *well-formed XML document* in the very next sentence, as if there were any other kind. But we are not here to criticize the prose.)

The `<termdef>` element identifies this as a term definition. The «id» attribute identifies this term definition uniquely within the document. The «term» attribute is the term being defined. This is also tagged using the `<term>` element where it appears in the text. This might appear redundant, but the DTD requires it. There are some cases where the two differ; for example, the XML specification states:

```
<p><termdef id="dt-root" term="Root Element">There is exactly one
element, called the <term>root</term>, or document element, no part of which
appears in the <termref def="dt-content">content</termref> of
any other element.</termdef>
```

I'm afraid I've never been sure as to whether the term being defined here is *root* or *root element*.

The `<termref>` element has a «def» attribute that must match the «id» attribute of some `<termdef>`. You find that confusing? Well so do I.

The template rule for the `<termdef>` marks the definition as such, and generates an HTML anchor, like this:

```
<!-- termdef: sentence or phrase defining a term -->
<xsl:template match="termdef">
  <xsl:text>[</xsl:text>
  <a name="{@id}" id="{@id}" title="{@term}">
    <xsl:text>Definition</xsl:text>
  </a>
  <xsl:text>: </xsl:text>
  <xsl:apply-templates/>
  <xsl:text>]</xsl:text>
</xsl:template>
```

The «id» and «name» attributes of the HTML `<a>` element are both used (by various browsers) to identify the element, and the «title» attribute identifies its role; it is not used by a conventional browser, but may be used, for example, by audio browsers.

The corresponding rule for the `<termref>` element generates a link to this anchor:

```
<!-- termref: reference to a defined term -->
<xsl:template match="termref">
  <a title="{key('ids', @def)/@term}">
    <xsl:attribute name="href">
      <xsl:call-template name="href.target">
        <xsl:with-param name="target" select="key('ids', @def)"/>
      </xsl:call-template>
    </xsl:attribute>
    <xsl:apply-templates/>
  </a>
</xsl:template>
```

This calls the named template «href.target» to produce the content of the «href» attribute. We've already seen this named template on page 1021. Note the use of the key() function to enable quick access to the target of the link: scanning the whole document, by using an expression such as «//termdef[@id= current()/@def]», would be hopelessly slow unless you're lucky enough to be using a processor that optimizes the construct.

The other rules that generate internal links are all very similar to this pair.

The links to a section are a little more complex because they require the section number to be computed. In the source XML document, the links look like this:

```
<p>Full definitions of the specific characters in each class
are given in <specref ref="CharClasses"/>.</p>
```

Here, «CharClasses» must match the «id» attribute of an element such as `<div1>`, `<div2>`, or `<div3>`. Originally, quite a range of different elements could act as the target of a `<specref>`, for example, an `<issue>` or a `<vcnote>`, but the code has been revised so that only `<divN>` and `<issue>` elements are still supported. The form of the link depends on the type of target, so the template rule contains an `<xsl:choose>` instruction that handles all the possibilities. It reads as follows:

```
<xsl:template match="specref">
  <xsl:variable name="target" select="key('ids', @ref)[1]"/>
  <xsl:choose>
    <xsl:when test="not($target)">
      <xsl:message>
        <xsl:text>specref to non-existent ID: </xsl:text>
        <xsl:value-of select="@ref"/>
      </xsl:message>
    </xsl:when>
    <xsl:when test="local-name($target)='issue'
                    or starts-with(local-name($target), 'div')">
      <xsl:apply-templates select="$target" mode="specref"/>
    </xsl:when>
    <xsl:otherwise>
      <xsl:message>  (error case: see below) </xsl:message>
    </xsl:otherwise>
  </xsl:choose>
</xsl:template>
```

This is another place where the code is substantially improved from earlier versions of the stylesheet. In previous versions, the `<xsl:choose>` contained a long list of choices, with different formatting code for each kind of target element. This has now been properly moved into one template rule for each kind of element, using «mode="specref"». However, there's still a strange omission. In principle, an overlay stylesheet ought to be able to add a new rule for references to another kind of element; for example, a reference to a function prototype in the XSLT specification. But the rewrite hasn't been done in a way that allows this — before calling `<xsl:apply-templates>`, it checks that the template is on the approved list. It would have been much better to put the error case in a fallback template rule defined with `<xsl:template match="*" mode="specref">`. (In fact, I wonder why there is no provision for a `<specref>` containing a reference to an `<inform-div1>`, that is, to a non-normative appendix. The stylesheet actually contains template rules for `<xsl:template match="inform-div1" mode="specref">`, and indeed for many other possible targets such as `<item>`, `<vcnote>`, `<label>`, and `<prod>`. This looks like unreachable code to me.)

Here are the template rules that can be invoked:

```
<xsl:template match="issue" mode="specref">
  <xsl:text>[</xsl:text>
  <a>
    <xsl:attribute name="href">
      <xsl:call-template name="href.target"/>
    </xsl:attribute>
```

```
      <b>
        <xsl:text>Issue </xsl:text>
        <xsl:apply-templates select="." mode="number"/>
        <xsl:text>: </xsl:text>
        <xsl:apply-templates select="head" mode="text"/>
      </b>
    </a>
    <xsl:text>]</xsl:text>
  </xsl:template>

  <xsl:template match="div1|div2|div3|div4|div5" mode="specref">
    <a>
      <xsl:attribute name="href">
        <xsl:call-template name="href.target"/>
      </xsl:attribute>
      <b>
        <xsl:apply-templates select="." mode="divnum"/>
        <xsl:apply-templates select="head" mode="text"/>
      </b>
    </a>
  </xsl:template>
```

The «href» attribute is generated using the named template «href.target», as before. For a reference to an <issue>, the text of the hyperlink contains the issue number and the title (the <head> element) of the issue. For references to <div1>, <div2>, and so on, the text of the link contains the section number and section heading of the target section.

I left out the part of the «match="specref"» template that handles the error case. Generally, this stylesheet does not do much validation of this kind, and it would probably be a good thing if it did more. Many errors in source documents, if they pass the checks performed by the DTD, are detected only because the HTML that's generated turns out to be invalid.

```
      <xsl:otherwise>
        <xsl:message>
          <xsl:text>Unsupported specref to </xsl:text>
          <xsl:value-of select="local-name($target)"/>
          <xsl:text> [</xsl:text>
          <xsl:value-of select="@ref"/>
          <xsl:text>] </xsl:text>
          <xsl:text> (Contact stylesheet maintainer).</xsl:text>
        </xsl:message>
        <b>
          <a>
            <xsl:attribute name="href">
              <xsl:call-template name="href.target">
                <xsl:with-param name="target" select="key('ids', @ref)"/>
              </xsl:call-template>
            </xsl:attribute>
            <xsl:text>???</xsl:text>
          </a>
        </b>
      </xsl:otherwise>
    </xsl:choose>
  </xsl:template>
```

Setting Out the Production Rules

Now we get to a more interesting area. The XML Recommendation contains syntax production rules, and these are marked up in some detail. A sequence of production rules is contained within a `<scrap>` element, and each rule is a `<prod>` element. Here is an example of a `<scrap>` that contains a single production rule:

```
<scrap lang='ebnf' id='document'>
    <head>Document</head>
    <prod id='NT-document'>
        <lhs>document</lhs>
        <rhs>
            <nt def='NT-prolog'>prolog</nt>
            <nt def='NT-element'>element</nt>
            <nt def='NT-Misc'>Misc</nt>*
        </rhs>
    </prod>
</scrap>
```

This is of course the production rule for an XML document, which appears in the specification as shown in Figure 18-4.

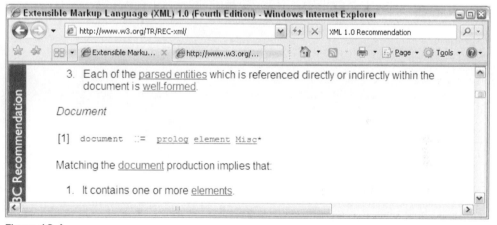

Figure 18-4

In some cases the production rules within a `<scrap>` are grouped into `<prodgroup>` elements, but this grouping is ignored in the output.

Here are the top-level template rules:

```
<!-- scrap: series of formal grammar productions -->
<!-- set up a <table> and handle children -->
<xsl:template match="scrap">
<xsl:apply-templates select="head"/>
  <table class="scrap" summary="Scrap">
    <xsl:apply-templates select="bnf | prod | prodgroup"/>
  </table>
</xsl:template>
```

```
<!-- create one <tbody> for each group -->
<xsl:template match="prodgroup">
  <tbody>
    <xsl:apply-templates/>
  </tbody>
</xsl:template>

<!-- prod: a formal grammar production -->
<!-- if not in a prodgroup, needs a <tbody> -->
<!-- has a weird content model; makes a table but there are no
     explicit rules; many different things can start a new row -->
<!-- process the first child in each row, and it will process the
     others -->
<xsl:template match="prod">
  <tbody>
    <xsl:apply-templates
      select="lhs |
              rhs[preceding-sibling::*[1][name()!='lhs']] |
              com[preceding-sibling::*[1][name()!='rhs']] |
              constraint[preceding-sibling::*[1][name()!='rhs']] |
              vc[preceding-sibling::*[1][name()!='rhs']] |
              wfc[preceding-sibling::*[1][name()!='rhs']]"/>
  </tbody>
</xsl:template>

<xsl:template match="prodgroup/prod">
  <xsl:apply-templates
    select="lhs |
            rhs[preceding-sibling::*[1][name()!='lhs']] |
            com[preceding-sibling::*[1][name()!='rhs']] |
            constraint[preceding-sibling::*[1][name()!='rhs']] |
            vc[preceding-sibling::*[1][name()!='rhs']] |
            wfc[preceding-sibling::*[1][name()!='rhs']]"/>
</xsl:template>
```

To understand this, let's first ignore the horrendous `select` expression that appears in the last two rules.

- ❑ The rule for the `<scrap>` element processes the `<head>` element to produce a heading and then outputs an HTML table, whose contents are generated by processing all the `<prodgroup>` and `<prod>` elements contained in the `<scrap>`.

- ❑ The rule also allows for a `<scrap>` to contain `<bnf>` elements. However, the document we're working with doesn't contain any, so we can ignore this.

- ❑ The rules are being rather pedantic by ensuring that the rows of the table are always contained in a `<tbody>` element. In practice, Web browsers don't insist on a `<tbody>` being present, and many HTML authors don't bother writing one, but technically the HTML specification requires it, and the W3C takes great pains to make sure that the documents it publishes are valid HTML. This means that when there is a `<prodgroup>` present, the `<tbody>` is generated at the level of the `<prodgroup>`; when there is a `<prod>` that is not contained in a `<prodgroup>` (that is, it is contained directly in the `<scrap>`), then the `<tbody>` is generated when processing the `<prod>` element; but when a `<prod>` is contained in a `<prodgroup>`, no additional `<tbody>` is produced.

Now let's look at the monster `select` expression. A production rule (`<prod>`) has one left-hand side (`<lhs>`), one or more right-hand sides (`<rhs>`), and one or more annotations (`<vc>`, `<wfc>`, or `<com>`). A `<vc>` element is used to refer to a validation constraint, a `<wfc>` element to refer to a well-formedness constraint, and a `<com>` element to refer to a comment. The XML specification does not use `<constraint>` elements, so we can ignore those.

A rule with one `<lhs>` element, two `<rhs>` elements, and three `<wfc>` annotations would be laid out in an HTML table like this:

[17]	lhs1	:: =	rhs1	
			rhs2	wfc1
				wfc2
				wfc3

As the comment says, the `select` expression is processing the children of the `<prod>` element that start a new row: here, lhs1, rhs2, wfc2, and wfc3. More precisely, the selected elements include every `<lhs>` element, any `<rhs>` element that is not immediately preceded by an `<lhs>` element, and any `<vc>`, `<wfc>`, or `<com>` element that is not immediately preceded by an `<rhs>` element. So, this template selects the elements that will start a new row, and calls `<xsl:apply-templates>` to process them.

We'll now look at the template rules that will match these elements. First, the `<lhs>`:

```
<!-- lhs: left-hand side of formal productions -->
<xsl:template match="lhs">
  <tr valign="baseline">
    <td>
      <xsl:if test="ancestor-or-self::*/@diff and $show.diff.markup != 0">
        <xsl:attribute name="class">
          <xsl:text>diff-</xsl:text>
          <xsl:value-of select="ancestor-or-self::*/@diff"/>
        </xsl:attribute>
      </xsl:if>
      <xsl:if test="../@id">
        <a name="{../@id}" id="{../@id}"/>
      </xsl:if>
      <xsl:number count="prod" level="any" from="spec" format="[1]"/>
      <xsl:text>   </xsl:text>
    </td>
    <td>
      <xsl:if test="ancestor-or-self::*/@diff and $show.diff.markup != 0">
        <xsl:attribute name="class">
          <xsl:text>diff-</xsl:text>
          <xsl:value-of select="ancestor-or-self::*/@diff"/>
        </xsl:attribute>
      </xsl:if>
      <code><xsl:apply-templates/></code>
    </td>
    <td>
      <xsl:if test="ancestor-or-self::*/@diff and $show.diff.markup != 0">
        <xsl:attribute name="class">
          <xsl:text>diff-</xsl:text>
          <xsl:value-of select="ancestor-or-self::*/@diff"/>
```

```
        </xsl:attribute>
      </xsl:if>
      <xsl:text>   ::=   </xsl:text>
    </td>
    <xsl:apply-templates select="following-sibling::*[1][name()='rhs']"/>
  </tr>
</xsl:template>
```

There's a great deal of clutter in this rule. The code outputs a table row (a `<tr>` element) and the first three cells in that table (`<td>` elements).

For each `<td>` element, there is a six-line `<xsl:if>` instruction that is concerned solely with coloring change-marked sections in the code: changes from one version to the next are marked by the presence of a «diff» attribute on this or some ancestor element, and the coloring happens only if the stylesheet parameter $show.diff.markup is enabled. This clutter could be reduced dramatically by replacing the six lines with a call such as the following, to return the relevant attribute node when required, or an empty sequence otherwise:

```
<xsl:call-template name="handle-diff"/>
```

The first cell contains an optional hyperlink anchor and a sequence number. The call on `<xsl:number>` using «level="any"» is a good example of how to generate a sequence of numbers that runs through the document. It creates a sequential number for each `<lhs>` element, that is, for each production rule. (Unfortunately, it is actually commented out in the current version of the stylesheet, supposedly because of a bug in one particular XSLT processor, and a less convenient technique is used instead. I decided on this occasion to publish the code as the author would have wanted it to be.)

In the second cell, the template calls `<xsl:apply-templates/>` to process the contents of the `<lhs>` element, which will generally just be the name of the syntactic term being defined. In the third cell it outputs the «::=» that separates the term from its definition. In various places it inserts nonbreaking space characters (« ») to achieve visual separation between the parts of the rule.

After producing these three cells, the template calls:

```
<xsl:apply-templates select="following-sibling::*[1][name()='rhs']"/>
```

This selects the immediately following sibling element, provided it is an `<rhs>` element, and applies the appropriate template rule. Actually, I think the `<lhs>` element is always followed immediately by an `<rhs>` element, so this could have been written rather more straightforwardly as:

```
<xsl:apply-templates select="following-sibling::rhs[1]"/>
```

As I mentioned before, I would normally write the predicate as «[self::rhs]» rather than «[name()= 'rhs']» to avoid namespace problems, and more particularly, to allow the optimizer to use indexes if it can.

As we will see, this `<xsl:apply-templates>` causes the other two cells to be added to the table row.

So let's look at the template rule for the `<rhs>` element. There are two cases to consider here: if the `<rhs>` immediately follows an `<lhs>` element, then it will appear in the same table row as the `<lhs>` element, but in all other cases, it will appear in a new row of its own, preceded by three empty table cells. I would probably have chosen to handle these two cases in two separate template rules, distinguishing the first case using a match pattern such as «match="rhs[preceding-sibling::*[1][self::lhs]]"», but the writer of this stylesheet chose to handle both cases in a single rule, like this:

```
<!-- rhs: right-hand side of a formal production -->
<!-- make a table cell; if it's not the first after an LHS, make a
     new row, too -->
<xsl:template match="rhs">
  <xsl:choose>
    <xsl:when test="preceding-sibling::*[1][name()='lhs']">
      <td>
        <xsl:if test="ancestor-or-self::*/@diff and $show.diff.markup != 0">
          <xsl:attribute name="class">
            <xsl:text>diff-</xsl:text>
            <xsl:value-of select="ancestor-or-self::*/@diff"/>
          </xsl:attribute>
        </xsl:if>
        <code><xsl:apply-templates/></code>
      </td>
      <xsl:apply-templates
        select="following-sibling::*[1][name()='com' or
                                        name()='constraint' or
                                        name()='vc' or
                                        name()='wfc']"/>
    </xsl:when>
    <xsl:otherwise>
      <tr valign="baseline">
        <td/><td/><td/>
        <td>
          <xsl:if test="ancestor-or-self::*/@diff and $show.diff.markup != 0">
            <xsl:attribute name="class">
              <xsl:text>diff-</xsl:text>
              <xsl:value-of select="ancestor-or-self::*/@diff"/>
            </xsl:attribute>
          </xsl:if>
          <code><xsl:apply-templates/></code>
        </td>
        <xsl:apply-templates
          select="following-sibling::*[1][name()='com' or
                                          name()='constraint' or
                                          name()='vc' or
                                          name()='wfc']"/>
      </tr>
    </xsl:otherwise>
  </xsl:choose>
</xsl:template>
```

Once again, the code is cluttered by the `<xsl:if>` instructions that generate change highlighting when required. It also contains a lot of repetition between the two branches of the `<xsl:choose>`.

What the code does is this:

❑ If the `<rhs>` is to appear on the same row as the `<lhs>`, it outputs a table cell (`<td>` element), colored to reflect any change markings necessary, whose contents are produced by calling `<xsl:apply-templates>` to process the children of the `<rhs>` element. It then calls

<xsl:apply-templates> to process the following sibling <vc>, <wfc>, <constraint>, or <com> element if there is one.

❏   If the <rhs> is to appear on a new row, it creates a new table row (<tr> element), and within this row it first outputs three blank table cells (<td> elements). It then outputs a table cell representing the <rhs> element itself and calls <xsl:apply-templates> to process the following sibling element, as in the previous case.

Some people prefer to avoid empty table cells by writing «<td> </td>», but that's really necessary only if the table has borders or a background color.

Finally, the last column contains the representation of a <vc>, <wfc>, <constraint>, or <com> element if there is one. The rules for these elements are all very similar, and I will show only one of them. The structure is very similar to that for the <rhs> element:

```
<!-- vc: validity check reference in a formal production -->
<xsl:template match="vc">
  <xsl:choose>
    <xsl:when test="preceding-sibling::*[1][name()='rhs']">
      <td>
        <xsl:if test="@diff and $show.diff.markup != 0">
          <xsl:attribute name="class">
            <xsl:text>diff-</xsl:text>
            <xsl:value-of select="@diff"/>
          </xsl:attribute>
        </xsl:if>
        <a>
          <xsl:attribute name="href">
            <xsl:call-template name="href.target">
              <xsl:with-param name="target" select="key('ids', @def)"/>
            </xsl:call-template>
          </xsl:attribute>
          <xsl:text>[VC: </xsl:text>
          <xsl:apply-templates select="key('ids', @def)/head" mode="text"/>
          <xsl:text>]</xsl:text>
        </a>
      </td>
    </xsl:when>
    <xsl:otherwise>
      <tr valign="baseline">
        <td/><td/><td/><td/>
        <td>
          <xsl:if test="@diff and $show.diff.markup != 0">
            <xsl:attribute name="class">
              <xsl:text>diff-</xsl:text>
              <xsl:value-of select="@diff"/>
            </xsl:attribute>
          </xsl:if>
          <a>
            <xsl:attribute name="href">
              <xsl:call-template name="href.target">
                <xsl:with-param name="target" select="key('ids', @def)"/>
              </xsl:call-template>
            </xsl:attribute>
```

```
                  <xsl:text>[VC: </xsl:text>
                  <xsl:apply-templates select="key('ids', @def)/head" mode="text"/>
                  <xsl:text>]</xsl:text>
               </a>
            </td>
         </tr>
      </xsl:otherwise>
   </xsl:choose>
</xsl:template>
```

After studying the previous rule, the basic structure should be familiar. But there is some extra code included in this rule, because the <vc> element is represented as a hyperlink to the description of a validity constraint held outside the table itself. The link is represented in the XML by a def attribute, and this is used directly to construct the HTML internal hyperlink. The displayed text of the link is formed by retrieving the element whose ID is equal to this def attribute, and displaying its text.

So much for formatting the production rules! This is by far the most complicated part of this stylesheet; the rest should be plain sailing. But before we move on, we should ask whether all this logic could have been written in a more straightforward way in XSLT 2.0.

I see this problem as an example of a positional grouping problem. Grouping problems are all concerned with turning a one-dimensional sequence of elements into a hierarchy, and the problem of arranging data in a table can often be understood as a grouping problem in which the hierarchic levels are the table, the rows, and the individual cells.

All grouping problems can be solved by answering two questions:

❑   How do you identify an element that can be used to represent the group as a whole (usually the first element of the group)?

❑   How do you then identify the remaining members of the same group?

We already have answers to these questions in the existing stylesheet: the group is a row of the table, and we have an XPath expression that selects elements that will be the first in a new row. The other elements in the row are then the following siblings, up to the next element that's a "new row" element.

So here is my XSLT 2.0 solution to this problem. First, in the two template rules for «match="prod"» and «match="prodgroup/prod"», we'll replace the complicated <xsl:apply-templates> instruction with a simple call on the named template «show.prod», with no parameters. This template looks like this:

```
<xsl:template name="show.prod">
  <xsl:for-each-group select="*" group-starting-with="
                lhs |
                rhs[preceding-sibling::*[1][not(self::lhs)]] |
                com[preceding-sibling::*[1][not(self::rhs)]] |
                constraint[preceding-sibling::*[1][not(self::rhs)]] |
                vc[preceding-sibling::*[1][not(self::rhs)] |
                wfc[preceding-sibling::*[1][not(self::rhs)]]]">
     <tr valign="baseline">
        <xsl:apply-templates select="." mode="padding"/>
        <xsl:apply-templates select="current-group()"/>
     </tr>
  </xsl:for-each-group>
</xsl:template>
```

Now, we define a set of simple template rules to produce the empty cells in each row, depending on the type of the first element in the row:

```
<xsl:template match="lhs" mode="padding"/>

<xsl:template match="rhs" mode="padding">
    <td/><td/><td/>
</xsl:template>

<xsl:template match="com|constraint|vc|wfc" mode="padding">
    <td/><td/><td/><td/>
</xsl:template>
```

And finally we provide one template rule for each kind of element, which simply outputs the content of the appropriate cells in the table. There is no longer any need for it to worry about what comes afterwards: that's taken care of by the iteration in the master «show.prod» template.

```
<xsl:template match="lhs">
    <td>
        <xsl:call-template name="show.diff"/>
        <xsl:if test="../@id">
            <a name="{../@id}" id="{../@id}"/>
        </xsl:if>
        <xsl:number count="prod" level="any" from="spec" format="[1]"/>
        <xsl:text>   </xsl:text>
    </td>
    <td>
        <xsl:call-template name="show.diff"/>
        <code><xsl:apply-templates/></code>
    </td>
    <td>
        <xsl:call-template name="show.diff"/>
        <xsl:text>   ::=   </xsl:text>
    </td>
</xsl:template>

<xsl:template match="rhs">
    <td>
        <xsl:call-template name="show.diff"/>
        <code><xsl:apply-templates/></code>
    </td>
</xsl:template>

<xsl:template match="vc">
    <td>
        <xsl:call-template name="show.diff"/>
        <a>
            <xsl:attribute name="href">
                <xsl:call-template name="href.target">
                    <xsl:with-param name="target" select="key('ids', @def)"/>
                </xsl:call-template>
            </xsl:attribute>
            <xsl:text>[VC: </xsl:text>
```

```
            <xsl:apply-templates select="key('ids', @def)/head" mode="text"/>
            <xsl:text>]</xsl:text>
        </a>
    </td>
</xsl:template>
```

As before, I left out the logic for `<wfc>`, `<com>`, and `<constraint>` elements, to avoid repetition. But I think you'll agree that the `<xsl:for-each-group>` instruction, while still requiring some thought, makes this tricky problem a lot easier to tackle than it was in XSLT 1.0.

For completeness, here is the «show.diff» template:

```
<xsl:template name="show.diff" as="attribute()?">
  <xsl:if test="ancestor-or-self::*/@diff and $show.diff.markup != 0">
      <xsl:attribute name="class"
                          select="concat('diff-', ancestor-or-self::*/@diff)"/>
  </xsl:if>
</xsl:template>
```

Finally, there's one other question that needs to be asked: Is it appropriate to be generating HTML `<table>` markup here at all? Good practice dictates that HTML tables should be used only for tabular information, and not to achieve manual control over the layout of the output page. I think one could argue this example either way. Certainly, use of CSS positioning would be an alternative worth considering.

Overlay Stylesheets

As I mentioned at the start, xmlspec.xsl is just one module in the stylesheet used to format the XML Recommendation. The xmlspec.xsl module is imported by diffspec.xsl, which in turn is imported by REC-xml.xsl. We will now take a look at these two "overlays", which modify the behavior of the base stylesheet.

diffspec.xsl

This stylesheet module is used to do change marking for documents such as the XML Recommendation. You can see an example of its output at http://www.w3.org/TR/REC-xml/REC-xml-20060816-review .html where it is used to show the changes between the third and fourth editions of the Recommendation.

For some of the W3C specifications, editors maintain change markup by hand as they make changes to documents. Typically, the markup looks like this:

```
<termdef id="dt-match" term="match">
   (Of strings or names:) Two strings or names being compared
   <phrase diff="del"><rfc2119>MUST</rfc2119> be</phrase>
   <phrase diff="add">are</phrase>
   identical. ...
</termdef>
```

In other cases, the change markup is generated automatically by running a comparison program (written in XSLT, naturally) against the two documents. I don't know which approach was used for the XML Recommendation, but the markup is the same either way, so it doesn't affect this stylesheet.

The way this module works is interesting. It contains template rules that override all other rules in the base stylesheet. For example, changes marked as additions («@diff="add"») are handled by this rule:

```
<xsl:template match="*[@diff='chg']">
  <xsl:choose>
    <xsl:when test="$show.diff.markup != 0">
      <xsl:call-template name="diff-markup">
       <xsl:with-param name="diff">chg</xsl:with-param>
      </xsl:call-template>
    </xsl:when>
    <xsl:otherwise>
       <xsl:apply-imports/>
    </xsl:otherwise>
  </xsl:choose>
</xsl:template>
```

This matches every element with the attribute «diff="chg"», indicating that the content has changed. If the global parameter $show.diff.markup is set to 0, to disable change marking, the template calls <xsl:apply-imports>, which, like a call on super() in an object-oriented program, invokes the base template rule in the imported stylesheet (in this case xmlspec.xsl). Otherwise, it invokes a named template diff-markup., which we will now examine. The template reads:

```
<xsl:template name="diff-markup">
  <xsl:param names="diff">off</xsl:param>
  <xsl:choose>
    <xsl:when test="ancestor::scrap">
      <!-- forget it, we can't add stuff inside tables -->
      <!-- handled in base stylesheet -->
      <xsl:apply-imports/>
    </xsl:when>
    <xsl:when test="self::gitem or self::bibl">
      <!-- forget it, we can't add stuff inside dls; handled below -->
      <xsl:apply-imports/>
    </xsl:when>
    <xsl:when test="ancestor-or-self::phrase">
      <span class="diff-{$diff}">
        <xsl:apply-imports/>
      </span>
    </xsl:when>
    <xsl:when test="ancestor::p and not(self::p)">
      <span class="diff-{$diff}">
        <xsl:apply-imports/>
      </span>
    </xsl:when>
    <xsl:when test="ancestor-or-self::affiliation">
      <span class="diff-{$diff}">
        <xsl:apply-imports/>
      </span>
    </xsl:when>
    <xsl:when test="ancestor-or-self::name">
      <span class="diff-{$diff}">
        <xsl:apply-imports/>
      </span>
    </xsl:when>
```

```
      <xsl:otherwise>
        <div class="diff-{$diff}">
          <xsl:apply-imports/>
        </div>
      </xsl:otherwise>
    </xsl:choose>
  </xsl:template>
```

This is pretty pragmatic code, and it almost certainly doesn't handle all possible cases. In effect, it recognizes that the «diff» attribute can occur in three different contexts: contexts where a <span> element can be added to the HTML, contexts where a <div> element can be added to the HTML, and contexts where nothing can be done. In the first two cases, the <div> or <span> element is added, with a «class» attribute that will invoke a CSS rule to cause the text to be displayed with a background color.

But the magic is in the <xsl:apply-imports> instruction, which says that having added a <div> or <span> element, the stylesheet should go on to process the element exactly as it would have done if the diffspec.xsl stylesheet module had not been invoked. The effect of this stylesheet module is thus entirely additive.

As well as the <xsl:template match="*[@diff='chg']"> rule, there are similar rules for «[@diff= "add"]» and «[@diff="del"]».

There are a few other points to note about this stylesheet module.

Firstly, it contains the declaration <xsl:import href="xmlspec.xsl"/>. This points up a nice little problem: How would one maintain a diffspec.xsl module that could be used as an overlay over a variety of different base stylesheets? To achieve this, the module could not import the underlying module, which means it could not use <xsl:apply-imports> to invoke the overridden template rules. An apparent solution would be to use a third module, xmlspec-diff.xsl, which imports both xmlspec.xsl and diffspec.xsl. Unfortunately, though, the rules for <xsl:apply-imports> don't allow this: this instruction will not consider all template rules of lower precedence, but only those in modules that have been directly imported. The new <xsl:next-match> instruction in XSLT 2.0 comes nicely to the rescue here.

Secondly, the stylesheet has a template rule, about 50 lines long, for <xsl:template match="spec">. This overrides the corresponding rule in the base stylesheet, and the only difference is that it outputs some text explaining the meaning of the change highlighting. Clearly duplicating so much code from the base stylesheet creates a problem in managing subsequent changes. There are a number of other ways to achieve the required effect. One way is to insert an <xsl:call-template> instruction to an empty template rule at the appropriate point in the base template; this can then be overridden in the overlay. If it is not possible to modify the base template, another solution is to write a template that invokes the base template by using <xsl:apply-imports>, capturing the results in a variable, and then perform a further transform on the contents of the variable. In this example, the XSLT 2.0 solution would look like this:

```
<xsl:template match="spec[$show-diff-markup=1]">
  <xsl:variable name="base-spec">
    <xsl:apply-imports/>
  </xsl:variable>
  <html>
    <xsl:copy-of select="$base-spec/html/head"/>
    <body>
      <div>
        <p>The presentation of this document has been augmented to identify
          changes from a previous version...</p>
```

```
        </div>
        <xsl:copy-of select="$base-spec/html/body/*"/>
      </body>
    </spec>
  </xsl:template>
```

REC-xml.xsl

The third module in the stylesheet is called `REC-xml.xsl`. Compared with `xmlspec.xsl`, this module is rather poorly documented. The thinking is apparently that `xmlspec.xsl` should be a generic stylesheet that applies to all the W3C specifications (or at any rate, all those that are authored in XML), while `REC-xml.xsl` is a customization for the XML Recommendation in particular.

Looking through the contents of this stylesheet, most of it appears to be rather pragmatic. For example, it recognizes that an `<author>` element can have a `role` attribute with values such as `"2e"`, `"3e"`, and `"4e"`, and thus allows the published output to distinguish between authors of each edition of the specification. The `role` attribute is permitted on pretty well any element in the DTD, and has no defined values; a comment in the DTD makes it fairly clear that it is intended as a general-purpose extensibility mechanism to allow document editors to add information that can't otherwise be captured.

There's another rule that causes production rules to be numbered manually (using an explicit `num` attribute in the source XML) rather than sequentially in order of appearance. This was done to allow production rules to have numbers such as [28a] and [28b] in revised editions of the specification, allowing existing productions to retain their established numbers.

Such changes are defensible, and one can see why they were made in a overlay rather than in the base stylesheet. Nevertheless, the accumulation of such changes over time can cause a significant change management problem. It doesn't even necessarily prevent the base stylesheet being forked, as we will see in the next section.

Stylesheets for Other Specifications

The stylesheet just presented is used for the XML specification. The stylesheets used for the XPath, XQuery, and XSLT specifications are slightly different, because these documents use additional element types beyond those used in the XML specification. In each case, the XML source document has an internal DTD subset that supplements the base DTD with some additional element types. For example, the XPath *Functions and Operators* document uses special tags to mark up function signatures, and the XSLT document has special tags to mark up the proformas used to summarize the syntax of each XSLT element.

In fact, the XSLT 2.0 specification is formatted using a stack of five stylesheet modules, as described in the following sections. This is a small subset of the total number of stylesheet modules used to produce the XSLT/XQuery family of specifications, which contains no less than 57 separate stylesheet modules (and the number is growing, as the production of errata to the original specs gets under way). The relationship between the five modules used for the XSLT specification is described by the import tree in Figure 18-5. The other modules, which we have no space to describe here, handle a wide variety of tasks:

❏   Many of the documents in the suite have a stylesheet for local customizations. The entire suite includes eight published Recommendations, a couple of specifications that are well advanced to becoming Recommendations, and numerous ancillary documents such as statements of requirements and use cases.

- ❑ Formatting of the specialized mathematical notation used in the XQuery formal semantics.

- ❑ Extraction of the XPath and XQuery specifications from a common base document, which contains markup indicating which parts apply to which language.

- ❑ Construction of an index of term definitions and section headings across the whole family of documents, to allow cross-document references to be maintained easily.

- ❑ Stylesheets to automate the comparison of document versions to create change markup.

- ❑ Stylesheets to maintain a common bibliography across the full range of documents, which is subsetted to form the reference section in each separate specification.

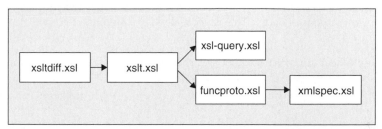

Figure 18-5

This collection of 57 modules doesn't even include the complex suite of XSLT stylesheets used to maintain the XQuery grammar: an XML definition of this grammar is used both to generate the production rules that appear in the various specifications and to construct the W3C reference parser (see `www.w3.org/2005/qt-applets/xqueryApplet.html`).

So, we will concentrate here on the production of the XSLT specification.

xslt.xsl

I developed most of this stylesheet module myself in my role as editor of the XSLT 2.0 specification (some parts were inherited from a similar stylesheet produced by James Clark). It refines the features available from the base stylesheet in three main ways:

- ❑ It handles additional markup that is special to the XSLT specification; for example, the proformas used for showing the structure of XSLT instructions, and the markup used for describing error conditions.

- ❑ It refines the presentation used for certain constructs, where the default presentation used in the base stylesheet didn't work well for this document. For example, the number of cross-references to other sections of the specification is so great that using a bold font for these became very distracting for the reader, so they were changed to use a normal font. Clearly, such changes need to be made with great discretion, but this is not the right place to discuss typography or editorial policy issues.

- ❑ It automates certain things that were not automated by the base stylesheets. For example, it provides an automatically generated glossary, and indexes of error conditions and outstanding issues; it also automates some of the generation of front material and hyperlinks.

In some cases, these changes have had cascading effects. For example, the fact that some sections of the specification are automatically generated means that the stylesheet (in places) operates in two phases.

The issues list that appears in earlier working drafts is generated as a temporary document using the markup from the `xmlspec` vocabulary, and this is then rendered into HTML by applying the standard template rules. Unfortunately, certain things break when this is done; for example, the standard `<specref>` template, shown earlier on page 1031, cannot handle a link from a `<specref>` element in a temporary document to a target element in the main source document — the use of the `key()` function assumes that both source and target are in the same tree. So, the `xslt.xsl` stylesheet contains a copy of the entire `<specref>` template rule with one line changed. (And inevitably, the structural improvements that have been made to the base template have not been migrated through to the copy.)

This is far from ideal, of course. It is always better to get the base stylesheet changed rather than forking the code, but this always takes time and is not possible when timescales are tight. It can then easily happen that differences between versions of the same template gradually accumulate, and it takes constant vigilance to prevent structural decay. This is not really any different, of course, from any other software endeavor.

The `xslt.xsl` stylesheet imports two other stylesheet modules, `funcproto.xsl` and `xsl-query.xsl`.

xsltdiff.xsl

This is a fork of the `diffspec.xsl` stylesheet described earlier in the chapter. It contains some refinements that were necessary (such as importing `xslt.xsl` instead of `xmlspec.xsl`) and other changes that the editor (that's me) found useful to give extra control, for example labeling of changes with the draft in which they were introduced, thus allowing any two versions of the spec to be differenced. It also handles change marking of some of the features that are unique to the XSLT specification.

This is actually the only stylesheet module that uses XSLT 2.0 — a natural consequence of the fact that while the specification was being drafted, the editor was one of the few people with access to an XSLT 2.0 processor. There are only a couple of XSLT 2.0 features used:

❑ Successive drafts were labelled A, B, C, . . . Z, ZA, ZB, so that the change marking code could detect all changes made since a particular draft with a simple string comparison. String ordering comparisons are not possible in XSLT 1.0 except by the cumbersome device of sorting.

❑ Some of the template rules take advantage of the ability in XSLT 2.0 to refer to global variables within a match pattern. Because change marking may be switched on or off by setting a global parameter, a template rule can be made conditional by using a pattern such as `<xsl:template match="*[@diff='chg' and $show.diff.markup='1']">`, which means that when the parameter is unset, the template rule never fires.

funcproto.xsl

This stylesheet module does a well-defined job: it formats the function signatures used in the XPath *Functions and Operators* specification and also in the XSLT specification. As with the XML production rules, these function signatures use a highly structured form of markup that is completely independent of the final presentation. For example, here is the function signature for the `format-date()` function:

```
<proto class="xslt" name="format-date" return-type="xs:string"
                          returnEmptyOk="yes">
    <arg name="value" type="xs:date" emptyOk="yes"/>
```

```
      <arg name="picture" type="xs:string"/>
      <arg name="language" type="xs:string" emptyOk="yes"/>
      <arg name="calendar" type="xs:string" emptyOk="yes"/>
      <arg name="country" type="xs:string" emptyOk="yes"/>
   </proto>
```

I would recommend taking a look at this stylesheet to see how it works (it's available in the downloads for this chapter). There are some interesting features, such as the use of a heuristic calculation that attempts to decide whether to use a single-line format for the function signature, or a multiline format. But I won't include any details here.

xsl-query.xsl

This stylesheet provides a customization of the `xmlspec.xsl` stylesheet that is used by all the specifications in the XSLT/XPath/XQuery family. It provides facilities to support fine-grained cross- references between the different specifications in this family, and to generate appendices such as error listings and glossaries.

Some of these facilities were introduced first in the XSLT specification, and were then adapted for use in other specifications; in some cases, the XSLT specification has changed to use the common capabilities, in other cases it has not. As with any sizable editorial operation, standards and processes are constantly in flux, and at any given point in time, there will be inconsistencies and overlaps. The fact that these exist in this family of stylesheets should be taken as positive evidence that the modular structure of the XSLT language can actually support this kind of change, which can never be synchronized totally across the whole organization. Changes are inevitably piloted in one area, then adopted and adapted in another, and at any one time the overall picture may appear slightly chaotic.

xmlspec.xsl

In theory, the `xmlspec.xsl` stylesheet module used at the base of the import tree for formatting the XSLT specification should be the same as the `xmlspec.xsl` described earlier in this chapter. Unfortunately, though, they aren't quite the same. There's no major difference — apart from the fact that XSLT is using the HTML version of the stylesheet rather than the XHTML version, the only differences are a few enhancements to the base stylesheet that haven't yet been migrated across. But change management is an issue here just as with any other software; and in some ways it's more difficult to maintain change control, because the code is so easy to tweak.

Summary

The case study presented in this chapter was of a real family of stylesheets, used for a real application, and not just developed for teaching purposes. It's perhaps slightly atypical in that much of it was written by XML and XSLT experts who developed the languages while they used them. However, it shares with many other projects the fact that the stylesheets were developed over a period of time by different individuals, that they were often working under time pressure, and that they had different coding styles. So, it's probably not that dissimilar from many other stylesheets used in document-formatting applications.

The phrase "document formatting" is crucial. The main tasks performed in this stylesheet are applying HTML display styles to different elements, generating hyperlinks, and formatting tables. These are all tasks that lend themselves to using the *rule-based* design pattern.

I think there are three main messages to come out of this study:

- ❑ Within an application that is doing very simple document formatting 90 percent of the time, it is possible to get benefits by using structured data for small parts of the information that have rich semantics — in this case, examples are the markup used for syntax productions, function prototypes, issue tracking, and error listings. The availability of XSLT really does enable you to use XML to represent the semantics of the data, uninfluenced by the way it is to appear on screen.

- ❑ Although most of this can be done reasonably easily using XSLT 1.0 facilities, as soon as the data gets complex, XSLT 2.0 features start to make a big impact.

- ❑ Within any complex publishing operation that's producing a large suite of documents, the key to success is not so much the detail of how individual stylesheets are coded but rather the overall structure of how many stylesheet modules there are, how they relate to each other, and how change is controlled.

The case study in the next chapter will be a very different kind of application — one that uses a highly structured data and displays it in a very different form from the way it arrives in the source document.

19

Case Study: A Family Tree

This chapter presents our second case study. Whereas the XML in the previous example fell firmly into the category of narrative (or document-oriented) XML, this chapter deals largely with data. However, as with many data-oriented XML applications, it is not rigid tabular data; rather, it is data with a very flexible structure with many complex linkages and with many fields allowed to repeat an arbitrary number of times. The data can also include structured text (document-oriented XML) in some of its elements.

The chosen application is to display a family tree, and the sample data we will use represents a small selection of information about the family of John F. Kennedy, president of the United States.

Because genealogy is for most people a hobby rather than a business, you may feel this example is a little frivolous. I think it would be a mistake to dismiss it that way, for several reasons:

❑   Genealogy is one of the most popular ways of using the Web for millions of people. Collaborative Internet-based genealogy in particular is rapidly growing, as witness the popularity of software such as PhpGedView (phpgedview.net) and can be seen as a classic example of the phenomenon sometimes called ''Web 2.0''. Catering to the information needs of consumers is a very serious business indeed, and whether consumers are interested in playing games, watching sport, making travel plans, or researching their family trees, the Web is in the business of helping them to do so. Genealogy is also one of the few areas where Web sites have built financial success by asking consumers to pay for content.

❑   Genealogical information presents some complex challenges in terms of managing richly structured data, and these same problems arise in many other disciplines such as geographic information systems, criminal investigation, epidemiology, and molecular biology. Data that fits neatly into rows and columns, to my mind, isn't interesting enough to be worth studying, and what's more, it's likely that the only reason it fits neatly into rows and columns is that a lot of important information has been thrown away in order to achieve that fit. With XML, we can do better.

❑   To write the application shown in this chapter, we have to tackle the problems of converting from non-XML legacy data formats to XML formats, and from one XML data model to another, which are absolutely typical of the data conversion problems encountered in every real-world application.

I could have used an example with invoices and requisitions and purchase orders. I believe that the techniques used in this worked example are equally applicable to many practical commercial problems, but that you will find a little excursion into the world of genealogy a pleasant relief from the day job.

Modeling a Family Tree

Genealogical data is complex for two main reasons:

- ❏ We want to record all the facts that we know about our ancestors, and many of these facts will not fit into a rigidly predefined schema. For those facts that follow a regular pattern, however, we want to use a structured representation so that we can analyze the data.

- ❏ The information we have is never complete, and it is never 100% accurate. Genealogy is always work-in-progress, and the information we need to manage includes everything from original source documents and oral evidence to the conjectures of other genealogists (not to mention Aunt Maud) whom we may or may not trust. In this respect it is similar to other investigative applications like crime detection and medical diagnosis.

One caveat before we start. Throughout this book I have been talking about tree models of XML, and I have been using words like parent and child, ancestor and descendant, in the context of these data trees. Don't imagine, though, that we can use this tree structure to represent a family tree directly. In fact, a family tree is not really a tree at all, because most children in real life have two parents, unlike XML elements where one parent is considered sufficient.

The structure of the family tree is quite different from the document tree used to represent it. And in this chapter, words like parent and child have their everyday meaning!

The GEDCOM Data Model

The established standard for representing genealogical data is known as GEDCOM, and data in this format is routinely exchanged between software packages and posted on the Internet. I will show some examples of this format later in the chapter.

Adoption of XML in genealogy has been slow, despite the obvious potential. In earlier editions of this book, I devised my own XML representation. However, in December 2002 the LDS Church (which maintains the GEDCOM specification) published a draft specification of GEDCOM XML, version 6.0. Although this draft hasn't been followed up by a final specification and is not yet widely supported by software products, it is this vocabulary that I shall use in this chapter. The specification is available at `http://www.familysearch.org/GEDCOM/GedXML60.pdf`. Further information about the use of XML in genealogy can be found on the XML Cover Pages at `http://xml.coverpages.org/genealogy.html`.

The GEDCOM XML spec includes a DTD rather than a schema. Several versions of this DTD are referenced from the XML Cover Pages; I have taken the one prepared by Lee Brown and have copied it for convenience as file `gedXML.dtd` in the download file for this chapter.

In defining version 6 of GEDCOM, the designers decided to do two things at the same time: to change the syntax of the data representation, so that it used XML instead of GEDCOM's earlier proprietary tagging syntax, and to change the data model, to fix numerous problems that had inhibited accurate data exchange between different software packages for years.

The three main objects in the new model are *individuals*, *events*, and *families*.

It might seem obvious what an individual is, but serious genealogists know that identifying individuals is actually one of the biggest problems: Is the Henry Kay who was born in Stannington in 1833 the same individual as the Henry Kay who married Emma Barber in Rotherham in 1855? (If you happen to know, please tell me.)

For this reason, the data is actually centered around the concept of an *event*. The main events of interest are births, marriages, and deaths, but there are many others; for example, emigration, writing a will, and a mention in a published book can all be treated as events. In earlier times, births and deaths were not systematically recorded, but baptisms and burials were, so these events assume a special importance. Events have a number of attributes:

❑ *The date of the event*: There are many complexities involved in recording historical dates, due to the use of different calendars, partial legibility, and varying precision.

❑ *The place of the event*: Again, this is not a simple data element. Places change their names over time, and place names are themselves structured information, with a structure that varies from one country to another. (Some software packages like to pretend that every event happens in a "city", but they are wrong. Even in the limited data used in this chapter, we have two deaths that occurred in the air, over international waters).

❑ *The participants in the event*: There may be any number of participants, and each has a role. For example, if the event is a marriage, then everyone who is known to have been present at the wedding can be regarded as a participant. Obvious roles include that of the bride, the groom, and the witnesses, but many records also provide the names of the father of the bride and the father of the groom, and this information has obvious genealogical significance. Moreover, it's important to record it even if it seems redundant, because it may help to resolve questions that are raised later when conflicting evidence emerges.

❑ *Evidence for the event*: This includes references to source information recording the event, and may include copies or transcripts of original documents.

Here is an example of an event from the Kennedy data set. I have included some additional information beyond that in the data we are using, to show some of the additional possibilities in the data model.

```
<EventRec Id="F1-6" Type="marriage" VitalType="marriage">
   <Participant>
      <Link Target="IndividualRec" Ref="I1"/>
      <Role>husband</Role>
   </Participant>
   <Participant>
      <Link Target="IndividualRec" Ref="I2"/>
      <Role>wife</Role>
   </Participant>
   <Participant>
      <Link Target="IndividualRec" Ref="I19"/>
      <Role>best man</Role>
   </Participant>
   <Date>12 SEP 1953</Date>
   <Place>
      <PlaceName>
         <PlacePart Type="country" Level="1">USA</PlacePart>
         <PlacePart Type="state" Level="2">RI</PlacePart>
         <PlacePart Type="city" Level="4">Newport</PlacePart>
      </PlaceName>
   </Place>
</EventRec>
```

This event is the marriage of John F. Kennedy to Jacqueline Lee Bouvier. Of course, the event information only makes sense by following the links to the participating individuals.

The properties of an individual include:

- ❑ Name (another potentially very complex data element, given the variety of conventions used in different places at different times). This element can be repeated, because a person can have different names at different times.

- ❑ Gender (male, female, or unknown; the model does not recognize this as an attribute that can change over time).

- ❑ Personal information: an open-ended set of information items about the person, each tagged with the type of information, optional date and place fields, and the actual information content. Certain types of personal information such as occupation, nationality, religion, and education are specifically recognized in the specification, but the list is completely open-ended.

The third fundamental object in the GEDCOM model is the family. A family is defined as a social group in which one individual takes the role of husband/father, another takes the role of wife/mother, and the others take the role of children. Any of the individuals may be absent or unknown, and the model is flexible as to the exact nature of the relationships: the parents, for example, are not necessarily married, and the children are not necessarily the biological children of the parents. An individual may be a member of several families, either consecutively or concurrently (membership in a family is not governed by dates).

There are actually three ways of representing relationships in the model. One way is through families, as described above. The second is through events: a birth event may record the person being born, the mother, and the father as participants in the event with corresponding roles. For certain key events, there are fixed roles with defined names (*principal, mother*, and *father* in this case). The third way is to use the properties of an individual: one can record as a property of an individual, for example, that his godfather was Winston Churchill. These variations are provided to reflect the variety of ways in which genealogical data becomes available. The genealogical research process starts by collecting raw data, which is usually data either about events or about individuals, and gradually builds from this to draw inferences about the identity of individuals and the way in which they relate to each other in families. The model has the crucial property that it allows imprecise information to be captured; for example, you can record that A and B were cousins without knowing precisely how they were related, and you can record that someone was the second of five children without knowing who the other children were. The ability to record this kind of information makes XML ideally suited to genealogical data management.

Apart from individual, event, and family, there are five other top-level object types in the GEDCOM model, but we won't be dealing with them in this chapter:

- ❑ A *group* is a collection of individuals related in some arbitrary way (for example, the individuals who were staying at a particular address on the night of a census).

- ❑ A *contact* is typically another genealogist, for example one who collaborates in the research on the individuals in this data set.

- ❑ A *source* is a document from which information has been obtained, such as a parish register or a will. It might also be a secondary source such as a published obituary.

- ❑ A *repository* is a place where source documents may be found, for example a library or a Web site, or the bottom drawer of your filing cabinet.

- ❑ An *LDS Ordinance* is an event of specific interest to the Church of Jesus Christ of Latter-day Saints (often called the Mormons), which is the organization that created the GEDCOM standard.

I'm not going to spend time discussing whether this is the perfect way of representing genealogical information. Many people have criticized the data model, either on technical grounds or from the point of view of political correctness. The new model in version 6 corrects many of the faults of the established version, without departing from it as radically as some people would have liked.

I would have liked to see some further changes — for example, some explicit ability to associate personal names with events rather than with individuals (I have an ancestor who is named Ada on her birth certificate but who was baptized as Edith). But with luck, the amount of change in the GEDCOM model is enough to fix the worst faults, but not so extensive that software products will need wholesale rewriting before they can support it.

Creating a Schema for GEDCOM 6.0

Because genealogical data is a perfect example of semi-structured data (it includes the full spectrum from raw images and sound recordings, through transcribed text, to fully structured and hyperlinked data) it is an ideal candidate for using an XML Schema to drive validation of the data and to produce XSLT stylesheets that are schema-aware. I have therefore produced a schema for GEDCOM 6.0, which I introduce in the next section.

My first step was to load the DTD into Stylus Studio and convert it to a schema. You could equally well do this using other tools such as XML Spy or oXygen. In fact Stylus Studio offers a choice of two converters, one of which is native to Stylus, the other a packaging of James Clark's `trang` program. I found that the native tool, with all options defaulted, did a very satisfactory job: the output is in the download directory as `rawschema-stylus.xsd`.

I then refined this schema by hand. The changes fell into the following categories:

- ❑ A number of the top-level elements have similar structure, in particular they all have children such as `ExternalID`, `Submitter`, `Note`, `Evidence`, `Enrichment`, and `Changed`. Because these common fields appear at the end, it's not possible to represent this in XML Schema by extending a common supertype, but the common data can be extracted into a named model group, which I called `CommonFields`. Similarly, complex types such as `BasicLinkType` and `ParentType` were created in cases where several elements have the same content model.

- ❑ Adding an import for the schema for the XML namespace, since the schema uses the `xml:lang` attribute.

- ❑ Adding simple type definitions for `GeneralDate` and `StandardDate`, as described below, and for other shared types such as `TimeType`.

An interesting feature of this data is that the schema is very permissive. For example, it specifies a default format for dates in the form «DD MMM YYYY» (such as «18 APR 1924»), which has long been the convention used by genealogists. However, it doesn't insist that the date of an event takes this form. It's quite OK, for example, to replace the last digit of the year by a question mark, perhaps to reflect the fact that the digit is difficult to decipher on an original manuscript. There are certain approved conventions such as preceding the date with «ABT» to indicate that the date is approximate, or «EST» to say that it is estimated, but there are no absolute rules. The golden rule in genealogy is that when you find information in a source document, you should be able to transcribe it as faithfully to the original as you possibly can, and a schema that imposes restrictions on your ability to do this is considered a bad thing. If you find an old church register in which a date of baptism is recorded as *Septuagesima 1582*, then you should be able to enter that in your database. I'll come back to the modeling of dates in the schema on page 1057.

Case Study: A Family Tree

In GEDCOM, there is no formal way of linking one file to another. XML, of course, creates wonderful opportunities to define how your family tree links to someone else's. But the linking isn't as easy as it sounds (nothing is, in genealogy) because of the problems of maintaining version integrity between two datasets that are changing independently. So I'll avoid getting into that area and stick to the model that has the whole family tree in one XML document.

The GEDCOM 6.0 Schema

Let's now take a quick look at some aspects of the XML Schema which I created for GEDCOM 6.0. In principle, because it's converted from the DTD, it covers all aspects of the specification; however, in improving the schema to describe the specification more precisely and more usefully, I concentrated on the parts that we are actually using in the application in this chapter: in particular, the three main object types individual, event, and family, and the three main properties, namely date, place, and personal name.

Individuals

Here is the element declaration for an `<IndividualRec>`:

```
<xs:element name='IndividualRec'>
  <xs:complexType>
    <xs:sequence>
      <xs:element ref='IndivName' minOccurs='0' maxOccurs='unbounded'/>
      <xs:element ref='Gender' minOccurs='0' maxOccurs='1'/>
      <xs:element ref='DeathStatus' minOccurs='0' maxOccurs='1'/>
      <xs:element ref='PersInfo' minOccurs='0' maxOccurs='unbounded'/>
      <xs:element ref='AssocIndiv' minOccurs='0' maxOccurs='unbounded'/>
      <xs:element ref='DupIndiv' minOccurs='0' maxOccurs='unbounded'/>
      <xs:group ref="CommonFields"/>
    </xs:sequence>
    <xs:attribute name='Id' type='xs:ID' use='required'/>
  </xs:complexType>
</xs:element>
```

IndivName gives the name of the individual. Gender has the obvious meaning; DeathStatus is for recording information such as "died in infancy" when no specific death event is known. PersInfo allows recording of arbitrary personal information such as occupation and religion. AssocIndiv is for links to related individuals where the relationships cannot be expressed directly through Family objects (for example, links to godparents). DupIndiv is interesting: it allows an assertion that this IndividualRec refers to the same individual as another IndividualRec. This is very useful when combining data sets compiled by different genealogists; merging the two records into one can be very difficult if there are inconsistencies in the data, and it can prove very difficult to unmerge the data later if they are found to be different individuals after all. Within the CommonFields group, which is also present in other top-level elements, ExternalID is for reference numbers that identify the individual in external databases; Submitter is the person who created this record; Note is for arbitrary comments; Evidence says where the information came from; Enrichment is for inline documentation such as photographs or transcripts of original documents, and Changed is for a change history of this record.

Most of these fields are optional and repeatable. Something I haven't captured in this schema is that the GEDCOM spec also says the structure is extensible; arbitrary namespaced elements may be inserted at any point in the structure. This is typically used to contain information specific to a particular product vendor, so that GEDCOM can be used to exchange data between users of that product with no loss of information. This can be handled in XML Schema by using wildcards, but only if they appear after other elements (this restriction disappears in XML Schema 1.1).

The Stylus Studio converter makes `IndividualRec` and all other elements into top-level element declarations in the schema. This isn't needed for validation, since in a GEDCOM file the `IndividualRec` will always be a child of the `<GEDCOM>` element. However, it makes this element name available in stylesheets, which is a great convenience; for example, I can write a function whose parameter is declared as `<xsl:param name="indi" as="schema-element(IndividualRec)"/>`.

Having made `IndividualRec` a top-level element declaration, there seems to be nothing that would be gained by **naming its** complex type as a top-level type definition. In general, the only types that are worth naming as **top-level** types are those that are used in more than one place, or at least look likely to be used in more than one place.

For the child elements of `IndividualRec`, the converter chose to use a global element declaration referring to a local (anonymous) type. There's nothing absolute about this; one could equally use a local element with a global type. As far as validation is concerned, you could also use a local element with an anonymous type, but this is not a good idea if you want to reference the schema from a stylesheet. When it comes to writing an XSLT stylesheet, it's important that where a data element such as `Date` appears in several places, it should either use a global element declaration or a global type definition, so that you can reference one or the other when you declare variables and parameters, and when you write match patterns.

There are no substitution groups in this model. They aren't needed, because the model has chosen to use generic elements like `<PersInfo>` rather than specialized types such as `<occupation>` and `<religion>`. The need for substitution groups generally arises when there are many elements that are structurally interchangeable.

Events

An event record has this structure:

```
<xs:element name='EventRec'>
  <xs:complexType>
    <xs:sequence>
      <xs:element ref='Participant' maxOccurs='unbounded'/>
      <xs:element ref='Date' minOccurs='0' maxOccurs='1'/>
      <xs:element ref='Place' minOccurs='0' maxOccurs='1'/>
      <xs:element ref='Religion' minOccurs='0' maxOccurs='1'/>
      <xs:group ref="CommonFields"/>
    </xs:sequence>
    <xs:attribute name='Id' type='xs:ID' use='required'/>
    <xs:attribute name='Type' type='xs:string' use='required'/>
    <xs:attribute name='VitalType' type='VitalTypeType' use='optional'/>
  </xs:complexType>
</xs:element>
```

The `Religion` element, of course, has a special place because so many of the events affecting our forebears were recorded by the religious authorities.

19

Case Study: A Family Tree

Case Study: A Family Tree

Families

The third object type we will look at is the *family*. Here is the definition:

```
<xs:element name='FamilyRec'>
  <xs:complexType>
    <xs:sequence>
      <xs:element ref='HusbFath' minOccurs='0' maxOccurs='1'/>
      <xs:element ref='WifeMoth' minOccurs='0' maxOccurs='1'/>
      <xs:element ref='Child' minOccurs='0' maxOccurs='unbounded'/>
      <xs:element ref='BasedOn' minOccurs='0' maxOccurs='1'/>
      <xs:group ref="CommonFields"/>
    </xs:sequence>
    <xs:attribute name='Id' type='xs:ID' use='required'/>
  </xs:complexType>
</xs:element>
```

Again, many of the fields are common with the other two object types. The elements HusbFath, WifeMoth, and Child play a crucial role in linking the data, so we'd better open them up:

```
<xs:element name='HusbFath' type="ParentType"/>

<xs:element name='WifeMoth' type="ParentType"/>

<xs:element name='Child' type="ChildType"/>

<xs:complexType name="BasicLinkType">
  <xs:sequence>
    <xs:element ref='Link'/>
  </xs:sequence>
</xs:complexType>

<xs:complexType name="ChildType">
  <xs:complexContent>
    <xs:extension base="BasicLinkType">
      <xs:sequence>
        <xs:element ref='ChildNbr' minOccurs='0' maxOccurs='1'/>
        <xs:element ref='RelToFath' minOccurs='0' maxOccurs='1'/>
        <xs:element ref='RelToMoth' minOccurs='0' maxOccurs='1'/>
      </xs:sequence>
    </xs:extension>
  </xs:complexContent>
</xs:complexType>

<xs:complexType name="ParentType">
  <xs:complexContent>
    <xs:extension base="BasicLinkType">
      <xs:sequence>
        <xs:element ref='FamilyNbr' minOccurs='0' maxOccurs='1'/>
      </xs:sequence>
    </xs:extension>
  </xs:complexContent>
</xs:complexType>
```

A `<ChildType>` element represents the participation of an individual in a family in the role of child. The `<Link>` identifies the individual concerned. The `<ChildNbr>` represents the position of that child in the family (1 for the eldest child, and so on); this allows for the fact that some of the children may be unknown. `<RelToFath>` and `<RelToMoth>` elements allow for detail about the relationship of the child to the father and mother; for example, the child may be the natural child of one parent and the adopted child of the other.

The `<ParentType>` element represents the participation of an individual in a family in the role of parent. The `<FamilyNbr>` element provides a sequence number; for example, it allows you to say that this family is the man's second marriage, which is useful if the dates of the marriages are not known.

Now let's look quickly at the three most common (and difficult) datatypes used for properties of these objects: dates, places, and personal names.

Dates

As we've seen, GEDCOM allows any character string to be used as a date. However, much of the presentation of data depends on analyzing dates wherever possible. How is this dilemma resolved?

The `Date` element referenced from the `Event` record has a complex type, defined like this:

```
<xs:complexType name="DateType">
  <xs:simpleContent>
    <xs:extension base="GeneralDate">
      <xs:attribute name="Calendar" type="xs:string"/>
    </xs:extension>
  </xs:simpleContent>
</xs:complexType>
```

That is to say, it is a complex type with simple content: the content is a `GeneralDate`, and the optional attribute indicates which calendar is used. The `GeneralDate` can be any character string, but certain formats such as «DD MMM YYYY» are recommended.

As far as validation is concerned, there isn't much point in defining a schema type for the pattern «DD MMM YYYY». However, it turns out that it can be useful to define this type even if it isn't used for validation. We can define the GEDCOM date format as a union type like this:

```
<xs:simpleType type="GeneralDate">
  <xs:union memberTypes="StandardDate xs:string">
</xs:simpleType>

<xs:simpleType type="StandardDate">
  <xs:restriction base="xs:string">
    <xs:pattern value=
"[0-9]?[0-9]\s(JAN|FEB|MAR|APR|MAY|JUN|JUL|AUG|SEP|OCT|NOV|DEC)\s[0-9]{4}"/>
  </xs:restriction>
</xs:simpleType>
```

This type is meaningless from the point of view of validation — all strings will be considered valid. But the effect is that a date that conforms to the «DD MMM YYYY» pattern will be labeled as a `StandardDate`, while one that doesn't will be labeled only as an `xs:string`. This will prove useful when we write our stylesheets, because it becomes very easy to separate standard dates from nonstandard dates when we want to perform operations like date formatting and sorting. In fact, I could have usefully split dates into three categories: simple exact dates like «4 MAR 1920»; inexact dates that conform to the GEDCOM syntax, such as «BEF JAN 1866» (meaning some time before January 1866); and arbitrary character strings whose interpretation is left purely to the reader.

Places

Place names have an internal structure, but the structure is highly variable. In many cases, components of the place name may be missing, and the part that is missing may be the major part rather than the minor part. For example, you might know that someone was born in Wolverton, England, without knowing which of the three towns of that name it refers to. The GEDCOM schema allows the place name to be entered as unstructured text but also allows individual components of the name to be marked up using a <PlacePart> element which can carry two attributes: Type, which can take values such as Country, City, or Parish to indicate what kind of place this is, and Level, which is a number that represents the relationship of this part of the place name to the other parts.

Personal Names

As with place names, personal names have a highly variable internal structure. The name can be written simply as a character string (within an <IndivName>) element, or the separate parts can be tagged using <NamePart> elements. As with place names, these have a completely open-ended structure. The Type attribute can be used to identify the name part as, for example, a surname or generation suffix, and the Level attribute can be used to indicate its relative importance, for example when used as a key for sorting and indexing.

Creating a Data File

Our next task is to create an XML file containing the Kennedy family tree in the appropriate format. I started by entering the data in a genealogy package, taking the information from public sources such as the Web site of the Kennedy museum. The package I use is called *The Master Genealogist*, and like all such software it is capable of outputting the data in GEDCOM 5.5 format. This is a file containing records that look something like this (it's included in the downloads for this chapter as kennedy.ged):

```
0 @I1@ INDI
1 NAME John Fitzgerald/Kennedy/
1 SEX M
1 BIRT
2 DATE 29 MAY 1917
2 PLAC Brookline, MA, USA
1 DEAT
2 DATE 22 NOV 1963
2 PLAC Dallas, TX, USA
2 NOTE Assassinated by Lee Harvey Oswald.
1 NOTE Educated at Harvard University.
2 CONT Elected Congressman in 1945
2 CONT aged 29; served three terms in the House of Representatives.
2 CONT Elected Senator in 1952. Elected President in 1960, the
2 CONT youngest ever President of the United States.
1 FAMS @F1@
1 FAMC @F2@
```

This isn't XML, of course, but it is a hierarchic data file containing tagged data, so it is a good candidate for converting into XML that looks like the document below. This doesn't conform to the GEDCOM 6.0 data model or schema, but it's a useful starting point.

```
<INDI ID="I1">
   <NAME>John Fitzgerald/Kennedy/</NAME>
   <SEX>M</SEX>
   <BIRT>
      <DATE>29 MAY 1917</DATE>
      <PLAC>Brookline, MA, USA</PLAC>
   </BIRT>
   <DEAT>
      <DATE>22 NOV 1963</DATE>
      <PLAC>Dallas, TX, USA</PLAC>
      <NOTE>Assassinated by Lee Harvey Oswald.<BR/></NOTE>
   </DEAT>
   <NOTE>Educated at Harvard University.
Elected Congressman in 1945
aged 29; served three terms in the House of Representatives.
Elected Senator in 1952. Elected President in 1960, the
youngest ever President of the United States.
   </NOTE>
   <FAMS REF="F1"/>
   <FAMC REF="F2"/>
</INDI>
```

Each record in a GEDCOM file has a unique identifier (in this case I1 – that's letter I, digit one), which is used to construct cross-references between records. Most of the information in this record is self-explanatory, except the <FAMS> and <FAMC> fields: <FAMS> is a reference to a <FAM> record representing a family in which this person is a parent, and <FAMC> is a reference to a family in which this person is a child.

The first stage in processing data is to do this conversion into XML, a process which we will examine in the next section.

Converting GEDCOM Files to XML

The main purpose of XSLT is to convert one XML document into another. But that's not all it can do; it can also generate structured text as the output, and in XSLT 2.0, there are new facilities to accept structured text files as the input. That's exactly what we need to do here.

We'll do this in two stages (splitting a complex transformation into a series of simpler transformations arranged in a pipeline is always a good idea). Since GEDCOM 5.5 is a hierarchic format that uses level numbers to represent the nesting, we will start by converting this mechanically to an XML representation. Then in the second phase, we will convert this first cut XML into XML that conforms to the GEDCOM 6.0 specification.

The source document is thus a text file containing records like this:

```
0 @I1@ INDI
1 NAME John Fitzgerald/Kennedy/
1 SEX M
1 BIRT
2 DATE 29 MAY 1917
2 PLAC Brookline, MA, USA
```

which needs to be converted into XML like this:

```
<INDI ID="I1">
   <NAME>John Fitzgerald/Kennedy/</NAME>
   <SEX>M</SEX>
   <BIRT>
       <DATE>29 MAY 1917</DATE>
       <PLAC>Brookline, MA, USA</PLAC>
   </BIRT>
</INDI>
```

The stylesheet that does this (`parse-gedcom.xsl`) is in fact a micropipeline in its own right, written as a series of variable declarations each one computing a new value from the value of the previous variable. It starts the usual way, and declares a parameter to accept the name of the input text document:

```
<xsl:transform version="2.0"
    xmlns:xsl="http://www.w3.org/1999/XSL/Transform"
    xmlns:xs="http://www.w3.org/2001/XMLSchema"
    exclude-result-prefixes="xs">

<xsl:output method="xml" indent="yes"/>

<xsl:param name="input" as="xs:string" required="yes"/>
```

The file identified by this parameter is then read using the XSLT 2.0 `unparsed-text()` function:

```
<xsl:variable name="input-text" as="xs:string"
              select="unparsed-text($input, 'iso-8859-1')"/>
```

I've actually cheated here. GEDCOM requires files to be encoded in a character set called ANSEL, otherwise ANSI Z39.47-1985, which is used for almost no other purpose. If ANSEL were a mainstream character encoding, it could be specified in the second argument of the `unparsed-text()` function call. In practice, however, it is rather unlikely that any XSLT 2.0 processor would support this encoding natively. Therefore, the conversion from ANSEL to a mainstream character encoding needs some extra logic. If you use Saxon, you can write a custom `UnparsedTextResolver` in Java to take care of low-level interfacing issues like this. This class can invoke a custom character-code converter in the form of a Java `Reader` — an example called `AnselInputReader` is supplied in the downloads for this chapter. (For detailed instructions, see the Saxon documentation.)

We can now split the input file into lines by using the XPath 2.0 `tokenize()` function. We use a separator that matches both Unix and Windows line endings:

```
<xsl:variable name="lines" as="xs:string*"
              select="tokenize($input-text, '\r?\n')"/>
```

The result is a sequence of strings (one for each line), and the next stage is to parse the individual lines. Each line in a GEDCOM file has up to five fields: a level number, an identifier, a tag, a cross-reference, and a value. We will create an XML `<line>` element representing the contents of the line, using attributes to represent each of these five components:

```
<xsl:variable name="parsed-lines" as="element(line)*">
  <xsl:for-each select="$lines">
    <xsl:analyze-string select="." flags="x"
```

```
            regex="^([0-9]+)\s*
                   (@([A-Za-z0-9]+)@)?\s*
                   ([A-Za-z]*)?\s*
                   (@([A-Za-z0-9]+)@)?
                   (.*)$">
    <xsl:matching-substring>
      <line level="{regex-group(1)}"
            ID="{regex-group(3)}"
            tag="{regex-group(4)}"
            REF="{regex-group(6)}"
            text="{regex-group(7)}"/>
    </xsl:matching-substring>
    <xsl:non-matching-substring>
      <xsl:message>Non-matching line "<xsl:value-of select="."/>"</xsl:message>
    </xsl:non-matching-substring>
  </xsl:analyze-string>
 </xsl:for-each>
</xsl:variable>
```

This code creates a `<line>` element for each line of the input file. The content of the elements is constructed by analyzing the text of the input line using a regular expression, where the five lines of the regex correspond to the five fields that may be present. The attribute «flags="x"» means that whitespace in the pattern is ignored, which allows the regex to be split into multiple lines for readability.

I describe this usage of `<xsl:analyze-string>` as a "single-match" usage, because the idea is that the regular expression matches the entire input string exactly once, and the `<xsl:non-matching-substring>` instruction is used only to catch errors. Within the `<xsl:matching-substring>` instruction, the content of the line is taken apart using the `regex-group()` function, which returns the part of the matching substring that matched the nth parenthesized subexpression within the regex. If the relevant part of the regex wasn't matched (for example, if the optional identifier was absent), then this returns a zero-length string, and our XSLT code then creates a zero-length attribute.

So we now have a sequence of XML elements each representing one line of the GEDCOM file, each containing attributes to represent the contents of the five fields in the input. It's useful when debugging to display the content of this intermediate variable, and I added a debugging template to the stylesheet (`<xsl:template name="debug"/>`) to enable this. If you run the stylesheet with this as the entry point, it displays the structure:

```
<?xml version="1.0" encoding="UTF-8"?>
<line level="0" ID="" tag="HEAD" REF="" text=""/>
<line level="1" ID="" tag="SOUR" REF="" text="TMG"/>
<line level="2" ID="" tag="VERS" REF="" text="4.0d"/>
<line level="1" ID="" tag="SUBM" REF="SUB1" text=""/>
<line level="1" ID="" tag="GEDC" REF="" text=""/>
<line level="2" ID="" tag="VERS" REF="" text="5.5"/>
<line level="2" ID="" tag="FORM" REF="" text="LINEAGE-LINKED"/>
```

The next stage is to convert this flat sequence into a hierarchy, in which lines with «level="1"» (for example) turn into XML elements that contain the corresponding «level="2"» lines.

Any problem that involves adding hierarchic levels to the result tree can be regarded as a grouping problem, and it should therefore be no surprise that we tackle it using the `<xsl:for-each-group>` instruction. A group in this case consists of a level N element together with the following elements up to the next one at level N. So this is a positional grouping rather than a value-based grouping. The option that we use to tackle this is the `group-starting-with` attribute, whose value is a match pattern that is used to recognize the first element in each group.

A single application of `<xsl:for-each-group>` creates one extra level in the result tree. In this example, we have a variable number of levels, so we want to apply the instruction a variable number of times. First, we group the overall sequence of `<line>` elements so that each level 0 line starts a new group. Within this group, we perform a further grouping so that each level 1 line starts a new group, and so on up to the maximum depth of the hierarchy. As one might expect, the process is recursive: we write a recursive template that performs the grouping at level N, and that calls itself to perform the level N+1 grouping. This is what it looks like:

```
<xsl:template name="process-level">
  <xsl:param name="population" required="yes" as="element()*"/>
  <xsl:param name="level" required="yes" as="xs:integer"/>
  <xsl:for-each-group select="$population"
                  group-starting-with="*[xs:integer(@level) eq $level]">
    <xsl:element name="{@tag}">
      <xsl:copy-of select="@ID[string(.)], @REF[string(.)]"/>
      <xsl:value-of select="normalize-space(@text)"/>
      <xsl:call-template name="process-level">
        <xsl:with-param name="population"
                        select="current-group()[position() != 1]"/>
        <xsl:with-param name="level"
                        select="$level + 1"/>
      </xsl:call-template>
    </xsl:element>
  </xsl:for-each-group>
</xsl:template>
```

In the recursive call I originally set the population parameter to «current-group() except .». This ought to work, but it produces incorrect output in Altova. Altova also fails to indent the output — this is reasonable, since the specification advises against indenting data that is known to contain mixed content.

When this is called to process all the `<line>` elements with the `$level` parameter set to zero, it forms one group for each line having the attribute «level="0"», containing that line and all the following lines up to the next one with «level="0"». It then processes each of these groups by creating an element to represent the level 0 line (the name of this element is taken from the GEDCOM tag, and its ID and REF attributes are copied unless they are empty), and constructs the content of this new element by means of a recursive call, processing all elements in the group except the first, and looking this time for level 1 lines as the ones that start a new group. The process continues until there are no lines at the next level (the `<xsl:for-each-group>` instruction does nothing if the population to be grouped is empty).

The remaining code in the stylesheet simply invokes this recursive template to process all the lines at level 0:

```
<xsl:template name="main" match="/">
  <xsl:call-template name="process-level">
    <xsl:with-param name="population" select="$parsed-lines"/>
    <xsl:with-param name="level" select="0"/>
  </xsl:call-template>
</xsl:template>
```

This main template represents the entry point to the stylesheet. I added the attribute «match="/"» because at the time of writing, the Altova XSLT 2.0 processor requires a source document to be supplied, even though it is not used. In principle, however, XSLT 2.0 allows a transformation to be invoked with no source document, by naming a template where execution is to start. I use the name «main» as a matter of convention.

In the previous edition of this book, I presented a different way of doing the GEDCOM-to-XML conversion which may still be of interest, so the necessary files are included in the downloads for this chapter. Instead of coding the logic in XSLT, I wrote it in Java. The Java code implements the Java interface `javax.xml.parsers.XMLReader`, which makes it look just like an XML parser, enabling it to feed data into an XSLT stylesheet exactly in the same way that a real XML parser does. The SAX2 parser for GEDCOM 5.5 is supplied with the sample files for this chapter on the Wrox Web site; it is named `GedcomParser`, and you can use it to process the input for a transformation using the `-x` flag on the Saxon command line. For completeness, to allow conversions in the reverse direction, I've also provided a SAX2 `ContentHandler` that accepts an XML result tree in the form of a sequence of SAX events, and serializes it in the GEDCOM notation. Along with these two classes are an `AnselInputStreamReader` and `AnselOutputStreamWriter` that handle the unusual character set used by GEDCOM.

Converting from GEDCOM 5.5 to 6.0

It's now time to look at the second stylesheet in the pipeline, which converts the raw XML obtained by mechanical conversion of the GEDCOM format into XML that conforms to the target GEDCOM 6.0 XML Schema. The stylesheet `ged55-to-6.xsl` doesn't handle the full job of GEDCOM conversion, but it does handle the subset that we're using in this demonstration. It starts like this:

```
<xsl:transform
  xmlns:xsl="http://www.w3.org/1999/XSL/Transform"
  xmlns:xs="http://www.w3.org/2001/XMLSchema"
  version="2.0"
>

<!-- This stylesheet converts from the XML representation GEDCOM 5.5
     to the GEDCOM 6.0 XML beta specification -->
<xsl:strip-space elements="*"/>
<xsl:output method="xml" indent="yes" encoding="iso-8859-1"/>

<!-- import the schema for the result vocabulary -->

<xsl:import-schema namespace="" schema-location="gedSchema.xsd"/>
```

I'm going to use a schema-aware stylesheet to tackle this conversion. I won't be using a schema for the input vocabulary (because I haven't written one), but I will be using the schema for the result document. I will also be validating the result document against this schema. The most noticeable effect of this is that mistakes in the stylesheet that cause incorrect output to be generated are reported immediately, and pinpointed to the line in the stylesheet that caused the error. As I developed this stylesheet, this happened dozens of times before I got it right, and diagnosing the errors proved far easier than using the conventional approach of generating the output, inspecting it for obvious faults, and then running it through a separate validation phase. I'll give some examples of this later on.

To run this example yourself, you will therefore need to install a schema-aware processor. At the time of writing, the the two candidates are Saxon-SA and the Altova XSLT 2.0 processor. Alternatively, because the only use of schema-aware processing is to validate the output, you can edit the stylesheet to remove the `<xsl:import-schema>` declaration and the «validation="strict"» attribute on the

`<xsl:result-document>` instruction, and it will then work with a basic XSLT 2.0 processor. However, later stylesheets in this chapter make rather deeper use of schema-aware transformation.

There is no «namespace» attribute on the `<xsl:import-schema>` declaration, because the schema has no target namespace.

Top-Level Processing

We can now get on with the top-level processing logic:

```
<xsl:param name="submitter" select="'Michael Kay'"/>

<xsl:template match="/">
  <xsl:result-document validation="strict">
    <GEDCOM>
      <HeaderRec>
        <FileCreation
            Date="{f:today()}"/>
        <Submitter>
          <Link Target="ContactRec" Ref="Contact-Submitter"/>
        </Submitter>
      </HeaderRec>
      <xsl:call-template name="families"/>
      <xsl:call-template name="individuals"/>
      <xsl:call-template name="events"/>
      <ContactRec Id="Contact-Submitter">
        <Name><xsl:value-of select="$submitter"/></Name>
      </ContactRec>
    </GEDCOM>
  </xsl:result-document>
</xsl:template>
```

This template rule establishes the outline of the result tree. The containing `<GEDCOM>` element will contain: a header record, which we generate here and now; then a set of family records, a set of individual records, and a set of events, which must appear in that order; and finally a contact record to indicate the originator of the data set, which must be present because the mandatory `<Submitter>` element in the header refers to it. The name of the submitter is defined by a stylesheet parameter, so you can set a different value if you use this stylesheet on your own data files. (The reason this field is called «Submitter» is historic: the original purpose of GEDCOM was to allow members of the LDS church to submit details of their ancestors to the church authorities.)

The instruction `<xsl:result-document validation="strict">` causes the result tree to be validated. The system will do this by looking in the imported schemas for an element declaration of the outermost element in the result tree (the `<GEDCOM>` element) and then ensuring that the rest of the result tree conforms to this element declaration. In the case of Saxon, this validation is done on the fly: each element is validated as soon as it is written to the result tree, which means that any validation errors can be reported in relation to the stylesheet instruction that wrote the incorrect data.

In the header I have generated only those fields that are mandatory. These include the file creation date, which must be in the format «DD MMM YYYY». I generated this using the user-defined function:

```
<xsl:function name="f:today" as="xs:string">
  <xsl:sequence select="format-date(current-date(), '[D1] [MN,*-3] [Y0001]')"/>
</xsl:function>
```

Creating Family Records

The `<FamilyRec>` elements in the result document correspond one-to-one with the `<FAM>` elements in the input, except that the event information is not included (it is output separately in `<EventRec>` elements, later). For example, the input element:

```
<FAM ID="F4">
    <HUSB REF="I3"/>
    <WIFE REF="I4"/>
    <CHIL REF="I2"/>
</FAM>
```

is translated to the output element

```
<FamilyRec Id="F4">
    <HusbFath>
        <Link Target="IndividualRec" Ref="I3"/>
    </HusbFath>
    <WifeMoth>
        <Link Target="IndividualRec" Ref="I4"/>
    </WifeMoth>
    <Child>
        <Link Target="IndividualRec" Ref="I2"/>
    </Child>
</FamilyRec>
```

Here is the code to do this:

```
<xsl:template name="families">
  <xsl:apply-templates select="/*/FAM"/>
</xsl:template>

<xsl:template match="FAM">
  <FamilyRec Id="{@ID}">
    <xsl:apply-templates select="HUSB, WIFE, CHIL"/>
  </FamilyRec>
</xsl:template>

<xsl:template match="FAM/HUSB">
  <HusbFath>
    <Link Target="IndividualRec" Ref="{@REF}"/>
  </HusbFath>
</xsl:template>

<xsl:template match="FAM/WIFE">
  <WifeMoth>
    <Link Target="IndividualRec" Ref="{@REF}"/>
  </WifeMoth>
</xsl:template>

<xsl:template match="FAM/CHIL">
  <Child>
    <Link Target="IndividualRec" Ref="{@REF}"/>
  </Child>
</xsl:template>
```

One point worth noting here is the use of «select="HUSB, WIFE, CHIL"» to ensure that the elements of the family appear in the right order in the output. The GEDCOM 6.0 schema is very strict about the order of elements, whereas GEDCOM 5.5 was more liberal. This expression selects a sequence containing zero-or-one HUSB elements, zero-or-one WIFE elements, and zero-or-more CHIL elements, and processes them in that order.

If the input GEDCOM file is invalid, for example if a FAM contains more than one WIFE element, then the output file will also be invalid, and this will cause a validation error to be reported by the XSLT processor.

Creating Individual Records

The code for mapping <INDI> records in the source to <IndividualRec> records in the result tree is similar in principle to the code for family records, though a little bit more complicated.

```
<xsl:template name="individuals">
  <xsl:apply-templates select="/*/INDI"/>
</xsl:template>

<xsl:template match="INDI">
  <IndividualRec Id="{@ID}">
    <xsl:apply-templates select="NAME, SEX, REFN, NOTE, CHAN"/>
  </IndividualRec>
</xsl:template>

<xsl:template match="INDI/NAME">
  <IndivName>
    <xsl:analyze-string select="." regex="/(.*?)/">
      <xsl:matching-substring>
        <xsl:text> </xsl:text>
        <NamePart Type="surname" Level="1">
          <xsl:value-of select="regex-group(1)"/>
        </NamePart>
        <xsl:text> </xsl:text>
      </xsl:matching-substring>
      <xsl:non-matching-substring>
        <xsl:value-of select="."/>
      </xsl:non-matching-substring>
    </xsl:analyze-string>
  </IndivName>
</xsl:template>
```

Note the code here for extracting the surname from the name using the <xsl:analyze-string> instruction. In GEDCOM 5.5 the surname is tagged by enclosing it between «/» characters; in 6.0, it is enclosed in a nested <NamePart> element. The 6.0 specification also allows tagging of other parts of the name, for example as a given name, a title, a generation suffix (such as «Jr») and so on, but as such fields aren't marked up in our source data, we can't generate them.

```
<xsl:template match="INDI/SEX">
  <Gender>
    <xsl:apply-templates/>
  </Gender>
</xsl:template>
```

```
<xsl:template match="INDI/REFN">
  <ExternalID Type="REFN" Id="{.}"/>
</xsl:template>

<xsl:template match="INDI/CHAN">
  <Changed Date="{DATE}" Time="00:00"/>
</xsl:template>

<xsl:template match="NOTE">
  <Note>
    <xsl:apply-templates/>
  </Note>
</xsl:template>

<xsl:template match="CONT">
  <xsl:text>&#x0a;</xsl:text>
  <xsl:value-of select="."/>
</xsl:template>
```

The rules for NOTE elements apply to such elements wherever they appear in a GEDCOM file, which is why the patterns specify «match="NOTE"» rather than «match="INDI/NOTE"»; for other elements, the rules may be specific to their use within an <INDI> record.

In the original GEDCOM file a NOTE can contain multiple lines, which are arranged like this:

```
1 NOTE Educated at Harvard University. Elected Congressman in 1945
2 CONT aged 29; served three terms in the House of Representatives.
2 CONT Elected Senator in 1952. Elected President in 1960, the
2 CONT youngest ever President of the United States.
```

In the direct conversion to XML, the note appears like this (except that there is no newline before the first <CONT> start tag):

```
<NOTE>Educated at Harvard University. Elected Congressman in 1945
<CONT>aged 29; served three terms in the House of Representatives.</CONT>
<CONT>Elected Senator in 1952. Elected President in 1960, the</CONT>
<CONT>youngest ever President of the United States.</CONT>
</NOTE>
```

The GEDCOM 6.0 specification allows only plain text in a <NOTE> element (it provides other elements for more complex information, such as a transcript of a will). So the ged55-to-6 conversion stylesheet preserves the line endings by inserting a newline character wherever a <CONT> element appeared. The final result is:

```
<Note>Educated at Harvard University. Elected Congressman in 1945
 aged 29; served three terms in the House of Representatives.
 Elected Senator in 1952. Elected President in 1960, the
 youngest ever President of the United States.
</Note>
```

The result isn't always satisfactory, because different genealogy packages that produce GEDCOM 5.5 vary widely in how they handle newlines and whitespace, but it works in this case.

A typical individual record after conversion looks like this:

```
<IndividualRec Id="I2">
   <IndivName>Jaqueline Lee
      <NamePart Type="surname" Level="1">Bouvier</NamePart>
   </IndivName>
   <IndivName>
      <NamePart Type="surname" Level="1">Kennedy</NamePart>
   </IndivName>
   <IndivName>
      <NamePart Type="surname" Level="1">Onassis</NamePart>
   </IndivName>
   <Gender>F</Gender>
   <ExternalID Type="REFN" Id="2"/>
   <Changed Date="13 JAN 2004" Time="00:00"/>
</IndividualRec>
```

GEDCOM 6.0 allows all the parts of an individual's name to be tagged indicating the type of the name, but it doesn't require it, and in our source data, there isn't enough information to achieve this. The `<ExternalID>` allows external reference numbers to be recorded; for example, it might be a stable reference number used to identify this record in a particular database. As with names, there's no limit on how many reference numbers can be stored — the idea is that the «Type» attribute distinguishes them.

Creating Event Records

The event records in the result tree correspond to events associated with individuals and families in the source data. As we've seen, the 6.0 data model treats events as first-class objects, which are linked to the individuals who participated in the event.

Our sample data set only includes a few different kinds of event: birth, marriage, divorce, death, and burial, and in the stylesheet we'll confine ourselves to handling these five, plus the other common event of baptism. We also handle the general EVEN tag, which is used in GEDCOM 5.5 for miscellaneous events. It should be obvious how the code can be extended to handle other events.

```
<xsl:template name="events">
  <xsl:apply-templates mode="event"
      select="/GED/INDI/(BIRT|BAPM|DEAT|BURI) | /GED/FAM/(MARR|DIV)" />
  <xsl:apply-templates select="/GED/(INDI|FAM)/EVEN"/>
</xsl:template>

<xsl:template match="*" mode="event">
  <xsl:variable name="id">
    <xsl:value-of select="../@ID"/>
    <xsl:text>-</xsl:text>
    <xsl:number count="*"/>
  </xsl:variable>
  <EventRec Id="{$id}">
    <xsl:copy-of select="$event-mapping/*[name()=name(current())]/@*"/>
    <xsl:apply-templates select="." mode="participants"/>
    <xsl:apply-templates select="DATE, PLAC, NOTE"/>
  </EventRec>
</xsl:template>
```

```
<xsl:variable name="event-mapping">
  <BIRT Type="birth" VitalType="birth"/>
  <BAPM Type="baptism" VitalType="birth"/>
  <DEAT Type="death" VitalType="death"/>
  <BURI Type="burial" VitalType="death"/>
  <MARR Type="marriage" VitalType="marriage"/>
  <DIV Type="divorce" VitalType="divorce"/>
</xsl:variable>

<xsl:template match="EVEN">
  <xsl:variable name="id">
    <xsl:value-of select="../@ID"/>
    <xsl:text>-</xsl:text>
    <xsl:number count="*"/>
  </xsl:variable>
  <EventRec Id="{$id}" Type="{TYPE}">
    <xsl:apply-templates select="." mode="participants"/>
    <xsl:apply-templates select="DATE, PLAC, NOTE"/>
  </EventRec>
</xsl:template>
```

This code identifies all the subelements of `<INDI>` and `<FAM>` that refer to events, and then processes these, creating one `<EventRec>` in the output for each. The identifier for the event is computed from the identifier of the containing `<INDI>` or `<FAM>` element plus a sequence number, and the attributes of the event are obtained from a look-up table based on the original element name. In the 6.0 model, the type of event (for example death or burial) is indicated by the «Type» attribute, whose values are completely open-ended. The optional «VitalType» attribute allows each event to be associated with one of the four key events of birth, death, marriage, and divorce: this means, for example, that the date of publication of an obituary can be used as an approximation for the date of death if no more accurate date is available, and that the announcement of banns can similarly be used to estimate the date of marriage.

The next two templates are used to generate the participants in an event. The first handles events associated with an individual, the second events associated with a couple (which come from the FAM record):

```
<xsl:template match="INDI/*" mode="participants">
  <Participant>
    <Link Target="IndividualRec" Ref="{../@ID}"/>
    <Role>principal</Role>
  </Participant>
</xsl:template>

<xsl:template match="FAM/*" mode="participants">
  <Participant>
    <Link Target="IndividualRec" Ref="{../HUSB/@REF}"/>
    <Role>husband</Role>
  </Participant>
  <Participant>
    <Link Target="IndividualRec" Ref="{../WIFE/@REF}"/>
    <Role>wife</Role>
  </Participant>
</xsl:template>
```

This leaves the handling of the date and place of the event. Both are potentially very complex information items. Dates, however, have changed little between GEDCOM 5.5 and 6.0, so they can be carried over unchanged.

```
<xsl:template match="DATE">
  <Date><xsl:apply-templates/></Date>
</xsl:template>
```

For place names, we can try to be a bit more clever. Many of the events in our data set occurred in the United States, and have a PLAC record of the form «somewhere, XX, USA», where XX is a two-letter code identifying a state. This format is predictable because *The Master Genealogist* captures place names in a structured way and generates this comma-separated format on output. We can recognize place names that follow this pattern, and use the regular-expression-handling capability of XSLT 2.0 to generate a more structured <Place> attribute. This records the country as USA, and the state as the two-letter code preceding the country name; anything before the state abbreviation is tokenized using commas as the delimiter, and the sequence of tokens is output in reverse order — note the calls on reverse() and tokenize() — using individual <PlacePart> elements in the output.

```
<xsl:template match="PLAC">
  <Place>
    <xsl:choose>
      <xsl:when test="matches(., '^.*,\s*[A-Z]{2},\s*USA\s*$')">
        <xsl:analyze-string select="."
                            regex="^(.*),\s*([A-Z]{{2}}),\s*USA\s*$">
          <xsl:matching-substring>
            <PlaceName>
              <PlacePart Type="country" Level="1">USA</PlacePart>
              <PlacePart Type="state" Level="2">
                <xsl:value-of select="regex-group(2)"/>
              </PlacePart>
              <xsl:for-each select="reverse(tokenize(regex-group(1), ','))">
                <PlacePart Level="{5+position()}">
                  <xsl:value-of select="normalize-space(.)"/>
                </PlacePart>
              </xsl:for-each>
            </PlaceName>
          </xsl:matching-substring>
          <xsl:non-matching-substring>
            <xsl:message>Error: string "<xsl:value-of select="."/>"
                      does not match regex</xsl:message>
          </xsl:non-matching-substring>
        </xsl:analyze-string>
      </xsl:when>
      <xsl:otherwise>
        <PlaceName><xsl:value-of select="."/></PlaceName>
      </xsl:otherwise>
    </xsl:choose>    </Place>
</xsl:template>
```

The effect of these rules is that we end up with event records of the form:

```
<EventRec Id="I2-5" Type="birth" VitalType="birth">
  <Participant>
    <Link Target="IndividualRec" Ref="I2"/>
```

```
        <Role>principal</Role>
    </Participant>
    <Date>28 JUL 1929</Date>
    <Place>
        <PlaceName>
            <PlacePart Type="country" Level="1">USA</PlacePart>
            <PlacePart Type="state" Level="2">NY</PlacePart>
            <PlacePart Level="6">Long Island</PlacePart>
            <PlacePart Level="7">Southampton</PlacePart>
        </PlaceName>
    </Place>
</EventRec>
```

The names "Long Island" and "Southampton" are classified as levels 6 and 7 because we don't know enough about them to classify them more accurately: levels up to 5 have reserved meanings, whereas 6 and above are available for arbitrary purposes. The ordering of levels is significant: higher levels are intended to represent a finer granularity of place name, which is why we have reversed the order of the original components of the name.

Debugging the Stylesheet

This completes the presentation of the stylesheet used to convert the data from GEDCOM 5.5 to 6.0 format. I'd like to add some notes, however, from my experience of developing this stylesheet. The vast majority of my errors in coding this stylesheet, unless they were basic XSLT or XPath errors, were detected as a result of the on-the-fly validation of the result document against its schema. These errors included:

- ❑ Leaving out required attributes
- ❑ Misspelling element names (for example, `ExternalId` for `ExternalID`)
- ❑ Generating elements in the wrong order
- ❑ Placing an element at the wrong level of nesting
- ❑ Generating an invalid value for an attribute

In the case of Saxon, a few of these errors are detected at stylesheet compile time, but most are reported while executing the stylesheet, and in nearly all cases the error message identifies exactly where the stylesheet is wrong. For example, if the code in the initial template is changed to read:

```
<Submitter>
    <Link Ref="Contact-Submitter"/>
</Submitter>
```

then the transformation fails with the message:

```
Validation error on line 27 of ged55-to-6.xsl:
  XTTE1510: Required attribute @Target is missing
  (See http://www.w3.org/TR/xmlschema-1/#cvc-complex-type clause 4)
```

This process caught quite a few basic XSLT coding errors. For example, I originally wrote:

```
<xsl:template match="FAM/CHIL">
  <Child>
    <Link Target="IndividualRec" Ref="@REF"/>
  </Child>
</xsl:template>
```

in which the curly braces around «@REF» have been omitted. This resulted in the error message:

```
Validation error on line 64 of ged55-to-6.xsl:
    The value '@REF' is not a valid NCName
```

The error message arises because in the absence of curly braces, the system has tried to use «@REF» as the literal value of the «Ref» attribute, and this is not allowed because the attribute is defined in the schema to have type IDREF, which is a subtype of NCName. An NCName cannot contain an «@» character.

Similarly, errors in the picture of the format-date() function call were picked up because they resulted in a string that did not match the picture defined in the schema for the StandardDate type.

However, schema validation of the result tree will not pick up all errors. I had some trouble, for example, getting the regular expression for matching place names right, but the errors simply resulted in the output file containing an empty <Place> element, which is allowed by the schema.

Displaying the Family Tree Data

What we want to do now is to write a stylesheet that displays the data in a GEDCOM file in HTML format. We want the display to look something like the following screenshot (see Figure 19-1).

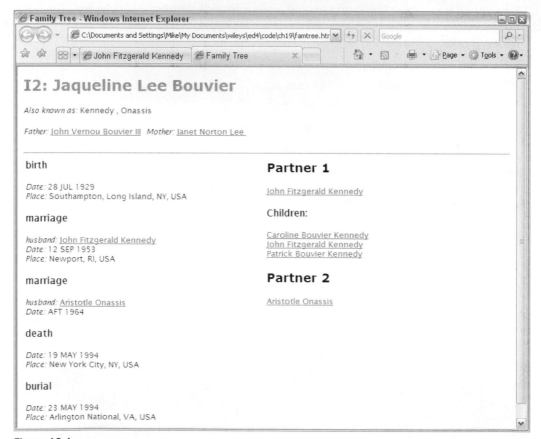

Figure 19-1

This shows all the details of one individual, with links to related individuals so that you can browse around the family tree. Of course one could attempt many more ambitious ways of displaying this data, and I would encourage you to do so: you can start with the small Kennedy data set included in the download for this book, and then continue with any other GEDCOM data set, perhaps one of your own family tree.

Because we will have one HTML page for each individual in the file, we have to think about how to create multiple HTML pages from a single XML input document. There are at least three ways of doing this:

❑ A bulk publishing process, in which you convert the XML input document into a set of HTML pages, and then publish these as static pages on the Web server. This has the benefit that you only incur the cost of transformation once. It minimizes your dependence on the facilities available from your Internet service provider, and it will work with any browser. However, it can take a lot of space on the server, and it can take a long time to upload if you have a slow connection.

❑ Generating HTML pages on demand in the server, using Java servlets or ASP pages. Again this will work with any browser, but this time you need to find an Internet service provider who allows you to run servlets or ASP pages.

❑ Downloading the entire XML file to the client, and generating the display there. This has the advantage that the data is only downloaded once, and the user can then browse it at leisure, with no further interaction with the server.

Unfortunately, at the time of writing the two major browsers (Firefox and Internet Explorer) both support XSLT 1.0 transformations, but neither yet supports XSLT 2.0. To get around this problem, I use a fallback stylesheet for this case that uses XSLT 1.0 only.

Another disadvantage is security; you have no way of filtering the data, for example to remove details of living persons, and you have no way to stop your entire XML file being copied by the user (for example, the user can View Source or can poke around in the browser cache).

The only real difference between the three cases, as far as the stylesheet is concerned, is that the hyperlinks will be generated differently.

We'll handle the differences by writing a generic stylesheet module containing all the common code for the three cases and then importing this into stylesheets that handle the variations. But we'll start by writing a stylesheet that displays one individual on one HTML page, and then we'll worry about the hyperlinks later.

The Stylesheet

We're ready to write a stylesheet, `person.xsl` that generates an HTML page showing the information relevant to a particular individual. This stylesheet will need to accept the `Id` of the required individual as a stylesheet parameter. If no value is supplied, we'll choose the first `<INDI>` record in the file. Here's how it starts:

```
<xsl:transform version="2.0"
    xmlns:xsl="http://www.w3.org/1999/XSL/Transform"
    xmlns:xs="http://www.w3.org/2001/XMLSchema"
    xmlns:ged="http://www.wrox.com/569090/gedcom"
    xmlns="http://www.w3.org/1999/xhtml"
    exclude-result-prefixes="xs ged">
```

```
<!-- import the schema for the GEDCOM 6.0 vocabulary -->

<xsl:import-schema namespace="" schema-location="gedSchema.xsd"/>

<!-- import the schema for the target XHTML vocabulary -->

<xsl:import-schema namespace="http://www.w3.org/1999/xhtml"
    schema-location="http://www.w3.org/2002/08/xhtml/xhtml1-transitional.xsd"/>

<xsl:output method="xhtml" indent="yes" encoding="iso-8859-1"/>
<!-- parameter to supply the Id of the person to be displayed.
     Default value is the Id of the first person in the data set -->

<xsl:param name="id" select="/*/IndividualRec[1]/@Id" as="xs:string"/>
```

The stylesheet defines four namespaces: the XSLT namespace, the schema namespace, a local namespace which is used only for the functions defined in this stylesheet module, and the XHTML namespace for the result tree. The schema and ged namespaces aren't needed in the output file, so the exclude-result-prefixes attribute is set to prevent them appearing.

I've chosen to generate the output in XHTML, so I've specified «method="xhtml"» in the <xsl:output> declaration, and I've imported the XHTML schema. This means that any attempt to generate incorrect XHTML can be reported immediately, while the stylesheet is running, and the offending instruction in the stylesheet can be pinpointed. I decided to use the transitional XHTML schema rather than the strict version of the schema, frankly out of laziness: the strict version is *very* strict indeed, and extra work would be needed on this stylesheet to make its output conform.

There's now a fair bit of preamble before we do any useful work. This is all designed to make the subsequent processing easier and faster. First we define some keys:

```
<!-- keys to allow records to be found by their Id -->

<xsl:key name="indi" match="IndividualRec" use="@Id"/>
<xsl:key name="fam" match="FamilyRec" use="@Id"/>

<!-- a key that locates the family record for a given child -->

<xsl:key name="family-of-child" match="FamilyRec" use="Child/Link/@Ref"/>

<!-- a key that locates the family records for a given parent -->

<xsl:key name="families-of-parent" match="FamilyRec"
        use="element(*,ParentType)/Link/@Ref"/>

<!-- a key to allow events to be found for a given individual -->

<xsl:key name="events-for-person" match="EventRec" use="Participant/Link/@Ref"/>
```

The main purpose of the keys is to make navigation around the structure faster. For a data model like GEDCOM, with many cross-references from one record to another, this can make a big difference. The first two keys allow records to be found given their unique identifiers (they are indexed on their Id attributes). The other three keys are there essentially to follow inverse relationships: a family contains links to the children in the family, and the first key enables us quickly to find the family with a link to a given child (in our data there will never be more than one, though GEDCOM allows it; for example, a child may be linked both to her birth parents and to her adoptive parents).

Having defined these keys, we now define some functions to make it easier to navigate around the data.

```
<!-- a function to get all the events for a given individual -->

<xsl:function name="ged:events-for-person" as="schema-element(EventRec)*">
  <xsl:param name="person" as="schema-element(IndividualRec)"/>
  <xsl:sequence select="$person/key('events-for-person', $person/@Id)"/>
</xsl:function>

<!-- a function to get the families in which a given individual is a spouse -->

<xsl:function name="ged:families-of-spouse" as="schema-element(FamilyRec)*">
  <xsl:param name="person" as="schema-element(IndividualRec)"/>
  <xsl:sequence select="$person/key('families-of-parent', $person/@Id)"/>
</xsl:function>

<!-- a function to get all the events for a couple -->

<xsl:function name="ged:events-for-couple" as="schema-element(EventRec)*">
  <xsl:param name="couple" as="schema-element(FamilyRec)"/>
  <xsl:sequence
    select="if ($couple/HusbFath and $couple/WifeMoth)
            then (ged:events-for-person(
                     $couple/key('indi', $couple/HusbFath/Link/@Ref))
                  intersect
                  ged:events-for-person(
                     $couple/key('indi', $couple/WifeMoth/Link/@Ref)))
            else ()"/>

</xsl:function>
```

This checks that the family record does indeed identify a couple (both parents are present), and then finds all the events in which both parties participate — note the use of the `intersect` operator to find the nodes that are present in two given node-sets.

```
<!-- function to get the birth date of an individual -->

<xsl:function name="ged:birth-date" as="element(*,DateType)">
  <xsl:param name="person" as="schema-element(IndividualRec)"/>
  <xsl:variable name="birth"
    select="ged:events-for-person($person)[@Type='birth']"/>
  <xsl:variable name="birth-vitals"
    select="ged:events-for-person($person)[@VitalType='birth']"/>
  <xsl:sequence select="(($birth, $birth-vitals)/Date)[1]"/>
</xsl:function>
```

This function is trying to accommodate some of the variety possible in the model. It first finds the person's birth event (there may be more than one if it has been recorded more than once). Then it selects the events whose `VitalType` is «birth»: this might include records such as baptism or the civil registration of birth (which careful genealogists will distinguish from the birth event itself). It returns the first one of these events that has a date associated with it.

```
<!-- function to get the estimated marriage date for a couple -->

<xsl:function name="ged:estimated-marriage-date" as="element(*, DateType)?">
  <xsl:param name="couple" as="schema-element(FamilyRec)"/>
  <xsl:variable name=   "marriage-vitals"
                as=      "schema-element(EventRec)*"
                select=  "ged:events-for-couple($couple)[@VitalType='marriage']"/>
  <xsl:variable name=   "marriage"
                as=      "schema-element(EventRec)*"
                select=  "$marriage-vitals[@Type='marriage']"/>
  <xsl:variable name=   "marriage-date"
                as=      "element(*, DateType)?"
                select=  "($marriage/Date, $marriage-vitals/Date)[1]"/>
  <xsl:sequence select="if ($marriage-date)
                        then $marriage-date
                        else ged:sort-dates($couple/Child/Link/@Ref/key('indi',.)/
                                 ged:birth-date(.))[1]"/>
</xsl:function>
```

This function attempts to determine when a couple (identified by a `FamilyRec`) were married. This is done solely so that an individual's partners can be listed in the right order, so the date does not have to be precise. The logic looks complicated, but all it does is find a dated marriage event if it can and otherwise to return the date of birth of the oldest child. The call on `ged:sort-dates()` is a forward reference to a function that we'll see later.

The next group of functions are concerned with formatting and sorting of dates. First a function to convert a date from GEDCOM format into ISO format:

```
<!-- function to convert a standard GEDCOM date (DD MMM YY) to an xs:date -->

<xsl:function name="ged:date-to-ISO" as="xs:date">
  <xsl:param name="date" as="StandardDate"/>
  <xsl:variable name="iso-date">
    <xsl:analyze-string select="$date"
                        regex="\s*([0-9]+)\s+([A-Z]+)\s+([0-9]+)\s*$">
      <xsl:matching-substring>
        <xsl:number value="regex-group(3)" format="0001"/>
        <xsl:text>-</xsl:text>
        <xsl:number value="index-of(('JAN', 'FEB', 'MAR', 'APR', 'MAY', 'JUN',
                                     'JUL', 'AUG', 'SEP', 'OCT', 'NOV', 'DEC'),
                                    regex-group(2))" format="01"/>
        <xsl:text>-</xsl:text>
        <xsl:number value="regex-group(1)" format="01"/>
      </xsl:matching-substring>
    </xsl:analyze-string>
  </xsl:variable>
  <xsl:sequence select="xs:date($iso-date)"/>
</xsl:function>
```

This function only works on a date in standard GEDCOM format «DD MMM YYYY». If you pass it a date in an extended form, such as «BEF 1870», the stylesheet will fail with a type error.

I've not attempted here to handle the problems of non-Gregorian calendars (which arise all the time with genealogical data). If the GEDCOM date represents a date in the Julian (or *Old Style*) calendar, then in theory it ought to be shifted by 10 or 11 days when converting it to an ISO date, because ISO dates are supposed always to be Gregorian.

```
<!-- function to format a standard GEDCOM date for display -->

<xsl:function name="ged:format-date" as="xs:string">
   <xsl:param name="date" as="StandardDate"/>
   <xsl:sequence select="format-date(ged:date-to-ISO($date), '[D] [MNn] [Y]')"/>
</xsl:function>
```

To format a date into the form «2 January 1931», we first convert the date to standard ISO representation (the xs:date type) and then call XSLT's format-date() function.

The next two functions are used for sorting dates:

```
<!-- function to get a sort key for GEDCOM dates -->

<xsl:function name="ged:date-sort-key" as="xs:string">
  <xsl:param name="date" as="element(*, DateType)"/>
  <xsl:sequence select="
        if (data($date) instance of StandardDate)
          then string(ged:date-to-ISO($date))
          else substring($date, string-length($date)-3)
        "/>
</xsl:function>

<!-- a function to sort a set of dates chronologically -->

<xsl:function name="ged:sort-dates" as="element(*, DateType)*">
  <xsl:param name="dates" as="element(*, DateType)*"/>
  <xsl:perform-sort select="$dates">
    <xsl:sort select="ged:date-sort-key(.)"/>
  </xsl:perform-sort>
</xsl:function>
```

We want to be able to sort standard dates such as «2 JAN 1931» chronologically, but we also want to be able to fit nonstandard dates such as «BEF 1870» into the sequence as best we can. To achieve this, I've chosen a sort key that uses the ISO conversion of the date in the case of standard dates (for example, «1931-01-02», and that uses the last four characters otherwise.

Sometimes we just want to display the year:

```
<!-- function to get the year from a GEDCOM date -->

<xsl:function name="ged:get-year" as="xs:string">
  <xsl:param name="date" as="element(*, DateType)"/>
  <xsl:sequence select="substring($date, string-length($date)-3)"/>
</xsl:function>
```

Finally, there's one more function we will be using, which converts a string so that the initial letter is a capital:

```
<!-- a function to capitalize the initial letter of a string -->

<xsl:function name="ged:initial-cap" as="xs:string">
  <xsl:param name="input" as="xs:string"/>
  <xsl:sequence select="concat(upper-case(substring($input, 1, 1)),
                               substring($input, 2))"/>
</xsl:function>
```

And that's the end of the preliminaries. Now we can get on with some actual template rules.

```
<xsl:template match="/">
  <xsl:if test="not(/* instance of schema-element(GEDCOM))">
    <xsl:message terminate="yes">Input document is not a
                               validated GEDCOM 6.0 file</xsl:message>
  </xsl:if>
  <xsl:result-document validation="strict">
    <xsl:variable name="person" select="key('indi', $id)"/>
    <xsl:apply-templates select="$person"/>
  </xsl:result-document>
</xsl:template>
```

The root template rule starts by testing to see if the outermost element of the source document is a GEDCOM element. It doesn't just test the name of the element: the sequence type descriptor «schema-element(GEDCOM)» also checks that the type annotation is appropriate. If the user supplies a source document that hasn't been validated, then this test will fail, even if the document is actually valid, and the stylesheet will proceed no further. If this check weren't present here, some strange and difficult-to-diagnose failures could occur later on, because we are relying on the type annotations being present in the input data.

The entire transformation is then wrapped inside an <xsl:result-document> instruction. This instruction is usually used only when producing multiple result trees, but in this case we're using it for the primary result tree, in order to request validation. It's not actually specifying what the type of the result document must be, only that it must be what it says it is: «validation="strict"» will cause a failure if the outermost element in the result tree isn't defined in some imported schema, or if the result tree isn't valid against that definition. In this case, the intent is to check that the result is valid XHTML.

The outline of the HTML page is produced when we process the selected <IndividualRec> element, as one might expect:

```
<xsl:template match="IndividualRec">
  <html>
    <head>
      <xsl:call-template name="css-style"/>
      <xsl:variable name="name">
        <xsl:apply-templates select="IndivName[1]"/>
      </xsl:variable>
      <title><xsl:value-of select="$name"/></title>
    </head>

    <body bgcolor="{if (Gender='M') then 'cyan' else 'pink'}">
```

```
<!-- Show name and parentage -->

      <h1><xsl:apply-templates select="IndivName[1]"/></h1>
      <xsl:if test="IndivName[2]">
        <p>
          <span class="label">Also known as: </span>
          <xsl:for-each select="IndivName[position() ge 2]">
            <xsl:apply-templates select="."/>
            <xsl:if test="position() ne last()">, </xsl:if>
          </xsl:for-each>
        </p>
      </xsl:if>
      <xsl:call-template name="show-parents"/>
      <hr/>

      <table>
        <tr>

          <!-- Show events and attributes -->

          <td width="50%" valign="top">
            <xsl:call-template name="show-events"/>
          </td>
          <td width="20%"/>

          <!-- Show children -->

          <td width="30%" valign="top">
            <xsl:call-template name="show-partners"/>
          </td>
        </tr>
      </table>

      <hr/>

      <!-- Show notes -->

      <xsl:for-each select="Note">
        <p class="text"><xsl:apply-templates mode="note"/></p>
        <xsl:if test="position() eq last()"><hr/></xsl:if>
      </xsl:for-each>

    </body>
  </html>
</xsl:template>
```

This template rule works through the process of generating the output page. Some observations:

❑   The title in the HTML header is generated by first creating a variable, and then copying the value of the variable to the `<title>` element. This is deliberate, it takes advantage of the standard template rules for generating a personal name, but the `<xsl:value-of>` instruction then removes the tags such as `<b>` that appear in the generated name, because these clutter the displayed title in some browsers.

❑   The background color of the page depends on the value of the person's `Gender` attribute. You might consider this to be an aesthetic abomination, in which case you are welcome to change it, but I left it in because it illustrates another XSLT technique. A more technical criticism is that strict XHTML doesn't allow the `<body>` element to have a `bgcolor` attribute: this will be reported as an error if you try to import the strict XHTML schema instead of the transitional one.

❑   The main task of generating the content of the page is split up and delegated to separate named templates, simply for reasons of modularity.

❑   There is no attempt to display all the data that GEDCOM allows to be included in, or referenced from, an `<INDI>` record, for example citations of sources, multimedia objects such as photographs, and the like. If such data is present it will simply be skipped.

I've chosen to use an internal CSS stylesheet to define styling information such as font sizes, and the task of generating this is delegated to the template named `css-style`. This generates fixed output, as follows:

```
<xsl:template name="css-style">
   <style type="text/css">

   H1 {
       font-family: Verdana, Helvetica, sans-serif;
       font-size: 18pt;
       font-weight: bold;
       color: "#FF0080"
   }

   H2 {
       font-family: Verdana, Helvetica, sans-serif;
       font-size: 14pt;
       font-weight: bold;
       color: black;
   }

   H3 {
       font-family: Lucida Sans, Helvetica, sans-serif;
       font-size: 11pt;
       font-weight: bold;
       color: black;
   }

   SPAN.label {
       font-family: Lucida Sans, Helvetica, sans-serif;
       font-size: 10pt;
       font-weight: normal;
       font-style: italic;
       color: black;     }

   P,LI,TD {
       font-family: Lucida Sans, Helvetica, sans-serif;
       font-size: 10pt;
       font-weight: normal;
       color: black;     }
```

```
P.text {
     font-family: Comic Sans MS, Helvetica, sans-serif;
     font-size: 10pt;
     font-weight: normal;
     color: black;     }


   </style>
</xsl:template>
```

It would have been quite possible, of course, to attach these attributes to the various HTML elements individually, or to incorporate them using XSLT attribute sets, but this way seems cleaner, and shows how XSLT and CSS can complement each other. In fact, it might have been even better to use an external CSS stylesheet, since a user displaying many of these HTML pages would then get more benefit from caching.

The next template displays the parents of the current individual, as hyperlinks:

```
<xsl:template name="show-parents">
  <xsl:variable name=    "parental-family"
                as=      "schema-element(FamilyRec)?"
                select= "key('family-of-child', @Id)[1]"/>

  <xsl:variable name=    "father"
                as=      "schema-element(IndividualRec)?"
                select= "key('indi', $parental-family/HusbFath/Link/@Ref)"/>

  <xsl:variable name=    "mother"
                as=      "schema-element(IndividualRec)?"
                select= "key('indi', $parental-family/WifeMoth/Link/@Ref)"/>
  <p>
    <xsl:if test="$father">
        <span class="label">Father: </span>
        <xsl:apply-templates select="$father/IndivName" mode="link"/> 
    </xsl:if>
    <xsl:if test="$mother">
        <span class="label">Mother: </span>
        <xsl:apply-templates select="$mother/IndivName" mode="link"/> 
    </xsl:if>
  </p>
</xsl:template>
```

The template starts by locating the <FamilyRec> element in which this person appears as a child. It does this using the «family-of-child» key defined earlier. Then it selects the <IndividualRec> records for the father and mother, these being the records pointed to by the <HusbFath> and <WifeMoth> fields of the <FamilyRec> record: this time the «indi» key is used.

If the data is not all present, for example if there is no <FamilyRec> element, or if the <FamilyRec> is missing a <HusbFath> and <WifeMoth> (no pedigree goes back to infinity), then the «$father» and or «$mother» variables will simply identify an empty sequence. The subsequent <xsl:if> instructions ensure that when this happens, the relevant label is omitted from the output.

The actual hyperlinks are generated by using <xsl:apply-templates> with «mode="link"»: this gets reused for all the other links on the page, and we'll see later how it works. The « » character reference outputs a nonbreaking space. It's actually simpler to do this than to output an ordinary space, which would require an <xsl:text> element. If you don't like numeric character references you can define an entity called «nbsp» in the <!DOCTYPE> declaration and then use « » in place of « ».

The next named template is used to display the list of events for an individual, such as birth, marriage and death.

```
<!-- Show the events for an individual -->
<xsl:template name="show-events">
  <xsl:variable name=   "subject"
                as=     "schema-element(IndividualRec)"
                select= "."/>

  <xsl:for-each select="ged:events-for-person(.)">
        <xsl:sort select="ged:date-sort-key(Date)"/>
        <h3><xsl:value-of select="ged:initial-cap(@Type)"/></h3>
        <p>
        <xsl:for-each select="Participant[Link/@Ref ne $subject/@Id]">
            <span class="label">
              <xsl:value-of select="ged:initial-cap(Role)"/>:
            </span>
            <xsl:apply-templates select="Link/@Ref/key('indi',.)/IndivName[1]"
                                 mode="link"/>

            <br/>
        </xsl:for-each>
        <xsl:if test="Date">
            <span class="label">Date: </span>
            <xsl:apply-templates select="Date"/><br/>
        </xsl:if>
        <xsl:if test="Place">
            <span class="label">Place: </span>
            <xsl:apply-templates select="Place"/><br/>
        </xsl:if>
        </p>
        <xsl:for-each select="Note">
            <p class="text"><xsl:apply-templates mode="note"/></p>
        </xsl:for-each>

  </xsl:for-each>
</xsl:template>
```

The events are located using the ged:events-for-person() function, and they are presented in an attempt at date order, achieved by calling the ged:date-sort-key() function that we saw earlier.

For each event the template displays the name of the event (in title case, for example «Birth»), the list of participants other than the subject of this page, the date and place of the event, and any notes recorded about the event. In each case this is done by applying the appropriate template rules.

The only part of the HTML display that remains is the right-hand panel, where we show information about a person's partner(s) and children. If multiple partners are recorded for an individual, we use headings such as "Partner 1", "Partner 2"; if there is only one, we omit the number.

The template looks like this:

```
<xsl:template name="show-partners">
  <xsl:variable name=  "subject"
                as=    "element(IndividualRec)"
                select= "."/>

  <xsl:variable name=  "partnerships"
                as=    "element(FamilyRec)*"
                select= "ged:families-of-spouse(.)"/>

  <xsl:for-each select="$partnerships">
    <xsl:sort select="ged:date-sort-key(ged:estimated-marriage-date(.))"/>

    <xsl:variable name=  "partner"
                  as=    "element(IndividualRec)?"
                  select= "key('indi', element(*, ParentType)/Link/@Ref)
                             except $subject"/>
    <xsl:variable name=  "partner-seq"
                  as=    "xs:integer?"
                  select= "position()[count($partnerships) ne 1]"/>
    <xsl:if test="$partner">
      <h2>Partner <xsl:value-of select="$partner-seq"/></h2>
      <p><xsl:apply-templates select="$partner/IndivName[1]" mode="link"/></p>
    </xsl:if>

    <xsl:if test="Child">
      <h3>Children:</h3>
      <p>
        <xsl:for-each select="Child">
          <xsl:sort select="ChildNbr"/>
          <xsl:sort select="ged:date-sort-key(
                              Link/@Ref/key('indi',.)/ged:birth-date(.))"/>

          <xsl:variable name=  "child"
                        as=    "element(IndividualRec)"
                        select= "Link/@Ref/key('indi',.)"/>

          <xsl:value-of select="ged:get-year(ged:birth-date($child))"/>
          <xsl:text> </xsl:text>
          <xsl:apply-templates select="$child/IndivName[1]" mode="link"/><br/>
        </xsl:for-each>
      </p>
    </xsl:if>
  </xsl:for-each>
</xsl:template>
```

As before, we try to list the partners in chronological order, based on the year of marriage. If this isn't known, there's not much we can do about it (I could have tried to use the `<FamilyNbr>` field, but it's not present in the data we are using). For each partnership, we list the partner's name, as a hyperlink, and then the children's names, again as hyperlinks. The children are found from the `<Child>` fields of the `<FamilyRec>` record, and they are listed in order of year of birth where this is known.

The expression «position()[count($partnerships) ne 1]» merits some explanation. It returns the value of position(), unless the number of partnerships is one, in which case it returns an empty sequence. The effect is that when there is only one partner we don't output ''Partner 1'' (which is not only inelegant, but might be thought presumptive!)

The next group of template rules is used to create the HTML hyperlinks:

```
<xsl:template match="IndivName" mode="link">
   <a>
     <xsl:attribute name="href">
        <xsl:call-template name="make-href"/>
     </xsl:attribute>
     <xsl:apply-templates/>
   </a>
</xsl:template>

<xsl:template match="NamePart[@Type='surname']">
    <xsl:text> </xsl:text>
    <span class="surname"><xsl:apply-templates/></span>
    <xsl:text> </xsl:text>
</xsl:template>

<xsl:template name="make-href">
    <xsl:value-of select="concat(../@Id, '.html')"/>
</xsl:template>
```

The «make-href» template is the only place where the form of a link is defined: in this case it consists of a relative URL reference to another HTML file, with a filename based on the individual's Id attribute, for example I27.html. This has been very deliberately isolated into a template all of its own, for reasons that will become clear later.

The stylesheet ends with the template rules for formatting dates, places, and notes:

```
<xsl:template match="PlaceName[PlacePart]">
  <xsl:variable name="sorted-parts" as="element()*">
    <xsl:perform-sort select="PlacePart">
      <xsl:sort select="@Level" order="descending"/>
    </xsl:perform-sort>
  </xsl:variable>
  <xsl:value-of select="$sorted-parts" separator=", "/>
</xsl:template>
```

The above rule sorts the parts of a date by the value of their Level attribute, and then outputs them in a comma-separated list. Note that we no longer need to specify that this is a numeric sort, the system can work this out from the schema.

```
<xsl:template match="Date[data(.) instance of StandardDate]">
  <xsl:value-of select="ged:format-date(data(.))"/>
</xsl:template>

<xsl:template match="Date">
  <xsl:value-of select="."/>
</xsl:template>
```

The above two rules handle standard dates and nonstandard dates respectively. We rely on the type annotation to distinguish the two cases. Note the call on «data(.)»: we want to test the type of the simple content of the <Date> element, not the type of the element itself. So we need to call the data() function to get the content.

The final rule, below, is for text nodes within a <Note> element. This uses the <xsl:analyze-string> instruction to replace newline characters by <br/> elements, so that the line endings are preserved in the browser's display.

```
<xsl:template match="text()" mode="note">
  <xsl:analyze-string select="." regex="\n">
    <xsl:matching-substring>
      <br/>
    </xsl:matching-substring>
    <xsl:non-matching-substring>
      <xsl:value-of select="."/>
    </xsl:non-matching-substring>
  </xsl:analyze-string>
</xsl:template>

</xsl:transform>
```

Putting It Together

We now have a stylesheet that can generate an HTML page for a single chosen individual. We don't yet have a working Web site!

As I suggested earlier, there are three ways you can work:

- ❏ You can do a batch conversion of the entire data file into a collection of linked static HTML pages held on the Web server.
- ❏ You can generate each page on demand from the server.
- ❏ You can generate pages dynamically at the client.

I'll show how to do all three; and in the second case, I'll describe two different implementations of the architecture, one using Java servlets and one using Microsoft ASP pages. The main differences among the three cases are in the way hyperlinks are constructed, and we'll achieve this by writing overlay stylesheets that change the relevant logic in the base stylesheet.

Publishing Static HTML

To generate HTML files for all the individuals in the data file, we need some kind of script that processes each individual in turn and produces a separate output file for each one. Here we can take advantage of the XSLT 2.0 capability to produce multiple output files from one input file. Many XSLT 1.0 products had a similar capability, but unfortunately each product used different syntax.

We'll need a new template for processing the root element, and because this must override the template defined in person.xsl, we'll need to use <xsl:import> to give the new template higher precedence.

Here is the complete stylesheet, publish.xsl, to do the bulk conversion. As well as generating an HTML page for each individual, it also creates an index page listing all the individuals grouped first by surname, then by the rest of the name.

```
<xsl:transform
  xmlns:xsl="http://www.w3.org/1999/XSL/Transform"
  xmlns="http://www.w3.org/1999/xhtml"
  version="2.0"
>
<xsl:import href="person.xsl"/>
<xsl:param name="dir" select="'.'"/>
<xsl:template match="/">
  <xsl:for-each select="*/IndividualRec">
    <xsl:result-document href="{$dir}/{@Id}.html" validation="strict">
      <xsl:apply-templates select="."/>
    </xsl:result-document>
  </xsl:for-each>
  <xsl:result-document href="{$dir}/index.html" validation="strict">
    <xsl:call-template name="make-index"/>
  </xsl:result-document>
</xsl:template>

<xsl:template name="make-index">
<html>
  <head>
      <title>Index of names</title>
  </head>
  <body>
  <h1>Index of names</h1>
  <xsl:for-each-group select="/*/IndividualRec/IndivName/NamePart[@Level=1]"
                      group-by=".">
    <xsl:sort select="current-grouping-key()"/>
    <h2><xsl:value-of select="current-grouping-key()"/></h2>
    <xsl:for-each select="current-group()">
      <p>
        <xsl:apply-templates select="ancestor::IndividualRec/IndivName[1]"
                             mode="link"/>
      </p>
    </xsl:for-each>
  </xsl:for-each-group>
  </body>
</html>
</xsl:template>
</xsl:transform>
```

In principle you should be able to run this stylesheet using any XSLT 2.0 schema-aware processor. At the time of writing, however, it doesn't work with Altova. It also hits a bug in regular expression handling when run using any version of Saxon-SA on .NET older than 9.0.0.2.

Assuming you have installed Saxon-SA and set up your classpath, and that you have downloaded the example files from the Wrox Web site, you should now create a new directory, copy the stylesheets and the XML data file into it, make this the current directory, and then run the command:

```
java com.saxonica.Transform -val:strict -t kennedy6.xml publish.xsl dir=d:\jfk
```

This assumes that the source files are in the current directory. The -val option is necessary to ensure that the source file is validated against its schema; the -t option is useful because it shows you exactly where the generated output files have been written. The dir=d:\jfk parameter gives the directory in which you want the HTML files to appear.

The specified directory should fill with HTML files. Double-click on the index.html file, and you should see an index of names. Click on any of the names to see the screen shown on page 1072, in glorious color. Then browse the data by following the relationships.

Generating HTML Pages from a Servlet

An alternative to bulk-converting the XML data into static HTML pages is to generate each HTML page on request. This requires execution of a stylesheet on the server, which in principle can be controlled using any server-side technology that will host XSLT: PHP, ASP.NET, Java servlets, or even raw CGI programs. However, as many of the available XSLT processors are written in Java, it turns out to be convenient to use servlets.

There's an element of wishful thinking here. If you're an individual wanting to set up a personal Web site, Java hosting tends to be rather expensive, and PHP is probably a more practical choice. Unfortunately however, the only practical ways to run XSLT 2.0 on a Web server at the time of writing involve installing either Java or .NET.

If you aren't familiar with servlet programming, it's probably best to skip this section, because there isn't space here to start from first principles. There are plenty of good books on the subject.

All the Java XSLT 1.0 processors (there have been at least five, though some are now rarely used) implement the JAXP API, which is described in Appendix E. This means you can write a servlet that works with any processor. Although the JAXP API currently only supports XSLT 1.0, there aren't that many differences at the API level between a 1.0 processor and a 2.0 processor, so you can use this API with minor tweaks to run an XSLT 2.0 processor such as Saxon.

We would like to accept incoming requests from the browser in the form:

```
http://www.myserver.com/..../GedServlet?tree=kennedy6&id=I1
```

However, for links between pages we can generate a relative URL to make the code independent of where the servlet is actually installed. This will be in the form:

```
GedServlet?tree=kennedy6&id=I1
```

The parameters included in the URL are firstly, the name of the data set to use (we'd like the server to be able to handle several concurrently), and secondly, the identifier of the individual to display.

So the first thing that we need to do is to generate hyperlinks in this format. We can do this by writing a new stylesheet module that imports person.xsl and overrides the template that generated the hyperlinks. We'll call this ged-servlet.xsl.

The ged-servlet.xsl stylesheet module is as follows. It has an extra parameter, which is the name of the tree we are interested in, because the same servlet ought to be able to handle requests for data from different family trees. And it overrides the «make-href» template with one that generates hyperlinks in the required format:

```
<xsl:transform version="2.0"
    xmlns:xsl="http://www.w3.org/1999/XSL/Transform">

<xsl:import href="person.xsl"/>
<xsl:param name="tree"/>

<xsl:template name="make-href">
    <xsl:value-of select="'GedServlet?tree=', $tree, '&amp;id=', ../@Id"
                  separator=""/>
</xsl:template>

</xsl:transform>
```

Note that in the XHTML document the ampersand in the URL will be represented as «&». People sometimes get anxious about this, but it's the correct representation and all browsers will accept it. Most will also accept an unescaped ampersand, which is what many HTML authors incorrectly write.

The stylesheet and the servlet interface could also be extended to generate an index of names, as in the previous example, but as that's a simple task I'll leave you to work that out for yourself.

The next task is to write the Java code of the servlet. The code below uses the JAXP interface with a minor extension to request the XSLT processor to perform validation of source documents.

```
import java.io.*;
import javax.servlet.*;
import javax.servlet.http.*;

import javax.xml.parsers.*;
import javax.xml.transform.*;
import javax.xml.transform.stream.*;

public class GedServlet extends HttpServlet {
```

The init() method of a servlet is called when the servlet is first initialized. In this method we set a system property to ensure that the XSLT processor we use is the schema-aware version of Saxon. In a production environment, it would be appropriate to read the values of this system properties from the web.xml configuration file.

```
    public void init(javax.servlet.ServletConfig conf)
            throws javax.servlet.ServletException {
        super.init (conf);
        System.setProperty("javax.xml.transform.TransformerFactory",
                        "com.saxonica.SchemaAwareTransformerFactory");
    }
```

The service() method of the servlet responds to an individual request from a user browser. It sets a StreamSource to the file identified by the tree parameter in the URL. It looks in its local data to see if the compiled stylesheet is already there; if not, it creates it. It then creates a Transformer, sets a couple of stylesheet parameters, and calls the JAXP transform() method to run the transformation, sending the result to the servlet output destination (which of course causes the result to appear at the browser).

```
/**
 * Respond to an HTTP request
 */

public void service(HttpServletRequest req, HttpServletResponse res)
        throws ServletException, IOException {
    res.setContentType("text/html");

    try {
        String clear = req.getParameter("clear");
        if (clear!=null && clear.equals("yes")) {
            resetData();
        }
        String family = req.getParameter("tree");
        Source source = new StreamSource(
            new File(getServletContext().getRealPath(
                        "/" + family + ".xml")));

        Result result = new StreamResult(res.getOutputStream());

        Templates style = getStyleSheet();
        Transformer transformer = style.newTransformer();
        transformer.setParameter("id", req.getParameter("id"));
        transformer.setParameter("tree", family);
        transformer.transform(source, result);

    } catch (Exception err) {
        PrintStream ps = new PrintStream(res.getOutputStream());
        ps.println("Error applying stylesheet: " + err.getMessage());
        err.printStackTrace(ps);
    }
}
```

When the stylesheet is first invoked, it is prepared and stored in memory as a `Templates` object. This method causes Saxon to validate the source document by setting the `SCHEMA_VALIDATION` property in the `TransformerFactory`: this attribute is specific to Saxon.

```
/**
 * Get the prepared stylesheet from memory; prepare it if necessary
 */
private synchronized Templates getStyleSheet()
throws TransformerConfigurationException {
    if (stylesheet == null) {
        File sheet = new File(getServletContext().getRealPath(
                            "/ged-servlet.xsl"));
        TransformerFactory factory = TransformerFactory.newInstance();
        factory.setAttribute(
            "http://saxon.sf.net/feature/schema-validation",
            new Integer(1));
        stylesheet = factory.newTemplates(new StreamSource(sheet));
    }
    return stylesheet;
}
```

The «factory.setAttribute()» line is specific to Saxon, and indicates that source documents are to be schema-validated. If you want your code to be portable across different XSLT processors (which is the whole point of using the JAXP interface), then it would be best to catch the IllegalArgumentException that's thrown when the processor doesn't recognize this particular attribute.

The rest is straightforward:

```
/**
 * Reset data held in memory
 */

private synchronized void resetData() {
    stylesheet = null;
}

private Templates stylesheet = null;
}
```

The XML file holding the family tree data must be in a file *tree*.xml where *tree* identifies the specific family tree, in our case kennedy6.xml. This must be in the home directory for the Web application containing the servlet, as defined by the configuration parameters for your Web server. The two stylesheet modules person.xsl and ged-servlet.xsl , and the schema gedSchema.xsd, must also be in this directory.

The servlet keeps in memory a copy of the compiled stylesheet (the JAXP Templates object): it makes this copy the first time it is needed.

It would also make sense to keep in memory a DOM Document object representing each family tree, to avoid overhead of parsing and validating the full XML document to display each individual. However, I haven't attempted to do that in this demonstration.

Installing and Configuring the Servlet

To run servlets you need to install a servlet container such as Tomcat, available from www.apache.org. For production use, Tomcat normally runs as an add-on to the Apache Web server, but for testing purposes, it also has an HTTP server of its own built in. There's no space here to go into all the details of installing a servlet container like Tomcat, but for quick reference, this section shows where I put the application files to get this example working.

Figure 19-2 shows the directory structure after installing Tomcat 6 (the details, of course, may vary).

Installing the software itself is very straightforward, but configuring it can be a little tricky. You need to follow the steps below:

1. Choose a root directory for your application. If you're just experimenting, it's simplest to use the preconfigured examples directory. On my machine that's in c:/lib/apache-tomcat-6.0.14/ webapps/examples. All the other file locations that follow are relative to this directory.

2. Place the Saxon JAR files where Tomcat can find them, typically in the WEB-INF/lib directory.

3. Place the Saxon-SA license key where Saxon will be able to find it, typically in the directory WEB-INF/classes.

4. Place the servlet code, GedServlet.class, in WEB-INF/classes, as shown in Figure 19-2.

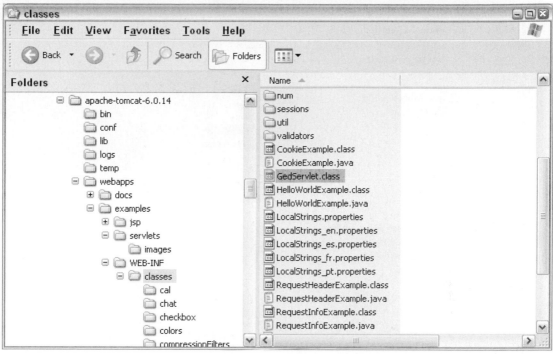

Figure 19-2

5. Edit the file WEB-INF/web.xml to record details of the servlet. Search for the `<servlet>` entry for the `HelloWorldExample`, and add the entry.

```
<servlet>
  <servlet-name>GedServlet</servlet-name>
  <servlet-class>GedServlet</servlet-class>
</servlet>
```

Similarly, search for the `<servlet-mapping>` entry for `HelloWorldExample`, and add:

```
<servlet-mapping>
  <servlet-name>GedServlet</servlet-name>
  <url-pattern>/servlets/servlet/GedServlet</url-pattern>
</servlet-mapping>
```

6. Add five data files to the application root directory, as shown in Figure 19-3: specifically, the two stylesheet modules ged-servlet.xsl and person.xsl, the two schema modules gedSchema.xsd and xhtml1-transitional.xsd, and the data file kennedy6.xml.

To start Tomcat up, double-click on the startup.bat file in the bin directory. This brings up an old-fashioned console that displays progress messages. Then, assuming you have defaulted everything in your configuration, open up your browser and enter the URL:

```
http://localhost:8080/
```

19

Case Study: A Family Tree

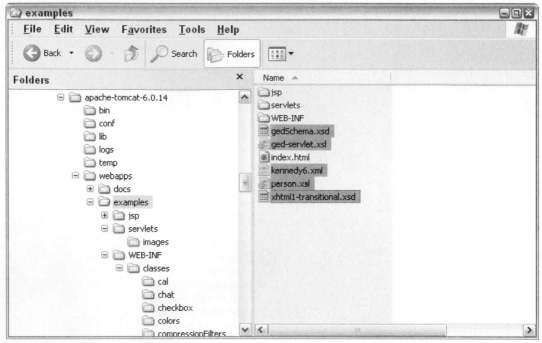

Figure 19-3

This will display Tomcat's home page: in the bottom-left corner is a link to `Servlets Examples`. Try one or two of the examples, for example Hello World, which should display «`Hello World!`» on your browser, to prove that Tomcat is working. If all is well, try:

```
http://localhost:8080/servlets/servlet/GedServlet?tree=kennedy6&id=I1
```

If things fail (and they probably will — servlets can be delicate animals), then you will probably see a summary message on the browser window, but the detailed diagnostics will be on the Tomcat console, or in its log files. Good luck!

Generating HTML Using ASP.NET Pages

If you work in a Microsoft environment, an alternative to writing Java servlets to perform server-side transformation is to control the process using an ASP.NET program. In this case you have a choice: you can use Microsoft's XSLT 1.0 processor, referred to by its assembly name `System.Xml.Xsl`, or you can use the Saxon processor in its .NET version. Microsoft have let it be known that they have an XSLT 2.0 processor under development, but it will be a while before it becomes publicly available.

When you can get by with XSLT 1.0, ASP.NET offers a handy `<asp:Xml>` control that you can use to invoke a transformation. You can simply write a page (say `transmog.aspx`) that looks something like this:

```
<%@ Page Language="C#" %>
<html>
    <head>
```

```
        <title>Transmogrification</title>
    </head>
    <body>
      <asp:Xml id="output" runat="server"
              DocumentSource="content.xml"
              TransformSource="stylesheet.xsl"/>
    </body>
  </html>
```

There's a lot more to the `<asp.Xml>` control than this, of course, but because it doesn't let you use XSLT 2.0, it's out of scope for this book.

If you choose the Saxon route, you will have to write a little bit more code. The stylesheet is exactly the same as on the Java platform: the only thing that's different is the controlling application. Saxon on the .NET platform has its own API, which was designed from first principles, taking some good ideas from both the Java and .NET worlds, but not copying either. The API is documented at http://www.saxonica.com/documentation/dotnetdoc/. The key steps are:

1. Create a Saxon `Processor`.

```
Processor processor = new Processor;
```

2. Create an XSLT Compiler.

```
XsltCompiler compiler = processor.NewXsltCompiler();
```

3. Compile the stylesheet; the result is an `XsltExecutable` object. Keep this in an application-level cache:

```
XsltExecutable executable = compiler.Compile();
```

4. Build the source document:

```
DocumentBuilder builder = processor.NewDocumentBuilder();
XdmDocument document =  builder.Build(inputStream);
```

5. Create a serializer for the result of the transformation, connecting this to the response object that represents the HTTP response:

```
Serializer serializer = new Serializer();
serializer.SetOutputWriter(Response.Output);
```

6. Run the transformation. Call the `Load()` method on the `XsltExecutable` to create an `XsltTransformer`. Supply any parameters using the `SetParameter()` method on the `XsltTransformer`, then run the transformation using its `Run()` method.

```
XsltTransformer transformer = executable.Load();
transformer.SetParameter(....);
transformer.Run(serializer);
```

Here's a complete example (`ged.aspx`). I've added some basic diagnostics, because until everything is configured correctly, it can be very hard to see what's going on. The «true» parameter to the `Processor()` call indicates that a schema-aware Saxon processor is required, and the code then checks for the failure that occurs when Saxon can't find the license file (don't do this in production, it's not very security-conscious!). I've also included code to display any XSLT compilation errors on the browser screen, because this is much more convenient than having them lost in a log file somewhere.

```
<%@ Page Debug="true" Language="C#" %>
<%@ Import Namespace="System" %>
<%@ Import Namespace="System.IO" %>
<%@ Import Namespace="Saxon.Api" %>

<script runat="server">

void Page_Load(Object sender, EventArgs e) {
    Uri sourceUri = new Uri(Server.MapPath(Request.QueryString["tree"] + ".xml"));
    Uri xsltUri = new Uri(Server.MapPath("ged-aspx.xsl"));
    Processor processor = new Processor(true);
    if (!processor.IsSchemaAware) {
        Response.Output.WriteLine("<p>Failed to load Saxon-SA (SAXON_HOME = " +
                    Environment.GetEnvironmentVariable("SAXON_HOME") + ")</p>");
    }
    DocumentBuilder builder = processor.NewDocumentBuilder();
    builder.SchemaValidationMode = SchemaValidationMode.Strict;
    XdmNode input = builder.Build(sourceUri);
    XsltCompiler compiler = processor.NewXsltCompiler();
    compiler.ErrorList = new ArrayList();
    XsltExecutable executable;
    try {
        executable = compiler.Compile(xsltUri);
    } catch (Exception err) {
        Response.Output.WriteLine("<p>Failed to compile stylesheet</p>");
        foreach (StaticError error in compiler.ErrorList) {
            Response.Output.WriteLine("<p>At line " + error.LineNumber + ": "
                                + error.Message + "</p>");
        }
        return;
    }
    XsltTransformer transformer = executable.Load();
    transformer.InitialContextNode = input;
    transformer.SetParameter(new QName("", "id"),
                        new XdmAtomicValue(Request.QueryString["id"]));
    transformer.SetParameter(new QName("", "tree"),
                        new XdmAtomicValue(Request.QueryString["tree"]));
    Serializer serializer = new Serializer();
    serializer.SetOutputWriter(Response.Output);
    transformer.Run(serializer);
}

</script>
```

This example makes no attempt to cache either the compiled stylesheet or the source document, which you would typically do by storing the `input` and/or `executable` objects in Application State.

The stylesheet that this uses, `ged-aspx.xsl`, is yet another overlay on the basic `person.xsl` code. This time it creates the hyperlinks like this:

```
<xsl:template name="make-href">
  <xsl:value-of select="'ged.aspx?tree=', $tree, '&amp;id=', ../@Id"
                separator=""/>
</xsl:template>
```

There's no space here for a detailed tutorial on ASP.NET. However, it may be worth listing briefly the steps I took to get this working, starting from scratch on a machine running Vista:

1. Activate IIS (Internet Information Server) — the software is already present on the machine, but it needs to be activated, which you can do via Control Panel ⇨ Programs ⇨ Turn Windows Features On and Off.

2. Create a simple static Web site (a single `index.html` page will do) to make sure IIS is working. (Start IIS manager, find the default Web site, and use Basic Settings to set the physical path to the directory holding the HTML files (say `d:/wwwroot`). Then enter `http://localhost/` in the browser.)

3. Download and install Microsoft .NET framework version 1.1.

4. Download and install Saxon-SA (version 9.0.0.2 or later), and obtain a free evaluation license from `http://www.saxonica.com/`. Install the Saxon DLL files in the Global Assembly Cache using the .NET framework administration tool in the Control Panel, and also copy them to (in our example) a directory `d:/wwwroot/bin/`. Place the `saxon-license.xml` file in the same `/bin` directory, and set the environment variable SAXON_HOME to `"d:/wwwroot"`.

5. Copy the files `kennedy6.xml`, `gedSchema.xsd`, `person.xsl`, `ged-aspx.xsl`, `xhtml1-transitional.xsd`, and `ged.aspx` to `d:/wwwroot`. All these files are in the download archive for this chapter.

6. Enter `http://localhost/ged.aspx?tree=kennedy6&id=I1` in the URL field of your browser.

Needless to say, there are quite a few things that can go wrong along the way, but these are popular technologies so there are some good tutorials available.

Generating HTML in the Browser

Finally, let's look at another way to display the family tree: namely, to download the whole XML file to the browser as a single chunk and then use client-side scripts to invoke stylesheet processing whenever the user clicks on a hyperlink.

The problem with this approach is that at the time of writing, there is no XSLT 2.0 processor available in either Internet Explorer or Firefox; both support XSLT 1.0 client-side transformation, but not yet 2.0. Hopefully, this situation will change in time, though there is always a drawback in running client-side applications because not all your users will be using the latest browser versions.

However, this book would not be complete if it didn't show you how to run transformations client-side, and for that purpose I have written an XSLT 1.0 version of the stylesheet.

My first attempt to do this was to produce the 1.0 version of the stylesheet as an overlay on the 2.0 version: that is, I wrote an XSLT 1.0 module in which every top-level declaration in the 2.0 stylesheet that contained constructs that would only run under XSLT 2.0 was replaced by a functionally equivalent 1.0 construct. My thinking was that the forward-compatibility rules in XSLT 1.0 would ensure that no errors were raised because of constructs in the unused part of the stylesheet. Unfortunately, it didn't prove possible to do this. To see why, look at the rule:

```
<xsl:template match="Date[data(.) instance of StandardDate]">
  <xsl:value-of select="ged:format-date(data(.))"/>
</xsl:template>
```

This uses XSLT 2.0 constructs (the `data()` function and the `"instance of"` operator) within the match pattern, and there is no way of overriding this with an XSLT 1.0 template rule in a way that an XSLT 1.0 processor will understand. Even the «use-when» attribute doesn't help, because an XSLT 1.0 processor won't understand it. So I simply copied the common code into the 1.0 module by cut-and-paste to create a freestanding XSLT 1.0 stylesheet, which is named `person10.xsl`. This stylesheet simply leaves out many of the more interesting aspects of the 2.0 version; for example, dates are output as they appear in the GEDCOM data, and no attempt is made to sort children or spouses in chronological order.

The next thing we need to do is to adapt the stylesheet to run in the browser. To do this, we need to write an HTML page containing JavaScript to invoke the transformation.

This particular example runs in Internet Explorer 6 or later. It won't run on Firefox, because it uses the Microsoft API to invoke the XSLT transformations. If you want to write pages that run under several different browsers, consider using the Sarissa package (`http://sarissa.sourceforge.net`) which provides a cross-product API.

If the XML file is large (family trees produced by serious genealogists often run to several megabytes) then this approach means the user is going to have to wait rather longer to see the first page of data. But the advantage is that once it's downloaded, browsing around the file can be done offline: there is no need to go back to the server to follow each link from one individual to another. This gives the user a lightning-fast response to navigation requests, and reduces the processing load and the number of hits on the server. Another benefit, given that many genealogists only have access to the limited Web space provided by a commercial ISP, is that no special code needs to be installed on the server.

This time, the transformation is controlled from JavaScript code on an HTML page `famtree.html`. The page itself reads as follows. The `<script>` elements contain client-side JavaScript code.

```
<html>
<head>
    <title>Family Tree</title>
    <style type="text/css">
        ... as before ...
    </style>
    <script>
        var source = null;
        var style = null;
        var transformer = null;

        function init() {
            source = new ActiveXObject("MSXML2.DOMDocument");
            source.async = false;
            source.load('kennedy.xml');

            style = new ActiveXObject("MSXML2.FreeThreadedDOMDocument");
            style.async = false;
            style.load('ms-person.xsl');

            transformer = new ActiveXObject("MSXML2.XSLTemplate");
            transformer.stylesheet = style.documentElement;
            refresh("I1");
        }
        function refresh(indi) {
            var xslproc = transformer.createProcessor();
```

```
            xslproc.input = source;
            xslproc.addParameter("id", indi, "");
            xslproc.transform();
            displayarea.innerHTML = xslproc.output;
     }       </script>
   <script for="window" event="onload">
       init();
   </script>
</head>
<body>
   <div id="displayarea"></div>
</body>
</html>
```

The CSS style definitions have **moved** from the XSLT stylesheet to the HTML page, but they are otherwise unchanged.

The init() function on this page is called when the page is loaded. It creates two DOM objects, one for the source XML and one for the stylesheet, and loads these using the relative URLs kennedy.xml and ms-person.xsl. It then compiles the stylesheet into an object which is rather confusingly called an XSLTemplate; this corresponds directly with the JAXP Templates object. Finally, it calls the refresh() function to display the individual with identifier I1.

I've taken a bit of a short cut here. There's no guarantee that a GEDCOM file will contain an individual with this identifier. A more carefully constructed application would display the first individual in the file, or an index of people.

The refresh() function creates an executable instance of the stylesheet by calling the createProcessor() method on the XSLTemplate object. It then sets the value of the global id parameter in the stylesheet, and applies the stylesheet to the source document by calling the transform() method. The HTML constructed by processing the stylesheet is then written to the contents of the <div id= "displayarea"> element in the body of the HTML page.

We can use the same stylesheet as before, again with modifications to the form of the hyperlinks. This time we want a hyperlink to another individual, I2 say, to take the form:

```
<a href="Javascript:refresh('I2')">Jaqueline Lee Bouvier</a>
```

When the user clicks on this hyperlink, the refresh() function is executed, which causes a new execution of the compiled stylesheet, against the same source document, but with a different value for the id parameter. The effect is that the contents of the page switches to display a different individual.

The ms-person.xsl stylesheet is written by importing the person10.xsl stylesheet, which is the XSLT 1.0 version of the person.xsl stylesheet presented earlier in this chapter, and then overriding the aspects we want to change. This time there are two changes: we want to change the form of the hyperlink, and we want to leave out the generation of the CSS style, because the necessary definitions are already present on the HTML page. Here is the stylesheet:

```
<xsl:transform
 xmlns:xsl="http://www.w3.org/1999/XSL/Transform"
 version="1.0"
>
```

```
<xsl:import href="person10.xsl"/>

<!-- Change the way hyperlinks are generated -->

<xsl:template name="make-href">
    <xsl:variable name="apos">'</xsl:variable>
    <xsl:value-of
          select="concat('Javascript:refresh(', $apos, ../@Id, $apos, ')')"/>
</xsl:template>

<!-- Suppress the generation of a CSS stylesheet -->

<xsl:template name="css-style"/>

</xsl:transform>
```

One slight infelicity in the resulting stylesheet is that it generates a full HTML page, complete with `<html>`, `<head>`, and `<body>` elements, and then inserts this as the content of a `<div>` element within an existing HTML page. Fortunately, Internet Explorer tolerates this abuse of the HTML specification rather well.

Summary

I hope this little excursion into the strange world of genealogical data models has given you some flavor of the power of XSLT as a manipulation and reporting tool for complex structured data. We've covered a lot of ground:

❑ Using XSLT to transform structured data that wasn't originally in XML format

❑ How to navigate your way around complex linked data within an XML document

❑ Several different ways of generating an interactive view of a large XML data set:

   ❑ Generating lots of static HTML pages in one go at publication time

   ❑ Generating HTML pages dynamically using either a Java servlet or a Microsoft ASP.NET page

   ❑ Generating HTML incrementally within the browser

The worked example in the next chapter will venture into even stranger territory, using XSLT to solve a chess problem. While genealogy has demonstrated how XSLT can be used to process complex data, the chess example will show something of the computational power of the language.

Case Study: Knight's Tour

This chapter contains the third (and last) of the XSLT case studies. It shows how XSLT can be used to calculate a knight's tour of the chessboard, in which the knight visits every square without ever landing on the same square twice.

New features in XSLT 2.0 make this kind of application much easier to write, which means that the stylesheet is almost a total rewrite of the XSLT 1.0 version.

Readers of previous editions of this book have reacted differently to this case study. Some have suggested that I should be less frivolous, and stick to examples that involve the processing of invoices and purchase orders, and the formatting of product catalogs. Others have welcomed the example as light relief from the comparatively boring programming tasks they are asked to do in their day job. A third group has told me that this example is absolutely typical of the challenges they face in building real Web sites. The Web, after all, does not exist only (or even primarily) to oil the wheels of big business. It is also there to provide entertainment.

Whatever your feelings about the choice of problem, I hope that by showing that it can be done I will convince you that XSLT has the computational power and flexibility to tackle any XML formatting and transformation challenge, and that as you study it, you will discover ideas that you can use a wide range of tasks that are more typical of your own programming assignments.

The Problem

The purpose of the stylesheet is to produce a knight's tour of the chessboard, in which each square is visited exactly once, as shown in the illustration overleaf. A knight can move to any square that is at the opposite corner of a 3×2 rectangle (see Figure 20-1).

The only input to the stylesheet is an indication of the starting square: in modern chess notation, the columns are denoted by the letters a–h starting from the left, and the rows by the numbers 1–8, starting at the bottom. We'll supply the starting square as a parameter to the stylesheet. The stylesheet doesn't need to get anything from the source document. In fact, with XSLT 2.0, there doesn't need to be a source document: the entry point to the stylesheet can be specified as a named template.

We'll build up the stylesheet piece by piece: you can find the complete stylesheet, `tour.xsl`, on the Wrox Web site.

Figure 20-1

The inspiration for this stylesheet came from Oren Ben-Kiki, who published a stylesheet for solving the eight-queens problem. The concept here is very similar, though the details are quite different.

The Algorithm

The strategy for getting the knight round the board is based on the observation that if a square hasn't been visited yet, and if it isn't the knight's final destination, then it had better have at least two unvisited squares that are a knight's move away from it, because there needs to be a way of getting in and another way of getting out. That means that if we can get to a square that's only got one exit left, we'd better go there now or we never will.

This suggests an approach where at each move, we look at all the squares we can jump to next, and choose the one that has fewest possible exits. It turns out that this strategy works, and always gets the knight round the board.

It's possible that this could lead the knight into a blind alley, especially in the case where two of the possible moves look equally good. In this case, the knight might need to retrace its steps and try a different route. In the version of the stylesheet that I published in the previous edition of this book, I included code to do this backtracking, but made the assertion that it was never actually used (though I couldn't prove why). Recently, one of my readers reported that if the knight starts on square f8, it does indeed take a wrong turning at move 58, and needs to retrace its steps. Moreover, this appears to be the only case where this happens.

The place I usually start design is with the data structures. Here the main data structure we need is the board itself. We need to know which squares the knight has visited, and so that we can print out the board at the end, we need to know the sequence in which they were visited. In XSLT 2.0 the obvious choice is to represent the board as a sequence of 64 integers: the value will be zero for a square that has not been visited, or a value in the range 1 to 64 representing the number of the move on which the knight arrived at this square.

In a conventional program this data structure would probably be held in a global variable and updated every time the knight moves. We can't do this in XSLT, because variables can't be updated. Instead, every time a function is called, it passes the current state of the board as a parameter, and when the knight moves, a new copy of the board is created, that differs from the previous one only in the details of one square.

It doesn't really matter which way the squares are numbered, but for the sake of convention we'll number them as shown in Figure 20-2.

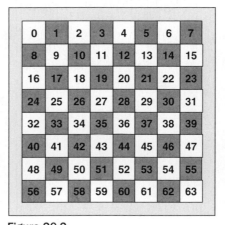

Figure 20-2

So if we number the rows 0–7, and the columns 0–7, the square number is given as «row * 8 + column», and then we add one if indexing into the sequence representing the board.

Having decided on the principal data structure, we can decide the broad structure of the program. There are three stages:

1. Prepare the initial data structures (the empty board with a knight placed on it, somewhere).
2. Calculate the tour.
3. Display the final state of the board.

Calculating the tour involves 63 steps, each one taking the form:

1. Find all the unvisited squares that the knight can move to from the current position.
2. For each one of these, count the number of exits (that is, the number of unvisited squares that can be reached from there).
3. Choose the square with the fewest exits, and move the knight there.

We're ready to start coding. The tricky bit, as you've probably already guessed, is that all the loops have to be coded using recursion. That takes a bit of getting used to at first, but it quickly becomes a habit.

The Initial Template

Let's start with the framework of top-level elements:

```
<xsl:transform
 xmlns:xsl="http://www.w3.org/1999/XSL/Transform"
 xmlns:xs="http://www.w3.org/2001/XMLSchema"
 xmlns:tour="http://www.wrox.com/5067/tour"
 exclude-result-prefixes="xs tour"
 version="2.0"
>

<xsl:output method="html" indent="yes"/>

<xsl:param name="start" select="'a1'" as="xs:string"/>

<!-- start-column is an integer in the range 0-7 -->

<xsl:variable name="start-column"
    select="number(translate(substring($start, 1, 1),
            'abcdefgh', '01234567'))"/>

<!-- start-row is an integer in the range 0-7, with zero at the top -->

<xsl:variable name="start-row"
    select="8 - number(substring($start, 2, 1))"/>

. . .

</xsl:transform>
```

All I'm doing here is declaring the global parameter, start, which defines the starting square, and deriving from it two global variables: a row number and column number.

Some observations:

❑   The parameter start has the default value a1. As this is a string-value, it needs to be in quotes; these quotes are additional to the quotes that surround the XML attribute. If I had written «select="a1"», the default value would be the string-value of the <a1> element child of the document root.

❑   The simplest way of converting the alphabetic column identifier (a–h) into a number (0–7) is to use the translate() function, which is described in Chapter 13.

❑   The row number is subtracted from 8 so that the lowest-numbered row is at the top, and so that row numbers start from zero. Numbering from zero makes it easier to convert between row and column numbers and a number for each square on the board in the range 0–63.

❑   I haven't yet checked that the supplied start square is valid. I'll do that in the initial template.

Now we can move on to the initial template. In XSLT 2.0 I can define the initial template as a named template, so that it can be invoked directly from the command line, without specifying a source document.

However, just in case you're using a processor that doesn't support this capability, it does no harm to define the template with «match="/"» as well.

The root template defines the stages of processing, as follows:

1. Validate the supplied parameter.

2. Set up the empty board and place the knight on it at the specified starting square.

3. Compute the knight's tour.

4. Print out the tour in HTML format.

These tasks are all delegated to stylesheet functions or templates, so the root template itself is quite simple:

```
<xsl:template name="main" match="/">

    <!-- This template controls the processing.
         It does not access the source document. -->

    <!-- Validate the input parameter -->

    <xsl:if test="not(matches($start, '^[a-h][1-8]$'))">
        <xsl:message terminate="yes"
                    select="Invalid start parameter: try say 'a1' or 'g6'"/>
    </xsl:if>

    <!-- Set up the empty board -->

    <xsl:variable name="empty-board" as="xs:integer*"
        select="for $i in (1 to 64) return 0"/>

    <!-- Place the knight on the board at the chosen starting position -->

    <xsl:variable name="initial-board" as="xs:integer*"
        select="tour:place-knight(1, $empty-board,
                                  $start-row * 8 + $start-column)"/>

    <!-- Evaluate the knight's tour -->

    <xsl:variable name="final-board" as="xs:integer*"
        select="tour:make-moves(2, $initial-board,
                                  $start-row * 8 + $start-column)"/>

    <!-- produce the HTML output -->

    <xsl:call-template name="print-board">
        <xsl:with-param name="board" select="$final-board"/>
    </xsl:call-template>

</xsl:template>
```

Notice the style of coding here, which uses a sequence of variables, each one computed from the value of the previous variable. Each variable is used only once, which means the variables aren't actually necessary: it would be possible to nest all the function calls inside each other, and express the whole calculation using one big XPath expression inside the call to the final `print-board` template. But in my view, writing the processing logic like this as a sequence of steps makes it much easier to explain what's going on. The «as» clauses, which define the type of each variable, also provide useful documentation. (I also found that while I was writing this code, the type checking provided by the «as» clauses caught many of my errors.)

The code for validating the `start` parameter uses a simple regular expression. The symbols «^» and «$» match the start and end of the input string, and the body of the regular expression specifies that the string must consist of a single letter in the range [a–h] followed by a single digit in the range [1–8]. If the parameter doesn't match, the stylesheet outputs a message using `<xsl:message>` and terminates.

Several of the variables (`empty-board`, `initial-board`, and `final-board`) represent a chessboard containing all or part of a knight's tour. Each of these variables is a sequence of 64 integers in the range 0 to 64. If the square has been visited, it contains a sequence number representing the order of visiting (1 for the start square, 2 for the next square visited, and so on). If the square has not been visited, the value is zero. The type «as="xs:integer*"» is actually much more liberal that this: it doesn't constrain the sequence to be of length 64, and it doesn't constrain the range of values to be 0 to 64. We could define a schema with a user-defined atomic type that allows only integers in the range 0 to 64, but it would seem overkill to import a schema just for this purpose, quite apart from the fact that the stylesheet would then work only with a schema-aware XSLT processor. Even then, restricting the size of the sequence to 64 is not something that the type system can achieve. Although list types can be defined in XML Schema to have a fixed length, this constraint can only be exploited in XSLT when validating an element or attribute node against this list type. Freestanding sequences of atomic values, like the ones being used here, cannot refer to a list type defined in the schema.

In parameters to function calls and in variables, squares on the board will always be represented by an integer in the range 0–63, which is calculated as $row * 8 + $column. When we use the square number to index the sequence that represents the board, we have to remember to add one.

The empty board is first initialized to a sequence of 64 zeroes, and the knight is then placed on its starting square by calling the function `place-knight`. Let's see how this function works.

Placing the Knight

This is a simple function:

```
<xsl:function name="tour:place-knight" as="xs:integer*">
    <!-- This function places a knight on the board at a given square.
         The returned value is the supplied board, modified to indicate
         that the knight reached a given square at a given move -->
    <xsl:param name="move" as="xs:integer"/>
    <xsl:param name="board" as="xs:integer*"/>
    <xsl:param name="square" as="xs:integer"/><!-- integer in range 0..63 -->
    <xsl:sequence select="
        for $i in 1 to 64 return
            if ($i = $square + 1) then $move else $board[$i]" />
</xsl:function>
```

This function takes three parameters: the number of this move, the current state of the chessboard, and the square on which the knight is to be placed. When it's called from the root template, the move number is always one, and the board is always empty, but I will use the same function again later with different arguments.

What the function does is to copy the whole supplied chessboard before and after the square where the knight is to be placed. This square itself is replaced by the move number. For example, if the tour starts at square a8 (which translates to square zero), then the first call on `place-knight()` will return a sequence containing a one followed by 63 zeroes.

I can't, of course, modify the supplied chessboard in situ. All variables in XSLT are immutable. Instead I create a new board as a modified copy of the original. The result of the function is a sequence representing the new state of the chessboard after placing the knight.

There are various ways the actual calculation of the new board could have been written here. Another possibility would be:

```
<xsl:sequence select="$board[position() = 1 to $square],
                       $move,
                       $board[position() = $square+2 to 64]"/>
```

and a third option would be:

```
<xsl:sequence select="insert-before(
                       remove($board, $square+1),
                       $square+1,
                       $move) "/>
```

Displaying the Final Board

I'll skip the function that computes the knight's tour for the moment, and describe the relatively easy task of outputting the final result as HTML. Like the rest of the stylesheet, this logic is greatly simplified in XSLT 2.0:

```
<xsl:template name="print-board">

    <!-- Output the board in HTML format -->

    <xsl:param name="board" as="xs:integer*" />

    <html>
    <head>
        <title>Knight's tour</title>
    </head>
    <body>
    <div align="center">
    <h1>Knight's tour starting at <xsl:value-of select="$start"/></h1>
    <table border="1" cellpadding="4" size="{count($board)}">
        <xsl:for-each select="0 to 7">
            <xsl:variable name="row" select="."/>
            <tr>
                <xsl:for-each select="0 to 7">
                    <xsl:variable name="column" select="."/>
                    <xsl:variable name="color"
```

```
                        select="if ((($row + $column) mod 2)=1)
                                then 'xffff44' else 'white'"/>
                    <td align="center" bgcolor="{$color}">
                      <xsl:value-of select="$board[$row * 8 + $column + 1]"/>
                    </td>
                  </xsl:for-each>
              </tr>
          </xsl:for-each>
      </table>
      </div>
      </body>
      </html>
  </xsl:template>
```

The template contains a little bit of logic to achieve the traditional checkerboard coloring of the squares, using the «mod» operator to test whether the sum of the row number and the column number is a multiple of 2.

The actual content of each square is the move number, extracted from the relevant item in the sequence representing the board.

Finding the Route

So much for the input and output of the stylesheet, now for the substance: the algorithm to calculate the knight's tour.

The basic algorithm we use is that at each move, we consider all the squares we could go to, and choose the one with the fewest exits. For example, if we are on c2 then we could move to a1, e1, a3, e3, b4, or d4, assuming they are all unvisited. Of these, the corner square a1 has only one exit, namely b3, and if we don't visit the corner square now, then we'll never get another chance later. It turns out that this strategy of always visiting the square with least exits nearly always succeeds in generating a complete knight's tour, though in the rare cases where it doesn't, the algorithm is resilient enough to backtrack and try a different route if the first one fails.

The root template makes a call on the function named «make-moves». This function, starting from any given start position, works out all the moves needed to complete the knight's tour. Of course, it does this by recursion, but unlike previous functions which called themselves directly, this one does so indirectly, via another function named «try-possible-moves».

The first thing the «make-moves» function does is to call the function «list-possible-moves» to construct a list of moves that are legal in the current situation. The result of this function, a list of moves, uses a very similar data structure to that of the chessboard itself. The list is represented as a sequence, and each possible move is represented by an integer whose value is the number of the square to which the knight travels. So in Figure 20-3, after move 5 the set of possible moves is the list (3, 19, 28, 30, 23). The list is in no particular order.

Having established the list of possible moves, the function then calls «try-possible-moves» to select one of these moves and execute it.

Here is the function. Its parameters are the number of this move (starting at move 2, because the knight's initial position is numbered 1), the state of the board before this move, and the number of the square on which the knight is currently sitting.

1106

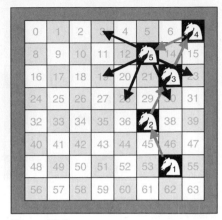

Figure 20-3

```
<xsl:function name="tour:make-moves" as="xs:integer*">

    <!-- This function takes the board in a given state,
         decides on the next move to make, and then calls itself
         recursively to make further moves, until the knight has completed
         his tour of the board. It returns the board in its final state. -->

    <xsl:param name="move" as="xs:integer" />
    <xsl:param name="board" as="xs:integer*" />
    <xsl:param name="square" as="xs:integer" />

    <!-- determine the possible moves that the knight can make -->

    <xsl:variable name="possible-move-list" as="xs:integer*"
        select="tour:list-possible-moves($board, $square)"/>

    <!-- try these moves in turn until one is found that works -->

    <xsl:sequence
        select="tour:try-possible-moves($move,
                                        $board,
                                        $square,
                                        $possible-move-list)"/>

</xsl:function>
```

Finding the Possible Moves

The next function to examine is «list-possible-moves». This takes as input the current state of the board and the position of the knight, and it produces a list of squares that the knight can move to. For a knight in the center of the board there are eight possible squares it can move to (as shown in Figure 20-4): those squares that are either two columns and one row, or two rows and one column, removed from the current row.

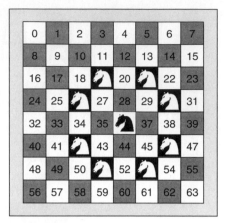

Figure 20-4

However, we have to consider the case where some of these squares are unavailable because they are off the edge of the board, and we also have to eliminate any squares that have already been visited. The logic I have used is simple, if verbose; it simply examines each of the eight candidate squares in turn:

```
<xsl:function name="tour:list-possible-moves" as="xs:integer*">

    <xsl:param name="board" as="xs:integer*" />
    <xsl:param name="square" as="xs:integer" />

    <xsl:variable name="row" as="xs:integer"
        select="$square idiv 8"/>
    <xsl:variable name="column" as="xs:integer"
        select="$square mod 8"/>

    <xsl:sequence select="
        (if ($row &gt; 1 and $column &gt; 0 and $board[($square - 17) + 1]=0)
            then $square - 17 else (),
         if ($row &gt; 1 and $column &lt; 7 and $board[($square - 15) + 1]=0)
            then $square - 15 else (),
         if ($row &gt; 0 and $column &gt; 1 and $board[($square - 10) + 1]=0)
            then $square - 10 else (),
         if ($row &gt; 0 and $column &lt; 6 and $board[($square - 6) + 1]=0)
            then $square - 6 else (),
         if ($row &lt; 6 and $column &gt; 0 and $board[($square + 15) + 1]=0)
            then $square + 15 else (),
         if ($row &lt; 6 and $column &lt; 7 and $board[($square + 17) + 1]=0)
            then $square + 17 else (),
         if ($row &lt; 7 and $column &gt; 1 and $board[($square + 6) + 1]=0)
            then $square + 6 else (),
         if ($row &lt; 7 and $column &lt; 6 and $board[($square + 10) + 1]=0)
            then $square + 10 else () )"
        />
</xsl:function>
```

An observation: not everyone is happy with the idea of writing a single XPath expression that is 16 lines long in the middle of a stylesheet. Some would prefer to write this code using XSLT instructions, using `<xsl:choose>`. I'm comfortable with the code as written, but you can express the same logic at the XSLT level if you prefer.

Another approach would be to try and capture all the logic in a single calculation, as follows:

```
for $r in (-2, -1, +1, +2),
    $c in (-(3-abs($r)), +(3-abs($r)))
return
    (($row+$r)*8 + ($column+$c) + 1)
        [($row+$r = 0 to 7 and $column+$c = 0 to 7]
        [$board[($row+$r)*8 + ($column+$c) + 1] eq 0]
```

So having found the possible moves we can make, we need to select one of them and make it. This is the job of the `try-possible-moves` function.

Trying the Possible Moves

In essence, this function is quite simple. As input it gets the current state of the board, the current position of the knight, the current move, and the list of moves that the knight can make from its current position. If there is at least one move that it can make, then it makes the best move it can find and returns the new state of the board; otherwise, it returns the special value « () » to indicate that it has failed, and that another path needs to be found.

```
<xsl:function name="tour:try-possible-moves" as="xs:integer*" >

    <xsl:param name="move" as="xs:integer" />
    <xsl:param name="board" as="xs:integer*" />
    <xsl:param name="square" as="xs:integer" />
    <xsl:param name="possible-moves" as="xs:integer*" />

    <xsl:sequence
        select="if (exists($possible-moves))
                then tour:make-best-move($move,
                                         $board,
                                         $square,
                                         $possible-moves)
                else ()"/>

        <!-- if there is no possible move, we return the special value ()
             as the final state of the board, to indicate to the caller
             that we got stuck -->
</xsl:function>
```

This depends, of course, on the function `make-best-move()`, which we will look at next. This function is a bit more complex, even though it delegates the task of finding the best move yet again, to another function called `find-best-move()`.

In fact, the first thing that this function does is to call `find-best-move()` to decide which move to make. It then makes a note of all the other possible moves, just in case it needs to backtrack (lazy evaluation comes in handy here: the variable `$other-possible-moves` won't be evaluated unless it's actually needed).

Then the function makes the selected move by placing the knight on the chosen square, using the `place-knight()` function that we saw earlier, and finally it makes a recursive call on `make-moves()`, which we've also seen earlier, to complete the rest of the tour from this new position.

If this final call returns a normal board, then we've finished, and the function exits, unwinding the whole stack down to the initial template, which can now print the final board and quit. However, if the final board is the special value «()», then backtracking is needed. This is done by calling `try-possible-moves()` with a reduced list of possible moves, that excludes the move that we've found to be a cul-de-sac.

```
<xsl:function name="tour:make-best-move" as="xs:integer*">
    <xsl:param name="move" as="xs:integer" />
    <xsl:param name="board" as="xs:integer*" />
    <xsl:param name="square" as="xs:integer" />
    <xsl:param name="possible-moves" as="xs:integer*" />

    <!-- if at least one move is possible, find the best one -->

    <xsl:variable name="best-move"
        select="tour:find-best-move($board, $possible-moves, 9, 999)"/>

    <!-- find the list of possible moves excluding the best one -->

    <xsl:variable name="other-possible-moves" as="xs:integer*"
        select="$possible-moves[. != $best-move]"/>

    <!-- update the board to make the move chosen as the best one -->

    <xsl:variable name="next-board" as="xs:integer*"
        select="tour:place-knight($move, $board, $best-move)"/>

    <!-- now make further moves using a recursive call,
         until the board is complete ->

    <xsl:variable name="final-board" as="xs:integer*"
        select = "if (exists($next-board[.=0]))
                    then tour:make-moves($move+1, $next-board, $best-move)
                    else $next-board"/>

    <!-- if the final board has the special value '()', we got stuck,
         and have to choose the next best of the possible moves.
         This is done by a recursive call. -->

    <xsl:sequence select="
        if (empty($final-board))
        then tour:try-possible-moves($move,
                                     $board,
                                     $square,
                                     $other-possible-moves)
        else $final-board"/>

</xsl:function>
```

Selecting the Best Move

The one thing remaining is to look at the template «find-best-move», which from a set of possible moves chooses the best one, namely the move to the square with fewest exits.

As always, the logic is recursive. We keep track of the best move so far, and the number of exits that the best move so far possesses. If the first move in the list (the *trial move*) is better than the best move so far, it replaces the previous best, and we then call the template to process the other moves in the list. The final output is the best move after examining the whole list.

To find the number of exits for a given move, we create a trial board, and make that move by calling the «place-knight» function described earlier. Using this board, we then call the «list-possible- moves» function, also described earlier, to see what moves would be available after the trial move. We aren't interested in the details of these moves, only in how many there are, which we can find out simply by examining the length of the list.

We can now calculate two variables: the best move so far and the least number of exits, based on whether the trial move is better than the previous best. If the move is the best one so far, it is output. Finally, the «find-best-move» function calls itself recursively to process the remaining moves in the list. On completion, the value returned by the function is the best move, that is, the square to which the knight should move next.

```
<xsl:function name="tour:find-best-move" as="xs:integer*" >

    <!-- This function finds from among the possible moves,
         the one with fewest exits. It calls itself recursively. -->

    <xsl:param name="board" as="xs:integer*" />
    <xsl:param name="possible-moves" as="xs:integer*" />
    <xsl:param name="fewest-exits" as="xs:integer" />
    <xsl:param name="best-so-far" as="xs:integer" />

    <!-- split the list of possible moves into the first move
         and the rest of the moves -->

    <xsl:variable name="trial-move" as="xs:integer"
        select="$possible-moves[1]"/>
    <xsl:variable name="other-possible-moves" as="xs:integer*"
        select="$possible-moves[position() gt 1]"/>

    <!-- try making the first move -->

    <xsl:variable name="trial-board" as="xs:integer*"
        select="tour:place-knight(99, $board, $trial-move)"/>

    <!-- see how many moves would be possible the next time -->

    <xsl:variable name="trial-move-exit-list" as="xs:integer*"
        select="tour:list-possible-moves($trial-board, $trial-move)"/>

    <xsl:variable name="number-of-exits" as="xs:integer"
        select="count($trial-move-exit-list)"/>
```

```
        <!-- determine whether this trial move has fewer exits than
             those considered up till now -->

        <xsl:variable name="minimum-exits" as="xs:integer"
             select="min(($number-of-exits, $fewest-exits))"/>

        <!-- determine which is the best move (the one with fewest exits)
             so far -->

        <xsl:variable name="new-best-so-far" as="xs:integer"
             select="if ($number-of-exits lt $fewest-exits)
                     then $trial-move
                     else $best-so-far"/>

        <!-- if there are other possible moves, consider them too,
             using a recursive call. Otherwise return the best move found. -->

        <xsl:sequence
            select="if (exists($other-possible-moves))
                    then tour:find-best-move($board, $other-possible-moves,
                                                $minimum-exits, $new-best-so-far)
                    else $new-best-so-far"/>

    </xsl:function>
```

And that's it.

Running the Stylesheet

To run the stylesheet, download it from `wrox.com` and execute it. No source document is needed. With Saxon, for example, try:

```
java -jar saxon9.jar -it:main -xsl:tour.xsl start=b6 >tour.html
```

The command line syntax shown here applies to Saxon 9.0 or later. However, if you want to run the stylesheet with an earlier version of Saxon you can do this simply by adapting the way the command line options are written.

The output of the stylesheet is written to the file `tour.html`, which you can then display in your browser.

Using the Altova XSLT 2.0 processor, the equivalent command line is:

```
altovaXML -xslt2 tour.xsl -in tour.xsl -out tour.html -param start='b6'
```

(At the time of writing, Altova does not provide any way of nominating an initial template as the entry point, so it is necessary to supply a dummy input document. The stylesheet is as good as any other.)

Observations

The knight's tour not a typical stylesheet, but it illustrates the computational power of the XSLT language, and in particular the essential part that recursion plays in any stylesheet that needs to do any non-trivial calculation or handle non-trivial data structures. And although you will probably never need to use XSLT to solve chess problems, you may just find yourself doing complex calculations to work out where best to place a set of images on a page, or how many columns to use to display a list of telephone numbers, or which of today's news stories should be featured most prominently given your knowledge of the user's preferences.

So if you're wondering why I selected this example, there are two answers: firstly, I enjoyed writing it, and secondly, I hope it persuaded you that there are no algorithms too complex to be written in XSLT.

The other thing that's worth noting about this stylesheet is how much it benefits from the new features in XSLT 2.0. In the first edition of this book, I published a version of this stylesheet that was written in pure XSLT 1.0; it used formatted character strings to represent all the data structures. In the second edition, I published a revised version that used temporary trees (as promised in the later-abandoned XSLT 1.1 specification) to hold the data structures. The following table shows the size of these three versions (in non-comment lines of code), revealing the extent to which the new language features contribute to making the stylesheet easier to write and easier to read. The table also shows the execution times in milliseconds of each version, using Saxon 9.0, which reveals that the XSLT 2.0 solution is also the fastest:

Version	Data structure	Lines of code	Execution time
1.0	character strings	276	75
1.1	temporary trees	267	220
2.0	sequences	59	37

In the previous edition of the book, the numbers reported in the last column (for Saxon 7.8 on a slower machine) were 580 ms, 1050 ms, and 900 ms, respectively. Repeating the measurements on my current machine with Saxon 7.8 gives figures of 180 ms, 360 ms, and 340 ms. At that stage in the development of Saxon, the native 2.0 constructs were significantly slower than the traditional XSLT 1.0 way of doing things. The position is now reversed — instead of being half the speed, the 2.0 solution is now twice as fast as the 1.0 code.

The earlier versions of the stylesheet are included in the download file under the names `tour10.xsl` and `tour11.xsl`. The file `ms-tour11.xsl` is a variant of `tour11.xsl` designed to work with Microsoft's MSXML3 and later processors.

Summary

If you haven't used functional programming languages before, then I hope that this chapter opened your eyes to a different way of programming. It's an extreme example of how XSLT can be used as a completely general-purpose language; but I don't think it's an unrealistic example, because I see an increasing number of cases where XSLT is being used for general-purpose programming tasks. The thing that characterizes XSLT applications is that their inputs and outputs are XML documents, but there should be no limits on the processing that can be carried out to transform the input to the output, and I hope this example convinces you that there are none.

In these last three chapters, I've presented three complete stylesheets, or collections of stylesheets, all similar in complexity to many of those you will have to write for real applications. I tried to choose three that were very different in character, reflecting three of the design patterns introduced in Chapter 17, namely:

❑ A rule-based stylesheet for converting a document containing semantic markup into HTML. In this stylesheet, most of the logic was concerned with generating the right HTML display style for each XML element, and with establishing tables of contents, section numbering, and internal hyperlinks, with some interesting logic for laying data out in a table.

❑   A navigational stylesheet for presenting selected information from a hierarchical data structure. This stylesheet was primarily concerned with following links with the XML data structure, and it was able to use the full power of XPath expression to achieve this. This stylesheet also gave us the opportunity to explore some of the systems issues surrounding XSLT: when and where to do the XML-to-HTML conversion, and how to handle data in non-XML legacy formats.

❑   A computational stylesheet for calculating the result of a moderately complex algorithm. This stylesheet demonstrated that even quite complex algorithms are quite possible to code in XSLT once you have mastered recursion. Such algorithms are much easier to implement in XSLT 2.0 than in XSLT 1.0, because of the ability to use sequences and temporary trees to hold working data.

Part IV

Appendices

XPath 2.0 Syntax Summary

This appendix summarizes the entire XPath 2.0 grammar. The tables in this appendix also act as an index: they identify the page where each construct is defined.

The way that the XPath grammar is presented in the W3C specification is influenced by the need to support the much richer grammar of XQuery. In this book, I have tried to avoid these complications.

The grammar is presented here for the benefit of users, not for implementors writing a parser (the W3C spec adopted the same approach in its final drafts). So there is no attempt to write the syntax rules in such a way that expressions can be parsed without lookahead or backtracking.

An interesting feature of the XPath grammar is that there are no reserved words. Words that have a special meaning in the language, because they are used as keywords («if», «for»), as operators («and», «except»), or as function names («not», «count») can also be used as the name of an element in a path expression. This means that the interpretation of a name depends on its context. The language uses several techniques to distinguish different roles for the same name:

❑ Operators such as «and» are distinguished from names used as element names or function names in a path expression by virtue of the token that precedes the name. In essence, if a word follows a token that marks the end of an expression, then the word must be an operator; otherwise, it must be some other kind of name.

❑ As an exception to the first rule, if a name follows «/», it is taken as an element name, not as an operator. To write «/ union /*», if you want the keyword treated as an operator, you must write the first operand in parentheses: «(/) union /*». Alternatively, write «/. union /*».

❑ Some operators such as «instance of» use a pair of keywords. This technique was adopted in XQuery for use at the start of a construct such as «declare function», but it's not actually needed for infix operators.

❑ Function names, together with the «if» keyword, are recognized by virtue of the following «(» token.

❑ Axis names are recognized by the following «::» token.

❑ The keywords «for» «some» and «every» are recognized by the following «$» token.

Whitespace and Comments

I have organized the rules in the appendix to make a clear distinction between tokens, which cannot contain internal whitespace, and non-terminals, which can contain whitespace between their individual tokens. This separation is not quite so clear in the W3C specification, which is another result of the complications caused by XQuery. (XQuery uses element constructors that mimic XML syntax, so it does not have such a clear separation between the lexical level of the language and the syntactic level.)

Whitespace is defined here as any sequence of space, tab, linefeed, and carriage return characters, and comments.

A comment in XPath starts with «(:» and ends with «:)». Comments may be nested, so any «(:» within a comment must be matched by a closing «:)». Comments may appear anywhere that whitespace is allowed.

Whitespace is required between two tokens if the first character of the second token could otherwise be construed as a continuation of the first token. So «price - discount» is three tokens, the «-» being a minus operator, while «price-discount» is a single token, the «-» being a hyphen within the element name. There is also a requirement to write a space between a number and an adjacent word, for example «if (a) then 3 else 4», because the «e» of «else» could otherwise be taken as introducing an exponent in a double. For consistency, this rule is applied even if the word begins with a letter other than «e».

Tokens

The definition of a token that I am using here is: a symbol that cannot contain separating whitespace. This means that my classification of which symbols are tokens is slightly different from the classification that appears in the W3C specification.

Simple tokens such as «+» and «and» are not included in this table; they simply appear anonymously in the syntax productions.

Symbol	Syntax	Page
IntegerLiteral	Digit+	page 530
DecimalLiteral	(«.» Digit+) | (Digit+ «.» Digit*)	page 530
DoubleLiteral	((«.» Digit+) | (Digit+ («.» Digit*)?)) («e» | «E») («+» | «-»)? Digit+	page 530
Digit	[0-9]	page 530
StringLiteral	(«"» ([^"]) * «"»)+ | («'» ([^']) * «'»)+	page 532
Wildcard	«*» | NCName«:*» | «*:»NCName	page 614
NCName	See XML Namespaces Recommendation	page 534
QName	See XML Namespaces Recommendation	page 534
Char	See XML Recommendation	page 534

Syntax Productions

These rules mainly use familiar notations: «*» for repetition, parentheses for grouping, «?» to indicate that the preceding construct is optional, «|» to separate alternatives. The rules are given in alphabetical order for ease of reference.

Simple tokens are represented using chevrons; for example, «@» in the first rule represents a literal at-symbol.

Symbol	Syntax	Page
AbbrevForwardStep	«@»? NodeTest	page 621
AbbrevReverseStep	«..»	page 621
AdditiveExpr	MultiplicativeExpr((«+» | «-») MultiplicativeExpr)*	page 572
AndExpr	ComparisonExpr («and» ComparisonExpr)*	page 594
AnyKindTest	«node» «(» «)»	page 616
AtomicType	QName	page 655
AttributeTest	BasicAttributeTest | SchemaAttributeTest	page 672
AxisStep	(ForwardStep | ReverseStep) PredicateList	page 606
BasicAttributeTest	«attribute» «(» (NameOrWildcard («,» TypeName) ?)? «)»	page 672
BasicElementTest	«element» «(» (NameOrWildCard(«,» TypeName «?»?) ?)? «)»	page 672
CastableExpr	CastExpr («castable» «as» SingleType)?	page 655
CastExpr	UnaryExpr («cast» «as» SingleType)?	page 655
CommentTest	«comment» «(» «)»	page 616
ComparisonExpr	RangeExpr ((ValueComp | GeneralComp | NodeComp) RangeExpr)?	page 582
ContextItemExpr	«.»	page 543
DocumentTest	«document-node» «(» ElementTest? «)»	page 616
ElementTest	BasicElementTest | SchemaElementTest	page 672
Expr	ExprSingle («,» ExprSingle)*	page 524
ExprSingle	ForExpr | QuantifiedExpr | IfExpr | OrExpr	page 524
FilterExpr	PrimaryExpr PredicateList	page 638
ForExpr	«for» «$» VarName «in» ExprSingle («,» «$» VarName «in» ExprSingle)* «return» ExprSingle	page 640
ForwardAxis	(«child» | «descendant» | «attribute» | «self» | «descendant-or-self» | «following-sibling» | «following» | «namespace») «::»	page 607

continued

Symbol	Syntax	Page
ForwardStep	(ForwardAxis NodeTest) | AbbrevForwardStep	page 606
FunctionCall	QName «(» (ExprSingle («,» ExprSingle)*)? «)»	page 544
GeneralComp	«=» | «!=» | «<» | «<=» | «>» | «>=»	page 582
IfExpr	«if» «(» Expr «)» «then» ExprSingle «else» ExprSingle	page 551
InstanceofExpr	TreatExpr («instance» «of» SequenceType)?	page 677
IntersectExceptExpr	InstanceOfExpr((«intersect» | «except») InstanceOfExpr)*	page 629
ItemType	AtomicType | KindTest | («item» «(» «)»)	page 668
KindTest	DocumentTest | ElementTest | AttributeTest | PITest | CommentTest | TextTest | AnyKindTest	page 616
Literal	NumericLiteral | StringLiteral	page 539
Multiplicative Expr	UnionExpr((«*» | «div» | «idiv» | «mod») UnionExpr)*	page 572
NameOrWildcard	QName | «*»	page 672
NameTest	QName | Wildcard	page 614
NodeComp	«is» | «<<» | «>>»	page 582
NodeTest	KindTest | NameTest	page 613
NumericLiteral	IntegerLiteral | DecimalLiteral | DoubleLiteral	page 539
OccurrenceIndicator	«?» | «*» | «+»	page 668
OrExpr	AndExpr («or» AndExpr)*	page 594
ParenthesizedExpr	«(» Expr? «)»	page 542
PathExpr	(«/» RelativePathExpr?) | («//» RelativePathExpr) | RelativePathExpr	page 625
PITest	«processing-instruction» «(» (NCName | StringLiteral)? «)»	page 616
Predicate	«[» Expr «]»	page 618
PredicateList	Predicate*	page 618
PrimaryExpr	Literal | VarRef | ParenthesizedExpr | ContextItemExpr | FunctionCall	page 539
QuantifiedExpr	(«some»| «every») «$» VarName «in» ExprSingle («,» «$» VarName «in» ExprSingle)* «satisfies» ExprSingle	page 646
RangeExpr	AdditiveExpr («to» AdditiveExpr)?	page 636
RelativePathExpr	StepExpr ((«/» | «//») StepExpr)*	page 625

Symbol	Syntax	Page
ReverseAxis	(«parent» | «ancestor» | «preceding-sibling» | «preceding» | «ancestor-or-self») «::»	page 607
ReverseStep	(ReverseAxis NodeTest) | AbbrevReverseStep	page 607
SchemaAttributeTest	«schema-attribute» «(» QName «)»	page 674
SchemaElementTest	«schema-element» «(» QName «)»	page 674
SequenceType	(ItemType OccurrenceIndicator?) | («empty-sequence» «(» «)»)	page 668
SingleType	AtomicType «?»?	page 655
StepExpr	AxisStep | FilterExpr	page 602
TextTest	«text» «(» «)»	page 616
TreatExpr	CastableExpr («treat» «as» SequenceType)?	page 678
TypeName	QName	page 672
UnaryExpr	(«+» | «-»)* PathExpr	page 572
UnionExpr	IntersectExceptExpr ((«union» | «|») IntersectExceptExpr)*	page 629
ValueComp	«eq» | «ne» | «lt» | «le» | «gt» | «ge»	page 582
VarRef	«$» QName	page 540

Operator Precedence

The following table lists the precedence of the XPath operators. Operators lower down the table bind more tightly than operators further up the table. So «A or B and C» means «A or (B and C)».

Precedence	Operator
1	«,»
2	«for», «some», «every», «if»
3	«or»
4	«and»
5	«eq», «ne», «lt», «le», «gt», «ge», «=», «!=», «<», «<=», «>», «>=», «is», «<<», «>>»
6	«to»
7	infix «+», infix «-»
8	«*», «div», «idiv», «mod»
9	«union», «|»
10	«intersect», «except»
11	«instance of»
12	«treat as»
13	«castable as»
14	«cast as»
15	unary «+», unary «-»
16	«/», «//»
17	«[]»

If two operators appear in the same row, then they are evaluated from left to right. So «A - B + C» means «(A - B) + C».

B

Error Codes

The XSLT and XPath specifications associate error codes with each error condition. There is an implicit assumption here that although the W3C specification defines no API for invoking XPath expressions, there will be such APIs defined elsewhere, and they will need some way of notifying the application what kind of error has occurred. The error codes may also appear in error messages output by an XSLT processor, though there is no guarantee of this.

Technically, error codes are QNames whose namespace is http://www.w3.org/2005/xqt-errors. The 8-character code that you usually see, such as XPTY0004, is the local part of the QName. This mechanism allows additional error codes defined by a product vendor or application writer to be allocated in a different namespace. If you detect an error at application level, you can call the error() function (see Chapter 13) to force an error to be raised, specifying the error code to be allocated.

There is no normative error message text associated with each error code, either in the specification or in this appendix: hopefully, real products will give error messages that are much more helpful than those in the specification, including an indication of where the error occurred. For each error, this appendix gives first a short description, then an explanation of possible causes. For the errors defined in the XPath and *Functions and Operators* specifications the short description is usually taken straight from the spec; for XSLT errors, the description in the spec is often quite long and technical, so the description given here is a gloss.

Experience with the XSLT and XQuery test suites suggests that different products will often report the same error in different ways, and for many error conditions there's more than one code listed that could describe it. However, understanding error messages when things go wrong can be one of the most baffling experiences while learning a new language, so I thought that listing the codes and trying to explain them would be a worthwhile use of the space.

Each error code has a two-letter type, a two-letter subtype, and a four-digit number. The types and subtypes are listed in the table below.

Type	Subtype	Meaning
FO	AR	Functions and Operators: Arithmetic
FO	CA	Functions and Operators: Casting
FO	CH	Functions and Operators: Character handling

continued

Type	Subtype	Meaning
FO	DC	Functions and Operators: Documents
FO	DT	Functions and Operators: Dates and Times
FO	ER	Functions and Operators: Error Function
FO	NS	Functions and Operators: Namespaces
FO	RG	Functions and Operators: Arguments
FO	RX	Functions and Operators: Regular Expressions
FO	TY	Functions and Operators: Typed Value Determination
XP	DY	XPath: Dynamic Errors
XP	ST	XPath: Static Errors
XP	TY	XPath: Type Errors
XT	DE	XSLT: Dynamic Errors
XT	MM	XSLT: `<xsl:message>`
XT	RE	XSLT: Recoverable Dynamic Errors
XT	SE	XSLT: Static Errors
XT	TE	XSLT: Type Errors

The error codes are listed in alphabetical order.

Functions and Operators (FO)

FOAR0001   *Division by zero*

This error can occur when using any of the operators «div», «idiv», or «mod» with integer or decimal arithmetic. With floating point arithmetic, division by zero results in positive or negative infinity.

FOAR0002   *Numeric operation overflow/underflow*

With floating point arithmetic, overflow and underflow conditions generally produce infinity or zero, but the implementation has the option of raising this error instead. With integer and decimal arithmetic, an implementation must produce this error if the result is outside the range of values that can be represented. The capacity of a decimal or integer value is implementation-defined, so an operation that succeeds with one implementation might raise this error with another.

FOCA0001   *Input value too large for decimal*

Used when casting to a decimal value from a float or double that is outside the implementation-defined limits supported by the xs:decimal data type.

FOCA0002   *Invalid lexical value*

Used when an invalid argument is passed to resolve-QName() or QName(), or when the float or double value NaN, INF, or -INF is cast to xs:decimal.

FOCA0003   *Input value too large for integer*

Raised when casting from an xs:decimal, xs:float, or xs:double to an xs:integer, if the value is outside the implementation-defined limits for the xs:integer data type.

FOCA0005   NaN *supplied as float/double value*

Used when multiplying or dividing a duration by a number, if the number supplied is NaN.

FOCA0006   *String to be cast to decimal has too many digits of precision*

Raised when casting from string to decimal if there are more digits than the system can represent accurately. The implementation has the option of raising this error or rounding the value.

FOCH0001   *Codepoint not valid*

Raised by the `codepoints-to-string()` function if the sequence of integers supplied includes a value that does not represent a legal XML character.

FOCH0002   *Unsupported collation*

Raised if the value of a collation argument of any function is not defined in the static context or is not supported by the implementation.

FOCH0003   *Unsupported normalization form*

The normalization form requested in a call to the `normalize-unicode()` function is one that the implementation does not support.

FOCH0004   *Collation does not support collation units*

Some collations can be used for comparing strings, but not for extracting substrings. This error is reported if the collation supplied to one of the functions `contains()`, `starts-with()`, `ends-with()`, `substring-before()`, or `substring-after()` is not able to split a string into substrings.

FODC0001   *No context document*

The functions `id()` and `idref()` operate within the document containing the context node. If there is no context item, or if the context item is not a node, or if the tree containing the context node is not rooted at a document node, then this error is raised.

FODC0002   *Error retrieving resource*

Indicates that a document requested using `doc()` or `document()` cannot be found or cannot be parsed as XML, or that `collection()` was called with no arguments when there is no default collection.

FODC0003   *Function stability not defined*

Repeated calls on `doc()`, `document()`, or `collection()` are required to return the same result each time unless the user explicitly waives this requirement. This error is raised if the implementation cannot return stable results perhaps because documents have been updated on disk.

FODC0004   *Invalid argument to* `collection()`

This error means that the URI passed to the `collection()` function is not a valid URI, or does not correspond to the URI of any known collection.

FODC0005   *Invalid argument to* `doc()` *or* `doc-available()`

Raised if the string passed as an argument to the `doc()` or `doc-available()` function is not a valid URI. Also raised for `doc()` if no document can be located with the

specified URI, or if the resource found at that URI cannot be parsed as an XML document.

FODT0001   *Overflow in date/time arithmetic*

Occurs when adding a duration to an `xs:date` or `xs:dateTime` value (or when subtracting), or when casting to a date/time value, if the result of the operation is outside the range supported for dates.

FODT0002   *Overflow/underflow in duration arithmetic*

Occurs when multiplying or dividing a duration by a number, or when casting to a duration, if the result is outside the range supported for the relevant duration data type.

FODT0003   *Invalid timezone value*

Indicates that the timezone supplied to `adjust-X-to-timezone()` is outside the range ±14 hours, or is not an integer number of minutes.

FOER0000   *Unidentified error*

Indicates that the `error()` function was called without supplying a more specific error code.

FONS0004   *No namespace found for prefix*

Raised by the `QName()` constructor and by the `resolve-QName()` function if the prefix in the supplied lexical QName cannot be resolved to a namespace URI.

FONS0005   *Base URI not defined in the static context*

Raised by the single-argument form of the `resolve-URI()` function if no base URI has been established in the static context. In XSLT, the base URI is taken from the stylesheet module containing the XPath expression, and this error suggests that the original location of this module is unknown.

FORG0001   *Invalid value for cast/constructor*

Means that the value passed to a constructor function or «cast as» expression is not a legal value (and cannot be converted to a legal value) for the target data type.

FORG0002   *Invalid argument to* `resolve-uri()`

This error occurs when either of the URIs passed to the `resolve-URI()` function is not a valid URI.

FORG0003   `zero-or-one()` *called with a sequence containing more than one item*

Calling the `zero-or-one()` function asserts that the argument is a sequence containing at most one item. If the assertion proves to be wrong, this error is raised.

FORG0004   `one-or-more()` *called with a sequence containing no items*

Calling the `one-or-more()` function asserts that the argument is a sequence containing at least one item. If the assertion proves to be wrong, this error is raised.

FORG0005 **`exactly-one()`** *called with a sequence containing zero or more than one item*

Calling the `exactly-one()` function asserts that the argument is a sequence containing exactly one item. If the assertion proves to be wrong, this error is raised.

FORG0006 *Invalid argument type*

Indicates that a value supplied to `boolean()`, `avg()`, `min()`, `max()`, or `sum()` is of a type that the function cannot handle, despite matching the function signature.

FORG0008 *Both arguments to* `dateTime()` *have a specified timezone*

If the two arguments of `dateTime()` both have a timezone, then the timezones must match.

FORG0009 *Error in resolving a relative URI against a base URI in* `resolve-uri()`

The second argument to `resolve-uri()`, if supplied, should be an absolute hierarchic URI.

FORX0001 *Invalid regular expression flags*

The flags supplied to `matches()`, `replace()`, and `tokenize()` must contain zero or more of the letters «s», «m», «i», and «x», in any order.

FORX0002 *Invalid regular expression*

Indicates that the regular expression passed to the function `matches()`, `replace()`, or `tokenize()` is not valid according to the rules given in Chapter 14.

FORX0003 *Regular expression matches zero-length string*

The functions `replace()` and `tokenize()` disallow use of a regular expression that would match a zero-length string. This rule exists because there is no obviously correct interpretation of what such a regular expression should mean.

FORX0004 *Invalid replacement string*

Indicates an error in the string supplied as the third argument of the `replace()` function. If the string contains a «\» character, this must be followed by either «\» or «$», and if the string contains a «$» that is not preceded by a «$», then it must be followed by a digit.

FOTY0012 *Argument node does not have a typed value*

Raised when the `data()` function is called supplying an element which according to the schema has element-only content. Such an element has no typed value. The call on `data()` might be implicit in some other operation that atomizes its operands.

XPDY0002 *Evaluation of an expression relies on some part of the dynamic context that has not been assigned a value*

For example, within a stylesheet function there is no context item, so a reference to «.» or `position()` will cause this error.

XPDY0050 *The dynamic type of the operand of a treat expression does not match the type specified by the treat expression*

The «treat as» expression is an assertion: when you say «$x treat as xs:integer», you are asserting that at runtime, the variable «$x» will contain an `xs:integer`. If you get it wrong, and the variable contains some other value, this is the error that will be reported.

Because «/» is defined using «treat as», this error also occurs if you use «/» when the context node is in a tree whose root is not a document node.

XPath Errors (XP)

XPST0001 *Analysis of an expression relies on some component of the static context that has not been assigned a value*

For example, using an unprefixed function name is an error if there is no default namespace for functions, and using the «=» operator is an error if there is no default collation.

XSLT defines default values for most components of the static context, making this error unlikely. But some aspects such as the static base URI need to be supplied by the user via the processor's API.

As with the static context, it's up to the host language to define whether the various parts of the dynamic context are given default values.

XPST0003 *An expression is not a valid instance of the XPath grammar*

This is an umbrella code that covers all XPath syntax errors.

XPST0005 *The static type assigned to an expression other than the expression «()» is* `empty-sequence()`

This error only occurs with static type checking, which makes it unlikely under XSLT. It is designed primarily to catch incorrect path expressions. For example, if the schema definition for element «para» does not allow it to contain element «head», then a processor that does static typing will reject the path expression «para/head» as an error.

XPST0008 *An expression refers to an element name, attribute name, schema type name, namespace prefix, or variable name that is not defined in the static context*

This means that you haven't declared the object that is referenced in the expression. This might be because you misspelled the name, or it might be because you got the namespace prefix wrong — if the name has a prefix, check that it refers to the correct namespace URI, and if it doesn't, check what the default namespace for that kind of name is.

XPST0010 *An expression refers to an axis that the implementation does not support*

Under XSLT this can only be the namespace axis; processors are not required to support this axis.

XPST0017 *The expanded QName and number of arguments in a function call do not match the name and arity of a function signature in the static context*

This error either means that the function you are calling has not been declared, or that you are calling it with the wrong number of arguments. Check the namespace.

XPST0021 *It is a dynamic error if a value in a cast expression cannot be cast to the required type*

Not all casts are allowed. For example, you cannot cast from an integer to a date. This error message means that you have attempted one of these disallowed casts. The casts that are allowed are described in Chapter 9 of this book.

XPST0051 *A QName used as an AtomicType in a SequenceType is not defined in the in-scope schema types as an atomic type*

This means you have used an expression such as «$x instance of mf:invoice» where the type

«mf:invoice» is either not defined at all or is a complex type, a list type, or a union type.

Perhaps you meant to write «$x instance of element(*, mf:invoice)».

XPST0080 *The target type of a cast or castable expression is* xs:NOTATION *or* xs:anyAtomicType

This is subtly different from XPST0051 because these two types are atomic. But they are abstract, so you cannot cast to them.

XPST0081 *A QName used in an expression contains a namespace prefix that cannot be expanded into a namespace URI using the statically known namespaces*

In other words, you have used a namespace prefix without first declaring it.

XPTY0004 *The value of an expression has a type that is not appropriate for the context in which the expression occurs*

A common error code. It will occur, for example, if you write «abs("a")», because the argument to abs() must be a number. Like other type errors, this may be detected either at compile time or at runtime.

XPTY0018 *The last step in a path expression contains both nodes and atomic values*

Any expression on the right-hand side of «/» must return either nodes or atomic values, not a mixture.

XPTY0019 *A step (other than the last step) in a path expression contains an atomic value*

Any expression on the left-hand side of «/» must return nodes, not atomic values.

XPTY0020 *In an axis step, the context item is not a node*

When you use an expression such as «title» or «@code» or «..» or «ancestor::chap», you are selecting nodes relative to the context node. If the context item is an atomic value, then these expressions can't be evaluated.

Note that even rooted path expressions (those starting with «/») require a context node, because they always select nodes within the same document that contains the context node.

XSLT Errors (XT)

XTDE0030 *The value of an attribute value template is invalid for that attribute*
For example, with `<xsl:message terminate="$z"/>`, the value of $z was "maybe."

XTDE0040 *When invoking a stylesheet by specifying an initial template, the name must match that of a named template in the stylesheet*

XTDE0045 *When invoking a stylesheet with an initial mode, the mode name must match the mode name of at least one* xsl:template *in the stylesheet*

XTDE0047 *When invoking a stylesheet, both an initial template and an initial mode were specified*

An initial template means you want to start by calling a named template, so the initial mode wouldn't be used.

XTDE0050 *When invoking a stylesheet, a value must be provided for every stylesheet parameter that specifies* required="yes"

XTDE0060 *When invoking a stylesheet by specifying an initial template, the initial template must not have any required parameters*

Any parameters you supply when starting the transformation are matched against global stylesheet parameters, not against the local parameters of the first template to be executed. These local parameters, if any, will always take their default values.

XTDE0160 *If the implementation does not support backward-compatible behavior, then instructions that invoke this behavior must not be evaluated*

XSLT processors are not required to support 1.0 mode. If you request it by setting «version="1.0"», and then evaluate an instruction with this setting in scope, the processor must report a fatal error.

XTDE0290 *Where the result of an XPath expression is required to be a lexical QName, the resulting name must have a prefix that is declared in the stylesheet*

This applies for example to the first argument of the key() function, or the third argument of format-number(). For some situations there is a more specific error code.

XTDE0410 *In the content of a new element node, attributes and namespaces must come before other kinds of node*

When you create a new element, you must write its attributes before you generate any child elements or text nodes. This rule is designed to allow streamed output: the processor knows when it sees the first child of an element that it will not see any more attributes, so it can write the start tag to the serializer. This can potentially reduce the delay before the user sees the first output emerging.

XTDE0420 *In the content of a new document node, there must be no attributes or namespaces*

Attributes and namespaces can be output to a result document only as part of the content of an element node.

XTDE0430 *In the content of a new element node, there must not be two namespace nodes that bind the same prefix to different URIs*

This will only happen if you create two conflicting namespaces deliberately. If there is an accidental clash, the system will sort it out by changing prefixes.

XTDE0440 *In the content of a new element node with a null namespace URI, there must be no namespace node that defines a default namespace*

This will only happen if you explicitly create or copy a namespace node equivalent to the declaration «xmlns="some-uri"». Perhaps you are doing this because you want the element to be in the «some-uri» namespace. The right way to put it in this namespace is at the time you create the element, typically by using the namespace attribute of <xsl:element>.

XTDE0560 *When* xsl:apply-imports *or* xsl:next-match *is evaluated, the current template rule must not be null*

The current template rule is null while evaluating a global variable or a stylesheet function; it is also null inside an <xsl:for-each> iteration.

XTDE0610 *When a template parameter is required because it has neither a* select *attribute nor content, but has an «as» attribute that does not allow the empty sequence, then the caller must supply a value*

If <xsl:param> has no «as» attribute, and no default is specified, then the default value is a zero-length string. If it has an «as» attribute, the "default default" is an empty sequence. But if the «as» attribute does not allow an empty sequence, for example «as="xs:date"», then the parameter is treated as a required parameter and it is an error to supply no value.

XTDE0640 *A stylesheet must have no circularities*

This describes a range of conditions, for example a global variable being defined in terms of itself, a key being defined in terms of itself, or a global variable being set by calling a function that references the global variable. XSLT processors must detect such errors, either at compile time or at runtime.

XTDE0700 *When a template has a parameter that specifies* required="yes", *the caller must supply a value*

XTDE0820 *The name attribute of* xsl:element *must evaluate to a valid lexical QName*

In XSLT 1.0 processors were allowed to ignore this error and continue without creating the offending element. In 2.0 it is fatal and must be reported.

XTDE0830 *When* `xsl:element` *has no* namespace *attribute, the QName produced by evaluating the* name *attribute must use a prefix that has been declared in the stylesheet*

This is true even if the name is computed at run-time. It's safest to specify the `namespace` attribute on `<xsl:element>` to avoid this error occuring.

XTDE0835 *The* namespace *attribute of* `xsl:element` *must evaluate to a valid* `xs:anyURI`

This is a change from XSLT 1.0, which specifically allowed you to use any string as a namespace name. However, the rules for what is a valid `xs:anyURI` are fairly liberal.

XTDE0850 *The* name *attribute of* `xsl:attribute` *must evaluate to a valid lexical QName*

See XTDE0820.

XTDE0855 *The* name *attribute of* `xsl:attribute` *must not evaluate to* `xmlns`.

You can't use `<xsl:attribute>` to create namespace declarations. Usually, namespace declarations take care of themselves if you specify the right namespace when creating your elements. On the rare occasions that you need to generate namespaces by hand, use `<xsl:namespace>`.

XTDE0860 *When* `xsl:attribute` *has no* namespace *attribute, the QName produced by evaluating the* name *attribute must use a prefix that has been declared*

See XTDE0830.

XTDE0865 *The* namespace *attribute of* `xsl:attribute` *must evaluate to a valid* `xs:anyURI`.

See XTDE0835.

XTDE0905 *The* name *attribute of* `xsl:processing-instruction` *must evaluate to a valid processing instruction name*

The name must be a valid NCName (no colon allowed), and it must not be «xml» in any combination of upper and lower case. (The XML declaration is not a processing instruction. To control the XML declaration in the result document, use the various attributes of `<xsl:output>`.)

XTDE0920 *The* name *attribute of* `xsl:namespace` *must evaluate to either a zero-length string or a valid* NCName *other than* «xmlns».

To generate «xmlns="abc"», the name attribute should be a zero-length string; to generate «xmlns:pfx="abc"», it should be "pfx".

XTDE0925 *In the result of* `xsl:namespace`, *the prefix* «xml» *can be used only with the XML namespace, and vice versa*

The XML namespace is automatically in-scope on every element, so you never need to generate it.

XTDE0930 *In the result of* `xsl:namespace`, *the namespace URI must not be a zero-length string*

The instruction generates a namespace node, not a namespace declaration or undeclaration. To force a namespace undeclaration to appear, use «[xsl:]inherit-namespaces="no"» when creating the element, with `<xsl:output method="xml" version="1.1"/>`.

XTDE0980 *The* value *attribute of* `xsl:number` *must evaluate to a sequence of non-negative integers*

A single positive integer is the more usual case.

XTDE1030 *The values of sort keys computed for* `xsl:sort` *must be comparable using* «lt»

For example, they must not be `xs:duration` or `xs:QName` values, and they must not use a mixture of different types such as strings and integers

XTDE1035 *The* collation *attribute of* `xsl:sort` *must be a collation recognized by the processor*

The collation URIs that are recognized will vary from one product to another. If you want your stylesheet to be portable, it's best to pass the collation URIs as the values of stylesheet parameters.

XTDE1110 *The* collation *attribute of* `xsl:for-each-group` *must be a collation recognized by the processor*

See XTDE1035.

XTDE1140 *The* regex *attribute of* `xsl:analyze-string` *must evaluate to a valid regular expression*

Remember that the `regex` attribute is an attribute value template, so any curly braces need to be doubled.

XTDE1145 *The* flags *attribute of* `xsl:analyze-string` *must evaluate to a valid set of flags*

The value must be a string containing one or more of «i», «m», «s», and «x».

XTDE1150 *The* regex *attribute of* `xsl:analyze-string` *must not evaluate to a regular expression that matches a zero-length string*

For example, «regex="[0-9]*"» matches the string "", so it is invalid. If "" is a legitimate input value, handle it separately.

XTDE1170 *The URI passed to* unparsed-text() *must contain no fragment identifier and must identify a resource containing text*

This covers a wide range of things that can go wrong when trying to read an external file.

XTDE1190 *The resource retrieved using* unparsed-text() *must be decodable using the specified encoding, and must decode to valid XML characters*

This rules out reading a binary file, which might contain bytes such as x00 that are not valid in XML.

XTDE1200 *If the second argument to* unparsed-text() *is omitted the processor must be able to infer the encoding, or the encoding must be UTF-8*

If the processor can't work out the encoding, then it will assume UTF-8, and if the file is not encoded in UTF-8 then it's quite likely that decoding will fail with this error.

XTDE1260 *The first argument to* key() *must be a valid lexical QName whose prefix has been declared and which identifies a key declaration in the stylesheet*

The value (even if computed at runtime, which is rare) must either be unprefixed or use a prefix that is declared at the point where the key() function is called, and it must match the name attribute of an <xsl:key> declaration.

XTDE1270 *The node supplied in the third argument of* key(), *or the context node if omitted, must be a node in a tree that is rooted at a document node*

To make life easier for implementors, key() can only be used to search within a complete document. You can search a subtree rooted at an element, as long as it is part of a complete document rooted at a document node.

XTDE1280 *The third argument to* format-number() *must be a valid lexical QName whose prefix has been declared and which identifies a decimal format declaration in the stylesheet*

That is, it must match the name attribute of an <xsl:decimal-format> declaration.

XTDE1310 *The second argument to* format-number() *must be a valid picture string*

For the rules, see the description of format-number() in Chapter 13.

XTDE1340 *The second argument to* format-date/time() *must be a valid picture string*

The rules are described under format-dateTime() in Chapter 13.

XTDE1350 *The picture string used for* format-date/time() *must not refer to components that are not available in the given type of value*

For example, you can't use «[MNn]» with format-time(), because a time does not have a month component.

XTDE1360 *The* current() *function must not be used within an expression that is evaluated when there is no context item*

Since current() refers to the value of the context item at the outermost level of the XPath expression, it's an error if there is no context item at that level.

XTDE1370 *When* unparsed-entity-uri() *is evaluated there must be a context node, and it must be in a tree rooted at a document node*

Unparsed entities can only occur in complete XML documents; this function searches the document in which the context node is to be found.

XTDE1380 *When* unparsed-entity-public-id() *is evaluated there must be a context node, and it must be in a tree rooted at a document node*

See XTDE1370.

XTDE1390 *The first argument of* system-property() *must be a valid lexical QName and its prefix must be declared*

The argument will usually be a string literal, and it will usually be a name in the XSLT namespace such as xsl:vendor. It doesn't have to be a prefixed name; you may be able to use a plain name to access operating system environment variables.

XTDE1400 *The first argument of* function-available() *must be a valid lexical QName and its prefix must be declared*

The name doesn't have to be prefixed; if it isn't, the default function namespace is assumed.

XTDE1425 *When an extension function is called the supplied arguments must satisfy the rules for the extension function, the extension function must not report an error, and the result must be convertible to an XPath value*

This is a catch-all for the things that can go wrong when you call an extension function.

XTDE1428 *The first argument of* type-available() *must be a valid lexical QName and its prefix must be declared*

The name doesn't have to be prefixed; in the absence of a prefix the value of xpath-default-namespace applies.

XTDE1440 *The first argument of* element-available() *must be a valid lexical QName and its prefix must be declared*

Typically, this will be a name either in the XSLT namespace, or in a namespace defined by the vendor for extensions.

XTDE1450 *An unrecognized extension instruction with no* xsl:fallback *children was encountered*

The processor knows that it is an extension instruction because its namespace was identified in [xsl:]extension-element-prefixes. But the processor doesn't know how to evaluate the instruction, and there is no fallback implementation.

XTDE1460 *The* format *attribute of* xsl:result-document *must evaluate to a valid lexical QName, its prefix must be declared, and it must match the name of an output definition in the stylesheet*

That is, it must match the name attribute of an <xsl:output> declaration (comparing the names as QNames).

XTDE1480 *The* xsl:result-document *instruction must not be evaluated in temporary output state*

This typically means that you called <xsl:result-document> while evaluating a variable or a function. This isn't allowed because producing a new output document is a kind of side effect.

XTDE1490 *A transformation must not generate two result trees with the same URI*

One output document would typically overwrite the other, and since order of execution is undefined, it's not clear which one would win. The processor might even try to write both at once, with fatal results.

XTDE1665 *When a basic (non-schema-aware) processor is used, the input document must not contain a node with a type annotation other than* xs:untyped *or* xs:untypedAtomic, *or an atomic value of a type which basic XSLT does not allow*

It's very likely that if your processor isn't schema-aware, then there's no way to create typed (validated) input documents, so this error condition will never arise. But it's there to cover the eventuality.

XTMM9000 *The* xsl:message *instruction was evaluated with* terminate="yes"

This isn't really an error, just a code that the system can use when the stylesheet terminates voluntarily.

XTRE0270 *An* xsl:strip-space *and* xsl:preserve-space *declaration define conflicting rules for the same element*

The processor can report this as an error, or can use whichever declaration comes last in the stylesheet.

XTRE0540 *There must not be two template rules that match the same node with the same mode, import precedence, and priority*

It's best not to have two template rules that match the same node, but if it happens, the processor has a choice. It can report a fatal error, or it can choose the template that comes last in the stylesheet, either silently or with a warning. If you see this error, it's best to make your intentions clear by setting the priority attribute on both templates to indicate which is preferred.

XTRE0795 *If the name of a constructed attribute is* xml:space *then the value must be* default *or* preserve.

The XML specification says that a value for xml:space other than these two is "erroneous", but it's not clear whether such a document is well formed or not; some XML parsers accept it and some don't. XSLT processors are allowed to report an error if you try to write such a value, but they can ignore the error if they prefer.

XTRE1160 *When a URI passed to* document() *contains a fragment identifier, the fragment identifier must be valid for the media type (which the processor must recognize) and must select a sequence of nodes*

A fragment identifier is the part of a URI after the «#» sign. The interpretation of a fragment identifier depends on the media type (=MIME type) of the resource. For «application/xml», the fragment is typically the value of an ID attribute, but this is only recognized if (a) the media type is known (usually from HTTP headers), and (b) ID attributes are notified by the XML parser.

XTRE1495 *A transformation must not generate two result trees with URIs that identify the same physical resource*

See also XTDE1490. If you write to two different URIs that refer to the same file (for example, file:/c:/temp.xml and file:/C:/TEMP.XML) the system is allowed to report an error, but it's likely that it won't notice, and the effect is then undefined.

XTRE1500 *A transformation must not write to and read from the same resource, whether or not the same URI is used*

This means you can't write a document using <xsl:result-document> and then immediately read it using the doc() function. This would make your stylesheet dependent on the order of execution; it would also be a sneaky way of introducing side effects. However, although this is defined as an error, processors are not obliged to catch it, and if you use a slightly different URI when reading and writing (see XTRE1495), you will probably get away with it.

XTRE1620 disable-output-escaping *was requested, but is not supported by the implementation*

This feature is deprecated in XSLT 2.0, and not all implementations support it. Try to find a cleaner design for the code. A processor that doesn't support this attribute can report a fatal error or a warning if you use it, or can simply ignore it.

XTRE1630 disable-output-escaping*was requested when writing to a result tree that is not being serialized*

The disable-output-escaping attribute is a request to the serializer. So if you're not serializing (for example, if you are writing the output to a DOM tree), then it can't be acted upon, which might mean that your code doesn't produce the desired effect. The processor can report the error or simply ignore the attribute.

XTSE0010 *An XSLT-defined element is used where it is not permitted, a required attribute is omitted, or the content of the element doesn't correspond to the permitted content*

This is a catch-all for structural errors in the stylesheet.

XTSE0020 *An attribute contains a value that is not permitted for that attribute*

Used when no more specific error is available.

XTSE0080 *A reserved namespace is used in the name of a named template, mode, attribute set, key, decimal format, variable, parameter, stylesheet function, output definition, or character map*

Reserved namespaces all start with http:// www.w3.org/; they are not available for user-defined names.

XTSE00090 *An element in the XSLT namespace has an attribute whose namespace is either null or the XSLT namespace, other than the attributes defined for this element*

This probably means you misspelled an attribute name in the stylesheet or forgot the correct name. You are allowed attributes beyond those defined in the spec if they are in your own (or the vendor's) namespace.

XTSE0110 *The value of the* version *attribute must be a valid* xs:decimal

Normal values are «version="1.0"» and «version="2.0"».

XTSE0125 *The* [xsl:]default-collation *attribute does not contain a URI that the implementation recognizes*

You can specify a list of URIs, and the system must recognize at least one of them. To ensure this, include http://www.w3.org/2005/xpath-functions/ collation/codepoint at the end of the list.

XTSE0130 *The* xsl:stylesheet *element has a child element with a null namespace URI*

Top-level elements can be in the XSLT namespace or a user or vendor namespace, but not in no namespace.

XTSE0150 *A literal result element used as the outermost element of a stylesheet has no* xsl:version *attribute*

This refers to the simplified stylesheet syntax; the outermost element must have an xsl:version attribute. This error could arise because you misspelled the XSLT namespace URI, or because you supplied a document that isn't a stylesheet at all.

XTSE0165 *The processor cannot retrieve a resource referenced by* xsl:include *or* xsl:import, *or that resource is not a valid stylesheet module*

A common reason for this is that you used a relative URI reference, and the base URI isn't known. Check your processor API for how to supply the base URI.

XTSE0170 xsl:include *must be a top-level element*

If you want a finer-grained inclusion mechanism, consider using XInclude, or external XML entities.

XTSE0180 *A stylesheet module directly or indirectly includes itself*

For example A includes B, B includes C, and C includes A. Just remove one of the includes.

XTSE0190 xsl:import *must be a top-level element*

XTSE0200 xsl:import *must precede all other children of the* xsl:stylesheet *element*

The reason for this is to ensure that imported declarations have lower import precedence than anything that comes after them.

XTSE0210 *A stylesheet module directly or indirectly imports itself*

For example A imports B, B includes C, and C includes A: there only needs to be one import in the cycle.

XTSE0215 *An* xsl:import-schema *element that contains an* xs:schema *element has a* schema-location *attribute, or its namespace conflicts with the* targetNamespace *of the contained schema*

This refers to the ability to write an inline schema directly within the <xsl:import-schema> element. In this case it's simplest to have no attributes on the <xsl:import-schema> element.

XTSE0220 *The schema constructed to support* xsl:import-schema *is not a valid schema*

This could be because you have imported a schema that isn't valid in itself, or because you have imported two schemas that aren't consistent with each other, if for example they contain duplicate definitions.

XTSE0260   *An XSLT element that is required to be empty has child elements or text nodes*

Examples of such elements are `<xsl:output>` and `<xsl:copy-of>`.

XTSE0265   *One stylesheet module sets* `input-type-annotations` *to* `strip,` *another to* `preserve.`

This is a rare case where a stylesheet module must be consistent with the modules it imports.

XTSE0280   *A prefix used in a QName in the stylesheet has not been declared*

This might be a prefixed variable, template, or mode name. The prefix needs to be declared in a name-space declaration on a containing element in the same stylesheet module.

XTSE0340   *The syntax of an XSLT pattern is incorrect*

Catch-all for syntax errors in the pattern supplied in the `match` attribute of `<xsl:template>`, or various other places where match patterns are used.

XTSE0350   *A left curly brace in an attribute value template has no matching right curly brace*

In an AVT, paired curly braces are used around an XPath expression; for example, «`name="chap{$ch}"`».

XTSE0370   *An unescaped right curly brace appears in an attribute value template*

If an attribute is defined as an AVT, then any curly braces forming a literal part of the attribute value must be doubled; for example, «`regex="#{{1,2}}"`».

XTSE0500   *An* `xsl:template` *element must have either a* `match` *attribute or a* `name` *attribute or both; if it has no* `match` *attribute, then* `mode` *and* `priority` *must be absent*

This is stricter than XSLT 1.0, where the `mode` and `priority` were ignored if there was no `match` attribute.

XTSE0530   *The* `priority` *attribute of* `xsl:template` *must be a valid* `xs:decimal`.

You can set `priority` to «`2.6`» or «`-100`», but not to «`1e6`» or «`3.1.5`».

XTSE0550   *The* `mode` *attribute of* `xsl:template` *is empty, contains duplicates, contains an invalid name, or contains* `#all` *as well as other names*

You can specify a list of valid modes, including `#default`. If the attribute is present, it must not be empty, and if you specify `#all`, then there must be no other mode-names present.

XTSE0580   *Two parameters of a template or function have the same name*

XTSE0620   *An* `xsl:variable`, `xsl:param`, *or* `xsl:with-param` *element with a* `select` *attribute is not empty*

You can provide a value using the `select` attribute or in a contained sequence constructor, but not both.

XTSE0630   *Stylesheet contains two global variables with the same name*

You can have two variables with the same name provided that they have different import precedence. Consider changing `xsl:include` to `xsl:import`.

XTSE0650   *The named template called by an* `xsl:call-template` *instruction has not been defined*

The QName appearing in the `name` attribute of `xsl:call-template` must match the `name` attribute of some `xsl:template` declaration in the stylesheet.

XTSE0660   *Stylesheet contains two named templates with the same name*

You can have two templates with the same name provided that they have different import precedence. Consider changing `xsl:include` to `xsl:import`.

XTSE0670   *Two* `xsl:with-param` *elements within the same instruction have the same name*

You can't supply two values for the same parameter. This rule applies even if one is a tunnel parameter and the other is not.

XTSE0680   *An* `xsl:call-template` *instruction supplies a non-tunnel parameter that is not declared in the template being called*

This is a new rule in XSLT 2.0 (in 1.0, the extra parameter was simply ignored).

XTSE0690   *An* `xsl:call-template` *instruction supplies no value for a parameter declared with* `required="yes"`.

XTSE0710   *An* `[xsl:]use-attribute-sets` *attribute is not a list of valid QNames, or contains a QName that doesn't match the name of any attribute set*

XTSE0720   *An attribute set directly or indirectly references itself via* `use-attribute-sets.`

For example, attribute set A has «`use-attribute-sets="B"`», and attribute set B has «`use-attribute-sets=A`».

XTSE0740   *A stylesheet function has an unprefixed name*

To distinguish user-defined functions from those in the standard function library, user-defined functions must always be in your own namespace, and must be declared using a prefix bound to that namespace. For example, `<xsl:function name="my:function">`, with the declaration «`xmlns:my="http://my.com/functions"`» on the `<xsl:stylesheet>` element.

XTSE0760 *A parameter to a stylesheet function specifies a default value*

In a function call, all arguments must be supplied by the caller, so it makes no sense for the `<xsl:function>` definition to provide a default value for an argument. The error means that the `<xsl:param>` element either has a `select` attribute, or is non-empty.

XTSE0770 *Stylesheet contains two functions with the same name and arity*

You are allowed two functions with the same name if they have different numbers of arguments, or if they have different import precedence. When overriding a function, use `xsl:import` rather than `xsl:include`.

XTSE0805 *An attribute on a literal result element is in the XSLT namespace but is not a permitted attribute*

Certain attribute such as `xsl:validation` and `xsl:type` can appear on literal result elements. Other attributes in the XSLT namespace are not permitted.

XTSE0808 *A namespace prefix used in* `exclude-result-prefixes` *has not been declared*

You can't exclude a namespace unless the namespace has been declared in the stylesheet.

XTSE0809 *The value* #default *is used in* `exclude-result-prefixes`, *but there is no default namespace*

XTSE0810 *Two* `xsl:namespace-alias` *declarations in the stylesheet specify the same namespace via their* `stylesheet-prefix` *attribute*

XTSE0812 *An* `xsl:namespace-alias` *declaration specifies a prefix in* `stylesheet-prefix` *or* `result-prefix` *that has not been declared*

XTSE0840 *The* `select` *attribute of* `xsl:attribute` *must be absent if the instruction has content*

In XSLT 2.0 you can specify the value of the new attribute using the `select` attribute, but the instruction must then be empty.

XTSE0870 *The* `select` *attribute of* `xsl:value-of` *must be present if the element is empty, and absent otherwise*

In XSLT 2.0 you can specify the value of the new text node in child instructions, but there must then be no `select` attribute.

XTSE0880 *The* `select` *attribute of* `xsl:processing-instruction` *must be absent if the instruction has content*

See XTSE0840.

XTSE0910 *The* `select` *attribute of* `xsl:namespace` *must be present if the instruction is empty, and absent otherwise, not counting any* `xsl:fallback` *children*

This is similar to other node-creating instructions, but because `<xsl:namespace>` is new in XSLT 2.0, it is allowed to have an `<xsl:fallback>` child which an XSLT 2.0 processor will ignore.

XTSE0940 *The* `select` *attribute of* `xsl:comment` *must be absent if the instruction has content*

See XTSE0840.

XTSE0975 *If the* `value` *attribute of* `xsl:number` *is present, then the* `select`, `level`, `count`, *and* `from` *attributes must all be absent*

Specifying the `value` attribute means you are using `<xsl:number>` only to format a number, not to get the section number of a node in the source document.

XTSE1015 *The* `select` *attribute of* `xsl:sort` *must be absent if the instruction has content*

In XSLT 2.0 you can compute the sort key using child instructions, but the `select` attribute must then be omitted.

XTSE1017 *The* `stable` *attribute of* `xsl:sort` *is allowed only on the first* `xsl:sort` *element*

This attribute indicates that items with duplicate sort keys should retain their original order. It is a property of the sort as a whole, not of an individual sort key, and is placed on the first `<xsl:sort>` element for convenience.

XTSE1040 *The* `select` *attribute of* `xsl:perform-sort` *must be absent if the instruction has content (other than* `xsl:sort` *and* `xsl:fallback`)

The sequence to be sorted can be computed either using the `select` attribute or using nested instructions, but not both.

XTSE1060 *Call to* `current-group()` *appears within a pattern*

XTSE1070 *Call to* `current-grouping-key()` *appears within a pattern*

XTSE1080 *Exactly one of the four* `attributes` `group-by`, `group-adjacent`, group-starting-with, *and* group-ending-with *must be present on* xsl:for-each-group.

XTSE1090   *The* collation *attribute of* xsl:for-each-group *cannot be used unless* group-by *or* group-adjacent *is specified*

For other cases, you can achieve the required effect using the default-collation attribute.

XTSE1130   *An* xsl:analyze-string *instruction must contain either* xsl:matching-substring *or* xsl:non-matching-substring *or both*

XTSE1205   *An* xsl:key *declaration must have either a* use *attribute or content, but not both*

In XSLT 2.0 you can compute the key value using nested instructions, but the use attribute must then be omitted.

XTSE1210   *The* collation *attribute of* xsl:key *is not a recognized collation*

XTSE1220   *Several* xsl:key *declarations with the same name specify different collations*

When you have several xsl:key declarations with the same name, they effectively define a single index, so the same collation must be used on all of them.

XTSE1290   *A decimal format contains two conflicting definitions for the same attribute*

This typically means that you have two <xsl:decimal-format> declarations with the same name (or both with no name) and they both define an attribute such as decimal-separator, but with different values.

XTSE1295   *The zero-digit in a decimal format is not a Unicode digit or is a digit whose value is not zero*

You can use non-ASCII digits, for example Indic, Tamil, or Thai digits, but the zero-digit symbol must be a character defined in the Unicode database to have a numeric value of zero.

XTSE1300   *In a decimal format, the various characters used in the picture string must have distinct values*

For example, you can't use «,» as the decimal separator if it is also used as the grouping separator, either explicitly or by default.

XTSE1430   *In* [xsl:]extension-element-prefixes, *a prefix is specified that has not been declared, or* #default *is used when there is no default namespace*

XTSE1505   *The* [xsl:]validation *and* [xsl:]type *attributes must not be present on the same element*

These attributes are mutually exclusive. If you know the type that you want to validate against, you don't need [xsl:]validation.

XTSE1520   *An* [xsl:]type *attribute is an invalid QName, uses an undeclared prefix, or does not match the name of any imported schema type*

XTSE1530   *The* type *attribute of* xsl:attribute *refers to a complex type*

Attributes must always have simple types.

XTSE1560   *An output definition specifies two conflicting values for the same attribute*

Typically, you have two xsl:output declarations that both specify the same name (or no name) and that have different values for some serialization property. If you want one to override the other, consider using xsl:import instead of xsl:include.

XTSE1570   *The* method *attribute of* xsl:output *must either be a prefixed QName, or one of* xml, html, xhtml, text.

If you want to use your own or a vendor-specific output method, then its name must be in a namespace.

XTSE1580   *Stylesheet contains two character maps with the same name*

If you want one to override the other, consider using xsl:import instead of xsl:include.

XTSE1590   *A* use-character-maps *attribute contains a QName that is not the name of any character map*

XTSE1600   *A character map references itself directly or indirectly*

For example, character map A has «use-character-maps="B"» while character map B has «use-character-maps="A"».

XTSE1650   *When a basic (non-schema-aware) XSLT processor is used, there must be no* xsl:import-schema *declaration*

This might be because you didn't invoke the processor in the right way to get schema-aware functionality, or you might be using a third-party stylesheet that was written to require a schema-aware processor.

XTSE1660   *When a basic (non-schema-aware) XSLT processor is used, there must be no* [xsl:]type *attribute, and the only permitted value for* [xsl:]validation *is* strip.

See XTSE1650.

XTTE0505   *The result of evaluating the content of* xsl:template *must match the required type*

If you specify an «as» attribute on xsl:template, then evaluating the template must deliver a value of the right type. Remember that new elements will be untyped unless you explicitly validate them.

XTTE0510 *When* xsl:apply-templates *has no* select *attribute, there must be a context node*

The default is to process the children of the context node, which fails if there is no context node.

XTTE0520 *The value of the* select *attribute of* xsl:apply-templates *must not contain atomic values*

You can only apply templates to nodes.

XTTE0570 *In a variable declaration, the value of the variable must match the declared type*

If you specify an «as» attribute on xsl:variable, then the value of the variable must match the specified type. Remember that this only declares the required type, it doesn't invoke automatic casting or validation.

XTTE0590 *The value supplied for a parameter of a template must match its declared type*

See XTTE0570.

XTTE0600 *The default value of a template parameter must match its declared type*

See XTTE0570.

XTTE0780 *The value returned by a stylesheet function must match its declared type*

See XTTE0505.

XTTE0790 *The value supplied for a parameter of a stylesheet function must match its declared type*

The rules for calling a user-defined function are the same as for a system function; the supplied arguments must match the declared types.

XTTE0950 *An* xsl:copy *or* xsl:copy-of *instruction is copying namespace-sensitive content using* validation="preserve", *without copying the necessary namespace nodes*

When you specify copy-namespaces="no" and validation="preserve", the absence of namespaces in the new copy could invalidate any QNames in the content of attributes or text nodes that have been copied.

XTTE0990 *When* xsl:number *has no* value *or* select *attribute, there must be a context node*

In the absence of these attributes, the default is «select="."», which requires a context node.

XTTE1000 *The* select *attribute of* xsl:number *must evaluate to a single node*

The message could mean that you have selected an atomic value, or a sequence of more than one node; more likely, you have selected an empty sequence.

XTTE1020 *Except in backward-compatibility mode, the value of a sort key must not contain more than one item*

XTTE1100 *The* group-adjacent *attribute of* xsl:for-each-group *must evaluate to a single item*

With group-by, a node can be assigned to multiple groups by calculating multiple grouping keys, but this isn't allowed with group-adjacent.

XTTE1120 *When* xsl:for-each-group *has a* group-starting-with *or* group-ending-with *attribute, the value of the* select *attribute must not contain atomic values*

These attributes are patterns that only match nodes, so the input (the grouping population) must consist entirely of nodes.

XTTE1510 *When* [xsl:]validation="strict" *is specified, the constructed content must be valid*

This is a catch-all error code for schema validation errors. Hopefully, the processor will provide more detailed information as to why the constructed content was found to be invalid against the schema.

XTTE1512 *When* [xsl:]validation="strict" *is specified, there must be a matching top-level element declaration in the schema*

Validation was not possible because no element declaration could be found for the root element. Check that the namespace is correct.

XTTE1515 *When* [xsl:]validation="lax" *is specified, the constructed content must have validity either "valid" or "unknown"*

This means that an element declaration was found (or perhaps there was an xsi:type attribute), so validation took place, but the content was invalid against the schema. See XTTE1510.

XTTE1540 *When* [xsl:]type *is specified, the created content must be valid against that type*

See also XTTE1510. This code is reported when validation was invoked against a named type.

XTTE1545 *An instruction with an* [xsl:]type *or* [xsl:]validation *attribute must not create a new attribute node with namespace-sensitive content*

This happens when you do validation at the level of an individual attribute node. If the attribute type is QName or NOTATION, validation is not possible because the attribute is not connected to any element, so there are no namespaces to check against.

XTTE1550   *When validation is done at document level, the document node must contain exactly one element child and no text nodes*

The XDM model allows document nodes with no children, multiple element children, or child text nodes, but such documents are never schema-valid.

XTTE1555   *When validation is done at document level, ID/IDREF constraints must be satisfied*

Specifically, ID values must be unique, and IDREF values must refer to an ID that exists within the document.

C

Backward Compatibility

The designers of XSLT 2.0 and XPath 2.0 took a great deal of care to ensure that existing code should continue to work unchanged as far as possible, and in my experience, moving forward to 2.0 rarely causes any compatibility problems. However, because there are so many new features, and particularly because of the changes in the type system, a few incompatibilities were inevitable. This appendix summarizes the areas where you are most likely to encounter problems. It's not a completely comprehensive list; for that, you should go to the relevant appendices of the W3C specifications for XSLT 2.0, XPath 2.0, and *Functions and Operators*. However, many of the incompatibilities described in those appendices are such obscure edge cases that you are very unlikely to encounter them in practice.

You can think of the transition from XSLT 1.0 to XSLT 2.0 as happening in three stages, though you may choose to do all three at once:

❑   The first stage takes the stylesheet unchanged, still specifying «version="1.0"», and runs it under an XSLT 2.0 processor instead of an XSLT 1.0 processor.

❑   The next stage is to change the stylesheet to specify «version="2.0"». This has the effect of switching off backward-compatibility mode.

❑   The final stage is to modify the stylesheet to take advantage of new facilities introduced in XSLT 2.0 and XPath 2.0; notably, the ability to validate the source documents against a schema.

There is potential for transition problems to occur at each of these three stages. The focus in this appendix, however, is on the first two stages, because once you start changing your stylesheet or your application, it's very much under your own control whether existing code keeps working.

In this appendix we'll treat the XSLT changes and the XPath changes together.

It's important to remember that we can only talk here about changes in the W3C language specification. The W3C specifications leave many options open to implementors, so there may be incompatible changes to products that are not described here. Some of these may be triggered by the change in language specification — for example, an API for passing parameters to a stylesheet may change to accommodate the larger number of data types allowed, or vendors may have dropped support for extension functions that duplicate XSLT 2.0 functionality. But that's entirely a matter for product vendors to sort out.

Stage 1: Backward-Compatibility Mode

This section describes the incompatibilities that can occur when you are running in backward-compatibilty mode enabled (that is, with a stylesheet that specifies «version="1.0"»). It is important to remember that even in this mode, you are using the XPath 2.0 data model rather than the XPath 1.0 data model and that this causes some inevitable differences.

XSLT 2.0 processors are not required to support backward-compatibility mode. If you request it (by specifying «version="1.0"»), then such a processor must report a fatal error. Alternatively (and this is what XML Spy does), your development environment may use the version attribute to decide whether to launch a 1.0 or a 2.0 processor.

Deprecated Facilities

The use of disable-output-escaping is now deprecated. It was always an optional feature in XSLT 1.0, and did not work in all environments (a notable example being the Firefox browser). The fact that it is deprecated in 2.0 means that more vendors may decide to drop support.

XPath 2.0 states that "the namespace axis is deprecated and need not be supported by a host language". XSLT, however, states that if backward-compatibility mode is in effect, then the namespace axis must be supported.

Error Handling

XSLT 1.0 described a large number of situations as "recoverable errors". Essentially this phrase means that if you (as the stylesheet author) do something questionable, the processor can either report an error or recover in a defined way.

In XSLT 2.0 many of these errors have become non-recoverable, so an XSLT 2.0 processor will behave like a 1.0 processor that reported the error. For example, if you try to create an attribute with an invalid name, or if you try to create an attribute for an element after creating its text content, the processor will now report an error — in 1.0, it might have simply ignored the attempt to create the attribute. These changes can trip you up if you were previously using an XSLT 1.0 processor that was forgiving about such errors.

In a few cases, XSLT 2.0 has standardized on the recovery behavior instead. So if you try to create a comment containing two adjacent hyphens, the processor will now insert a space between the hyphens.

Some other errors remain recoverable at processor discretion: notable examples are having two template rules that match the same node and calling the document() function to retrieve a document that doesn't exist. Different processors may behave differently in these situations.

There is one particular case where the behavior in 2.0 (even in backward-compatibility mode) is different from both the error behavior and the recovery behavior in 1.0. This arises if you try to supply an element node when constructing the value of a new attribute node, for example:

```
<xsl:attribute name="a">
  <e>23</e>
</xsl:attribute>
```

In 1.0 this either would cause an error or would give you an empty attribute. In 2.0, the new attribute is created, and its value is «23» (the result of atomizing the element).

XSLT 2.0 is also stricter about error conditions that can be detected statically. For example, in XSLT 1.0 if an <xsl:template> instruction had a priority attribute and no match attribute, the priority attribute was simply ignored. In 2.0, it is reported as an error. This also applies to inconsistent combinations of attributes on <xsl:number>.

XSLT 1.0 explicitly said that it wasn't an error to use an arbitrary string (for example «!*?$») as a namespace — that is, there's no requirement that it should be a valid URI. The 2.0 spec wriggles on this point. Element and attribute names are QNames, and QNames are defined in XML Schema as containing an xs:anyURI and an xs:NCName, so it's no longer possible to say there are no rules about what the namespace can be. However, both the XML Schema spec and the XSLT 2.0 spec leave implementations latitude as to how much checking should be done. As it happens, XML Schema 1.1 is moving in the direction of allowing any string to be used as an xs:anyURI value.

Comparing Strings

In XSLT 1.0 testing for equality between two strings performed a strict comparison of the codepoints of the characters in the two strings. There was no flexibility to treat "XML" and "xml" as being equal. Sorting, however, was left very much up to the implementation: two different products would probably sort the same set of strings differently. There was no «<» operator to compare strings, and no min() or max() function.

This changes significantly in XSLT 2.0 and XPath 2.0, though the amount of backward incompatibility depends to a considerable extent on choices made by the vendor. The «=» operator, when comparing two strings, now uses the default collation. How the default collation is defined is up to the implementor, but it isn't necessarily the Unicode codepoint collation. Nor is it necessarily the same collation as is used by default to support <xsl:sort>.

Sort keys defined using <xsl:sort> (in the absence of «data-type="text"») are now compared using their actual data type, rather than being converted to strings. This will only affect you in the unlikely event that your stylesheet defines a numeric key (for example, «@length mod 100») and you actually wanted it to be sorted as a string rather than a number.

Numeric Formats

XPath 2.0 has (in effect) four numeric data types: double, float, decimal, and integer, whereas XPath 1.0 made do with one type, double. Literals that were interpreted as doubles in XPath 1.0 (such as «3.5» or «17») may be interpreted as decimals or integers in XPath 2.0. However, when backward-compatibility mode is selected, all arithmetic is still done in double-precision floating point.

Very large and very small floating point numbers are now output using scientific notation (or the programmer's variant of scientific notation); for example, 1.5E-9. If this output format isn't acceptable, you can use the format-number() function to control the format you want.

There are some changes to the specification of format-number(). In most cases these are tightening up a specification that was previously rather vague in certain areas, but the result of this is that a conformant XSLT 2.0 processor may do things differently from the way that your favorite 1.0 processor interpreted the specification. These changes are caused by the fact that XSLT 1.0 defined format-number() in terms of an old version of the Java DecimalFormat class, and this dependency has now been removed.

There are also changes to the rules for converting strings to numbers. Strings containing a leading plus sign are now recognized (previously they were treated as NaN), as are the strings «INF» and «-INF» for positive and negative infinity, replacing «Infinity» and «-Infinity».

1141

Other XPath Changes

Constructs such as «A = B = C», or «A < B < C» were allowed in XPath 1.0 but are disallowed in XPath 2.0. This is because their actual meaning was wildly different from their intuitive meaning, making them a probable cause of bugs. For example, in XPath 1.0 «1 = 2 = 0» is true, because «(1 = 2)» is false, and «false() = 0» is true.

The XPath 1.0 lexical rules allowed you to write «10div 3» with no space before the «div»; in 2.0, the space is required.

Using an empty sequence as input to an arithmetic operator in 2.0 (in an expression such as «@x+1», where there is no «x» attribute) gives an empty sequence; in 1.0 it gave NaN.

Serialization Changes

The rules for the serializer have become stricter, which means that the format of the output produced by your chosen processor may need to change, or it might have to report errors where it didn't do so in the past.

One particular rule, which caused a lot of controversy, is that an HTML serializer is now required to report an error if your result tree contains a character in the range 128–159. These characters essentially mean nothing in Unicode; they are permitted in XML, but not in HTML. In practice, if your output contains such a character, the chances are it was copied from the input; and the reason it appeared in the input was probably because Windows codepage 1251 uses characters in this range. If the XML document properly declares that it is using this codepage, then no problem arises, because these characters will be converted to their Unicode equivalents, but if it allows the XML parser to misinterpret the encoding as (say) ISO-8859-1, the conversion to Unicode is done incorrectly, and results in invalid HTML. Because browsers are rather tolerant of invalid HTML, it's quite likely this has been going on for years without anyone noticing, but an XSLT 2.0 serializer will put a stop to it.

The 2.0 rules have also become stricter in regard to the interpretation of «indent="yes"». There are more rules now about where the processor is allowed to insert whitespace. The result may be that the pretty printing is not quite as pretty as it used to be.

Stage 2: Setting version="2.0"

The next stage in your transition to XSLT 2.0 is to switch off backward-compatibility mode by setting the version attribute in the <xsl:stylesheet> element to «2.0». This section looks at what changes you should be prepared for when you do this. I'll assume here that you have fixed any problems that arose during stage 1.

The First Node Rule

The most common incompatibilities relate to the dropping of the rule that you can supply a node-set where a single value is expected, and the system will use the first node in the node-set.

In XSLT this arises when a sequence containing more than one value is supplied to:

❑   The select attribute of <xsl:value-of>
❑   The value of an attribute value template

❑   The `value` attribute of `<xsl:number>`

❑   The value of a sort key

In all these cases XSLT 1.0 discards any selected node after the first. In the first three cases, XSLT 2.0 outputs all the values, with an appropriate separator. In the final case XSLT 2.0 reports an error.

In XPath 2.0, if a sequence containing more than one value is supplied in a context where a single value is expected (notably as an operand of an arithmetic expression or as an argument to a function where a singleton is expected), then an error (XPTY0004) is reported.

If your stylesheets fall foul of this change when you switch backward compatibility off, it's easy to fix. If the current code is, for example, `<xsl:value-of select="//item"/>`, change it to `<xsl:value-of select="(//item)[1]"/>`. Remember to use parentheses where necessary.

Type Checking of Function Arguments

With a few exceptions such as the `string()`, `number()`, and `concat()` functions, XPath 2.0 will not implicitly convert a supplied value to the required type. This means, for example, that you can no longer do «`starts-with($x, '-')`» to test whether the number $x is negative: you must first convert it to a string. The conversion still occurs, however, if the value is `untypedAtomic`.

This also applies to operators such as the arithmetic operators. The remedy is to do an explicit conversion to the required type using a constructor function or cast, as described in Chapter 11.

Comparison Operators

In XPath 1.0, the operands of «`<`» and «`>`» were automatically converted to numbers, and a numeric comparison was performed. If either value could not be converted to a number, the result would be `false`. In XPath 2.0, this conversion no longer happens, unless one of the values is `untypedAtomic` and the other is a number. So the comparison «`@price > 20`» still does a numeric comparison, but assuming the document is untyped, «`@price > @discount`» now does a string comparison.

In XPath 1.0, if either of the operands of «`<`», «`>`», «`=`», or any of the other comparison operators was a boolean value, the other operand would be converted to a boolean value. This is no longer the case: instead, the comparison has the same existential semantics as usual. For example, «`@married = true()`» in XPath 1.0 would test if the attribute `married` exists; in 2.0 it tests whether the result of atomizing the attribute is equal to the value `true()`.

Arithmetic

Arithmetic operations in XPath 2.0 may be carried out using integer, decimal, or single- or double-precision floating point. This means the result may be slightly different from XPath 1.0, which always used double-precision floating point. XPath 2.0 in backward-compatibility mode also uses double-precision floating point for all arithmetic.

The Empty Sequence

In XPath 1.0, if an empty node-set was used as an operand to a function or operator that expected a string, it was automatically converted to the zero-length string. Similarly, if the operator or function expected a number, it was automatically converted to NaN (not a number).

1143

In XPath 2.0 the functions in the core library that expect a string argument reproduce this behavior. This is not a built-in feature of the language, it is simply part of the way these particular functions are specified, but this is sufficient to prevent compatibility problems.

However, the corresponding change for numeric operators and functions has not been made. For example, if the attribute A does not exist, then the expression «@A+1» returned NaN under XPath 1.0, but returns an empty sequence under XPath 2.0. If you output this value by converting it to a string, the result will be a zero-length string instead of the string «NaN».

Although the empty sequence plays a significant role as a null value in XPath 2.0, most practical expressions are unaffected by the change.

Error Semantics for «and» and «or»

In XPath 1.0 it was defined, in the case of an expression such as «A and B», that B would not be evaluated if A was false. Similarly, with «A or B», B would not be evaluated if A was true.

This meant that you could safely write an expression such as:

```
($cols = 0) or ($n div $cols > 100)
```

XPath 2.0 no longer gives this guarantee. The operands of «and» and «or» can now be evaluated in either order, or in parallel. In the example above, this means that the division might be evaluated, and cause an error, in the case where $cols is zero.

To be sure of avoiding this failure, you need to rewrite the expression as:

```
if ($cols = 0)
then true()
else ($n div $cols > 100)
```

The reason this change was made is that changing the order of evaluation of expressions within a predicate is a common technique used by database optimizers to take maximum advantage of indexes present in a database. The existing rule in XPath 1.0 prevented many such optimizations. This of course is more likely to affect XQuery than XPath implementations, but the rule was changed in both languages to keep them consistent. A vendor who wishes to offer the maximum level of backward compatibility can of course continue to implement boolean expressions in the same way as XPath 1.0.

I think it's unlikely that many existing stylesheets or freestanding XPath expressions will be affected by this change, if only because runtime errors in XPath 1.0 are extremely rare: most programming mistakes in XPath 1.0 produce either a syntax error, or wrong answers, but not a runtime failure.

Other XSLT Differences

XSLT 2.0 reports a compile-time error if an `<xsl:call-template>` instruction supplies a value for a parameter that is not declared in the called template. XSLT 1.0 simply ignored the extra parameter.

With the `key()` function, XSLT 1.0 converted both the stored value and the supplied value to strings before comparison. XSLT 2.0 compares them without conversion. If they are of different types, they are regarded as not matching (and untypedAtomic is treated as string). So a call on «key('k', 12)» will no longer match an unvalidated element such as `<a>12</a>`.

Stage 3: Adding a Schema

The output that an XSLT 2.0 stylesheet produces for a given source document can change if you validate the source document before transforming it. This section lists some of the changes that might occur:

❏ By default, when a source document is validated, whitespace text nodes will be stripped if they appear in elements with element-only content, that is, elements defined in the schema as having a complex type without mixed content. (In fact, this is also likely to happen if the source document is validated against a DTD). In XSLT 1.0, in principle, all whitespace was retained. Some processors such as MSXML, however, were notable for breaking the rules.

❏ Processing a source document using a schema will cause attribute nodes with default values to be added to the tree, and will cause element nodes with default values to acquire a value. These extra nodes will be visible to the XSLT stylesheet.

❏ Because data is now typed rather than untyped, errors may be reported. For example, if an attribute `birthDate` is defined in the schema to have type `xs:date`, then the expression «`substring(@birthDate, 1, 4)`» will fail with a type error, because the `substring()` function can be applied only to a string. The remedy is to convert the value to a string explicitly, using the `string()` function or a cast.

❏ The results of comparisons may change. The most noticeable effect will be with list-valued elements and attributes, where a comparison (using «=» or any of the other general comparison operators) now tests each item in the list of values independently, rather than testing the string value of the containing node as a whole.

❏ The results of sorting may change. For example, if the sort key has type «`xs:dayTime Duration`», then the values will be compared as durations, not as strings.

❏ Atomizing an element with element-only content is an error. This error can only arise when you have a schema, because without a schema, all elements are considered to have mixed content. An example of an expression that does this is «`contains(invoice, "overdue")`», which checks for the presence of the string «`overdue`» anywhere in the text of an invoice. To make this work after applying a schema, you need to extract the string value of the invoice explicitly, by writing «`contains(string(invoice), "overdue")`».

Summary

XSLT 2.0 is not 100% backward compatible with version 1.0. Most stylesheets will convert with no changes at all, but a few will need tweaking. Moving a large application from XSLT 1.0 to 2.0 is an exercise that needs to be carefully planned, with detailed regression testing carried out to catch any obscure corner cases that might not show up immediately with the first few test runs.

Microsoft XSLT Processors

This appendix contains summary information about Microsoft's XSLT processors.

At the time of writing, Microsoft does not yet have an XSLT 2.0 processor, so the information in this appendix all relates to its XSLT 1.0 products. In view of this, I am not including a comprehensive specification of Microsoft's APIs, merely an outline of their structure. The reference information can be found in Microsoft's own documentation, or in books that concentrate on XSLT 1.0 processing.

The best information available on Microsoft's future plans comes in a blog posting released just after XSLT 2.0 was finalized, at `http://blogs.msdn.com/xmlteam/archive/2007/01/29/xslt-2-0.aspx`. All this really does is to confirm that Microsoft has a development team in place to work on an implementation, but this represents a significant turnaround given that two years earlier Microsoft was saying it thought XQuery would meet all the requirements, and more recently that the way forward was its proprietary *Linq to XML* language. It's likely to be 2009 at the earliest before we see a full product release, though hopefully there will be previews earlier than this.

> *The announcement suggests Saxon on .NET as an interim solution. A recommendation from Microsoft is not something I would have dared to hope for when I started out on the project!*

Microsoft offers two families of products, with completely different APIs. The XSLT processor in the MSXML family comes as standard with Internet Explorer, though it is also available as a freestanding component and is delivered as part of the Office suite. In the current Microsoft jargon, this runs ''on the native stack'', that is, it is compiled into machine code and calls the Windows APIs, rather than relying on the .NET platform. More recently, the `System.Xml.Xsl` package has become available as part of the .NET framework. This appendix gives a brief outline of both these product families.

In the early days it was frequently reported that MSXML was faster than the .NET processor, and that it conformed more closely to the W3C specifications. As far as I can tell, neither of these criticisms is now valid. Both processors offer excellent performance, and few serious conformance issues are reported for either product (the main one being MSMXL's cavalier attitude toward whitespace).

MSXML

MSXML is a package that includes a number of core XML technologies: XML parsing with SAX and DOM interfaces, XSLT transformation, and XML Schema validation. Microsoft has released several versions of the product. The original beta version 1.0 was quickly superseded by version 2.0, which was supplied with the final release of Internet Explorer 5.

MSXML3 became a production release in October 2000 and was included as a standard part of Internet Explorer 6. You will sometimes see it referred to as MSXSL, that being more accurately the name of a command line interface which is available as a free MSDN download.

MSXML4, 5, and 6 followed, with fairly minor enhancements as far as the XSLT part of the product was concerned. However, MSXML3 is still in use, partly because of the installed base of IE6 users, and partly because it was the last version that retained support for Microsoft's obsolete WD-xsl dialect. WD-xsl was first shipped in 1998 before XSLT 1.0 was finalized, and you still occasionally come across stylesheets written in this variant of the language: you can recognize them because they use the namespace URI `http://www.w3.org/TR/WD-xsl`.

You can find download links for MSXML by going to `http://msdn.microsoft.com/xml`. The current version of the Software Development Kit (SDK) includes support for MSXML versions 3, 4, 5, and 6, recognizing that many developers need to test with multiple versions of the runtime.

The objects, methods, properties, and events available with the MSXML3 parser are listed in the Help file that comes with the SDK. I have only included here the parts of the interface that are relevant to XSLT and XPath processing.

Objects

The objects of particular interest to XSLT and XPath processing are listed below:

Object	Description
IXMLDOMDocument	The root of an XML document
IXMLDOMNode	Any node in the DOM
IXMLDOMNodeList	A collection of Node objects
IXMLDOMParseError	Details of the last parse error that occurred
IXMLDOMSelection	A selection of nodes
IXSLProcessor	An execution of an XSLT stylesheet
IXSLTemplate	A compiled XSLT stylesheet in memory

These objects are described in the sections that follow.

IXMLDOMDocument and IXMLDOMDocument2

The IXMLDOMDocument class inherits all the properties and methods of IXMLDOMNode. IXMLDOMDocument2 is a later version of the interface, introducing a few extra properties and methods. This section lists the additional methods and properties of relevance to XSLT and XPath processing, in other words, all the methods and properties that are not also present on IXMLDOMNode, which is described on page 1150.

Additional Methods

The methods particularly relevant to XPath and XSLT processing are described in detail below.

The validate() and setProperty() methods actually belong to the IXMLDOMDocument2 interface, which is an extension to IXMLDOMDocument introduced with MSXML version 2.6.

Name	Returns	Description
abort	(Nothing)	When a document is being loaded asynchronously, abort() can be called at any time to abandon the process.
load	Boolean	Loads document from the specified XML source. The argument is normally a string containing a URL. Clears out any existing content of the Document object, and replaces it with the result of parsing the XML source. Returns True if successful, False otherwise.
loadXML	Boolean	Loads the document from a string containing the text of an XML document. Clears out any existing content of the Document object, and replaces it with the result of parsing the XML string. Returns True if successful, False otherwise.
save	(Nothing)	Saves the document to a specified destination. The destination is usually a filename, given as a string. The effect is to serialize the Document in XML format as a file. It is also possible to specify various other objects as a destination, for example, it can be another Document object, in which case the document is duplicated.
setProperty	(Nothing)	Sets various system properties. The most important properties are: ❑ SelectionLanguage. This takes the value «XPath» (the MSXML4 default) or «XSLPattern» (the default for MSXML3). This affects the syntax used in the expression passed to the selectNodes() and selectSingleNode() methods. If you want to use XPath 1.0 syntax you must set this property to «XPath». The value «XSLPattern» refers to the old Microsoft-specific WD-xsl dialect. ❑ SelectionNamespaces. The value of this property should be a space-separated list of namespace declarations, for example: «xmlns:a="http://a.com/" xmlns:b="http://b.com/"» These define the namespace prefixes that can be used within any expression passed to the selectNodes() and selectSingleNode() methods.
validate	(Nothing)	Validates the document, using the current DTD or schema.

Additional Properties

Name	Type	Description
async	Boolean	True if the document is to be loaded asynchronously.
parseError	IXMLDOMParseError	The last parser error.
readyState	Long	Current state of readiness for use. Used when loading asynchronously. The values are Uninitialized (0), Loading (1), Loaded (2), Interactive (3), and Completed (4).
validateOnParse	Boolean	Requests validation of the document against its DTD or schema.

IXMLDOMNode

This object represents a node in the document tree. Note that the tree conforms to the DOM model, which is not always the same as the XPath model described in Chapter 2; for example, the way namespaces are modeled is different, and text nodes are not necessarily normalized.

There are subclasses of IXMLDOMNode for all the different kinds of node found in the tree. I have not included descriptions of all these, since they are not directly relevant to XSLT and XPath processing. The only subclass I have included is IXMLDOMDocument, which can be regarded as representing either the whole document or its root node, depending on your point of view.

Methods

The methods available on IXMLDOMNode that are relevant to XSLT and XPath processing are listed below. Most often, these methods will be applied to the root node (the DOM Document object), but they can be applied to any node.

Name	Returns	Description
selectNodes	IXMLDOMNodeList	Executes an XPath expression and returns a list of matching nodes.
selectSingleNode	IXMLDOMNode	Executes an XPath expression and returns the first matching node.
transformNode	String	Applies a stylesheet to the subtree rooted at this node, returning the result as a string. The argument identifies the XSLT stylesheet. This will usually be a Document, but it may be a Node representing an embedded stylesheet within a Document. The serialized result of the transformation is returned as a string of characters (the <xsl:output> encoding is ignored).
transformNodeToObject	(Nothing)	Applies a stylesheet to the subtree, placing the result into a supplied document or stream. The difference between this and transformNode() is that the destination of the transformation is supplied as a second argument. This will usually be a Document. It may also be a Stream.

Properties

The most useful properties are listed below. Properties whose main purpose is to navigate through the document are not listed here, because navigation can be achieved more easily using XPath expressions.

Name	Type	Description
baseName	String	The local name of the node, excluding any namespace prefix.
namespaceURI	String	The namespace URI.
nodeName	String	The name of the node, including its namespace prefix if any. Note that unlike the XPath model, unnamed nodes are given conventional names such as "#document", "#text", and "#comment".

continued

Name	Type	Description
nodeTypeString	String	Returns the type of node in string form. For example, `"element"`, `"attribute"`, or `"comment"`.
nodeValue	Variant	The value stored in the node. This is not the same as the XPath string value; for elements, it is always null.
prefix	String	The prefix for the namespace applying to the node.
text	String	Text contained by this node (like the XPath string value).
xml	String	XML representation of the node and its descendants.

IXMLDOMNodeList

This object represents a list of nodes. For our present purposes, we are interested in this object because it is the result of the selectNodes() method.

An IXMLDOMNodeList is returned as a result of the selectNodes() method: it contains the list of nodes selected by the supplied XPath expression. You can process all the nodes in the list either by using the nextNode() method or by direct indexing using the item property.

Methods

Name	Returns	Description
item	IXMLDOMNode	item(N) gets the node at position N.
nextNode	IXMLDOMNode	Gets the next node.
reset	(Nothing)	Resets the current position.

Properties

Name	Type	Description
length	Long	Identifies the number of nodes in the collection.

IXMLDOMParseError

This object is accessible through the parseError property of the IXMLDOMDocument interface.

Properties

Name	Type	Description
errorCode	Long	The error code.
filepos	Long	The character position of the error within the XML document.
line	Long	The line number of the error.
linepos	Long	The character position in the line containing the error.
reason	String	Explanation of the error.

continued

Name	Type	Description
srcText	String	The XML text in error.
url	String	The URL of the offending document.

IXMLDOMSelection

This object represents a selection of nodes. It is returned as the result of the selectNodes() method when the target document implements the IXMLDOMDocument2 interface.

It's simplest to think of this object as a stored expression that returns a list of nodes on demand. It's rather like a relational view: You don't need to know whether the results are actually stored, or whether they are obtained as required.

This interface extends the IXMLDOMNodeList interface.

Methods

Name	Returns	Description
clone	IXMLDOMSelection	Produces a copy of this IXMLDOMSelection.
getProperty	String	Returns the value of a named property such as SelectionLanguage.
item	IXMLDOMNode	item(N) gets the node at position N.
matches	IXMLDOMNode	Tests whether the given node is a member of the set of nodes (returns null if no match; otherwise, the node from which the selection succeeds).
nextNode	IXMLDOMNode	Gets the next node.
reset	(Nothing)	Resets the current position.

Properties

Name	Type	Description
context	IXMLDOMNode	Establishes the context node for evaluating the expression. Changing the context node implicitly resets the current list of nodes, replacing it with a new list.
expr	String	The XPath expression that determines the nodes selected. This can be changed at any time; doing so implicitly resets the current list of nodes, replacing it with a new list.
length	Long	Identifies the number of nodes in the collection.

IXSLProcessor

An IXSLProcessor object represents a single execution of a stylesheet to transform a source document.

The object is normally created by calling the createProcessor() method of an IXSLTemplate object.

The transformation is achieved by calling the `transform()` method.

Methods

Name	Returns	Description
addParameter	(Nothing)	Sets the value of a stylesheet parameter. The first argument is the local name of the parameter, the second is the parameter value, and the third is the namespace URI (usually ""). The value can be a boolean, a number, or a string, or a `Node` or `NodeList`.
reset	(Nothing)	Resets the state of the processor and aborts the current transform.
setStartMode	(Nothing)	Sets the initial mode. There are two arguments, representing the local name and the namespace URI parts of the mode name.
transform	Boolean	Applies the stylesheet (from which this `XSLProcessor` was derived) to the source document identified in the input property. The result tree is accessible through the output property. If the source document is being loaded asynchronously, a return value of `False` means that the transformation needs to wait until more input is available. It can be resumed by calling `transform()` again later. The current state of the transformation can be determined from the `readyState` property.

Properties

Name	Type	Description
input	Variant	XML source document to transform. This is normally supplied as a DOM `Document`, but it may also be a `Node`. The input can also be supplied as an `IStream`.
output	Variant	Output of the transformation. If you don't supply an output object, the processor will create a `String` to hold the output, which you can read using this property. If you prefer, you can supply an object such as a DOM `Document`, a DOM `Node`, or an `IStream` to receive the output.
ownerTemplate	IXSLTemplate	The `XSLTemplate` object used to create this processor object.
readyState	Long	The current state of the transformation. This will be `READYSTATE_COMPLETE` (3) when the transformation is finished.
startMode	String	Name of the initial mode. See `setStartMode()` method above.
startModeURI	String	Namespace of the initial mode. See `setStartMode()` method above.
stylesheet	IXMLDOMNode	The current stylesheet being used.

IXSLTemplate

An `IXSLTemplate` object represents a compiled stylesheet in memory. If you want to use the same stylesheet more than once, then creating an `IXSLTemplate` and using it repeatedly is more efficient than using the raw stylesheet repeatedly using `transformNode()`.

Methods

Name	Returns	Description
createProcessor	IXSLProcessor	Creates an IXSLProcessor object. This method should only be called after the stylesheet property has been set to associate the IXSLTemplate object with a stylesheet. It creates an IXSLProcessor object, which can then be used to initiate a transformation of a given source document.

Properties

Name	Type	Description
stylesheet	IXMLDOMNode	Identifies the stylesheet from which this IXSLTemplate is derived.

Setting this property causes the specified stylesheet to be compiled; this IXSLTemplate object is the reusable representation of the compiled stylesheet.

The DOM Node representing the stylesheet will normally be a DOM Document object, but it may be an Element representing an embedded stylesheet.

The document identified by the stylesheet property must be a free-threaded document object.

Putting it Together

The example in this section shows one way of controlling a transformation using MSXML from within JavaScript on an HTML page.

Example: Using Client-Side JScript to Transform a Document

This example demonstrates the way that you can load, parse, and transform an XML document using client-side JScript in Internet Explorer. You can run this simply by loading the page default.html using the IE browser (version 5 or higher). When you first load it, you may see a security warning, depending on your browser security settings. If this happens, right-click on the message and select "Allow blocked content".

The example shows an HTML page with two buttons on it. The user can click on either of the buttons to select how the data should be displayed. The effect of clicking either button is to apply the corresponding stylesheet to the source XML document.

XML Source

The XML source file for this example is tables_data.xml. It defines several tables (real tables, the kind you sit at to have your dinner), each looking like this:

```
<tables>
<table>
   <table-name>Conference</table-name>
   <number-of-legs>4</number-of-legs>
   <table-top-material type="laminate">Ash</table-top-material>
```

```
        <table-shape>Oblong</table-shape>
        <retail-price currency="USD">1485</retail-price>
    </table>
    . . .
    </tables>
```

Stylesheet

There are two stylesheet files, `tables_list.xsl` and `tables_catalog.xsl`. Since this example is designed to show the JScript used to control the transformation rather than the XSLT transformation code itself, I won't list them here.

HTML page

The page `default.htm` contains some simple styling information for the HTML page, then the JScript code that loads the XML and XSL documents, checks for errors, and performs the transformation. Notice that the `transformFiles` function takes the name of a stylesheet as a parameter, which allows you to specify the stylesheet you want to use at runtime:

```
<html>
<head>
<style type="text/css">
        body {font-family:Tahoma,Verdana,Arial,sans-serif;
              font-size:14px}
        head {font-family:Tahoma,Verdana,Arial,sans-serif;
              font-size:18px; font-weight:bold}
</style>

<script language="JScript">
function transformFiles(strStylesheetName) {

    // get a reference to the results DIV element
    var objResults = document.all['divResults'];

    // create two new document instances
    var objXML = new ActiveXObject('MSXML2.DOMDocument.3.0');
    var objXSL = new ActiveXObject('MSXML2.DOMDocument.3.0');

    // set the parser properties
    objXML.validateOnParse = true;
    objXSL.validateOnParse = true;

    // load the XML document and check for errors
    objXML.load('tables_data.xml');
    if (objXML.parseError.errorCode != 0) {
        // error found so show error message and stop
        objResults.innerHTML = showError(objXML)
        return false;
    }

    // load the XSL stylesheet and check for errors
     objXSL.load(strStylesheetName);
```

```
        if (objXSL.parseError.errorCode != 0) {
           // error found so show error message and stop
          objResults.innerHTML = showError(objXSL)
          return false;
        }

        // all must be OK, so perform transformation
        strResult = objXML.transformNode(objXSL);

        // and display the results in the DIV element
        objResults.innerHTML = strResult;
        return true;
    }
```

Provided that there are no errors, the function performs the transformation using the XML file `tables_data.xml` and the stylesheet whose name is specified as the `strStylesheet Name` parameter when the function is called.

The result of the transformation is inserted into the `<div>` element that has the `id` attribute value «`divResults`». You'll later see where this is defined in the HTML.

If either of the `load` calls fails, perhaps due to a badly formed document, a function named `showError` is called. This function takes a reference to the document where the error was found, and returns a string describing the nature of the error. This error message is then displayed on the page instead of the result of the transformation:

```
function showError(objDocument)
    // create the error message
    var strError = new String;
    strError = 'Invalid XML file !<BR />'
            + 'File URL: ' + objDocument.parseError.url + '<BR />'
            + 'Line No.: ' + objDocument.parseError.line + '<BR />'
            + 'Character: ' + objDocument.parseError.linepos + '<BR />'
            + 'File Position: ' + objDocument.parseError.filepos + '<BR />'
            + 'Source Text: ' + objDocument.parseError.srcText + '<BR />'
            + 'Error Code: ' + objDocument.parseError.errorCode + '<BR />'
            + 'Description: ' + objDocument.parseError.reason
    return strError;
}

//-->
</script>
```

The remainder of the file is the HTML that creates the visible part of the page. The opening `<body>` element specifies an `onload` attribute that causes the `transformFiles()` function in our script section to run once the page has finished loading:

```
. . .
</head>
<body onload="transformFiles('tables_list.xsl')">
<p><span class="head">Transforming an XML Document using
      the client-side code</span></p>
. . .
```

Because it uses the value «tables_list.xsl» for the parameter to the function, this stylesheet is used for the initial display. This shows the data in tabular form.

The next thing in the page is the code that creates the two HTML <button> elements, marked Catalog and Simple List. The onclick attributes of each one simply execute the transform-Files() function again, each time specifying the appropriate stylesheet name:

```
. . .
View the tables as a   <button onclick="transformFiles
    ('tables_catalog.xsl')">Catalog</button>
  or as a  
<button onclick="transformFiles('tables_list.xsl')">Simple List</button>
<hr />
```

Finally, at the end of the code, you can see the definition of the <div> element into which the function inserts the results of the transformation.

```
<!-- to insert the results of parsing the object model -->
<div id="divResults"></div>
</body>

</html>
```

Output

When the page is first displayed, it looks like Figure D-1.

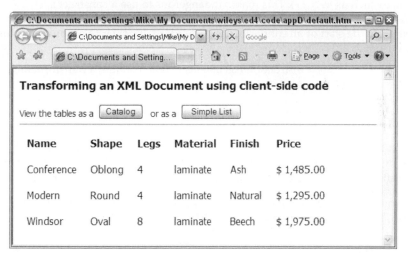

Figure D-1

Click the *Catalog* button, and you will see an alternative graphical presentation of the same data, achieved by applying the other stylesheet.

Restrictions

Microsoft claims full compliance with XSLT 1.0 and XPath 1.0, although there are one or two gray areas where its interpretation of the specification may cause stylesheets to be less than 100% portable. These include:

❑ Handling of whitespace nodes. The normal way of supplying input to Microsoft's XSLT processor is in the form of a DOM, and the default option in MSXML3 for building a DOM is to remove whitespace text nodes as the text is parsed. The result is that `<xsl:preserve-space>` in the stylesheet has no effect, because by the time the XSLT processor gets to see the data, there are no whitespace text nodes left to preserve. If you want conformant behavior in this area, set the `preserveWhitespace` property of the `DOMDocument` object to `True`, before loading the document. The same applies to the stylesheet; if you want to use `<xsl:text>` to control output of whitespace, particularly when generating output in a space-sensitive format such as comma-separated values, then load the stylesheet with `preserveWhitespace` set to `True`. It's not possible to preserve whitespace, unfortunately, when stylesheets are loaded into the browser using the `<?xml-stylesheet?>` processing instruction.

❑ Normalization of text nodes. XSLT and XPath specify that adjacent text nodes in the tree are always merged into a single node. MSXML uses a DOM as its internal data structure, and the DOM does not impose the same rule. Although MSXML does a good job at creating a correct XPath view of the underlying DOM tree, this is one area where the mapping is incomplete. The two common cases where adjacent text nodes are not merged are firstly, when one of the text nodes represents the contents of a CDATA section in the source XML, and secondly, when one of them represents the expanded text of an entity reference (other than the built-in entity references such as «<»). This makes it dangerous to use a construct such as `<xsl:value-of select="text()"/>` because MSXML will return only the first of the text nodes, that is, the text up to the start of an entity or CDATA boundary. It's safer to output the value of an element by writing `<xsl:value-of select="."/>`.

❑ The `<xsl:message>` instruction has no effect when running a transformation in the browser, unless you specify «terminate="yes"».

System.Xml

`System.Xml` is the XML infrastructure within Microsoft's .NET framework. It provides support for XML 1.0, XML Namespaces 1.0, XSLT 1.0, XPath 1.0, DOM level 1 and level 2, and XML Schema. The API is completely different from the older MSXML products described in the earlier part of this appendix.

Within this framework, the .NET namespace `System.Xml.Xsl` provides the API for XSLT processing, while `System.Xml.Xpath` provides the XPath API.

XPathDocument

This class represents a document optimized for XPath and XSLT processing. An instance of this class can be created by directly loading XML from a file:

```
XPathDocument doc = new XPathDocument("source.xml");
```

Other constructors are available, allowing the document to be constructed from a `Stream`, a `TextReader`, or an `XmlReader`. Some of the constructors have a second parameter allowing you to specify whether whitespace text nodes should be stripped or preserved.

An XPathDocument implements the interface IXPathNavigable, described below.

XmlNode

This class represents a node in the .NET implementation of the DOM. Because it supports the DOM data model as well as the XPath data model, it is likely to be less efficient for XPath and XSLT processing than the XPathDocument object.

There are subclasses of XmlNode for the different node kinds; for example, XmlElement, XmlAttribute, and so on.

This class, like XPathDocument, implements the IXPathNavigable interface. This means that any software written to use the IXPathNavigable interface can use either an XPathDocument or an XmlNode document as the data source.

One of the subclasses of XmlNode is System.Xml.XmlDataDocument, which supports an XML view of data in a relational database. This allows the XSLT processor to run directly against relational data.

IXPathNavigable

This is a very small but very significant interface, with a single method, CreateNavigator. This method returns an XPathNavigator object that can be used to process the underlying data, treating it as an implementation of the XPath data model.

For example:

```
XPathDocument doc = new XPathDocument("source.xml");
XPathNavigator nav = doc.CreateNavigator();
```

XPathNavigator

The XPathNavigator object holds a current position within a tree, and provides methods to extract properties of the node at that position and to move the current position to another related node. If the data source is implemented as an XPathDocument, there is actually no object representing the node itself, which makes the model very efficient because small objects have a high overhead.

Because an XPathNavigator is capable of returning all the information in the XPath data model, it acts as an abstraction of a source document, and any object that implements the XPathNavigator interface can be used as a source document for an XSLT transformation.

XslTransform

The class System.Xml.Xsl.XslTransform is used to perform an XSLT transformation. The basic sequence of operations is:

- ❏ Create an XslTransform object.
- ❏ Use the Load method to load (and compile) the stylesheet.
- ❏ Use the Transform method to perform the transformation.

There are different variants of the `Load` method that allow the stylesheet to be loaded by supplying a URL, by nominating an `XmlReader` to read the stylesheet and perform XML parsing, or by supplying an `XPathNavigator` or `IXPathNavigable` that locates the stylesheet within an existing document in memory.

If you want to go through all the stages of loading a stylesheet, you can write:

```
XPathDocument ss = new XPathDocument("stylesheet.xsl");
XPathNavigator nav = doc.createNavigator();
XslTransform trans = new XslTransform();
trans.Load(nav);
```

The options to supply a URL or an `XmlReader` as input to the `Load` method can be seen as shortcuts to this process.

The `Transform` method has a very large number of different overloaded variants. Essentially it takes four arguments: the source document to be transformed, the values supplied for stylesheet parameters, the destination for the result document, and an `XmlResolver` that is used to resolve URI references supplied to the `document()` function. The number of variations of this method is due to the fact that both the source and the destination can be supplied in a number of different ways, and these are supported in all combinations.

❑ The source document can be supplied by giving a URL, or in the form of an `IXPathNavigable` or `XPathNavigator` object.

❑ Stylesheet parameters are supplied in an `XsltArgumentList` object. This allows parameter values to be added using an `AddParam()` method. Parameters of type boolean, number, and string can be supplied using the `Boolean`, `Double`, and `String` classes; a parameter of type `node-set` can be supplied in the form of an `XPathNavigator`.

❑ The output destination can be given as an `XmlWriter`, a `TextWriter`, or a `Stream`. Alternatively, instead of supplying the output destination as an argument, the `Transform()` method can return an `XmlReader`, which means that the calling application can use the transformation results in the same way as it would use the output of an XML parser.

❑ An `XmlResolver` can be supplied. Like the `URIResolver` in the JAXP interface, this object is used to fetch a document when supplied with a URI. This allows you to implement your own URI schemes or to use your own catalogs to find a local copy of required documents such as stylesheet modules, schemas, or DTDs.

For example:

```
// Load a stylesheet

XslTransform trans = new XslTransform();
trans.Load("stylesheet.xsl");

// Load a source document
XPathDocument source = new XPathDocument("source.xml");

// Set the current date and time as a stylesheet parameter
XsltArgumentList args = new XsltArgumentList();
DateTime now = DateTime.Now;
args.AddParam("date", "", now.ToString());
```

```
// Create an XmlTextWriter for the output
XmlTextWriter writer = new XmlTextWriter(Console.Out);

// Perform the transformation (no XmlResolver is supplied)
xslt.Transform(source, args, writer, null);
writer.Close();
```

Summary

This appendix summarized the application programming interfaces available for using Microsoft's two XSLT product families: the MSXML product line, and the System.Xml framework classes for .NET. For full information about these APIs, you will need to go to Microsoft's documentation, but the summary given here has hopefully given you a good introduction.

As you've seen, Microsoft has promised an XSLT 2.0 processor but it's unlikely to be completed until 2009 at the earliest.

JAXP: The Java API for Transformation

JAXP is a Java API for controlling various aspects of XML processing, including parsing, validation, and XSLT transformation. This appendix concentrates on the transformation API. During its development this was known as TrAX (Transformation API for XML) — you will still see this term used occasionally.

JAXP is well supported by all the Java XML processors. The benefit of JAXP is that it allows you to write Java applications that invoke XSLT transformations without committing your application to a particular XSLT processor. At one time, there were five different Java processors you could choose from (xt, Saxon, Xalan, Oracle, or jd.xslt) but for most people now the choice has whittled down to Xalan and Saxon (though both these products have a choice of processors within the same product family). JAXP works so well that I have come across users who were running Saxon when they thought they were using Xalan, or vice versa. It's a good idea to include the following instruction in your initial template so that you avoid this mistake:

```
<xsl:comment>
    Created using <xsl:value-of select="system-property('xsl:vendor')"/>
</xsl:comment>
```

The version numbers for JAXP are irritatingly out of sync with those of the JDK. The following table shows the correspondence:

JAXP version	JDK version	New Functionality
1.2	JDK 1.4	XML Parsing (SAX and DOM) and Transformation
1.3	JDK 1.5 (Java 5)	Schema processing; XPath processing; DOM level 3
1.4	JDK 1.6 (Java 6)	Pull parsing (StAX)

Generally, a new version of JAXP has also been made available as a freestanding component for use with the earlier version of the JDK, so for example you can install JAXP 1.3 on a JDK 1.4 system. But the installation process tends to be messy and error-prone, so it's best avoided unless you have no choice.

JAXP as yet does not explicitly support XSLT 2.0 or XPath 2.0 processing; you have to make do with APIs that were designed for version 1.0 of these specifications. This means there are many aspects of XSLT processing that you cannot control directly; for example, you cannot run a transformation that starts at a named template and uses no source document, and there is no standard way to specify the new serialization options that are defined in XSLT 2.0. As Appendix F explains, Saxon has defined its own API extensions to get around these limitations.

The JAXP Parser API

JAXP 1.2 defined two sets of interfaces: interfaces for XML parsing, in package javax.xml.parsers, and interfaces for XML transformation (that is, TrAX) in package javax.xml.transform and its subsidiary packages. (JAXP 1.3 adds interfaces for schema validation, for XPath processing, and more.) Although the parser APIs could be regarded as being out of scope for this book, applications will often use both together, so I shall start by quickly reviewing the two parser APIs, covering SAX parsing and DOM parsing. The StAX specification for pull parsing included in JAXP 1.4 provides a third option, but this is currently of rather specialized interest, so I will say no more about it. You can find an overview at http://java.sun.com/webservices/docs/1.6/tutorial/doc/SJSXP2.html.

The JAXP interfaces do not supersede the SAX and DOM interfaces, which are described in many XML reference books. Rather, they supplement them with facilities that are (or were at one time) lacking in both SAX and DOM, namely the ability to select a SAX or DOM parser to do the processing, and to set options such as specifying whether you want a validating or non-validating parser, and whether you want namespace processing to be performed.

I'll look at the two parts of the interface, SAX and DOM, separately.

JAXP Support for SAX

JAXP 1.2 supports SAX2, but remains backward compatible with earlier versions that supported SAX1. In the interests of brevity, I will leave out the features that are relevant only to SAX1.

javax.xml.parsers.SAXParserFactory

The first thing an application must do is to obtain a SAXParserFactory, which it can do by calling the static method SAXParserFactory.newInstance(). Different vendors of SAX parsers will each implement their own subclass of SAXParserFactory, and this call determines which vendor's parser your application will end up using. If there are several available, the one that is used is based on the following decision process:

1. Use the value of the system property javax.xml.parsers.SAXParserFactory if it is available. You can typically set system properties using the -D option on the Java command line, or by calling System.setProperty() from your application.

2. Look for a properties file $JAVA_HOME/lib/jaxp.properties, and within this file, for the property named javax.xml.parsers.SAXParserFactory.

3. Use the services API, which is part of the JAR specification. This effectively means that the parser that is used will be the first one to be found on your classpath.

The theory is that when you install a particular SAX parser, it will contain a file within its .jar archive that causes that particular parser to be the default, so if you don't do anything to select a specific parser, the one chosen will depend on the order of files and directories on your class path. In practice there can be a number of complications, which we'll discuss later when talking about the analogous Transformer-Factory interface.

The default parser in Sun's JDK 1.4 was the Crimson parser, but this changed in Java 5 to Xerces 2. There was a time when Java users split their loyalties between half a dozen decent parsers, but these days Xerces 2 has cornered the market, and there is very little reason to choose anything different.

Once you have obtained a `SAXParserFactory`, you can use a number of methods to configure it. Finally, you can call the `newSAXParser()` method to return a `SAXParser`. The methods available are as follows. I haven't listed the exceptions that are thrown: you can get these from the JavaDoc.

Method	Description
boolean getFeature(String)	Determines whether the parser factory is configured to support a particular feature. The names of features correspond to those defined in SAX2 for the XMLReader class.
boolean isNamespaceAware()	Determines whether parsers produced using this factory will be namespace-aware.
boolean isValidating()	Determines whether parsers produced using this factory will perform XML validation.
static SAXParserFactory newInstance()	Produces a SAXParserFactory for a specific vendor's parser, decided according to the rules given above.
SAXParser newSAXParser()	Returns a SAXParser that can be used to perform parsing. This is a wrapper around the SAX2 XMLReader object.
void setFeature(String, boolean)	Sets a particular feature on or off. The names of features correspond to those defined in SAX2 for the XMLReader class.
void setNamespaceAware(boolean)	Indicates whether parsers produced using this factory are required to be namespace aware.
void setValidating(boolean)	Indicates whether parsers produced using this factory are required to perform XML validation.

The `SAXParserFactory` class was introduced in JAXP 1.0 because the SAX 1 specification itself provided no means of requesting a parser. This was fixed in SAX 2 with the introduction of the `XMLReaderFactory` class. So now you have a choice of two factories. Arguably the `XMLReaderFactory` does the job better. I wouldn't put it quite as strongly as Elliotte Rusty Harold:

> `SAXParserFactory` [is] a hideous, evil monstrosity of a class that should be hung, shot, beheaded, drawn and quartered, burned at the stake, buried in unconsecrated ground, dug up, cremated, and the ashes tossed in the Tiber while the complete cast of Wicked sings "Ding dong, the witch is dead."

But one thing that `SAXParserFactory` got badly wrong is that by default, the parser that is selected is not namespace-aware. Even if your particular document is not using namespaces, you should always set this property because almost all applications written to use SAX expect to receive events in the form that a namespace-aware parser supplies them.

javax.xml.parsers.SAXParser

A `SAXParser` is obtained using the `newSAXParser()` method of a `SAXParserFactory`. A `SAXParser` is a wrapper around a SAX2 `XMLReader`. You can use the `getXMLReader()` method to get the underlying `XMLReader`, but in simple cases you won't need to, since you can perform a parse and nominate a handler for all the parsing events using this class alone.

The methods relevant to SAX2 parsers are:

Method	Description
Object getProperty(String)	Gets the named property of the underlying SAX2 XMLReader.
XMLReader getXMLReader()	Gets the underlying SAX2 XMLReader.
boolean isNamespaceAware()	Determines whether the underlying SAX2 XMLReader is namespace-aware.
boolean isValidating()	Determines whether the underlying SAX2 XMLReader performs XML validation.
void parse(File, DefaultHandler)	Parses the contents of the specified file, passing all parsing events to the specified event handler. Normally, of course, this will not actually be a SAX2 DefaultHandler, but a user-defined subclass of DefaultHandler written to process selected events.
void parse(InputSource, DefaultHandler)	Parses the contents of the specified SAX InputSource, passing all parsing events to the specified event handler.
void parse(InputStream, DefaultHandler)	Parses the contents of the specified InputStream, passing all parsing events to the specified event handler. The third argument contains a System ID that will be used for resolving relative URIs contained in the XML source.
void parse(InputStream, DefaultHandler, String)	Parses the contents of the specified InputStream, passing all parsing events to the specified event handler. Note that in this case the System ID of the input is unknown, so the parser has no way of resolving relative URIs.
void parse(String, DefaultHandler)	Parses the XML document identified by the URI in the first argument, passing all parsing events to the specified event handler.
void setProperty(String, Object)	Sets a property of the underlying SAX2 XMLReader.

JAXP Support for DOM

JAXP 1.2 was aligned with DOM level 2, while JAXP 1.3 introduced support for DOM level 3 (for once, the numbers make sense). The main innovation in DOM level 2 was support for XML namespaces; DOM level 3 added many non-core features designed primarily for the browser world, but the main features of interest for XSLT users were the introduction of data typing for nodes, and tests on node identity.

Unfortunately Sun made an exception to their usual backward-compatibility policies when DOM level 3 was introduced, allowing a new version of the interface that invalidated existing implementations. This can cause no end of trouble in upgrading, especially in the case of a product like Saxon that tries to implement DOM interfaces while running on different JDK versions simultaneously.

The DOM interface itself defines methods for constructing a tree programmatically, and methods for navigating around a tree, but it does not define any way of constructing a DOM tree by parsing a source XML document. JAXP is designed to plug this gap.

The architecture of the interface is very similar to the SAX case:

1. First, call the static method DocumentBuilderFactory.newInstance() to get a Document-BuilderFactory representing one particular vendor's DOM implementation.

2. Then use the newDocumentBuilder() method on this DocumentBuilderFactory to obtain a DocumentBuilder.

3. Finally, call one of the various parse() methods on the DocumentBuilder to obtain a DOM Document object.

javax.xml.parsers.DocumentBuilderFactory

The first thing an application must do is obtain a DocumentBuilderFactory, which it can do by calling the static method DocumentBuilderFactory.newInstance(). Different vendors of DOM implementations will each implement their own subclass of DocumentBuilderFactory, and this call determines which implementation your application will end up using. If there are several available, the one that is used is based on the following decision process:

1. Use the value of the system property javax.xml.parsers.DocumentBuilderFactory if it is available. You can typically set system properties using the --D option on the Java command line, or by calling System.setProperty() from your application.

2. Look for a properties file $JAVA_HOME/lib/jaxp.properties, and within this file, for the property named:

       javax.xml.parsers.DocumentBuilderFactory

3. Use the services API, which is part of the JAR specification. In practice, this means that the DOM implementation used will be the first one found on the classpath.

It is likely that when you install a particular DOM implementation, it will contain a file in its .jar archive that makes that particular implementation the default, so if you don't do anything to select a specific implementation, the one chosen will depend on the order of files and directories on your class path.

As with SAX, the default parser changed from Crimson to Xerces 2 with the introduction of Java 5.

Once you have a DocumentBuilderFactory, you can use a number of methods to configure it. Finally, you can call the newDocumentBuilder() method to return a DocumentBuilder. The methods available are:

Method	Description
Object getAttribute(String)	Gets information about the properties of the underlying implementation
boolean isCoalescing()	Determines whether the resulting DocumentBuilder will merge CDATA nodes into their adjacent text nodes
boolean isExpandEntityReferences()	Determines whether the resulting DocumentBuilder will expand entity references and merge their content into the adjacent text nodes

continued

1167

Method	Description
`boolean isIgnoringComments()`	Determines whether the resulting `DocumentBuilder` will ignore comments in the source XML
`boolean isIgnoringElement ContentWhitespace()`	Determines whether the resulting `DocumentBuilder` will ignore whitespace in element content
`boolean isNamespaceAware()`	Determines whether the resulting `DocumentBuilder` is namespace aware
`boolean isValidating()`	Determines whether the resulting `DocumentBuilder` will validate the XML source
`DocumentBuilder newDocumentBuilder()`	Returns a new `DocumentBuilder` configured as specified by previous calls
`static DocumentBuilderFactory newInstance()`	Returns a vendor-specific `DocumentBuilderFactory` selected according to the rules given above
`setAttribute(String, Object)`	Sets vendor-specific properties on the underlying implementation
`void setCoalescing(boolean)`	Determines whether the resulting `DocumentBuilder` will merge CDATA nodes into their adjacent text nodes
`void setExpandEntityReferences (boolean)`	Determines whether the resulting `DocumentBuilder` will expand entity references and merge their content into the adjacent text nodes
`void setIgnoringComments (boolean)`	Determines whether the resulting `DocumentBuilder` will ignore comments in the source XML
`void setIgnoringElementContent Whitespace(boolean)`	Determines whether the resulting `DocumentBuilder` will ignore whitespace in element content
`void setNamespaceAware(boolean)`	Determines whether the resulting `DocumentBuilder` is namespace aware
`void setValidating(boolean)`	Determines whether the resulting `DocumentBuilder` will validate the XML source

javax.xml.parsers.DocumentBuilder

A `DocumentBuilder` is always obtained by calling the `newDocumentBuilder()` method of a `Document-BuilderFactory`.

A `DocumentBuilder` performs the task of parsing a source XML document and returning the resulting instance of `org.w3.dom.Document`, containing the root of a tree representation of the document in memory.

The source document is specified in similar ways to the input for a SAX parser. This doesn't mean that a `DocumentBuilder` has to use a SAX parser to do the actual parsing: some will work this way and others won't. It's defined this way to avoid unnecessary differences between the SAX and DOM approaches.

> You might be aware that in the Microsoft DOM implementation, the `Document` class has a method `load()` that parses a source XML file and constructs a `Document` object. This is a Microsoft extension; there is no corresponding method in the W3C DOM definition. This `DocumentBuilder` class fills the gap.

The methods available are:

Method	Description
boolean isNamespaceAware()	Indicates whether the parser understands XML namespaces.
boolean isValidating()	Indicates whether the parser validates the XML source.
Document newDocument()	Returns a new Document object with no content. The returned Document can be populated using DOM methods such as createElement().
Document parse(File)	Parses the XML in the supplied file, and returns the resulting Document object.
Document parse(InputSource)	Parses the XML in the supplied SAX InputSource, and returns the resulting Document object.
Document parse(InputStream)	Parses the XML in the supplied InputStream, and returns the resulting Document object. Note that the System ID of the source document will be unknown, so it will not be possible to resolve any relative URIs contained in the document.
Document parse(InputStream, String)	Parses the XML in the supplied InputStream, and returns the resulting Document object. The second argument supplies the System ID of the source document, which will be used to resolve any relative URIs contained in the document.
Document parse(String)	Parses the XML in the document identified by the supplied URI, and returns the resulting Document object.
void setEntityResolver (EntityResolver)	Supplies a SAX EntityResolver to be used during the parsing.
void setErrorHandler (Error Handler)	Supplies a SAX ErrorHandler to be used during the parsing.

The JAXP Transformation API

The previous sections provided a summary of the classes and methods defined in JAXP to control XML parsing. This section covers the classes and methods used to control XSLT transformation.

These classes are designed so they could be used with transformation mechanisms other than XSLT; for example, they could in principle be used to invoke XQuery (however, a different API called XQJ is under development for XQuery, which has more in common with JDBC). But XSLT is the primary target and is the one we will concentrate on.

There is one other kind of transformation that's worth mentioning, however, and this is an identity transformation in which the result represents a copy of the source. JAXP provides explicit support for identity transformations. These are more useful than they might appear, because JAXP defines three ways of supplying the source document (SAX, DOM, or lexical XML) and three ways of capturing the result document (SAX, DOM, or lexical XML), so an identity transformation can be used to convert any of these inputs to any of the outputs. For example, it can take SAX input and produce a lexical XML file as output, or it can take DOM input and produce a stream of SAX events as output. An implementation of JAXP can also support additional kinds of Source and Result objects if it chooses.

This allows the ''unofficial'' document models such as JDOM, DOM4J, and XOM to coexist within the JAXP framework.

JAXP is also designed to control a composite transformation consisting of a sequence of transformation steps, each defined by an XSLT stylesheet in its own right. To do this, it builds on the SAX2 concept of an `XMLFilter`, which takes an input document as a stream of SAX events and produces its output as another stream of SAX events. Any number of such filters can be arranged end to end in a pipeline to define a composite transformation.

As with the JAXP `SAXParser` and `DocumentBuilder` interfaces, JAXP allows the specific XSLT implementation to be selected using a `TransformerFactory` object. Typically, the XSLT vendors will each provide their own subclass of `TransformerFactory`.

For performance reasons, the API separates the process of compiling a stylesheet from the process of executing it. A stylesheet can be compiled once and executed many times against different source documents, perhaps concurrently in different threads. The compiled stylesheet, following Microsoft's MSXML nomenclature, is known as a `Templates` object. To keep simple things simple, however, there are also methods that combine the two processes of compilation and execution into a single call.

The classes defined in the `javax.xml.transform` package fall into several categories:

Category	Class or interface	Description
Principal classes	TransformerFactory	Selects and configures a vendor's implementation
	Templates	Represents a compiled stylesheet in memory
	Transformer	Represents a single execution of a stylesheet to transform a source document into a result
	SAXTransformerFactory	Allows a transformation to be packaged as a SAX XMLFilter
	Source	Represents the input to a transformation
	Result	Represents the output of a transformation
Source classes	SAXSource	Transformation input in the form of a SAX event stream
	DOMSource	Transformation input in the form of a DOM Document
	StreamSource	Transformation input in the form of a serial XML document
Result classes	SAXResult	Transformation output in the form of a SAX event stream
	DOMResult	Transformation output in the form of a DOM Document
	StreamResult	Transformation output in the form of a serial XML document (or HTML, or a plain text file)
Helper classes	URIResolver	User-supplied object that takes a URI contained in the stylesheet (for example, in the document() function) and fetches the relevant document as a Source object

continued

Category	Class or interface	Description
	`ErrorListener`	User-supplied object that is notified of warnings and errors. The `ErrorListener` reports these conditions to the user and decides whether to continue processing.
	`SourceLocator`	Used primarily to identify where in the stylesheet an error occurred.
	`DOMLocator`	Subclass of `SourceLocator`, used when the source was a DOM.
	`OutputKeys`	A collection of constants defining the names of properties for serial output files.
Error classes	`Transformer ConfigurationException`	Generally denotes an error in the stylesheet that is detected at compile time.
	`TransformerException`	A failure occurring in the course of executing a transformation.
	`TransformerFactory ConfigurationError`	A failure to configure the `Transformer`.

In the following sections I will describe each of these classes, in alphabetical order of the class name (ignoring the name of the package).

javax.xml.transform.dom.DOMLocator

A `DOMLocator` is used to identify the location of an error when the document is supplied in the form of a DOM. This object will normally be created by the processor when an error occurs, and can be accessed using the `getLocator()` method of the relevant `Exception` object. It specializes `SourceLocator`, providing one additional method:

Method	Description
`org.w3c.dom.Node getOriginatingNode()`	Returns the node at which the error or other event is located

javax.xml.transform.dom.DOMResult

Supplying a `DOMResult` as the result of a transformation indicates that the output is to be written to a DOM in memory. This object will normally be created by the application and supplied to the processor as the second argument of the `Transformer.transform()` method.

The `DOMResult` identifies a `Node` (which will generally be a `Document` or an `Element`, or possibly a `DocumentFragment`) to hold the results of the transformation. The children of the root in the result tree will become children of this `Node` in the DOM. If no `Node` is supplied by the application, the system will create a `Document` node, which can be retrieved using `getNode()`.

Many XSLT processors will support DOM output, but it is not mandatory. If the processor does support it, then calling `getFeature(DOMResult.FEATURE)` on the `TransformerFactory` will return `true`.

If the XSLT stylesheet outputs text using «disable-output-escaping="yes"», then this text will be preceded in the tree by a processing instruction named by the constant `Result.PI_DISABLE_`

OUTPUT_ESCAPING, and followed by another processing instruction named by the constant Result.PI_ ENABLE_OUTPUT_ESCAPING.

The class has five constructors allowing different combinations of the same three parameters:

❑ node, the node that will become the parent of the new tree. This must be a Document, an Element, or a DocumentFragment.

❑ nextSibling (new in JDK 1.5), indicating where in a sequence of existing nodes the new tree should be inserted.

❑ systemId, identifying the system identifier of the document, which will typically be used as its base URI.

The methods on the class are simply getters and setters for the same three properties.

javax.xml.transform.dom.DOMSource

A DOMSource packages a DOM Document as a Source, so it can be supplied as input to a transformation.

The DOMSource object will normally be created by the application and supplied to the processor as the first argument of the Transformer.transform() method. It can also be used to identify the stylesheet document, in which case it will be supplied as a parameter to TransformerFactory.newTemplates().

It is a good idea to call setSystemId() to supply a base URI for the document, so that relative URIs (for example, those used in the document() function) can be resolved. The DOM itself does not hold this information, so it must be supplied extraneously.

The DOMSource can identify any node in the DOM; it does not have to be the Document node. For example, when you use a DOMSource to identify a stylesheet, this might be a stylesheet embedded within another document, in which case the DOMSource would identify the <xsl:stylesheet> element node. When you supply a node other than the Document node as input to the transform() method, the effect is not specified very clearly, but it is probably intended that it should behave like the transformNode() method in MSXML3. This means that the entire document containing the identified node forms the input to the transformation, but the transformation starts by looking for a template rule that matches the specified node, rather than the one that matches the root node.

Note that there are two different ways XSLT processors might handle the supplied document. They might create the XPath tree model as a view or wrapper around the DOM tree, or they might make a copy. The difference between these approaches will become apparent if the stylesheet makes calls to external Java functions that attempt to manipulate the tree as a DOM. It will also, of course, affect performance. Generally, it is best to supply input as a stream or SAX source if you can. Don't construct a DOM specially in order to supply it as input to a transformation, as you might do if you are used to the Microsoft MSXML API. Most implementations will have an internal tree model that is designed to optimize transformation speed, and this will often run several times faster than the same transformation using the DOM.

Not every XSLT processor will support DOM input. If the processor does so, then calling getFeature(DOMSource.FEATURE) on the TransformerFactory will return true.

The class has three constructors:

```
DOMSource()
DOMSource(Node)
DOMSource(Node, String)
```

Its methods are listed below:

Method	Description
Node getNode()	Gets the starting node of this DOMSource
String getSystemId()	Gets the system identifier (that is, base URI) for resolving relative URIs
void setNode(Node)	Sets the starting node of this DOMSource
setSystemId(String)	Gets the system identifier (that is, base URI) for resolving relative URIs

javax.xml.transform.ErrorListener

ErrorListener is an interface; if you want to do your own error handling you can write a class that implements this interface and supply it to the setErrorListener() methods of the Transformer Factory or Transformer class. The ErrorListener will be notified of both compile-time and runtime errors.

The class is modeled on the SAX ErrorHandler interface, and recognizes three categories of errors: warnings, errors, and fatal errors. After a warning, the transformation can proceed to a successful conclusion; after an error, the processor can continue for the purpose of finding further errors, but in the end it will fail, and after a fatal error, it will stop immediately.

Each method can throw an exception to cause processing to stop immediately, even where the processor is prepared to continue.

Some processors (Xalan in particular) report the output of <xsl:message> to the ErrorListener. If «terminate="no"» is specified, the message is treated as a warning; if «terminate="yes"» is specified, it is treated as a fatal error. JAXP doesn't dictate how <xsl:message> is handled, and other processors do it differently.

If no ErrorListener is supplied, errors will be reported on the standard System.err output stream.

The methods are listed below. Each method can throw a TransformerException, to terminate processing.

Method	Description
void error(TransformerException)	Handles an error
void fatalError(TransformerException)	Handles a fatal error
void warning(TransformerException)	Handles a warning

javax.xml.transform.OutputKeys

This class defines a set of constant strings used to represent the standard output properties defined in the <xsl:output> element. This list hasn't yet been updated to support the new properties found in XSLT 2.0. (If you're using Saxon, the missing constants can be found in class net.sf.saxon.event.SaxonOutputKeys).

The names of these constants are:

```
CDATA_SECTION_ELEMENTS
DOCTYPE_PUBLIC
DOCTYPE_SYSTEM
ENCODING
```

```
INDENT
MEDIA_TYPE
METHOD
OMIT_XML_DECLARATION
STANDALONE
VERSION
```

They correspond in the obvious way to the attributes of the `<xsl:output>` element.

These constants are useful when you call methods such as `getOutputProperty()` and `setOutputProperty()` on the `Transformer` object.

javax.xml.transform.Result

`Result` is an interface; it exists as an abstraction of the three classes `SAXResult`, `DOMResult`, and `StreamResult`, which are different ways of representing an XML output destination. This allows any of these different kinds of destination to be supplied as the second argument to the `Transformer` `.transform()` method. Implementations can also define other kinds of `Result` objects if they wish.

This class defines the two static constants `PI_DISABLE_OUTPUT_ESCAPING` and `PI_ENABLE OUTPUT_ ESCAPING` which are the names of the processing instructions generated as a result of setting «disable-output-escaping="yes"» on the `<xsl:text>` or «xsl:value-of» instruction in the stylesheet.

The interface defines two methods, allowing any of the different types of `Result` to have a system identifier (or base URI):

Method	Description
String getSystemId()	Gets the system identifier
void setSystemId()	Sets the system identifier

javax.xml.transform.sax.SAXResult

Specifying a `SAXResult` as the output of the transformation causes the result tree produced by the transformation to be fed to a user-supplied SAX2 `ContentHandler` as a sequence of SAX events, just as if the events came from an XML parser. The `SAXResult` object holds a reference to this `ContentHandler`, and also to a `String` containing a system identifier. (This system identifier might be made available to the `ContentHandler` code as part of the `Locator` object, though the specification doesn't make it clear that this is what should happen.)

Many XSLT processors will support SAX output, but it is not mandatory. If the processor does support it, then calling `getFeature(SAXResult.FEATURE)` on the `TransformerFactory` will return `true`.

There are several potential difficulties with supplying XSLT output to a `ContentHandler`:

❑   What happens about `disable-output-escaping`? The JAXP specification solves this by saying that any text output using `disable-output-escaping="yes"` will be preceded by a processing instruction named by the constant `Result.PI_DISABLE_OUTPUT_ESCAPING`, and followed by another processing instruction named by the constant `Result.PI_ENABLE_ OUTPUT_ESCAPING`.

❑   What happens to comments in the result tree? JAXP solves this by allowing the `SAXResult` to hold a `LexicalHandler` as well as a `ContentHandler`. Comments can then be notified to the `LexicalHandler`.

❑ What happens if the result tree is not a well-formed document? The SAX `ContentHandler` interface is designed to receive a stream of events representing a well-formed document, and many `ContentHandlers` will fail (gracefully or otherwise) if they are sent anything else. However, as you saw in Chapter 2, the output of an XSLT transformation needs only to be well balanced. Unfortunately, the JAXP specification doesn't answer this question. (Saxon allows any sequence of events to be sent to the `ContentHandler`, whether it represents a well-formed sequence or not, unless the additional attribute `saxon:require-well-formed="yes"` is present on the `<xsl:output>` declaration.)

The class has two constructors:

```
SAXResult()
SAXResult(org.xml.sax.ContentHandler)
```

and the following methods:

Method	Description
org.xml.sax.ContentHandler getHandler()	Gets the `ContentHandler`
org.xml.sax.ext.LexicalHandler getLexicalHandler()	Gets the `LexicalHandler`
String getSystemId()	Gets the system identifier (base URI)
void setHandler (org.xml.sax.ContentHandler)	Sets the `ContentHandler` that is to receive events representing the result tree
void setHandler (org.xml.sax.ext.LexicalHandler)	Sets the `LexicalHandler` that is to receive lexical events (notably, comments) representing the result tree
void setSystemId()	Sets the system identifier (base URI)

javax.xml.transform.sax.SAXSource

A `SAXSource` is a `Source`, so it is one of the possible inputs you can supply to the `Transformer` `.transform()` method (when it represents a source XML document) or to the `TransformerFactory` `.newTemplates()` method (when it represents a stylesheet).

Essentially, a `SAXSource` is the combination of a SAX parser (`XMLReader`) and a SAX `InputSource`, which can be a URI, a binary input stream, or a character input stream. A `SAXSource` delivers the source document in the form of a stream of SAX events. Usually it will achieve this by parsing XML held in a file or somewhere in memory, but by defining your own implementations of `XMLReader` and/or `InputSource`, you can supply the SAX events from anywhere; for example, you can generate them as the result of an SQL query or an LDAP directory search, or you could use an `XMLFilter` that modifies the events coming through from a real XML parser before passing them on to the transformation.

If no `XMLReader` is supplied, the system will use a default one. It may do this using the rules for the `javax.xml.parsers.SAXParserFactory` class described earlier in this appendix, but this is not guaranteed.

Not every XSLT processor will support SAX input. If the processor does so, then calling `getFeature` `(SAXSource.FEATURE)` on the `TransformerFactory` will return `true`.

There are three constructors:

```
SAXSource()
SAXSource(InputSource)
SAXSource(XMLReader, InputSource)
```

plus the following methods:

Method	Description
InputSource getInputSource()	Gets the SAX InputSource.
String getSystemId()	Gets the System Identifier used for resolving relative URIs.
XMLReader getXMLReader()	Gets the XMLReader (the parser) if one has been set.
void setInputSource(org.xml.sax.InputSource)	Sets the SAX InputSource.
void setSystemId(String)	Sets a System Identifier that can be used to resolve relative URIs.
void setXMLReader(XMLReader)	Sets the XMLReader (the parser) to be used.
static org.xml.sax.InputSource sourceToInputSource(Source source)	This static method attempts to construct a SAX InputSource from any kind of Source object. It will return null if this isn't possible.

javax.xml.transform.sax.SAXTransformerFactory

This class is a subclass of TransformerFactory that provides three additional facilities:

❑   The ability to construct a SAX ContentHandler (called a TemplatesHandler), which will accept a stream of SAX events representing a stylesheet, and on completion return a Templates object for this stylesheet.

❑   The ability to construct a SAX ContentHandler (called a TransformerHandler) that will accept a stream of SAX events representing a source document, and on completion automatically apply a given stylesheet to that source document.

❑   The ability to construct a SAX XMLFilter based on a particular stylesheet: the XMLFilter performs the same SAX-to-SAX transformation as the equivalent Transformer would perform, but using the interfaces defined for an XMLFilter. This makes it possible to insert this transformation filter into a pipeline of filters.

These facilities were made optional because it was assumed that not every JAXP processor will support them; in practice, all mainstream implementations do.

❑   If getFeature(SAXTransformerFactory.FEATURE) returns true, then the implementation's TransformerFactory will be a SAXTransformerFactory.

❑   If getFeature(SAXTransformerFactory.FEATURE_XMLFILTER) returns true, then the two newXMLFilter() methods can be used.

If a SAXTransformerFactory is available at all, then it will always be produced as a result of calling TransformerFactory.newInstance().

The class has the following methods, in addition to those of `TransformerFactory`:

Method	Description
`TemplatesHandler newTemplatesHandler()`	Creates and returns a `TemplatesHandler`. The `TemplatesHandler` can be supplied with a stream of SAX events representing the contents of a stylesheet.
`TransformerHandler newTransformerHandler()`	Creates and returns a `TransformerHandler`. The `TransformerHandler` will perform an identity transformation on the XML source document that is supplied to it in the form of a stream of SAX events.
`TransformerHandler newTransformerHandler(Source)`	Creates and returns a `TransformerHandler`. The `Source` identifies a document containing a stylesheet. The `TransformerHandler` will perform the transformation defined by this stylesheet, on the XML source document that is supplied to it in the form of a stream of SAX events.
`TransformerHandler newTransformerHandler(Templates)`	Creates and returns a `TransformerHandler`. The `Templates` argument identifies a compiled stylesheet. The `TransformerHandler` will perform the transformation defined by this stylesheet, on the XML source document that is supplied to it in the form of a stream of SAX events.
`org.sax.xml.XMLFilter newXMLFilter(Source)`	Creates and returns an `XMLFilter`. The `Source` identifies a document containing a stylesheet. The resulting `XMLFilter` will perform the transformation defined by this stylesheet.
`org.sax.xml.XMLFilter newXMLFilter(Templates)`	Creates and returns an `XMLFilter`. The `Templates` argument identifies a compiled stylesheet. The resulting `XMLFilter` will perform the transformation defined by this stylesheet.

javax.xml.transform.Source

`Source` is an interface; it exists as an abstraction of the three classes `SAXSource`, `DOMSource`, and `StreamSource`, which are different ways of representing an XML document. This allows any of these different kinds of object to be supplied as the source document to the `Transformer.transform()` method, or as the stylesheet to the `TransformerFactory.newTemplates()` method.

The interface defines two methods, allowing any of the different types of `Source` to have a system identifier. Specifying a system identifier on a `Source` object is important, because it will be used as the base URI when relative URIs within the `Source` are resolved.

Method	Description
`String getSystemId()`	Gets the system identifier
`void setSystemId()`	Sets the system identifier

javax.xml.transform.SourceLocator

`SourceLocator` is an interface modeled on the SAX `Locator` interface. A `SourceLocator` is used to indicate where in the stylesheet an error occurred. Normally, a `SourceLocator` will be produced by the XSLT processor, and the application will access it using the `TransformerException.getLocator()` method.

The methods available are:

Method	Description
int getColumnNumber()	Returns the column number of the location if known, or -1 if not
int getLineNumber()	Returns the line number of the location if known, or -1 if not
String getPublicId()	Returns the public identifier of the document, if available, or null if not
String getSystemId()	Returns the system identifier of the document, if available, or null if not

You can supply a StreamResult as the result of a transformation if you want the result tree to be serialized. The format of the resulting file will be XML, HTML, or plain text, depending on the output method defined using <xsl:output> or the Transformer methods setOutputProperty() and setOutputProperties(). With an XSLT 2.0 engine, XHTML output will also be supported.

Note that if you supply a Writer (which represents a stream of characters rather than bytes), then the XSLT processor will ignore the encoding attribute specified on <xsl:output>. The way in which characters are translated to bytes in this situation depends on how the Writer is configured, and not on the XSLT serializer. One consequence of this is that because the Writer knows nothing about XML, it will not be able to replace characters that aren't available in the chosen encoding by XML character references of the form «€».

StreamResult is defined analogously to StreamSource, which in turn is based on the SAX InputSource class. A StreamResult may be a file (represented by a URL or a Java File object), or a character stream (Writer), or a byte stream (OutputStream).

Most XSLT processors will support stream output, but it is not mandatory. If the processor does support it, then calling getFeature(StreamResult.FEATURE) on the TransformerFactory will return true.

Although the output destination can be expressed as a URI, this must be a writable destination. In practice, this usually means it should be a URI that uses the «file:» prefix, but it could potentially be an FTP or WebDAV destination. If you're running the processor in an applet, writing the output to a file is probably not feasible. The specification doesn't say what happens if you supply a relative URI, but since relative URIs are not allowed in a SAX InputSource, on which this class is modeled, it's best to avoid them. Some processors might interpret a relative URI as being relative to the current directory.

The class has constructors for each of the possible output destinations. The constructor for a String expects the string to contain a system identifier (URL).

```
StreamResult()
StreamResult(File)
StreamResult(java.io.OutputStream)
StreamResult(String)
StreamResult(java.io.Writer)
```

The methods are straightforward:

Method	Description
java.io.OutputStream getOutputStream()	Gets the binary output stream
String getSystemId()	Gets the system identifier

continued

Method	Description
`java.io.Writer getWriter()`	Gets the `Writer` (character output stream)
`void setOutputStream` `(java.io.OutputStream)`	Sets the binary output stream
`void setSystemId(java.io.File)`	Sets output to go to the specified file, by setting the system identifier to the URL of this file
`void setSystemId(String)`	Specifies the system identifier of the output, as a URL
`void setWriter(java.io.Writer)`	Specifies the `Writer` (character output stream) to receive the output

javax.xml.transform.stream.StreamSource

A `StreamSource` represents XML input in the form of a character or byte stream. It is modeled on the SAX `InputSource` class; the only reason `StreamSource` is necessary is that `InputSource` does not implement the `Source` interface, so it cannot be supplied directly as the input to methods such as `Transformer.transform(Source, Result)`.

Most XSLT processors will support stream input, but it is not mandatory. If the processor does support it, then `getFeature(StreamSource.FEATURE)` will return `true`.

If input is from a byte stream (`InputStream`) or character stream (`Reader`), it is a good idea to call `setSystemId()` to supply a URI for the document, so that relative URIs (for example, those used in the `document()` function) can be resolved. The stream itself does not hold this information, so it must be supplied extraneously.

The constructors are as follows:

```
StreamSource()
StreamSource(java.io.File)
StreamSource(java.io.InputStream)
StreamSource(java.io.InputStream, String)
StreamSource(java.io.Reader)
StreamSource(java.io.Reader, String)
StreamSource(String)
```

In each case, the effect is the same as using the default constructor followed by the relevant `setXXX()` method. The `String` argument is always a system identifier for the document.

With earlier JAXP releases I advised against supplying a `java.io.File` object, because the conversion to a URI was buggy. This seems to have been fixed in recent versions.

The methods are straightforward:

Method	Description
`java.io.InputStream getInputStream()`	Gets the supplied `InputStream`
`String getPublicId()`	Gets the supplied Public Identifier

continued

Method	Description
`java.io.Reader getReader()`	Gets the supplied `Reader`
`String getSystemId()`	Gets the system identifier
`void setInput-Stream(java.io.InputStream)`	Supplies an `InputStream`
`void setPublicId(String)`	Supplies a Public Identifier
`void setReader(java.io.Reader)`	Supplies a `Reader`
`void setSystemId(java.io.File)`	Supplies a `File` from which a system identifier can be obtained
`void setSystemId(String)`	Supplies a system identifier (a URL)

javax.xml.transform.Templates

`Templates` is an interface representing a compiled stylesheet. Compiled stylesheets cannot be saved directly to disk (unless the processor provides extensions to enable this), but they are held in memory and can be used as often as required. To use a `Templates` object to perform a transformation, first create a `Transformer` by calling its `newTransformer()` method, then configure the `Transformer` as required (for example, setting its parameters and output properties), and then run the transformation using the `Transformer.transform()` method.

The methods available on the `Templates` object are:

Method	Description
`java.util.Properties getOutputProperties()`	Returns a `Properties` object representing the names and values of the output properties defined using `<xsl:output>` elements in the stylesheet. The keys of these properties will be strings defined in the `OutputKeys` class; the values will be the values defined in the stylesheet. Note that output properties that are determined dynamically will not be returned. For example, if the `method` attribute of `<xsl:output>` is defaulted, the system doesn't know at compile time whether the output will be XML or HTML.
`Transformer newTransformer()`	Creates a `Transformer` object, which can be used to effect the transformation defined in this stylesheet.

javax.xml.transform.sax.TemplatesHandler

The `TemplatesHandler` interface represents a specialized SAX `ContentHandler` that treats the stream of SAX events supplied to it as the contents of a stylesheet. When the full document has been supplied, the stylesheet is compiled, and the compiled stylesheet can be retrieved using the `getTemplates()` method.

This provides an alternative to calling `TransformerFactory.newTemplates()` and supplying a `SAXSource` as the source of the stylesheet. The case for using a `TemplatesHandler` arises when the source of the SAX events is something other than a SAX `XMLReader`; for example, when the stylesheet is the output of another transformation, in which case the source of the SAX events is a JAXP `Transformer`. In this situation the `TemplatesHandler` can be wrapped into a `SAXResult` and used as the `Result` of the earlier transformation.

A `TemplatesHandler` is always created using the `newTemplatesHandler()` method of a `SAXTransformer-Factory`. It provides the following methods in addition to those defined in the SAX `ContentHandler` interface:

Method	Description
`String getSystemId()`	Gets the system identifier of the stylesheet.
`Templates getTemplates()`	Returns the `Templates` object created by compiling the supplied document as a stylesheet.
`void setSystemId(String)`	Sets the system identifier of the stylesheet. A system identifier is needed if relative URIs (for example in `<xsl:include>` or `<xsl:import>` elements) need to be resolved.

javax.xml.transform.Transformer

A `Transformer` represents the collection of resources needed to perform a transformation of a `Source` to a `Result`. This includes the compiled stylesheet, the parameter values, and the output properties, as well as details such as an `ErrorListener` and a `URIResolver`.

This interface is analogous to the `IXSLProcessor` class in Microsoft's MSXML API.

A `Transformer` is always created by calling the `newTransformer()` method of either the `Templates` object, or the `TransformerFactory` object.

A transformer can be used to perform more than one transformation, but it is not thread-safe: You should not start one transformation until another has finished. If you want to perform several transformations in parallel, obtain several `Transformers` from the same `Templates` object.

The principal method is `transform()`, which takes two arguments, representing the `Source` and the `Result`. There are several different kinds of `Source` defined, and several kinds of `Result`. These are described elsewhere in this appendix.

The full set of methods is as follows.

Method	Description
`void clearParameters()`	Clears all parameters set using `setParameter()`.
`ErrorListener getErrorListener()`	Gets the `ErrorListener` for this transformation.
`java.util.Properties getOutputProperties()`	Gets the output properties defined for this transformation. This will be a combination of those defined in the stylesheet and those defined using `setOutputProperty()` and `setOutput Properties()`.
`String getOutputProperty(String)`	Gets a specific output property defined for this transformation. The argument should be one of the constants defined in `OutputKeys`, or a vendor-specific property name.
`Object getParameter(String)`	Gets the value of a parameter defined for this transformation.

continued

Method	Description
URIResolver getURIResolver()	Gets the URIResolver used for this transformation, or null if none has been supplied.
void setErrorListener (ErrorListener)	Sets the ErrorListener to be used to handle errors reported during this transformation.
void setOutputProperties(java.util.Properties)	Sets output properties for the result of this transformation. These properties override any values set using <xsl:output> in the stylesheet. The property names will normally be constants defined in OutputKeys, or vendor-defined properties, but they can also be user-defined properties provided they are namespace-qualified. Names are namespace-qualified using the «{uri}localname» notation, in the same way as parameters.
void setOutputProperty(String, String)	Sets the value of a specific output property for the result of this transformation.
void setParameter(String, Object)	Supplies a parameter for the transformation. The first argument corresponds to the parameter name, as defined in a global <xsl:param> element in the stylesheet; if this is namespace-qualified, it should be written in the form «urilocal-name». The second argument is the parameter value. It's not defined in the JAXP specification what the mapping from Java objects to XPath data types is. Using a String, a Double, a Boolean, or a DOM Node is likely to work in most processors, but beyond this, it depends on the implementation.
void setURIResolver (URIResolver)	Sets the URIResolver to be used to resolve all URIs encountered during this transformation, especially when evaluating the document() function.
void transform(Source, Result)	Performs the transformation. Source and Result are interfaces, allowing a wide range of different types of Source and Result to be supplied.

javax.xml.transform.TransformerConfigurationException

This class defines a compile-time error, generally an error in the stylesheet. It is a subclass of TransformerException and has the same methods as its parent class, TransformerException.

There are several constructors defined, but since this object will usually be created by the XSLT processor itself, I won't list them here.

javax.xml.transform.TransformerException

A TransformerException represents an error that might be detected either at compile time or at runtime. The exception may contain any or all of the following:

❑   A message explaining the error.

❑   A nested exception, generally containing additional information about this error. (Actually, despite the name getException(), this need not be an Exception object; it can be any Throwable, allowing an Error as well as an Exception.)

❏ A `SourceLocator`, indicating where in the stylesheet the error occurred.

❏ A cause. This is likely to be the same as the nested exception. Nested exceptions were intro-duced in JAXP before they became a standard Java feature in JDK 1.4, which is why there are two methods that appear to do the same thing.

There are several constructors defined, but since this object will usually be created by the XSLT processor itself, I won't list them here.

The methods available are:

Method	Description
Throwable getCause()	Gets the cause of the exception, if any
Throwable getException()	Gets the nested exception, if any
String getLocationAsString()	Constructs a `String` representing the location of the error
SourceLocator getLocator()	Gets the `SourceLocator`, if any, that identifies where the error occurred
String getMessageAndLocation()	Constructs a `String` that combines information about the error and information about where it occurred
void initCause(Throwable)	Sets the cause of this exception
void setLocator (SourceLocator)	Sets a `SourceLocator` identifying where the error occurred

javax.xml.transform.TransformerFactory

Like the `SAXParserFactory` and `DocumentBuilderFactory` in the `javax.xml.parsers` package, described in the first part of this appendix, this factory class enables you to select a specific vendor's XSLT imple-mentation.

The first thing an application must do is obtain a `TransformerFactory`, which it can do by calling the static method `TransformerFactory.newInstance()`. Different vendors of XSLT processors will each implement their own subclass of `TransformerFactory`, and this method call determines which vendor's processor your application will end up using. If there are several available, the one that is used is based on the following decision process:

1. Use the value of the system property `javax.xml.transform.TransformerFactory` if it is avail-able. You can set system properties using the -D option on the Java command line, or by calling `System.setProperty()` from your application.

2. Look for a properties file `$JAVA_HOME/lib/jaxp.properties`, and within this file, for the property named `javax.xml.parsers.TransformerFactory`.

3. Use the services API, which is part of the JAR specification. This generally means that the first processor found on the classpath will be used.

The theory is that when you install a particular XSLT processor, it will contain a file in its `.jar` archive that makes that particular processor the default, so if you don't do anything to select a specific processor, the one chosen will depend on the order of files and directories on your class path. Unfortunately the practice can be rather different, because you don't always have control over the classpath, especially in a complex application server environment.

Relying on a search of the classpath has two other disadvantages. Firstly, it is expensive; if the transformation is a short one then it can take longer to find a transformer than to run it. Secondly, it is error-prone; it's difficult to be sure that your application will keep working when small and apparently unrelated configuration changes are made. Although it's a good thing to write your application in such a way that it will potentially work with any XSLT processor, it's a bad thing to allow it to run with an XSLT processor that it hasn't been tested with.

If you're writing an application that's designed to work only with Saxon, and you don't mind having compile-time references to Saxon classes in your code, then I would recommend bypassing the call to `TransformerFactory.newInstance()`, and simply calling «`new net.sf.saxon .TransformerFactoryImpl()`» instead. Alternatively, call «`System.setProperty("javax.xml .transform.TransformerFactory", "net.sf.saxon.TransformerFactoryImpl")`». But remember that this setting will affect everything running in the same Java VM.

For Saxon-SA, the name of the class is `com.saxonica.SchemaAwareTransformerFactory`.

The latest JAXP release, included in Java 6, provides a new version of the `TransformerFactory .newInstance()` method that allows you to specify the name of the implementation class as a parameter to the call. This avoids the side effects of setting the system property.

Java includes a copy of Xalan in its core libraries. This doesn't stop you using any of the techniques above to load a different XSLT processor, such as Saxon. What can be slightly tricky, however, is to use a later version of Xalan than the one included with the JDK. The easiest way to achieve this is to copy `xalan.jar` into a specially recognized directory for endorsed code, such as `j2sdk1.5.0/jre/lib/endorsed/ xalan.jar`.

Once you have got a `TransformerFactory`, you can use a number of methods to configure it. Finally, you can call the `newTemplates()` method to compile a stylesheet, or call the `new Transformer()` method to obtain a `Transformer` directly (if you only want to use the compiled stylesheet once).

The methods available are shown below.

Method	Description
Source getAssociatedStyleSheet(Source doc, String media, String title, String charset)	Within the XML source document identified by the Source argument, finds the `<?xml-stylesheet ?>` processing instruction corresponding to the `media`, `title`, and `charset` parameters (any of which may be null), and returns a `Source` representing this stylesheet.
Object getAttribute(String)	Gets a vendor-specific configuration property.
ErrorListener getErrorListener()	Gets the default error listener that will be used for transformations. If none has been set, this will be a vendor-supplied `ErrorListener`.
boolean getFeature(String)	Gets information about the features supported by this implementation. Features are defined by constants within other classes; for example, `getFeature(SAXResult .FEATURE)` returns `true` if the processor supports output to a SAX `ContentHandler`.

continued

Method	Description
URIResolver getURIResolver()	Gets the default URIResolver that will be used for transformations.
static TransformerFactory newInstance()	Returns an instance of the vendor-specific Transformer-Factory, selected according to the rules given above.
Templates newTemplates(Source)	Compiles the stylesheet provided in the given Source, returning a Templates object as a representation of the compiled stylesheet.
Transformer newTransformer()	Creates a Transformer that will perform an identity transformation.
Transformer newTransformer(Source)	A shortcut method equivalent to calling newTemplates (Source).newTransformer().
void setAttribute(String, Object)	Sets a vendor-specific configuration property.
void setErrorListener (ErrorListener)	Defines the ErrorListener to be used for error handling.
void setURIResolver(URIResolver)	Defines the URIResolver to be used for resolving URIs contained in the stylesheet or source document.

javax.xml.transform.TransformerFactoryConfigurationError

A TransformerFactoryConfigurationError (the specification writers must be good typists) represents an error in configuring the XSLT processor, as distinct from an error in the stylesheet itself.

Note that this is an Error rather than an Exception, which means that an application is not expected to take any recovery action.

The only methods available are:

Method	Description
String getMessage()	Gets the error message
Exception getException()	Gets any nested exception

javax.xml.transform.sax.TransformerHandler

The TransformerHandler interface is a specialization of the SAX ContentHandler. It is an object that receives SAX events representing a source document and performs a transformation on this source document, writing the results of the transformation to a given Result object.

The TransformerHandler interface extends three SAX event-handling interfaces: the ContentHandler, the LexicalHandler, and the DTDHandler. It needs to act as a LexicalHandler so that it can handle comments in the source document, and it needs to act as a DTDHandler so that it can ignore comments in the DTD and find out about unparsed entity declarations in the DTD.

Using a TransformerHandler is an alternative to creating a Transformer and using a SAXSource to define the input document. This alternative approach is particularly useful when the source of SAX events is something other than a SAX XMLReader. For example, the source of SAX events might be another JAXP transformation, or it might be any other piece of software that allows a `ContentHandler` to be nominated to receive results.

A `TransformerHandler` is always created using the `newTransformerHandler()` method of a `SAXTransformerFactory`.

In addition to the methods defined in the SAX `ContentHandler`, `LexicalHandler`, and `DTDHandler` interfaces, a `TransformerHandler` offers the following methods:

Method	Description
String getSystemId()	Gets the system identifier defined for the source document.
Transformer getTransformer()	Gets the underlying Transformer. This can be used to set parameters and output properties for the transformation.
void setResult(Result)	Sets the output destination for the transformation.
void setSystemId(String)	Sets the system identifier for the source document. This will be used as a base URI to resolve any relative URIs contained in the document.

javax.xml.transform.URIResolver

`URIResolver` is an interface; you can write a class that implements this interface and supply it to the `setURIResolver()` method of the `TransformerFactory` or `Transformer` class. The `URIResolver` supplied to the `TransformerFactory` is used to handle a URI encountered at compile time in an `<xsl:include>` or `<xsl:import>` declaration, while the `URIResolver` supplied to the `Transformer` is used at runtime to handle the `document()` function. The `URIResolver` can treat the URI any way it likes, and it returns the required document as a `Source` object: typically a `SAXSource`, a `DOMSource`, or a `StreamSource`.

For example, if the stylesheet called «`document('db:employee=517541')`», your `URIResolver` could interpret this URI as a database query and return an XML document containing the results of the query.

Technically, this interface is rather poorly named. The Internet RFCs distinguish the process of *resolving* a relative URI against a base URI, which is essentially a syntactic operation on two character strings, from the process of *dereferencing* the resulting absolute URI, which typically sends a request over the wires to retrieve some resource. Although the `URIResolver` is passed the relative URI and base URI as separate arguments, it would be bad practice to resolve the relative URI in a nonstandard way. The real power of the `URIResolver` is its ability to control how the absolute URI is dereferenced.

The interface defines only one method:

Method	Description
Source resolve(String, String)	The first argument is a relative URI, the second is the base URI against which it is resolved. The method returns a Source containing the requested document, or throws a Transformer-Exception if it cannot retrieve it. It may also return null, indicating that the default URIResolver should be used.

There is a practical problem that the JAXP interface does not address, namely the XSLT rule that if you call the `document()` function twice to fetch the same absolute URI, the same document should be returned each time. Since the URIResolver accepts the relative URI and base URI as separate arguments, but does not actually return an absolute URI, it's not entirely clear whether it is the responsibility *of the processor or the* URIResolver *to enforce this rule, especially when the URI is in a format that the XSLT processor itself does not recognize, as in the example above.*

Note also that the arguments are supplied in the opposite order to those of the Java java.net.URI *class.*

Examples of JAXP Transformations

This section provides some simple examples of applications that use the JAXP API in different ways to control a transformation.

Example 1: Transformation Using Files

This example (FileTransform.java) performs a single transformation, reading the source document and stylesheet from files, and sending the XML output to another file.

```
import javax.xml.transform.*;
import javax.xml.transform.stream.*;
import java.io.File;

public class FileTransform {

    public static void main(String[] args) throws Exception {
        StreamSource source = new StreamSource(new File(args[0]));
        StreamSource style = new StreamSource(new File(args[1]));
        StreamResult out = new StreamResult(new File(args[2]));

        TransformerFactory factory = TransformerFactory.newInstance();
        Transformer t = factory.newTransformer(style);
        t.transform(source, out);
    }
}
```

This is a minimal JAXP application.

At one time I was reluctant to supply File objects to the JAXP StreamSource and StreamResult constructors, because the filename-to-URI conversion was buggy. In recent releases the problems seem to have been fixed.

Assuming you have installed the Sun Java JDK, you can compile this application by the command:

```
javac FileTransform.java
```

This assumes that the directory containing the Java source file is the current directory. Once you have compiled the code, you can run it from the command line, for example:

```
java FileTransform source.xml style.xsl out.html
```

Of course, this is not a very professionally written application. It will fall over with a stack trace if incorrect arguments are supplied, if either of the input files doesn't exist, or if errors occur during the transformation; but it's a start. My aim in these examples is to show how the main JAXP classes work, not to teach you professional Java programming.

Because some people like to type examples exactly as they are written in the book, the folder containing the Java applications also contains specimen XML and XSL files called source.xml and style.xsl.

1187

So if you make this folder your current directory, you should be able to type the command line above exactly as shown. But, of course, the Java application will handle any source file and any stylesheet. The stylesheet `style.xsl` uses the construct shown at the start of this chapter to place in the output file a comment identifying which XSLT processor was used. So by experimenting with different classpath settings you should be able to satisfy yourself that this code works with multiple XSLT processors.

Example 2: Supplying Parameters and Output Properties

This example, `Parameters.java`, enhances the previous example:

❑ It allows a stylesheet parameter to be supplied from the command line.

❑ It modifies the output properties defined in the stylesheet.

❑ It directs the output to `System.out` instead of a file.

The `main()` method of the enhanced application looks like this:

```java
public static void main(String[] args) throws Exception {
    StreamSource source = new StreamSource(new File(args[0]));
    StreamSource style = new StreamSource(new File(args[1]));
    String title = args[2];

    TransformerFactory factory = TransformerFactory.newInstance();
    Transformer t = factory.newTransformer(style);
    t.setParameter("title", title);
    t.setOutputProperty(OutputKeys.INDENT, "no");
    t.transform(source, new StreamResult(System.out));
}
```

This version of the program can be run using a command such as the following. The third argument on the command line (written in quotes because it contains spaces) is now a parameter value for the stylesheet, instead of the output filename.

```
java Parameters source.xml style.xsl "New organization structure"
```

Comparing the output with that of the previous example, note that the HTML is no longer indented, and that the contents of the `<title>` and `<h1>` elements have changed. And, of course, the output is written to the console this time.

Example 3: Holding Documents in Memory

In this example we will hold both the stylesheet and the source document in memory so that they can be used repeatedly. In principle, this would allow us to run different source documents past the same stylesheet, or to use different stylesheets to transform the same source document, but in practice, to keep the example simple, we'll use the same source document and stylesheet repeatedly, changing only the parameters to the transformation. We'll do one transformation using each of the parameters supplied on the command line.

To keep the source document in memory, create a DOM. One way of doing this would be to use the `DocumentBuilder` class defined in the first section of this appendix. But I'd prefer to stick to using the `javax.xml.transform` interfaces in these examples, so I'll do it in a different way. JAXP makes it very easy to do an identity transform, and to build the DOM — all you need is an identity transform that takes the serial file as input and produces the DOM as output.

You could also keep the stylesheet in memory as a DOM, but this would mean validating and compiling it each time it is used. It's better to keep the compiled stylesheet, that is, the `Templates` object.

The main program of this example (`Repeat.java`) looks like this:

```
public static void main(String[] args) throws Exception {
    StreamSource source = new StreamSource(new File(args[0]));
    StreamSource style = new StreamSource(new File(args[1]));

    TransformerFactory factory = TransformerFactory.newInstance();
    // Build a DOM using an identity transform
    Transformer builder = factory.newTransformer();
    DOMResult result = new DOMResult();
    builder.transform(source, result);
    Document doc = (Document)result.getNode();

    // Compile the stylesheet
    Templates templates = factory.newTemplates(style);

    // do one transformation for each parameter supplied
    for (int i=2; i<args.length; i++) {
        Transformer t = templates.newTransformer();
        System.out.println("======= TITLE = " + args[i] + "=======");
        t.setParameter("title", args[i]);
        t.transform(new StreamSource(source), new StreamResult(System.out));
    }
}
```

You can run this application from the command line with a command such as:

```
java Repeat source.xml style.xsl one two three four
```

This will run the transformation four times, producing output HTML with the title set to «one», «two», «three», and «four» in turn.

This application is quite unrealistic, but the same principle of keeping source documents and stylesheets in memory can often be used to achieve significant performance benefits in a servlet environment, such as the application described in Chapter 19.

Example 4: Using the <?xml-stylesheet?> Processing Instruction

The previous examples have all specified the source document and the stylesheet separately. However, as you saw in Chapter 3, it is possible for a source XML document to identify its preferred stylesheet using an <?xml-stylesheet?> processing instruction at the start of the source XML. This example shows how to extract the relevant stylesheet using the JAXP API: specifically, the getAssociatedStyle sheet() method provided by the TransformerFactory object.

The main() method of this example (Associated.java) is:

```
public static void main(String[] args) throws Exception {
    StreamSource source = new StreamSource(new File(args[0]));
```

```
        TransformerFactory factory = TransformerFactory.newInstance();

        // Get the associated stylesheet for the source document
        Source style = factory.getAssociatedStylesheet(source, null, null, null);

        // Use this to do the transformation

        Transformer t = factory.newTransformer(style);
        t.transform(source, new StreamResult(System.out));
    }
```

Specifying null values for the media, title, and charset arguments of `getAssociatedStylesheet()` selects the default stylesheet for the document. If the document has multiple `<?xml-stylesheet?>` processing instructions, it is possible to use these parameters to choose more selectively.

You can run this example with the command:

```
java Associated source.xml
```

This example illustrates a difference between the Saxon and Xalan implementations of JAXP. If you run this example on a source document that has no `<?xml-stylesheet?>` processing instruction, Saxon throws a `TransformerConfigurationException`, whereas Xalan returns `null` from the `getAssociatedStylesheet()` method. The JAXP specification, as often happens, is silent on the question. In production code, it would be best to check for both conditions.

Example 5: A SAX Pipeline

It can often be useful to place an XSLT transformation within a SAX pipeline. A pipeline consists of a series of stages, each of which implements the SAX2 interface `XMLFilter`. The filters are connected together so that each filter looks like a SAX2 `ContentHandler` (a receiver of SAX events) to the previous stage in the pipeline, and looks like an `XMLReader` (a supplier of SAX events) to the following stage. Some of these filters might be XSLT filters, others might be written in Java or implemented using other tools.

In our example (`Pipeline.java`) we will use a pipeline that contains a source (the XML parser), three filters, and a sink (a serializer). The first filter will be a Java-written `XMLFilter` whose job is to convert all the element names in the document to upper-case, recording the original name in an attribute. The second filter is an XSLT transformation that copies some elements through unchanged and removes others, based on the value of another attribute. The final filter is another Java-written `XMLFilter` that restores the element names to their original form.

I've invented this example for the purpose of illustration, but there is some rationale behind it. In XML, upper-case and lower-case are distinct, so `<b>` and `<B>` are quite distinct element names. But the legacy of HTML means you may sometimes want to do a transformation in which `<b>` and `<B>` are handled in the same way. This isn't easy to achieve in XSLT (it's easier in XSLT 2.0, but still clumsy), so it makes sense to do the pre- and post-processing in Java.

Start with the two Java-written `XMLFilter` classes. These are written as subclasses of the SAX helper class `XMLFilterImpl`. You only need to implement the `startElement()` and `endElement()` methods; the other methods simply pass the events through unchanged.

The prefilter looks like this. It normalizes the name of the element to lower-case, and saves the supplied local name and QName as additional attributes.

```
private class PreFilter extends XMLFilterImpl {

    public void startElement (String uri, String localName,
                                     String qName, Attributes atts)
    throws SAXException {
        String newLocalName = localName.toLowerCase();
        String newQName = qName.toUpperCase();
        AttributesImpl newAtts =
            (atts.getLength()>0 ?
                new AttributesImpl(atts) :
                new AttributesImpl());
        newAtts.addAttribute("", "old-local-name",
                    "old-local-name", "CDATA", localName);
        newAtts.addAttribute("", "old-qname",
                    "old-qname", "CDATA", qName);
        super.startElement(uri, newLocalName, newQName, newAtts);
    }

    public void endElement (String uri, String localName,
                                   String qName)
    throws SAXException {
        String newLocalName = localName.toLowerCase();
        String newQName = qName.toUpperCase();
        super.endElement(uri, newLocalName, newQName);
    }
}
```

The postfilter is very similar; the only difference is that because the original element name is needed by the endElement() code as well as startElement(), the startElement() code (which gets the names from the attribute list) saves them on a stack where endElement can pick them up later.

```
private class PostFilter extends XMLFilterImpl {

    public Stack stack;

    public void startDocument() throws SAXException {
        stack = new Stack();
        super.startDocument();
    }

    public void startElement (String uri, String localName, String qName,
                              Attributes atts)
    throws SAXException {
        String originalLocalName = localName;
        String originalQName = qName;
        AttributesImpl newAtts = new AttributesImpl();
        for (int i=0; i<atts.getLength(); i++) {
            String name = atts.getQName(i);
            String val = atts.getValue(i);
            if (name.equals("old-local-name")) {
                originalLocalName = val;
            } else if (name.equals("old-qname")) {
                originalQName = val;
            } else {
```

```
                        newAtts.addAttribute(
                                        atts.getURI(i),
                                        atts.getLocalName(i),
                                        name,
                                        atts.getType(i),
                                        val);
                }
        }
        super.startElement(uri, originalLocalName, originalQName, newAtts);
        stack.push(originalLocalName);
        stack.push(originalQName);
    }

    public void endElement (String uri, String localName, String qName)
    throws SAXException {
        String originalQName = (String)stack.pop();
        String originalLocalName = (String)stack.pop();
        super.endElement(uri, originalLocalName, originalQName);
    }
}
```

Now you can build the pipeline, which actually has five components:

1. The XML `parser` itself, which you can get using the `ParserFactory` mechanism described at the start of this appendix.

2. The prefilter.

3. The XSLT transformation, constructed using the stylesheet held in `filter.xsl`.

4. The postfilter.

5. The serializer. The serializer is obtained from the `TransformerFactory` and is actually a `TransformerHandler` that performs an identity transformation with a `StreamResult` as its output.

As with any SAX2 pipeline, the first stage is an `XMLReader`, the last is a `ContentHandler`, and each of the intermediate stages is an `XMLFilter`. Each stage is linked to the previous stage using `setParent()`, except that the `ContentHandler` at the end is linked in by calling `setContentHandler()` on the last `XMLFilter`. Finally, the pipeline is activated by calling the `parse()` method on the last `XMLFilter`, which in our case is the postfilter.

Here is the code that builds the pipeline and runs a supplied source file through it:

```
public void run(String input) throws Exception {
    StreamSource source = new StreamSource(new File(input));
    File style = new File("filter.xsl");

    TransformerFactory factory = TransformerFactory.newInstance();
    if (!factory.getFeature(SAXTransformerFactory.FEATURE_XMLFILTER)) {
        System.err.println("SAX Filters are not supported");
    } else {
        SAXParserFactory parserFactory = SAXParserFactory.newInstance();
        parserFactory.setNamespaceAware(true);
        XMLReader parser = parserFactory.newSAXParser().getXMLReader();
```

```
            SAXTransformerFactory saxFactory = (SAXTransformerFactory)factory;
            XMLFilter pre = new PreFilter();

            // substitute your chosen SAX2 parser here, or use the
            // SAXParserFactory to get one
            pre.setParent(parser);
            XMLFilter filter = saxFactory.newXMLFilter(new StreamSource(style));
            filter.setParent(pre);

            XMLFilter post = new PostFilter();
            post.setParent(filter);

            TransformerHandler serializer = saxFactory.newTransformerHandler();
            serializer.setResult(new StreamResult(System.out));
            Transformer trans = serializer.getTransformer();
            trans.setOutputProperty(OutputKeys.METHOD, "xml");
            trans.setOutputProperty(OutputKeys.INDENT, "yes");
            post.setContentHandler(serializer);
            post.parse(source.getSystemId());
        }
    }
```

For the example I've given the class a trivial main program as follows:

```
public static void main(String[] args) throws Exception {
    new Pipeline().run(args[0]);
}
```

And you can execute it as:

```
java Pipeline mixed-up.xml
```

The results are sent to standard output.

Summary

In this appendix I have given an overview of the JAXP interfaces.

I started, for the sake of completeness, with a quick tour of the JAXP facilities for controlling SAX and DOM parsers, found in package `javax.xml.parsers`.

I then gave detailed descriptions of the classes and methods in the package `javax.xml.transform` and its subsidiary packages.

Finally, I showed some simple examples of JAXP in action. Although the applications chosen were very simple, they illustrate the range of possibilities for using Java and JAXP to integrate XSLT components into a powerful application architecture.

Saxon

Saxon is an implementation of XSLT 2.0 produced by the author of this book, Michael Kay. Saxon also includes XQuery and XML Schema processors. The product runs on two platforms, Java and .NET, and it exists in two versions: an open source product Saxon-B, which implements the basic conformance level of the XSLT specification, and a commercial product Saxon-SA, which adds schema-aware processing. All versions can be obtained by following links from `http://saxon.sf.net/`.

There is also an older version of Saxon available, version 6.5, which implements XSLT 1.0. This appendix is concerned only with the XSLT 2.0 processor.

The Java version of Saxon requires JDK 1.4 or a later Java release, and there are no other dependencies. The .NET version is produced by cross-compiling the Java code into the Intermediate Language (IL) used by the .NET platform, using the IKVMC cross-compiler produced by Jeroen Frijters (`http://www.ikvm.net`). This runs on .NET version 1.1 or 2.0.

There are three ways of running Saxon:

❑   You can run it from within a product that provides a graphical user interface. Saxon doesn't come with its own GUI, but it is integrated into a number of development environments such as Stylus Studio (`stylusstudio.com`) and oXygen (`oxygenxml.com`), and it can be configured as an external processor for use within XML Spy (`altova.com`). If you just want to experiment with Saxon, the quickest way to get started is probably to download Kernow (`kernowforsaxon.sf.net`). As long as you have Java installed (J2SE 6), you don't need to install anything else — Saxon comes bundled with Kernow.

❑   You can run Saxon from the command line, either on Java or .NET. This is described in the next section.

❑   You can invoke Saxon from within your Java or .NET application. On Java, Saxon implements the standard JAXP interfaces described in Appendix E, though if you want to get the full benefits of the product, then you'll need to understand how Saxon extends these interfaces (JAXP in its current form was designed with XSLT 1.0 in mind). On the .NET platform, Saxon has its own API, which is outlined on page 1203.

Saxon doesn't come with an installer, so whether you use the Java or .NET product, it's essentially a question of unzipping the distributed files into a directory of your own choosing. For details, see the Getting Started documentation at `http://www.saxonica.com/documentation`.

For Java, the most likely place to slip up is in setting the classpath. This is largely because Java doesn't give you much help when you get it wrong. Either you can set the classpath using the -cp option on the command line when you run Saxon or you can set it in the CLASSPATH environment variable. To do this on Windows, go to Settings ⇨ Control Panel ⇨ System ⇨ Advanced ⇨ Environment Variables. If there is already an environment variable called CLASSPATH, click Edit to change its value, adding the new entries separated by semicolons from the existing entries. Otherwise, click New either under User Variables if you want to change the settings only for the current user, or under System Variables if you want to change settings for all users. Enter CLASSPATH as the name of the variable, and a list of directories and/or .jar files, separated by semicolons, as the value.

For the .NET product, unless you're just playing with Saxon very casually from the command line, you should install the DLL files in the General Assembly Cache. There's a batch script provided to do this; you only need to run it once. On Vista it's probably easier to do it using the .NET framework administration tool which can be reached via the Control Panel.

If you're using the schema-aware product Saxon-SA, then you'll need to obtain a license key from Saxonica. It comes with instructions for how to install it.

Using Saxon from the Command Line

If you are using Saxon on a Windows platform (and even more so if you are running on a Mac), then you may not be accustomed to using the command line to run applications. You can do this from the standard MS-DOS console that comes with Windows, but I wouldn't recommend it because it's too difficult to correct your typing mistakes and to stop output from scrolling off the screen. It is far better to install a text editor that includes a Windows-friendly command line capability. If you're familiar with Unix tools, then you may want to install Cygwin (cygwin.com). I quite like the console plugin for the open-source jEdit editor (from jedit.org), mainly because it has good Unicode support, but for general editing I usually use UltraEdit (ultraedit.com) which has a basic-but-adequate capability for launching command line applications.

The command line can be considered in two halves:

```
command options
```

The command part causes the Saxon XSLT processor to be invoked, and the options are then passed to Saxon to control what the XSLT transformation actually does.

For Java, the simplest form of the command is:

```
java -jar saxon9.jar [options]
```

This works provided that java is on your PATH, and saxon9.jar is in the current directory. If either of these conditions isn't true, you may need to add a full path so that the Java VM and/or Saxon can be located.

Although the -jar form of the command is very convenient, it is also very restricted, because it does not allow code to be loaded from anywhere other than the specified JAR file. For anything more complicated (for example, a stylesheet that uses extension functions, or one that access DOM, JDOM, or XOM files, or one that uses schema-aware processing), you will need to use a form of command that uses the classpath. You can either set the classpath within the command line itself:

```
java -cp c:\saxon\saxon9.jar;c:\saxon\saxon9-dom.jar net.sf.saxon.Transform [options]
```

or you can set the CLASSPATH environment variable and omit the -cp option:

```
java net.sf.saxon.Transform [options]
```

Here `net.sf.saxon.Transform` is the entry point that tells Java to load the Saxon XSLT transformer. If you get a message indicating that this class wasn't found, it means there is something wrong with your classpath.

For .NET the situation is somewhat simpler. Either make the directory containing the Saxon executables (including `Transform.exe`) the current directory, or add it to the system PATH variable. Then use the command:

```
Transform [options]
```

The options are the same whichever form of the command you use, and are described below. For a more detailed explanation, see the Saxon documentation. This table relates to Saxon 9.0 and later; earlier versions used a slightly different format.

Option	Description
`-a`	Use the `<?xml-stylesheet?>` processing instruction in the source document to identify the stylesheet to be used. The stylesheet argument should then be omitted.
`-c:filename`	Requests use of a stylesheet that has been previously compiled using the `net.sf.saxon.Compile` command.
`-cr:classname`	Sets a user-defined resolver for collection URIs.
`-dtd:on|off`	Sets DTD validation on or off.
`-expand:on|off`	The value `off` suppresses expansion of attribute defaults defined in the DTD or schema.
`-explain[:filename]`	Requests output showing how the code has been optimized. The output is sent to the console unless a filename is supplied.
`-ext:on|off`	The value `off` prevents calls on extension functions.
`-im:modename`	Starts execution in the named mode.
`-it:template`	Specifies the name of the initial template. The transformation will start by evaluating this named template.
`-l:on|off`	Switches line numbering on (or off) for the source document. Line numbers are accessible through the extension function `saxon:line-number()`, or from a trace listener.
`-m:classname`	Specifies the name of a Java class used to process the output of `<xsl:message>` instructions.
`-o:filename`	Defines a file to contain the primary output of the transformation. Filenames for secondary output files (created using `<xsl:result-document>`) will be interpreted relative to the location of this primary output file.
`-or:classname`	Sets a user-defined resolver for secondary output files.
`-outval:recover|fatal`	Indicates whether validation failures found when validating the result document should be treated as fatal or recoverable.

continued

F

Saxon

Option	Description
-p:on|off	The value on means that query parameters such as «val=strict» are recognized in URIs passed to the doc() and document() functions.
-r:classname	Sets a JAXP URIResolver, used to resolve all URIs used in <xsl:include>, <xsl:import>, or in the doc() and document() functions.
-repeat:N	Runs the same transformation N times. Useful for performance measurement.
-s:filename	Specifies the principal source document.
-sa	Requests schema-aware processing.
-strip: all|none|ignorable	Requests stripping of all whitespace, or none, or "ignorable" whitespace (whitespace in elements defined by the DTD or schema to have element-only content).
-t	Displays information about the Saxon and Java versions in use, and progress messages indicating which files are being processed and how long the key stages of processing took.
-T[:classname]	Traces execution of the stylesheet. Each instruction is traced as it is executed, identifying the instruction and the current location in the source document by line number. If a classname is supplied, trace output is sent to a user-supplied TraceListener.
-TJ	Traces the loading of Java extension functions. This is a useful debugging aid if you are having problems in this area.
-tree:tiny|linked	Chooses the implementation of the XDM tree model.
-u	Indicates that the names of the source document and stylesheet are URLs rather than filenames.
-val:strict|lax	Requests strict or lax schema-based validation of all source documents. This option is available only with Saxon-SA.
-versmsg:on|off	Setting this to off suppresses the warning message that appears when running against a 1.0 stylesheet.
-warnings: silent|recover|fatal	Indicates how XSLT-defined recoverable errors are to be handled. Either recover silently; or output a warning message and continue; or treat the error as fatal.
-x:classname	Defines the XML parser to be used for the source document, and for any additional document loaded using the document() function.
-xi	Enable XInclude processing (if the XML parser supports it).
-xsl:filename	The stylesheet to be applied.
-xmlversion:1.0|1.1	Indicates whether the XML 1.0 or 1.1 rules for the syntax of names (etc) should be used.
-y:classname	Defines the XML parser to be used for processing stylesheet documents and schema documents.

You can specify values for global parameters defined in the stylesheet using a `keyword=value` notation; for example:

```
Transform -s:source.xml -xsl:style.xsl param1=value1 param2=value2
```

If the parameter names have a non-null namespace, you can use Clark notation for expanded names; for example, «{namespace-uri}local-name». The parameter values are interpreted as strings. If the string contains a space, you should enclose it in quotes; for example, «param1="John Brown"». They are passed to the stylesheet as `xs:untypedAtomic` values, which means that if the `<xsl:param>` element declares a type such as `xs:integer` or `xs:string`, the value will be converted automatically to the required type, provided that the value is valid for that type.

If you want to pass an XML document as a parameter to the stylesheet, you can do this by prefixing the parameter name with «+» and supplying the name of the XML file as the parameter value. For example:

```
Transform -s:source.xml -xsl:style.xsl +lookup=lookup.xml
```

The XML contained in `lookup.xml` will be parsed, and the document node of the resulting tree will be passed to the stylesheet as the value of the stylesheet parameter named «lookup».

You can also override `<xsl:output>` attributes using a similar notation, but prefixing the keyword with «!». For example, to get indented output write:

```
Transform -s:source.xml -xsl:style.xsl !indent=yes
```

Using Saxon from a Java Application

When calling Saxon from Java, you have a choice between using the JAXP interface defined in Appendix E, or one of Saxon's native interfaces. Saxon 9.0 introduces a new Java interface called s9api (pronounced "snappy") that is designed to eliminate some of the limitations and inconsistencies of the JAXP interfaces, but JAXP is still available if you need to keep your application portable. Although Saxon itself works with JDK 1.4, to use the s9api interface you will need Java 5 or later, because it takes advantage of features like the generic collection classes.

I will first describe how to use Saxon's implementation of the JAXP interfaces, and then take a look at the s9api design.

Using Saxon via JAXP Interfaces

JAXP interfaces are summarized in Appendix E, and you can find full specifications in the Sun Javadoc documentation: go to `http://java.sun.com/j2se/1.5.0/docs/api/index.html`, and look for the packages `javax.xml.transform`, `javax.xml.validation`, and `javax.xml.xpath`. These three packages allow you to:

❑ Compile an XSLT stylesheet and run a transformation

❑ Load a schema and validate a source document

❑ Compile and run XPath expressions

These are described briefly in the following sections.

Running XSLT Transformations

The JAXP transformation API allows you to compile a stylesheet into a `Templates` object, which can then be used repeatedly (in series or in multiple threads) to process different source documents through the same stylesheet. This can greatly improve throughput on a Web server. Saxon supplies a sample application to achieve this, in the form of a Java servlet.

Saxon implements the whole of the `javax.xml.transform` package, including the `dom`, `sax`, and `stream` subpackages, both for input and output. It also implements the `SAXTransformerFactory`, which allows you to do the transformation as part of a SAX pipeline. If you want to use Saxon with the DOM you need to have `saxon9-dom.jar` on the classpath.

The implementation of `TransformerFactory` in Saxon-B is the class `net.sf.saxon.TransformerFactory-Impl`, and this is used in the examples below. The equivalent in Saxon-SA is `com.saxonica.SchemaAware-TransformerFactory`.

The `saxon9.jar` package includes a services file that has the effect of causing the JAXP `Transformer-Factory` to choose Saxon as the default XSLT processor. However, it can be tricky to ensure that Saxon is loaded, given that the JDK includes an XSLT implementation (Xalan) as a standard component. The best policy, if you require Saxon because your stylesheet is written in XSLT 2.0, is to select it explicitly. There are several ways this can be achieved:

❑   If you don't mind your code having a compile-time reference to Saxon classes, the simplest, fastest, and most robust approach is to replace the call:

```
factory = TransformerFactory.newInstance();
```

by:

```
factory = new net.sf.saxon.TransformerFactoryImpl();
```

❑   You can choose Saxon by setting the Java system property named `javax.xml.transform.TransformerFactory` to the value `net.sf.saxon.TransformerFactoryImpl`. Use the `-D` option on the Java command when you invoke your application. Note that this goes before the name of the class to be executed:

```
java -Djavax.xml.transform.TransformerFactory=
        net.sf.saxon.TransformerFactoryImpl com.my-com.appl.Program
```

This all goes on one line. In practice of course you won't want to type this more than once, so create a batch file or shell script using your text editor, and invoke this instead.

❑   Create a file called `jaxp.properties` within the directory `$JAVA_HOME/lib` (where `$JAVA_HOME` is the directory containing your Java installation), and include in this file a line of the form `key=value`, where `key` is the property key `javax.xml.transform .TransformerFactory` and `value` is the Saxon class `net.sf.saxon .TransformerFactoryImpl`.

❑   Put the call:

```
System.setProperty ("javax.xml.transform.TransformerFactory",
            "net.sf.saxon.TransformerFactoryImpl")
```

in your application, to be executed at runtime. This technique is useful if you want to run several different JAXP processors from the same application, perhaps in order to compare their results or to benchmark their performance.

❑   In Java 6 you can call:

```
TransformerFactory.newInstance("net.sf.saxon.TransformerFactoryImpl", null)
```

If you are still having trouble, try setting the Java system property `jaxp.debug` to «1». This gives diagnostic information about the loading process.

The `TransformerFactory` interface in JAXP has a method `setAttribute()`, which allows processor-dependent configuration options to be set. Saxon offers a large number of such options, corresponding to all the options on the command line and a few more. Details are in the Saxon Javadoc documentation at `http://www.saxonica.com/documentation/javadoc/index.html`. The names of the attributes and a description of their purpose can be found in the specification of the class `net.sf.saxon.FeatureKeys`.

As well as accepting the standard three kinds of `Source` object defined in JAXP, that is, `StreamSource`, `SAXSource`, and `DOMSource`, a Saxon transformation can also take other kinds of input. Saxon's tree model uses an interface `net.sf.saxon.om.NodeInfo` to represent a node, and because this interface extends the JAXP `Source` interface, any `NodeInfo` can be used as the source of a transformation. If you want to use a document as input to several transformations, you can build the tree once using the factory method `Configuration.buildDocument()`, and then supply the returned `NodeInfo` to the Transformer's `transform()` method. You can also construct a `NodeInfo` as a wrapper around a DOM, JDOM, DOM4J, or XOM document, and supply this wrapper to the transformer in the same way. As well as supplying the primary input to the transformation, all these techniques can be used to supply additional documents as the values of stylesheet parameters (just supply a `Source` as the argument to the Transformer's `setParameter()` method), or documents read using the `doc()` or `document()` functions (you can return any kind of `Source` from the user-supplied `URIResolver`).

The Schema Validation API

Saxon-SA supports the schema validation API defined in package `javax.xml.validation`. It provides an implementation of the `SchemaFactory` interface (`com.saxonica.jaxp.SchemaValidatorImpl`), which is currently in a separate package and JAR file for the benefit of JDK 1.4 users — this part of the JAXP API appears first in JDK 1.5. This allows you to load a schema, and to validate instance documents in either streaming (SAX) mode, or while building a DOM tree. Both these options are only really useful if you want to do freestanding validation.

Because the JAXP transformation API was designed for XSLT 1.0, it doesn't provide any direct way to request validation of the source document for a transformation, so Saxon provides its own mechanism. In fact, it provides several. One approach is to set a system-wide switch indicating that all source documents should be validated strictly or laxly. This can be done by calling `setAttribute(FeatureKeys.SCHEMA_VALIDATION, Validation.STRICT)` on the `TransformerFactory` object. If you want to control validation on a per-document basis, then you can create an `AugmentedSource` object with the appropriate options set. `AugmentedSource` is a JAXP Source object, so it can be used as input to a transformation, and as the name suggests it bundles together an underlying `Source` object with a number of parameters indicating how the source should be processed — one of these being an option to request schema validation.

Using XPath Expressions in Saxon

Another JAXP component introduced in JDK 1.5 is the interface for evaluating XPath expressions. Saxon implements this one too, allowing the source object to be either a native Saxon tree, or a DOM, JDOM, XOM, or DOM4J tree wrapped in a Saxon `NodeInfo` wrapper.

Unfortunately the JAXP XPath API suffers a number of weaknesses. It is designed for XPath 1.0 rather than 2.0, which means it cannot handle the full range of data types that XPath 2.0 supports. I would therefore be strongly inclined to recommend using Saxon's s9api interface instead, which is described in the next section. There is also a legacy API in package `net.sf.saxon.sxpath` which you can use if you need it to work on JDK 1.4. This is modeled on the JAXP API, but has many differences of detail.

The s9api Interface

Saxon's s9api interface for Java was newly introduced in Saxon 9.0, strongly influenced by the success of the API provided on the .NET platform. The design aims were:

❑ To provide a consistent approach to XSLT, XQuery, XPath, and XML Schema processing

❑ To avoid the clutter caused by conforming to a ragbag of legacy interfaces and by exposing implementation-level classes

❑ To provide a greater level of type safety, partly achieved by exploiting new Java 5 language features such as generics

The starting point for an application is to create an instance of `Processor` (all classes are in package `net.sf.saxon.s9api`). This provides a few system-wide configuration options, acts as an owner of shared resources, and provides factory methods for other functionality.

Whether you are running XSLT, XQuery, or XPath, you follow the same sequence of steps:

1. Create a compiler for the appropriate language, using one of the three factory methods `newXslt-Compiler()`, `newXQueryCompiler()`, and `newXPathCompiler()` defined on the `Processor` class.

2. Set properties on the compiler defining the static context for the compilation, and any other compile time options. For example, in the case of XPath this includes the base URI, the declared namespaces, and the external variables available to the XPath expression.

3. Call the `compile()` method on the compiler. This creates a corresponding executable (`Xslt Executable`, `XQueryExecutable`, or `XPathExecutable`) which represents the compiled program or expression as an object in (potentially shared) memory. The principle in each case is that you only compile the object once, and you can run it as often as you like in the same thread or in different threads.

4. Load the executable, by calling its `load()` method, which returns a runtime object called variously the `XsltTransformer`, `XQueryEvaluator`, or `XPathSelector`.

5. Configure the runtime object by setting options that affect a single evaluation (that is, the dynamic evaluation context). This typically includes the node to be used as the initial context node, the runtime values of variables/parameters, and serialization options.

6. Finally, run the transformation or query by calling one of the following methods:

   ❑ `transform()` for XSLT

   ❑ `evaluate()`, `iterator()`, or `run()` for XQuery

   ❑ `evaluate()`, `evaluateSingle()`, or `iterator()` for XPath

The `Processor` also allows you to obtain a `DocumentBuilder`, which is used for building source documents in tree form, and a `SchemaManager`, which can be used to load schema documents into a central pool of schema definitions, which are then shared by all operations running under the control of the same `Processor`.

The s9api package includes a set of classes for representing objects defined in the XDM data model, and reflecting the XDM type hierarchy:

- ❏ XdmValue (a sequence of items)
- ❏ XdmItem (a node or atomic value)
- ❏ XdmNode (a node)
- ❏ XdmAtomicValue (an atomic value)

and these classes provide methods for converting between the XDM objects and native Java objects.

The result of a query or XPath expression can be returned as an XdmValue; alternatively, the relevant runtime objects implement the Java Iterable<XdmItem> interface, so you can process the results like this:

```
XPathCompiler compiler = processor.newXPathCompiler();
XPathSelector selector = compiler.compile("//book[price > 20]").load();
XDMNode doc = processor.newDocumentBuilder().build(new StreamSource("in.xml"))
selector.setContextItem(doc);
for (XdmItem item : selector) {
    System.out.println("<li>" + item + "</li>");
}
```

The result of performing a transformation (or a validation) can be sent to any kind of Destination object. This is analogous to the JAXP Result object, except that it is possible to implement your own kinds of Destination. The system allows you to choose a number of possible destinations:

- ❏ To serialize the output, send it to a Serializer.
- ❏ To send it to a SAX ContentHandler, choose a SAXDestination.
- ❏ If you want the result tree as an XdmNode, choose an XdmDestination.
- ❏ If you want a DOM document node, use a DOMDestination.
- ❏ If you want to validate the output against a schema, send it to a SchemaValidator, which can be constructed from the SchemaManager.
- ❏ If you want to apply a further transformation, the XsltTransformer class is also an implementation of XdmDestination.

Using Saxon from a .NET Application

There is no equivalent to the JAXP interface on .NET, so Saxon provides its own APIs. (It could have attempted to emulate the APIs in the System.Xml.Xsl namespace, but as these are concrete classes rather than interfaces, it would still be difficult to write applications that work interchangeably with Saxon or with the native XSLT 1.0 processor in .NET.). Applications can of course be written in any .NET language, for example C# or VB.NET.

The API follows a three-stage Compile/Load/Go model. If you read the previous section describing s9api, then this will already be familiar, because s9api was modeled on the .NET interface. The steps are as follows:

1. Create a Processor object. This contains global Saxon configuration information.
2. Create an XsltCompiler object. This contains compile-time options for processing a stylesheet.

3.   Compile the stylesheet to create an XsltExecutable object. The XsltExecutable represents the compiled stylesheet, and can be used as often as you like, in multiple threads concurrently.

4.   Each time you want to run a transformation, load the stylesheet from the XsltExecutable to create an XsltTransformer. The XsltTransformer is generally used once only. You can set parameters that affect this transformation, and then call the Run() method to perform the transformation.

The source document is built by creating a DocumentBuilder and calling its Build() method: the input can come from a URI, a stream, an XmlNode, or an XmlReader. It is then supplied by setting the Initial ContextNode property of the XsltTransformer.

The result destination is supplied as an argument of the Run() method, and may be any XmlDestination object. One kind of destination is a Serializer; you can create a Serializer and initialize it with settings of the various output properties such as indent and encoding, which override any values supplied in the stylesheet. Alternatively, you can supply a TextWriterDestination which bridges to the .NET world by feeding the output to a .NET TextWriter, or you can supply an XdmDestination to get the result in the form of a Saxon tree, or a DomDestination to get it in the form of a System.Xml DOM node.

Here is an example showing a simple transformation (the full code is in ShowAccount.cs):

```csharp
public static void SimpleTransformation(String sourceUri, String xsltUri) {

    // Create a Processor instance
    Processor processor = new Processor();

    // Load the source document
    XdmNode input = processor.NewDocumentBuilder().Build(new Uri(sourceUri));

    // Create a transformer for the stylesheet
    XsltTransformer transformer =
        processor.NewXsltCompiler().Compile(new Uri(xsltUri)).Load();

    // Set the root node of the source document to be the initial context node
    transformer.InitialContextNode = input;

    // Set a parameter to the transformation
    transformer.SetParameter(new QName("", "", "greeting"),
                             new XdmAtomicValue("hello"));

    // Create a serializer
    Serializer serializer = new Serializer();
    serializer.SetOutputWriter(Console.Out);
    serializer.SetOutputProperty(Serializer.INDENT, "yes");

    // Transform the source XML to Console.Out
    transformer.Run(serializer);
}
```

The API also allows you to control schema validation of source documents, and to evaluate XPath and XQuery expressions. The APIs for XPath and XQuery use the same Compile/Load/Go metaphor, and the method names are chosen to be as consistent as possible.

Saxon Tree Models

Saxon defines an internal interface, the NodeInfo interface, to represent the XPath data model, and the product is capable of transforming any data source that supplies an implementation of this interface. There are several implementations of this interface available:

❑ The default is the Tiny Tree, which as the name implies, is optimized for space, but also turns out to be the fastest implementation under many circumstances.

❑ The Linked Tree is a more conventional tree, which is sometimes faster to navigate than the Tiny Tree but takes longer to build and occupies more space. Saxon uses this model internally for stylesheets and schemas.

❑ There is an implementation of NodeInfo that wraps a standard level-3 DOM.

❑ There are further implementations of NodeInfo that wrap a JDOM tree, a XOM tree, or a DOM4J tree.

If none of these is suitable, you can in principle write your own. For example, you could write an implementation of NodeInfo that fetches the underlying data from a relational database.

Although Saxon allows an input document to be supplied as a DOM, processing a DOM is much slower than processing Saxon's native tree implementations. Unless your input already exists in the form of a DOM, it's better to supply a StreamSource or SAXSource and let Saxon build the tree itself. If you want to build the tree yourself so that it can be used more than once, Saxon supplies a method Configuration.buildDocument(). The Configuration is a Saxon object that underpins the TransformerFactory, and if you are running any kind of complex workload, you will probably want to manipulate it explicitly rather than via JAXP interfaces.

In the .NET API, nodes are represented by the .NET class XdmNode. This is a simple wrapper around the Java NodeInfo object.

Extensibility

In this section, I will describe the facilities Saxon provides for user-written extension functions, and also the way that Saxon handles collations. Following this, I'll look at a few of the extension functions that come ready-supplied with the Saxon product.

For all these extensions, the namespace prefix «saxon» needs to be declared as «xmlns:saxon= "http://saxon.sf.net/"». Don't forget the trailing «/».

Try to avoid using extension functions that have side effects: Saxon (especially Saxon-SA) has an aggressive optimizer that will often rearrange expressions into a very different form from the way they were originally written, and this can make side effects very unpredictable. The most common trap is to call such a function in the `select` expression of `<xsl:variable>`. Such a function will usually not be called until the variable is first referenced, and if the variable is never referenced, the function will probably never be called at all.

Writing Extension Functions in Java

Saxon allows you to write extension functions in Java. The facilities can be extensively customized, but the simplest approach is to use a namespace URI in the function name that reflects the name of the Java class. For example:

```
<xsl:variable name="today"
              select="Date:new()"
              xmlns:Date="java:java.util.Date"/>
```

This returns an XPath value that is a wrapper for a Java object of class `java.util.Date`. Saxon maps Java classes into the XPath type hierarchy (as a new kind of atomic value), so you can declare the type of this value as:

```
<xsl:variable name="today"
              select="Date:new()"
              xmlns:Date="java:java.util.Date"
              as="class:java.util.Date"
              xmlns:class="http://saxon.sf.net/java-type"/>
```

Saxon looks for methods in the specified class that have the right name and the right number of arguments, and if there is more than one, it tries to find the one that is the best fit to the arguments supplied. For convenience, a hyphenated XPath name such as `get-random-number()` is mapped to the camelCased Java name `getRandomNumber()`.

The above example uses the function name `new()` to call a constructor on the specified class. It is also possible to call static methods in the same way, by using the actual method name. If you want to call an instance-level method (that is, a non-static method), you can do this by supplying the relevant object as an extra first argument, thus:

```
<xsl:value-of select="Date:toString($today)"/>
```

where `$today` was defined as in the previous example. Public fields in the instance can be accessed as if they were zero-argument methods.

If you have problems with Saxon being unable to locate the classes and methods you want to call, try the `-TJ` option on the command line, which gives you detailed diagnostics. Remember that Saxon will only look for classes that are on the classpath, and (a common pitfall) that the classpath is effectively empty if you invoke Java using the `-jar` option on the command line. Also remember that the class and method must both be public.

Writing Extension Functions under .NET

When you run Saxon under .NET, it is still possible to invoke external Java classes such as `java.util.Date`, provided they are in the standard system library. That's because Saxon itself relies on having the full

Java library available, cross-compiled into IL. (The version currently used is the GNU Classpath library, though this may move to OpenJDK in the future.)

Loading your own Java code dynamically is a bit more tricky, and the best way is probably to use IKVMC to compile it to a .NET assembly, in which case you can load it in the same way as .NET code written in any other language.

Saxon uses the same basic technique to load a .NET assembly as it uses for Java code: the namespace URI in the function call, which should be prefixed «clitype:», is used to identify the assembly and class to be invoked, and the local part of the function name identifies the method or property. Generally speaking, if the assembly has already been loaded by the application, then it's sufficient to supply the type name. For example, the following displays the name of the current user:

```
<xsl:value-of select="env:UserName()" xmlns:env="clitype:System.Environment"/>
```

If it's necessary to load the assembly dynamically, then more information is needed. This is supplied in the form of query parameters to the URI. To load a class Employee from the Payroll assembly held in the Global Assembly Cache with a particular version number and strong name, you might use a call such as:

```
<xsl:value-of select="emp:GetSalary($empnr)" xmlns:emp=
"clitype:Acme.Payroll.Employee?asm=payroll;version=5.0.0.1;sn=abcd0123cdef9876"/>
```

Collations

One of the new features in XSLT 2.0 and XPath 2.0 is that all comparison and sorting of strings can be controlled using collations. This is because the rules for sorting and comparison vary from one language (and one application) to another. Collations are identified using a URI; like namespace URIs, these are not expected to identify real resources on the Web, but simply act as globally unique identifiers.

The specifications say nothing about how collation URIs are established or what they mean, so each product has to devise its own naming scheme. This section explains how it's done in Saxon.

Both Java and .NET offer extensive support for defining collations, so the approach that Saxon adopts is to provide a parameterized URI that identifies the required properties of the collation, which are then used to obtain a collator object from the underlying platform to perform the string comparisons. The collation URI takes the general form:

```
http://saxon.sf.net/collation?keyword=value;keyword=value;...
```

The parameters you are most likely to use are lang, which defines the required language (for example, «lang=sv» selects Swedish), ignore-case (values «yes» and «no»), which defines whether the difference between upper case and lower case is significant, and ignore-modifiers (values «yes» and «no»), which defines whether accents should be ignored. Other options available include case-order (values «upper-first» and «lower-first»), which determines whether upper-case letters precede lower-case ones or vice versa, and alphanumeric (values «yes» and «no»), which if set causes any sequence of digits to be interpreted as a number, so for example «iso-10646» will sort after «iso-646».

Generally, if you are matching words in natural language text, you should ignore differences such as case and accents (a low-strength collation), while for sorting, a high-strength collation is appropriate: This will ensure that words that differ only in their accents are sorted in the correct way, even though they might compare as equal in a search.

For other parameters that you can include in a Saxon collation URI, see the product documentation. If you want the ultimate in control, the collation URI can identify a user-written implementation of the «java.lang.Comparator» interface.

Because collation URIs are unlikely to be portable across implementations, it's a good idea to define them as stylesheet parameters. For example, you can define a stylesheet parameter:

```
<xsl:param name="sorting-collation"
  select="'http://saxon.sf.net/collation?lang=de;ignore-modifiers=yes'"/>
```

and then use this in a sort, by specifying:

```
<xsl:sort select="value" collation="{$sorting-collation}"/>
```

You could also define the collation using a conditional expression, using the system-property() function to determine which vendor's XSLT processor is currently in use.

The «[xsl]:default-collation» attribute, which applies to everything in its scope except <xsl:sort> elements, can specify a list of collation URIs, and a processor will use the first one that it recognizes. You can specify http://www.w3.org/2005/xpath-functions/collation/codepoint as the last item in the list to provide a fallback that every processor is obliged to recognize.

Extensions

The XSLT specification provides a number of mechanisms allowing extensions to be implemented in a vendor namespace, and Saxon has exploited these to the full. As well as providing extensibility mechanisms allowing you to extend the capabilities of the product, Saxon includes quite a few built-in extensions. These fall into a number of categories, described in the following sections.

Serialization Extensions

Saxon provides a number of extra serialization properties, with names in the Saxon namespace, that you can use on the <xsl:output> declaration and the <xsl:result-document> instruction. The two most common options are shown below.

Property	Value and Meaning
saxon:indent-spaces	An integer, determines the level of indentation when «indent="yes"».
saxon:character-representation	Indicates how non-ASCII characters should be represented. For «method="xml"», this only affects characters outside the chosen encoding, and the values are «hex» and «decimal». For HTML, two values are allowed; for example, «entity;hex», which indicates that non-ASCII characters within the encoding should use named entities if possible; those outside the encoding should use hex character references.

Extension Attributes

Extension attributes are attributes in the Saxon namespace that can be added to XSLT instructions. Processors other than Saxon will ignore these attributes. The table below gives examples.

Attribute	Value and Meaning
saxon:memo-function	When «saxon:memo-function="yes"» is present on an <xsl:function> element, Saxon remembers the result of evaluating the function, and uses the saved result if the function is called again with the same arguments.
saxon:explain	When «saxon:explain="yes"» is present on an <xsl:template> or <xsl:function> element, Saxon outputs an XML representation of the compiled code showing what optimizations it has applied. (The same output is available for the entire stylesheet using the -explain option on the command line.)
saxon:read-once	This option is used to signal to Saxon that a document read using the document() function will only be used once; this acts as a hint that streamed execution can be used, avoiding the need to build the tree representation of the document in memory.

Extension Instructions

Extension instructions are elements in the Saxon namespace that perform a similar role to XSLT instructions. If you use any of these instructions, your stylesheet must contain the attribute «extension-element-prefixes="saxon"». You can use <xsl:fallback> elements to indicate how processors other than Saxon should behave when these instructions are encountered. Examples of extension instructions are:

Instruction	Meaning
saxon:assign	Modifies the value of a variable. Not recommended, as the effect can be very unpredictable.
saxon:call-template	Same as <xsl:call-template> except that the template name can be computed at runtime.
saxon:doctype	Constructs a DTD to include in the output document.
saxon:entity-ref	Creates an entity reference in the serialized output.

Saxon also provides a set of extension instructions sql:connect, sql:query, sql:insert, sql:delete, and sql:update, allowing data to be read from and written to relational databases. These are in the namespace «/net.sf.saxon.sql.SQLElementFactory» and are described at http://www.saxonica.com/documentation/sql-extension/intro.html.

Extension Functions

The largest category of extensions are additional functions provided in the Saxon namespace. Chapter 16 contains advice on how to call extension functions without sacrificing portability of your stylesheet.

Examples of these functions are shown in the table below, grouped according to their intended purpose. Some of them are available only in Saxon-SA.

Functions	Purpose
saxon:parse() saxon:serialize() saxon:compile-stylesheet() saxon:transform()	Allow parsing, serialization, and transformation of documents to be controlled from within a stylesheet. Useful when input or output documents contain nested documents within CDATA sections.
saxon:analyze-string() saxon:for-each-group() saxon:format-date() saxon:format-number() saxon:generate-id() saxon:index() saxon:find() saxon:namespace-node() etc.	Provide equivalents of XSLT capabilities for the benefit of XQuery users.
saxon:base64Binary-to-octets() saxon:base64Binary-to-string() saxon:hexBinary-to-octets() saxon:hexBinary-to-string()	Allow manipulation of base64 binary values (found for example in LDAP directories) and hexBinary values.
saxon:path() saxon:line-number() saxon:system-id() saxon:type-annotation()	Provide information about the current node in the source document, for use in diagnostics.
saxon:try()	Allows dynamic errors to be caught.
saxon:eval() saxon:evaluate() saxon:evaluate-node() saxon:expression()	Allow evaluation of XPath expressions constructed dynamically from strings or read from a source document. See next section for a use case.

The evaluate() Extension

Many of the new facilities included in XSLT 2.0, including multiple output files, grouping facilities, and stylesheet functions, were first pioneered as Saxon extensions. Saxon also copied extensions that were first introduced elsewhere: the ubiquitous node-set() extension function, for example, appeared first in James Clark's xt processor, as did extensions to find the intersection or difference between two node-sets. Saxon went further than most XSLT processors in providing a wide range of extensions built in to the product. However, most of these have been superseded by standard features in XSLT 2.0.

The most important extension that remains, which has sadly not made it into XSLT 2.0 even though it has been copied by several other processors, is the ability to evaluate a dynamically constructed XPath expression. This extension has been adopted, in restricted form, as the dyn:evaluate() function within EXSLT (see www.exslt.org). Here I will describe the Saxon implementation of this functionality.

In standard XSLT (even in 2.0), there is no way of constructing an XPath expression at runtime from a string. This makes it difficult to do things that are very familiar to SQL programmers; for example, building a query from the values of parameters read from a form, or sorting a table on a column selected by the user. It also makes it impossible to interpret XPath expressions held as part of the text of the source document, perhaps implementing a subset of the XPointer specification for defining links between documents. The Saxon stored expression concept fills this gap: you can use the `saxon:expression()` extension function to create a stored expression from a string, and `saxon:eval()` to evaluate the stored expression; or you can combine these two operations into one using the `saxon:evaluate()` function.

The table below describes these functions in more detail.

Function	Explanation
expression (string)	This function constructs a stored expression from the XPath expression contained in the supplied string. The stored expression can be evaluated later using the `saxon:eval()` function.
	If the XPath expression contains namespace prefixes, these are resolved at the time the stored expression is created, not at the time it is subsequently evaluated. They are always resolved relative to namespaces declared in the stylesheet.
	The expression may contain references to the variables $p1 to $p9. The values of these variables are supplied when the expression is subsequently evaluated.
eval(expression, variables...)	This function evaluates a stored expression supplied in the first argument. The stored expression is constructed using the `saxon:expression()` function. The second and subsequent arguments (which are optional) provide values that will be bound to the variables $p1..$p9 used within the stored expression.
	The context node, position, and size for evaluating the expression are those that apply to the stylesheet at the point where `eval()` is called.
evaluate(string, variables...)	This function combines the effect of `saxon:expression()` and `saxon:eval()` into a single call: That is, it prepares the expression and immediately evaluates it.
evaluate-node(node)	This function can be used when reading an XPath expression stored in a source XML document. It is similar to `saxon:evaluate()`, except that namespace bindings are taken from the node where the expression is written, rather than from the stylesheet; this node is also used as the context node. This version does not allow reference to parameters.

Allowing XPath queries to be constructed dynamically gives a number of benefits:

❑ You can construct a query such as «//book[author="Kay" and publisher="Wrox"]», from the values of stylesheet parameters supplied at runtime.

❑ You can easily change the sort order used in an `<xsl:sort>` element based on parameters supplied at runtime.

❑ You can allow XPath expressions to be used within the source document, for example to define hyperlinks between documents, and you can write code in your stylesheet to follow these links.

❏   You can implement higher-order functions in which an expression is passed as a parameter to a function.

❏   You can use XPath expressions to define business rules in a separate document.

The following example demonstrates the last of these techniques.

Example: Using saxon:evaluate( ) to Apply Business Rules

In this example, we imagine a call center that is charging customers for the calls they make. We want to prepare the account for a period, listing all the calls and calculating the total charge.

Source

The list of calls is in the file `calls.xml`, as follows:

```
<calls>
<call date="2001-01-15" time="08.15" duration="17"/>
<call date="2001-01-16" time="10.42" duration="8"/>
<call date="2001-01-18" time="17.42" duration="5"/>
<call date="2001-01-18" time="22.10" duration="06"/>
<call date="2001-01-24" time="12.19" duration="41"/>
<call date="2001-01-25" time="06.40" duration="13"/>
<call date="2001-01-27" time="11.15" duration="26"/>
</calls>
```

We want to put the business rules for calculating the charges in a separate document. Of course, these rules could go in the stylesheet, but this isn't very good practice; mixing business rules and presentation rules in one place doesn't give the right separation of responsibilities. Instead, we'll put the relevant formula in a separate document `tariff.xml`, in the form of an XPath expression. This calculates the total charge, with different rates per minute during the working day and outside office hours:

```
<tariff>
    sum(call[@time &gt;= 08.00 and @time &lt; 18.00]/@duration) * 1.50 +
    sum(call[@time &lt; 08.00 or @time &gt;= 18.00]/@duration) * 2.50
</tariff>
```

Stylesheet

Most of the stylesheet (`account.xsl`) is conventional, and is concerned with displaying the information. When it comes to calculating the total charges, however, the stylesheet reads the XPath expression containing the relevant formula from the `tariff.xml` document and evaluates it (using `saxon:evaluate()`) in the context of the source document.

F

Saxon

```
<?xml version="1.0"?>
<xsl:stylesheet xmlns:xsl="http://www.w3.org/1999/XSL/Transform"
                xmlns:saxon="http://saxon.sf.net/"
                version="1.0">

<xsl:template match="/">
  <html>
    <head>
      <title>Account for period ending
             <xsl:value-of select="(//@date)[last()]"/></title>
    </head>
    <body>
      <h1>Account for period ending
             <xsl:value-of select="(//@date)[last()]"/></h1>
      <xsl:apply-templates/>
    </body>
  </html>
</xsl:template>

<xsl:template match="calls">
  <table>
    <tr>
      <th width="100">Date</th>
      <th width="100">Time</th>
      <th width="100">Duration</th>
    </tr>
    <xsl:apply-templates/>
  </table>
  <xsl:variable name="total"
                select="saxon:evaluate(document('tariff.xml'))"/>
  <p>Total charges for the period:
      <xsl:value-of select="format-number($total, '$###0.00')"/>
  </p>
</xsl:template>

<xsl:template match="call">
  <tr>
    <td><xsl:value-of select="@date"/></td>
    <td><xsl:value-of select="@time"/></td>
    <td><xsl:value-of select="@duration"/></td>
  </tr>
</xsl:template>

</xsl:stylesheet>
```

An observation on this stylesheet: This was first written to work with XSLT 1.0. In principle, it could be rewritten to use the facilities for arithmetic on dates, times, and durations provided in XSLT 2.0. However, little would be gained by doing so. Converting the application to use these facilities would require times to be written as «xs:time('08:00:00')» rather than as «08.00», which would also create a dependency on the declaration of the namespace prefix «xs». Also, multiplying a duration by a number in XPath 2.0 returns a duration, not a cost. Just because the facilities are provided doesn't mean that you have to use them, and in this case, it seems simpler not to.

To run this stylesheet, make the directory containing the downloaded files for this chapter the current directory, and enter:

```
java -jar c:\saxon\saxon9.jar -s:calls.xml -xsl:account.xsl -o:bill.html
```

Output

The output of this stylesheet (bill.html) appears in the browser as shown in Figure F-1.

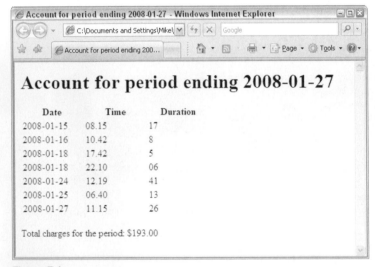

Figure F-1

Summary

This appendix describes how to install and use the Saxon product, and how to invoke it from a Java or .NET application. It also describes some of the facilities provided by Saxon that go beyond the XSLT 2.0 specification itself.

Altova

Altova is the company that produces the popular XMLSpy toolkit. Among its many capabilities this includes an XSLT 2.0 processor, which can be used either as part of XMLSpy or on its own from the command line or via one of a number of application programming interfaces. XMLSpy is commercial software that can be purchased from www.altova.com.

Altova's XSLT 2.0 processor is available as a free (but not open source) download from the same site — it is part of a package called AltovaXML that also includes an XML validating parser, an XML Schema processor, an XQuery engine, and an XSLT 1.0 processor. The XQuery and XSLT 2.0 processors are both schema-aware. Although the product is internally a COM component, APIs are offered for COM, Java, and .NET.

As well as the XSLT 2.0 processor itself, XMLSpy also includes an interactive XSLT debugger and a profiler for performance analysis.

Both products run on Windows only. The version described in this chapter is the 2008 edition.

Running from within XMLSpy

An example showing how to run a simple "Hello World" stylesheet from within XMLSpy was given in Chapter 1 (see page 11).

Remember that XMLSpy includes both an XSLT 1.0 and an XSLT 2.0 processor, and the one it uses depends on the «version» attribute in your <xsl:stylesheet> element. If you are writing an XSLT 2.0 stylesheet and you get error messages referring to unrecognized functions or instructions, check that you haven't inadvertently specified «version="1.0"».

When you click F10 (or the relevant icon or menu item) to fire off a transformation, the only thing you are asked for is the filename of the source document to be transformed. If you want to supply parameters to the transformation, there is a separate dialog box for this: select the menu item XSL/XQuery, then XSL Parameters/XQuery Variables. The value of the parameter is interpreted as an XPath expression, so if you want to supply a simple string, then it has to be in quotes.

There's no option to start the transformation without a source document, with a named template, or in a named mode; in fact, there are no other options at all. This also applies when the processor is launched from the command line or using the API. Instead, use the XSLT 1.0 technique of adding «match="/"» to the entry template (remember that a template can have both a `match` attribute and a `name` attribute), and supply a dummy input document.

Using Tools ⇨ Options ⇨ XSL, you can configure XMLSpy to use a different transformation engine. You can either select MSXML (versions 3, 4, or 6), or you can connect to an external processor (for example, Saxon) by giving a template for its command line interface. This can be useful if you want to check that your stylesheets work with more than one processor, or if you want a second opinion when you get an error message that you don't understand. This feature also caters to people who want to use XMLSpy to develop stylesheets and then to use a different engine for live deployment.

Conformance

You may find suggestions on the web that the Altova processor is less than fully conformant with the W3C Recommendations. However, the level of conformance has been steadily improving with each successive release, and the 2008 release has very few restrictions that are likely to affect the typical user. Most of the gaps that were present in the 2007 version have been plugged, for example `format-date()` is now fully supported, and `upper-case()` and `lower-case()` now work with the full Unicode character set. We've tested most of the examples in this book against both Saxon and Altova, and where we found a problem, we've pointed it out.

Altova supports all of the optional features of the XSLT 2.0 specification, including schema awareness, serialization, the namespace axis, `disable-output-escaping`, and backward compatibility. (Backward compatibility is not normally invoked when running inside XMLSpy, because XMLSpy chooses an XSLT 1.0 processor when you specify «version="1.0"». However, you can force the issue by importing an XSLT 1.0 stylesheet module into an XSLT 2.0 module, and it handles this correctly.)

One remaining area where Altova warns you about significant differences in behavior is in the area of whitespace handling. Like the Microsoft MSXML parser, the Altova XML parser strips whitespace text nodes from the source document before XSLT processing starts; unlike the Microsoft parser, there doesn't appear to be anything you can do to prevent this.

There are two problems this can cause:

- ❏ In the first case, you aren't actually interested in the boundary whitespace, so it doesn't matter that it has been removed, except that your stylesheet was written on the assumption that it was there, so it stops working. The best answer here is to add the declaration `<xsl:strip-space elements="*"/>` so that every processor strips the unwanted whitespace, and then make any necessary changes to your code. In many cases the only impact will be that the inter-element whitespace is no longer copied to the output, making the output less legible. You can fix this by adding `<xsl:output indent="yes"/>`.

- ❏ In other cases, the whitespace might really be meaningful. This happens most often with mixed content, that is, with narrative documents. If your document contains two adjacent bold words with a space between them, like this:

  ```
  <p>It was a <b>long</b> <b>hard</b> winter</p>
  ```

  then you don't want the space to disappear. Altova's only suggestion for dealing with this problem is to modify the source document, by moving the space character inside one of the two adjacent elements. (If you want to do this with XSLT, of course, you will need to use a processor that doesn't strip whitespace....)

Extensions and Extensibility

As far as I have been able to determine, Altova includes no built-in extensions in its product, that is, no extra functions or top-level declarations in a vendor-defined namespace.

There also appear to be no facilities for creating user-defined extensions, that is, callouts to code written in languages such as Java and JavaScript.

The `doc()` and `document()` functions generally work as you would expect. Like many Microsoft products (but unlike Saxon), they generally interpret "URI" in the specifications to mean "URI or Windows filename", so strings like «c:\temp\data.xml» are accepted in places where a URI is expected. There's no ability to work with a user-supplied URI resolver or catalog to redirect URI references to local copies (if you need this, consider using the `collection()` function instead — see below).

If a schema can be found for the document, then the document is validated against it, but if no schema can be found, or if the document is not valid against the schema, then the call succeeds anyway and returns an untyped document. However, if no document can be found, or if the document is not well formed, then a fatal error is reported. As far as I can tell, the only reliable way of ensuring that a schema is found when validating input documents is to include a reference to the schema within the document itself, using an «xsi:schemaLocation» or «xsi:noNamespaceSchemaLocation» attribute. Importing a schema into the stylesheet isn't enough. The same rules appear to apply to the principal input document to the transformation. (You might note the tentative prose in this paragraph — this area of the product is not well documented, and I had to do quite a few experiments to work out what it was doing.)

This means that if you want to force the input to be valid, you can use the instruction:

```
<xsl:copy-of select="/" validation="strict"/>
```

In this case, it seems that the schema must be imported into the stylesheet; identifying it within an «xsi:schemaLocation» attribute in the document that you are validating doesn't work.

The `collection()` function in the 2008 release has been enhanced to provide facilities similar to the two ways of defining a collection in Saxon. The collection URI can either identify an XML file used as a catalog to contain a list of the files in the collection, or you can specify a filename with wildcards; for example, «collection('c:/data/*.xml')» to process all the XML files in a directory. The default collection (the one you get when you call `collection()` with no arguments) is always empty.

AltovaXML only supports a single collating sequence, namely Unicode codepoint collation.

The Command Line Interface

The command line interface to AltovaXML is very uncluttered.

The product installs by default into the directory c:\Program Files\Altova\Altova\AltovaXML2008. It doesn't add this directory to the PATH environment variable, so I will assume you have either done this by hand, or that you have made it your current directory. The command to transform a document is then:

```
AltovaXML -xslt2 style.xsl -in source.xml [-out output.html] [options]
```

Apart from one option, `-xslstack`, which is used to control the amount of space allocated to variables on the stack, the options are used to provide parameters to the transformation (values for `<xsl:param>` declarations). The format is:

```
-param name=expression
```

where the `-param` keyword is repeated before each parameter. The value of the parameter is given in the form of an XPath expression, so for a boolean parameter you might write «`-param debug=true()`». Unfortunately, this means you need to understand the way that the command line interpreter handles spaces and quotes. To supply a string value for a parameter, write it between single quotes; for example, «`-param city='Paris'`». These quotes are the XPath quotes that surround a string literal. If the value contains a space, surround it with double quotes, for example «`-param value="2 + 2"`». These are directed at the command line interpreter. To supply a string value that contains a space, you need both sets of quotes, thus: «`-param city=" 'Los Angeles' "`».

Using the API

AltovaXML offers three APIs, for COM, Java, and .NET applications. The underlying implementation is a COM object, and the Java and .NET interfaces are simply thin wrappers over the COM interface. The server is automatically registered as a COM object during product installation, but you can also register it (or unregister it) manually if you need to. See the reference manual for details. A single server supports concurrent clients, whether they are doing XML validation, XSLT processing, or XQuery processing.

The APIs are thoroughly documented in the reference manual that comes with the product. They are fairly straightforward. Generally, they take raw XML as input and produce raw XML as output; they don't interface with other XML-related components such as the Microsoft or Java DOM. There is no attempt to conform to externally defined API specifications such as JAXP in the Java world.

The COM API

A COM application starts by invoking:

```
Set altova = CreateObject("AltovaXML.Application")
```

This object contains four subsidiary objects available via its properties: their names are `XMLValidator`, `XSLT1`, `XSLT2`, and `XQuery`. Let's look briefly at the `XMLValidator` and `XSLT2` objects.

XMLValidator

The `XMLValidator` is used to test whether an XML document is well formed, and whether it is valid against a schema and/or DTD.

The source document can be loaded either by specifying a filename (or URI) or by supplying the XML content as a string, as shown in the following two examples:

```
Set altova = CreateObject("Altova.Application");
altova.XMLValidator.InputXMLFileName = "c:\data\books.xml"
altova.XMLValidator.InputXmlFromText = "<foo><bar/></foo>"
```

There are analogous properties to supply a DTD or a schema document either as a filename or as a string: `DTDFileName`, `DTDFromText`, `SchemaFileName`, `SchemaFromText`.

You can then test whether the document is well formed by using the `IsWellFormed` property, you can check it against a DTD or schema referenced from within the instance by using the `IsValid` property, and you can check it against an externally-supplied DTD or schema by using the property `IsValidWith-ExternalSchemaOrDTD`. I wasn't able to find in the documentation any way to return the document after validation (that is, with defaults expanded and with type annotations). There is a property, `Last-ErrorMessage`, which provides a rudimentary way of returning error information to the application.

XSLT2

The XSLT2 object similarly has properties to load the source document and stylesheet either by giving a filename (or URI) or by supplying the content as a string. These properties are `InputXMLFileName`, `InputXMLFromText`, `XSLFileName`, and `XSLFromText`.

You can specify the values of stylesheet parameters by calling the method `AddExternalParameter`. The value is supplied in the form of an XPath expression, which is evaluated with the input document as the context node. This means that if you want to supply a string as the value, you need to put it in quotes.

There are two methods provided to run the transformation: `Execute`, which runs the stylesheet and serializes the result to a specified output file, and `ExecuteAndGetResultAsString`, which returns the serialized result as a string.

Putting this together, you can run a transformation like this:

```
Set altova = CreateObject("Altova.Application");
altova.XSLT2.InputXMLFileName = "c:\data\books.xml"
altova.XSLT2.XSLFileName = "c:\data\books.xsl"
altova.XSLT2.AddExternalParameter "date" "current-date()"
altova.XSLT2.Execute "c:\data\output.html"
```

The Java API

The Java API is provided as a thin layer above the underlying COM engine. It makes no attempt to implement JAXP interfaces or to integrate with any other XML components in the Java environment: if you want to mix Altova processing with other components, the only way to interface them is via lexical XML (that is, XML stored as a file or as a string).

First step is:

```
IAltovaXMLFactory factory = AltovaXMLFactory.getInstance():
```

Following which you can get a validator or an XSLT 2.0 processor as follows:

```
XMLValidator validator = (XMLValidator)factory.getXMLValidatorInstance();
XSLT2 transformer = (XSLT2)factory.getXSLT2Instance();
```

The source document, schema, and stylesheet are supplied to these objects using methods that map directly onto the COM properties described earlier: `setInputXMLFileName()`, `setInputXMLFromText()`, `setSchemaFileName()`, `setSchemaFromText()`, `setXSLTFileName()`, `setXSLTFromText()`.

The schema validator supports the methods that map directly to the underlying COM object: `isWell-Formed()`, `isValid()`, `isValidWithExternalSchemaOrDTD()`, and `getLastErrorMessage()`.

Similarly the XSLT2 processor supports methods `addExternalParameter()`, `execute()`, `executeAnd-GetResultAsString()`, and `getLastErrorMessage()`.

G

Altova

1219

One thing that requires a little care is the need to explicitly disconnect from the COM server when a task is finished. For this purpose, both the XMLValidator and the XSLT2 object provide a method release-Instance(). Unless you call this, the COM server will be left running. You can quickly find yourself with multiple instances of this process tying up all your memory.

The .NET API

If the Java API is a thin layer over the COM interface, the .NET API is waif-like. In fact, when you get beyond the top-level marketing statements, there isn't really a separate API at all; the way you call Altova from a .NET application is the same way that you invoke any other COM object, by making direct use of the .NET capabilities to call COM interfaces. Which, to be fair, is all that you need.

If you're not familiar with how to import a COM object into a .NET application built using Visual Studio, the Altova documentation gives a helpful summary of the steps you need to take.

Summary

I've tried hard in this short appendix to stick to factual information about Altova's product; it's tempting at the end of the chapter to give a personal assessment, but it would inevitably be biased and I will resist the temptation. Try it out, and make your own judgment. Don't make the mistake, however, of judging it solely from what people have said publicly about earlier releases: as I have stated, the level of conformance to the W3C specifications has improved with each release and in the 2008 version looks quite solid.

At the time of writing, Altova, Gestalt, and Saxon are the only finished XSLT 2.0 processors on the market, so there's no harm in trying all three and seeing how they compare against your particular requirements. They are very different products.

Glossary

This glossary gathers together some of the more common technical terms used in this book. Most of these terms are defined in the XSLT or XPath specifications, but some of them are borrowed from XML or other standards in the XML family, and one or two have been invented for the purposes of this book. So for each definition, I also tell you where the term comes from.

The definitions in all cases are my own; in some cases, the original specifications have a much more formal definition, but in other cases they are surprisingly vague.

Where a definition contains references to other terms defined in the glossary, these terms are written in italics.

Ancestor Axis (*XPath*)   The ancestor *axis* selects the *parent* of the *context node*, its *parent*, and so on, up to and including the *root node*. This *axis* is a *reverse axis*.

Ancestor-or-Self Axis (*XPath*)   The ancestor-or-self *axis* selects the *context node* followed by all the nodes on the *ancestor axis*. This *axis* is a *reverse axis*.

Arity (*XPath*)   The arity of a *function* is the number of *parameters* defined in the function signature; for example, the arity of the function true() is zero, while the two versions of the contains() function have arity two and three, respectively.

Atomic Value (*XPath*)   An atomic value is an *item* such as an integer, a *string*, a date, or a *boolean*. Specifically, it is an instance of the class xs:anyAtomicType, which includes all *simple types* (as defined in XML Schema) that are not *list types* or *union types*.

Atomization (*XPath*)   Atomization is a process that takes an arbitrary *sequence*, containing a mixture of *nodes* and *atomic values*, and creates a new *sequence* in which each of the nodes is replaced by its *typed value*. *Atomic values* appearing in the input sequence are retained in the result sequence unchanged.

Attribute (*XML*)   A name = value pair appearing in an *element*'s start *tag*; for example, «category="grocery"».

Attribute Axis (*XPath*)   The attribute *axis* selects all the *attributes* of the *context node*. If the *context node* is not an *element*, the *axis* will be empty.

Attribute Declaration (*Schema*)   An attribute declaration is a *schema component* corresponding to an <xs:attribute> element in a *schema document*: it defines constraints on the values of *attributes* having a particular name. It may be a global attribute declaration (if it is defined at the top level of a schema) or a local attribute declaration (if defined within the structure of a *complex type*).

Attribute Node (*XPath*)   A *node* in a tree that represents an *attribute* in an XML *document*. There will be an attribute node attached to an *element node* for each *attribute* defined in the start *tag* of the corresponding *element* in the original XML *document*, other than an attribute acting as a *namespace declaration*. There will also be attribute nodes for attributes given a default value in the *document type definition* or *schema*. The *string value* of the *node* is the value of the attribute; its *typed value* is the result of *validating* the string value against the relevant *type definition* in a *schema*.

Attribute Set (*XSLT*) A named collection of `<xsl:attribute>` *instructions*, which when invoked using the `use-attribute-sets` attribute of `<xsl:element>` or `<xsl:copy>`, or the `xsl:use-attribute-sets` attribute of a *literal result element*, generates a set of *attribute nodes* to be added to the result sequence.

Attribute Value Template (*XSLT*) An attribute value template is an *attribute* in the *stylesheet* that can contain both fixed and variable parts. The fixed parts are written as ordinary characters, while the variable parts are written between curly braces; for example, «`file="{$dir}/{$fname}.html"`» would evaluate to «`file="out/page.html"`» if the variables `$dir` and `$fname` have the values «`out`» and «`page`», respectively. Attribute value templates can be used for any attribute of a *literal result element*, but on XSLT elements they can be used only for those attributes that explicitly allow them.

Axis (*XPath*) An axis is a direction of travel through the *tree*. Starting from a particular *context node*, an axis defines a list of *nodes* reached from that origin. For example, the *ancestor axis* returns the parent, grandparent, and so on up to the root of the tree, while the *following sibling* axis returns all the *nodes* that appear after the *context node* and share the same parent.

Base URI (*XPath*) Every *node* has an associated base URI. For an element, this is the absolute URI of the XML external *entity* containing the element's start and end *tags* (most often, of course, this will be the document entity). For other node types, it is defined by reference to an associated *element node*, typically its parent. The base URI of an element can also be set explicitly by using the `xml:base` attribute. The base URI of a node is used when expanding a relative URI defined in that node; for example, a relative URI in an `href` attribute is considered to be relative to the base URI of the parent element.

Every XPath expression also has a base URI defined as part of its *static context*. For an XPath expression contained in a *stylesheet*, this is the base URI of the stylesheet element containing the XPath expression. In non-XSLT contexts, it's up to the host environment to specify a base URI for the expression.

Boolean (*XPath*) One of the allowed data *types* for the value of an XPath expression. It takes the value true or false.

Built-In Template Rule (*XSLT*) A *template rule* that is not explicitly defined in the *stylesheet*, but that is implicitly available to process a *node* if there is no explicit template rule that matches it.

Built-In Type (*Schema*) The XML Schema specification defines a number of built-in *simple types* that are available for use, without any need to declare them in a schema. These include 19 *primitive types* (such as `xs:string` and `xs:date`), 20 built-in derived atomic types (including `xs:integer` and `xs:ID`), and 3 built-in *list types* (`xs:NMTOKENS`, `xs:IDREFS`, and `xs:ENTITIES`).

Cast (*XPath*) An *expression* that converts an *atomic value* of one *type* to an atomic value of a different type.

CDATA Section (*XML*) A sequence of characters in an XML document enclosed between the delimiters «`![CDATA[`» and «`]]`»; within a CDATA section all characters represent text content rather than markup, except for the sequence «`]]`».

Character Map (*XSLT*) A rule for translating characters in a *result tree* into different characters (or strings) in the serialized output.

Character Reference (*XML*) A representation of a character using its decimal or hexadecimal Unicode value; for example, «`&#10;`» or «`&#x21A4;`». Normally used for characters that are difficult or impossible to enter directly at the keyboard. Character references appear in lexical XML documents, but in the *XDM* data model, they are replaced by the characters that they represent.

Child Axis (*XPath*) The child axis selects all the immediate children of the *context node*. These can include *elements*, *text nodes*, *comments*, and *processing instructions*, but not *attributes* or *namespace nodes*. This is a *forwards axis*.

Codepoint (*Unicode*) A numeric value identifying a Unicode character.

Codepoint Collation (*XPath*) A *collation* that compares and sorts strings strictly according to the numeric values of the *codepoints* making up the characters of the string.

Collation (*XPath*) A set of rules for comparing strings. A collation can be used to decide whether two strings are equal, to decide how they should be ordered, and to decide whether one string is a substring of another. Different collations are needed to satisfy the needs of different languages or different applications. In XPath and XSLT a collation is identified by a *URI*. Except for the *codepoint collation*, the URIs used to identify collations are defined by the implementation.

Comment (*XML*) Markup in an XML document that is conventionally used to carry extraneous information that is not part of the document proper. Written between the delimiters «`<!--`» and «`-->`».

Comment Node (*XPath*) A *node* in a *tree* representing an XML *comment*. The *string value* of the node is the text of the comment.

Complex Type (*Schema*) A *schema type* that describes the structure of *elements* that may have *child* elements or *attributes*. If the type permits attributes but not child elements, it is referred to as a complex type with simple content.

Constructor Function (*XPath*) A *function* that constructs an *atomic value* of a particular *type*. The function has the same name as the target *atomic type*, and always takes a single argument. A constructor function is created automatically for every *atomic type*, including user-defined atomic types. An example of a call on a constructor function is «xs:date("2008-02-29")». The semantics of constructor functions are defined by reference to the rules for *cast* expressions.

Context Item (*XPath*) The *item* currently being processed; part of the *dynamic context*. Certain XSLT instructions and XPath expressions place a new context item on the stack, and revert to the previous context item when the instruction or expression has been evaluated. The XSLT instructions <xsl:apply-templates> and <xsl:for-each> change the context item, as do the XPath expressions «E1/E2» and «E1[E2]». The context item can be retrieved using the expression «.».

Context Node (*XPath*) If the *context item* is a *node*, then the context node is the same thing as the context item. If the context item is not a node, then the context node is undefined.

Context Position (*XPath*) When a *sequence* of *items* is processed in an *expression* of the form «E1/E2» or «E1[E2]», or by an <xsl:for-each> or <xsl:apply-templates> *instruction* in XSLT, each item in the sequence in turn becomes the *context item*, and the context position identifies the position of the context item in the sequence being processed. The context position determines the value of the position() function, and is also used in evaluating a numeric *predicate* such as «[1]».

Context Size (*XPath*) When a *sequence* of *items* is processed in an *expression* of the form «E1/E2» or «E1[E2]», or by an <xsl:for-each> or <xsl:apply-templates> *instruction* in XSLT, each item in the sequence in turn becomes the *context item*, and the context size identifies the number of items in the sequence being processed. The context size determines the value of the last() function.

Current Mode (*XSLT*) When a *template rule* is invoked, the *mode* used in the <xsl:apply-templates> *instruction* that invoked it is called the current mode. A further call of <xsl:apply-templates> within this *template rule* can specify «mode="#current"» to continue processing in the current mode.

Current Template Rule (*XSLT*) When <xsl:apply-templates> selects a *template rule* to process a particular *node*, that template rule becomes the current template rule. It remains the current template rule through calls of <xsl:call-template>, but not through calls of <xsl:for-each>. The current template rule is used only in deciding which template rule to invoke when <xsl:apply-imports> is called.

Data Model (*XPath*) The *XDM* data model is a description of the kinds of objects that can be manipulated by XPath *expressions*, and their properties and relationships. Examples of such objects are *sequences*, *items*, *atomic values*, *nodes*, and *trees*. (Sometimes the term *data model* is used loosely to refer to a specific object, such as the tree representation of a particular document).

Declaration (*XSLT*) A declaration is a top-level *element* in a *stylesheet module* (that is, a *child* element of the <xsl:stylesheet> element), other than a user-defined data element, which is ignored by the XSLT processor.

Default Namespace Declaration (*XML*) This takes the form of an XML *attribute* xmlns="uri". It declares that within its scope, an *element* name with no explicit prefix will be associated with a particular *namespace URI*. The default namespace is used only for element names; other objects with no *prefix* (for example, attributes) have a null namespace URI.

Descendant Axis (*XPath*) The descendant *axis* selects all the *children* of the *context node*, their children, and so on, in *document order*. This is a *forwards axis*.

Descendant-or-Self Axis (*XPath*) The descendant-or-self *axis* selects the *context node* followed by all the *nodes* on the *descendant axis*. This is a *forwards axis*.

Document (*XML*) A parsed entity that conforms to the XML syntax for a Document is said to be a *well-formed document*; a document that also obeys the rules in its *document type definition* is said to be *valid*. In XSLT and XPath the term *document* is often used to refer to the *tree* representation of a document, that is, a *document node* together with all the *nodes* that have this document node as an *ancestor*.

Document Element (*XML*) The outermost *element* of a *document*, the one that contains all other elements. The XML standard also refers to this as the root element, but it must not be confused with the *root node* in the XPath tree model: the *root node* is usually the *document node* that is the *parent* of the document element, which represents the document itself.

Document Node (*XDM*) If the *tree* represents a well-formed XML *document*, the *root node* will be a *document node* with exactly one *element node* as a child, representing the *document element*, and no *text nodes* as children. In other cases, it may have zero or more *element node* children, and zero or more *text node* children: I refer to such a document as being *well balanced*. In both cases, the *root node* may also have *comment nodes* and *processing instruction nodes* as children.

Document Order (*XDM*)   The *nodes* in a *sequence* can always be sorted into document order. For *elements* from the same *document*, document order is the same as the order of the start *tags* in the original source. In terms of the tree structure, a node is ordered after its *preceding siblings*, and these are ordered after their *parent* node. The ordering of *attribute* and *namespace nodes*, and of nodes from different source *documents*, is only partially defined.

Document Type Definition (DTD) (*Xml*)   The definition of the structure of an XML *document*, or a collection of XML *documents*. May be split into an external subset, held in a separate file, and an internal subset, embedded within the document itself.

Dynamic Context (*XPath*)   The dynamic context of an XPath *expression* is the total collection of information available to the XPath engine at evaluation time. This includes the *context item*, *context position*, and *context size*, the values of all *variables*, and the contents of all *documents* that can be accessed by their *URI*, using functions such as doc() and document().

Dynamic Error (*XPath*)   A dynamic error is an error detected during the evaluation phase, as distinct from a *static error*, which is detected at compile time. Technically, *type errors* (which may be detected either at compile time or at runtime) form a separate third category.

Dynamic errors defined in XSLT are classified as being either recoverable or nonrecoverable. In the case of recoverable errors, the processor is allowed either to report the error or to recover in a defined way and continue processing, or both.

Effective Boolean Value (*XPath*)   The effective boolean value of an *expression* is used when the expression appears in a context where a choice needs to be made; for example, the condition in an XPath conditional *expression* or an XSLT <xsl:if> *instruction*. The effective boolean value of a *sequence* is false if the sequence is empty, or if it contains a singleton *atomic value* that is the *boolean* false, a zero-length string, a number equal to zero, or NaN; in most other cases, the effective boolean value is true. For some sequences (for example a sequence of more than one atomic value, or a single date), there is no effective boolean value, and using such an expression in a boolean context causes an error.

Effective Value (*XSLT*)   The effective value of an *attribute* in an XSLT *stylesheet* is the value after

expanding any *attribute value template*; for example, given the instruction <xsl:message terminate="{$term}"/>, the effective value of the «terminate» attribute is the value of the $term variable.

Element (*XML*)   A logical unit within an XML document, delimited by start and end *tags*, for example <publisher>Wrox </publisher>; an empty element may also be written in abbreviated form, for example <publisher name="Wrox"/>.

Element Declaration (*Schema*)   An element declaration is a *schema component* that corresponds to an <xs:element> *element* in a *schema*: it defines the structure of *elements* having a particular name. It may be a global element declaration (if it is defined at the top level of a schema) or a local element declaration (if defined within the structure of a *complex type*).

Element Node (*XDM*)   A *node* in a *tree* that represents an *element* in an XML *document*. The *parent* of the element node is either the containing element or the *document node* of the tree; its *children* are the element nodes, *text nodes*, *comment nodes*, and *processing instruction nodes* derived from the immediate content of the XML element.

Embedded Stylesheet Module (*XSLT*)   A *stylesheet module* that does not constitute an entire XML *document* in its own right, but is embedded as an <xsl:stylesheet> element within some larger XML (or perhaps non-XML) document.

Empty Sequence (*XDM*)   An empty sequence is a *sequence* containing no *items*. It can be written as «()» in XPath.

Entity Reference (*XML*)   A reference to an internal or external *entity*, generally in the form «&name;». Note that numeric references of the form « » are correctly referred to as *character references* rather than entity references.

Entity (*XML*)   A physical unit of information that may be referenced within an XML *document*. Internal entities are embedded within the document in its *Document Type Definition*; external entities are generally held as a separate file. A parsed entity contains text with XML markup; an *unparsed entity* contains binary data. A general entity contains material for inclusion in the document; a parameter entity contains material for inclusion in the Document Type Definition.

Expanded QName (*XDM*)   The term QName is sometimes used to mean a QName as written in source XML documents, that is a construct of the form «prefix:local-name», and it is sometimes used to mean the (namespace-uri, local-name) pair that this represents. Within the XSLT 2.0 and XPath 2.0

specifications the preferred usage is *lexical QName* for the first construct, and *expanded QName* for the second. These terms are not consistent across the full range of XML specifications.

There is no standard convention for displaying an expanded QName, though in some interfaces such as JAXP, expanded QNames are written in the form «{namespace-uri}local-name». This is sometimes referred to as Clark notation.

Expression (*XPath*)   An XPath construct that can be evaluated to yield a value, which will always be a *sequence* (of *nodes* and/or *atomic values*). In XSLT, expressions are used in many contexts such as the select attribute of <xsl:for-each>, <xsl:value-of>, and <xsl:variable>, and the test attribute of <xsl:if> and <xsl:when>. Expressions are also used between curly braces in *attribute value templates*.

Extension Attribute (*XSLT*)   An *attribute* in a vendor- or user-defined *namespace* used on an XSLT *element* in the *stylesheet*. Such attributes may be used to control behavior that would otherwise be implementation defined, or to provide extra control over *serialization*.

Extension Function (*XSLT*)   A *function* defined by a product vendor, a user, or a third party, which can be called from within an XPath *expression*. The XSLT specification defines how extension functions are called but not how they are implemented.

Extension Instruction (*XSLT*)   An *element* within a *sequence constructor* that is defined by a product vendor, a user, or a third party but otherwise behaves like an XSLT *instruction*. The XSLT specification defines how extension instructions are evaluated but not how they are implemented. In XSLT 1.0, extension instructions were referred to as extension elements.

Facet (*Schema*)   A facet is a constraint placed on the values of a *simple type* in the *schema*. For example, the pattern facet (not to be confused with XSLT *patterns*) constrains the value to match a given *regular expression*, while the maxInclusive facet defines the largest permitted value.

Final Result Tree (*XSLT*)   A *tree* that is constructed by a *stylesheet* and acts as an output of the transformation (as distinct from a *temporary tree* that can be further processed by the transformation).

Following Axis (*XPath*)   The following *axis* selects all the *nodes* that follow the *context node* in *document order* with the exception of *attribute* and *namespace* nodes, and the node's own *descendants*. This is a *forwards axis*.

Following Sibling Axis (*XPath*)   The following sibling *axis* selects all the *nodes* that follow the *context node* in

document order and that share the same *parent* node. This is a *forwards axis*.

Forwards Axis (*XPath*)   An *axis* containing a *sequence* of *nodes* that follow the *context node* in *document order*. Within a *predicate* of an axis *step* that uses a forwards axis (for example, «following-sibling::x[3]»), position numbers count the nodes in *document order*.

Function (*XPath*)   A procedure that can be called from within an XPath *expression*; it takes arguments and returns a result. Functions cannot be defined using XPath, only invoked from XPath. A function is either a core function defined in the XPath or XSLT recommendations, or a *stylesheet function* defined using an <xsl:function> declaration in XSLT, or an *extension function* provided by the vendor or the user. Functions may also be defined using XQuery. A function has a name (which is a *QName*), a signature defining the types expected for its arguments and the return type, and an implementation.

Global Variable (*XSLT*)   A *variable* defined in a top-level <xsl:variable> element. Global variables are available anywhere in the *stylesheet* (including in other *stylesheet modules*), unless masked by a *local variable* or *range variable* of the same name, or a global variable of the same name and higher *import precedence*.

ID (*XML*)   An *attribute* of type ID has a value that is unique within the *document* (that is, different from any other ID attribute). It is an ID by virtue of being declared as such in the *DTD* or *Schema*, or by being named xml:id. It is guaranteed to be unique only if the document is *valid* (XSLT is not constrained to operate only on valid documents). *Elements* can be accessed using their ID by means of the id() function.

Import Precedence (*XSLT*)   A *stylesheet module* that is loaded using <xsl:import> has lower import precedence than the *stylesheet module* doing the importing. The import precedence affects all the top-level *declarations* in that stylesheet, and is used when deciding which top-level elements to use. For example, if two *global variables* have the same name, the one with higher import precedence is used.

Initial Template (*XSLT*)   The first *template* to be evaluated when a *stylesheet* is activated. This may be defined by nominating a *named template* from the invoking API, or it may be selected by applying *template rules* to an initial node supplied in the API (typically, by default, the *document node* of the principal source document).

In-Scope Namespaces (*XPath*)   Any *element node* has a set of *namespace declarations* that are in scope for the element: these are represented by the *namespace nodes* for that element. An XPath *expression* also has a set of in-scope namespaces in its *static context*. For XPath expressions in an XSLT *stylesheet module*, the in-scope namespaces for the expression are the namespaces that are in-scope for the *element* in the *stylesheet* that contains the XPath expression, augmented with the namespace defined in the `[xsl:]xpath-default-namespace` attribute if present. In non-XSLT contexts, it is up to the host environment to define how the *static context* for an XPath expression is established.

Instruction (*XSLT*) One of a number of XSLT *elements* that is permitted to appear directly within a *sequence constructor*; for example, `<xsl:variable>`, `<xsl:choose>`, and `<xsl:message>`. Not all XSLT elements are instructions; for example `<xsl:param>` and `<xsl:when>` are not; this is because these can appear in a defined context only.

Item (*XDM*) An item is either an *atomic value* or a *node*.

Item Type (*XPath*) An item type describes the type allowed for *items* within a *sequence*. This is either `item()`, which allows any item; an *atomic type*; or a node type. Node types define the kind of node (for example *element*, *attribute*, or *comment*) plus, optionally, constraints on the name of the node and on its *type annotation*, which will always be a *schema type*.

Lexical QName (*XPath*) A *QName* written in its lexical form: either a simple unprefixed name or a construct of the form «prefix:local-name». See also *expanded QName*.

List Type (*Schema*) A *simple type* that allows a space-separated sequence of values to be written. For example, the type `xs:NMTOKENS` permits the value `"red green blue"`. When an *element* or *attribute* is annotated with a list type, its *typed value* in XPath is a *sequence* containing the individual *items*.

Literal Result Element (*XSLT*) A literal result element is an *element* appearing within a *sequence constructor* in a *stylesheet* that is not an XSLT *instruction* or an *extension instruction*. When the sequence constructor is evaluated a new *element node* is added to the result sequence, and its content (which is also a *sequence constructor*) is evaluated to form the content of the newly constructed element.

Local Variable (*XSLT*) A *variable* defined within a *sequence constructor*. A local variable is accessible only from the *following siblings* of the `<xsl:variable>` element that defines the variable, and from their *descendants*. This is analogous to the normal rule in block-structured programming languages.

Mode (*XSLT*) Modes partition the set of *template rules* in a *stylesheet*, so that the same *nodes* can be processed more than once using different rules each time. The mode named on the call of `<xsl:apply-templates>`

must match the mode named on the `<xsl:template>` element that is invoked.

Named Template (*XSLT*) An `<xsl:template>` element in the *stylesheet* with a `name` attribute. A named template may be invoked using an `<xsl:call-template>` *instruction*.

Namespace (*XML Namespaces*) A named collection of names. The namespace is named using a *URI* (or in the 1.1 specification, an *IRI*), which is intended to be formed in such a way as to ensure global uniqueness, but which, in practice, may be almost any string. Within a particular region of a *document*, a namespace is also identified by a shorthand name called a *prefix*; different prefixes can be used to refer to the same namespace in different *documents* or even within the same document. A name (of an *element* or *attribute* in XML, and of a *variable, template, function, mode*, and so on in XSLT) belongs to a specific namespace, and two names can be considered equivalent only if they belong to the same namespace.

Namespace Axis (*XPath*) The namespace *axis* selects all the *namespace nodes* belonging to the *context node*. If the context node is not an *element node*, the axis will be empty. For element nodes, there is one *namespace node* for every *namespace* that is in scope for the element, whether it relates to a *namespace declaration* that was defined on this element or on a containing element. This is a *forwards axis*. The namespace axis is retained in XPath 2.0, but it is deprecated: applications requiring namespace information should instead use the functions `in-scope-prefixes()` and `namespace-for-prefix()`.

Namespace Declaration (*XML Namespaces*) A construct in an XML *document* that declares that within a particular region of the document, a given *namespace prefix* will be used to refer to the *namespace* with a particular *URI*. There are two forms of namespace declaration: `xmlns="uri"` to declare the default namespace (the one with a null prefix), and `xmlns:prefix="uri"` to declare a namespace with a non-null prefix. Both are written in the form of XML *attributes* and apply to the *element* they are on and all *descendant* elements, unless overridden.

Namespace Fixup (*Xslt*) Namespace fixup is the process of adding *namespace nodes* to a newly constructed *element node* to ensure that all the namespaces actually used by the element are properly declared.

Namespace Node (*XPath*) A *node* in a *tree* that represents the binding of a *namespace prefix* to a *namespace URI*. A namespace node belongs to an element called its *parent*: it applies only to that element and not to any *descendant* elements.

Namespace Prefix (*Xml Namespaces*) A short name used to identify a *namespace* within a particular region of an XML *document*, so called because it is most often used as the prefix of a *lexical QName* (the part before the colon). Different prefixes can be used to identify the same namespace, and in different contexts the same prefix can be used to identify different namespaces.

Namespace URI (*XML Namespaces*)   A *URI* used to identify a *namespace*. Namespace URIs are unusual in that there is no actual resource that can be obtained using the URI; the URI is simply a unique identifier. In practice, any string can be used as a namespace URI, though «http://» URLs are often used to give some prospect of uniqueness. Technically, the XML Namespaces specification refers to this concept as a *namespace name*, and in version 1.1 the namespace name can be an IRI, which unlike a URI allows non-ASCII characters. However, the term namespace URI is in widespread use despite the fact that practical products allow any string to be used.

NaN (*XPath*)   Not a number. This is one of the possible values of a *variable* whose data *type* is float or double. It results from an operation whose result is not numeric, for example «number('apple')».

Node (*XDM*)   An object forming part of a *tree*. There are seven kinds of node: *attribute nodes, comment nodes, document nodes, element nodes, namespace nodes, processing instruction nodes,* and *text nodes*. Nodes have properties including a name, a *string value*, a *typed value*, and a *base URI*. Every kind of node except a document node may have a *parent* node; document nodes and element nodes may have children; element nodes may have attributes and namespaces.

Node Kind (*XDM*)   Nodes are classified into seven kinds: *attribute nodes, comment nodes, document nodes, element nodes, namespace nodes, processing instruction nodes,* and *text nodes*.

Number (*XDM*)   In XPath 2.0, the term *number* is used as a generic term for the three primitive types deci-mal, double, and float, and their subtypes (including integer).

Output Method (*XSLT*)   XSLT 2.0 defines four output methods, xml, html, xhtml, and text. The output method controls the way in which the result tree is output (or *serialized*) as a stream of characters or bytes.

Parameter (*XSLT*)   A variable whose value is supplied by the caller. A *stylesheet* parameter is a *global variable* whose value can be set (in a vendor-defined way) when the stylesheet is executed. A *template* parameter is defined within an <xsl:template> element, and its value can be set when the template is invoked using <xsl:apply-templates> or <xsl:call-template>. A *function* parameter is

defined within an <xsl:function> element, and is set by evaluating the arguments in an XPath function call.

Parent Axis (*XPath*)   The parent *axis* selects the *node* that is the parent of the *context node*, assuming it has a parent. Since this axis selects at most one node, it doesn't matter whether it is considered as a *forwards axis* or as a *reverse axis*.

Particle (*Schema*)   In the language of XML Schema, a particle is a component part of the definition of the structure of a *complex type*. A particle may be an *element declaration*, or a wildcard that allows elements from defined namespaces, or a sequence or choice compositor with a defined substructure.

Path Expression (*XPath*)   A path expression is an *expression* that selects a *sequence* of *nodes* in a *tree*. It defines a sequence of *steps* that define navigation paths from the *context node* to further nodes. The final result is the sequence of nodes reached by following each of the steps in turn. For example, the path expression «../@code» has two steps: the first step selects the parent of the context node, and the second step selects the «code» attribute of the selected parent. The nodes in the result of a path expression are always returned in *document order*, with duplicates removed.

Pattern (*XSLT*)   A construct that defines a condition that a *node* either satisfies or does not satisfy. The syntax for a pattern is a subset of the syntax for an XPath *expression*. Patterns are used in only four XSLT elements: <xsl:template>, <xsl:key>, <xsl:number>, and <xsl:for-each-group>.

Precedence (*XSLT*)   See *Import Precedence*.

Preceding Axis (*XPath*)   The preceding *axis* selects all the *nodes* that precede the *context node* within the same *tree*, with the exception of *attribute* and *namespace* nodes, and the node's own *ancestors*. This is a *reverse axis*.

Preceding Sibling Axis (*XPath*)   The preceding sibling *axis* selects all the *nodes* that precede the *context node* and that share the same parent node. This is a *reverse axis*.

Predicate (*XPath*)   An *expression* used to filter which *nodes* are selected by a particular *step* in a *path expression* or to select a subset of the *items* in a *sequence*. A boolean expression selects the items for which the predicate is true; a numeric expression selects the item at the position given by the value of the expression, for example «[1]» selects the first item.

Prefix (*XML Namespaces*)   See *Namespace Prefix*.

Primitive Type (*Schema*)   The XML Schema specification defines 19 primitive types. In the XPath model these are defined as subtypes of the abstract type xs:anyAtomicType, which contains all atomic values. The 19 primitive types are `boolean`, `string`, `decimal`, `double`, `float`, `QName`, `anyURI`, `hex-Binary`, `base64Binary`, `date`, `time`, `dateTime`, `gYear`, `gYearMonth`, `gMonth`, `gMonthDay`, `gDay`, `duration`, and `NOTATION`. XPath in effect adds `untypedAtomic` to this list, representing values that have not been *validated* against any *schema*.

Principal Node Kind (*XPath*)   Every *axis* has a principal *node kind*. For most axes, the principal node kind is *elements*. For the *attribute axis*, the principal node kind is *attribute*, and for the *namespace axis*, it is *namespace*. The principal node kind determines the kind of nodes selected by the node test «`*`»; for example, «`following-siblings::*`» selects elements, while «`namespace::*`» selects *namespace nodes*.

Priority (*XSLT*)   Every *template rule* has a priority. The priority is expressed as a number (which may be a decimal number such as «`3.5`»). The priority may be specified explicitly, using the `priority` attribute of the `<xsl:template>` element; if it is omitted a default priority is allocated based on the *pattern*. The priority is used to decide which *template rule* to evaluate when several template rules match the same *node*: a rule with numerically higher priority is used in preference to one with lower priority.

Processing Instruction (*XML*)   An item in an XML *document* that is conventionally used to carry instructions to the software that receives the document and processes it. Written between the delimiters «`<?`» and «`?>`». Note that the XML declaration at the start of a document, and the text declaration at the start of an external parsed entity, are not processing instructions even though they use the same delimiters.

Processing Instruction Node (*XDM*)   A *node* in a *tree* representing an XML *processing instruction*.

Promotion (*XPath*)   The type-checking rules for *function* calling in XPath, and also for arithmetic operators and comparison operators, allow numeric values to be used where a different numeric type is expected. The operation of converting the supplied *number* to the required type (for example, integer to double) is known as promotion. Similarly, any URI values can be promoted to `string` values.

QName (*XML Namespaces*)   A qualified name. It is either a simple name (an NCName) or a name preceded by a namespace prefix and a colon. See also *lexical QName* and *expanded QName*.

Range Variable (*XPath*)   A *variable* declared in a «`for`», «`some`», or «`every`» expression, which is bound to each *item* in a *sequence* in turn; for example, the variable `$i` in «`for $i in 1 to 5 return $i*$i`».

Regular Expression (*XPath*)   A regular expression is a pattern that *strings* may or may not match. Regular expressions can be used in the three functions `matches()`, `replace()`, and `tokenize()` defined in XPath, and in the `<xsl:analyze-string>` *instruction* in XSLT. Regular expressions also appear in the pattern *facet* of *simple type* definitions in XML Schema.

Result Tree (*XSLT*)   The output of a *stylesheet*. A stylesheet defines a transformation from a source tree to a result tree. XSLT 2.0 allows multiple result trees to be created. The final stage of processing is normally to *serialize* the result tree as a stream of characters or bytes; this is controlled by the selected *output method*.

Reverse Axis (*XPath*)   An *axis* containing a *sequence* of *nodes* that precede the *context node* in *document order*. Within a *predicate* of an axis *step* that uses a reverse axis (for example, «`preceding-sibling::x[position() = 1 to 3]`»), position numbers count the nodes in reverse *document order*. However, as with any other axis step, the result of the expression is in forwards *document order*. So this *expression* returns the last three «`x`» nodes before the context node, in document order.

Root Node (*XPath*)   The topmost *node* in a *tree*; any *node* that has no *parent*. In XPath 2.0, any kind of node may be a root node. A root node that represents a complete XML document is now referred to as a *document node*.

Schema (*Schema*)   In this book the term *schema*, unless otherwise specified, always means a schema defined using the W3C XML Schema language. A schema can be regarded as a collection of *element declarations*, *attribute declarations*, and *type definitions*. A *schema document*, by contrast, is the XML *document* rooted at an `<xs:schema>` element (which one might regard as containing one module of a schema).

Schema Component (*Schema*)   A generic term for *element declarations*, *attribute declarations*, and *type definitions*.

Schema Type (*XDM*)   A type as defined in XML Schema: either a *complex type* or a *simple type*. The type may be named, or it may be anonymous. The term includes both *built-in types* (such as `xs:integer`) and user-defined types.

Self Axis (*XPath*)   The self *axis* contains a single *node*, the *context node*. It makes no difference whether it is regarded as a *forwards axis* or a *reverse axis*. The *principal node kind* of the self axis is *elements*, which means that when the context node is an *attribute*, an axis *step* of the form «`self::*`» or «`self::xyz`» will not select that attribute.

Sequence (*XPath*)   A sequence in the XPath *data model* is an ordered collection of *items*. The items may be *atomic values* or references to *nodes* in a *tree*. A sequence containing no items is referred to as the *empty sequence*. Sequences have no identity of their own; two sequences containing the same items cannot be distinguished.

Sequence Constructor (*XSLT*) A sequence of XSLT *instructions, extension instructions, literal result elements*, and *text nodes*, forming the content of an `<xsl:template>` element or of various other elements in the *stylesheet*. When the sequence constructor is evaluated, any *instructions* and *extension instructions* are evaluated according to the rules for each one, while any *literal result elements* and *text nodes* are copied to the result sequence. In most cases, the result sequence will be used to form the content of a new *node* in a *result tree*, but this depends on the instruction that contains the sequence constructor.

Sequence Type (*XPath*) A sequence type is a definition that constrains the permitted values of a *sequence*. It has two parts: an *item type*, which constrains the type of the *items* in the sequence, and a cardinality, which constrains the number of items in the sequence. The cardinality may be zero-or-one, exactly-one, zero-or-more, or one-or-more.

Serialization (*XSLT*) Serialization is the reverse of parsing: it takes a *document* represented as a *tree* in the XPath *data model*, and converts it into a lexical XML document.

Simple Type (*Schema*) A simple type in XML Schema describes values that can be written as text, with no embedded markup. Simple types divide into *atomic types, list types*, and *union types*. *Attributes* always have a simple type; the content of an *element* may be either a simple or a *complex type*. XML Schema defines a number of built-in simple types, but further simple types can be defined in a user-written *schema*.

Simplified Stylesheet Module (*XSLT*) A simplified stylesheet module is a *stylesheet module* consisting solely of a *literal result element* which is evaluated using the root of the source document as the *context node*.

Source Document (*XPath*) The principal source document is the XML document to which the stylesheet is being applied. Secondary source documents can be loaded using the `document()` function.

Static Context (*XPath*) The static context of an XPath *expression* is the total collection of information available to the XPath engine at compile time. This includes the *namespace declarations* that are in scope, the names and types of declared *variables*, the *base URI* of the expression, and the *collations* that are available.

Static Error (*XPath*) A static error is an error detected during the analysis phase, that is, at compile time.

Static Type (*XPath*) Every *expression* (and sub-expression) has a static type. This is a *sequence type*, representing the best possible inference that can be made about the dynamic type of the value that will be returned when the expression is evaluated. For example, the static type of the expression «@*» might be «attribute()*». In an XPath processor that implements strict static typing, a *type error* will be reported if the static type of an expression is not a subtype of the type required by the context in which the expression is used.

Step (*XPath*) A step is used within a *path expression* to navigate from one *node* to a *sequence* of related nodes. The most common kind of step is an axis step, which is defined by an *axis*, giving the direction of navigation; a node test, which defines constraints on the type of and names of the target nodes; and zero or more *predicates*, which define arbitrary constraints that the target nodes must satisfy.

String (*XPath*) One of the allowed data types for the value of an XPath expression. It is a sequence of zero or more Unicode characters (the same character set as is used in XML).

String Value (*XDM*) Every *node* has a string value. For a *text node* the string value is the textual content; for an *element* it is the concatenation of the string values of its *descendant* text nodes (that is, the textual content of the element after stripping all markup). The string value of a node can be obtained using the `string()` function.

Stylesheet (*XSLT*) A stylesheet represents the contents of one or more *stylesheet modules*, consisting of a principal stylesheet module and other modules that are reachable from the principal module using `<xsl:include>` and `<xsl:import>` declarations.

Stylesheet Function (*XSLT*) A *function* defined in a *stylesheet* using an `<xsl:function>` declaration. Like other *functions*, a stylesheet function is called using a function call in an XPath *expression*.

Stylesheet Module (*XSLT*) A stylesheet module is defined by a single `<xsl:stylesheet>` or `<xsl:transform>` element, usually comprising the whole of an XML document, or it may be a *simplified stylesheet* whose root is a *literal result element* with an `xsl:version` attribute.

Tag (*XML*) Often used incorrectly to mean *element*. An element `<a href="u">...</a>` has two tags, the start tag `<a href="u">` and the end tag `</a>`. Empty elements may be written with a single tag `<a/>`.

Template (*XSLT*) An `<xsl:template>` element in the *stylesheet*, together with its content. See also *named template*. (XSLT 1.0 had a different definition for this term, but XSLT 2.0 has bowed to popular usage.)

Template Rule (*XSLT*)   An `<xsl:template>` *declaration* in the *stylesheet* with a `match` attribute. A template rule may be invoked using the `<xsl:apply-templates>` *instruction*; for each selected *node*, the appropriate template rule is determined based on a number of criteria, including the match *pattern* and the template rule's *import precedence* and *priority*.

Temporary Tree (*XSLT*)   A *tree* constructed in the course of processing a stylesheet, by evaluating a nonempty `<xsl:variable>` element. The value of the *variable* is the *document node* at the root of the temporary tree.

Text Node (*XDM*)   A *node* in a *tree* representing character data (called PCDATA in XML) within an XML *document*. Adjacent text nodes will always be merged into a single node. *Character references* and *entity references* occurring within the original text will have been replaced by their expansions.

Top-Level Element (*XSLT*)   An *element* in a *stylesheet* that is an immediate child of the `<xsl:stylesheet>` element.

Tree (*XDM*)   An abstract data structure representing the information content of an XML *document*. The tree always has a single *root node* (which contrary to the botanical analogy, is always depicted at the top). The structure of nodes in the tree need not follow the rules for a *well-formed* document in XML; for example, there may be several *element nodes* as children of the root. In XPath 2.0 the root of a tree need not be a *document node*. It is possible to have an element node as the root. It is also possible for any other kind of node (for example, an attribute node) to be parentless, in which case it acts as the root of a tree in which it is the only node.

Tunnel Parameter (*XSLT*)   A tunnel *parameter* is a parameter to an XSLT *template* that is passed transparently via any called *templates* until eventually reaching the template that actually uses its value.

Type (*XPath*)   In the context of XPath values, the term type means *sequence type*. In the context of nodes validated against a schema, it means *schema type*.

Type Annotation (*XDM*)   Every *element node* and *attribute node* has a type annotation. The type annotation identifies a *schema type*, which may be a *simple type* or a *complex type*. Type annotations are added to nodes as a consequence of *validation* against a *schema*. An element node that has not been validated against any schema is annotated with the special type `xs:untyped`, while an attribute node that has not been validated is annotated as `xs:untypedAtomic`.

Type Definition (*Schema*)   A type definition is a *schema component* that defines a *simple type* or a *complex type*.

Typed Value (*XDM*)   The typed value of a node is in general a *sequence* of *atomic values*. It represents the result of analyzing the textual content of the *node* against the *schema definition* for that node, during the process of *validation*.

Type Error (*XPath*)   A type error occurs when the value used as input to some operation is not of the *type* required by that operation; for example, when a string is used as an argument to an arithmetic operator. Type errors may be detected either at compile time or at runtime. A system that implements strict *static type* checking will report type errors at compile time pessimistically, that is, it will report an error if there is any possibility that the runtime value will have the wrong type.

Unparsed Entity (*XML*)   An unparsed entity is an *entity* declared in the *document type definition* with an associated notation. Such entities are unparsed because they generally contain binary data such as images, rather than XML. Two functions, `unparsed-entity-uri()` and `unparsed-entity-public-id()`, are available in XSLT to access the unparsed entities associated with a source document. However, it is not possible to create unparsed entities in a result document.

Union Type (*Schema*)   A union type is a *simple type* that allows a choice of alternatives. For example, a union type might allow an *attribute* to contain either a decimal value, or the string `"N/A"`.

URI (*RFC 3986*)   Uniform Resource Identifier: a generalization of the URLs (Uniform Resource Locators) used to uniquely address resources such as Web pages on the Internet.

Validation (*XSLT*)   Validation in XSLT 2.0 is the process of assessing a *tree* against a *schema*. If the tree is not valid against the schema, the transformation fails; if it is valid, then each *element node* and *attribute node* in the tree acquires a *type annotation* identifying the *schema type* against which it was found to be valid.

Variable (*XPath*)   A named value. Variables in XPath and XSLT differ from variables in procedural programming language in that there is no assignment statement.

Variable Binding (*XSLT*)   The declaration of a *variable*, in an `<xsl:variable>` or `<xsl:param>` element, in conjunction with the current value of that variable.

Variable Reference (*XPath*)   A reference to a *variable* within an *expression*, in the form `$name`.

Well-Balanced (*XML Fragment Interchange*)   An XML fragment is well-balanced if there is an end tag that matches every start tag. This is a less strict constraint than being *well formed*: a well-balanced fragment does not have to have a single element that encloses all the others. XSLT and XPath are defined so that they will work on any *trees* representing a well-balanced XML fragment. The XML and XSLT standards don't use this terminology; instead they refer to the rules for an *external general parsed entity*.

Well Formed (*XML*)   A *document* is well formed if it follows the syntax rules in the XML specification. These include the rule that there must be a single outermost *element* that encloses all others. The XML output of an XSLT stylesheet is not required to be well formed, only to be *well balanced*.

Whitespace (*XML*)   Whitespace is any contiguous sequence of tab, carriage return, newline, and space characters. A whitespace node is a *text node* whose *string value*

consists solely of whitespace. (The XML specification spells this as two words, *white space*, but I prefer a single word, because using *white* as a qualifying adjective suggests that white space is to be contrasted with red space and green space, which of course is not the case.)

XDM   The data model used by XSLT, XPath, and XQuery. Every value in XDM is a sequence of items; an item is either an atomic value or a node.

XPath 1.0 Compatibility Mode (*XPath*)   A mode of executing XPath 2.0 expressions that attempts to provide the maximum possible level of backward compatibility with XPath 1.0. In XSLT, this mode is selected by specifying «version="1.0"» in the stylesheet.

H

Glossary

Index

G

K

L